American Payroll Association

2006 Edition

By Michael P. O'Toole, Esq.
Senior Director of Publications and Government Relations

In the preparation of this text, every effort has been made to offer the most current, correct, and clearly understandable information possible. Nonetheless, inadvertent errors can occur, and tax rules and regulations are constantly changing.

This text is intended to provide authoritative information in regard to the subject matter covered and can be used as a training tool. As such, it is not an evaluation device upon which to base performance reviews and/or promotions.

This material is distributed with the understanding that the publisher and author are not engaged in rendering legal, accounting, or other professional services. If legal advice or other professional assistance is required, the service of your attorney or certified public accountant should be sought. Readers are encouraged to consult with appropriate professional advisors for advice concerning specific matters before making decisions affecting their individual operations. The publisher disclaims any responsibility for positions taken by practitioners in their individual cases or for any misunderstanding on the part of readers. The information in this text is current as of its publication date of February 1, 2006.

Please visit our Web site at www.americanpayroll.org

ISBN: 1-930471-74-2

Printed in the United States

ANSWER KEY

Table of Contents

SECTION 1: THE EMPLOYER-EMPLOYEE RELATIONSHIP

Review Questions

1. The factors used in determining whether an employer has the right to direct or control the financial aspects of a worker's activities (i.e., whether the worker can suffer a profit or loss) include:

    *   Whether the worker has made a significant financial investment in performing the work
    *   Whether the worker has business expenses that are unreimbursed
    *   Whether the worker makes his or her services available to the general market
    *   Whether the worker is paid on a regularly recurring basis or by the job

2. The four categories of statutory employees are:

    *   Agent-drivers or commission-drivers
    *   Full-time life insurance salespersons
    *   Homeworkers
    *   Traveling or city salespersons

3. The two categories of statutory nonemployees are:

    *   Qualified real estate agents
    *   Direct sellers

4. Temporary workers are hired, screened, and trained by the temporary help agency to provide services for clients. They are employees of the temporary help agency, which sets their wages and has the sole right to hire and fire. The agency is also responsible for all payroll taxes.

    Leased employees are hired, trained, and qualified by a leasing company, which provides workers for a client company. The client pays a fee to the leasing company to cover the cost of payroll, benefits, etc.

5. Employers should make sure they are dealing with a financially secure and reputable company before entering into a contract, since the temporary help agency or leasing company's financial failure could lead to the client company becoming liable for any withholding or employment taxes that remain unpaid.

6. a. The three parts of the ABC test are:

    *   The worker is free from control or direction in performing the work both by agreement and in reality (Absence of control).
    *   The work is performed outside the usual course of the company's business or away from any of the employer's facilities (Business—unusual and/or away).
    *   The worker is customarily engaged in an independent trade, occupation, or business (Customarily independent contractor).

    b. The ABC test is used by many states to determine a worker's employment status under state unemployment insurance laws.

7. Form I-9 is used to verify that an individual has the legal right to work in the United States. The Immigration Reform and Control Act of 1986 makes it illegal for an employer to hire an unauthorized worker.

8. Although the client company may have the right to hire and fire the workers, set wage levels, and supervise their work, the workers are generally employees of the leasing company, which is responsible for withholding federal income tax and social security and Medicare taxes, as well as paying the employer's share of social security, Medicare, and FUTA taxes.

9. The factors courts and the DOL consider when making an employment status determination under the FLSA include:

   - how much control the employer has over how the work is performed;
   - whether the worker has the chance to make a profit or risks a loss based on how skillfully the work is performed;
   - whether the worker invests in tools or materials required to perform the work or hires helpers;
   - whether the work requires a special skill;
   - how permanent the working relationship is; and
   - whether the work performed is an integral part of the employer's business operation.

10. Employers would rather use workers who are not employees to perform services for them because employers must withhold income and employment taxes from employees' wages, and match the withheld employment taxes with their own funds. Employers also must pay federal and state unemployment taxes based on their employees' wages. If a worker is an employee, most companies have their own list of benefits and other entitlements that are provided to employees but not to independent contractors.

11. A social security card without employment restrictions is proof of an employee's authorization to work in the U.S., but not proof of identity.

12. Factors that the IRS does not consider important in making worker classification determinations include part-time or full-time work, the location of the work, and hours of work.

13. The employer must report each new hire's name, address, and social security number, as well as the employer's name, address, and federal employer identification number.

14. In general, employers must report new hires within 20 calendar days of the date of hire. Employers that report magnetically or electronically must send 2 transmissions per calendar month which are 12-16 days apart.

True or False Questions

1. True

2. False   Their earnings must consist solely of commissions to be exempt from FUTA.

3. True

4. False   If telemarketers work under the direction and control of a company, they are employees of that company.

5. True

6. True

7. True

8. False   The IRS relies first on the common law right to control test in making worker status determinations.

9. False   Managers and executives are classified as employees, except under most wage-hour and labor relations laws.

10. True

11. True

12. True

13. False   Part-time employees are covered under the federal payroll tax laws if they meet the common law test for employment status.

14. True

15. False   Employers cannot demand specific documents to prove an employee's eligibility to work. New hires can produce any approved documents that prove identity and work authorization.

16. False   The IRS cannot require an employer to show that more than 25% of its industry treated similarly situated workers as independent contractors.

17. True

18. True

19. False   Multistate employers can designate one state in which they have employees as the state to which they will report all new hires.

Multiple Choice Questions

1.	c	7.	c
2.	b	8.	c
3.	a	9.	a
4.	b	10.	a
5.	c	11.	c
6.	b	12.	c

SECTION 2: FEDERAL AND STATE WAGE-HOUR LAWS

Review Questions

1. The five major areas regulated by the Fair Labor Standards Act are:

    - Minimum wage
    - Overtime
    - Child labor
    - Equal pay
    - Recordkeeping

2. Under enterprise coverage, all the employees of a business are covered by the FLSA so long as at least two employees of the business are engaged in interstate commerce or involved in the production of goods or services for interstate commerce, and the business has annual gross sales of at least $500,000. Individual employees can be covered even if the business is not a covered enterprise if the employee is engaged in interstate commerce or the production of goods for interstate commerce.

3. Exempt employees do not have to be paid the required minimum wage or overtime pay, and the employer does not have to keep certain records detailing their work, while nonexempt employees must be paid the required minimum wage and overtime pay and the employer must keep detailed records of their work hours and wage payments.

4. The time limit is two years after the alleged violation or three years if the violation was willful.

5. The plan is called the "Belo" plan, named after the company involved in the Supreme Court's decision, and the plan guarantees a fixed salary for irregular hours that includes a set amount of overtime pay.

6. "Compensable time" is defined as all hours during which the employee is under the employer's control, even if the time is unproductive, so long as the time spent is for the employer's benefit.

7. The following categories of employees make up the "white collar" exemption under the FLSA:

    - Administrative
    - Executive
    - Professional
    - Computer-related professional
    - Outside sales employees

8. The following questions must be answered to properly calculate overtime pay:

    - What is the employee's workweek?
    - What constitutes hours worked?
    - What payments made to the employee are considered wages?
    - What is the employee's regular rate of pay?

9. The regular rate of pay is an hourly rate of pay determined by dividing the total regular pay actually earned for the workweek by the total number of hours worked. For salaried non-exempt employees, the regular rate of pay is the employee's salary divided by the number of hours the salary is intended to compensate.

10. Yes. In order for the computer professional exemption to apply to an hourly paid employee, the employee would have to be paid at least $27.63 per hour.

11. To qualify as an administrative employee:

- The employee's primary duty must be the performance of office or nonmanual work directly related to the management or general business operations of the employer or the employer's customers; and
- The employee's primary duty must include the exercise of discretion and independent judgment regarding matters of significance.

12. The following conditions must be met for an employer to apply the tip credit to the minimum wage:

- The employee must be a "tipped employee," which is an employee working in an occupation in which he or she regularly receives at least $30 per month in tips.
- The employee must receive at least as much in tips as the credit taken by the employer.
- The employee must be informed about the tip credit provisions of the law before the credit is taken.
- All tips received by the employee must be kept by the employee, although tip pooling may be required among employees who are customarily and regularly tipped.
- Credit card tips must be given to the employee by the next payday.

13. All the following conditions must be met for attendance at meetings, lectures, seminars, and training sessions to be considered nonwork time:

- The meeting, lecture, etc., is not held during the employee's regular work hours.
- Attendance is voluntary.
- The meeting, lecture, etc., is not directly related to the employee's job.
- The employee does not perform any productive work for the employer while attending.

14. No minors under age 18 can work in a job that has been declared hazardous by the Wage and Hour Division. Some minors age 16 and 17 are exempt from these restrictions under student learner or apprenticeship programs, or under an exception for loading paper balers and compactors.

15. Employers can be fined up to $11,000 for each violation of the child labor restrictions that causes the death or serious injury of a minor.

True or False Questions

1. False   Employers must comply with whichever law is more beneficial to the employee.

2. True

3. True

4. False   An important sounding job title does not exempt an employee from the minimum wage and overtime pay provisions of the FLSA. The employee's actual duties and salary must meet the tests of the exemption.

Answer Key

5. True

6. True

7. True

8. False   The FLSA does not require overtime pay for hours worked on Sunday, unless the total hours worked for the workweek exceed 40.

9. False   Under the FLSA, employers are not required to give rest periods to employees. However, rest periods may be required by state law.

10. False   Bona fide meal periods during which the employee is completely relieved from duty are not working time.

11. False   The FLSA does not require the employer to pay for hours not worked because of illness.

12. True

13. False   To determine gross earnings, the total overtime earnings are added to the total regular earnings.

14. True

15. False   The Oregon state minimum hourly wage is higher than the federal minimum wage, so Sharon must be paid the state minimum wage of $7.50.

16. True

17. True

18. True

19. True

20. False   Taxicab drivers are only exempt from the overtime pay requirements.

21. True

22. False   In addition to wages paid in the form of cash, employees may be paid in other forms as well. They may be paid partly in room, board, or other facilities provided by the employer. These facilities must primarily benefit the employee, not the employer, in order to be classified as wages.

23. True

24. False   Where service charges are automatically added to customers' bills and then turned over to the employee, these amounts are not tips and are considered wages when determining whether the minimum wage has been paid.

25. False   When employees are required to wear uniforms that cannot be worn as regular "street clothing" and their cost and maintenance would put the employee below the minimum hourly wage, the employer must pay for the purchase, cleaning, and repair of the uniforms. If the uniform can be worn off the job, the employer need not reimburse the employee, even if the employee's wages go below the minimum.

Multiple Choice Questions

1.	b	6.	b
2.	b	7.	b
3.	d	8.	d
4.	d	9.	b
5.	a	10.	b

Problems

1. Step 1: Calculate total earnings due if overtime pay is required for hours worked over 8 in a day.

   Regular pay: $10 x 85 hours = $850
   Overtime hours: [5 x (9-8)] + [4 x (10-8)] = 13
   Overtime premium: 0.5 x $10 x 13 hours = $65
   Total earnings: $850 + $65 = $915

   Step 2: Calculate total earnings due if overtime pay is required for hours worked over 80 in the 14-day work period.

   Regular pay: $10 x 85 hours = $850
   Overtime hours: 85 - 80 = 5
   Overtime premium: 0.5 x $10 x 5 = $25
   Total earnings: $850 + $25 = $875

   Step 3: David must be paid the higher of the result in Step 1 or 2—$915.

2. Regular pay: $7 x 47 hours = $329
   Overtime hours: 47 - 40 = 7
   Overtime premium: 0.5 x $7 x 7 = $24.50
   Total earnings: $329 + $24.50 = $353.50

3. Regular pay: $12 x 42 hours = $504
   Overtime hours: 42 - 40 = 2
   Overtime premium: 0.5 x $12 x 2 = $12
   Total earnings: $504 + $12 = $516

4. Regular pay: ($10 + $1) x 45 hours = $495
   Overtime hours: 45 - 40 = 5
   Overtime premium: 0.5 x $11 x 5 = $27.50
   Total earnings: $495 + $27.50 = $522.50

5. Regular pay: ($10 x 44 hours) + $38 bonus = $478
   Regular rate of pay: $478 ÷ 44 hours = $10.86
   Overtime hours: 44 - 40 = 4
   Overtime premium: 0.5 x $10.86 x 4 = $21.72
   Total earnings: $478 + $21.72 = $499.72

6. Regular pay: $8.50 x 48 = $408
   Overtime hours: 48 - 40 = 8
   Overtime premium: 0.5 x $8.50 x 8 = $34
   Discretionary bonus: $100
   Total earnings: $408 + $34 + $100 = $542

7. Regular pay: ($10 x 24 hours) + ($12 x 20 hours) $240 + $240 = $480
    Regular rate of pay: $480 ÷ 44 hours = $10.91
    Overtime hours: 44 - 40 = 4
    Overtime premium: 0.5 x $10.91 x 4 = $21.82
    Total earnings: $480 + $21.82 = $501.82

8. Regular rate of pay: $520 ÷ 40 hours = $13
    Regular pay: $13 x 49 hours = $637
    Overtime hours: 49 - 40 = 9
    Overtime premium: 0.5 x $13 x 9 = $58.50
    Total earnings: $637 + $58.50 = $695.50

9. Regular rate of pay: $23,400 ÷ (52 x 40) = $11.25
    Regular pay: $11.25 x 48 hours = $540
    Overtime hours: 48 - 40 = 8
    Overtime premium: 0.5 x $11.25 x 8 = $45
    Total earnings: $540 + $45 = $585

10. Yearly earnings: $1,500 x 12 = $18,000
    Regular rate of pay: $18,000 ÷ (52 x 40) = $8.65
    Regular pay: $8.65 x 49 hours = $423.85
    Overtime hours: 49 - 40 = 9
    Overtime premium: 0.5 x $8.65 x 9 = $38.93
    Total earnings: $423.85 + $38.93 = $462.78

11. Yearly earnings: $1,000 x 24 = $24,000
    Regular rate of pay: $24,000 ÷ (52 x 32) = $14.42
    Regular pay: $14.42 x 42 = $605.64
    Overtime hours: 42 - 40 = 2
    Overtime premium: 0.5 x $14.42 x 2 = $14.42
    Total earnings: $605.64 + $14.42 = $620.06

12. Yearly earnings: $1,500 x 12 = $18,000
    Regular rate of pay: $18,000 ÷ (52 x 35) = $9.89
    Regular pay: $9.89 x 43 hours = $425.27
    Overtime hours: 43 - 40 = 3
    Overtime premium: 0.5 x $9.89 x 3 = $14.84
    Total earnings: $425.27 + $14.84 = $440.11

13. Regular piecework earnings: $0.50 x 840 units = $420
    Regular rate of pay: $420 ÷ 46 hours = $9.13
    Overtime hours: 46 - 40 = 6
    Overtime premium: 0.5 x $9.13 x 6 = $27.39
    Total earnings: $420 + $27.39 = $447.39

14. Regular piecework earnings: $2 x 326 units = $652
    Production bonus: $0.50 x 26 units = $13
    Regular rate of pay: ($652 + $13) ÷ 43 hours = $15.47
    Overtime hours: 43 - 40 = 3
    Overtime premium: 0.5 x $15.47 x 3 = $23.21
    Total earnings: $652 + $13 + $23.21 = $688.21

15. Regular piecework earnings: $0.30 x 1,560 units = $468
    Overtime piece rate: $0.30 x 1.5 = $0.45
    Overtime earnings: $0.45 x 212 = $95.40
    Total earnings: $468 + $95.40 = $563.40

SECTION 3: TAXABLE AND NONTAXABLE COMPENSATION

Review Questions

1. The following conditions must be met for an employer to use the vehicle cents-per-mile method of valuing an employee's personal use of an employer-provided car.

   - The employer must expect the employee to regularly use the vehicle while conducting the employer's business, or the vehicle must actually be driven at least 10,000 miles and be used primarily by employees.

   - The fair market value of the vehicle cannot exceed $15,000 for cars placed in service in 2006.

   - If the employee pays for fuel, the mileage rate is reduced by $.055 per mile.

2. A benefit whose value is so small that accounting for it would be unreasonable or impracticable.

3. The three special valuation methods are:

   - Annual lease value method
   - Vehicle cents-per-mile method
   - Commuting method

4. a. $90,000 - $50,000 = $40,000

   b. $.15 per $1,000 of the taxable value of the coverage

5. $2,000. If the employer provides more than $2,000 in group-term life insurance to an employee's dependent, the value of the total amount including the first $2,000 becomes taxable to the employee. However, if the difference between the Table I value of the insurance and the amount paid by the employee in after-tax dollars is considered de minimis, then there is no income for the employee.

6. Taxable: When the employer has a nonaccountable plan because it does not require the employee to substantiate business travel expenses and to return any amount not spent by the employee on business within a reasonable period of time.

   Nontaxable: When the employer has an accountable plan and the employee is required to substantiate business travel expenses and refund the balance of the advance not used within a reasonable period of time.

7. Yes. The method allowed by the IRS is called "grossing-up."

8. Outplacement services are not included in employees' income under the following circumstances:

   - The employer derives a substantial business benefit from providing the outplacement services other than providing the compensation (e.g., a positive corporate image, an attractive benefit that encourages new hires).

- The employees do not have the choice of accepting cash rather than the outplacement services (e.g., a higher severance payment if the services are refused).

- The employees would be able to deduct the cost of the outplacement services as a business expense on their personal tax returns.

9. In the private sector, a control employee is an employee who:

   - is a corporate officer earning at least $85,000 in 2006 (indexed annually);
   - is a director;
   - earns at least $175,000 in 2006 (indexed annually); or
   - is a 1% owner.

   In the public sector, a control employee is an employee who:

   - is an elected official; or
   - earns more than a federal employee at Executive Level V ($133,900 in 2006).

10. The two types of deductible job-related moving expenses are:

    - transportation and storage of household goods, and
    - expenses of moving the employee and his or her family from the old home to the new home (not meals)

11. If a reimbursement is made under an "accountable plan," the amount reimbursed is excluded from income and is not subject to federal income tax withholding or social security, Medicare, and FUTA taxes. If the reimbursement is made under a "nonaccountable plan," the reimbursement or the excess amount is included in income and is subject to federal income tax withholding and social security, Medicare, and FUTA taxes.

12. If an employer regularly fails to comply with the requirements for reimbursing or advancing amounts paid or incurred by employees for business expenses, the IRS will consider this a "pattern of abuse" and will treat all payments as being made under a nonaccountable plan.

13. Five years.

14. When a manufacturer pays a bonus to sales employees working for a retailer to get them to "push" its products, the bonus is not wages because it is being paid by a third party, not the employer (for services performed for the third party), and is not subject to federal income tax withholding or social security, Medicare, and FUTA taxes. The bonus is taxable income to the sales employees, however, and must be reported on their personal income tax return.

15. Exclusion limitation: The excluded amount of dependent care assistance cannot exceed $5,000 in a year or the employee's earned income for the year, whichever is less.

    When expenses are incurred: An employer's dependent care expenses are treated as incurred when the care is provided, not when payments are made to the employee or third party.

    Written plan: The dependent care assistance program must be a separate, written plan of the employer and it must be designed solely for the employees' benefit.

    No discrimination: The program must not discriminate in favor of highly compensated employees.

Notification: Eligible employees must receive reasonable notification of the availability and terms of the program.

Annual statement: The employer must give the employee a statement each year by January 31 showing the dependent care assistance provided by the employer during the previous year (Box 10 of Form W-2).

16. When companies change ownership, key executives are often provided with "golden parachutes" to soften their landing should they be terminated by the new owner. The tax law defines a "parachute payment" as compensation that is paid to an officer, shareholder, or highly compensated employee only after a change in corporate ownership or control and that is at least three times the employee's average compensation during the five most recent tax years.

True or False Questions

1. False   The Internal Revenue Code does not define the term "fringe benefits," although it includes several examples.

2. True

3. False   The goods or services must be offered for sale to customers in the employer's line of business in which the employee normally works.

4. True

5. True

6. True

7. False   Cellular phones in company-provided cars are not included in a vehicle's fair market value if they are necessary to the employer's business.

8. True

9. False   The annual lease value does not include the value of employer-provided fuel.

10. False   If an employee uses a company aircraft for business and personal use, the value of the personal use is included in the employee's income.

11. True

12. True

13. True

14. False   During the 12-month period immediately following the move, the employee must work for at least 39 weeks in the general location of the new workplace. The employee does not have to work for the same employer for 39 weeks, nor do the 39 weeks have to be consecutive.

15. False   Cash gifts or gift certificates with a cash value are never de minimis fringes. They are included in income and are taxable to the employee.

16. True

17. False   Scholarships and fellowships covering tuition and related fees are excluded from an individual's income if the individual is a candidate for a degree at an educational institution.

18. True

19. True

20. True

21. True

22. True

23. False   Gifts provided to employees must be included in the employees' income unless they can be excluded as a de minimis fringe benefit or as a gift between relatives that is not based on the employer-employee relationship.

24. False   This exclusion was repealed in 1996.

25. True

26. False   Special rules and limitations apply to combined business and pleasure travel outside the United States. Even though the trip is primarily for business, if the trip has any element of pleasure, the cost of traveling to and from the destination must be allocated between the business and personal portions of the trip.

27. False   To deduct travel expenses, an employee must be in travel status. The employee must usually be away from home "overnight." Overnight does not literally mean 24 hours. It is a period of time longer than an ordinary work day during which rest or relief from work is required. The deduction may also be available to employees who travel from their residence to a temporary work location and return home on the same day.

28. True

29. True

30. True

Multiple Choice Questions

1.	c	10.	b
2.	d	11.	a
3.	b	12.	a
4.	d	13.	b
5.	a	14.	d
6.	b	15.	b
7.	a	16.	b
8.	c	17.	a
9.	d		

Problems

1. Annual lease value = $3,600
   Taxable amount: $3,600 x 40% = $1,440

2. Personal use: 100% - 70% = 30%
   Personal mileage: 12,000 miles x .30 = 3,600 miles
   Taxable amount: (3,600 miles x $0.445) = $1,602.00

3. Step 1: 2 x $35,000 = $70,000
   Step 2: $70,000 - $50,000 = $20,000
   Step 3: $20,000 ÷ $1,000 = 20
   Step 4: Bill is 39 years old as of 12-31-06
   Step 5: $0.09 x 20 = $1.80 monthly taxable coverage

4. Step 1: 2 x $38,000 = $76,000
   Step 2: $76,000 - $50,000 = $26,000
   Step 3: $26,000 ÷ $1,000 = 26
   Step 4: Bill is 39 years old as of 12-31-06
   Step 5: $0.09 x 26 = $2.34 monthly taxable coverage
   Step 6: $2.34 - $2.00 = $0.34 monthly taxable coverage for May - December

5. a. Total tax % = 25% + 5% + 6.2% + 1.45% = 37.65%
   Gross-up % = 100% - 37.65% = 62.35%
   Gross earnings = $4,500 ÷ .6235 = $7,217.32

   To check:
   FITW = 25% x $7,217.32 = $1,804.33
   SITW = 5% x $7,217.32 = $360.87
   Soc. Sec. = 6.2% x $7,217.32 = $447.47
   Medicare = 1.45% x $7,217.32 = $104.65

   $7,217.32 - $1,804.33 - $360.87 - $447.47 - $104.65 = $4,500.00

   b. Soc. Sec. tax on $1,500 = .062 x $1,500 = $93
   Total to be grossed-up = $4,500 + $93 = $4,593
   Total tax % = 25% + 5% + 1.45% = 31.45%
   Gross-up % = 100% - 31.45% = 68.55%
   Gross earnings = $4,593 ÷ .6855 = $6,700.22

   To check:
   FITW = 25% x $6,700.22 = $1,675.06
   SITW = 5% x $6,700.22 = $335.01
   Soc. Sec. = 6.2% x $1,500 = $93.00
   Medicare = 1.45% x $6,700.22 = $97.15

   $6,700.22 - $1,675.06 - $335.01 - $93.00 - $97.15 = $4,500.00

6. Total tax % = 25% + 3.5% + 6.2% + 1.45% = 36.15%
    Gross-up % = 100% - 36.15% = 63.85%

    a. Gross earnings = $6,000 ÷ .6385 = $9,397.02
    b. FITW = 25% x $9,397.02 =   - 2,349.25
    c. SITW = 3.5% x $9,397.02 =   - 328.90
    d. Soc. Sec. = 6.2% x $9,397.02 =   - 582.62
    e. Medicare = 1.45% x $9,397.02 =   - 136.25
    f. Check: $6,000.00

7. Moving, packing, and storage = $2,800.00
    Travel expenses during move (no meals):
              $1,500 - $150 =   + 1,350.00
    Total qualified reimbursement $4,150.00

SECTION 4: HEALTH, ACCIDENT, AND RETIREMENT BENEFITS

Review Questions

1. Family and Medical Leave Act.

2. Cafeteria plan.

3. Only if the §401(k) plan existed prior to the effective date of the Tax Reform Act of 1986.

4. 12 weeks

5. The status changes that allow a cafeteria plan to permit an employee to change a cafeteria plan benefit election during the year are:

   - marital status changes – marriage, divorce, death of spouse, legal separation, or annulment
   - changes in the number of dependents – birth, adoption, placement for adoption, or death of a dependent
   - employment status changes (applies to employee, spouse, or dependent) – termination or commencement of employment, strike or lockout, starting or ending an unpaid leave of absence, change in worksite, change from full-time to part-time, exempt to nonexempt, or salaried to hourly status
   - change in dependent status – any event that causes an employee's dependent to become covered or lose coverage (e.g., attainment of a certain age, student status)
   - residence change – a change in the place of residence of the employee, spouse, or dependent
   - adoptions – the commencement or termination of an adoption proceeding

6. Cafeteria plans must satisfy the following three nondiscrimination tests:

   - eligibility test
   - contributions and benefits test
   - concentration test

7. The three major types of health insurance plans offered by employers are:

   - traditional health insurance (fee-for-service)
   - Health Maintenance Organizations
   - Preferred Provider Organizations

8. "The diagnosis, cure, mitigation, treatment, or prevention of disease, or for the purpose of affecting any structure or function of the body."

9. To be nondiscriminatory in terms of eligibility, a self-insured health insurance plan must benefit:

   - at least 70% of all employees;
   - at least 80% of all employees who are eligible to participate in the plan (if at least 70% of all employees are eligible to participate); or
   - a classification of employees that the Secretary of the Treasury finds not to be discriminatory.

In terms of benefits, a self-insured plan is nondiscriminatory if all the benefits provided to highly compensated employees are provided to all other participating employees. Plans may have limits on benefits, but they must be uniform for all participants when based on employer contributions and must not be proportionately based on employee compensation.

10. Sick pay may take many forms, but its essential purpose is to replace the wages of an employee who cannot work because of a nonjob-related illness or injury. Workers' compensation, however, deals with payments to employees who cannot work because of job-related injuries or illness.

11. Information an employer should provide a third-party payer of sick pay includes:

    • the total wages paid by the employer to the employee during the calendar year before the third party begins making payments (helps determine whether the social security and FUTA wage bases have been met);

    • the last month in which the employee worked for the employer (helps determine how long the third party is responsible for social security and Medicare taxes); and

    • employee contributions made to the cost of the insurance after taxes have been withheld (helps determine how much of each disability payment is taxable).

12. While an employer's business generally determines its classification code, and the more dangerous the business the higher the dollar value assigned to that code, some employees may be assigned a different or less costly code because of the duties they perform. Employees who work exclusively in an office, outside salespeople, and drivers and their helpers may be assigned a "standard exception classification." Such classifications generally carry a significantly lower dollar value than other employee classifications.

13. A pre-tax contribution is one that is made from an employee's wages before the taxes on those wages are calculated, while an after-tax contribution is made after the tax is calculated. A pre-tax contribution will result in higher take-home pay for the employee.

14. The payroll department must maintain accurate records of:

    • hours worked
    • compensation earned
    • date of birth
    • date of hire

15. A defined contribution plan sets up individual accounts for each employee, with a set amount being contributed into the account by the employer and/or the employee periodically. The employee's retirement benefit depends on the amount of money in his or her account at retirement, which is determined by the contribution amounts and any investment gains or losses. Other characteristics of defined contribution plans include:

    • the plan provides for a contribution formula involving the employer and/or the employees
    • employer contributions are made no less frequently than annually (usually more often)
    • being able to see how much is in their accounts makes the plan easy to understand for employees
    • no need for actuarial calculations
    • annual reports must be filed with the IRS and the Department of Labor

True or False Questions

1. True

2. True

3. False A pre-tax contribution will result in more take-home pay for the employee.

4. True

5. False In this case, cafeteria plans are exempt from the nondiscrimination tests.

6. True

7. True

8. False Only the premium portion of overtime is excluded.

9. False Employers can require eligible employees to use any paid vacation, personal, sick, medical, or family leave as part of the 12-week guaranteed leave.

10. True

11. True

12. False Employer contributions to an accident or health insurance plan for the benefit of its employees and their spouses and dependents are not wages and are not subject to federal income tax withholding or social security, Medicare, and FUTA taxes.

13. True

14. True

15. True

16. True

17. True

18. False The general rules for depositing withheld federal income, social security, and Medicare taxes do apply to sick pay, although the party liable for depositing the taxes may change.

19. True

20. True

21. True

22. True

23. False Once selected, benefits cannot be changed during the plan year unless the cafeteria plan permits the employee to make a change if there is a change in status that causes the employee or the employee's spouse or dependent to lose or gain coverage under the plan, or premiums or coverage are significantly altered by the insurance carrier or the employer.

24. True

Multiple Choice Questions

1.	c	13.	b
2.	c	14.	c
3.	b	15.	b
4.	c	16.	d
5.	b	17.	c
6.	a	18.	d
7.	c	19.	a
8.	a	20.	c
9.	b	21.	b
10.	d	22.	c
11.	d	23.	c
12.	c	24.	c

Problems

1. a. $1,000 x 6 months x 60% = $3,600
   b. $1,000 x 10 months x 60% = $6,000

2. a. $900 x 6 months x $2/_3$ = $3,600
   b. $900 x 7 months x $2/_3$ = $4,200
   c. $900 x 7 months x $1/_3$ = $2,100

3. a. If the contribution is pre-tax:

Regular wages	$600.00
Medical and dental	- 25.00
FITW ($600 - 25) x 15%	- 86.25
Soc. Sec. ($600 - 25) x 6.2%	- 35.65
Medicare ($600 - 25) x 1.45%	- 8.34
SITW $86.25 x 10%	- 8.63
Net Pay:	$436.13

   b. If the contribution is after-tax:

Regular wages	$600.00
FITW ($600 x 15%)	- 90.00
Soc. Sec. ($600 x 6.2%)	- 37.20
Medicare ($600 x 1.45%)	- 8.70
SITW ($90 x 10%)	- 9.00
Medical and dental	- 25.00
Net Pay:	$430.10

4. a. §408(k)
   b. §501(c)(18)(D)
   c. §457
   d. §403(b)
   e. §401(k)
   f. §401(a)
   g. §408(p)

5. a. $7,500 — the lesser of 15% x $50,000 ($7,500) or $15,000 (annual dollar limit effective for 2006).
   b. $15,000 — the lesser of 15% x $120,000 ($18,000) or $15,000 (annual dollar limit effective for 2006).

6. $4,000 — the lesser of $27,500 x 100% or $4,000 annual dollar limit.

7. a. Federal income taxable wages

Gross wages ($18,000 ÷ 24):	$750.00
Cafeteria plan ($25 ÷ 2):	- 12.50
§401(k) plan ($750 x .05):	- 37.50
Taxable wages:	$700.00

   b. Social security taxable wages

Gross wages ($18,000 ÷ 24):	$750.00
Cafeteria plan ($25 ÷ 2):	-12.50
Taxable wages	$737.50

   c. Medicare taxable wages

Gross wages ($18,000 ÷ 24):	$750.00
Cafeteria plan ($25 ÷ 2):	- 12.50
Taxable wages:	$737.50

   d. FUTA taxable wages

Gross wages ($18,000 ÷ 24):	$750.00
Cafeteria plan ($25 ÷ 2):	-12.50
Taxable wages:	$737.50

8. a. Federal income taxable wages

Gross wages:	$1,760.00
Cafeteria plan:	- 75.00
§401(k) plan ($1,760 x .075):	- 132.00
Taxable wages:	$1,553.00

   b. Social security taxable wages

Gross wages:	$1,760.00
Cafeteria plan:	-75.00
Taxable wages:	$1,685.00

   c. Medicare taxable wages

Gross wages:	$1,760.00
Cafeteria plan:	-75.00
Taxable wages:	$1,685.00

   d. FUTA taxable wages

Gross wages:	$1,760.00
Cafeteria plan:	-75.00
Taxable wages:	$1,685.00

Answer Key

9. Gross wages: $650.00
    Cafeteria plan ($650 x 6%):   -39.00
    Taxable wages: $611.00

    FITW ($611.00 x 15%)   - 91.65
    Soc. Sec. ($611.00 x 6.2%):   - 37.88
    Medicare ($611.00 x 1.45%):   -8.86
    Net Pay: $472.61

10. Gross wages: $500.00
    Cafeteria plan: - 10.00
    §401(k) plan ($500 x 6%):   - 30.00
    FITW [$500 - ($10 + $30)] x 15%:   - 69.00
    Soc. Sec. [($500 - $10) x 6.2%]:   - 30.38
    Medicare [($500 - $10) x 1.45%]:   - 7.11
    Net pay: $353.51

SECTION 5: PAYING THE EMPLOYEE

Review Questions

1. State laws govern how often employers must pay employees.

2. Advantages of direct deposit for an employer include:

   * prevents lost and stolen checks
   * employees do not have to take time out of their work day to cash or deposit their paycheck
   * employers do not have to file/store cashed checks and related documents
   * better control of check stock

   Disadvantages of direct deposit for an employer include:

   * direct deposit is not a paperless system, since employers still may have to provide employees with a written statement of hours worked and deductions from gross pay
   * direct deposit cannot be made mandatory in most states
   * employer cannot dictate the financial institution that the employee uses in most states
   * employer's loss of interest on payroll funds before paychecks clear

3. State escheat laws govern the treatment of unclaimed paychecks. Under these laws, employers are generally required to:

   * try to locate and contact the employee
   * file an annual report with the state that includes the employee's name, last known address, amount of the check, and the related payday
   * hold the checks for a certain length of time before turning them over to the state as abandoned property

4. Prenotification involves sending zero dollar amounts through the ACH network as a test before the first actual direct deposit for an employee. If such a "prenote" is used (it is an optional procedure), it must be sent at least 6 business days before any actual pay is sent through the network. This is a test of the accuracy of the information in the authorization agreement.

5. Authorization agreements (where they are in paper form) still must be signed and checked for accuracy, and employees using direct deposit must be given statements on payday showing the compensation they earned and the deductions taken for the pay period. Some employers do use electronic pay statements in meeting that requirement.

6. The main problem is whether to recompute weekly or biweekly paychecks for exempt salaried employees who are earning a certain amount annually. Employers are free to reduce exempt salaried employees' pay when faced with an extra pay period, so long as there is no contract guaranteeing a certain amount of pay each weekly or biweekly pay period and the employee's pay is not reduced below the minimum required by state or federal law. Employers may also face a hostile reaction from salaried employees whose pay is reduced in this manner.

7. The following is a list of states that do not allow compulsory direct deposit:

Alaska	Illinois	New York
Arizona*	Indiana	Oklahoma*
Arkansas*	Iowa*	Oregon
California	Kansas	Pennsylvania
Colorado	Maryland	Rhode Island
Connecticut	Michigan*	Utah*
Delaware	Minnesota*	Vermont
Dist. of Col.	Montana	Virginia
Florida	Nevada	West Virginia
Georgia	New Hampshire	Wyoming
Hawaii*	New Jersey	
Idaho	New Mexico	

* There are limited exceptions to this general rule in these states.

8. The following is a list of states where the employee must incur no added fees:

Arizona	Kentucky	North Dakota
Colorado	Louisiana	Oregon
Connecticut	Maryland	South Carolina
Delaware	Michigan	Tennessee
Dist. of Col.	Minnesota	Texas
Hawaii	Montana	Utah
Idaho	Nevada	Vermont
Illinois	New Hampshire	Virginia
Iowa	New Mexico	Washington
Kansas	New York	Wisconsin

9. The following are the steps involved in establishing an electronic funds transfer:

- The employee must give authorization for direct deposit by designating the financial institution(s) to which the employee's pay will be transferred, the type of account to which the pay will be transferred, the number of the account, and the financial institution's routing number

- The employer prepares an automated file of direct deposit records which is sent to a financial institution with the ability to process the file, known as the Originating Depository Financial Institution (ODFI).

- The ODFI processes the file through the Automated Clearing House (ACH) operator.

- The ACH operator processes electronic payments between the ODFI and the financial institutions designated by the employees to receive the payments and coordinates the financial settlement between the participating financial institutions.

- The Receiving Depository Financial Institutions (RDFI) designated by the employees accept the electronic payments and post them to their customers' (the employees') accounts.

- On payday, the employees receive an information statement containing the same data that would have been shown on the pay stub, had the employee been paid by check.

10. Disadvantages for an employer in paying employees by paycheck include:

- lost or stolen checks
- unclaimed or uncashed checks
- employee time off needed to cash checks
- storage of cashed checks and related documents
- early preparation of vacation checks
- reconciliation of bank account with outstanding checks

True or False Questions

1. False   These matters are left up to the individual states.

2. True

3. False   Most states have a separate set of rules governing when employees must be paid when they separate from employment, either through discharge, layoff, or resignation.

4. False   More than 15 states have no statutory provisions dealing with paying wages owed to deceased employees.

5. True

6. True

7. False   A biweekly salary is paid every two weeks.

8. True

9. True

10. False   There is no minimum number required. Each state has its own regulations and requirements regarding mandatory direct deposit.

11. False   The FLSA does not regulate the frequency of wage payments. Each state regulates when employees must be paid.

12. True

Multiple Choice Questions

1.	c	8.	c
2.	b	9.	a
3.	a	10.	b
4.	b	11.	c
5	c	12.	b
6.	c		
7.	c		

SECTION 6: WITHHOLDING TAXES

Review Questions

1. Employee's Withholding Allowance Certificate

2. Employers must retain each employee's Form W-4 for at least four years after the date the last tax return was due using information from the form.

3. Constructive payment indicates the point of time when an employee has the ability to control the payments for services from an employer.

4. The date of actual or constructive payment is important because it determines when wages are taxed and reported and at what rates.

5. A Form W-4 filed by a newly hired employee must be put into effect by the employer for the first wage payment after the form is filed.

6. Form W-4 tells the employer how many withholding allowances the employee is claiming. The number of allowances helps determine the amount of federal income tax to withhold from the employee's wages. Form W-4 also notifies the employer that the employee is claiming exempt from withholding. In addition, it may indicate that the employee wants an additional dollar amount withheld beyond the amount that is calculated on the withholding allowances claimed.

7. In order to be exempt from withholding, the employee must certify that:

   - he or she had a right to a refund of all federal income tax withheld in the prior year because the employee had no tax liability,

   - he or she expects to have no tax liability in the current year, and

   - he or she cannot be claimed as a dependent on someone else's income tax return if the employee will have more than $850 in income (including at least $300 in nonwage income) in 2006.

8. The employer must submit Form W-4 to the IRS in the following situations:

   - the IRS directs the employer to do so in a written notice to the employer; or

   - the IRS directs the employer to do so in published guidance, such as a revenue procedure.

9. Types of payments that may be treated as supplemental wage payments include:

   - bonuses
   - prizes
   - awards
   - commissions
   - backpay awards
   - retroactive pay
   - overtime pay
   - severance or dismissal pay
   - payments for unused annual leave

- tips
- reimbursements for nondeductible moving expenses
- reimbursements for employee business expenses under a nonaccountable plan

10. The withholding exemption generally would apply to the supplemental wages as well, so no withholding for federal income tax would be done. However, if the current supplemental wage payment brings the total of the employee's year-to-date supplemental wages over $1,000,000, the excess must be taxed at the highest marginal tax rate (35% in 2006), and the employee's clam of exemption on Form W-4 is ignored.

11. Generally all nonperiodic payments of all or any portion of the balance of a recipient's account in a qualified deferred compensation plan are eligible rollover distributions other than:

   - substantially equal periodic payments made over the lifetime or life expectancy of the employee or his or her beneficiary, or made for a specified period of at least 10 years,

   - any minimum distribution that is required under IRC §401(a)(9) regarding qualified plans,

   - distributions not included in gross income (e.g., return of an employee's after-tax contributions), except for net unrealized appreciation of employer securities,

   - returns of amounts deferred under a §401(k) or §403(b) plan that exceed the elective deferral limits,

   - loans treated as deemed distributions,

   - dividends paid on employer securities, or

   - distributions of the cost of current life insurance coverage.

12. Payers must generally withhold 28% of reportable nonpayroll payments during 2006 if payees fail to furnish payers with their taxpayer identification number or the IRS notifies them to withhold. This withholding is referred to as backup withholding.

13. To be eligible for advance earned income credit for 2006, an employee must meet all of the following requirements:

   - The employee's earned income and adjusted gross income must be less than $32,001 ($34,001 if the employee is married filing jointly).

   - The employee must have at least one qualifying child who is supported by the employee.

   - The employee must not file his or her personal income tax return as a married individual filing separately.

   - The employee must file Form W-5 before any advance payments can be made.

14. Employers must put the first Form W-5 filed by an employee for a calendar year into effect for the first payroll period ending on or after the date the form is filed with them.

15. Employers must provide notification of the right to the earned income credit by giving the employees one of the following:

- Copy B of Form W-2, *Wage and Tax Statement* (IRS-supplied forms have the required EIC statement on the back; substitutes used for this purpose must have the required statement on the back of the employee copy),

- Notice 797, *Possible Federal Tax Refund Due to the Earned Income Credit*, or

- a written statement with the exact same wording as Notice 797.

True or False Questions

1. True

2. False   Wages are considered constructively paid only if they are made available to the employee without "substantial limitation or restriction."

3. True

4. True

5. True

6. False   Under the principle of constructive payment, an employee is considered to have been paid wages when they are actually or constructively paid, not when they are earned or payable.

7. True

8. False   The required rate for backup withholding in 2006 is 28%.

9. True

10. True

11. True

12. True

13. False   Employees cannot indicate on their W-4 form that they wish to have a flat amount of tax withheld rather than an amount based on the number of withholding allowances that can be claimed.

14. True

15. True

16. False   For wage payments equalling or exceeding the maximum amount, the percentage method of withholding must be used.

17. True

18. True

19. True

20. True

Multiple Choice Questions

1.	b	12.	d
2.	a	13.	d
3.	b	14.	b
4.	b	15.	a
5.	a	16.	b
6.	b	17.	d
7.	b	18.	b
8.	c	19.	d
9.	b	20.	a
10.	b	21.	b
11.	a		

Problems

1. a.
Semimonthly wages ($1,800 ÷ 2):	$900.00
Allowance value:	-137.50
Wages subject to withholding:	$762.50
Percentage method formula:	-417.00
	345.50
	x .15
	$ 51.83
	+30.70
FITW:	$ 82.53

b.
Monthly wages ($42,500 ÷ 12):	$3,541.67
Allowance value ($275.00 x 3):	- 825.00
Wages subject to withholding:	2,716.67
Percentage method formula:	- 1,908.00
	808.67
	x .15
	$121.30
	+124.10
FITW:	$245.40

c.
Weekly wages ($27,500 ÷ 52):	$528.85
Allowance value ($63.46 x 2):	- 126.92
Wages subject to withholding:	401.93
Percentage method formula:	- 192.00
	209.93
	x .15
	$ 31.49
	+14.10
FITW:	$ 45.59

2. a.
Quarterly wages ($72,000 ÷ 4):	$18,000.00
Allowance value ($825.00 x 4):	-3,300.00
Wages subject to withholding:	14,700.00
Percentage method formula:	-5,725.00
	8,975.00
	x .15
	$ 1,346.25
	+372.50
FITW:	$1,718.75

b. Weekly wages [($2,650 x 12) ÷ 52]: $611.54
Allowance value: - 63.46
Wages subject to withholding: 548.08
Percentage method formula: - 192.00
356.08
x .15
$ 53.41
+14.10
FITW: $ 67.51

c. Biweekly wages ($53,000 ÷ 26): $2,038.46
Allowance value ($126.92 x 3): -380.76
Wages subject to withholding: 1,657.70
Percentage method formula: - 881.00
776.70
x .15
$116.51
+57.30
FITW: 173.81

3. $24.00

4. Annual wages = $1,200 x 26 payroll periods = $31,200

Withholding using the percentage method:

Gross wages: $31,200.00
Allowance value ($3,300 x 3): - 9,900.00
Wages subject to withholding: $21,300.00
Percentage method formula: - 8,000.00
$13,300.00
x .10
$1,330.00

Withholding per payroll period = $1,330.00 ÷ 26 = $51.15

5. Annual wages = $6,000 x 12 payroll periods = $72,000

Withholding using the percentage method:

Gross wages: $72,000.00
Allowance value ($3,300 x 2): - 6,600.00
Wages subject to withholding: $65,400.00
Percentage method formula: -32,240.00
$33,160.00
x .25
8,290.00
+ 4,071.00
$12,361.00

Withholding per payroll period = $12,361.00 ÷ 12 = $1,030.08

6. $2,000 x 25% = $500

7. a. FITW on regular wages = $15
   b. FITW on supplemental wages = $1,000 x 25% = $250
   c. FITW on total wages $15 + $250 = $265

8. Total of latest wages and bonus ($1,200 + $750) = $1,950
    FITW on total amount (wage-bracket method) =   287
    FITW from latest wage payment =   - 129
    FITW from supplemental wage payment = $ 158

9. a. Using the flat rate method:
        FITW on regular wages = $ 67
        FITW on supplemental wages ($100 x 25%) =   + 25
        Total FITW = $67 + $25 = $ 92

    b. Using the aggregate method:
        FITW on $700 ($600 in regular wages plus $100 bonus) = $84

10. Gross semimonthly wages $950.00
    Federal income tax withheld   - 20.00
    State income tax withheld   - 28.50
    Social security tax withheld   - 58.90
    Medicare tax withheld   - 13.78
    Advance EIC payments   +44.00
    Net pay $872.82

11. Social security: $430 x 6.2% = $26.66

    Medicare: $430 x 1.45% = $6.24

12. Weekly wages: $36,000 ÷ 52 = $692.31

    Social security: $692.31 x 6.2% = $42.92

    Medicare: $692.31 x 1.45% = $10.04

13. Social security wage limit: $94,200
    Wages paid to date ($2,025 x 46):   -93,150
    Social security taxable wages this pay: 1,050
                                                      x 6.2%
    Social security tax to withhold: $ 65.10

    Medicare taxable wages this pay: $2,025
                                                      x 1.45%
    Medicare tax to withhold: $29.36

14. Social security wage limit: $94,200
    Wages paid to date ($8,300 x 11):   -91,300
    Social security taxable wages this pay: 2,900
                                                      x 6.2%
    Social security tax to withhold: $ 179.80

    Medicare taxable wages this pay: $8,300
                                                      x 1.45%
    Medicare tax to withhold: $ 120.35

SECTION 7: UNEMPLOYMENT INSURANCE

Review Questions

1. The normal credit against FUTA tax liability equals the amount of an employer's required contributions that are timely paid into a certified state unemployment insurance fund. It is also called the 90% credit because the amount of the credit is limited to 90% of the basic 6.0% FUTA tax rate.

2. The following individuals can sign an employer's Form 940:

   - the individual owning the business if it is a sole proprietorship,
   - the president, vice president, or other principal corporate officer, if the employer is a corporation (including a limited liability company treated as a corporation),
   - an authorized member or partner of an unincorporated association or partnership (including a limited liability company treated as a partnership) having knowledge of the organization's affairs
   - the owner, if it is a single member limited liability company treated as a disregarded entity, or
   - a fiduciary if the employer is a trust or estate.

3. A Form 940 that is mailed through the U.S. Postal Service is considered filed at the time it is postmarked by the U.S. Postal Service.

4. Employers that cease doing business must file a Form 940 for the portion of the last calendar year they were in business and check Box b in the upper right hand corner of page 1 indicating no future returns will be filed. The employer must also attach a statement to the form including the following information: the location where required records will be kept; who is responsible for keeping the records; and the name and address of the purchaser of the business or the fact that there was no purchaser or that the purchaser's name is unknown.

5. Unless there is reasonable cause and no willful neglect, late payment of tax owed as shown on Form 940 results in an "addition to tax," the amount of which depends on how late the payment is made. The amounts are:

   - 5% of any unpaid tax shown on the return (after accounting for credits) for each month or fraction of a month that the payment is late, up to a maximum of 25%, and

   - an additional 0.5% per month of any unpaid tax that is not shown on the return but for which the IRS has issued a notice and demand, if the tax is not paid within 21 calender days days of the notice and demand (10 business days if the amount is at least $100,000), up to a maximum of 25%.

6. The four factors used by employers in allocating employees who work in more than one state for purposes of unemployment insurance are:

   - Are services "localized?"
   - Does the employee have a "base of operations?"
   - Is there a "place of direction or control?"
   - What is the employee's "state of residence?"

7. The following employers are not subject to FUTA tax:

   - federal, state, and local government employers, including their political subdivisions,

   - Indian tribes; and

   - nonprofit religious, charitable, or educational organizations that are tax-exempt.

8. Following is a list of several FUTA exempt payments:

   - sick or disability pay paid more than six calendar months after the last month the employee worked for an employer;

   - sickness or injury payments made under a state workers' compensation law or a law in the nature of a workers' compensation law;

   - payments made under a deferred compensation plan, except elective deferrals to the plan;

   - noncash payments to an employee for work done outside the employer's trade or business;

   - qualified moving expense reimbursements;

   - death or disability retirement benefits;

   - noncash payments to agricultural workers;

   - reimbursements for, or provision of deductible dependent care assistance;

   - value of group-term life insurance coverage;

   - value of deductible meals and lodging provided by the employer;

   - wages owed to a deceased employee and paid to a beneficiary after the year of the employee's death; and

   - tips not reported by an employee to an employer (generally if less that $20 a month).

9. Following is a list of several types of employment that are exempt from FUTA:

   - work on a foreign ship outside the U.S.;

   - work done by full-time students for the school where they attend classes or for an organized camp;

   - work performed as student nurses or hospital interns;

   - life insurance agents who receive only commissions;

   - newspaper deliverers under age 18 who deliver directly to customers;

   - certain nonimmigrant aliens working under F, J, M or Q visas;

   - work performed for a spouse or child;

   - work performed by a child under age 21 for his or her parents;

- work performed by an inmate of a penal institution;

- work performed by an election worker who is paid less than $1,300 in 2006;

- work performed by alien agricultural workers under an H-2A visa; and

- work performed by statutory nonemployees.

10. Employers that make an error on Form 940 need to file an amended return. They do this by filing a new Form 940 for the year being amended with the correct numbers. Box a in the upper right corner of page 1 indicating an amended return should be checked. The form should be accompanied by a statement as to why the amended return is necessary.

11. The four methods used to determine an employer's unemployment insurance experience rating are:

   - Reserve ratio
   - Benefit ratio
   - Benefit-wage ratio
   - Payroll stabilization

12. The voluntary contribution option is often made unavailable to:

   - new employers,
   - negative reserve balance employers, and
   - employers that have not paid state taxes on time.

13. When faced with a claim for unemployment benefits, the employer should:

   - be complete and truthful in listing the grounds for an employee's termination when responding to forms and notices from the unemployment benefits agency;

   - document any and all evidence of misconduct that may be needed to challenge a claim for benefits;

   - respond to notices and requests for information within the time frame allowed;

   - detail any final payments made to terminated employees, since they may disqualify the employee, at least temporarily; and

   - urge the unemployment agency to make sure the claimant is looking for work.

14. The following standards must be met for employees to be eligible for unemployment benefits:

   - earning a certain amount of wages in the "base period";

   - being involuntarily unemployed for reasons other than misconduct connected with their work;

   - filing a claim for benefits;

   - registering for work with the state employment security office;

- being physically and mentally able to work;

- be looking for and available for work (other than during time spent on job training or jury duty);

- not being unemployed because of a labor dispute other than a lockout;

- being truthful in applying for benefits.

True or False Questions

1. True

2. True

3. False   The employer receives the normal credit for timely payments it makes.

4. True

5. False   Nonprofit and public sector employers may choose the direct reimbursement method or the experience-rated method to satisfy their state unemployment insurance liability.

6. True

7. True

8. True

9. False   The employer must file Form 940 annually, no later than January 31 following the close of the calendar year.

10. True

11. False   If the employer's FUTA tax liability is more than $500, a deposit is required.

12. False   If the FUTA tax deposit due date falls on a Saturday, the deposit is due on the next business day.

13. True

14. False   FUTA tax is based on the first $7,000 in wages paid to each employee in 2006.

15. True

16. True

17. False   If an employee works for more than one employer, the wage limit must be applied to the wages paid by each employer.

18. True

19. False   Employers that have a great deal of turnover generally have a higher experience rate.

20. True

21. False   The period for which a terminated employee is eligible to claim benefits is known as the "benefit year."

22. True

23. False   Employees whose hours are reduced are also eligible, so long as they are not earning more than the weekly benefit amount.

Multiple Choice Questions

1.	a	10.	b
2.	c	11.	b
3.	b	12.	c
4.	a	13.	c
5.	d	14.	d
6.	b	15.	c
7.	c	16.	a
8.	a	17.	b
9.	c	18.	b

Problems

1. a. $14,000 x .008 = $112

   b. No, because the liability did not exceed $500.

2. a. $70,000 x .008 = $560

   b. $70,000 x .032 = $2,240

   c. $560 + $2,240 = $2,800

3. a. $7,000 x 5 x 6.2% = $2,170

   b. $7,000 x 5 x 5.4% = $1,890

   c. $2,170 - $1,890 = $280

4. Six employees earned $7,000 or more during the first quarter.

   Taxable wages:
   $7,000 x 6 = $42,000
                        + 6,000
                        + 3,150
                        + 4,600
                        + 5,400
   Total taxable wages: $61,150

   1st quarter FUTA liability = $61,150 x .008 = $489.20

5. a. $6,000 x .049 = $294

   b. $1,000 x .049 = $49

   c. $7,000 x .008 = $56

6. a. $6,600 x .008 = $52.80

   b. $7,000 x .008 = $56

7. a. Gross FUTA tax:

Total wages paid during 2005: $72,680 - $1,700 =	$70,980.00
Wages paid in excess of $7,000:	-26,230.00
Total taxable wages:	44,750.00
Rate of tax:	x 6.2%
Amount of gross FUTA tax:	$ 2,774.50

   b. State tax credit:

Total taxable wages:	$44,750.00
Credit against tax:	x 5.4%
Total credit:	$ 2,416.50

   c. Net FUTA tax: $2,774.50 - $2,416.50 = $358

8. Four employees earned $7,000 or more during the first quarter.

Taxable wages:	
David Jones	$ 7,000
Sheryl Smith	7,000
Johnny Foster	7,000
Melissa Denney	5,400
Jackie Stewart	7,000
Kathy Jensen	4,300
Paul Thornton	2,600
Total	$40,300

   1st quarter FUTA tax liability: $40,300 x .008 = $322.40

9. See the completed Form 940 on pages 38 and 39.

10. a.   First quarter:

$1,800 x 10 x 3 months = $ 54,000
$2,000 x 6 x 3 months =   36,000
$1,000 x 4 x 3 months =   12,000
FUTA taxable wages: $102,000

Net 1st quarter FUTA tax: $102,000 x .008 = $816

Second quarter:

$1,600 x 10 x 1 month = $16,000
$1,000 x 6 x 1 month =   6,000
$1,000 x 4 x 3 months =   12,000
FUTA taxable wages: $34,000

Net 2nd quarter FUTA tax: $34,000 x .008 = $272

Third quarter:

$1,000 x 4 x 1 month = $4,000

Net 3rd quarter FUTA tax: $4,000 x .008 = $32

b.   Taxable wages   FUTA Tax

   1st Quarter $102,000
   2nd Quarter   34,000
   3rd Quarter   4,000
   Total $140,000 x 2.2% =$3,080

Less year-to-date liability   -1,120
($816 + $272 + $32)
4th quarter liability $1,960

11. See the completed Form 940 on pages 40 and 41, and the completed Schedule A on page 42.

12. See the completed Form 940 on pages 43 and 44, and the completed Schedule A on page 45.

Problem 9

Form 940 for 2006: Employer's Annual Federal Unemployment (FUTA) Tax Return
999999

Department of the Treasury — Internal Revenue Service   OMB No. 1545-0028

Employer identification number (EIN) 2 2 - 3 4 1 2 3 4 5

Name (*not your trade name*): Fine Arts

Trade name (*if any*):

Address: 31 West Street

Number   10/26/2005 1:45 PM   Suite or room number

Tulsa, OK   OK   98243

City   State   ZIP code

Type of Return (Check all that apply)
- a. Amended
- b. Successor employer
- c. No payments to employees in 2006.
- d. Final: Business closed or stopped paying wages

Read the separate instructions before you fill out this form. Please type or print within the boxes.

1. If you were required to pay your state unemployment tax in ...

   1a. **One** state only, write the state abbreviation .... 1a O K

   - OR -

   1b. **More than one** state (You are a multi-state employer) ... 1b ☐ Check here. Fill out Schedule A

2. If you paid wages in [Name of State], a state that is subject to CREDIT REDUCTION ... 2 ☐ Check here. Fill out Schedule A (Form 940), Part 2.

Part 2: Determine your FUTA wages for 2006. If any line does NOT apply, leave it blank.

3. Total payments to all employees	3	69000 . 00
4. Payments exempt from FUTA tax	4	.

Check all that apply: 4a ☐ Fringe benefits   4c ☐ Retirement/Pension   4e ☐ Other
4b ☐ Group term life insurance   4d ☐ Dependent care

5. Total of payments made to each employee in excess of $7,000	5	27000 . 00
6. Subtotal (line 4 + line 5 = line 6)	6	27000 . 00
7. Total taxable FUTA wages (line 3 – line 6 = line 7)	7	42000 . 00
8. FUTA tax before adjustments (line 7 x .008 = line 8)	8	336 . 00

Part 3: Determine your adjustments. If any line does NOT apply, leave it blank.

9. If ALL of the FUTA wages you paid were excluded from state unemployment tax (line 7 x .054 = line 9) Then go to line 12.	9	.
10. If SOME of the FUTA wages you paid were excluded from state unemployment tax, OR you paid ANY state unemployment tax late (after the due date for filing Form 940), fill out the worksheet in the instructions. Enter the amount from line 7 of the worksheet onto line 10.	10	.
11. If credit reduction applies, enter the amount from line 3 of Schedule A (Form 940)	11	.

Part 4: Determine your FUTA tax for 2006. If any line does NOT apply, leave it blank.

12. Total FUTA tax after adjustments (lines 8 + 9 + 10 + 11 = line 12)	12	336 . 00
13. FUTA tax deposited for the year, including any payment applied from a prior year	13	336 . 00
14. Balance due (line 12 – line 13 = line 14) • If line 14 is more than $500, you must deposit your tax. • If line 14 is $500 or less and you pay by check, make your check payable to the United States Treasury and write your EIN, *Form 940*, and 2006 on the check.	14	.
15. Overpayment (If line 13 is more than line 12, enter the difference on line 15 and check a box below.)	15	.

Check one: ☐ Apply overpayment to next return. ☐ Send a refund.

Next ➡

▶ **You MUST fill out both pages of this form and SIGN it.**

For Privacy Act and Paperwork Reduction Act Notice, see the back of Form 940-V: Payment Voucher.   Cat. No. 112340   Form **940** (2006)

Problem 9 continued

Name (not your trade name) Fine Arts	**Employer identification number (EIN)** 2 2 - 3 4 1 2 3 4 5

Part 5: Report your FUTA tax liability by quarter only if line 12 is more than $500. If not, go to Part 6.

16. Report the amount of your FUTA tax liability for each quarter; do NOT enter the amount you deposited. If you had no liability for a quarter, leave the line blank.

16a.	1st quarter	(January 1 – March 31)	16a	110.40
16b.	2nd quarter	(April 1 – June 30)	16b	122.40
16c.	3rd quarter	(July 1 – September 30)	16c	61.60
16d.	4th quarter	(October 1 – December 31)	16d	41.60

17. **Total tax liability for the year** (lines 16a + 16b + 16c + 16d = line 17) .... **17**   336.00   Total must equal line 12.

Part 6: May we speak with your third-party designee?

Do you want to allow an employee, a paid tax preparer, or another person to discuss this return with the IRS? See the instructions for details.

☐ Yes.   Designee's name....

Select a 5-digit Personal Identification Number (PIN) to use when talking to IRS...... ☐ ☐ ☐ ☐ ☐

☑ No

Part 7: Sign here

You MUST fill out both pages of this form and SIGN it.

Under penalties of perjury, I declare that I have examined this return, including accompanying schedules and statements, and to the best of my knowledge and belief, it is true, correct, and complete, and that no part of any payment made to a state unemployment fund claimed as a credit was, or is to be, deducted from the payments made to employees.

✗ Sign your name here

Print your name here

Print your title here

Date   /   /

Best daytime phone ( )

Part 8: For paid preparers only (optional)

If you were paid to prepare this return and are not an employee of the business that is filing this return, you may choose to fill out Part 8.

Paid Preparer's name......

Paid Preparer's signature.

☐ Check if you are self employed

Preparer's SSN/PTIN ...

Date ...   /   /

Draft

Firm's name......

Street address ...

City ....   State ......

Firm's EIN ......

ZIP code ....

Problem 11

Form 940 for 2006: Employer's Annual Federal Unemployment (FUTA) Tax Return

999999

Department of the Treasury — Internal Revenue Service   OMB No. 1545-0028

Employer identification number (EIN)   8 6 - 2 3 4 5 6 7 8

Name (*not your trade name*)   Conrow Lumber Company

Trade name (*if any*)

Address   1234 San Francisco Street

Number   Suite or room number

San Francisco   CA   56789

City   State   ZIP code

Type of Return (Check all that apply)

- [ ] a. Amended
- [ ] b. Successor employer
- [ ] c. No payments to employees in 2006.
- [ ] d. Final: Business closed or stopped paying wages

Read the separate instructions before you fill out this form. Please type or print within the boxes.

1. If you were required to pay your state unemployment tax in ...

1a. *One* **state only,** write the state abbreviation .... 1a [ ][ ]

- OR -

1b. *More than one* state (You are a multi-state employer) ... 1b [✓] Check here. Fill out Schedule A

2. If you paid wages in [Name of State], a state that is subject to CREDIT REDUCTION ... 2 [ ] Check here. Fill out Schedule A (Form 940), Part 2.

Part 2: Determine your FUTA wages for 2006. If any line does NOT apply, leave it blank.

3.	Total payments to all employees	3	600000 . 00
4.	Payments exempt from FUTA tax	4	.

Check all that apply: **4a** [ ] Fringe benefits   **4c** [ ] Retirement/Pension   **4e** [ ] Other

4b [ ] Group term life insurance   **4d** [ ] Dependent care

5.	Total of payments made to each employee in excess of $7,000	5	460000.00
6.	Subtotal (line 4 + line 5 = line 6)	6	460000.00
7.	Total taxable FUTA wages (line 3 – line 6 = line 7)	7	140000.00
8.	FUTA tax before adjustments (line 7 x .008 = line 8)	8	1120.00

Part 3: Determine your adjustments. If any line does NOT apply, leave it blank.

9. If ALL of the FUTA wages you paid were excluded from state unemployment tax (line 7 x .054 = line 9) Then go to line 12. .... 9 | . |

10. If SOME of the FUTA wages you paid were excluded from state unemployment tax, OR you paid ANY state unemployment tax late (after the due date for filing Form 940), fill out the worksheet in the instructions. Enter the amount from line 7 of the worksheet onto line 10. .... 10 | . |

11. If credit reduction applies, enter the amount from line 3 of Schedule A (Form 940) .... 11 | . |

Part 4: Determine your FUTA tax for 2006. If any line does NOT apply, leave it blank.

12.	Total FUTA tax after adjustments (lines 8 + 9 + 10 + 11 = line 12)	12	1120.00
13.	FUTA tax deposited for the year, including any payment applied from a prior year	13	1120.00

14. Balance due (line 12 – line 13 = line 14)
- If line 14 is more than $500, you must deposit your tax.
- If line 14 is $500 or less and you pay by check, make your check payable to the United States Treasury and write your EIN, *Form 940,* and *2006* on the check.   14 | . |

15. Overpayment (If line 13 is more than line 12, enter the difference on line 15 and check a box below.)   15 | . |

Check one: [ ] Apply overpayment to next return.   [ ] Send a refund.

▶ **You MUST fill out both pages of this form and SIGN it.**   Next ➡

For Privacy Act and Paperwork Reduction Act Notice, see the back of Form 940-V: Payment Voucher.   Cat. No. 112340   Form **940** (2006)

Problem 11 continued

999999

Name (not your trade name) Conrow Lumber Company	Employer identification number (EIN) 8 6 - 2 3 4 5 6 7 8

Part 5: Report your FUTA tax liability by quarter only if line 12 is more than $500. If not, go to Part 6.

16. Report the amount of your FUTA tax liability for each quarter; do NOT enter the amount you deposited. If you had no liability for a quarter, leave the line blank.

16a.	1st quarter	(January 1 – March 31)	16a	896.00
16b.	2nd quarter	(April 1 – June 30)	16b	112.00
16c.	3rd quarter	(July 1 – September 30)	16c	56.00
16d.	4th quarter	(October 1 – December 31)	16d	56.00

17. **Total tax liability for the year** (lines 16a + 16b + 16c + 16d = line 17) 17   1120.00   Total must equal line 12.

Part 6: May we speak with your third-party designee?

Do you want to allow an employee, a paid tax preparer, or another person to discuss this return with the IRS? See the instructions for details.

☐ Yes.   Designee's name....

Select a 5-digit Personal Identification Number (PIN) to use when talking to IRS ..... ☐ ☐ ☐ ☐ ☐

☑ No

Part 7: Sign here

You MUST fill out both pages of this form and SIGN it.

Under penalties of perjury, I declare that I have examined this return, including accompanying schedules and statements, and to the best of my knowledge and belief, it is true, correct, and complete, and that no part of any payment made to a state unemployment fund claimed as a credit was, or is to be, deducted from the payments made to employees.

X   **Sign your name here**

Print your name here

Print your title here

Date   /   /

Best daytime phone ( )

Part 8: For paid preparers only (optional)

If you were paid to prepare this return and are not an employee of the business that is filing this return, you may choose to fill out Part 8.

Paid Preparer's name ....

Preparer's SSN/PTIN .....

Paid Preparer's signature .

Date ..... / /

☐ Check if you are self employed

Draft

Firm's name .....

Firm's EIN .....

Street address .....

City .....

State .....

ZIP code .....

Form **940** (2006)

Problem 11 continued

Schedule A (Form 940) for 2006:
Multi-State Employer and Credit Reduction Information

Department of the Treasury
Internal Revenue Service

999999

OMB No. 1545-0028

Employer identification number (EIN) 8 6 – 2 3 4 5 6 7 8

Name (*not your trade name*) Conrow Lumber Company

About this schedule:

- You must fill out Schedule A, Form 940 (*Employer's Annual Federal Unemployment Tax Return*) if you were required to pay your state unemployment tax in **more than one state** or if you paid wages in any state that is subject to **credit reduction.**
- Attach Schedule A to your Form 940 and file

For more information, read the Instructions for Schedule A (Form 940).

Part 1:   Fill out this part if you were required to pay state unemployment taxes in more than one state. If any states do NOT apply to you, leave them blank.

1. Check the box for every state in which you were required to pay state unemployment tax this year. For a list of state names and their abbreviations, see the Instructions for Schedule A (Form 940).

AK	CO	GA	IN	MD	MS	NH	OH	SC	VA	WY
AL	CT	HI	KS	MI	MT	NJ	OK	SD	VT	PR
AR	DC	IA	KY	MN	NC	NM	OR	TN	WA	VI
✓ AZ	DE	ID	LA	MO	ND	NV	PA	TX	WI	
✓ CA	FL	IL	MA	ME	NE	NY	RI	UT	WV	

Part 2:   Fill out this part to tell us about wages you paid in any state that is subject to credit reduction. If any lines do NOT apply, leave them blank.

2. If you paid wages in any of these states …

2a-b. [Name of State] Total taxable FUTA wages paid in [state] **2a.** [   ] x .00x = line 2b **2b** [   ]

2c-d. [Name of State] Total taxable FUTA wages paid in [state] **2c.** [   ] x .00x = line 2d **2d** [   ]

2e-f. [Name of State] Total taxable FUTA wages paid in [state] **2e.** [   ] x .00x = line 2f **2f** [   ]

2g-h. [Name of State] Total taxable FUTA wages paid in [state] **2g.** [   ] x .00x = line 2h **2h** [   ]

2i-j. [Name of State] Total taxable FUTA wages paid in [state] **2i.** [   ] x .00x = line 2j **2j** [   ]

3. Total credit reduction (Lines 2b + 2d + 2f + 2h + 2j = line 3) .... **3** [   ]

Enter the amount from line 3 onto line 11 of Form 940.

Problem 12

Form 940 for 2006: Employer's Annual Federal Unemployment (FUTA) Tax Return

Department of the Treasury — Internal Revenue Service   OMB No. 1545-0028

999999

Employer identification number (EIN)   8 2 – 4 0 2 0 3 0 4

Name (*not your trade name*)   MiloSuisse Textured Yarns

Trade name (*if any*)

Address   1000 East State Street

Number

Campton   FL   13579

City   State   ZIP code

Type of Return (Check all that apply)

- ☐ a. Amended
- ☐ b. Successor employer
- ☐ c. No payments to employees in 2006.
- ☐ d. Final: Business closed or stopped paying wages

Read the separate instructions before you fill out this form. Please type or print within the boxes.

1. If you were required to pay your state unemployment tax in ...

   1a. **One state only**, write the state abbreviation .... 1a ☐☐
   - OR -
   1b. **More than one** state (You are a multi-state employer) ... 1b ☑ Check here. Fill out Schedule A

2. If you paid wages in [Name of State], a state that is subject to CREDIT REDUCTION ... 2 ☐ Check here. Fill out Schedule A (Form 940), Part 2.

Part 2: Determine your FUTA wages for 2006. If any line does NOT apply, leave it blank.

3. Total payments to all employees	3	995500.00
4. Payments exempt from FUTA tax	4	56000.00

Check all that apply: 4a ☑ Fringe benefits   4c ☐ Retirement/Pension   4e ☐ Other
4b ☑ Group term life insurance   4d ☐ Dependent care

5. Total of payments made to each employee in excess of $7,000	5	589500.00
6. Subtotal (line 4 + line 5 = line 6)	6	645500.00
7. Total taxable FUTA wages (line 3 – line 6 = line 7)	7	350000.00
8. FUTA tax before adjustments (line 7 x .008 = line 8)	8	2800.00

Part 3: Determine your adjustments. If any line does NOT apply, leave it blank.

9. If ALL of the FUTA wages you paid were excluded from state unemployment tax (line 7 x .054 = line 9) Then go to line 12.	9	.
10. If SOME of the FUTA wages you paid were excluded from state unemployment tax, OR you paid ANY state unemployment tax late (after the due date for filing Form 940), fill out the worksheet in the instructions. Enter the amount from line 7 of the worksheet onto line 10.	10	.
11. If credit reduction applies, enter the amount from line 3 of Schedule A (Form 940)	11	.

Part 4: Determine your FUTA tax for 2006. If any line does NOT apply, leave it blank.

12. Total FUTA tax after adjustments (lines 8 + 9 + 10 + 11 = line 12)	12	2800.00
13. FUTA tax deposited for the year, including any payment applied from a prior year	13	2800.00

14. Balance due (line 12 – line 13 = line 14)
   - If line 14 is more than $500, you must deposit your tax.
   - If line 14 is $500 or less and you pay by check, make your check payable to the United States Treasury and write your EIN, *Form 940*, and *2006* on the check.

	14	.
15. Overpayment (If line 13 is more than line 12, enter the difference on line 15 and check a box below.)	15	.

Check one: ☐ Apply overpayment to next return.
☐ Send a refund.   Next ➡

▶ **You MUST fill out both pages of this form and SIGN it.**

For Privacy Act and Paperwork Reduction Act Notice, see the back of Form 940-V: Payment Voucher.   Cat. No. 112340   Form **940** (2006)

Problem 12 continued

999999

Name (not your trade name) MiloSuisse Textured Yarns	Employer identification number (EIN) 8 2 - 4 0 2 0 3 0 4

Part 5: Report your FUTA tax liability by quarter only if line 12 is more than $500. If not, go to Part 6.

16. Report the amount of your FUTA tax liability for each quarter; do NOT enter the amount you deposited. If you had no liability for a quarter, leave the line blank.

16a.	1st quarter	(January 1 – March 31)	16a	1350.00
16b.	2nd quarter	(April 1 – June 30)	16b	950.00
16c.	3rd quarter	(July 1 – September 30)	16c	350.00
16d.	4th quarter	(October 1 – December 31)	16d	150.00

17. Total tax liability for the year (lines 16a + 16b + 16c + 16d = line 17) .... 17 | 2800.00 | Total must equal line 12.

Part 6: May we speak with your third-party designee?

Do you want to allow an employee, a paid tax preparer, or another person to discuss this return with the IRS? See the instructions for details.

☐ Yes. Designee's name.....

Select a 5-digit Personal Identification Number (PIN) to use when talking to IRS...... ☐☐☐☐☐

☑ No

Part 7: Sign here

You MUST fill out both pages of this form and SIGN it.

Under penalties of perjury, I declare that I have examined this return, including accompanying schedules and statements, and to the best of my knowledge and belief, it is true, correct, and complete, and that no part of any payment made to a state unemployment fund claimed as a credit was, or is to be, deducted from the payments made to employees.

X **Sign your name here** | Print your name here |
| Print your title here |

Date | / / | Best daytime phone | ( )

Part 8: For paid preparers only (optional)

If you were paid to prepare this return and are not an employee of the business that is filing this return, you may choose to fill out Part 8.

Paid Preparer's name....... | Preparer's SSN/PTIN ...
Paid Preparer's signature | Date.......... | / /

☐ Check if you are self employed

Draft

Firm's name.............. | Firm's EIN ....
Street address ....
City | State | ZIP code ....

Page **2**

Form **940** (2006)

Problem 12 continued

Schedule A (Form 940) for 2006:
Multi-State Employer and Credit Reduction Information

Department of the Treasury
Internal Revenue Service

999999

OMB No. 1545-0028

Employer identification number (EIN) 8 2 - 4 0 2 0 3 0 4

Name (*not your trade name*) MiloSuisse Textured Yarns

About this schedule:

- You must fill out Schedule A, Form 940 (*Employer's Annual Federal Unemployment Tax Return*) if you were required to pay your state unemployment tax in **more than one state** or if you paid wages in any state that is subject to **credit reduction**.
- Attach Schedule A to your Form 940 and file ~~10/26/2005 1:50 PM~~

For more information, read the Instructions for Schedule A (Form 940).

Part 1: Fill out this part if you were required to pay state unemployment taxes in more than one state. If any states do NOT apply to you, leave them blank.

1. Check the box for every state in which you were required to pay state unemployment tax this year. For a list of state names and their abbreviations, see the Instructions for Schedule A (Form 940).

Checked: MS, AZ, CA, FL

Part 2: Fill out this part to tell us about wages you paid in any state that is subject to credit reduction. If any lines do NOT apply, leave them blank.

2. If you paid wages in any of these states ...

2a-b. [Name of State] Total taxable FUTA wages paid in [state] 2a.	x .00x = line 2b	2b.
2c-d. [Name of State] Total taxable FUTA wages paid in [state] 2c.	x .00x = line 2d	2d.
2e-f. [Name of State] Total taxable FUTA wages paid in [state] 2e.	x .00x = line 2f	2f.
2g-h. [Name of State] Total taxable FUTA wages paid in [state] 2g.	x .00x = line 2h	2h.
2i-j. [Name of State] Total taxable FUTA wages paid in [state] 2i.	x .00x = line 2j	2j.

3. Total credit reduction (Lines 2b+ 2d+ 2f +2h+ 2j = line 3) 3

Enter the amount from line 3 onto line 11 of Form 940.

SECTION 8: DEPOSITING AND REPORTING WITHHELD TAXES

Review Questions

1. Monthly depositors must deposit their accumulated tax liability for each calendar month by the 15th of the following month.

   Semiweekly depositors must deposit their payroll tax liability for wages paid on Wednesday, Thursday and Friday by the following Wednesday. The payroll tax liability for wages paid on Saturday, Sunday, Monday, and Tuesday must be paid by the following Friday.

   If an employer's accumulated payroll tax liability reaches $100,000 on any day during a monthly or semiweekly deposit period, the liability must be deposited by the close of the next banking day.

2. Under the "shortfall" rule, employers are not penalized for depositing a small amount less than the entire amount of their deposit obligation. An employer satisfies its deposit obligation if the shortfall is no more than the greater of $100 or 2% of the entire amount due and the shortfall is made up by the appropriate "make-up" date.

3. Deposits that are mailed through the U.S. Postal Service are considered timely if postmarked at least two days before the due date. However, deposits of $20,000 or more made by a semiweekly depositor must be received by the deposit due date. This rule also applies to private delivery services if they have qualified under IRS rules as "designated".

4. Form 8109 is a Federal Tax Deposit Coupon, and it is used to deposit withheld federal income and employment taxes (among other taxes) with a financial institution that is authorized to accept federal tax deposits.

5. Individuals who are responsible for collecting, accounting for, and paying over withheld income and employment taxes and who willfully fail to do so are subject to an additional penalty equal to the total amount of the taxes owed. This is known as the "Trust Fund Recovery Penalty" or the "100% penalty."

6. If a Form W-2c cannot be delivered to an employee after a reasonable effort to do so has been made, the employer must keep the form for four years.

7. Employers that fail to withhold or deposit taxes or file returns on time may be required by the IRS to report employment taxes monthly on Form 941-M rather than quarterly.

8. Take the following steps to obtain an EIN by phone:

   - complete Form SS-4 before calling;

   - call 800-829-4933;

   - provide the requested information from Form SS-4; and

   - if requested by the IRS representative, mail or fax Form SS-4 within 24 hours to the Tele-TIN unit at the service center address provided by the representative.

9. The lookback period is the 12-month period running from July 1 of the second previous year through June 30 of the previous year.

10. March 5, 2006 through June 30, 2006.

11. Mark's deposit obligation as of July 14 is $110,000. It must be deposited by the close of the next banking day (Monday, July 17). Mark becomes a semiweekly depositor for the rest of 2006 and all of 2007.

12. The following are the penalties for not making payroll tax deposits on time:

    • 2% of the undeposited amount if it is deposited within 5 days of the due date;

    • 5% of the undeposited amount if it is deposited within 6-15 days of the due date;

    • 10% of the undeposited amount if it is deposited more than 15 days after the due date; or

    • 15% of the undeposited amount if it is not paid within 10 days after the employer receives its first IRS delinquency notice or on the same day that a notice and demand for payment is received.

13. An employer that will no longer be in business and will not be paying wages subject to federal income withholding, social security, and Medicare taxes should do the following:

    • check the box on Line 16 when completing its last Form 941 indicating that it will not file any returns in the future;

    • enter the date that final wages were paid;

    • attach a statement showing the address where the employer's records will be kept, the name of the person keeping the records, and, if the business has been sold or transferred, the name and address of the new owner and the date of the sale or transfer;

    • file the Form 941 by the end of the first month after the end of the quarter during which the employer stopped paying wages; and

    • file Schedule D (Form 941), *Report of Discrepancies Caused by Acquisitions, Statutory Mergers, or Consolidations*, if the employer is no longer in business as the result of a statutory merger or consolidation, or if it qualifies as a predecessor or successor after an acquisition.

14. Enter on Line 7a the difference between the total security and Medicare taxes on Line 5d and the amount actually withheld from employees' wages and paid by the employer that is due to rounding to the nearest penny.

15. Schedule B records an employer's payroll tax liability, not its deposits. Semiweekly depositors at any time during a quarter must file a Schedule B with Form 941.

16. Form 945, *Annual Return of Withheld Federal Income Tax.*

17. Unless an employer has reasonable cause and is not guilty of willful neglect, late filing of Form 941 or other employment tax returns results in an "addition to tax," the amount of which depends on how late the return is filed. The amount is: 5% of the amount of tax required to be shown on the return (after accounting for deposits and credits) for each month or fraction of a month that the return is late, to a maximum of 25% (15% per month to a maximum of 75% of the unpaid tax if the late filing is fraudulent).

18. The purpose of backup withholding is to ensure that income tax is paid on income reported on Form 1099.

19. The amounts compared by the SSA include:

   - social security wages,
   - social security tips,
   - Medicare wages and tips, and
   - advance earned income credit payments.

20. The general penalties for failure to file information returns on time and with correct information are as follows:

   - $15 per return if the failure to file or provide correct information is corrected within 30 days after the due date, with a maximum penalty of $75,000 a year ($25,000 for small businesses);

   - $30 per return if the failure to file or provide correct information is corrected more than 30 days after the due date but before August 1 of the same year the return is due, with a maximum penalty of $150,000 a year ($50,000 for small businesses); and

   - $50 per return if the failure to file or provide correct information is not corrected by August 1, with a maximum penalty of $250,000 ($100,000 for small businesses).

True or False Questions

1. False   Employees with less than $200,000 in total tax deposits in 2004 do not have to use EFTPS in 2006 unless they were required to use it in 2005.

2. False   New employers are classified as monthly depositors.

3. False   At least 98% of the tax liability (or the liability - $100, if that is less) must be deposited to avoid a late payment penalty.

4. True

5. True

6. False   Form SS-4 is filed with the IRS, not the SSA.

7. False   This scenario creates 2 separate deposit obligations that must be satisfied by the same day.

8. True

9. False   For calendar year 2006, the payroll tax deposit lookback period is July 1, 2004 - June 30, 2005.

10. False   The employer is a monthly depositor for 2006 because its total payroll tax liability for the 2006 lookback period is less than $50,000.

11. True

12. False   Deposits by U.S. mail are considered timely if postmarked at least two days before the due date, although deposits of $20,000 or more made by semiweekly depositors must be received by the deposit due date.

13. True

14. True

15. False   The employer has the option to either deposit the amount or pay it with Form 941.

16. True

17. False   When recovering undercollections from employees, each employee must be treated separately, so an overcollection of taxes from one employee cannot be used to offset an undercollection from another.

18. True

19. False   Allocated tips should not be included in Box 1, 5, or 7 of Form W-2, but they should be included in Box 8.

20. False   In general, employers wishing to use substitute W-2 forms should not send a sample to the IRS or SSA for approval prior to use.

21. True

22. True

23. False   Nonprofit organizations engaged in a trade or business are not exempt from Form 1099 reporting requirements.

24. False   Forms 1099 must be sent to the IRS Service Center listed on the 1099 series instructions.

25. True

Multiple Choice Questions

1.	c	14.	b
2.	d	15.	b
3.	a	16.	d
4.	d	17.	b
5.	c	18.	d
6.	c	19.	c
7.	b	20.	d
8.	b	21.	a
9.	a	22.	c
10.	d	23.	a
11.	b	24.	c
12.	c	25.	b
13.	a		

Problems

1. J   Sick pay not included as income
    C   Value of group-term life insurance over $50,000
    E   Section 403(b) elective deferrals
    Q   Nontaxable combat pay
    D   Section 401(k) elective deferrals
    G   Section 457(b) elective deferrals
    W   Health savings account contributions
    T   Adoption benefits
    AA   Designated Roth contributions to a Section 401(k) plan
    P   Excludable moving expense reimbursements paid to employees
    F   Section 408(k)(6) elective deferrals
    H   Section 501(c)(18)(D) elective deferrals
    Y   Deferrals under a Section 409A nonqualified deferred compensation plan
    B   Uncollected Medicare tax on tips
    R   Medical savings account contributions
    A   Uncollected social security tax on tips
    V   Nonstatutory stock options
    BB   Designated Roth contributions to Section 403(b) plan
    L   Nontaxable part of employee business expense reimbursements
    K   Tax on excess golden parachute payments
    Z   Income under Section 409A on a nonqualified deferred compensation plan
    M   Uncollected social security tax on value of group-term life insurance coverage over $50,000
    N   Uncollected Medicare tax on value of group-term life insurance coverage over $50,000
    S   SIMPLE retirement account contributions

2. See the completed Form 941 on page 51—52.

3. See the completed Form 941 on page 53—54.

4. See the completed Form 941 and Schedule B on pages 55—57.

5. See the completed Forms W-2 and Form W-3 on pages 58—60.

6. a. No penalty is imposed for 13 of the failures to provide correct information (i.e., the greater of 10 or 0.5% x 2,600 = 13).

    Late returns subject to penalty: 40 - 13 = 27

    b. 27 x $30 = $810 since the corrections were made more than 30 days after the due date (March 31) but before August 1.

7. a. No penalty is imposed for 10 of the failures to provide correct information (i.e., the greater of 10 or 0.5% x 1,400 = 7).

    Late returns subject to penalty: 30 - 10 = 20

    b. 20 x $30 = $600 since the corrections were made more than 30 days after the due date (March 31) but before August 1.

8. (50 x $50 maximum penalty) = $2,500 since the returns were filed after August 1.

9. 380 - 249 = 131 returns subject to penalty.

Problem 2

Form 941 for 2005: Employer's Quarterly Federal Tax Return

(Rev. January 2005)

Department of the Treasury — Internal Revenue Service

9901

OMB No. 1545-0029

Employer identification number ☐☐ – ☐☐☐☐☐☐☐

Name *(not your trade name)* Allied Steel Products

Trade name *(if any)*

Address

Number | Street | Suite or room number

City | State | ZIP code

Report for this Quarter ...
(Check one.)

☐ **1:** January, February, March

☐ **2:** April, May, June

☐ **3:** July, August, September

☑ **4:** October, November, December

Read the separate instructions before you fill out this form. Please type or print within the boxes.

Part 1: Answer these questions for this quarter.

1 Number of employees who received wages, tips, or other compensation for the pay period including: *Mar. 12 (Quarter 1), June 12 (Quarter 2), Sept. 12 (Quarter 3), Dec. 12 (Quarter 4)* — **1** — 18

2 Wages, tips, and other compensation — **2** — 83254 . 90

3 Total income tax withheld from wages, tips, and other compensation — **3** — 8991 . 49

4 If no wages, tips, and other compensation are subject to social security or Medicare tax . . ☐ Check and go to line 6.

5 Taxable social security and Medicare wages and tips:

	Column 1		Column 2
5a Taxable social security wages	83254 . 90	× .124 =	10323 . 61
5b Taxable social security tips	.	× .124 =	.
5c Taxable Medicare wages & tips	83254 . 90	× .029 =	2414 . 39

5d Total social security and Medicare taxes (*Column 2*, lines 5a + 5b + 5c = line 5d) . **5d** — 12738 . 00

6 Total taxes before adjustments (lines 3 + 5d = line 6) . . . . **6** — 21729 . 49

7 Tax adjustments (If your answer is a negative number, write it in brackets.):

7a Current quarter's fractions of cents . . . . — .

7b Current quarter's sick pay . . . . — .

7c Current quarter's adjustments for tips and group-term life insurance — .

7d Current year's income tax withholding (Attach Form 941c) . . — .

7e Prior quarters' social security and Medicare taxes (Attach Form 941c) — .

7f Special additions to federal income tax (reserved use) . . . . — .

7g Special additions to social security and Medicare (reserved use) — .

7h Total adjustments (Combine all amounts: lines 7a through 7g.) . . . . . **7h** — .

8 Total taxes after adjustments (Combine lines 6 and 7h.) . . . . **8** — 21729 . 49

9 Advance earned income credit (EIC) payments made to employees . . . . . **9** — .

10 Total taxes after adjustment for advance EIC (lines 8 – 9 = line 10) . . . . . **10** — 21729 . 49

11 Total deposits for this quarter, including overpayment applied from a prior quarter . . **11** — 21729 . 49

12 Balance due (lines 10 – 11 = line 12) Make checks payable to the *United States Treasury* . **12** — .

13 Overpayment (If line 11 is more than line 10, write the difference here.) — . Check one ☐ Apply to next return. ☐ Send a refund.

Next ➡

For Privacy Act and Paperwork Reduction Act Notice, see the back of the Payment Voucher.

Cat. No. 17001Z   Form **941** (Rev. 1-2005)

Problem 2 continued

9902

Name *(not your trade name)* Allied Steel Products	Employer identification number

Part 2: Tell us about your deposit schedule for this quarter.

If you are unsure about whether you are a monthly schedule depositor or a semiweekly schedule depositor, see *Pub. 15 (Circular E)*, section 11.

14 ☐☐ Write the state abbreviation for the state where you made your deposits OR write "MU" if you made your deposits in *multiple* states.

15 Check one: ☐ Line 10 is less than $2,500. Go to Part 3.

☑ You were a monthly schedule depositor for the entire quarter. Fill out your tax liability for each month. Then go to Part 3.

Tax liability:	Month 1	9654 . 87	
	Month 2	5866 . 35	
	Month 3	6208 . 27	
	Total	21729 . 49	Total must equal line 10.

☐ You were a semiweekly schedule depositor for any part of this quarter. Fill out *Schedule B (Form 941): Report of Tax Liability for Semiweekly Schedule Depositors*, and attach it to this form.

Part 3: Tell us about your business. If a question does NOT apply to your business, leave it blank.

16 If your business has closed and you do not have to file returns in the future . . . . ☐ Check here, and

enter the final date you paid wages ☐ / / .

17 If you are a seasonal employer and you do not have to file a return for every quarter of the year . . ☐ Check here.

Part 4: May we contact your third-party designee?

Do you want to allow an employee, a paid tax preparer, or another person to discuss this return with the IRS? See the instructions for details.

☐ Yes. Designee's name

Phone ( ) – Personal Identification Number (PIN) ☐☐☐☐☐

☑ No.

Part 5: Sign here

Under penalties of perjury, I declare that I have examined this return, including accompanying schedules and statements, and to the best of my knowledge and belief, it is true, correct, and complete.

X

Sign your name here

Print name and title

Date / / Phone ( ) –

Part 6: For paid preparers only *(optional)*

Preparer's signature

Firm's name

Address _____ EIN _____

_____ ZIP code _____

Date / / Phone ( ) – SSN/PTIN _____

☐ Check if you are self-employed.

Form **941** (Rev. 1-2005)

Problem 3

Form **941 for 2005:** Employer's Quarterly Federal Tax Return

(Rev. January 2005)   Department of the Treasury — Internal Revenue Service

9901

OMB No. 1545-0029

Employer identification number ☐☐ – ☐☐☐☐☐☐☐

Name *(not your trade name)*   Value Carpet Center

Trade name *(if any)*

Address

Number   Street   Suite or room number

City   State   ZIP code

Report for this Quarter ...
(Check one.)

☐ **1:** January, February, March

☐ **2:** April, May, June

☑ **3:** July, August, September

☐ **4:** October, November, December

Read the separate instructions before you fill out this form. Please type or print within the boxes.

Part 1: Answer these questions for this quarter.

1	Number of employees who received wages, tips, or other compensation for the pay period including: *Mar. 12* (Quarter 1), *June 12* (Quarter 2), *Sept. 12* (Quarter 3), *Dec. 12* (Quarter 4) **1**	
2	Wages, tips, and other compensation **2**	36000 . 00
3	Total income tax withheld from wages, tips, and other compensation **3**	5800 . 00
4	If no wages, tips, and other compensation are subject to social security or Medicare tax . . ☐ Check and go to line 6.	
5	Taxable social security and Medicare wages and tips:	

	Column 1		Column 2	
5a Taxable social security wages	34000 . 00	× .124 =	4216 . 00	
5b Taxable social security tips	.	× .124 =	.	
5c Taxable Medicare wages & tips	36000 . 00	× .029 =	1044 . 00	

5d Total social security and Medicare taxes (*Column 2,* lines 5a + 5b + 5c = line 5d) . . **5d**		5260 . 00
6 Total taxes before adjustments (lines 3 + 5d = line 6) **6**		11060 . 00

7 Tax adjustments (If your answer is a negative number, write it in brackets.):

7a Current quarter's fractions of cents	.
7b Current quarter's sick pay	.
7c Current quarter's adjustments for tips and group-term life insurance	.
7d Current year's income tax withholding (Attach Form 941c) . .	.
7e Prior quarters' social security and Medicare taxes (Attach Form 941c)	.
7f Special additions to federal income tax (reserved use)	.
7g Special additions to social security and Medicare (reserved use)	.

7h Total adjustments (Combine all amounts: lines 7a through 7g.) **7h**		.
8 Total taxes after adjustments (Combine lines 6 and 7h.) **8**		11060 . 00
9 Advance earned income credit (EIC) payments made to employees **9**		1200 . 00
10 Total taxes after adjustment for advance EIC (lines 8 – 9 = line 10) **10**		9860 . 00
11 Total deposits for this quarter, including overpayment applied from a prior quarter . . . **11**		9860 . 00
12 Balance due (lines 10 – 11 = line 12) Make checks payable to the *United States Treasury* . **12**		.
13 Overpayment (If line 11 is more than line 10, write the difference here.)	.	Check one ☐ Apply to next return. ☐ Send a refund.

Next ➡

For Privacy Act and Paperwork Reduction Act Notice, see the back of the Payment Voucher.   Cat. No. 17001Z   Form **941** (Rev. 1-2005)

Problem 3 continued

9902

Name *(not your trade name)*	Employer identification number
Value Carpet Center	

Part 2: Tell us about your deposit schedule for this quarter.

If you are unsure about whether you are a monthly schedule depositor or a semiweekly schedule depositor, see *Pub. 15 (Circular E),* section 11.

14 ☐ ☐ Write the state abbreviation for the state where you made your deposits OR write "MU" if you made your deposits in *multiple* states.

15 Check one: ☐ **Line 10 is less than $2,500.** Go to Part 3.

☑ **You were a monthly schedule depositor for the entire quarter. Fill out your tax liability for each month.** Then go to Part 3.

Tax liability:	Month 1	3500 . 00
	Month 2	3500 . 00
	Month 3	2860 . 00
	Total	9860 . 00 Total must equal line 10.

☐ **You were a semiweekly schedule depositor for any part of this quarter.** Fill out *Schedule B (Form 941): Report of Tax Liability for Semiweekly Schedule Depositors,* and attach it to this form.

Part 3: Tell us about your business. If a question does NOT apply to your business, leave it blank.

16 If your business has closed and you do not have to file returns in the future . . . . ☐ Check here, and

enter the final date you paid wages [/ /] .

17 If you are a seasonal employer and you do not have to file a return for every quarter of the year . . ☐ Check here.

Part 4: May we contact your third-party designee?

Do you want to allow an employee, a paid tax preparer, or another person to discuss this return with the IRS? See the instructions for details.

☐ Yes. Designee's name _____

Phone ( ) – ___ Personal Identification Number (PIN) ☐ ☐ ☐ ☐ ☐

☑ No.

Part 5: Sign here

Under penalties of perjury, I declare that I have examined this return, including accompanying schedules and statements, and to the best of my knowledge and belief, it is true, correct, and complete.

X

Sign your name here	
Print name and title	
Date	/ / Phone ( ) –

Part 6: For paid preparers only *(optional)*

Preparer's signature	
Firm's name	
Address		EIN	
		ZIP code	
Date	/ / Phone ( ) –	SSN/PTIN	

☐ Check if you are self-employed.

Form **941** (Rev. 1-2005)

Problem 4

Form **941 for 2005:** **Employer's Quarterly Federal Tax Return**   9901
(Rev. January 2005)   Department of the Treasury — Internal Revenue Service
                                                                        OMB No. 1545-0029

Employer identification number | 4 | 3 | — | 1 | 2 | 3 | 4 | 5 | 6 | 7 |

Name *(not your trade name)*   Bimms & Ferrow, Inc.

Trade name *(if any)*

Address   3456 Mid West Street
           Number   Street   Suite or room number

           Kansas City | KS | 25783
           City   State   ZIP code

Report for this Quarter ...
(Check one.)

☐ 1: January, February, March
☐ 2: April, May, June
☑ 3: July, August, September
☐ 4: October, November, December

Read the separate instructions before you fill out this form. Please type or print within the boxes.

Part 1: Answer these questions for this quarter.

1 Number of employees who received wages, tips, or other compensation for the pay period
  including: *Mar. 12* (Quarter 1), *June 12* (Quarter 2), *Sept. 12* (Quarter 3), *Dec. 12* (Quarter 4)   1 | |

2 Wages, tips, and other compensation . . . . 2 | 2400000 . 00 |

3 Total income tax withheld from wages, tips, and other compensation . . . . . . 3 | 360000 . 00 |

4 If no wages, tips, and other compensation are subject to social security or Medicare tax . . ☐ Check and go to line 6.

5 Taxable social security and Medicare wages and tips:

	Column 1		Column 2	
5a Taxable social security wages	2000000 . 00	× .124 =	248000 . 00	
5b Taxable social security tips	.	× .124 =	.	
5c Taxable Medicare wages & tips	2400000 . 00	× .029 =	69600 . 00	

5d Total social security and Medicare taxes (*Column 2*, lines 5a + 5b + 5c = line 5d) . . 5d | 317600 . 00 |

6 Total taxes before adjustments (lines 3 + 5d = line 6) . . . . 6 | 677600 . 00 |

7 **Tax adjustments** (If your answer is a negative number, write it in brackets.):

7a Current quarter's fractions of cents . . . . | . |

7b Current quarter's sick pay . . . . | . |

7c Current quarter's adjustments for tips and group-term life insurance | . |

7d Current year's income tax withholding (Attach Form 941c) . . | . |

7e Prior quarters' social security and Medicare taxes (Attach Form 941c) | . |

7f Special additions to federal income tax (reserved use) . . . . | . |

7g Special additions to social security and Medicare (reserved use) | . |

7h Total adjustments (Combine all amounts: lines 7a through 7g.) . . . . . . 7h | . |

8 Total taxes after adjustments (Combine lines 6 and 7h.) . . . . 8 | 677600 . 00 |

9 Advance earned income credit (EIC) payments made to employees . . . . . . 9 | . |

10 Total taxes after adjustment for advance EIC (lines 8 – 9 = line 10) . . . . . . 10 | 677600 . 00 |

11 Total deposits for this quarter, including overpayment applied from a prior quarter . . 11 | 677600 . 00 |

12 Balance due (lines 10 – 11 = line 12) Make checks payable to the *United States Treasury* . . 12 | . |

13 Overpayment (If line 11 is more than line 10, write the difference here.) | . | Check one ☐ Apply to next return.
                                                                                          ☐ Send a refund.

                                                                                          Next ➡

For Privacy Act and Paperwork Reduction Act Notice, see the back of the Payment Voucher.   Cat. No. 17001Z   Form **941** (Rev. 1-2005)

Problem 4 continued

Name *(not your trade name)*	Employer identification number
Bimms & Ferrow, Inc.	43-1234567

Part 2: Tell us about your deposit schedule for this quarter.

If you are unsure about whether you are a monthly schedule depositor or a semiweekly schedule depositor, see *Pub. 15 (Circular E)*, section 11.

14 [K] [S] Write the state abbreviation for the state where you made your deposits OR write "MU" if you made your deposits in *multiple* states.

15 Check one: ☐ Line 10 is less than $2,500. Go to Part 3.

☐ You were a monthly schedule depositor for the entire quarter. Fill out your tax liability for each month. Then go to Part 3.

Tax liability: Month 1 [.]

Month 2 [.]

Month 3 [.]

Total [.] Total must equal line 10.

☑ You were a semiweekly schedule depositor for any part of this quarter. Fill out *Schedule B (Form 941): Report of Tax Liability for Semiweekly Schedule Depositors,* and attach it to this form.

Part 3: Tell us about your business. If a question does NOT apply to your business, leave it blank.

16 If your business has closed and you do not have to file returns in the future . . . . ☐ Check here, and

enter the final date you paid wages [/ /] .

17 If you are a seasonal employer and you do not have to file a return for every quarter of the year . . ☐ Check here.

Part 4: May we contact your third-party designee?

Do you want to allow an employee, a paid tax preparer, or another person to discuss this return with the IRS? See the instructions for details.

☐ Yes. Designee's name [ ]

Phone ( ) – Personal Identification Number (PIN) ☐☐☐☐☐

☑ No.

Part 5: Sign here

Under penalties of perjury, I declare that I have examined this return, including accompanying schedules and statements, and to the best of my knowledge and belief, it is true, correct, and complete.

X

Sign your name here [ ]

Print name and title [ ]

Date [/ /] Phone ( ) –

Part 6: For paid preparers only *(optional)*

Preparer's signature [ ]

Firm's name [ ]

Address [ ] EIN [ ]

[ ] ZIP code [ ]

Date [/ /] Phone ( ) – SSN/PTIN [ ]

☐ Check if you are self-employed.

Page **2** Form **941** (Rev. 1-2005)

Problem 4 continued

Schedule B (Form 941):
Report of Tax Liability for Semiweekly Schedule Depositors
(Rev. January 2005)   Department of the Treasury — Internal Revenue Service

9903

OMB No. 1545-0029

Employer identification number   4 3 — 1 2 3 4 5 6 7

Name *(not your trade name)*   Bimms & Ferrow, Inc.

Report for this Quarter ...
(Check one.)

[ ] **1:** January, February, March

[ ] **2:** April, May, June

[✓] **3:** July, August, September

[ ] **4:** October, November, December

Use this schedule to show your tax liability for the quarter; DO NOT use it to show your deposits. You must fill out this form and attach it to Form 941 (or Form 941-SS) if you are a semiweekly schedule depositor or became one because your accumulated tax liability on any day was $100,000 or more. Write your daily tax liability on the numbered space that corresponds to the date wages were paid. See Section 11 in *Pub. 15 (Circular E), Employer's Tax Guide,* for details.

Month 1

#		#		#		#		Tax liability for Month 1
1		9		17		25		
2		10		18		26		228400 . 00
3		11		19		27		
4		12		20		28		
5		13		21		29		
6		14		22		30		
7		15	114200 . 00	23		31	114200 . 00	
8		16		24				

Month 2

#		#		#		#		Tax liability for Month 2
1		9		17		25		
2		10		18		26		226400 . 00
3		11		19		27		
4		12		20		28		
5		13		21		29		
6		14		22		30		
7		15	113600 . 00	23		31	112800 . 00	
8		16		24				

Month 3

#		#		#		#		Tax liability for Month 3
1		9		17		25		
2		10		18		26		222800 . 00
3		11		19		27		
4		12		20		28		
5		13		21		29		
6		14		22		30	110900 . 00	
7		15	111900 . 00	23		31		
8		16		24				

Fill in your total liability for the quarter (Month 1 + Month 2 + Month 3) = Total tax liability for the quarter ▶
Total must equal line 10 on Form 941 (or line 8 on Form 941-SS).

Total liability for the quarter

677600 . 00

For Paperwork Reduction Act Notice, see separate instructions.   Cat. No. 11967Q   Schedule B (Form 941) Rev. 1-2005

Problem 5

a Control number	22222	Void ☐	For Official Use Only ► OMB No. 1545-0008	

b Employer identification number (EIN) 12-3456789		1 Wages, tips, other compensation 39500.00	2 Federal income tax withheld 5925.00
c Employer's name, address, and ZIP code		3 Social security wages 42500.00	4 Social security tax withheld 2635.00
Sanchez Corporation		5 Medicare wages and tips 42500.00	6 Medicare tax withheld 616.25
640 San Francisco St., Ste. 6		7 Social security tips	8 Allocated tips
Sacramento, CA 35123			
d Employee's social security number 486-11-3245		9 Advance EIC payment	10 Dependent care benefits 1000.00
e Employee's first name and initial David V	Last name Sandoval	Suff.	11 Nonqualified plans	12a See instructions for box 12 D 3000.00
		13 Statutory employee ☐ Retirement plan ☑ Third-party sick pay ☐	12b
4213 Central Avenue		14 Other	12c
Sacramento, CA 35814			12d
f Employee's address and ZIP code			

15 State CA	Employer's state ID number 985-4321	16 State wages, tips, etc. 39500.00	17 State income tax 1777.50	18 Local wages, tips, etc.	19 Local income tax	20 Locality name

Form **W-2** Wage and Tax Statement **2006**

Department of the Treasury—Internal Revenue Service

Copy A For Social Security Administration — Send this entire page with Form W-3 to the Social Security Administration; photocopies are **not** acceptable.

For Privacy Act and Paperwork Reduction Act Notice, see back of Copy D.

Cat. No. 10134D

Do Not Cut, Fold, or Staple Forms on This Page — Do Not Cut, Fold, or Staple Forms on This Page

a Control number	22222	Void ☐	For Official Use Only ► OMB No. 1545-0008	

b Employer identification number (EIN) 12-3456789		1 Wages, tips, other compensation 28481.50	2 Federal income tax withheld 4272.33
c Employer's name, address, and ZIP code		3 Social security wages 30481.50	4 Social security tax withheld 1889.85
Sanchez Corporation		5 Medicare wages and tips 30481.50	6 Medicare tax withheld 441.98
640 San Francisco St., Ste. 6		7 Social security tips	8 Allocated tips
Sacramento, CA 35123			
d Employee's social security number 234-56-7890		9 Advance EIC payment	10 Dependent care benefits
e Employee's first name and initial William T	Last name Foster	Suff.	11 Nonqualified plans	12a See instructions for box 12 C 481.50
		13 Statutory employee ☐ Retirement plan ☑ Third-party sick pay ☐	12b D 2000.00
123 University Heights		14 Other	12c
Sacramento, CA 35111			12d
f Employee's address and ZIP code			

15 State CA	Employer's state ID number 985-4321	16 State wages, tips, etc. 28481.50	17 State income tax 1281.67	18 Local wages, tips, etc.	19 Local income tax	20 Locality name

Form **W-2** Wage and Tax Statement **2006**

Department of the Treasury—Internal Revenue Service

Copy A For Social Security Administration — Send this entire page with Form W-3 to the Social Security Administration; photocopies are **not** acceptable.

For Privacy Act and Paperwork Reduction Act Notice, see back of Copy D.

Cat. No. 10134D

Do Not Cut, Fold, or Staple Forms on This Page — Do Not Cut, Fold, or Staple Forms on This Page

Problem 5 continued

a Control number	22222	Void ☐	For Official Use Only ▶ OMB No. 1545-0008	

b Employer identification number (EIN) 12-3456789		1 Wages, tips, other compensation 31800.00	2 Federal income tax withheld 4770.00

c Employer's name, address, and ZIP code Sanchez Corporation 640 San Francisco St., Ste. 6 Sacramento, CA 35123	3 Social security wages 34200.00	4 Social security tax withheld 2120.40

5 Medicare wages and tips 34200.00 — 6 Medicare tax withheld 495.90

7 Social security tips — 8 Allocated tips

d Employee's social security number 987-65-4321 — 9 Advance EIC payment — 10 Dependent care benefits

e Employee's first name and initial Helen G — Last name Roseville — Suff. — 11 Nonqualified plans — 12a See instructions for box 12 D 2400.00

7000 Mount Pleasant Road — 13 Statutory employee ☐ Retirement plan ☑ Third-party sick pay ☐ — 12b

Sacramento, CA 35900 — 14 Other Auto 1800.00 Ed Asst 2500.00 — 12c — 12d

f Employee's address and ZIP code

15 State CA Employer's state ID number 985-4321	16 State wages, tips, etc. 31800.00	17 State income tax 1431.00	18 Local wages, tips, etc.	19 Local income tax	20 Locality name

Form **W-2** Wage and Tax Statement   **2006**   Department of the Treasury—Internal Revenue Service

Copy A For Social Security Administration — Send this entire page with Form W-3 to the Social Security Administration; photocopies are **not** acceptable.   Cat. No. 10134D

For Privacy Act and Paperwork Reduction Act Notice, see back of Copy D.

Do Not Cut, Fold, or Staple Forms on This Page — Do Not Cut, Fold, or Staple Forms on This Page

---

a Control number	22222	Void ☐	For Official Use Only ▶ OMB No. 1545-0008	

b Employer identification number (EIN) 12-3456789		1 Wages, tips, other compensation 18000.00	2 Federal income tax withheld 2700.00

c Employer's name, address, and ZIP code Sanchez Corporation 640 San Francisco St., Ste. 6 Sacramento, CA 35123	3 Social security wages 19000.00	4 Social security tax withheld 1178.00

5 Medicare wages and tips 19000.00 — 6 Medicare tax withheld 275.50

7 Social security tips — 8 Allocated tips

d Employee's social security number 246-80-1357 — 9 Advance EIC payment 624.00 — 10 Dependent care benefits

e Employee's first name and initial Beryl — Last name Horstmann — Suff. — 11 Nonqualified plans — 12a See instructions for box 12 D 1000.00

1212 Forest Ridge Drive — 13 Statutory employee ☐ Retirement plan ☑ Third-party sick pay ☐ — 12b

Sacramento, CA 35196 — 14 Other Ed Asst 800.00 — 12c — 12d

f Employee's address and ZIP code

15 State CA Employer's state ID number 985-4321	16 State wages, tips, etc. 18000.00	17 State income tax 540.00	18 Local wages, tips, etc.	19 Local income tax	20 Locality name

Form **W-2** Wage and Tax Statement   **2006**   Department of the Treasury—Internal Revenue Service

Copy A For Social Security Administration — Send this entire page with Form W-3 to the Social Security Administration; photocopies are **not** acceptable.   Cat. No. 10134D

For Privacy Act and Paperwork Reduction Act Notice, see back of Copy D.

Do Not Cut, Fold, or Staple Forms on This Page — Do Not Cut, Fold, or Staple Forms on This Page

Problem 5 continued

DO NOT STAPLE

a Control number	**33333**	For Official Use Only ▶ OMB No. 1545-0008

b Kind of Payer ▶		
941 ✓	Military ☐	943 ☐	944 ☐
CT-1 ☐	Hshld. emp. ☐	Medicare govt. emp. ☐	Third-party sick pay ☐

1 Wages, tips, other compensation 117781.50	**2** Federal income tax withheld 17667.23	
3 Social security wages 126181.50	**4** Social security tax withheld 7823.25	
c Total number of Forms W-2 4	**d** Establishment number	**5** Medicare wages and tips 126181.50	**6** Medicare tax withheld 1829.63
e Employer identification number (EIN) 12-3456789		**7** Social security tips	**8** Allocated tips
f Employer's name Sanchez Corporation		**9** Advance EIC payments 624.00	**10** Dependent care benefits 1000.00
640 San Francisco St., Ste. 6		**11** Nonqualified plans	**12** Deferred compensation 8400.00
Sacramento, CA 35123		**13** For third-party sick pay use only	
g Employer's address and ZIP code		**14** Income tax withheld by payer of third-party sick pay	
h Other EIN used this year			
15 State	Employer's state ID number	**16** State wages, tips, etc.	**17** State income tax
CA	985-4321	117781.50	5030.17
		18 Local wages, tips, etc.	**19** Local income tax
Contact person		Telephone number ( )	For Official Use Only
Email address		Fax number ( )	

Under penalties of perjury, I declare that I have examined this return and accompanying documents, and, to the best of my knowledge and belief, they are true, correct, and complete.

Signature ▶   Title ▶   Date ▶

Form **W-3** Transmittal of Wage and Tax Statements   **2006**   Department of the Treasury
Internal Revenue Service

Send this entire page with the entire Copy A page of Form(s) W-2 to the Social Security Administration. Photocopies are not acceptable.

Do not send any payment (cash, checks, money orders, etc.) with Forms W-2 and W-3.

What's New

New checkbox for box b on Form W-3. Use the "944" checkbox in box b if you file Form 944, Employer's Annual Federal Tax Return. Form 944 for 2006 is a newly developed form.

Magnetic media filing is discontinued. The Social Security Administration (SSA) will no longer accept any magnetic media reporting of Forms W-2.

Reminder

Separate instructions. See the 2006 Instructions for Forms W-2 and W-3 for information on completing this form.

Purpose of Form

Use Form W-3 to transmit Copy A of Form(s) W-2, Wage and Tax Statement. Make a copy of Form W-3 and keep it with Copy D (For Employer) of Form(s) W-2 for your records. Use Form W-3 for the correct year. **File Form W-3 even if only one Form W-2 is being filed.** If you are filing Form(s) W-2 electronically, **do not** file Form W-3.

When To File

File Form W-3 with Copy A of Form(s) W-2 by February 28, 2007.

Where To File

Send this entire page with the entire Copy A page of Form(s) W-2 to:

> **Social Security Administration**
> **Data Operations Center**
> **Wilkes-Barre, PA 18769-0001**

Note. *If you use "Certified Mail" to file, change the ZIP code to "18769-0002." If you use an IRS-approved private delivery service, add "ATTN: W-2 Process, 1150 E. Mountain Dr." to the address and change the ZIP code to "18702-7997." See Publication 15 (Circular E), Employer's Tax Guide, for a list of IRS-approved private delivery services.*

For Privacy Act and Paperwork Reduction Act Notice, see back of Copy D of Form W-2.

Cat. No. 10159Y

SECTION 9: OTHER DEDUCTIONS FROM PAY

Review Questions

1. According to Form 668-W, when determining take-home pay the employer should allow the payroll deductions that were in effect when the levy notice was received.

2. Employers that fail to withhold and pay over an amount not exempt from levy after receiving Form 668-W are liable for the full amount required to be withheld, plus interest from the wage payment date. In addition, the employer is liable for a penalty equal to 50% of the amount recoverable by the IRS after the failure to withhold and remit.

3. CCPA stands for Consumer Credit Protection Act. It provides the legal framework around which state child support withholding laws have been constructed and limits the amount that can be withheld for child support.

4. When the law of the state where the employee works requires that health insurance be deducted to determine the employee's disposable earnings.

5. Yes. Payments to independent contractors constitute property subject to a child support withholding order.

6. The federal garnishment maximum applies no matter how many garnishments are received for an employee. If the maximum is already being withheld when a second garnishment is received, nothing may be withheld for that garnishment.

7. The lesser of the amount stated on the garnishment order up to 15% of an employee's disposable earnings or the excess of the employee's disposable earnings over 30 times the federal minimum wage may be garnished to satisfy a delinquent federal agency loan unless the employee consents in writing to a higher amount.

8. 50%, because it is more beneficial to the employee.

9. Following are some of the voluntary deductions which are not subtracted from earnings in calculating disposable pay:

   - health insurance premiums (unless state law says otherwise)
   - life insurance premiums
   - union dues
   - retirement plan contributions
   - United Way contributions
   - other charitable contributions
   - savings plan deductions, etc.

10. Under a medical child support order, a noncustodial parent is required to provide health insurance for the child by enrolling the child in the parent's employer-sponsored health insurance plan. The order may also provide for automatic enrollment of the child if the parent fails to accomplish the enrollment.

11. Under these requirements, each state's laws must:

- prohibit insurers from denying medical insurance under a parent's coverage to a child because the child was born out of wedlock, is not a dependent on the parent's income tax return, or does not live with the parent or in the insurer's service area;

- where a qualified medical child support order exists, require insurers and employers to allow the parent to enroll the child without restrictions, and to enroll the child themselves if the parent does not do it;

- where a qualified medical child support order exists, require employers to withhold the employee's share of health insurance premiums and pay it to the insurer;

- require insurers to make it easier for custodial parents to submit and collect on claims where the noncustodial parent's insurer carries the child's coverage; and

- permit state Medicaid agencies to garnish an employee's wages so the state can be reimbursed for payments made to the employee on behalf of a child who is eligible for Medicaid.

True or False Questions

1. False — You must use the table for married filing separate with one exemption if the employee does not submit a statement of filing status and exemptions.

2. False — The Consumer Credit Protection Act imposes a lower limit depending on the amount of the employee's disposable earnings in relation to the minimum wage, and various state laws also have more severe restrictions.

3. False — The exempt amount is subtracted from the employee's "take-home pay."

4. True

5. True

6. False — Employers are liable for the full amount required to be withheld.

7. True

8. False — Voluntary deductions are not subtracted from gross pay to determine disposable earnings, which only take into account deductions required by law, but they are subtracted to determine take-home pay.

9. False — An employer is only required to garnish an employee's wages by order of a court, not the creditor.

10. True

11. True

12. True

13. True

14. True

Answer Key

15. True

16. True

17. False   Employers must withhold child support from payments made to independent contractors when required to do so by order of a court or state child support enforcement agency.

18. False   Government employees are subject to child and spousal support withholding orders on the same basis as private sector employees.

19. False   Employers are prohibited by the CCPA from terminating an employee because the employee's earnings have been subjected to garnishment for any one indebtedness.

20. True

Multiple Choice Questions

1.	c	9.	a
2.	b	10.	b
3.	d	11.	c
4.	b	12.	a
5.	c	13.	b
6.	d	14.	d
7.	c	15.	a
8.	c		

Problems

1. Continue withholding according to the order unless and until you receive notification in writing from the court or issuing agency that a change is necessary.

2. John's take-home pay: $351.75
   ($500.00 - $148.25)
   Exempt amount: -162.50
   (Taken from 2006 table)
   Amount subject to levy: $189.25

3. Matthew's take-home pay: $1,150.20
   ($2,000.00 - $849.80)
   Exempt amount: -979.17
   (Taken from 2006 table)
   Amount subject to levy: $ 171.03

4. a. David's take-home pay: $2,258.75
   ($3,500.00 - $1,241.25)
   Exempt amount: - 1,408.33
   (Taken from 2006 table)
   Amount subject to levy: $850.42

   b. David's new take-home pay: $2,263.75
   ($3,500.00 - $1,306.25 + $70.00)
   Exempt amount: -1,683.33
   (Taken from 2006 table)
   Amount subject to levy: $580.42

Note: David's §401(k) deduction changed from $70 to $140 when he changed his elective deferral rate from 2% to 4%. His health insurance deduction increased from $50 to $70 when the premiums were raised. In figuring David's take-home pay, the employer cannot deduct the $70 increase in the §401(k) deduction because it was the result of a voluntary increase. The $20 increase in the health insurance deduction may be counted because it was the result of an increase in the cost of coverage, not a change in coverage chosen by the employee.

   c. David's net pay after changes:
      Net pay = Exempt amount - §401(k) deduction increase
      Net pay = $1,683.33 - $70.00 = $1,613.33

5. Gross pay ($5.50 x 40): $220.00
    Federal income tax: - 33.00
    State income tax: - 3.30
    Social security tax: - 13.64
    Medicare tax: - 3.19
    Disposable earnings: $166.87

6. Regular pay ($7.50 x 48): $360.00
    Overtime premium (0.5 x $7.50 x 8): +30.00
    Gross pay: 390.00
    Federal income tax ($390 x 15%): - 58.50
    State income tax ($390 x 3%)   - 11.70
    Social security tax ($390 x 6.2%): - 24.18
    Medicare tax ($390 x 1.45%):   - 5.66
    Disposable earnings: $289.96

7. Week one:
    Regular pay ($10.00 x 43): $430.00
    Overtime premium (0.5 x $10 x 3): + 15.00
    Total: 445.00

    Week two:
    Regular pay ($10.00 x 39):   390.00
    Total earnings (2 weeks):   835.00

    Federal income tax ($835 x 15%): -125.25
    State income tax ($835 x 3%):   - 25.05
    Social security tax ($835 x 6.2%): - 51.77
    Medicare tax ($835 x 1.45%):   - 12.11
    Disposable earnings: $620.82

8. The lesser of:
    $320.00 x 25% = $80 or
    $320 - $154.50 = $165.50

Therefore, the maximum amount of Jane's disposable earnings that can be garnished is $80.

9. | | |
    |---|---:|
    | Gross pay: | $2,600.00 |
    | Federal income tax ($2,600 x 15%): | - 390.00 |
    | State income tax ($2,600 x 7.5%): | - 195.00 |
    | Social security tax ($2,600 x 6.2%): | - 161.20 |
    | Medicare tax ($2,600 x 1.45%): | - 37.70 |
    | Disposable pay: | $1,816.10 |

    The lesser of:
    $1,816.10 x 25% = $454.03 or
    $1,816.10 - $334.75 = $1,481.35

    Therefore, the maximum amount of Don's disposable earnings that can be garnished is $454.03. However, since $150 of Don's disposable earnings are already subject to a child support withholding order and a federal tax levy, only $304.03 is subject to garnishment ($454.03 - $150).

SECTION 10: RECORDKEEPING AND RECORD RETENTION

Review Questions

1. Where employees are exempt from overtime pay requirements for time spent receiving remedial education, the employer must keep, in addition to other required records, records of the hours spent by each employee receiving such remedial education and the wages paid for those hours.

2. Willful violations of the recordkeeping requirements can bring a criminal penalty of up to $10,000 and/or imprisonment for up to 6 months, although a jail sentence can be imposed only for second and subsequent convictions.

3. These records must be kept for at least four years after the due date of the tax (or the date the tax is paid, if later) for the return period to which the records relate.

4. 3 days

5. Following is a list of the records that must be kept for three years after the last date of entry for each covered employee under the FLSA:

   • name, as it appears on the employee's social security card;

   • home address, including apartment number, if any, and Zip code;

   • date of birth, if under age 19;

   • sex and occupation (for use in determining Equal Pay Act compliance);

   • the beginning of the employee's workweek (time and day);

   • regular rate of pay for overtime weeks, the basis for determining the rate, and any payments excluded from the regular rate;

   • hours worked each workday and workweek;

   • straight-time earnings (including straight-time pay for overtime hours);

   • overtime premium earnings;

   • additions to and deductions from wages for each pay period;

   • total wages paid for each pay period; and

   • date of payment and the pay period covered.

6. Following is a list of records that must be kept for at least two years from their last date of entry under the FLSA:

   • basic employment and earning records that support the data for each nonexempt employee's hours of work, basis for determining wages, and wages paid (e.g., time or production cards);

- order, shipping, and billing records showing customer orders, shipping and delivery records, and customer billings; and

- records substantiating additions to or deductions from employees' wages, including purchase orders, operating cost records, wage assignments, and garnishments.

7. In addition to other required records, hospitals and residential care facilities whose employees have a work period of 14 consecutive days (rather than 7 for other employees) must keep records of the time and day on which the 14-day period begins, hours worked each day and each 14-day period, and straight-time and overtime premium earnings paid in each 14-day period. They also must keep a copy of the written agreement between the hospital and the employee allowing use of the 14-day work period or a memorandum summarizing its terms if the agreement is oral.

8. Employers that use the tip credit to pay part of a tipped employee's minimum wage must keep, in addition to other required records, the following:

- some notation of the records showing that the employee's wages are determined partly by tips;

- the amount reported by the employee to the employer as tips (weekly or monthly), which may be taken from IRS Form 4070;

- the amount of the tip credit taken by the employer;

- hours worked and straight-time earnings for time worked other than as a tipped employee; and

- hours worked and straight-time earnings for time worked as a tipped employee.

9. The procedures are generally aimed at achieving one goal—making it easy for the IRS to determine the employer's correct tax liability.

10. Employers must retain the completed Form I-9, *Employment Eligibility Verification,* for at least three years after the date of hire or one year after the date of termination, whichever is later.

11. The advantages of micromedia storage over paper storage include:

- less space needed for storage
- reduced storage costs
- less chance of losing individual documents
- increased durability

12. The main problem is one of quality control—the camera may not photograph 100% of every document, the image may be partially unreadable, and verification of the image after it develops can be a time-consuming process.

13. Whatever method an employer uses to create and preserve its employment and payroll records, it should have a policy governing record retention, retrieval, and destruction. The written policy should clearly state how long records are to be retained (and how the containers should be labeled), how they can be retrieved (especially important if records are stored off site), and when and how they should be disposed of.

Answer Key

True or False Questions

1. False   Payroll records may be retained in any form, including microfilm, microfiche, paper, or computerized.

2. True

3. False   72 hours.

4. True

5. False   The employer remains ultimately responsible for the recordkeeping requirements.

6. True

7. False   Certain records relating to overtime pay requirements need not be kept for exempt "white collar" employees. However, employers must include in their records the basis on which wages are paid so that each employee's total earnings for each pay period can be calculated.

8. True

9. True

10. False   The records required by the FLSA may be stored by the employer either at the work site or at a central location where its records are customarily maintained.

11. True

12. False   Form W-4 must be retained by the employer for four years.

13. True

14. True

15. False   The various federal and state laws generally do not require that records be kept in any particular form and often specifically allow record retention on microfilm or microfiche.

Multiple Choice Questions

1.	a	6.	b
2.	d	7.	b
3.	b	8.	a
4.	c	9.	b
5.	d	10.	c

SECTION 11: PAYROLL ACCOUNTING

Review Questions

1. Management, stockholders, investors, employees, and auditors would be interested in the financial records of a business.

2. Subsidiary ledgers are used for a single type of account and are subordinate to the general ledger. For example, entries documenting payroll expenses and liabilities may be contained in a subsidiary ledger known as the Payroll Register. Other subsidiary ledgers that contain entries for several accounts might include Accounts Payable, Accounts Receivable, and Fixed Assets.

3. In most companies, a "chart of accounts" lists each account by name and number, with the number being used to identify accounts in a manual or computerized system.

4. Asset, Liability, Expense, Revenue, and Equity.

5. If payroll expenses are recorded functionally, entries must be based on the processes supported by the expenses (e.g., manufacturing, sales, administration). This means that the payroll would have to be distributed into different labor distribution expense accounts and a separate Labor Distribution Subsidiary Ledger would have to be kept. Recording payroll expenses by type of pay can be done where the payroll register breaks down employees' wages into regular and overtime pay.

6. Internal controls

7. Under accrual accounting, revenue is recognized and recorded when earned and expenses are recognized and recorded when incurred. Accrual entries are made at the end of an accounting period to estimate payroll expenses and liabilities incurred between the end of the last payroll period and the accounting period end.

8. Accruals generally are estimates, so they must be corrected by reversing entries during the next accounting period when the actual expenses and liabilities are recorded.

9. In preparing to file quarterly Form 941, and annual Form 940, employers should verify the following:

   • that FUTA, social security, and Medicare tax deposits for the quarter equal the current tax rates for each, multiplied by the taxable wages for each;

   • the total Form 941 tax deposits for the quarter equal the liability section for Form 941 (Line 11 of Form 941 equals Line 15 of Form 941 or the "Total liability for the quarter" line of Schedule B, whichever applies), although monthly depositors may pay their lawful $100 or 2% deposit shortfall with Form 941, in which case total deposits would not equal the liability;

   • total FUTA tax deposits equal Part 4, Line 13 and Part 5, Line 17 of Form 940.

10. Earnings per share show the company's net income divided by the weighted average number of outstanding shares of stock.

11. The purposes of an external audit include:

    - to determine the accuracy of financial statements,

    - to depict the company's financial condition and determine whether the notes to financial statements accurately summarize the company's accounting policies and procedures,

    - to guard against any possible conflict of interest,

    - to safeguard the company's assets, and

    - to provide an objective opinion as to the fairness of the financial statements.

12. The job of a company's internal auditor is to review the efficiency of the organization's internal control procedures and to identify weaknesses in the controls.

13. A balance sheet is a statement of the financial position of a business at a specific period in time. It is an itemized list showing the business's assets, liabilities, and owner's equity.

14. Revenue has the effect of increasing owner's equity.

15. Expenses have the effect of decreasing owner's equity.

16. The journal is used to list all the necessary information about a transaction in one place. The journal is the first accounting record of business transactions and is therefore referred to as a record of original entry.

True or False Questions

1. True

2. True

3. False   Payroll taxes are always reported on a calendar year basis.

4. False   The income statement summarizes the organization's revenues, expenses, and earnings for the current and preceding fiscal years.

5. True

6. False   Accounts payable are liabilities.

7. False   Assets must equal liabilities plus owner's equity.

8. False   The property owned by a business is known as assets.

9. True

10. True

11. True

12. True

13. True

14. True

15. False   Revenue appears on the income statement.

16. True

17. True

18. True

19. True

20. True

21. False   The general ledger is the record of final entry.

22. False   The payroll expense journal will debit an expense account for the labor costs (salary expense) and credit a liability account (accrued salaries/wages).

23. True

24. False   Payroll checks that cannot be delivered should be returned to a department other than payroll and be locked up until the employee returns and can receive the check.

25. True

26. True

Multiple Choice Questions

1.	b	12.	d
2.	c	13.	d
3.	a	14.	c
4.	d	15.	c
5.	a	16.	b
6.	a	17.	b
7.	a	18.	b
8.	b	19.	d
9.	c	20.	d
10.	b	21.	d
11.	a		

Problems

1. a. Cash   <u>Asset</u>
   b. Loan payable to a bank <u>Liability</u>
   c. Delivery equipment <u>Asset</u>
   d. Account payable to a creditor <u>Liability</u>
   e. Office furniture <u>Asset</u>
   f. Owner's financial interest <u>Owner's Equity</u>
   g. Petty cash <u>Asset</u>
   h. Mortgage payable to a bank <u>Liability</u>
   i. FUTA taxes payable <u>Liability</u>

2.

	Accounts	Income Statement	Balance Sheet
a.	Accounts payable		✓
b.	Accounts receivable		✓
c.	Advertising expense	✓	
d.	Cash		✓
e.	Salaries payable		✓
f.	Duplicating equipment		✓
g.	Paul Morris, capital		✓
h.	Miscellaneous expense	✓	
i.	Office furniture		✓
j.	Rent expense	✓	

3. a. Accounts receivable   Debit
   b. Social security tax payable   Credit
   c. Sales   Credit
   d. Sales tax payable   Credit
   e. Accounts payable   Credit
   f. Wage garnishments payable   Credit
   g. Payroll taxes expense   Debit
   h. Professional fees payable   Credit
   i. Freight expense   Debit
   j. Life insurance premiums payable Credit

4.

Date	Item	Debit	Credit
Jan 7, 2006	Wages/salary expense	$50,000.00	
	Social security tax payable		$ 3,100.00
	Medicare tax payable		725.00
	Federal income tax payable		7,500.00
	State income tax payable		750.00
	City income tax payable		375.00
	Life insurance premiums payable		200.00
	Health insurance premiums payable		120.00
	Credit union contributions payable		100.00
	Savings Bond deductions payable		350.00
	Wages/salaries payable		36,780.00

5.

Date	Item	Debit	Credit
Jan 21, 2006	Payroll taxes expense	$ 4,460.00	
	Social security tax payable		$ 2,480.00
	Medicare tax payable		580.00
	FUTA tax payable		320.00
	SUTA tax payable		1,080.00

6.

a.

Date	Item	Debit	Credit
Jan 21, 2006	Wages/salaries expense	$30,000.00	
	Social security tax payable		$ 1,860.00
	Medicare tax payable		435.00
	Federal income tax payable		4,500.00
	Wages/salaries payable		23,205.00

b.

Jan 21, 2006	Payroll taxes expense	$ 3,345.00	
	Social security tax payable		$ 1,860.00
	Medicare tax payable		435.00
	FUTA tax payable		240.00
	SUTA tax payable		810.00

c.

Jan 25, 2006	Wages/salaries payable	$23,205.00	
	Cash		$23,205.00

7.

Date	Item	Debit	Credit
Jan 7, 2006	Wages/salaries expense	$16,400.00	
	Social security tax payable		$ 1,016.80
	Medicare tax payable		237.80
	Federal income tax payable		2,460.00
	State income tax payable		246.00
	Life insurance premiums payable		30.00
	Health insurance premiums payable		22.00
	Wages/salaries payable		12,387.40
Jan 7, 2006	Payroll taxes expense	$ 1,828.60	
	Social security tax payable		$ 1,016.80
	Medicare tax payable		237.80
	FUTA tax payable		131.20
	SUTA tax payable		442.80
Jan 7, 2006	Wages/salaries payable	$12,387.40	
	Cash		$12,387.40

8.

a.

Date	Item	Debit	Credit
Aug 24, 2006	Accrued payroll expense	$80,000.00	
	Accrued payroll liability		$80,000.00

To record the estimated salaries due from Aug. 21 - Aug. 24

Date	Item	Debit	Credit
Aug 24, 2006	Accrued payroll tax expense	$9,160.00	
	Accrued social security tax payable		$ 4,960.00
	Accrued Medicare tax payable		1,160.00
	Accrued FUTA tax payable		640.00
	Accrued SUTA tax payable		2,400.00

To record the estimated payroll tax expenses on wages from Aug. 21 - Aug. 24.

b.

Date	Item	Debit	Credit
Aug. 25, 2006	Accrued payroll liability	$80,000.00	
	Accrued payroll expense		$80,000.00

To record the reversal of the estimated salaries from Aug. 21 - Aug. 24.

Date	Item	Debit	Credit
Aug. 25, 2006	Accrued social security tax payable		$ 4,960.00
	Accrued Medicare tax payable	$ 1,160.00	
	Accrued FUTA tax payable	640.00	
	Accrued SUTA tax payable	2,400.00	
	Accrued payroll tax expense		9,160.00

To record the reversal of the estimated payroll tax expenses from Aug. 21 - Aug. 24.

9. a.

Item	Debit	Credit
Vacation expense	$4,000	
Vacation liability payable		$4,000

To record the employees' accrual of vacation leave for the month of January.

b.

Item	Debit	Credit
Vacation liability payable	$ 900	
Cash		$ 900

To record the employees' actual use of vacation leave.

SECTION 12: PAYROLL SYSTEMS AND TECHNOLOGY

Review Questions

1. Other company systems that interface with payroll include:

   - human resources,
   - benefits,
   - accounting,
   - bank reconciliation,
   - direct deposit,
   - time and attendance, and
   - general ledger.

2. Commonly used payroll system edits include:

   - warning that a check is being generated for a terminated employee,
   - report for new hires,
   - error message when no check is generated for an active employee,
   - error message for negative net pay,
   - error message for negative deductions,
   - report when compensation exceeds certain amounts,
   - report for excessive overtime (or any overtime in some companies), and
   - report when rate of pay changes.

3. The payroll department's customers include:

   - employees,
   - other departments
   - upper management, and
   - federal, state and local government agencies

4. Reasons why an integrated payroll, human resources, and benefits system would benefit a company include:

   - streamlining functions that make up the highest percentage of cost in most organizations,

   - storing complete data in a single separate database, which means that the information needed to make intelligent business decisions is readily available, and

   - significant improvements in existing systems are often impossible, because most of their time and energy is spent supporting necessary interfaces among the existing systems' databases.

5. Representatives of the following departments should be included on the system selection and implementation project team:

   - payroll,
   - human resources/personnel,
   - benefits,
   - accounting,
   - tax,

- budget/finance,
- data processing/MIS, and
- facilities.

6. A successful automated payroll system must:

- provide for compliance with federal, state, and local withholding, depositing, and reporting requirements,

- issue timely and accurate paychecks and/or make accurate direct deposits,

- maintain adequate records of all data and transactions,

- prepare internal reports, and

- guarantee the security of the system.

7. Slow response time to needed changes and emergency requirements.

8. Advantages of using an in-house computer payroll system include:

- control of the system

- convenient access

- downtime can be reduced

- system security

- scheduling flexibility

- interactive applications

9. Disadvantages of using vendor-supplied software include:

- specific needs may not be met

- possibly slow changes

- extensive training needed

- lengthy processing

- improper fit

10. Advantages of using customized software include:

- special needs are met

- the employer has control

- there is increased flexibility

- training needs are reduced

11. A Current Situation Analysis should include the following components:

    - documentation of all paper flow into/out of the current system,

    - documentation of the procedures for maintenance, including who is called, response time, and average downtime,

    - identify who receives information from the payroll system, how often, and whether they are using it,

    - along with the end users, identify and prioritize complaints, problems, and restrictions,

    - identify any actual or potential compliance problems,

    - document any manual processes that might be eliminated by automation, and

    - identify all costs of the current system—tax updates, corporate policy changes, computer time, paper, system shutdowns, etc.

12. A Request for Proposal should include the following:

    - the employer's purpose in issuing the proposal,

    - specific payroll information—size, frequency, union vs. nonunion, salaried and hourly,

    - functional requirements of a new system now and in the future,

    - number of fields required for earnings and deductions,

    - whether human resources and benefits will be integrated with the payroll system and what interfaces will be required,

    - training needs and whether this should be included in the bid,

    - level of support (maintenance) expected,

    - contract terms and conditions, and

    - instructions to vendor on how to submit proposal.

13. Common mistakes made during selection of a new payroll system include:

    - not including representatives of all the potential user departments,

    - failing to provide enough time for project team members to work on their system selection duties,

    - failing to prioritize needs and desires,

    - making decisions without sufficient input,

- failing to consider all the costs associated with a new system,

- making on-site visits only to customers referred by a vendor or service bureau,

- failing to thoroughly check for signs of obsolescence,

- failing to negotiate performance guarantees, and

- not considering future company needs—shortsightedness.

14. Four environmental concerns that need to be addressed regarding new system hardware are:

- need for climate controlled rooms,

- power surges, or spikes,

- dirt, and

- humidity.

True or False Questions

1. True

2. True

3. True

4. True

5. False   Documentation is a very important part of a company's overall control mechanisms.

6. True

7. True

8. False   Off-the-shelf software is almost never able to be modified to a user's unique needs.

9. True

10. False   The employer's own staff is responsible for maintaining and keeping its software up to date.

11. False   The initial step in selecting a new payroll system is to put together a project team or task force.

12. True

13. False   The final test before going live with a new system is called parallel testing.

14. True

15. True

Multiple Choice Questions

1.	b	9.	a
2.	b	10.	c
3.	a	11.	d
4.	b	12.	b
5.	b	13.	d
6.	b	14.	c
7.	b	15.	a
8.	d		

SECTION 13: MANAGING A PAYROLL DEPARTMENT

Review Questions

1. Tasks and relationships.

2. The fundamental skills that most managers must master to be successful include:

   - strategic planning/organizing,
   - staffing,
   - giving directions,
   - controlling progress, and
   - reporting to upper management.

3. Activities that must be defined during the planning and organizing process include:

   - goals and objectives,
   - the time frame, and
   - the subtasks.

4. In developing a job description, the payroll manager must answer the five following questions:

   - What are the educational requirements needed to perform the job?

   - What knowledge/skills must the applicant have before being offered the job?

   - What training opportunities can be offered to the new employee?

   - What is the level of supervision required on the job?

   - How much necessary communication and interaction with other employees will be necessary?

5. Interview questions should be open-ended and force applicants to explain past behavior rather than questions that call for one word answers.

6. If their delegation is unsuccessful, they must do the work themselves, which tends to result in unfulfilled employees and burned out managers.

7. Four communication skills managers must possess when directing employees are:

   - listening,
   - providing feedback,
   - coaching, and
   - leading.

8. Three qualities that can help make a payroll manager a strong leader include:

   - having a vision,
   - building team support, and
   - seeking partners.

9. Often the best performers are driven by a personal need to succeed and be the best rather than by money or other incentives.

10. Possible rewards for employees who have demonstrated leadership potential include:

    *   public recognition,
    *   promotion to supervisory positions,
    *   leadership roles (projects, teams or tasks), and
    *   taking them into your confidence (seeking their input).

11. A payroll manager's report to upper management should have the following characteristics:

    *   include only the relevant information,
    *   the information should be produced in a timely manner, and
    *   it should be written clearly but briefly.

12. There are several things the payroll manager can do to ensure that the lessons a crisis has taught are not forgotten:

    *   conduct a meeting of the team to discuss the crisis and determine which of the problems that occurred during the crisis are preventable;

    *   initiate a plan to prevent those problems that can be prevented from reoccurring;

    *   list the successful results of the crisis management operation and include them in a "Crisis File" for future reference;

    *   list all the issues that were not satisfactorily resolved and formulate procedures to resolve them; and

    *   express your appreciation to your staff once again for their hard work during the crisis.

13. The four combinations of time categories should be:

    *   urgent and important—crisis management, immediate attention needed;

    *   not urgent but important—planning and prevention activities;

    *   urgent but not important—pressing activities that may be easy to accomplish; and

    *   not urgent and not important—easily accomplished, time-wasting activities.

14. Following are the characteristics that define effective teams and team players:

    *   the team has clear and specific goals and objectives,

    *   team meetings have a relaxed atmosphere where members can offer help and share experiences;

    *   each member has a role in reaching the team's goals;

    *   team members listen without judging and with interest in what others are saying;

    *   there is civilized disagreement among team members, who criticize constructively;

    *   decisions are reached by a consensus of support, not unanimity, with even disagreeing members pledging to support the final decision;

- there is open communication and trust among members;

- each member has a clear assignment;

- all members are responsible for the team's success or failure;

- the team builds networks with employees outside the team and asks for their feedback;

- the team contains a diversity of employee styles—contributors, collaborators, communicators, and challengers; and

- the team performs a formal or informal self-assessment.

15. When conducting performance appraisals, managers often make these common mistakes:

- guilt over negative evaluations,
- no accountability for the manager, and
- improper application of standards

16. Some of the forms of guidance in interpreting tax laws, other than IRS regulations, include:

- Revenue Procedures
- Revenue Rulings
- Private Letter Rulings
- Publications
- Announcements, Notices, and News Releases
- Field Service Advice, Service Center Advice, Internal Legal Memoranda

17. Union contract obligations can affect the following areas of payroll processing:

- dues checkoffs,
- fringe benefit contributions,
- upcoming layoffs,
- wage increases,
- probationary employees, and
- overtime and other premium pay.

18. Once the type of meeting has been determined, the manager leading the meeting should take the following steps:

- prepare an agenda,
- keep the meeting on track,
- promote participation, and
- keep written records.

19. The four stages of team development are:

- forming,
- storming,
- norming, and
- performing.

Answer Key

True or False Questions

1. False   Most payroll managers achieve their position because of their technical proficiency.

2. True

3. True

4. True

5. False   Timely completion of subtasks will lead to attainment of the objectives.

6. True

7. False   At all times during the hiring process—from job analysis through interviewing and orientation, the payroll manager must keep in mind the legal requirements surrounding the process.

8. True

9. False   The payroll manager must decide which employee will be assigned the responsibility for each task or portion of a task in the department.

10. False   Use a different training method before resorting to discipline.

11. False   Training can improve skills and knowledge, not attitude.

12. True

13. True

14. True

15. True

16. True

17. True

18. False   Counseling should not be used by a payroll manager when an employee has a severe personal problem. The employee should be referred to an appropriate employee counseling program if the employer has an Employee Assistance Program.

19. False   While most payroll managers do not like to think about it, crisis management is one of the most important leadership tests they will have.

20. True

21. False   Managers who are constantly moving from crisis to crisis, or who fail to delegate properly, have no time to focus on the payroll department's overall mission of quality service or their own personal goals and objectives.

22. True

23. False   Performance evaluations are a formal way of giving feedback. They provide a form and written record of how employees are performing relative to present goals that are designed to help the department and company meet their overall business goals.

24. True

25. False   The final stage of team development is performing.

Multiple Choice Questions

1.	c	11.	c
2.	b	12.	d
3.	a	13.	b
4.	c	14.	c
5.	d	15.	d
6.	a	16.	b
7.	d	17.	a
8.	c	18.	c
9.	d	19.	d
10.	a	20.	c

SECTION 14: PAYROLL FOR U.S. EMPLOYEES ABROAD AND ALIENS IN THE U.S.

Review Questions

1. Reasonable housing expenses do not include the following:

    - telephone and cable television charges,
    - capital expenditures such as mortgage payments or furniture,
    - cost of domestic labor such as a maid or gardener, and
    - lavish or extravagant expenses under the circumstances.

2. An employee's tax home is the location of his or her regular place of business. If there is none, the employee's tax home is where the employee regularly lives.

3. Whether an expatriate employee is a bona fide resident of a foreign country depends on the following factors:

    - whether the employee brings his or her family and they intend to make the foreign country their home for the duration of the assignment;

    - purchase of a home or signing a long-term lease in the foreign country;

    - involvement in the culture and social life of the foreign country;

    - the terms of the employment agreement regarding the foreign assignment; and

    - the type of visa or residence permit secured by the employee.

4. This test is met if the expatriate employee has a foreign tax home and is physically present in a foreign country (or countries) for 330 full days during any consecutive 12-month period.

5. Foreign earned income is income earned by an employee from sources within a foreign country while that employee has a foreign tax home and qualifies for the foreign earned income exclusion under the bona fide residence or physical presence test. Earned income includes all compensation, such as wages, salaries, commissions, bonuses, tax reimbursements, cost of living allowances, educational reimbursements, professional fees, etc., paid for personal services rendered, including noncash payments.

6. Totalization agreements are agreements between the U.S. and another country under which expatriate employees working "temporarily" in the foreign country would be subject to U.S. social security tax only. Wages earned by employees working "permanently" in the foreign country would be subject only to the foreign country's social security taxes. The reverse is also true for foreign employees working in the U.S.

7. Income tax treaty benefits include:

    *   nondiscrimination clauses allowing resident aliens to qualify for the foreign earned income and housing cost exclusions under the bona fide residence test as well as the physical presence test;

    *   a partial or total exemption from taxation by the foreign country for an employee's wages for personal services performed in the treaty country if the employee's stay is short and certain other requirements are met;

    *   wages received by a U.S. teacher or professor in a treaty country are exempt from foreign taxes under most treaties for temporary periods of up to 2 or 3 years;

    *   amounts received by U.S. residents for study, research, or business and technical training are generally exempt from the treaty country's income tax; and

    *   to avoid double taxation, tax treaties provide for credits and deductions to reduce taxes imposed by the foreign country.

8. An education allowance is added compensation for an expatriate so the employee can send his or her children to a private or boarding school.

9. Tax protection plans attempt to guarantee that the employee will be reimbursed by the employer to the extent that the employee's combined income and social security taxes in the U.S. and the foreign country exceed the amount the employee would have paid if living and working in the U.S.

10. Tax equalization plans ensure that all expatriates continue to incur a tax burden equal to what they would incur if they were living and working in the U.S., regardless of the actual foreign tax liability.

11. The following factors generally indicate an employee's domicile:

    *   where the employee votes;

    *   where the employee maintains a residence;

    *   where the employee's immediate family lives and where children attend school;

    *   whether the employee owns a new abode or has a short-term lease;

    *   where the employee returns after vacations or other leaves from work;

    *   the state issuing the employee's driver's license; and

    *   where bank accounts and business associations are maintained.

12. Some of the factors that generally indicate residency include:

    *   physical presence;

    *   where family members live and children attend school;

    *   where the employee works, has business interests, and owns property; and

    *   where bank accounts and business interests are maintained.

13. Under the Internal Revenue Code, an alien qualifies as a resident if he or she meets either one of two tests—the lawful permanent resident test or the substantial presence test.

14. The substantial presence test to determine an alien's tax status requires the following:

    - that the alien be present in the U.S. for at least 31 days during the current calendar year; and

    - that the total of the number of days of U.S. presence during the current calendar year, plus one-third of the U.S. days during the first preceding calendar year, plus one-sixth of the U.S. days during the second preceding calendar year, be at least 183 days (no rounding allowed—fractions must be used).

15. The specific conditions that must be satisfied for the "commercial traveler" exemption to apply are as follows:

    - the nonresident alien employee is in the U.S. for no more than a total of 90 days during the taxable year;

    - compensation received for work performed in the U.S. totals no more than $3,000 during the taxable year; and

    - the nonresident alien is employed by: a U.S. employer in a foreign country or a U.S. possession or by a foreign employer not engaged in a trade or business in the U.S.

True or False Questions

1. True

2. False   The total exclusion is up to the first $80,000 of foreign earned income in 2006.

3. True

4. False   For purposes of the §911 exclusions, all territories of the U.S., including Guam, are not considered foreign countries.

5. True

6. True

7. False   Travel and living expense reimbursements for employees on a temporary foreign assignment may be excluded from income as reimbursed employee business travel expenses if they are provided under an accountable plan.

8. True

9. True

10. False   Reimbursements for nondeductible moving expenses incurred for a move from the U.S. to a foreign country are included in foreign earned income.

11. True

12. True

13. False   The foreign earned income exclusion is available to each spouse to the extent that each spouse actually has foreign earned income.

14. True

15. True

16. True

17. True

18. False   Employers cannot require nonresident aliens to produce their social security cards as proof of authorization to work in the U.S. The alien can produce any approved document to show work authorization.

19. False   In general, social security and Medicare taxes apply to all wages paid for work performed in the U.S., regardless of the citizenship or residency status of the employee (unless exempted by a totalization agreement).

20. True

21. True

22. True

Multiple Choice Questions

1.	c	11.	a	
2.	b	12.	c	
3.	d	13.	c	
4.	b	14.	a	
5.	c	15.	c	
6.	d	16.	b	
7.	b	17.	d	
8.	b	18.	d	
9.	d	19.	a	
10.	b	20.	c	

SECTION 15: PREPARING FOR THE CPP EXAM

Practice Test Number 1

1.	a	14.	b
2.	c	15.	a
3.	a	16.	c
4.	c	17.	a
5.	b	18.	c
6.	b	19.	b
7.	c	20.	c
8.	a	21.	c
9.	c	22.	c
10.	c	23.	c
11.	b	24.	c
12.	d	25.	b
13.	c		

Practice Test Number 2

1.	c	14.	a
2.	a	15.	d
3.	b	16.	b
4.	d	17.	a
5.	b	18.	c
6.	d	19.	a
7.	d	20.	a
8.	d	21.	b
9.	d	22.	d
10.	d	23.	d
11.	d	24.	c
12.	c	25.	b
13.	c		

Practice Test Number 3

1.	c	14.	b
2.	d	15.	b
3.	b	16.	d
4.	a	17.	c
5.	c	18.	c
6.	b	19.	c
7.	c	20.	b
8.	d	21.	c
9.	a	22.	c
10.	a	23.	c
11.	a	24.	b
12.	c	25.	c
13.	a		

Practice Test Number 4

1.	c	14.	d
2.	b	15.	c
3.	a	16.	c
4.	d	17.	a
5.	a	18.	b
6.	d	19.	b
7.	a	20.	c
8.	b	21.	b
9.	d	22.	c
10.	a	23.	a
11.	c	24.	d
12.	b	25.	b
13.	a		

APPENDIX—FEDERAL WITHHOLDING TABLES, FORMS, AND INSTRUCTIONS

TABLE OF CONTENTS

Appendix

If the number of withholding allowances is:	ALLOWANCE TABLE FOR WAGES PAID IN 2006							
	And wages are paid –							
	WEEKLY	BIWEEKLY	SEMI-MONTHLY	MONTHLY	QUARTERLY	SEMI-ANNUALLY	ANNUALLY	DAILY OR MISC.
	The total amount of withholding allowances for the payroll period is:							
0	$ -	$ -	$ -	$ -	$ -	$ -	$ -	$ -
1	63.46	126.92	137.50	275.00	825.00	1,650.00	3,300.00	12.69
2	126.92	253.84	275.00	550.00	1,650.00	3,300.00	6,600.00	25.38
3	190.38	380.76	412.50	825.00	2,475.00	4,950.00	9,900.00	38.07
4	253.84	507.68	550.00	1,100.00	3,300.00	6,600.00	13,200.00	50.76
5	317.30	634.60	687.50	1,375.00	4,125.00	8,250.00	16,500.00	63.45
6	380.76	761.52	825.00	1,650.00	4,950.00	9,900.00	19,800.00	76.14
7	444.22	888.44	962.50	1,925.00	5,775.00	11,550.00	23,100.00	88.83
8	507.68	1,015.36	1,100.00	2,200.00	6,600.00	13,200.00	26,400.00	101.52
9	571.14	1,142.28	1,237.50	2,475.00	7,425.00	14,850.00	29,700.00	114.21
10	634.60	1,269.20	1,375.00	2,750.00	8,250.00	16,500.00	33,000.00	126.90

Tables for Percentage Method of Withholding
(For Wages Paid in 2006)

TABLE 1—WEEKLY Payroll Period

(a) SINGLE person (including head of household)—		(b) MARRIED person—	
If the amount of wages (after subtracting withholding allowances) is:	The amount of income tax to withhold is:	If the amount of wages (after subtracting withholding allowances) is:	The amount of income tax to withhold is:
Not over $51	$0	Not over $154	$0

Over—	But not over—			of excess over—	Over—	But not over—			of excess over—
$51	—$192	. .	10%	—$51	$154	—$440	. .	10%	—$154
$192	—$620	. .	$14.10 plus 15%	—$192	$440	—$1,308	. .	$28.60 plus 15%	—$440
$620	—$1,409	. .	$78.30 plus 25%	—$620	$1,308	—$2,440	. .	$158.80 plus 25%	—$1,308
$1,409	—$3,013	. .	$275.55 plus 28%	—$1,409	$2,440	—$3,759	. .	$441.80 plus 28%	—$2,440
$3,013	—$6,508	. .	$724.67 plus 33%	—$3,013	$3,759	—$6,607	. .	$811.12 plus 33%	—$3,759
$6,508	. . . . .		$1,878.02 plus 35%	—$6,508	$6,607	. . . . .		$1,750.96 plus 35%	—$6,607

TABLE 2—BIWEEKLY Payroll Period

(a) SINGLE person (including head of household)—		(b) MARRIED person—	
If the amount of wages (after subtracting withholding allowances) is:	The amount of income tax to withhold is:	If the amount of wages (after subtracting withholding allowances) is:	The amount of income tax to withhold is:
Not over $102	$0	Not over $308	$0

Over—	But not over—			of excess over—	Over—	But not over—			of excess over—
$102	—$385	. .	10%	—$102	$308	—$881	. .	10%	—$308
$385	—$1,240	. .	$28.30 plus 15%	—$385	$881	—$2,617	. .	$57.30 plus 15%	—$881
$1,240	—$2,817	. .	$156.55 plus 25%	—$1,240	$2,617	—$4,881	. .	$317.70 plus 25%	—$2,617
$2,817	—$6,025	. .	$550.80 plus 28%	—$2,817	$4,881	—$7,517	. .	$883.70 plus 28%	—$4,881
$6,025	—$13,015	. .	$1,449.04 plus 33%	—$6,025	$7,517	—$13,213	. .	$1,621.78 plus 33%	—$7,517
$13,015	. . . . .		$3,755.74 plus 35%	—$13,015	$13,213	. . . . .		$3,501.46 plus 35%	—$13,213

TABLE 3—SEMIMONTHLY Payroll Period

(a) SINGLE person (including head of household)—		(b) MARRIED person—	
If the amount of wages (after subtracting withholding allowances) is:	The amount of income tax to withhold is:	If the amount of wages (after subtracting withholding allowances) is:	The amount of income tax to withhold is:
Not over $110	$0	Not over $333	$0

Over—	But not over—			of excess over—	Over—	But not over—			of excess over—
$110	—$417	. .	10%	—$110	$333	—$954	. .	10%	—$333
$417	—$1,343	. .	$30.70 plus 15%	—$417	$954	—$2,835	. .	$62.10 plus 15%	—$954
$1,343	—$3,052	. .	$169.60 plus 25%	—$1,343	$2,835	—$5,288	. .	$344.25 plus 25%	—$2,835
$3,052	—$6,527	. .	$596.85 plus 28%	—$3,052	$5,288	—$8,144	. .	$957.50 plus 28%	—$5,288
$6,527	—$14,100	. .	$1,569.85 plus 33%	—$6,527	$8,144	—$14,315	. .	$1,757.18 plus 33%	—$8,144
$14,100	. . . . .		$4,068.94 plus 35%	—$14,100	$14,315	. . . . .		$3,793.61 plus 35%	—$14,315

TABLE 4—MONTHLY Payroll Period

(a) SINGLE person (including head of household)—		(b) MARRIED person—	
If the amount of wages (after subtracting withholding allowances) is:	The amount of income tax to withhold is:	If the amount of wages (after subtracting withholding allowances) is:	The amount of income tax to withhold is:
Not over $221	$0	Not over $667	$0

Over—	But not over—			of excess over—	Over—	But not over—			of excess over—
$221	—$833	. .	10%	—$221	$667	—$1,908	. .	10%	—$667
$833	—$2,687	. .	$61.20 plus 15%	—$833	$1,908	—$5,670	. .	$124.10 plus 15%	—$1,908
$2,687	—$6,104	. .	$339.30 plus 25%	—$2,687	$5,670	—$10,575	. .	$688.40 plus 25%	—$5,670
$6,104	—$13,054	. .	$1,193.55 plus 28%	—$6,104	$10,575	—$16,288	. .	$1,914.65 plus 28%	—$10,575
$13,054	—$28,200	. .	$3,139.55 plus 33%	—$13,054	$16,288	—$28,629	. .	$3,514.29 plus 33%	—$16,288
$28,200	. . . . .		$8,137.73 plus 35%	—$28,200	$28,629	. . . . .		$7,586.82 plus 35%	—$28,629

Tables for Percentage Method of Withholding (Continued)
(For Wages Paid in 2006)

TABLE 5—QUARTERLY Payroll Period

(a) SINGLE person (including head of household)—

If the amount of wages (after subtracting withholding allowances) is:		The amount of income tax to withhold is:	
Not over $663		$0	
Over—	**But not over—**		**of excess over—**
$663	—$2,500 .	. 10%	—$663
$2,500	—$8,060 .	. $183.70 plus 15%	—$2,500
$8,060	—$18,313 .	. $1,017.70 plus 25%	—$8,060
$18,313	—$39,163 .	. $3,580.95 plus 28%	—$18,313
$39,163	—$84,600 .	. $9,418.95 plus 33%	—$39,163
$84,600	. . . . .	. $24,413.16 plus 35%	—$84,600

(b) MARRIED person—

If the amount of wages (after subtracting withholding allowances) is:		The amount of income tax to withhold is:	
Not over $2,000		$0	
Over—	**But not over—**		**of excess over—**
$2,000	—$5,725 .	. 10%	—$2,000
$5,725	—$17,010 .	. $372.50 plus 15%	—$5,725
$17,010	—$31,725 .	. $2,065.25 plus 25%	—$17,010
$31,725	—$48,863 .	. $5,744.00 plus 28%	—$31,725
$48,863	—$85,888 .	. $10,542.64 plus 33%	—$48,863
$85,888	. . . . .	. $22,760.89 plus 35%	—$85,888

TABLE 6—SEMIANNUAL Payroll Period

(a) SINGLE person (including head of household)—

If the amount of wages (after subtracting withholding allowances) is:		The amount of income tax to withhold is:	
Not over $1,325		$0	
Over—	**But not over—**		**of excess over—**
$1,325	—$5,000 .	. 10%	—$1,325
$5,000	—$16,120 .	. $367.50 plus 15%	—$5,000
$16,120	—$36,625 .	. $2,035.50 plus 25%	—$16,120
$36,625	—$78,325 .	. $7,161.75 plus 28%	—$36,625
$78,325	—$169,200 .	. $18,837.75 plus 33%	—$78,325
$169,200	. . . . .	. $48,826.50 plus 35%	—$169,200

(b) MARRIED person—

If the amount of wages (after subtracting withholding allowances) is:		The amount of income tax to withhold is:	
Not over $4,000		$0	
Over—	**But not over—**		**of excess over—**
$4,000	—$11,450 .	. 10%	—$4,000
$11,450	—$34,020 .	. $745.00 plus 15%	—$11,450
$34,020	—$63,450 .	. $4,130.50 plus 25%	—$34,020
$63,450	—$97,725 .	. $11,488.00 plus 28%	—$63,450
$97,725	—$171,775 .	. $21,085.00 plus 33%	—$97,725
$171,775	. . . . .	. $45,521.50 plus 35%	—$171,775

TABLE 7—ANNUAL Payroll Period

(a) SINGLE person (including head of household)—

If the amount of wages (after subtracting withholding allowances) is:		The amount of income tax to withhold is:	
Not over $2,650		$0	
Over—	**But not over—**		**of excess over—**
$2,650	—$10,000 .	. 10%	—$2,650
$10,000	—$32,240 .	. $735.00 plus 15%	—$10,000
$32,240	—$73,250 .	. $4,071.00 plus 25%	—$32,240
$73,250	—$156,650 .	. $14,323.50 plus 28%	—$73,250
$156,650	—$338,400 .	. $37,675.50 plus 33%	—$156,650
$338,400	. . . . .	. $97,653.00 plus 35%	—$338,400

(b) MARRIED person—

If the amount of wages (after subtracting withholding allowances) is:		The amount of income tax to withhold is:	
Not over $8,000		$0	
Over—	**But not over—**		**of excess over—**
$8,000	—$22,900 .	. 10%	—$8,000
$22,900	—$68,040 .	. $1,490.00 plus 15%	—$22,900
$68,040	—$126,900 .	. $8,261.00 plus 25%	—$68,040
$126,900	—$195,450 .	. $22,976.00 plus 28%	—$126,900
$195,450	—$343,550 .	. $42,170.00 plus 33%	—$195,450
$343,550	. . . . .	. $91,043.00 plus 35%	—$343,550

TABLE 8—DAILY or MISCELLANEOUS Payroll Period

(a) SINGLE person (including head of household)—

If the amount of wages (after subtracting withholding allowances) divided by the number of days in the payroll period is:		The amount of income tax to withhold per day is:	
Not over $10.20		$0	
Over—	**But not over—**		**of excess over—**
$10.20	—$38.50 .	. 10%	—$10.20
$38.50	—$124.00 .	. $2.83 plus 15%	—$38.50
$124.00	—$281.70 .	. $15.66 plus 25%	—$124.00
$281.70	—$602.50 .	. $55.09 plus 28%	—$281.70
$602.50	—$1,301.50 .	. $144.91 plus 33%	—$602.50
$1,301.50	. . . . .	. $375.58 plus 35%	— $1,301.50

(b) MARRIED person—

If the amount of wages (after subtracting withholding allowances) divided by the number of days in the payroll period is:		The amount of income tax to withhold per day is:	
Not over $30.80		$0	
Over—	**But not over—**		**of excess over—**
$30.80	—$88.10 .	. 10%	—$30.80
$88.10	—$261.70 .	. $5.73 plus 15%	—$88.10
$261.70	—$488.10 .	. $31.77 plus 25%	—$261.70
$488.10	—$751.70 .	. $88.37 plus 28%	—$488.10
$751.70	—$1,321.30 .	. $162.18 plus 33%	—$751.70
$1,321.30	. . . . .	. $350.15 plus 35%	— $1,321.30

SINGLE Persons—WEEKLY Payroll Period

(For Wages Paid in 2006)

If the wages are—		And the number of withholding allowances claimed is—										
At least	But less than	0	1	2	3	4	5	6	7	8	9	10
		The amount of income tax to be withheld is—										
$0	$55	$0	$0	$0	$0	$0	$0	$0	$0	$0	$0	$0
55	60	1	0	0	0	0	0	0	0	0	0	0
60	65	1	0	0	0	0	0	0	0	0	0	0
65	70	2	0	0	0	0	0	0	0	0	0	0
70	75	2	0	0	0	0	0	0	0	0	0	0
75	80	3	0	0	0	0	0	0	0	0	0	0
80	85	3	0	0	0	0	0	0	0	0	0	0
85	90	4	0	0	0	0	0	0	0	0	0	0
90	95	4	0	0	0	0	0	0	0	0	0	0
95	100	5	0	0	0	0	0	0	0	0	0	0
100	105	5	0	0	0	0	0	0	0	0	0	0
105	110	6	0	0	0	0	0	0	0	0	0	0
110	115	6	0	0	0	0	0	0	0	0	0	0
115	120	7	0	0	0	0	0	0	0	0	0	0
120	125	7	1	0	0	0	0	0	0	0	0	0
125	130	8	1	0	0	0	0	0	0	0	0	0
130	135	8	2	0	0	0	0	0	0	0	0	0
135	140	9	2	0	0	0	0	0	0	0	0	0
140	145	9	3	0	0	0	0	0	0	0	0	0
145	150	10	3	0	0	0	0	0	0	0	0	0
150	155	10	4	0	0	0	0	0	0	0	0	0
155	160	11	4	0	0	0	0	0	0	0	0	0
160	165	11	5	0	0	0	0	0	0	0	0	0
165	170	12	5	0	0	0	0	0	0	0	0	0
170	175	12	6	0	0	0	0	0	0	0	0	0
175	180	13	6	0	0	0	0	0	0	0	0	0
180	185	13	7	0	0	0	0	0	0	0	0	0
185	190	14	7	1	0	0	0	0	0	0	0	0
190	195	14	8	1	0	0	0	0	0	0	0	0
195	200	15	8	2	0	0	0	0	0	0	0	0
200	210	16	9	3	0	0	0	0	0	0	0	0
210	220	18	10	4	0	0	0	0	0	0	0	0
220	230	19	11	5	0	0	0	0	0	0	0	0
230	240	21	12	6	0	0	0	0	0	0	0	0
240	250	22	13	7	0	0	0	0	0	0	0	0
250	260	24	14	8	1	0	0	0	0	0	0	0
260	270	25	16	9	2	0	0	0	0	0	0	0
270	280	27	17	10	3	0	0	0	0	0	0	0
280	290	28	19	11	4	0	0	0	0	0	0	0
290	300	30	20	12	5	0	0	0	0	0	0	0
300	310	31	22	13	6	0	0	0	0	0	0	0
310	320	33	23	14	7	1	0	0	0	0	0	0
320	330	34	25	15	8	2	0	0	0	0	0	0
330	340	36	26	17	9	3	0	0	0	0	0	0
340	350	37	28	18	10	4	0	0	0	0	0	0
350	360	39	29	20	11	5	0	0	0	0	0	0
360	370	40	31	21	12	6	0	0	0	0	0	0
370	380	42	32	23	13	7	1	0	0	0	0	0
380	390	43	34	24	14	8	2	0	0	0	0	0
390	400	45	35	26	16	9	3	0	0	0	0	0
400	410	46	37	27	17	10	4	0	0	0	0	0
410	420	48	38	29	19	11	5	0	0	0	0	0
420	430	49	40	30	20	12	6	0	0	0	0	0
430	440	51	41	32	22	13	7	0	0	0	0	0
440	450	52	43	33	23	14	8	1	0	0	0	0
450	460	54	44	35	25	15	9	2	0	0	0	0
460	470	55	46	36	26	17	10	3	0	0	0	0
470	480	57	47	38	28	18	11	4	0	0	0	0
480	490	58	49	39	29	20	12	5	0	0	0	0
490	500	60	50	41	31	21	13	6	0	0	0	0
500	510	61	52	42	32	23	14	7	1	0	0	0
510	520	63	53	44	34	24	15	8	2	0	0	0
520	530	64	55	45	35	26	16	9	3	0	0	0
530	540	66	56	47	37	27	18	10	4	0	0	0
540	550	67	58	48	38	29	19	11	5	0	0	0
550	560	69	59	50	40	30	21	12	6	0	0	0
560	570	70	61	51	41	32	22	13	7	1	0	0
570	580	72	62	53	43	33	24	14	8	2	0	0
580	590	73	64	54	44	35	25	16	9	3	0	0
590	600	75	65	56	46	36	27	17	10	4	0	0

SINGLE Persons—WEEKLY Payroll Period
(For Wages Paid in 2006)

If the wages are—		And the number of withholding allowances claimed is—										
At least	But less than	0	1	2	3	4	5	6	7	8	9	10
		The amount of income tax to be withheld is—										
$600	$610	$76	$67	$57	$47	$38	$28	$19	$11	$5	$0	$0
610	620	78	68	59	49	39	30	20	12	6	0	0
620	630	80	70	60	50	41	31	22	13	7	0	0
630	640	82	71	62	52	42	33	23	14	8	1	0
640	650	85	73	63	53	44	34	25	15	9	2	0
650	660	87	74	65	55	45	36	26	17	10	3	0
660	670	90	76	66	56	47	37	28	18	11	4	0
670	680	92	77	68	58	48	39	29	20	12	5	0
680	690	95	79	69	59	50	40	31	21	13	6	0
690	700	97	81	71	61	51	42	32	23	14	7	1
700	710	100	84	72	62	53	43	34	24	15	8	2
710	720	102	86	74	64	54	45	35	26	16	9	3
720	730	105	89	75	65	56	46	37	27	18	10	4
730	740	107	91	77	67	57	48	38	29	19	11	5
740	750	110	94	78	68	59	49	40	30	21	12	6
750	760	112	96	80	70	60	51	41	32	22	13	7
760	770	115	99	83	71	62	52	43	33	24	14	8
770	780	117	101	85	73	63	54	44	35	25	16	9
780	790	120	104	88	74	65	55	46	36	27	17	10
790	800	122	106	90	76	66	57	47	38	28	19	11
800	810	125	109	93	77	68	58	49	39	30	20	12
810	820	127	111	95	79	69	60	50	41	31	22	13
820	830	130	114	98	82	71	61	52	42	33	23	14
830	840	132	116	100	84	72	63	53	44	34	25	15
840	850	135	119	103	87	74	64	55	45	36	26	17
850	860	137	121	105	89	75	66	56	47	37	28	18
860	870	140	124	108	92	77	67	58	48	39	29	20
870	880	142	126	110	94	79	69	59	50	40	31	21
880	890	145	129	113	97	81	70	61	51	42	32	23
890	900	147	131	115	99	84	72	62	53	43	34	24
900	910	150	134	118	102	86	73	64	54	45	35	26
910	920	152	136	120	104	89	75	65	56	46	37	27
920	930	155	139	123	107	91	76	67	57	48	38	29
930	940	157	141	125	109	94	78	68	59	49	40	30
940	950	160	144	128	112	96	80	70	60	51	41	32
950	960	162	146	130	114	99	83	71	62	52	43	33
960	970	165	149	133	117	101	85	73	63	54	44	35
970	980	167	151	135	119	104	88	74	65	55	46	36
980	990	170	154	138	122	106	90	76	66	57	47	38
990	1,000	172	156	140	124	109	93	77	68	58	49	39
1,000	1,010	175	159	143	127	111	95	79	69	60	50	41
1,010	1,020	177	161	145	129	114	98	82	71	61	52	42
1,020	1,030	180	164	148	132	116	100	84	72	63	53	44
1,030	1,040	182	166	150	134	119	103	87	74	64	55	45
1,040	1,050	185	169	153	137	121	105	89	75	66	56	47
1,050	1,060	187	171	155	139	124	108	92	77	67	58	48
1,060	1,070	190	174	158	142	126	110	94	78	69	59	50
1,070	1,080	192	176	160	144	129	113	97	81	70	61	51
1,080	1,090	195	179	163	147	131	115	99	83	72	62	53
1,090	1,100	197	181	165	149	134	118	102	86	73	64	54
1,100	1,110	200	184	168	152	136	120	104	88	75	65	56
1,110	1,120	202	186	170	154	139	123	107	91	76	67	57
1,120	1,130	205	189	173	157	141	125	109	93	78	68	59
1,130	1,140	207	191	175	159	144	128	112	96	80	70	60
1,140	1,150	210	194	178	162	146	130	114	98	83	71	62
1,150	1,160	212	196	180	164	149	133	117	101	85	73	63
1,160	1,170	215	199	183	167	151	135	119	103	88	74	65
1,170	1,180	217	201	185	169	154	138	122	106	90	76	66
1,180	1,190	220	204	188	172	156	140	124	108	93	77	68
1,190	1,200	222	206	190	174	159	143	127	111	95	79	69
1,200	1,210	225	209	193	177	161	145	129	113	98	82	71
1,210	1,220	227	211	195	179	164	148	132	116	100	84	72
1,220	1,230	230	214	198	182	166	150	134	118	103	87	74
1,230	1,240	232	216	200	184	169	153	137	121	105	89	75
1,240	1,250	235	219	203	187	171	155	139	123	108	92	77

$1,250 and over   Use Table 1(a) for a **SINGLE person** on page 36. Also see the instructions on page 34.

MARRIED Persons—WEEKLY Payroll Period
(For Wages Paid in 2006)

If the wages are—		And the number of withholding allowances claimed is—										
At least	But less than	0	1	2	3	4	5	6	7	8	9	10
		The amount of income tax to be withheld is—										
$0	$125	$0	$0	$0	$0	$0	$0	$0	$0	$0	$0	$0
125	130	0	0	0	0	0	0	0	0	0	0	0
130	135	0	0	0	0	0	0	0	0	0	0	0
135	140	0	0	0	0	0	0	0	0	0	0	0
140	145	0	0	0	0	0	0	0	0	0	0	0
145	150	0	0	0	0	0	0	0	0	0	0	0
150	155	0	0	0	0	0	0	0	0	0	0	0
155	160	0	0	0	0	0	0	0	0	0	0	0
160	165	1	0	0	0	0	0	0	0	0	0	0
165	170	1	0	0	0	0	0	0	0	0	0	0
170	175	2	0	0	0	0	0	0	0	0	0	0
175	180	2	0	0	0	0	0	0	0	0	0	0
180	185	3	0	0	0	0	0	0	0	0	0	0
185	190	3	0	0	0	0	0	0	0	0	0	0
190	195	4	0	0	0	0	0	0	0	0	0	0
195	200	4	0	0	0	0	0	0	0	0	0	0
200	210	5	0	0	0	0	0	0	0	0	0	0
210	220	6	0	0	0	0	0	0	0	0	0	0
220	230	7	1	0	0	0	0	0	0	0	0	0
230	240	8	2	0	0	0	0	0	0	0	0	0
240	250	9	3	0	0	0	0	0	0	0	0	0
250	260	10	4	0	0	0	0	0	0	0	0	0
260	270	11	5	0	0	0	0	0	0	0	0	0
270	280	12	6	0	0	0	0	0	0	0	0	0
280	290	13	7	0	0	0	0	0	0	0	0	0
290	300	14	8	1	0	0	0	0	0	0	0	0
300	310	15	9	2	0	0	0	0	0	0	0	0
310	320	16	10	3	0	0	0	0	0	0	0	0
320	330	17	11	4	0	0	0	0	0	0	0	0
330	340	18	12	5	0	0	0	0	0	0	0	0
340	350	19	13	6	0	0	0	0	0	0	0	0
350	360	20	14	7	1	0	0	0	0	0	0	0
360	370	21	15	8	2	0	0	0	0	0	0	0
370	380	22	16	9	3	0	0	0	0	0	0	0
380	390	23	17	10	4	0	0	0	0	0	0	0
390	400	24	18	11	5	0	0	0	0	0	0	0
400	410	25	19	12	6	0	0	0	0	0	0	0
410	420	26	20	13	7	1	0	0	0	0	0	0
420	430	27	21	14	8	2	0	0	0	0	0	0
430	440	28	22	15	9	3	0	0	0	0	0	0
440	450	29	23	16	10	4	0	0	0	0	0	0
450	460	31	24	17	11	5	0	0	0	0	0	0
460	470	32	25	18	12	6	0	0	0	0	0	0
470	480	34	26	19	13	7	0	0	0	0	0	0
480	490	35	27	20	14	8	1	0	0	0	0	0
490	500	37	28	21	15	9	2	0	0	0	0	0
500	510	38	29	22	16	10	3	0	0	0	0	0
510	520	40	30	23	17	11	4	0	0	0	0	0
520	530	41	32	24	18	12	5	0	0	0	0	0
530	540	43	33	25	19	13	6	0	0	0	0	0
540	550	44	35	26	20	14	7	1	0	0	0	0
550	560	46	36	27	21	15	8	2	0	0	0	0
560	570	47	38	28	22	16	9	3	0	0	0	0
570	580	49	39	30	23	17	10	4	0	0	0	0
580	590	50	41	31	24	18	11	5	0	0	0	0
590	600	52	42	33	25	19	12	6	0	0	0	0
600	610	53	44	34	26	20	13	7	1	0	0	0
610	620	55	45	36	27	21	14	8	2	0	0	0
620	630	56	47	37	28	22	15	9	3	0	0	0
630	640	58	48	39	29	23	16	10	4	0	0	0
640	650	59	50	40	31	24	17	11	5	0	0	0
650	660	61	51	42	32	25	18	12	6	0	0	0
660	670	62	53	43	34	26	19	13	7	0	0	0
670	680	64	54	45	35	27	20	14	8	1	0	0
680	690	65	56	46	37	28	21	15	9	2	0	0
690	700	67	57	48	38	29	22	16	10	3	0	0
700	710	68	59	49	40	30	23	17	11	4	0	0
710	720	70	60	51	41	32	24	18	12	5	0	0
720	730	71	62	52	43	33	25	19	13	6	0	0
730	740	73	63	54	44	35	26	20	14	7	1	0

MARRIED Persons—WEEKLY Payroll Period
(For Wages Paid in 2006)

If the wages are—		And the number of withholding allowances claimed is—										
At least	But less than	0	1	2	3	4	5	6	7	8	9	10
		The amount of income tax to be withheld is—										
$740	$750	$74	$65	$55	$46	$36	$27	$21	$15	$8	$2	$0
750	760	76	66	57	47	38	28	22	16	9	3	0
760	770	77	68	58	49	39	30	23	17	10	4	0
770	780	79	69	60	50	41	31	24	18	11	5	0
780	790	80	71	61	52	42	33	25	19	12	6	0
790	800	82	72	63	53	44	34	26	20	13	7	1
800	810	83	74	64	55	45	36	27	21	14	8	2
810	820	85	75	66	56	47	37	28	22	15	9	3
820	830	86	77	67	58	48	39	29	23	16	10	4
830	840	88	78	69	59	50	40	31	24	17	11	5
840	850	89	80	70	61	51	42	32	25	18	12	6
850	860	91	81	72	62	53	43	34	26	19	13	7
860	870	92	83	73	64	54	45	35	27	20	14	8
870	880	94	84	75	65	56	46	37	28	21	15	9
880	890	95	86	76	67	57	48	38	29	22	16	10
890	900	97	87	78	68	59	49	40	30	23	17	11
900	910	98	89	79	70	60	51	41	32	24	18	12
910	920	100	90	81	71	62	52	43	33	25	19	13
920	930	101	92	82	73	63	54	44	35	26	20	14
930	940	103	93	84	74	65	55	46	36	27	21	15
940	950	104	95	85	76	66	57	47	38	28	22	16
950	960	106	96	87	77	68	58	49	39	30	23	17
960	970	107	98	88	79	69	60	50	41	31	24	18
970	980	109	99	90	80	71	61	52	42	33	25	19
980	990	110	101	91	82	72	63	53	44	34	26	20
990	1,000	112	102	93	83	74	64	55	45	36	27	21
1,000	1,010	113	104	94	85	75	66	56	47	37	28	22
1,010	1,020	115	105	96	86	77	67	58	48	39	29	23
1,020	1,030	116	107	97	88	78	69	59	50	40	31	24
1,030	1,040	118	108	99	89	80	70	61	51	42	32	25
1,040	1,050	119	110	100	91	81	72	62	53	43	34	26
1,050	1,060	121	111	102	92	83	73	64	54	45	35	27
1,060	1,070	122	113	103	94	84	75	65	56	46	37	28
1,070	1,080	124	114	105	95	86	76	67	57	48	38	29
1,080	1,090	125	116	106	97	87	78	68	59	49	40	30
1,090	1,100	127	117	108	98	89	79	70	60	51	41	32
1,100	1,110	128	119	109	100	90	81	71	62	52	43	33
1,110	1,120	130	120	111	101	92	82	73	63	54	44	35
1,120	1,130	131	122	112	103	93	84	74	65	55	46	36
1,130	1,140	133	123	114	104	95	85	76	66	57	47	38
1,140	1,150	134	125	115	106	96	87	77	68	58	49	39
1,150	1,160	136	126	117	107	98	88	79	69	60	50	41
1,160	1,170	137	128	118	109	99	90	80	71	61	52	42
1,170	1,180	139	129	120	110	101	91	82	72	63	53	44
1,180	1,190	140	131	121	112	102	93	83	74	64	55	45
1,190	1,200	142	132	123	113	104	94	85	75	66	56	47
1,200	1,210	143	134	124	115	105	96	86	77	67	58	48
1,210	1,220	145	135	126	116	107	97	88	78	69	59	50
1,220	1,230	146	137	127	118	108	99	89	80	70	61	51
1,230	1,240	148	138	129	119	110	100	91	81	72	62	53
1,240	1,250	149	140	130	121	111	102	92	83	73	64	54
1,250	1,260	151	141	132	122	113	103	94	84	75	65	56
1,260	1,270	152	143	133	124	114	105	95	86	76	67	57
1,270	1,280	154	144	135	125	116	106	97	87	78	68	59
1,280	1,290	155	146	136	127	117	108	98	89	79	70	60
1,290	1,300	157	147	138	128	119	109	100	90	81	71	62
1,300	1,310	158	149	139	130	120	111	101	92	82	73	63
1,310	1,320	161	150	141	131	122	112	103	93	84	74	65
1,320	1,330	163	152	142	133	123	114	104	95	85	76	66
1,330	1,340	166	153	144	134	125	115	106	96	87	77	68
1,340	1,350	168	155	145	136	126	117	107	98	88	79	69
1,350	1,360	171	156	147	137	128	118	109	99	90	80	71
1,360	1,370	173	158	148	139	129	120	110	101	91	82	72
1,370	1,380	176	160	150	140	131	121	112	102	93	83	74
1,380	1,390	178	162	151	142	132	123	113	104	94	85	75
1,390	1,400	181	165	153	143	134	124	115	105	96	86	77

$1,400 and over   Use Table 1(b) for a **MARRIED person** on page 36. Also see the instructions on page 34.

SINGLE Persons—BIWEEKLY Payroll Period

(For Wages Paid in 2006)

If the wages are—		And the number of withholding allowances claimed is—										
At least	But less than	0	1	2	3	4	5	6	7	8	9	10
		The amount of income tax to be withheld is—										
$0	$105	$0	$0	$0	$0	$0	$0	$0	$0	$0	$0	$0
105	110	1	0	0	0	0	0	0	0	0	0	0
110	115	1	0	0	0	0	0	0	0	0	0	0
115	120	2	0	0	0	0	0	0	0	0	0	0
120	125	2	0	0	0	0	0	0	0	0	0	0
125	130	3	0	0	0	0	0	0	0	0	0	0
130	135	3	0	0	0	0	0	0	0	0	0	0
135	140	4	0	0	0	0	0	0	0	0	0	0
140	145	4	0	0	0	0	0	0	0	0	0	0
145	150	5	0	0	0	0	0	0	0	0	0	0
150	155	5	0	0	0	0	0	0	0	0	0	0
155	160	6	0	0	0	0	0	0	0	0	0	0
160	165	6	0	0	0	0	0	0	0	0	0	0
165	170	7	0	0	0	0	0	0	0	0	0	0
170	175	7	0	0	0	0	0	0	0	0	0	0
175	180	8	0	0	0	0	0	0	0	0	0	0
180	185	8	0	0	0	0	0	0	0	0	0	0
185	190	9	0	0	0	0	0	0	0	0	0	0
190	195	9	0	0	0	0	0	0	0	0	0	0
195	200	10	0	0	0	0	0	0	0	0	0	0
200	205	10	0	0	0	0	0	0	0	0	0	0
205	210	11	0	0	0	0	0	0	0	0	0	0
210	215	11	0	0	0	0	0	0	0	0	0	0
215	220	12	0	0	0	0	0	0	0	0	0	0
220	225	12	0	0	0	0	0	0	0	0	0	0
225	230	13	0	0	0	0	0	0	0	0	0	0
230	235	13	0	0	0	0	0	0	0	0	0	0
235	240	14	1	0	0	0	0	0	0	0	0	0
240	245	14	1	0	0	0	0	0	0	0	0	0
245	250	15	2	0	0	0	0	0	0	0	0	0
250	260	15	3	0	0	0	0	0	0	0	0	0
260	270	16	4	0	0	0	0	0	0	0	0	0
270	280	17	5	0	0	0	0	0	0	0	0	0
280	290	18	6	0	0	0	0	0	0	0	0	0
290	300	19	7	0	0	0	0	0	0	0	0	0
300	310	20	8	0	0	0	0	0	0	0	0	0
310	320	21	9	0	0	0	0	0	0	0	0	0
320	330	22	10	0	0	0	0	0	0	0	0	0
330	340	23	11	0	0	0	0	0	0	0	0	0
340	350	24	12	0	0	0	0	0	0	0	0	0
350	360	25	13	0	0	0	0	0	0	0	0	0
360	370	26	14	1	0	0	0	0	0	0	0	0
370	380	27	15	2	0	0	0	0	0	0	0	0
380	390	28	16	3	0	0	0	0	0	0	0	0
390	400	30	17	4	0	0	0	0	0	0	0	0
400	410	31	18	5	0	0	0	0	0	0	0	0
410	420	33	19	6	0	0	0	0	0	0	0	0
420	430	34	20	7	0	0	0	0	0	0	0	0
430	440	36	21	8	0	0	0	0	0	0	0	0
440	450	37	22	9	0	0	0	0	0	0	0	0
450	460	39	23	10	0	0	0	0	0	0	0	0
460	470	40	24	11	0	0	0	0	0	0	0	0
470	480	42	25	12	0	0	0	0	0	0	0	0
480	490	43	26	13	0	0	0	0	0	0	0	0
490	500	45	27	14	1	0	0	0	0	0	0	0
500	520	47	28	15	3	0	0	0	0	0	0	0
520	540	50	31	17	5	0	0	0	0	0	0	0
540	560	53	34	19	7	0	0	0	0	0	0	0
560	580	56	37	21	9	0	0	0	0	0	0	0
580	600	59	40	23	11	0	0	0	0	0	0	0
600	620	62	43	25	13	0	0	0	0	0	0	0
620	640	65	46	27	15	2	0	0	0	0	0	0
640	660	68	49	30	17	4	0	0	0	0	0	0
660	680	71	52	33	19	6	0	0	0	0	0	0
680	700	74	55	36	21	8	0	0	0	0	0	0
700	720	77	58	39	23	10	0	0	0	0	0	0
720	740	80	61	42	25	12	0	0	0	0	0	0
740	760	83	64	45	27	14	1	0	0	0	0	0
760	780	86	67	48	29	16	3	0	0	0	0	0
780	800	89	70	51	32	18	5	0	0	0	0	0

SINGLE Persons—BIWEEKLY Payroll Period

(For Wages Paid in 2006)

If the wages are—		And the number of withholding allowances claimed is—										
At least	But less than	0	1	2	3	4	5	6	7	8	9	10
		The amount of income tax to be withheld is—										
$800	$820	$92	$73	$54	$35	$20	$7	$0	$0	$0	$0	$0
820	840	95	76	57	38	22	9	0	0	0	0	0
840	860	98	79	60	41	24	11	0	0	0	0	0
860	880	101	82	63	44	26	13	1	0	0	0	0
880	900	104	85	66	47	28	15	3	0	0	0	0
900	920	107	88	69	50	31	17	5	0	0	0	0
920	940	110	91	72	53	34	19	7	0	0	0	0
940	960	113	94	75	56	37	21	9	0	0	0	0
960	980	116	97	78	59	40	23	11	0	0	0	0
980	1,000	119	100	81	62	43	25	13	0	0	0	0
1,000	1,020	122	103	84	65	46	27	15	2	0	0	0
1,020	1,040	125	106	87	68	49	30	17	4	0	0	0
1,040	1,060	128	109	90	71	52	33	19	6	0	0	0
1,060	1,080	131	112	93	74	55	36	21	8	0	0	0
1,080	1,100	134	115	96	77	58	39	23	10	0	0	0
1,100	1,120	137	118	99	80	61	42	25	12	0	0	0
1,120	1,140	140	121	102	83	64	45	27	14	1	0	0
1,140	1,160	143	124	105	86	67	48	29	16	3	0	0
1,160	1,180	146	127	108	89	70	51	32	18	5	0	0
1,180	1,200	149	130	111	92	73	54	35	20	7	0	0
1,200	1,220	152	133	114	95	76	57	38	22	9	0	0
1,220	1,240	155	136	117	98	79	60	41	24	11	0	0
1,240	1,260	159	139	120	101	82	63	44	26	13	1	0
1,260	1,280	164	142	123	104	85	66	47	28	15	3	0
1,280	1,300	169	145	126	107	88	69	50	31	17	5	0
1,300	1,320	174	148	129	110	91	72	53	34	19	7	0
1,320	1,340	179	151	132	113	94	75	56	37	21	9	0
1,340	1,360	184	154	135	116	97	78	59	40	23	11	0
1,360	1,380	189	157	138	119	100	81	62	43	25	13	0
1,380	1,400	194	162	141	122	103	84	65	46	27	15	2
1,400	1,420	199	167	144	125	106	87	68	49	30	17	4
1,420	1,440	204	172	147	128	109	90	71	52	33	19	6
1,440	1,460	209	177	150	131	112	93	74	55	36	21	8
1,460	1,480	214	182	153	134	115	96	77	58	39	23	10
1,480	1,500	219	187	156	137	118	99	80	61	42	25	12
1,500	1,520	224	192	161	140	121	102	83	64	45	27	14
1,520	1,540	229	197	166	143	124	105	86	67	48	29	16
1,540	1,560	234	202	171	146	127	108	89	70	51	32	18
1,560	1,580	239	207	176	149	130	111	92	73	54	35	20
1,580	1,600	244	212	181	152	133	114	95	76	57	38	22
1,600	1,620	249	217	186	155	136	117	98	79	60	41	24
1,620	1,640	254	222	191	159	139	120	101	82	63	44	26
1,640	1,660	259	227	196	164	142	123	104	85	66	47	28
1,660	1,680	264	232	201	169	145	126	107	88	69	50	31
1,680	1,700	269	237	206	174	148	129	110	91	72	53	34
1,700	1,720	274	242	211	179	151	132	113	94	75	56	37
1,720	1,740	279	247	216	184	154	135	116	97	78	59	40
1,740	1,760	284	252	221	189	157	138	119	100	81	62	43
1,760	1,780	289	257	226	194	162	141	122	103	84	65	46
1,780	1,800	294	262	231	199	167	144	125	106	87	68	49
1,800	1,820	299	267	236	204	172	147	128	109	90	71	52
1,820	1,840	304	272	241	209	177	150	131	112	93	74	55
1,840	1,860	309	277	246	214	182	153	134	115	96	77	58
1,860	1,880	314	282	251	219	187	156	137	118	99	80	61
1,880	1,900	319	287	256	224	192	160	140	121	102	83	64
1,900	1,920	324	292	261	229	197	165	143	124	105	86	67
1,920	1,940	329	297	266	234	202	170	146	127	108	89	70
1,940	1,960	334	302	271	239	207	175	149	130	111	92	73
1,960	1,980	339	307	276	244	212	180	152	133	114	95	76
1,980	2,000	344	312	281	249	217	185	155	136	117	98	79
2,000	2,020	349	317	286	254	222	190	159	139	120	101	82
2,020	2,040	354	322	291	259	227	195	164	142	123	104	85
2,040	2,060	359	327	296	264	232	200	169	145	126	107	88
2,060	2,080	364	332	301	269	237	205	174	148	129	110	91
2,080	2,100	369	337	306	274	242	210	179	151	132	113	94

$2,100 and over   Use Table 2(a) for a **SINGLE person** on page 36. Also see the instructions on page 34.

MARRIED Persons—BIWEEKLY Payroll Period
(For Wages Paid in 2006)

If the wages are—		And the number of withholding allowances claimed is—										
At least	But less than	0	1	2	3	4	5	6	7	8	9	10
		The amount of income tax to be withheld is—										
$0	$250	$0	$0	$0	$0	$0	$0	$0	$0	$0	$0	$0
250	260	0	0	0	0	0	0	0	0	0	0	0
260	270	0	0	0	0	0	0	0	0	0	0	0
270	280	0	0	0	0	0	0	0	0	0	0	0
280	290	0	0	0	0	0	0	0	0	0	0	0
290	300	0	0	0	0	0	0	0	0	0	0	0
300	310	0	0	0	0	0	0	0	0	0	0	0
310	320	1	0	0	0	0	0	0	0	0	0	0
320	330	2	0	0	0	0	0	0	0	0	0	0
330	340	3	0	0	0	0	0	0	0	0	0	0
340	350	4	0	0	0	0	0	0	0	0	0	0
350	360	5	0	0	0	0	0	0	0	0	0	0
360	370	6	0	0	0	0	0	0	0	0	0	0
370	380	7	0	0	0	0	0	0	0	0	0	0
380	390	8	0	0	0	0	0	0	0	0	0	0
390	400	9	0	0	0	0	0	0	0	0	0	0
400	410	10	0	0	0	0	0	0	0	0	0	0
410	420	11	0	0	0	0	0	0	0	0	0	0
420	430	12	0	0	0	0	0	0	0	0	0	0
430	440	13	0	0	0	0	0	0	0	0	0	0
440	450	14	1	0	0	0	0	0	0	0	0	0
450	460	15	2	0	0	0	0	0	0	0	0	0
460	470	16	3	0	0	0	0	0	0	0	0	0
470	480	17	4	0	0	0	0	0	0	0	0	0
480	490	18	5	0	0	0	0	0	0	0	0	0
490	500	19	6	0	0	0	0	0	0	0	0	0
500	520	20	8	0	0	0	0	0	0	0	0	0
520	540	22	10	0	0	0	0	0	0	0	0	0
540	560	24	12	0	0	0	0	0	0	0	0	0
560	580	26	14	1	0	0	0	0	0	0	0	0
580	600	28	16	3	0	0	0	0	0	0	0	0
600	620	30	18	5	0	0	0	0	0	0	0	0
620	640	32	20	7	0	0	0	0	0	0	0	0
640	660	34	22	9	0	0	0	0	0	0	0	0
660	680	36	24	11	0	0	0	0	0	0	0	0
680	700	38	26	13	0	0	0	0	0	0	0	0
700	720	40	28	15	2	0	0	0	0	0	0	0
720	740	42	30	17	4	0	0	0	0	0	0	0
740	760	44	32	19	6	0	0	0	0	0	0	0
760	780	46	34	21	8	0	0	0	0	0	0	0
780	800	48	36	23	10	0	0	0	0	0	0	0
800	820	50	38	25	12	0	0	0	0	0	0	0
820	840	52	40	27	14	1	0	0	0	0	0	0
840	860	54	42	29	16	3	0	0	0	0	0	0
860	880	56	44	31	18	5	0	0	0	0	0	0
880	900	59	46	33	20	7	0	0	0	0	0	0
900	920	62	48	35	22	9	0	0	0	0	0	0
920	940	65	50	37	24	11	0	0	0	0	0	0
940	960	68	52	39	26	13	1	0	0	0	0	0
960	980	71	54	41	28	15	3	0	0	0	0	0
980	1,000	74	56	43	30	17	5	0	0	0	0	0
1,000	1,020	77	58	45	32	19	7	0	0	0	0	0
1,020	1,040	80	61	47	34	21	9	0	0	0	0	0
1,040	1,060	83	64	49	36	23	11	0	0	0	0	0
1,060	1,080	86	67	51	38	25	13	0	0	0	0	0
1,080	1,100	89	70	53	40	27	15	2	0	0	0	0
1,100	1,120	92	73	55	42	29	17	4	0	0	0	0
1,120	1,140	95	76	57	44	31	19	6	0	0	0	0
1,140	1,160	98	79	60	46	33	21	8	0	0	0	0
1,160	1,180	101	82	63	48	35	23	10	0	0	0	0
1,180	1,200	104	85	66	50	37	25	12	0	0	0	0
1,200	1,220	107	88	69	52	39	27	14	1	0	0	0
1,220	1,240	110	91	72	54	41	29	16	3	0	0	0
1,240	1,260	113	94	75	56	43	31	18	5	0	0	0
1,260	1,280	116	97	78	59	45	33	20	7	0	0	0
1,280	1,300	119	100	81	62	47	35	22	9	0	0	0
1,300	1,320	122	103	84	65	49	37	24	11	0	0	0
1,320	1,340	125	106	87	68	51	39	26	13	1	0	0
1,340	1,360	128	109	90	71	53	41	28	15	3	0	0
1,360	1,380	131	112	93	74	55	43	30	17	5	0	0

MARRIED Persons—BIWEEKLY Payroll Period
(For Wages Paid in 2006)

If the wages are–		And the number of withholding allowances claimed is—										
At least	But less than	0	1	2	3	4	5	6	7	8	9	10
		The amount of income tax to be withheld is—										
$1,380	$1,400	$134	$115	$96	$77	$58	$45	$32	$19	$7	$0	$0
1,400	1,420	137	118	99	80	61	47	34	21	9	0	0
1,420	1,440	140	121	102	83	64	49	36	23	11	0	0
1,440	1,460	143	124	105	86	67	51	38	25	13	0	0
1,460	1,480	146	127	108	89	70	53	40	27	15	2	0
1,480	1,500	149	130	111	92	73	55	42	29	17	4	0
1,500	1,520	152	133	114	95	76	57	44	31	19	6	0
1,520	1,540	155	136	117	98	79	60	46	33	21	8	0
1,540	1,560	158	139	120	101	82	63	48	35	23	10	0
1,560	1,580	161	142	123	104	85	66	50	37	25	12	0
1,580	1,600	164	145	126	107	88	69	52	39	27	14	1
1,600	1,620	167	148	129	110	91	72	54	41	29	16	3
1,620	1,640	170	151	132	113	94	75	56	43	31	18	5
1,640	1,660	173	154	135	116	97	78	58	45	33	20	7
1,660	1,680	176	157	138	119	100	81	61	47	35	22	9
1,680	1,700	179	160	141	122	103	84	64	49	37	24	11
1,700	1,720	182	163	144	125	106	87	67	51	39	26	13
1,720	1,740	185	166	147	128	109	90	70	53	41	28	15
1,740	1,760	188	169	150	131	112	93	73	55	43	30	17
1,760	1,780	191	172	153	134	115	96	76	57	45	32	19
1,780	1,800	194	175	156	137	118	99	79	60	47	34	21
1,800	1,820	197	178	159	140	121	102	82	63	49	36	23
1,820	1,840	200	181	162	143	124	105	85	66	51	38	25
1,840	1,860	203	184	165	146	127	108	88	69	53	40	27
1,860	1,880	206	187	168	149	130	111	91	72	55	42	29
1,880	1,900	209	190	171	152	133	114	94	75	57	44	31
1,900	1,920	212	193	174	155	136	117	97	78	59	46	33
1,920	1,940	215	196	177	158	139	120	100	81	62	48	35
1,940	1,960	218	199	180	161	142	123	103	84	65	50	37
1,960	1,980	221	202	183	164	145	126	106	87	68	52	39
1,980	2,000	224	205	186	167	148	129	109	90	71	54	41
2,000	2,020	227	208	189	170	151	132	112	93	74	56	43
2,020	2,040	230	211	192	173	154	135	115	96	77	58	45
2,040	2,060	233	214	195	176	157	138	118	99	80	61	47
2,060	2,080	236	217	198	179	160	141	121	102	83	64	49
2,080	2,100	239	220	201	182	163	144	124	105	86	67	51
2,100	2,120	242	223	204	185	166	147	127	108	89	70	53
2,120	2,140	245	226	207	188	169	150	130	111	92	73	55
2,140	2,160	248	229	210	191	172	153	133	114	95	76	57
2,160	2,180	251	232	213	194	175	156	136	117	98	79	60
2,180	2,200	254	235	216	197	178	159	139	120	101	82	63
2,200	2,220	257	238	219	200	181	162	142	123	104	85	66
2,220	2,240	260	241	222	203	184	165	145	126	107	88	69
2,240	2,260	263	244	225	206	187	168	148	129	110	91	72
2,260	2,280	266	247	228	209	190	171	151	132	113	94	75
2,280	2,300	269	250	231	212	193	174	154	135	116	97	78
2,300	2,320	272	253	234	215	196	177	157	138	119	100	81
2,320	2,340	275	256	237	218	199	180	160	141	122	103	84
2,340	2,360	278	259	240	221	202	183	163	144	125	106	87
2,360	2,380	281	262	243	224	205	186	166	147	128	109	90
2,380	2,400	284	265	246	227	208	189	169	150	131	112	93
2,400	2,420	287	268	249	230	211	192	172	153	134	115	96
2,420	2,440	290	271	252	233	214	195	175	156	137	118	99
2,440	2,460	293	274	255	236	217	198	178	159	140	121	102
2,460	2,480	296	277	258	239	220	201	181	162	143	124	105
2,480	2,500	299	280	261	242	223	204	184	165	146	127	108
2,500	2,520	302	283	264	245	226	207	187	168	149	130	111
2,520	2,540	305	286	267	248	229	210	190	171	152	133	114
2,540	2,560	308	289	270	251	232	213	193	174	155	136	117
2,560	2,580	311	292	273	254	235	216	196	177	158	139	120
2,580	2,600	314	295	276	257	238	219	199	180	161	142	123
2,600	2,620	317	298	279	260	241	222	202	183	164	145	126
2,620	2,640	321	301	282	263	244	225	205	186	167	148	129
2,640	2,660	326	304	285	266	247	228	208	189	170	151	132
2,660	2,680	331	307	288	269	250	231	211	192	173	154	135
2,680	2,700	336	310	291	272	253	234	214	195	176	157	138

$2,700 and over Use Table 2(b) for a **MARRIED person** on page 36. Also see the instructions on page 34.

SINGLE Persons—SEMIMONTHLY Payroll Period
(For Wages Paid in 2006)

If the wages are—		And the number of withholding allowances claimed is—										
At least	But less than	0	1	2	3	4	5	6	7	8	9	10
		The amount of income tax to be withheld is—										
$0	$115	$0	$0	$0	$0	$0	$0	$0	$0	$0	$0	$0
115	120	1	0	0	0	0	0	0	0	0	0	0
120	125	1	0	0	0	0	0	0	0	0	0	0
125	130	2	0	0	0	0	0	0	0	0	0	0
130	135	2	0	0	0	0	0	0	0	0	0	0
135	140	3	0	0	0	0	0	0	0	0	0	0
140	145	3	0	0	0	0	0	0	0	0	0	0
145	150	4	0	0	0	0	0	0	0	0	0	0
150	155	4	0	0	0	0	0	0	0	0	0	0
155	160	5	0	0	0	0	0	0	0	0	0	0
160	165	5	0	0	0	0	0	0	0	0	0	0
165	170	6	0	0	0	0	0	0	0	0	0	0
170	175	6	0	0	0	0	0	0	0	0	0	0
175	180	7	0	0	0	0	0	0	0	0	0	0
180	185	7	0	0	0	0	0	0	0	0	0	0
185	190	8	0	0	0	0	0	0	0	0	0	0
190	195	8	0	0	0	0	0	0	0	0	0	0
195	200	9	0	0	0	0	0	0	0	0	0	0
200	205	9	0	0	0	0	0	0	0	0	0	0
205	210	10	0	0	0	0	0	0	0	0	0	0
210	215	10	0	0	0	0	0	0	0	0	0	0
215	220	11	0	0	0	0	0	0	0	0	0	0
220	225	11	0	0	0	0	0	0	0	0	0	0
225	230	12	0	0	0	0	0	0	0	0	0	0
230	235	12	0	0	0	0	0	0	0	0	0	0
235	240	13	0	0	0	0	0	0	0	0	0	0
240	245	13	0	0	0	0	0	0	0	0	0	0
245	250	14	0	0	0	0	0	0	0	0	0	0
250	260	14	1	0	0	0	0	0	0	0	0	0
260	270	15	2	0	0	0	0	0	0	0	0	0
270	280	16	3	0	0	0	0	0	0	0	0	0
280	290	17	4	0	0	0	0	0	0	0	0	0
290	300	18	5	0	0	0	0	0	0	0	0	0
300	310	19	6	0	0	0	0	0	0	0	0	0
310	320	20	7	0	0	0	0	0	0	0	0	0
320	330	21	8	0	0	0	0	0	0	0	0	0
330	340	22	9	0	0	0	0	0	0	0	0	0
340	350	23	10	0	0	0	0	0	0	0	0	0
350	360	24	11	0	0	0	0	0	0	0	0	0
360	370	25	12	0	0	0	0	0	0	0	0	0
370	380	26	13	0	0	0	0	0	0	0	0	0
380	390	27	14	0	0	0	0	0	0	0	0	0
390	400	28	15	1	0	0	0	0	0	0	0	0
400	410	29	16	2	0	0	0	0	0	0	0	0
410	420	30	17	3	0	0	0	0	0	0	0	0
420	430	32	18	4	0	0	0	0	0	0	0	0
430	440	33	19	5	0	0	0	0	0	0	0	0
440	450	35	20	6	0	0	0	0	0	0	0	0
450	460	36	21	7	0	0	0	0	0	0	0	0
460	470	38	22	8	0	0	0	0	0	0	0	0
470	480	39	23	9	0	0	0	0	0	0	0	0
480	490	41	24	10	0	0	0	0	0	0	0	0
490	500	42	25	11	0	0	0	0	0	0	0	0
500	520	45	26	12	0	0	0	0	0	0	0	0
520	540	48	28	14	1	0	0	0	0	0	0	0
540	560	51	30	16	3	0	0	0	0	0	0	0
560	580	54	33	18	5	0	0	0	0	0	0	0
580	600	57	36	20	7	0	0	0	0	0	0	0
600	620	60	39	22	9	0	0	0	0	0	0	0
620	640	63	42	24	11	0	0	0	0	0	0	0
640	660	66	45	26	13	0	0	0	0	0	0	0
660	680	69	48	28	15	1	0	0	0	0	0	0
680	700	72	51	30	17	3	0	0	0	0	0	0
700	720	75	54	33	19	5	0	0	0	0	0	0
720	740	78	57	36	21	7	0	0	0	0	0	0
740	760	81	60	39	23	9	0	0	0	0	0	0
760	780	84	63	42	25	11	0	0	0	0	0	0
780	800	87	66	45	27	13	0	0	0	0	0	0
800	820	90	69	48	29	15	1	0	0	0	0	0
820	840	93	72	51	31	17	3	0	0	0	0	0

SINGLE Persons—SEMIMONTHLY Payroll Period
(For Wages Paid in 2006)

If the wages are–		And the number of withholding allowances claimed is—										
At least	But less than	0	1	2	3	4	5	6	7	8	9	10
		The amount of income tax to be withheld is—										
$840	$860	$96	$75	$54	$34	$19	$5	$0	$0	$0	$0	$0
860	880	99	78	57	37	21	7	0	0	0	0	0
880	900	102	81	60	40	23	9	0	0	0	0	0
900	920	105	84	63	43	25	11	0	0	0	0	0
920	940	108	87	66	46	27	13	0	0	0	0	0
940	960	111	90	69	49	29	15	1	0	0	0	0
960	980	114	93	72	52	31	17	3	0	0	0	0
980	1,000	117	96	75	55	34	19	5	0	0	0	0
1,000	1,020	120	99	78	58	37	21	7	0	0	0	0
1,020	1,040	123	102	81	61	40	23	9	0	0	0	0
1,040	1,060	126	105	84	64	43	25	11	0	0	0	0
1,060	1,080	129	108	87	67	46	27	13	0	0	0	0
1,080	1,100	132	111	90	70	49	29	15	2	0	0	0
1,100	1,120	135	114	93	73	52	32	17	4	0	0	0
1,120	1,140	138	117	96	76	55	35	19	6	0	0	0
1,140	1,160	141	120	99	79	58	38	21	8	0	0	0
1,160	1,180	144	123	102	82	61	41	23	10	0	0	0
1,180	1,200	147	126	105	85	64	44	25	12	0	0	0
1,200	1,220	150	129	108	88	67	47	27	14	0	0	0
1,220	1,240	153	132	111	91	70	50	29	16	2	0	0
1,240	1,260	156	135	114	94	73	53	32	18	4	0	0
1,260	1,280	159	138	117	97	76	56	35	20	6	0	0
1,280	1,300	162	141	120	100	79	59	38	22	8	0	0
1,300	1,320	165	144	123	103	82	62	41	24	10	0	0
1,320	1,340	168	147	126	106	85	65	44	26	12	0	0
1,340	1,360	171	150	129	109	88	68	47	28	14	0	0
1,360	1,380	176	153	132	112	91	71	50	30	16	2	0
1,380	1,400	181	156	135	115	94	74	53	32	18	4	0
1,400	1,420	186	159	138	118	97	77	56	35	20	6	0
1,420	1,440	191	162	141	121	100	80	59	38	22	8	0
1,440	1,460	196	165	144	124	103	83	62	41	24	10	0
1,460	1,480	201	168	147	127	106	86	65	44	26	12	0
1,480	1,500	206	172	150	130	109	89	68	47	28	14	0
1,500	1,520	211	177	153	133	112	92	71	50	30	16	2
1,520	1,540	216	182	156	136	115	95	74	53	33	18	4
1,540	1,560	221	187	159	139	118	98	77	56	36	20	6
1,560	1,580	226	192	162	142	121	101	80	59	39	22	8
1,580	1,600	231	197	165	145	124	104	83	62	42	24	10
1,600	1,620	236	202	168	148	127	107	86	65	45	26	12
1,620	1,640	241	207	173	151	130	110	89	68	48	28	14
1,640	1,660	246	212	178	154	133	113	92	71	51	30	16
1,660	1,680	251	217	183	157	136	116	95	74	54	33	18
1,680	1,700	256	222	188	160	139	119	98	77	57	36	20
1,700	1,720	261	227	193	163	142	122	101	80	60	39	22
1,720	1,740	266	232	198	166	145	125	104	83	63	42	24
1,740	1,760	271	237	203	169	148	128	107	86	66	45	26
1,760	1,780	276	242	208	173	151	131	110	89	69	48	28
1,780	1,800	281	247	213	178	154	134	113	92	72	51	30
1,800	1,820	286	252	218	183	157	137	116	95	75	54	33
1,820	1,840	291	257	223	188	160	140	119	98	78	57	36
1,840	1,860	296	262	228	193	163	143	122	101	81	60	39
1,860	1,880	301	267	233	198	166	146	125	104	84	63	42
1,880	1,900	306	272	238	203	169	149	128	107	87	66	45
1,900	1,920	311	277	243	208	174	152	131	110	90	69	48
1,920	1,940	316	282	248	213	179	155	134	113	93	72	51
1,940	1,960	321	287	253	218	184	158	137	116	96	75	54
1,960	1,980	326	292	258	223	189	161	140	119	99	78	57
1,980	2,000	331	297	263	228	194	164	143	122	102	81	60
2,000	2,020	336	302	268	233	199	167	146	125	105	84	63
2,020	2,040	341	307	273	238	204	170	149	128	108	87	66
2,040	2,060	346	312	278	243	209	174	152	131	111	90	69
2,060	2,080	351	317	283	248	214	179	155	134	114	93	72
2,080	2,100	356	322	288	253	219	184	158	137	117	96	75
2,100	2,120	361	327	293	258	224	189	161	140	120	99	78
2,120	2,140	366	332	298	263	229	194	164	143	123	102	81

$2,140 and over   Use Table 3(a) for a **SINGLE person** on page 36. Also see the instructions on page 34.

MARRIED Persons—SEMIMONTHLY Payroll Period
(For Wages Paid in 2006)

If the wages are—		And the number of withholding allowances claimed is—										
At least	But less than	0	1	2	3	4	5	6	7	8	9	10
		The amount of income tax to be withheld is—										
$0	$270	$0	$0	$0	$0	$0	$0	$0	$0	$0	$0	$0
270	280	0	0	0	0	0	0	0	0	0	0	0
280	290	0	0	0	0	0	0	0	0	0	0	0
290	300	0	0	0	0	0	0	0	0	0	0	0
300	310	0	0	0	0	0	0	0	0	0	0	0
310	320	0	0	0	0	0	0	0	0	0	0	0
320	330	0	0	0	0	0	0	0	0	0	0	0
330	340	0	0	0	0	0	0	0	0	0	0	0
340	350	1	0	0	0	0	0	0	0	0	0	0
350	360	2	0	0	0	0	0	0	0	0	0	0
360	370	3	0	0	0	0	0	0	0	0	0	0
370	380	4	0	0	0	0	0	0	0	0	0	0
380	390	5	0	0	0	0	0	0	0	0	0	0
390	400	6	0	0	0	0	0	0	0	0	0	0
400	410	7	0	0	0	0	0	0	0	0	0	0
410	420	8	0	0	0	0	0	0	0	0	0	0
420	430	9	0	0	0	0	0	0	0	0	0	0
430	440	10	0	0	0	0	0	0	0	0	0	0
440	450	11	0	0	0	0	0	0	0	0	0	0
450	460	12	0	0	0	0	0	0	0	0	0	0
460	470	13	0	0	0	0	0	0	0	0	0	0
470	480	14	0	0	0	0	0	0	0	0	0	0
480	490	15	1	0	0	0	0	0	0	0	0	0
490	500	16	2	0	0	0	0	0	0	0	0	0
500	520	18	4	0	0	0	0	0	0	0	0	0
520	540	20	6	0	0	0	0	0	0	0	0	0
540	560	22	8	0	0	0	0	0	0	0	0	0
560	580	24	10	0	0	0	0	0	0	0	0	0
580	600	26	12	0	0	0	0	0	0	0	0	0
600	620	28	14	0	0	0	0	0	0	0	0	0
620	640	30	16	2	0	0	0	0	0	0	0	0
640	660	32	18	4	0	0	0	0	0	0	0	0
660	680	34	20	6	0	0	0	0	0	0	0	0
680	700	36	22	8	0	0	0	0	0	0	0	0
700	720	38	24	10	0	0	0	0	0	0	0	0
720	740	40	26	12	0	0	0	0	0	0	0	0
740	760	42	28	14	0	0	0	0	0	0	0	0
760	780	44	30	16	2	0	0	0	0	0	0	0
780	800	46	32	18	4	0	0	0	0	0	0	0
800	820	48	34	20	6	0	0	0	0	0	0	0
820	840	50	36	22	8	0	0	0	0	0	0	0
840	860	52	38	24	10	0	0	0	0	0	0	0
860	880	54	40	26	12	0	0	0	0	0	0	0
880	900	56	42	28	14	1	0	0	0	0	0	0
900	920	58	44	30	16	3	0	0	0	0	0	0
920	940	60	46	32	18	5	0	0	0	0	0	0
940	960	62	48	34	20	7	0	0	0	0	0	0
960	980	64	50	36	22	9	0	0	0	0	0	0
980	1,000	67	52	38	24	11	0	0	0	0	0	0
1,000	1,020	70	54	40	26	13	0	0	0	0	0	0
1,020	1,040	73	56	42	28	15	1	0	0	0	0	0
1,040	1,060	76	58	44	30	17	3	0	0	0	0	0
1,060	1,080	79	60	46	32	19	5	0	0	0	0	0
1,080	1,100	82	62	48	34	21	7	0	0	0	0	0
1,100	1,120	85	65	50	36	23	9	0	0	0	0	0
1,120	1,140	88	68	52	38	25	11	0	0	0	0	0
1,140	1,160	91	71	54	40	27	13	0	0	0	0	0
1,160	1,180	94	74	56	42	29	15	1	0	0	0	0
1,180	1,200	97	77	58	44	31	17	3	0	0	0	0
1,200	1,220	100	80	60	46	33	19	5	0	0	0	0
1,220	1,240	103	83	62	48	35	21	7	0	0	0	0
1,240	1,260	106	86	65	50	37	23	9	0	0	0	0
1,260	1,280	109	89	68	52	39	25	11	0	0	0	0
1,280	1,300	112	92	71	54	41	27	13	0	0	0	0
1,300	1,320	115	95	74	56	43	29	15	1	0	0	0
1,320	1,340	118	98	77	58	45	31	17	3	0	0	0
1,340	1,360	121	101	80	60	47	33	19	5	0	0	0
1,360	1,380	124	104	83	63	49	35	21	7	0	0	0
1,380	1,400	127	107	86	66	51	37	23	9	0	0	0
1,400	1,420	130	110	89	69	53	39	25	11	0	0	0

Appendix

MARRIED Persons—SEMIMONTHLY Payroll Period
(For Wages Paid in 2006)

If the wages are—		And the number of withholding allowances claimed is—										
At least	But less than	0	1	2	3	4	5	6	7	8	9	10
		The amount of income tax to be withheld is—										
$1,420	$1,440	$133	$113	$92	$72	$55	$41	$27	$13	$0	$0	$0
1,440	1,460	136	116	95	75	57	43	29	15	2	0	0
1,460	1,480	139	119	98	78	59	45	31	17	4	0	0
1,480	1,500	142	122	101	81	61	47	33	19	6	0	0
1,500	1,520	145	125	104	84	63	49	35	21	8	0	0
1,520	1,540	148	128	107	87	66	51	37	23	10	0	0
1,540	1,560	151	131	110	90	69	53	39	25	12	0	0
1,560	1,580	154	134	113	93	72	55	41	27	14	0	0
1,580	1,600	157	137	116	96	75	57	43	29	16	2	0
1,600	1,620	160	140	119	99	78	59	45	31	18	4	0
1,620	1,640	163	143	122	102	81	61	47	33	20	6	0
1,640	1,660	166	146	125	105	84	63	49	35	22	8	0
1,660	1,680	169	149	128	108	87	66	51	37	24	10	0
1,680	1,700	172	152	131	111	90	69	53	39	26	12	0
1,700	1,720	175	155	134	114	93	72	55	41	28	14	0
1,720	1,740	178	158	137	117	96	75	57	43	30	16	2
1,740	1,760	181	161	140	120	99	78	59	45	32	18	4
1,760	1,780	184	164	143	123	102	81	61	47	34	20	6
1,780	1,800	187	167	146	126	105	84	64	49	36	22	8
1,800	1,820	190	170	149	129	108	87	67	51	38	24	10
1,820	1,840	193	173	152	132	111	90	70	53	40	26	12
1,840	1,860	196	176	155	135	114	93	73	55	42	28	14
1,860	1,880	199	179	158	138	117	96	76	57	44	30	16
1,880	1,900	202	182	161	141	120	99	79	59	46	32	18
1,900	1,920	205	185	164	144	123	102	82	61	48	34	20
1,920	1,940	208	188	167	147	126	105	85	64	50	36	22
1,940	1,960	211	191	170	150	129	108	88	67	52	38	24
1,960	1,980	214	194	173	153	132	111	91	70	54	40	26
1,980	2,000	217	197	176	156	135	114	94	73	56	42	28
2,000	2,020	220	200	179	159	138	117	97	76	58	44	30
2,020	2,040	223	203	182	162	141	120	100	79	60	46	32
2,040	2,060	226	206	185	165	144	123	103	82	62	48	34
2,060	2,080	229	209	188	168	147	126	106	85	64	50	36
2,080	2,100	232	212	191	171	150	129	109	88	67	52	38
2,100	2,120	235	215	194	174	153	132	112	91	70	54	40
2,120	2,140	238	218	197	177	156	135	115	94	73	56	42
2,140	2,160	241	221	200	180	159	138	118	97	76	58	44
2,160	2,180	244	224	203	183	162	141	121	100	79	60	46
2,180	2,200	247	227	206	186	165	144	124	103	82	62	48
2,200	2,220	250	230	209	189	168	147	127	106	85	65	50
2,220	2,240	253	233	212	192	171	150	130	109	88	68	52
2,240	2,260	256	236	215	195	174	153	133	112	91	71	54
2,260	2,280	259	239	218	198	177	156	136	115	94	74	56
2,280	2,300	262	242	221	201	180	159	139	118	97	77	58
2,300	2,320	265	245	224	204	183	162	142	121	100	80	60
2,320	2,340	268	248	227	207	186	165	145	124	103	83	62
2,340	2,360	271	251	230	210	189	168	148	127	106	86	65
2,360	2,380	274	254	233	213	192	171	151	130	109	89	68
2,380	2,400	277	257	236	216	195	174	154	133	112	92	71
2,400	2,420	280	260	239	219	198	177	157	136	115	95	74
2,420	2,440	283	263	242	222	201	180	160	139	118	98	77
2,440	2,460	286	266	245	225	204	183	163	142	121	101	80
2,460	2,480	289	269	248	228	207	186	166	145	124	104	83
2,480	2,500	292	272	251	231	210	189	169	148	127	107	86
2,500	2,520	295	275	254	234	213	192	172	151	130	110	89
2,520	2,540	298	278	257	237	216	195	175	154	133	113	92
2,540	2,560	301	281	260	240	219	198	178	157	136	116	95
2,560	2,580	304	284	263	243	222	201	181	160	139	119	98
2,580	2,600	307	287	266	246	225	204	184	163	142	122	101
2,600	2,620	310	290	269	249	228	207	187	166	145	125	104
2,620	2,640	313	293	272	252	231	210	190	169	148	128	107
2,640	2,660	316	296	275	255	234	213	193	172	151	131	110
2,660	2,680	319	299	278	258	237	216	196	175	154	134	113
2,680	2,700	322	302	281	261	240	219	199	178	157	137	116
2,700	2,720	325	305	284	264	243	222	202	181	160	140	119
2,720	2,740	328	308	287	267	246	225	205	184	163	143	122

$2,740 and over   Use Table 3(b) for a **MARRIED person** on page 36. Also see the instructions on page 34.

SINGLE Persons—MONTHLY Payroll Period

(For Wages Paid in 2006)

If the wages are—		And the number of withholding allowances claimed is—										
At least	But less than	0	1	2	3	4	5	6	7	8	9	10
		The amount of income tax to be withheld is—										
$0	$220	$0	$0	$0	$0	$0	$0	$0	$0	$0	$0	$0
220	230	0	0	0	0	0	0	0	0	0	0	0
230	240	1	0	0	0	0	0	0	0	0	0	0
240	250	2	0	0	0	0	0	0	0	0	0	0
250	260	3	0	0	0	0	0	0	0	0	0	0
260	270	4	0	0	0	0	0	0	0	0	0	0
270	280	5	0	0	0	0	0	0	0	0	0	0
280	290	6	0	0	0	0	0	0	0	0	0	0
290	300	7	0	0	0	0	0	0	0	0	0	0
300	320	9	0	0	0	0	0	0	0	0	0	0
320	340	11	0	0	0	0	0	0	0	0	0	0
340	360	13	0	0	0	0	0	0	0	0	0	0
360	380	15	0	0	0	0	0	0	0	0	0	0
380	400	17	0	0	0	0	0	0	0	0	0	0
400	420	19	0	0	0	0	0	0	0	0	0	0
420	440	21	0	0	0	0	0	0	0	0	0	0
440	460	23	0	0	0	0	0	0	0	0	0	0
460	480	25	0	0	0	0	0	0	0	0	0	0
480	500	27	0	0	0	0	0	0	0	0	0	0
500	520	29	1	0	0	0	0	0	0	0	0	0
520	540	31	3	0	0	0	0	0	0	0	0	0
540	560	33	5	0	0	0	0	0	0	0	0	0
560	580	35	7	0	0	0	0	0	0	0	0	0
580	600	37	9	0	0	0	0	0	0	0	0	0
600	640	40	12	0	0	0	0	0	0	0	0	0
640	680	44	16	0	0	0	0	0	0	0	0	0
680	720	48	20	0	0	0	0	0	0	0	0	0
720	760	52	24	0	0	0	0	0	0	0	0	0
760	800	56	28	1	0	0	0	0	0	0	0	0
800	840	60	32	5	0	0	0	0	0	0	0	0
840	880	65	36	9	0	0	0	0	0	0	0	0
880	920	71	40	13	0	0	0	0	0	0	0	0
920	960	77	44	17	0	0	0	0	0	0	0	0
960	1,000	83	48	21	0	0	0	0	0	0	0	0
1,000	1,040	89	52	25	0	0	0	0	0	0	0	0
1,040	1,080	95	56	29	1	0	0	0	0	0	0	0
1,080	1,120	101	60	33	5	0	0	0	0	0	0	0
1,120	1,160	107	66	37	9	0	0	0	0	0	0	0
1,160	1,200	113	72	41	13	0	0	0	0	0	0	0
1,200	1,240	119	78	45	17	0	0	0	0	0	0	0
1,240	1,280	125	84	49	21	0	0	0	0	0	0	0
1,280	1,320	131	90	53	25	0	0	0	0	0	0	0
1,320	1,360	137	96	57	29	2	0	0	0	0	0	0
1,360	1,400	143	102	61	33	6	0	0	0	0	0	0
1,400	1,440	149	108	67	37	10	0	0	0	0	0	0
1,440	1,480	155	114	73	41	14	0	0	0	0	0	0
1,480	1,520	161	120	79	45	18	0	0	0	0	0	0
1,520	1,560	167	126	85	49	22	0	0	0	0	0	0
1,560	1,600	173	132	91	53	26	0	0	0	0	0	0
1,600	1,640	179	138	97	57	30	2	0	0	0	0	0
1,640	1,680	185	144	103	62	34	6	0	0	0	0	0
1,680	1,720	191	150	109	68	38	10	0	0	0	0	0
1,720	1,760	197	156	115	74	42	14	0	0	0	0	0
1,760	1,800	203	162	121	80	46	18	0	0	0	0	0
1,800	1,840	209	168	127	86	50	22	0	0	0	0	0
1,840	1,880	215	174	133	92	54	26	0	0	0	0	0
1,880	1,920	221	180	139	98	58	30	3	0	0	0	0
1,920	1,960	227	186	145	104	62	34	7	0	0	0	0
1,960	2,000	233	192	151	110	68	38	11	0	0	0	0
2,000	2,040	239	198	157	116	74	42	15	0	0	0	0
2,040	2,080	245	204	163	122	80	46	19	0	0	0	0
2,080	2,120	251	210	169	128	86	50	23	0	0	0	0
2,120	2,160	257	216	175	134	92	54	27	0	0	0	0
2,160	2,200	263	222	181	140	98	58	31	3	0	0	0
2,200	2,240	269	228	187	146	104	63	35	7	0	0	0
2,240	2,280	275	234	193	152	110	69	39	11	0	0	0
2,280	2,320	281	240	199	158	116	75	43	15	0	0	0
2,320	2,360	287	246	205	164	122	81	47	19	0	0	0
2,360	2,400	293	252	211	170	128	87	51	23	0	0	0
2,400	2,440	299	258	217	176	134	93	55	27	0	0	0

SINGLE Persons—MONTHLY Payroll Period

(For Wages Paid in 2006)

If the wages are—		And the number of withholding allowances claimed is—										
At least	But less than	0	1	2	3	4	5	6	7	8	9	10
		The amount of income tax to be withheld is—										
$2,440	$2,480	$305	$264	$223	$182	$140	$99	$59	$31	$4	$0	$0
2,480	2,520	311	270	229	188	146	105	64	35	8	0	0
2,520	2,560	317	276	235	194	152	111	70	39	12	0	0
2,560	2,600	323	282	241	200	158	117	76	43	16	0	0
2,600	2,640	329	288	247	206	164	123	82	47	20	0	0
2,640	2,680	335	294	253	212	170	129	88	51	24	0	0
2,680	2,720	343	300	259	218	176	135	94	55	28	0	0
2,720	2,760	353	306	265	224	182	141	100	59	32	4	0
2,760	2,800	363	312	271	230	188	147	106	65	36	8	0
2,800	2,840	373	318	277	236	194	153	112	71	40	12	0
2,840	2,880	383	324	283	242	200	159	118	77	44	16	0
2,880	2,920	393	330	289	248	206	165	124	83	48	20	0
2,920	2,960	403	336	295	254	212	171	130	89	52	24	0
2,960	3,000	413	344	301	260	218	177	136	95	56	28	1
3,000	3,040	423	354	307	266	224	183	142	101	60	32	5
3,040	3,080	433	364	313	272	230	189	148	107	65	36	9
3,080	3,120	443	374	319	278	236	195	154	113	71	40	13
3,120	3,160	453	384	325	284	242	201	160	119	77	44	17
3,160	3,200	463	394	331	290	248	207	166	125	83	48	21
3,200	3,240	473	404	337	296	254	213	172	131	89	52	25
3,240	3,280	483	414	345	302	260	219	178	137	95	56	29
3,280	3,320	493	424	355	308	266	225	184	143	101	60	33
3,320	3,360	503	434	365	314	272	231	190	149	107	66	37
3,360	3,400	513	444	375	320	278	237	196	155	113	72	41
3,400	3,440	523	454	385	326	284	243	202	161	119	78	45
3,440	3,480	533	464	395	332	290	249	208	167	125	84	49
3,480	3,520	543	474	405	338	296	255	214	173	131	90	53
3,520	3,560	553	484	415	346	302	261	220	179	137	96	57
3,560	3,600	563	494	425	356	308	267	226	185	143	102	61
3,600	3,640	573	504	435	366	314	273	232	191	149	108	67
3,640	3,680	583	514	445	376	320	279	238	197	155	114	73
3,680	3,720	593	524	455	386	326	285	244	203	161	120	79
3,720	3,760	603	534	465	396	332	291	250	209	167	126	85
3,760	3,800	613	544	475	406	338	297	256	215	173	132	91
3,800	3,840	623	554	485	416	348	303	262	221	179	138	97
3,840	3,880	633	564	495	426	358	309	268	227	185	144	103
3,880	3,920	643	574	505	436	368	315	274	233	191	150	109
3,920	3,960	653	584	515	446	378	321	280	239	197	156	115
3,960	4,000	663	594	525	456	388	327	286	245	203	162	121
4,000	4,040	673	604	535	466	398	333	292	251	209	168	127
4,040	4,080	683	614	545	476	408	339	298	257	215	174	133
4,080	4,120	693	624	555	486	418	349	304	263	221	180	139
4,120	4,160	703	634	565	496	428	359	310	269	227	186	145
4,160	4,200	713	644	575	506	438	369	316	275	233	192	151
4,200	4,240	723	654	585	516	448	379	322	281	239	198	157
4,240	4,280	733	664	595	526	458	389	328	287	245	204	163
4,280	4,320	743	674	605	536	468	399	334	293	251	210	169
4,320	4,360	753	684	615	546	478	409	340	299	257	216	175
4,360	4,400	763	694	625	556	488	419	350	305	263	222	181
4,400	4,440	773	704	635	566	498	429	360	311	269	228	187
4,440	4,480	783	714	645	576	508	439	370	317	275	234	193
4,480	4,520	793	724	655	586	518	449	380	323	281	240	199
4,520	4,560	803	734	665	596	528	459	390	329	287	246	205
4,560	4,600	813	744	675	606	538	469	400	335	293	252	211
4,600	4,640	823	754	685	616	548	479	410	341	299	258	217
4,640	4,680	833	764	695	626	558	489	420	351	305	264	223
4,680	4,720	843	774	705	636	568	499	430	361	311	270	229
4,720	4,760	853	784	715	646	578	509	440	371	317	276	235
4,760	4,800	863	794	725	656	588	519	450	381	323	282	241
4,800	4,840	873	804	735	666	598	529	460	391	329	288	247
4,840	4,880	883	814	745	676	608	539	470	401	335	294	253
4,880	4,920	893	824	755	686	618	549	480	411	343	300	259
4,920	4,960	903	834	765	696	628	559	490	421	353	306	265
4,960	5,000	913	844	775	706	638	569	500	431	363	312	271
5,000	5,040	923	854	785	716	648	579	510	441	373	318	277
5,040	5,080	933	864	795	726	658	589	520	451	383	324	283

$5,080 and over   Use Table 4(a) for a **SINGLE person** on page 36. Also see the instructions on page 34.

MARRIED Persons—MONTHLY Payroll Period
(For Wages Paid in 2006)

If the wages are–		And the number of withholding allowances claimed is—										
At least	But less than	0	1	2	3	4	5	6	7	8	9	10
		The amount of income tax to be withheld is—										
$0	$540	$0	$0	$0	$0	$0	$0	$0	$0	$0	$0	$0
540	560	0	0	0	0	0	0	0	0	0	0	0
560	580	0	0	0	0	0	0	0	0	0	0	0
580	600	0	0	0	0	0	0	0	0	0	0	0
600	640	0	0	0	0	0	0	0	0	0	0	0
640	680	0	0	0	0	0	0	0	0	0	0	0
680	720	3	0	0	0	0	0	0	0	0	0	0
720	760	7	0	0	0	0	0	0	0	0	0	0
760	800	11	0	0	0	0	0	0	0	0	0	0
800	840	15	0	0	0	0	0	0	0	0	0	0
840	880	19	0	0	0	0	0	0	0	0	0	0
880	920	23	0	0	0	0	0	0	0	0	0	0
920	960	27	0	0	0	0	0	0	0	0	0	0
960	1,000	31	4	0	0	0	0	0	0	0	0	0
1,000	1,040	35	8	0	0	0	0	0	0	0	0	0
1,040	1,080	39	12	0	0	0	0	0	0	0	0	0
1,080	1,120	43	16	0	0	0	0	0	0	0	0	0
1,120	1,160	47	20	0	0	0	0	0	0	0	0	0
1,160	1,200	51	24	0	0	0	0	0	0	0	0	0
1,200	1,240	55	28	0	0	0	0	0	0	0	0	0
1,240	1,280	59	32	4	0	0	0	0	0	0	0	0
1,280	1,320	63	36	8	0	0	0	0	0	0	0	0
1,320	1,360	67	40	12	0	0	0	0	0	0	0	0
1,360	1,400	71	44	16	0	0	0	0	0	0	0	0
1,400	1,440	75	48	20	0	0	0	0	0	0	0	0
1,440	1,480	79	52	24	0	0	0	0	0	0	0	0
1,480	1,520	83	56	28	1	0	0	0	0	0	0	0
1,520	1,560	87	60	32	5	0	0	0	0	0	0	0
1,560	1,600	91	64	36	9	0	0	0	0	0	0	0
1,600	1,640	95	68	40	13	0	0	0	0	0	0	0
1,640	1,680	99	72	44	17	0	0	0	0	0	0	0
1,680	1,720	103	76	48	21	0	0	0	0	0	0	0
1,720	1,760	107	80	52	25	0	0	0	0	0	0	0
1,760	1,800	111	84	56	29	1	0	0	0	0	0	0
1,800	1,840	115	88	60	33	5	0	0	0	0	0	0
1,840	1,880	119	92	64	37	9	0	0	0	0	0	0
1,880	1,920	123	96	68	41	13	0	0	0	0	0	0
1,920	1,960	129	100	72	45	17	0	0	0	0	0	0
1,960	2,000	135	104	76	49	21	0	0	0	0	0	0
2,000	2,040	141	108	80	53	25	0	0	0	0	0	0
2,040	2,080	147	112	84	57	29	2	0	0	0	0	0
2,080	2,120	153	116	88	61	33	6	0	0	0	0	0
2,120	2,160	159	120	92	65	37	10	0	0	0	0	0
2,160	2,200	165	124	96	69	41	14	0	0	0	0	0
2,200	2,240	171	130	100	73	45	18	0	0	0	0	0
2,240	2,280	177	136	104	77	49	22	0	0	0	0	0
2,280	2,320	183	142	108	81	53	26	0	0	0	0	0
2,320	2,360	189	148	112	85	57	30	2	0	0	0	0
2,360	2,400	195	154	116	89	61	34	6	0	0	0	0
2,400	2,440	201	160	120	93	65	38	10	0	0	0	0
2,440	2,480	207	166	124	97	69	42	14	0	0	0	0
2,480	2,520	213	172	130	101	73	46	18	0	0	0	0
2,520	2,560	219	178	136	105	77	50	22	0	0	0	0
2,560	2,600	225	184	142	109	81	54	26	0	0	0	0
2,600	2,640	231	190	148	113	85	58	30	3	0	0	0
2,640	2,680	237	196	154	117	89	62	34	7	0	0	0
2,680	2,720	243	202	160	121	93	66	38	11	0	0	0
2,720	2,760	249	208	166	125	97	70	42	15	0	0	0
2,760	2,800	255	214	172	131	101	74	46	19	0	0	0
2,800	2,840	261	220	178	137	105	78	50	23	0	0	0
2,840	2,880	267	226	184	143	109	82	54	27	0	0	0
2,880	2,920	273	232	190	149	113	86	58	31	3	0	0
2,920	2,960	279	238	196	155	117	90	62	35	7	0	0
2,960	3,000	285	244	202	161	121	94	66	39	11	0	0
3,000	3,040	291	250	208	167	126	98	70	43	15	0	0
3,040	3,080	297	256	214	173	132	102	74	47	19	0	0
3,080	3,120	303	262	220	179	138	106	78	51	23	0	0
3,120	3,160	309	268	226	185	144	110	82	55	27	0	0
3,160	3,200	315	274	232	191	150	114	86	59	31	4	0
3,200	3,240	321	280	238	197	156	118	90	63	35	8	0

Appendix

MARRIED Persons—MONTHLY Payroll Period
(For Wages Paid in 2006)

If the wages are—		And the number of withholding allowances claimed is—										
At least	But less than	0	1	2	3	4	5	6	7	8	9	10
		The amount of income tax to be withheld is—										
$3,240	$3,280	$327	$286	$244	$203	$162	$122	$94	$67	$39	$12	$0
3,280	3,320	333	292	250	209	168	127	98	71	43	16	0
3,320	3,360	339	298	256	215	174	133	102	75	47	20	0
3,360	3,400	345	304	262	221	180	139	106	79	51	24	0
3,400	3,440	351	310	268	227	186	145	110	83	55	28	0
3,440	3,480	357	316	274	233	192	151	114	87	59	32	4
3,480	3,520	363	322	280	239	198	157	118	91	63	36	8
3,520	3,560	369	328	286	245	204	163	122	95	67	40	12
3,560	3,600	375	334	292	251	210	169	127	99	71	44	16
3,600	3,640	381	340	298	257	216	175	133	103	75	48	20
3,640	3,680	387	346	304	263	222	181	139	107	79	52	24
3,680	3,720	393	352	310	269	228	187	145	111	83	56	28
3,720	3,760	399	358	316	275	234	193	151	115	87	60	32
3,760	3,800	405	364	322	281	240	199	157	119	91	64	36
3,800	3,840	411	370	328	287	246	205	163	123	95	68	40
3,840	3,880	417	376	334	293	252	211	169	128	99	72	44
3,880	3,920	423	382	340	299	258	217	175	134	103	76	48
3,920	3,960	429	388	346	305	264	223	181	140	107	80	52
3,960	4,000	435	394	352	311	270	229	187	146	111	84	56
4,000	4,040	441	400	358	317	276	235	193	152	115	88	60
4,040	4,080	447	406	364	323	282	241	199	158	119	92	64
4,080	4,120	453	412	370	329	288	247	205	164	123	96	68
4,120	4,160	459	418	376	335	294	253	211	170	129	100	72
4,160	4,200	465	424	382	341	300	259	217	176	135	104	76
4,200	4,240	471	430	388	347	306	265	223	182	141	108	80
4,240	4,280	477	436	394	353	312	271	229	188	147	112	84
4,280	4,320	483	442	400	359	318	277	235	194	153	116	88
4,320	4,360	489	448	406	365	324	283	241	200	159	120	92
4,360	4,400	495	454	412	371	330	289	247	206	165	124	96
4,400	4,440	501	460	418	377	336	295	253	212	171	130	100
4,440	4,480	507	466	424	383	342	301	259	218	177	136	104
4,480	4,520	513	472	430	389	348	307	265	224	183	142	108
4,520	4,560	519	478	436	395	354	313	271	230	189	148	112
4,560	4,600	525	484	442	401	360	319	277	236	195	154	116
4,600	4,640	531	490	448	407	366	325	283	242	201	160	120
4,640	4,680	537	496	454	413	372	331	289	248	207	166	124
4,680	4,720	543	502	460	419	378	337	295	254	213	172	130
4,720	4,760	549	508	466	425	384	343	301	260	219	178	136
4,760	4,800	555	514	472	431	390	349	307	266	225	184	142
4,800	4,840	561	520	478	437	396	355	313	272	231	190	148
4,840	4,880	567	526	484	443	402	361	319	278	237	196	154
4,880	4,920	573	532	490	449	408	367	325	284	243	202	160
4,920	4,960	579	538	496	455	414	373	331	290	249	208	166
4,960	5,000	585	544	502	461	420	379	337	296	255	214	172
5,000	5,040	591	550	508	467	426	385	343	302	261	220	178
5,040	5,080	597	556	514	473	432	391	349	308	267	226	184
5,080	5,120	603	562	520	479	438	397	355	314	273	232	190
5,120	5,160	609	568	526	485	444	403	361	320	279	238	196
5,160	5,200	615	574	532	491	450	409	367	326	285	244	202
5,200	5,240	621	580	538	497	456	415	373	332	291	250	208
5,240	5,280	627	586	544	503	462	421	379	338	297	256	214
5,280	5,320	633	592	550	509	468	427	385	344	303	262	220
5,320	5,360	639	598	556	515	474	433	391	350	309	268	226
5,360	5,400	645	604	562	521	480	439	397	356	315	274	232
5,400	5,440	651	610	568	527	486	445	403	362	321	280	238
5,440	5,480	657	616	574	533	492	451	409	368	327	286	244
5,480	5,520	663	622	580	539	498	457	415	374	333	292	250
5,520	5,560	669	628	586	545	504	463	421	380	339	298	256
5,560	5,600	675	634	592	551	510	469	427	386	345	304	262
5,600	5,640	681	640	598	557	516	475	433	392	351	310	268
5,640	5,680	687	646	604	563	522	481	439	398	357	316	274
5,680	5,720	696	652	610	569	528	487	445	404	363	322	280
5,720	5,760	706	658	616	575	534	493	451	410	369	328	286
5,760	5,800	716	664	622	581	540	499	457	416	375	334	292
5,800	5,840	726	670	628	587	546	505	463	422	381	340	298
5,840	5,880	736	676	634	593	552	511	469	428	387	346	304

$5,880 and over — Use Table 4(b) for a **MARRIED person** on page 36. Also see the instructions on page 34.

A-21

SINGLE Persons—DAILY OR MISCELLANEOUS Payroll Period

(For Wages Paid in 2006)

If the wages are—		And the number of withholding allowances claimed is—										
At least	But less than	0	1	2	3	4	5	6	7	8	9	10
		The amount of income tax to be withheld is—										
$0	$12	$0	$0	$0	$0	$0	$0	$0	$0	$0	$0	$0
12	15	0	0	0	0	0	0	0	0	0	0	0
15	18	1	0	0	0	0	0	0	0	0	0	0
18	21	1	0	0	0	0	0	0	0	0	0	0
21	24	1	0	0	0	0	0	0	0	0	0	0
24	27	2	0	0	0	0	0	0	0	0	0	0
27	30	2	1	0	0	0	0	0	0	0	0	0
30	33	2	1	0	0	0	0	0	0	0	0	0
33	36	2	1	0	0	0	0	0	0	0	0	0
36	39	3	1	0	0	0	0	0	0	0	0	0
39	42	3	2	0	0	0	0	0	0	0	0	0
42	45	4	2	1	0	0	0	0	0	0	0	0
45	48	4	2	1	0	0	0	0	0	0	0	0
48	51	4	3	1	0	0	0	0	0	0	0	0
51	54	5	3	2	0	0	0	0	0	0	0	0
54	57	5	3	2	1	0	0	0	0	0	0	0
57	60	6	4	2	1	0	0	0	0	0	0	0
60	63	6	4	3	1	0	0	0	0	0	0	0
63	66	7	5	3	2	0	0	0	0	0	0	0
66	69	7	5	3	2	1	0	0	0	0	0	0
69	72	8	6	4	2	1	0	0	0	0	0	0
72	75	8	6	4	3	1	0	0	0	0	0	0
75	78	9	7	5	3	2	0	0	0	0	0	0
78	81	9	7	5	3	2	1	0	0	0	0	0
81	84	9	8	6	4	2	1	0	0	0	0	0
84	87	10	8	6	4	2	1	0	0	0	0	0
87	90	10	8	7	5	3	1	0	0	0	0	0
90	93	11	9	7	5	3	2	1	0	0	0	0
93	96	11	9	7	6	4	2	1	0	0	0	0
96	99	12	10	8	6	4	2	1	0	0	0	0
99	102	12	10	8	6	5	3	1	0	0	0	0
102	105	13	11	9	7	5	3	2	0	0	0	0
105	108	13	11	9	7	5	4	2	1	0	0	0
108	111	13	12	10	8	6	4	2	1	0	0	0
111	114	14	12	10	8	6	4	3	1	0	0	0
114	117	14	12	11	9	7	5	3	2	0	0	0
117	120	15	13	11	9	7	5	3	2	1	0	0
120	123	15	13	11	10	8	6	4	2	1	0	0
123	126	16	14	12	10	8	6	4	3	1	0	0
126	129	17	14	12	10	9	7	5	3	2	0	0
129	132	17	15	13	11	9	7	5	3	2	1	0
132	135	18	15	13	11	9	8	6	4	2	1	0
135	138	19	16	14	12	10	8	6	4	2	1	0
138	141	20	16	14	12	10	8	7	5	3	2	0
141	144	20	17	15	13	11	9	7	5	3	2	1
144	147	21	18	15	13	11	9	7	6	4	2	1
147	150	22	19	16	14	12	10	8	6	4	2	1
150	153	23	19	16	14	12	10	8	6	5	3	1
153	156	23	20	17	15	13	11	9	7	5	3	2
156	159	24	21	18	15	13	11	9	7	5	4	2
159	162	25	22	18	15	14	12	10	8	6	4	2
162	165	26	22	19	16	14	12	10	8	6	4	3
165	168	26	23	20	17	14	13	11	9	7	5	3
168	171	27	24	21	18	15	13	11	9	7	5	3
171	174	28	25	21	18	15	13	12	10	8	6	4
174	177	29	25	22	19	16	14	12	10	8	6	4
177	180	29	26	23	20	17	14	12	11	9	7	5
180	183	30	27	24	21	17	15	13	11	9	7	5
183	186	31	28	24	21	18	15	13	11	10	8	6
186	189	32	28	25	22	19	16	14	12	10	8	6
189	192	32	29	26	23	20	16	14	12	10	8	7
192	195	33	30	27	24	20	17	15	13	11	9	7
195	198	34	31	27	24	21	18	15	13	11	9	7
198	201	35	31	28	25	22	19	16	14	12	10	8
201	204	35	32	29	26	23	19	16	14	12	10	8
204	207	36	33	30	27	23	20	17	15	13	11	9
207	210	37	34	30	27	24	21	18	15	13	11	9
210	213	38	34	31	28	25	22	18	15	14	12	10
213	216	38	35	32	29	26	22	19	16	14	12	10
216	219	39	36	33	30	26	23	20	17	14	13	11

SINGLE Persons—DAILY OR MISCELLANEOUS Payroll Period
(For Wages Paid in 2006)

If the wages are—		And the number of withholding allowances claimed is—										
At least	But less than	0	1	2	3	4	5	6	7	8	9	10
		The amount of income tax to be withheld is—										
$219	$222	$40	$37	$33	$30	$27	$24	$21	$18	$15	$13	$11
222	225	41	37	34	31	28	25	21	18	15	13	12
225	228	41	38	35	32	29	25	22	19	16	14	12
228	231	42	39	36	33	29	26	23	20	17	14	12
231	234	43	40	36	33	30	27	24	21	17	15	13
234	237	44	40	37	34	31	28	24	21	18	15	13
237	240	44	41	38	35	32	28	25	22	19	16	14
240	243	45	42	39	36	32	29	26	23	20	16	14
243	246	46	43	39	36	33	30	27	24	20	17	15
246	249	47	43	40	37	34	31	27	24	21	18	15
249	252	47	44	41	38	35	31	28	25	22	19	16
252	255	48	45	42	39	35	32	29	26	23	19	16
255	258	49	46	42	39	36	33	30	27	23	20	17
258	261	50	46	43	40	37	34	30	27	24	21	18
261	264	50	47	44	41	38	34	31	28	25	22	19
264	267	51	48	45	42	38	35	32	29	26	22	19
267	270	52	49	45	42	39	36	33	30	26	23	20
270	273	53	49	46	43	40	37	33	30	27	24	21
273	276	53	50	47	44	41	37	34	31	28	25	22
276	279	54	51	48	45	41	38	35	32	29	25	22
279	282	55	52	48	45	42	39	36	33	29	26	23
282	285	56	52	49	46	43	40	36	33	30	27	24
285	288	56	53	50	47	44	40	37	34	31	28	25
288	291	57	54	51	48	44	41	38	35	32	28	25
291	294	58	55	51	48	45	42	39	36	32	29	26
294	297	59	55	52	49	46	43	39	36	33	30	27
297	300	60	56	53	50	47	43	40	37	34	31	28
300	303	61	57	54	51	47	44	41	38	35	31	28
303	306	61	58	54	51	48	45	42	39	35	32	29
306	309	62	59	55	52	49	46	42	39	36	33	30
309	312	63	60	56	53	50	46	43	40	37	34	31
312	315	64	60	57	54	50	47	44	41	38	34	31
315	318	65	61	58	54	51	48	45	42	38	35	32
318	321	66	62	59	55	52	49	45	42	39	36	33
321	324	67	63	59	56	53	49	46	43	40	37	34
324	327	67	64	60	57	53	50	47	44	41	37	34
327	330	68	65	61	58	54	51	48	45	41	38	35
330	333	69	65	62	58	55	52	48	45	42	39	36
333	336	70	66	63	59	56	52	49	46	43	40	37
336	339	71	67	64	60	56	53	50	47	44	40	37
339	341	71	68	64	61	57	54	51	47	44	41	38
341	343	72	68	65	61	58	54	51	48	45	42	38
343	345	73	69	65	62	58	55	52	48	45	42	39
345	347	73	70	66	62	59	55	52	49	46	43	39
347	349	74	70	67	63	59	56	53	49	46	43	40
349	351	74	71	67	64	60	56	53	50	47	44	40
351	353	75	71	68	64	61	57	54	50	47	44	41
353	355	75	72	68	65	61	58	54	51	48	45	41
355	357	76	72	69	65	62	58	55	51	48	45	42
357	359	76	73	69	66	62	59	55	52	49	46	42
359	361	77	73	70	66	63	59	56	52	49	46	43
361	363	78	74	70	67	63	60	56	53	50	47	43
363	365	78	75	71	67	64	60	57	53	50	47	44
365	367	79	75	72	68	64	61	57	54	51	48	44
367	369	79	76	72	69	65	61	58	54	51	48	45
369	371	80	76	73	69	66	62	58	55	52	49	45
371	373	80	77	73	70	66	63	59	55	52	49	46
373	375	81	77	74	70	67	63	60	56	53	50	46
375	377	81	78	74	71	67	64	60	57	53	50	47
377	379	82	78	75	71	68	64	61	57	54	51	47
379	381	83	79	75	72	68	65	61	58	54	51	48
381	383	83	80	76	73	69	65	62	58	55	52	48
383	385	84	80	77	73	70	66	62	59	55	52	49
385	387	84	81	77	74	70	67	63	59	56	53	49
387	389	85	81	78	74	71	67	64	60	56	53	50
389	391	85	82	78	75	71	68	64	61	57	54	50

$391 and over   Use Table 8(a) for a **SINGLE person** on page 37. Also see the instructions on page 34.

MARRIED Persons—DAILY OR MISCELLANEOUS Payroll Period
(For Wages Paid in 2006)

If the wages are—		And the number of withholding allowances claimed is—										
At least	But less than	0	1	2	3	4	5	6	7	8	9	10
		The amount of income tax to be withheld is—										
$0	$27	$0	$0	$0	$0	$0	$0	$0	$0	$0	$0	$0
27	30	0	0	0	0	0	0	0	0	0	0	0
30	33	0	0	0	0	0	0	0	0	0	0	0
33	36	0	0	0	0	0	0	0	0	0	0	0
36	39	1	0	0	0	0	0	0	0	0	0	0
39	42	1	0	0	0	0	0	0	0	0	0	0
42	45	1	0	0	0	0	0	0	0	0	0	0
45	48	2	0	0	0	0	0	0	0	0	0	0
48	51	2	1	0	0	0	0	0	0	0	0	0
51	54	2	1	0	0	0	0	0	0	0	0	0
54	57	2	1	0	0	0	0	0	0	0	0	0
57	60	3	2	0	0	0	0	0	0	0	0	0
60	63	3	2	1	0	0	0	0	0	0	0	0
63	66	3	2	1	0	0	0	0	0	0	0	0
66	69	4	2	1	0	0	0	0	0	0	0	0
69	72	4	3	1	0	0	0	0	0	0	0	0
72	75	4	3	2	0	0	0	0	0	0	0	0
75	78	5	3	2	1	0	0	0	0	0	0	0
78	81	5	4	2	1	0	0	0	0	0	0	0
81	84	5	4	3	1	0	0	0	0	0	0	0
84	87	5	4	3	2	0	0	0	0	0	0	0
87	90	6	5	3	2	1	0	0	0	0	0	0
90	93	6	5	4	2	1	0	0	0	0	0	0
93	96	7	5	4	3	1	0	0	0	0	0	0
96	99	7	5	4	3	2	0	0	0	0	0	0
99	102	8	6	4	3	2	1	0	0	0	0	0
102	105	8	6	5	3	2	1	0	0	0	0	0
105	108	8	7	5	4	2	1	0	0	0	0	0
108	111	9	7	5	4	3	2	0	0	0	0	0
111	114	9	7	6	4	3	2	1	0	0	0	0
114	117	10	8	6	5	3	2	1	0	0	0	0
117	120	10	8	6	5	4	2	1	0	0	0	0
120	123	11	9	7	5	4	3	1	0	0	0	0
123	126	11	9	7	6	4	3	2	0	0	0	0
126	129	12	10	8	6	5	3	2	1	0	0	0
129	132	12	10	8	6	5	4	2	1	0	0	0
132	135	13	11	9	7	5	4	3	1	0	0	0
135	138	13	11	9	7	5	4	3	2	0	0	0
138	141	13	12	10	8	6	5	3	2	1	0	0
141	144	14	12	10	8	6	5	4	2	1	0	0
144	147	14	12	11	9	7	5	4	3	1	0	0
147	150	15	13	11	9	7	5	4	3	2	0	0
150	153	15	13	11	10	8	6	4	3	2	1	0
153	156	16	14	12	10	8	6	5	3	2	1	0
156	159	16	14	12	10	9	7	5	4	3	1	0
159	162	17	15	13	11	9	7	5	4	3	2	0
162	165	17	15	13	11	9	8	6	4	3	2	1
165	168	17	16	14	12	10	8	6	5	3	2	1
168	171	18	16	14	12	10	8	7	5	4	2	1
171	174	18	16	15	13	11	9	7	5	4	3	1
174	177	19	17	15	13	11	9	7	6	4	3	2
177	180	19	17	15	14	12	10	8	6	5	3	2
180	183	20	18	16	14	12	10	8	6	5	4	2
183	186	20	18	16	14	13	11	9	7	5	4	3
186	189	21	19	17	15	13	11	9	7	6	4	3
189	192	21	19	17	15	13	12	10	8	6	5	3
192	195	22	20	18	16	14	12	10	8	6	5	4
195	198	22	20	18	16	14	12	11	9	7	5	4
198	201	22	21	19	17	15	13	11	9	7	5	4
201	204	23	21	19	17	15	13	11	10	8	6	4
204	207	23	21	20	18	16	14	12	10	8	6	5
207	210	24	22	20	18	16	14	12	10	9	7	5
210	213	24	22	20	19	17	15	13	11	9	7	5
213	216	25	23	21	19	17	15	13	11	9	8	6
216	219	25	23	21	19	18	16	14	12	10	8	6
219	222	26	24	22	20	18	16	14	12	10	8	7
222	225	26	24	22	20	18	17	15	13	11	9	7
225	228	26	25	23	21	19	17	15	13	11	9	7
228	231	27	25	23	21	19	17	16	14	12	10	8
231	234	27	25	24	22	20	18	16	14	12	10	8

MARRIED Persons—DAILY OR MISCELLANEOUS Payroll Period
(For Wages Paid in 2006)

If the wages are—		And the number of withholding allowances claimed is—										
At least	But less than	0	1	2	3	4	5	6	7	8	9	10
		The amount of income tax to be withheld is—										
$234	$237	$28	$26	$24	$22	$20	$18	$16	$15	$13	$11	$9
237	240	28	26	24	23	21	19	17	15	13	11	9
240	243	29	27	25	23	21	19	17	15	14	12	10
243	246	29	27	25	23	22	20	18	16	14	12	10
246	249	30	28	26	24	22	20	18	16	14	13	11
249	252	30	28	26	24	22	21	19	17	15	13	11
252	255	31	29	27	25	23	21	19	17	15	13	12
255	258	31	29	27	25	23	21	20	18	16	14	12
258	261	31	30	28	26	24	22	20	18	16	14	12
261	264	32	30	28	26	24	22	20	19	17	15	13
264	267	33	30	29	27	25	23	21	19	17	15	13
267	270	33	31	29	27	25	23	21	19	18	16	14
270	273	34	31	29	28	26	24	22	20	18	16	14
273	276	35	32	30	28	26	24	22	20	18	17	15
276	279	36	33	30	28	27	25	23	21	19	17	15
279	282	36	33	31	29	27	25	23	21	19	17	16
282	285	37	34	31	29	27	26	24	22	20	18	16
285	288	38	35	32	30	28	26	24	22	20	18	16
288	291	39	36	32	30	28	26	25	23	21	19	17
291	294	39	36	33	31	29	27	25	23	21	19	17
294	297	40	37	34	31	29	27	25	24	22	20	18
297	300	41	38	35	32	30	28	26	24	22	20	18
300	303	42	39	35	32	30	28	26	24	23	21	19
303	306	42	39	36	33	31	29	27	25	23	21	19
306	309	43	40	37	34	31	29	27	25	23	22	20
309	312	44	41	38	34	31	30	28	26	24	22	20
312	315	45	42	38	35	32	30	28	26	24	22	21
315	318	45	42	39	36	33	30	29	27	25	23	21
318	321	46	43	40	37	34	31	29	27	25	23	21
321	324	47	44	41	37	34	31	29	28	26	24	22
324	327	48	45	41	38	35	32	30	28	26	24	22
327	330	48	45	42	39	36	33	30	28	27	25	23
330	333	49	46	43	40	37	33	31	29	27	25	23
333	336	50	47	44	40	37	34	31	29	27	26	24
336	339	51	48	44	41	38	35	32	30	28	26	24
339	341	51	48	45	42	39	35	32	30	28	26	24
341	343	52	49	46	42	39	36	33	30	29	27	25
343	345	52	49	46	43	40	36	33	31	29	27	25
345	347	53	50	47	43	40	37	34	31	29	27	25
347	349	53	50	47	44	41	37	34	31	29	28	26
349	351	54	51	48	44	41	38	35	32	30	28	26
351	353	54	51	48	45	42	38	35	32	30	28	26
353	355	55	52	49	45	42	39	36	33	30	28	27
355	357	55	52	49	46	43	39	36	33	31	29	27
357	359	56	53	50	46	43	40	37	34	31	29	27
359	361	56	53	50	47	44	40	37	34	31	29	27
361	363	57	54	51	47	44	41	38	35	32	30	28
363	365	57	54	51	48	45	41	38	35	32	30	28
365	367	58	55	52	48	45	42	39	36	32	30	28
367	369	58	55	52	49	46	42	39	36	33	31	29
369	371	59	56	53	49	46	43	40	37	33	31	29
371	373	59	56	53	50	47	43	40	37	34	31	29
373	375	60	57	54	50	47	44	41	38	34	31	30
375	377	60	57	54	51	48	44	41	38	35	32	30
377	379	61	58	55	51	48	45	42	39	35	32	30
379	381	61	58	55	52	49	45	42	39	36	33	30
381	383	62	59	56	52	49	46	43	40	36	33	31
383	385	62	59	56	53	50	46	43	40	37	34	31
385	387	63	60	57	53	50	47	44	41	37	34	31
387	389	63	60	57	54	51	47	44	41	38	35	32
389	391	64	61	58	54	51	48	45	42	38	35	32
391	393	64	61	58	55	52	48	45	42	39	36	33
393	395	65	62	59	55	52	49	46	43	39	36	33
395	397	65	62	59	56	53	49	46	43	40	37	34
397	399	66	63	60	56	53	50	47	44	40	37	34
399	401	66	63	60	57	54	50	47	44	41	38	35

$401 and over   Use Table 8(b) for a **MARRIED person** on page 37. Also see the instructions on page 34.

Tables for Percentage Method of Advance EIC Payments
(For Wages Paid in 2006)

Table 1. WEEKLY Payroll Period

(a) SINGLE or HEAD OF HOUSEHOLD			(b) MARRIED Without Spouse Filing Certificate			(c) MARRIED With Both Spouses Filing Certificate		
If the amount of wages (before deducting withholding allowances) is:		The amount of payment to be made is:	If the amount of wages (before deducting withholding allowances) is:		The amount of payment to be made is:	If the amount of wages (before deducting withholding allowances) is:		The amount of payment to be made is:
Over—	But not over—		Over—	But not over—		Over—	But not over—	
$0	$155	20.40% of wages	$0	$155	20.40% of wages	$0	$77	20.40% of wages
$155	$284	$32	$155	$323	$32	$77	$161	$16
$284		$32 less 9.588% of wages in excess of $284	$323		$32 less 9.588% of wages in excess of $323	$161		$16 less 9.588% of wages in excess of $161

Table 2. BIWEEKLY Payroll Period

(a) SINGLE or HEAD OF HOUSEHOLD			(b) MARRIED Without Spouse Filing Certificate			(c) MARRIED With Both Spouses Filing Certificate		
If the amount of wages (before deducting withholding allowances) is:		The amount of payment to be made is:	If the amount of wages (before deducting withholding allowances) is:		The amount of payment to be made is:	If the amount of wages (before deducting withholding allowances) is:		The amount of payment to be made is:
Over—	But not over—		Over—	But not over—		Over—	But not over—	
$0	$310	20.40% of wages	$0	$310	20.40% of wages	$0	$155	20.40% of wages
$310	$569	$63	$310	$646	$63	$155	$323	$32
$569		$63 less 9.588% of wages in excess of $569	$646		$63 less 9.588% of wages in excess of $646	$323		$32 less 9.588% of wages in excess of $323

Table 3. SEMIMONTHLY Payroll Period

(a) SINGLE or HEAD OF HOUSEHOLD			(b) MARRIED Without Spouse Filing Certificate			(c) MARRIED With Both Spouses Filing Certificate		
If the amount of wages (before deducting withholding allowances) is:		The amount of payment to be made is:	If the amount of wages (before deducting withholding allowances) is:		The amount of payment to be made is:	If the amount of wages (before deducting withholding allowances) is:		The amount of payment to be made is:
Over—	But not over—		Over—	But not over—		Over—	But not over—	
$0	$336	20.40% of wages	$0	$336	20.40% of wages	$0	$168	20.40% of wages
$336	$617	$69	$336	$700	$69	$168	$350	$34
$617		$69 less 9.588% of wages in excess of $617	$700		$69 less 9.588% of wages in excess of $700	$350		$34 less 9.588% of wages in excess of $350

Table 4. MONTHLY Payroll Period

(a) SINGLE or HEAD OF HOUSEHOLD			(b) MARRIED Without Spouse Filing Certificate			(c) MARRIED With Both Spouses Filing Certificate		
If the amount of wages (before deducting withholding allowances) is:		The amount of payment to be made is:	If the amount of wages (before deducting withholding allowances) is:		The amount of payment to be made is:	If the amount of wages (before deducting withholding allowances) is:		The amount of payment to be made is:
Over—	But not over—		Over—	But not over—		Over—	But not over—	
$0	$673	20.40% of wages	$0	$673	20.40% of wages	$0	$336	20.40% of wages
$673	$1,234	$137	$673	$1,400	$137	$336	$700	$69
$1,234		$137 less 9.588% of wages in excess of $1,234	$1,400		$137 less 9.588% of wages in excess of $1,400	$700		$69 less 9.588% of wages in excess of $700

Tables for Percentage Method of Advance EIC Payments (Continued)
(For Wages Paid in 2006)

Table 5. QUARTERLY Payroll Period

(a) SINGLE or HEAD OF HOUSEHOLD		(b) MARRIED Without Spouse Filing Certificate		(c) MARRIED With Both Spouses Filing Certificate	
If the amount of wages (before deducting withholding allowances) is:	The amount of payment to be made is:	If the amount of wages (before deducting withholding allowances) is:	The amount of payment to be made is:	If the amount of wages (before deducting withholding allowances) is:	The amount of payment to be made is:
Over— But not over—		Over— But not over—		Over— But not over—	
$0 $2,020	20.40% of wages	$0 $2,020	20.40% of wages	$0 $1,010	20.40% of wages
$2,020 $3,702	$412	$2,020 $4,202	$412	$1,010 $2,101	$206
$3,702	$412 less 9.588% of wages in excess of $3,702	$4,202	$412 less 9.588% of wages in excess of $4,202	$2,101	$206 less 9.588% of wages in excess of $2,101

Table 6. SEMIANNUAL Payroll Period

(a) SINGLE or HEAD OF HOUSEHOLD		(b) MARRIED Without Spouse Filing Certificate		(c) MARRIED With Both Spouses Filing Certificate	
If the amount of wages (before deducting withholding allowances) is:	The amount of payment to be made is:	If the amount of wages (before deducting withholding allowances) is:	The amount of payment to be made is:	If the amount of wages (before deducting withholding allowances) is:	The amount of payment to be made is:
Over— But not over—		Over— But not over—		Over— But not over—	
$0 $4,040	20.40% of wages	$0 $4,040	20.40% of wages	$0 $2,020	20.40% of wages
$4,040 $7,405	$824	$4,040 $8,405	$824	$2,020 $4,202	$412
$7,405	$824 less 9.588% of wages in excess of $7,405	$8,405	$824 less 9.588% of wages in excess of $8,405	$4,202	$412 less 9.588% of wages in excess of $4,202

Table 7. ANNUAL Payroll Period

(a) SINGLE or HEAD OF HOUSEHOLD		(b) MARRIED Without Spouse Filing Certificate		(c) MARRIED With Both Spouses Filing Certificate	
If the amount of wages (before deducting withholding allowances) is:	The amount of payment to be made is:	If the amount of wages (before deducting withholding allowances) is:	The amount of payment to be made is:	If the amount of wages (before deducting withholding allowances) is:	The amount of payment to be made is:
Over— But not over—		Over— But not over—		Over— But not over—	
$0 $8,080	20.40% of wages	$0 $8,080	20.40% of wages	$0 $4,040	20.40% of wages
$8,080 $14,810	$1,648	$8,080 $16,810	$1,648	$4,040 $8,405	$824
$14,810	$1,648 less 9.588% of wages in excess of $14,810	$16,810	$1,648 less 9.588% of wages in excess of $16,810	$8,405	$824 less 9.588% of wages in excess of $8,405

Table 8. DAILY or MISCELLANEOUS Payroll Period

(a) SINGLE or HEAD OF HOUSEHOLD		(b) MARRIED Without Spouse Filing Certificate		(c) MARRIED With Both Spouses Filing Certificate	
If the wages divided by the number of days in such period (before deducting withholding allowances) are:	The amount of payment to be made is the following amount multiplied by the number of days in such period:	If the wages divided by the number of days in such period (before deducting withholding allowances) are:	The amount of payment to be made is the following amount multiplied by the number of days in such period:	If the wages divided by the number of days in such period (before deducting withholding allowances) are:	The amount of payment to be made is the following amount multiplied by the number of days in such period:
Over— But not over—		Over— But not over—		Over— But not over—	
$0 $31	20.40% of wages	$0 $31	20.40% of wages	$0 $15	20.40% of wages
$31 $56	$6	$31 $64	$6	$15 $32	$3
$56	$6 less 9.588% of wages in excess of $56	$64	$6 less 9.588% of wages in excess of $64	$32	$3 less 9.588% of wages in excess of $32

Tables for Wage Bracket Method of Advance EIC Payments (For Wages Paid in 2006)

WEEKLY Payroll Period

SINGLE or HEAD OF HOUSEHOLD

At least	But less than	Payment to be made	At least	But less than	Payment to be made	At least	But less than	Payment to be made	At least	But less than	Payment to be made	At least	But less than	Payment to be made
$0	$5	$0	$65	$70	$13	$130	$135	$27	$350	$360	$24	$480	$490	$12
5	10	1	70	75	14	135	140	28	360	370	24	490	500	11
10	15	2	75	80	15	140	145	29	370	380	23	500	510	10
15	20	3	80	85	16	145	150	30	380	390	22	510	520	9
20	25	4	85	90	17	150	155	31	390	400	21	520	530	8
25	30	5	90	95	18	155	280	32	400	410	20	530	540	7
30	35	6	95	100	19	280	290	31	410	420	19	540	550	6
35	40	7	100	105	20	290	300	30	420	430	18	550	560	5
40	45	8	105	110	21	300	310	29	430	440	17	560	570	4
45	50	9	110	115	22	310	320	28	440	450	16	570	580	3
50	55	10	115	120	23	320	330	27	450	460	15	580	590	2
55	60	11	120	125	24	330	340	26	460	470	14	590	600	1
60	65	12	125	130	26	340	350	25	470	480	13	600	610	1
												610	- - -	0

MARRIED Without Spouse Filing Certificate

At least	But less than	Payment to be made	At least	But less than	Payment to be made	At least	But less than	Payment to be made	At least	But less than	Payment to be made	At least	But less than	Payment to be made
$0	$5	$0	$65	$70	$13	$130	$135	$27	$390	$400	$24	$520	$530	$12
5	10	1	70	75	14	135	140	28	400	410	23	530	540	11
10	15	2	75	80	15	140	145	29	410	420	22	540	550	10
15	20	3	80	85	16	145	150	30	420	430	21	550	560	9
20	25	4	85	90	17	150	155	31	430	440	21	560	570	8
25	30	5	90	95	18	155	320	32	440	450	20	570	580	7
30	35	6	95	100	19	320	330	31	450	460	19	580	590	6
35	40	7	100	105	20	330	340	30	460	470	18	590	600	5
40	45	8	105	110	21	340	350	29	470	480	17	600	610	4
45	50	9	110	115	22	350	360	28	480	490	16	610	620	3
50	55	10	115	120	23	360	370	27	490	500	15	620	630	2
55	60	11	120	125	24	370	380	26	500	510	14	630	640	1
60	65	12	125	130	26	380	390	25	510	520	13	640	- - -	0

MARRIED With Both Spouses Filing Certificate

At least	But less than	Payment to be made	At least	But less than	Payment to be made	At least	But less than	Payment to be made	At least	But less than	Payment to be made	At least	But less than	Payment to be made
$0	$5	$0	$35	$40	$7	$70	$75	$14	$210	$220	$10	$280	$290	$4
5	10	1	40	45	8	75	160	15	220	230	9	290	300	3
10	15	2	45	50	9	160	170	15	230	240	8	300	310	2
15	20	3	50	55	10	170	180	14	240	250	7	310	320	1
20	25	4	55	60	11	180	190	13	250	260	6	320	- - -	0
25	30	5	60	65	12	190	200	12	260	270	5			
30	35	6	65	70	13	200	210	11	270	280	4			

BIWEEKLY Payroll Period

SINGLE or HEAD OF HOUSEHOLD

At least	But less than	Payment to be made	At least	But less than	Payment to be made	At least	But less than	Payment to be made	At least	But less than	Payment to be made	At least	But less than	Payment to be made
$0	$5	$0	$55	$60	$11	$110	$115	$22	$165	$170	$34	$220	$225	$45
5	10	1	60	65	12	115	120	23	170	175	35	225	230	46
10	15	2	65	70	13	120	125	24	175	180	36	230	235	47
15	20	3	70	75	14	125	130	26	180	185	37	235	240	48
20	25	4	75	80	15	130	135	27	185	190	38	240	245	49
25	30	5	80	85	16	135	140	28	190	195	39	245	250	50
30	35	6	85	90	17	140	145	29	195	200	40	250	255	51
35	40	7	90	95	18	145	150	30	200	205	41	255	260	52
40	45	8	95	100	19	150	155	31	205	210	42	260	265	53
45	50	9	100	105	20	155	160	32	210	215	43	265	270	54
50	55	10	105	110	21	160	165	33	215	220	44	270	275	55

(continued on next page)

BIWEEKLY Payroll Period

SINGLE or HEAD OF HOUSEHOLD

Wages— At least	But less than	Payment to be made	Wages— At least	But less than	Payment to be made	Wages— At least	But less than	Payment to be made	Wages— At least	But less than	Payment to be made	Wages— At least	But less than	Payment to be made
$275	$280	$56	$635	$645	$56	$785	$795	$42	$935	$945	$27	$1,085	$1,095	$13
280	285	57	645	655	55	795	805	41	945	955	26	1,095	1,105	12
285	290	58	655	665	54	805	815	40	955	965	25	1,105	1,115	11
290	295	59	665	675	53	815	825	39	965	975	25	1,115	1,125	10
295	300	60	675	685	52	825	835	38	975	985	24	1,125	1,135	9
300	305	61	685	695	51	835	845	37	985	995	23	1,135	1,145	8
305	310	62	695	705	50	845	855	36	995	1,005	22	1,145	1,155	7
310	565	63	705	715	49	855	865	35	1,005	1,015	21	1,155	1,165	6
565	575	63	715	725	48	865	875	34	1,015	1,025	20	1,165	1,175	5
575	585	62	725	735	48	875	885	33	1,025	1,035	19	1,175	1,185	4
585	595	61	735	745	47	885	895	32	1,035	1,045	18	1,185	1,195	3
595	605	60	745	755	46	895	905	31	1,045	1,055	17	1,195	1,205	2
605	615	59	755	765	45	905	915	30	1,055	1,065	16	1,205	1,215	2
615	625	58	765	775	44	915	925	29	1,065	1,075	15	1,215	1,225	1
625	635	57	775	785	43	925	935	28	1,075	1,085	14	1,225	- - -	0

MARRIED Without Spouse Filing Certificate

Wages— At least	But less than	Payment to be made	Wages— At least	But less than	Payment to be made	Wages— At least	But less than	Payment to be made	Wages— At least	But less than	Payment to be made	Wages— At least	But less than	Payment to be made
$0	$5	$0	$130	$135	$27	$260	$265	$53	$795	$805	$48	$1,055	$1,065	$23
5	10	1	135	140	28	265	270	54	805	815	47	1,065	1,075	22
10	15	2	140	145	29	270	275	55	815	825	46	1,075	1,085	21
15	20	3	145	150	30	275	280	56	825	835	45	1,085	1,095	20
20	25	4	150	155	31	280	285	57	835	845	44	1,095	1,105	19
25	30	5	155	160	32	285	290	58	845	855	43	1,105	1,115	18
30	35	6	160	165	33	290	295	59	855	865	42	1,115	1,125	18
35	40	7	165	170	34	295	300	60	865	875	41	1,125	1,135	17
40	45	8	170	175	35	300	305	61	875	885	41	1,135	1,145	16
45	50	9	175	180	36	305	310	62	885	895	40	1,145	1,155	15
50	55	10	180	185	37	310	645	63	895	905	39	1,155	1,165	14
55	60	11	185	190	38	645	655	63	905	915	38	1,165	1,175	13
60	65	12	190	195	39	655	665	62	915	925	37	1,175	1,185	12
65	70	13	195	200	40	665	675	61	925	935	36	1,185	1,195	11
70	75	14	200	205	41	675	685	60	935	945	35	1,195	1,205	10
75	80	15	205	210	42	685	695	59	945	955	34	1,205	1,215	9
80	85	16	210	215	43	695	705	58	955	965	33	1,215	1,225	8
85	90	17	215	220	44	705	715	57	965	975	32	1,225	1,235	7
90	95	18	220	225	45	715	725	56	975	985	31	1,235	1,245	6
95	100	19	225	230	46	725	735	55	985	995	30	1,245	1,255	5
100	105	20	230	235	47	735	745	54	995	1,005	29	1,255	1,265	4
105	110	21	235	240	48	745	755	53	1,005	1,015	28	1,265	1,275	3
110	115	22	240	245	49	755	765	52	1,015	1,025	27	1,275	1,285	2
115	120	23	245	250	50	765	775	51	1,025	1,035	26	1,285	1,295	1
120	125	24	250	255	51	775	785	50	1,035	1,045	25	1,295	- - -	0
125	130	26	255	260	52	785	795	49	1,045	1,055	24			

MARRIED With Both Spouses Filing Certificate

Wages— At least	But less than	Payment to be made	Wages— At least	But less than	Payment to be made	Wages— At least	But less than	Payment to be made	Wages— At least	But less than	Payment to be made	Wages— At least	But less than	Payment to be made
$0	$5	$0	$65	$70	$13	$130	$135	$27	$390	$400	$24	$520	$530	$12
5	10	1	70	75	14	135	140	28	400	410	23	530	540	11
10	15	2	75	80	15	140	145	29	410	420	22	540	550	10
15	20	3	80	85	16	145	150	30	420	430	21	550	560	9
20	25	4	85	90	17	150	155	31	430	440	21	560	570	8
25	30	5	90	95	18	155	320	32	440	450	20	570	580	7
30	35	6	95	100	19	320	330	31	450	460	19	580	590	6
35	40	7	100	105	20	330	340	30	460	470	18	590	600	5
40	45	8	105	110	21	340	350	29	470	480	17	600	610	4
45	50	9	110	115	22	350	360	28	480	490	16	610	620	3
50	55	10	115	120	23	360	370	27	490	500	15	620	630	2
55	60	11	120	125	24	370	380	26	500	510	14	630	640	1
60	65	12	125	130	26	380	390	25	510	520	13	640	- - -	0

SEMIMONTHLY Payroll Period

SINGLE or HEAD OF HOUSEHOLD

At least	But less than	Payment to be made	At least	But less than	Payment to be made	At least	But less than	Payment to be made	At least	But less than	Payment to be made	At least	But less than	Payment to be made
$0	$5	$0	$140	$145	$29	$280	$285	$57	$775	$785	$53	$1,055	$1,065	$26
5	10	1	145	150	30	285	290	58	785	795	52	1,065	1,075	25
10	15	2	150	155	31	290	295	59	795	805	51	1,075	1,085	24
15	20	3	155	160	32	295	300	60	805	815	50	1,085	1,095	23
20	25	4	160	165	33	300	305	61	815	825	49	1,095	1,105	22
25	30	5	165	170	34	305	310	62	825	835	48	1,105	1,115	21
30	35	6	170	175	35	310	315	63	835	845	47	1,115	1,125	20
35	40	7	175	180	36	315	320	64	845	855	46	1,125	1,135	19
40	45	8	180	185	37	320	325	65	855	865	45	1,135	1,145	18
45	50	9	185	190	38	325	330	66	865	875	44	1,145	1,155	17
50	55	10	190	195	39	330	335	67	875	885	43	1,155	1,165	16
55	60	11	195	200	40	335	615	68	885	895	42	1,165	1,175	15
60	65	12	200	205	41	615	625	68	895	905	41	1,175	1,185	14
65	70	13	205	210	42	625	635	67	905	915	40	1,185	1,195	13
70	75	14	210	215	43	635	645	66	915	925	39	1,195	1,205	12
75	80	15	215	220	44	645	655	65	925	935	38	1,205	1,215	11
80	85	16	220	225	45	655	665	64	935	945	37	1,215	1,225	10
85	90	17	225	230	46	665	675	63	945	955	36	1,225	1,235	9
90	95	18	230	235	47	675	685	62	955	965	35	1,235	1,245	8
95	100	19	235	240	48	685	695	61	965	975	34	1,245	1,255	8
100	105	20	240	245	49	695	705	60	975	985	33	1,255	1,265	7
105	110	21	245	250	50	705	715	59	985	995	32	1,265	1,275	6
110	115	22	250	255	51	715	725	58	995	1,005	31	1,275	1,285	5
115	120	23	255	260	52	725	735	57	1,005	1,015	31	1,285	1,295	4
120	125	24	260	265	53	735	745	56	1,015	1,025	30	1,295	1,305	3
125	130	26	265	270	54	745	755	55	1,025	1,035	29	1,305	1,315	2
130	135	27	270	275	55	755	765	54	1,035	1,045	28	1,315	1,325	1
135	140	28	275	280	56	765	775	54	1,045	1,055	27	1,325	- - -	0

MARRIED Without Spouse Filing Certificate

At least	But less than	Payment to be made	At least	But less than	Payment to be made	At least	But less than	Payment to be made	At least	But less than	Payment to be made	At least	But less than	Payment to be made
$0	$5	$0	$140	$145	$29	$280	$285	$57	$860	$870	$52	$1,140	$1,150	$26
5	10	1	145	150	30	285	290	58	870	880	51	1,150	1,160	25
10	15	2	150	155	31	290	295	59	880	890	50	1,160	1,170	24
15	20	3	155	160	32	295	300	60	890	900	50	1,170	1,180	23
20	25	4	160	165	33	300	305	61	900	910	49	1,180	1,190	22
25	30	5	165	170	34	305	310	62	910	920	48	1,190	1,200	21
30	35	6	170	175	35	310	315	63	920	930	47	1,200	1,210	20
35	40	7	175	180	36	315	320	64	930	940	46	1,210	1,220	19
40	45	8	180	185	37	320	325	65	940	950	45	1,220	1,230	18
45	50	9	185	190	38	325	330	66	950	960	44	1,230	1,240	17
50	55	10	190	195	39	330	335	67	960	970	43	1,240	1,250	16
55	60	11	195	200	40	335	700	68	970	980	42	1,250	1,260	15
60	65	12	200	205	41	700	710	68	980	990	41	1,260	1,270	14
65	70	13	205	210	42	710	720	67	990	1,000	40	1,270	1,280	13
70	75	14	210	215	43	720	730	66	1,000	1,010	39	1,280	1,290	12
75	80	15	215	220	44	730	740	65	1,010	1,020	38	1,290	1,300	11
80	85	16	220	225	45	740	750	64	1,020	1,030	37	1,300	1,310	10
85	90	17	225	230	46	750	760	63	1,030	1,040	36	1,310	1,320	9
90	95	18	230	235	47	760	770	62	1,040	1,050	35	1,320	1,330	8
95	100	19	235	240	48	770	780	61	1,050	1,060	34	1,330	1,340	7
100	105	20	240	245	49	780	790	60	1,060	1,070	33	1,340	1,350	6
105	110	21	245	250	50	790	800	59	1,070	1,080	32	1,350	1,360	5
110	115	22	250	255	51	800	810	58	1,080	1,090	31	1,360	1,370	4
115	120	23	255	260	52	810	820	57	1,090	1,100	30	1,370	1,380	4
120	125	24	260	265	53	820	830	56	1,100	1,110	29	1,380	1,390	3
125	130	26	265	270	54	830	840	55	1,110	1,120	28	1,390	1,400	2
130	135	27	270	275	55	840	850	54	1,120	1,130	27	1,400	1,410	1
135	140	28	275	280	56	850	860	53	1,130	1,140	27	1,410	- - -	0

SEMIMONTHLY Payroll Period

MARRIED With Both Spouses Filing Certificate

Wages— At least	But less than	Payment to be made	Wages— At least	But less than	Payment to be made	Wages— At least	But less than	Payment to be made	Wages— At least	But less than	Payment to be made	Wages— At least	But less than	Payment to be made
$0	$5	$0	$70	$75	$14	$140	$145	$29	$430	$440	$26	$570	$580	$12
5	10	1	75	80	15	145	150	30	440	450	25	580	590	11
10	15	2	80	85	16	150	155	31	450	460	24	590	600	10
15	20	3	85	90	17	155	160	32	460	470	23	600	610	9
20	25	4	90	95	18	160	165	33	470	480	22	610	620	8
25	30	5	95	100	19	165	350	34	480	490	21	620	630	8
30	35	6	100	105	20	350	360	33	490	500	20	630	640	7
35	40	7	105	110	21	360	370	32	500	510	19	640	650	6
40	45	8	110	115	22	370	380	31	510	520	18	650	660	5
45	50	9	115	120	23	380	390	31	520	530	17	660	670	4
50	55	10	120	125	24	390	400	30	530	540	16	670	680	3
55	60	11	125	130	26	400	410	29	540	550	15	680	690	2
60	65	12	130	135	27	410	420	28	550	560	14	690	700	1
65	70	13	135	140	28	420	430	27	560	570	13	700	- - -	0

MONTHLY Payroll Period

SINGLE or HEAD OF HOUSEHOLD

Wages— At least	But less than	Payment to be made	Wages— At least	But less than	Payment to be made	Wages— At least	But less than	Payment to be made	Wages— At least	But less than	Payment to be made	Wages— At least	But less than	Payment to be made
$0	$5	$0	$220	$225	$45	$440	$445	$90	$660	$665	$135	$1,640	$1,650	$97
5	10	1	225	230	46	445	450	91	665	670	136	1,650	1,660	97
10	15	2	230	235	47	450	455	92	670	1,230	137	1,660	1,670	96
15	20	3	235	240	48	455	460	93	1,230	1,240	137	1,670	1,680	95
20	25	4	240	245	49	460	465	94	1,240	1,250	136	1,680	1,690	94
25	30	5	245	250	50	465	470	95	1,250	1,260	135	1,690	1,700	93
30	35	6	250	255	51	470	475	96	1,260	1,270	134	1,700	1,710	92
35	40	7	255	260	52	475	480	97	1,270	1,280	133	1,710	1,720	91
40	45	8	260	265	53	480	485	98	1,280	1,290	132	1,720	1,730	90
45	50	9	265	270	54	485	490	99	1,290	1,300	131	1,730	1,740	89
50	55	10	270	275	55	490	495	100	1,300	1,310	130	1,740	1,750	88
55	60	11	275	280	56	495	500	101	1,310	1,320	129	1,750	1,760	87
60	65	12	280	285	57	500	505	102	1,320	1,330	128	1,760	1,770	86
65	70	13	285	290	58	505	510	103	1,330	1,340	127	1,770	1,780	85
70	75	14	290	295	59	510	515	104	1,340	1,350	126	1,780	1,790	84
75	80	15	295	300	60	515	520	105	1,350	1,360	125	1,790	1,800	83
80	85	16	300	305	61	520	525	106	1,360	1,370	124	1,800	1,810	82
85	90	17	305	310	62	525	530	107	1,370	1,380	123	1,810	1,820	81
90	95	18	310	315	63	530	535	108	1,380	1,390	122	1,820	1,830	80
95	100	19	315	320	64	535	540	109	1,390	1,400	121	1,830	1,840	79
100	105	20	320	325	65	540	545	110	1,400	1,410	120	1,840	1,850	78
105	110	21	325	330	66	545	550	111	1,410	1,420	120	1,850	1,860	77
110	115	22	330	335	67	550	555	112	1,420	1,430	119	1,860	1,870	76
115	120	23	335	340	68	555	560	113	1,430	1,440	118	1,870	1,880	75
120	125	24	340	345	69	560	565	114	1,440	1,450	117	1,880	1,890	74
125	130	26	345	350	70	565	570	115	1,450	1,460	116	1,890	1,900	73
130	135	27	350	355	71	570	575	116	1,460	1,470	115	1,900	1,910	73
135	140	28	355	360	72	575	580	117	1,470	1,480	114	1,910	1,920	72
140	145	29	360	365	73	580	585	118	1,480	1,490	113	1,920	1,930	71
145	150	30	365	370	74	585	590	119	1,490	1,500	112	1,930	1,940	70
150	155	31	370	375	75	590	595	120	1,500	1,510	111	1,940	1,950	69
155	160	32	375	380	77	595	600	121	1,510	1,520	110	1,950	1,960	68
160	165	33	380	385	78	600	605	122	1,520	1,530	109	1,960	1,970	67
165	170	34	385	390	79	605	610	123	1,530	1,540	108	1,970	1,980	66
170	175	35	390	395	80	610	615	124	1,540	1,550	107	1,980	1,990	65
175	180	36	395	400	81	615	620	125	1,550	1,560	106	1,990	2,000	64
180	185	37	400	405	82	620	625	126	1,560	1,570	105	2,000	2,010	63
185	190	38	405	410	83	625	630	128	1,570	1,580	104	2,010	2,020	62
190	195	39	410	415	84	630	635	129	1,580	1,590	103	2,020	2,030	61
195	200	40	415	420	85	635	640	130	1,590	1,600	102	2,030	2,040	60
200	205	41	420	425	86	640	645	131	1,600	1,610	101	2,040	2,050	59
205	210	42	425	430	87	645	650	132	1,610	1,620	100	2,050	2,060	58
210	215	43	430	435	88	650	655	133	1,620	1,630	99	2,060	2,070	57
215	220	44	435	440	89	655	660	134	1,630	1,640	98	(Continued on next page)		

MONTHLY Payroll Period

SINGLE or HEAD OF HOUSEHOLD

Wages— At least	But less than	Payment to be made	Wages— At least	But less than	Payment to be made	Wages— At least	But less than	Payment to be made	Wages— At least	But less than	Payment to be made	Wages— At least	But less than	Payment to be made
$2,070	$2,080	$56	$2,190	$2,200	$45	$2,310	$2,320	$33	$2,430	$2,440	$22	$2,550	$2,560	$10
2,080	2,090	55	2,200	2,210	44	2,320	2,330	32	2,440	2,450	21	2,560	2,570	9
2,090	2,100	54	2,210	2,220	43	2,330	2,340	31	2,450	2,460	20	2,570	2,580	8
2,100	2,110	53	2,220	2,230	42	2,340	2,350	30	2,460	2,470	19	2,580	2,590	7
2,110	2,120	52	2,230	2,240	41	2,350	2,360	29	2,470	2,480	18	2,590	2,600	6
2,120	2,130	51	2,240	2,250	40	2,360	2,370	28	2,480	2,490	17	2,600	2,610	5
2,130	2,140	50	2,250	2,260	39	2,370	2,380	27	2,490	2,500	16	2,610	2,620	4
2,140	2,150	50	2,260	2,270	38	2,380	2,390	27	2,500	2,510	15	2,620	2,630	4
2,150	2,160	49	2,270	2,280	37	2,390	2,400	26	2,510	2,520	14	2,630	2,640	3
2,160	2,170	48	2,280	2,290	36	2,400	2,410	25	2,520	2,530	13	2,640	2,650	2
2,170	2,180	47	2,290	2,300	35	2,410	2,420	24	2,530	2,540	12	2,650	2,660	1
2,180	2,190	46	2,300	2,310	34	2,420	2,430	23	2,540	2,550	11	2,660	- - -	0

MARRIED Without Spouse Filing Certificate

Wages— At least	But less than	Payment to be made	Wages— At least	But less than	Payment to be made	Wages— At least	But less than	Payment to be made	Wages— At least	But less than	Payment to be made	Wages— At least	But less than	Payment to be made
$0	$5	$0	$230	$235	$47	$460	$465	$94	$1,430	$1,440	$134	$1,890	$1,900	$89
5	10	1	235	240	48	465	470	95	1,440	1,450	133	1,900	1,910	89
10	15	2	240	245	49	470	475	96	1,450	1,460	132	1,910	1,920	88
15	20	3	245	250	50	475	480	97	1,460	1,470	131	1,920	1,930	87
20	25	4	250	255	51	480	485	98	1,470	1,480	130	1,930	1,940	86
25	30	5	255	260	52	485	490	99	1,480	1,490	129	1,940	1,950	85
30	35	6	260	265	53	490	495	100	1,490	1,500	128	1,950	1,960	84
35	40	7	265	270	54	495	500	101	1,500	1,510	127	1,960	1,970	83
40	45	8	270	275	55	500	505	102	1,510	1,520	126	1,970	1,980	82
45	50	9	275	280	56	505	510	103	1,520	1,530	125	1,980	1,990	81
50	55	10	280	285	57	510	515	104	1,530	1,540	124	1,990	2,000	80
55	60	11	285	290	58	515	520	105	1,540	1,550	123	2,000	2,010	79
60	65	12	290	295	59	520	525	106	1,550	1,560	122	2,010	2,020	78
65	70	13	295	300	60	525	530	107	1,560	1,570	121	2,020	2,030	77
70	75	14	300	305	61	530	535	108	1,570	1,580	120	2,030	2,040	76
75	80	15	305	310	62	535	540	109	1,580	1,590	119	2,040	2,050	75
80	85	16	310	315	63	540	545	110	1,590	1,600	118	2,050	2,060	74
85	90	17	315	320	64	545	550	111	1,600	1,610	117	2,060	2,070	73
90	95	18	320	325	65	550	555	112	1,610	1,620	116	2,070	2,080	72
95	100	19	325	330	66	555	560	113	1,620	1,630	115	2,080	2,090	71
100	105	20	330	335	67	560	565	114	1,630	1,640	114	2,090	2,100	70
105	110	21	335	340	68	565	570	115	1,640	1,650	113	2,100	2,110	69
110	115	22	340	345	69	570	575	116	1,650	1,660	112	2,110	2,120	68
115	120	23	345	350	70	575	580	117	1,660	1,670	112	2,120	2,130	67
120	125	24	350	355	71	580	585	118	1,670	1,680	111	2,130	2,140	66
125	130	26	355	360	72	585	590	119	1,680	1,690	110	2,140	2,150	66
130	135	27	360	365	73	590	595	120	1,690	1,700	109	2,150	2,160	65
135	140	28	365	370	74	595	600	121	1,700	1,710	108	2,160	2,170	64
140	145	29	370	375	75	600	605	122	1,710	1,720	107	2,170	2,180	63
145	150	30	375	380	77	605	610	123	1,720	1,730	106	2,180	2,190	62
150	155	31	380	385	78	610	615	124	1,730	1,740	105	2,190	2,200	61
155	160	32	385	390	79	615	620	125	1,740	1,750	104	2,200	2,210	60
160	165	33	390	395	80	620	625	126	1,750	1,760	103	2,210	2,220	59
165	170	34	395	400	81	625	630	128	1,760	1,770	102	2,220	2,230	58
170	175	35	400	405	82	630	635	129	1,770	1,780	101	2,230	2,240	57
175	180	36	405	410	83	635	640	130	1,780	1,790	100	2,240	2,250	56
180	185	37	410	415	84	640	645	131	1,790	1,800	99	2,250	2,260	55
185	190	38	415	420	85	645	650	132	1,800	1,810	98	2,260	2,270	54
190	195	39	420	425	86	650	655	133	1,810	1,820	97	2,270	2,280	53
195	200	40	425	430	87	655	660	134	1,820	1,830	96	2,280	2,290	52
200	205	41	430	435	88	660	665	135	1,830	1,840	95	2,290	2,300	51
205	210	42	435	440	89	665	670	136	1,840	1,850	94	2,300	2,310	50
210	215	43	440	445	90	670	1,400	137	1,850	1,860	93	2,310	2,320	49
215	220	44	445	450	91	1,400	1,410	136	1,860	1,870	92	2,320	2,330	48
220	225	45	450	455	92	1,410	1,420	135	1,870	1,880	91	2,330	2,340	47
225	230	46	455	460	93	1,420	1,430	135	1,880	1,890	90	(Continued on next page)		

MONTHLY Payroll Period

MARRIED Without Spouse Filing Certificate

Wages— At least	But less than	Payment to be made	Wages— At least	But less than	Payment to be made	Wages— At least	But less than	Payment to be made	Wages— At least	But less than	Payment to be made	Wages— At least	But less than	Payment to be made
$2,340	$2,350	$46	$2,440	$2,450	$37	$2,540	$2,550	$27	$2,640	$2,650	$18	$2,740	$2,750	$8
2,350	2,360	45	2,450	2,460	36	2,550	2,560	26	2,650	2,660	17	2,750	2,760	7
2,360	2,370	44	2,460	2,470	35	2,560	2,570	25	2,660	2,670	16	2,760	2,770	6
2,370	2,380	43	2,470	2,480	34	2,570	2,580	24	2,670	2,680	15	2,770	2,780	5
2,380	2,390	42	2,480	2,490	33	2,580	2,590	23	2,680	2,690	14	2,780	2,790	4
2,390	2,400	42	2,490	2,500	32	2,590	2,600	22	2,690	2,700	13	2,790	2,800	3
2,400	2,410	41	2,500	2,510	31	2,600	2,610	21	2,700	2,710	12	2,800	2,810	2
2,410	2,420	40	2,510	2,520	30	2,610	2,620	20	2,710	2,720	11	2,810	2,820	1
2,420	2,430	39	2,520	2,530	29	2,620	2,630	19	2,720	2,730	10	2,820	- - -	0
2,430	2,440	38	2,530	2,540	28	2,630	2,640	19	2,730	2,740	9			

MARRIED With Both Spouses Filing Certificate

Wages— At least	But less than	Payment to be made	Wages— At least	But less than	Payment to be made	Wages— At least	But less than	Payment to be made	Wages— At least	But less than	Payment to be made	Wages— At least	But less than	Payment to be made
$0	$5	$0	$140	$145	$29	$280	$285	$57	$860	$870	$52	$1,140	$1,150	$26
5	10	1	145	150	30	285	290	58	870	880	51	1,150	1,160	25
10	15	2	150	155	31	290	295	59	880	890	50	1,160	1,170	24
15	20	3	155	160	32	295	300	60	890	900	50	1,170	1,180	23
20	25	4	160	165	33	300	305	61	900	910	49	1,180	1,190	22
25	30	5	165	170	34	305	310	62	910	920	48	1,190	1,200	21
30	35	6	170	175	35	310	315	63	920	930	47	1,200	1,210	20
35	40	7	175	180	36	315	320	64	930	940	46	1,210	1,220	19
40	45	8	180	185	37	320	325	65	940	950	45	1,220	1,230	18
45	50	9	185	190	38	325	330	66	950	960	44	1,230	1,240	17
50	55	10	190	195	39	330	335	67	960	970	43	1,240	1,250	16
55	60	11	195	200	40	335	700	68	970	980	42	1,250	1,260	15
60	65	12	200	205	41	700	710	68	980	990	41	1,260	1,270	14
65	70	13	205	210	42	710	720	67	990	1,000	40	1,270	1,280	13
70	75	14	210	215	43	720	730	66	1,000	1,010	39	1,280	1,290	12
75	80	15	215	220	44	730	740	65	1,010	1,020	38	1,290	1,300	11
80	85	16	220	225	45	740	750	64	1,020	1,030	37	1,300	1,310	10
85	90	17	225	230	46	750	760	63	1,030	1,040	36	1,310	1,320	9
90	95	18	230	235	47	760	770	62	1,040	1,050	35	1,320	1,330	8
95	100	19	235	240	48	770	780	61	1,050	1,060	34	1,330	1,340	7
100	105	20	240	245	49	780	790	60	1,060	1,070	33	1,340	1,350	6
105	110	21	245	250	50	790	800	59	1,070	1,080	32	1,350	1,360	5
110	115	22	250	255	51	800	810	58	1,080	1,090	31	1,360	1,370	4
115	120	23	255	260	52	810	820	57	1,090	1,100	30	1,370	1,380	4
120	125	24	260	265	53	820	830	56	1,100	1,110	29	1,380	1,390	3
125	130	26	265	270	54	830	840	55	1,110	1,120	28	1,390	1,400	2
130	135	27	270	275	55	840	850	54	1,120	1,130	27	1,400	1,410	1
135	140	28	275	280	56	850	860	53	1,130	1,140	27	1,410	- - -	0

DAILY Payroll Period

SINGLE or HEAD OF HOUSEHOLD

Wages— At least	But less than	Payment to be made	Wages— At least	But less than	Payment to be made
$0	$5	$0	$65	$75	$5
5	10	1	75	85	4
10	15	2	85	95	3
15	20	3	95	105	2
20	25	4	105	115	1
25	30	5	115	- - -	0
30	55	6			
55	65	6			

MARRIED Without Spouse Filing Certificate

Wages— At least	But less than	Payment to be made	Wages— At least	But less than	Payment to be made
$0	$5	$0	$70	$80	$5
5	10	1	80	90	4
10	15	2	90	100	3
15	20	3	100	110	2
20	25	4	110	120	1
25	30	5	120	- - -	0
30	60	6			
60	70	6			

MARRIED With Both Spouses Filing Certificate

Wages— At least	But less than	Payment to be made	Wages— At least	But less than	Payment to be made
$0	$5	$0	$30	$40	$2
5	10	1	40	50	1
10	15	2	50	- - -	0
15	30	3			

Department of Homeland Security
U.S. Citizenship and Immigration Services

OMB No. 1615-0047; Expires 03/31/07

Employment Eligibility Verification

INSTRUCTIONS

PLEASE READ ALL INSTRUCTIONS CAREFULLY BEFORE COMPLETING THIS FORM.

Anti-Discrimination Notice. It is illegal to discriminate against any individual (other than an alien not authorized to work in the U.S.) in hiring, discharging, or recruiting or referring for a fee because of that individual's national origin or citizenship status. It is illegal to discriminate against work eligible individuals. Employers **CANNOT** specify which document(s) they will accept from an employee. The refusal to hire an individual because of a future expiration date may also constitute illegal discrimination.

Section 1- Employee.

All employees, citizens and noncitizens, hired after November 6, 1986, must complete Section 1 of this form at the time of hire, which is the actual beginning of employment. **The employer is responsible for ensuring that Section 1 is timely and properly completed.**

Preparer/Translator Certification. The Preparer/Translator Certification must be completed if Section 1 is prepared by a person other than the employee. A preparer/translator may be used only when the employee is unable to complete Section 1 on his/her own. However, the employee must still sign Section 1 personally.

Section 2 - Employer.

For the purpose of completing this form, the term "employer" includes those recruiters and referrers for a fee who are agricultural associations, agricultural employers or farm labor contractors.

Employers must complete Section 2 by examining evidence of identity and employment eligibility within three (3) business days of the date employment begins. If employees are authorized to work, but are unable to present the required document(s) within three business days, they must present a receipt for the application of the document(s) within three business days and the actual document(s) within ninety (90) days. However, if employers hire individuals for a duration of less than three business days, Section 2 must be completed at the time employment begins. **Employers must record: 1)** document title; **2)** issuing authority; **3)** document number, **4)** expiration date, if any; and **5)** the date employment begins. Employers must sign and date the certification. Employees must present original documents. Employers may, but are not required to, photocopy the document(s) presented. These photocopies may only be used for the verification process and must be retained with the I-9. **However, employers are still responsible for completing the I-9.**

Section 3 - Updating and Reverification.

Employers must complete Section 3 when updating and/or reverifying the I-9. Employers must reverify employment eligibility of their employees on or before the expiration date recorded in Section 1. Employers **CANNOT** specify which document(s) they will accept from an employee.

- If an employee's name has changed at the time this form is being updated/reverified, complete Block A.

- If an employee is rehired within three (3) years of the date this form was originally completed and the employee is still eligible to be employed on the same basis as previously indicated on this form (updating), complete Block B and the signature block.

- If an employee is rehired within three (3) years of the date this form was originally completed and the employee's work authorization has expired **or** if a current employee's work authorization is about to expire (reverification), complete Block B and:

— examine any document that reflects that the employee is authorized to work in the U.S. (see List A **or** C),

— record the document title, document number and expiration date (if any) in Block C, and

— complete the signature block.

Photocopying and Retaining Form I-9. A blank I-9 may be reproduced, provided both sides are copied. The Instructions must be available to all employees completing this form. Employers must retain completed I-9s for three (3) years after the date of hire or one (1) year after the date employment ends, whichever is later.

For more detailed information, you may refer to the Department of Homeland Security (DHS) Handbook for Employers, (Form M-274). You may obtain the handbook at your local U.S. Citizenship and Immigration Services (USCIS) office.

Privacy Act Notice. The authority for collecting this information is the Immigration Reform and Control Act of 1986, Pub. L. 99-603 (8 USC 1324a).

This information is for employers to verify the eligibility of individuals for employment to preclude the unlawful hiring, or recruiting or referring for a fee, of aliens who are not authorized to work in the United States.

This information will be used by employers as a record of their basis for determining eligibility of an employee to work in the United States. The form will be kept by the employer and made available for inspection by officials of the U.S. Immigration and Customs Enforcement, Department of Labor and Office of Special Counsel for Immigration Related Unfair Employment Practices.

Submission of the information required in this form is voluntary. However, an individual may not begin employment unless this form is completed, since employers are subject to civil or criminal penalties if they do not comply with the Immigration Reform and Control Act of 1986.

Reporting Burden. We try to create forms and instructions that are accurate, can be easily understood and which impose the least possible burden on you to provide us with information. Often this is difficult because some immigration laws are very complex. Accordingly, the reporting burden for this collection of information is computed as follows: **1)** learning about this form, 5 minutes; **2)** completing the form, 5 minutes; and **3)** assembling and filing (recordkeeping) the form, 5 minutes, for an average of 15 minutes per response. If you have comments regarding the accuracy of this burden estimate, or suggestions for making this form simpler, you can write to U.S. Citizenship and Immigration Services, Regulatory Management Division, 111 Massachusetts Avenue, N.W., Washington, DC 20529. OMB No. 1615-0047.

NOTE: This is the 1991 edition of the Form I-9 that has been rebranded with a current printing date to reflect the recent transition from the INS to DHS and its components.

EMPLOYERS MUST RETAIN COMPLETED FORM I-9
PLEASE DO NOT MAIL COMPLETED FORM I-9 TO ICE OR USCIS

Form I-9 (Rev. 05/31/05)Y

Department of Homeland Security
U.S. Citizenship and Immigration Services

OMB No. 1615-0047; Expires 03/31/07
Employment Eligibility Verification

Please read instructions carefully before completing this form. The instructions must be available during completion of this form. ANTI-DISCRIMINATION NOTICE: It is illegal to discriminate against work eligible individuals. Employers CANNOT specify which document(s) they will accept from an employee. The refusal to hire an individual because of a future expiration date may also constitute illegal discrimination.

Section 1. Employee Information and Verification. To be completed and signed by employee at the time employment begins.

Print Name: Last	First	Middle Initial	Maiden Name

Address (Street Name and Number)	Apt. #	Date of Birth (month/day/year)

City	State	Zip Code	Social Security #

I am aware that federal law provides for imprisonment and/or fines for false statements or use of false documents in connection with the completion of this form.

I attest, under penalty of perjury, that I am (check one of the following):
☐ A citizen or national of the United States
☐ A Lawful Permanent Resident (Alien #) A _____
☐ An alien authorized to work until ___/___/___
(Alien # or Admission #) _____

Employee's Signature	Date (month/day/year)

Preparer and/or Translator Certification. (To be completed and signed if Section 1 is prepared by a person other than the employee.) I attest, under penalty of perjury, that I have assisted in the completion of this form and that to the best of my knowledge the information is true and correct.

Preparer's/Translator's Signature	Print Name

Address (Street Name and Number, City, State, Zip Code)	Date (month/day/year)

Section 2. Employer Review and Verification. To be completed and signed by employer. Examine one document from List A OR examine one document from List B and one from List C, as listed on the reverse of this form, and record the title, number and expiration date, if any, of the document(s).

List A	OR	List B	AND	List C
Document title: _____		_____		_____
Issuing authority: _____		_____		_____
Document #: _____		_____		_____
Expiration Date (if any): ___/___/___		___/___		___/___
Document #: _____				
Expiration Date (if any): ___/___/___				

CERTIFICATION - I attest, under penalty of perjury, that I have examined the document(s) presented by the above-named employee, that the above-listed document(s) appear to be genuine and to relate to the employee named, that the employee began employment on (month/day/year) ___/___/___ and that to the best of my knowledge the employee is eligible to work in the United States. (State employment agencies may omit the date the employee began employment.)

Signature of Employer or Authorized Representative	Print Name	Title

Business or Organization Name	Address (Street Name and Number, City, State, Zip Code)	Date (month/day/year)

Section 3. Updating and Reverification. To be completed and signed by employer.

A. New Name (if applicable)	B. Date of rehire (month/day/year) (if applicable)

C. If employee's previous grant of work authorization has expired, provide the information below for the document that establishes current employment eligibility.

Document Title:_____   Document #: _____   Expiration Date (if any): ___/___/___

I attest, under penalty of perjury, that to the best of my knowledge, this employee is eligible to work in the United States, and if the employee presented document(s), the document(s) I have examined appear to be genuine and to relate to the individual.

Signature of Employer or Authorized Representative	Date (month/day/year)

NOTE: This is the 1991 edition of the Form I-9 that has been rebranded with a current printing date to reflect the recent transition from the INS to DHS and its components.

Form I-9 (Rev. 05/31/05)Y Page 2

LISTS OF ACCEPTABLE DOCUMENTS

LIST A		LIST B		LIST C
Documents that Establish Both Identity and Employment Eligibility	**OR**	**Documents that Establish Identity**	**AND**	**Documents that Establish Employment Eligibility**

LIST A — Documents that Establish Both Identity and Employment Eligibility

1. U.S. Passport (unexpired or expired)

2. Certificate of U.S. Citizenship *(Form N-560 or N-561)*

3. Certificate of Naturalization *(Form N-550 or N-570)*

4. Unexpired foreign passport, with *I-551 stamp or* attached *Form I-94* indicating unexpired employment authorization

5. Permanent Resident Card or Alien Registration Receipt Card with photograph *(Form I-151 or I-551)*

6. Unexpired Temporary Resident Card *(Form I-688)*

7. Unexpired Employment Authorization Card *(Form I-688A)*

8. Unexpired Reentry Permit *(Form I-327)*

9. Unexpired Refugee Travel Document *(Form I-571)*

10. Unexpired Employment Authorization Document issued by DHS that contains a photograph *(Form I-688B)*

LIST B — Documents that Establish Identity

1. Driver's license or ID card issued by a state or outlying possession of the United States provided it contains a photograph or information such as name, date of birth, gender, height, eye color and address

2. ID card issued by federal, state or local government agencies or entities, provided it contains a photograph or information such as name, date of birth, gender, height, eye color and address

3. School ID card with a photograph

4. Voter's registration card

5. U.S. Military card or draft record

6. Military dependent's ID card

7. U.S. Coast Guard Merchant Mariner Card

8. Native American tribal document

9. Driver's license issued by a Canadian government authority

For persons under age 18 who are unable to present a document listed above:

10. School record or report card

11. Clinic, doctor or hospital record

12. Day-care or nursery school record

LIST C — Documents that Establish Employment Eligibility

1. U.S. social security card issued by the Social Security Administration *(other than a card stating it is not valid for employment)*

2. Certification of Birth Abroad issued by the Department of State *(Form FS-545 or Form DS-1350)*

3. Original or certified copy of a birth certificate issued by a state, county, municipal authority or outlying possession of the United States bearing an official seal

4. Native American tribal document

5. U.S. Citizen ID Card *(Form I-197)*

6. ID Card for use of Resident Citizen in the United States *(Form I-179)*

7. Unexpired employment authorization document issued by DHS *(other than those listed under List A)*

Illustrations of many of these documents appear in Part 8 of the Handbook for Employers (M-274)

Form I-9 (Rev. 05/31/05)Y Page 3

| Form **SS-4**
(Rev. December 2001)
Department of the Treasury
Internal Revenue Service | **Application for Employer Identification Number**
(For use by employers, corporations, partnerships, trusts, estates, churches, government agencies, Indian tribal entities, certain individuals, and others.)
► See separate instructions for each line. ► Keep a copy for your records. | EIN

OMB No. 1545-0003 |

Type or print clearly.

1 Legal name of entity (or individual) for whom the EIN is being requested

2 Trade name of business (if different from name on line 1)	**3** Executor, trustee, "care of" name
4a Mailing address (room, apt., suite no. and street, or P.O. box)	**5a** Street address (if different) (Do not enter a P.O. box.)
4b City, state, and ZIP code	**5b** City, state, and ZIP code

6 County and state where principal business is located

7a Name of principal officer, general partner, grantor, owner, or trustor	**7b** SSN, ITIN, or EIN

8a **Type of entity** (check only one box)

☐ Sole proprietor (SSN) _____

☐ Partnership

☐ Corporation (enter form number to be filed) ► _____

☐ Personal service corp.

☐ Church or church-controlled organization

☐ Other nonprofit organization (specify) ► _____

☐ Other (specify) ►

☐ Estate (SSN of decedent) _____

☐ Plan administrator (SSN) _____

☐ Trust (SSN of grantor) _____

☐ National Guard   ☐ State/local government

☐ Farmers' cooperative   ☐ Federal government/military

☐ REMIC   ☐ Indian tribal governments/enterprises

Group Exemption Number (GEN) ► _____

8b If a corporation, name the state or foreign country (if applicable) where incorporated

State	Foreign country

9 **Reason for applying** (check only one box)

☐ Started new business (specify type) ► _____

☐ Hired employees (Check the box and see line 12.)

☐ Compliance with IRS withholding regulations

☐ Other (specify) ►

☐ Banking purpose (specify purpose) ► _____

☐ Changed type of organization (specify new type) ► _____

☐ Purchased going business

☐ Created a trust (specify type) ► _____

☐ Created a pension plan (specify type) ► _____

10 Date business started or acquired (month, day, year)	**11** Closing month of accounting year

12 First date wages or annuities were paid or will be paid (month, day, year). **Note:** *If applicant is a withholding agent, enter date income will first be paid to nonresident alien. (month, day, year)* . . . . ►

13 Highest number of employees expected in the next 12 months. **Note:** *If the applicant does not expect to have any employees during the period, enter "-0-."* . . . . ►	Agricultural	Household	Other

14 Check **one** box that best describes the principal activity of your business.

☐ Construction   ☐ Rental & leasing   ☐ Transportation & warehousing

☐ Real estate   ☐ Manufacturing   ☐ Finance & insurance

☐ Health care & social assistance   ☐ Wholesale–agent/broker

☐ Accommodation & food service   ☐ Wholesale–other   ☐ Retail

☐ Other (specify)

15 Indicate principal line of merchandise sold; specific construction work done; products produced; or services provided.

16a Has the applicant ever applied for an employer identification number for this or any other business? . . . . ☐ Yes   ☐ No

Note: *If "Yes," please complete lines 16b and 16c.*

16b If you checked "Yes" on line 16a, give applicant's legal name and trade name shown on prior application if different from line 1 or 2 above.

Legal name ►   Trade name ►

16c Approximate date when, and city and state where, the application was filed. Enter previous employer identification number if known.

Approximate date when filed (mo., day, year)	City and state where filed	Previous EIN

Third Party Designee	Complete this section **only** if you want to authorize the named individual to receive the entity's EIN and answer questions about the completion of this form.	
	Designee's name	Designee's telephone number (include area code) ( )
	Address and ZIP code	Designee's fax number (include area code) ( )

Under penalties of perjury, I declare that I have examined this application, and to the best of my knowledge and belief, it is true, correct, and complete.

Applicant's telephone number (include area code)
(   )

Name and title (type or print clearly) ►

Applicant's fax number (include area code)
(   )

Signature ►   Date ►

For Privacy Act and Paperwork Reduction Act Notice, see separate instructions.   Cat. No. 16055N   Form **SS-4** (Rev. 12-2001)

Form SS-4 (Rev. 12-2001)   Page **2**

Do I Need an EIN?

File Form SS-4 if the applicant entity does not already have an EIN but is required to show an EIN on any return, statement, or other document.[1] **See also the separate instructions for each line on Form SS-4.**

IF the applicant...	AND...	THEN...
Started a new business	Does not currently have (nor expect to have) employees	Complete lines 1, 2, 4a–6, 8a, and 9–16c.
Hired (or will hire) employees, including household employees	Does not already have an EIN	Complete lines 1, 2, 4a–6, 7a–b (if applicable), 8a, 8b (if applicable), and 9–16c.
Opened a bank account	Needs an EIN for banking purposes only	Complete lines 1–5b, 7a–b (if applicable), 8a, 9, and 16a–c.
Changed type of organization	Either the legal character of the organization or its ownership changed (e.g., you incorporate a sole proprietorship or form a partnership)[2]	Complete lines 1–16c (as applicable).
Purchased a going business[3]	Does not already have an EIN	Complete lines 1–16c (as applicable).
Created a trust	The trust is other than a grantor trust or an IRA trust[4]	Complete lines 1–16c (as applicable).
Created a pension plan as a plan administrator[5]	Needs an EIN for reporting purposes	Complete lines 1, 2, 4a–6, 8a, 9, and 16a–c.
Is a foreign person needing an EIN to comply with IRS withholding regulations	Needs an EIN to complete a Form W-8 (other than Form W-8ECI), avoid withholding on portfolio assets, or claim tax treaty benefits[6]	Complete lines 1–5b, 7a–b (SSN or ITIN optional), 8a–9, and 16a–c.
Is administering an estate	Needs an EIN to report estate income on Form 1041	Complete lines 1, 3, 4a–b, 8a, 9, and 16a–c.
Is a withholding agent for taxes on non-wage income paid to an alien (i.e., individual, corporation, or partnership, etc.)	Is an agent, broker, fiduciary, manager, tenant, or spouse who is required to file **Form 1042,** Annual Withholding Tax Return for U.S. Source Income of Foreign Persons	Complete lines 1, 2, 3 (if applicable), 4a–5b, 7a–b (if applicable), 8a, 9, and 16a–c.
Is a state or local agency	Serves as a tax reporting agent for public assistance recipients under Rev. Proc. 80-4, 1980-1 C.B. 581[7]	Complete lines 1, 2, 4a–5b, 8a, 9, and 16a–c.
Is a single-member LLC	Needs an EIN to file **Form 8832,** Classification Election, for filing employment tax returns, **or** for state reporting purposes[8]	Complete lines 1–16c (as applicable).
Is an S corporation	Needs an EIN to file **Form 2553,** Election by a Small Business Corporation[9]	Complete lines 1–16c (as applicable).

[1] For example, a sole proprietorship or self-employed farmer who establishes a qualified retirement plan, or is required to file excise, employment, alcohol, tobacco, or firearms returns, must have an EIN. **A partnership, corporation, REMIC (real estate mortgage investment conduit), nonprofit organization (church, club, etc.), or farmers' cooperative must use an EIN for any tax-related purpose even if the entity does not have employees.**

[2] However, **do not** apply for a new EIN if the existing entity only **(a)** changed its business name, **(b)** elected on Form 8832 to change the way it is taxed (or is covered by the default rules), or **(c)** terminated its partnership status because at least 50% of the total interests in partnership capital and profits were sold or exchanged within a 12-month period. (The EIN of the terminated partnership should continue to be used. See Regulations section 301.6109-1(d)(2)(iii).)

[3] Do not use the EIN of the prior business unless you became the "owner" of a corporation by acquiring its stock.

[4] However, IRA trusts that are required to file **Form 990-T,** Exempt Organization Business Income Tax Return, must have an EIN.

[5] A plan administrator is the person or group of persons specified as the administrator by the instrument under which the plan is operated.

[6] Entities applying to be a Qualified Intermediary (QI) need a QI-EIN even if they already have an EIN. **See Rev. Proc. 2000-12.**

[7] See also *Household employer* on page 4. **(Note:** State or local agencies may need an EIN for other reasons, e.g., hired employees.)

[8] Most LLCs **do not** need to file Form 8832. See **Limited liability company (LLC)** on page 4 for details on completing Form SS-4 for an LLC.

[9] An existing corporation that is electing or revoking S corporation status should use its previously-assigned EIN.

Instructions for Form SS-4

Department of the Treasury
Internal Revenue Service

(Rev. September 2003)

For use with Form SS-4 (Rev. December 2001)
Application for Employer Identification Number.
Section references are to the Internal Revenue Code unless otherwise noted.

General Instructions

Use these instructions to complete **Form SS-4,** Application for Employer Identification Number. Also see **Do I Need an EIN?** on page 2 of Form SS-4.

Purpose of Form

Use Form SS-4 to apply for an employer identification number (EIN). An EIN is a nine-digit number (for example, 12-3456789) assigned to sole proprietors, corporations, partnerships, estates, trusts, and other entities for tax filing and reporting purposes. The information you provide on this form will establish your business tax account.

*An EIN is for use in connection with your business activities only. Do **not** use your EIN in place of your social security number (SSN).*

Items To Note

Apply online. You can now apply for and receive an EIN online using the internet. See **How To Apply** below.

File only one Form SS-4. Generally, a sole proprietor should file only one Form SS-4 and needs only one EIN, regardless of the number of businesses operated as a sole proprietorship or trade names under which a business operates. However, if the proprietorship incorporates or enters into a partnership, a new EIN is required. Also, each corporation in an affiliated group must have its own EIN.

EIN applied for, but not received. If you do not have an EIN by the time a return is due, write "Applied For" and the date you applied in the space shown for the number. **Do not** show your SSN as an EIN on returns.

If you do not have an EIN by the time a tax deposit is due, send your payment to the Internal Revenue Service Center for your filing area as shown in the instructions for the form that you are filing. Make your check or money order payable to the "United States Treasury" and show your name (as shown on Form SS-4), address, type of tax, period covered, and date you applied for an EIN.

How To Apply

You can apply for an EIN online, by telephone, by fax, or by mail depending on how soon you need to use the EIN. Use only one method for each entity so you do not receive more than one EIN for an entity.

Online. You can receive your EIN by internet and use it immediately to file a return or make a payment. Go to the

IRS website at **www.irs.gov/businesses** and click on **Employer ID Numbers** under **topics.**

Telephone. You can receive your EIN by telephone and use it immediately to file a return or make a payment. Call the IRS at **1-800-829-4933.** (International applicants must call 215-516-6999.) The hours of operation are 7:00 a.m. to 10:00 p.m. The person making the call must be authorized to sign the form or be an authorized designee. See **Signature** and **Third Party Designee** on page 6. Also see the **TIP** below.

If you are applying by telephone, it will be helpful to complete Form SS-4 before contacting the IRS. An IRS representative will use the information from the Form SS-4 to establish your account and assign you an EIN. Write the number you are given on the upper right corner of the form and sign and date it. Keep this copy for your records.

If requested by an IRS representative, mail or fax (facsimile) the signed Form SS-4 (including any Third Party Designee authorization) within 24 hours to the IRS address provided by the IRS representative.

*Taxpayer representatives can apply for an EIN on behalf of their client and request that the EIN be faxed to their **client** on the same day. **Note:** By using this procedure, you are authorizing the IRS to fax the EIN without a cover sheet.*

Fax. Under the Fax-TIN program, you can receive your EIN by fax within 4 business days. Complete and fax Form SS-4 to the IRS using the Fax-TIN number listed on page 2 for your state. A long-distance charge to callers outside of the local calling area will apply. Fax-TIN numbers can only be used to apply for an EIN. **The numbers may change without notice.** Fax-TIN is available 24 hours a day, 7 days a week.

Be sure to provide your fax number so the IRS can fax the EIN back to you. **Note:** By using this procedure, you are authorizing the IRS to fax the EIN without a cover sheet.

Mail. Complete Form SS-4 at least 4 to 5 weeks before you will need an EIN. Sign and date the application and mail it to the service center address for your state. You will receive your EIN in the mail in approximately 4 weeks. See also **Third Party Designee** on page 6.

Call 1-800-829-4933 to verify a number or to ask about the status of an application by mail.

Cat. No. 62736F

Where To Fax or File

If your principal business, office or agency, or legal residence in the case of an individual, is located in:	Call the Fax-TIN number shown or file with the "Internal Revenue Service Center" at:
Connecticut, Delaware, District of Columbia, Florida, Georgia, Maine, Maryland, Massachusetts, New Hampshire, New Jersey, New York, North Carolina, Ohio, Pennsylvania, Rhode Island, South Carolina, Vermont, Virginia, West Virginia	Attn: EIN Operation P. O. Box 9003 Holtsville, NY 11742-9003 Fax-TIN 631-447-8960
Illinois, Indiana, Kentucky, Michigan	Attn: EIN Operation Cincinnati, OH 45999 Fax-TIN 859-669-5760
Alabama, Alaska, Arizona, Arkansas, California, Colorado, Hawaii, Idaho, Iowa, Kansas, Louisiana, Minnesota, Mississippi, Missouri, Montana, Nebraska, Nevada, New Mexico, North Dakota, Oklahoma, Oregon, Puerto Rico, South Dakota, Tennessee, Texas, Utah, Washington, Wisconsin, Wyoming	Attn: EIN Operation Philadelphia, PA 19255 Fax-TIN 215-516-3990
If you have no legal residence, principal place of business, or principal office or agency in any state:	Attn: EIN Operation Philadelphia, PA 19255 Telephone 215-516-6999 Fax-TIN 215-516-3990

How To Get Forms and Publications

Phone. You can order forms, instructions, and publications by phone 24 hours a day, 7 days a week. Call 1-800-TAX-FORM (1-800-829-3676). You should receive your order or notification of its status within 10 workdays.

Personal computer. With your personal computer and modem, you can get the forms and information you need using the IRS website at **www.irs.gov** or File Transfer Protocol at **ftp.irs.gov**.

CD-ROM. For small businesses, return preparers, or others who may frequently need tax forms or publications, a CD-ROM containing over 2,000 tax products (including many prior year forms) can be purchased from the National Technical Information Service (NTIS).

To order **Pub. 1796,** Federal Tax Products on CD-ROM, call **1-877-CDFORMS** (1-877-233-6767) toll free or connect to **www.irs.gov/cdorders**.

Tax Help for Your Business

IRS-sponsored Small Business Workshops provide information about your Federal and state tax obligations.

For information about workshops in your area, call 1-800-829-4933.

Related Forms and Publications

The following **forms** and **instructions** may be useful to filers of Form SS-4:
• **Form 990-T,** Exempt Organization Business Income Tax Return
• **Instructions for Form 990-T**
• **Schedule C (Form 1040),** Profit or Loss From Business
• **Schedule F (Form 1040),** Profit or Loss From Farming
• **Instructions for Form 1041 and Schedules A, B, D, G, I, J, and K-1,** U.S. Income Tax Return for Estates and Trusts
• **Form 1042,** Annual Withholding Tax Return for U.S. Source Income of Foreign Persons
• **Instructions for Form 1065,** U.S. Return of Partnership Income
• **Instructions for Form 1066,** U.S. Real Estate Mortgage Investment Conduit (REMIC) Income Tax Return
• **Instructions for Forms 1120 and 1120-A**
• **Form 2553,** Election by a Small Business Corporation
• **Form 2848,** Power of Attorney and Declaration of Representative
• **Form 8821,** Tax Information Authorization
• **Form 8832,** Entity Classification Election
For more **information** about filing Form SS-4 and related issues, see:
• **Circular A,** Agricultural Employer's Tax Guide (Pub. 51)
• **Circular E,** Employer's Tax Guide (Pub. 15)
• **Pub. 538,** Accounting Periods and Methods
• **Pub. 542,** Corporations
• **Pub. 557,** Exempt Status for Your Organization
• **Pub. 583,** Starting a Business and Keeping Records
• **Pub. 966,** Electronic Choices for Paying ALL Your Federal Taxes
• **Pub. 1635,** Understanding Your EIN
• **Package 1023,** Application for Recognition of Exemption Under Section 501(c)(3) of the Internal Revenue Code
• **Package 1024,** Application for Recognition of Exemption Under Section 501(a)

Specific Instructions

Print or type all entries on Form SS-4. Follow the instructions for each line to expedite processing and to avoid unnecessary IRS requests for additional information. Enter "N/A" (nonapplicable) on the lines that do not apply.

Line 1—Legal name of entity (or individual) for whom the EIN is being requested. Enter the legal name of the entity (or individual) applying for the EIN exactly as it appears on the social security card, charter, or other applicable legal document.

Individuals. Enter your first name, middle initial, and last name. If you are a sole proprietor, enter your individual name, not your business name. Enter your business name on line 2. Do not use abbreviations or nicknames on line 1.

Trusts. Enter the name of the trust.

Estate of a decedent. Enter the name of the estate.

Partnerships. Enter the legal name of the partnership as it appears in the partnership agreement.

Corporations. Enter the corporate name as it appears in the corporation charter or other legal document creating it.

Plan administrators. Enter the name of the plan administrator. A plan administrator who already has an EIN should use that number.

Line 2—Trade name of business. Enter the trade name of the business if different from the legal name. The trade name is the "doing business as " (DBA) name.

 *Use the full legal name shown on line 1 on all tax returns filed for the entity. (However, if you enter a trade name on line 2 and choose to use the trade name instead of the legal name, enter the trade name on **all returns** you file.) To prevent processing delays and errors, **always** use the legal name only (or the trade name only) on **all** tax returns.*

Line 3—Executor, trustee, "care of" name. Trusts enter the name of the trustee. Estates enter the name of the executor, administrator, or other fiduciary. If the entity applying has a designated person to receive tax information, enter that person's name as the "care of" person. Enter the individual's first name, middle initial, and last name.

Lines 4a-b—Mailing address. Enter the mailing address for the entity's correspondence. If line 3 is completed, enter the address for the executor, trustee or "care of" person. Generally, this address will be used on all tax returns.

 *File **Form 8822**, Change of Address, to report any subsequent changes to the entity's mailing address.*

Lines 5a-b—Street address. Provide the entity's physical address **only** if different from its mailing address shown in lines 4a-b. **Do not** enter a P.O. box number here.

Line 6—County and state where principal business is located. Enter the entity's primary **physical** location.

Lines 7a-b—Name of principal officer, general partner, grantor, owner, or trustor. Enter the first name, middle initial, last name, and SSN of **(a)** the principal officer if the business is a corporation, **(b)** a general partner if a partnership, **(c)** the owner of an entity that is disregarded as separate from its owner (disregarded entities owned by a corporation enter the corporation's name and EIN), or **(d)** a grantor, owner, or trustor if a trust.

If the person in question is an **alien individual** with a previously assigned individual taxpayer identification number (ITIN), enter the ITIN in the space provided and submit a copy of an official identifying document. If

necessary, complete **Form W-7,** Application for IRS Individual Taxpayer Identification Number, to obtain an ITIN.

You are **required** to enter an SSN, ITIN, or EIN unless the only reason you are applying for an EIN is to make an entity classification election (see Regulations sections 301.7701-1 through 301.7701-3) and you are a nonresident alien with no effectively connected income from sources within the United States.

Line 8a—Type of entity. Check the box that best describes the type of entity applying for the EIN. If you are an alien individual with an ITIN previously assigned to you, enter the ITIN in place of a requested SSN.

 *This is not an election for a tax classification of an entity. See **Limited liability company (LLC)** on page 4.*

Other. If not specifically listed, check the "Other" box, enter the type of entity and the type of return, if any, that will be filed (for example, "Common Trust Fund, Form 1065" or "Created a Pension Plan"). Do not enter "N/A." If you are an alien individual applying for an EIN, see the **Lines 7a-b** instructions above.

● **Household employer.** If you are an individual, check the "Other" box and enter "Household Employer" and your SSN. If you are a state or local agency serving as a tax reporting agent for public assistance recipients who become household employers, check the "Other" box and enter "Household Employer Agent." If you are a trust that qualifies as a household employer, you do not need a separate EIN for reporting tax information relating to household employees; use the EIN of the trust.

● **QSub.** For a qualified subchapter S subsidiary (QSub) check the "Other" box and specify "QSub."

● **Withholding agent.** If you are a withholding agent required to file Form 1042, check the "Other" box and enter "Withholding Agent."

Sole proprietor. Check this box if you file Schedule C, C-EZ, or F (Form 1040) and have a qualified plan, or are required to file excise, employment, alcohol, tobacco, or firearms returns, or are a payer of gambling winnings. Enter your SSN (or ITIN) in the space provided. If you are a nonresident alien with no effectively connected income from sources within the United States, you do not need to enter an SSN or ITIN.

Corporation. This box is for any corporation **other than a personal service corporation.** If you check this box, enter the income tax form number to be filed by the entity in the space provided.

 *If you entered "1120S" after the "Corporation" checkbox, the corporation **must** file Form 2553 **no later than the 15th day of the 3rd month of the tax year the election is to take effect.** Until Form 2553 has been received and approved, you will be considered a Form 1120 filer. See the Instructions for Form 2553.*

Personal service corp. Check this box if the entity is a personal service corporation. An entity is a personal service corporation for a tax year only if:

-3-

- The principal activity of the entity during the testing period (prior tax year) for the tax year is the performance of personal services substantially by employee-owners, and
- The employee-owners own at least 10% of the fair market value of the outstanding stock in the entity on the last day of the testing period.

Personal services include performance of services in such fields as health, law, accounting, or consulting. For more information about personal service corporations, see the Instructions for Forms 1120 and 1120-A and Pub. 542.

Other nonprofit organization. Check this box if the nonprofit organization is other than a church or church-controlled organization and specify the type of nonprofit organization (for example, an educational organization).

 *If the organization also seeks tax-exempt status, you **must** file either Package 1023 or Package 1024. See Pub. 557 for more information.*

If the organization is covered by a group exemption letter, enter the four-digit **group exemption number (GEN).** (Do not confuse the GEN with the nine-digit EIN.) If you do not know the GEN, contact the parent organization. Get Pub. 557 for more information about group exemption numbers.

Plan administrator. If the plan administrator is an individual, enter the plan administrator's SSN in the space provided.

REMIC. Check this box if the entity has elected to be treated as a real estate mortgage investment conduit (REMIC). See the Instructions for Form 1066 for more information.

Limited liability company (LLC). An LLC is an entity organized under the laws of a state or foreign country as a limited liability company. For Federal tax purposes, an LLC may be treated as a partnership or corporation or be disregarded as an entity separate from its owner.

By **default,** a domestic LLC with only one member is **disregarded** as an entity separate from its owner and must include all of its income and expenses on the owner's tax return (e.g., **Schedule C (Form 1040)**). Also by default, a domestic LLC with two or more members is treated as a partnership. A domestic LLC may file Form 8832 to avoid either default classification and elect to be classified as an association taxable as a corporation. For more information on entity classifications (including the rules for foreign entities), see the instructions for Form 8832.

 Do not *file Form 8832 if the LLC accepts the default classifications above. **However, if the LLC will be electing S Corporation status, it must timely file both Form 8832 and Form 2553.***

Complete Form SS-4 for LLCs as follows:
- A single-member domestic LLC that accepts the default classification (above) does not need an EIN and generally should not file Form SS-4. Generally, the LLC should use the name and EIN of its **owner** for all Federal tax purposes. However, the reporting and payment of employment taxes for employees of the LLC may be made using the name and EIN of **either** the owner or the LLC as explained in Notice 99-6. You can find Notice 99-6 on page 12 of Internal Revenue Bulletin 1999-3 at **www.irs.gov/pub/irs-irbs/irb99-03.pdf. (Note:** If the LLC applicant indicates in box 13 that it has employees or expects to have employees, the owner (whether an individual or other entity) of a single-member domestic LLC will also be assigned its own EIN (if it does not already have one) even if the LLC will be filing the employment tax returns.)
- A single-member, domestic LLC that accepts the default classification (above) and wants an EIN for filing employment tax returns (see above) or non-Federal purposes, such as a state requirement, must check the "Other" box and write "Disregarded Entity" or, when applicable, "Disregarded Entity—Sole Proprietorship" in the space provided.
- A multi-member, domestic LLC that accepts the default classification (above) must check the "Partnership" box.
- A domestic LLC that will be filing Form 8832 to elect corporate status must check the "Corporation" box and write in "Single-Member" or "Multi-Member" immediately below the "form number" entry line.

Line 9—Reason for applying. Check only **one** box. Do not enter "N/A."

Started new business. Check this box if you are starting a new business that requires an EIN. If you check this box, enter the type of business being started. **Do not** apply if you already have an EIN and are only adding another place of business.

Hired employees. Check this box if the existing business is requesting an EIN because it has hired or is hiring employees and is therefore required to file employment tax returns. **Do not** apply if you already have an EIN and are only hiring employees. For information on employment taxes (e.g., for family members), see Circular E.

 You may be required to make electronic deposits of all depository taxes (such as employment tax, excise tax, and corporate income tax) using the Electronic Federal Tax Payment System (EFTPS). See section 11, Depositing Taxes, of Circular E and Pub. 966.

Created a pension plan. Check this box if you have created a pension plan and need an EIN for reporting purposes. Also, enter the type of plan in the space provided.

 Check this box if you are applying for a trust EIN when a new pension plan is established. In addition, check the "Other" box in line 8a and write "Created a Pension Plan" in the space provided.

Banking purpose. Check this box if you are requesting an EIN for banking purposes only, and enter the banking purpose (for example, a bowling league for

-4-

depositing dues or an investment club for dividend and interest reporting).

Changed type of organization. Check this box if the business is changing its type of organization. For example, the business was a sole proprietorship and has been incorporated or has become a partnership. If you check this box, specify in the space provided (including available space immediately below) the type of change made. For example, "From Sole Proprietorship to Partnership."

Purchased going business. Check this box if you purchased an existing business. **Do not** use the former owner's EIN unless you became the "owner" of a corporation by acquiring its stock.

Created a trust. Check this box if you created a trust, and enter the type of trust created. For example, indicate if the trust is a nonexempt charitable trust or a split-interest trust.

Exception. Do **not** file this form for certain grantor-type trusts. The trustee does not need an EIN for the trust if the trustee furnishes the name and TIN of the grantor/owner and the address of the trust to all payors. See the Instructions for Form 1041 for more information.

 Do not check this box if you are applying for a trust EIN when a new pension plan is established. Check "Created a pension plan."

Other. Check this box if you are requesting an EIN for any other reason; and enter the reason. For example, a newly-formed state government entity should enter "Newly-Formed State Government Entity" in the space provided.

Line 10—Date business started or acquired. If you are starting a new business, enter the starting date of the business. If the business you acquired is already operating, enter the date you acquired the business. If you are changing the form of ownership of your business, enter the date the new ownership entity began. Trusts should enter the date the trust was legally created. Estates should enter the date of death of the decedent whose name appears on line 1 or the date when the estate was legally funded.

Line 11—Closing month of accounting year. Enter the last month of your accounting year or tax year. An accounting or tax year is usually 12 consecutive months, either a calendar year or a fiscal year (including a period of 52 or 53 weeks). A calendar year is 12 consecutive months ending on December 31. A fiscal year is either 12 consecutive months ending on the last day of any month other than December or a 52-53 week year. For more information on accounting periods, see Pub. 538.

Individuals. Your tax year generally will be a calendar year.

Partnerships. Partnerships must adopt one of the following tax years:
- The tax year of the majority of its partners,
- The tax year common to all of its principal partners,
- The tax year that results in the least aggregate deferral of income, or
- In certain cases, some other tax year.

See the Instructions for Form 1065 for more information.

REMICs. REMICs must have a calendar year as their tax year.

Personal service corporations. A personal service corporation generally must adopt a calendar year unless:
- It can establish a business purpose for having a different tax year, or
- It elects under section 444 to have a tax year other than a calendar year.

Trusts. Generally, a trust must adopt a calendar year except for the following:
- Tax-exempt trusts,
- Charitable trusts, and
- Grantor-owned trusts.

Line 12—First date wages or annuities were paid or will be paid. If the business has or will have employees, enter the date on which the business began or will begin to pay wages. If the business does not plan to have employees, enter "N/A."

Withholding agent. Enter the date you began or will begin to pay income (including annuities) to a nonresident alien. This also applies to individuals who are required to file Form 1042 to report alimony paid to a nonresident alien.

Line 13—Highest number of employees expected in the next 12 months. Complete each box by entering the number (including zero ("-0-")) of "Agricultural," "Household," or "Other" employees expected by the applicant in the next 12 months. For a definition of agricultural labor (farmwork), see Circular A.

Lines 14 and 15. Check the **one** box in line 14 that best describes the principal activity of the applicant's business. Check the "Other" box (and specify the applicant's principal activity) if none of the listed boxes applies.

Use line 15 to describe the applicant's principal line of business in more detail. For example, if you checked the "Construction" box in line 14, enter additional detail such as "General contractor for residential buildings" in line 15.

Construction. Check this box if the applicant is engaged in erecting buildings or other structures, (e.g., streets, highways, bridges, tunnels). The term "Construction" also includes special trade contractors, (e.g., plumbing, HVAC, electrical, carpentry, concrete, excavation, etc. contractors).

Real estate. Check this box if the applicant is engaged in renting or leasing real estate to others; managing, selling, buying or renting real estate for others; or providing related real estate services (e.g., appraisal services).

Rental and leasing. Check this box if the applicant is engaged in providing tangible goods such as autos, computers, consumer goods, or industrial machinery and equipment to customers in return for a periodic rental or lease payment.

Manufacturing. Check this box if the applicant is engaged in the mechanical, physical, or chemical transformation of materials, substances, or components

-5-

into new products. The assembling of component parts of manufactured products is also considered to be manufacturing.

Transportation & warehousing. Check this box if the applicant provides transportation of passengers or cargo; warehousing or storage of goods; scenic or sight-seeing transportation; or support activities related to these modes of transportation.

Finance & insurance. Check this box if the applicant is engaged in transactions involving the creation, liquidation, or change of ownership of financial assets and/or facilitating such financial transactions; underwriting annuities/insurance policies; facilitating such underwriting by selling insurance policies; or by providing other insurance or employee-benefit related services.

Health care and social assistance. Check this box if the applicant is engaged in providing physical, medical, or psychiatric care using licensed health care professionals or providing social assistance activities such as youth centers, adoption agencies, individual/ family services, temporary shelters, etc.

Accommodation & food services. Check this box if the applicant is engaged in providing customers with lodging, meal preparation, snacks, or beverages for immediate consumption.

Wholesale–agent/broker. Check this box if the applicant is engaged in arranging for the purchase or sale of goods owned by others or purchasing goods on a commission basis for goods traded in the wholesale market, usually between businesses.

Wholesale–other. Check this box if the applicant is engaged in selling goods in the wholesale market generally to other businesses for resale on their own account.

Retail. Check this box if the applicant is engaged in selling merchandise to the general public from a fixed store; by direct, mail-order, or electronic sales; or by using vending machines.

Other. Check this box if the applicant is engaged in an activity not described above. Describe the applicant's principal business activity in the space provided.

Lines 16a-c. Check the applicable box in line 16a to indicate whether or not the entity (or individual) applying for an EIN was issued one previously. Complete lines 16b and 16c **only** if the "Yes" box in line 16a is checked. If the applicant previously applied for **more than one** EIN, write "See Attached" in the empty space in line 16a and attach a separate sheet providing the line 16b and 16c information for each EIN previously requested.

Third Party Designee. Complete this section **only** if you want to authorize the named individual to receive the entity's EIN and answer questions about the completion of Form SS-4. The designee's authority terminates at the time the EIN is assigned and released to the designee. **You must complete the signature area for the authorization to be valid.**

Signature. When required, the application must be signed by **(a)** the individual, if the applicant is an individual, **(b)** the president, vice president, or other

principal officer, if the applicant is a corporation, **(c)** a responsible and duly authorized member or officer having knowledge of its affairs, if the applicant is a partnership, government entity, or other unincorporated organization, or **(d)** the fiduciary, if the applicant is a trust or an estate. Foreign applicants may have any duly-authorized person, (e.g., division manager), sign Form SS-4.

Privacy Act and Paperwork Reduction Act Notice. We ask for the information on this form to carry out the Internal Revenue laws of the United States. We need it to comply with section 6109 and the regulations thereunder which generally require the inclusion of an employer identification number (EIN) on certain returns, statements, or other documents filed with the Internal Revenue Service. If your entity is required to obtain an EIN, you are required to provide all of the information requested on this form. Information on this form may be used to determine which Federal tax returns you are required to file and to provide you with related forms and publications.

We disclose this form to the Social Security Administration for their use in determining compliance with applicable laws. We may give this information to the Department of Justice for use in civil and criminal litigation, and to the cities, states, and the District of Columbia for use in administering their tax laws. We may also disclose this information to Federal and state agencies to enforce Federal nontax criminal laws and to combat terrorism.

We will be unable to issue an EIN to you unless you provide all of the requested information which applies to your entity. Providing false information could subject you to penalties.

You are not required to provide the information requested on a form that is subject to the Paperwork Reduction Act unless the form displays a valid OMB control number. Books or records relating to a form or its instructions must be retained as long as their contents may become material in the administration of any Internal Revenue law. Generally, tax returns and return information are confidential, as required by section 6103.

The time needed to complete and file this form will vary depending on individual circumstances. The estimated average time is:

Recordkeeping	6 min.
Learning about the law or the form	22 min.
Preparing the form	46 min.
Copying, assembling, and sending the form to the IRS	20 min.

If you have comments concerning the accuracy of these time estimates or suggestions for making this form simpler, we would be happy to hear from you. You can write to the Tax Products Coordinating Committee, Western Area Distribution Center, Rancho Cordova, CA 95743-0001. **Do not** send the form to this address. Instead, see **How To Apply** on page 1.

SOCIAL SECURITY ADMINISTRATION
Application for a Social Security Card

Applying for a Social Security Card is easy <u>AND</u> it is free!

USE THIS APPLICATION TO APPLY FOR:
- An **original** Social Security card
- A **duplicate** Social Security card (same name and number)
- A **corrected** Social Security card (name change and same number)
- A **change of information** on your record other than your name (no card needed)

IMPORTANT: You MUST provide the required evidence or we cannot process the application. Follow the instructions below to provide the information and evidence we need.

STEP 1 Read pages 1 through 3 which explain how to complete the application and what evidence we need.

STEP 2 Complete and sign the application using BLUE or BLACK ink. Do not use pencil or other colors of ink. Please print legibly.

STEP 3 Submit the completed and signed application with all required evidence to any Social Security office.

HOW TO COMPLETE THIS APPLICATION

Most items on the form are self-explanatory. Those that need explanation are discussed below. The numbers match the numbered items on the form. If you are completing this form for someone else, please complete the items as they apply to that person.

2. Show the address where you can receive your card 10 to 14 days from now.

3. If you check "Legal Alien **Not** Allowed to Work," you need to provide a document from the government agency requiring your Social Security number that explains why you need a number and that you meet all of the requirements for the benefit or service except for the number. A State or local agency requirement must conform with Federal law.

    If you check "Other," you need to provide proof you are entitled to a federally-funded benefit for which a Social Security number is required as a condition for you to receive payment.

5. Providing race/ethnic information is voluntary. However, if you do give us this information, it helps us prepare statistical reports on how Social Security programs affect people. We do not reveal the identities of individuals.

6. Show the month, day and full (4 digit) year of birth, for example, "1998" for year of birth.

8.B. Show the mother's Social Security number only if you are applying for an original Social Security card for a child under age 18. You may leave this item blank if the mother does not have a number or you do not know the mother's number. We will still be able to assign a number to the child.

9.B. Show the father's Social Security number only if you are applying for an original Social Security card for a child under age 18. You may leave this item blank if the father does not have a number or you do not know the father's number. We will still be able to assign a number to the child.

13. If the date of birth you show in item 6 is different from the date of birth you used on a prior application for a Social Security card, show the date of birth you used on the prior application and submit evidence of age to support the date of birth in item 6.

16. You **must** sign the application yourself if you are age 18 or older and are physically and mentally capable. If you are under age 18, you may also sign the application if you are physically and mentally capable. If you cannot sign your name, you should sign with an "X" mark and have two people sign as witnesses in the space beside the mark. If you are physically or mentally incapable of signing the application, generally a parent, close relative, or legal guardian may sign the application. Call us if you need clarification about who can sign.

ABOUT YOUR DOCUMENTS

- We need **ORIGINAL** documents or **copies certified by the custodian of the record.** We will return your documents after we have seen them.

- **We cannot accept photocopies or notarized copies of documents.**

- If your documents do not meet this requirement, we cannot process your application.

DOCUMENTS WE NEED

To apply for an **ORIGINAL CARD** (you have NEVER been assigned a Social Security number before), we need at least 2 documents as proof of:

- **Age,**
- **Identity, and**
- **U.S. citizenship or lawful alien status.**

To apply for a **DUPLICATE CARD** (same number, same name), we need proof of **identity.**

To apply for a **CORRECTED CARD** (same number, different name), we need proof of **identity.** We need one or more documents which identify you by the OLD NAME on our records and your NEW NAME. Examples include: a marriage certificate, divorce decree, or a court order that changes your name. Or we can accept two identity documents - one in your old name and one in your new name. (See IDENTITY, for examples of identity documents.)

IMPORTANT: If you are applying for a duplicate or corrected card and were **born outside the U.S.**, we also need proof of U.S. citizenship or lawful alien status. (See U.S. CITIZENSHIP or ALIEN STATUS for examples of documents you can submit.)

AGE: We prefer to see your birth certificate. However, we can accept another document that shows your age. Some of the other documents we can accept are:

- Hospital record of your birth (created at the time of your birth)
- Religious record showing your age made before you were 3 months old
- Passport
- Adoption record (the adoption record must indicate that the birth data was taken from the original birth certificate)

Call us for advice if you cannot obtain one of these documents.

IDENTITY: We must see a document in the name you want shown on the card. The identity document must be of recent issuance so that we can determine your continued existence. We prefer to see a document with a photograph. However, we can generally accept a non-photo identity document if it has enough information to identify you (e.g., your name, as well as age, date of birth or parents' names). **WE CANNOT ACCEPT A BIRTH CERTIFICATE, HOSPITAL SOUVENIR BIRTH CERTIFICATE, SOCIAL SECURITY CARD OR CARD STUB, OR SOCIAL SECURITY RECORD** as evidence of identity. Some documents we can accept are:

- Driver's license
- Employee ID card
- Passport
- Marriage or divorce record
- Adoption record (only if not being used to establish age)
- Health insurance card (not a Medicare card)
- Military record
- Life insurance policy
- School ID card

As evidence of identity for infants and young children, we can accept :

- Doctor, clinic, hospital record
- Daycare center, school record
- Religious record (e.g., baptismal record)

IMPORTANT: If you are **applying for a card on behalf of someone else**, you must provide evidence that establishes your authority to sign the application on behalf of the person to whom the card will be issued. In addition, we must see proof of identity for both you and the person to whom the card will be issued.

U. S. CITIZENSHIP: We can accept most documents that show you were born in the U.S. If you are a U.S. citizen born outside the U.S., show us a U.S. consular report of birth, a U.S. passport, a Certificate of Citizenship, or a Certificate of Naturalization.

ALIEN STATUS: We need to see an unexpired document issued to you by the Department of Homeland Security (DHS) showing your immigration status, such as Form I-551, I-94, I-688B, or I-766. We CANNOT accept a receipt showing you applied for the document. If you are not authorized to work in the U.S., we can issue you a Social Security card if you are lawfully here and need the number for a valid nonwork reason. (See HOW TO COMPLETE THIS APPLICATION, Item 3.) Your card will be marked to show you cannot work. If you do work, we will notify DHS.

To **CHANGE INFORMATION** on your record other than your name, we need proof of:

- **Identity**, and
- **Another document which supports the change** (for example, a birth certificate to change your date and/or place of birth or parents' names).

HOW TO SUBMIT THIS APPLICATION

In most cases, you can mail this application with your evidence documents to any Social Security office. We will return your documents to you. If you do not want to mail your original documents, take them with this application to the nearest Social Security office.

EXCEPTION: If you are age 12 or older and have never been assigned a number before, you must apply in person.

If you have any questions about this form, or about the documents we need, please contact any Social Security office. A telephone call will help you make sure you have everything you need to apply for a card or change information on your record. You can find your nearest office in your local phone directory or on our website at www.socialsecurity.gov.

THE PAPERWORK/PRIVACY ACT AND YOUR APPLICATION

The Privacy Act of 1974 requires us to give each person the following notice when applying for a Social Security number.

Sections 205(c) and 702 of the Social Security Act allow us to collect the facts we ask for on this form.

We use the facts you provide on this form to assign you a Social Security number and to issue you a Social Security card. You do not have to give us these facts, however, without them we cannot issue you a Social Security number or a card. Without a number, you may not be able to get a job and could lose Social Security benefits in the future.

The Social Security number is also used by the Internal Revenue Service for tax administration purposes as an identifier in processing tax returns of persons who have income which is reported to the Internal Revenue Service and by persons who are claimed as dependents on someone's Federal income tax return.

We may disclose information as necessary to administer Social Security programs, including to appropriate law enforcement agencies to investigate alleged violations of Social Security law; to other government agencies for administering entitlement, health, and welfare programs such as Medicaid, Medicare, veterans benefits, military pension, and civil service annuities, black lung, housing, student loans, railroad retirement benefits, and food stamps; to the Internal Revenue Service for Federal tax administration; and to employers and former employers to properly prepare wage reports. We may also disclose information as required by Federal law, for example, to the Department of Homeland Security, to identify and locate aliens in the U.S.; to the Selective Service System for draft registration; and to the Department of Health and Human Services for child support enforcement purposes. We may verify Social Security numbers for State motor vehicle agencies that use the number in issuing drivers licenses, as authorized by the Social Security Act. Finally, we may disclose information to your Congressional representative if they request information to answer questions you ask him or her.

We may use the information you give us when we match records by computer. Matching programs compare our records with those of other Federal, State, or local government agencies to determine whether a person qualifies for benefits paid by the Federal government. The law allows us to do this even if you do not agree to it.

Explanations about these and other reasons why information you provide us may be used or given out are available in Social Security offices. If you want to learn more about this, contact any Social Security office.

This information collection meets the requirements of 44 U.S.C. §3507, as amended by Section 2 of the Paperwork Reduction Act of 1995. You do not need to answer these questions unless we display a valid Office of Management and Budget control number. We estimate that it will take about 8.5 to 9 minutes to read the instructions, gather the facts, and answer the questions. **SEND THE COMPLETED FORM TO YOUR LOCAL SOCIAL SECURITY OFFICE. The office is listed under U. S. Government agencies in your telephone directory or you may call Social Security at 1-800-772-1213.** *You may send comments on our time estimate above to: SSA, 1338 Annex Building, Baltimore, MD 21235-6401.* **Send only comments relating to our time estimate to this address, not the completed form.**

SOCIAL SECURITY ADMINISTRATION
Application for a Social Security Card

Form Approved
OMB No. 0960-0066

1

NAME → TO BE SHOWN ON CARD	First	Full Middle Name	Last
FULL NAME AT BIRTH IF OTHER THAN ABOVE	First	Full Middle Name	Last
OTHER NAMES USED			

2 MAILING ADDRESS →
Do Not Abbreviate

Street Address, Apt. No., PO Box, Rural Route No.

City	State	Zip Code

3 CITIZENSHIP →
(Check One)

☐ U.S. Citizen   ☐ Legal Alien Allowed To Work   ☐ Legal Alien **Not** Allowed To Work (See Instructions On Page 1)   ☐ Other (See Instructions On Page 1)

4 SEX →   ☐ Male   ☐ Female

5 RACE/ETHNIC DESCRIPTION →
(Check One Only - Voluntary)

☐ Asian, Asian-American or Pacific Islander   ☐ Hispanic   ☐ Black (Not Hispanic)   ☐ North American Indian or Alaskan Native   ☐ White (Not Hispanic)

6 DATE OF BIRTH _____ Month, Day, Year

7 PLACE OF BIRTH _____ (Do Not Abbreviate) City   State or Foreign Country   FCI   Office Use Only

8

A. MOTHER'S MAIDEN NAME →	First	Full Middle Name	Last Name At Her Birth

B. MOTHER'S SOCIAL SECURITY NUMBER → ☐☐☐ – ☐☐ – ☐☐☐☐

9

A. FATHER'S NAME →	First	Full Middle Name	Last

B. FATHER'S SOCIAL SECURITY NUMBER → ☐☐☐ – ☐☐ – ☐☐☐☐

10 Has the applicant or anyone acting on his/her behalf ever filed for or received a Social Security number card before?

☐ Yes (If "yes", answer questions 11-13.)   ☐ No (If "no", go on to question 14.)   ☐ Don't Know (If "don't know", go on to question 14.)

11 Enter the Social Security number previously assigned to the person listed in item 1. → ☐☐☐ – ☐☐ – ☐☐☐☐

12 Enter the name shown on the most recent Social Security card issued for the person listed in item 1. →

First	Middle Name	Last

13 Enter any different date of birth if used on an earlier application for a card. → _____ Month, Day, Year

14 TODAY'S DATE _____ Month, Day, Year

15 DAYTIME PHONE NUMBER (___) _____ Area Code   Number

I declare under penalty of perjury that I have examined all the information on this form, and on any accompanying statements or forms, and it is true and correct to the best of my knowledge.

16 YOUR SIGNATURE ►

17 YOUR RELATIONSHIP TO THE PERSON IN ITEM 1 IS:
☐ Self   ☐ Natural Or Adoptive Parent   ☐ Legal Guardian   ☐ Other (Specify) _____

DO NOT WRITE BELOW THIS LINE (FOR SSA USE ONLY)

NPN			DOC	NTI	CAN		ITV
PBC	EVI	EVA	EVC	PRA	NWR	DNR	UNIT

EVIDENCE SUBMITTED	SIGNATURE AND TITLE OF EMPLOYEE(S) REVIEWING EVIDENCE AND/OR CONDUCTING INTERVIEW
	_____ DATE
	DCL _____ DATE

Form **SS-5** (10-2003)   EF (12-2004)   Destroy Prior Editions   Page 5

| Form **SS-8**
(Rev. June 2003)
Department of the Treasury
Internal Revenue Service | **Determination of Worker Status
for Purposes of Federal Employment Taxes
and Income Tax Withholding** | OMB No. 1545-0004 |

| Name of firm (or person) for whom the worker performed services | Worker's name |

| Firm's address (include street address, apt. or suite no., city, state, and ZIP code) | Worker's address (include street address, apt. or suite no., city, state, and ZIP code) |

| Trade name | Telephone number (include area code)
(   ) | Worker's social security number |

| Telephone number (include area code)
(   ) | Firm's employer identification number | Worker's employer identification number (if any) |

If the worker is paid by a firm other than the one listed on this form for these services, enter the name, address, and employer identification number of the payer.

Important Information Needed To Process Your Request

We must have your permission to disclose your name and the information on this form and any attachments to other parties involved with this request. **Do we have your permission to disclose this information?** . . . . ☐ Yes ☐ No

If you answered "No" or did not mark a box, we will not process your request and will not issue a determination.

You must answer ALL items OR mark them "Unknown" or "Does not apply." If you need more space, attach another sheet.

A This form is being completed by: ☐ Firm ☐ Worker; for services performed _____ to _____ .
                   (beginning date)   (ending date)

B Explain your reason(s) for filing this form (e.g., you received a bill from the IRS, you believe you received a Form 1099 or Form W-2 erroneously, you are unable to get worker's compensation benefits, you were audited or are being audited by the IRS). -----------------------------------

----

C Total number of workers who performed or are performing the same or similar services _____ .

D How did the worker obtain the job? ☐ Application ☐ Bid ☐ Employment Agency ☐ Other (specify) _____

E Attach copies of all supporting documentation (contracts, invoices, memos, Forms W-2, Forms 1099, IRS closing agreements, IRS rulings, etc.). In addition, please inform us of any current or past litigation concerning the worker's status. If no income reporting forms (Form 1099-MISC or W-2) were furnished to the worker, enter the amount of income earned for the year(s) at issue $ _____ .

F Describe the firm's business. --

G Describe the work done by the worker and provide the worker's job title. ----------------------------------

----

H Explain why you believe the worker is an employee or an independent contractor. ----------------------------

----

I Did the worker perform services for the firm before getting this position? . . . . ☐ Yes ☐ No ☐ N/A

If "Yes," what were the dates of the prior service? ---

If "Yes," explain the differences, if any, between the current and prior service. -----------------------------

----

J If the work is done under a written agreement between the firm and the worker, attach a copy (preferably signed by both parties). Describe the terms and conditions of the work arrangement. ----------------------------------

----

For **Privacy Act and Paperwork Reduction Act Notice, see page 5.**   Cat. No. 16106T   Form **SS-8** (Rev. 6-2003)

Form SS-8 (Rev. 6-2003)   Page **2**

Part I   Behavioral Control

1. What specific training and/or instruction is the worker given by the firm? ....

2. How does the worker receive work assignments? ....

3. Who determines the methods by which the assignments are performed? ....

4. Who is the worker required to contact if problems or complaints arise and who is responsible for their resolution? ....

5. What types of reports are required from the worker? Attach examples. ....

6. Describe the worker's daily routine (i.e., schedule, hours, etc.). ....

7. At what location(s) does the worker perform services (e.g., firm's premises, own shop or office, home, customer's location, etc.)? ....

8. Describe any meetings the worker is required to attend and any penalties for not attending (e.g., sales meetings, monthly meetings, staff meetings, etc.).

9. Is the worker required to provide the services personally? . . . . ☐ **Yes**   ☐ **No**

10. If substitutes or helpers are needed, who hires them? ....

11. If the worker hires the substitutes or helpers, is approval required? . . . . ☐ **Yes**   ☐ **No**
    If "Yes," by whom? ....

12. Who pays the substitutes or helpers? ....

13. Is the worker reimbursed if the worker pays the substitutes or helpers? . . . . ☐ **Yes**   ☐ **No**
    If "Yes," by whom?

Part II   Financial Control

1. List the supplies, equipment, materials, and property provided by each party:
   The firm ....
   The worker ....
   Other party ....

2. Does the worker lease equipment? . . . . ☐ **Yes**   ☐ **No**
   If "Yes," what are the terms of the lease? (Attach a copy or explanatory statement.) ....

3. What expenses are incurred by the worker in the performance of services for the firm? ....

4. Specify which, if any, expenses are reimbursed by:
   The firm ....
   Other party ....

5. Type of pay the worker receives: ☐ Salary   ☐ Commission   ☐ Hourly Wage   ☐ Piece Work
   ☐ Lump Sum   ☐ Other (specify) ....
   If type of pay is commission, and the firm guarantees a minimum amount of pay, specify amount $ _____ .

6. Is the worker allowed a drawing account for advances? . . . . ☐ **Yes**   ☐ **No**
   If "Yes," how often? ....
   Specify any restrictions. ....

7. Whom does the customer pay? . . . . ☐ Firm   ☐ Worker
   If worker, does the worker pay the total amount to the firm? ☐ **Yes**   ☐ **No**   If "No," explain. ....

8. Does the firm carry worker's compensation insurance on the worker? . . . . ☐ **Yes**   ☐ **No**

9. What economic loss or financial risk, if any, can the worker incur beyond the normal loss of salary (e.g., loss or damage of equipment, material, etc.)? ....

Form **SS-8** (Rev. 6-2003)

Part III **Relationship of the Worker and Firm**

1   List the benefits available to the worker (e.g., paid vacations, sick pay, pensions, bonuses). ---------------------------

2   Can the relationship be terminated by either party without incurring liability or penalty? . . . . ☐ **Yes**   ☐ **No**
    If "No," explain your answer. --

3   Does the worker perform similar services for others? . . . . ☐ **Yes**   ☐ **No**
    If "Yes," is the worker required to get approval from the firm? . . . . ☐ **Yes**   ☐ **No**
4   Describe any agreements prohibiting competition between the worker and the firm while the worker is performing services or during any later
    period. Attach any available documentation. ---

5   Is the worker a member of a union? . . . . ☐ **Yes**   ☐ **No**
6   What type of advertising, if any, does the worker do (e.g., a business listing in a directory, business cards, etc.)? Provide copies, if applicable.
    ----

7   If the worker assembles or processes a product at home, who provides the materials and instructions or pattern? ---------------------

8   What does the worker do with the finished product (e.g., return it to the firm, provide it to another party, or sell it)? ---------------------

9   How does the firm represent the worker to its customers (e.g., employee, partner, representative, or contractor)? ---------------------

10   If the worker no longer performs services for the firm, how did the relationship end? ---------------------------------

Part IV **For Service Providers or Salespersons**—Complete this part if the worker provided a service directly to
customers or is a salesperson.

1   What are the worker's responsibilities in soliciting new customers? --

2   Who provides the worker with leads to prospective customers? ---
3   Describe any reporting requirements pertaining to the leads. --

4   What terms and conditions of sale, if any, are required by the firm? ---
5   Are orders submitted to and subject to approval by the firm? . . . . ☐ **Yes**   ☐ **No**
6   Who determines the worker's territory? ---
7   Did the worker pay for the privilege of serving customers on the route or in the territory? . . . . ☐ **Yes**   ☐ **No**
    If "Yes," whom did the worker pay? ---
    If "Yes," how much did the worker pay? . . . . $ _____ .
8   Where does the worker sell the product (e.g., in a home, retail establishment, etc.)? --------------------------------

9   List the product and/or services distributed by the worker (e.g., meat, vegetables, fruit, bakery products, beverages, or laundry or dry cleaning
    services). If more than one type of product and/or service is distributed, specify the principal one. ------------------------

10   Does the worker sell life insurance full time? . . . . ☐ **Yes**   ☐ **No**
11   Does the worker sell other types of insurance for the firm? . . . . ☐ **Yes**   ☐ **No**
    If "Yes," enter the percentage of the worker's total working time spent in selling other types of insurance. . . . _____ %
12   If the worker solicits orders from wholesalers, retailers, contractors, or operators of hotels, restaurants, or other similar
    establishments, enter the percentage of the worker's time spent in the solicitation. . . . . _____ %
13   Is the merchandise purchased by the customers for resale or use in their business operations? . . . . ☐ **Yes**   ☐ **No**
    Describe the merchandise and state whether it is equipment installed on the customers' premises. -------------------

Part V **Signature** (see page 4)

Under penalties of perjury, I declare that I have examined this request, including accompanying documents, and to the best of my knowledge and belief, the facts
presented are true, correct, and complete.

Signature ▶ _____   Title ▶ _____   Date ▶ _____
             (Type or print name below)

Form **SS-8** (Rev. 6-2003)

General Instructions

Section references are to the Internal Revenue Code unless otherwise noted.

Purpose

Firms and workers file Form SS-8 to request a determination of the status of a worker for purposes of Federal employment taxes and income tax withholding.

A Form SS-8 determination may be requested only in order to resolve Federal tax matters. If Form SS-8 is submitted for a tax year for which the statute of limitations on the tax return has expired, a determination letter will not be issued. The statute of limitations expires 3 years from the due date of the tax return or the date filed, whichever is later.

The IRS does not issue a determination letter for proposed transactions or on hypothetical situations. We may, however, issue an information letter when it is considered appropriate.

Definition

Firm. For the purposes of this form, the term "firm" means any individual, business enterprise, organization, state, or other entity for which a worker has performed services. The firm may or may not have paid the worker directly for these services. **If the firm was not responsible for payment for services, be sure to enter the name, address, and employer identification number of the payer on the first page of Form SS-8 below the identifying information for the firm and the worker.**

The SS-8 Determination Process

The IRS will acknowledge the receipt of your Form SS-8. Because there are usually two (or more) parties who could be affected by a determination of employment status, the IRS attempts to get information from all parties involved by sending those parties blank Forms SS-8 for completion. The case will be assigned to a technician who will review the facts, apply the law, and render a decision. The technician may ask for additional information from the requestor, from other involved parties, or from third parties that could help clarify the work relationship before rendering a decision. The IRS will generally issue a formal determination to the firm or payer (if that is a different entity), and will send a copy to the worker. A determination letter applies only to a worker (or a class of workers) requesting it, and the decision is binding on the IRS. In certain cases, a formal determination will not be issued. Instead, an information letter may be issued. Although an information letter is advisory only and is not binding on the IRS, it may be used to assist the worker to fulfill his or her Federal tax obligations.

Neither the SS-8 determination process nor the review of any records in connection with the determination constitutes an examination (audit) of any Federal tax return. If the periods under consideration have previously been examined, the SS-8 determination process will not constitute a reexamination under IRS reopening procedures. Because this is not an examination of any Federal tax return, the appeal rights available in connection with an examination do not apply to an SS-8 determination. However, if you disagree with a determination and you have additional information concerning the work relationship that you believe was not previously considered, you may request that the determining office reconsider the determination.

Completing Form SS-8

Answer all questions as completely as possible. Attach additional sheets if you need more space. Provide information for all years the worker provided services for the firm. Determinations are based on the entire relationship between the firm and the worker.

Additional copies of this form may be obtained by calling 1-800-829-4933 or from the IRS website at **www.irs.gov.**

Fee

There is no fee for requesting an SS-8 determination letter.

Signature

Form SS-8 must be signed and dated by the taxpayer. A stamped signature will not be accepted.

The person who signs for a corporation must be an officer of the corporation who has personal knowledge of the facts. If the corporation is a member of an affiliated group filing a consolidated return, it must be signed by an officer of the common parent of the group.

The person signing for a trust, partnership, or limited liability company must be, respectively, a trustee, general partner, or member-manager who has personal knowledge of the facts.

Where To File

Send the completed Form SS-8 to the address listed below for the firm's location. However, for cases involving Federal agencies, send Form SS-8 to the Internal Revenue Service, Attn: CC:CORP:T:C, Ben Franklin Station, P.O. Box 7604, Washington, DC 20044.

Firm's location:	Send to:
Alaska, Arizona, Arkansas, California, Colorado, Hawaii, Idaho, Illinois, Iowa, Kansas, Minnesota, Missouri, Montana, Nebraska, Nevada, New Mexico, North Dakota, Oklahoma, Oregon, South Dakota, Texas, Utah, Washington, Wisconsin, Wyoming, American Samoa, Guam, Puerto Rico, U.S. Virgin Islands	Internal Revenue Service SS-8 Determinations P.O. Box 630 Stop 631 Holtsville, NY 11742-0630
Alabama, Connecticut, Delaware, District of Columbia, Florida, Georgia, Indiana, Kentucky, Louisiana, Maine, Maryland, Massachusetts, Michigan, Mississippi, New Hampshire, New Jersey, New York, North Carolina, Ohio, Pennsylvania, Rhode Island, South Carolina, Tennessee, Vermont, Virginia, West Virginia, all other locations not listed	Internal Revenue Service SS-8 Determinations 40 Lakemont Road Newport, VT 05855-1555

Instructions for Workers

If you are requesting a determination for more than one firm, complete a separate Form SS-8 for each firm.

 Form SS-8 is not a claim for refund of social security and Medicare taxes or Federal income tax withholding.

If the IRS determines that you are an employee, you are responsible for filing an amended return for any corrections related to this decision. A determination that a worker is an employee does not necessarily reduce any current or prior tax liability. For more information, call 1-800-829-1040.

Time for filing a claim for refund. Generally, you must file your claim for a credit or refund within 3 years from the date your original return was filed or within 2 years from the date the tax was paid, whichever is later.

Filing Form SS-8 does not prevent the expiration of the time in which a claim for a refund must be filed. If you are concerned about a refund, and the statute of limitations for filing a claim for refund for the year(s) at issue has not yet expired, you should file **Form 1040X,** Amended U.S. Individual Income Tax Return, to protect your statute of limitations. File a separate Form 1040X for each year.

On the Form 1040X you file, do not complete lines 1 through 24 on the form. Write "Protective Claim" at the top of the form, sign and date it. In addition, you should enter the following statement in Part II, Explanation of Changes to Income, Deductions, and Credits: "Filed Form SS-8 with the Internal Revenue Service Office in (Holtsville, NY; Newport, VT; or Washington, DC; as appropriate). By filing this protective claim, I reserve the right to file a claim for any refund that may be due after a determination of my employment tax status has been completed."

Filing Form SS-8 does not alter the requirement to timely file an income tax return. Do not delay filing your tax return in anticipation of an answer to your SS-8 request. In addition, if applicable, do not delay in responding to a request for payment while waiting for a determination of your worker status.

Instructions for Firms

If a **worker** has requested a determination of his or her status while working for you, you will receive a request from the IRS to complete a Form SS-8. In cases of this type, the IRS usually gives each party an opportunity to present a statement of the facts because any decision will affect the employment tax status of the parties. Failure to respond to this request will not prevent the IRS from issuing a determination letter based on the information he or she has made available so that the worker may fulfill his or her Federal tax obligations. However, the information that you provide is extremely valuable in determining the status of the worker.

If **you** are requesting a determination for a particular class of worker, complete the form for **one** individual who is representative of the class of workers whose status is in question. If you want a written determination for more than one class of workers, complete a separate Form SS-8 for one worker from each class whose status is typical of that class. A written determination for any worker will apply to other workers of the same class if the facts are not materially different for these workers. Please provide a list of names and addresses of all workers potentially affected by this determination.

If you have a reasonable basis for not treating a worker as an employee, you may be relieved from having to pay employment taxes for that worker under section 530 of the 1978 Revenue Act. However, this relief provision cannot be considered in conjunction with a Form SS-8 determination because the determination does not constitute an examination of any tax return. For more information regarding section 530 of the 1978 Revenue Act and to determine if you qualify for relief under this section, you may visit the IRS website at **www.irs.gov**.

Privacy Act and Paperwork Reduction Act Notice. We ask for the information on this form to carry out the Internal Revenue laws of the United States. This information will be used to determine the employment status of the worker(s) described on the form. Subtitle C, Employment Taxes, of the Internal Revenue Code imposes employment taxes on wages. Sections 3121(d), 3306(a), and 3401(c) and (d) and the related regulations define employee and employer for purposes of employment taxes imposed under Subtitle C. Section 6001 authorizes the IRS to request information needed to determine if a worker(s) or firm is subject to these taxes. Section 6109 requires you to provide your taxpayer identification number. Neither workers nor firms are required to request a status determination, but if you choose to do so, you must provide the information requested on this form. Failure to provide the requested information may prevent us from making a status determination. If any worker or the firm has requested a status determination and you are being asked to provide information for use in that determination, you are not required to provide the requested information. However, failure to provide such information will prevent the IRS from considering it in making the status determination. Providing false or fraudulent information may subject you to penalties. Routine uses of this information include providing it to the Department of Justice for use in civil and criminal litigation, to the Social Security Administration for the administration of social security programs, and to cities, states, and the District of Columbia for the administration of their tax laws. We may also disclose this information to Federal and state agencies to enforce Federal nontax criminal laws and to combat terrorism. We may provide this information to the affected worker(s) or the firm as part of the status determination process.

You are not required to provide the information requested on a form that is subject to the Paperwork Reduction Act unless the form displays a valid OMB control number. Books or records relating to a form or its instructions must be retained as long as their contents may become material in the administration of any Internal Revenue law. Generally, tax returns and return information are confidential, as required by section 6103.

The time needed to complete and file this form will vary depending on individual circumstances. The estimated average time is: **Recordkeeping,** 22 hrs.; **Learning about the law or the form,** 47 min.; and **Preparing and sending the form to the IRS,** 1 hr., 11 min. If you have comments concerning the accuracy of these time estimates or suggestions for making this form simpler, we would be happy to hear from you. You can write to the Tax Products Coordinating Committee, Western Area Distribution Center, Rancho Cordova, CA 95743-0001. **Do not** send the tax form to this address. Instead, see **Where To File** on page 4.

Appendix

Social Security Administration

Form Approved
OMB No. 0960-0565

EMPLOYER REPORT OF SPECIAL WAGE PAYMENTS

PART I - TO BE COMPLETED BY SSA/EMPLOYER:

Tax Year	Employee Name	Employee's SSN	SSA Claim Number *(To be completed by SSA)*

Employer	Address

PART 2 - TO BE COMPLETED BY EMPLOYER:

Employees are sometime paid wages *in a year* subsequent to the year that the wages were earned. The most common types of payments are accumulated (for prior years) vacation pay or sick pay paid after retirement; deferred compensation; severance pay (when paid on account of retirement) and bonuses--paid pursuant to a prior agreement or contract.

Wages which are earned in a year prior to the year they are paid usually do not affect benefits payable under the Social Security annual earnings test. However, for the Social Security Administration to pay benefits accurately, these prior year amounts must be reported to us. The above named individual has filed for Social Security benefits. To ensure that correct Social Security benefits are paid, please complete the information below and return this form to the Social Security Administration. (Please see reverse side for instructions for the completion of this form.)

1. Employer Identification Number (EIN)	2. Retirement date (MM/DD/YYYY)	3. Date employee last performed services (MM/DD/YYYY)

If the dates in items 2 and 3 are not the same, please explain the difference.

4. For wages paid to the employee in the "tax year" (see Part I above), enter the amount that was for services performed prior to the tax year; or was not attributable to services rendered during the tax year; or was paid on account of retirement: ⟶ $_____

Check the type(s) of wages paid in the tax year but for services performed in a prior year or were paid on account of retirement.

☐ Vacation Pay   ☐ Sick Pay   ☐ Severance Pay

☐ Bonus   ☐ Deferred Compensation

☐ Other *(Explain)* _____

5. Will payments listed in item "4" be made for years after the tax year?   ☐ Yes   ☐ No

If answered Yes, please show the amounts and years in which these amounts will be paid, if known.

Amount	Year	Amount	Year

6. Nonqualified deferred compensation and section 457 plans only. If payments and deferrals occurred during the tax year, enter the amount of wages earned by the employee during the tax year. $_____

Signature ▶

Title	Date	Phone Number (_ _ _) _ _ _ _ - _ _ _ _ _

Form **SSA-131** (8-2001) Destroy Prior Editions EF (06-2002)   (Over)

EMPLOYER INSTRUCTIONS FOR COMPLETING SPECIAL WAGE PAYMENT FORM

1. Provide the EIN that was used or will be used to report the employee's wages on the Form W-2.

2. Enter the date the employee retired. Enter "Not Retired" if the employee has not retired.

3. Enter the date that the employee last performed services; was not expected to return to work; and was not subject to recall to render additional services. This date should be the same as or earlier than the date in item "2." Enter "Not Retired" if the employee has not retired.

4. Enter the wages that were paid to the employee in the tax year that were for services that were performed in years prior to the tax year or that were paid on account of retirement.

   Examples (not all inclusive) of payments to be included:

   - Payments in lieu of vacation that were earned in a year prior to the tax year.

   - Accumulated sick payments which were paid in a lump sum based on "retirement" as the sole condition of payment.

   - Accumulated sick payments paid at or after the date in item 3, which were earned in a year prior to the tax year.

   - Payments "on account of retirement"--dismissal, severance or termination pay paid because of retirement.

   - Bonuses which are paid pursuant to a prior contract, agreement or promise causing the employee to expect such payments regularly; or announced to induce the employee to work more steadily, rapidly or efficiently or to remain with the employer.

   - Stock Options.

   Do not include in item "4" payments:

   - For annual, sick, holiday or vacation pay if used (absence from work) prior to the date of retirement (earlier of items "2" or "3").

   - That were reported or will be reported under "Nonqualified Plans" on the Form W-2.

   - That were deducted from the employee's wages and paid to a deferred compensation plan (e.g., 401k).

   - Employees health and dental plan benefits (non-covered/non-taxable for Social Security Wages).

   - Bonuses *earned* and *paid* in the tax year.

5. Check whether payments listed in item 4 will be made for years after the tax year. If yes, please show the amounts and years in which these will be paid, if known.

6. **Nonqualified deferred compensation and section 457 plans only.** If you were unable to report nonqualified deferred compensation or section 457 plan payments and deferrals (contributions) on Form W-2 because both payments and deferrals occurred during the year, show the amount of wages **earned** by the employee during the tax year. Generally, the wages earned will be the compensation reported in block 1 of Form W-2 less payments from a nonqualified deferred compensation (or 457) plan, but including any amounts deferred under the plan during the tax year (See IRS Publication 957).

Paperwork/Privacy Act Notice: This report is authorized by regulation 20 CFR 404.702. The information that you provide will be used in making a determination regarding the amount of Social Security benefits payable to the above named individual. While your response is voluntary, if you do not respond we may not be able to make a correct determination regarding the amount of Social Security benefits payable to the above named individual for the year in question.

We may also use the information you give us when we match records by computer. Matching programs compare our records with those of other Federal, State, or local government agencies. Many agencies may use matching programs to find or prove that a person qualifies for benefits paid by the Federal Government. The law allows us to do this even if you do not agree to it.

Explanations about these and other reasons why information you provide us may be used or given out are available in Social Security Offices. If you want to learn more about this, contact any Social Security Office.

PAPERWORK REDUCTION ACT: This information collection meets the clearance requirements of 44 U.S.C. §3507, as amended by Section 2 of the Paperwork Reduction Act of 1995. You are not required to answer these questions unless we display a valid Office of Management and Budget control number. We estimate that it will take you about 20 minutes to read the instructions, gather the necessary facts, and answer the questions.

Form **SSA-131** (8-2001) EF (06-2002)

Statement Concerning Your Employment in a Job
Not Covered by Social Security

Employee Name _____   **Employee ID #** _____

Employer Name _____   **Employer ID#** _____

Your earnings from this job are not covered under Social Security. When you retire, or if you become disabled, you may receive a pension based on earnings from this job. If you do, and you are also entitled to a benefit from Social Security based on either your own work or the work of your husband or wife, or former husband or wife, your pension may affect the amount of the Social Security benefit you receive. Your Medicare benefits, however, will not be affected. Under the Social Security law, there are two ways your Social Security benefit amount may be affected.

Windfall Elimination Provision

Under the Windfall Elimination Provision, your Social Security retirement or disability benefit is figured using a modified formula when you are also entitled to a pension from a job where you did not pay Social Security tax. As a result, you will receive a lower Social Security benefit than if you were not entitled to a pension from this job. For example, if you are age 62 in 2005, the maximum monthly reduction in your Social Security benefit as a result of this provision is $313.50. This amount is updated annually. This provision reduces, but does not totally eliminate, your Social Security benefit. For additional information, please refer to the Social Security publication, "Windfall Elimination Provision."

Government Pension Offset Provision

Under the Government Pension Offset Provision, any Social Security spouse or widow(er) benefit to which you become entitled will be offset if you also receive a Federal, State or local government pension based on work where you did not pay Social Security tax. The offset reduces the amount of your Social Security spouse or widow(er) benefit by two-thirds of the amount of your pension.

For example, if you get a monthly pension of $600 based on earnings that are not covered under Social Security, two-thirds of that amount, $400, is used to offset your Social Security spouse or widow(er) benefit. If you are eligible for a $500 widow(er) benefit, you will receive $100 per month from Social Security, $500 - $400 = $100. Even if your pension is high enough to totally offset your spouse or widow(er) Social Security benefit, you are still eligible for Medicare at age 65. For additional information, please refer to the Social Security publication, "Government Pension Offset."

For More Information

Social Security publications and additional information, including information about exceptions to each provision, are available at www.socialsecurity.gov. You may also call toll free 1-800-772-1213, or, for the deaf or hard of hearing, call the TTY number 1-800-325-0778, or contact your local Social Security office.

I certify that I have received Form SSA-1945 that contains information about the possible effects of the Windfall Elimination Provision and the Government Pension Offset Provision on my potential future Social Security benefits.

Signature of Employee _____   **Date** _____

Form **SSA-1945 (11-2004)** **(Expires January, 2006)**

**Information about Social Security Form SSA-1945,
Statement Concerning Your Employment in a Job Not Covered by Social Security**

New legislation [Section 419(c) of Public Law 108-203, the Social Security Protection Act of 2004] requires State and local government employers to provide a statement to employees hired January 1, 2005 or later in a job not covered under Social Security. The statement explains how a pension from that job could affect future Social Security benefits to which they may become entitled.

Form SSA-1945, **Statement Concerning Your Employment in a Job Not Covered by Social Security**, is the document that employers should use to meet the requirements of the law. The SSA-1945 explains the potential effects of two provisions in the Social Security law for workers who also receive a pension based on their work in a job not covered by Social Security. The Windfall Elimination Provision can affect the amount of a worker's Social Security retirement or disability benefit. The Government Pension Offset Provision can affect any possible Social Security benefit entitlement as a spouse or an ex-spouse.

Employers must:
- Give the statement to the employee prior to the start of employment;
- Get the employee's signature on the form; and
- Submit a copy of the signed form to the pension paying agency.

Social Security will not be setting any additional guidelines for the use of this form.

Copies of the SSA-1945 are available online at the Social Security website, www.socialsecurity.gov/form1945. Paper copies can be requested by email at **oplm.oswm.rqct.orders@ssa.gov** or by fax at 410-965-2037. The request must include the name, complete address and telephone number of the employer. Forms will not be sent to a post office box. Also, if appropriate, include the name of the person to whom the forms are to be delivered. The forms are available in packages of 25. Please refer to Inventory Control Number (ICN) 276950 when ordering.

a Control number	22222	Void ☐	For Official Use Only ▶ OMB No. 1545-0008		

b Employer identification number (EIN)		1 Wages, tips, other compensation	2 Federal income tax withheld
c Employer's name, address, and ZIP code		3 Social security wages	4 Social security tax withheld
		5 Medicare wages and tips	6 Medicare tax withheld
		7 Social security tips	8 Allocated tips
d Employee's social security number		9 Advance EIC payment	10 Dependent care benefits

e Employee's first name and initial	Last name	Suff.	11 Nonqualified plans	12a See instructions for box 12
			13 Statutory employee ☐ Retirement plan ☐ Third-party sick pay ☐	12b
			14 Other	12c
				12d
f Employee's address and ZIP code				

15 State	Employer's state ID number	16 State wages, tips, etc.	17 State income tax	18 Local wages, tips, etc.	19 Local income tax	20 Locality name

Form **W-2** Wage and Tax Statement   **2006**

Department of the Treasury—Internal Revenue Service

Copy A For Social Security Administration — Send this entire page with Form W-3 to the Social Security Administration; photocopies are **not** acceptable.

For Privacy Act and Paperwork Reduction Act Notice, see back of Copy D.

Cat. No. 10134D

Do Not Cut, Fold, or Staple Forms on This Page — Do Not Cut, Fold, or Staple Forms on This Page

a Control number	22222		OMB No. 1545-0008		
b Employer identification number (EIN)				1 Wages, tips, other compensation	2 Federal income tax withheld
c Employer's name, address, and ZIP code				3 Social security wages	4 Social security tax withheld
				5 Medicare wages and tips	6 Medicare tax withheld
				7 Social security tips	8 Allocated tips
d Employee's social security number				9 Advance EIC payment	10 Dependent care benefits
e Employee's first name and initial Last name Suff.				11 Nonqualified plans	12a Code
				13 Statutory employee Retirement plan Third-party sick pay	12b Code
				14 Other	12c Code
					12d Code
f Employee's address and ZIP code					

15 State	Employer's state ID number	16 State wages, tips, etc.	17 State income tax	18 Local wages, tips, etc.	19 Local income tax	20 Locality name

Form **W-2** **Wage and Tax Statement**

2006

Department of the Treasury—Internal Revenue Service

Copy 1—For State, City, or Local Tax Department

a Control number			OMB No. 1545-0008		Safe, accurate, FAST! Use	IRS *e~file*	Visit the IRS website at *www.irs.gov/efile*.

b Employer identification number (EIN)	1 Wages, tips, other compensation	2 Federal income tax withheld
c Employer's name, address, and ZIP code	3 Social security wages	4 Social security tax withheld
	5 Medicare wages and tips	6 Medicare tax withheld
	7 Social security tips	8 Allocated tips
d Employee's social security number	9 Advance EIC payment	10 Dependent care benefits
e Employee's first name and initial Last name Suff.	11 Nonqualified plans	12a See instructions for box 12
	13 Statutory employee Retirement plan Third-party sick pay	12b
	14 Other	12c
		12d
f Employee's address and ZIP code		

15 State Employer's state ID number	16 State wages, tips, etc.	17 State income tax	18 Local wages, tips, etc.	19 Local income tax	20 Locality name

Form **W-2** **Wage and Tax Statement**   **2006**   Department of the Treasury—Internal Revenue Service

Copy B—To Be Filed With Employee's FEDERAL Tax Return.
This information is being furnished to the Internal Revenue Service.

Notice to Employee

Refund. Even if you do not have to file a tax return, you should file to get a refund if box 2 shows federal income tax withheld or if you can take the earned income credit.

Earned income credit (EIC). You must file a tax return if any amount is shown in box 9.

You may be able to take the EIC for 2006 if: **(a)** you do not have a qualifying child and you earned less than $12,120 ($14,120 if married filing jointly), **(b)** you have one qualifying child and you earned less than $32,001 ($34,001 if married filing jointly), or **(c)** you have more than one qualifying child and you earned less than $36,348 ($38,348 if married filing jointly). You and any qualifying children must have valid social security numbers (SSNs). You cannot take the EIC if your investment income is more than $2,800. **Any EIC that is more than your tax liability is refunded to you, but only if you file a tax return.** If you have at least one qualifying child, you may get as much as $1,648 of the EIC in advance by completing Form W-5, Earned Income Credit Advance Payment Certificate, and giving it to your employer.

Clergy and religious workers. If you are not subject to social security and Medicare taxes, see Publication 517, Social Security and Other Information for Members of the Clergy and Religious Workers.

Corrections. If your name, SSN, or address is incorrect, correct Copies B, C, and 2 and ask your employer to correct your employment record. Be sure to ask the employer to file Form W-2c, Corrected Wage and Tax Statement, with the Social Security Administration (SSA) to correct any name, SSN, or money amount error reported to the SSA on Form W-2. If your name and SSN are correct but are not the same as shown on your social security card, you should ask for a new card at any SSA office or call 1-800-772-1213.

Credit for excess taxes. If you had more than one employer in 2006 and more than $5,840.40 in social security and/or Tier I railroad retirement (RRTA) taxes were withheld, you may be able to claim a credit for the excess against your federal income tax. If you had more than one railroad employer and more than $3,075.60 in Tier II RRTA tax was withheld, you also may be able to claim a credit. See your Form 1040 or Form 1040A instructions and Publication 505, Tax Withholding and Estimated Tax.

(Also see *Instructions for Employee* on the back of Copy C.)

a Control number		OMB No. 1545-0008	This information is being furnished to the Internal Revenue Service. If you are required to file a tax return, a negligence penalty or other sanction may be imposed on you if this income is taxable and you fail to report it.	
b Employer identification number (EIN)			1 Wages, tips, other compensation	2 Federal income tax withheld
c Employer's name, address, and ZIP code			3 Social security wages	4 Social security tax withheld
			5 Medicare wages and tips	6 Medicare tax withheld
			7 Social security tips	8 Allocated tips
d Employee's social security number			9 Advance EIC payment	10 Dependent care benefits
e Employee's first name and initial Last name Suff.			11 Nonqualified plans	12a See instructions for box 12
			13 Statutory employee Retirement plan Third-party sick pay	12b
			14 Other	12c
				12d
f Employee's address and ZIP code				

15 State	Employer's state ID number	16 State wages, tips, etc.	17 State income tax	18 Local wages, tips, etc.	19 Local income tax	20 Locality name

Form **W-2** Wage and Tax Statement

Copy C—For EMPLOYEE'S RECORDS (see Notice to Employee on back of Copy B.)

2006

Department of the Treasury—Internal Revenue Service

Safe, accurate, FAST! Use

Instructions for Employee (also see Notice to Employee, on back of Copy B)

Box 1. Enter this amount on the wages line of your tax return.

Box 2. Enter this amount on the federal income tax withheld line of your tax return.

Box 8. This amount is **not** included in boxes 1, 3, 5, or 7. For information on how to report tips on your tax return, see your Form 1040 instructions.

Box 9. Enter this amount on the advance earned income credit payments line of your Form 1040 or Form 1040A.

Box 10. This amount is the total dependent care benefits that your employer paid to you or incurred on your behalf (including amounts from a section 125 (cafeteria) plan). Any amount over $5,000 also is included in box 1. You **must** complete Schedule 2 (Form 1040A) or Form 2441, Child and Dependent Care Expenses, to compute any taxable and nontaxable amounts.

Box 11. This amount is: **(a)** reported in box 1 if it is a distribution made to you from a nonqualified deferred compensation or nongovernmental section 457(b) plan or **(b)** included in box 3 and/or 5 if it is a prior year deferral under a nonqualified or section 457(b) plan that became taxable for social security and Medicare taxes this year because there is no longer a substantial risk of forfeiture of your right to the deferred amount.

Box 12. The following list explains the codes shown in box 12. You may need this information to complete your tax return. Elective deferrals (codes D, E, F, and S) and designated Roth contributions (codes **AA** and **BB**) under all plans are generally limited to a total of $15,000 ($10,000 if you only have SIMPLE plans; $18,000 for section 403(b) plans if you qualify

for the 15-year rule explained in Pub. 571). Deferrals under code G are limited to $15,000. Deferrals under code H are limited to $7,000.

However, if you were at least age 50 in 2006, your employer may have allowed an additional deferral of up to $5,000 ($2,500 for section 401(k)(11) and 408(p) SIMPLE plans). This additional deferral amount is not subject to the overall limit on elective deferrals. For code G, the limit on elective deferrals may be higher for the last three years before you reach retirement age. Contact your plan administrator for more information. Amounts in excess of the overall elective deferral limit must be included in income. See the "Wages, Salaries, Tips, etc." line instructions for Form 1040.

Note. *If a year follows code D, E, F, G, H, or S, you made a make-up pension contribution for a prior year(s) when you were in military service. To figure whether you made excess deferrals, consider these amounts for the year shown, not the current year. If no year is shown, the contributions are for the current year.*

A—Uncollected social security or RRTA tax on tips. Include this tax on Form 1040. See "Total Tax" in the Form 1040 instructions.

B—Uncollected Medicare tax on tips. Include this tax on Form 1040. See "Total Tax" in the Form 1040 instructions.

C—Taxable cost of group-term life insurance over $50,000 (included in boxes 1, 3 (up to social security wage base), and 5)

D—Elective deferrals to a section 401(k) cash or deferred arrangement. Also includes deferrals under a SIMPLE retirement account that is part of a section 401(k) arrangement.

E—Elective deferrals under a section 403(b) salary reduction agreement

(continued on back of Copy 2)

a Control number				
	OMB No. 1545-0008			
b Employer identification number (EIN)		1 Wages, tips, other compensation	2 Federal income tax withheld	
c Employer's name, address, and ZIP code		3 Social security wages	4 Social security tax withheld	
		5 Medicare wages and tips	6 Medicare tax withheld	
		7 Social security tips	8 Allocated tips	
d Employee's social security number		9 Advance EIC payment	10 Dependent care benefits	
e Employee's first name and initial Last name Suff.		11 Nonqualified plans	12a	
		13 Statutory employee Retirement plan Third-party sick pay	12b	
		14 Other	12c	
			12d	
f Employee's address and ZIP code				

15 State Employer's state ID number	16 State wages, tips, etc.	17 State income tax	18 Local wages, tips, etc.	19 Local income tax	20 Locality name

Form **W-2** **Wage and Tax Statement**   **2006**   Department of the Treasury—Internal Revenue Service

Copy 2—To Be Filed With Employee's State, City, or Local Income Tax Return.

Instructions for Employee *(continued from back of Copy C)*

F—Elective deferrals under a section 408(k)(6) salary reduction SEP

G—Elective deferrals and employer contributions (including nonelective deferrals) to a section 457(b) deferred compensation plan

H—Elective deferrals to a section 501(c)(18)(D) tax-exempt organization plan. See "Adjusted Gross Income" in the Form 1040 instructions for how to deduct.

J—Nontaxable sick pay (information only, not included in boxes 1, 3, or 5)

K—20% excise tax on excess golden parachute payments. See "Total Tax" in the Form 1040 instructions.

L—Substantiated employee business expense reimbursements (nontaxable)

M—Uncollected social security or RRTA tax on taxable cost of group-term life insurance over $50,000 (former employees only). See "Total Tax" in the Form 1040 instructions.

N—Uncollected Medicare tax on taxable cost of group-term life insurance over $50,000 (former employees only). See "Total Tax" in the Form 1040 instructions.

P—Excludable moving expense reimbursements paid directly to employee (not included in boxes 1, 3, or 5)

Q—Nontaxable combat pay. See the instructions for Form 1040 or Form 1040A for details on reporting this amount.

R—Employer contributions to your Archer MSA. Report on Form 8853, Archer MSAs and Long-Term Care Insurance Contracts.

S—Employee salary reduction contributions under a section 408(p) SIMPLE (not included in box 1)

T—Adoption benefits (not included in box 1). You **must** complete Form 8839, Qualified Adoption Expenses, to compute any taxable and nontaxable amounts.

V—Income from exercise of nonstatutory stock option(s) (included in boxes 1, 3 (up to social security wage base), and 5)

W—Employer contributions to your Health Savings Account. Report on Form 8889, Health Savings Accounts (HSAs).

Y—Deferrals under a section 409A nonqualified deferred compensation plan.

Z—Income under section 409A on a nonqualified deferred compensation plan. This amount is also included in box 1. It is subject to an additional 20% tax plus interest. See "Total Tax" in the Form 1040 instructions.

AA—Designated Roth contributions to a section 401(k) plan.

BB—Designated Roth contributions under a section 403(b) salary reduction agreement.

Box 13. If the "Retirement plan" box is checked, special limits may apply to the amount of traditional IRA contributions that you may deduct.

Note: *Keep **Copy C** of Form W-2 for at least 3 years after the due date for filing your income tax return. However, to help **protect your social security benefits,** keep Copy C until you begin receiving social security benefits, just in case there is a question about your work record and/or earnings in a particular year. Review the information shown on your annual (for workers over 25) Social Security Statement.*

a Control number		Void ☐	OMB No. 1545-0008		
b Employer identification number (EIN)				**1** Wages, tips, other compensation	**2** Federal income tax withheld
c Employer's name, address, and ZIP code				**3** Social security wages	**4** Social security tax withheld
				5 Medicare wages and tips	**6** Medicare tax withheld
				7 Social security tips	**8** Allocated tips
d Employee's social security number				**9** Advance EIC payment	**10** Dependent care benefits
e Employee's first name and initial Last name Suff.				**11** Nonqualified plans	**12a** See instructions for box 12
				13 Statutory employee ☐ Retirement plan ☐ Third-party sick pay ☐	**12b**
				14 Other	**12c**
					12d
f Employee's address and ZIP code					

15 State Employer's state ID number	16 State wages, tips, etc.	17 State income tax	18 Local wages, tips, etc.	19 Local income tax	20 Locality name

Form **W-2** **Wage and Tax Statement**

2006

Department of the Treasury—Internal Revenue Service

Copy D—For Employer.

For Privacy Act and Paperwork Reduction Act Notice, see back of Copy D.

Employers, Please Note—

Specific information needed to complete Form W-2 is given in a separate booklet titled 2006 Instructions for Forms W-2 and W-3. You can order those instructions and additional forms by calling 1-800-TAX-FORM (1-800-829-3676). You can also get forms and instructions from the IRS website at *www.irs.gov*.

Caution. *Because the SSA processes paper forms by machine, you cannot file with the SSA Forms W-2 and W-3 that you print from the IRS website. Instead, you can use the SSA website at* www.socialsecurity.gov/ employer/bsohbnew.htm *to create and file electronically "fill-in" versions of Forms W-2 and W-3.*

Due dates. Furnish Copies B, C, and 2 to the employee generally by January 31, 2007.

File Copy A with the SSA generally by February 28, 2007. Send all Copies A with Form W-3, Transmittal of Wage and Tax Statements. However, if you file electronically, the due date is April 2, 2007.

Privacy Act and Paperwork Reduction Act Notice. We ask for the information on Forms W-2 and W-3 to carry out the Internal Revenue laws of the United States. We need it to figure and collect the right amount of tax. Section 6051 and its regulations require you to furnish wage and tax statements to employees and to the Social Security Administration. Section 6109 requires you to provide your employer identification number (EIN). If you fail to provide this information in a timely manner, you may be subject to penalties.

You are not required to provide the information requested on a form that is subject to the Paperwork Reduction Act unless the form displays a valid OMB control number. Books or records relating to a form or its instructions must be retained as long as their contents may become material in the administration of any Internal Revenue law.

Generally, tax returns and return information are confidential, as required by section 6103. However, section 6103 allows or requires the Internal Revenue Service to disclose or give the information shown on your return to others as described in the Code. For example, we may disclose your tax information to the Department of Justice for civil and/or criminal litigation, and to cities, states, and the District of Columbia for use in administering their tax laws. We may also disclose this information to other countries under a tax treaty, to federal and state agencies to enforce federal nontax criminal laws, or to federal law enforcement and intelligence agencies to combat terrorism.

The time needed to complete and file these forms will vary depending on individual circumstances. The estimated average times are: **Form W-2**—30 minutes, and **Form W-3**—28 minutes. If you have comments concerning the accuracy of these time estimates or suggestions for making these forms simpler, we would be happy to hear from you. You can write to the Internal Revenue Service, Tax Products Coordinating Committee, SE:W:CAR:MP:T:T:SP, 1111 Constitution Ave. NW, IR-6406, Washington, DC 20224. **Do not** send Forms W-2 and W-3 to this address. Instead, see *Where to file* in the Instructions for Forms W-2 and W-3.

DO NOT STAPLE

a Control number 33333	For Official Use Only ▶ OMB No. 1545-0008		
b Kind of Payer	☐ 941 ☐ Military ☐ 943 ☐ 944 ☐ CT-1 ☐ Hshld. emp. ☐ Medicare govt. emp. ☐ Third-party sick pay	**1** Wages, tips, other compensation	**2** Federal income tax withheld
		3 Social security wages	**4** Social security tax withheld
c Total number of Forms W-2	d Establishment number	**5** Medicare wages and tips	**6** Medicare tax withheld
e Employer identification number (EIN)		**7** Social security tips	**8** Allocated tips
f Employer's name		**9** Advance EIC payments	**10** Dependent care benefits
		11 Nonqualified plans	**12** Deferred compensation
		13 For third-party sick pay use only	
		14 Income tax withheld by payer of third-party sick pay	
g Employer's address and ZIP code			
h Other EIN used this year			
15 State Employer's state ID number		**16** State wages, tips, etc.	**17** State income tax
		18 Local wages, tips, etc.	**19** Local income tax
Contact person		Telephone number ( )	For Official Use Only
Email address		Fax number ( )	

Under penalties of perjury, I declare that I have examined this return and accompanying documents, and, to the best of my knowledge and belief, they are true, correct, and complete.

Signature ▶   Title ▶   Date ▶

Form **W-3** Transmittal of Wage and Tax Statements   **2006**   Department of the Treasury Internal Revenue Service

Send this entire page with the entire Copy A page of Form(s) W-2 to the Social Security Administration. Photocopies are not acceptable.

Do not send any payment (cash, checks, money orders, etc.) with Forms W-2 and W-3.

What's New

New checkbox for box b on Form W-3. Use the "944" checkbox in box b if you file Form 944, Employer's Annual Federal Tax Return. Form 944 for 2006 is a newly developed form.

Magnetic media filing is discontinued. The Social Security Administration (SSA) will no longer accept any magnetic media reporting of Forms W-2.

Reminder

Separate instructions. See the 2006 Instructions for Forms W-2 and W-3 for information on completing this form.

Purpose of Form

Use Form W-3 to transmit Copy A of Form(s) W-2, Wage and Tax Statement. Make a copy of Form W-3 and keep it with Copy D (For Employer) of Form(s) W-2 for your records. Use Form W-3 for the correct year. **File Form W-3 even if only one Form W-2 is being filed.** If you are filing Form(s) W-2 electronically, **do not** file Form W-3.

When To File

File Form W-3 with Copy A of Form(s) W-2 by February 28, 2007.

Where To File

Send this entire page with the entire Copy A page of Form(s) W-2 to:

**Social Security Administration
Data Operations Center
Wilkes-Barre, PA 18769-0001**

Note. *If you use "Certified Mail" to file, change the ZIP code to "18769-0002." If you use an IRS-approved private delivery service, add "ATTN: W-2 Process, 1150 E. Mountain Dr." to the address and change the ZIP code to "18702-7997." See Publication 15 (Circular E), Employer's Tax Guide, for a list of IRS-approved private delivery services.*

For Privacy Act and Paperwork Reduction Act Notice, see back of Copy D of Form W-2.

Cat. No. 10159Y

20**06**

Department of the Treasury
Internal Revenue Service

Instructions for Forms W-2 and W-3

Wage and Tax Statement and
Transmittal of Wage and Tax Statements

Section references are to the Internal Revenue Code unless otherwise noted.

What's New

New code AA, box 12. We added code **AA** to report designated Roth contributions to a section 401(k) plan. For more information, see *Designated Roth contributions* on page 5.

New code BB, box 12. We added code **BB** to report designated Roth contributions under a section 403(b) salary reduction agreement. For more information, see *Designated Roth contributions* on page 5.

New Form 944. We added a checkbox for Form 944, Employer's Annual Federal Tax Return, to box b of Form W-3. Form 944 for 2006 is a newly developed form. References to Form 944 have been included as appropriate.

Suffix entry, box e. We added a separate entry field to box e (employee's name) on Form W-2 for employee suffix names such as "Jr." or "Sr." For more information, see *Boxes e and f—Employee's name and address* on page 9.

Employee instructions added to Copy 2. We made the employee instructions on the back of Copy C easier to read by increasing their type size and continuing the instructions on the back of Copy 2.

Reminders

Electronic payee statements. If your employees give their consent, you may be able to furnish Copies B, C, and 2 of Forms W-2 to your employees electronically. See Pub. 15-A, Employer's Supplemental Tax Guide, for additional information.

Elimination of magnetic media as a filing method. The last year for filing Forms W-2 on tapes and cartridges was tax year 2004 (forms timely filed with the SSA in 2005). The last year for filing Forms W-2 on diskette was tax year 2005 (forms timely filed with the SSA in 2006).

Nonqualified deferred compensation plans. Section 409A, added by the American Jobs Creation Act of 2004, provides that all amounts deferred under a nonqualified deferred compensation (NQDC) plan for all taxable years are currently includible in gross income unless certain requirements are satisfied. See *Nonqualified deferred compensation plans* on page 7.

Extended due date for electronic filers. If you file your 2006 Forms W-2 with the Social Security Administration (SSA) electronically, the due date is extended to April 2, 2007. For information on how to file electronically, see *Electronic reporting* on page 3.

Online filing of Forms W-2 and W-3. File Forms W-2 and W-3 electronically by visiting SSA's Employer Reporting Instructions and Information website at *www.socialsecurity.gov/employer*, selecting "Electronically File Your W-2s", and logging into "Business Services Online (BSO)." SSA's "Create Forms W-2 Online" option allows you to create "fill-in" versions of Forms W-2 for filing with the SSA and to print out copies of the forms for filing with state or local governments, distribution to your employees, and for your records. Form W-3 will be created for you based on your Forms W-2. Also see *Online wage reporting* on page 2.

Substitute forms. If you are not using the official IRS form to furnish Form W-2 to employees or to file with the SSA, you may use an acceptable substitute form that complies with the rules in Pub. 1141, General Rules and Specifications for Substitute Forms W-2 and W-3. Pub. 1141, which is revised annually, is a revenue procedure that explains the requirements for format and content of substitute Forms W-2 and W-3. **Your substitute forms must comply with the requirements in Pub. 1141.**

Earned income credit (EIC) notice. You must notify employees who have no income tax withheld that they may be able to claim an income tax refund because of the EIC. You can do this by using the official IRS Form W-2 with the EIC notice on the back of Copy B or a substitute Form W-2 with the same statement. You must give your employee Notice 797, Possible Federal Tax Refund Due to the Earned Income Credit (EIC), or your own statement that contains the same wording if (a) you use a substitute Form W-2 that does not contain the EIC notice, (b) you are not required to furnish Form W-2, or (c) you do not furnish a timely Form W-2 to your employee. For more information, see section 10 in Pub. 15 (Circular E).

Distributions from governmental section 457(b) plans of state and local agencies. Generally, report **distributions after December 31, 2001** from section 457(b) plans of state and local agencies on Form 1099-R, Distributions From Pensions, Annuities, Retirement or Profit-Sharing Plans, IRAs, Insurance Contracts, etc. See Notice 2003-20 for details. You can find Notice 2003-20 on page 894 of Internal Revenue Bulletin 2003-19 at *www.irs.gov/pub/irs-irbs/irb03-19.pdf*.

Cat. No. 25979S

Need Help?

Information reporting customer service site. The IRS operates a centralized customer service site to answer questions about reporting on Forms W-2, W-3, 1099, and other information returns. If you have questions about reporting on these forms, call 1-866-455-7438 (toll free), Monday through Friday, 8:30 a.m. to 4:30 p.m. Eastern time. If you have questions about electronic filing of Forms W-2, contact the SSA at 1-800-772-6270 or visit the SSA website at *www.socialsecurity.gov/employer.*

Help for people with disabilities. Telephone help is available using TTY/TDD equipment. If you have questions about reporting on information returns—Forms 1096, 1098, 1099, 5498, W-2, W-2G, and W-3, you may call 304-267-3367. For any other tax information, call 1-800-829-4059.

Online wage reporting. Using a personal computer and a modem, you can access SSA's Business Services Online (BSO) to electronically report wage data. To obtain information regarding filing wage data electronically with SSA or to access BSO, visit the SSA's Employer Reporting Instructions and Information website at *www.socialsecurity.gov/employer.* Call the SSA at 1-888-772-2970 if you experience problems using any of the services within BSO.

The website includes information on electronic filing, some IRS and SSA publications, and general topics of interest about annual wage reporting. You can also use BSO to ask questions about wage reporting.

Employers can also electronically file MMREF-1 wage reports. See *Electronic reporting* on page 3.

Employment tax information. Detailed employment tax information is given in:
- Pub. 15 (Circular E), Employer's Tax Guide,
- Pub. 15-A, Employer's Supplemental Tax Guide,
- Pub. 15-B, Employer's Tax Guide to Fringe Benefits, and
- Pub. 51 (Circular A), Agricultural Employer's Tax Guide.

You can also call the IRS with your employment tax questions at 1-800-829-4933 (hours of operation are Monday through Friday 8:00 a.m to 8:00 p.m. local time) or visit the IRS website at *www.irs.gov* and type "Employment Taxes" in the *Keyword/Search Terms* box.

How To Get Forms and Publications

Personal computer. You can access the IRS website 24 hours a day, 7 days a week at *www.irs.gov* to:
- Download forms, instructions, and publications;
- See answers to frequently asked tax questions.
- Search publications on-line by topic or keyword.
- Send us comments or request help by email.
- Sign up to receive local and national tax news by email.

 Do not file Copy A of Forms W-2, W-3, W-2c, and W-3c downloaded from the IRS website with the SSA. They are provided for informational purposes only. A penalty of $50 per information return may be imposed for filing such forms that cannot be scanned.

CD. Order Pub. 1796, IRS Tax Products on CD, and get:
- Current year forms, instructions, and publications;
- Prior year forms, instructions, and publications;
- Popular tax forms that can be filled in electronically, printed out for submission, and saved for recordkeeping; and
- The Internal Revenue Bulletin.

Purchase the CD on the Internet at *www.irs.gov/cdorders* from the National Technical Information Service (NTIS) or from the Government Printing Office (GPO) at *www.bookstore.gpo.gov/irs.* You can also purchase the CD by calling 1-877-CDFORMS (1-877-233-6767) toll free.

By phone and in person. You can order forms and publications by calling 1-800-TAX-FORM (1-800-829-3676). You can also get most forms and publications at your local IRS office.

Common Errors on Forms W-2

Forms W-2 provide information to your employees, the SSA, the IRS, and state and local governments. Avoid making the following errors, which cause processing delays.

Do not:
- Use ink that is too light to make entries. Use only black ink.
- Make entries that are too small or too large. Use 12-point Courier font, if possible.
- Add dollar signs to the money-amount boxes. They have been removed from Copy A and are not required.
- Inappropriately check the "Retirement plan" checkbox in box 13. See *Retirement plan* on page 13.
- Misformat the employee's name in box e. Enter the employee's first name and middle initial in the first box, his or her surname in the second box, and his or her suffix in the third box.

General Instructions for Forms W-2 and W-3

Who must file Form W-2. Employers must **file** Form W-2 for wages paid to each employee from whom:
- Income, social security, or Medicare tax was withheld or
- Income tax would have been withheld if the employee had claimed no more than one withholding allowance or had not claimed exemption from withholding on Form W-4, Employee's Withholding Allowance Certificate.

Also, every employer engaged in a trade or business who pays remuneration for services performed by an employee, including noncash payments, must **furnish** a Form W-2 to each employee even if the employee is related to the employer.

If you are required to file 250 or more Forms W-2, see *Electronic reporting* on page 3.

Who must file Form W-3. Anyone required to file Form W-2 must file Form W-3 to transmit Copy A of Forms W-2. Make a copy of Form W-3; keep it and Copy D (For Employer) of Forms W-2 with your records for 4 years. Be sure to use Form W-3 for the correct year. If you are filing Forms W-2 electronically, see *Electronic reporting* on page 3.

Household employers, even those with only one household employee, must file Form W-3 if filing a paper Form W-2. On Form W-3 check the "Hshld. emp." checkbox in box b. For more information, see Schedule H (Form 1040), Household Employment Taxes, and its separate instructions. **You must have an EIN.** See *Box b—Employer identification number (EIN)* on page 9.

Who may sign Form W-3. A transmitter or sender (including a service bureau, reporting agent, paying agent, or disbursing agent) may sign Form W-3 (or use its PIN on electronic filings) for the employer or payer only if the sender:
- Is authorized to sign by an agency agreement (either oral, written, or implied) that is valid under state law and
- Writes "For (name of payer)" next to the signature (paper Form W-3 only).

If an authorized sender signs for the payer, the payer is still responsible for filing, when due, a correct and complete

Form W-3 and related Forms W-2, and is subject to any penalties that result from not complying with these requirements. Be sure that the payer's name and employer identification number (EIN) on Forms W-2 and W-3 are the same as those used on the Form 941, Employer's Quarterly Federal Tax Return, Form 943, Employer's Annual Federal Tax Return for Agricultural Employees, Form 944, Employer's Annual Federal Tax Return, Form CT-1, Employer's Annual Railroad Retirement Tax Return, or Schedule H (Form 1040) filed by or for the payer.

When to file. File Copy A of Form W-2 with the entire page of Form W-3 by February 28, 2007. However, if you file electronically, the due date is April 2, 2007. You may owe a penalty for each Form W-2 that you file late. See *Penalties* on page 8. If you terminate your business, see *Terminating a business* on page 7.

Extension to file. You may request an automatic extension of time to file Form W-2 with the SSA by sending Form 8809, Application for Extension of Time To File Information Returns, to the address shown on Form 8809. You must request the extension before the due date of Forms W-2. You will have an additional 30 days to file. See Form 8809 for details.

 Even if you request an extension to file Form W-2, you must still furnish Form W-2 to your employees by January 31, 2007. But see Extension to furnish Forms W-2 to employees *below.*

Where to file. File the entire Copy A page of Form W-2 with the entire page of Form W-3 at the following address:

Social Security Administration
Data Operations Center
Wilkes-Barre, PA 18769-0001

 If you use "Certified Mail" to file, change the ZIP code to "18769-0002." If you use an IRS-approved private delivery service, add "ATTN: W-2 Process, 1150 E. Mountain Dr." to the address and change the ZIP code to "18702-7997." See Pub. 15 (Circular E) for a list of IRS-approved private delivery services.

 Do not send cash, checks, money orders, etc. with the Forms W-2 and W-3 that you submit to the SSA. Do not use the address above to file electronically. See SSA's MMREF-1, Magnetic Media Reporting and Electronic Filing, for the electronic filing address. Employment tax forms (for example, Form 941 or Form 943), remittances, and Forms 1099 must be sent to the IRS.

Send Copy 1 of Form W-2 to your state, city, or local tax department. For more information concerning Copy 1 (including how to complete boxes 15-20), contact your state, city, or local tax department.

Shipping and mailing. If you file more than one type of employment tax form, please group Forms W-2 of the same type with a separate Form W-3 for each type, and send them in separate groups. See the specific instructions for box b of Form W-3 on page 14.

Prepare and file Forms W-2 either alphabetically by employees' last names or numerically by employees' social security numbers. **Please do not staple or tape Form W-3 to the related Forms W-2 or Forms W-2 to each other.** These forms are machine read. Staple holes or tears interfere with machine reading. Also, **do not fold Forms W-2 and W-3.** Send the forms to the SSA in a flat mailing.

Electronic reporting. If you are required to file 250 or more Forms W-2, you must file them electronically unless the IRS granted you a waiver. You may be charged a penalty if you fail to file electronically when required.

Elimination of magnetic media as a filing method. The last year for filing on tapes and cartridges was tax year 2004 (forms timely filed with the SSA in 2005). The last year for filing on diskette was tax year 2005 (forms timely filed with the SSA in 2006).

 You are encouraged to file electronically even if you are filing fewer than 250 Forms W-2. Small submitters may be able to file Forms W-2 online. For more information, visit SSA's Employer Reporting Instructions and Information website at www.socialsecurity.gov/employer *and select "Business Services Online Tutorial."*

You may request a waiver on Form 8508, Request for Waiver From Filing Information Returns Electronically/ Magnetically. Submit Form 8508 to the IRS at least 45 days before the due date of Form W-2. See Form 8508 for filing information.

 If you file electronically, do not file the same returns on paper.

Electronic reporting specifications for Form W-2 are in the SSA's MMREF-1, a publication that can be downloaded by accessing SSA's Employer Reporting Instructions and Information website at *www.socialsecurity.gov/employer* and selecting "Forms and publications." You can also get electronic specifications by calling SSA's Employer Reporting Branch at 1-800-772-6270.

Reporting instructions for electronic filing differ in a few situations from paper reporting instructions. For example, electronic filers may enter more than four items in box 12 in one individual's wage report, but paper filers are limited to four entries in box 12 on Copy A of each Form W-2.

Furnishing Copies B, C, and 2 to employees. Furnish Copies B, C, and 2 of Form W-2 to your employees, generally, by January 31, 2007. You will meet the "furnish" requirement if the form is properly addressed and mailed on or before the due date.

If employment ends before December 31, 2006, you may furnish copies to the employee at any time after employment ends, but no later than January 31, 2007. If an employee asks for Form W-2, give him or her the completed copies within 30 days of the request or within 30 days of the final wage payment, whichever is later. However, if you terminate your business, see *Terminating a business* on page 7.

You may furnish Forms W-2 to employees on IRS official forms or on acceptable substitute forms. See *Substitute forms* on page 1. **Be sure that the Forms W-2 you provide to employees are clear and legible and comply with the requirements in Pub. 1141.**

Extension to furnish Forms W-2 to employees. You may request an extension of time to furnish Forms W-2 to employees by sending a letter to:

IRS–Enterprise Computing Center–Martinsburg
Information Reporting Program
Attn: Extension of Time Coordinator
240 Murall Drive
Kearneysville, WV 25430

Mail your letter on or before the due date for furnishing Forms W-2 to employees. It must include:
• Your name and address,
• Your employer identification number (EIN),
• A statement that you are requesting an extension to furnish "Forms W-2" to employees,
• Reason for delay, and
• Your signature or that of your authorized agent.

Undeliverable Forms W-2. Keep for four years any employee copies of Forms W-2 that you tried to deliver but

-3-

could not. **Do not send undeliverable Forms W-2 to the SSA.**

Taxpayer identification numbers (TINs). Employers use an **employer identification number** (EIN) (00-0000000). Employees use a **social security number** (SSN) (000-00-0000). When you list a number, please separate the nine digits properly to show the kind of number. Do not accept an individual taxpayer identification number (ITIN) for employment purposes. For more information, see section 4 of Pub. 15 (Circular E).

The IRS uses SSNs to check the payments that you report against the amounts shown on the employees' tax returns. The SSA uses SSNs to record employees' earnings for future social security and Medicare benefits. **When you prepare Form W-2, be sure to show the correct SSN for each employee.** For information on verification of SSNs, see section 4 of Pub. 15 (Circular E).

Special Reporting Situations for Form W-2

Adoption benefits. Amounts paid or expenses incurred by an employer for qualified adoption expenses under an adoption assistance program are not subject to income tax withholding and are not reportable in box 1. However, these amounts (including adoption benefits **paid** from a section 125 (cafeteria) plan, but not including adoption benefits forfeited from a cafeteria plan) are subject to social security, Medicare, and railroad retirement taxes and must be reported in boxes 3 and 5. Also, the total amount must be reported in box 12 with code **T.**

See Notice 97-9, 1997-1 C.B. 365, for more information on adoption benefits. You can find Notice 97-9 on page 35 of Internal Revenue Bulletin 1997-2 at *www.irs.gov/pub/ irs-irbs/irb97-02.pdf.* Advise your employees to get Pub. 968, Tax Benefits for Adoption.

Agent reporting. Generally, an agent who has an approved Form 2678, Employer Appointment of Agent, should enter the agent's name as the employer in box c of Form W-2, and file only one Form W-2 for each employee. However, if the agent (a) is acting as an agent for two or more employers or is an employer and is acting as an agent for another employer and (b) pays social security wages for more than one employer in excess of the wage base to an individual, special reporting for payments to that employee is needed.

If both (a) and (b) above apply, the agent must file separate Forms W-2 for the affected employee reflecting the wages paid by each employer. On each Form W-2, the agent should enter the following in box c of Form W-2:

> (Name of agent)
> Agent for (name of employer)
> Address of agent

Each Form W-2 should reflect the EIN of the **agent** in box b. An agent files one Form W-3 for all of the Forms W-2 and enters its own information in boxes e, f, and g of Form W-3 as it appears on the agent's related employment tax returns (for example, Form 941). Enter the client-employer's EIN in box h of Form W-3 if the Forms W-2 relate to only one employer (other than the agent); if not, leave box h blank. See Rev. Proc. 70-6, 1970-1 C.B. 420, for procedures to be followed in applying to be an agent.

TIP *Generally, an agent is not responsible for refunding excess social security or railroad retirement (RRTA) tax on employees. If an employee worked for more than one employer during 2006 and had more than $5,840.40 in social security and Tier I RRTA tax withheld (or* more than $3,075.60 in Tier II RRTA tax withheld), he or she should claim the excess on the appropriate line of Form 1040 or Form 1040A.

Archer MSA. An **employer's** contribution to an employee's Archer MSA is not subject to income tax withholding, or social security, Medicare, or railroad retirement taxes if it is reasonable to believe at the time of the payment that the contribution will be excludable from the employee's income. However, if it is not reasonable to believe at the time of payment that the contribution will be excludable from the employee's income, employer contributions are subject to income tax withholding and social security and Medicare taxes (or railroad retirement taxes, if applicable) and must be reported in boxes 1, 3, and 5.

You must report all employer contributions to an Archer MSA in box 12 of Form W-2 with code **R.** Employer contributions to an Archer MSA that are not excludable from the income of the employee also must be reported in box 1.

An **employee's** contributions to an Archer MSA are includible in income as wages and are subject to income tax withholding and social security and Medicare taxes (or railroad retirement taxes, if applicable). Employee contributions are deductible, within limits, on the employee's Form 1040.

See Notice 96-53, 1996-2 C.B. 219 and Pub. 969, Health Savings Accounts and Other Tax-Favored Health Plans, for more information. You can find Notice 96-53 on page 5 of Internal Revenue Bulletin 1996-51 at *www.irs.gov/pub/ irs-irbs/irb96-51.pdf.*

Clergy and religious workers. For certain members of the clergy and religious workers who are not subject to social security and Medicare taxes as employees, boxes 3 and 5 of Form W-2 should be left blank. You may include a minister's parsonage and/or utilities allowance in box 14. For information on the rules that apply to ministers and certain other religious workers, see Pub. 517, Social Security and Other Information for Members of the Clergy and Religious Workers, and *Section 4—Religious Exemptions* in Pub. 15-A.

Corrections. Use the current version of Form W-2c, Corrected Wage and Tax Statement, to correct errors (such as incorrect name, SSN, or amount) on a previously filed Form W-2.

If the SSA issues your employee a replacement card after a name change, or a new card with a different social security number after a change in alien work status, file a Form W-2c to correct the name/SSN reported on the most recently filed Form W-2. It is not necessary to correct the prior years if the previous name and number were used for the years prior to the most recently filed Form W-2.

File Form W-3c, Transmittal of Corrected Wage and Tax Statements, whenever you file a Form W-2c with the SSA, even if you are only filing a Form W-2c to correct an employee's name or SSN. However, see *Incorrect address on employee's Form W-2* on page 5 for information on correcting an employee's address. See the Instructions for Forms W-2c and W-3c if an error was made on a previously filed Form W-3.

If you discover an error on Form W-2 after you issue it to your employee but before you send it to the SSA, check the **"Void"** box at the top of the incorrect Form W-2 on Copy A. Prepare a new Form W-2 with the correct information, and send Copy A to the SSA. Write "CORRECTED" on the **employee's** new copies (B, C, and 2), and furnish them to the employee. If the "Void" Form W-2 is on a page with a correct Form W-2, send the entire page to the SSA. The "Void" form will not be processed. **Do not** write "CORRECTED" on Copy A of Form W-2.

-4-

If you are making an adjustment in 2006 to correct social security and Medicare taxes for a prior year, you must file Form 941c, Supporting Statement To Correct Information, with your Form 941, Form 943, or Form 944 in the return period that you find the error, and issue the employee a Form W-2c for the prior year. If you are correcting social security or Medicare wages or tips, also file the entire Copy A page of Form W-2c and Form W-3c with the SSA to correct the social security records and **any other items** on the original Form W-2 (or previously filed Form W-2c) that were in error.

Incorrect address on employee's Form W-2. If you filed a Form W-2 with the SSA showing an incorrect address for the employee but all other information on Form W-2 is correct, **do not file Form W-2c with the SSA merely to correct the address.**

However, if the address was incorrect on the Form W-2 furnished to the employee, **you must do one of the following:**
- Issue a new, corrected Form W-2 to the employee, including the new address. Indicate "REISSUED STATEMENT" on the new copies. **Do not send Copy A to the SSA.**
- Issue a Form W-2c to the employee showing the correct address in box f and all other correct information. **Do not send Copy A to the SSA.**
- Mail the Form W-2 with the incorrect address to the employee in an envelope showing the correct address or otherwise deliver it to the employee.

Deceased employee's wages. If an employee dies during the year, you must report the accrued wages, vacation pay, and other compensation paid after the date of death.

If you made the **payment in the same year that the employee died**, you must withhold social security and Medicare taxes on the payment and report the payment on the employee's Form W-2 only as social security and Medicare wages to ensure proper social security and Medicare credit is received.

On the employee's Form W-2, show the payment as social security wages (box 3) and Medicare wages and tips (box 5) and the social security and Medicare taxes withheld in boxes 4 and 6. **Do not show the payment in box 1.**

If you made the **payment after the year of death,** do not report it on Form W-2, and do not withhold social security and Medicare taxes.

Whether the payment is made in the year of death or after the year of death, you also must report it in box 3 of Form 1099-MISC, Miscellaneous Income, for the payment to the estate or beneficiary. Use the name and taxpayer identification number (TIN) of the payment recipient on Form 1099-MISC.

Example. Before Employee A's death on June 15, 2006, A was employed by Employer X and received $10,000 in wages on which federal income tax of $1,500 was withheld. When A died, X owed A $2,000 in wages and $1,000 in accrued vacation pay. The total of $3,000 (less the social security and Medicare taxes withheld) was paid to A's estate on July 20, 2006. Because X made the payment during the year of death, X must withhold social security and Medicare taxes on the $3,000 payment and must complete Form W-2 as follows:
- **Box d** – Employee A's SSN
- **Box e** – Employee A's name
- **Box f** – Employee A's address
- **Box 1** – 10000.00 (does not include the $3,000 accrued wages and vacation pay)
- **Box 2** – 1500.00
- **Box 3** – 13000.00 (includes the $3,000 accrued wages and vacation pay)

- **Box 4** – 806.00 (6.2% of the amount in box 3)
- **Box 5** – 13000.00 (includes the $3,000 accrued wages and vacation pay)
- **Box 6** – 188.50 (1.45% of the amount in box 5)

 Employer X also must complete Form 1099-MISC as follows:

- **Boxes for:** Recipient's name, address, and TIN—The estate's name, address, and TIN
- **Box 3:** 3000.00 (Even though amounts were withheld for social security and Medicare taxes, the gross amount is reported here.)

If Employer X made the payment after the year of death, the $3,000 would **not** be subject to social security and Medicare taxes and would **not** be shown on Form W-2. However, the employer would still file Form 1099-MISC.

Designated Roth contributions. New section 402A, added by the Economic Growth and Tax Reconciliation Act of 2001, provides that a participant in a section 401(k) plan or under a 403(b) salary reduction agreement that includes a qualified Roth contribution program may elect to make designated Roth contributions to the plan or program in lieu of elective deferrals. Designated Roth contributions are subject to income tax withholding and social security and Medicare taxes (and railroad retirement taxes, if applicable) and must be reported in boxes 1, 3, and 5.

The Act requires separate reporting of the yearly designated Roth contributions. Designated Roth contributions to 401(k) plans will be reported using code **AA** in box 12; designated Roth contributions under 403(b) salary reduction agreements will be reported using code **BB** in box 12. For reporting instructions, see *Code AA* and *Code BB* on page 13.

Educational assistance programs. A $5,250 exclusion for employer-provided educational assistance applies to benefits provided to your employees under an educational assistance program. See Pub. 970, Tax Benefits for Education, and section 2 of Pub. 15-B for more information. Also see *Box 1 – Wages, tips, other compensation* on page 9.

Election workers. Report on Form W-2 payments of $600 or more to election workers for services performed in state, county, and municipal elections. File Form W-2 for payments of less than $600 paid to election workers if social security and Medicare taxes were withheld under a section 218 (Social Security Act) agreement. **Do not** report election worker payments on Form 1099-MISC.

If the election worker is employed in another capacity with the same government entity, see Rev. Rul. 2000-06 on page 512 of Internal Revenue Bulletin 2000-06 at *www.irs.gov/pub/irs-irbs/irb00-06.pdf.*

Employee business expense reimbursements. Reimbursements to employees for business expenses must be reported as follows:
- Generally, payments made under an **accountable plan** are excluded from the employee's gross income and are not reported on Form W-2. However, if you pay a per diem or mileage allowance and the amount paid exceeds the amount treated as substantiated under IRS rules, you must report as wages on Form W-2 the amount in excess of the amount treated as substantiated. The excess amount is subject to income tax withholding and social security and Medicare taxes. Report the amount treated as substantiated (that is, the nontaxable portion) in box 12 using code **L**. See *Code L – Substantiated employee business expense reimbursements* on page 12.
- Payments made under a **nonaccountable plan** are reported as wages on Form W-2 and are subject to income tax withholding and social security and Medicare taxes.

-5-

For more information on accountable plans, nonaccountable plans, amounts treated as substantiated under a per diem or mileage allowance, the standard mileage rate, the per diem substantiation method, and the high-low substantiation method, see Pub. 463, Travel, Entertainment, Gift, and Car Expenses; Pub. 1542, Per Diem Rates; and section 5 of Pub. 15 (Circular E).

Employee's taxes paid by employer. If you paid your employee's share of social security and Medicare taxes rather than deducting them from the employee's wages, you must include these payments as wages subject to income tax withholding and social security, Medicare, and federal unemployment (FUTA) taxes. Generally, this increase in your employee's wages for your payment of the employee's social security and Medicare taxes is also subject to employee social security and Medicare taxes. The amount to include as wages is determined by using the formula contained in the discussion of *Employee's Portion of Taxes Paid by Employer* in section 7 of Pub. 15 (Circular E).

 This does not apply to household and agricultural employers. If you pay a household or agricultural employee's social security and Medicare taxes, you must include these payments in the employee's wages. However, the wage increase due to the tax payments is not subject to social security, Medicare, or FUTA taxes. For information on completing Forms W-2 and W-3 in this situation, see the Instructions for Schedule H (Form 1040), Household Employers and section 4 of Pub. 51 (Circular A).

Fringe benefits. Include all taxable fringe benefits in box 1 of Form W-2 as wages, tips, and other compensation and, if applicable, in boxes 3 and 5 as social security and Medicare wages. Although not required, you may include the total value of fringe benefits in box 14 (or on a separate statement). However, if you provided your employee a vehicle and included 100% of its annual lease value in the employee's income, you **must** separately report this value to the employee in box 14 (or on a separate statement). The employee can then figure the value of any business use of the vehicle and report it on Form 2106, Employee Business Expenses. Also see Pub. 15-B for more information.

⚠ *If you used the commuting rule or the vehicle cents-per-mile rule to value the personal use of the vehicle, you cannot include 100% of the value of the use of the vehicle in the employee's income. See Pub. 15-B.*

Golden parachute payments. Include any golden parachute payments in boxes 1, 3, and 5 of Form W-2. Withhold income, social security, and Medicare taxes as usual and report them in boxes 2, 4, and 6, respectively. Excess parachute payments are also subject to a 20% excise tax. If the excess payments are considered wages, withhold the 20% excise tax and include it in box 2 as income tax withheld. Also report the excise tax in box 12 with code **K**. For definitions and additional information, see Regulations section 1.280G-1 and Rev. Proc. 2003-68. You can find Rev. Proc. 2003-68 on page 398 of Internal Revenue Bulletin 2003-34 at *www.irs.gov/pub/irs-irbs/irb03-34.pdf.*

Government employers. Federal, state, and local agencies have two options for reporting their employees' wages that are subject only to Medicare tax for part of the year and full social security and Medicare taxes for part of the year.

Option one (which the SSA prefers) is to file a single Form W-2 reflecting the employees' wages for the entire year, even if only part of the year's wages were subject to both social security and Medicare taxes. The Form W-3 must have the "941" box checked in box b. The wages in box 5 must be equal to or greater than the wages in box 3 on Form W-2.

Option two is to file two Forms W-2 and two Forms W-3. File one Form W-2 for wages subject to Medicare tax only. Be sure to check the "Medicare govt. emp." box in box b of Form W-3. File the second Form W-2 for wages subject to both social security and Medicare taxes with the "941" box checked in box b of Form W-3. The wages in box 5 on each Form W-2 must be equal to or greater than the wages in box 3 on that same Form W-2.

Group-term life insurance. If you paid for group-term life insurance over $50,000 for an employee or a former employee, you must report the taxable cost of excess coverage, determined by using the table in section 2 of Pub. 15-B, in boxes 1, 3, and 5 of Form W-2. Also, show the amount in box 12 with code **C**. For employees, you must withhold social security and Medicare taxes, but not income tax. Former employees must pay the employee part of social security and Medicare taxes on the taxable cost of group-term life insurance over $50,000 on Form 1040. You are not required to collect those taxes. However, you must report the uncollected social security tax with code **M** and the uncollected Medicare tax with code **N** in box 12 of Form W-2.

Health Savings Account (HSA). An **employer's** contribution to an employee's Health Savings Account (HSA) is not subject to income tax withholding, or social security, Medicare, or railroad retirement taxes (or FUTA tax) if it is reasonable to believe at the time of the payment that the contribution will be excludable from the employee's income. However, if it is not reasonable to believe at the time of payment that the contribution will be excludable from the employee's income, employer contributions are subject to income tax withholding and social security and Medicare taxes (or railroad retirement taxes, if applicable) and must be reported in boxes 1, 3, and 5 (and on Form 940, Employer's Annual Federal Unemployment (FUTA) Tax Return).

You must report all employer contributions to an HSA in box 12 of Form W-2 with code **W**. Employer contributions to an HSA that are not excludable from the income of the employee also must be reported in box 1.

An **employee's** contributions to an HSA are includible in income as wages and are subject to income tax withholding and social security and Medicare taxes (or railroad retirement taxes, if applicable). Employee contributions are deductible, within limits, on the employee's Form 1040. For more information about HSAs, see Notice 2004-2 and Notice 2004-50. You can find Notice 2004-2 on page 269 of Internal Revenue Bulletin 2004-2 at *www.irs.gov/pub/irs-irbs/irb04-02.pdf.* You can find Notice 2004-50 on page 196 of Internal Revenue Bulletin 2004-33 at *www.irs.gov/pub/irs-irbs/irb04-33.pdf.* Also see Form 8889, Health Savings Accounts (HSAs), and Pub. 969.

Lost Form W-2—reissued statement. If an employee loses a Form W-2, write "REISSUED STATEMENT" on the new copy and furnish it to the employee. You do not have to add "Reissued Statement" on Forms W-2 provided to employees electronically. **Do not send Copy A of the reissued Form W-2 to the SSA.** Employers are not prohibited (by the Internal Revenue Code) from charging a fee for the issuance of a duplicate Form W-2.

Moving expenses. Report moving expenses as follows:
• Qualified moving expenses that an employer paid to a third party on behalf of the employee (for example, to a moving company) and services that an employer furnished in kind to an employee are not reported on Form W-2.
• Qualified moving expense reimbursements paid directly to an employee by an employer are reported only in box 12 of Form W-2 with code **P**.
• Nonqualified moving expense reimbursements are reported in boxes 1, 3, and 5 of Form W-2. These amounts

-6-

are subject to income tax withholding and social security and Medicare taxes.

Nonqualified deferred compensation plans. Section 409A, added by the American Jobs Creation Act of 2004, provides that all amounts deferred under a nonqualified deferred compensation (NQDC) plan for all tax years are currently includible in gross income unless certain requirements are met. If section 409A requires an amount to be included in gross income, the section imposes a substantial additional tax. Section 409A, generally, is effective with respect to amounts deferred in tax years beginning after December 31, 2004, but deferrals made prior to that year may be subject to section 409A under some circumstances.

The Act requires reporting of the **yearly deferrals** (plus earnings) under a section 409A nonqualified deferred compensation plan, using code **Y** in box 12.

Income included under section 409A from a nonqualified deferred compensation plan will be reported in box 1, and in box 12 using code **Z**. This income is also subject to an additional tax reported on Form 1040. For more information, see section 5 of Pub. 15-A.

Railroad employers. Railroad employers must file Form W-2 to report their employees' wages and income tax withholding in boxes 1 and 2. Electronic reporting may be required; see *Electronic reporting* on page 3.

If an employee is covered by social security and Medicare, also complete boxes 3, 4, 5, 6, and 7 of Form W-2 to show the social security and Medicare wages and the amounts withheld for social security and Medicare taxes. On the Form W-3 used to transmit these Forms W-2, check the "941" box in box b.

For employees covered by RRTA tax, you also must report the Tier I and Tier II taxes withheld in box 14 of Form W-2. Label them "Tier I tax" and "Tier II tax." Boxes 3, 4, 5, 6, and 7 apply only to covered social security and Medicare employees and are not to be used to report railroad retirement wages and taxes. On the Form W-3 used to transmit these Forms W-2, check the "CT-1" box in box b.

Repayments. If an employee repays you for wages received in error, do not offset the repayments against current year's wages unless the repayments are for amounts received in error in the current year. Repayments made in the current year, but related to a prior year or years, must be repaid in gross, not net, and require special tax treatment by employees in some cases. You may advise the employee of the total repayments made during the current year and the amount (if any) related to prior years. This information will help the employee account for such repayments on his or her federal income tax return.

If the repayment was for a prior year, you must file Form W-2c with the SSA to correct only social security and Medicare wages and taxes. **Do not correct "Wages" in box 1 on Form W-2c for the amount paid in error.** For information on reporting adjustments to Form 941, Form 943, or Form 944, see section 13 of Pub. 15 (Circular E) or section 9 of Pub. 51 (Circular A).

TIP *Tell your employee that the wages paid in error in a prior year remain taxable to him or her for that year. This is because the employee received and had use of those funds during that year. The employee is not entitled to file an amended return (Form 1040X) to recover the income tax on these wages. Instead, the employee is entitled to a deduction (or a credit, in some cases) for the repaid wages on his or her Form 1040 for the year of repayment.*

Scholarship and fellowship grants. Give a Form W-2 to each recipient of a scholarship or fellowship grant only if you are reporting amounts includible in income under section 117(c) (relating to payments for teaching, research, or other services required as a condition for receiving the qualified scholarship). Also see Pub. 15-A and Pub. 970. These payments are subject to income tax withholding. However, their taxability for social security and Medicare taxes depends on the nature of the employment and the status of the organization. See *Students* in section 15 of Pub. 15 (Circular E).

Sick pay. If you had employees who received sick pay in 2006 from an insurance company or other third-party payer and the third party notified you of the amount of sick pay involved, you may be required to report the information on the employees' Forms W-2. If the insurance company or other third-party payer did not notify you in a timely manner about the sick pay payments, it must prepare Forms W-2 and W-3 for your employees showing the sick pay. For specific reporting instructions, see *Sick Pay Reporting* in section 6 of Pub. 15-A.

SIMPLE retirement account. An **employee's** salary reduction contributions to a SIMPLE (savings incentive match plan for employees) retirement account are not subject to income tax withholding but are subject to social security, Medicare, and railroad retirement taxes. Do not include an employee's contribution in box 1 but do include it in boxes 3 and 5. An employee's total contribution also must be included in box 12 with code **D** or **S**.

An **employer's** matching or nonelective contribution to an employee's SIMPLE is not subject to income tax withholding or social security, Medicare, or railroad retirement taxes and is not to be shown on Form W-2.

See Notice 98-4, 1998-1 C.B. 269, for more information on SIMPLE retirement accounts. You can find Notice 98-4 on page 25 of Internal Revenue Bulletin 1998-2 at *www.irs.gov/pub/irs-irbs/irb98-02.pdf*.

Successor/predecessor employers. If you buy or sell a business during the year, see Rev. Proc. 2004-53 for information on who must file Forms W-2 and employment tax returns. You can find Rev. Proc. 2004-53 on page 320 of Internal Revenue Bulletin 2004-34 at *www.irs.gov/pub/ irs-irbs/irb04-34.pdf*.

Terminating a business. If you terminate your business, you must provide Forms W-2 to your employees for the calendar year of termination by the due date of your final Form 941. You must also file Forms W-2 with the SSA by the last day of the month that follows the due date of your final Form 941. If filing on paper, make sure you obtain Forms W-2 and W-3 preprinted with the correct year. If filing electronically, make sure your software has been updated for the current tax year.

However, if any of your employees are immediately employed by a successor employer, see *Successor/ predecessor employers* above. Also, see Rev. Proc. 96-57, 1996-2 C.B. 389 for information on automatic extensions for furnishing Forms W-2 to employees and filing Forms W-2. You can find Rev. Proc. 96-57 on page 14 of Internal Revenue Bulletin 1996-53 at *www.irs.gov/pub/irs-irbs/ irb96-53.pdf*.

TIP *Get Schedule D (Form 941), Report of Discrepancies Caused by Acquisitions, Statutory Mergers, or Consolidations, for information on reconciling wages and taxes reported on Forms W-2 with amounts reported on Forms 941, Form 943, or Form 944.*

USERRA makeup amounts to a pension plan. If an employee returned to your employment after military service and certain makeup amounts were contributed to a pension plan for a prior year(s) under the Uniformed Services Employment and Reemployment Rights Act of 1994 (USERRA), report the prior year contributions separately in

-7-

box 12. See the *TIP* above *Code D* on page 12. You also may report certain makeup amounts in box 14. See *Box 14—Other* on page 13.

Instead of reporting in box 12 (or box 14), **you may choose to provide a separate statement to your employee showing USERRA makeup contributions.** The statement must identify the type of plan, the year(s) to which the contributions relate, and the amount contributed for each year.

Penalties

The following penalties generally apply to the person required to file Form W-2. The penalties apply to paper filers as well as to electronic filers.

 Use of a reporting agent or other third-party payroll service provider does not relieve an employer of the responsibility to ensure that Forms W-2 are furnished to employees and are filed correctly and on time.

Failure to file correct information returns by the due date. If you fail to file a correct Form W-2 by the due date and cannot show reasonable cause, you may be subject to a penalty as provided under section 6721. The penalty applies if you:
- Fail to file timely,
- Fail to include all information required to be shown on Form W-2,
- Include incorrect information on Form W-2,
- File on paper when you were required to file electronically,
- Report an incorrect TIN,
- Fail to report a TIN, or
- Fail to file paper Forms W-2 that are machine readable.

The amount of the penalty is based on when you file the correct Form W-2. The penalty is:
- **$15** per Form W-2 if you correctly file within 30 days (by March 30 if the due date is February 28); maximum penalty $75,000 per year ($25,000 for small businesses, defined later).
- **$30** per Form W-2 if you correctly file more than 30 days after the due date but by August 1; maximum penalty $150,000 per year ($50,000 for small businesses).
- **$50** per Form W-2 if you file after August 1 or you do not file required Forms W-2; maximum penalty $250,000 per year ($100,000 for small businesses).

 If you do not file corrections and you do not meet any of the exceptions to the penalty stated below, the penalty is $50 per information return.

Exceptions to the penalty. The following are exceptions to the failure to file correction information returns penalty:

1. The penalty will not apply to any failure that you can show was due to reasonable cause and not to willful neglect. In general, you must be able to show that your failure was due to an event beyond your control or due to significant mitigating factors. You must also be able to show that you acted in a responsible manner and took steps to avoid the failure.

2. An inconsequential error or omission is not considered a failure to include correct information. An inconsequential error or omission does not prevent or hinder the SSA/IRS from processing the Form W-2, from correlating the information required to be shown on the form with the information shown on the payee's tax return, or from otherwise putting the form to its intended use. **Errors and omissions that are never inconsequential are those relating to:**
- A TIN,
- A payee's surname, and

- Any money amounts.

3. **De minimis rule for corrections.** Even though you cannot show reasonable cause, the penalty for failure to file correct Forms W-2 will not apply to a certain number of returns if you:
- Filed those Forms W-2 on or before the required filing date,
- Either failed to include all of the information required on the form or included incorrect information, and
- Filed corrections of these forms by August 1.

If you meet all of the conditions above, the penalty for filing incorrect information returns (including Form W-2) will not apply to the greater of 10 information returns (including Form W-2) or ½ of 1% of the total number of information returns (including Form W-2) that you are required to file for the calendar year.

Lower maximum penalties for small businesses. For purposes of the lower maximum penalties shown in parentheses above, you are a small business if your average annual gross receipts for the three most recent tax years (or for the period that you were in existence, if shorter) ending before the calendar year in which the Forms W-2 were due are $5 million or less.

Intentional disregard of filing requirements. If any failure to file a correct Form W-2 is due to intentional disregard of the filing or correct information requirements, the penalty is at least $100 per Form W-2 with no maximum penalty.

Failure to furnish correct payee statements. If you fail to provide correct payee statements (Forms W-2) to your employees and you cannot show reasonable cause, you may be subject to a penalty. The penalty applies if you fail to provide the statement by January 31, if you fail to include all information required to be shown on the statement, or if you include incorrect information on the statement.

The penalty is $50 per statement, no matter when the correct statement is furnished, with a maximum of $100,000 per year. The penalty is not reduced for furnishing a correct statement by August 1.

Exception. An inconsequential error or omission is not considered a failure to include correct information. An inconsequential error or omission cannot reasonably be expected to prevent or hinder the payee from timely receiving correct information and reporting it on his or her income tax return or from otherwise putting the statement to its intended use. **Errors and omissions that are never inconsequential are those relating to:**
- A dollar amount,
- A significant item in a payee's address, and
- The appropriate form for the information provided, such as whether the form is an acceptable substitute for the official IRS form.

Intentional disregard of payee statement requirements. If any failure to provide a correct payee statement (Form W-2) to an employee is due to intentional disregard of the requirements to furnish a correct payee statement, the penalty is at least $100 per Form W-2 with no maximum penalty.

Civil damages for fraudulent filing of Forms W-2. If you willfully file a fraudulent Form W-2 for payments that you claim you made to another person, that person may be able to sue you for damages. You may have to pay $5,000 or more.

Specific Instructions for Form W-2

How to complete Form W-2. Form W-2 is a six-part form. **Please ensure that all copies are legible.** Send Copy A to

-8-

the SSA; Copy 1 to your state, city, or local tax department; and Copies B, C, and 2 to your employee. Keep Copy D, and a copy of Form W-3, with your records for 4 years.

Type the entries on Form W-2 using black ink in 12-point Courier font, if possible. Because Copy A is read by machine, handwritten entries or the use of inks other than black to make entries on the form hinder processing by the SSA. Do not use script type, inverted font, italics, or dual case alpha characters. It is important that entries in the boxes do not cross one or more of the vertical or horizontal lines that separate the boxes. Please do not erase, whiteout, or strike over an entry. **Make all dollar entries on Copy A without the dollar sign and comma but with the decimal point (00000.00). Show the cents portion of the money amounts.** If a box does not apply, leave it blank.

Send the whole Copy A page of Form W-2 with Form W-3 to the SSA even if one of the Forms W-2 on the page is blank or void. Do not staple Forms W-2 together or to Form W-3. Also, if possible, please file Forms W-2 either alphabetically by employees' last names or numerically by employees' SSNs. This will help the SSA locate specific forms.

Calendar year basis. The entries on Form W-2 must be based on wages paid during the calendar year. Use Form W-2 for the correct tax year. For example, if the employee worked from December 21, 2006, through January 3, 2007, and the wages for that period were paid on January 5, 2007, include those wages on the 2007 Form W-2.

Multiple forms. If necessary, you can issue more than one Form W-2 to an employee. For example, you may need to report more than four coded items in box 12 or you may want to report other compensation on a second form. If you issue a second Form W-2, complete boxes b, c, d, e, and f with the same information as on the first Form W-2. Show any items that were not included on the first Form W-2 in the appropriate boxes. Also, see the *TIP* below *Box 12—Codes* on page 11.

Do not report the same federal tax data to the SSA on more than one Copy A.

 *For **each** Form W-2 showing an amount in box 3 or box 7, make certain that box 5 equals or exceeds the sum of boxes 3 and 7.*

Box a—Control number. You may use this box to identify individual Forms W-2. **Make certain that entries do not cross over into the form identification box (22222).** You do not have to use this box.

Void. Check this box when an error is made on Form W-2 and you are voiding it because you are going to complete a new Form W-2. **Be careful not to include any amounts shown on "Void" forms in the totals that you enter on Form W-3.** See *Corrections* on page 4.

Box b—Employer identification number (EIN). Show the employer identification number (EIN) assigned to you by the IRS (00-0000000). This should be the same number that you used on your federal employment tax returns (Form 941, Form 943, Form 944, Form CT-1, or Schedule H (Form 1040)). Do not use a prior owner's EIN. If you do not have an EIN when filing Forms W-2, enter "Applied For" in box b; do not use your SSN. You can get an EIN by filing Form SS-4, Application for Employer Identification Number. Also see *Agent reporting* on page 4.

Box c—Employer's name, address, and ZIP code. This entry should be the same as shown on your Form 941, Form 943, Form 944, Form CT-1, or Schedule H (Form 1040). Also see *Agent reporting* on page 4.

Box d—Employee's social security number. Enter the number shown on the employee's social security card. If the employee does not have a card, he or she should apply for

one by completing Form SS-5, Application for a Social Security Card.

If the employee has applied for a card but the number is not received in time for filing, enter "Applied For" in box d on paper Forms W-2 filed with the SSA. (Enter zeros (000-00-0000) if Form W-2 is filed electronically with the SSA.)

Ask the employee to inform you of the number and name as they are shown on the social security card when it is received. Then correct your previous report by filing Form W-2c showing the employee's SSN. If the employee needs to change his or her name from that shown on the card, the employee should call the SSA at 1-800-772-1213.

Boxes e and f—Employee's name and address. Enter the name as shown on your employee's social security card (first, middle initial, last). Generally, do not enter "Jr.," "Sr.," etc. in the "Suff." box on Copy A **unless** the suffix appears on the card. However, SSA still prefers that you do not enter the suffix on Copy A. If the name does not fit, you may show first name initial, middle initial, and last name (and ignore the vertical line). If the name has changed, the employee must get a corrected card from any SSA office. Use the name on the original card until you see the corrected one. **Do not show titles or academic degrees, such as "Dr.," "RN," or "Esq.," at the beginning or end of the employee's name.**

Include in the address the number, street, apartment or suite number (or P.O. box number if mail is not delivered to a street address). For a foreign address, give the information in the following order: city, province or state, and country. Follow the country's practice for entering the postal code. Do not abbreviate the country name.

Third-party payers of sick pay filing third-party sick pay recap Forms W-2 and W-3 must enter "Third-Party Sick Pay Recap" in place of the employee's name in box e. Also, **do not** enter the employee's SSN in box d. See *Sick Pay Reporting* in section 6 of Pub. 15-A.

Box 1—Wages, tips, other compensation. Show the total wages, tips, and other compensation, before any payroll deductions, that you paid to your employee during the year. Do not include elective deferrals, except section 501(c)(18) contributions. **Include the following:**

1. Total wages, bonuses (including signing bonuses), prizes, and awards paid to employees during the year. See *Calendar year basis* above.
2. Total noncash payments, including certain fringe benefits. See *Fringe benefits* on page 6.
3. Total **tips** reported by the employee to the employer (not allocated tips).
4. Certain employee business expense reimbursements (see *Employee business expense reimbursements* on page 5).
5. The cost of **accident and health insurance** premiums for 2% or more shareholder-employees paid by an S corporation.
6. Taxable benefits from a **section 125 (cafeteria) plan** (that is, employee chooses cash).
7. Employee contributions to an Archer MSA.
8. Employer contributions to an Archer MSA if includible in the income of the employee. See *Archer MSA* on page 4.
9. Employer contributions for **qualified long-term care services** to the extent that such coverage is provided through a flexible spending or similar arrangement.
10. Taxable cost of group-term life insurance in excess of $50,000. See *Group-term life insurance* on page 6.
11. Unless excludable under *Educational assistance programs* (see page 5), payments for non-job-related education expenses or for payments under a nonaccountable plan. See Pub. 970.

-9-

12. The amount includible as wages because you paid your employee's share of taxes. See *Employee's taxes paid by employer* on page 6.

13. All other compensation, including certain scholarship and fellowship grants (see page 7). Other compensation includes taxable amounts that you paid to your employee from which federal income tax was not withheld. You may show other compensation on a separate Form W-2. See *Multiple forms* on page 9.

14. **Distributions** to an employee or former employee from a nonqualified deferred compensation plan (including a rabbi trust) or a **nongovernmental** section 457(b) plan.

15. Amounts includible in income under section 457(f) because the amounts are no longer subject to a substantial risk of forfeiture.

16. Payments to statutory employees who are subject to social security and Medicare taxes but not subject to federal income tax withholding must be shown in box 1 as other compensation. See *Statutory employee* on page 13.

17. Cost of current insurance protection under a **compensatory split-dollar** life insurance arrangement.

18. **Employee** contributions to a **Health Savings Account (HSA).**

19. Employer contributions to a **Health Savings Account (HSA)** if includible in the income of the employee. See *Health Savings Account (HSA)* on page 6.

20. Amounts includible in income **under a nonqualified deferred compensation plan** because of section 409A. See *Nonqualified deferred compensation plans* on page 7.

21. Designated Roth contributions made to a section 401(k) plan or under a section 403(b) salary reduction agreement. See *Designated Roth contributions* on page 5.

Box 2—Federal income tax withheld. Show the total federal income tax withheld from the employee's wages for the year (do not reduce the wages by any advance EIC payments made to the employee). Include the 20% excise tax withheld on excess parachute payments. See *Golden parachute payments* on page 6.

Box 3—Social security wages. Show the total wages paid (before payroll deductions) subject to employee social security tax but **not** including **social security tips** and **allocated tips.** See *Box 7—Social security tips* and *Box 8—Allocated tips* below. Generally, noncash payments are considered to be wages. Include employee business expense reimbursements reported in box 1. If you paid the employee's share of social security and Medicare taxes rather than deducting them from wages, see *Employee's taxes paid by employer* on page 6. The **total** of boxes 3 and 7 cannot exceed $94,200 (2006 maximum social security wage base). Include in box 5 any amounts reported in box 3.

Report in box 3 elective deferrals to certain **qualified** cash or deferred compensation arrangements and to retirement plans described in box 12 (codes **D, E, F, G,** and **S**) even though the deferrals are not includible in box 1. Also report in box 3 designated Roth contributions made to a section 401(k) plan or under a section 403(b) salary reduction agreement described in box 12 (codes **AA** and **BB**).

Amounts deferred under a **nonqualified or section 457(b) plan** must be included in boxes 3 and/or 5 as social security and/or Medicare wages as of the later of when the services giving rise to the deferral are performed or when there is no substantial forfeiture risk of the rights to the deferred amount. Include elective and nonelective deferrals for purposes of section 457(b) plans.

Also include in box 3:

• Signing bonuses an employer pays for signing or ratifying an employment contract. See Rev. Rul. 2004-109. You can find Rev. Rul. 2004-109 on page 958 of Internal Revenue Bulletin 2004-50 at *www.irs.gov/pub/irs-irbs/irb04-50.pdf.*

• Taxable cost of group-term life insurance over $50,000 included in box 1. See *Group-term life insurance* on page 6.

• Cost of accident and health insurance premiums for 2% or more shareholder-employees paid by an S corporation, but only if not excludable under section 3121(a)(2)(B).

• Employee and nonexcludable employer contributions to an MSA or HSA. See *Archer MSA* on page 4 and *Health Savings Account (HSA)* on page 6.

• Employee contributions to a SIMPLE retirement account. See *SIMPLE retirement account* on page 7.

• Adoption benefits. See *Adoption benefits* on page 4.

Box 4—Social security tax withheld. Show the total employee social security tax (not your share) withheld, including social security tax on tips. Do not reduce this amount by any advance EIC payments made to the employee. For 2006, the amount should not exceed $5,840.40 ($94,200 × 6.2%). Include only taxes withheld (or paid by you for the employee) for 2006 wages and tips. If you paid your employee's share, see *Employee's taxes paid by employer* on page 6.

Box 5—Medicare wages and tips. The wages and tips subject to Medicare tax are the same as those subject to social security tax (boxes 3 and 7) except that there is no wage base limit for Medicare tax. Enter the total Medicare wages and tips in box 5. Be sure to enter tips that the employee reported even if you did not have enough employee funds to collect the Medicare tax for those tips. See *Box 3—Social security wages* above for payments to report in this box. If you paid your employee's share of taxes, see *Employee's taxes paid by employer* on page 6.

If you are a federal, state, or local agency with employees paying only the 1.45% Medicare tax, enter the Medicare wages in this box. See *Government employers* on page 6.

Example of how to report social security and Medicare wages. You paid your employee $140,000 in wages. Enter in box 3 (social security wages) 94200.00 but enter in box 5 (Medicare wages and tips) 140000.00. There is no limit on the amount reported in box 5. If the amount of wages paid was $94,200 or less, the amounts entered in boxes 3 and 5 would be the same.

Box 6—Medicare tax withheld. Enter the total employee Medicare tax (not your share) withheld. Include only tax withheld for 2006 wages and tips. Do not reduce this amount by any advance EIC payments made to the employee. If you paid your employee's share of the taxes, see *Employee's taxes paid by employer* on page 6.

Box 7—Social security tips. Show the tips that the employee reported to you even if you did not have enough employee funds to collect the social security tax for the tips. **The total of boxes 3 and 7 should not be more than $94,200** (the maximum social security wage base for 2006). Report all tips in box 1 along with wages and other compensation. Include any tips reported in box 7 in box 5 also.

Box 8—Allocated tips. If you are a large food or beverage establishment, show the tips allocated to the employee. See the Instructions for Form 8027, Employer's Annual Information Return of Tip Income and Allocated Tips. **Do not include this amount in boxes 1, 3, 5, or 7.**

Box 9—Advance EIC payment. Show the total paid to the employee as advance earned income credit (EIC) payments.

Box 10—Dependent care benefits. Show the total dependent care benefits under a dependent care assistance program (section 129) paid or incurred by you for your employee. Include the fair market value (FMV) of employer-provided or employer-sponsored day-care facilities and amounts paid or incurred for dependent care assistance in a section 125 (cafeteria) plan. Report all

-10-

amounts paid or incurred (regardless of any employee forfeitures), including those in excess of the $5,000 exclusion. This may include (a) the FMV of benefits provided in kind by the employer, (b) an amount paid directly to a day-care facility by the employer or reimbursed to the employee to subsidize the benefit, or (c) benefits from the pre-tax contributions made by the employee to a section 125 dependent care flexible spending account. Include any amounts over $5,000 in boxes 1, 3, and 5. For more information, see Pub. 15-B.

TIP *An employer that amends its cafeteria plan to provide a grace period for dependent care assistance may continue to rely on Notice 89-111, by reporting in Box 10 of Form W-2 the salary reduction amount elected by the employee for the year for dependent care assistance (plus any employer matching contributions attributable to dependent care).*

Box 11—Nonqualified plans. The purpose of box 11 is for the SSA to determine if any part of the amount reported in box 1 or boxes 3 and/or 5 was earned in a prior year. The SSA uses this information to verify that they have properly applied the social security earnings test and paid the correct amount of benefits.

TIP *Reporting in box 11 is unaffected by the changes made by the American Jobs Creation Act of 2004.*

Show **distributions** to an employee from a nonqualified plan or a **nongovernmental** section 457(b) plan. Also report these distributions in box 1. **Make only one entry in this box.** Distributions from governmental section 457(b) plans must be reported on Form 1099-R, Distributions From Pensions, Annuities, Retirement or Profit-Sharing Plans, IRAs, Insurance Contracts, etc., not in box 1 of Form W-2.

If you did not make distributions this year, show deferrals (plus earnings) under a nonqualified or any section 457(b) plan that became taxable for social security and Medicare taxes during the year (but were for prior year services) because the deferred amounts were no longer subject to a substantial risk of forfeiture. Also report these amounts in boxes 3 (up to the social security wage base) and box 5. **Do not report in box 11 deferrals that are included in boxes 3 and/or 5 and that are for current year services (such as those that have no risk of forfeiture).**

 If you made distributions and are also reporting any deferrals in box 3 and/or 5, do not complete box 11. See Pub. 957, Reporting Back Pay and Special Wage Payments to the Social Security Administration, and Form SSA-131, Employer Report of Special Wage Payments, for instructions on reporting these and other kinds of compensation earned in prior years. However, do not file Form SSA-131 if this situation applies but the employee will not be age 62 or older by the end of that year.

Unlike qualified plans, nonqualified deferred compensation plans do not meet the qualification requirements for tax-favored status. Nonqualified plans include those arrangements traditionally viewed as deferring the receipt of current compensation. Accordingly, welfare benefit plans, stock option plans, and plans providing dismissal pay, termination pay, or early retirement pay are not nonqualified plans.

Report distributions from nonqualified or section 457 plans to beneficiaries of deceased employees on Form 1099-R, not on Form W-2.

Military employers must report military retirement payments on Form 1099-R.

TIP *Do not report special wage payments, such as accumulated sick pay or vacation pay, in box 11. For more information on reporting special wage payments, see Pub. 957.*

Box 12—Codes. Complete and code this box for all items described below. Note that the codes do not relate to where they should be entered for boxes 12a-12d on Form W-2. For example, if you are only required to report code D in box 12, you can enter code **D** and the amount in **box 12a** of Form W-2. Do not report in box 12 any items that are not listed as codes **A–BB**. Also, do not report in box 12 section 414(h)(2) contributions (relating to certain state or local government plans). Instead, use box 14 for these items and any other information that you wish to give to your employee. For example, union dues and uniform payments may be reported in box 14.

TIP *On Copy A (Form W-2), do not enter more than four items in box 12. If more than four items need to be reported in box 12, use a separate Form W-2 to report the additional items (but enter no more than four items on each Copy A (Form W-2)). On all other copies of Form W-2 (Copies B, C, etc.), you may enter more than four items in box 12 when using an approved substitute Form W-2. See* Multiple forms *on page 9.*

Use the IRS code designated below for the item that you are entering, followed by the dollar amount for that item. Even if only one item is entered, you must use the IRS code designated for that item. Enter the code using a capital letter. Leave at least one space blank after the code, and enter the dollar amount on the same line. Use decimal points but not dollar signs or commas. For example, if you are reporting $5,300.00 in elective deferrals to a section 401(k) plan, the entry would be **D 5300.00** (not A 5300.00 even though it is the first or only entry in this box). **Report the IRS code to the left of the vertical line in boxes 12a-d and money amount to the right of the vertical line.**

See the *Form W-2 Reference Guide for Box 12 Codes* on page 16. See also the detailed instructions below for each code.

Code A—Uncollected social security or RRTA tax on tips. Show the employee social security or Railroad Retirement Tax Act (RRTA) tax on all of the employee's tips that you could not collect because the employee did not have enough funds from which to deduct it. Do not include this amount in box 4.

Code B—Uncollected Medicare tax on tips. Show the employee Medicare tax or RRTA Medicare tax on tips that you could not collect because the employee did not have enough funds from which to deduct it. Do not include this amount in box 6.

Code C—Taxable cost of group-term life insurance over $50,000. Show the taxable cost of group-term life insurance coverage over $50,000 provided to your employee (including a former employee). See *Group-term life insurance* on page 6. Also include this amount in boxes 1, 3 (up to the social security wage base), and 5.

Codes D through H, S, Y, AA, and BB. Use these codes to show elective deferrals and designated Roth contributions made to the plans listed. Do not report amounts for other types of plans. See below for an example of reporting elective deferrals to a section 401(k) plan.

The amount reported as elective deferrals and designated Roth contributions is only the part of the employee's salary (or other compensation) that he or she did not receive because of the deferrals or designated Roth contributions. Only elective deferrals and designated Roth contributions should be reported in box 12 for all coded plans; except, when using code **G** for section 457(b) plans, include both elective and nonelective deferrals.

-11-

For employees who were 50 years of age or older at any time during the year and made elective deferral and/or designated Roth "catch-up" contributions, report the elective deferrals and the elective deferral "catch-up" contributions as a **single sum** in box 12 using the appropriate code, and the designated Roth contributions and designated Roth "catch-up" contributions as a **single sum** in box 12 using the appropriate code.

TIP *If any elective deferrals, salary reduction amounts, or nonelective contributions to a section 457(b) plan during the year are makeup amounts under the Uniformed Services Employment and Reemployment Rights Act of 1994 (USERRA) for a prior year, you must enter the prior year contributions separately. Beginning with the earliest year, enter the code, the year, and the amount. For example, elective deferrals of $2,250 for 2004 and $1,250 for 2005 under USERRA to a section 401(k) plan are reported in box 12 as follows:*

D 04 2250.00, D 05 1250.00. The 2006 contribution of $7,000 does not require a year designation; enter it as D 7000.00. Report the code (and year for prior year USERRA contributions) to the left of the vertical line in boxes 12a-d.

The following are not elective deferrals and may be reported in box 14, but not in box 12:
- Nonelective employer contributions made on behalf of an employee.
- After-tax contributions that are not designated Roth contributions, such as voluntary contributions to a pension plan that are deducted from an employee's pay. See the instructions below in codes **AA** and **BB** for reporting designated Roth contributions.
- Required employee contributions.
- Employer matching contributions.

Code D—Elective deferrals to a section 401(k) cash or deferred arrangement (plan). Also show deferrals under a SIMPLE retirement account that is part of a section 401(k) arrangement.

Example of reporting elective deferrals and designated Roth contributions to a section 401(k) plan. For 2006, Employee A (age 45) elected to defer $15,500 to a section 401(k) plan, made a designated Roth contribution of $1,000 to the plan, and made a voluntary (non-Roth) after-tax contribution of $600. In addition, the employer, on A's behalf, made a qualified nonelective contribution of $2,000 to the plan and a nonelective profit-sharing employer contribution of $3,000.

The total elective deferral of $15,500 is reported in box 12 with code **D** (D 15500.00) and the designated Roth contribution is reported in box 12 with code **AA** (AA 1000.00). Even though the 2006 limit for elective deferrals and designated Roth contributions is $15,000, the employer must separately report the total amount of $15,500 and $1,000 in box 12. The excess is not reported in box 1. The return of excess salary deferrals and excess designated Roth contributions, including earnings on both, is reported on Form 1099-R.

The $600 voluntary after-tax contribution may be reported in box 14 (this is optional) but not in box 12. The $2,000 nonelective contribution and the $3,000 nonelective profit-sharing employer contribution are not required to be reported on Form W-2, but may be reported in box 14.

Check the "Retirement plan" box in box 13.

Code E—Elective deferrals under a section 403(b) salary reduction agreement.

Code F—Elective deferrals under a section 408(k)(6) salary reduction SEP.

Code G—Elective deferrals and employer contributions (including nonelective deferrals) to any governmental or nongovernmental section 457(b) deferred compensation plan. Do not report either section 457(b) or section 457(f) amounts that are subject to a substantial risk of forfeiture.

Code H—Elective deferrals to a section 501(c)(18)(D) tax-exempt organization plan. Be sure to include this amount in box 1 as wages. The employee will deduct the amount on his or her Form 1040.

Code J—Nontaxable sick pay. Show any sick pay that was paid by a third-party and was **not** includible in income (and **not** shown in boxes 1, 3, and 5) because the employee contributed to the sick pay plan.

Code K—20% excise tax on excess golden parachute payments. If you made excess "golden parachute" payments to certain key corporate employees, report the 20% excise tax on these payments. If the excess payments are considered to be wages, report the 20% excise tax withheld as income tax withheld in box 2.

Code L—Substantiated employee business expense reimbursements. Use this code only if you reimbursed your employee for employee business expenses using a per diem or mileage allowance and the amount that you reimbursed exceeds the amount treated as substantiated under IRS rules. See *Employee business expense reimbursements* on page 5.

Report in box 12 **only** the amount treated as substantiated (such as the nontaxable part). In boxes 1, 3 (up to the social security wage base), and 5, include the part of the reimbursement that is more than the amount treated as substantiated.

Code M—Uncollected social security or RRTA tax on taxable cost of group-term life insurance over $50,000 (for former employees). If you provided your former employees (including retirees) more than $50,000 of group-term life insurance coverage for periods during which an employment relationship no longer exists, enter the amount of uncollected social security or RRTA tax on the coverage in box 12. Also see *Group-term life insurance* on page 6.

Code N—Uncollected Medicare tax on taxable cost of group-term life insurance over $50,000 (for former employees). If you provided your former employees (including retirees) more than $50,000 of group-term life insurance coverage for periods during which an employment relationship no longer exists, enter the amount of uncollected Medicare tax or RRTA Medicare tax on the coverage in box 12. Also see *Group-term life insurance* on page 6.

Code P—Excludable moving expense reimbursements paid directly to employee. Show the total moving expense reimbursements that you paid directly to your employee for qualified (deductible) moving expenses. See *Moving expenses* on page 6.

Code Q—Nontaxable combat pay. If you are a military employer, report any nontaxable combat pay in box 12.

Code R—Employer contributions to an Archer MSA. Show any employer contributions to an Archer MSA. See *Archer MSA* on page 4.

Code S—Employee salary reduction contributions under a section 408(p) SIMPLE. Show deferrals under a section 408(p) salary reduction SIMPLE retirement account. However, if the SIMPLE is part of a section 401(k) arrangement, use code **D**. If you are reporting prior year contributions under USERRA, see the *TIP* above *Code D* above.

Code T—Adoption benefit. Show the total that you paid or reimbursed for qualified adoption expenses furnished to your employee under an adoption assistance

-12-

program. Also include adoption benefits paid or reimbursed from the pre-tax contributions made by the employee to a section 125 (cafeteria) plan. However, do not include adoption benefits forfeited from a section 125 (cafeteria) plan. Report all amounts including those in excess of the $10,960 exclusion.

Code V—Income from the exercise of nonstatutory stock option(s). Show the spread (that is, the fair market value of stock over the exercise price of option(s) granted to your employee with respect to that stock) from your employee's (or former employee's) exercise of nonstatutory stock option(s). Include this amount in boxes 1, 3 (up to the social security wage base), and 5.

This reporting requirement does not apply to the exercise of a statutory stock option, or the sale or disposition of stock acquired pursuant to the exercise of a statutory stock option. For more information concerning stock options, see Pub. 15-B.

Code W—Employer contributions to a Health Savings Account (HSA). Show any employer contributions (including amounts the employee elected to contribute using a section 125 (cafeteria) plan) to a Health Savings Account (HSA). See *Health Savings Account (HSA)* on page 6.

Code Y—Deferrals under a section 409A nonqualified deferred compensation plan. Include current year deferrals under a section 409A nonqualified deferred compensation plan. Any earnings during the year on current year and prior year deferrals must also be reported here. See *Nonqualified deferred compensation plans* on page 7.

Code Z—Income under section 409A on a nonqualified deferred compensation plan. Show any income under section 409A on a nonqualified deferred compensation plan that was included in box 1. This income is also subject to an additional tax reported on the employee's Form 1040. See *Nonqualified deferred compensation plans* on page 7.

Code AA—Designated Roth contributions to a section 401(k) plan. Use this code to report designated Roth contributions to a section 401(k) plan. Do not use this code to report elective deferrals under code **D**. See *Designated Roth contributions* on page 5.

Code BB—Designated Roth contributions under a section 403(b) salary reduction agreement. Use this code to report designated Roth contributions under a section 403(b) salary reduction agreement. Do not use this code to report elective deferrals under code **E**. See *Designated Roth contributions* on page 5.

Box 13—Checkboxes. Check all boxes that apply.
• *Statutory employee.* Check this box for statutory employees whose earnings are subject to social security and Medicare taxes but not subject to federal income tax withholding. Do not check this box for common-law employees. There are workers who are independent contractors under the common-law rules but are treated by statute as employees. They are called statutory employees.

1. A driver who distributes beverages (other than milk), or meat, vegetable, fruit, or bakery products; or who picks up and delivers laundry or dry cleaning if the driver is your agent or is paid on commission.

2. A full-time life insurance sales agent whose principal business activity is selling life insurance or annuity contracts, or both, primarily for one life insurance company.

3. An individual who works at home on materials or goods that you supply and that must be returned to you or to a person you name if you also furnish specifications for the work to be done.

4. A full-time traveling or city salesperson who works on your behalf and turns in orders to you from wholesalers,

retailers, contractors, or operators of hotels, restaurants, or other similar establishments. The goods sold must be merchandise for resale or supplies for use in the buyer's business operation. The work performed for you must be the salesperson's principal business activity.

For details on statutory employees and common-law employees, see section 1 in Pub. 15-A.
• *Retirement plan.* Check this box if the employee was an "active participant" (for any part of the year) in any of the following:

1. A qualified pension, profit-sharing, or stock-bonus plan described in section 401(a) (including a 401(k) plan).

2. An annuity plan described in section 403(a).

3. An annuity contract or custodial account described in section 403(b).

4. A simplified employee pension (SEP) plan described in section 408(k).

5. A SIMPLE retirement account described in section 408(p).

6. A trust described in section 501(c)(18).

7. A plan for federal, state, or local government employees or by an agency or instrumentality thereof (other than a section 457(b) plan).

Generally, an employee is an **active participant** if covered by (a) a defined benefit plan for any tax year that he or she is eligible to participate or (b) a defined contribution plan (for example, a section 401(k) plan) for any tax year that employer or employee contributions (or forfeitures) are added to his or her account. For additional information on employees who are eligible to participate in a plan, contact your plan administrator. For details on the active participant rules, see Notice 87-16, 1987-1 C.B. 446, Notice 98-49, 1998-2 C.B. 365, section 219(g)(5), and Pub. 590, Individual Retirement Arrangements (IRAs). You can find Notice 98-49 on page 5 of Internal Revenue Bulletin 1998-38 at *www.irs.gov/pub/irs-irbs/irb98-38.pdf.*

 Do not check this box for contributions made to a nonqualified or section 457(b) plan.

• *Third-party sick pay.* Check this box **only** if you are a third-party sick pay payer filing a Form W-2 for an insured's employee or are an employer reporting sick pay payments made by a third party. See *Sick Pay Reporting* in section 6 of Pub. 15-A.

Box 14—Other. The lease value of a vehicle provided to your employee and reported in box 1 must be reported here or on a separate statement to your employee. You may also use this box for any other information that you want to give to your employee. **Please label each item.** Examples include state disability insurance taxes withheld, union dues, uniform payments, health insurance premiums deducted, nontaxable income, educational assistance payments, or a member of the clergy's parsonage allowance and utilities. In addition, you may enter the following contributions to a pension plan: (a) nonelective employer contributions made on behalf of an employee, (b) voluntary after-tax contributions (but not designated Roth contributions) that are deducted from an employee's pay, (c) required employee contributions, and (d) employer matching contributions.

If you are reporting prior year contributions under USERRA (see the *TIP* above *Code D* on page 12 and *USERRA makeup amounts to a pension plan* on page 7), you may report in box 14 makeup amounts for nonelective employer contributions, voluntary after-tax contributions, required employee contributions, and employer matching contributions. Report such amounts separately for each year. Railroad employers, see page 7.

-13-

Boxes 15 through 20—State and local income tax information. Use these boxes to report state and local income tax information. Enter the two-letter abbreviation for the name of the state. The employer's state ID numbers are assigned by the individual states. The state and local information boxes can be used to report wages and taxes for two states and two localities. Keep each state's and locality's information separated by the broken line. If you need to report information for more than two states or localities, prepare a second Form W-2. See *Multiple forms* on page 9. Contact your state or locality for specific reporting information.

Specific Instructions for Form W-3

How to complete Form W-3. The instructions under *How to complete Form W-2* on page 8 generally apply to Form W-3. **Darkly type all entries, if possible.**

 Amounts reported on related employment tax forms (for example, Form W-2, Form 941, Form 943, or Form 944) should agree with the amounts reported on Form W-3. If there are differences, you may be contacted by the IRS and SSA. You should retain a reconciliation for future reference. See Reconciling Forms W-2, W-3, 941, 943, 944, CT-1, and Schedule H (Form 1040) *on page 15.*

Box a—Control number. This is an optional box that you may use for numbering the whole transmittal. **Make certain that entries do not cross over into the form identification number box (33333).**

Box b—Kind of Payer. Check the box that applies to you. Check **only one box** unless the second, checked box is "Third-party sick pay." **If you have more than one type of Form W-2, send each type** (except "Third-party sick pay") **with a separate Form W-3.** (The "Third-party sick pay" indicator box does not designate a separate kind of payer.)

941. Check this box if you file Form 941, Employer's Quarterly Federal Tax Return, and no other category (except "Third-party sick pay") applies. A church or church organization should check this box even if it is not required to file Form 941 or Form 944.

Military. Check this box if you are a **military employer** sending Forms W-2 for members of the uniformed services.

943. Check this box if you are an **agricultural employer** and file Form 943, Employer's Annual Federal Tax Return for Agricultural Employees, and you are sending Forms W-2 for agricultural employees. For nonagricultural employees, send their Forms W-2 with a separate Form W-3, checking the appropriate box.

944. Check this box if you file Form 944, Employer's Annual Federal Tax Return, and no other category (except "Third-party sick pay") applies.

CT-1. Check this box if you are a **railroad employer** sending Forms W-2 for employees covered under the Railroad Retirement Tax Act (RRTA). **Do not show employee RRTA tax in boxes 3 through 7.** These boxes are only for social security and Medicare information. If you also have employees who are subject to social security and Medicare taxes, send that group's Forms W-2 with a separate Form W-3 and check the "941" box on that Form W-3.

Hshld. emp. Check this box if you are a **household employer** sending Forms W-2 for household employees and you did not include the household employee's taxes on Form 941, Form 944, or Form 943.

Medicare govt. emp. Check this box if you are a U.S., state, or local agency filing Forms W-2 for employees subject only to the 1.45% Medicare tax. See *Government employers* on page 6.

Third-party sick pay. Check this box **and** another box such as the "941" box if you are a third-party sick pay payer (or are reporting sick pay payments made by a third party) filing Forms W-2 with the "Third-party sick pay" checkbox in box 13 checked. **File a single Form W-3 for the regular and "Third-party sick pay" Forms W-2.** See *941* above.

Box c—Total number of Forms W-2. Show the number of **completed** individual Forms W-2 that you are transmitting with this Form W-3. Do not count "Void" Forms W-2.

Box d—Establishment number. You may use this box to identify separate establishments in your business. You may file a separate Form W-3, with Forms W-2, for each establishment even if they all have the same EIN; or you may use a single Form W-3 for all Forms W-2 of the same type.

Box e—Employer identification number (EIN). If you received a preprinted Form W-3 from the IRS with Pub. 393, Federal Employment Tax Forms, or Pub. 2184, Alternative Ways To Get Employment Tax Forms and Instructions, verify that your employer identification number (EIN) is correct. Make any necessary corrections on the form.

If you did not receive a form with a preprinted EIN, enter the nine-digit EIN assigned to you by the IRS. The number should be the same as shown on your Form 941, Form 943, Form 944, Form CT-1, or Schedule H (Form 1040) and in the following format: 00-0000000. **Do not use a prior owner's EIN.** See *Box h—Other EIN used this year* below.

If you do not have an EIN when filing your Form W-3, enter "Applied For" in box e, not your social security number, and see *Box b—Employer identification number (EIN)* on page 9.

Box f—Employer's name. If you are not using a preprinted Form W-3, enter the same name as shown on your Form 941, Form 943, Form 944, or Form CT-1. Make any necessary corrections on your preprinted Form W-3.

Box g—Employer's address and ZIP code. If you are not using a preprinted Form W-3, enter your address. Make any necessary corrections on your preprinted Form W-3.

Box h—Other EIN used this year. If you have used an EIN (including a prior owner's EIN) on Form 941, Form 943, Form 944, or Form CT-1 submitted for 2006 that is different from the EIN reported on Form W-3 in box e, enter the other EIN used. Agents generally report the employer's EIN in box h. See *Agent reporting* on page 4.

Contact person, telephone number, fax number, and email address. Please enter this information for use by the SSA if any questions arise during processing.

 The amounts to enter in boxes 1 through 19, described below, are totals from only the Forms W-2 that you are sending with this Form W-3.

Boxes 1 through 10. Enter the totals reported in boxes 1 through 10 on the Forms W-2.

Box 11—Nonqualified plans. Enter the total reported in box 11 on Forms W-2.

Box 12—Deferred compensation. Enter one total of all amounts reported with codes **D–H, S, Y, AA, and BB** in box 12 on Forms W-2. Do not enter a code.

Box 13—For third-party sick pay use only. Third-party payers of sick pay (or employers using the optional rule for Form W-2 described in section 6 of Pub. 15-A) filing third-party sick pay recap Forms W-2 and W-3 must enter "Third-Party Sick Pay Recap" in this box.

Box 14—Income tax withheld by payer of third-party sick pay. Complete this box only if you are the employer and have employees who had income tax withheld on third-party payments of sick pay. Show the total income tax withheld by third-party payers on payments to all of your

-14-

employees. Although this tax is included in the box 2 total, it must be separately shown here.

Box 15—State/Employer's state ID number. Enter the two-letter abbreviation for the name of the state being reported on Form(s) W-2. Also enter your state-assigned ID number. If the Forms W-2 being submitted with this Form W-3 contain wage and income tax information from more than one state, enter an "X" under "State" and do not enter any state ID number.

Boxes 16–19. Enter the total of state/local wages and income tax shown in their corresponding boxes on the Forms W-2 included with this Form W-3. If the Forms W-2 show amounts from more than one state or locality, report them as one sum in the appropriate box on Form W-3. **Please verify that the amount reported in each box is an accurate total of the Forms W-2.**

Reconciling Forms W-2, W-3, 941, 943, 944, CT-1, and Schedule H (Form 1040)

Reconcile the amounts shown in boxes 2, 3, 5, 7, and 9 from **all** 2006 Forms W-3 with their respective amounts from the 2006 **yearly** totals from the quarterly Forms 941, or Form 943, Form 944, Form CT-1 (box 2 only), and Schedule H (Form 1040). When there are discrepancies between amounts reported on Forms W-2 and W-3 filed with the SSA and on Form 941, Form 943, Form 944, Form CT-1, or Schedule H (Form 1040) filed with the IRS, we must contact you to resolve the discrepancies. **To help reduce discrepancies on Forms W-2:**

● Report bonuses as wages **and** as social security and Medicare wages on Forms W-2 and Form 941/943/944/ Schedule H (Form 1040).
● Report both social security and Medicare wages and taxes separately on Forms W-2, W-3, and 941/943/944/ Schedule H (Form 1040).
● Report social security taxes withheld on Form W-2 in box 4, not in box 3.
● Report Medicare taxes withheld on Form W-2 in box 6, not in box 5.

● Make sure that the social security wage amount for each employee does not exceed the annual social security wage base limit ($94,200 for 2006).
● Do not report noncash wages that are not subject to social security or Medicare taxes as social security or Medicare wages.
● If you use an EIN on any quarterly Form 941 for the year (or annual Form 943/944/CT-1/Schedule H (Form 1040)) that is different from the EIN reported in box e on Form W-3, enter the other EIN in box h on Form W-3.

To reduce the discrepancies between amounts reported on Forms W-2, W-3, and Form 941/943/944/ CT-1/Schedule H (Form 1040):
● Be sure that the amounts on Form W-3 are the total amounts from Forms W-2.
● Reconcile Form W-3 with your four quarterly Forms 941 (or annual Form 943/944/CT-1/Schedule H (Form 1040)) by comparing amounts reported for:

1. Income tax withholding (box 2).
2. Social security wages, Medicare wages and tips, and social security tips (boxes 3, 5, and 7). Form W-3 should include Form 941 or Form 943/Form 944/Schedule H (Form 1040) adjustments only for the current year. If the Form 941, Form 943, or Form 944 adjustments include amounts for a prior year, do not report those prior year adjustments on the current year Forms W-2 and W-3.
3. Social security and Medicare taxes (boxes 4 and 6). The amounts shown on the four quarterly Forms 941 (or annual Form 943/Form 944/Schedule H (Form 1040)), including current year adjustments, should be approximately twice the amounts shown on Form W-3.
4. Advance EIC payment (box 9).

Amounts reported on Forms W-2, W-3, and 941/943/944/ CT-1/Schedule H (Form 1040) may not match for valid reasons. If they do not match, you should determine that the reasons are valid. **Keep your reconciliation in case there are inquiries from the IRS or the SSA.**

-15-

Form W-2 Reference Guide for Box 12 Codes (See the box 12 instructions.)

A	Uncollected social security or RRTA tax on tips	**H**	Elective deferrals to a section 501(c)(18)(D) tax-exempt organization plan	**R**	Employer contributions to an Archer MSA
B	Uncollected Medicare tax on tips	**J**	Nontaxable sick pay	**S**	Employee salary reduction contributions under a section 408(p) SIMPLE
C	Taxable cost of group-term life insurance over $50,000	**K**	20% excise tax on excess golden parachute payments		
				T	Adoption benefits
D	Elective deferrals to a section 401(k) cash or deferred arrangement (including a SIMPLE 401(k) arrangement)	**L**	Substantiated employee business expense reimbursements (federal rate)	**V**	Income from exercise of nonstatutory stock option(s)
				W	Employer contributions to an employee's Health Savings Account (HSA)
E	Elective deferrals under a section 403(b) salary reduction agreement	**M**	Uncollected social security or RRTA tax on taxable cost of group-term life (for former employees)	**Y**	Deferrals under a section 409A nonqualified deferred compensation plan
F	Elective deferrals under a section 408(k)(6) salary reduction SEP	**N**	Uncollected Medicare tax on taxable cost of group-term life insurance over $50,000 (for former employees)	**Z**	Income under section 409A on a nonqualified deferred compensation plan
G	Elective deferrals and employer contributions (including nonelective deferrals) to a section 457(b) deferred compensation plan (state and local government and tax-exempt employers)	**P**	Excludable moving expense reimbursements paid directly to employee	**AA**	Designated Roth contributions to a section 401(k) plan
		Q	Nontaxable combat pay	**BB**	Designated Roth contributions under a section 403(b) salary reduction agreement

Index

-16-

DO NOT CUT, FOLD, OR STAPLE THIS FORM

a Tax year/Form corrected ___/ W-2 ___	44444	For Official Use Only ▶ OMB No. 1545-0008	
b Employee's correct SSN		c Corrected name (if checked enter correct name in **box e** and **complete box i**) ☐	d Employer's Federal EIN

e Employee's first name and initial	Last name	g Employer's name, address, and ZIP code

f Employee's address and ZIP code

Complete boxes h and/or i only if incorrect on last form filed. ▶	h Employee's **incorrect** SSN	i Employee's name (as **incorrectly** shown on previous form)

Note: Only complete money fields that are being corrected (except MQGE).

Previously reported	Correct information	Previously reported	Correct information
1 Wages, tips, other compensation	1 Wages, tips, other compensation	2 Federal income tax withheld	2 Federal income tax withheld
3 Social security wages	3 Social security wages	4 Social security tax withheld	4 Social security tax withheld
5 Medicare wages and tips	5 Medicare wages and tips	6 Medicare tax withheld	6 Medicare tax withheld
7 Social security tips	7 Social security tips	8 Allocated tips	8 Allocated tips
9 Advance EIC payment	9 Advance EIC payment	10 Dependent care benefits	10 Dependent care benefits
11 Nonqualified plans	11 Nonqualified plans	12a See instructions for box 12	12a See instructions for box 12
13 Statutory employee Retirement plan Third-party sick pay	13 Statutory employee Retirement plan Third-party sick pay	12b	12b
14 Other (see instructions)	14 Other (see instructions)	12c	12c
		12d	12d

State Correction Information

Previously reported	Correct information	Previously reported	Correct information
15 State / Employer's state ID number	15 State / Employer's state ID number	15 State / Employer's state ID number	15 State / Employer's state ID number
16 State wages, tips, etc.	16 State wages, tips, etc.	16 State wages, tips, etc.	16 State wages, tips, etc.
17 State income tax	17 State income tax	17 State income tax	17 State income tax

Locality Correction Information

18 Local wages, tips, etc.	18 Local wages, tips, etc.	18 Local wages, tips, etc.	18 Local wages, tips, etc.
19 Local income tax	19 Local income tax	19 Local income tax	19 Local income tax
20 Locality name	20 Locality name	20 Locality name	20 Locality name

For Privacy Act and Paperwork Reduction Act Notice, see separate instructions.

Form **W-2c** (Rev. 12-2002) **Corrected Wage and Tax Statement** Cat. No. 61437D

Copy A—For Social Security Administration
Department of the Treasury
Internal Revenue Service

Notice to Employee

This is a corrected **Form W-2,** Wage and Tax Statement, (or Form W-2AS, W-2CM, W-2GU, or W-2VI) for the tax year shown in box a. If you have filed an income tax return for the year shown, you may have to file an amended return. Compare amounts on this form with those reported on your income tax return. If the corrected amounts change your U.S. income tax, file **Form 1040X,** Amended U.S. Individual Income Tax Return, with Copy B of this Form W-2c to amend the return you already filed.

If you have not filed your return for the year shown in box a, attach Copy B of the original Form W-2 you received from your employer and Copy B of this Form W-2c to your return when you file it.

For more information, contact your nearest Internal Revenue Service office. Employees in American Samoa, Commonwealth of the Northern Mariana Islands, Guam, or the U.S. Virgin Islands should contact their local taxing authority for more information.

Employers, Please Note:

Specific information needed to complete Form W-2c is given in the separate **Instructions for Forms W-2c and W-3c** (December 2002). You can order those instructions and additional forms by calling 1-800-TAX-FORM (1-800-829-3676). You can also get forms and instructions from the IRS Web Site at **www.irs.gov.**

DO NOT CUT, FOLD OR STAPLE

| a Tax year/Form corrected .... / W-___ | 55555 | For Official Use Only ▶ OMB No. 1545-0008 | |

b Employer's name, address, and ZIP code

c Kind of Payer ▶
941/941-SS ☐ Military ☐ 943 ☐ Sec. 218 ☐
CT-1 ☐ Hshld. emp. ☐ Medicare govt. emp. ☐ Third-party sick pay ☐

| **d** Number of Forms W-2c | **e** Employer's Federal EIN | **f** Establishment number | **g** Employer's state ID number |
| Complete boxes h, i, or j **only** if incorrect on last form filed. | **h** Employer's **incorrect** Federal EIN | **i** **Incorrect** establishment number | **j** Employer's **incorrect** state ID number |

Total of amounts previously reported as shown on enclosed Forms W-2c.	Total of corrected amounts as shown on enclosed Forms W-2c.	Total of amounts previously reported as shown on enclosed Forms W-2c.	Total of corrected amounts as shown on enclosed Forms W-2c.
1 Wages, tips, other compensation	1 Wages, tips, other compensation	2 Federal income tax withheld	2 Federal income tax withheld
3 Social security wages	3 Social security wages	4 Social security tax withheld	4 Social security tax withheld
5 Medicare wages and tips	5 Medicare wages and tips	6 Medicare tax withheld	6 Medicare tax withheld
7 Social security tips	7 Social security tips	8 Allocated tips	8 Allocated tips
9 Advance EIC payments	9 Advance EIC payments	10 Dependent care benefits	10 Dependent care benefits
11 Nonqualified plans	11 Nonqualified plans	12a-d (Coded items)	12a-d (Coded items)
14 Inc. tax W/H by 3rd party sick pay payer	14 Inc. tax W/H by 3rd party sick pay payer		
16 State wages, tips, etc.	16 State wages, tips, etc.	17 State income tax	17 State income tax
18 Local wages, tips, etc.	18 Local wages, tips, etc.	19 Local income tax	19 Local income tax

Explain decreases here:

Has an adjustment been made on an employment tax return filed with the Internal Revenue Service? ☐ Yes ☐ No
If "Yes," give date the return was filed ▶

Under penalties of perjury, I declare that I have examined this return, including accompanying documents, and, to the best of my knowledge and belief, it is true, correct, and complete.

Signature ▶   Title ▶   Date ▶

Contact person   Telephone number ( )   For Official Use Only

E-mail address   Fax number ( )

Purpose of Form

Use this form to transmit Copy A of **Form(s) W-2c,** Corrected Wage and Tax Statement (Rev. 12-2002). Make a copy of Form W-3c and keep it with Copy D (For Employer) of Forms W-2c for your records. File Form W-3c even if only one Form W-2c is being filed or if those Forms W-2c are being filed only to correct an employee's name or social security number (SSN). See the separate **Instructions for Forms W-2c and W-3c** (Rev. December 2002) for information on completing this form.

When To File

File this form and Copy A of Form(s) W-2c with the Social Security Administration as soon as possible after you discover an error on Forms W-2, W-2AS, W-2GU, W-2CM, or W-2VI. Also provide Copies B, C, and 2 of Form W-2c to your employees as soon as possible.

Where To File

If you use the U.S. Postal Service, send Forms W-2c and W-3c to the following address:

**Social Security Administration
Data Operations Center
P.O. Box 3333
Wilkes-Barre, PA 18767-3333**

If you use a carrier other than the U.S. Postal Service, send Forms W-2c and W-3c to the following address:

**Social Security Administration
Data Operations Center
Attn: W-2c Process
1150 E. Mountain Drive
Wilkes-Barre, PA 18702-7997**

Form **W-3c** (Rev. 12-2002) **Transmittal of Corrected Wage and Tax Statements** Department of the Treasury Internal Revenue Service
For Privacy Act and Paperwork Reduction Act Notice, see separate instructions. Cat. No. 10164R

Instructions for Forms W-2c and W-3c

(Rev. December 2002)

Department of the Treasury
Internal Revenue Service

Items To Note

New magnetic/electronic reporting requirement. If you are required to file 250 or more Forms W-2c during a calendar year, you must now file them on magnetic media (or electronically) unless the IRS granted you a waiver. You may be charged a penalty if you fail to file on magnetic media (or electronically) when required. See also **Magnetic media/electronic reporting** below.

For purposes of the magnetic media/electronic requirement, only Forms W-2 for the immediate prior year are taken into account. Also, if an employer must file 200 Forms W-2c for the immediate prior year in March and then discovers that another 100 Forms W-2c for the **same year** must be filed in August, only the 100 Forms W-2c that are filed in August must be filed on magnetic media or electronically.

You may request a waiver on **Form 8508,** Request for Waiver From Filing Information Returns Magnetically. Submit Form 8508 to the IRS at least 45 days before you file Forms W-2c. See Form 8508 for filing information.

Revised Forms W-2c and W-3c. We revised **Form W-2c,** Corrected Wage and Tax Statement, to provide boxes for the correction of state and local tax information. We also added other Federal boxes that appear on **Form W-2,** Wage and Tax Statement. As a result, Form W-2c is now printed one per page.

We revised **Form W-3c,** Transmittal of Corrected Wage and Tax Statements, by adding a new box (box 14) "Inc. tax W/H by 3rd party sick pay payer." Use box 14 to correct the amount reported in box 14 of **Form W-3,** Transmittal of Wage and Tax Statements.

Copy A of Form W-2c and Form W-3c are now printed in red dropout ink to enhance their scanning capabilities. After June 30, 2003 **do not** use prior versions of Forms W-2c and W-3c.

Substitute forms. If you are not using the official IRS form to furnish Form W-2c to employees or to file with the SSA, you may use an acceptable substitute form that complies with the rules in **Pub. 1223,** General Rules and Specifications for Substitute Forms W-2c and W-3c. Pub. 1223 is a revenue procedure that explains the requirements for format and content of substitute Forms W-2c and W-3c. **Your substitute forms must comply with the requirements in Pub. 1223.**

General Instructions

Purpose of forms. Use Form W-2c to correct errors on Forms W-2, W-2c, W-2AS, W-2GU, W-2CM, or W-2VI filed with the SSA. Also use Form W-2c to provide corrected Forms W-2, W-2AS, W-2GU, W-2CM, or W-2VI to employees.

Do not use Form W-2c to report back pay. Instead, see **Pub. 957,** Reporting Back Pay and Special Wage Payments to the Social Security Administration, and **Form SSA-131,** Employer Report of Special Wage Payments.

Do not use Form W-2c to correct **Form W-2G,** Certain Gambling Winnings. Instead, see the Instructions for Forms 1099, 1098, 5498, and W-2G.

Use Form W-3c to send Copy A of Form W-2c to the Social Security Administration (SSA). Form W-3c is required to be filed with a single Form W-2c as well as with multiple Forms W-2c. You may file Form W-3c separately if you are simply correcting your EIN on a previously filed Form W-3 or **W-3SS,** Transmittal of Wage and Tax Statements (for Forms W-2AS, W-2GU, W-2CM, and W-2VI).

Where to file Forms W-2c and W-3c. If you use the **U.S. Postal Service,** send Forms W-2c and W-3c to:

   Social Security Administration
   Data Operations Center
   P.O. Box 3333
   Wilkes-Barre, PA 18767-3333.

If you use a **carrier other than the U.S. Postal Service,** send Forms W-2c and W-3c to:

   Social Security Administration
   Data Operations Center
   Attn: W-2c Process
   1150 E. Mountain Drive
   Wilkes-Barre, PA 18702-7997.

TIP *Do not send **Form W-2,** to either of these addresses. Instead, see the **Instructions for Forms W-2 and W-3.***

When to file. File Forms W-2c and W-3c as soon as possible after you discover an error. Also provide Form W-2c to employees as soon as possible.

How to file. You may file Forms W-2c and W-3c on paper. Please type all entries using dark or black ink in **12-point Courier font,** if possible, and make sure all copies are legible. See the **Instructions for Forms W-2 and W-3** for more information.

If any item shows a dollar change and one of the amounts is zero, enter "-0-." Do not leave the box blank.

Magnetic media or electronic reporting. If you are required to file 250 or more Forms W-2c during a calendar year, you must file them on magnetic media or electronically unless the IRS granted you a waiver. See **New magnetic/electronic reporting requirement** above.

To submit Forms W-2c on magnetic media or electronically, contact the Employer Service Liaison Officer (ESLO) for your state. Call 1-800-772-6270 for your ESLO's phone number. Employers in the U.S. Virgin Islands may call 787-766-5574. Employers in American Samoa and Guam may call 510-970-8247.

Specifications for filing Form W-2c on magnetic media or electronically are contained in SSA's **MMREF-2,** Magnetic Media Reporting and Electronic Filing of W-2c Information. You can download MMREF-2 by visiting the SSA Web Site at **www.socialsecurity.gov/employer.** You can also order a copy of MMREF-2 by calling SSA's Employer Reporting Branch at 1-800-772-6270.

If you file fewer than 250 forms W-2c, they are not required to be filed on magnetic media or electronically; however, doing so will enhance the timeliness and accuracy of forms processing.

Cat. No. 25978H

Shipping and mailing. If you have a large number of forms, you may send them in separate packages. Show your name and employer identification number (EIN) on each package. Number them in order (1 of 4, 2 of 4, etc.), and place Form W-3c in package 1. Show the number of packages at the bottom of Form W-3c below the title. You must send Forms W-2c and W-3c by First-Class Mail.

Who may sign Form W-3c. Generally, employers must sign Form W-3c. However, the transmitter or sender (including a service bureau, paying agent, or disbursing agent) may sign Form W-3c for the employer or payer only if the sender:
• Is authorized to sign by an agency agreement (either oral, written, or implied) that is valid under state law and
• Writes "For (name of payer)" next to the signature.

Even though an authorized sender signs for the payer, the payer still has the responsibility for making sure the Form W-3c and attachments are filed correctly and timely. The payer is subject to any penalties that result from not complying with these requirements.

Online Wage Reporting. Using a personal computer and a modem, you can access SSA's Business Services Online (BSO) to electronically report wage data. To obtain information regarding filing wage data electronically with SSA or to access BSO, visit the SSA Web Site at **www.socialsecurity.gov/employer**. Call the SSA at 1-888-772-2970 if you experience problems using any of the services within BSO.

Information available includes magnetic media filing information, some IRS and SSA publications, information on electronic filing, and general topics of interest about annual wage reporting. You can also use BSO to ask questions about wage reporting.

Special Situations

Correcting more than one kind of form. You must use a **separate** Form W-3c for each type of Form W-2 (i.e., W-2, W-2c, W-2AS, W-2GU, W-2CM, or W-2VI) being corrected. You must also use a separate Form W-3c for each kind of payer in box c (unless the second, checked box is the "Third-party sick pay" indicator). If you are correcting more than one kind of form, please group forms of the same kind, and send them in separate groups.

Correcting an employee's name and/or SSN only. If you are correcting only an employee's name and/or SSN, complete Form W-2c through box i, as appropriate. Do not complete boxes 1 through 20. Advise your employee to correct the SSN and/or name on his or her original Form W-2.

If your employee is given a new social security card following an adjustment to his or her resident status that shows a different name or SSN, file a Form W-2c for the most current year only.

To correct an incorrect tax year or EIN on Form W-2, file one Form W-2c showing the incorrect tax year or EIN and reducing the previously-reported money amounts to zero and a second Form W-2c reporting the money amounts (showing zeros in the "Previously reported" columns) in the correct year or with the correct EIN.

Employee's incorrect address on Form W-2. If you filed a Form W-2 with the SSA showing an incorrect address for the employee but all other information on the Form W-2 is correct, **do not** file Form W-2c with the SSA merely to correct the address.

However, if the address was incorrect on the Form W-2 furnished to the employee, **you must do one of the following:**

• Issue a new, corrected Form W-2 to the employee including the new address. Indicate "REISSUED STATEMENT" on the new copies. **Do not send Copy A to the SSA.**
• Issue a Form W-2c to the employee showing the correct address in box f and all other correct information. **Do not send Copy A to the SSA.**
• Mail the Form W-2 with the incorrect address to the employee in an envelope showing the correct address or otherwise deliver it to the employee.

Correcting more than one Form W-2 for an employee. There are two ways to prepare a correction for an employee who received more than one Form W-2 under the **same** employer identification number (EIN) for the tax year. You can: **(a)** consider all the Forms W-2 when determining the amounts to enter on Form W-2c as shown in **Example 1** below, or **(b)** file a single Form W-2c to correct only the incorrect Form W-2 (see **Example 2**). However, state, local, and Federal government employers who are preparing corrections for Medicare Qualified Government Employment (MQGE) employees must also follow the instructions in the **CAUTION** under **Boxes 5 and 6** on page 3.

Example 1. Mary Smith received two Forms W-2 for tax year 2002 under the **same** EIN. One form **incorrectly** reported social security wages of $30,000 and the second correctly reported social security wages of $20,000. A single Form W-2c filed to change the $30,000 to $25,000 (correct amount) would show $50,000 in box 3 under "Previously reported" and $45,000 in box 3 under "Correct information."

Example 2. The facts are the same as in the first example. However, you may choose to correct only the incorrect Form W-2 by filing a Form W-2c that shows $30,000 in box 3 under "Previously reported" and $25,000 in box 3 under "Correct information."

Repayments. If an employee repays you for wages received in error in a prior year, file Form W-2c to correct only social security and Medicare wages and tax. **Do not** correct wages reported in box 1 for the amount paid in error. Report an adjustment on **Form 941,** Employer's Quarterly Federal Tax Return (or 941-SS, 943, or CT-1) for the period during which the repayment was made to recover the social security and Medicare taxes. Instead of making an adjustment on Form 941 (or 941-SS, 943, or CT-1) you may file a claim for these taxes using **Form 843,** Claim for Refund and Request for Abatement. You may not make an adjustment for income tax withholding because the wages were paid in a prior year.

TIP *Please tell your employee that the wages paid in error in a prior year remain taxable to him or her for that year. This is because the employee received and had use of those funds during that year. The employee is not entitled to file an amended return (**Form 1040X,** Amended, U.S. Individual Income Tax Return) to recover the income tax on these wages. Instead, the employee is entitled to a deduction (or a credit, in some cases) for the repaid wages on his or her Form 1040 for the year of repayment.*

Undeliverable Forms W-2c. Keep for 4 years any employee copies of Forms W-2c that you tried to deliver but could not. **Do not send undeliverable Forms W-2c to the SSA.**

Specific Instructions for Form W-2c

Box a—Tax year/Form corrected. If you are correcting Form W-2, enter **all four digits** of the year of the form you are correcting. If you are correcting Form W-2c, W-2AS, W-2GU, W-2CM, or W-2VI, enter **all four digits** of the year you are correcting, and **also enter** "c," "AS," "GU," "CM," or "VI" to designate the form you are correcting. For example, "2001" and "GU" shows that you are correcting a 2001 Form W-2GU.

Box b—Employee's correct SSN. You must enter the employee's correct SSN even if it was correct on the original Form W-2.

Box c—Corrected name. Check this box **only** if the employee's name on Form W-2 (or on a prior Form W-2c) was incorrect. If you check this box, you **must** also enter the employee's **correct** name in box e and show his or her previously reported, **incorrect** name in box i.

Box d—Employer's Federal EIN. Show the correct EIN assigned to you by the IRS in the format 00-0000000.

Boxes e and f—Employee's name, address, and ZIP code. Enter the employee's correct name and address. See the **Instructions for Forms W-2 and W-3** for name formatting information. If you are correcting the name, check the "Corrected name" box in box c and also complete box i.

Box g—Employer's name, address, and ZIP code. This entry should be the same as shown on your Form 941, **943,** Employer's Annual Return for Agricultural Employees, **CT-1,** Employer's Annual Railroad Retirement Tax Return, or **Schedule H (Form 1040),** Household Employment Taxes.

The IRS will **not** use Form W-2c to update your address of record. To change your address, file **Form 8822,** Change of Address. To get Form 8822, or any other IRS form, call 1-800-TAX-FORM (1-800-829-3676) or visit the IRS Web Site at **www.irs.gov.**

Boxes h and i. Complete these boxes **only** if you are correcting an employee's SSN or name.

Boxes 1–20. For the items you are changing, enter under "Previously reported" the amount reported on the original Form W-2 or on a prior Form W-2c. Enter under "Correct information" the correct amount.

Do not make an entry in any of these boxes on **Copy A** unless you are making a change. However, see **CAUTION** below.

Box 2—Federal income tax withheld. Use this box only to make corrections because of an **administrative error.** (An administrative error occurs **only** if the amount you entered in box 2 of the incorrect Form W-2 was not the amount you actually withheld.) If correcting Forms W-2AS, W-2GU, W-2CM, or W-2VI, box 2 is for income tax withheld for the applicable possession.

Boxes 5 and 6. Complete these boxes to correct Medicare wages and tips and Medicare tax withheld. State, local, or Federal government employers should also use these boxes to correct MQGE wages. Box 5 must equal or exceed the sum of boxes 3 and 7 for 1991 and later years.

 *A state, local, or Federal government employer correcting only social security wages and/or social security tips (boxes 3 and/or 7) for an MQGE employee for **1991 and later years** must also complete Medicare wages and tips in box 5. Enter the total Medicare wages and tips, including MQGE-only wages, even if there is no change to the total Medicare wages and tips previously reported.*

Boxes 8–11. Use these boxes to correct allocated tips, an advance EIC payment, dependent care benefits, or deferrals and distributions relating to nonqualified plans.

Box 12–Codes. Complete these boxes to correct any of the coded items shown on Form W-2. Examples include uncollected social security and/or Medicare taxes on tips, taxable cost of group-term life insurance coverage over $50,000, elective deferrals (codes D through H and S, box 12), sick pay not includible as income, and employee business expenses. See the **Instructions for Form W-2**

and W-3 for the proper format to use in reporting coded items from box 12.

If a single Form W-2c does not provide enough blank spaces for corrections, use additional Forms W-2c.

Box 13. Check the boxes in box 13, under "Previously reported," as they were checked on the original Form W-2; under "Correct information," check them as they should have been checked. For example, if you checked the "Retirement plan" box on the original Form W-2 by mistake, check the "Retirement plan" box in box 13 under "Previously reported," but do not check the "Retirement plan" box in box 13 under "Correct information."

Box 14. Use this box to correct items reported in **box 14** of the original Form W-2 or on a prior Form W-2c. If possible, complete box 14 on Copies B, C, 1, and 2 of Form W-2c only, **not** on Copy A.

Boxes 15-20—State/local taxes. If your **only** changes to the original Form W-2 are to state or local data, **do not send Copy A of Form W-2c to the SSA.** Just send Form W-2c to the appropriate state or local agency and furnish copies to your employees.

Correcting state information. Contact your state or locality for specific reporting information.

Specific Instructions for Form W-3c

Please do not staple or tape the Forms W-2c to Form W-3c or to each other. File a separate Form W-3c for each tax year, for each type of form, and for each kind of payer except "Third-party sick pay." (The "Third-party sick pay" indicator box does not designate a **separate** kind of payer.) **Make a copy** of Form W-3c for your records.

Form W-3c can be filed **alone** (without Forms W-2c) to correct your EIN on a previously filed Form W-3. If the EIN is the only change you need to make, complete only boxes a, b, e, f, and h, and sign the form.

In the money boxes (except box 12- see **Boxes 1–12 and 14** on page 4) of Form W-3c, total the amounts from each box and column on the Forms W-2c you are sending.

Box a—Tax year/Form corrected. Enter **all four digits** of the year of the form you are correcting and the type of form you are correcting. For the type of form, enter "2," "2c," "2AS," "2GU," "2CM," "2VI," "3," "3c," or "3SS." For example, entering "2001" and "2" indicates that all the forms being corrected are 2001 Forms W-2.

Box b—Employer's name, address, and ZIP code. This should be the same as shown on your Form 941, 943, CT-1, or Schedule H (Form 1040). Include the suite, room, or other unit number after the street address. If the Post Office does not deliver mail to the street address and you use a P.O. box, show the P.O. box number instead of the street address.

 *The IRS will not use Form W-3c to update your address of record. If you wish to change your address, file Form 8822. To get this or any other IRS form, call 1-800-TAX-FORM (1-800-829-3676) or visit the IRS Web Site at **www.irs.gov.***

Box c—Kind of Payer. Check the applicable box. If your previous Form W-3 or W-3SS was checked incorrectly, report your prior, incorrect payer type in the "Explain decreases here:" area below box 19.

941/941-SS. Check this box if you file Form 941 or 941-SS and no other category (except "Third-party sick pay," if applicable) applies.

Military. Check this box if you are a military employer correcting Forms W-2 for members of the uniformed services.

-3-

943. Check this box if you file Form 943 and you are correcting Forms W-2 for agricultural employees. For nonagricultural employees, send Forms W-2c with a separate Form W-3c, generally with the 941/941-SS box checked.

Section 218. Check this box if you are a state or local government employer correcting 1986 or earlier Forms W-2 for employees covered under section 218 of the Social Security Act. You must also enter your employer's SSA number ("69–") in the shaded "corrected" box below box 12a-d (in box 14 on Form W-2c).

CT-1. Check this box if you are a railroad employer correcting Forms W-2 for employees covered under the Railroad Retirement Tax Act (RRTA). If you also have to correct forms of employees who are subject to social security and Medicare taxes, complete a separate Form W-3c with the 941/941-SS box checked instead.

Hshld. emp. Check this box if you are a household employer correcting Forms W-2 for household employees and you file Schedule H (Form 1040) (or Form 942 before 1995). If you also have to correct forms of employees who are not household employees, complete a separate Form W-3c.

Medicare govt. emp. Check this box if you are a U.S., state, or local agency filing corrections for employees subject only to Medicare taxes.

Third-party sick pay. Check this box **and** another box such as the "941/941-SS" box if you are a third-party sick pay payer (or are an employer reporting sick pay payments made by a third party) correcting Forms W-2 and the "Third-party sick pay" box in box 13 of Form W-2c under "Correct information" is checked. **File a single Form W-3c for the regular and "Third-party sick pay"** Forms W-2c.

Box d—Number of Forms W-2c. Show the number of individual Forms W-2c filed with this Form W-3c or enter "-0-" if you are correcting only a previously filed Form W-3 or Form W-3SS.

Box e—Employer's Federal EIN. Enter the correct number assigned to you by the IRS in the following format: 00-0000000. If you are correcting your EIN, enter the incorrect EIN you used in box h.

Box f—Establishment number. You may use this box to identify separate establishments in your business. You may file a separate Form W-3c, with Forms W-2c, for each establishment or you may use a single Form W-3c for all Forms W-2c. You do not have to complete this item; it is optional.

Box g—Employer's state ID number. You are not required to complete this box. This number is assigned by the individual state where your business is located. However, you may want to complete this item if you use copies of this form for your state returns.

Box h—Employer's incorrect Federal EIN. Your correct number must appear in box e. Make an entry here **only** if the number on the original form was incorrect.

Box i—Incorrect establishment number. You may use this box to correct an establishment number.

Box j—Employer's incorrect state ID number. Use this box to make any corrections to your previously reported state ID number.

Boxes 1–12 and 14. Enter the totals of each box and each column from Forms W-2c. For box 12, enter **only** the total of codes D through H and S.

Boxes 16–19. If your **only** changes to the Forms W-2c and W-3c are to the state and local data, **do not** send either Copy A of Form W-2c or Form W-3c to the SSA. Just send the forms to the appropriate state or local agency. Furnish copies of Form W-2c to your employees.

Explain decreases here. Explain any **decreases** to amounts "Previously reported." Also report here your previous, **incorrect** entry in box c, "Kind of Payer." Enclose (but do not attach) additional sheets explaining your decreases, if necessary.

Signature. Sign and date the form. Also enter your title, phone number, and the name of a person to contact. If you have a fax number and/or e-mail address, enter them. If you are not the employer, see *Who may sign Form W-3c,* on page 2.

Privacy Act and Paperwork Reduction Act Notice. We ask for the information on Forms W-2c and W-3c to carry out the Internal Revenue laws of the United States. We need it to figure and collect the right amount of tax. Section 6051 of the Internal Revenue Code and its regulations require you to furnish wage and tax statements to employees and to the Social Security Administration. Section 6109 of the Code requires you to provide your employer identification number.

You are not required to provide the information requested on a form that is subject to the Paperwork Reduction Act unless the form displays a valid OMB control number. Books or records relating to a form or its instructions must be retained as long as their contents may become material in the administration of any Internal Revenue law.

Generally, tax returns and return information are confidential, as required by section 6103. However, section 6103 allows or requires the Internal Revenue Service to disclose or give the information shown on your return to others as described in the Code. For example, we may disclose your tax information to the Department of Justice for civil and criminal litigation, and to cities, states, and the District of Columbia for use in administrating their tax laws. We may also disclose this information to Federal and state agencies to enforce Federal nontax criminal laws and to combat terrorism.

The time needed to complete and file these forms will vary depending on individual circumstances. The estimated average times are: **Form W-2c**—40 minutes; **Form W-3c**—51 minutes. If you have comments concerning the accuracy of these time estimates or suggestions for making these forms simpler, we would be happy to hear from you. You can write to the Tax Forms Committee, Western Area Distribution Center, Rancho Cordova, CA 95743-0001. **Do not** send these tax forms to this address. Instead, see **Where to file Forms W-2c and W-3c** on page 1.

Form W-4 (2006)

Purpose. Complete Form W-4 so that your employer can withhold the correct federal income tax from your pay. Because your tax situation may change, you may want to refigure your withholding each year.

Exemption from withholding. If you are exempt, complete only lines 1, 2, 3, 4, and 7 and sign the form to validate it. Your exemption for 2006 expires February 16, 2007. See Pub. 505, Tax Withholding and Estimated Tax.

Note. You cannot claim exemption from withholding if (a) your income exceeds $850 and includes more than $300 of unearned income (for example, interest and dividends) and (b) another person can claim you as a dependent on their tax return.

Basic instructions. If you are not exempt, complete the **Personal Allowances Worksheet** below. The worksheets on page 2 adjust your withholding allowances based on itemized deductions, certain credits, adjustments to income, or two-earner/two-job situations. Complete all worksheets that apply. However, you may claim fewer (or zero) allowances.

Head of household. Generally, you may claim head of household filing status on your tax return only if you are unmarried and pay more than 50% of the costs of keeping up a home for yourself and your dependent(s) or other qualifying individuals. See line E below.

Tax credits. You can take projected tax credits into account in figuring your allowable number of withholding allowances. Credits for child or dependent care expenses and the child tax credit may be claimed using the **Personal Allowances Worksheet** below. See Pub. 919, How Do I Adjust My Tax Withholding, for information on converting your other credits into withholding allowances.

Nonwage income. If you have a large amount of nonwage income, such as interest or dividends, consider making estimated tax payments using Form 1040-ES, Estimated Tax for Individuals. Otherwise, you may owe additional tax.

Two earners/two jobs. If you have a working spouse or more than one job, figure the total number of allowances you are entitled to claim on all jobs using worksheets from only one Form W-4. Your withholding usually will be most accurate when all allowances are claimed on the Form W-4 for the highest paying job and zero allowances are claimed on the others.

Nonresident alien. If you are a nonresident alien, see the Instructions for Form 8233 before completing this Form W-4.

Check your withholding. After your Form W-4 takes effect, use Pub. 919 to see how the dollar amount you are having withheld compares to your projected total tax for 2006. See Pub. 919, especially if your earnings exceed $130,000 (Single) or $180,000 (Married).

Recent name change? If your name on line 1 differs from that shown on your social security card, call 1-800-772-1213 to initiate a name change and obtain a social security card showing your correct name.

Personal Allowances Worksheet (Keep for your records.)

A Enter "1" for **yourself** if no one else can claim you as a dependent . . . . **A** _____

B Enter "1" if:
- You are single and have only one job; or
- You are married, have only one job, and your spouse does not work; or
- Your wages from a second job or your spouse's wages (or the total of both) are $1,000 or less.

B _____

C Enter "1" for your **spouse**. But, you may choose to enter "-0-" if you are married and have either a working spouse or more than one job. (Entering "-0-" may help you avoid having too little tax withheld.) . . . . **C** _____

D Enter number of **dependents** (other than your spouse or yourself) you will claim on your tax return . . . . . . **D** _____

E Enter "1" if you will file as **head of household** on your tax return (see conditions under **Head of household** above) . **E** _____

F Enter "1" if you have at least $1,500 of **child or dependent care expenses** for which you plan to claim a credit . . **F** _____
(**Note.** Do **not** include child support payments. See **Pub. 503**, Child and Dependent Care Expenses, for details.)

G **Child Tax Credit** (including additional child tax credit):
- If your total income will be less than $55,000 ($82,000 if married), enter "2" for each eligible child.
- If your total income will be between $55,000 and $84,000 ($82,000 and $119,000 if married), enter "1" for each eligible child plus "1" **additional** if you have four or more eligible children.

G _____

H Add lines A through G and enter total here. (**Note.** This may be different from the number of exemptions you claim on your tax return.) ▶ **H** _____

For accuracy, complete all worksheets that apply.
- If you plan to **itemize or claim adjustments to income** and want to reduce your withholding, see the **Deductions and Adjustments Worksheet** on page 2.
- If you have **more than one job** or are **married and you and your spouse both work** and the combined earnings from all jobs exceed $35,000 ($25,000 if married) see the **Two-Earner/Two-Job Worksheet** on page 2 to avoid having too little tax withheld.
- If **neither** of the above situations applies, **stop here** and enter the number from line H on line 5 of Form W-4 below.

- - - - - - - - - - - - - - - - **Cut here and give Form W-4 to your employer. Keep the top part for your records.** - - - - - - - - - - - - - - -

Form **W-4**

Department of the Treasury
Internal Revenue Service

Employee's Withholding Allowance Certificate

▶ **Whether you are entitled to claim a certain number of allowances or exemption from withholding is subject to review by the IRS. Your employer may be required to send a copy of this form to the IRS.**

OMB No. 1545-0074

2006

1 Type or print your first name and middle initial.	Last name	2 Your social security number

Home address (number and street or rural route)

3 ☐ Single ☐ Married ☐ Married, but withhold at higher Single rate.
Note. If married, but legally separated, or spouse is a nonresident alien, check the "Single" box.

City or town, state, and ZIP code

4 If your last name differs from that shown on your social security card, check here. You must call 1-800-772-1213 for a new card. ▶ ☐

5 Total number of allowances you are claiming (from line **H** above **or** from the applicable worksheet on page 2) **5** _____

6 Additional amount, if any, you want withheld from each paycheck . . . . **6** $ _____

7 I claim exemption from withholding for 2006, and I certify that I meet **both** of the following conditions for exemption.
- Last year I had a right to a refund of **all** federal income tax withheld because I had **no** tax liability **and**
- This year I expect a refund of **all** federal income tax withheld because I expect to have **no** tax liability.
If you meet both conditions, write "Exempt" here . . . . ▶ **7** _____

Under penalties of perjury, I declare that I have examined this certificate and to the best of my knowledge and belief, it is true, correct, and complete.

Employee's signature
(Form is not valid unless you sign it.) ▶

Date ▶

8 Employer's name and address (Employer: Complete lines 8 and 10 only if sending to the IRS.)	9 Office code (optional)	10 Employer identification number (EIN)

For Privacy Act and Paperwork Reduction Act Notice, see page 2.

Cat. No. 10220Q

Form **W-4** (2006)

Appendix

Deductions and Adjustments Worksheet

Note. Use this worksheet *only* if you plan to itemize deductions, claim certain credits, or claim adjustments to income on your 2006 tax return.

1   Enter an estimate of your 2006 itemized deductions. These include qualifying home mortgage interest, charitable contributions, state and local taxes, medical expenses in excess of 7.5% of your income, and miscellaneous deductions. (For 2006, you may have to reduce your itemized deductions if your income is over \$150,500 (\$75,250 if married filing separately). See *Worksheet 3* in Pub. 919 for details.) . . .   1 \$ _____

2   Enter: { \$10,300 if married filing jointly or qualifying widow(er)
             \$ 7,550 if head of household
             \$ 5,150 if single or married filing separately }   . . . .   2 \$ _____

3   **Subtract** line 2 from line 1. If line 2 is greater than line 1, enter "-0-" . . . .   3 \$ _____

4   Enter an estimate of your 2006 adjustments to income, including alimony, deductible IRA contributions, and student loan interest   4 \$ _____

5   **Add** lines 3 and 4 and enter the total. (Include any amount for credits from *Worksheet 7* in Pub. 919) .   5 \$ _____

6   Enter an estimate of your 2006 nonwage income (such as dividends or interest) . . . .   6 \$ _____

7   **Subtract** line 6 from line 5. Enter the result, but not less than "-0-" . . . .   7 \$ _____

8   **Divide** the amount on line 7 by \$3,300 and enter the result here. Drop any fraction . . . . . .   8 _____

9   Enter the number from the **Personal Allowances Worksheet,** line H, page 1 . . . .   9 _____

10 **Add** lines 8 and 9 and enter the total here. If you plan to use the **Two-Earner/Two-Job Worksheet,** also enter this total on line 1 below. Otherwise, **stop here** and enter this total on Form W-4, line 5, page 1.   10 _____

Two-Earner/Two-Job Worksheet (See *Two earners/two jobs* on page 1.)

Note. Use this worksheet *only* if the instructions under line H on page 1 direct you here.

1   Enter the number from line H, page 1 (or from line 10 above if you used the **Deductions and Adjustments Worksheet**)   1 _____

2   Find the number in **Table 1** below that applies to the **LOWEST** paying job and enter it here . . . .   2 _____

3   If line 1 is **more than or equal to** line 2, subtract line 2 from line 1. Enter the result here (if zero, enter "-0-") and on Form W-4, line 5, page 1. **Do not** use the rest of this worksheet . . . .   3 _____

Note. If line 1 is *less than* line 2, enter "-0-" on Form W-4, line 5, page 1. Complete lines 4–9 below to calculate the additional withholding amount necessary to avoid a year-end tax bill.

4   Enter the number from line 2 of this worksheet . . . .   4 _____

5   Enter the number from line 1 of this worksheet . . . .   5 _____

6   **Subtract** line 5 from line 4 . . . .   6 _____

7   Find the amount in **Table 2** below that applies to the **HIGHEST** paying job and enter it here . . . .   7 \$ _____

8   **Multiply** line 7 by line 6 and enter the result here. This is the additional annual withholding needed . .   8 \$ _____

9   Divide line 8 by the number of pay periods remaining in 2006. For example, divide by 26 if you are paid every two weeks and you complete this form in December 2005. Enter the result here and on Form W-4, line 6, page 1. This is the additional amount to be withheld from each paycheck . . . .   9 \$ _____

Table 1: Two-Earner/Two-Job Worksheet

Married Filing Jointly						All Others	
If wages from **HIGHEST** paying job are—	AND, wages from **LOWEST** paying job are—	Enter on line 2 above	If wages from **HIGHEST** paying job are—	AND, wages from **LOWEST** paying job are—	Enter on line 2 above	If wages from **LOWEST** paying job are—	Enter on line 2 above
\$0 - \$42,000	\$0 - \$4,500	0	\$42,001 and over	32,001 - 38,000	6	\$0 - \$6,000	0
	4,501 - 9,000	1		38,001 - 46,000	7	6,001 - 12,000	1
	9,001 - 18,000	2		46,001 - 55,000	8	12,001 - 19,000	2
	18,001 and over	3		55,001 - 60,000	9	19,001 - 26,000	3
				60,001 - 65,000	10	26,001 - 35,000	4
\$42,001 and over	\$0 - \$4,500	0		65,001 - 75,000	11	35,001 - 50,000	5
	4,501 - 9,000	1		75,001 - 95,000	12	50,001 - 65,000	6
	9,001 - 18,000	2		95,001 - 105,000	13	65,001 - 80,000	7
	18,001 - 22,000	3		105,001 - 120,000	14	80,001 - 90,000	8
	22,001 - 26,000	4		120,001 and over	15	90,001 - 120,000	9
	26,001 - 32,000	5				120,001 and over	10

Table 2: Two-Earner/Two-Job Worksheet

Married Filing Jointly		All Others	
If wages from **HIGHEST** paying job are—	Enter on line 7 above	If wages from **HIGHEST** paying job are—	Enter on line 7 above
\$0 - \$60,000	\$500	\$0 - \$30,000	\$500
60,001 - 115,000	830	30,001 - 75,000	830
115,001 - 165,000	920	75,001 - 145,000	920
165,001 - 290,000	1,090	145,001 - 330,000	1,090
290,001 and over	1,160	330,001 and over	1,160

 Printed on recycled paper

Form **W-4P**

Department of the Treasury
Internal Revenue Service

Withholding Certificate for Pension or Annuity Payments

OMB No. 1545-0074

20**06**

Purpose. Form W-4P is for U.S. citizens, resident aliens, or their estates who are recipients of pensions, annuities (including commercial annuities), and certain other deferred compensation. Use Form W-4P to tell payers the correct amount of federal income tax to withhold from your payment(s). You also may use Form W-4P to choose (a) not to have any federal income tax withheld from the payment (except for eligible rollover distributions, or payments to U.S. citizens delivered outside the United States or its possessions) or (b) to have an additional amount of tax withheld.

Your options depend on whether the payment is periodic, nonperiodic, or an eligible rollover distribution, as explained on pages 3 and 4. Your previously filed Form W-4P will remain in effect if you do not file a Form W-4P for 2006.

What do I need to do? Complete lines **A** through **G** of the **Personal Allowances Worksheet.** Use the additional worksheets on page 2 to adjust your withholding allowances for itemized deductions, adjustments to income, certain credits, or multiple pensions/more-than-one-income situations. If you do not want any income tax withheld (see *Purpose* above), you can skip the worksheets and go directly to the Form W-4P below.

Sign this form. Form W-4P is not valid unless you sign it.

Personal Allowances Worksheet (Keep for your records.)

A Enter "1" for **yourself** if no one else can claim you as a dependent . . . . **A** _____

B Enter "1" if:
- You are single and have only one pension; or
- You are married, have only one pension, and your spouse has no income subject to withholding; or
- Your income from a second pension or a job, or your spouse's pension or wages (or the total of all) is $1,000 or less.

. . . . . **B** _____

C Enter "1" for your **spouse.** But, you may choose to enter "-0-" if you are married and have either a spouse who has income subject to withholding or you have more than one source of income subject to withholding. (Entering "-0-" may help you avoid having too little tax withheld.) . . . . **C** _____

D Enter number of **dependents** (other than your spouse or yourself) you will claim on your tax return . . . . **D** _____

E Enter "1" if you will file as **head of household** on your tax return . . . . **E** _____

F **Child Tax Credit** (including additional child tax credit):
- If your total income will be less than $55,000 ($82,000 if married), enter "2" for each eligible child.
- If your total income will be between $55,000 and $84,000 ($82,000 and $119,000 if married), enter "1" for each eligible child plus "1" **additional** if you have four or more eligible children . . . . **F** _____

G Add lines A through F and enter total here. (**Note.** *This may be different from the number of exemptions you claim on your tax return.*) . . . . ▶ **G** _____

For accuracy, **complete all worksheets that apply.**
- If you plan to **itemize or claim adjustments to income** and want to reduce your withholding, see the **Deductions and Adjustments Worksheet** on page 2.
- If you have more than one source of income subject to withholding or a spouse with income subject to withholding **and** your combined income from all sources exceeds $35,000 ($25,000 if married), see the **Multiple Pensions/More-Than-One-Income Worksheet** on page 2 to avoid having too little tax withheld.
- If **neither** of the above situations applies, **stop here** and enter the number from line G on line 2 of Form W-4P below.

- - - - - - - - - - Cut here and give Form W-4P to the payer of your pension or annuity. Keep the top part for your records. - - - - - - - - - -

Form **W-4P**

Department of the Treasury
Internal Revenue Service

Withholding Certificate for Pension or Annuity Payments

▶ For Privacy Act and Paperwork Reduction Act Notice, see page 4.

OMB No. 1545-0074

20**06**

Type or print your full name.	Your social security number

Home address (number and street or rural route)	Claim or identification number (if any) of your pension or annuity contract
City or town, state, and ZIP code	

Complete the following applicable lines.

1 Check here if you **do not want any** federal income tax withheld from your pension or annuity. (Do not complete lines 2 or 3.) ▶ ☐

2 Total number of allowances and marital status you are claiming for withholding from each **periodic** pension or annuity payment. (You may also designate an additional dollar amount on line 3.) . . . . ▶ ☐ (Enter number of allowances.)

Marital status: ☐ Single ☐ Married ☐ Married, but withhold at higher "Single" rate

3 Additional amount, if any, you want withheld from each pension or annuity payment. (**Note.** *For periodic payments, you cannot enter an amount here without entering the number (including zero) of allowances on line 2.*) . . ▶ $ _____

Your signature ▶	Date ▶

Cat. No. 10225T

Form **W-4P** (2006)

Form W-4P (2006)   Page **2**

Deductions and Adjustments Worksheet

Note. *Use this worksheet **only** if you plan to itemize deductions, claim certain credits, or claim adjustments to income on your 2006 tax return.*

1 Enter an estimate of your 2006 itemized deductions. These include qualifying home mortgage interest, charitable contributions, state and local taxes, medical expenses in excess of 7.5% of your income, and miscellaneous deductions. (For 2006, you may have to reduce your itemized deductions if your income is over $150,500 ($75,250 if married filing separately). See *Worksheet 3* in Pub. 919 for details.) . .   **1** $ _____

2 Enter: { $10,300 if married filing jointly or qualifying widow(er)
$ 7,550 if head of household
$ 5,150 if single
$ 5,150 if married filing separately } . . . .   **2** $ _____

3 **Subtract** line 2 from line 1. If line 2 is greater than line 1, enter "-0-" . . . .   **3** $ _____

4 Enter an estimate of your 2006 adjustments to income, including alimony, deductible IRA contributions, and student loan interest . . . .   **4** $ _____

5 **Add** lines 3 and 4 and enter the total. (Include any credit amounts from *Worksheet 7* in Pub. 919.) .   **5** $ _____

6 Enter an estimate of your 2006 income not subject to withholding (such as dividends or interest) . .   **6** $ _____

7 **Subtract** line 6 from line 5. Enter the result, but not less than "-0-" . . . .   **7** $ _____

8 **Divide** the amount on line 7 by $3,300 and enter the result here. Drop any fraction. . . . . . .   **8** _____

9 Enter the number from the **Personal Allowances Worksheet,** line G, page 1 . . . .   **9** _____

10 **Add** lines 8 and 9 and enter the total here. If you use the **Multiple Pensions/More-Than-One-Income Worksheet,** also enter this total on line 1 below. Otherwise, **stop here** and enter this total on Form W-4P, line 2, page 1 . . . .   **10** _____

Multiple Pensions/More-Than-One-Income Worksheet

Note. *Complete only if the instructions under line G, page 1, direct you here. This applies if you (and your spouse if married filing a joint return) have more than one source of income subject to withholding (such as more than one pension, or a pension and a job, or you have a pension and your spouse works).*

1 Enter the number from line G, page 1 (or from line 10 above if you used the **Deductions and Adjustments Worksheet**) **1** _____

2 Find the number in **Table 1** below that applies to the **LOWEST** paying pension or job and enter it here   **2** _____

3 If line 1 is **more than or equal to** line 2, subtract line 2 from line 1. Enter the result here (if zero, enter "-0-") and on Form W-4P, line 2, page 1. **Do not** use the rest of this worksheet . . . .   **3** _____

Note. *If line 1 is **less than** line 2, enter "-0-" on Form W-4P, line 2, page 1. Complete lines 4–9 below to calculate the additional withholding amount necessary to avoid a year-end tax bill.*

4 Enter the number from line 2 of this worksheet . . . .   **4** _____

5 Enter the number from line 1 of this worksheet . . . .   **5** _____

6 Subtract line 5 from line 4 . . . .   **6** _____

7 Find the amount in **Table 2** below that applies to the **HIGHEST** paying pension or job and enter it here   **7** $ _____

8 **Multiply** line 7 by line 6 and enter the result here. This is the additional annual withholding needed .   **8** $ _____

9 **Divide** line 8 by the number of pay periods remaining in 2006. For example, divide by 12 if you are paid every month and you complete this form in December 2005. Enter the result here and on Form W-4P, line 3, page 1. This is the additional amount to be withheld from each payment . . . .   **9** $ _____

Table 1: Multiple Pensions/More-Than-One-Income Worksheet

Married Filing Jointly						All Others	
If amount from **HIGHEST** paying pension or job is—	AND, amount from **LOWEST** paying pension or job is—	Enter on line 2 above	If amount from **HIGHEST** paying pension or job is—	AND, amount from **LOWEST** paying pension or job is—	Enter on line 2 above	If amount from **LOWEST** paying pension or job is—	Enter on line 2 above
$0 - $42,000	$0 - $4,500	0	$42,001 and over	$32,001 - $38,000	6	$0 - $6,000	0
	4,501 - 9,000	1		38,001 - 46,000	7	6,001 - 12,000	1
	9,001 - 18,000	2		46,001 - 55,000	8	12,001 - 19,000	2
	18,001 and over	3		55,001 - 60,000	9	19,001 - 26,000	3
				60,001 - 65,000	10	26,001 - 35,000	4
$42,001 and over	$0 - $4,500	0		65,001 - 75,000	11	35,001 - 50,000	5
	4,501 - 9,000	1		75,001 - 95,000	12	50,001 - 65,000	6
	9,001 - 18,000	2		95,001 - 105,000	13	65,001 - 80,000	7
	18,001 - 22,000	3		105,001 - 120,000	14	80,001 - 90,000	8
	22,001 - 26,000	4		120,001 and over	15	90,001 - 120,000	9
	26,001 - 32,000	5				120,001 and over	10

Table 2: Multiple Pensions/More-Than-One-Income Worksheet

Married Filing Jointly		All Others	
If amount from **HIGHEST** paying pension or job is—	Enter on line 7 above	If amount from **HIGHEST** paying pension or job is—	Enter on line 7 above
$0 - $60,000	$500	$0 - $30,000	$500
60,001 - 115,000	830	30,001 - 75,000	830
115,001 - 165,000	920	75,001 - 145,000	920
165,001 - 290,000	1,090	145,001 - 330,000	1,090
290,001 and over	1,160	330,001 and over	1,160

Additional Instructions

Section references are to the Internal Revenue Code.

When should I complete the form? Complete Form W-4P and give it to the payer as soon as possible. Get Pub. 919, How Do I Adjust My Tax Withholding, to see how the dollar amount you are having withheld compares to your projected total federal income tax for 2006. You may also use the Withholding Calculator on the IRS website at *www.irs.gov/individuals* for help in determining how many withholding allowances to claim on your Form W-4P.

Multiple pensions/more than one income. To figure the number of allowances that you may claim, combine allowances and income subject to withholding from all sources on one worksheet. You may file a Form W-4P with each pension payer, but do not claim the same allowances more than once. Your withholding will usually be more accurate if you claim all allowances on the Form W-4P for the highest source of income subject to withholding.

Other income. If you have a large amount of income from other sources not subject to withholding (such as interest, dividends, or capital gains), consider making estimated tax payments using Form 1040-ES, Estimated Tax for Individuals. Call 1-800-TAX-FORM (1-800-829-3676) to get Form 1040-ES and Pub. 505, Tax Withholding and Estimated Tax. You can also get forms and publications from the IRS website at *www.irs.gov*.

Note. Social security and railroad retirement payments may be includible in income. See Form W-4V, Voluntary Withholding Request, for information on voluntary withholding from these payments.

Withholding From Pensions and Annuities

Generally, federal income tax withholding applies to the taxable part of payments made from pension, profit-sharing, stock bonus, annuity, and certain deferred compensation plans; from individual retirement arrangements (IRAs); and from commercial annuities. The method and rate of withholding depends on (a) the kind of payment you receive, (b) whether the payments are delivered outside the United States or its possessions, and (c) whether the recipient is a nonresident alien individual, a nonresident alien beneficiary, or a foreign estate. Qualified distributions from a Roth IRA are nontaxable and, therefore, not subject to withholding. See page 4 for special withholding rules that apply to payments outside the United States and payments to foreign persons.

Because your tax situation may change from year to year, you may want to refigure your withholding each year. You can change the amount to be withheld by using lines 2 and 3 of Form W-4P.

Choosing not to have income tax withheld. You (or in the event of death, your beneficiary or estate) can choose not to have federal income tax withheld from your payments by using line 1 of Form W-4P. For an estate, the election to have no income tax withheld may be made by the executor or personal representative of the decedent. Enter the estate's EIN in the area reserved for "Your social security number" on Form W-4P.

You may not make this choice for eligible rollover distributions. *See Eligible rollover distribution—20% withholding* on page 4.

Caution. *There are penalties for not paying enough federal income tax during the year, either through withholding or estimated tax payments. New retirees, especially, should see Pub. 505. It explains your estimated tax requirements and describes penalties in detail. You may be able to avoid quarterly estimated tax payments by having enough tax withheld from your pension or annuity using Form W-4P.*

Periodic payments. Withholding from periodic payments of a pension or annuity is figured in the same manner as withholding from wages. Periodic payments are made in installments at regular intervals over a period of more than 1 year. They may be paid annually, quarterly, monthly, etc.

If you want federal income tax to be withheld, you must designate the number of withholding allowances on line 2 of Form W-4P and indicate your marital status by checking the appropriate box. Under current law, you cannot designate a specific dollar amount to be withheld. However, you can designate an additional amount to be withheld on line 3.

If you do not want any federal income tax withheld from your periodic payments, check the box on line 1 of Form W-4P and submit the form to your payer. However, see *Payments to Foreign Persons and Payments Outside the United States* on page 4.

Caution. *If you do not submit Form W-4P to your payer, the payer must withhold on periodic payments as if you are married claiming three withholding allowances. Generally, this means that tax will be withheld if your pension or annuity is at least $1,480 a month.*

If you submit a Form W-4P that does not contain your correct taxpayer identification number (TIN), the payer must withhold as if you are single claiming zero withholding allowances even if you choose not to have federal income tax withheld.

There are some kinds of periodic payments for which you cannot use Form W-4P because they are already defined as wages subject to federal income tax withholding. These payments include retirement pay for service in the U.S. Armed Forces and payments from certain nonqualified deferred compensation plans and deferred compensation plans of exempt organizations described in section 457. Your payer should be able to tell you whether Form W-4P applies.

For periodic payments, your Form W-4P stays in effect until you change or revoke it. Your payer must notify you each year of your right to choose not to have federal income tax withheld (if permitted) or to change your choice.

Nonperiodic payments—10% withholding. Your payer must withhold at a flat 10% rate from nonperiodic payments (but see *Eligible rollover distribution—20% withholding* on page 4) **unless** you choose not to have federal income tax withheld. Distributions from an IRA that are payable on demand are treated as nonperiodic payments. You can choose not to have federal income tax withheld from a nonperiodic payment (if permitted) by submitting Form W-4P (containing your correct TIN) to your payer and checking the box on line 1. Generally, your choice not to have federal income tax withheld will apply to any later payment from the same plan. You cannot use line 2 for nonperiodic payments. But you may use line 3 to specify an additional amount that you want withheld.

Caution. *If you submit a Form W-4P that does not contain your correct TIN, the payer cannot honor your request not to have income tax withheld and must withhold 10% of the payment for federal income tax.*

Appendix

Eligible rollover distribution—20% withholding.
Distributions you receive from qualified pension or annuity plans (for example, 401(k) pension plans, IRAs, and section 457(b) plans maintained by a governmental employer) or tax-sheltered annuities that are eligible to be rolled over tax free to an IRA or qualified plan are subject to a flat 20% federal withholding rate. The 20% withholding rate is required, and you cannot choose not to have income tax withheld from eligible rollover distributions. Do not give Form W-4P to your payer unless you want an additional amount withheld. Then, complete line 3 of Form W-4P and submit the form to your payer.

Note. The payer will not withhold federal income tax if the entire distribution is transferred by the plan administrator in a direct rollover to a traditional IRA, qualified pension plan, governmental section 457(b) plan (if allowed by the plan), or tax-sheltered annuity.

Distributions that are (a) required by law, (b) one of a specified series of equal payments, or (c) qualifying "hardship" distributions are **not** "eligible rollover distributions" and are not subject to the mandatory 20% federal income tax withholding. See Pub. 505 for details. See also *Nonperiodic payments—10% withholding* on page 3.

Changing Your "No Withholding" Choice

Periodic payments. If you previously chose not to have federal income tax withheld and you now want withholding, complete another Form W-4P and submit it to your payer. If you want federal income tax withheld at the rate set by law (married with three allowances), write "Revoked" next to the checkbox on line 1 of the form. If you want tax withheld at any different rate, complete line 2 on the form.

Nonperiodic payments. If you previously chose not to have federal income tax withheld and you now want withholding, write "Revoked" next to the checkbox on line 1 and submit Form W-4P to your payer.

Payments to Foreign Persons and Payments Outside the United States

Unless you are a nonresident alien, withholding (in the manner described above) is required on any periodic or nonperiodic payments that are delivered to you outside the United States or its possessions. You cannot choose not to have federal income tax withheld on line 1 of Form W-4P. See Pub. 505 for details.

In the absence of a tax treaty exemption, nonresident aliens, nonresident alien beneficiaries, and foreign estates generally are subject to a 30% federal withholding tax under section 1441 on the taxable portion of a periodic or nonperiodic pension or annuity payment that is from U.S. sources. However, most tax treaties provide that private pensions and annuities are exempt from withholding and tax. Also, payments from certain pension plans are exempt from withholding even if no tax treaty applies. See Pub. 515, Withholding of Tax on Nonresident Aliens and Foreign Entities, and Pub. 519, U.S. Tax Guide for Aliens, for details. A foreign person should submit Form W-8BEN, Certificate of Foreign Status of Beneficial Owner for United States Tax Withholding, to the payer before receiving any payments. The Form W-8BEN must contain the foreign person's TIN.

Statement of Federal Income Tax Withheld From Your Pension or Annuity

By January 31 of next year, your payer will furnish a statement to you on Form 1099-R, Distributions From Pensions, Annuities, Retirement or Profit-Sharing Plans, IRAs, Insurance Contracts, etc., showing the total amount of your pension or annuity payments and the total federal income tax withheld during the year. If you are a foreign person who has provided your payer with Form W-8BEN, your payer instead will furnish a statement to you on Form 1042-S, Foreign Person's U.S. Source Income Subject to Withholding, by March 15 of next year.

Privacy Act and Paperwork Reduction Act Notice

We ask for the information on this form to carry out the Internal Revenue laws of the United States. You are required to provide this information only if you want to (a) request federal income tax withholding from periodic pension or annuity payments based on your withholding allowances and marital status, (b) request additional federal income tax withholding from your pension or annuity, (c) choose not to have federal income tax withheld, when permitted, or (d) change or revoke a previous Form W-4P. To do any of the aforementioned, you are required by sections 3405(e) and 6109 and their regulations to provide the information requested on this form. Failure to provide this information may result in inaccurate withholding on your payment(s).

Routine uses of this information include giving it to the Department of Justice for civil and criminal litigation, and to cities, states, and the District of Columbia for use in administering their tax laws. We may also disclose this information to other countries under a tax treaty, to federal and state agencies to enforce federal nontax criminal laws, or to federal law enforcement and intelligence agencies to combat terrorism.

You are not required to provide the information requested on a form that is subject to the Paperwork Reduction Act unless the form displays a valid OMB control number. Books or records relating to a form or its instructions must be retained as long as their contents may become material in the administration of any Internal Revenue law. Generally, tax returns and return information are confidential, as required by section 6103.

The average time and expenses required to complete and file this form will vary depending on individual circumstances. For estimated averages, see the instructions for your income tax return.

If you have suggestions for making this form simpler, we would be happy to hear from you. See the instructions for your income tax return.

Printed on recycled paper

Form **W-4S**	**Request for Federal Income Tax Withholding From Sick Pay**	OMB No. 1545-0074
Department of the Treasury Internal Revenue Service	► **Give this form to the third-party payer of your sick pay.**	20**06**

Type or print your first name and middle initial.	Last name	Your social security number

Home address (number and street or rural route)

City or town, state, and ZIP code

Claim or identification number (if any) . . . .

I request federal income tax withholding from my sick pay payments. I want the following amount to be withheld from each payment. (See **Worksheet** below.) . . . . $

Employee's signature ►   Date ►

------------------- **Cut here and give the top part of this form to the payer. Keep the lower part for your records.** -------------------

Worksheet (Keep for your records. Do not send to the Internal Revenue Service.)

1 Enter amount of adjusted gross income that you expect in 2006 . . . . **1**

2 If you plan to itemize deductions on Schedule A (Form 1040), enter the estimated total of your deductions. For 2006, you may have to reduce your itemized deductions if your income is over $150,500 ($75,250 if married filing separately). See Pub. 919, How Do I Adjust My Tax Withholding, for details. Call 1-800-829-3676 or visit the IRS website at *www.irs.gov* to order forms and publications. If you do not plan to itemize deductions, enter the standard deduction. (See the instructions on page 2 for the standard deduction amount, including additional amounts for age and blindness.) **2**

3 Subtract line 2 from line 1 . . . . **3**

4 Exemptions. Multiply $3,300 by the number of personal exemptions. For 2006, your personal exemption(s) amount is reduced if your income is over $150,500 if single, $225,750 if married filing jointly or qualifying widow(er), $112,875 if married filing separately, or $188,150 if head of household. See Pub. 919 for details. **4**

5 Subtract line 4 from line 3 . . . . **5**

6 Tax. Figure your tax on line 5 by using the 2006 Tax Rate Schedule X, Y, or Z on page 2. Do not use the Tax Table or Tax Rate Schedule X, Y, or Z in the 2005 Form 1040, 1040A, or 1040EZ instructions . . . **6**

7 Credits (child tax and higher education credits, credit for child and dependent care expenses, etc.) . . . **7**

8 Subtract line 7 from line 6 . . . . **8**

9 Estimated federal income tax withheld and to be withheld from other sources (including amounts withheld due to a prior Form W-4S) during 2006 or paid with Form 1040-ES **9**

10 Subtract line 9 from line 8 . . . . **10**

11 Enter the number of sick pay payments you expect to receive this year to which this Form W-4S will apply **11**

12 Divide line 10 by line 11. Round to the nearest dollar. This is the amount that should be withheld from each sick pay payment. Be sure it meets the requirements for the amount that should be withheld, as explained under *Amount to be withheld* below. If it does, enter this amount on Form W-4S above **12**

General Instructions

Purpose of form. Give this form to the third-party payer of your sick pay, such as an insurance company, if you want federal income tax withheld from the payments. You are not required to have federal income tax withheld from sick pay paid by a third party. However, if you choose to request such withholding, Internal Revenue Code sections 3402(o) and 6109 and their regulations require you to provide the information requested on this form. Do not use this form if your employer (or its agent) makes the payments because employers are already required to withhold income tax from sick pay.

Note. If you receive sick pay under a collective bargaining agreement, see your union representative or employer.

Definition. Sick pay is a payment that you receive:

● Under a plan to which your employer is a party and
● In place of wages for any period when you are temporarily absent from work because of your sickness or injury.

Amount to be withheld. Enter on this form the amount that you want withheld from each payment. The amount that you enter:

● Must be in whole dollars (for example, $35, not $34.50).
● Must be at least $4 per day, $20 per week, or $88 per month based on your payroll period.
● Must not reduce the net amount of each sick pay payment that you receive to less than $10.

For payments larger or smaller than a regular full payment of sick pay, the amount withheld will be in the same proportion as your regular withholding from sick pay. For example, if your regular full payment of $100 a week normally has $25 (25%) withheld, then $20 (25%) will be withheld from a partial payment of $80.

Caution. Generally, you may be subject to a penalty if your tax payments during the year are not at least 90% of the tax shown on your tax return. For exceptions and details, see Pub. 505, Tax Withholding and Estimated Tax. You may pay tax during the year through withholding or estimated tax payments or both. To avoid a penalty, make sure that you have enough tax withheld or make estimated tax payments using Form 1040-ES, Estimated Tax for Individuals. You may estimate your federal income tax liability by using the worksheet above.

(continued on back)

For Paperwork Reduction Act Notice, see page 2.   Cat. No. 10226E   Form **W-4S** (2006)

Sign this form. Form W-4S is not valid unless you sign it.

Statement of income tax withheld. After the end of the year, you will receive a Form W-2, Wage and Tax Statement, reporting the taxable sick pay paid and federal income tax withheld during the year. These amounts are reported to the Internal Revenue Service.

Changing your withholding. Form W-4S remains in effect until you change or revoke it. You may do this by giving a new Form W-4S or a written notice to the payer of your sick pay. To revoke your previous Form W-4S, complete a new Form W-4S and write "Revoked" in the money amount box, sign it, and give it to the payer.

Specific Instructions for Worksheet

You may use the worksheet on page 1 to estimate the amount of federal income tax that you want withheld from each sick pay payment. Use your tax return for last year and the worksheet as a basis for estimating your tax, tax credits, and withholding for this year.

You may not want to use Form W-4S if you already have your total tax covered by estimated tax payments or other withholding.

If you expect to file a joint return, be sure to include the income, deductions, credits, and payments of both yourself and your spouse in figuring the amount you want withheld.

Caution. If any of the amounts on the worksheet change after you give Form W-4S to the payer, you may use a new Form W-4S to request a change in the amount withheld.

Line 2—Deductions

Itemized deductions. You may have to reduce your itemized deductions if your income is over $150,500 ($75,250 if married filing separately). See Pub. 919 for details.

Standard deduction. For 2006, the standard deduction amounts are:

Filing Status	Standard Deduction
Married filing jointly or qualifying widow(er).	$10,300*
Head of household	$7,550*
Single	$5,150*
Married filing separately	$5,150*

*If you are age 65 or older or blind, add to the standard deduction amount the additional amount that applies to you as shown in the next paragraph. If you can be claimed as a dependent on another person's return, see *Limited standard deduction for dependents* below.

Additional amount for the elderly or blind. An additional standard deduction of $1,000 is allowed for a married individual (filing jointly or separately) or qualifying widow(er) who is 65 or older or blind, $2,000 if 65 or older **and** blind. If both spouses are 65 or older or blind, an additional $2,000 is allowed on a joint return ($2,000 on a separate return if you can claim an exemption for your spouse). If both spouses are 65 or older **and** blind, an additional $4,000 is allowed on a joint return ($4,000 on a separate return if you can claim an exemption for your spouse). An additional $1,250 is allowed for an unmarried individual (single or head of household) who is 65 or older or blind, $2,500 if 65 or older **and** blind.

Limited standard deduction for dependents. If you can be claimed as a dependent on another person's return, your standard deduction is the greater of: (a) $850 or (b) your earned income plus $300 (up to the regular standard deduction for your filing status). If you are 65 or older or blind, see Pub. 505 for additional amounts that you may claim.

Certain individuals not eligible for standard deduction. For the following individuals, the standard deduction is zero.

- A married individual filing a separate return if either spouse itemizes deductions.
- A nonresident alien individual.
- An individual filing a return for a period of less than 12 months because of a change in his or her annual accounting period.

Line 7—Credits

Include on this line any tax credits that you are entitled to claim, such as the child tax and higher education credits, credit for child and dependent care expenses, earned income credit, or credit for the elderly or the disabled.

Line 9—Tax Withholding and Estimated Tax

Enter the federal income tax that you expect will be withheld this year on income other than sick pay and any payments that you made using Form 1040-ES. Include any federal income tax withheld from wages and pensions.

2006 Tax Rate Schedules

Schedule X—Single

If line 5 is: Over—	But not over—	The tax is:		of the amount over—
$0	$7,550	$0	10%	$0
7,550	30,650	$755.00 +	15%	7,550
30,650	74,200	4,220.00 +	25%	30,650
74,200	154,800	15,107.50 +	28%	74,200
154,800	336,550	37,675.50 +	33%	154,800
336,550	and greater	97,653.00 +	35%	336,550

Schedule Z—Head of household

If line 5 is: Over—	But not over—	The tax is:		of the amount over—
$0	$10,750	$0	10%	$0
10,750	41,050	$1,075.00 +	15%	10,750
41,050	106,000	5,620.00 +	25%	41,050
106,000	171,650	21,857.50 +	28%	106,000
171,650	336,550	40,239.50 +	33%	171,650
336,550	and greater	94,656.50 +	35%	336,550

Schedule Y-1—Married filing jointly or Qualifying widow(er)

If line 5 is: Over—	But not over—	The tax is:		of the amount over—
$0	$15,100	$0	10%	$0
15,100	61,300	$1,510.00 +	15%	15,100
61,300	123,700	8,440.00 +	25%	61,300
123,700	188,450	24,040.00 +	28%	123,700
188,450	336,550	42,170.00 +	33%	188,450
336,550	and greater	91,043.00 +	35%	336,550

Schedule Y-2—Married filing separately

If line 5 is: Over—	But not over—	The tax is:		of the amount over—
$0	$7,550	$0	10%	$0
7,550	30,650	$755.00 +	15%	7,550
30,650	61,850	4,220.00 +	25%	30,650
61,850	94,225	12,020.00 +	28%	61,850
94,225	168,275	21,085.00 +	33%	94,225
168,275	and greater	45,521.50 +	35%	168,275

Paperwork Reduction Act Notice. We ask for the information on this form to carry out the Internal Revenue laws of the United States.

You are not required to provide the information requested on a form that is subject to the Paperwork Reduction Act unless the form displays a valid OMB control number. Books or records relating to a form or its instructions must be retained as long as their contents may become material in the administration of any Internal Revenue law. Generally, tax returns and return information are confidential, as required by Code section 6103.

The average time and expenses required to complete and file this form will vary depending on individual circumstances. For estimated averages, see the instructions for your income tax return.

If you have suggestions for making this form simpler, we would be happy to hear from you. See the instructions for your income tax return.

 Printed on recycled paper

20**06** Form W-5

**Department of the Treasury
Internal Revenue Service**

Instructions

Purpose of Form

Use Form W-5 if you are eligible to get part of the earned income credit (EIC) in advance with your pay and choose to do so. See *Who Is Eligible To Get Advance EIC Payments?* below. The amount you can get in advance generally depends on your wages. If you are married, the amount of your advance EIC payments also depends on whether your spouse has filed a Form W-5 with his or her employer. However, your employer cannot give you more than $1,648 throughout 2006 with your pay. You will get the rest of any EIC you are entitled to when you file your tax return and claim the EIC.

If you do not choose to get advance payments, you can still claim the EIC on your 2006 tax return.

What Is the EIC?

The EIC is a credit for certain workers. It reduces the tax you owe. It may give you a refund even if you do not owe any tax.

Who Is Eligible To Get Advance EIC Payments?

You are eligible to get advance EIC payments if **all three** of the following apply.

1. You expect to have at least one qualifying child and to be able to claim the credit using that child. If you do not expect to have a qualifying child, you may still be eligible for the EIC, but you cannot receive advance EIC payments. See *Who Is a Qualifying Child?* below.

2. You expect that your 2006 earned income and adjusted gross income (AGI) will each be less than $32,001 ($34,001 if you expect to file a joint return for 2006). Include your spouse's income if you plan to file a joint return. As used on this form, earned income does not include amounts inmates in penal institutions are paid for their work, amounts received as

a pension or annuity from a nonqualified deferred compensation plan or a nongovernmental section 457 plan, or nontaxable earned income.

3. You expect to be able to claim the EIC for 2006. To find out if you may be able to claim the EIC, answer the questions on page 2.

How To Get Advance EIC Payments

If you are eligible to get advance EIC payments, fill in the 2006 Form W-5 at the bottom of this page. Then, detach it and give it to your employer. If you get advance payments, you must file a 2006 Form 1040 or 1040A income tax return.

You may have only one Form W-5 in effect at one time. If you and your spouse are both employed, you should file separate Forms W-5.

This Form W-5 expires on December 31, 2006. If you are eligible to get advance EIC payments for 2007, you must file a new Form W-5 next year.

TIP You may be able to get a larger credit when you file your 2006 return. For details, see *Additional Credit* on page 3.

Who Is a Qualifying Child?

A qualifying child is any child who meets all three of the following conditions.

1. The child is your:

Son, daughter, stepchild, foster child, brother, sister, stepbrother, stepsister, or a descendant of any of them (for example, your grandchild, niece, or nephew).

Note. An adopted child is always treated as your own child. An adopted child includes a child lawfully placed with you for legal adoption. A foster child is any child placed with you by an authorized placement agency or by judgment, decree, or other order of any court of competent jurisdiction.

(continued on page 3)

▼ *Give the bottom part to your employer; keep the top part for your records.* ▼

- Detach here -

Form **W-5**	**Earned Income Credit Advance Payment Certificate**	OMB No. 1545-0074
Department of the Treasury Internal Revenue Service	▶ Use the current year's certificate only. ▶ Give this certificate to your employer. ▶ This certificate expires on December 31, 2006.	20**06**

Print or type your full name	Your social security number

Note. *If you get advance payments of the earned income credit for 2006, you **must** file a 2006 federal income tax return. To get advance payments, you **must** have a qualifying child and your filing status must be any status **except** married filing a separate return.*

1 I expect to have a qualifying child and be able to claim the earned income credit for 2006 using that child. I do not have another Form W-5 in effect with any other current employer, and I choose to get advance EIC payments . . . . ☐ **Yes** ☐ **No**

2 Check the box that shows your expected filing status for 2006:

    ☐ Single, head of household, or qualifying widow(er)   ☐ Married filing jointly

3 If you are married, does your spouse have a Form W-5 in effect for 2006 with any employer?. . . . . ☐ **Yes** ☐ **No**

Under penalties of perjury, I declare that the information I have furnished above is, to the best of my knowledge, true, correct, and complete.

Signature ▶   Date ▶

Cat. No. 10227P

Questions To See if You May Be Able To Claim the EIC for 2006

⚠ **CAUTION** You **cannot** claim the EIC if you file either Form 2555 or Form 2555-EZ (relating to foreign earned income) for 2006. You also **cannot** claim the EIC if you are a nonresident alien for any part of 2006 unless you are married to a U.S. citizen or resident, file a joint return, and elect to be taxed as a resident alien for all of 2006.

1 Do you expect to have a qualifying child? Read *Who Is a Qualifying Child?* that starts on page 1 before you answer this question. If the child is married, be sure you also read *Married child* on page 3.

☐ **No.** (STOP) You may be able to claim the EIC but you **cannot** get advance EIC payments.

☐ **Yes.** *Continue.*

⚠ **CAUTION** If the child meets the conditions to be a qualifying child for both you and another person, see *Qualifying child of more than one person* on page 3.

2 Do you expect your 2006 filing status to be married filing a separate return?

☐ **Yes.** (STOP) You **cannot** claim the EIC.

☐ **No.** *Continue.*

(TIP) If you expect to file a joint return for 2006, include your spouse's income when answering questions 3 and 4.

3 Do you expect that your 2006 earned income and AGI will each be less than: $32,001 ($34,001 if married filing jointly) if you expect to have 1 qualifying child; $36,348 ($38,348 if married filing jointly) if you expect to have 2 or more qualifying children?

☐ **No.** (STOP) You **cannot** claim the EIC.

☐ **Yes.** *Continue.* But remember, you **cannot** get advance EIC payments if you expect your 2006 earned income or AGI will be $32,001 ($34,001 or more if married filing jointly) or more.

4 Do you expect that your 2006 investment income will be more than $2,800? For most people, investment income is the total of their taxable interest, ordinary dividends, capital gain distributions, and tax-exempt interest. However, if you plan to file a 2006 Form 1040, see the 2005 Form 1040 instructions to figure your investment income.

☐ **Yes.** (STOP) You **cannot** claim the EIC.

☐ **No.** *Continue.*

5 Do you expect that you, or your spouse if filing a joint return, will be a qualifying child of another person for 2006?

☐ **Yes.** You **cannot** claim the EIC.

☐ **No.** You may be able to claim the EIC.

2. At the end of 2006, the child is under age 19, or under age 24 and a student, or any age and permanently and totally disabled. A student is a child who during any 5 months of 2006 (a) was enrolled as a full-time student at a school or (b) took a full-time, on-farm training course given by a school or a state, county, or local government agency. A school includes a technical, trade, or mechanical school. It does not include an on-the-job training course, correspondence school, or Internet school.

3. The child lives with you in the United States for over half of 2006. But you do not have to meet this condition if (a) the child was born or died during the year and your home was this child's home for the entire time he or she was alive in 2006, or (b) the child is presumed by law enforcement authorities to have been kidnapped by someone who is not a family member and the child lived with you for over half of the part of the year before he or she was kidnapped.

Note. Temporary absences, such as for school, vacation, medical care, or detention in a juvenile facility, count as time lived at home. Members of the military on extended active duty outside the United States are considered to be living in the United States.

Married child. A child who is married at the end of 2006 is a qualifying child only if:

1. You may claim him or her as your dependent, or

2. You are the custodial parent and would be able to claim the child as your dependent, but the noncustodial parent claims the child as a dependent because:

a. You signed Form 8332, Release of Claim to Exemption for Child of Divorced or Separated Parents, or a similar statement, agreeing not to claim the child for 2006, or

b. You have a pre-1985 divorce decree or separation agreement that allows the noncustodial parent to claim the child and he or she gives at least $600 for the child's support in 2006.

Other rules may apply. See Pub. 501, Exemptions, Standard Deduction, and Filing Information, for more information on children of divorced or separated parents.

Qualifying child of more than one person. If the child meets the conditions to be a qualifying child of more than one person, only one person may treat that child as a qualifying child for 2006. If you and someone else have the same qualifying child, you and the other person(s) can decide which of you, if otherwise eligible, will take all the following tax benefits based on the qualifying child: the child's dependency exemption, the child tax credit, head of household filing status, the credit for child and dependent care expenses, and the EIC. The other person cannot take any of the five tax benefits unless he or she has a different qualifying child.

If you and the other person cannot agree and more than one person claims the EIC or other benefits listed above using the same child, the tie-breaker rule applies. See Pub. 596, Earned Income Credit, Table 2. When More Than One Person Claims EIC Using Same Child (Tie-Breaker Rule) and the Instructions for Form 1040 or 1040A.

Caution. A qualifying child whom you use to claim the EIC must have a valid social security number unless he or she is born and dies in 2006.

What if My Situation Changes?

If your situation changes after you give Form W-5 to your employer, you will probably need to file a new Form W-5. For example, you must file a new Form W-5 if any of the following applies for 2006.

● You no longer expect to have a qualifying child. Check "No" on line 1 of your new Form W-5.

● You no longer expect to be able to claim the EIC for 2006. Check "No" on line 1 of your new Form W-5.

● You no longer want advance payments. Check "No" on line 1 of your new Form W-5.

● Your spouse files Form W-5 with his or her employer. Check "Yes" on line 3 of your new Form W-5.

Note. If you get advance EIC payments and find you are not eligible for the EIC, you must pay back these payments when you file your 2006 federal income tax return.

Additional Information

How To Claim the EIC

If you are eligible, claim the EIC on your 2006 tax return. See your 2006 tax return instruction booklet.

Additional Credit

You may be able to claim a larger credit when you file your 2006 Form 1040 or Form 1040A because your employer cannot give you more than $1,648 throughout the year with your pay. You may also be able to claim a larger credit if you have more than one qualifying child. But you must file your 2006 tax return to claim any additional credit.

Printed on recycled paper

Form **W-7**	Application for IRS Individual	
(Rev. January 2006)	**Taxpayer Identification Number**	OMB No. 1545-0074
Department of the Treasury Internal Revenue Service	▶ See instructions. ▶ For use by individuals who are not U.S. citizens or permanent residents.	

An IRS individual taxpayer identification number (ITIN) is for federal tax purposes only.

FOR IRS USE ONLY

Before you begin:
- **Do not submit** this form if you have, or are eligible to obtain, a U.S. social security number (SSN).
- *Getting an ITIN does not change your immigration status or your right to work in the United States and does not make you eligible for the earned income credit.*

Reason you are submitting Form W-7. Read the instructions for the box you check. **Caution:** If you check box **b, c, d, e,** or **g, you must file a tax return with Form W-7 unless you meet one of the exceptions** (see instructions).

- **a** ☐ Nonresident alien required to obtain ITIN to claim tax treaty benefit
- **b** ☐ Nonresident alien filing a U.S. tax return
- **c** ☐ U.S. resident alien **(based on days present in the United States)** filing a U.S. tax return
- **d** ☐ Dependent of U.S. citizen/resident alien ⎫ Enter name and SSN/ITIN of U.S. citizen/resident alien (see instructions) ▶ ----------------
- **e** ☐ Spouse of U.S. citizen/resident alien ⎭ --
- **f** ☐ Nonresident alien student, professor, or researcher filing a U.S. tax return
- **g** ☐ Dependent/spouse of a nonresident alien holding a U.S. visa
- **h** ☐ Other (see instructions) ▶ --

Additional information for **a** and **f:** Enter treaty country ▶ _____ and treaty article number ▶ _____

Name (see instructions)	**1a** First name	Middle name	Last name
Name at birth if different . . ▶	**1b** First name	Middle name	Last name

Applicant's mailing address

2 Street address, apartment number, or rural route number. **If you have a P.O. box, see page 4.**

City or town, state or province, and country. Include ZIP code or postal code where appropriate.

Foreign address (if different from above) (see instructions)

3 Street address, apartment number, or rural route number. **Do not use a P.O. box number.**

City or town, state or province, and country. Include ZIP code or postal code where appropriate.

Birth information	**4** Date of birth (month / day / year) / /	Country of birth	City and state or province (optional)	**5** ☐ Male ☐ Female

Other information

6a Country(ies) of citizenship	**6b** Foreign tax I.D. number (if any)	**6c** Type of U.S. visa (if any), number, and expiration date

6d Identification document(s) submitted (see instructions)

☐ Passport ☐ Driver's license/State I.D. ☐ USCIS documentation ☐ Other ----------------

Issued by: _____ No.: _____ Exp. date: / / Entry date in U.S. / /

6e Have you previously received a U.S. temporary taxpayer identification number (TIN) or employer identification number (EIN)?

☐ **No/Do not know.** Skip line 6f.
☐ **Yes.** Complete line 6f. If more than one, list on a sheet and attach to this form (see instructions).

6f Enter: TIN or EIN ▶ -- and
Name under which it was issued ▶ _____

6g Name of college/university or company (see instructions) ------------------------------
City and state _____ Length of stay _____

Sign Here

Under penalties of perjury, I (applicant/delegate/acceptance agent) declare that I have examined this application, including accompanying documentation and statements, and to the best of my knowledge and belief, it is true, correct, and complete. I authorize the IRS to disclose to my acceptance agent returns or return information necessary to resolve matters regarding the assignment of my IRS individual taxpayer identification number (ITIN), including any previously assigned taxpayer identifying number.

Signature of applicant (if delegate, see instructions)	Date (month / day / year) / /	Phone number ( )

Keep a copy for your records.

Name of delegate, if applicable (type or print)	Delegate's relationship to applicant	☐ Parent ☐ Court-appointed guardian ☐ Power of Attorney

Acceptance Agent's Use ONLY

Signature	Date (month / day / year) / /	Phone ( )
		Fax ( )
Name and title (type or print)	Name of company	EIN

For Paperwork Reduction Act Notice, see page 4.   Cat. No. 10229L   Form **W-7** (Rev. 1-2006)

General Instructions

Purpose of Form

Use Form W-7 to apply for an IRS individual taxpayer identification number (ITIN). An ITIN is a nine-digit number issued by the U.S. Internal Revenue Service (IRS) to individuals who are required for U.S. tax purposes to have a U.S. taxpayer identification number but who do not have, and are not eligible to obtain, a social security number (SSN).

The ITIN is for federal tax purposes only. It does not entitle you to social security benefits and does not change your immigration status or your right to work in the United States. Also, individuals filing tax returns using an ITIN are not eligible for the earned income credit (EIC).

SSNs. Do not complete Form W-7 if you have an SSN or you are eligible to obtain an SSN. You are eligible for an SSN if you are a U.S. citizen or if you have been admitted by the United States for permanent residence or U.S. employment.

If you have an application for an SSN pending, do not file Form W-7. Complete Form W-7 only if the Social Security Administration (SSA) notifies you that an SSN cannot be issued.

To obtain an SSN, see Form SS-5, Application for a Social Security Card. To get Form SS-5 or to find out if you are eligible to obtain an SSN, go to *www.socialsecurity.gov* or contact an SSA office.

Who Must Apply

Any individual who is not eligible to obtain an SSN but who must furnish a taxpayer identification number must apply for an ITIN on Form W-7. Examples include the following.

• A nonresident alien individual eligible to obtain the benefit of reduced withholding under an income tax treaty. See Pub. 515, Withholding of Tax on Nonresident Aliens and Foreign Entities.

• A nonresident alien individual not eligible for an SSN who is required to file a U.S. tax return or who is filing a U.S. tax return only to claim a refund.

• A nonresident alien individual not eligible for an SSN who elects to file a joint U.S. tax return with a spouse who is a U.S. citizen or resident.

• A U.S. resident alien (based on the substantial presence test) who files a U.S. tax return but who is not eligible for an SSN. For information about the substantial presence test, see Pub. 519, U.S. Tax Guide for Aliens.

• An alien spouse claimed as an exemption on a U.S. tax return who is not eligible to obtain an SSN.

• An alien individual eligible to be claimed as a dependent on a U.S. tax return but who is not eligible to obtain an SSN. To determine if an alien individual is eligible to be claimed as a dependent on a U.S. tax return, see Pub. 501, Exemptions, Standard Deduction, and Filing Information, and Pub. 519.

• A nonresident alien student, professor, or researcher who is required to file a U.S. tax return but who is not eligible for an SSN.

• A dependent/spouse of a nonresident alien holding a U.S. visa who is not eligible for an SSN.

ITIN not needed for Forms 4868, 1040-ES, or 1040-ES(NR). If you are filing an application for an extension of time to file using Form 4868, or making an estimated tax payment using Form 1040-ES or Form 1040-ES(NR), do not file Form W-7 with these forms. Enter "ITIN TO BE REQUESTED" wherever your SSN or ITIN is requested. An ITIN will be issued only after you file a tax return and meet all other requirements.

Additional Information

Publications. For details on resident and nonresident alien status, see Pub. 519.

For details on individuals who can be claimed as dependents and on obtaining an SSN for a dependent, see Pub. 501.

These publications are available free from the IRS. To order the publications, call 1-800-TAX-FORM (1-800-829-3676) if you are in the United States. If you have a foreign address, write to:

National Distribution Center
P.O. Box 8903
Bloomington, IL 61702-8903

You can also get these publications on the IRS website at *www.irs.gov*.

Telephone help. If, after reading these instructions and our free publications, you are not sure how to complete your application or have additional questions, call 1-800-829-1040 if you are in the United States. If you are outside the United States, you can contact our overseas offices in London or Paris.

How To Apply

Your application must include all of the following.

1. Your completed Form W-7.

2. Your original, completed tax return(s) for which the ITIN is needed. Attach Form W-7 to the front of your tax return. After your Form W-7 has been processed, the IRS will assign an ITIN to the return and process the return. The tax return will be processed as if it were filed at the address listed in the tax return instructions. Do not send a copy of the return to any other IRS office.

If you are not required to file a tax return or if you fail to file a completed tax return with your Form W-7, you will not be issued an ITIN, unless one of the exceptions explained on page 3 applies. If an exception applies, include instead the documents described under that exception.

3. The original documents, or certified or notarized copies of documents, that substantiate the information provided on the Form W-7. The supporting documentation must be consistent with the applicant's information provided on Form W-7. For example, the name, date of birth, and country of citizenship must be the same as on Form W-7, lines 1a, 4, and 6a.

If you submit an original valid passport (or a notarized or certified copy of a valid passport), you do not need to submit any other documents from the list below. Otherwise, you must submit at least two or more of the documents listed below. The documents must be current and verify your identity (that is, contain your name). At least one document must contain your photograph and one must support your claim of foreign status. Do not attach expired documents.

a. National identification card (must show photo, name, current address, date of birth, and expiration date).

b. U.S. driver's license.

c. Civil birth certificate.

d. Foreign driver's license.

e. U.S. state identification card.

f. Foreign voter's registration card.

g. U.S. military identification card.

h. Foreign military identification card.

i. U.S. visa issued by the U.S. Department of State.

j. U.S. Citizenship and Immigration Services (USCIS) photo identification.

k. Medical records (dependents only).

l. School records (dependents and/or students only).

You can submit copies of original documents if the copies are:

• Certified by the issuing agency or official custodian of the original record, or

• Notarized by a U.S. notary public legally authorized within his or her local jurisdiction to certify that the document is a true copy of the original. To do this, the notary must see the valid, unaltered original document and verify that the copy conforms to the original. U.S. notaries public are available at U.S. embassies and consulates worldwide. Foreign notaries are acceptable as outlined by the Hague Convention.

Original documents you submit will be returned to you. You do not need to provide a return envelope. If your original documents are not returned within 60 days, you can call the IRS (see *Telephone help* on this page). Copies of documents will not be returned.

Keep a copy of your application for your records.

Appendix

When To Apply

Complete and attach Form W-7 when you file the tax return for which the ITIN is needed. However, if you meet one of the exceptions on this page, complete and submit Form W-7 as soon as possible after you determine you are covered by that exception.

Allow 4 to 6 weeks for the IRS to notify you in writing of your ITIN. If you have not received your ITIN or correspondence at the end of the 6-week period, you can call the IRS to find out the status of your application (see *Telephone help* on page 2).

Where To Apply

By mail. Mail Form W-7, your tax return (or other documents required by an exception on this page), and the documentation listed in item (3) under *How To Apply* on page 2 to:

> Internal Revenue Service
> Philadelphia Service Center
> ITIN Unit
> P.O. Box 447
> Bensalem, PA 19020

 Do not use the mailing address in the instructions for your tax return.

In person. You can apply for an ITIN by bringing your completed forms and documentation to any IRS Taxpayer Assistance Center in the United States and most IRS offices abroad. Before applying at an IRS office abroad, find out if that office accepts Form W-7 applications.

Through acceptance agent. You can also apply through an acceptance agent authorized by the IRS. An acceptance agent can help you complete and file Form W-7. To obtain a list of agents, visit the IRS website at *www.irs.gov*.

Specific Instructions

If you are completing this form for someone else, answer the questions as they apply to that person.

Reason For Applying

You must check the box to indicate the reason you are completing Form W-7. If more than one box applies to you, check the box that best explains your reason for submitting Form W-7.

 If you check box b, c, d, e, or g, you must file a completed tax return by attaching it to Form W-7. You must do this even if the ITIN is for a spouse or dependent. If you are applying for more than one ITIN for the same return (such as for a spouse or dependent), attach all Forms W-7 to the same return.

a. Nonresident alien required to obtain ITIN to claim tax treaty benefit. Certain nonresident aliens must obtain an ITIN to claim a tax treaty benefit even if they do not have to file a U.S. tax return. If you check this box to claim the benefits of a U.S. income tax treaty with a foreign country, also check box h. On the dotted line next to box h, enter "Exception 1" or "Exception 2," whichever applies (see this page). Also enter the name of the treaty country and treaty article number in the appropriate entry spaces below box h. Also attach the documents required under whichever exception applies. For more details on tax treaties, see Pub. 901, U.S. Tax Treaties.

b. Nonresident alien filing a U.S. tax return. This category includes:

● A nonresident alien who must file a U.S. tax return to report income effectively or not effectively connected with the conduct of a trade or business in the United States, and

● A nonresident alien who is filing a U.S. tax return only to obtain a refund.

c. U.S. resident alien (based on days present in the United States) filing a U.S. tax return. A foreign individual living in the United States who does not have permission to work from the USCIS, and is thus ineligible for an SSN, may still be required to file a U.S. tax return. These individuals must check this box.

d. Dependent of U.S. citizen/resident alien. This is an individual who can be claimed as a dependent on a U.S. tax return and is not eligible to obtain an SSN.

e. Spouse of U.S. citizen/resident alien. This category includes:

● A nonresident alien husband or wife who is not filing a U.S. tax return (including a joint return) and who is not eligible to obtain an SSN but who, as a spouse, can be claimed as an exemption, and

● A nonresident alien electing to file a U.S. tax return jointly with a spouse who is a U.S. citizen or resident.

f. Nonresident alien student, professor, or researcher filing a U.S. tax return. This is an individual who has not abandoned his or her residence in a foreign country and who is a bona fide student, professor, or researcher coming temporarily to the United States solely to attend classes at a recognized institution of education, to teach, or to perform research. If you check this box, you must complete lines 6c and 6g, provide your passport with a valid U.S. visa, and a letter from an official of the school or institution stating that you have not been offered, and have not secured other employment. If applicable, enter the name of the treaty country and the treaty article number in the appropriate entry spaces below box h.

g. Dependent/spouse of a nonresident alien holding a U.S. visa. This is an individual who can be claimed as a dependent or a spouse on a U.S. tax return and who is unable, or not eligible, to obtain an SSN and has entered the United States with a nonresident holding a U.S. visa. For example, the primary visa holder has a B-1 visa; the dependent or spouse has a B-2 visa.

h. Other. If the reason for your ITIN request is not described in a through g, check this box. Describe in detail your reason for requesting an ITIN and attach supporting documents. If any of the following exceptions apply to you, you will not need to attach a tax return to your Form W-7. Check box h and enter the number of the exception that applies (for example, "Exception 3") on the dotted line next to box h.

Exception 1. **Passive income—treaty benefits (box a) or third party withholding (box h).** To obtain an ITIN under this exception, you must include documentation with the Form W-7 showing you own an asset that generates income subject to information reporting or withholding requirements. Examples include:

● Evidence that you opened an interest bearing account with a financial institution and you have an ownership interest in that account, and

● For a partnership interest—the partnership agreement together with the partnership's EIN or other evidence that the partnership is conducting business in the United States.

Exception 2. **Other income (wages, salary, compensation)— treaty benefits (box a).**

 Applicants with a U.S. visa that is valid for employment should first apply for an SSN with the Social Security Administration (SSA). You are not eligible for an ITIN if you are eligible to obtain an SSN.

If you are an individual receiving pay for personal services, your Form W-7 will be processed if you provide proof that your application for an SSN (Form SS-5) was rejected by the SSA and include a Form 8233, Exemption From Withholding on Compensation for Independent (and Certain Dependent) Personal Services of a Nonresident Alien Individual.

If you are a nonresident alien visitor with gaming winnings, your Form W-7 will be processed if submitted through the appropriate gaming official serving as an acceptance agent.

Exception 3. **Third party reporting— mortgage interest (box h).** To obtain an ITIN under this exception, you must include documentation with the Form W-7 showing evidence of a home mortgage loan on real property located in the United States.

Exception 4. **Disposition by foreign person of U.S. real property interest (box h).** If a transferor or transferee does not have a taxpayer identification number, and an amount withheld is due, attach completed Forms 8288, U.S. Withholding Tax Return for Dispositions by Foreign Persons of U.S. Real Property Interests, and 8288-A, Statement of Wihtholding on Dispositions by Foreign Persons of U.S. Real Property Interests, to the completed Form W-7.

If you are applying for a withholding certificate to reduce or eliminate withholding on dispositions of U.S. real property, you must attach a copy of the contract for sale and a completed application for a withholding certificate to the completed Form W-7. The application for a withholding certificate must comply with the provisions of Regulations sections 1.1445-3 and 1.1445-6 and Rev. Proc. 2000-35, 2000-35 I.R.B. 211. You can find Rev. Proc. 2000-35 on page 211 of Internal Revenue Bulletin 2000-35 at *www.irs.gov/pub/irs-irbs/irb00-35.pdf.* You may be able to use Form 8288-B, Application for Withholding Certificate for Dispositions by Foreign Persons of U.S. Real Property Interests, for this purpose. See Form 8288-B for details.

Line Instructions

Enter N/A (not applicable) on all lines that do not apply to you. Do not leave any lines blank.

Line 1a. Enter your legal name on line 1a as it appears on your documents. This entry should reflect your name as it will appear on a U.S. tax return.

 Your ITIN will be established using this name. If you do not use this name on the U.S. tax return, the processing of the U.S. tax return may be delayed.

Line 1b. Enter your name as it appears on your birth certificate if it is different from your entry on line 1a.

Line 2. Enter your complete mailing address on line 2. This is the address the IRS will use to return your original documents and send written notification of your ITIN.

Note. If the U.S. Postal Service will not deliver mail to your physical location, enter the U.S. Postal Service's post office box number for your mailing address. Contact your local U.S. Post Office for more information. Do not use a post office box owned and operated by a private firm or company.

Line 3. Enter your complete foreign address in the country where you permanently or normally reside if it is different from the address on line 2. If you no longer have a permanent residence, due to your relocation to the United States, enter only the foreign country where you last resided on line 3. If you are claiming a benefit under an income tax treaty with the United States, line 3 must show the treaty country.

 Do not use a post office box or an "in care of" (c/o) address. If you do, your application will be rejected.

Line 4. To be eligible for an ITIN, your birth country must be recognized as a foreign country by the U.S. Department of State.

Line 6a. Enter the country or countries (in the case of dual citizenship) in which you are a citizen. Enter the complete country name; do not abbreviate.

Line 6b. If your country of residence for tax purposes has issued you a tax identification number, enter that number on line 6b. For example, if you are a resident of Canada, enter your Canadian Social Insurance Number.

Line 6c. Enter only U.S. nonimmigrant visa information. Include the USCIS classification, number of the U.S. visa, and the expiration date in month/day/year format. For example, if you have a B-1/B-2 visa with the number 123456 that has an expiration date of December 31, 2006, enter "B-1/B-2," "123456," and "12/31/2006" in the entry space.

Note. If the visa has been issued under a "duration of stay" label by USCIS, enter "D/S" as the expiration date.

Line 6d. Check the box indicating the type of document(s) you are submitting for identification. You must submit documents as explained in item (3) under *How To Apply* on page 2. Enter the name of the state or country or other issuer, the identification number (if any) appearing on the document(s), the expiration date, and the date on which you entered the United States. Dates must be entered in the month/day/year format. Also, you may be required to provide a certified translation of foreign language documents.

Note. Any visa information shown on a passport must be entered on line 6c.

Line 6e. If you ever received a temporary taxpayer identification number (TIN) or an employer identification number (EIN), check the "Yes" box and complete line 6f. If you never had a temporary TIN or an EIN, or you do not know your temporary TIN, check the "No/Do not know" box.

A temporary TIN is a nine-digit number issued by the IRS to persons who file a return or make a payment without providing a TIN. You would have been issued this number if you filed a U.S. tax return and did not have a social security number. This temporary TIN will appear on any correspondence the IRS sent you concerning that return.

An EIN is a nine-digit number (for example, 12-3456789) assigned by the IRS to businesses, such as sole proprietorships.

Line 6f. If you have both a temporary TIN and an EIN, attach a separate sheet listing both. If you were issued more than one temporary TIN, attach a separate sheet listing all the temporary TINs you received.

Line 6g. If you checked reason f, you must enter the name of the educational institution and the city and state in which it is located. You must also enter your length of stay in the United States.

If you are temporarily in the United States for business purposes, you must enter the name of the company with whom you are conducting your business and the city and state in which it is located. You must also enter your length of stay in the United States.

Signature. You must sign Form W-7. However, if the applicant is a minor under 14 years of age, a delegate (parent or court-appointed guardian) should sign for him or her. Type or print the delegate's name in the space provided and check the appropriate box that indicates his or her relationship to the applicant. If the delegate is signing as a court-appointed guardian, attach a copy of the court-appointment papers showing the legal guardianship.

If the applicant is 14 years of age or over, the applicant can appoint an authorized agent to sign. The authorized agent must print his or her name in the space provided for the name of the delegate and attach Form 2848, Power of Attorney and Declaration of Representative.

Paperwork Reduction Act Notice. We ask for the information on this form to carry out the Internal Revenue laws of the United States. You are required to give us the information. We need it to ensure that you are complying with these laws and to allow us to figure and collect the right amount of tax.

You are not required to provide the information requested on a form that is subject to the Paperwork Reduction Act unless the form displays a valid OMB control number. Books or records relating to a form or its instructions must be retained as long as their contents may become material in the administration of any Internal Revenue law. Generally, tax returns and return information are confidential, as required by Internal Revenue Code section 6103.

The average time and expenses required to complete and file this form will vary depending on individual circumstances. For the estimated averages, see the instructions for your income tax return.

If you have suggestions for making this form simpler, we would be happy to hear from you. See the instructions for your income tax return.

Form W-8BEN

(Rev. December 2000)

Department of the Treasury
Internal Revenue Service

Certificate of Foreign Status of Beneficial Owner for United States Tax Withholding

▶ Section references are to the Internal Revenue Code.   ▶ See separate instructions.
▶ Give this form to the withholding agent or payer. Do not send to the IRS.

OMB No. 1545-1621

Do not use this form for:

Instead, use Form:

- A U.S. citizen or other U.S. person, including a resident alien individual W-9
- A person claiming an exemption from U.S. withholding on income effectively connected with the conduct of a trade or business in the United States W-8ECI
- A foreign partnership, a foreign simple trust, or a foreign grantor trust (see instructions for exceptions) . . . . W-8ECI or W-8IMY
- A foreign government, international organization, foreign central bank of issue, foreign tax-exempt organization, foreign private foundation, or government of a U.S. possession that received effectively connected income or that is claiming the applicability of section(s) 115(2), 501(c), 892, 895, or 1443(b) (see instructions) . . . . W-8ECI or W-8EXP

Note: *These entities should use Form W-8BEN if they are claiming treaty benefits or are providing the form only to claim they are a foreign person exempt from backup withholding.*

- A person acting as an intermediary W-8IMY

Note: *See instructions for additional exceptions.*

Part I   Identification of Beneficial Owner (See instructions.)

1 Name of individual or organization that is the beneficial owner	2 Country of incorporation or organization

3   Type of beneficial owner: ☐ Individual   ☐ Corporation   ☐ Disregarded entity   ☐ Partnership   ☐ Simple trust

☐ Grantor trust   ☐ Complex trust   ☐ Estate   ☐ Government   ☐ International organization

☐ Central bank of issue   ☐ Tax-exempt organization   ☐ Private foundation

4   Permanent residence address (street, apt. or suite no., or rural route). **Do not use a P.O. box or in-care-of address.**

City or town, state or province. Include postal code where appropriate.	Country (do not abbreviate)

5   Mailing address (if different from above)

City or town, state or province. Include postal code where appropriate.	Country (do not abbreviate)

6 U.S. taxpayer identification number, if required (see instructions) ☐ SSN or ITIN ☐ EIN	7 Foreign tax identifying number, if any (optional)

8   Reference number(s) (see instructions)

Part II   Claim of Tax Treaty Benefits (if applicable)

9   I certify that (check all that apply):

a ☐ The beneficial owner is a resident of .... within the meaning of the income tax treaty between the United States and that country.

b ☐ If required, the U.S. taxpayer identification number is stated on line 6 (see instructions).

c ☐ The beneficial owner is not an individual, derives the item (or items) of income for which the treaty benefits are claimed, and, if applicable, meets the requirements of the treaty provision dealing with limitation on benefits (see instructions).

d ☐ The beneficial owner is not an individual, is claiming treaty benefits for dividends received from a foreign corporation or interest from a U.S. trade or business of a foreign corporation, and meets qualified resident status (see instructions).

e ☐ The beneficial owner is related to the person obligated to pay the income within the meaning of section 267(b) or 707(b), and will file Form 8833 if the amount subject to withholding received during a calendar year exceeds, in the aggregate, $500,000.

10   **Special rates and conditions** (if applicable—see instructions): The beneficial owner is claiming the provisions of Article .... of the treaty identified on line 9a above to claim a .... % rate of withholding on (specify type of income): ....

Explain the reasons the beneficial owner meets the terms of the treaty article: --

----

Part III   Notional Principal Contracts

11 ☐ I have provided or will provide a statement that identifies those notional principal contracts from which the income is **not** effectively connected with the conduct of a trade or business in the United States. I agree to update this statement as required.

Part IV   Certification

Under penalties of perjury, I declare that I have examined the information on this form and to the best of my knowledge and belief it is true, correct, and complete. I further certify under penalties of perjury that:

- I am the beneficial owner (or am authorized to sign for the beneficial owner) of all the income to which this form relates,
- The beneficial owner is not a U.S. person,
- The income to which this form relates is not effectively connected with the conduct of a trade or business in the United States or is effectively connected but is not subject to tax under an income tax treaty, **and**
- For broker transactions or barter exchanges, the beneficial owner is an exempt foreign person as defined in the instructions.

Furthermore, I authorize this form to be provided to any withholding agent that has control, receipt, or custody of the income of which I am the beneficial owner or any withholding agent that can disburse or make payments of the income of which I am the beneficial owner.

Sign Here ▶

Signature of beneficial owner (or individual authorized to sign for beneficial owner)	Date (MM-DD-YYYY)	Capacity in which acting

For Paperwork Reduction Act Notice, see separate instructions.   Cat. No. 25047Z   Form **W-8BEN** (Rev. 12-2000)

Instructions for Form W-8BEN

(Rev. January 2003)

Department of the Treasury
Internal Revenue Service

(Use with the December 2000 revision of Form W-8BEN.)

Certificate of Foreign Status of Beneficial Owner for United States Tax Withholding

Section references are to the Internal Revenue Code unless otherwise noted.

General Instructions

Note: *For definitions of terms used throughout these instructions, see* **Definitions** *on pages 2 and 3.*

A change to note. We added **Nonresident alien who becomes a resident alien** to the instructions for line 10 on page 5. This new section requires the use of Form W-9 in certain circumstances. See page 5 for details.

Purpose of form. Foreign persons are subject to U.S. tax at a 30% rate on income they receive from U.S. sources that consists of:

- Interest (including certain original issue discount (OID));
- Dividends;
- Rents;
- Royalties;
- Premiums;
- Annuities;
- Compensation for, or in expectation of, services performed;
- Substitute payments in a securities lending transaction; or
- Other fixed or determinable annual or periodical gains, profits, or income.

This tax is imposed on the gross amount paid and is generally collected by withholding on that amount. A payment is considered to have been made whether it is made directly to the beneficial owner or to another person, such as an intermediary, agent, or partnership, for the benefit of the beneficial owner.

If you receive certain types of income, you must provide Form W-8BEN to:
- Establish that you are not a U.S. person;
- Claim that you are the beneficial owner of the income for which Form W-8BEN is being provided; and
- If applicable, claim a reduced rate of, or exemption from, withholding as a resident of a foreign country with which the United States has an income tax treaty.

You may also be required to submit Form W-8BEN to claim an exception from domestic information reporting and backup withholding for certain types of income that are not subject to foreign-person withholding. Such income includes:
- Broker proceeds.
- Short-term (183 days or less) original issue discount (OID).
- Bank deposit interest.
- Foreign source interest, dividends, rents, or royalties.

- Proceeds from a wager placed by a nonresident alien individual in the games of blackjack, baccarat, craps, roulette, or big-6 wheel.

You may also use Form W-8BEN to certify that income from a notional principal contract is not effectively connected with the conduct of a trade or business in the United States.

A withholding agent or payer of the income may rely on a properly completed Form W-8BEN to treat a payment associated with the Form W-8BEN as a payment to a foreign person who beneficially owns the amounts paid. If applicable, the withholding agent may rely on the Form W-8BEN to apply a reduced rate of withholding at source.

Provide Form W-8BEN to the withholding agent or payer before income is paid or credited to you. Failure to provide a Form W-8BEN when requested may lead to withholding at a 30% rate (foreign-person withholding) or the backup withholding rate.

Note: *For additional information and instructions for the withholding agent, see the* **Instructions for the Requester of Forms W-8BEN, W-8ECI, W-8EXP, and W-8IMY.**

Who must file. You must give Form W-8BEN to the withholding agent or payer if you are a foreign person and you are the beneficial owner of an amount subject to withholding. Submit Form W-8BEN when requested by the withholding agent or payer whether or not you are claiming a reduced rate of, or exemption from, withholding.

Do not use Form W-8BEN if:
- You are a U.S. citizen (even if you reside outside the United States) or other U.S. person (including a resident alien individual). Instead, use **Form W-9,** Request for Taxpayer Identification Number and Certification.
- You are a disregarded entity with a single owner that is a U.S. person and you are not a hybrid entity claiming treaty benefits. Instead, provide Form W-9.
- You are a nonresident alien individual who claims exemption from withholding on compensation for independent or dependent personal services performed in the United States. Instead, provide **Form 8233,** Exemption from Withholding on Compensation for Independent (and Certain Dependent) Personal Services of a Nonresident Alien Individual, or **Form W-4,** Employee's Withholding Allowance Certificate.
- You are receiving income that is effectively connected with the conduct of a trade or business in the United

Cat. No. 25576H

States. Instead, provide **Form W-8ECI,** Certificate of Foreign Person's Claim for Exemption From Withholding on Income Effectively Connected With the Conduct of a Trade or Business in the United States. If any of the income for which you have provided a Form W-8BEN becomes effectively connected, this is a change in circumstances and Form W-8BEN is no longer valid. You must file Form W-8ECI. See **Change in circumstances** below.

• You are filing for a foreign government, international organization, foreign central bank of issue, foreign tax-exempt organization, foreign private foundation, or government of a U.S. possession claiming the applicability of section 115(2), 501(c), 892, 895, or 1443(b). Instead, provide **Form W-8EXP,** Certificate of Foreign Government or Other Foreign Organization for United States Tax Withholding. However, you should use Form W-8BEN if you are claiming treaty benefits or are providing the form only to claim you are a foreign person exempt from backup withholding. You should use Form W-8ECI if you received effectively connected income (for example, income from commercial activities).

• You are a foreign flow-through entity, other than a hybrid entity, claiming treaty benefits. Instead, provide **Form W-8IMY,** Certificate of Foreign Intermediary, Foreign Flow-Through Entity, or Certain U.S. Branches for United States Tax Withholding. However, if you are a partner, beneficiary, or owner of a flow-through entity and you are not yourself a flow-through entity, you may be required to furnish a Form W-8BEN to the flow-through entity.

• You are a reverse hybrid entity transmitting beneficial owner documentation provided by your interest holders to claim treaty benefits on their behalf. Instead, provide Form W-8IMY.

• You are a withholding foreign partnership or a withholding foreign trust. A withholding foreign partnership or a withholding foreign trust is a foreign partnership or trust that has entered into a withholding agreement with the IRS under which it agrees to assume primary withholding responsibility for each partner's, beneficary's, or owner's distributive share of income subject to withholding that is paid to the partnership or trust. Instead, provide Form W-8IMY.

• You are acting as an intermediary (that is, acting not for your own account, but for the account of others as an agent, nominee, or custodian). Instead, provide Form W-8IMY.

Giving Form W-8BEN to the withholding agent. Do not send Form W-8BEN to the IRS. Instead, give it to the person who is requesting it from you. Generally, this will be the person from whom you receive the payment or who credits your account. Give Form W-8BEN to the person requesting it before the payment is made to you or credited to your account. If you do not provide this form, the withholding agent may have to withhold at a 30% rate (foreign-person withholding) or backup withholding rate. If you receive more than one type of income from a single withholding agent for which you claim different benefits, the withholding agent may, at its option, require you to submit a Form W-8BEN for each different type of income. Generally, a separate Form W-8BEN must be given to each withholding agent.

Note: *If you own the income or account jointly with one or more other persons, the income or account will be treated by the withholding agent as owned by a foreign person if Forms W-8BEN are provided by all of the owners. If the withholding agent receives a Form W-9 from any of the joint owners, the payment must be treated as made to a U.S. person.*

Change in circumstances. If a change in circumstances makes any information on the Form W-8BEN you have submitted incorrect, you must notify the withholding agent or payer within 30 days of the change in circumstances and you **must** file a new Form W-8BEN or other appropriate form.

If you use Form W-8BEN to certify that you are a foreign person, a change of address to an address in the United States is a change in circumstances. Generally, a change of address within the same foreign country or to another foreign country is not a change in circumstances. However, if you use Form W-8BEN to claim treaty benefits, a move to the United States or outside the country where you have been claiming treaty benefits is a change in circumstances. In that case, you must notify the withholding agent or payer within 30 days of the move.

If you become a U.S. citizen or resident after you submit Form W-8BEN, you are no longer subject to the 30% foreign-person withholding rate. You must notify the withholding agent or payer within 30 days of becoming a U.S. citizen or resident. You may be required to provide a Form W-9. For more information, see Form W-9 and instructions.

Expiration of Form W-8BEN. Generally, a Form W-8BEN provided without a U.S. taxpayer identification number (TIN) will remain in effect for a period starting on the date the form is signed and ending on the last day of the third succeeding calendar year, unless a change in circumstances makes any information on the form incorrect. For example, a Form W-8BEN signed on September 30, 2003, remains valid through December 31, 2006. A Form W-8BEN furnished with a U.S. TIN will remain in effect until a change in circumstances makes any information on the form incorrect, provided that the withholding agent reports on Form 1042-S at least one payment annually to the beneficial owner who provided the Form W-8BEN. See the instructions for line 6 on page 4 for circumstances under which you **must** provide a U.S. TIN.

Definitions

Beneficial owner. For payments other than those for which a reduced rate of withholding is claimed under an income tax treaty, the beneficial owner of income is generally the person who is required under U.S. tax principles to include the income in gross income on a tax return. A person is not a beneficial owner of income, however, to the extent that person is receiving the income as a nominee, agent, or custodian, or to the extent the person is a conduit whose participation in a transaction is disregarded. In the case of amounts paid that do not constitute income, beneficial ownership is determined as if the payment were income.

Foreign partnerships, foreign simple trusts, and foreign grantor trusts are not the beneficial owners of income paid to the partnership or trust. The beneficial owners of income paid to a foreign partnership are generally the

-2-

partners in the partnership, provided that the partner is not itself a partnership, foreign simple or grantor trust, nominee or other agent. The beneficial owners of income paid to a foreign simple trust (that is, a foreign trust that is described in section 651(a)) are generally the beneficiaries of the trust, if the beneficiary is not a foreign partnership, foreign simple or grantor trust, nominee or other agent. The beneficial owners of a foreign grantor trust (that is, a foreign trust to the extent that all or a portion of the income of the trust is treated as owned by the grantor or another person under sections 671 through 679) are the persons treated as the owners of the trust. The beneficial owners of income paid to a foreign complex trust (that is, a foreign trust that is not a foreign simple trust or foreign grantor trust) is the trust itself.

The beneficial owner of income paid to a foreign estate is the estate itself.

Note: *A payment to a U.S. partnership, U.S. trust, or U.S. estate is treated as a payment to a U.S. payee that is not subject to 30% foreign-person withholding. A U.S. partnership, trust, or estate should provide the withholding agent with a Form W-9.*

Foreign person. A foreign person includes a nonresident alien individual, a foreign corporation, a foreign partnership, a foreign trust, a foreign estate, and any other person that is not a U.S. person. It also includes a foreign branch or office of a U.S. financial institution or U.S. clearing organization if the foreign branch is a qualified intermediary. Generally, a payment to a U.S. branch of a foreign person is a payment to a foreign person.

Nonresident alien individual. Any individual who is not a citizen or resident of the United States is a nonresident alien individual. An alien individual meeting either the "green card test" or the "substantial presence test" for the calendar year is a resident alien. Any person not meeting either test is a nonresident alien individual. Additionally, an alien individual who is a resident of a foreign country under the residence article of an income tax treaty, or an alien individual who is a resident of Puerto Rico, Guam, the Commonwealth of the Northern Mariana Islands, the U.S. Virgin Islands, or American Samoa is a nonresident alien individual. See **Pub. 519,** U.S. Tax Guide for Aliens, for more information on resident and nonresident alien status.

Note: *Even though a nonresident alien individual married to a U.S. citizen or resident alien may choose to be treated as a resident alien for certain purposes (for example, filing a joint income tax return), such individual is still treated as a nonresident alien for withholding tax purposes on all income except wages.*

Flow-through entity. A flow-through entity is a foreign partnership (other than a withholding foreign partnership), a foreign simple or foreign grantor trust (other than a withholding foreign trust), or, for payments for which a reduced rate of withholding is claimed under an income tax treaty, any entity to the extent the entity is considered to be fiscally transparent (see below) with respect to the payment by an interest holder's jurisdiction.

Hybrid entity. A hybrid entity is any person (other than an individual) that is treated as fiscally transparent (see below) in the United States but is not treated as fiscally transparent by a country with which the United States

has an income tax treaty. Hybrid entity status is relevant for claiming treaty benefits. See the instructions for line 9c on page 5.

Reverse hybrid entity. A reverse hybrid entity is any person (other than an individual) that is not fiscally transparent under U.S. tax law principles but that is fiscally transparent under the laws of a jurisdiction with which the United States has an income tax treaty. See the instructions for line 9c on page 5.

Fiscally transparent entity. An entity is treated as fiscally transparent with respect to an item of income for which treaty benefits are claimed to the extent that the interest holders in the entity must, on a current basis, take into account separately their shares of an item of income paid to the entity, whether or not distributed, and must determine the character of the items of income as if they were realized directly from the sources from which realized by the entity. For example, partnerships, common trust funds, and simple trusts or grantor trusts are generally considered to be fiscally transparent with respect to items of income received by them.

Disregarded entity. A business entity that has a single owner and is not a corporation under Regulations section 301.7701-2(b) is disregarded as an entity separate from its owner.

Amounts subject to withholding. Generally, an amount subject to withholding is an amount from sources within the United States that is fixed or determinable annual or periodical (FDAP) income. FDAP income is all income included in gross income, including interest (as well as OID), dividends, rents, royalties, and compensation. FDAP income does not include most gains from the sale of property (including market discount and option premiums).

Withholding agent. Any person, U.S. or foreign, that has control, receipt, or custody of an amount subject to withholding or who can disburse or make payments of an amount subject to withholding is a withholding agent. The withholding agent may be an individual, corporation, partnership, trust, association, or any other entity, including (but not limited to) any foreign intermediary, foreign partnership, and U.S. branches of certain foreign banks and insurance companies. Generally, the person who pays (or causes to be paid) the amount subject to withholding to the foreign person (or to its agent) must withhold.

Specific Instructions

Note: *A hybrid entity should give Form W-8BEN to a withholding agent only for income for which it is claiming a reduced rate of withholding under an income tax treaty. A reverse hybrid entity should give Form W-8BEN to a withholding agent only for income for which **no** treaty benefit is being claimed.*

Part I

Line 1. Enter your name. If you are a disregarded entity with a single owner who is a foreign person and you are not claiming treaty benefits as a hybrid entity, this form should be completed and signed by your foreign single owner. If the account to which a payment is made or credited is in the name of the disregarded entity, the

-3-

foreign single owner should inform the withholding agent of this fact. This may be done by including the name and account number of the disregarded entity on line 8 (reference number) of the form. However, if you are a disregarded entity that is claiming treaty benefits as a hybrid entity, this form should be completed and signed by you.

Line 2. If you are a corporation, enter the country of incorporation. If you are another type of entity, enter the country under whose laws you are created, organized, or governed. If you are an individual, enter N/A (for "not applicable").

Line 3. Check the **one** box that applies. By checking a box, you are representing that you qualify for this classification. You must check the box that represents your classification (for example, corporation, partnership, trust, estate, etc.) under U.S. tax principles. **Do not** check the box that describes your status under the law of the treaty country. If you are a partnership or disregarded entity receiving a payment for which treaty benefits are being claimed, you **must** check the "Partnership" or "Disregarded entity" box. If you are a sole proprietor, check the "Individual" box, not the "Disregarded entity" box.

 Only entities that are tax-exempt under section 501 should check the "Tax-exempt organizations" box. Such organizations should use Form W-8BEN only if they are claiming a reduced rate of withholding under an income tax treaty or some code exception other than section 501. Use Form W-8EXP if you are claiming an exemption from withholding under section 501.

Line 4. Your permanent residence address is the address in the country where you claim to be a resident for purposes of that country's income tax. If you are giving Form W-8BEN to claim a reduced rate of withholding under an income tax treaty, you must determine your residency in the manner required by the treaty. **Do not** show the address of a financial institution, a post office box, or an address used solely for mailing purposes. If you are an individual who does not have a tax residence in any country, your permanent residence is where you normally reside. If you are not an individual and you do not have a tax residence in any country, the permanent residence address is where you maintain your principal office.

Line 5. Enter your mailing address only if it is different from the address you show on line 4.

Line 6. If you are an individual, you are generally required to enter your social security number (SSN). To apply for an SSN, get **Form SS-5** from a Social Security Administration (SSA) office or, if in the United States, you may call the SSA at 1-800-772-1213. Fill in Form SS-5 and return it to the SSA.

If you do not have an SSN and are not eligible to get one, you must get an individual taxpayer identification number (ITIN). **To apply for an ITIN,** file **Form W-7** with the IRS. It usually takes 4-6 weeks to get an ITIN.

Note: *An ITIN is for tax use only. It does not entitle you to social security benefits or change your employment or immigration status under U.S. law.*

If you are not an individual or you are an individual who is an employer or who is engaged in a U.S. trade or

business as a sole proprietor, you must enter an employer identification number (EIN). If you do not have an EIN, you should apply for one on **Form SS-4,** Application for Employer Identification Number. If you are a disregarded entity claiming treaty benefits as a hybrid entity, enter **your** EIN.

You **must** provide a U.S. taxpayer identification number (TIN) if you are:

   1. Claiming an exemption from withholding under section 871(f) for certain annuities received under qualified plans, or

   2. A foreign grantor trust with 5 or fewer grantors, or

   3. Claiming benefits under an income tax treaty.

However, a U.S. TIN is not required to be shown in order to claim treaty benefits on the following items of income:

- Dividends and interest from stocks and debt obligations that are actively traded;
- Dividends from any redeemable security issued by an investment company registered under the Investment Company Act of 1940 (mutual fund);
- Dividends, interest, or royalties from units of beneficial interest in a unit investment trust that are (or were upon issuance) publicly offered and are registered with the SEC under the Securities Act of 1933; and
- Income related to loans of any of the above securities.

Note: *You may want to obtain and provide a U.S. TIN on Form W-8BEN even though it is not required. A Form W-8BEN containing a U.S. TIN remains valid for as long as your status and the information relevant to the certifications you make on the form remain unchanged provided at least one payment is reported to you annually on Form 1042-S.*

Line 7. If your country of residence for tax purposes has issued you a tax identifying number, enter it here. For example, if you are a resident of Canada, enter your Social Insurance Number.

Line 8. This line may be used by the filer of Form W-8BEN or by the withholding agent to whom it is provided to include any referencing information that is useful to the withholding agent in carrying out its obligations. For example, withholding agents who are required to associate the Form W-8BEN with a particular Form W-8IMY may want to use line 8 for a referencing number or code that will make the association clear. A beneficial owner may use line 8 to include the number of the account for which he or she is providing the form. A foreign single owner of a disregarded entity may use line 8 to inform the withholding agent that the account to which a payment is made or credited is in the name of the disregarded entity (see instructions for line 1 starting on page 3).

Part II

Line 9a. Enter the country where you claim to be a resident for income tax treaty purposes. For treaty purposes, a person is a resident of a treaty country if the person is a resident of that country under the terms of the treaty.

Line 9b. If you are claiming benefits under an income tax treaty, you must have a U.S. TIN unless one of the exceptions listed in the line 6 instructions above applies.

-4-

Line 9c. An entity (but not an individual) that is claiming a reduced rate of withholding under an income tax treaty must represent that it **(a)** derives the item of income for which the treaty benefit is claimed and **(b)** meets the limitation on benefits provisions contained in the treaty, if any.

An item of income may be derived by either the entity receiving the item of income or by the interest holders in the entity or, in certain circumstances, both. An item of income paid to an entity is considered to be derived by the entity only if the entity is not fiscally transparent under the laws of the entity's jurisdiction with respect to the item of income. An item of income paid to an entity shall be considered to be derived by the interest holder in the entity only if **(a)** the interest holder is not fiscally transparent in its jurisdiction with respect to the item of income and **(b)** the entity is considered to be fiscally transparent under the laws of the interest holder's jurisdiction with respect to the item of income. An item of income paid directly to a type of entity specifically identified in a treaty as a resident of a treaty jurisdiction is treated as derived by a resident of that treaty jurisdiction.

If an entity is claiming treaty benefits on its own behalf, it should complete Form W-8BEN. If an interest holder in an entity that is considered fiscally transparent in the interest holder's jurisdiction is claiming a treaty benefit, the interest holder should complete Form W-8BEN on its own behalf and the fiscally transparent entity should associate the interest holder's Form W-8BEN with a Form W-8IMY completed by the entity.

Note: *An income tax treaty may not apply to reduce the amount of any tax on an item of income received by an entity that is treated as a domestic corporation for U.S. tax purposes. Therefore, neither the domestic corporation nor its shareholders are entitled to the benefits of a reduction of U.S. income tax on an item of income received from U.S. sources by the corporation.*

To determine whether an entity meets the limitation on benefits provisions of a treaty, you must consult the specific provisions or articles under the treaties. Income tax treaties are available on the IRS Web Site at **www.irs.gov**.

Note: *If you are an entity that derives the income as a resident of a treaty country, you may check this box if the applicable income tax treaty does not contain a "limitation on benefits" provision.*

Line 9d. If you are a foreign corporation claiming treaty benefits under an income tax treaty that entered into force before January 1, 1987 (and has not been renegotiated) on **(a)** U.S. source dividends paid to you by another foreign corporation or **(b)** U.S. source interest paid to you by a U.S. trade or business of another foreign corporation, you must generally be a "qualified resident" of a treaty country. See section 884 for the definition of interest paid by a U.S. trade or business of a foreign corporation ("branch interest") and other applicable rules.

In general, a foreign corporation is a qualified resident of a country if one or more of the following applies:
• It meets a 50% ownership and base erosion test.
• It is primarily and regularly traded on an established securities market in its country of residence or the United States.

• It carries on an active trade or business in its country of residence.
• It gets a ruling from the IRS that it is a qualified resident.
    See Regulations section 1.884-5 for the requirements that must be met to satisfy each of these tests.

 If you are claiming treaty benefits under an income tax treaty entered into force after December 31, 1986, **do not** *check box 9d. Instead, check box 9c.*

Line 9e. Check this box if you are related to the withholding agent within the meaning of section 267(b) or 707(b) and the aggregate amount subject to withholding received during the calendar year exceeds $500,000. Additionally, you must file **Form 8833,** Treaty-Based Return Position Disclosure Under Section 6114 or 7701(b).

Line 10

Line 10 must be used **only** if you are claiming treaty benefits that require that you meet conditions not covered by the representations you make in lines 9a through 9e. However, this line should always be completed by foreign students and researchers claiming treaty benefits. See **Scholarship and fellowship grants** below for more information.

Additional examples of persons who should complete this line are:

1. Exempt organizations claiming treaty benefits under the exempt organization articles of the treaties with Canada, Mexico, Germany, and the Netherlands.

2. Foreign corporations that are claiming a preferential rate applicable to dividends based on ownership of a specific percentage of stock.

3. Persons claiming treaty benefits on royalties if the treaty contains different withholding rates for different types of royalties.

This line is generally not applicable to claiming treaty benefits under an interest or dividends (other than dividends subject to a preferential rate based on ownership) article of a treaty.

Nonresident alien who becomes a resident alien. Generally, only a nonresident alien individual may use the terms of a tax treaty to reduce or eliminate U.S. tax on certain types of income. However, most tax treaties contain a provision known as a "saving clause." Exceptions specified in the saving clause may permit an exemption from tax to continue for certain types of income even after the recipient has otherwise become a U.S. resident alien for tax purposes. The individual must use Form W-9 to claim the tax treaty benefit. See the instructions for Form W-9 for more information. Also see **Nonresident alien student or researcher who becomes a resident alien** on page 6 for an example.

Scholarship and fellowship grants. A nonresident alien student (including a trainee or business apprentice) or researcher who receives noncompensatory scholarship or fellowship income may use Form W-8BEN to claim benefits under a tax treaty that apply to reduce or eliminate U.S. tax on such income. **No Form W-8BEN is required unless a treaty benefit is being claimed.** A nonresident alien student or researcher who receives compensatory scholarship or fellowship income must use

Form 8233 to claim any benefits of a tax treaty that apply to that income. The student or researcher must use Form W-4 for any part of such income for which he or she is not claiming a tax treaty withholding exemption. **Do not use Form W-8BEN for compensatory scholarship or fellowship income. See Compensation for Dependent Personal Services** in the Instructions for Form 8233.

Note: *If you are a nonresident alien individual who received noncompensatory scholarship or fellowship income and personal services income (including compensatory scholarship or fellowship income) from the same withholding agent, you may use Form 8233 to claim a tax treaty withholding exemption for part or all of both types of income.*

Completing lines 4 and 9a. Most tax treaties that contain an article exempting scholarship or fellowship grant income from taxation require that the recipient be a resident of the other treaty country at the time of, or immediately prior to, entry into the United States. Thus, a student or researcher may claim the exemption even if he or she no longer has a permanent address in the other treaty country after entry into the United States. If this is the case, you may provide a U.S. address on line 4 and still be eligible for the exemption if all other conditions required by the tax treaty are met. You must also identify on line 9a the tax treaty country of which you were a resident at the time of, or immediately prior to, your entry into the United States.

Completing line 10. You must complete line 10 if you are a student or researcher claiming an exemption from taxation on your scholarship or fellowship grant income under a tax treaty.

Nonresident alien student or researcher who becomes a resident alien. You must use Form W-9 to claim an exception to a saving clause. See **Nonresident alien who becomes a resident alien** on page 5 for a general explanation of saving clauses and exceptions to them.

Example. Article 20 of the U.S.-China income tax treaty allows an exemption from tax for scholarship income received by a Chinese student temporarily present in the United States. Under U.S. law, this student will become a resident alien for tax purposes if his or her stay in the United States exceeds 5 calendar years. However, paragraph 2 of the first protocol to the U.S.-China treaty (dated April 30, 1984) allows the provisions of Article 20 to continue to apply even after the Chinese student becomes a resident alien of the United States. A Chinese student who qualifies for this exception (under paragraph 2 of the first protocol) and is relying on this exception to claim an exemption from tax on his or her scholarship or fellowship income would complete Form W-9.

Part III

If you check this box, you must provide the withholding agent with the required statement for income from a notional principal contract that is to be treated as income not effectively connected with the conduct of a trade or business in the United States. You should update this statement as often as necessary. A new Form W-8BEN is not required for each update provided the form otherwise remains valid.

Part IV

Form W-8BEN must be signed and dated by the beneficial owner of the income, or, if the beneficial owner is not an individual, by an authorized representative or officer of the beneficial owner. If Form W-8BEN is completed by an agent acting under a duly authorized power of attorney, the form must be accompanied by the power of attorney in proper form or a copy thereof specifically authorizing the agent to represent the principal in making, executing, and presenting the form. **Form 2848,** Power of Attorney and Declaration of Representative, may be used for this purpose. The agent, as well as the beneficial owner, may incur liability for the penalties provided for an erroneous, false, or fraudulent form.

Broker transactions or barter exchanges. Income from transactions with a broker or a barter exchange is subject to reporting rules and backup withholding unless Form W-8BEN or a substitute form is filed to notify the broker or barter exchange that you are an exempt foreign person.

You are an exempt foreign person for a calendar year in which: **(a)** you are a nonresident alien individual or a foreign corporation, partnership, estate, or trust; **(b)** you are an individual who has not been, and does not plan to be, present in the United States for a total of 183 days or more during the calendar year; and **(c)** you are neither engaged, nor plan to be engaged during the year, in a U.S. trade or business that has effectively connected gains from transactions with a broker or barter exchange.

Paperwork Reduction Act Notice. We ask for the information on this form to carry out the Internal Revenue laws of the United States. You are required to provide the information. We need it to ensure that you are complying with these laws and to allow us to figure and collect the right amount of tax.

You are not required to provide the information requested on a form that is subject to the Paperwork Reduction Act unless the form displays a valid OMB control number. Books or records relating to a form or its instructions must be retained as long as their contents may become material in the administration of any Internal Revenue law. Generally, tax returns and return information are confidential, as required by section 6103.

The time needed to complete and file this form will vary depending on individual circumstances. The estimated average time is: **Recordkeeping,** 5 hr., 58 min.; **Learning about the law or the form,** 3 hr., 46 min.; **Preparing and sending the form to IRS,** 4 hr., 2 min.

If you have comments concerning the accuracy of these time estimates or suggestions for making this form simpler, we would be happy to hear from you. You can write to the Tax Forms Committee, Western Area Distribution Center, Rancho Cordova, CA 95743-0001. **Do not** send Form W-8BEN to this office. Instead, give it to your withholding agent.

-6-

Form **W-9**	**Request for Taxpayer**	Give form to the
(Rev. November 2005)	**Identification Number and Certification**	requester. Do not
Department of the Treasury Internal Revenue Service		send to the IRS.

Print or type — See Specific Instructions on page 2.

Name (as shown on your income tax return)

Business name, if different from above

Check appropriate box: ☐ Individual/ Sole proprietor ☐ Corporation ☐ Partnership ☐ Other ▶ ---------------   ☐ Exempt from backup withholding

Address (number, street, and apt. or suite no.)

Requester's name and address (optional)

City, state, and ZIP code

List account number(s) here (optional)

Part I   Taxpayer Identification Number (TIN)

Enter your TIN in the appropriate box. The TIN provided must match the name given on Line 1 to avoid backup withholding. For individuals, this is your social security number (SSN). However, for a resident alien, sole proprietor, or disregarded entity, see the Part I instructions on page 3. For other entities, it is your employer identification number (EIN). If you do not have a number, see *How to get a TIN* on page 3.

Note. If the account is in more than one name, see the chart on page 4 for guidelines on whose number to enter.

Social security number

or

Employer identification number

Part II   Certification

Under penalties of perjury, I certify that:

1. The number shown on this form is my correct taxpayer identification number (or I am waiting for a number to be issued to me), and

2. I am not subject to backup withholding because: (a) I am exempt from backup withholding, or (b) I have not been notified by the Internal Revenue Service (IRS) that I am subject to backup withholding as a result of a failure to report all interest or dividends, or (c) the IRS has notified me that I am no longer subject to backup withholding, and

3. I am a U.S. person (including a U.S. resident alien).

Certification instructions. You must cross out item 2 above if you have been notified by the IRS that you are currently subject to backup withholding because you have failed to report all interest and dividends on your tax return. For real estate transactions, item 2 does not apply. For mortgage interest paid, acquisition or abandonment of secured property, cancellation of debt, contributions to an individual retirement arrangement (IRA), and generally, payments other than interest and dividends, you are not required to sign the Certification, but you must provide your correct TIN. (See the instructions on page 4.)

Sign Here   Signature of U.S. person ▶   Date ▶

Purpose of Form

A person who is required to file an information return with the IRS, must obtain your correct taxpayer identification number (TIN) to report, for example, income paid to you, real estate transactions, mortgage interest you paid, acquisition or abandonment of secured property, cancellation of debt, or contributions you made to an IRA.

U.S. person. Use Form W-9 only if you are a U.S. person (including a resident alien), to provide your correct TIN to the person requesting it (the requester) and, when applicable, to:

1. Certify that the TIN you are giving is correct (or you are waiting for a number to be issued),

2. Certify that you are not subject to backup withholding, or

3. Claim exemption from backup withholding if you are a U.S. exempt payee.

In 3 above, if applicable, you are also certifying that as a U.S. person, your allocable share of any partnership income from a U.S. trade or business is not subject to the withholding tax on foreign partners' share of effectively connected income.

Note. If a requester gives you a form other than Form W-9 to request your TIN, you must use the requester's form if it is substantially similar to this Form W-9.

For federal tax purposes, you are considered a person if you are:

● An individual who is a citizen or resident of the United States,

● A partnership, corporation, company, or association created or organized in the United States or under the laws of the United States, or

● Any estate (other than a foreign estate) or trust. See Regulations sections 301.7701-6(a) and 7(a) for additional information.

Special rules for partnerships. Partnerships that conduct a trade or business in the United States are generally required to pay a withholding tax on any foreign partners' share of income from such business. Further, in certain cases where a Form W-9 has not been received, a partnership is required to presume that a partner is a foreign person, and pay the withholding tax. Therefore, if you are a U.S. person that is a partner in a partnership conducting a trade or business in the United States, provide Form W-9 to the partnership to establish your U.S. status and avoid withholding on your share of partnership income.

The person who gives Form W-9 to the partnership for purposes of establishing its U.S. status and avoiding withholding on its allocable share of net income from the partnership conducting a trade or business in the United States is in the following cases:

● The U.S. owner of a disregarded entity and not the entity,

Cat. No. 10231X   Form **W-9** (Rev. 11-2005)

Appendix

- The U.S. grantor or other owner of a grantor trust and not the trust, and

- The U.S. trust (other than a grantor trust) and not the beneficiaries of the trust.

Foreign person. If you are a foreign person, do not use Form W-9. Instead, use the appropriate Form W-8 (see Publication 515, Withholding of Tax on Nonresident Aliens and Foreign Entities).

Nonresident alien who becomes a resident alien. Generally, only a nonresident alien individual may use the terms of a tax treaty to reduce or eliminate U.S. tax on certain types of income. However, most tax treaties contain a provision known as a "saving clause." Exceptions specified in the saving clause may permit an exemption from tax to continue for certain types of income even after the recipient has otherwise become a U.S. resident alien for tax purposes.

If you are a U.S. resident alien who is relying on an exception contained in the saving clause of a tax treaty to claim an exemption from U.S. tax on certain types of income, you must attach a statement to Form W-9 that specifies the following five items:

1. The treaty country. Generally, this must be the same treaty under which you claimed exemption from tax as a nonresident alien.

2. The treaty article addressing the income.

3. The article number (or location) in the tax treaty that contains the saving clause and its exceptions.

4. The type and amount of income that qualifies for the exemption from tax.

5. Sufficient facts to justify the exemption from tax under the terms of the treaty article.

Example. Article 20 of the U.S.-China income tax treaty allows an exemption from tax for scholarship income received by a Chinese student temporarily present in the United States. Under U.S. law, this student will become a resident alien for tax purposes if his or her stay in the United States exceeds 5 calendar years. However, paragraph 2 of the first Protocol to the U.S.-China treaty (dated April 30, 1984) allows the provisions of Article 20 to continue to apply even after the Chinese student becomes a resident alien of the United States. A Chinese student who qualifies for this exception (under paragraph 2 of the first protocol) and is relying on this exception to claim an exemption from tax on his or her scholarship or fellowship income would attach to Form W-9 a statement that includes the information described above to support that exemption.

If you are a nonresident alien or a foreign entity not subject to backup withholding, give the requester the appropriate completed Form W-8.

What is backup withholding? Persons making certain payments to you must under certain conditions withhold and pay to the IRS 28% of such payments (after December 31, 2002). This is called "backup withholding." Payments that may be subject to backup withholding include interest, dividends, broker and barter exchange transactions, rents, royalties, nonemployee pay, and certain payments from fishing boat operators. Real estate transactions are not subject to backup withholding.

You will not be subject to backup withholding on payments you receive if you give the requester your correct TIN, make the proper certifications, and report all your taxable interest and dividends on your tax return.

Payments you receive will be subject to backup withholding if:

1. You do not furnish your TIN to the requester,

2. You do not certify your TIN when required (see the Part II instructions on page 4 for details),

3. The IRS tells the requester that you furnished an incorrect TIN,

4. The IRS tells you that you are subject to backup withholding because you did not report all your interest and dividends on your tax return (for reportable interest and dividends only), or

5. You do not certify to the requester that you are not subject to backup withholding under 4 above (for reportable interest and dividend accounts opened after 1983 only).

Certain payees and payments are exempt from backup withholding. See the instructions below and the separate Instructions for the Requester of Form W-9.

Also see *Special rules regarding partnerships* on page 1.

Penalties

Failure to furnish TIN. If you fail to furnish your correct TIN to a requester, you are subject to a penalty of $50 for each such failure unless your failure is due to reasonable cause and not to willful neglect.

Civil penalty for false information with respect to withholding. If you make a false statement with no reasonable basis that results in no backup withholding, you are subject to a $500 penalty.

Criminal penalty for falsifying information. Willfully falsifying certifications or affirmations may subject you to criminal penalties including fines and/or imprisonment.

Misuse of TINs. If the requester discloses or uses TINs in violation of federal law, the requester may be subject to civil and criminal penalties.

Specific Instructions

Name

If you are an individual, you must generally enter the name shown on your income tax return. However, if you have changed your last name, for instance, due to marriage without informing the Social Security Administration of the name change, enter your first name, the last name shown on your social security card, and your new last name.

If the account is in joint names, list first, and then circle, the name of the person or entity whose number you entered in Part I of the form.

Sole proprietor. Enter your individual name as shown on your income tax return on the "Name" line. You may enter your business, trade, or "doing business as (DBA)" name on the "Business name" line.

Limited liability company (LLC). If you are a single-member LLC (including a foreign LLC with a domestic owner) that is disregarded as an entity separate from its owner under Treasury regulations section 301.7701-3, enter the owner's name on the "Name" line. Enter the LLC's name on the "Business name" line. Check the appropriate box for your filing status (sole proprietor, corporation, etc.), then check the box for "Other" and enter "LLC" in the space provided.

Other entities. Enter your business name as shown on required federal tax documents on the "Name" line. This name should match the name shown on the charter or other legal document creating the entity. You may enter any business, trade, or DBA name on the "Business name" line.

Note. You are requested to check the appropriate box for your status (individual/sole proprietor, corporation, etc.).

Exempt From Backup Withholding

If you are exempt, enter your name as described above and check the appropriate box for your status, then check the "Exempt from backup withholding" box in the line following the business name, sign and date the form.

Generally, individuals (including sole proprietors) are not exempt from backup withholding. Corporations are exempt from backup withholding for certain payments, such as interest and dividends.

Note. If you are exempt from backup withholding, you should still complete this form to avoid possible erroneous backup withholding.

Exempt payees. Backup withholding is not required on any payments made to the following payees:

1. An organization exempt from tax under section 501(a), any IRA, or a custodial account under section 403(b)(7) if the account satisfies the requirements of section 401(f)(2),

2. The United States or any of its agencies or instrumentalities,

3. A state, the District of Columbia, a possession of the United States, or any of their political subdivisions or instrumentalities,

4. A foreign government or any of its political subdivisions, agencies, or instrumentalities, or

5. An international organization or any of its agencies or instrumentalities.

Other payees that may be exempt from backup withholding include:

6. A corporation,

7. A foreign central bank of issue,

8. A dealer in securities or commodities required to register in the United States, the District of Columbia, or a possession of the United States,

9. A futures commission merchant registered with the Commodity Futures Trading Commission,

10. A real estate investment trust,

11. An entity registered at all times during the tax year under the Investment Company Act of 1940,

12. A common trust fund operated by a bank under section 584(a),

13. A financial institution,

14. A middleman known in the investment community as a nominee or custodian, or

15. A trust exempt from tax under section 664 or described in section 4947.

The chart below shows types of payments that may be exempt from backup withholding. The chart applies to the exempt recipients listed above, 1 through 15.

IF the payment is for . . .	THEN the payment is exempt for . . .
Interest and dividend payments	All exempt recipients except for 9
Broker transactions	Exempt recipients 1 through 13. Also, a person registered under the Investment Advisers Act of 1940 who regularly acts as a broker
Barter exchange transactions and patronage dividends	Exempt recipients 1 through 5
Payments over $600 required to be reported and direct sales over $5,000 [1]	Generally, exempt recipients 1 through 7 [2]

[1] See Form 1099-MISC, Miscellaneous Income, and its instructions.

[2] However, the following payments made to a corporation (including gross proceeds paid to an attorney under section 6045(f), even if the attorney is a corporation) and reportable on Form 1099-MISC are not exempt from backup withholding: medical and health care payments, attorneys' fees; and payments for services paid by a federal executive agency.

Part I. Taxpayer Identification Number (TIN)

Enter your TIN in the appropriate box. If you are a resident alien and you do not have and are not eligible to get an SSN, your TIN is your IRS individual taxpayer identification number (ITIN). Enter it in the social security number box. If you do not have an ITIN, see *How to get a TIN* below.

If you are a sole proprietor and you have an EIN, you may enter either your SSN or EIN. However, the IRS prefers that you use your SSN.

If you are a single-owner LLC that is disregarded as an entity separate from its owner (see *Limited liability company (LLC)* on page 2), enter your SSN (or EIN, if you have one). If the LLC is a corporation, partnership, etc., enter the entity's EIN.

Note. See the chart on page 4 for further clarification of name and TIN combinations.

How to get a TIN. If you do not have a TIN, apply for one immediately. To apply for an SSN, get Form SS-5, Application for a Social Security Card, from your local Social Security Administration office or get this form online at *www.socialsecurity.gov*. You may also get this form by calling 1-800-772-1213. Use Form W-7, Application for IRS Individual Taxpayer Identification Number, to apply for an ITIN, or Form SS-4, Application for Employer Identification Number, to apply for an EIN. You can apply for an EIN online by accessing the IRS website at *www.irs.gov/businesses* and clicking on Employer ID Numbers under Related Topics. You can get Forms W-7 and SS-4 from the IRS by visiting *www.irs.gov* or by calling 1-800-TAX-FORM (1-800-829-3676).

If you are asked to complete Form W-9 but do not have a TIN, write "Applied For" in the space for the TIN, sign and date the form, and give it to the requester. For interest and dividend payments, and certain payments made with respect to readily tradable instruments, generally you will have 60 days to get a TIN and give it to the requester before you are subject to backup withholding on payments. The 60-day rule does not apply to other types of payments. You will be subject to backup withholding on all such payments until you provide your TIN to the requester.

Note. Writing "Applied For" means that you have already applied for a TIN or that you intend to apply for one soon.

Caution: *A disregarded domestic entity that has a foreign owner must use the appropriate Form W-8.*

Appendix

Part II. Certification

To establish to the withholding agent that you are a U.S. person, or resident alien, sign Form W-9. You may be requested to sign by the withholding agent even if items 1, 4, and 5 below indicate otherwise.

For a joint account, only the person whose TIN is shown in Part I should sign (when required). Exempt recipients, see *Exempt From Backup Withholding* on page 2.

Signature requirements. Complete the certification as indicated in 1 through 5 below.

1. Interest, dividend, and barter exchange accounts opened before 1984 and broker accounts considered active during 1983. You must give your correct TIN, but you do not have to sign the certification.

2. Interest, dividend, broker, and barter exchange accounts opened after 1983 and broker accounts considered inactive during 1983. You must sign the certification or backup withholding will apply. If you are subject to backup withholding and you are merely providing your correct TIN to the requester, you must cross out item 2 in the certification before signing the form.

3. Real estate transactions. You must sign the certification. You may cross out item 2 of the certification.

4. Other payments. You must give your correct TIN, but you do not have to sign the certification unless you have been notified that you have previously given an incorrect TIN. "Other payments" include payments made in the course of the requester's trade or business for rents, royalties, goods (other than bills for merchandise), medical and health care services (including payments to corporations), payments to a nonemployee for services, payments to certain fishing boat crew members and fishermen, and gross proceeds paid to attorneys (including payments to corporations).

5. Mortgage interest paid by you, acquisition or abandonment of secured property, cancellation of debt, qualified tuition program payments (under section 529), IRA, Coverdell ESA, Archer MSA or HSA contributions or distributions, and pension distributions. You must give your correct TIN, but you do not have to sign the certification.

What Name and Number To Give the Requester

For this type of account:	Give name and SSN of:
1. Individual	The individual
2. Two or more individuals (joint account)	The actual owner of the account or, if combined funds, the first individual on the account [1]
3. Custodian account of a minor (Uniform Gift to Minors Act)	The minor [2]
4. a. The usual revocable savings trust (grantor is also trustee)	The grantor-trustee [1]
b. So-called trust account that is not a legal or valid trust under state law	The actual owner [1]
5. Sole proprietorship or single-owner LLC	The owner [3]

For this type of account:	Give name and EIN of:
6. Sole proprietorship or single-owner LLC	The owner [3]
7. A valid trust, estate, or pension trust	Legal entity [4]
8. Corporate or LLC electing corporate status on Form 8832	The corporation
9. Association, club, religious, charitable, educational, or other tax-exempt organization	The organization
10. Partnership or multi-member LLC	The partnership
11. A broker or registered nominee	The broker or nominee
12. Account with the Department of Agriculture in the name of a public entity (such as a state or local government, school district, or prison) that receives agricultural program payments	The public entity

[1] List first and circle the name of the person whose number you furnish. If only one person on a joint account has an SSN, that person's number must be furnished.

[2] Circle the minor's name and furnish the minor's SSN.

[3] You must show your individual name and you may also enter your business or "DBA" name on the second name line. You may use either your SSN or EIN (if you have one). If you are a sole proprietor, IRS encourages you to use your SSN.

[4] List first and circle the name of the legal trust, estate, or pension trust. (Do not furnish the TIN of the personal representative or trustee unless the legal entity itself is not designated in the account title.) Also see *Special rules regarding partnerships* on page 1.

Note. If no name is circled when more than one name is listed, the number will be considered to be that of the first name listed.

Privacy Act Notice

Section 6109 of the Internal Revenue Code requires you to provide your correct TIN to persons who must file information returns with the IRS to report interest, dividends, and certain other income paid to you, mortgage interest you paid, the acquisition or abandonment of secured property, cancellation of debt, or contributions you made to an IRA, or Archer MSA or HSA. The IRS uses the numbers for identification purposes and to help verify the accuracy of your tax return. The IRS may also provide this information to the Department of Justice for civil and criminal litigation, and to cities, states, the District of Columbia, and U.S. possessions to carry out their tax laws. We may also disclose this information to other countries under a tax treaty, to federal and state agencies to enforce federal nontax criminal laws, or to federal law enforcement and intelligence agencies to combat terrorism.

You must provide your TIN whether or not you are required to file a tax return. Payers must generally withhold 28% of taxable interest, dividend, and certain other payments to a payee who does not give a TIN to a payer. Certain penalties may also apply.

Instructions for the Requester of Form W-9
(Rev. November 2005)
Request for Taxpayer Identification Number and Certification

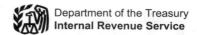
Department of the Treasury
Internal Revenue Service

Section references are to the Internal Revenue Code unless otherwise noted.

What's New

Partnerships subject to withholding under section 1446 may require signed Forms W-9 from its U.S. partners to overcome any presumptions of foreign status and to avoid withholding on the partner's allocable share of the partnership's effectively connected taxable income. For more information, see Regulations section 1.1446-1(c). The final regulations are published as Treasury Decision 9200 on page 1158 of Internal Revenue Bulletin 2005-23 and are available at *www.irs.gov/pub/irs-irbs/irb05-23.pdf*.

Reminders

● The backup withholding rate is 28% for reportable payments.
● The IRS website offers TIN Matching e-services for payers to validate name and TIN combinations. See *Taxpayer Identification Number (TIN) Matching* on page 4.

How Do I Know When To Use Form W-9?

Use Form W-9 to request the taxpayer identification number (TIN) of a U.S. person (including a resident alien) and to request certain certifications and claims for exemption. (See Purpose of Form on Form W-9.) Withholding agents may require signed Forms W-9 from U.S. exempt recipients to overcome any presumptions of foreign status. For federal purposes, a U.S. person includes but is not limited to:

● An individual who is a citizen or resident of the United States,
● A partnership, corporation, company, or association created or organized in the United States or under the laws of the United States,
● Any estate (other than a foreign estate) or trust. See Regulations section 301.7701-6(a) for additional information.

For partnerships subject to withholding under section 1446, see *What's New* above.

Advise foreign persons to use the appropriate Form W-8. See Pub. 515, Withholding of Tax on Nonresident Aliens and Foreign Entities, for more information and a list of the W-8 forms.

Also, a nonresident alien individual may, under certain circumstances, claim treaty benefits on scholarships and fellowship grant income. See Pub. 515 or Pub. 519, U.S. Tax Guide for Aliens, for more information.

Electronic Submission of Forms W-9

Requesters may establish a system for payees and payees' agents to submit Forms W-9 electronically, including by fax. A requester is anyone required to file an information return. A payee is anyone required to provide a taxpayer identification number (TIN) to the requester.

Payee's agent. A payee's agent can be an investment advisor (corporation, partnership, or individual) or an introducing broker. An investment advisor must be registered with the Securities Exchange Commission (SEC) under the Investment Advisers Act of 1940. The introducing broker is a broker-dealer that is regulated by the SEC and the National Association of Securities Dealers, Inc., and that is not a payer. Except for a broker who acts as a payee's agent for "readily tradable instruments," the advisor or broker must show in writing to the payer that the payee authorized the advisor or broker to transmit the Form W-9 to the payer.

Electronic system. Generally, the electronic system must:
● Ensure the information received is the information sent, and document all occasions of user access that result in the submission;
● Make reasonably certain that the person accessing the system and submitting the form is the person identified on Form W-9, the investment advisor, or the introducing broker;
● Provide the same information as the paper Form W-9;
● Be able to supply a hard copy of the electronic Form W-9 if the Internal Revenue Service requests it; and
● Require as the final entry in the submission an electronic signature by the payee whose name is on Form W-9 that authenticates and verifies the submission. The electronic signature must be under penalties of perjury and the perjury statement must contain the language of the paper Form W-9.

 For Forms W-9 that are not required to be signed, the electronic system need not provide for an electronic signature or a perjury statement.

For more details, see the following.
● Announcement 98-27, is on page 30 of Internal Revenue Bulletin (I.R.B.)1998-15 available at *www.irs.gov/pub/irs-irbs/irb98-15.pdf*.
● Announcement 2001-91 on page 221 of I.R.B. 2001-36 available at *www.irs.gov/pub/irs-irbs/irb01-36.pdf*.

Cat. No. 20479P

Individual Taxpayer Identification Number (ITIN)

Form W-9 (or an acceptable substitute) is used by persons required to file information returns with the IRS to get the payee's (or other person's) correct name and TIN. For individuals, the TIN is generally a social security number (SSN).

However, in some cases, individuals who become U.S. resident aliens for tax purposes are not eligible to obtain an SSN. This includes certain resident aliens who must receive information returns but who cannot obtain an SSN.

These individuals must apply for an ITIN on Form W-7, Application for IRS Individual Taxpayer Identification Number, unless they have an application pending for an SSN. Individuals who have an ITIN must provide it on Form W-9.

Substitute Form W-9

You may develop and use your own Form W-9 (a substitute Form W-9) if its content is substantially similar to the official IRS Form W-9 and it satisfies certain certification requirements.

You may incorporate a substitute Form W-9 into other business forms you customarily use, such as account signature cards. However, the certifications on the substitute Form W-9 must clearly state (as shown on the official Form W-9) that under penalties of perjury:

1. The payee's TIN is correct,
2. The payee is not subject to backup withholding due to failure to report interest and dividend income, and
3. The payee is a U.S. person.

You may not:

1. Use a substitute Form W-9 that requires the payee, by signing, to agree to provisions unrelated to the required certifications, or
2. Imply that a payee may be subject to backup withholding unless the payee agrees to provisions on the substitute form that are unrelated to the required certifications.

A substitute Form W-9 that contains a separate signature line just for the certifications satisfies the requirement that the certifications be clearly stated.

If a single signature line is used for the required certifications and other provisions, the certifications must be highlighted, boxed, printed in bold-face type, or presented in some other manner that causes the language to stand out from all other information contained on the substitute form. Additionally, the following statement must be presented to stand out in the same manner as described above and must appear immediately above the single signature line:

"The Internal Revenue Service does not require your consent to any provision of this document other than the certifications required to avoid backup withholding."

If you use a substitute form, you are encouraged (but not required) to provide Form W-9 instructions to the payee. However, if the IRS has notified the payee that backup withholding applies, then you must instruct the payee to strike out the language in the certification that relates to underreporting. This instruction can be given orally or in writing. See item 2 of the Certification on Form W-9. For more information, see Revenue Procedure 83-89,1983-2, C.B. 613; amplified by Revenue Procedure 96-26 which is on page 22 of I.R.B. 1996-8 at *www.irs.gov/pub/irs-irbs/irb96-08.pdf*.

TIN Applied for

For interest and dividend payments and certain payments with respect to readily tradable instruments, the payee may return a properly completed, signed Form W-9 to you with "Applied For" written in Part I. This is an "awaiting- TIN" certificate. The payee has 60 calendar days, from the date you receive this certificate, to provide a TIN. If you do not receive the payee's TIN at that time, you must begin backup withholding on payments.

Reserve rule. You must backup withhold on any reportable payments made during the 60-day period if a payee withdraws more than $500 at one time, unless the payee reserves 28 percent of all reportable payments made to the account.

Alternative rule. You may also elect to backup withhold during this 60-day period, after a 7-day grace period, under one of the two alternative rules discussed below.

Option 1. Backup withhold on any reportable payments if the payee makes a withdrawal from the account after the close of 7 business days after you receive the awaiting-TIN certificate. Treat as reportable payments all cash withdrawals in an amount up to the reportable payments made from the day after you receive the awaiting-TIN certificate to the day of withdrawal.

Option 2. Backup withhold on any reportable payments made to the payee's account, regardless of whether the payee makes any withdrawals, beginning no later than 7 business days after you receive the awaiting-TIN certificate.

 The 60-day exemption from backup withholding does not apply to any payment other than interest, dividends, and certain payments relating to readily tradable instruments. Any other reportable payment, such as nonemployee compensation, is subject to backup withholding immediately, even if the payee has applied for and is awaiting a TIN.

Even if the payee gives you an awaiting-TIN certificate, you must backup withhold on reportable interest and dividend payments if the payee does not certify, under penalties of perjury, that the payee is not subject to backup withholding.

Payees Exempt From Backup Withholding

Even if the payee does not provide a TIN in the manner required, you are not required to backup withhold on any payments you make if the payee is:

1. An organization exempt from tax under section 501(a), any IRA, or a custodial account under

section 403(b)(7) if the account satisfies the requirements of section 401(f)(2),

    2. The United States or any of its agencies or instrumentalities,

    3. A state, the District of Columbia, a possession of the United States, or any of their political subdivisions or instrumentalities,

    4. A foreign government or any of its political subdivisions, agencies, or instrumentalities, or

    5. An international organization or any of its agencies or instrumentalities.

    Other payees that may be exempt from backup withholding include:

    6. A corporation,

    7. A foreign central bank of issue,

    8. A dealer in securities or commodities required to register in the United States, the District of Columbia, or a possession of the United States,

    9. A futures commission merchant registered with the Commodity Futures Trading Commission,

    10. A real estate investment trust,

    11. An entity registered at all times during the tax year under the Investment Company Act of 1940,

    12. A common trust fund operated by a bank under section 584(a),

    13. A financial institution,

    14. A middleman known in the investment community as a nominee or custodian, or

    15. A trust exempt from tax under section 664 or described in section 4947.

    The following types of payments are exempt from backup withholding as indicated for items 1 through 15 above.

Interest and dividend payments. All listed payees are exempt except the payee in item 9.

Broker transactions. All payees listed in items 1 through 13 are exempt. A person registered under the Investment Advisers Act of 1940 who regularly acts as a broker is also exempt.

Barter exchange transactions and patronage dividends. Only payees listed in items 1 through 5 are exempt.

Payments reportable under sections 6041 and 6041A. Only payees listed in items 1 through 7 are generally exempt.

    However, the following payments made to a corporation (including gross proceeds paid to an attorney under section 6045(f), even if the attorney is a corporation) and reportable on Form 1099-MISC, Miscellaneous Income, are not exempt from backup withholding.

- Medical and health care payments.
- Attorneys' fees.
- Payments for services paid by a federal executive agency. (See Revenue Ruling 2003-66 on page 1115 in I.R.B. 2003-26 at *www.irs.gov/pub/irs-irbs/irb03-26.pdf*.)

Payments Exempt From Backup Withholding

Payments that are not subject to information reporting also are not subject to backup withholding. For details, see sections 6041, 6041A, 6042, 6044, 6045, 6049, 6050A, and 6050N, and their regulations. The following payments are generally exempt from backup withholding.

Dividends and patronage dividends
- Payments to nonresident aliens subject to withholding under section 1441.
- Payments to partnerships not engaged in a trade or business in the United States and that have at least one nonresident alien partner.
- Payments of patronage dividends not paid in money.
- Payments made by certain foreign organizations.
- Section 404(k) distributions made by an ESOP.

Interest payments
- Payments of interest on obligations issued by individuals. However, if you pay $600 or more of interest in the course of your trade or business to a payee, you must report the payment. Backup withholding applies to the reportable payment if the payee has not provided a TIN or has provided an incorrect TIN.
- Payments of tax-exempt interest (including exempt-interest dividends under section 852).
- Payments described in section 6049(b)(5) to nonresident aliens.
- Payments on tax-free covenant bonds under section 1451.
- Payments made by certain foreign organizations.
- Mortgage or student loan interest paid to you.

Other types of payment
- Wages.
- Distributions from a pension, annuity, profit-sharing or stock bonus plan, any IRA, an owner-employee plan, or other deferred compensation plan.
- Distributions from a medical or health savings account and long-term care benefits.
- Certain surrenders of life insurance contracts.
- Distribution from qualified tuition programs or Coverdell ESAs.
- Gambling winnings if regular gambling winnings withholding is required under section 3402(q). However, if regular gambling winnings withholding is not required under section 3402(q), backup withholding applies if the payee fails to furnish a TIN.
- Real estate transactions reportable under section 6045(e).
- Cancelled debts reportable under section 6050P.
- Fish purchases for cash reportable under section 6050R.
- Certain payment card transactions if the payment is made on or after January 1, 2005, by a qualified payment card agent (as described in Rev. Proc. 2004-42 and Regulations section 31.3406(g)-1(f) and if the requirements under Regulations section 31.3406(g)-1(f) are met. Rev. Proc. 2004-42 is on page 121 of I.R.B. 2004-31 which is available at *www.irs.gov/pub/irs-irbs/irb04-31.pdf*.

-3-

Joint Foreign Payees

If the first payee listed on an account gives you a Form W-8 or a similar statement signed under penalties of perjury, backup withholding applies unless:

    1. Every joint payee provides the statement regarding foreign status, or

    2. Any one of the joint payees who has not established foreign status gives you a TIN.

    If any one of the joint payees who has not established foreign status gives you a TIN, use that number for purposes of backup withholding and information reporting.

    For more information on foreign payees, see the Instructions for the Requester of Forms W-8BEN, W-8ECI, W-8EXP, and W-8IMY.

Names and TINs To Use for Information Reporting

Show the full name and address as provided on Form W-9 on the information return filed with the IRS and on the copy furnished to the payee. If you made payments to more than one payee or the account is in more than one name, enter on the first name line only the name of the payee whose TIN is shown on the information return. You may show the names of any other individual payees in the area below the first name line.

Sole proprietor. Enter the individual's name on the first name line. On the second name line, enter the business name or "doing business as (DBA)" if provided. You may not enter only the business name. For the TIN, you may enter either the individual's SSN or the employer identification number (EIN) of the business. However, the IRS encourages you to use the SSN.

LLC. For an LLC that is disregarded as an entity separate from its owner, you must show the owner's name on the first name line. On the second name line, you may enter the LLC's name. Use the owner's TIN.

Notices From the IRS

The IRS will send you a notice if the payee's name and TIN on the information return you filed do not match the IRS's records. (*See Taxpayer Identification Number (TIN) Matching* below.) You may have to send a "B" notice to the payee to solicit another TIN. Pub. 1281 contains copies of the two types of "B" notices.

Taxpayer Identification Number (TIN) Matching

TIN Matching allows a payer or authorized agent who is required to file Forms 1099-B, DIV, INT, MISC, OID, and /or PATR to match TIN and name combinations with IRS records before submitting the forms to the IRS. TIN Matching is one of the e-services products that is offered, and is accessible through the IRS website. Go to *www.irs.gov* and search for "e-services." It is anticipated that payers who validate the TIN and name combinations before filing information returns will receive fewer backup withholding (CP2100) "B"notices and penalty notices.

Additional Information

For more information on backup withholding, see Pub. 1281, Backup Withholding for Missing and Incorrect Name/TIN(s).

Form **668-D** (Rev. December 2001)	Department of the Treasury —— Internal Revenue Service ## Release of Levy/Release of Property from Levy

To	Taxpayer(s)
	Identifying Number(s)

A notice of levy was served on you and demand was made for the surrender of:

☐ all property, rights to property, money, credits and bank deposits of the taxpayer(s) named above, except as provided in 6332(c) of the Internal Revenue Code—"Special Rule For Banks." See the back of this form regarding this exception.

☐ wages, salary and other income, now owed to or becoming payable to the taxpayer(s) named above.

The box checked below applies to the levy we served on you.

Release of Levy

☐ Under the provisions of Internal Revenue Code section 6343, all property, rights to property, money, credits, and bank deposits of the taxpayer(s) named above are released from the levy.

☐ Under the provisions of Internal Revenue Code section 6343, all wages, salary and other income now owed to or becoming payable to the taxpayer(s) named above are released from the levy.

Release of Property from Levy

☐ Under the provisions of Internal Revenue Code section 6343, all property, rights to property, money, credits, and bank deposits greater than $ _____ are released from the levy. The levy now attaches only to this amount.

☐ The last payment we received from you was $ _____ dated _____ . The amount the taxpayer still owes is $ _____ . When this amount is paid to the Internal Revenue Service, the levy is released. If you sent us a payment after the last payment date shown, subtract that from the amount you send now.

☐ Under the provisions of Internal Revenue Code section 6343, all wages, salary and other income ☐ **greater than** ☐ **less than** $ _____ each _____ now owed to or becoming payable to the taxpayer(s) named above are released from the levy.

Dated at _____ _____
(Place) (Date)

Signature	Telephone Number	Title

Part 1— To Addressee   Cat. No. 20450C   www.irs.gov   Form **668-D** (Rev. 12-2001)

Appendix

Excerpts from the Internal Revenue Code

Sec. 6332 Surrender of Property Subject to Levy

(c) **Special Rule for Banks.**—Any bank *(as defined in section 408(n)) shall surrender (subject to an attachment or execution under judicial process) any deposits (including interest thereon)* in such bank only after 21 days after service of levy.

* * * * * * *

Sec. 6343. Authority to Release Levy and Return Property

(a) **Release of Levy and Notice of Release.**—

(1) **In general.**—Under regulations prescribed by the Secretary, the Secretary shall release the levy upon all, or part of, the property or rights to property levied upon and shall promptly notify the person upon whom such levy was made *(if any)* that such levy has been released if—

(A) the liability for which such levy was made is satisfied or becomes unenforceable by reason of lapse of time,

(B) release of such levy will facilitate the collection of such liability,

(C) the taxpayer has entered into an agreement under section 6159 to satisfy such liability by means of installment payments, unless such agreement provides otherwise,

(D) the Secretary has determined that such levy is creating an economic hardship due to the financial condition of the taxpayer, or

(E) the fair market value of the property exceeds such liability and release of the levy on a part of such property could be made without hindering the collection of such liability.

For purposes of subparagraph (C), the Secretary is not required to release such levy if such release would jeopardize the secured creditor status of the Secretary.

(2) **Expedited determination of certain business property.**—In the case of any tangible personal property essential in carrying on the trade or business of the taxpayer, the Secretary shall provide for an expedited determination under paragraph (1) if levy on such tangible personal property would prevent the taxpayer from carrying on such trade or business.

(3) **Subsequent levy.**—The release of levy on any property under paragraph (1) shall not prevent any subsequent levy on such property.

(b) **Return of property.**—

If the Secretary determines that property has been wrongfully levied upon, it shall be lawful for the Secretary to return . . . an amount equal to the amount of money levied upon . . . any time before the expiration of 9 months from the date of such levy . . . .

(d) **Return of Property in Certain Cases.**—If—

(1) any property has been levied upon, and

(2) the Secretary determines that—

(A) the levy on such property was premature or otherwise not in accordance with administrative procedures of the Secretary,

(B) the taxpayer has entered into an agreement under section 6159 to satisfy the tax liability for which the levy was imposed by means of installment payments, unless such agreement provides otherwise,

(C) the return of such property will facilitate the collection of the tax liability, or

(D) with the consent of the taxpayer or the Taxpayer Advocate, the return of such property would be in the best interests of the taxpayer (as determined by the Taxpayer Advocate) and the United States,

the provisions of subsection (b) shall apply in the same manner as if such property had been wrongly levied upon, except that no interest shall be allowed . . . .

Form **668-D** (Rev. 12-2001)

Form **668-D**
(Rev. December 2001)

Department of the Treasury — Internal Revenue Service
Release of Levy/Release of Property from Levy

To	Taxpayer(s)
	Identifying Number(s)

A notice of levy was served on you and demand was made for the surrender of:

☐ all property, rights to property, money, credits and bank deposits of the taxpayer(s) named above, except as provided in 6332(c) of the Internal Revenue Code—"Special Rule For Banks." See the back of this form regarding this exception.

☐ wages, salary and other income, now owed to or becoming payable to the taxpayer(s) named above.

The box checked below applies to the levy we served on you.

Release of Levy

☐ Under the provisions of Internal Revenue Code section 6343, all property, rights to property, money, credits, and bank deposits of the taxpayer(s) named above are released from the levy.

☐ Under the provisions of Internal Revenue Code section 6343, all wages, salary and other income now owed to or becoming payable to the taxpayer(s) named above are released from the levy.

Release of Property from Levy

☐ Under the provisions of Internal Revenue Code section 6343, all property, rights to property, money, credits, and bank deposits greater than $ _____ are released from the levy. The levy now attaches only to this amount.

☐ The last payment we received from you was $ _____ dated _____ . The amount the taxpayer still owes is $ _____ . When this amount is paid to the Internal Revenue Service, the levy is released. If you sent us a payment after the last payment date shown, subtract that from the amount you send now.

☐ Under the provisions of Internal Revenue Code section 6343, all wages, salary and other income ☐ **greater than** ☐ **less than** $ _____ each _____ now owed to or becoming payable to the taxpayer(s) named above are released from the levy.

Dated at _____   _____
(Place)   (Date)

Signature	Telephone Number	Title

Part 2— For Taxpayer   Cat. No. 20450C   www.irs.gov   Form **668-D** (Rev. 12-2001)

Excerpts from the Internal Revenue Code

Sec. 6332 Surrender of Property Subject to Levy

(c) **Special Rule for Banks.**—Any bank *(as defined in section 408(n)) shall surrender (subject to an attachment or execution under judicial process) any deposits (including interest thereon)* in such bank only after 21 days after service of levy.

* * * * * * *

Sec. 6343. Authority to Release Levy and Return Property

(a) **Release of Levy and Notice of Release.**—

(1) **In general.**—Under regulations prescribed by the Secretary, the Secretary shall release the levy upon all, or part of, the property or rights to property levied upon and shall promptly notify the person upon whom such levy was made *(if any)* that such levy has been released if—

(A) the liability for which such levy was made is satisfied or becomes unenforceable by reason of lapse of time,

(B) release of such levy will facilitate the collection of such liability,

(C) the taxpayer has entered into an agreement under section 6159 to satisfy such liability by means of installment payments, unless such agreement provides otherwise,

(D) the Secretary has determined that such levy is creating an economic hardship due to the financial condition of the taxpayer, or

(E) the fair market value of the property exceeds such liability and release of the levy on a part of such property could be made without hindering the collection of such liability.

For purposes of subparagraph (C), the Secretary is not required to release such levy if such release would jeopardize the secured creditor status of the Secretary.

(2) **Expedited determination of certain business property.**—In the case of any tangible personal property essential in carrying on the trade or business of the taxpayer, the Secretary shall provide for an expedited determination under paragraph (1) if levy on such tangible personal property would prevent the taxpayer from carrying on such trade or business.

(3) **Subsequent levy.**—The release of levy on any property under paragraph (1) shall not prevent any subsequent levy on such property.

(b) **Return of property.**—

If the Secretary determines that property has been wrongfully levied upon, it shall be lawful for the Secretary to return . . . an amount equal to the amount of money levied upon . . . any time before the expiration of 9 months from the date of such levy . . . .

(d) **Return of Property in Certain Cases.**—If—

(1) any property has been levied upon, and

(2) the Secretary determines that—

(A) the levy on such property was premature or otherwise not in accordance with administrative procedures of the Secretary,

(B) the taxpayer has entered into an agreement under section 6159 to satisfy the tax liability for which the levy was imposed by means of installment payments, unless such agreement provides otherwise,

(C) the return of such property will facilitate the collection of the tax liability, or

(D) with the consent of the taxpayer or the Taxpayer Advocate, the return of such property would be in the best interests of the taxpayer (as determined by the Taxpayer Advocate) and the United States,

the provisions of subsection (b) shall apply in the same manner as if such property had been wrongly levied upon, except that no interest shall be allowed . . . .

Form **668-D** (Rev. 12-2001)

Form **668-D** (Rev. December 2001)	Department of the Treasury — Internal Revenue Service **Release of Levy/Release of Property from Levy**

To	Taxpayer(s)
	Identifying Number(s)

A notice of levy was served on you and demand was made for the surrender of:

☐ all property, rights to property, money, credits and bank deposits of the taxpayer(s) named above, except as provided in 6332(c) of the Internal Revenue Code—"Special Rule For Banks." See the back of this form regarding this exception.

☐ wages, salary and other income, now owed to or becoming payable to the taxpayer(s) named above.

The box checked below applies to the levy we served on you.

Release of Levy

☐ Under the provisions of Internal Revenue Code section 6343, all property, rights to property, money, credits, and bank deposits of the taxpayer(s) named above are released from the levy.

☐ Under the provisions of Internal Revenue Code section 6343, all wages, salary and other income now owed to or becoming payable to the taxpayer(s) named above are released from the levy.

Release of Property from Levy

☐ Under the provisions of Internal Revenue Code section 6343, all property, rights to property, money, credits, and bank deposits greater than $ _____ are released from the levy. The levy now attaches only to this amount.

☐ The last payment we received from you was $ _____ dated _____ . The amount the taxpayer still owes is $ _____ . When this amount is paid to the Internal Revenue Service, the levy is released. If you sent us a payment after the last payment date shown, subtract that from the amount you send now.

☐ Under the provisions of Internal Revenue Code section 6343, all wages, salary and other income ☐ **greater than** ☐ **less than** $ _____ each _____ now owed to or becoming payable to the taxpayer(s) named above are released from the levy.

Dated at _____ _____
(Place) (Date)

Signature	Telephone Number	Title

Part 3— IRS Copy   Cat. No. 20450C   www.irs.gov   Form **668-D** (Rev. 12-2001)

Appendix

Excerpts from the Internal Revenue Code

Sec. 6332 Surrender of Property Subject to Levy

(c) **Special Rule for Banks.**—Any bank *(as defined in section 408(n))* shall surrender *(subject to an attachment or execution under judicial process)* any deposits *(including interest thereon)* in such bank only after 21 days after service of levy.

* * * * * * *

Sec. 6343. Authority to Release Levy and Return Property

(a) **Release of Levy and Notice of Release.**—

(1) **In general.**—Under regulations prescribed by the Secretary, the Secretary shall release the levy upon all, or part of, the property or rights to property levied upon and shall promptly notify the person upon whom such levy was made *(if any)* that such levy has been released if—

(A) the liability for which such levy was made is satisfied or becomes unenforceable by reason of lapse of time,

(B) release of such levy will facilitate the collection of such liability,

(C) the taxpayer has entered into an agreement under section 6159 to satisfy such liability by means of installment payments, unless such agreement provides otherwise,

(D) the Secretary has determined that such levy is creating an economic hardship due to the financial condition of the taxpayer, or

(E) the fair market value of the property exceeds such liability and release of the levy on a part of such property could be made without hindering the collection of such liability.

For purposes of subparagraph (C), the Secretary is not required to release such levy if such release would jeopardize the secured creditor status of the Secretary.

(2) **Expedited determination of certain business property.**—In the case of any tangible personal property essential in carrying on the trade or business of the taxpayer, the Secretary shall provide for an expedited determination under paragraph (1) if levy on such tangible personal property would prevent the taxpayer from carrying on such trade or business.

(3) **Subsequent levy.**—The release of levy on any property under paragraph (1) shall not prevent any subsequent levy on such property.

(b) **Return of property.**—

If the Secretary determines that property has been wrongfully levied upon, it shall be lawful for the Secretary to return . . . an amount equal to the amount of money levied upon . . . any time before the expiration of 9 months from the date of such levy . . . .

(d) **Return of Property in Certain Cases.**—If—

(1) any property has been levied upon, and

(2) the Secretary determines that—

(A) the levy on such property was premature or otherwise not in accordance with administrative procedures of the Secretary,

(B) the taxpayer has entered into an agreement under section 6159 to satisfy the tax liability for which the levy was imposed by means of installment payments, unless such agreement provides otherwise,

(C) the return of such property will facilitate the collection of the tax liability, or

(D) with the consent of the taxpayer or the Taxpayer Advocate, the return of such property would be in the best interests of the taxpayer (as determined by the Taxpayer Advocate) and the United States,

the provisions of subsection (b) shall apply in the same manner as if such property had been wrongly levied upon, except that no interest shall be allowed . . . .

Form **668-D** (Rev. 12-2001)

A-125

Form **668-W(c)(DO)** (Rev. July 2002)	Department of the Treasury – Internal Revenue Service **Notice of Levy on Wages, Salary, and Other Income**

DATE:

REPLY TO:

TELEPHONE NUMBER
OF IRS OFFICE:

NAME AND ADDRESS OF TAXPAYER:

TO:

IDENTIFYING NUMBER*(S)*:

Kind of Tax	Tax Period Ended	Unpaid Balance of Assessment	Statutory Additions	Total
			Total Amount Due ▶	

We figured the interest and late payment penalty to _____

THIS ISN'T A BILL FOR TAXES YOU OWE. THIS IS A NOTICE OF LEVY TO COLLECT MONEY OWED BY THE TAXPAYER NAMED ABOVE.

The Internal Revenue Code provides that there is a lien for the amount shown above. Although we have given the notice and demand required by the Code, the amount owed hasn't been paid. This levy requires you to turn over to us: (1) this taxpayer's wages and salary that have been earned but not paid, as well as wages and salary earned in the future until this levy is released, and (2) this taxpayer's other income that you have now or for which you are obligated.

We levy this money to the extent it isn't exempt, as shown in the instructions. Don't offset money this person owes you without contacting us at the telephone number shown above for instructions.

If you don't owe money to this taxpayer, please call us at the telephone number at the top of this form. Instead of calling us you may complete the back of Part 3, attach it as a cover to the rest of this form, and return all parts to IRS in the enclosed envelope.

If you do owe money to this taxpayer, please see the back of this page for instructions on how to act on this notice.

Signature of Service Representative	Title

Part 1 — For Employer or other Addressee   Catalog No. 15703I   www.irs.gov   Form **668-W(c)(DO)** (Rev. 7-2002)

IF MONEY IS DUE THIS TAXPAYER

Give the taxpayer Parts 2, 3, 4 and 5, as soon as you receive this levy. Part of the taxpayer's wages, salary, or other income is exempt from levy. To claim exemptions, the taxpayer must complete and sign the Statement of Exemptions and Filing Status on Parts 3, 4, and 5 and return Parts 3 and 4 to you within 3 work days after you receive this levy. The taxpayer's instructions for completing the Statement of Exemptions and Filing Status are on the back of Part 5.

Send us the taxpayer's take home pay minus the exempt amount which is described below, on the same dates that payments are made, or are due, to the taxpayer. Unless we tell you that a deduction should not be allowed, allow the taxpayer's payroll deductions which were in effect when you received this levy in determining the take home pay. Do not allow the taxpayer to take new voluntary payroll deductions while this levy is in effect. The method of payment to the taxpayer, for example, direct deposit, has no bearing on take home pay. Direct deposit is not considered a payroll deduction.

When you send us your check, **complete the back of Part 3 of this form,** attach it to the check, and mail them to us in the enclosed envelope. **Make your check payable to United States Treasury. Please write on the check (not on a detachable stub) the taxpayer's name, identifying number**(s)**, kind of tax, and tax periods shown on Part 1, and the words "LEVY PROCEEDS."**

This levy remains in effect for all wages and salary for personal services until we send you a release of levy. Wages and salary include fees, commissions, and bonuses. If more than one payment is necessary to satisfy the levy, send additional payments to the Internal Revenue Service address shown on your copy of this levy, and make out your check as described above.

This levy remains in effect for benefit and retirement income if the taxpayer has a current fixed right to future payments, until we send you a release of levy.

For income other **than wages and salary, and benefit and retirement income as described above, this levy is effective only for funds you owe the taxpayer now.** We may issue another levy if necessary. However, this levy attaches to all obligations you owe the taxpayer at the time you receive it, even though you plan to make the payment at a later date.

INSTRUCTIONS FOR FIGURING THE AMOUNT EXEMPT FROM THIS LEVY

There are three steps in figuring the amount exempt from this levy.

1. When you receive the completed Parts 3 and 4 from the taxpayer, use item 1 of the enclosed table (Publication 1494) to figure how much wages, salary, or other income is exempt from this levy. Find the correct block on the table using the taxpayer's filing status, number of personal exemptions claimed, and pay period. Be sure you allow one exemption for the taxpayer, in addition to one for each person listed on Parts 3 and 4, unless, "I cannot claim myself as an exemption," is written next to the taxpayer's signature. If no Social Security Number is provided for a personal exemption, do not allow that exemption, unless "Less than six months old" is written in the space for that person's Social Security Number. If you don't receive the completed Parts 3 and 4, then the exempt amount is what would be exempt if the taxpayer had returned them indicating married filing separate and only the taxpayer is claimed as a personal exemption. Don't use the information on the taxpayer's Form W-4, Employee's Withholding Allowance Certificate, to determine the amount that is exempt from this levy. That information can be different from what is filed on the employee's individual income tax return.

2. If the taxpayer, or the taxpayer's spouse, is at least 65 years old and/or blind, an additional amount is exempt from this levy. To claim this, the taxpayer counts one for each of the following: (a) the taxpayer is 65 or older, (b) the taxpayer is blind, (c) the taxpayer's spouse is 65 or older, and (d) the taxpayer's spouse is blind. Then, this total (up to 4) is entered next to "ADDITIONAL STANDARD DEDUCTION" on the Statement of Exemptions and Filing Status. If the taxpayer has entered a number in this space, use item 2 of the enclosed table to figure the additional amount exempt from this levy.

3. The amount the taxpayer needs to pay support, established by a court or an administrative order, for minor children is also exempt from the levy, but the court or administrative order must have been made before the date of this levy. These children can't be claimed as personal exemptions on Parts 3, 4, and 5.

If the taxpayer's exemptions, filing status, or eligibility for additional standard deduction change while this levy is in effect, the taxpayer may give you a new statement to change the amount that is exempt. You can get more forms from an IRS office. If you are sending payments for this levy next year, the amount that is exempt doesn't change merely because the amount that all taxpayers can deduct for exemptions, filing status, and additional standard deductions on individual income tax returns changes for the new year. However, if the taxpayer asks you to recompute the exempt amount in the new year by submitting a new Statement of Exemptions and Filing Status, even though there may be no change from the prior statement, you may use the new year's exemption table. This change applies to levies you already have as well as this one. If you are asked to recompute the exempt amount and you don't have the new year's exemption table, you may order one by calling 1-800-829-3676. Ask for Publication 1494. This publication is also available at our internet site www.irs.gov The taxpayer submits the information under penalties of perjury, and it is subject to verification by the Internal Revenue Service.

Form **668-W(c)(DO)** (Rev. 7-2002)

Form **668-W(c)(DO)** (Rev. July 2002)	Department of the Treasury – Internal Revenue Service **Notice of Levy on Wages, Salary, and Other Income**

DATE:

REPLY TO:

TELEPHONE NUMBER
OF IRS OFFICE:

NAME AND ADDRESS OF TAXPAYER:

TO:

IDENTIFYING NUMBER*(S)*:

Kind of Tax	Tax Period Ended	Unpaid Balance of Assessment	Statutory Additions	Total
			Total Amount Due ▶	

We figured the interest and late payment penalty to _____

Although we asked you to pay the amount you owe, it is still not paid.

This is your copy of a Notice of Levy we have sent to collect the unpaid amount. We will send other levies if we don't get sufficient funds to pay the total amount you owe.

This levy requires the person who received it to turn over to us: your wages and salary that have been earned but not paid, as well as wages and salary earned in the future until the levy is released; and (2) your other income that the person has now or is obligated to pay you. This money is levied to the extent it isn't exempt, as explained on the back of Part 5 of this form.

If you decide to pay the amount you owe now, please **bring** a guaranteed payment *(cash, cashier's check, or money order)* to the nearest IRS office with this form, so we can tell the person who received this levy not to send us your money. Make checks and money orders payable to United States Treasury. If you mail your payment instead of bringing it to us, we may not have time to stop the person who received this levy from sending us your money.

If you have any questions or want to arrange payment before other levies are issued, please call or write us. If you write to us, please include your telephone number and the best time for us to call you.

Please see the back of Part 5 for instructions.

Signature of Service Representative	Title

Appendix

Excerpts from the Internal Revenue Code

Sec. 6331. LEVY AND DISTRAINT.

(b) **Seizure and Sale of Property.**—The term "levy" as used in this title includes the power of distraint and seizure by any means. Except as otherwise provided in subsection (e), a levy shall extend only to property possessed and obligations existing at the time thereof. In any case in which the Secretary may levy upon property or rights to property, he may seize and sell such property or rights to property (whether real or personal, tangible or intangible).

(c) **Successive Seizures.**—Whenever any property or right to property upon which levy has been made by virtue of subsection (a) is not sufficient to satisfy the claim of the United States for which levy is made, the Secretary may, thereafter, and as often as may be necessary, proceed to levy in like manner upon any other property liable to levy of the person against whom such claim exists, until the amount due from him, together with all expenses, is fully paid.

(e) **Continuing Levy on Salary and Wages.**—The effect of a levy on salary or wages payable to or received by a taxpayer shall be continuous from the date such levy is first made until such levy is released under Section 6343.

Sec. 6332. SURRENDER OF PROPERTY SUBJECT TO LEVY.

(a) **Requirement.**— Except as otherwise provided in this section, any person in possession of (or obligated with respect to) property or rights to property subject to levy upon which a levy has been made shall, upon demand of the Secretary, surrender such property or rights (or discharge such obligation) to the Secretary, except such part of the property or rights as is, at the time of such demand, subject to an attachment or execution under any judicial process.

(d) **Enforcement of Levy.**

(1) **Extent of personal liability.**—Any person who fails or refuses to surrender any property or rights to property, subject to levy, upon demand by the Secretary, shall be liable in his own person and estate to the United States in a sum equal to the value of the property or rights not so surrendered, but not exceeding the amount of taxes for the collection of which such levy has been made, together with costs and interest on such sum at the underpayment rate established under section 6621 from the date of such levy (or, in the case of a levy described in section 6331 (d)(3), from the date such person would otherwise have been obligated to pay over such amounts to the taxpayer). Any amount (other than costs) recovered under this paragraph shall be credited against the tax liability for the collection of which such levy was made.

(2) **Penalty for violation.**—In addition to the personal liability imposed by paragraph (1), if any person required to surrender property or rights to property fails or refuses to surrender such property or rights to property without reasonable cause, such person shall be liable for a penalty equal to 50 percent of the amount recoverable under paragraph (1). No part of such penalty shall be credited against the tax liability for the collection of which such levy was made.

(e) **Effect of honoring levy.**—Any person in possession of (or obligated with respect to) property or rights to property subject to levy upon which a levy has been made who, upon demand by the Secretary, surrenders such property or rights to property (or discharges such obligation) to the Secretary (or who pays a liability under subsection (d)(1)) shall be discharged from any obligation or liability to the delinquent taxpayer and any other person with respect to such property or rights to property arising from such surrender or payment.

Sec. 6333. PRODUCTION OF BOOKS.

If a levy has been made or is about to be made on any property, or right to property, any person having custody or control of any books or records, containing evidence or statements relating to the property or right to property subject to levy, shall, upon demand of the Secretary exhibit such books or records to the Secretary.

Sec. 6334. PROPERTY EXEMPT FROM LEVY.

(a) **Enumeration.**—There shall be exempt from levy

(4) **Unemployment benefits.**—Any amount payable to an individual with respect to his unemployment (including any portion thereof payable with respect to dependents) under an unemployment compensation law of the United States, of any State, or of the District of Columbia or of the Commonwealth of Puerto Rico.

(6) **Certain annuity and pension payments.**—Annuity or pension payments under the Railroad Retirement Act, benefits under the Railroad Unemployment Insurance Act, special pension payments received by a person whose name has been entered on the Army, Navy, Air Force, and Coast Guard Medal of Honor roll (38 U.S.C. 562), and annuities based on retired or retainer pay under chapter 73 of title 10 of the United States Code.

(7) **Workmen's compensation.**— Any amount payable to an individual as workmen's compensation (including any portion thereof payable with respect to dependents) under a workmen's compensation law of the United States, any State, the District of Columbia, or the Commonwealth of Puerto Rico.

(8) **Judgments for support of minor children.**—If the taxpayer is required by judgment of a court of competent jurisdiction, entered prior to the date of levy, to contribute to the support of his minor children, so much of his salary, wages, or other income as is necessary to comply with such judgment.

(9) **Minimum exemption for wages, salary and other income.**—Any amount payable to or received by an individual as wages or salary for personal services, or as income derived from other sources, during any period, to the extent that the total of such amounts payable to or received by him during such period does not exceed the applicable exempt amount determined under subsection (d).

(10) **Certain service-connected disability payments.**—Any amount payable to an individual as a service-connected (within the meaning of section 101(16) of title 38, United States Code) disability benefit under–
(A) subchapter II, III, IV, V, or VI of chapter 11 of such title 38, or
(B) Chapter 13, 21, 23, 31, 32, 34, 35, 37, or 39 of such title 38.

(11) **Certain public assistance payments.**—Any amount payable to an individual as a recipient of public assistance under-
(A) title IV or title XVI (relating to supplemental security income for the aged,

blind, and disabled) of the Social Security Act, or
(B) State or local government public assistance or public welfare programs for which eligibility is determined by a needs or income test.

(12) **Assistance Under Job Training Partnership Act.**—Any amount payable to a participant under the Job Training Partnership Act (29 U.S.C. 1501 *et seq.*) from funds appropriated pursuant to such Act.

(d) **Exempt Amount of Wages, Salary, or Other Income.**–

(1) **Individuals on weekly basis.**—In the case of an individual who is paid or receives all of his wages, salary, and other income on a weekly basis, the amount of the wages, salary, and other income payable to or received by him during any week which is exempt from levy under subsection (a) (9) shall be the exempt amount.

(2) **Exempt Amount.**—For purposes of paragraph (1), the term "exempt amount" means an amount equal to–
(A) the sum of–
(I) the standard deduction, and
(II) the aggregate amount of the deductions for personal exemptions allowed the taxpayer under section 151 in the taxable year in which such levy occurs, divided by
(B) 52.

Unless the taxpayer submits to the Secretary a written and properly verified statement specifying the facts necessary to determine the proper amount under subparagraph (A), subparagraph (A) shall be applied as if the taxpayer were a married individual filing a separate return with only 1 personal exemption.

(3) **Individuals on basis other than weekly.**—In the case of any individual not described in paragraph (1), the amount of wages, salary, and other income payable to or received by him during any applicable pay period or other fiscal period (as determined under regulations prescribed by the Secretary) which is exempt from levy under subsection (a) (9) shall be an amount (determined under such regulations) which as nearly as possible will result in the same total exemption from levy for such individual over a period of time as he would have under paragraph (1) if (during such period of time) he were paid or received such wages, salary and other income on a regular weekly basis.

Sec. 6343. AUTHORITY TO RELEASE LEVY AND RETURN PROPERTY.

(a) Release of Levy and Notice of Release.–

(1) **In General.**—Under regulations prescribed by the Secretary, the Secretary shall release the levy upon all, or part of, the property or rights to property levied upon and shall promptly notify the person upon whom such levy was made *(if any)* that such levy has been released if–

(A) the liability for which such levy was made is satisfied or becomes unenforceable by reason of lapse of time,

(B) release of such levy will facilitate the collection of such liability,

(C) the taxpayer has entered into an agreement under section 6159 to satisfy such liability by means of installment payments, unless such agreement provides otherwise.

(D) the Secretary has determined that such levy is creating an economic hardship due to the financial condition of the taxpayer, or

(E) the fair market value of the property exceeds such liability and release of the levy on a part of such property could be made without hindering the collection of such liability.

For purposes of subparagraph (C), the Secretary is not required to release such levy if such release would jeopardize the secured creditor status of the Secretary.

(2) **Expedited determination on certain business property.**—In the case of any tangible personal property essential in carrying on the trade or business of the taxpayer, the Secretary shall provide for an expedited determination under paragraph (1) if levy on such tangible personal property would prevent the taxpayer from carrying on such trade or business.

(3) **Subsequent levy.**—The release of levy on any property under paragraph (1) shall not prevent any subsequent levy on such property.

(b) **Return of Property.**—If the Secretary determines that property has been wrongfully levied upon, it shall be lawful for the Secretary to return-

(1) the specific property levied upon,
(2) an amount of money equal to the amount of money levied upon, or
(3) an amount of money equal to the amount of money received by the United States from a sale of such property.

Property may be returned at any time. An amount equal to the amount of money levied upon or received from such sale may be returned at any time before the expiration of 9 months from the date of such levy. For purposes of paragraph (3), if property is declared purchased by the United States at a sale pursuant to section 6335(e) (relating to manner and conditions of sale), the United States shall be treated as having received an amount of money equal to the minimum price determined pursuant to such section or (if larger) the amount received by the United States from the resale of such property.

(d) RETURN OF PROPERTY IN CERTAIN CASES-IF–

(1) any property has been levied upon, and
(2) the Secretary determines that–

(A) the levy on such property was premature or otherwise not in accordance with administrative procedures of the Secretary,

(B) the taxpayer has entered into an agreement under section 6159 to satisfy the tax liability for which the levy was imposed by means of installment payments, unless such agreement provides otherwise,

(C) the return of such property will facilitate the collection of the tax liability, or

(D) with the consent of the taxpayer or the National Taxpayer Advocate, the return of such property would be in the best interest of the taxpayer (as determined by the National Taxpayer Advocate) and the United States,

the provisions of subsection (b) shall apply in the same manner as if such property had been wrongly levied upon, except that no interest shall be allowed under subsection (c).

Form **668-W(c)(DO)** (Rev. 7-2002)

| Form **668-W(c)(DO)** | Department of the Treasury – Internal Revenue Service |
| (Rev. July 2002) | **Notice of Levy on Wages, Salary, and Other Income** |

DATE:

REPLY TO:

TELEPHONE NUMBER
OF IRS OFFICE:

NAME AND ADDRESS OF TAXPAYER:

TO:

IDENTIFYING NUMBER*(S)*:

Kind of Tax	Tax Period Ended	Unpaid Balance of Assessment	Statutory Additions	Total

Employer or Other Addressee: Please complete the back of this page.   **Total Amount Due** ▶

We figured the interest and late payment penalty to _____

Statement of Exemptions and Filing Status *(To be completed by taxpayer; instructions are on the back of Part 5)*

My filing status for my income tax return is *(check one):*   ❏ Single;   ❏ Married Filing a Joint Return;
❏ Married Filing a Separate Return;   ❏ Head of Household; or   ❏ Qualifying Widow*(er)* with dependent child

ADDITIONAL STANDARD DEDUCTION: _____ *(Enter amount only if you or your spouse is at least 65 and/or blind.)*

I certify that I can claim the people named below as personal exemptions on my income tax return and that none are claimed on another Notice of Levy.
No one I have listed is my minor child to whom (as required by court or administrative order) I make support payments that are already exempt from levy.
I understand the information I have provided may be verified by the Internal Revenue Service. Under penalties of perjury, I declare that this statement of
exemptions and filing status is true.

Name *(Last, First, Middle Initial)*	Relationship *(Husband, Wife, Son, Daughter, etc.)*	Social Security Number *(SSN)*

Taxpayer's Signature	Date

Part 3 — Return to IRS

Form **668-W(c)(DO)** (Rev. 7-2002)

A-130

Appendix

PLEASE REMOVE THIS PAGE BEFORE COMPLETING IT.

TAXPAYER'S NAME*(S)* _____

IDENTIFYING NUMBER*(S)*
(as shown on the front) _____

SECTION 1.— Levy Acknowledgment

Signature of person responding   _____

Printed name of person responding   _____

Your telephone number   (   ) _____

Date and time this levy received   _____

SECTION 2.— Levy Results *(Check all applicable boxes.)*

☐   Check attached in the amount of $ _____

☐   Additional checks will be sent:

☐   _____ *(weekly, bi-weekly, monthly, etc.)*

☐   _____ approximate amount of each payment

☐   Taxpayer no longer employed here, as of _____ (date).

☐   Remarks

SECTION 3.— Additional Information *(Please complete this section if this levy does not attach any funds.)*

Taxpayer's latest address, if different from the one on this levy. _____

_____

Taxpayer's telephone number (   ) _____

Name and address of taxpayer's employer: _____
   (if different from addressee)

Other information you believe may help us:

Form **668-W(c)(DO)** (Rev. 7-2002)

Form **668-W(c)(DO)** (Rev. July 2002)	Department of the Treasury – Internal Revenue Service **Notice of Levy on Wages, Salary, and Other Income**

DATE:

REPLY TO:

TELEPHONE NUMBER
OF IRS OFFICE:

NAME AND ADDRESS OF TAXPAYER:

TO:

IDENTIFYING NUMBER(S):

Kind of Tax	Tax Period Ended	Unpaid Balance of Assessment	Statutory Additions	Total
			Total Amount Due ▶	

We figured the interest and late payment penalty to _____

Statement of Exemptions and Filing Status *(To be completed by taxpayer; instructions are on the back of Part 5)*

My filing status for my income tax return is *(check one)*: ☐ Single; ☐ Married Filing a Joint Return;
☐ Married Filing a Separate Return; ☐ Head of Household; or ☐ Qualifying Widow*(er)* with dependent child

ADDITIONAL STANDARD DEDUCTION: _____ *(Enter amount only if you or your spouse is at least 65 and/or blind.)*

I certify that I can claim the people named below as personal exemptions on my income tax return and that none are claimed on another Notice of Levy.
No one I have listed is my minor child to whom (as required by court or administrative order) I make support payments that are already exempt from levy.
I understand the information I have provided may be verified by the Internal Revenue Service. Under penalties of perjury, I declare that this statement of
exemptions and filing status is true.

Name *(Last, First, Middle Initial)*	Relationship *(Husband, Wife, Son, Daughter, etc.)*	Social Security Number *(SSN)*

Taxpayer's Signature	Date

Part 4 — For Employer or other Addressee to keep after Taxpayer completes   Form **668-W(c)(DO)** (Rev. 7-2002)

Appendix

Excerpts from the Internal Revenue Code

Sec. 6331. LEVY AND DISTRAINT.

(b) **Seizure and Sale of Property.**–The term "levy" as used in this title includes the power of distraint and seizure by any means. Except as otherwise provided in subsection (e), a levy shall extend only to property possessed and obligations existing at the time thereof. In any case in which the Secretary may levy upon property or rights to property, he may seize and sell such property or rights to property (whether real or personal, tangible or intangible).

(c) **Successive Seizures.**–Whenever any property or right to property upon which levy has been made by virtue of subsection (a) is not sufficient to satisfy the claim of the United States for which levy is made, the Secretary may, thereafter, and as often as may be necessary, proceed to levy in like manner upon any other property liable to levy of the person against whom such claim exists, until the amount due from him, together with all expenses, is fully paid.

(e) **Continuing Levy on Salary and Wages.**–The effect of a levy on salary or wages payable to or received by a taxpayer shall be continuous from the date such levy is first made until such levy is released under Section 6343.

Sec. 6332. SURRENDER OF PROPERTY SUBJECT TO LEVY.

(a) **Requirement.**– Except as otherwise provided in this section, any person in possession of (or obligated with respect to) property or rights to property subject to levy upon which a levy has been made shall, upon demand of the Secretary, surrender such property or rights (or discharge such obligation) to the Secretary, except such part of the property or rights as is, at the time of such demand, subject to an attachment or execution under any judicial process.

(d) **Enforcement of Levy.**

(1) **Extent of personal liability.**–Any person who fails or refuses to surrender any property or rights to property, subject to levy, upon demand by the Secretary, shall be liable in his own person and estate to the United States in a sum equal to the value of the property or rights not so surrendered, but not exceeding the amount of taxes for the collection of which such levy has been made, together with costs and interest on such sum at the underpayment rate established under section 6621 from the date of such levy (or, in the case of a levy described in section 6331 (d)(3), from the date such person would otherwise have been obligated to pay over such amounts to the taxpayer). Any amount (other than costs) recovered under this paragraph shall be credited against the tax liability for the collection of which such levy was made.

(2) **Penalty for violation.**–In addition to the personal liability imposed by paragraph (1), if any person required to surrender property or rights to property fails or refuses to surrender such property or rights to property without reasonable cause, such person shall be liable for a penalty equal to 50 percent of the amount recoverable under paragraph (1). No part of such penalty shall be credited against the tax liability for the collection of which such levy was made.

(e) **Effect of honoring levy.**–Any person in possession of (or obligated with respect to) property or rights to property subject to levy upon which a levy has been made who, upon demand by the Secretary, surrenders such property or rights to property (or discharges such obligation) to the Secretary (or who pays a liability under subsection (d)(1)) shall be discharged from any obligation or liability to the delinquent taxpayer and any other person with respect to such property or rights to property arising from such surrender or payment.

Sec. 6333. PRODUCTION OF BOOKS.

If a levy has been made or is about to be made on any property, or right to property, any person having custody or control of any books or records, containing evidence or statements relating to the property or right to property subject to levy, shall, upon demand of the Secretary exhibit such books or records to the Secretary.

Sec. 6334. PROPERTY EXEMPT FROM LEVY.

(a) **Enumeration.**–There shall be exempt from levy

(4) **Unemployment benefits.**–Any amount payable to an individual with respect to his unemployment (including any portion thereof payable with respect to dependents) under an unemployment compensation law of the United States, of any State, or of the District of Columbia or of the Commonwealth of Puerto Rico.

(6) **Certain annuity and pension payments.**–Annuity or pension payments under the Railroad Retirement Act, benefits under the Railroad Unemployment Insurance Act, special pension payments received by a person whose name has been entered on the Army, Navy, Air Force, and Coast Guard Medal of Honor roll (38 U.S.C. 562), and annuities based on retired or retainer pay under chapter 73 of title 10 of the United States Code.

(7) **Workmen's compensation.**– Any amount payable to an individual as workmen's compensation (including any portion thereof payable with respect to dependents) under a workmen's compensation law of the United States, any State, the District of Columbia, or the Commonwealth of Puerto Rico.

(8) **Judgments for support of minor children.**–If the taxpayer is required by judgment of a court of competent jurisdiction, entered prior to the date of levy, to contribute to the support of his minor children, so much of his salary, wages, or other income as is necessary to comply with such judgment.

(9) **Minimum exemption for wages, salary and other income.**–Any amount payable to or received by an individual as wages or salary for personal services, or as income derived from other sources, during any period, to the extent that the total of such amounts payable to or received by him during such period does not exceed the applicable exempt amount determined under subsection (d).

(10) **Certain service-connected disability payments.**–Any amount payable to an individual as a service-connected (within the meaning of section 101(16) of title 38, United States Code) disability benefit under-

(A) subchapter II, III, IV, V, or VI of chapter 11 of such title 38, or

(B) Chapter 13, 21, 23, 31, 32, 34, 35, 37, or 39 of such title 38.

(11) **Certain public assistance payments.**–Any amount payable to an individual as a recipient of public assistance under-

(A) title IV or title XVI (relating to supplemental security income for the aged, blind, and disabled) of the Social Security Act, or

(B) State or local government public assistance or public welfare programs for which eligibility is determined by a needs or income test.

(12) **Assistance Under Job Training Partnership Act.**–Any amount payable to a participant under the Job Training Partnership Act (29 U.S.C. 1501 *et seq.*) from funds appropriated pursuant to such Act.

(d) **Exempt Amount of Wages, Salary, or Other Income.**–

(1) **Individuals on weekly basis.**–In the case of an individual who is paid or receives all of his wages, salary, and other income on a weekly basis, the amount of the wages, salary, and other income payable to or received by him during any week which is exempt from levy under subsection (a) (9) shall be the exempt amount.

(2) **Exempt Amount.**–For purposes of paragraph (1), the term "exempt amount" means an amount equal to–

(A) the sum of–

(I) the standard deduction, and

(II) the aggregate amount of the deductions for personal exemptions allowed the taxpayer under section 151 in the taxable year in which such levy occurs, divided by

(B) 52.

Unless the taxpayer submits to the Secretary a written and properly verified statement specifying the facts necessary to determine the proper amount under subparagraph (A), subparagraph (A) shall be applied as if the taxpayer were a married individual filing a separate return with only 1 personal exemption.

(3) **Individuals on basis other than weekly.**–In the case of any individual not described in paragraph (1), the amount of wages, salary, and other income payable to or received by him during any applicable pay period or other fiscal period (as determined under regulations prescribed by the Secretary) which is exempt from levy under subsection (a) (9) shall be an amount (determined under such regulations) which as nearly as possible will result in the same total exemption from levy for such individual over a period of time as he would have under paragraph (1) if (during such period of time) he were paid or received such wages, salary and other income on a regular weekly basis.

Sec. 6343. AUTHORITY TO RELEASE LEVY AND RETURN PROPERTY.

(a) Release of Levy and Notice of Release.–

(1) **In General.**–Under regulations prescribed by the Secretary, the Secretary shall release the levy upon all, or part of, the property or rights to property levied upon and shall promptly notify the person upon whom such levy was made *(if any)* that such levy has been released if–

(A) the liability for which such levy was made is satisfied or becomes unenforceable by reason of lapse of time,

(B) release of such levy will facilitate the collection of such liability,

(C) the taxpayer has entered into an agreement under section 6159 to satisfy such liability by means of installment payments, unless such agreement provides otherwise.

(D) the Secretary has determined that such levy is creating an economic hardship due to the financial condition of the taxpayer, or

(E) the fair market value of the property exceeds such liability and release of the levy on a part of such property could be made without hindering the collection of such liability.

For purposes of subparagraph (C), the Secretary is not required to release such levy if such release would jeopardize the secured creditor status of the Secretary.

(2) **Expedited determination on certain business property.**–In the case of any tangible personal property essential in carrying on the trade or business of the taxpayer, the Secretary shall provide for an expedited determination under paragraph (1) if levy on such tangible personal property would prevent the taxpayer from carrying on such trade or business.

(3) **Subsequent levy.**–The release of levy on any property under paragraph (1) shall not prevent any subsequent levy on such property.

(b) **Return of Property.**–If the Secretary determines that property has been wrongfully levied upon, it shall be lawful for the Secretary to return-

(1) the specific property levied upon,

(2) an amount of money equal to the amount of money levied upon, or

(3) an amount of money equal to the amount of money received by the United States from a sale of such property.

Property may be returned at any time. An amount equal to the amount of money levied upon or received from such sale may be returned at any time before the expiration of 9 months from the date of such levy. For purposes of paragraph (3), if property is declared purchased by the United States at a sale pursuant to section 6335(e) (relating to manner and conditions of sale), the United States shall be treated as having received an amount of money equal to the minimum price determined pursuant to such section or (if larger) the amount received by the United States from the resale of such property.

(d) RETURN OF PROPERTY IN CERTAIN CASES-IF–

(1) any property has been levied upon, and

(2) the Secretary determines that–

(A) the levy on such property was premature or otherwise not in accordance with administrative procedures of the Secretary,

(B) the taxpayer has entered into an agreement under section 6159 to satisfy the tax liability for which the levy was imposed by means of installment payments, unless such agreement provides otherwise,

(C) the return of such property will facilitate the collection of the tax liability, or

(D) with the consent of the taxpayer or the National Taxpayer Advocate, the return of such property would be in the best interest of the taxpayer (as determined by the National Taxpayer Advocate) and the United States,

the provisions of subsection (b) shall apply in the same manner as if such property had been wrongly levied upon, except that no interest shall be allowed under subsection (c).

Form **668-W(c)(DO)** (Rev. 7-2002)

Form **668-W(c)(DO)**	Department of the Treasury – Internal Revenue Service
(Rev. July 2002)	**Notice of Levy on Wages, Salary, and Other Income**

DATE:

REPLY TO:

TELEPHONE NUMBER
OF IRS OFFICE:

NAME AND ADDRESS OF TAXPAYER:

TO:

IDENTIFYING NUMBER(S):

Kind of Tax	Tax Period Ended	Unpaid Balance of Assessment	Statutory Additions	Total
			Total Amount Due ▶	

We figured the interest and late payment penalty to _____

Statement of Exemptions and Filing Status *(To be completed by taxpayer; instructions are on the back of Part 5)*

My filing status for my income tax return is *(check one):* ☐ Single; ☐ Married Filing a Joint Return; ☐ Married Filing a Separate Return; ☐ Head of Household; or ☐ Qualifying Widow*(er)* with dependent child

ADDITIONAL STANDARD DEDUCTION: _____ *(Enter amount only if you or your spouse is at least 65 and/or blind.)*

I certify that I can claim the people named below as personal exemptions on my income tax return and that none are claimed on another Notice of Levy. No one I have listed is my minor child to whom (as required by court or administrative order) I make support payments that are already exempt from levy. I understand the information I have provided may be verified by the Internal Revenue Service. Under penalties of perjury, I declare that this statement of exemptions and filing status is true.

Name *(Last, First, Middle Initial)*	Relationship *(Husband, Wife, Son, Daughter, etc.)*	Social Security Number *(SSN)*

Taxpayer's Signature	Date

Part 5 — For Taxpayer to keep   Form **668-W(c)(DO)** (Rev. 7-2002)

A-134

Instructions to the Taxpayer

A levy was served on the person named on the front of this form. The information you provide on this form will be used by that person to figure the amount of your income that is exempt from levy.

Please complete Parts 3, 4, and 5. First, indicate your filing status by checking one of the five blocks on the Statement of Exemptions and Filing Status. Then, list each person that you can claim as an exemption on your income tax return not claimed on another Notice of Levy on Wages, Salary, and Other Income. Include each person's relationship to you and Social Security Number. If the person is less than six months old and does not have a number yet, write "Less than six months old" in the Social Security Number column. If you are claimed as a dependent by someone else, write "I can't claim an exemption for myself" next to your signature on the statement. Be sure to complete, sign and date all copies of the statement.

The amount of your income that is exempt from this levy each week can be figured by adding the standard deduction you can claim on your income tax return and the amount you claim on it for exemptions. Then, this total is divided by 52.

If you or your spouse is at least 65 years old and/or blind, you can claim the additional standard deduction which increases the amount exempt from this levy. Count one for each of the following: (a) you are 65 or older, (b) you are blind, (c) your spouse is 65 or older, and (d) your spouse is blind. Enter this total (up to 4) to the right of "ADDITIONAL STANDARD DEDUCTION" on Parts 3, 4, and 5.

Also, if you are required by a court or administrative order *(made before the date of this levy)* to support your minor children, then the amount needed to pay the support established by a court or administrative order is also exempt from the levy, and these minor children can't be listed as exemptions.

Keep Parts 2 and 5 for your records. Give Parts 3 and 4 to your employer within 3 work days after you receive them. If you do not give the completed statement to your employer, then your exempt amount will be figured as if your filing status is married filing separate with only one exemption, plus the amount for paying child support established by a court or administrative order. If you subsequently submit a Statement of Exemptions and Filing Status to your employer, your exempt amount will be adjusted to correspond to your statement.

If the number of your exemptions or your filing status change while this levy is in effect, please file another Statement of Exemptions and Filing Status with the person on whom this levy was served. You can get more forms from an Internal Revenue Service office.

In addition, if this levy is still in effect next year and if the standard deduction and amount deductible for personal exemptions change in the new year for all taxpayers, you may submit a new Statement of Exemptions and Filing Status, even though there may be no change from the prior statement. Submitting a new Statement of Exemptions and Filing Status will allow your employer to use the new year's exemption table (Publication 1494).

The information you provide is submitted under penalties of perjury and may be verified by the Internal Revenue Service.

Form **668-W(c)(DO)** (Rev. 7-2002)

| Form **668-W(c)(DO)** | Department of the Treasury – Internal Revenue Service |
| (Rev. July 2002) | **Notice of Levy on Wages, Salary, and Other Income** |

DATE:

REPLY TO:

TELEPHONE NUMBER
OF IRS OFFICE:

NAME AND ADDRESS OF TAXPAYER:

TO:

IDENTIFYING NUMBER*(S)*:

Kind of Tax	Tax Period Ended	Unpaid Balance of Assessment	Statutory Additions	Total
			Total Amount Due ▶	

We figured the interest and late payment penalty to _____

THIS ISN'T A BILL FOR TAXES YOU OWE. THIS IS A NOTICE OF LEVY TO COLLECT MONEY OWED BY THE TAXPAYER NAMED ABOVE.

The Internal Revenue Code provides that there is a lien for the amount shown above. Although we have given the notice and demand required by the Code, the amount owed hasn't been paid. This levy requires you to turn over to us: (1) this taxpayer's wages and salary that have been earned but not paid, as well as wages and salary earned in the future until this levy is released, and (2) this taxpayer's other income that you have now or for which you are obligated.

We levy this money to the extent it isn't exempt, as shown in the instructions. Don't offset money this person owes you without contacting us at the telephone number shown above for instructions.

If you don't owe money to this taxpayer, please call us at the telephone number at the top of this form. Instead of calling us you may complete the back of Part 3, attach it as a cover to the rest of this form, and return all parts to IRS in the enclosed envelope.

If you do owe money to this taxpayer, please see the back of this page for instructions on how to act on this notice.

Signature of Service Representative	Title

Part 6 — IRS File Copy   Catalog No. 15703I   www.irs.gov   Form **668-W(c)(DO)** (Rev. 7-2002)

Form 673
(Rev. January 2006)
Department of the Treasury
Internal Revenue Service

Statement for Claiming Exemption From Withholding on Foreign Earned Income Eligible for the Exclusion(s) Provided by Section 911

OMB No. 1545-0074

The following statement, when completed and furnished by a citizen of the United States to his or her employer, permits the employer to exclude from income tax withholding all or a part of the wages paid for services performed outside the United States.

Name *(please print or type)*

Social security number

Part I   Qualification Information for Foreign Earned Income Exclusion

I expect to qualify for the foreign earned income exclusion under either the bona fide residence or physical presence test for calendar year _____ or other tax year beginning _____ and ending _____ .

Please check applicable box:

☐ **Bona Fide Residence Test**

I am a citizen of the United States. I have been a bona fide resident of and my tax home has been located in _____ (foreign country or countries) for an uninterrupted period which includes an entire tax year that began on _____ , 20 _____ .
(date)

I expect to remain a bona fide resident and retain my tax home in a foreign country (or countries) until the end of the tax year for which this statement is made. Or, if not that period, from the date of this statement until _____ , 20 _____ .
(date within tax year)

I have not submitted a statement to the authorities of any foreign country named above that I am not a resident of that country. Or, if I made such a statement, the authorities of that country thereafter made a determination to the effect that I am a resident of that country.

Based on the facts in my case, I have good reason to believe that for this period of foreign residence I will satisfy the tax home and the bona fide foreign resident requirements prescribed by section 911(d)(1)(A) of the Internal Revenue Code and qualify for the exclusion Code section 911(a) allows.

☐ **Physical Presence Test**

I am a citizen of the United States. Except for occasional absences that will not disqualify me for the benefit of section 911(a) of the Internal Revenue Code, I expect to be present in and maintain my tax home in _____ (foreign country or countries) for a 12-month period that includes the entire tax year _____ . Or, if not the entire year, for the part of the tax year beginning on _____ , 20 _____ , and ending on _____ , 20 _____ .

Based on the facts in my case, I have good reason to believe that for this period of presence in a foreign country or countries, I will satisfy the tax home and the 330 full-day requirements within a 12-month period under section 911(d)(1)(B).

Part II   Estimated Housing Cost Amount for Foreign Housing Exclusion

1 Rent .	1	
2 Utilities (other than telephone charges) .	2	
3 Real and personal property insurance .	3	
4 Occupancy tax not deductible under section 164 .	4	
5 Nonrefundable fees paid for securing a leasehold .	5	
6 Household repairs .	6	
7 **Estimated qualified housing expenses.** Add lines 1 through 6 .	7	
8 Estimated base housing amount for qualifying period .	8	
9 Subtract line 8 from line 7. This is your estimated housing cost amount .	9	

Part III   Certification

Under penalties of perjury, I declare that I have examined the information on this form and to the best of my knowledge and belief it is true, correct, and complete. I further certify under penalties of perjury that:

● The estimated housing cost amount entered in Part II, plus the amount reported on any other statements outstanding with other employers, is not more than my total estimated housing cost amount.

● If I become disqualified for the exclusions, I will immediately notify my employer and advise what part, if any, of the period for which I am qualified.

I understand that any exemption from income tax withholding permitted by reason of furnishing this statement is not a determination by the Internal Revenue Service that any amount paid to me for any services performed during the tax year is excludable from gross income under the provisions of Code section 911(a).

Your Signature   Date

For Paperwork Reduction Act Notice, see back of form.   Cat. No. 10183Y   Form **673** (Rev. 1-2006)

Instructions

Information for Employee

File Form 673 with your U.S. employer to claim an exemption from U.S. income tax withholding on wages earned abroad to the extent of the foreign earned income exclusion and foreign housing exclusion. Your employer will then withhold the correct amount of federal income tax from your pay.

Even though you may qualify for the foreign earned income exclusion, you must file Form 2555, Foreign Earned Income, or Form 2555-EZ, Foreign Earned Income Exclusion, with your Form 1040, U.S. Individual Income Tax Return, to claim your exclusion. You must file Form 2555 to claim the foreign housing exclusion.

Information for Employer

Once you have received Form 673 completed by the employee, you may discontinue withholding of U.S. income tax on those wages that qualify for the exclusion(s). If for any reason you believe the employee will not qualify for the exclusion(s), you should disregard Form 673.

Note. If you have questions about the exclusion(s), see Pub. 54, Tax Guide for U.S. Citizens and Resident Aliens Abroad.

Paperwork Reduction Act Notice

We ask for the information on this form to carry out the Internal Revenue laws of the United States. If you want to claim an exemption from withholding, you are required to give this form (or similar statement) to your employer.

You are not required to provide the information requested on a form that is subject to the Paperwork Reduction Act unless the form displays a valid OMB control number. Books or records relating to a form or its instructions must be retained as long as their contents may become material in the administration of any Internal Revenue law. Generally, tax returns and return information are confidential, as required by Code section 6103.

The average time and expenses required to complete and file this form will vary depending on individual circumstances. For the estimated averages, see the instructions for your income tax return.

If you have suggestions for making this form simpler, we would be happy to hear from you. See the instructions for your income tax return.

Form **843**
(Rev. November 2005)
Department of the Treasury
Internal Revenue Service

Claim for Refund and Request for Abatement

▶ See separate instructions.

OMB No. 1545-0024

Use Form 843 only if your claim involves **(a)** *one of the taxes shown on line 3a or* **(b)** *a refund or abatement of interest, penalties, or additions to tax on line 4a.*

Do not *use Form 843 if your claim is for—*
- *An overpayment of income taxes;*
- *A refund for nontaxable use (or sales) of fuel; or*
- *An overpayment of excise taxes reported on Form(s) 11-C, 720, 730, or 2290.*

Type or print		
Name of claimant	Your SSN or ITIN	
Address (number, street, and room or suite no.)	Spouse's SSN or ITIN	
City or town, state, and ZIP code	Employer identification number (EIN)	
Name and address shown on return if different from above	Daytime telephone number ( )	

1   **Period.** Prepare a separate Form 843 for each tax period

From   /   /   to   /   /

2   Amount to be refunded or abated
$

3a   Type of tax, penalty, or addition to tax:
☐ Employment   ☐ Estate   ☐ Gift   ☐ Excise (see instructions)
☐ Penalty—IRC section ▶ _____

b   Type of return filed (see instructions):
☐ 706   ☐ 709   ☐ 940   ☐ 941   ☐ 943   ☐ 945   ☐ 990-PF   ☐ 4720   ☐ Other (specify)

4a   Request for abatement or refund of:
☐ Interest as a result of IRS errors or delays.
☐ A penalty or addition to tax as a result of erroneous advice from the IRS.

b   Dates of payment ▶ _____

5   **Explanation and additional claims.** Explain why you believe this claim should be allowed, and show the computation of your tax refund or abatement of interest, penalty, or addition to tax. If you need more space, attach additional sheets.

Signature. If you are filing Form 843 to request a refund or abatement relating to a joint return, both you and your spouse must sign the claim. Claims filed by corporations must be signed by a corporate officer authorized to sign, and the signature must be accompanied by the officer's title.

Under penalties of perjury, I declare that I have examined this claim, including accompanying schedules and statements, and, to the best of my knowledge and belief, it is true, correct, and complete.

Signature (Title, if applicable. Claims by corporations must be signed by an officer.)   Date

---

Signature   Date

For Privacy Act and Paperwork Reduction Act Notice, see separate instructions.   Cat. No. 10180R   Form **843** (Rev. 11-2005)

Instructions for Form 843

Department of the Treasury
Internal Revenue Service

(Rev. November 2005)

Claim for Refund and Request for Abatement

Section references are to the Internal Revenue Code.

General Instructions

Purpose of Form

Use Form 843 to file a claim for refund of certain overpaid taxes, interest, penalties, and additions to tax.

Use Form 843 to request the following.

• A refund of employment taxes when you reported and paid more federal income tax on your employment tax return than you actually withheld from an employee.

• A refund of excess tier 2 RRTA tax when you had more than one railroad employer for the year and your total tier 2 RRTA tax withheld or paid for the year was more than the tier 2 limit. See the instructions for line 3a.

• A refund of social security or Medicare taxes that were withheld in error. If you are a nonresident alien student, see Pub. 519 for specific instructions.

• A refund under section 6715 for misuse of dyed fuel.

• Abatement or refund of interest or penalties under section 6404(e) or 6404(f) relating to excise taxes.

• Abatement of an overassessment (or the unpaid portion of an overassessment) if more than the correct amount of tax (except income, estate, and gift tax), interest, additions to tax, or penalties have been assessed.

Generally, you must file a separate Form 843 for each tax period and each type of tax. Exceptions are provided for certain claims in the line 4 instructions beginning on this page.

Do not use Form 843 when you should use a different tax form. For example, do not file Form 843 to request:

• A refund or abatement of your income tax. Individuals must use Form 1040X, Amended U.S. Individual Income Tax Return. Corporations that filed Form 1120 or 1120-A must use Form 1120X, Amended U.S. Corporation Income Tax Return. Other income tax filers should file a claim on the appropriate amended tax return.

• A refund of excess tier 1 RRTA tax. Instead, use Form 1040 or 1040A.

• A refund relating to excise taxes reported on Forms 11-C, 720, 730, or 2290. See Form 720X, Amended Quarterly Federal Excise Tax Return; Form 4136, Credit for Federal Tax Paid on Fuels; Form 8849, Claim for Refund of Excise Taxes; Schedule C (Form 720), Quarterly Federal Excise Tax Return; Pub. 378, Fuel Tax Credits and Refunds; and Pub. 510, Excise Taxes, for information on the appropriate forms to use to claim the various excise tax refunds.

• A refund of the required payment under section 7519. Instead, file Form 8752, Required Payment or Refund Under Section 7519.

Who May File

You may file Form 843 or your agent may file it for you. If your agent files, the original or a copy of Form 2848, Power of Attorney and Declaration of Representative, must be attached. You must sign Form 2848 and authorize the representative to act on your behalf for the purposes of the request. See the Instructions for Form 2848 for more information.

If you are filing as a legal representative for a decedent whose return you filed, attach to Form 843 a statement that you filed the return and you are still acting as the representative. If you did not file the decedent's return, attach certified copies of letters testamentary, letters of administration, or similar evidence to show your authority. File Form 1310, Statement of Person Claiming Refund Due a Deceased Taxpayer, with Form 843 if you are the legal representative of a decedent.

Specific Instructions

SSN or ITIN. Enter your social security number (SSN) or IRS individual taxpayer identification number (ITIN). If you are filing Form 843 relating to a joint return, enter the SSNs or ITINs for both you and your spouse.

Line 3

Line 3a. Check the appropriate box to show the type of tax, penalty, or addition to tax. If you are filing a claim for refund or request for abatement of an assessed penalty, check the box and enter the applicable Internal

Revenue Code (IRC) section. Generally, you can find the IRC section on the Notice of Assessment you receive from the service center.

Excess tier 2 RRTA tax. Complete lines 1 and 2. On line 3a, check the box for "Employment" tax. Skip lines 3b, 4a, and 4b. In the space for line 5, identify the claim as "Excess Tier 2 RRTA" and show your computation of the refund. You must also attach copies of your Forms W-2 for the year to Form 843. See the worksheet in Pub. 505, Tax Withholding and Estimated Tax, to help you figure the excess amount.

Line 3b. Check the appropriate box to show the type of return, if any, that you filed.

 You must attach Form 941c, Supporting Statement To Correct Information, or an equivalent statement, if you are claiming a refund of taxes reported on Form 941, 941-M, 941-SS, 943, or 945.

Line 4

Requesting Abatement or Refund of Interest Under Section 6404(e)

Section 6404(e) gives the IRS the authority to abate interest when the additional interest is attributable to IRS errors or delays.

Section 6404(e) applies only if there was an unreasonable error or delay in performing a managerial or ministerial act (defined below and on page 2). The taxpayer cannot have caused any significant aspect of the error or delay. In addition, section 6404(e) relates only to taxes for which a notice of deficiency is required by section 6212(a). This includes income taxes, generation-skipping transfer taxes, estate and gift taxes, and certain excise taxes imposed by IRC chapter 41, 42, 43, or 44. Section 6404(e) does not allow abatement of interest for employment taxes or other excise taxes. See Pub. 556, Examination of Returns, Appeal Rights, and Claims of Refund, for more information.

Managerial act. The term "managerial act" means an administrative act that occurs during the processing of your case involving the temporary or permanent loss of records or the

Cat. No. 11200I

exercise of judgment or discretion relating to management of personnel. A decision regarding the proper application of federal tax law is not a managerial act. See Regulations section 301.6404-2 for more information.

Ministerial act. The term "ministerial act" means a procedural or mechanical act that does not involve the exercise of judgment or discretion and that occurs during the processing of your case after all prerequisites of the act, such as conferences and review by supervisors, have taken place. A decision regarding the proper application of federal tax law is not a ministerial act. See Regulations section 301.6404-2 for more information.

How To Request an Abatement of Interest

Request an abatement of interest by writing "Request for Abatement of Interest Under Section 6404(e)" at the top of Form 843.

Complete lines 1 through 3. Check the first box on line 4a. On line 4b, show the dates of any payment of interest or tax liability for the tax period involved.

On line 5 state:
- The type of tax involved,
- When you were first notified by the IRS in writing about the deficiency or payment,
- The specific period for which you are requesting abatement of interest,
- The circumstances of your case, and
- The reasons why you believe that failure to abate the interest would result in grossly unfair treatment.

Multiple tax years. File only one Form 843 if the interest assessment resulted from the IRS's error or delay in performing a single managerial or ministerial act affecting a tax assessment for multiple tax years or types of tax (for example, where 2 or more tax years were under examination).

Where to file. File Form 843 with the Internal Revenue Service Center where you filed your return.

Requesting Abatement or Refund of a Penalty or Addition to Tax as a Result of Written Advice

Section 6404(f) gives the IRS the authority to abate any portion of a penalty or addition to tax attributable to erroneous advice furnished to you in writing by an officer or employee of the IRS, acting in his or her official capacity.

The IRS will abate the penalty or addition to tax only if:
1. You reasonably relied on the written advice,
2. The written advice was in response to a specific written request you (or your representative who met the requirements of Regulations section 301.6404-3(b)(3)) made for advice, and
3. The penalty or addition to tax did not result from your failure to provide the IRS with adequate or accurate information.

How To Request an Abatement or Refund of a Penalty or an Addition to Tax

Request an abatement or refund of a penalty or addition to tax because of erroneous written advice by writing "Request for Abatement of Penalty or Addition to Tax Under Section 6404(f)" at the top of Form 843.

Complete lines 1 through 3. Check the appropriate box on line 4a. On line 4b, enter the date of payment if the penalty or addition to tax has been paid.

You must attach copies of the following information to Form 843:
1. Your written request for advice;
2. The erroneous written advice you relied on that was furnished to you by the IRS; and
3. The report, if any, of tax adjustments identifying the penalty or addition to tax, and the item(s) relating to the erroneous advice.

When to file. An abatement of any penalty or addition to tax under this section will be allowed only if:
- You submit the request for abatement within the period allowed for collection of the penalty or addition to tax, or
- You paid the penalty or addition to tax, within the period allowed for claiming a credit or refund of such penalty or addition to tax.

Where to file. If the erroneous advice received relates to an item on a federal tax return, send Form 843 to the Internal Revenue Service Center where your return was filed. If the erroneous advice does not relate to an item on a federal tax return, send Form 843 to the service center where your return was filed for the tax year you relied on the advice.

Line 5

Explain in detail your reasons for filing this claim and show your computation for the credit, refund, or abatement. If you attach an additional sheet(s), include your name and SSN, ITIN, or EIN on it. Also, attach appropriate supporting evidence.

Privacy Act and Paperwork Reduction Act Notice. We ask for the information on this form to carry out the Internal Revenue laws of the United States. Sections 6402 and 6404 state the conditions under which you may file a claim for refund and request for abatement of certain taxes, penalties, and interest. Form 843 may be used to file your claim. Section 6109 requires that you disclose your taxpayer identification number (TIN). Routine uses of this information include providing it to the Department of Justice for civil and criminal litigation and to cities, states, and the District of Columbia for use in administering their tax laws. We may also give this information to Federal and state agencies to enforce Federal nontax criminal laws and to combat terrorism. You are not required to claim a refund or request an abatement; however, if you choose to do so you are required to provide the information requested on this form. Failure to provide all of the requested information may delay or prevent processing your claim or request; providing false or fraudulent information may subject you to civil or criminal penalties.

You are not required to provide the information requested on a form that is subject to the Paperwork Reduction Act unless the form displays a valid OMB control number. Books or records relating to a form or its instructions must be retained as long as their contents may become material in the administration of any Internal Revenue law. Generally, tax returns and return information are confidential, as required by section 6103.

The time needed to complete and file this form will vary depending on individual circumstances. The estimated average time is:

Recordkeeping . . . . 26 min.
Learning about the law or the form . . . . 18 min.
Preparing the form . . . . 35 min.
Copying, assembling, and sending the form to the IRS . . 20 min.

If you have comments concerning the accuracy of these time estimates or suggestions for making this form simpler, we would be happy to hear from you. You can write to the Internal Revenue Service, Tax Products Coordinating Committee, SE:W:CAR:MP:T:T:SP, 1111 Constitution Ave. NW, IR-6406, Washington, DC 20224. Do not send the form to this address. Instead, see *Where to file* on this page.

-2-

Form 940 for 2006: Employer's Annual Federal Unemployment (FUTA) Tax Return

Department of the Treasury — Internal Revenue Service   OMB No. 1545-0028

999999

Employer identification number (EIN)

Name (*not your trade name*)

Trade name (*if any*)

Address

Number   Street   Suite or room number

City   State   ZIP code

Vision Draft
10/26/2005 1:45 PM

Type of Return (Check all that apply)

- a. Amended
- b. Successor employer
- c. No payments to employees in 2006.
- d. Final: Business closed or stopped paying wages

Read the separate instructions before you fill out this form. Please type or print within the boxes.

1. If you were required to pay your state unemployment tax in ...

    1a. **One** state only, write the state abbreviation 1a
    - OR -
    1b. **More than one** state (You are a multi-state employer) ... 1b ☐ Check here. Fill out Schedule A

2. If you paid wages in [Name of State], a state that is subject to CREDIT REDUCTION ... 2 ☐ Check here. Fill out Schedule A (Form 940), Part 2.

Part 2: Determine your FUTA wages for 2006. If any line does NOT apply, leave it blank.

3. Total payments to all employees 3

4. Payments exempt from FUTA tax 4

    Check all that apply: **4a** ☐ Fringe benefits   **4c** ☐ Retirement/Pension   **4e** ☐ Other

    4b ☐ Group term life insurance   **4d** ☐ Dependent care

5. Total of payments made to each employee in excess of $7,000 5

6. **Subtotal** (line 4 + line 5 = line 6) 6

7. **Total taxable FUTA wages** (line 3 – line 6 = line 7) 7

8. **FUTA tax before adjustments** (line 7 x .008 = line 8). 8

Part 3: Determine your adjustments. If any line does NOT apply, leave it blank.

9. If ALL of the FUTA wages you paid were excluded from state unemployment tax
(line 7 x .054 = line 9) Then go to line 12. 9

10. If SOME of the FUTA wages you paid were excluded from state unemployment tax, OR you
paid ANY state unemployment tax late (after the due date for filing Form 940), fill out the worksheet
in the instructions. Enter the amount from line 7 of the worksheet onto line 10. 10

11. If credit reduction applies, enter the amount from line 3 of Schedule A (Form 940) 11

Part 4: Determine your FUTA tax for 2006. If any line does NOT apply, leave it blank.

12. **Total FUTA tax after adjustments** (lines 8 + 9 + 10 + 11 = line 12) 12

13. FUTA tax deposited for the year, including any payment applied from a prior year 13

14. **Balance due** (line 12 – line 13 = line 14)
    - If line 14 is more than $500, you must deposit your tax.
    - If line 14 is $500 or less and you pay by check, make your check payable to the United States
    Treasury and write your EIN, *Form 940*, and *2006* on the check. 14

15. **Overpayment** (If line 13 is more than line 12, enter the difference on line 15 and check a box below.) 15

Check one: ☐ Apply overpayment to next return.
            ☐ Send a refund.

▶ **You MUST fill out both pages of this form and SIGN it.**

Next ➡

For Privacy Act and Paperwork Reduction Act Notice, see the back of Form 940-V: Payment Voucher.   Cat. No. 112340   Form **940** (2006)

999999

Name (not your trade name)	Employer identification number (EIN)

Part 5: Report your FUTA tax liability by quarter only if line 12 is more than $500. If not, go to Part 6.

16. Report the amount of your FUTA tax liability for each quarter; do NOT enter the amount you deposited. If you had no liability for a quarter, leave the line blank.

16a. **1st quarter** (January 1 – March 31) .... 16a [·]

16b. **2nd quarter** (April 1 – June 30) .... 16b [·]

16c. **3rd quarter** (July 1 – September 30) .... 16c [·]

16d. **4th quarter** (October 1 – December 31) .... 16d [·]

17. **Total tax liability for the year** (lines 16a + 16b + 16c + 16d = line 17) .... 17 [·]   Total must equal line 12.

Part 6: May we speak with your third-party designee?

Do you want to allow an employee, a paid tax preparer, or another person to discuss this return with the IRS? See the instructions for details.

[ ] Yes. Designee's name....[_____]

Select a 5-digit Personal Identification Number (PIN) to use when talking to IRS........ [ ][ ][ ][ ][ ]

[ ] No

Part 7: Sign here

You MUST fill out both pages of this form and SIGN it.

Under penalties of perjury, I declare that I have examined this return, including accompanying schedules and statements, and to the best of my knowledge and belief, it is true, correct, and complete, and that no part of any payment made to a state unemployment fund claimed as a credit was, or is to be, deducted from the payments made to employees.

✗ **Sign your name here** [_____]

Print your name here [_____]

Print your title here [_____]

Date [/ /]

Best daytime phone [( )]

Part 8: For paid preparers only (optional)

If you were paid to prepare this return and are not an employee of the business that is filing this return, you may choose to fill out Part 8.

Paid Preparer's name...... [_____]   Preparer's SSN/PTIN ... [_____]

Paid Preparer's signature . [_____]   Date.................... [/ /]

[ ] Check if you are self employed

Draft

Firm's name.............. [_____]   Firm's EIN .... [_____]

Street address .... [_____]

City ...... [_____] State...... [____]   ZIP code............. [_____]

Form **940** (2006)

Vision Draft 10/31/2005 3:42 PM

Instructions for Form 940 for 2006:
Employer's Annual Federal Unemployment (FUTA) Tax Return

What's New

We've revised the form and instructions

You may notice a number of changes in Form 940, *Employer's Annual Federal Unemployment (FUTA) Tax Return*. We revised the form and instructions so they are easier for you to read and fill out. At the same time, the new design makes the forms easier and faster for us to process. Now we can optically scan the forms and will capture data more accurately and efficiently than before. Please read both the form and instructions carefully to become familiar with the changes.

The redesigned Form 940 replaces previous versions of both Form 940-EZ and Form 940. We have replaced two forms with one simplified form that should make preparing your tax return easier. If you filed Form 940-EZ before, you must now use the redesigned Form 940.

A new schedule is available for multi-state employers and employers in states that are subject to credit reduction. In addition to the changes on the Form 940, we developed Schedule A (Form 940), *Multi-State Employer and Credit Reduction Information*. You must use Schedule A (Form 940) if you paid wages to employees in more than 1 state or if you paid wages in any state that is subject to credit reduction.

We've also developed a new worksheet for you to use if some of the wages you paid were excluded from state unemployment tax or if you paid any state unemployment tax late. On page 9, you'll find an easier, all-inclusive worksheet that you can use to compute the adjustment if you paid state tax late. You must also use this worksheet to figure the adjustment for additional FUTA tax if your state does not require you to pay state unemployment tax on all your employees, for example, if wages paid to your corporate officers are excluded from state unemployment tax.

You can file and pay electronically...

Using electronic options available from the Internal Revenue Service (IRS) can make filing a return and paying your federal tax easier. You can use e-file to file a return and Electronic Federal Tax Payment System (EFTPS) to make deposits or pay in full whether you rely on a tax professional or prepare your own taxes.

- For e-file, visit www.irs.gov for additional information.

- For EFTPS, visit www.eftps.gov or call EFTPS Customer Service at 1-800-555-4477.

Photographs of missing children

IRS is a proud partner with the National Center for Missing and Exploited Children. Photographs of missing children selected by the Center may appear in instructions on pages that would otherwise be blank. You can help bring these children home by looking at the photographs and calling 1-800-THE-LOST (1-800-843-5678) if you recognize a child.

General Instructions:
Understanding Form 940

What's the Purpose of Form 940?

Use Form 940 to report your annual Federal Unemployment Tax Act (FUTA) tax. Together with state unemployment tax systems, the FUTA tax provides funds for paying unemployment compensation to workers who have lost their jobs. Most employers pay both a federal and a state unemployment tax. Only employers pay FUTA tax. Do not collect or deduct FUTA tax from your employees' wages.

The FUTA tax applies to the first $7,000 of taxable wages you pay to each employee during a calendar year.

These instructions give you some background information about the Form 940. They tell you who must file the form, how to fill it out line by line, and when and where to file it.

Who Must File Form 940?

Except as noted below, if you answer *Yes* to either one of these questions, you must file Form 940:

- Did you pay wages of $1,500 or more to employees in any calendar quarter during 2005 or 2006?

- Did you have one or more employees for at least some part of a day in any 20 or more different weeks in 2005 or 20 or more different weeks in 2006? Count all full-time, part-time, and temporary employees. However, if your business is a partnership, do not count its partners.

If your business was sold or transferred during the year, each employer who answered *Yes* to at least one question above must file Form 940. However, do not include any wages paid by the other employer unless you are a successor employer. For details, see *Type of Return, Successor Employer* on page 5.

If you received a preprinted Form 940 and are not liable for FUTA tax for 2006 because you made no payments to employees in 2006, check box *c* in the top corner of the form. Then go to Part 7, sign the form, and file it with the IRS.

Appendix

If you will not be liable for filing Form 940 in the future because your business has closed or because you stopped paying wages, check box *d* in the top right corner of the form. See *Type of Return, Final* on page 5 for more information.

For employers of household employees ...

If you are a household employer, you must pay FUTA tax on wages that you paid to your household employees only if you paid cash wages of $1,000 or more (for all household employees) in any calendar quarter in 2005 or 2006.

A *household employee* performs household work in a:

• private home,

• local college club, or

• local chapter of a college fraternity or sorority.

Generally, employers of household employees should file Schedule H (Form 1040) instead of Form 940.

However, if you have other employees in addition to household employees, you can choose to include the FUTA taxes for your household employees on the Form 940 instead of filing Schedule H (Form 1040). If you choose to include household employees on your Form 940, you must also file Form 941, *Employer's Quarterly Federal Tax Return,* Form 943, *Employer's Annual Federal Tax Return for Agricultural Employees,* or Form 944, *Employer's Annual Federal Tax Return* to report social security, Medicare, and withheld federal income taxes for your household employees.

See Pub. 926, *Household Employer's Tax Guide,* for more information.

For agricultural employers ...

File Form 940 if you answer *Yes* to either of these questions:

• Did you pay cash wages of $20,000 or more to farmworkers during any calendar quarter in 2005 or 2006?

• Did you employ 10 or more farmworkers during some part of the day (whether or not at the same time) during any 20 or more different weeks in 2005 or 20 or more different weeks in 2006?

Count wages you paid to aliens who were admitted to the United States temporarily to perform farmwork (these workers are also known as workers with H-2(A) visas). Wages paid to "H-2(A) visa workers" are not subject to FUTA tax.

See Pub. 51, (Circular A), *Agricultural Employer's Tax Guide,* for more information.

For Indian tribal governments ...

After December 20, 2000, a federally recognized Indian tribal government employer (including any subdivision, subsidiary, or wholly owned business enterprise) that participates in its state unemployment tax system and complies with applicable state law, is exempt from FUTA tax and does not have to file Form 940. For more information, see Internal Revenue code section 3309(d).

For nonprofit organizations ...

Religious, educational, and charitable organizations described in section 501 (c)(3) and exempt from tax under section 501(a) are not subject to FUTA tax and do not have to file Form 940.

For employers of state and local government employees...

Employers of state and local government employees are not subject to FUTA tax and do not have to file Form 940.

When Must You File Form 940?

The due date for filing Form 940 for 2006 is January 31, 2007. However, if you deposited all your FUTA tax when it was due, you may file Form 940 by February 12, 2007.

If we receive your return after the due date, we will treat your return as if you filed it on time if the envelope containing your return is properly addressed, contains sufficient postage, and is mailed First Class or sent by an IRS-designated delivery service on or before the due date. However, if you do not follow these guidelines, we will consider your return filed when it is actually received. For a list of designated delivery services, see Pub. 15 (Circular E), *Employer's Tax Guide.*

Where Should You File?

Where you file depends on whether you include a payment with your form.

If you are in...		Without a payment...	With a payment...
Connecticut	New Jersey	IRS	IRS
Delaware	New York	Cincinnati, OH	P.O. Box 105887
District of	North Carolina	45999-0046	Atlanta, GA
Columbia	Ohio		30348-5887
Illinois	Pennsylvania		
Indiana	Rhode Island		
Kentucky	South Carolina		
Maine	Vermont		
Maryland	Virginia		
Massachusetts	West Virginia		
Michigan	Wisconsin		
New Hampshire			

Need help? Call us at **1-800-829-4933** or visit our web site **at www.irs.gov.**

If you are in...		Without a payment...	With a payment...
Alabama	Missouri	IRS Ogden, UT 84201-0046	IRS P.O. Box 660095 Dallas, TX 75266-0095
Alaska	Montana		
Arizona	Nebraska		
Arkansas	Nevada		
California	New Mexico		
Colorado	North Dakota		
Florida	Oklahoma		
Georgia	Oregon		
Hawaii	South Dakota		
Idaho	Tennessee		
Iowa	Texas		
Kansas	Utah		
Louisiana	Washington		
Minnesota	Wyoming		
Mississippi			
Puerto Rico U.S. Virgin Islands		IRS Philadelphia, PA 19255-0046	IRS P.O. Box 80105 Cincinnati, OH 45280-0005
If the location of your legal residence, principal place of business, office, or agency is not listed ...		IRS Philadelphia, PA 19255-0046	IRS Philadelphia, PA 19255-0046
EXCEPTION for exempt organizations, Federal, State and Local Governments, and Indian Tribal Governments, regardless of your location		IRS Ogden, UT 84201-0046	IRS P.O. Box 660095 Dallas, TX 75266-0095

 Private delivery services cannot deliver to P.O. boxes.

Depositing Your FUTA Tax

When Must You Deposit Your FUTA Tax?

Although Form 940 covers a calendar year, you may have to deposit your FUTA tax before you file your return. Generally, if your FUTA tax is more than $500 for the calendar year, you must deposit at least one quarterly payment for the year. Deposit your FUTA tax by the last day of the month after the end of the quarter.

You must determine when to deposit your tax based on the amount of your quarterly tax liability. If your FUTA tax is $500 or less in a quarter, carry it over to the next quarter. Continue carrying your tax liability over until your cumulative tax is more than $500. At that point, you must deposit your tax for the quarter. However, if your tax for the next quarter is less than $500, you are not required to deposit your tax again until the cumulative amount reaches $500.

Fourth quarter liabilities. If your FUTA tax for the 4th quarter (plus any undeposited amounts from earlier quarters, including credit reduction liabilities) is more than $500, deposit the entire amount by January 31, 2007. If it is $500 or

less, you can either deposit the amount or pay it with your Form 940 by January 31, 2007. **You must include liabilities owed for credit reduction with your 4th quarter deposit.**

When to deposit your FUTA tax	
If your undeposited FUTA tax is more than $500 on ...	Deposit your tax by ...
March 31	April 30
June 30	July 31
September 30	October 31
December 31	January 31

 If any deposit due date falls on a Saturday, Sunday, or legal holiday, you may deposit on the next business day.

How Do You Figure Your Quarterly Payment?

You owe a FUTA tax of 6.2% (.062) on the first $7,000 of wages that you paid to each employee during a calendar year. Most employers receive a maximum credit of up to 5.4% (.054) against this FUTA tax. Every quarter, you must calculate how much of the first $7,000 of each employee's annual wages you paid during that quarter.

Figure your tax liability

Before you can figure the amount to deposit, figure your FUTA tax liability for the quarter. To figure your tax liability, add the first $7,000 of each employee's annual wages you paid during a quarter, then multiply that amount by .008.

The .008 tax rate is based on your receiving the maximum credit against FUTA taxes. You are entitled to the maximum credit if you paid all state unemployment tax by the due date of your Form 940 or if you were not required to pay state unemployment tax during a calendar year due to your state experience rate.

Example:

During the first quarter, you have 3 employees: Employees A, B, and C. You paid $11,000 to Employee A, $2,000 to Employee B, and $4,000 to Employee C during the quarter.

To figure your quarterly liability, add the first $7,000 of each employee's wages:

	$7,000	Employee A's wages subject to FUTA tax
	$2,000	Employee B's wages subject to FUTA tax
+	$4,000	Employee C's wages subject to FUTA tax
	$13,000	Total wages subject to FUTA tax for quarter

	$13,000	Total wages subject to FUTA tax for quarter
X	.008	Tax rate (based on maximum credit)
	$ 104.00	Your quarterly liability

In this example, you do not have to make a deposit because the total is $500 or less for the quarter. However, you must carry this liability over to the next quarter.

Instructions for Form 940: *Employer's Annual Federal Unemployment Tax Return*

Draft

page 3

Appendix

If any wages subject to FUTA tax are not subject to state unemployment tax, you may be required to deposit your FUTA tax at a higher rate. For instance, in certain states, wages paid to corporate officers, certain payments of sick pay by unions, and certain fringe benefits are excluded from state unemployment tax. **Note:** If all of the wages you paid were excluded from state unemployment tax, you must deposit your FUTA tax at the 6.2% (.062) rate.

Example:

Employee A and Employee B are corporate officers whose wages are excluded from state unemployment tax. Employee C's wages are not excluded from state unemployment tax. You paid $11,000 to Employee A, $2,000 to Employee B and $4,000 to Employee C.

$ 9,000 Total FUTA wages for Employees A and B in 1st quarter
X .062 Tax rate
　$558 Your quarterly liability for Employees A and B

$4,000 Total FUTA wages subject to state unemployment tax
x .008 Tax rate (based on maximum credit)
$32.00 Your quarterly liability for Employee C

　$558 Your quarterly liability for Employees A and B
+　 32 Your quarterly liability for Employee C
　$590 Your tax liability

In this example, you must deposit $590 by April 30.

How Must You Deposit Your Tax?

You may pay your FUTA tax electronically by using EFTPS or by depositing your tax with an authorized financial institution (for example, a commercial bank that is qualified to accept federal tax deposits). The financial institution will send IRS a record of your payment to credit to your business account.

You may deposit your FUTA tax using EFTPS

To expedite your deposit and confirm that IRS has received your payment, you may choose to deposit your tax using EFTPS. To enroll, call 1-800-555-4477 or visit the EFTPS website at www.eftps.gov.

If your business is new, IRS will automatically pre-enroll you in EFTPS when you apply for an employer identification number (EIN). If you choose to deposit your tax using EFTPS, follow the instructions on your EIN package to activate your enrollment.

You may be required to use EFTPS. In some cases, **you may be required** to deposit your tax using EFTPS. For instance, you must use EFTPS in 2007 if:

- The total payments of your employment tax, excise tax, and corporate income tax were more than $200,000 for 2005; or
- You were required to use EFTPS in 2006.

 To make your EFTPS payments on time, you must initiate the transaction at least 1 business day before the date the deposit is due.

If you do not use EFTPS, use Form 8109, *Federal Tax Deposit (FTD) Coupon,* when you deposit your tax. **Do not mail your payments directly to IRS.** If you were required to use EFTPS and you use Form 8109 instead, you may be subject to a 10% penalty.

If you are a new employer and would like to receive an FTD coupon booklet, call 1-800-829-4933. Please allow 5 to 6 weeks for delivery.

How Can You Avoid Penalties and Interest?

Penalties and interest are assessed at a rate set by law on taxes paid late, returns filed late or incorrectly, insufficient payments made, and failure to pay using EFTPS (when required).

You can avoid paying penalties and interest if you:

- deposit or pay your tax when it is due, using EFTPS if required; and
- file your completed Form 940 accurately and on time.

If you receive a notice about penalty and interest after you file this return, send us an explanation and we will determine if you meet reasonable-cause criteria. Do not attach an explanation when you file your Form 940.

How Can You Amend a Return?

You can use Form 940 to amend a return that you previously filed. If you are amending a return for a prior year, use the prior year's Form 940, if possible.

Follow these steps:

- Check the amended return box in the top right corner of Form 940, page 1, box *a.*
- Fill in all the amounts that should have been on the original form.
- Sign the form.
- Attach an explanation of why you are amending your return. For example, tell us if you are filing to claim credit for tax paid to your state unemployment fund after the due date of Form 940.
- File the amended return with the IRS office where you filed the original return.
- Do not mail your amended form to a P.O. box, even if you include a payment.

Need help? Call us at **1-800-829-4933** or visit our web site **at www.irs.gov.**

Completing Your Form 940

Follow these guidelines to correctly fill out the form

To help us accurately scan and process your form, please follow these guidelines:

- Make sure your business name and EIN are on every page of the form and any attachments.

- If you type or use a computer to fill out your form, use a 12-point Courier font, if possible.

- Make sure you enter dollars to the left of the preprinted decimal point and cents to the right.

- Do not use dollar signs or decimal points. Commas are optional.

- You may choose to round your figures to the nearest dollar, rather than reporting cents on this form. If you do choose to round, you must round all entries. To round, follow these steps: If the amount is $.49 or less, add nothing to the dollar figure. If the amount is between $.50 and $.99, increase the dollar figure by $1.00. (For example, $1.49 becomes $1.00 and $2.50 becomes $3.00.) If you use 2 or more figures to calculate an entry on the form, use cents in your calculations and round the answer only.

- If you have a line with the value of zero, leave it blank.

Employer Identification Number (EIN), Name, Trade name, and Address

Review your business information at the top of the form

If you pay a tax preparer to fill out Form 940, make sure the preparer shows your business name and EIN **exactly** as they appear on the preprinted form we sent you.

If you are using a copy of Form 940 that has your business name and address preprinted at the top of the form, check to make sure that the information is correct. Carefully review your EIN to make sure that it exactly matches the EIN assigned to your business by the IRS. If any information is incorrect, cross it out and type or print the correct information. See *Tell us if you change your name or address* below.

If you are not using a preprinted Form 940, type or print your EIN, name, and address in the spaces provided. You must enter your name and EIN here and on page 2. Do not use your social security number or individual taxpayer identification number (ITIN) as your EIN. Enter the business (legal) name that you used when you applied for your EIN on Form SS-4, *Application for Employer Identification Number.* For example, if you are a sole proprietor, enter "Ronald Smith" on the "Name" line and "Ron's Cycles" on the Trade Name line. Leave the "Trade Name" line blank if it is the same as your "Name."

Employer Identification Number (EIN). The IRS monitors tax filings and payments by using a numerical system to identify taxpayers and to make sure that businesses comply with federal tax laws. A unique 9-digit EIN is assigned to all corporations, partnerships, and some sole proprietors. Businesses that need an EIN must apply for a number and use it throughout the life of the business on all tax returns, payments, and reports.

Your business should have only one EIN. If you have more than one and are unsure which one to use, call 1-800-829-4933 to verify your correct EIN.

If you do not have an EIN, apply for one by:

- Visiting the IRS website at www.irs.gov/smallbiz and filling out Form SS-4, *Application for Employer Identification Number,*

- Calling 1-800-829-4933 and applying by telephone, or

- Writing to the address on Form SS-4, *Application for Employer Identification Number.*

If you do not have an EIN by the time a return is due, write *"Applied For"* and the date you applied in the space shown for the EIN on pages 1 and 2 of your return.

 Always be sure the EIN on the form you file exactly matches the EIN that IRS assigned to your business. Do not use your social security number on forms that ask for an EIN. Filing a Form 940 with an incorrect EIN or using another business' EIN may result in penalties and delays in processing your return.

Tell us if you change your name or address

Notify the IRS immediately if you change your business name or address.

- If your business name changes, write to the IRS office where you would send your return if you had no payment. See *Where Should You File?* on page 2. See Pub. 1635, *Understanding Your EIN* for general information on EINs.

- If your address changes, complete and mail Form 8822, *Change of Address.*

Type of Return

Review the box at the top of the form. If any line applies to you, check the appropriate box to tell us which type of return you are filing. You may need to check more than one box.

a. Amended — If this is an amended return that you are filing to correct a return that you previously filed, check box *a.*

b. Successor employer — If you are a successor employer and you are reporting wages or claiming state tax that a

Appendix

previous employer paid before you acquired the business, check box *b*.

A *successor employer* is an employer who:

- acquires a unit of another owner's trade or business or all or most of the property used in the trade or business of another owner, and

- immediately after the acquisition, employs one or more people who were employed by the previous owner.

c. **No payments to employees in 2006** — If you are not liable for FUTA tax for 2006 because you made no payments to employees in 2006, check box *c* Then go to Part 7, sign the form, and file it with the IRS.

d. **Final: Business closed or stopped paying wages** — If this is a final return because you went out of business or stopped paying wages and you will not be liable for filing Form 940 in the future, check box *d*.

How you can get more help

If you want more information about this form, see Pub. 15 (Circular E), *Employer's Tax Guide*, visit our website at www.irs.gov, or call 1-800-829-4933.

For a list of related employment tax topics, visit the IRS website at www.irs.gov and type "Employment Tax" in the keyword search box.

Specific Instructions:
Part 1: Tell us about your return

If any line in Part 1 does not apply, leave it blank.

1. **If you were required to your state unemployment tax in ...**

1a. One state only...

If you were required to pay state unemployment tax in one state only, on line 1a enter the two-letter Postal Service abbreviation for the state where you paid your tax.

1b. More than one state (you are a multi-state employer) ...

If you were required to pay state unemployment tax in more than one state, check the box in line 1b. Then fill out Part 1 of Schedule A (Form 940), and attach it to your Form 940.

2. **If you paid wages in XXX, a state that is subject to credit reduction ...**

A state that has not repaid money it borrowed from the federal government to pay unemployment benefits is called *a credit reduction state*. The U.S. Department of Labor determines which states are credit reduction states.

If you paid wages that are subject to the unemployment tax laws of a credit reduction state, you may have to pay more FUTA tax when filing your Form 940.

For 2006, XXX is a credit reduction state. If you paid wages subject to the unemployment tax laws of the state of XXX, check the box on line 2 and fill out Part 2 of Schedule A (Form 940). (See instructions for line 9 before completing Part 2, Schedule A, Form 940.)

Part 2: Determine your FUTA wages for 2006

If any line in Part 2 does not apply, leave it blank.

3. **Total payments to all employees**

Report the total payments that you made during the calendar year for the services of all employees, even if the payments are not taxable for FUTA. Your method of payment does not determine whether payments are wages. You may have paid wages hourly, daily, weekly, monthly, or yearly. You may have paid wages for piecework or as a percentage of profits. Include:

- **Compensation**, such as:
  - Salaries, wages, commissions, fees, bonuses, vacation allowances, and amounts you paid to full-time, part-time, or temporary employees

- **Fringe benefits**, such as:
  - Sick pay (including third-party sick pay if liability is transferred to the employer). For details on sick pay, see Pub. 15-A, *Employer's Supplemental Tax Guide*.
  - The value of goods, lodging, food, clothing, and non-cash fringe benefits
  - Section 125 (cafeteria) plan benefits

- **Retirement/Pension**, such as:
  - Employer contributions to a 401(k) plan, payments to an Archer MSA, payments under adoption assistance programs, and contributions to SIMPLE retirement accounts (including elective salary reduction contributions)
  - Amounts deferred under a non-qualified deferred compensation plan

- **Other payments**, such as:
  - Tips of $20 or more in a month that your employees reported to you
  - Payments made by a previous employer to the employees of a business you acquired

For details, see section 5 of Pub. 15-A, *Employer's Supplemental Tax Guide.*

Example:

You had 3 employees. You paid $44,000 to Employee A, $8.000 to Employee B, and $16,000 to Employee C.

$44,000	Amount paid to Employee A
$8,000	Amount paid to Employee B
+ $16,000	Amount paid to Employee C
$68,000	Total payments to employees. You would enter this amount on line 3.

4. Payments exempt from FUTA tax

Some payments are exempt from FUTA tax because the payments are not included in the definition of wages or the services are not included in the definition of employment. You should only report an amount as exempt from FUTA on line 4 if you included the amount on line 3.

Payments exempt from FUTA tax may include:

- **Fringe benefits**, such as:
  - The value of certain meals and lodging
  - Contributions to accident or health plans for employees, including certain employer payments to a Health Savings Account or an Archer MSA
  - Employer reimbursements (including payments to a third party) for qualified moving expenses, to the extent that these expenses would otherwise be deductible by the employee
  - Payments for benefits excluded under section 125 (cafeteria) plans

For more information about these and other payments for fringe benefits that may be exempt from FUTA tax, see Pub. 15-B, *Employer's Tax Guide to Fringe Benefits.*

- **Group term life insurance**. For more information, see Pub. 15-B, *Employer's Tax Guide to Fringe Benefits*.

- **Retirement/Pension**, such as employer contributions to a qualified plan, including a SIMPLE retirement account (other than elective salary reduction contributions) and a 401(k) plan.

- **Dependent care**, such as payments (up to $5,000 per employee, $2,500 if married filing separately) for a qualifying person's care that allows your employees to work and that would be excludable by the employee under section 129.

- **Other payments**, such as:
  - All non-cash payments and certain cash payments for agricultural labor, and all payments to "H-2(A)"

visa workers. See *For agricultural employers* on page 2 or Pub. 51 (Circular A), *Agricultural Employer's Tax Guide.*

- Payments made under a workers' compensation law because of a work-related injury or sickness. See sec. 6 of Pub. 15-A, *Employer's Supplemental Tax Guide.*

- Payments for domestic services if you did not pay cash wages of $1,000 or more (for all domestic employees) in any calendar quarter in 2005 or 2006. See Pub. 926, *Household Employer's Tax Guide.*

- Payments for services provided to you by your parent, spouse, or child under the age of 21. See sec. 3 of Pub. 15 (Circular E), *Employer's Tax Guide.*

- Payments for certain fishing activities. See Pub. 595, *Tax Highlights for Commercial Fishermen.*

- Payments to certain statutory employees. See sec. 1 of Pub. 15-A, *Employer's Supplemental Tax Guide.*

See section 3306 and its related regulations for more information about FUTA taxation of retirement plan contributions, dependent care payments, and other payments.

If you enter an amount on line 4, check the appropriate boxes on lines 4a–4e to show the type of exempt payment you made.

Example:

You had 3 employees. You paid $44,000 to Employee A including $2,000 in health insurance benefits. You paid $8,000 to Employee B, including $500 in retirement benefits. You paid $16,000 to Employee C, including $2,000 in health and retirement benefits.

$ 2,000	Health insurance benefits for Employee A
500	Health insurance benefits for Employee B
+ 2,000	Health and retirement benefits for Employee C
$4,500	Total exempt payments. You would enter this amount on line 4 and check boxes 4a and 4c.

5. Total of payments made to each employee in excess of $7,000

Only the first $7,000 of taxable FUTA payments that you make to each employee in a calendar year is subject to FUTA tax. This $7,000 is called the *FUTA wage base.*

Add the amount of taxable FUTA payments you made to each employee in excess of $7,000 for the calendar year. Then add those excess amounts. Enter the total on line 5.

Again following our example:
You had 3 employees. You paid $44,000 to Employee A, $8,000 to Employee B, and $16,000 to Employee C, including a total of $4,500 in exempt payments for all three employees.

Employees	A	B	C
Payments to employees	44,000	8,000	16,000
- Exempt payments	2,000	500	2,000
- FUTA wage base	7,000	7,000	7,000
	35,000	500	7,000

```
   35,000
      500
 +  7,000
   42,500  Total payments in excess of $7,000 to all
           employees. You would enter this amount on line 5.
```

If you are a successor employer ... When you calculate the $7,000 FUTA wage base for each employee, you may count the payments that the other employer made to the employees who continue to work for you only if:

• The other employer was required to file Form 940, and

• You report payments the other employer made on line 3.

Add the payments that the other employer made in the calendar year to the payments you paid in the same calendar year and subtract any excess FUTA payments that you both made.

Example for successor employers:
During the calendar year, the other employer paid $5,000 to Employee A. You acquired the business, kept Employee A, and paid an additional $3,000 in wages during the rest of the year.

```
   $5,000  Payments by other employer
 +  3,000  Payments by you
   $8,000  Total payments to Employee A. Report this on line 3.

   $8,000  Total payments to Employee A
 -  7,000  FUTA wage base
   $1,000  Total of payments to Employee A in excess of $7,000

   $1,000  Excess payments to employee A
 +  5,000  Taxable FUTA wages reported by other employer
   $6,000  You would enter this amount on line 5
```

6. Subtotal
To calculate your subtotal,

```
    line 4
 + _line 5_
    line 6
```

7. Total taxable FUTA wages
To calculate your total taxable FUTA wages,

```
    line 3
 - _line 6_
    line 7
```

8. FUTA tax before adjustments
To calculate your total FUTA tax before adjustments,

```
    line 7
 x _.008_
    line 8
```

Part 3: Determine your adjustments

If any line in Part 3 does not apply, leave it blank.

9. If ALL of the FUTA wages you paid were excluded from state unemployment tax:

```
    line 7
 x _.054_
    line 9
```

If you were not required to pay state unemployment tax because all of the wages you paid were excluded from state unemployment tax, you must pay FUTA tax at the 6.2% (.062) rate. For example, if your state unemployment tax law excludes wages paid to corporate officers or employees in specific occupations, and the only wages you paid were to corporate officers or employees in those specific occupations, you must pay FUTA tax on those wages at the full FUTA rate of 6.2% (.062).

If line 9 applies to you, lines 11 and 12 do not apply; leave lines 10 and 11 BLANK. Do not fill out the worksheet or complete Part 2, Schedule A (Form 940).

10. If SOME of the FUTA wages you paid were excluded from state unemployment tax or you paid ANY state unemployment tax late, fill out the worksheet on the next page. The worksheet takes you step by step through the process of figuring your credit. On page 10, you'll find an example of how to use it. Do not fill out the worksheet if line 9 is more than zero (see instructions above).

Before you fill out the worksheet, gather the following information:

• Taxable FUTA wages (from line 7 of Form 940),

• Taxable state unemployment wages,

• The experience rates assigned to you by the states where you paid wages,

• The amount of state unemployment taxes you paid on time (*On time* means that you paid the state unemployment taxes on or before the due date for filing Form 940), and

• The amount of state unemployment taxes you paid late (*Late* means after the due date for filing Form 940).

For line 3 of the worksheet:

• If any of the experience rates assigned to you were less than 5.4% for all or part of the calendar year, you must list each assigned rate separately on the worksheet.

• If you were assigned 6 or more experience rates that were less than 5.4% for all or part of the calendar year, use another sheet to compute the additional credits. Then include those additional credits in the line 3 total.

After you complete the worksheet, enter the amount from line 7 from the worksheet onto line 10 of Form 940. Do not attach the worksheet to your Form 940. Keep it with your records.

Worksheet

Use this worksheet to figure your credit if:
- ▶ some of the wages you paid were excluded from state unemployment tax, OR
- ▶ you paid any state unemployment tax late.

For this worksheet, do not round your figures.

Before you can properly fill out this worksheet, you will need to gather this information:
- ■ Taxable FUTA wages (from line 7 of Form 940)
- ■ Taxable state unemployment wages
- ■ The experience rates assigned to you by the states where you paid wages
- ■ The amount of state unemployment taxes you paid on time (*ON TIME* means that you paid the state unemployment taxes on or before the due date for filing the Form 940.)
- ■ The amount of state unemployment taxes you paid late (*LATE* means after the due date for filing Form 940.)

1. **Maximum allowable credit** — Enter line 7 from Form 940 here: [_____.___] x .054 = line 1   **1** [_____.___]

Compute your credit:

2. **Credit for timely state unemployment tax payments** — How much did you pay on time?   **2** [_____.___]

- ■ If line 2 is **equal to or more** than line 1, **STOP here.** (STOP) You have completed the worksheet. Enter zero on line 10 of Form 940.
- ■ If line 2 is **less than** line 1, continue this worksheet.

3. **Additional credit** — Were ALL of your assigned experience rates 5.4% or more?

- ■ If **yes,** enter zero on line 3. Then go to line 4 of this worksheet.
- ■ If **no,** fill out the computations below. List ONLY THOSE STATES for which your assigned experience rate for all or part of the calendar year was less than 5.4%.

State	Computation rate The difference between 5.4% (.054) and your assigned experience rate. .054 − .XXX (assigned rate) = computation rate		Taxable state unemployment wages at assigned experience rate	Additional credit
1. _____	_____._	x	_____.__	= _____.__
2. _____	_____._	x	_____.__	= _____.__
3. _____	_____._	x	_____.__	= _____.__
4. _____	_____._	x	_____.__	= _____.__
5. _____	_____._	x	_____.__	= _____.__

If you need more lines, use another sheet and include those additional credits in the total. **Total** [_____.___]
Enter the total onto line 3.

3 [_____.___]

4. **Subtotal** (Line 2 + line 3 = line 4)   **4** [_____.___]

- ■ If line 4 is **equal to or more** than line 1, **STOP here.** (STOP) You have completed the worksheet. Enter zero on line 10 of Form 940.
- ■ If line 4 is **less than** line 1, continue this worksheet.

5. **Credit for paying state unemployment taxes late**

5a. **What is your remaining allowable credit?** (Line 1 − line 4 = line 5a)   **5a** [_____.___]

5b. **How much state unemployment tax did you pay late?**   **5b** [_____.___]

5c. **Which is smaller, line 5a or line 5b?** Enter the smaller number here.   **5c** [_____.___]

5d. **Your allowable credit for paying state unemployment taxes late** (Line 5c x .90 = line 5d)   **5d** [_____.___]

6. **Your FUTA credit** (Lines 4 + line 5d = line 6)   **6** [_____.___]

- ■ If line 6 is **equal to or more** than line 1, **STOP here.** (STOP) You have completed the worksheet. Enter zero on line 10 of Form 940.
- ■ If line 6 is **less than** line 1, continue this worksheet.

7. **Your adjustment** (Lines 1 − line 6 = line 7)   Enter line 7 onto line 10 of Form 940.   **7** [_____.___]

Do not attach this worksheet to your Form 940. Keep it for your records.

Instructions for Form 940: *Employer's Annual Federal Unemployment Tax Return*   **Draft**   page 9

Appendix

Need help? Call us at **1-800-829-4933** or visit our web site **at www.irs.gov.**

Example for using the worksheet:

You had 3 employees, 2 are corporate officers whose wages were not subject to state unemployment tax. You paid some state tax on time, some late, and some remains unpaid. Here are the records:

Taxable FUTA wages (line 7 from Form 940): $21,000.00
Taxable state unemployment wages: $ 7,000.00
Experience rate for 2006: 4.1%
State unemployment tax paid on time: $100.00
State unemployment tax paid late: $78.00
State unemployment tax not paid: $100.00

1. Maximum allowable credit (line 7 from Form 940)
$ 21,000.00
x _____.054
$1,134.00   1. $1,134.00

2. Credit for timely state unemployment tax payment   2. $100.00

3. Additional credit   3. $91.00
.054
- .041 (your experience rate) x .013
.013 $ 91.00 $7,000

4. Subtotal (line 2 + line 3)   4. $19,100.00
$100
+ 91
$191

5. Credit for paying state unemployment taxes late

5a. Remaining allowable credit   5a. $943.00
$1,134.00
- 191.00
$ 943.00

5b. State unemployment tax paid late   5b. $78.00

5c. Which is smaller? Line 5a or line 5b? 5c. $78.00

5d. Allowable credit   5d. $70.20
$78.00
x .90
$70.20

6. Your FUTA credit (line 4 + line 5d)   6. $261.20
$191.00
+ 70.20
$261.20

7. Your adjustment (line 1 - line 6)   7. $872.80
$1,134.00
- 261.20
$872.80 **You would enter this amount onto line 10 of Form 940.**

11. If credit reduction applies ...

If you paid wages in a state that is subject to credit reduction, enter the amount from line 3 of Schedule A (Form 940) onto line 11 of Form 940. However, see the instructions for line 9 before entering an amount here.

Part 4: Determine your FUTA tax for 2006

If any line in Part 4 does not apply, leave it blank.

12. Total FUTA tax after adjustments

Add the amounts shown on lines 8, 9, 10, and 11 and enter the result on line 12.

line 8
line 9
line 10
+ line 11
line 12

 If line 9 is more than zero, lines 10 and 11 must be zero.

13. FUTA tax deposited for the year

Enter the amount of total FUTA tax that you deposited for the year, including any overpayment that you applied from a prior year. For the 4th quarter only, include any tax from credit reduction.

14. Balance due

line 12
- line 13
line 14

If line 13 is less than line 12, enter the difference on line 14.

If line 14 is:

- More than $500, you must deposit your tax. See *Depositing Your FUTA Tax*, on page 3.

- $500 or less, you can either deposit your tax or pay the amount of tax owed with your return.

- Less than $1, you do not have to pay it.

 If you do not deposit as required and pay your tax with Form 940, you may be subject to a penalty.

Instructions for Form 940: *Employer's Annual Federal Unemployment Tax Return*   Draft   page 10

A-153

How to pay. You may pay using EFTPS, check, money order, or credit card.

- If you pay using EFTPS, file your return using the "without a payment" address on page 2 under *Where should you file?*

- If you pay using a check or money order, make it payable to *United States Treasury*. Be sure to write your EIN, *Form 940*, and *2006* on your check or money order. Complete Form 940-V, *Payment Voucher*, and enclose it with your return, using the "With a payment" address on page 2 under *"Where should you file?"*

- *If you pay by credit card, …*

15. Overpayment

If line 13 is more than line 12, enter the difference on line 15.

If you deposited more than the FUTA tax due for the year, you may choose to have us either:

- Apply the refund to your next return, or
- Send you the refund.

Check the appropriate box in line 15 to tell us which option you select. If you do not check either box, we will automatically refund your overpayment. We may apply your overpayment to any past due tax account you have.

If line 15 is less than $1, we will send you a refund or apply it to your next return only if you ask for it in writing.

Part 5: Report your FUTA tax liability by quarter only if line 12 is more than $500

Fill out Part 5 only if line 12 is more than $500. If line 12 is $500 or less, leave Part 5 blank and go to Part 6.

16. Report the amount of your FUTA tax liability for each quarter

Enter the amount of your FUTA tax liability for each quarter on lines 16a-d. **Do not** enter the amount you deposited. If you had no liability for a quarter, leave the line blank.

16a. 1ˢᵗ quarter (from January 1 to March 31)

16b. 2ⁿᵈ quarter (from April 1 to June 30)

16c. 3ʳᵈ quarter (from July 1 to September 30)

16d. 4ᵗʰ quarter (from October 1 to December 31). In the 4ᵗʰ quarter, include any tax from credit reduction.

Example:
You paid wages on March 28 and your FUTA tax on those wages is $200. You were not required to make a deposit on April 30 because your accumulated FUTA tax was $500 or less.

You would enter $200 in line 16a because your liability for the 1ˢᵗ quarter is $200.

17. Total tax liability for the year

To calculate your total tax liability for the year,

$$\begin{array}{r} \text{line 16a} \\ \text{line 16b} \\ \text{line 16c} \\ +\ \underline{\text{line 16d}} \\ \text{line 17} \end{array}$$

Your total tax liability for the year **must equal** line 12. If line 17 does not match line 12, you should carefully review your computations to determine the reason for the discrepancy.

Part 6: May we speak with your third-party designee?

If you want to allow an employee, your paid tax preparer, or another person to discuss your Form 940 with the IRS, check the *Yes* box. Then write the name of the person you choose (*your designee*). Be sure to give us the specific name of a person — not the name of the firm who prepared your tax reports.

Have your designee select a 5-digit Personal Identification Number (PIN) that he or she must use as identification when talking to IRS about your form.

By checking *Yes*, you authorize us to talk to your designee about any questions that we may have while we process your return. Your authorization applies only to this form, for this year; it does not apply to other forms or other tax years.

You are authorizing your designee to:

- give us any information that is missing from your return,

- ask us for information about processing your return, and

- respond to certain IRS notices that you have shared with your designee about math errors and preparing your return. We will **not** send notices to your designee.

You are **NOT** authorizing your designee to:

- receive any refund check,

- bind you to anything (including additional tax liability), or

- otherwise represent you before the IRS.

Appendix

The authorization will automatically expire 1 year after the due date for filing your Form 940 (regardless of extensions). If you or your designee want to end the authorization before it expires, write to the IRS office where you filed your return.

If you want to expand your designee's authorization or if you want us to send your designee copies of your notices, see Pub. 947, *Practice Before the IRS and Power of Attorney*.

Part 7: Sign here

You must fill out both pages of the form and sign it. Failure to sign will delay processing your return.

In Part 7, sign your name and print your name and title. Then enter the date and the best daytime telephone number, including area code.

Who Must Sign Form 940?

Form 940 must be signed as follows.

- Sole proprietorship— The individual who owns the business.

- Corporation (including an LLC treated as a corporation) — The president, vice president, or other principal officer.

- Partnership (including a limited liability company (LLC) treated as a partnership) or unincorporated organization— A responsible and duly authorized member or officer having knowledge of its affairs.

- Single member LLC treated as a disregarded entity — The owner of the LLC.

- Trust or estate — The fiduciary.

If you have filed a valid power of attorney, your duly authorized agent may also sign your Form 940.

Part 8: For paid preparers only (optional)

Paid preparers may choose to fill out Part 8 if they were paid to prepare this return and are not an employee of the business that is filing this return. Do not fill out Part 8 if you are filing the return as a reporting agent and have a valid Form 8655, *Reporting Agent Authorization*, on file with the IRS.

You are not required to complete this section.

If you are a paid preparer and you choose to fill out Part 8, sign in the space provided. Give the employer the return to file with IRS and include a copy of the return for the business' records.

Write your Social Security Number (SSN) or your Preparer Tax Identification Number (PTIN) in the spaces provided. Include your complete address.

If you work for a firm, write the firm's name and the EIN of your firm.

How to Order Forms and Publications from IRS

Call 1-800-TAX-FORM or 1-800-829-3676

Visit our web site at www.irs.gov

Other IRS Publications You May Need

- Form 8109, *Federal Tax Deposit (FTD) Coupon*

- Form 8655, *Reporting Agent Authorization*

- Form 8822, *Change of Address*.

- Form 941, *Employer's Quarterly Federal Tax Return*

- Form 943, *Employer's Annual Federal Tax Return for Agricultural Employees*

- Form SS-4, *Application for Employer Identification Number*

- Publication 15 (Circular E), *Employer's Tax Guide*.

- Publication 15-A, *Employer's Supplemental Tax Guide*

- Publication 1635, *Understanding Your EIN*

- Publication 51, *Circular A, Agricultural Employer's Tax Guide*

- Publication 521, *Moving Expenses*

- Publication 595, *Tax Highlights for Commercial Fishermen*

- Publication 926, *Household Employer's Tax Guide*

- Publication 947, *Practice Before the IRS and Power of Attorney*

- Schedule A (Form 940), *Multi-State Employer and Credit Reduction Information*

- Schedule H (Form 1040), *Household Employment Taxes*

Instructions for Form 940: *Employer's Annual Federal Unemployment Tax Return*

Draft

page 12

Schedule A (Form 940) for 2006:

Multi-State Employer and Credit Reduction Information

Department of the Treasury
Internal Revenue Service

999999

OMB No. 1545-0028

Vision Draft
10/26/2005 1:50 PM

Employer identification number (EIN)

Name (*not your trade name*)

About this schedule:

- You must fill out Schedule A, Form 940 (*Employer's Annual Federal Unemployment Tax Return)* if you were required to pay your state unemployment tax in **more than one state** or if you paid wages in any state that is subject to **credit reduction**.
- Attach Schedule A to your Form 940 and file it with your return.

For more information, read the Instructions for Schedule A (Form 940).

Part 1: **Fill out this part if you were required to pay state unemployment taxes in more than one state. If any states do NOT apply to you, leave them blank.**

1. **Check the box for every state in which you were required to pay state unemployment tax this year.** For a list of state names and their abbreviations, see the Instructions for Schedule A (Form 940).

AK	CO	GA	IN	MD	MS	NH	OH	SC	VA	WY
AL	CT	HI	KS	MI	MT	NJ	OK	SD	VT	PR
AR	DC	IA	KY	MN	NC	NM	OR	TN	WA	VI
AZ	DE	ID	LA	MO	ND	NV	PA	TX	WI	
CA	FL	IL	MA	ME	NE	NY	RI	UT	WV	

Part 2: **Fill out this part to tell us about wages you paid in any state that is subject to credit reduction. If any lines do NOT apply, leave them blank.**

2. If you paid wages in any of these states …

2a-b. **[Name of State]** Total taxable FUTA wages paid in [state] **2a.** _____ . x .00x = line 2b **2b** _____ .

2c-d. **[Name of State]** Total taxable FUTA wages paid in [state] **2c.** _____ . x .00x = line 2d **2d** _____ .

2e-f. **[Name of State]** Total taxable FUTA wages paid in [state] **2e.** _____ . x .00x = line 2f **2f** _____ .

2g-h. **[Name of State]** Total taxable FUTA wages paid in [state] **2g.** _____ . x .00x = line 2h **2h** _____ .

2i-j. **[Name of State]** Total taxable FUTA wages paid in [state] **2i.** _____ . x .00x = line 2j **2j** _____ .

3. **Total credit reduction** (Lines 2b+ 2d+ 2f +2h+ 2j = line 3) .... **3** _____ .

Enter the amount from line 3 onto line 11 of Form 940.

Instructions for Schedule A (Form 940) for 2006:

Multi-State Employer and Credit Reduction Information

Specific Instructions: Completing Schedule A (Form 940)

Part 1: Fill out this part if you were required to pay state unemployment taxes in more than one state.

1. **Check the box for every state in which you were required to pay state unemployment taxes this year,**

Note: Make sure that you have applied for a state unemployment number for your business. If you do not have an unemployment account number from a state in which you paid wages, contact the local state office to receive one and enter *Applied For* on the appropriate line for the state.

For ease of reference, here is a list of the states and territories and their 2-letter postal abbreviations:

State	Postal Abbreviation	State	Postal Abbreviation
Alabama	AL	Montana	MT
Alaska	AK	Nebraska	NE
Arizona	AZ	Nevada	NV
Arkansas	AR	New Hampshire	NH
California	CA	New Jersey	NJ
Colorado	CO	New Mexico	NM
Connecticut	CT	New York	NY
Delaware	DE	North Carolina	NC
District of Columbia	DC	North Dakota	ND
Florida	FL	Ohio	OH
Georgia	GA	Oklahoma	OK
Hawaii	HI	Oregon	OR
Idaho	ID	Pennsylvania	PA
Illinois	IL	Puerto Rico	PR
Indiana	IN	Rhode Island	RI
Iowa	IA	South Carolina	SC
Kansas	KS	South Dakota	SD
Kentucky	KY	Tennessee	TN
Louisiana	LA	Texas	TX
Maine	ME	Utah	UT
Maryland	MD	Vermont	VT
Massachusetts	MA	Virginia	VA
Michigan	MI	Virgin Islands	VI
Minnesota	MN	Washington	WA
Mississippi	MS	West Virginia	WV
Missouri	MO	Wisconsin	WI
		Wyoming	WY

Part 2: Fill out this part to tell us about wages you paid in any state that is subject to credit reduction.

2. **You are subject to credit reduction, if you paid wages in any state listed.**

If you paid wages in any states that are subject to credit reduction, find the lines where the states are listed.

In the first box, enter the total taxable FUTA wages that you paid in that state. (Note: The FUTA wage base for all states is $7,000.) Do not use your state unemployment wages here.

Then multiply the total taxable FUTA wages by the number shown.

Enter your answer in the box at the end of the line.

3. **Total credit reduction**

To calculate the total credit reduction,

line 2b
line 2d
line 2f
line 2h
+ line 2j
line 3

Then enter the amount from line 3 onto line 11 of Form 940.

Attach Schedule A to Form 940 when you file your return.

Form **941 for 2005:** Employer's Quarterly Federal Tax Return

(Rev. January 2005)

Department of the Treasury — Internal Revenue Service

9901

OMB No. 1545-0029

Employer identification number ☐☐ — ☐☐☐☐☐☐☐

Name *(not your trade name)*

Trade name *(if any)*

Address

Number   Street   Suite or room number

City   State   ZIP code

Report for this Quarter ...
(Check one.)

☐ **1:** January, February, March

☐ **2:** April, May, June

☐ **3:** July, August, September

☐ **4:** October, November, December

Read the separate instructions before you fill out this form. Please type or print within the boxes.

Part 1: Answer these questions for this quarter.

1 Number of employees who received wages, tips, or other compensation for the pay period including: *Mar. 12* (Quarter 1), *June 12* (Quarter 2), *Sept. 12* (Quarter 3), *Dec. 12* (Quarter 4) **1**

2 Wages, tips, and other compensation **2**

3 Total income tax withheld from wages, tips, and other compensation **3**

4 If no wages, tips, and other compensation are subject to social security or Medicare tax . . ☐ Check and go to line 6.

5 Taxable social security and Medicare wages and tips:

	Column 1		Column 2
5a Taxable social security wages		× .124 =	
5b Taxable social security tips		× .124 =	
5c Taxable Medicare wages & tips		× .029 =	

5d Total social security and Medicare taxes (*Column 2,* lines 5a + 5b + 5c = line 5d) . . **5d**

6 Total taxes before adjustments (lines 3 + 5d = line 6) **6**

7 Tax adjustments (If your answer is a negative number, write it in brackets.):

7a Current quarter's fractions of cents . . . .

7b Current quarter's sick pay . . . .

7c Current quarter's adjustments for tips and group-term life insurance

7d Current year's income tax withholding (Attach Form 941c) . . .

7e Prior quarters' social security and Medicare taxes (Attach Form 941c)

7f Special additions to federal income tax (reserved use) . . . . .

7g Special additions to social security and Medicare (reserved use)

7h Total adjustments (Combine all amounts: lines 7a through 7g.) **7h**

8 Total taxes after adjustments (Combine lines 6 and 7h.) **8**

9 Advance earned income credit (EIC) payments made to employees **9**

10 Total taxes after adjustment for advance EIC (lines 8 – 9 = line 10) **10**

11 Total deposits for this quarter, including overpayment applied from a prior quarter . . . **11**

12 Balance due (lines 10 – 11 = line 12) Make checks payable to the *United States Treasury* . . **12**

13 Overpayment (If line 11 is more than line 10, write the difference here.) _____ Check one ☐ Apply to next return.
☐ Send a refund.

Next ➡

For Privacy Act and Paperwork Reduction Act Notice, see the back of the Payment Voucher.

Cat. No. 17001Z   Form **941** (Rev. 1-2005)

9902

Name *(not your trade name)*	Employer identification number

Part 2: Tell us about your deposit schedule for this quarter.

If you are unsure about whether you are a monthly schedule depositor or a semiweekly schedule depositor, see *Pub. 15 (Circular E)*, section 11.

14 ☐☐ Write the state abbreviation for the state where you made your deposits OR write "MU" if you made your deposits in *multiple* states.

15 Check one: ☐ Line 10 is less than $2,500. Go to Part 3.

☐ You were a monthly schedule depositor for the entire quarter. Fill out your tax liability for each month. Then go to Part 3.

Tax liability: Month 1 ☐ .

Month 2 ☐ .

Month 3 ☐ .

Total ☐ . Total must equal line 10.

☐ You were a semiweekly schedule depositor for any part of this quarter. Fill out *Schedule B (Form 941): Report of Tax Liability for Semiweekly Schedule Depositors,* and attach it to this form.

Part 3: Tell us about your business. If a question does NOT apply to your business, leave it blank.

16 If your business has closed and you do not have to file returns in the future . . . . ☐ Check here, and

enter the final date you paid wages ☐ / / .

17 If you are a seasonal employer and you do not have to file a return for every quarter of the year . . ☐ Check here.

Part 4: May we contact your third-party designee?

Do you want to allow an employee, a paid tax preparer, or another person to discuss this return with the IRS? See the instructions for details.

☐ Yes. Designee's name ☐

Phone ( ) – Personal Identification Number (PIN) ☐☐☐☐☐

☐ No.

Part 5: Sign here

Under penalties of perjury, I declare that I have examined this return, including accompanying schedules and statements, and to the best of my knowledge and belief, it is true, correct, and complete.

✗

Sign your name here ☐

Print name and title ☐

Date / / Phone ( ) –

Part 6: For paid preparers only *(optional)*

Preparer's signature		
Firm's name		
Address		EIN
		ZIP code
Date / / Phone ( ) –		SSN/PTIN

☐ Check if you are self-employed.

Form **941** (Rev. 1-2005)

Form 941-V,
Payment Voucher

Purpose of Form

Complete Form 941-V if you are making a payment with Form 941, Employer's Quarterly Federal Tax Return. We will use the completed voucher to credit your payment more promptly and accurately, and to improve our service to you.

If you have your return prepared by a third party and make a payment with that return, please provide this payment voucher to the return preparer.

Making Payments With Form 941

Make your payment with Form 941 **only if:**

● Your net taxes for the quarter (line 10 on Form 941) are less than $2,500 and you are paying in full with a timely filed return or

● You are a monthly schedule depositor making a payment in accordance with the Accuracy of Deposits Rule. (See section 11 of Pub. 15 (Circular E), Employer's Tax Guide, for details.) This amount may be $2,500 or more.

Otherwise, you must deposit the amount at an authorized financial institution or by electronic funds transfer. (See section 11 of Pub. 15 (Circular E) for deposit instructions.) Do not use the Form 941-V payment voucher to make federal tax deposits.

Caution. *If you pay amounts with Form 941 that should have been deposited, you may be subject to a penalty. See* Deposit Penalties *in section 11 of Pub. 15 (Circular E).*

Specific Instructions

Box 1—Employer identification number (EIN). If you do not have an EIN, apply for one on Form SS-4, Application for Employer Identification Number, and write "Applied For" and the date you applied in this entry space.

Box 2—Amount paid. Enter the amount paid with Form 941.

Box 3—Tax period. Darken the capsule identifying the quarter for which the payment is made. Darken only one capsule.

Box 4—Name and address. Enter your name and address as shown on Form 941.

● Enclose your check or money order made payable to the "United States Treasury." Be sure also to enter your EIN, "Form 941," and the tax period on your check or money order. Do not send cash. Please do not staple this voucher or your payment to the return (or to each other).

● Detach the completed voucher and send it with your payment and Form 941 to the address provided in the Instructions for Form 941.

Note. You must also complete the entity information above Part 1 on Form 941.

▼ **Detach Here and Mail With Your Payment and Tax Return.** ▼   Form **941-V** (2005)

– –

Form **941-V** Department of the Treasury Internal Revenue Service	**Payment Voucher** ▶ **Do not staple or attach this voucher to your payment.**	OMB No. 1545-0029 20**05**

1 Enter your employer identification number (EIN).	**2** Enter the amount of your payment. ▶	Dollars	Cents

3 Tax period		**4** Enter your business name (individual name if sole proprietor).
⟋ 1st Quarter	⟋ 3rd Quarter	Enter your address.
⟋ 2nd Quarter	⟋ 4th Quarter	Enter your city, state, and ZIP code.

Appendix

Privacy Act and Paperwork Reduction Act Notice.
We ask for the information on this form to carry out the Internal Revenue laws of the United States. We need it to figure and collect the right amount of tax. Subtitle C, Employment Taxes, of the Internal Revenue Code imposes employment taxes on wages, including income tax withholding. This form is used to determine the amount of the taxes that you owe. Section 6011 requires you to provide the requested information if the tax is applicable to you. Section 6109 requires you to provide your employer identification number (EIN). If you fail to provide this information in a timely manner, you may be subject to penalties and interest.

You are not required to provide the information requested on a form that is subject to the Paperwork Reduction Act unless the form displays a valid OMB control number. Books and records relating to a form or instructions must be retained as long as their contents may become material in the administration of any Internal Revenue law.

Generally, tax returns and return information are confidential, as required by section 6103. However, section 6103 allows or requires the IRS to disclose or give the information shown on your tax return to others as described in the Code. For example, we may disclose your tax information to the Department of Justice for civil and criminal litigation, and to cities, states, and the District of Columbia for use in administering their tax laws. We may also disclose this information to other countries under a tax treaty, to federal and state agencies to enforce federal nontax criminal laws, or to federal law enforcement and intelligence agencies to combat terrorism.

The time needed to complete and file this form will vary depending on individual circumstances. The estimated average time is:

For Form 941:

Recordkeeping	12 hr., 39 min.
Learning about the law or the form . .	40 min.
Preparing the form	1 hr., 49 min.
Copying, assembling, and sending the form to the IRS	16 min.

For Form 941TeleFile:

Recordkeeping	5 hr., 30 min.
Learning about the law or the Tax Record	18 min.
Preparing the Tax Record	24 min.
TeleFile phone call	11 min.

If you have comments concerning the accuracy of these time estimates or suggestions for making this form simpler, we would be happy to hear from you. You can write to: Internal Revenue Service, Tax Products Coordinating Committee, SE:W:CAR:MP:T:T:SP, 1111 Constitution Ave. NW, IR-6406, Washington, DC 20224. **Do not** send Form 941 to this address.

 Printed on recycled paper

Instructions for Form 941

(Rev. April 2005)

**Department of the Treasury
Internal Revenue Service**

For use with Form 941 (Rev. January 2005)

Employer's Quarterly Federal Tax Return

Section references are to the Internal Revenue Code unless otherwise indicated.

What's New

Change to the procedure for submitting copies of Form W-4. The Treasury Department issued temporary and proposed regulations, effective April 14, 2005, eliminating the requirement that employers routinely send copies of potentially questionable Forms W-4, Employee's Withholding Allowance Certificate, to the IRS.

The temporary and proposed regulations also provide guidance about substitute forms developed by employers or submitted by employees. For more information, see Treasury Decision 9196. You can find Treasury Decision 9196 in Internal Revenue Bulletin 2005-19, dated May 9, 2005, at *www.irs.gov/pub/irs-irbs/irb05-19.pdf.*

Revised form and instructions. You may notice a number of changes in Form 941. We revised the form and instructions in January 2005 so that they are easier for you to read and fill out. At the same time, the new design makes the forms easier and faster for us to process. Now we can optically scan the forms and will capture data more accurately and efficiently than before. Please read both the form and instructions carefully to become familiar with the many changes.

If you have comments or suggestions for improving the form or instructions, we would be happy to hear from you. Write to the address shown in the *Privacy Act and Paperwork Reduction Act Notice* on the back of Form 941-V, Payment Voucher.

New form for reporting discrepancies between Forms 941 and Forms W-2. We recently developed Schedule D (Form 941), Report of Discrepancies Caused by Acquisitions, Statutory Mergers, or Consolidations. You may use Schedule D (Form 941) to explain the discrepancies between Forms W-2 and Forms 941 in the totals of social security wages, Medicare wages and tips, social security tips, federal income tax withheld, and advance earned income credit (EIC) payments caused by acquisitions, statutory mergers, or consolidations.

Social security wage base for 2005. Do not withhold social security tax after an employee reaches $90,000 in social security wages. (There is no limit on the amount of wages subject to Medicare tax.)

Electronic Filing and Payment

Now, more than ever before, businesses can enjoy the benefits of filing and paying their federal taxes electronically. Whether you rely on a tax professional or handle your own taxes, IRS offers you convenient programs to make it easier. Spend less time and worry on taxes and more time running your business. Use e-file and Electronic Federal Tax Payment System (EFTPS) to your benefit.
● For e-file, visit *www.irs.gov* for additional information.
● For EFTPS, visit *www.eftps.gov* or call EFTPS Customer Service at 1-800-555-4477.

Use the electronic options available from IRS and make filing and paying taxes easier.

941TeleFile Discontinued

After the second quarter of 2005, you will no longer be able to file your employment tax return by telephone using 941TeleFile. The IRS encourages you to file your Form 941 using other convenient and easy IRS e-file options. Please visit us at *www.irs.gov* and click on the e-file logo located in the lower-right corner. File your "Zero Wage" Forms 941 using IRS e-file, if possible.

Photographs of Missing Children

The Internal Revenue Service is a proud partner with the National Center for Missing and Exploited Children. Photographs of missing children selected by the Center may appear in instructions on pages that would otherwise be blank. You can help bring these children home by looking at the photographs and calling 1-800-THE-LOST (1-800-843-5678) if you recognize a child.

General Instructions: Understanding Form 941

Purpose of Form 941

These instructions give you some background information about Form 941, Employer's Quarterly Federal Tax Return. They tell you who must fill out the form, how to fill it out line by line, and when and where to file it. If you want more in-depth information about payroll tax topics relating to Form 941, see Pub. 15 (Circular E), Employer's Tax Guide, visit the IRS website at *www.irs.gov*, or call 1-800-829-4933.

Federal law requires you, as an employer, to withhold taxes from your employees' paychecks. Each time you pay wages, you must withhold – or take out of your employees' paychecks – certain amounts for federal income tax, social security tax, and Medicare tax (payroll taxes). Under the withholding system, taxes withheld from your employees are credited to your employees in payment of their tax liabilities.

Federal law also requires employers to pay any liability for the employer's portion of social security and Medicare taxes. This portion of social security and Medicare taxes is not withheld from employees.

Use Form 941 to report:
● payroll taxes for the quarter;
● current quarter's adjustments to social security and Medicare taxes for fractions of cents, sick pay, tips, and group-term life insurance; and
● prior quarters' adjustments to payroll taxes.

Do not use the Form 941 to report backup withholding or income tax withholding on **nonpayroll** payments such as pensions, annuities, and gambling winnings. Report these types of withholding on Form 945, Annual Return of Withheld Federal Income Tax.

Cat. No. 14625L

Who Must File Form 941?

If you are an employer, you must file a quarterly Form 941 to report:
- wages you have paid,
- tips your employees have received,
- federal income tax you withheld,
- both the employer's and the employee's share of social security and Medicare taxes, and
- advance earned income tax credit (EIC) payments.

After you file your first Form 941, you must file a return for each quarter even if you have no taxes to report. However, see *Exceptions* below.

Exceptions

Special rules apply to some employers.
- **Seasonal employers** are not required to file a Form 941 for quarters when they have no tax liability because they have paid no wages. To tell the IRS that you will not file a return for one or more quarters during the year, check the box on line 17 **every quarter** you file the form. See section 12 of Pub. 15 (Circular E) for more information.
- Employers of **household employees** do not usually file Form 941. See Pub. 926, Household Employer's Tax Guide, and Schedule H (Form 1040), Household Employment Taxes, for more information.
- Employers of **farm employees** do not usually file Form 941. See Form 943, Employer's Annual Tax Return for Agricultural Employees, and Pub. 51 (Circular A), Agricultural Employer's Tax Guide.

What if you reorganize or close your business?

If you sell or transfer your business . . .

If you sell or transfer your business, you and the new owner must each file a Form 941 for the quarter in which the transfer occurred. Report only the wages you paid.

When two businesses merge, the continuing firm must file a return for the quarter in which the change took place and the other firm should file a **final return**.

Changing from one form of business to another—such as from a sole proprietorship to a partnership or corporation—is considered a transfer. See section 1 of Pub. 15 (Circular E). If a transfer occurs, you may need a new employer identification number (EIN). Attach a statement to your return with:
- the new owner's name (or the new name of the business),
- whether the business is now a sole proprietorship, partnership, or corporation;
- the kind of change that occurred (a sale or transfer);
- the date of the change; and
- the name of the person keeping the payroll records and the address where those records will be kept.

If your business has closed . . .

If you go out of business or stop paying wages to your employees, you must file a **final return.** To tell the IRS that the form for a particular quarter is your final return, check the box on line 16 and enter the date that you last paid wages. Also attach a statement to your return showing the name of the person keeping the payroll records and the address where those records will be kept.

See the Instructions for Forms W-2 and W-3 for information about earlier dates for the expedited furnishing and filing of Forms W-2 when a final Form 941 is filed.

If you participated in a statutory merger or consolidation, or qualify for predecessor-successor status due to an acquisition, you should generally file Schedule D (Form 941), Report of Discrepancies Caused by Acquisitions, Statutory Mergers, or Consolidations. See the Instructions for Schedule D (Form 941) to determine whether you should file Schedule D (Form 941) and when you should file it.

When Must You File?

File your initial Form 941 for the quarter in which you first paid wages that are subject to social security and Medicare taxes or subject to federal income tax withholding. See the table below titled, *When To File Form 941.*

Then you must file for every quarter after that—every 3 months—even if you have no taxes to report (unless you are a seasonal employer or are filing your final return. See *Seasonal employers* on page 1 and *If your business has closed . . .* above).

File Form 941 only once for each quarter. If you filed electronically, do not also file a paper Form 941. For more information about filing Form 941 electronically, see *Electronic Filing and Payment* on page 1.

When To File Form 941

Your Form 941 is due by the last day of the month that follows the end of the quarter.		
The Quarter Includes . . .	Quarter Ends	Form 941 Is Due
1. January, February, March	March 31	April 30
2. April, May, June	June 30	July 31
3. July, August, September	September 30	October 31
4. October, November, December	December 31	January 31

For example, generally you must report wages you pay during the first quarter—which is January through March—by April 30th. If you made deposits in full payment of your taxes for a quarter, you have 10 more days after the due dates shown above to file your Form 941.

We consider your form filed on time if it is properly addressed and mailed First-Class or if it is sent by an IRS-designated delivery service on or before the due date. See Pub. 15 (Circular E) for more information on IRS-designated delivery services.

If any due date for filing shown above falls on a Saturday, Sunday, or legal holiday, you may file your return on the next business day.

How Should You Complete Form 941?

Review Your Business Information at the Top of the Form

If you are using a copy of Form 941 that has your business name and address preprinted at the top of the form, check to make sure that the information is correct. Carefully review your EIN to make sure that it exactly matches the EIN assigned to your business by the IRS. If any information is incorrect, cross it out and type or print the correct information. See also *If you change your name or address...* on page 3.

If you pay a tax preparer to fill out Form 941, make sure the preparer uses your business name and EIN **exactly** as they appear on the preprinted form we sent you.

If you are not using a preprinted Form 941, type or print your EIN, name, and address in the spaces provided. You **must** enter your name and EIN here and on the back of page 2 even if you complete and return Form 941-V, Payment Voucher. **Do not** use your social security number (SSN) or individual taxpayer identification number (ITIN).

Generally, enter the business (legal) name that you used when you applied for your EIN on Form SS-4, Application for Employer Identification Number. For example, if you are a sole proprietor, enter "Ronald Smith" on the "Name" line and "Ron's Cycles" on the "Trade name" line. Leave the "Trade name" line blank if it is the same as your "Name."

Employer identification number. To make sure that businesses comply with federal tax laws, the IRS monitors tax filings and payments by using a numerical system to identify taxpayers. A unique 9-digit employer identification number (EIN) is assigned to all corporations, partnerships, and some sole proprietors. Businesses needing an EIN must apply for a number and use it throughout the life of the business on all tax returns, payments, and reports.

Your business should have only one EIN. If you have more than one and are not sure which one to use, check with the IRS office where you file your returns "Without a payment." If you do not have an EIN, apply for one from the IRS by mail, by telephone, by fax, or by visiting the IRS website at *www.irs.gov/smallbiz*. Request Form SS-4, Application for Employer Identification Number. If you do not have an EIN by the time a return is due, write "Applied For" and the date you applied in the space shown for the number.

 Always be sure the EIN on the form you file exactly matches the EIN that IRS assigned to your business. Do not use your social security number on forms that ask for an EIN. Filing a Form 941 with an incorrect EIN or using another business's EIN may result in penalties and delays in processing your return.

If you change your name or address... Notify the IRS **immediately** if you change your business name or address.
• Write to the IRS office where you would file your return "Without a payment" to notify the IRS of any name change. (Get Pub. 1635, Understanding Your EIN, to see if you need to also apply for a new EIN.)
• Complete and mail Form 8822, Change of Address, for any address change.

Check the Box for the Quarter
In the box at the top of the form, check the appropriate box of the quarter for which you are filing. Make sure that the quarter checked is the same as shown on any attached Schedule B (Form 941), Report of Tax Liability for Semiweekly Schedule Depositors.

Completing and Filing the Form
Make entries on Form 941 as follows to enable accurate scanning and processing.
• Use 12-point Courier font (if possible) for all entries if you are typing or using a computer to fill out your form.
• Omit dollar signs and decimal points. Commas are optional. (Report dollars to the left of the preprinted decimal point and cents to the right of it.)
• Leave blank any data field (except line 10) with a value of zero.
• Enter negative amounts in parentheses (if possible).
• Enter your name and EIN on **all** pages and attachments. (Filers using the IRS-preaddressed Form 941 are not required to enter their name and EIN on page 2.)

Other Forms That You Must Use
Give each eligible employee Notice 797, Possible Federal Tax Refund Due to the Earned Income Credit (EIC). Then each eligible employee who wishes to receive any advance earned income credit (EIC) payments must give you a completed Form W-5, Earned Income Credit Advance Payment Certificate. For more information, see section 10 of Pub. 15 (Circular E) and also Pub. 596, Earned Income Credit.

Reconciling Forms 941 and Form W-3
The IRS matches amounts reported on your four quarterly Forms 941 with Form W-2 amounts totaled on your yearly Form W-3, Transmittal of Wage and Tax Statements. If the amounts do not agree, you may be contacted by the IRS. The reconciled amounts are:
• income tax withholding,
• social security wages,
• social security tips,
• Medicare wages and tips, and
• advance earned income credit (EIC) payments.

For more information, see section 12 of Pub. 15 (Circular E). See also the Instructions for Schedule D (Form 941), Report of Discrepancies Caused by Acquisitions, Statutory Mergers, or Consolidations.

Depositing Your Taxes: When Must You Deposit Your Taxes?

Determine if you are a monthly or semiweekly schedule depositor for the quarter.
The IRS uses two different sets of deposit rules to determine when businesses must deposit their social security, Medicare, and withheld federal income taxes. These schedules tell you when a deposit is due after you have a payday.

Your deposit schedule is not determined by how often you pay your employees. Your deposit schedule depends on the total tax liability you reported on Form 941 during the previous four-quarter **lookback period** (July 1 of the second preceding calendar year through June 30 of last year). See section 11 of Pub. 15 (Circular E) for details.

Before the beginning of each calendar year, determine which type of deposit schedule you must use. If you reported:
• $50,000 or less in taxes during the lookback period, you are a **monthly schedule depositor**. Check the appropriate box on line 15 and, if your tax liability for the quarter is $2,500 or more, fill out the tax liability for each month in the quarter.
• more than $50,000 of taxes for the lookback period, you are a **semiweekly schedule depositor**. Check the appropriate box on line 15 and, if your tax liability for the quarter was $2,500 or more, fill out Schedule B (Form 941) and attach it to Form 941 when you submit it.

 See section 11 of Pub. 15 (Circular E) for the Next Day Deposit Rule on taxes of $100,000 or more accumulated on any day during the deposit period.

How Must You Deposit Your Taxes?

You may be required to deposit the income taxes you withheld and both the employer and employee social security taxes and Medicare taxes. If your total taxes after adjustment for advance EIC (line 10) are:
• **Less than $2,500 for the quarter.** You are not required to make a deposit, and you may pay the taxes in full with a timely filed return. However, if you are unsure that your taxes will be less than $2,500 for the quarter, deposit your taxes using the appropriate rules (above) to avoid failure to deposit penalties.
• **$2,500 or more for the quarter.** You must deposit your taxes by using the Electronic Federal Tax Payment System (EFTPS) or by depositing them at a financial institution that is authorized to accept federal tax deposits (that is, authorized depository) with Form 8109, Federal Tax Deposit

-3-

Coupon. See section 11 of Pub. 15 (Circular E) for more information.

 EFTPS is an easy, safe, and convenient way for all employers to make their tax deposits. Using EFTPS helps eliminate errors commonly made on federal tax deposit (FTD) coupons. **Some taxpayers are required to use EFTPS to deposit their taxes.** *See section 11 of Pub. 15 (Circular E) for details.*

What About Penalties and Interest?

Avoiding penalties and interest

You can avoid paying penalties and interest if you:

- deposit your taxes when they are due using EFTPS if required,
- file your fully completed Form 941 on time,
- report your tax liability accurately,
- submit valid checks to the IRS, and
- give accurate Forms W-2 to employees and file Copies A of Form W-2 with the Social Security Administration (SSA) on time and accurately.

If your deposit is late and you have a reasonable cause, attach an explanation to your return. We will review it when we process your form and, if you meet the reasonable cause requirements, penalties may be abated. (However, do not attach an explanation for late filing to copies of Form W-2 filed with the SSA.) Penalties and interest are charged on taxes paid late and returns filed late at a rate set by law. See sections 11 and 12 of Pub. 15 (Circular E) for details.

Use Form 843, Claim for Refund and Request for Abatement, to request abatement of assessed penalties or interest. **Do not** request abatement of assessed penalties or interest on Form 941 or Form 941c, Supporting Statement To Correct Information.

 A trust fund recovery penalty may apply if income, social security, and Medicare taxes that must be withheld are not withheld or paid. The penalty is the full amount of the unpaid trust fund tax. This penalty may apply when these unpaid taxes cannot be collected from the employer or business. The trust fund recovery penalty may be imposed on all people the IRS determines to be responsible for collecting, accounting for, and paying these taxes, and who acted willfully in not doing so. For details, see section 11 of Pub. 15 (Circular E).

Where Should You File?

Where you file depends on whether you include a payment with your form.

If you are in . . .		Without a payment . . .	With a payment . . .
Connecticut	New Jersey	Internal Revenue Service Cincinnati, OH 45999-0005	Internal Revenue Service P.O. Box 105703 Atlanta, GA 30348-5703
Delaware	New York		
District of Columbia	North Carolina		
Illinois	Ohio		
Indiana	Pennsylvania		
Kentucky	Rhode Island		
Maine	South Carolina		
Maryland	Vermont		
Massachusetts	Virginia		
Michigan	West Virginia		
New Hampshire	Wisconsin		

If you are in . . .		Without a payment . . .	With a payment . . .
Alabama	Missouri	Internal Revenue Service Ogden, UT 84201-0005	Internal Revenue Service P.O. Box 660264 Dallas, TX 75266-0264
Alaska	Montana		
Arizona	Nebraska		
Arkansas	Nevada		
California	New Mexico		
Colorado	North Dakota		
Florida	Oklahoma		
Georgia	Oregon		
Hawaii	South Dakota		
Idaho	Tennessee		
Iowa	Texas		
Kansas	Utah		
Louisiana	Washington		
Minnesota	Wyoming		
Mississippi			
No legal residence or principal place of business in any state		Internal Revenue Service Philadelphia, PA 19255-0005	Internal Revenue Service P.O. Box 80106 Cincinnati, OH 45280-0006
Special rule for Exempt Organizations, Federal, State and Local Governmental Entities, and Indian Tribal Governmental Entities, regardless of location		Internal Revenue Service Ogden, UT 84201-0046	Internal Revenue Service P.O. Box 660264 Dallas, TX 75266-0264

 Your filing or payment address may have changed from prior years. If you are using an IRS-provided envelope, use only the labels and envelope provided with this tax package. Do not send Form 941 or any payments to the Social Security Administration (SSA).

Specific Instructions:

Part 1: Answer these questions for this quarter.

1. Number of employees who received wages, tips, or other compensation this quarter

Tell us the number of employees you paid for the pay period including March 12, June 12, September 12, or December 12 **for the quarter indicated** at the top of the return. Do not include:

- household employees,
- employees who received no pay for the pay period,
- pensioners, or
- active members of the Armed Forces.

 If you enter "250" or more on line 1, you must file Forms W-2 electronically or on magnetic diskette. For details, call the SSA at 1-800-772-6270 or visit SSA's Employer Reporting Instructions and Information website at www.socialsecurity.gov/employer.

2. Wages, tips, and other compensation

Enter amounts on line 2 that would also be included in box 1 of your employees' Forms W-2. See the Instructions for Forms W-2 and W-3 for details.

If you are an insurance company, do not include sick pay that you paid to policyholders' employees here if you gave the policyholders timely notice of the payments.

3. Total income tax withheld from wages, tips, and other compensation

Enter the income tax that you withheld (or were required to withhold) from your employees on this quarter's wages, tips, taxable fringe benefits, and supplemental unemployment

-4-

compensation benefits. Also include here any excise taxes that you were required to withhold on golden parachute payments (section 4999).

If you are an insurance company, enter the income tax that you withheld (or were required to withhold) on third-party sick pay here.

4. If no wages, tips, and compensation on line 2 are subject to social security or Medicare tax . . .

If no wages, tips, and compensation on line 2 are subject to social security or Medicare tax, check the box on line 4. If this question does not apply to you, leave the box blank. For more information about exempt wages, see section 15 of Pub. 15 (Circular E) and section 4 of Pub. 15-A, Employer's Supplemental Tax Guide.

 If you are a government employer, wages that you pay are not automatically exempt from social security and Medicare taxes. Your employees may be covered by law or by a voluntary Section 218 Agreement with SSA. For more information, see Pub. 963, Federal-State Reference Guide.

5. Taxable social security and Medicare wages and tips

5a.   Taxable social security wages. Report the total wages, sick pay, or fringe benefits subject to social security taxes that you paid to your employees during the quarter. For this purpose, sick pay includes payments made by an insurance company to your employees for which you received timely notice from the insurance company. See Section 6 in Pub. 15-A for more information about sick pay reporting.

Enter the amount before deductions. **Do not** include tips on this line. For information on types of wages subject to social security taxes, see section 5 of Pub. 15 (Circular E).

The rate of social security tax on taxable wages is 6.2 percent (.062) each for the employer and employee or 12.4 percent (.124) for both. Stop paying social security tax on and reporting an employee's wages on line 5a when the employee's taxable wages (including tips) reach $90,000 during 2005. However, continue to withhold income and Medicare taxes for the whole year on wages and tips even when the social security wage base of $90,000 has been reached.

$$\begin{array}{r} \text{line 5a (column 1)} \\ \underline{\text{x}\qquad .124} \\ \text{line 5a (column 2)} \end{array}$$

5b.   Taxable social security tips. Enter all tips your employees reported to you during the quarter until the total of the tips and wages for an employee reach $90,000 in 2005. Do this even if you were unable to withhold the employee tax of 6.2%.

An employee must report cash tips to you, including tips you paid the employee for charge customers, totaling $20 or more in a month by the 10th of the next month. Employees may use Form 4070, Employee's Report of Tips to Employer, or submit a written statement or electronic tip record.

Do not include allocated tips on this line. Instead, report them on Form 8027, Employer's Annual Information Return of Tip Income and Allocated Tips. Allocated tips are not reportable on Form 941 and are not subject to withholding of income, social security, or Medicare taxes.

$$\begin{array}{r} \text{line 5b (column 1)} \\ \underline{\text{x}\qquad .124} \\ \text{line 5b (column 2)} \end{array}$$

5c.   Taxable Medicare wages and tips. Report all wages, tips, sick pay, and taxable fringe benefits that are subject to Medicare tax. Unlike social security wages, there is no limit on the amount of wages subject to Medicare tax.

Include all tips your employees reported during the quarter, even if you were unable to withhold the employee tax of 1.45%.

$$\begin{array}{r} \text{line 5c (column 1)} \\ \underline{\text{x}\qquad .029} \\ \text{line 5c (column 2)} \end{array}$$

For more information, see section 6 of Pub. 15 (Circular E).

5d.   Total social security and Medicare taxes. Add social security tax, social security tips tax, and Medicare tax.

$$\begin{array}{r} \text{line 5a (column 2)} \\ \text{line 5b (column 2)} \\ \underline{+\quad \text{line 5c (column 2)}} \\ \text{line 5d} \end{array}$$

6. Total taxes before adjustments

Add the total income tax withheld from wages, tips, and other compensation and total social security and Medicare taxes before adjustments.

$$\begin{array}{r} \text{line 3} \\ \underline{+\quad \text{line 5d}} \\ \text{line 6} \end{array}$$

7. Adjustments

Current period adjustments. In certain cases, you must adjust the amounts you reported as social security and Medicare taxes in column 2 of lines 5a, 5b, and 5c to figure your correct tax liability for this quarter's Form 941. See section 13 of Pub. 15 (Circular E). **Do not** attach Form 941c or an equivalent statement for current period adjustments.

If you need to adjust any amount previously reported on lines 7a-7c, use line 7e to report the adjustment and attach Form 941c or an equivalent statement with an explanation.

7a.   Current quarter's fractions of cents. Enter adjustments for fractions of cents (due to rounding) relating to the employee share of social security and Medicare taxes withheld. The employee share (one-half) of amounts shown in column 2 of lines 5a-5c may differ slightly from amounts actually withheld from employees' paychecks due to the rounding of social security and Medicare taxes based on statutory rates.

7b.   Current quarter's sick pay. Enter the adjustment for the employee share of social security and Medicare taxes that were withheld by your third-party sick pay payer.

7c.   Current quarter's adjustments for tips and group-term life insurance. Enter adjustments for:
• any uncollected employee share of social security and Medicare taxes on tips and
• the uncollected employee share of social security and Medicare taxes on group-term life insurance premiums paid for former employees.

Prior period adjustments. Use lines 7d-7g to adjust amounts reported on **previous returns.** If you need to report both an increase and a decrease for the same line, show only the difference.

Adjustments you report here change your tax liability and your tax deposits. You will have to take these adjustments into account on line 15 as Tax liability: Month 1; Month 2; Month 3 or on Schedule B (Form 941). You **must** explain any adjustments that you make on Form 941c, Supporting Statement to Correct Information, or in an equivalent statement.

-5-

Form 941c is **not** an amended return but is a statement providing the necessary information and certifications for adjustments shown on lines 7d-7g. **Do not** file Form 941c separately from Form 941. See also section 13 of Pub. 15 (Circular E).

7d. Current year's income tax withholding. Enter adjustments for the **current year's** income tax withholding. For example, if you made a mistake when withholding income tax from wages that were **paid in earlier quarters of the same calendar year,** adjust it here. However, see the CAUTION below for adjustment of a prior year's "administrative error" that may also be shown on line 7d.

You cannot adjust or claim a refund or credit for any overpayment of income tax that you withheld or deducted from your employees in a previous year because employees use the amount shown on Form W-2 as a credit when they file their income tax returns.

 Do not adjust income tax withholding for quarters in previous years unless you do it to correct an administrative error. An administrative error happened if the amount you entered on Form 941 was not the same amount you actually withheld. For example, when the total amount of income tax actually withheld was not reported correctly on Form 941 because of a mathematical or transposition error, the difference is an administrative error. The administrative error adjustment corrects the amounts reported on the Form 941 to agree with the amount actually withheld from the employee. Remember to attach an explanation for the adjustment.

7e. Prior quarters' social security and Medicare taxes. Enter adjustments for prior quarters' social security and Medicare taxes. For example, if you made a mistake when reporting social security and Medicare taxes on previously filed Forms 941, adjust it here. If you need to report both an underpayment and an overpayment, show only the net difference.

 If you are adjusting an employee's social security or Medicare wages or tips for a prior year, you must also file Form W-2c, Corrected Wage and Tax Statement, and Form W-3c, Transmittal of Corrected Wage and Tax Statements.

7f. Special additions to federal income tax. This line is reserved for employers with special circumstances. Use this line **only** if the IRS has sent you a notice instructing you to do so.

7g. Special additions to social security and Medicare. This line is reserved for employers with special circumstances. Use this line **only** if the IRS has sent you a notice instructing you to do so.

7h. Total adjustments. Combine all adjustments shown on lines 7a through 7g and enter the result here.

8. Total Taxes After Adjustments

Combine the amounts shown on lines 6 and 7h and enter the result here.

9. Advance Earned Income Credit (EIC) Payments Made to Employees

Enter the amount of the advance earned income credit (EIC) payments that you made to your employees. Eligible employees may choose to receive part of the EIC as an advance payment. Those who expect to have a qualifying child must give you a completed Form W-5 stating they expect to qualify for the EIC. Once the employee gives you a signed and completed Form W-5 you must make the advance EIC payments starting with the employee's next wage payment. Advance EIC payments are generally made from withheld income tax and employee and employer social

security and Medicare taxes. See section 10 of Pub. 15 (Circular E) and Pub. 596, Earned Income Credit.

If the amount of your advance EIC payments is more than your total taxes after adjustments (line 8) for the quarter, you may claim a refund of the overpayment or elect to have the credit applied to your return for the next quarter. Attach a statement to your Form 941 identifying the amount of excess payments and the pay periods in which you paid it. See section 10 of Pub. 15 (Circular E).

10. Total Taxes After Adjustment for Advance EIC

Calculate your total taxes as shown below.

$$\frac{\begin{array}{r}\text{line 8}\\ -\quad \text{line 9}\end{array}}{\text{line 10}}$$

- **If line 10 is less than $2,500, you may pay the full amount with a timely filed return** because you were not required to deposit. See section 11 of Pub. 15 (Circular E) for information and rules about federal tax deposits.
- **If line 10 is $2,500 or more for the quarter,** you must deposit your tax liabilities by using the Electronic Federal Tax Payment System (EFTPS) or at an authorized financial institution with Form 8109. The amount shown on line 10 **must** equal the "Total" shown on Form 941, line 15 or the "Total liability for the quarter" shown on Schedule B (Form 941).

 *If you are a **semiweekly depositor,** you must complete Schedule B (Form 941). If you fail to complete and submit Schedule B (Form 941), IRS will assert deposit penalties based on available information.*

11. Total Deposits for This Quarter

Enter your deposits for this quarter, including any deposits that you were required to make to cover prior period liabilities resulting from adjustments shown on line 7. Also include in the amount shown any overpayment from a previous period that you applied to this return.

12. Balance Due

You do not have to pay if line 12 is under $1. Generally, you should have a balance due only if your total taxes after adjustment for advance EIC for the quarter (line 10) are less than $2,500. (However, see section 11 of Pub. 15 (Circular E) for information about payments made under the **accuracy of deposits rule**.)

You may pay the amount shown on line 12 using EFTPS. If you do so, file your return using the "Without a payment" address on page 4 under *Where should you file?* and **do not** file Form 941-V, Payment Voucher.

If line 10 is $2,500 or more and you have deposited all taxes when due, line 12 ("Balance due") should be zero.

$$\frac{\begin{array}{r}\text{line 10}\\ -\quad \text{line 11}\end{array}}{\text{line 12}}$$

 If you do not deposit as required and, instead, pay the taxes with Form 941, you may be subject to a penalty.

13. Overpayment

If line 11 is more than line 10, write the amount in line 13. **Never** make an entry in both lines 12 and 13.

If you deposited more than the correct amount for a quarter, you can choose to have us either refund the overpayment or apply it to your next return. Check the appropriate box in line 13. If you do not check either box, we will automatically refund the overpayment. We may apply

-6-

your overpayment to any past due tax account that is shown in our records under your EIN.

If line 13 is under $1, we will send a refund or apply it to your next return only if you ask us in writing to do so.

Part 2: Tell us about your deposit schedule for this quarter.

14. State abbreviation

In the spaces provided, write the two-digit U.S. Postal Service abbreviation for the state where you deposit your taxes using Form 8109 or initiate EFTPS transfers. IRS uses the state shown to determine banking days for purposes of deposit due dates. Official state holidays for the state shown are not counted as banking days. If you deposit in multiple states, enter "MU" in the spaces provided.

When you deposit in multiple states, IRS cannot determine what portion of your liability was affected by a state holiday and may propose a deposit penalty for one or more of the states where you made deposits. If you receive a notice and your deposit due date was extended because of a state bank holiday, respond to the notice citing the state holiday and applicable deposit amount.

15. Check one:

- If line 10 is less than $2,500, check the appropriate box in line 15 and go to Part 3.
- If you reported $50,000 or less in taxes during the lookback period (see below), you are a **monthly schedule depositor** unless the *$100,000 Next-Day Deposit Rule* discussed in section 11 of Pub. 15 (Circular E) applies. Check the appropriate box on line 15 and fill out your tax liability for each month in the quarter.

+	Month 1
+	Month 2
+	Month 3
Total tax liability for the quarter	

Note that your total tax liability for the quarter must equal your total taxes shown on line 10. If it does not, your tax deposits and payments may not be counted as timely.

You are a **monthly schedule depositor** for the calendar year if the amount of your Form 941 taxes reported for the lookback period is $50,000 or less. The **lookback period** is the four consecutive quarters ending on June 30 of the prior year. For 2005, the lookback period begins July 1, 2003, and ends June 30, 2004. For details on the deposit rules, see section 11 of Pub. 15 (Circular E).

 *This is a summary of your monthly **tax liability**, not a summary of deposits you made. If you do not properly report your liabilities when required or if you are a semiweekly schedule depositor and report your liabilities on line 15 instead of on Schedule B (Form 941), you may be assessed an "averaged" failure-to-deposit (FTD) penalty. See Deposit Penalties in section 11 of Pub. 15 (Circular E) for more information.*

- If you reported more than $50,000 of taxes for the lookback period (see above), you are a **semiweekly schedule depositor.** Check the appropriate box on line 15.

You **must** complete Schedule B (Form 941) and submit it with your Form 941. **Do not** use Schedule B (Form 941) if you are a monthly schedule depositor.

Reporting adjustments on line 15. If your tax liability for any month is negative (for example, if you are adjusting an overreported liability in a prior period), do not enter a negative amount for the month. Instead, enter zero for the

month and subtract that negative amount from your tax liability for the next month.

Here's an example:
Pine Co. discovered on February 6, 2005, that it overreported social security tax on a prior quarter return by $2,500. Its Form 941 taxes for the first quarter of 2005 were:

January	=	$2,000
February	=	$2,000
March	=	$2,000

Pine Co. reports liabilities on line 15 as follows:

Month 1	=	$2,000
Month 2	=	0
Month 3	=	+$1,500
Total		$3,500

The prior period adjustment ($2,500) offsets the $2,000 liability for February and the excess $500 must be used to offset March liabilities. Since the error was not discovered until February, it does not affect January liabilities reported in Month 1 of line 15.

Using the above example, if the overreported social security tax on a prior quarter return had been $10,000, Pine Co. could carry the excess negative adjustment of $6,000 ($10,000 – $2,000 – $2,000) to the next quarter. Pine Co. would only report $4,000 of the adjustment on line 7e because line 10 must equal the total shown in line 15. See Form 941c for reporting requirements and information on the option of filing a claim for refund of overpaid employment taxes.

Part 3: Tell us about your business.

In Part 3, answer only those questions that apply to your business. If the questions do not apply, leave them blank and go to Part 4.

16. If Your Business Has Closed . . .

If you go out of business or stop paying wages, you must file a **final return**. To tell IRS that a particular Form 941 is your final return, check the box on line 16 and enter the date you last paid wages in the space provided. For additional filing requirements, see *If your business has closed...* on page 2.

17. If You Are a Seasonal Employer . . .

If you hire employees seasonally—such as for summer or winter only—check the box on line 17. Checking the box tells IRS not to expect four Forms 941 from you throughout the year because you have not paid wages regularly.

IRS will mail you two forms once a year after March 1. Generally, we will not ask about unfiled returns if you file at least one return showing tax due each year. However, you must check the box **every time** you file a Form 941.

Also, when you fill out Form 941, be sure to check the box on the top of the form that corresponds to the quarter reported.

Part 4: May we contact your third-party designee?

If you want to allow an employee, a paid tax preparer, or another person to discuss your Form 941 with the IRS, check the "Yes" box in Part 4. Then tell us the name, phone number, and the five-digit personal identification number (PIN) of the specific person to contact—not the name of the firm who prepared your tax return. The designee may choose any five numbers as his or her PIN.

By checking "Yes," you authorize IRS to call the person you named (your designee) with any questions we may have while we process your return. You also authorize your designee to:
• give us any information that is missing from your return,
• call us for information about processing your return, and
• respond to certain IRS notices that you have shared with your designee about math errors and return preparation. IRS will **not** send notices to your designee.

You are **not authorizing** your designee to bind you to anything (including additional tax liability) or to otherwise represent you before the IRS. If you want to expand your designee's authorization, see Pub. 947, Practice Before the IRS and Power of Attorney.

The authorization will automatically **expire** one year from the due date (without regard to extensions) for filing your Form 941. If you or your designee want to terminate the authorization, write to the IRS office for your locality using the "Without a payment" address under *Where Should You File* on page 4.

Part 5: Sign here— Who Must Sign the Form 941?

Form 941 must be signed as follows.
• **Sole proprietorship—** The individual who owns the business.
• **Corporation (including an LLC treated as a corporation)—** The president, vice president, or other principal officer.
• **Partnership (including an LLC treated as a partnership) or unincorporated organization—** A responsible and duly authorized member or officer having knowledge of its affairs.
• **Single member limited liability company (LLC) treated as a disregarded entity—** The owner of the limited liability company (LLC).
• **Trust or estate—** The fiduciary.

Form 941 may also be signed by a duly authorized agent of the taxpayer if a valid power of attorney has been filed.

Part 6: For Paid Preparers Only (optional)

Complete Part 6 if you were paid to prepare Form 941 and are not an employee of the filing entity. Sign in the space provided and give the filer a copy of the return in addition to the copy to be filed with the IRS. Do not complete Part 6 if you are filing the return as a reporting agent and have a valid Form 8655, Reporting Agent Authorization, on file with the IRS. You are not required to complete this section.

How to Order Forms and Publications from the IRS

 Call 1-800-829-3676.

 Visit the IRS website at *www.irs.gov*.

Other IRS Products You May Need

- Form SS-4, Application for Employer Identification Number
- Form W-2, Wage and Tax Statement
- Form W-2c, Corrected Wage and Tax Statement
- Form W-3, Transmittal of Wage and Tax Statements
- Form W-3c, Transmittal of Corrected Wage and Tax Statements
- Form W-4, Employee's Withholding Allowance Certificate
- Form W-5, Earned Income Credit Advance Payment Certificate
- Form 940, Employer's Annual Federal Unemployment (FUTA) Tax Return
- Form 941c, Supporting Statement to Correct Information
- Form 943, Employer's Annual Federal Tax Return for Agricultural Employees
- Form 945, Annual Return of Withheld Federal Income Tax
- Form 4070, Employee's Report of Tips to Employer
- Form 8027, Employer's Annual Information Return of Tip Income and Allocated Tips
- Instructions for Forms W-2 and W-3
- Notice 797, Possible Federal Tax Refund Due to the Earned Income Credit (EIC)
- Pub. 15 (Circular E), Employer's Tax Guide
- Pub. 15-A, Employer's Supplemental Tax Guide
- Pub. 15-B, Employer's Tax Guide to Fringe Benefits
- Pub. 51, (Circular A), Agricultural Employer's Tax Guide
- Pub. 596, Earned Income Credit
- Pub. 926, Household Employer's Tax Guide
- Pub. 947, Practice Before the IRS and Power of Attorney
- Schedule B (Form 941), Report of Tax Liability for Semiweekly Schedule Depositors
- Schedule D (Form 941), Report of Discrepancies Caused by Acquisitions, Statutory Mergers, or Consolidations
- Schedule H (Form 1040), Household Employment Taxes

-8-

Schedule B (Form 941):

Report of Tax Liability for Semiweekly Schedule Depositors

(Rev. January 2005)   Department of the Treasury — Internal Revenue Service

9903

OMB No. 1545-0029

Employer identification number   ☐☐ – ☐☐☐☐☐☐☐

Name *(not your trade name)*

Report for this Quarter ...
(Check one.)

☐ **1:** January, February, March

☐ **2:** April, May, June

☐ **3:** July, August, September

☐ **4:** October, November, December

Use this schedule to show your tax liability for the quarter; DO NOT use it to show your deposits. You must fill out this form and attach it to Form 941 (or Form 941-SS) if you are a semiweekly schedule depositor or became one because your accumulated tax liability on any day was $100,000 or more. Write your daily tax liability on the numbered space that corresponds to the date wages were paid. See Section 11 in *Pub. 15 (Circular E), Employer's Tax Guide,* for details.

Month 1

1	9	17	25	**Tax liability for Month 1**
2	10	18	26	
3	11	19	27	
4	12	20	28	
5	13	21	29	
6	14	22	30	
7	15	23	31	
8	16	24		

Month 2

1	9	17	25	**Tax liability for Month 2**
2	10	18	26	
3	11	19	27	
4	12	20	28	
5	13	21	29	
6	14	22	30	
7	15	23	31	
8	16	24		

Month 3

1	9	17	25	**Tax liability for Month 3**
2	10	18	26	
3	11	19	27	
4	12	20	28	
5	13	21	29	
6	14	22	30	
7	15	23	31	
8	16	24		

Fill in your total liability for the quarter (Month 1 + Month 2 + Month 3) = Total tax liability for the quarter ▶

Total must equal line 10 on Form 941 (or line 8 on Form 941-SS).

Total liability for the quarter

For Paperwork Reduction Act Notice, see separate instructions.   Cat. No. 11967Q   Schedule B (Form 941) Rev. 1-2005

Instructions for Schedule B (Form 941)

Department of the Treasury
Internal Revenue Service

(Rev. January 2005)

Report of Tax Liability for Semiweekly Schedule Depositors

General Instructions:

Purpose of Schedule B (Form 941)

These instructions tell you about Schedule B (Form 941), Report of Tax Liability for Semiweekly Schedule Depositors. To determine if you are a "semiweekly depositor," visit the IRS website at *www.irs.gov*. Also see Pub. 15 (Circular E), Employer's Tax Guide, or Pub. 80 (Circular SS), Federal Tax Guide for Employers in the U.S. Virgin Islands, Guam, American Samoa, and the Commonwealth of the Northern Mariana Islands.

What Is Schedule B (Form 941)?

Federal law requires you as an employer to withhold taxes from your employees' paychecks. Each time you pay wages, you must withhold – or take out of your employees' paychecks – certain amounts for federal income tax, social security tax, and Medicare tax (payroll taxes). Under the withholding system, taxes withheld from your employees are credited to your employees in payment of their tax liabilities.

Federal law also requires employers to pay any liability for the employer's portion of social security and Medicare taxes. This portion of social security and Medicare taxes is not withheld from employees.

Schedule B (Form 941) accompanies Form 941, Employer's Quarterly Federal Tax Return, or Form 941-SS, Employer's Quarterly Federal Tax Return (American Samoa, Guam, the Commonwealth of the Northern Mariana Islands, and the U.S. Virgin Islands), that you use to report your payroll taxes and adjustments.

On Schedule B, list your **tax liability** for each day. Include:
- the income tax you withheld from your employees' paychecks and
- both employee and employer Medicare and social security taxes.

Note. Subtract any advance earned income credit payments from your tax liability.

Do not use the Schedule B (Form 941) to show federal tax deposits. Deposit information is taken from your deposit coupons (Form 8109, Federal Tax Deposit Coupon) or from the Electronic Federal Tax Payment System (EFTPS).

 IRS uses Schedule B (Form 941) to determine if you have deposited your federal employment tax liabilities on time. If you do not properly complete and file your Schedule B (Form 941) with Form 941 or 941-SS, IRS may propose an "averaged" failure-to-deposit penalty. See Deposit Penalties *in section 11 of Pub. 15 (Circular E) for more information.*

Who Must file Schedule B (Form 941)?

File Schedule B (Form 941) if you are:
- a semiweekly schedule depositor or
- a monthly schedule depositor who accumulated a tax liability of $100,000 or more on any given day in the reporting period.

See *$100,000 Next-Day Deposit Rule* in section 11 of Pub. 15 (Circular E) for important details.

 Do not complete Schedule B (Form 941) if you have a tax liability that is less than $2,500 (after you subtract any advance earned income credit (EIC) payment) during the quarter and you pay in full with a return that you file on time.

When Must You File?

Attach your Schedule B (Form 941) to your Form 941 or Form 941-SS and file it every quarter when that Form 941 or Form 941-SS is due. For more information, see section 12 of Pub. 15 (Circular E), the Instructions for Form 941, or the Instructions for Form 941-SS.

Specific Instructions:

Completing Schedule B (Form 941)

Fill in Your Business Information
Carefully fill in your employer identification number (EIN) and name at the top of the schedule. Make sure that they exactly match the name of your business and the EIN that IRS assigned to your business and also agree with the name and EIN shown on the attached Form 941 or Form 941-SS.

 Always be sure the EIN on the schedule you file exactly matches the EIN that IRS assigned to your business. Do not use your social security number on forms that ask for an EIN. Filing a Schedule B (Form 941) with an incorrect EIN, or using the EIN of another business, may result in penalties and delays in processing your return.

Check the Box for the Quarter
In the box at the top of the schedule, check the appropriate box of the quarter for which you are filing this schedule. Make sure that the quarter checked on the top of the Schedule B (Form 941) matches the quarter checked on your Form 941 or Form 941-SS.

Fill in Your Tax Liability by Month
Schedule B (Form 941) is divided into the 3 months that make up a quarter of a year. Each month has 31 numbered spaces that correspond to the dates of a typical month. Write your tax liabilities in the spaces that correspond to the dates you **paid** wages to your employees, not the date payroll deposits were made.

For example, if your payroll period ended on December 31, 2004, and you **paid** the wages for that period on January 7, 2005, you would:
- go to Month 1 (because January is the first month of the quarter) and
- write your tax liability on line 7 (because line 7 represents the seventh day of the month).

 Make sure you have checked the appropriate box on line 15 of Form 941 to show that you are a semiweekly schedule depositor.

Cat. No. 38683X

Total Liability for the Quarter

To find your total liability for the quarter, add your monthly tax liabilities.

```
        Tax Liability for Month 1
      + Tax Liability for Month 2
      + Tax Liability for Month 3
        Total Liability for the Quarter
```

Your total liability for the quarter must equal line 10 on Form 941 or line 8 on Form 941-SS.

Here are some examples.

- Employer A is a **semiweekly** schedule depositor who pays wages for each month on the last day of the month. On December 21, 2005, Employer A also paid its employees year-end bonuses (subject to employment taxes). Because Employer A is a semiweekly schedule depositor, Employer A must record employment tax liabilities on Schedule B (Form 941). For the 4th quarter (October, November, December), Employer A should report tax liability in this way—

Month	Lines for dates wages were paid
1 (October)	line 31 (pay day, last day of the month)
2 (November)	line 30 (pay day, last day of the month)
3 (December)	lines 21 (bonus paid) + 31 (pay day)

- Employer B is a **semiweekly** schedule depositor who pays employees every other Friday. Employer B accumulated a $20,000 employment tax liability on each of these pay dates: 1/14/05, 1/28/05, 2/11/05, 2/25/05, 3/11/05, and 3/25/05. Since Employer B is a semiweekly schedule depositor, Employer B must record tax liabilities on Schedule B in this way—

Month	Lines for dates wages were paid
1 (January)	lines 14 and 28
2 (February)	lines 11 and 25
3 (March)	lines 11 and 25

- Employer C is a new business and **monthly** schedule depositor for 2005. Employer C pays wages every Friday and has accumulated a $2,000 employment tax liability on 1/14/05 and a $110,000 liability on 1/21/05 and on every subsequent Friday during 2005. Under the deposit rules, employers **become semiweekly schedule depositors** on the day after any day they accumulate $100,000 or more of tax liability in a deposit period. (See section 11 of Pub. 15 (Circular E) or section 8 of Pub. 80 (Circular SS) for details.)

Because Employer C accumulated $112,000 on 1/12/05, Employer C became a semiweekly schedule depositor on the next day and must complete Schedule B (Form 941) and file it with Form 941 or Form 941-SS. Employer C should record tax liabilities in this way—

Month	Dates wages were paid	Amount to record
1 (January)	line 14	$2,000
1 (January)	lines 21, 28	$110,000
2 (February)	lines 4, 11, 18, 25	$110,000
3 (March)	lines 4, 11, 18, 25	$110,000

Prior Period Adjustments

On Schedule B (Form 941), you must take into account adjustments to correct errors on prior period returns. See lines 7d-7g of post-2004 Forms 941; lines 7e and 7g of post-2004 Forms 941-SS. (For pre-2005 Forms 941 and 941-SS, see lines 4 and 9.)

- If the adjustment corrects an **underreported** liability in a prior quarter, include the adjustment amount in the total liability reported for the entry space that corresponds to the date you discovered the error.

- If the adjustment corrects an **overreported** liability, use the adjustment amount to offset subsequent liabilities until it is used up.

Example. On 1/21/05, Employer D discovered that social security tax was over-reported by $10,000 on a prior quarter return. Employer D paid wages on 1/14/05, 1/21/05, 1/28/05, and 2/4/05 and had a $5,000 tax liability for each of those pay dates. On Schedule B (Form 941), Employer D must report a $5,000 liability on 1/14/05 for Month 1 using line 14. Since the adjustment for the $10,000 over-reported liability offsets the 1/21/05 and 1/28/05 liability, Employer D does not deposit or report these two $5,000 liabilities on Schedule B (Form 941). Employer D must report the $5,000 liability for 2/4/05 on Month 2 using line 4. (See section 13 of Pub. 15 (Circular E) for details on reporting adjustments to correct errors on prior period returns.)

How to Order Forms and Publications from the IRS

 Call 1-800-829-3676

Visit the IRS website at *www.irs.gov*

Other IRS Products You May Need

- Form 941, Employer's Quarterly Federal Tax Return
- Form 941-SS, Employer's Quarterly Federal Tax Return (American Samoa, Guam, the Commonwealth of the Northern Marianas Islands, and the U.S. Virgin Islands)
- Pub. 15 (Circular E), Employer's Tax Guide
- Pub. 80 (Circular SS), Federal Tax Guide for Employers in the U.S. Virgin Islands, Guam, American Samoa, and the Commonwealth of the Northern Mariana Islands.

Paperwork Reduction Act Notice

We ask for the information on Schedule B (Form 941) to carry out the Internal Revenue laws of the United States. You are required to give us the information. We need it to ensure that you are complying with these laws and to allow us to figure and collect the right amount of tax.

You are not required to provide the information requested on a form that is subject to the Paperwork Reduction Act unless the form displays a valid OMB control number. Books or records relating to a form or its instructions must be retained as long as their contents may become material in the administration of any Internal Revenue law. Generally, tax returns and return information are confidential, as required by Code section 6103.

The time needed to complete and file Schedule B (Form 941) will vary depending on individual circumstances. The estimated average time is 2 hours, 53 minutes.

If you have comments concerning the accuracy of this time estimate or suggestions for making Schedule B (Form 941) simpler, we would be happy to hear from you. You can write to: Internal Revenue Service, Tax Products Coordinating Committee, SE:W:CAR:MP:T:T:SP, 1111 Constitution Ave. NW, IR-6406, Washington, DC 20224.

Do not send the Schedule B (Form 941) to this address. Instead, see *Where Should You File?* in the Form 941 or Form 941-SS instructions.

-2-

Schedule D (Form 941):

Report of Discrepancies Caused by Acquisitions, Statutory Mergers, or Consolidations

(Rev. March 2005)   Department of the Treasury—Internal Revenue Service

OMB No. 1545-0029

Employer Identification Number (EIN) ☐☐ — ☐☐☐☐☐☐☐

Name *(not your trade name)*

Trade name *(if any)*

Address

Number   Street   Suite or room number

City   State   ZIP code

Phone number ( ) —

Tax Year of Discrepancies (Fill in)

☐☐☐☐   Format: YYYY

Type of Submission (Check one)

☐ Original

☐ Corrected

About this schedule

Each year the Internal Revenue Service (IRS) and the Social Security Administration (SSA) compare the totals on your Forms 941, *Employer's Quarterly Federal Tax Return,* with the totals on Forms W-2, *Wage and Tax Statement,* to verify that:

- the wages you reported on Forms 941 match those you reported on Forms W-2 (Copy A) so that your employees' social security earnings records are complete for benefit purposes; and
- you have paid the appropriate taxes.

Generally, the totals on your Forms W-2 (Copy A) should equal the totals you reported on Forms 941. Use this schedule if discrepancies exist between the totals you reported on those forms ONLY as a result of an acquisition, statutory merger, or consolidation. **In many cases, the information on this schedule should help the IRS resolve discrepancies without contacting you.** If you are an eligible employer who elects to use the alternate procedure set forth in Rev. Proc. 2004-53, explained in the instructions, you should file this schedule.

Read the separate instructions before you fill out this schedule.

Part 1: Answer these background questions.

1. Are you filing this schedule —

☐ after a statutory merger or consolidation? (See Rev. Rul. 62-60, 1962-1 C.B. 186 and Rev. Proc. 2004-53, 2004-34 I.R.B. 320.)

You are either: ☐ an acquired corporation or
☐ a surviving corporation.

OR

☐ after an acquisition and you are using the alternate procedure under Rev. Proc. 2004-53, 2004-34 I.R.B. 320?

You are either: ☐ a predecessor or
☐ a successor.

2. The effective date of the statutory merger/consolidation or acquisition is . . . . . . ☐☐ / ☐☐ / ☐☐☐☐

MM / DD / YYYY

3. The OTHER PARTY in this transaction is . . .

Other party's EIN ☐☐ — ☐☐☐☐☐☐☐

Other party's name

Trade name *(if any)*

Address

Number   Street   Suite or room number

City   State   ZIP code

Phone number ( ) —

Next ➡

For Paperwork Reduction Act Notice, see separate instructions.   Cat. No. 38791Y   **Schedule D (Form 941)** Rev. 3-2005

Your EIN ☐☐ – ☐☐☐☐☐☐☐

Name (not your trade name) _____

Other party's EIN ☐☐ – ☐☐☐☐☐☐☐

Tax Year of Discrepancies (Fill in)
☐☐☐☐ Format: YYYY

Part 2: Tell us about the discrepancies with your returns.

	Column A		Column B		Column C
	Amount you reported to IRS for the tax year	−	**Amount you reported to SSA for the tax year**	=	**The difference**
	Totals from Forms 941 as corrected by any Forms 941c		Totals from Forms W-2 (Copy A) as corrected by any Forms W-2c (Copy A)		
4. social security wages		−		=	
5. Medicare wages and tips		−		=	
6. social security tips		−		=	
7. federal income tax withheld		−		=	
8. advance earned income credit (EIC) payments		−		=	

If you are filing for one transaction only, STOP here. If you are filing for more than one transaction, go to Part 3.

Part 3: Fill this part out ONLY if you are filing more than one Schedule D (Form 941) for any calendar year.

9. File one Schedule D (Form 941) for each separate transaction. This is schedule ☐ of ☐ . (Example: *This is schedule 1 of 3.*)

	Column A		Column B		Column C
	Amount you reported to IRS for the tax year for the employees affected by the transaction reported on this Schedule D (Form 941)	−	**Amount you reported to SSA for the tax year for the employees affected by the transaction reported on this Schedule D (Form 941)**	=	**The difference**
	Totals from Forms 941 as corrected by any Forms 941c		Totals from Forms W-2 (Copy A) as corrected by any Forms W-2c (Copy A)		
10. social security wages		−		=	
11. Medicare wages and tips		−		=	
12. social security tips		−		=	
13. federal income tax withheld		−		=	
14. advance earned income credit (EIC) payments		−		=	

Instructions for Schedule D (Form 941)

(Rev. March 2005)

Department of the Treasury
Internal Revenue Service

Report of Discrepancies Caused by Acquisitions, Statutory Mergers, or Consolidations

General Instructions

Understanding Schedule D (Form 941)

These instructions tell you about Schedule D (Form 941), Report of Discrepancies Caused by Acquisitions, Statutory Mergers, or Consolidations. Employers can use Schedule D (Form 941) to explain certain discrepancies (caused by acquisitions, statutory mergers, and consolidations) between Forms W-2 (Copy A) and Forms 941 for the totals of social security wages, Medicare wages and tips, social security tips, federal income tax withheld, and advance earned income credit (EIC) payments.

What Is Schedule D (Form 941)?

Each year the Internal Revenue Service (IRS) and the Social Security Administration (SSA) compare the totals on your Forms 941 with the totals from your Forms W-2, Wage and Tax Statement (Copy A), to verify that:
• the wages you reported on Forms 941 match those you reported on Forms W-2 (Copy A) so that your employees' social security earnings records are complete for benefit purposes and
• you have paid the appropriate taxes.

Generally, the totals of all your Forms W-2 (Copy A) should equal the aggregate quarterly totals you reported on Forms 941. Use Schedule D (Form 941) if discrepancies exist between the totals you reported on those forms **only** as a result of an acquisition, statutory merger, or consolidation.

 IRS uses Schedule D (Form 941) to determine if you have reported your wages and tax liabilities correctly. In many cases, the information on Schedule D (Form 941) helps the IRS resolve discrepancies without contacting you.

Who Should File Schedule D (Form 941)?

You **do not** need to file a Schedule D (Form 941) for every merger, acquisition, or other reorganization that occurs. File Schedule D (Form 941) **only** for those acquisitions, statutory mergers or consolidations that create discrepancies between Forms W-2 (Copy A) and Forms 941 in the totals of:
• social security wages,
• Medicare wages and tips,
• social security tips,
• federal income tax withheld, and
• advance EIC payments.

 Each *party to an applicable transaction (see below) files its own Schedule D (Form 941).*

File Schedule D (Form 941) for:
• a statutory merger,
• a consolidation, or
• an acquisition for which you are using the alternate procedure under Rev. Proc. 2004-53. You can find Rev. Proc. 2004-53 on page 320 of Internal Revenue Bulletin 2004-34 at *www.irs.gov/pub/irs-irbs/irb04-34.pdf.*

Do NOT file a Schedule D for:
• an acquisition for which you are using the standard procedure under Rev. Proc. 2004-53 or
• an acquisition that is **not** a statutory merger or consolidation and that does **not** qualify under the predecessor-successor rules. See *Acquisitions that Qualify Under the Predecessor-Successor Rules,* on page 2, for a complete discussion of the predecessor-successor rules.

Types of Mergers and Acquisitions

Mergers, acquisitions, and other reorganizations generally fall into one of three categories for purposes of reporting employment taxes.

1. Statutory mergers and consolidations,
2. Acquisitions that qualify under the predecessor-successor rules (see *Acquisitions that Qualify Under the Predecessor-Successor Rules* on page 2), or
3. Other acquisitions that are not statutory mergers or consolidations and that **do not** qualify under the predecessor-successor rules (see *Acquisitions that Qualify Under the Predecessor-Successor Rules* on page 2).

Statutory Mergers and Consolidations

If you are the **surviving** corporation after a statutory merger or consolidation, you should file Schedule D (Form 941) to provide:
• the date of the statutory merger or consolidation;
• the name, trade name (doing business as or d/b/a), address, and employer identification number (EIN) of the acquired corporation; and
• an explanation of any discrepancies between Forms W-2 (Copy A) and Forms 941 in the totals of social security wages, Medicare wages and tips, social security tips, federal income tax withheld, and advance EIC payments.

Cat. No. 38789M

If you are the **acquired** corporation after a statutory merger or consolidation and you are filing a final Form 941, you should file Schedule D (Form 941) to provide:
- the date of the statutory merger or consolidation;
- the name, trade name (doing business as or d/b/a), address, and EIN of the surviving corporation; and
- an explanation of any discrepancies between Forms W-2 (Copy A) and Forms 941 in the totals of social security wages, Medicare wages and tips, social security tips, federal income tax withheld, and advance EIC payments.

Rev. Rul. 62-60, 1962-1 C.B. 186, provides that, for employment tax purposes, the "resultant" corporation (now called a "surviving" corporation) resulting from a statutory merger or consolidation is the same employer and taxpayer as the "absorbed" corporation (now called an "acquired" corporation). The predecessor-successor rules described in Rev. Proc. 2004-53 do not apply to these transactions.

However, Rev. Proc. 2004-53 provides for using Schedule D (Form 941) by a surviving corporation or an acquired corporation to report information after a statutory merger or consolidation **only** where there is a discrepancy. If the surviving corporation completes and files Schedule D (Form 941) to explain discrepancies between the totals on Forms W-2 (Copy A) and the totals on Forms 941, filing Schedule D (Form 941) will also provide notice of a statutory merger or consolidation under Rev. Rul. 62-60.

Acquisitions that Qualify Under Predecessor-Successor Rules

Acquisitions that qualify under the predecessor-successor rules are acquisitions in which a **successor** employer:
- acquires substantially all the property used in a trade or business of another employer (predecessor) or in a separate unit of a trade or business of a predecessor and
- in connection with and directly after the acquisition (but during the same calendar year) employs individuals who immediately before the acquisition were employed in the trade or business of the predecessor.

These acquisitions satisfy the conditions for predecessor-successor status set forth in section 3121(a)(1) of the Internal Revenue Code and section 31.3121(a)(1)-1(b) of the Employment Tax Regulations.

Rev. Proc. 2004-53 contains the rules that apply to employment tax reporting in a predecessor-successor situation. Two procedures can be used in an acquisition that qualifies as a predecessor-successor situation.
- **Standard procedure**—**Do not** file Schedule D (Form 941). No discrepancies should exist between the totals of the Forms W-2 (Copy A) and the totals of the Forms 941 as a result of the acquisition.
- **Alternate procedure**—**Each** party in the transaction should file Schedule D (Form 941). Forms W-2 (Copy A) filed by the successor may include amounts reported on Forms 941 filed by the predecessor.

Other Acquisitions

If you completed other acquisitions that are not statutory mergers or consolidations and that do not qualify under the predecessor-successor rules, no discrepancies should exist as a result of the acquisition. Rev. Rul. 62-60 and Rev. Proc. 2004-53 do not apply to such transactions. **Do not** file Schedule D (Form 941) for such transactions.

When Should You File?

You should file Schedule D (Form 941):
- no later than the due date of your Form 941 for the first quarter of the year **after** the calendar year of the transaction or
- with your final Form 941, if your final Form 941 is due before the first quarter of the year after the calendar year of the transaction.

For example, if the transaction occurred in the third quarter of 2005 and your business is continuing to operate, you would file Schedule D (Form 941) with your Form 941 for the first quarter of 2006. However, if your business is not continuing to operate during 2005, you would file Schedule D (Form 941) with your final Form 941.

How Should You File?

Schedule D (Form 941) was designed to be filed electronically (after March 31, 2006) with your electronic submission of Form 941. Electronic filing of Schedule D (Form 941) enables IRS to process information on the form more efficiently and accurately.

However, you may file Schedule D (Form 941) on paper if necessary. When filing on paper, **do not** attach Schedule D (Form 941) to your Form 941. Instead, file Schedule D (Form 941) **separately** using the following address.

> **Stop 815G—Team 301**
> **Internal Revenue Service**
> **201 Rivercenter Blvd.**
> **Covington, KY 41011**

Do not use this address to file Form 941. See *Where Should You File?* in the Instructions for Form 941 for the filing address of Form 941.

Specific Instructions

Completing Schedule D (Form 941)

Your Business Information

Carefully fill in your employer identification number (EIN), name, trade name (doing business as or d/b/a), and complete address at the top of the schedule.

 Always be sure the EIN on the Schedule D (Form 941) that you file exactly matches the EIN that IRS assigned to your business.

-2-

Tax Year of Discrepancies

In the box at the top of the schedule, write the **tax year** (not the quarter) in which the discrepancies occurred. Write the tax year using **four digits**. For example, if the transaction occurred on March 22, 2005, write "2005" in the box.

Make sure you fill in the correct tax year so that you can reconcile the information appropriately. The tax year must be the same as the calendar year that you write in Part 1, line 2.

 *Be sure to **fill in** your EIN, business name, other party's EIN, and the tax year of the discrepancies on the top of page 2 as well.*

Type of Submission

Check the appropriate box to show whether this form is the "Original" Schedule D (Form 941) for a specific transaction or corrects (mark "Corrected") a Schedule D (Form 941) that you previously submitted.

Part 1: Answer these background questions.

1. Check the appropriate box to explain the type of transaction for which you are submitting Schedule D (Form 941). See *Types of Mergers and Acquisitions* on page 1 for details.

File Schedule D (Form 941) after either:
- a statutory merger or consolidation (Check whether you are an **acquired corporation** or a **surviving corporation**.) or
- an acquisition for which you are using the alternate procedure under Rev. Proc. 2004-53. (Check whether you are a **predecessor** or a **successor**.)

2. Fill in the effective date of the transaction in the box. Make sure that you write the month, day, and year in this format: **MM/DD/YYYY**. The year must be the same as the calendar year that you write in the box at the top of the schedule.

3. Fill in the contact information about the OTHER PARTY in the transaction by including the other party's EIN, name, trade name (doing business as or d/b/a), complete address, and phone number. **Verify** the other party's EIN to make sure it is correct.

Part 2: Tell us about the discrepancies with your returns.

4-8. Gather your information about the social security wages, Medicare wages and tips, social security tips, federal income tax withheld, and advance earned income credit (EIC) payments that you reported. When entering money amounts from your Forms 941 and W-2 (Copy A) on lines 4 -14, you may round to the nearest dollar. Do not show dollar signs but do use commas as appropriate. Show an amount (even if it is zero) for each column of a line.

In Column A, fill in the amount you reported to the IRS for the tax year for each of the items. Add the totals from

all Forms 941, as corrected by any Forms 941c, and write your answers on the appropriate lines.

In Column B, fill in the amount you reported to SSA for each of the items. Add the totals from all Forms W-2 (Copy A), as corrected by any Forms W-2c (Copy A), and write your answers on the appropriate lines.

Calculate the differences between the entries in the columns:

$$\begin{array}{r} \text{Column A} \\ - \ \underline{\text{Column B}} \\ \text{Column C} \end{array}$$

Enter any negative result in parentheses, if possible. For example, if line 6, Column A is "-0-" and line 6, Column B is "6,000," write "(6,000)" in line 6, Column C.

 *If no Forms W-2 (Copy A) were filed by **you**, write "-0-" in column B, "Amount you reported to SSA for the tax year."*

If you are filing for one transaction only, STOP here. If you are filing for more than one transaction, go to Part 3.

Part 3: Fill this part out ONLY if you are filing more than one Schedule D (Form 941) for any calendar year.

If you are filing only one Schedule D (Form 941) for the calendar year, leave this part blank.

When more than one statutory merger, consolidation, or acquisition occurs during a calendar year, file a **separate** Schedule D (Form 941) for each transaction. Complete Part 3 for each transaction. For instance, if you have 11 different transactions in a calendar year, you need to file 11 different Schedules D (Form 941). Part 2 would be the same for each schedule. Part 3 would show one of the 11 transactions. For example, the amount entered in Part 2 on line 4 for Column C should equal the total of all 11 entries in Part 3 on line 10 for Column C.

9. Show the number of schedules that you are filing for the year and identify which schedule this is. For example, if you had three different transactions in a calendar year and you are filing a Schedule D (Form 941) to describe the second transaction, fill in "2" and "3" so that the sentence reads: "This is schedule 2 of 3. "

10-14. For purposes of Part 3, Columns A and B, the term "employees affected by the transaction reported on this Schedule D" means those employees who received wages that were reported on Forms 941 filed by one employer but whose wages were reported on Form W-2 (Copy A) filed by another employer as a result of this particular transaction. Report the totals for social security wages, Medicare wages and tips, social security tips, federal income tax withheld, and advance earned income credit (EIC) payments.

In Column A, fill in the amount you reported to the IRS for the tax year for employees affected by the transaction reported on this Schedule D (Form 941) for each of the items. Add the totals from all your Forms 941, as corrected by any Forms 941c, and write your answers on the appropriate lines.

-3-

In Column B, fill in the amount you reported to SSA for the tax year for employees affected by the transaction reported on this Schedule D (Form 941) for each of the items. Add the totals from all Forms W-2 (Copy A), as corrected by any Forms W-2c (Copy A), and write your answers on the appropriate lines.

Calculate the differences between the entries in the columns:

$$\begin{array}{r} \text{Column A} \\ - \underline{\text{Column B}} \\ \text{Column C} \end{array}$$

Enter any negative result in parentheses, if possible. For example, if line 12, Column A is "-0-" and line 12, Column B is "6,000," write "(6,000)" in line 12, Column C.

 If no Forms W-2 (Copy A) were filed by you, write "-0-" in Column B, "Amount you reported to SSA for the tax year."

Paperwork Reduction Act Notice

We ask for the information on Schedule D (Form 941) to carry out the Internal Revenue laws of the United States. If you file this form, you are required to give us the information requested. We need it to ensure that you are complying with these laws and to allow us to figure and collect the right amount of tax.

You are not required to provide the information requested on a form that is subject to the Paperwork Reduction Act unless the form displays a valid OMB control number. Books or records relating to a form or its instructions must be retained as long as their contents may become material in the administration of any Internal Revenue law. Generally, tax returns and return information are confidential, as required by section 6103 of the Internal Revenue Code.

The time needed to complete and file Schedule D (Form 941) will vary depending on individual circumstances. The estimated average time is: **Recordkeeping,** 11 hr., 43 min.; **Learning about the law or the form,** 18 min.; **Preparing, copying, assembling, and sending the form to the IRS,** 30 min. If you have comments concerning the accuracy of this time estimate or suggestions for making Schedule D (Form 941) simpler, we would be happy to hear from you. You can write to: Internal Revenue Service, Tax Products Coordinating Committee, SE:W:CAR:MP:T:T:SP, 1111 Constitution Ave. NW, IR-6406, Washington, DC 20224. **Do not** send Schedule D (Form 941) to this address. Instead, see *Where Should You File?* on page 2.

-4-

Form **941c**	**Supporting Statement To Correct Information**	OMB No. 1545-0256
(Rev. October 2003) Department of the Treasury Internal Revenue Service	**Do Not File Separately** ▶ File with Forms 941, 941-M, 941-SS, 943, 945, or Form 843.	Page No.

Name	Employer identification number

Telephone number (optional)	**A** This form supports adjustments to: **Check only one box.** (see instructions) ☐ Form 941 ☐ Form 941-SS ☐ Form 945 ☐ Form 941-M ☐ Form 943

B This form is **attached to** and filed with the return for the period ending (month, year) ▶	**C** Enter the date that you discovered the error(s) reported on this form. (If you are making more than one correction and the errors were not discovered at the same time, explain in Part V.) . . . . . ▶

Part I **Signature and Certification** (You **must** complete this part for the IRS to process your adjustments for overpayments.) Skip Part I if all of your adjustments are underpayments. **(Part I applies to wages only.)**

I certify that **Forms W-2c,** Corrected Wage and Tax Statement, have been filed (as necessary) with the Social Security Administration, and that (check appropriate boxes):

☐ All overcollected income taxes for the current calendar year and all social security and Medicare taxes for the current and prior calendar years have been **repaid** to employees. For claims of overcollected employee social security and Medicare taxes in earlier years, a written statement has been obtained from each employee stating that the employee has not claimed and will not claim refund or credit of the amount of the overcollection.

☐ All affected employees have given their **written consent** to the allowance of this credit or refund. For claims of overcollected employee social security and Medicare taxes in earlier years, a written statement has been obtained from each employee stating that the employee has not claimed and will not claim refund or credit of the amount of the overcollection.

☐ The social security tax and Medicare tax adjustments represent the **employer's share only.** An attempt was made to locate the employee(s) affected, but the affected employee(s) could not be located or will not comply with the certification requirements.

☐ None of this refund or credit was withheld from employee wages.

Sign Here

Signature ▶	Title ▶	Date ▶

Part II **Income Tax Withholding (Including Backup Withholding) Adjustment**

	(a) Period Corrected (For quarterly returns, enter date quarter ended. For annual returns, enter year.)	(b) Withheld Income Tax Previously Reported for Period	(c) Correct Withheld Income Tax for Period	(d) Withheld Income Tax Adjustment
1				
2				
3				
4				
5	**Net withheld income tax adjustment.** If more than one page, enter total of **all** columns (d) on first page only. Enter here and on the **appropriate** line of the return with which you file this form. ▶	5		

Part III **Social Security Tax Adjustment** (Use the tax rate in effect during the period(s) corrected. You must also complete Part IV.)

	(a) Period Corrected (For quarterly returns, enter date quarter ended. For annual returns, enter year.)	(b) Wages Previously Reported for Period	(c) Correct Wages for Period	(d) Tips Previously Reported for Period	(e) Correct Tips for Period	(f) Social Security Tax Adjustment
1						
2						
3						
4						
5	**Totals.** If more than one page, enter totals on first page only . ▶					
6	**Net social security tax adjustment.** If more than one page, enter total of **all** columns (f) on first page only. Enter here and on the appropriate line of the return with which you file this form . . ▶	6				
7	**Net wage adjustment.** If more than one page, enter total of **all** lines 7 on first page only. If line 5(c) is smaller than line 5(b), enter difference in parentheses . . . . ▶	7				
8	**Net tip adjustment.** If more than one page, enter total of **all** lines 8 on first page only. If line 5(e) is smaller than line 5(d), enter difference in parentheses . . . . ▶	8				

For Paperwork Reduction Act Notice, see page 4.   Cat. No. 11242O   Form **941c** (Rev. 10-2003)

Part IV   Medicare Tax Adjustment

(a) Period Corrected (For quarterly returns, enter date quarter ended. For annual returns, enter year.)	(b) Wages and Tips Previously Reported for Period	(c) Correct Wages and Tips for Period	(d) Medicare Tax Adjustment
1			
2			
3			
4			

5 **Totals.** If more than one page, enter totals on first page only ▶

6 **Net Medicare tax adjustment.** If more than one page, enter total of **all** columns (d) on first page only. Enter here and on the appropriate line of the return with which you file this form ▶ **6**

7 **Net wage and tip adjustment.** If more than one page, enter total of **all** lines 7 on first page only. If line 5(c) is smaller than line 5(b), enter difference in parentheses ▶ **7**

Part V   **Explanation of Adjustments**

General Instructions

Purpose of form. Use Form 941c to provide background information and certifications supporting **prior period** adjustments to income, social security, and Medicare taxes reported on Form 941, 941-M, 941-SS, 943, or 945. File it with the tax return on which you are claiming the adjustment (Form 941, 943, 945, etc.). You may use Form 941c even though you filed the original return on magnetic media or electronically.

Do not use Form 941c as a supporting statement for current period adjustments (e.g., adjustment for uncollected employee share of social security and Medicare taxes on tips). **No supporting statement is required for the fractions-of-cents and third-party sick pay adjustments.** See your form instructions.

Income tax withholding errors. Generally, you are **not** permitted to correct income tax withholding errors made in a **prior calendar year.** However, you may make an adjustment to correct an **administrative error** in a prior year. Refer to **Circular E (Pub. 15),** Employer's Tax Guide, for more information on correcting administrative errors.

More information. See Circular E (Pub. 15), **Circular A (Pub. 51),** Agricultural Employer's Tax Guide, or your form instructions for more information about adjustments.

How to use Form 941c. Form 941c is **not** an amended return and **must never be filed separately.** You must make adjustments on the return (e.g., Form 941) for the period during which you **discovered** the error. There is no limit to the number of adjustments that you can make, and these adjustments can be for corrections to more than one prior period. However, if you filed two or more types of tax returns that need correction (for example, Form 941 and Form 943), use a **separate** Form 941c for each type of return. The net adjustment increases or decreases your tax liability for the period in which the error was discovered and adjusted.

If your adjustment(s) results in an overpayment, you may apply for a refund using **Form 843,** Claim for Refund and Request for Abatement, instead of making an adjustment as discussed above. If you choose to file Form 843, you will receive a refund check (with interest) instead of reducing your current employment tax liability (no interest). When filing Form 843, attach Form 941c or an equivalent statement.

If you did not file a return for one or more return periods, **do not** use Form 941c to report the information. Instead, file the required returns.

Corrections not required. You are not required to correct errors previously reported on the Summary of Federal Tax Liability (e.g., line 17, Form 941, or line 15, Form 943) or on Schedule B (Form 941), Form 943-A or Form 945-A. Also, you are not required to correct amounts previously reported on lines 1 or 2 of Form 941 or Form 941-M; or line 1 of Form 941-SS or Form 943.

Statute of limitations. Generally, you may make an adjustment only within three years of the return due date or the date the return was filed, whichever is later. For purposes of the statute of limitations, the due date of Forms 941, 941-M, 941-SS, 943, and 945 is April 15 of the year after the close of the tax year. For example, the four quarterly Forms 941 filed for 2001 are all treated as due on April 15, 2002. If they were filed on or before April 15, 2002, adjustments could be made for any of the quarterly returns for 2001 until April 15, 2005.

Specific Instructions

Complete all applicable columns on the line for each return period that you are correcting. Show the total amount paid to all employees, not the amount for each individual employee. If you need more space, use additional Forms 941c. If you use additional Forms 941c as continuation pages, be sure that the total and net adjustment lines on the first form include the totals from the continuation pages. These lines are line 5 of Part II, lines 5 through 8 of Part III, and lines 5 through 7 of Part IV.

Line A. Check the box for the return that you are adjusting. Check **only** one box. Use a **separate** Form 941c for each type of return (e.g., Form 941 and Form 945).

Line B. Show the return period in which you are reporting tax adjustment(s). For example, if you are making an adjustment on Form 941 for the quarter ending June 30, 2003, enter 06-2003. File Form 941c with the return for this period. **Do not** show the return period(s) being corrected in this entry space.

Line C. Enter the date that you **discovered** the error(s). If you are making more than one correction and the errors were not discovered at the same time, leave line C blank and explain in Part V. The date that you discover the error(s) is the date that your tax liability increases or decreases. Your deposits for this date must be adjusted accordingly. See the related return instructions for more information.

Part I—Signature and certification. Part I applies to wages only. If any adjustment is for an overpayment, it cannot be processed unless you check at least one box in Part I and you sign the certification. If you obtained written consents or statements from some employees but you could not locate or secure the cooperation of the remaining employees, check **both** the second and third boxes. Provide a summary in Part V of the amount of the adjustments for both the employees who provided statements and for those who did not.

You may make an adjustment for both the employer and employee shares of social security and Medicare taxes for those employees who provided the required written statement. But you may make adjustments for only the employer's share for those employees who did not provide statements.

Part II—Income tax withholding (including backup withholding) adjustment. Use this part to correct income tax withholding (including backup withholding) information that you previously reported. Show the total amount of tax withheld, not the amount withheld from each individual.

After the end of the year, you **cannot adjust** the amounts reported as **income tax withheld** (including backup withholding) **unless** it is to correct an **administrative error.** An administrative error is any error that does not change the amount of income tax that was actually withheld. For example, if the total income tax actually withheld was incorrectly reported due to a mathematical computation or transposition error, this is an administrative error.

Except to correct an administrative error, you will **not** be allowed a refund or credit for any **prior year** overpayment of income tax withheld (including backup withholding). This is because the amount of withholding shown on **Form W-2,** Wage and Tax Statement, **Form W-2G,** Certain Gambling Winnings, or Form 1099, is used as a credit on the employee's or income recipient's income tax return (Form 1040, etc.). If you are making an administrative error adjustment for a period during a prior calendar year, provide an explanation in Part V.

Part III—Social security tax adjustment. Use this part to correct social security wages and tips information that you reported in an earlier period. You may make corrections to social security taxes reported in prior calendar years as long as the statute of limitations has not expired (see **Statute of limitations** on page 3). If you are **reducing** social security taxes, be sure to read and check the appropriate boxes in Part I.

Because Form W-2 is used by the Social Security Administration (SSA) to post an employee's social security wages and tips to his or her earnings record, you must file a **Form W-2c,** Corrected Wage and Tax Statement, with the SSA and give copies to the employee for any social security correction made after you filed his or her Form W-2 with the SSA. **Do not** send Form 941c (or a copy) to the SSA with Form(s) W-2c.

Part IV—Medicare tax adjustment. Use this part to correct Medicare wages and tips information that you reported in an earlier period. You may make corrections to Medicare taxes reported in prior calendar years as long as the statute of limitations has not expired (see **Statute of limitations** on page 3). If you are **reducing** Medicare taxes, be sure to read and check the appropriate boxes in Part I.

You must file a Form W-2c with the SSA and give copies to the employee for any Medicare correction made after you filed Form W-2 with the SSA.

Paperwork Reduction Act Notice. We ask for the information on this form to carry out the Internal Revenue laws of the United States. You are required to give us the information. We need it to ensure that you are complying with these laws and to allow us to figure and collect the right amount of tax.

You are not required to provide the information requested on a form that is subject to the Paperwork Reduction Act unless the form displays a valid OMB control number. Books or records relating to a form or its instructions must be retained as long as their contents may become material in the administration of any Internal Revenue law. Generally, tax returns and return information are confidential, as required by Code section 6103.

The time needed to complete and file this form will vary depending on individual circumstances. The estimated average time is 9 hours and 12 minutes.

If you have comments concerning the accuracy of this time estimate or suggestions for making this form simpler, we would be happy to hear from you. You can write to the IRS at the address shown in the Privacy Act and Paperwork Reduction Act Notice in the instructions of the tax return with which you file this form.

Form **941-M for 2005:** Employer's Monthly Federal Tax Return

(Rev. March 2005) Department of the Treasury — Internal Revenue Service

OMB No. 1545-0718

▶ **Do not** file this form unless instructed to do so by the IRS.

Employer identification number [ ][ ] – [ ][ ][ ][ ][ ][ ]

Name (not your trade name)

Trade name (if any)

Address

Number Street Suite or room number

City State ZIP code

Report for this Month ...
(Check ONE month only.)

☐ Jan. ☐ Feb. ☐ March

☐ April ☐ May ☐ June

☐ July ☐ August ☐ Sept.

☐ Oct. ☐ Nov. ☐ Dec.

Read the separate instructions before you fill out this form. Please type or print within the boxes.

Part 1: Answer these questions for this month.

1 Number of employees who received wages, tips, or other compensation for the pay period including: *Mar. 12* (Quarter 1), *June 12* (Quarter 2), *Sept. 12* (Quarter 3), *Dec. 12* (Quarter 4) **1**

2 Wages, tips, and other compensation **2**

3 Total income tax withheld from wages, tips, and other compensation **3**

4 If no wages, tips, and other compensation are subject to social security or Medicare tax . . ☐ Check and go to line 6.

5 Taxable social security and Medicare wages and tips:

	Column 1		Column 2
5a Taxable social security wages		× .124 =	
5b Taxable social security tips		× .124 =	
5c Taxable Medicare wages & tips		× .029 =	

5d Total social security and Medicare taxes (*Column 2,* lines 5a + 5b + 5c = line 5d) . **5d**

6 Total taxes before adjustments (lines 3 + 5d = line 6) **6**

7 Tax adjustments (If your answer is a negative number, write it in brackets.):

7a Current month's fractions of cents . . . .

7b Current month's sick pay . . . .

7c Current month's adjustments for tips and group-term life insurance

7d Current year's income tax withholding (Attach Form 941c) . . .

7e Prior quarters' social security and Medicare taxes (Attach Form 941c)

7f Special additions to federal income tax (reserved use) . . . . .

7g Special additions to social security and Medicare (reserved use)

7h Total adjustments (Combine all amounts: lines 7a through 7g.) **7h**

8 Total taxes after adjustments (Combine lines 6 and 7h.) **8**

9 Advance earned income credit (EIC) payments made to employees **9**

10 Total taxes after adjustment for advance EIC (lines 8 – 9 = line 10) **10**

11 Total deposits for this month, including overpayment applied from a prior month . . . **11**

12 Balance due (lines 10 – 11 = line 12) Make checks payable to the *United States Treasury* . . **12**

13 Overpayment (If line 11 is more than line 10, write the difference here.) Check one ☐ Apply to next return.
☐ Send a refund.

Next ➡

For Privacy Act and Paperwork Reduction Act Notice, see the separate instructions. Cat. No. 17013R Form **941-M** (Rev. 3-2005)

Name *(not your trade name)*		Employer identification number

Part 2: Tell us about your deposit schedule for this month.

14 Record of Federal Tax Liability and Deposits (Read the instructions for this line.)

	Tax Liability	Amount Deposited		Tax Liability	Amount Deposited		Tax Liability	Amount Deposited
Overpayment from previous month . . . . ▶								
1			12			23		
2			13			24		
3			14			25		
4			15			26		
5			16			27		
6			17			28		
7			18			29		
8			19			30		
9			20			31		
10			21					
11			22					

a Total tax liability for the month (must equal line 10) **14a**

b Total deposits for the month (including overpayment from previous month) . . . **14b**

15 Copy the amount shown on line 14b to line 11.

Part 3: Tell us about your business. If a question does NOT apply to your business, leave it blank.

16 If your business has closed and you do not have to file returns in the future . . . . ☐ Check here, and

enter the final date you paid wages ☐ / /

17 If you are a seasonal employer and you do not have to file a return for every month of the year . . . ☐ Check here.

Part 4: May we contact your third-party designee?

Do you want to allow an employee, a paid tax preparer, or another person to discuss this return with the IRS? See the instructions for details.

☐ **Yes.** Designee's name

Phone ( ) – Personal Identification Number (PIN) ☐ ☐ ☐ ☐ ☐

☐ **No.**

Part 5: Sign here

Under penalties of perjury, I declare that I have examined this return, including accompanying schedules and statements, and to the best of my knowledge and belief, it is true, correct, and complete.

X

Sign your name here

Print name and title

Date / / Phone ( ) –

Part 6: For paid preparers only *(optional)*

Preparer's signature

Firm's name

Address

EIN

ZIP code

Date / / Phone ( ) – SSN/PTIN

☐ Check if you are self-employed.

Form **941-M** (Rev. 3-2005)

Instructions for Form 941-M

 Department of the Treasury
Internal Revenue Service

(Rev. March 2005)

Employer's Monthly Federal Tax Return

Section references are to the Internal Revenue Code unless otherwise indicated.

What's New

Revised form and instructions. We revised Form 941-M and the Instructions for Form 941-M to conform with the redesign of Form 941 and the Instructions for Form 941.

Social security wage base for 2005. Stop withholding social security tax after an employee reaches **$90,000** in taxable wages. (There is no limit on the amount of wages subject to Medicare tax.)

General Instructions

Purpose of form. Use Form 941-M to report monthly: (a) income tax you withheld from wages, tips, distributions from **nonqualified** pension plans (including nongovernmental section 457(b) plans), supplemental unemployment compensation benefits, and third-party payments of sick pay; and (b) social security and Medicare taxes. If you report just one kind of tax, fill in only the lines that apply.

 *This form is **not** for general public use and should **only** be filed directly with an IRS compliance representative.*

Who must file. File Form 941-M if you are required to report income taxes withheld, social security taxes, and Medicare taxes on a monthly basis by an IRS compliance representative. The IRS may require monthly returns on this form and payments of tax from any employer who has not complied with the requirements for the filing of returns or the paying or depositing of taxes reported on quarterly returns. **Do not** file monthly returns unless you received written notification from the IRS to do so. A preaddressed return envelope and blank Form 941-M will be mailed to you before your first monthly return is due and for each month thereafter. If you no longer expect to pay amounts subject to tax reportable on Form 941-M, check the box on line 16 and enter the date that you last paid wages.

When to file. Form 941-M for any month is due by the 15th day of the following month. If the due date for filing a return falls on a Saturday, Sunday, or legal holiday, you may file the return on the next business day.

Where to file. File Form 941-M, with any payment due, **using the preaddressed envelope** furnished to you. Keep a duplicate Form 941-M for your records.

Forms W-4. You are required to send to the IRS copies of any Forms W-4 received during the month from employees still employed by you at the end of the month claiming: (a) more than 10 withholding allowances or (b) exemption from income tax withholding if their wages are expected to exceed $200 a week. For details, see section 9 of Pub. 15 (Circular E), Employer's Tax Guide. Do not send any Forms W-4P or W-4S to the IRS.

Form W-5. Each eligible employee wishing to receive any advance earned income credit (EIC) payments must give you a completed Form W-5, Earned Income Credit Advance Payment Certificate. The employer's requirement to notify certain employees about the EIC can be met by giving each eligible employee Notice 797, Possible Federal Tax Refund Due to the Earned Income Credit (EIC). See section 10 of Pub. 15 (Circular E) and Pub. 596, Earned Income Credit (EIC), for more information.

Form W-2. By January 31, furnish Forms W-2 to employees who worked for you during the previous year. If an employee stops working for you before the end of the year, furnish Form W-2 to the employee any time after employment ends but no later than January 31 of the following year. However, if the employee asks you for Form W-2, furnish the completed form within 30 days after the request or the final wage payment, whichever is later. Send Copy A of all Forms W-2, Wage and Tax Statement, issued for the year with a Form W-3, Transmittal of Wage and Tax Statements, filed on paper, or reports filed on magnetic diskette, to the Social Security Administration (SSA) by the last day of February. If you file Forms W-2 electronically (not by magnetic diskette) file them with SSA by the last day of March.

 If you file a final return on Form 941-M, you are also required to furnish Form W-2 to your employees by the last day of the month in which the final Form 941-M is due. File Copy A of Forms W-2 and Form W-3 with the Social Security Administration by the last day of the month following the month your final Form 941-M was due. See the Instructions for Forms W-2 and W-3 for details

Penalties and interest. There are penalties for filing a return late and paying or depositing taxes late, unless there is reasonable cause. If you file or pay late, attach an explanation to your return. There are also penalties for failure to: (a) furnish Forms W-2 to employees and file copies with the SSA and (b) deposit taxes when required. (Do not attach an explanation of why the return is late to Forms W-2 sent to the SSA.) In addition, there are penalties for willful failure to file returns and pay taxes when due and for filing false returns or submitting bad checks. Interest is charged on taxes paid late at the rate set by law. See Pub. 15 (Circular E) for additional information.

 A trust fund recovery penalty may apply if income, social security, and Medicare taxes that must be withheld are not withheld or are not paid. This penalty is the full amount of any unpaid trust fund tax. This penalty may apply to you if these unpaid taxes cannot be immediately collected from the employer or business. The trust fund recovery penalty may be imposed on all persons who are determined by the IRS to be responsible for collecting, accounting for, and paying over these taxes, and who acted willfully in not doing so.

*A **responsible person** can be an officer or employee of a corporation, a partner or employee of a partnership, an accountant, a volunteer director/trustee, or any employee of a sole proprietorship. A responsible person also may include one who signs checks for the business or otherwise has authority to cause the spending of business funds. **Willfully** means voluntary, consciously, and intentionally.*

Related publications. Pub. 15 (Circular E) explains the rules for withholding, paying, depositing, and reporting federal income tax, social security and Medicare taxes, and federal unemployment (FUTA) tax on wages. See Pub. 15-A, Employer's Supplemental Tax Guide, for information on sick pay paid by third-party payers. Pub. 51 (Circular A), Agricultural Employer's Tax Guide, explains rules for employers of farmworkers. These publications are available by calling 1-800-TAX-FORM (1-800-829-3676). See Pub. 15 (Circular E) for additional methods of obtaining forms and publications.

Reconciliation of Forms 941-M and W-3. Certain amounts reported on the monthly Forms 941-M for the year should agree with the Form W-2 totals reported on Form W-3. **The amounts that should agree are:** income tax withholding, social security

Cat. No. 39535W

wages, social security tips, Medicare wages and tips, and the advance earned income credit (EIC).

If the totals do not agree, the IRS may require you to explain the differences and correct any errors. See section 12 of Pub. 15 (Circular E) for details.

Specific Instructions

Part 1: Answer these questions for this month

Line 1—Number of employees. For March, June, September, and December, report the number of employees you paid for the pay period that includes the 12th of the month. Leave line 1 blank for all other months. Do not include household employees, employees who received no pay during the pay period, pensioners, or active members of the Armed Forces. An entry of 250 or more on line 1 indicates that you must file Forms W-2 electronically or on magnetic diskette. Call the SSA at 1-800-772-6270 or access the SSA website at *www.socialsecurity.gov/employer* for more information on electronic or magnetic diskette filing of Forms W-2.

Line 2—Wages, tips, and other compensation. Enter amounts on line 2 that would also be included in box 1 of your employees' Form W-2. See the Instructions for Forms W-2 and W-3 for details.

If you get timely notice from your insurance carrier concerning the amount of third-party sick pay that it paid to your employees, include the sick pay on line 2.

Line 3—Total income tax withheld from wages, tips, and other compensation. Enter the income tax that you withheld (or were required to withhold) on wages, tips, taxable fringe benefits, sick pay, other compensation, and supplemental unemployment compensation benefits. Also include here any excise taxes that you were required to withhold on golden parachute payments (section 4999).

Line 4—If no wages, tips, or other compensation are subject to social security or Medicare tax. If no wages, tips, or compensation on line 2 are subject to social security or Medicare tax, check the box on line 4. If this question does not apply to you, leave the box blank. For more information about exempt wages, see section 15 of Pub. 15 (Circular E) and section 4 of Pub. 15-A, Employer's Supplemental Tax Guide.

Line 5a—Taxable social security wages. Enter the total wages subject to social security taxes that you paid to your employees during the month. Also include any sick pay and taxable fringe benefits subject to social security taxes. Enter the amount before deductions. Do not include tips on this line. Stop reporting for any employee whose wages (including tips) reach $90,000 for 2005. However, continue to withhold **income tax** for the whole year on wages and tips even when the limit of $90,000 is reached. See the **Line 5c** instructions for Medicare wages and tips.

Line 5b—Taxable social security tips. Enter all tips that your employees reported during the month until tips and wages for an employee reach $90,000 in 2005. Do this even if you were not able to withhold the employee tax (6.2%). Report the uncollected employee's share of social security tax on line 7c. Also see section 6 of Pub. 15 (Circular E).

An employee must report to you cash tips, including tips you paid the employee for charge customers, totaling $20 or more in a month by the 10th day of the next month. The employee may use Form 4070, Employee's Report of Tips to Employer, or give you a written statement.

Do not include allocated tips on this line. Instead, report them on Form 8027, Employer's Annual Information Return of Tip Income and Allocated Tips. Allocated tips are not reportable on Form 941-M and are not subject to withholding of income, social security, or Medicare tax.

Line 5c—Taxable Medicare wages and tips. Report all wages and tips subject to Medicare tax. Also include any sick pay and taxable fringe benefits subject to Medicare tax. See section 5 in Pub. 15 (Circular E) for information on types of wages subject to Medicare tax. If none of the payments are subject to Medicare tax, enter "-0-."

Include all tips that your employees reported during the month, even if you were not able to withhold the employee tax (1.45%). Report the uncollected employee's share of Medicare tax on line 7c. Also see section 6 of Pub. 15 (Circular E).

Line 7—Tax adjustments. See the Instructions for Form 941 for more information.

Current period adjustments. In certain cases, amounts reported as social security and Medicare taxes on lines 5a–5c must be adjusted to arrive at your correct tax liability. See section 13 of Pub. 15 (Circular E) for information on the following adjustments:

- Fractions-of-cents adjustment.
- Adjustment for the **employee share** of social security and Medicare taxes withheld by a third-party sick pay payer.
- Adjustment for the uncollected **employee share** of social security and Medicare taxes on tips.
- Adjustment for the **employee share** of social security and Medicare taxes on group-term life insurance premiums paid for former employees.

Prior period adjustments. Use lines 7d–7g to correct errors in taxes reported on an earlier return, including errors from a previous month of the current quarter. For example, if you are correcting an error in social security and Medicare taxes reported on your July 2005 Form 941-M and you found the error in September 2005, report the adjustment using line 7e of your September 2005 Form 941-M.

If you report both an underpayment and an overpayment, show only the net difference.

Explain any prior period adjustments on an attached Form 941c, Supporting Statement To Correct Information.

Line 9—Advance earned income credit (EIC) payments made to employees. Enter advance EIC payments made to employees. Your eligible employees may elect to receive part of the EIC as an advance payment. Eligible employees who have a qualifying child must give you a completed Form W-5 stating that they qualify for the EIC. Once the employee gives you a signed and completed Form W-5, you must make the advance EIC payments. Advance EIC payments are generally made from withheld income tax and employee and employer social security and Medicare taxes. See section 10 of Pub. 15 (Circular E) and Pub. 596 for more information on advance EIC payments and eligibility requirements.

If the amount of your advance EIC payments exceeds your total taxes (line 8) for the month, you may claim a refund of the overpayment or elect to have the credit applied to your return for the following month. Provide a statement with your return identifying the amount of excess payment(s) and the pay period(s) in which it was paid. See section 10 of Pub. 15 (Circular E).

Line 12—Undeposited taxes due. You do not have to pay if line 15 is under $1.

 If you fail to make deposits as required and instead pay the taxes with Form 941-M, you may be subject to a penalty.

Line 13—Overpayment. If you deposited more than the correct amount for a month, you can have the overpayment refunded (applies only to March, June, September, and December Forms 941-M) or applied to your next return. Show any amount applied in the Record of Federal Tax Liability and Deposits on your next return. If line 13 is under $1, we will send a refund or apply it to your next return only on written request

-2-

Part 2: Tell us about your deposit schedule for this month

Special deposit account. Do not make deposits using the Electronic Federal Tax Payment System (EFTPS) or Form 8109, Federal Tax Deposit Coupon, and **do not** complete line 14, Record of Federal Tax Liability and Deposits, if you are required to have a special deposit account under section 7512(b). If you have received, by hand delivery, Form 2481, Notice To Make Special Deposits of Taxes, you are required to deposit in a separate bank account any taxes collected or required by law to be collected. Your deposit must be made not later than the end of the **second banking day** after any taxes were required to be collected from your employees. The taxes deposited must be kept in the account until paid with any employer tax that may be due. The account must be designated as a special fund in trust for the United States, payable to the "United States Treasury" by you as trustee. For the definition of the term "bank," see Form 2481.

Federal tax deposits. If you are not required to have a special deposit account, in general, you must deposit your tax liability at an authorized financial institution with Form 8109 or by using EFTPS. For more information on the deposit rules and the electronic deposit requirements, see section 11 of Pub. 15 (Circular E).

Line 14—Record of Federal Tax Liability and Deposits. If you are required to deposit taxes using the Federal Tax Deposit System, complete both columns of the record. In the tax liability column, include income tax withheld plus both the employer and employee shares of social security and Medicare taxes minus advance EIC payment (if any) for each date of payment (payday). Enter each deposit amount in the numbered entry space corresponding to the date of deposit.

Line 14a—Total tax liability for the month. The amount of this line must equal line 10 (Total taxes after adjustment for advance EIC). Otherwise, you may be subject to a penalty for failure to make deposits of taxes.

Part 3: Tell us about your business

In Part 3, answer only those questions that apply to your business. If a question does not apply, leave it blank and go to Part 4.

Line 16—If Your Business Has Closed . . .

If you go out of business or stop paying wages, you must file a **final return**. To tell IRS that a particular Form 941 is your final return, check the box on line 16 and enter the date you last paid wages in the space provided.

Line 17—If You Are a Seasonal Employer . . .

If you hire employees seasonally—such as for summer or winter only—check the box on line 17. Checking the box tells IRS not to expect Form 941-M from you every month because you have not paid wages regularly. However, you must check the box **every time** you file a Form 941-M. Also, be sure to check the box in the upper right corner of page 1 of Form 941-M that corresponds to the month reported.

Part 4: May we contact your third-party designee?

If you want to allow an employee, a paid tax preparer, or another person to discuss your Form 941-M with the IRS, check the "Yes" box in Part 4. Then tell us the name, phone number, and the five-digit personal identification number (PIN) of the specific person to contact—not the name of the firm who prepared your tax return. The designee may choose any five numbers as his or her PIN.

By checking "Yes," you authorize IRS to call the person you named (your designee) with any questions we may have while we process your return. You also authorize your designee to:
• give us any information that is missing from your return,
• call us for information about processing your return, and
• respond to certain IRS notices that you have shared with your designee about math errors and return preparation. IRS will **not** send notices to your designee.

You are **not authorizing** your designee to bind you to anything (including additional tax liability) or to otherwise represent you before the IRS. If you want to expand your designee's authorization, see Pub. 947, Practice Before the IRS and Power of Attorney.

The authorization will automatically **expire** one year from the due date for filing your Form 941-M. If you or your designee want to terminate the authorization, write to the IRS office for your locality using the "Without a payment" address under *Where Should You File* on page 4 in the instructions for Form 941.

Part 5: Sign here—
Who Must Sign the Form 941?

Form 941-M must be signed as follows.

• **Sole proprietorship—** The individual who owns the business.

• **Corporation (including an LLC treated as a corporation)—** The president, vice president, or other principal officer.

• **Partnership (including an LLC treated as a partnership) or unincorporated organization—** A responsible and duly authorized member or officer having knowledge of its affairs.

• **Single member limited liability company (LLC) treated as a disregarded entity—** The owner of the limited liability company (LLC).

• **Trust or estate—** The fiduciary.

Form 941-M may also be signed by a duly authorized agent of the taxpayer if a valid power of attorney has been filed.

Part 6: For Paid Preparers Only (optional)

Complete Part 6 if you were paid to prepare Form 941-M and are not an employee of the filing entity. Sign in the space provided and give the filer a copy of the return in addition to the copy to be filed with the IRS. Do not complete Part 6 if you are filing the return as a reporting agent and have a valid Form 8655, Reporting Agent Authorization, on file with the IRS. You are not required to complete this section.

How to Order Forms and Publications from the IRS

 Call 1-800-829-3676.

 Visit the IRS website at *www.irs.gov*.

-3-

Privacy Act and Paperwork Reduction Act Notice

We ask for the information on Form 941-M to carry out the Internal Revenue laws of the United States. We need it to figure and collect the right amount of tax. Subtitle C, Employment Taxes, of the Internal Revenue Code imposes employment taxes on wages, including income tax withholding. Form 941-M is used to determine the amount of the taxes that you owe. Section 6011 requires you to provide the requested information if the tax is applicable to you. Section 6109 requires you to provide your employer identification number (EIN). If you fail to provide this information in a timely manner, you may be subject to penalties and interest. If you do not file this information, or provide incomplete or fraudulent information, you may be subject to penalties and/or criminal prosecution.

You are not required to provide the information requested on a form that is subject to the Paperwork Reduction Act unless the form displays a valid OMB control number. Books or records relating to a form or its instructions must be retained as long as their contents may become material in the administration of any Internal Revenue law.

Generally, tax returns and return information are confidential, as required by section 6103. However, section 6103 allows or requires the IRS to disclose or give the information shown on your tax return to others as described in the Code. For example, we may disclose your tax information to the Department of Justice for civil and criminal litigation, and to cities, states, and the District of Columbia for use in administering their tax laws. We may also disclose this information to other countries under a tax treaty, to federal and state agencies to enforce federal nontax criminal laws, or to federal law enforcement and intelligence agencies to combat terrorism.

The time needed to complete and file Form 941-M will vary depending on individual circumstances. The estimated average time is: Recordkeeping, 14 hrs., 35 min.; Learning about the law or the form, 1 hr., 0 min.; Preparing, copying, assembling, and sending the form to the IRS, 1 hr., 16 min. If you have comments concerning the accuracy of these time estimates or suggestions for making this form simpler, we would be happy to hear from you. You can write to: Internal Revenue Service, Tax Products Coordinating Committee, SE:W:CAR:MP:T:T:SP, 1111 Constitution Ave. NW, IR-6406, Washington DC 20224.

Do not send Form 941-M to this address. Instead, use the preaddressed envelope furnished to you.

Appendix

Form **943**

Department of the Treasury
Internal Revenue Service

Employer's Annual Federal Tax Return for Agricultural Employees

▶ See the separate Instructions for Form 943 for information on completing this return.

OMB No. 1545-0035

2005

Enter state code for state in which deposits were made **only** if different from state in address to the right ▶ (see the separate instructions). If you do not have to file returns in the future, check here . . . . ▶ ☐

Name (as distinguished from trade name)	Calendar year
Trade name, if any	Employer identification number (EIN)
Address (number and street)	City, state, and ZIP code

If address is different from prior return, check here. ▶ ☐

1	Number of agricultural employees employed in the pay period that includes March 12, 2005 ▶	1
2	Total wages subject to social security tax (see separate instructions) 2	
3	Social security tax (multiply line 2 by 12.4% (.124))	3
4	Total wages subject to Medicare tax (see separate instructions) . . . 4	
5	Medicare tax (multiply line 4 by 2.9% (.029)).	5
6	Federal income tax withheld (see separate instructions)	6
7	Total taxes before adjustments (add lines 3, 5, and 6)	7
8	Adjustment to taxes (see separate instructions).	8
9	Total taxes (line 7 as adjusted by line 8)	9
10	Advance earned income credit (EIC) payments made to employees, if any (see separate instructions)	10
11	Net taxes (subtract line 10 from line 9)	11
12	**Total deposits** for 2005, including overpayment applied from 2004 return. . . .	12
13	**Balance due** (subtract line 12 from line 11) (see separate instructions) . . . . . ▶	13
14	**Overpayment** If line 12 is more than line 11, enter here ▶ $ and check if to be: ☐ Applied to next return or ☐ Refunded.

● All filers: If line 11 is less than $2,500, **do not** complete line 15 or Form 943-A.
● Semiweekly schedule depositors: Complete Form 943-A and check here ▶ ☐   ● Monthly schedule depositors: Complete line 15 and check here ▶ ☐

| 15 | **Monthly Summary of Federal Tax Liability. (Do not** complete if you were a semiweekly schedule depositor.) |

	Tax liability for month		Tax liability for month		Tax liability for month
A January		F June		K November	
B February		G July		L December	
C March		H August		M Total liability for year (add lines A through L)	
D April		I September			
E May		J October			

Third-Party Designee
Do you want to allow another person to discuss this return with the IRS (see separate instructions)? ☐ **Yes.** Complete the following. ☐ **No.**
Designee's name ▶   Phone no. ▶ (   )   Personal identification number (PIN) ▶ ☐☐☐☐☐

Sign Here
Under penalties of perjury, I declare that I have examined this return, including accompanying schedules and statements, and to the best of my knowledge and belief, it is true, correct, and complete.
Signature ▶   Print Your Name and Title ▶   Date ▶

For Privacy Act and Paperwork Reduction Act Notice, see the separate instructions.   ▼ DETACH HERE ▼   Cat. No. 11252K   Form **943** (2005)

- -

Form **943-V**
Department of the Treasury
Internal Revenue Service

Payment Voucher

▶ Use this voucher when making a payment with your return.

2005

Do not send cash and do not staple your payment to this voucher. Make your check or money order payable to the "United States Treasury." Be sure to enter your employer identification number (EIN), "Form 943," and "2005" on your payment.

1 Enter your employer identification number (EIN).	2 Enter the amount of your payment. ▶	Dollars	Cents
	3 Enter your business name (individual name for sole proprietors).		
	Enter your address.		
	Enter your city, state, and ZIP code.		

A-189

Instructions for Form 943-V, Payment Voucher

Purpose of Form

Complete Form 943-V, Payment Voucher, if you are making a payment with Form 943, Employer's Annual Federal Tax Return for Agricultural Employees. We will use the completed voucher to credit your payment more promptly and accurately, and to improve our service to you.

If you have your return prepared by a third party and make a payment with that return, please provide Form 943-V to the return preparer.

Making Payment With Form 943

Make a payment with your 2005 Form 943 **only if:**

● Your net taxes for the year (line 11 on Form 943) are less than $2,500 and the taxes are paid in full with a timely filed return or

● You are a monthly schedule depositor making a payment in accordance with the *Accuracy of Deposits Rule.* (See section 7 of Pub. 51 (Circular A), Agricultural Employer's Tax Guide, for details.) This amount may be $2,500 or more.

Otherwise, you must deposit the amount at an authorized financial institution or by electronic funds transfer. (See section 7 of Pub. 51 (Circular A) for deposit instructions.) **Do not** use Form 943-V to make federal tax deposits.

Caution. *If you pay an amount with Form 943 that should have been deposited, you may be subject to a penalty. See* Deposit Penalties *in section 7 of Pub. 51 (Circular A).*

Specific Instructions

Box 1—Employer identification number (EIN). If you do not have an EIN, apply for one on Form SS-4, Application for Employer Identification Number, and write "Applied For" and the date you applied in this entry space.

Box 2—Amount paid. Enter the amount paid with Form 943.

Box 3—Name and address. Enter your business name and address as shown on Form 943.

● Enclose your check or money order made payable to the "United States Treasury." Be sure also to enter your EIN, "Form 943," and "2005" on your check or money order. Do not send cash. Do not staple Form 943-V or your payment to the return (or to each other).

● Detach Form 943-V and send it with your payment and Form 943 to the address provided in the separate Instructions for Form 943.

Note. You **must** also complete the entity information above line 1 on Form 943.

2005

Department of the Treasury
Internal Revenue Service

Instructions for Form 943

Employer's Annual Federal Tax Return for Agricultural Employees

Section references are to the Internal Revenue Code unless otherwise noted.

What's New

Alternative signature method. Effective with returns filed after June 30, 2005, corporate officers or duly authorized agents may sign Form 943 by rubber stamp, mechanical device, or computer software program. For details and required documentation, see Rev. Proc. 2005-39. You can find Rev. Proc. 2005-39 on page 82 of Internal Revenue Bulletin 2005-28 at *www.irs.gov/pub/irs-irbs/irb05-28.pdf*.

Social security wage base for 2006. Stop withholding social security tax after an employee reaches the social security wage base for taxable wages. See *What's New* in Pub. 51 (Circular A), Agricultural Employer's Tax Guide, for the 2006 social security wage base.

Reminders

Correcting Form 943. If you discover an error on a previously filed Form 943, make the correction using Form 943 for the year in which you discovered the error and attach Form 941c, Supporting Statement to Correct Information. For example, in October 2005, you discover that you underreported $10,000 in social security and Medicare wages on your 2004 Form 943. Correct the error by showing $1,530 (15.3% × $10,000) on line 8 of your 2005 Form 943 and attaching a completed Form 941c. For details, see *Line 8—Adjustment to taxes* on page 3.

Electronic payment. Now, more than ever before, businesses can enjoy the benefits of paying their federal taxes electronically. Whether you rely on a tax professional or handle your own taxes, IRS offers you convenient programs to make it easier.

Spend less time and worry on taxes and more time running your business. Use Electronic Federal Tax Payment System (EFTPS) to your benefit.

For EFTPS, visit *www.eftps.gov* or call EFTPS Customer Service at 1-800-555-4477.

Use the electronic options available from IRS and make paying taxes easier.

How to get forms and publications. You can get most IRS forms and publications by accessing the IRS website at *www.irs.gov* or by calling the IRS at 1-800-TAX-FORM (1-800-829-3676).

Telephone help. You can call the IRS toll free at 1-800-829-4933 to order FTD coupons (Forms 8109) and for answers to your questions about completing Form 943, tax deposit rules, or obtaining an employer identification number (EIN).

Photographs of Missing Children

The Internal Revenue Service is a proud partner with the National Center for Missing and Exploited Children. Photographs of missing children selected by the Center may appear in instructions on pages that would otherwise be blank. You can help bring these children home by looking at the photographs and calling 1-800-THE-LOST (1-800-843-5678) if you recognize a child.

General Instructions

Purpose of form. Use Form 943 to report federal income tax withheld and employer and employee social security and Medicare taxes on wages paid to farmworkers.

If you have household employees working in your private home on your farm operated for a profit, they are not considered to be farm employees. To report social security, Medicare, and federal income tax withholding on the wages of household employees, you may either:
● File Schedule H (Form 1040), Household Employment Taxes, with your Form 1040 or
● Include the wages with your farm employees' wages on Form 943.

If you paid wages to a household employee in a home that is not on a for-profit farm, you must report the taxes on Schedule H. If you paid wages to other nonfarm workers, do not report these on Form 943. Report them on Form 941, Employer's Quarterly Federal Tax Return. See Pub. 926, Household Employer's Tax Guide, for more information about household employees.

Who must file. File Form 943 if you paid wages to one or more farmworkers and the wages were subject to social security and Medicare taxes or federal income tax withholding under the tests discussed below. For definitions of farmworkers and wages, see Pub. 51 (Circular A), Agricultural Employer's Tax Guide.

The $150 test or the $2,500 test. All cash wages that you pay to farmworkers are subject to social security and Medicare taxes and federal income tax withholding for any calendar year that you meet either of these tests:
● You pay an employee cash wages of $150 or more in a year for farmwork.
● The total (cash and noncash) wages that you pay to all farmworkers is $2,500 or more.

If the $2,500-or-more test for the group is not met, the $150-or-more test for an individual still applies.

Exceptions. Special rules apply to certain hand-harvest laborers who receive less than $150 in annual cash wages. For more information, see section 4 of Pub. 51 (Circular A).

When to file. For 2005, file Form 943 by January 31, 2006. However, if you made deposits on time in full payment of the taxes due for the year, you may file the return as late as February 10, 2006.

Final return. If you stop paying wages during the year and do not expect to pay wages again, file a final return for 2005. Be sure to mark the box above line 1 on the form indicating that you do not have to file returns in the

Cat. No. 25976L

future. If you later become liable for any of the taxes, notify the IRS.

Forms W-2 and W-3. By January 31, 2006, give Form W-2 to each employee who was working for you at the end of 2005. If an employee stops working for you before the end of the year, give him or her Form W-2 any time after employment ends but no later than January 31 of the following year. If the employee asks you for Form W-2, give him or her the completed form within 30 days of the request or the last wage payment, whichever is later.

Filing on paper forms. By February 28, 2006, send Copy A of all Forms W-2 with Form W-3 to the Social Security Administration (SSA) (if less than 250 paper forms). The address is in the Instructions for Forms W-2 and W-3.

Filing electronically. Visit the Social Security Administration's Employer Reporting Instructions and Information website at *www.socialsecurity.gov/employer* for information about electronic filing of Forms W-2. If you file electronically (not magnetic media), the due date is March 31, 2006.

Filing on magnetic media. If you are required to file 250 or more Forms W-2, you must file them on magnetic diskette (or electronically) instead of filing Copy A of Form W-2. See the Instructions for Forms W-2 and W-3 for more information. The due date for filing forms with the SSA on diskette is February 28, 2006.

Where to file. Find the state of your legal residence, principal place of business, office, or agency in the table that follows. Send your return to the "Internal Revenue Service" at the address listed for your location. No street address is needed.

Note. Where you file depends on whether or not you are including a payment. Be sure to use the correct address.

Connecticut, Delaware, District of Columbia, Illinois, Indiana, Kentucky, Maine, Maryland, Massachusetts, Michigan, New Hampshire, New Jersey, New York, North Carolina, Ohio, Pennsylvania, Rhode Island, South Carolina, Vermont, Virginia, West Virginia, Wisconsin	
Return without payment: Cincinnati, OH 45999-0008	**Return with payment:** P.O. Box 105094 Atlanta, GA 30348-5094

Alabama, Alaska, Arizona, Arkansas, California, Colorado, Florida, Georgia, Hawaii, Idaho, Iowa, Kansas, Louisiana, Minnesota, Mississippi, Missouri, Montana, Nebraska, Nevada, New Mexico, North Dakota, Oklahoma, Oregon, South Dakota, Tennessee, Texas, Utah, Washington, Wyoming	
Return without payment: Ogden, UT 84201-0008	**Return with payment:** P.O. Box 660587 Dallas, TX 75266-0587

If you have no legal residence or principal place of business in any state:	
Return without payment: Philadelphia, PA 19255-8526	**Return with payment:** P.O. Box 80107 Cincinnati, OH 45280-0007

Exception for exempt organizations and government entities. If you are filing Form 943 for an exempt organization or government entity (federal, state, local, or Indian tribal government), use the following addresses regardless of your location:
- *Return without payment:* Ogden, UT 84201-0008
- *Return with payment:* P.O. Box 660587, Dallas, TX 75266-0587

Reconciliation of Form 943 to Forms W-2 and W-3. Certain amounts reported on Form 943 for 2005 should

agree with the Form W-2, Wage and Tax Statement, totals reported on the 2005 Form W-3, Transmittal of Wage and Tax Statements. The amounts from Form 943 that should agree with the related boxes on Form W-3 are: federal income tax withheld (line 6 versus box 2), social security wages (line 2 versus box 3), Medicare wages and tips (line 4 versus box 5), and advance earned income credit payments (line 10 versus box 9). If the totals do not agree, the IRS may require you to explain any differences and correct any errors. Keep all records that show why the totals do not match. For more information, see section 12 of Pub. 51 (Circular A).

Depositing taxes. If your net taxes (line 11) are $2,500 or more for the year, you generally must deposit your tax liabilities at an authorized financial institution using Form 8109, Federal Tax Deposit Coupon, or by using the Electronic Federal Tax Payment System (EFTPS). See section 7 of Pub. 51 (Circular A), Agricultural Employer's Tax Guide, for information and rules concerning federal tax deposits and to determine your status as a monthly or semiweekly schedule depositor.

Penalties and interest. There are penalties for filing a return late and for paying or depositing taxes late, unless there is reasonable cause. There are also penalties for failure to (a) furnish Forms W-2 to employees and file copies with the SSA or (b) deposit taxes when required. See Pub. 51 (Circular A) for more information. In addition, there are penalties for willful failure to file returns and pay taxes when due and for filing false returns or submitting bad checks. Interest is charged on taxes paid late at the rate set by law.

If federal income, social security, and Medicare taxes that must be withheld (that is, trust fund taxes) are not withheld or are not paid to the United States Treasury, the trust fund recovery penalty may apply. The penalty is 100% of the unpaid trust fund tax. This penalty may apply to you if these unpaid taxes cannot be immediately collected from the employer or business. The trust fund recovery penalty may be imposed on all persons who are determined by the IRS to be responsible for collecting, accounting for, and paying over these taxes, and who acted willfully in not doing so. See section 7 of Pub. 51 (Circular A) for more information.

Preprinted name, EIN, and address. If your preprinted name, EIN, or address on Form 943 is not correct, cross it out and type or print the correct information. However, do not change any of the preprinted information on your Form 943-V, Payment Voucher.

Zero Wage return. If you received a preprinted Form 943 in the mail from the IRS and are not required to file because you paid no wages subject to social security or Medicare tax and withheld no federal income tax, write "NONE" on line 11, sign the return, and file it with the IRS. If you will not have to file Form 943 in the future, also check the box above line 1 at the left of your name and address.

Specific Instructions

State code. If you made your deposits by FTD coupon (Form 8109) or by using an EFTPS bank account in a state other than that shown in your address on Form 943, enter the state code for the state where you made deposits or initiated EFTPS transfers in the box provided in the upper-left corner of Form 943. Use the Postal Service two-letter state abbreviation as the state code.

-2-

Enter the code "MU" in the state code box if you deposit in more than one state. If you deposit in the same state as shown in your address, do not make an entry in this box.

Line 1—Number of agricultural employees. Enter the number of agricultural employees on your payroll during the pay period that included March 12, 2005. Do not include household employees, persons who received no pay during the pay period, pensioners, or members of the Armed Forces.

An entry of 250 or more on line 1 indicates that you must file Forms W-2 electronically or on magnetic diskette. Call the SSA at 1-800-772-6270 or access the SSA's Employer Reporting Instructions and Information website at *www.socialsecurity.gov/employer* for more information on electronic or diskette filing requirements.

Line 2—Total wages subject to social security tax. Enter the total cash wages subject to social security tax that you paid to your employees for farmwork during the calendar year. Enter the amount before deductions. Cash wages include checks, money orders, etc. Do not include (a) the value of noncash items such as food or lodging or (b) pay for services other than farmwork. See section 3 of Pub. 51 (Circular A) for more information. Do not report an employee's social security wages over $90,000 for 2005.

Line 4—Total wages subject to Medicare tax. Enter the total cash wages subject to Medicare tax that you paid to your employees for farmwork during the calendar year. Enter the amount before deductions. Do not include (a) the value of noncash items such as food or lodging or (b) pay for services other than farmwork. There is no limit on the amount of wages subject to Medicare tax.

Line 6—Federal income tax withheld. Enter federal income tax withheld on wages paid to your employees. Generally, you must withhold federal income tax from employees from whom you withhold social security and Medicare taxes. See sections 5 and 13 of Pub. 51 (Circular A) for more information on withholding rules.

Line 8—Adjustment to taxes. Use line 8 to:
• Adjust for rounding of fractions of cents,
• Correct errors in social security and Medicare taxes reported on a prior year return, and
• Correct an administrative error in reporting federal income tax withholding on a prior year return. See section 9 in Pub. 51 (Circular A). Use parentheses (if possible) to show a decrease to the amounts reported on lines 3 or 5.

Fractions of cents. If there is a small difference between net taxes (line 11) and total deposits (line 12), it may be caused by rounding to the nearest cent each time you computed payroll. This rounding occurs when you figure the amount of social security and Medicare tax to be withheld from each employee's wages. See Pub. 51 (Circular A) for details. If the fractions of cents adjustment is the only entry on line 8, write "Fractions Only" in the margin of Form 943.

Prior year adjustments. Prior year adjustments include errors in social security and Medicare taxes reported on earlier returns. If you report both an underpayment and an overpayment, show only the difference.

Because any amount shown on line 8 increases or decreases your tax liability, the adjustment must also be included on your Monthly Summary of Federal Tax Liability on Form 943 (line 15) or Form 943-A, Agricultural Employer's Record of Federal Tax Liability. For details on how to report adjustments on the Monthly Summary of

Federal Tax Liability, see the instructions for line 15, later, or the instructions for Form 943-A.

Explain any prior year adjustments on Form 941c, Supporting Statement To Correct Information, or attach a statement that shows the same information. Enter on Form 941c or include in the statement the total wages for all of your employees as previously reported and as corrected. **Do not** file Form 941c (or statement) separately from Form 943.

If you are adjusting an employee's social security or Medicare wages for a prior year, you must also file Form W-2c, Corrected Wage and Tax Statement, and Form W-3c, Transmittal of Corrected Wage and Tax Statements, with the Social Security Administration. You can get these from the IRS by calling 1-800-829-3676.

Federal income tax adjustments. Generally, you cannot adjust amounts reported as federal income tax withheld in a prior calendar year unless it is to correct an administrative error. An administrative error occurs if the amount that you entered on the return is not the amount that you actually withheld. See section 9 of Pub. 51 (Circular A) for details.

Line 9—Total taxes. Combine lines 7 and 8; enter the result on line 9.

Line 10—Advance earned income credit (EIC) payments made to employees. Employees who are eligible can receive advance earned income credit (EIC) payments with their wages by giving you Form W-5, Earned Income Credit Advance Payment Certificate, annually. For more information, see sections 6 and 14 of Pub. 51 (Circular A).

Line 12—Total deposits. Enter the total amount deposited for the year, including any overpayment from 2004, as shown in your records.

Line 13—Balance due. You do not have to pay if line 13 is under $1.

Generally, you should show a balance due on line 13 only if your net tax liability for the year (line 11) is less than $2,500. However, see section 7 of Pub. 51 (Circular A) regarding payments made under the "accuracy of deposits" rule.

 If you fail to make deposits as required and instead pay the taxes with Form 943, you may be subject to a penalty.

Line 14—Overpayment. If you deposited more than the correct amount for the year, you can have the overpayment refunded or applied to your next return.

 If line 14 is under $1, we will send you a refund or apply it to your next return only on written request.

Line 15—Monthly Summary of Federal Tax Liability. This is a summary of your yearly tax liability, not a summary of deposits made. If line 11 is less than $2,500, **do not** complete line 15 or Form 943-A.

Complete line 15 only if you were a **monthly schedule depositor** for the entire year and line 11 is $2,500 or more. The amount entered on line 15M must equal the amount reported on line 11. See section 7 of Pub. 51 (Circular A) for details on the deposit rules. You are a monthly schedule depositor for the calendar year if the amount of your Form 943 taxes (line 9) reported for the lookback period is not more than $50,000. The lookback period is the second calendar year preceding the current calendar year. For example, the lookback period for 2006 is 2004.

-3-

If you were a semiweekly schedule depositor during any part of the year, do not complete line 15. Instead, complete Form 943-A.

Reporting adjustments on line 15. If your net adjustment during a month is negative (for example, correcting an overreported liability in a prior period) and it exceeds your total liability for the month, do not enter a negative amount for the month. Instead, enter "-0-" for the month and carry over the unused portion of the adjustment to the next month.

For example, Pine Tree Farm discovered on February 6, 2005, that it overreported social security tax on its 2004 Form 943 by $2,500. Its Form 943 taxes for the first 3 months of 2005 were: January—$2,000; February—$2,000; and March—$2,000. Pine Tree Farm should complete line 15 by entering "2,000" on line A, "-0-" on line B, and "1,500" on line C.

The prior period adjustment ($2,500) offsets the $2,000 liability for February and the excess $500 must be used to offset the March liabilities. Since the error was not discovered until February, it does not affect January liabilities reported on line A.

Additional information. Pub. 51 (Circular A) has information that you may need about social security, Medicare, federal unemployment (FUTA), withheld federal income taxes, and the advance earned income credit. It includes tables showing the federal income tax to withhold from an employee's wages.

Third-Party Designee. If you want to allow any individual, corporation, firm, organization, or partnership to discuss your 2005 Form 943 with the IRS, check the "Yes" box in the Third-Party Designee section of the return. Also, enter the name, phone number, and any five numbers that the designee chooses as his or her personal identification number (PIN). The authorization applies only to the tax form upon which it appears.

By checking the "Yes" box, you are authorizing the IRS to call the designee to answer any questions relating to the information reported on your tax return. You are also authorizing the designee to:
• Exchange information concerning your tax return with the IRS and
• Request and receive written tax return information relating to your tax return including copies of specific notices, correspondence, and account transcripts.

You are not authorizing the designee to receive any refund check, bind you to anything (including additional tax liability), or otherwise represent you before the IRS. If you want to expand the designee's authorization or desire automatic issuances of copies of notices, see Pub. 947, Practice Before the IRS and Power of Attorney.

The Third-Party Designee authorization is substantially equivalent to Form 8821, Tax Information Authorization, but automatically expires one year from the due date (without regard to extensions) for filing your 2005 Form 943. If you or your designee desire to terminate the authorization, a written statement conveying your wish to revoke the authorization should be submitted to the IRS service center where the return was processed.

Who must sign. Form 943 must be signed as follows:
• **Sole proprietorship**—The individual who owns the business.
• **Corporation** (including an LLC treated as a corporation)— The president, vice president, or other principal officer.

• **Partnership** (including an LLC treated as a partnership) **or unincorporated organization**— A responsible and duly authorized member or officer having knowledge of its affairs.
• **Single member limited liability company (LLC) treated as a disregarded entity**— The owner of the limited liability company (LLC).
• **Trust or estate**—The fiduciary.

Form 943 may also be signed by a duly authorized agent of the taxpayer if a valid power of attorney has been filed.

Privacy Act and Paperwork Reduction Act Notice. We ask for the information on Forms 943, 943-A, and 943-V to carry out the Internal Revenue laws of the United States. We need it to figure and collect the right amount of tax. Subtitle C, Employment Taxes, of the Internal Revenue Code imposes employment taxes on wages, including income tax withholding. These forms are used to report the amount of taxes that you owe. Section 6011 requires you to provide the requested information if the tax applies to you. Section 6109 requires you to provide your employer identification number (EIN). If you fail to provide this information in a timely manner, you may be subject to penalties and interest.

You are not required to provide the information requested on a form that is subject to the Paperwork Reduction Act unless the form displays a valid OMB control number. Books or records relating to a form or its instructions must be retained as long as their contents may become material in the administration of any Internal Revenue law.

Generally, tax returns and return information are confidential, as required by Code section 6103. However, section 6103 allows or requires the Internal Revenue Service to disclose or give the information shown on your return to others as described in the Code. For example, we may disclose your tax information to the Department of Justice for civil and criminal litigation, and to cities, states, and the District of Columbia for use in administering their tax laws. We may also disclose this information to federal and state agencies to enforce federal nontax criminal laws, or to federal law enforcement and intelligence agencies to combat terrorism.

The time needed to complete and file these forms will vary depending on individual circumstances. The estimated average time for **Form 943** is: Recordkeeping, 10 hr., 31 min.; Learning about the law or the form, 40 min.; Preparing the form, 1 hr., 47 min.; Copying, assembling, and sending the form to the IRS, 16 min. The estimated average time for **Form 943-A** is: Recordkeeping, 8 hr., 22 min.; Preparing and sending the form to the IRS, 8 min. The estimated average time for **Form 943-V** is 20 min. If you have comments concerning the accuracy of these time estimates or suggestions for making these forms simpler, we would be happy to hear from you. You can write to the Internal Revenue Service, Tax Products Coordinating Committee, SE:W:CAR:MP:T:T:SP, 1111 Constitution Ave. NW, IR-6406, Washington, DC 20224. **Do not** send Form 943 to this address. Instead, see *Where to file* on page 2.

Form **943-A**	Agricultural Employer's Record of	
(Rev. July 2001)	**Federal Tax Liability**	OMB No. 1545-0035
Department of the Treasury Internal Revenue Service	▶ File with Form 943.	

Name (as shown on Form 943)	Employer identification number

You must complete this form if you are required to deposit on a semiweekly schedule, or if your tax liability during any month is $100,000 or more. Show tax liability here, not deposits. (The IRS gets deposit data from FTD coupons or EFTPS.)

A. Daily Tax Liability—January				B. Daily Tax Liability—February				C. Daily Tax Liability—March			
1		16		1		16		1		16	
2		17		2		17		2		17	
3		18		3		18		3		18	
4		19		4		19		4		19	
5		20		5		20		5		20	
6		21		6		21		6		21	
7		22		7		22		7		22	
8		23		8		23		8		23	
9		24		9		24		9		24	
10		25		10		25		10		25	
11		26		11		26		11		26	
12		27		12		27		12		27	
13		28		13		28		13		28	
14		29		14		29		14		29	
15		30		15				15		30	
		31								31	
A Total liability for month ▶				**B** Total liability for month ▶				**C** Total liability for month ▶			

D. Daily Tax Liability—April				E. Daily Tax Liability—May				F. Daily Tax Liability—June			
1		16		1		16		1		16	
2		17		2		17		2		17	
3		18		3		18		3		18	
4		19		4		19		4		19	
5		20		5		20		5		20	
6		21		6		21		6		21	
7		22		7		22		7		22	
8		23		8		23		8		23	
9		24		9		24		9		24	
10		25		10		25		10		25	
11		26		11		26		11		26	
12		27		12		27		12		27	
13		28		13		28		13		28	
14		29		14		29		14		29	
15		30		15		30		15		30	
						31					
D Total liability for month ▶				**E** Total liability for month ▶				**F** Total liability for month ▶			

General Instructions

Purpose of form. Use this form to report your tax liability (income tax withheld plus both employee and employer social security and Medicare taxes minus any advance earned income credit payments) on a daily basis. **Do not** show Federal tax deposits here. The IRS gets deposit data from the deposit coupons (Forms 8109) or from the Electronic Federal Tax Payment System (EFTPS). Do not report taxes on wages paid to nonfarm workers on this form. Taxes on wages paid to nonfarm workers are reported on **Form 941,** Employer's Quarterly Federal Tax Return.

Caution. *Form 943-A is used by the IRS to determine if you have timely deposited your Form 943 tax liabilities. If you are a semiweekly schedule depositor and fail to properly complete and file Form 943-A with Form 943, the IRS will* not be able to process your return and will have to contact you for the missing information.

Who must file. Semiweekly schedule depositors are required to complete and file Form 943-A with **Form 943,** Employer's Annual Tax Return for Agricultural Employees. Monthly schedule depositors who accumulate $100,000 or more during any month (after which they become semiweekly schedule depositors) must also complete and file Form 943-A. **Do not** file this form if you are a monthly schedule depositor for the entire year or if your net taxes for the year (line 11, Form 943) are less than $2,500.

Note. *If you use this form, do not complete line 15 on Form 943.*

For Privacy Act and Paperwork Reduction Act Notice, see the separate Instructions for Form 943.   Cat. No. 17030C   Form **943-A** (Rev. 7-2001)

Form 943-A (Rev. 7-2001)

G. Daily Tax Liability—July				H. Daily Tax Liability—August				I. Daily Tax Liability—September			
1		16		1		16		1		16	
2		17		2		17		2		17	
3		18		3		18		3		18	
4		19		4		19		4		19	
5		20		5		20		5		20	
6		21		6		21		6		21	
7		22		7		22		7		22	
8		23		8		23		8		23	
9		24		9		24		9		24	
10		25		10		25		10		25	
11		26		11		26		11		26	
12		27		12		27		12		27	
13		28		13		28		13		28	
14		29		14		29		14		29	
15		30		15		30		15		30	
		31				31				30	

G Total liability for month ▶   H Total liability for month ▶   I Total liability for month ▶

J. Daily Tax Liability—October				K. Daily Tax Liability—November				L. Daily Tax Liability—December			
1		16		1		16		1		16	
2		17		2		17		2		17	
3		18		3		18		3		18	
4		19		4		19		4		19	
5		20		5		20		5		20	
6		21		6		21		6		21	
7		22		7		22		7		22	
8		23		8		23		8		23	
9		24		9		24		9		24	
10		25		10		25		10		25	
11		26		11		26		11		26	
12		27		12		27		12		27	
13		28		13		28		13		28	
14		29		14		29		14		29	
15		30		15		30		15		30	
		31				30				31	

J Total liability for month ▶   K Total liability for month ▶   L Total liability for month ▶

M Total tax liability for year (add lines A through L) . . . . ▶

Specific Instructions

The total tax liability for the year (line M) must equal net taxes on Form 943 (line 11).

Each numbered entry space corresponds to dates during the year. Report your tax liabilities on this form corresponding to the dates of each wage payment, **not** to when payroll liabilities are accrued. Enter the monthly totals on lines **A, B, C, D, E, F, G, H, I, J, K,** and **L.** Enter the total for the year on line **M.**

Example. Employer F is a semiweekly schedule depositor. Employer F accumulated a tax liability of $3,000 on its January 11 and January 25 paydays. In the January column, Employer F must enter $3,000 on lines 11 and 25.

See **Deposit Requirements** in **Circular A,** Agricultural Employer's Tax Guide (Pub. 51), for more information.

Adjustments. Semiweekly schedule depositors must take into account on Form 943-A adjustments to correct prior year returns (reported on line 8 of Form 943). If the adjustment was made to correct an **underreported liability** in a prior year, report the adjustment on the entry space corresponding to the date the error was discovered.

If the adjustment corrects an **overreported liability** in a prior year, use the adjustment amount as a credit to offset current year tax liabilites until it is used up. For example, Employer A discovered on January 12 that it overreported social security tax on a prior year Form 943 by $10,000. It paid wages on January 5, 12, 19, and 26, and had a $5,000 tax liability for each of those pay dates. In column A (for January), Employer A must report $5,000 on line 5. The adjustment for the $10,000 overreported tax liability is used to offset the January 12 and 19 tax liabilities, so these two $5,000 tax liabilities are not reported on Form 943-A and are not deposited. The $5,000 tax liability for January 26 must be reported on line 26 of column A. See Circular A for more information on reporting adjustments to correct errors on prior year returns.

Form **944 for Tax Year 2006:** Employer's Annual Federal Tax Return

Department of the Treasury — Internal Revenue Service

OMB No. XXXX-XXXX

Employer identification number (EIN)

Name *(not your trade name)*

Trade name *(if any)*

Address

Number   Street   Suite or room number

City   State   ZIP code

Who Must File Form 944

You must file annual Form 944 instead of filing quarterly Forms 941 **only if the IRS notified you in writing.**

Read the separate instructions before you fill out this form. Please type or print within the boxes.

Part 1: Answer these questions for 2006.

1 Wages, tips, and other compensation   1

2 Total income tax withheld from wages, tips, and other compensation   2

3 If no wages, tips, and other compensation are subject to social security or Medicare tax .   3 ☐ Check and go to line 5.

4 Taxable social security and Medicare wages and tips:

Column 1   Column 2

4a Taxable social security wages   × .124 =

4b Taxable social security tips   × .124 =

4c Taxable Medicare wages & tips   × .029 =

4d Total social security and Medicare taxes (*Column 2,* lines 4a + 4b + 4c = 4d) 4d

5 Total taxes before adjustments (line 2 + line 4d = line 5)   5

6 Tax adjustments (If your answer is a negative number, write it in parentheses.):
(See instructions for each line.)

6a Current year's adjustments (See instructions) 6a

6b Prior years' income tax adjustments (See instructions. Attach Form 941c.) 6b

6c Prior years' social security and Medicare tax adjustments (See instructions. Attach Form 941c.) 6c

6d Special additions to federal income tax (reserved use). Attach Form 941c 6d

6e Special additions to social security and Medicare taxes (reserved use). Attach Form 941c 6e

6f Total adjustments (Combine all amounts: lines 6a through 6e.) 6f

7 Total taxes after adjustments (Combine lines 5 and 6f.)   7

Caution: If line 7 is more than $1,000, beginning the first quarter of 2007 you must file Form 941 instead of filing Form 944.

8 Advance earned income credit (EIC) payments made to employees   8

9 Total taxes after adjustment for advance EIC (line 7 – line 8 = line 9)   9

10 Total deposits for this year, including overpayment applied from a prior year   10

11 Balance due (If line 9 is more than line 10, write the difference here.) Make your check payable to the *United States Treasury* and write your EIN, *Form 944,* and *2006* on the check   11

12 Overpayment (If line 10 is more than line 9, write the difference here.):   12   Check one ☐ Apply to next return. ☐ Send a refund.

▶ You MUST fill out both pages of this form and SIGN it.

Next ➡

For Privacy Act and Paperwork Reduction Act Notice, see the back of the payment voucher.   Cat. No. 39316N   Form **944** (2006)

Name *(not your trade name)*	Employer identification number (EIN)

Part 2: Tell us about your tax liability for 2006.

13 Check one: ☐ Line 9 is less than $2,500. Go to line 15.

☐ Line 9 is $2,500 or more, fill out the tax liability for each month.

	Jan.		Apr.		Jul.		Oct.
13a	___ .	**13d**	___ .	**13g**	___ .	**13j**	___ .
	Feb.		May		Aug.		Nov.
13b	___ .	**13e**	___ .	**13h**	___ .	**13k**	___ .
	Mar.		Jun.		Sep.		Dec.
13c	___ .	**13f**	___ .	**13i**	___ .	**13l**	___ .

Total liability for year (Add lines a through l). Total must equal line 9. **13m** ___ .

14 ☐☐ If you made deposits of taxes reported on this form, write the state abbreviation for the state where you made your deposits OR write *MU* if you made your deposits in *multiple* states.

Part 3: Tell us about your business. If question 15 does NOT apply to your business, leave it blank.

15 If your business has closed or you have stopped paying wages

☐ Check here and enter the final date you paid wages. ___ / ___ / ___

Part 4: May we speak with your third-party designee?

Do you want to allow an employee, a paid tax preparer, or another person to discuss this return with the IRS? (See the instructions for details.)

☐ Yes. Designee's name _____

Select a 5-digit Personal Identification Number (PIN) to use when talking to IRS ☐ ☐ ☐ ☐ ☐

☐ No.

Part 5: Sign here.

You MUST fill out both pages of this form and SIGN it.

Under penalties of perjury, I declare that I have examined this return, including accompanying schedules and statements, and to the best of my knowledge and belief, it is true, correct, and complete.

✗ **Sign your name here**		Print your name here	
		Print your title here	
Date ___ / ___ / ___		Best daytime phone (___) ___ – ___	

Part 6: For paid preparers only *(optional)*

If you were PAID to prepare this return and are not an employee of the business that is filing this return, you may choose to fill out Part 6.

Paid Preparer's name		Preparer's SSN/PTIN	
Paid Preparer's signature		Date	___ / ___ / ___
☐ Check if you are self employed			
Firm's name		Firm's EIN	
Address			
City		State	ZIP code

Page **2**

Form **944** (2006)

Form 945

Department of the Treasury
Internal Revenue Service

Annual Return of Withheld Federal Income Tax

▶ For withholding reported on Forms 1099 and W-2G.
▶ See separate instructions. For more information on income tax withholding, see Pub. 15 (Circ. E) and Pub. 15-A.
Please type or print.

OMB No. 1545-1430

2005

Enter state code for state in which deposits were made **only** if different from state in address to the right ▶ (see the instructions).

Name (as distinguished from trade name)

Trade name, if any

Address (number and street)

Calendar year

Employer identification number (EIN)

City, state, and ZIP code

If address is different from prior return, check here. ▶

A If you **do not have to file** returns in the future, check here ▶ ☐ and enter date final payments made. ▶ ....

1	Federal income tax withheld from pensions, annuities, IRAs, gambling winnings, etc.	**1**
2	Backup withholding	**2**
3	Adjustment to correct administrative errors (see the instructions)	**3**
4	**Total taxes.** If $2,500 or more, this must equal line 8M below or line M of Form 945-A . . .	**4**
5	Total deposits for 2005 from your records, including overpayment applied from 2004 return	**5**
6	**Balance due** (subtract line 5 from line 4) (see the instructions)	**6**

7 **Overpayment.** If line 4 is less than line 5, enter overpayment here ▶ $ _____ and check if to be:

☐ Applied to next return **or** ☐ Refunded.

- **All filers:** If line 4 is less than $2,500, **do not** complete line 8 **or** Form 945-A.
- **Semiweekly schedule depositors:** Complete **Form 945-A** and check here if line 4 is $2,500 or more . . . . . ▶ ☐
- **Monthly schedule depositors:** Complete **line 8, entries A through M,** and check here if line 4 is $2,500 or more . ▶ ☐

8 **Monthly Summary of Federal Tax Liability.** (Complete Form 945-A instead, if you were a semiweekly schedule depositor.)

	Tax liability for month		Tax liability for month		Tax liability for month
A January		**F** June		**K** November. . . .	
B February . .		**G** July		**L** December. . . .	
C March		**H** August . . .		**M** Total liability for	
D April		**I** September. . .		year (add lines **A**	
E May		**J** October . . .		through **L**). . . .	

Third-Party Designee

Do you want to allow another person to discuss this return with the IRS (see the instructions)? ☐ **Yes.** Complete the following. ☐ **No.**

Designee's name ▶

Phone no. ▶ (   )

Personal identification number (PIN) ▶

Sign Here

Under penalties of perjury, I declare that I have examined this return, including accompanying schedules and statements, and to the best of my knowledge and belief, it is true, correct, and complete.

Signature ▶

Print Your Name and Title ▶

Date ▶

For Privacy Act and Paperwork Reduction Act Notice, see the separate instructions.

Cat. No. 14584B

Form **945** (2005)

Form 945-V,
Payment Voucher

Purpose of Form

Complete Form 945-V if you are making a payment with Form 945, Annual Return of Withheld Federal Income Tax. We will use the completed voucher to credit your payment more promptly and accurately, and to improve our service to you.

If you have your return prepared by a third party and make a payment with that return, please provide Form 945-V to the return preparer.

Making Payments With Form 945

Make a payment with your 2005 Form 945 **only if:**

• Your total taxes for the year (line 4 on Form 945) are less than $2,500 and you are paying in full with a timely filed return or

• You are a monthly schedule depositor making a payment in accordance with the *Accuracy of Deposits Rule.* See section 11 of Pub. 15 (Circular E), Employer's Tax Guide, for details. This amount may be $2,500 or more.

Otherwise, you are required to deposit the amount at an authorized financial institution or by electronic funds transfer. See section 11 of Pub. 15 (Circular E) for deposit instructions. Do not use the Form 945-V payment voucher to make federal tax deposits.

Caution. *If you pay amounts with Form 945 that should have been deposited, you may be subject to a penalty. See* Deposit Penalties *in section 11 of Pub. 15 (Circular E).*

Specific Instructions

Box 1—Employer identification number (EIN). If you do not have an EIN, apply for one on Form SS-4, Application for Employer Identification Number, and write "Applied For" and the date you applied in this entry space.

Box 2—Amount paid. Enter the amount paid with Form 945.

Box 3—Name and address. Enter your business name and address as shown on Form 945.

• Enclose your check or money order made payable to the "United States Treasury." Be sure to enter your EIN, "Form 945," and "2005" on your check or money order. Do not send cash. Do not staple this voucher or your payment to the return (or to each other).

• Detach the completed Form 945-V and send it with your payment and Form 945 to the address provided in the Instructions for Form 945.

Note. You **must** also complete the entity information above line A on Form 945.

▼ **Detach Here and Mail With Your Payment and Form 945.** ▼

Form 945-V	Payment Voucher	OMB No. 1545-1430
Department of the Treasury Internal Revenue Service	▶ Use this voucher when making a payment with Form 945.	2005

1 Enter your employer identification number (EIN).

2 **Enter the amount of your payment** . . ▶ | Dollars | Cents

3 Enter your business name (individual name if sole proprietor).

Enter your address.

Enter your city, state, and ZIP code.

20**05**

Department of the Treasury
Internal Revenue Service

Instructions for Form 945

Annual Return of Withheld Federal Income Tax

Section references are to the Internal Revenue Code unless otherwise noted.

What's New

Alternative signature method. Effective with returns filed after June 30, 2005, corporate officers or duly authorized agents may sign Form 945 by rubber stamp, mechanical device, or computer software program. For details and required documentation, see Rev. Proc. 2005-39. You can find Rev. Proc. 2005-39 on page 82 of Internal Revenue Bulletin 2005-28 at *www.irs.gov/pub/ irs-irbs/irb05-28.pdf.*

Reminders

Additional information. Pub. 15 (Circular E), Employer's Tax Guide, explains the rules for withholding, depositing, and reporting federal income tax. Pub. 15-A, Employer's Supplemental Tax Guide, includes information on federal income tax withholding from pensions, annuities, and Indian gaming profits. For information on withholding from gambling winnings, see the Instructions for Forms W-2G and 5754.

For a list of employment tax products, visit the IRS website at *www.irs.gov* and type "Employment Tax" in the *Keyword Search* box.

Correcting Form 945. If you discover an error on a previously filed Form 945, make the correction using Form 945 for the year in which you discovered the error and attach Form 941c, Supporting Statement to Correct Information. For example, in October 2005, you discover that you underreported $1,000 ($5,000 reported when $6,000 was actually withheld) in withheld federal income tax on your 2004 Form 945. Correct the error by showing $1,000 on line 3 of your 2005 Form 945 and attaching a completed Form 941c. For details, see *Line 3— Adjustment to correct administrative errors* on page 3.

Electronic payment. Now, more than ever before, businesses can enjoy the benefits of paying their federal taxes electronically. Whether you rely on a tax professional or handle your own taxes, IRS offers you convenient programs to make paying taxes easier.

Spend less time and worry on taxes and more time running your business. Use Electronic Federal Tax Payment System (EFTPS) to your benefit.

For more information about EFTPS, visit *www.eftps.gov* or call EFTPS Customer Service at 1-800-555-4477.

How to get forms and publications. You can get most IRS forms and publications by accessing the IRS website at *www.irs.gov* or by calling the IRS at 1-800-TAX-FORM (1-800-829-3676).

Telephone help. You can call the IRS toll free at 1-800-829-4933 to order FTD coupons (Form 8109) and for answers to your questions about completing Form 945, tax deposit rules, or obtaining an employer identification number (EIN).

Photographs of Missing Children

The Internal Revenue Service is a proud partner with the National Center for Missing and Exploited Children. Photographs of missing children selected by the Center may appear in instructions on pages that would otherwise be blank. You can help bring these children home by looking at the photographs and calling 1-800-THE-LOST (1-800-843-5678) if you recognize a child.

General Instructions

Purpose of form. Use Form 945 to report withheld federal income tax from nonpayroll payments. **Nonpayroll payments** include the following:

- Pensions (including **governmental** section 457(b) plan distributions), annuities, and IRA distributions
- Military retirement
- Gambling winnings
- Indian gaming profits
- Voluntary withholding on certain government payments
- Backup withholding

Report all federal income tax withholding from nonpayroll payments or distributions annually on one Form 945. **Do not** file more than one Form 945 for any calendar year.

All federal income tax withholding reported on Forms 1099 (for example, Form 1099-R or 1099-MISC) or Form W-2G must be reported on Form 945. **Do not** report federal income tax withholding from wages on Form 945.

All employment taxes and federal income tax withholding reported on Form W-2, Wage and Tax Statement, must be reported on Form 941 (or Form 943 for agricultural employees), Schedule H (Form 1040) for household employees, or Form CT-1 for railroad employees.

Do not report on Form 945 federal income tax withheld on distributions to participants from nonqualified plans (including **nongovernmental** section 457(b) plans) and some other deferred compensation arrangements that are treated as wages and are reported on Form W-2. Report such withholding on Form 941. See Pub. 15 (Circular E) for more information.

Who must file. If you withhold federal income tax (including backup withholding) from nonpayroll payments, you must file Form 945. See *Purpose of form* above. You are not required to file Form 945 for those years in which you do not have a nonpayroll tax liability. **Do not** report on Form 945 withholding that is required to be reported on Form 1042, Annual Withholding Tax Return for U.S. Source Income of Foreign Persons.

Where to file. In the list on page 2, find the location of your legal residence, principal place of business, office, or agency. Send your return to the **Internal Revenue Service** at the address listed for your location. No street address is needed.

Cat. No. 20534D

Where you file depends on whether or not you are including a payment with the return.

Connecticut, Delaware, District of Columbia, Illinois, Indiana, Kentucky, Maine, Maryland, Massachusetts, Michigan, New Hampshire, New Jersey, New York, North Carolina, Ohio, Pennsylvania, Rhode Island, South Carolina, Vermont, Virginia, West Virginia, Wisconsin

Return without payment:	Return with payment:
	P.O. Box 105092
Cincinnati, OH 45999-0042	Atlanta, GA 30348-5092

Alabama, Alaska, Arizona, Arkansas, California, Colorado, Florida, Georgia, Hawaii, Idaho, Iowa, Kansas, Louisiana, Minnesota, Mississippi, Missouri, Montana, Nebraska, Nevada, New Mexico, North Dakota, Oklahoma, Oregon, South Dakota, Tennessee, Texas, Utah, Washington, Wyoming

Return without payment:	Return with payment:
	P.O. Box 660443
Ogden, UT 84201-0042	Dallas, TX 75266-0443

If you have no legal residence or principal place of business in any state—

Return without payment:	Return with payment:
	P.O. Box 80108
Philadelphia, PA 19255-0042	Cincinnati, OH 45280-0008

Exception for exempt organizations and government entities. If you are filing Form 945 for an exempt organization or government entity (federal, state, local, or Indian tribal government), use the following addresses, regardless of your location:

Return without payment: Ogden, UT 84201-0042.

Return with payment: P.O. Box 660443, Dallas, TX 75266-0443.

When to file. For 2005, file Form 945 by January 31, 2006. However, if you made deposits on time in full payment of the taxes for the year, you may file the return by February 10, 2006. Your return will be considered timely filed if it is properly addressed and mailed First-Class or sent by an IRS-designated private delivery service on or before the due date. See Pub. 15 (Circular E) for more information on IRS-designated private delivery services.

Employer identification number (EIN). If you do not have an EIN, you may apply for one online. Go to the IRS website at *www.irs.gov/businesses/small* and click on the "Employer ID Numbers (EINs)" link. You may also apply for an EIN by calling 1-800-829-4933. Or, you can fax or mail Form SS-4, Application for Employer Identification Number, to the IRS.

Note. If you are reporting withholding on pension distributions, be sure to be consistent in using the same name and EIN for all reporting and depositing of taxes (for example, on Forms 945, 1099-R, and 8109/EFTPS). Filing Form 945 with an incorrect name and EIN or failure to use the same name and EIN in all reporting and depositing of taxes may result in penalties and delays in processing your return.

Penalties and interest. There are penalties for filing Form 945 late and for paying or depositing taxes late, unless there is reasonable cause. See section 11 of Pub. 15 (Circular E) for more information on deposit penalties. There are also penalties for failure to furnish information returns (for example, Forms 1099-MISC, 1099-R, or W-2G) to payees and failure to file copies with the IRS.

 If amounts that must be withheld are not withheld or are not deposited or paid to the United States Treasury, the **trust fund recovery penalty** *may apply. The penalty is the full amount of any unpaid trust fund tax. This penalty may apply when these unpaid taxes cannot be immediately collected from the employer or business. The trust fund recovery penalty may be imposed on all persons who are determined by the IRS to have been responsible for collecting, accounting for, and paying over these taxes, and who acted willfully in not doing so. "Willfully" in this case means voluntarily, consciously, and intentionally. A responsible person acts willfully if the person knows that the required actions are not taking place.*

Voluntary income tax withholding. States must allow **unemployment compensation** recipients to elect to have federal income tax withheld at a 10% rate in 2006. Recipients paid under the Railroad Unemployment Insurance Act may also elect withholding at a 10% rate in 2006.

Recipients of any of the following federal payments may request federal income tax withholding in 2006 at a rate of 7%, 10%, 15%, or 25% on:
- Social security and Tier 1 railroad retirement benefits,
- Certain crop disaster payments, and
- Commodity Credit Corporation loans.

The payee may request withholding on Form W-4V, Voluntary Withholding Request, or you may develop your own substitute form. Any voluntary withholding on these payments must be reported on Form 945 (and on Form 1099-G) and is subject to the deposit rules.

Depositing Withheld Taxes

Deposit all nonpayroll (Form 945) withheld federal income tax, including backup withholding, by using the Electronic Federal Tax Payment System (EFTPS) or by depositing at an authorized institution using Form 8109, Federal Tax Deposit Coupon. Some taxpayers are required to use EFTPS to deposit their taxes (see *Electronic deposit requirement* on page 3). Combine all Form 945 taxes for deposit purposes. **Do not** combine deposits for Forms 941, 943, or CT-1 with deposits for Form 945. If you deposit using Form 8109, be sure to darken the space for Form "945" on Form 8109.

Generally, the deposit rules that apply to Form 941 also apply to Form 945. However, because Form 945 is an annual return, the rules for determining your deposit schedule (discussed below) are different from those for Form 941. See section 11 of Pub. 15 (Circular E) for a detailed discussion of the deposit rules.

Determining your deposit schedule. There are two deposit schedules—**monthly** or **semiweekly**—for determining when you must deposit withheld federal income tax. These schedules tell you when a deposit is due after a tax liability arises (that is, you make a payment subject to federal income tax withholding, including backup withholding). Before the beginning of each calendar year, you must determine which of the two deposit schedules you must use.

For 2006, you are a monthly schedule depositor for Form 945 if the total tax reported on your 2004 Form 945 (line 4) was $50,000 or less. If the total tax reported for 2004 exceeded $50,000, you are a semiweekly schedule depositor.

-2-

If you are a monthly schedule depositor and accumulate a $100,000 liability or more on any day during a calendar month, your deposit schedule changes to semiweekly for the remainder of the year and for the following year. For more information, see the $100,000 Next-Day Deposit Rule *in section 11 of Pub. 15 (Circular E).*

Electronic deposit requirement. You must make electronic deposits of all depository taxes (such as employment tax, withheld income tax, excise tax, and corporate income tax) using the Electronic Federal Tax Payment System (EFTPS) in 2006 if:
- The total deposits of such taxes in 2004 were more than $200,000 or
- You were required to use EFTPS in 2005.

If you are required to use EFTPS and use Form 8109 instead, you may be subject to a 10% penalty. Using EFTPS is voluntary, but you must enroll in EFTPS before you can use it. To get more information or to enroll in EFTPS, visit the EFTPS website at *www.eftps.gov* or call 1-800-555-4477.

Specific Instructions

State code. If you made your deposits using Form 8109 or by using an EFTPS bank account in a state other than that shown in your address on Form 945, enter the state code for the state where you made deposits or initiated EFTPS transfers in the box provided in the upper left corner of Form 945. Use the Postal Service two-letter state abbreviation as the state code. Enter the code "MU" in the state code box if you deposit in more than one state. If you deposit in the **same state** as shown in your address, **do not** make an entry in this box.

Line A—Final return. If you go out of business or end operations and you will not be required to file Form 945 in the future, file a final return. Be sure to check the box in line A and enter the date that final nonpayroll payments were made.

Line 1—Federal income tax withheld. Enter the federal income tax that you withheld (or were required to withhold) from pensions (including distributions from **governmental** section 457(b) plans), annuities, IRA distributions, military retirement, Indian gaming profits, and gambling winnings (regular gambling withholding only). Also enter any voluntary amount that you withheld on certain government payments. If you are required to report federal income tax withholding on Forms 1099 (for example, Form 1099-R or Form W-2G), you must report the federal income tax withheld on Form 945.

Note. Federal income tax withholding reported on Form W-2 **must** be reported on Form 941, Form 943, Form 944 or Schedule H (Form 1040), as appropriate.

Line 2—Backup withholding. Enter any backup withholding, including backup withholding on gambling winnings.

Regulated investment companies (RICs) and real estate investment trusts (REITs) must report any backup withholding on Form 945 in the year that the dividends are actually paid. This includes January payments of dividends declared during October, November, and December of the prior year. See the Instructions for Form 1099-DIV for special reporting requirements.

Line 3—Adjustment to correct administrative errors. You cannot make an adjustment on Form 945 to correct federal income tax withholding or backup withholding reported in a prior calendar year **unless** it is to correct an **administrative error**. An administrative error occurs if the amount you entered on Form 945 is not the amount that you actually withheld. For example, if the total federal income tax actually withheld was incorrectly reported on Form 945 due to a math or transposition error, this is an administrative error. The administrative error adjustment corrects the amount reported on Form 945 to agree with the amount actually withheld from nonpayroll payments.

You must report an adjustment to correct an administrative error on Form 945 in the year in which you discover the error. If the net adjustment is negative (reducing your tax liability), enclose the amount reported on line 3 in parentheses (if possible).

You will not be allowed a refund or credit for any prior year's overpayment of federal income tax that you withheld from a payee. This is because the payees use the amount of withholding shown on the information return (for example, Form 1099-R) as a credit when filing their income tax returns.

If you are making an adjustment(s) to correct a prior year administrative error, report the net adjustment (including adjustments to federal income tax withholding **and** backup withholding) on line 3. Complete Form 941c, Supporting Statement To Correct Information, or an equivalent statement, and file it with Form 945 to provide the required information on the adjustment(s). Be sure to identify the adjustment(s) in the *Explanation of Adjustments* (Part V of Form 941c) as correcting an administrative error and provide a description of the error(s). **Do not** file Form 941c separately from Form 945.

Reporting adjustments on line 8 or on Form 945-A. The amount of the adjustment(s) also must be taken into account in the Monthly Summary of Federal Tax Liability (line 8) or on Form 945-A, Annual Record of Federal Tax Liability. If the adjustment increases your tax liability, include the adjustment with any other amount on the entry space for the date that you discovered the error and increase any required deposit by the adjustment amount. If the adjustment decreases your tax liability, use the adjustment amount as a credit to offset subsequent liabilities on line 8 or Form 945-A until it is used up. For more information, see section 13 of Pub. 15 (Circular E). The Pub. 15 (Circular E) instructions for making adjustments refer to Form 941 but also apply to Form 945 adjustments.

 If you are not required to complete line 8 or Form 945-A because your total taxes are less than $2,500, do not show adjustments on line 8 or on Form 945-A.

Line 4—Total taxes. Add lines 1 and 2 and add or subtract any net adjustment on line 3. If total taxes are $2,500 or more, the amount reported on line 4 must equal the total liability for the year reported on line 8M of the Monthly Summary of Federal Tax Liability, or line M of Form 945-A.

Line 5—Total deposits. Enter your total Form 945 deposits for the year, including any overpayment applied from your 2004 return.

Line 6—Balance due. You do not have to pay if line 6 is under $1. Generally, you should have a balance due only if your total taxes for the year (line 4) are less than $2,500. If you made payments under the accuracy of deposits rule, see section 11 of Pub. 15 (Circular E). Enter your EIN, "Form 945," and "2005" on your check or money order and make it payable to the "United States Treasury." If line 4 is $2,500 or more and you deposited all taxes when due, the amount on line 6 should be zero.

-3-

If you fail to make required deposits (using EFTPS or Form 8109, as required) and instead pay these amounts with your return, you may be subject to a penalty.

Line 7—Overpayment. If you deposited more than the correct amount for the year, you can have the overpayment refunded or applied to your next return by checking the appropriate box. The IRS may apply your overpayment to any past due tax account under your EIN. If line 7 is under $1, we will send a refund or apply it to your next return only on written request.

Line 8—Monthly Summary of Federal Tax Liability.

 This is a summary of your monthly tax liability, not a summary of deposits made. If line 4 is less than $2,500, do not complete line 8 or Form 945-A.

Complete line 8 **only** if you were a **monthly schedule depositor** for the entire year and line 4 is $2,500 or more. See *Determining your deposit schedule* on page 2.

 The amount entered on line 8M must equal the amount reported on line 4.

Report your liabilities on Form 945-A instead of on line 8 if:
• You were a **semiweekly schedule depositor** during 2005. **Do not** complete entries A through M of line 8. Instead, complete and file Form 945-A with Form 945.
• You were a **monthly schedule depositor** for 2005 and during any month you accumulated nonpayroll taxes of $100,000 or more. Because this converted you to a semiweekly schedule depositor for the remainder of 2005 (and for 2006), you must report your liabilities on Form 945-A for the entire year. **Do not** complete entries A through M of line 8. For more information, see the *$100,000 Next-Day Deposit Rule* in section 11 of Pub. 15 (Circular E).

Third-Party Designee. If you want to allow any individual, corporation, firm, organization, or partnership to discuss your 2005 Form 945 with the IRS, check the "Yes" box in the Third-Party Designee section of Form 945. Also, enter the name, phone number, and any five numbers that the designee chooses as his or her personal identification number (PIN). The authorization applies only to the tax form upon which it appears.

By checking the "Yes" box, you are **authorizing** the IRS to call the designee to answer any questions relating to the information reported on your tax return. You are also authorizing the designee to:
• Exchange information concerning your tax return with the IRS and
• Request and receive written tax return information relating to your tax return including copies of specific notices, correspondence, and account transcripts.

You are **not authorizing** the designee to receive any refund check, bind you to anything (including additional tax liability), or otherwise represent you before the IRS. If you want to expand the designee's authorization or desire automatic issuances of copies of notices, see Pub. 947, Practice Before the IRS and Power of Attorney.

The Third-Party Designee authorization is substantially equivalent to Form 8821, Tax Information Authorization, but automatically **expires** one year from the due date (without regard to extensions) for filing your 2005 Form 945. If you or your designee desire to terminate the authorization, a written statement conveying your wish to revoke the authorization should be submitted to the IRS service center where the return was processed.

Who must sign. Form 945 must be signed as follows:
• **Sole proprietorship** — The individual who owns the business.
• **Corporation** (including an LLC treated as a corporation) — The president, vice president, or other principal officer.
• **Partnership** (including an LLC treated as a partnership) **or unincorporated organization** — A responsible and duly authorized member or officer having knowledge of its affairs.
• **Single member limited liability company (LLC) treated as a disregarded entity** — The owner of the limited liability company (LLC).
• **Trust or estate** — The fiduciary.

Form 945 may also be signed by a duly authorized agent of the taxpayer if a valid power of attorney has been filed.

Privacy Act and Paperwork Reduction Act Notice. We ask for the information on Form 945 to carry out the Internal Revenue laws of the United States. We need it to figure and collect the right amount of tax. Sections 3402, 3405, and 3406 of the Internal Revenue Code require taxpayers to pay over to the IRS federal income tax withheld from certain nonpayroll payments and distributions, including backup withholding. Form 945 is used to determine the amount of the taxes that you owe. Section 6011 requires you to provide the requested information if the tax applies to you. Section 6109 requires you to provide your employer identification number (EIN). If you fail to provide this information in a timely manner, you may be subject to penalties and interest.

You are not required to provide the information requested on a form that is subject to the Paperwork Reduction Act unless the form displays a valid OMB control number. Books or records relating to a form or its instructions must be retained as long as their contents may become material in the administration of any Internal Revenue law.

Generally, tax returns and return information are confidential, as required by section 6103. However, section 6103 allows or requires the Internal Revenue Service to disclose or give the information shown on your tax return to others described in the Code. For example, we may disclose your tax information to the Department of Justice for civil and criminal litigation, and to cities, states, and the District of Columbia for use in administering their tax laws. We may also disclose this information to other countries under a tax treaty, to federal and state agencies to enforce federal nontax criminal laws, or to federal law enforcement and intelligence agencies to combat terrorism.

The time needed to complete and file Form 945 will vary depending on individual circumstances. The estimated average time is: **Recordkeeping,** 7 hr., 9 min.; **Learning about the law or the form,** 47 min.; and **Preparing and sending the form to the IRS,** 56 min. If you have comments concerning the accuracy of these time estimates or suggestions for making Form 945 simpler, we would be happy to hear from you. You can write to the Internal Revenue Service, Tax Products Coordinating Committee, SE:W:CAR:MP:T:T:SP, 1111 Constitution Ave. NW, IR-6406, Washington, DC 20224. **Do not** send Form 945 to this address. Instead, see *Where to file* on page 1.

-4-

Form **945-A**
(Rev. August 2003)

Department of the Treasury
Internal Revenue Service

Annual Record of Federal Tax Liability

► File with Form 945 or CT-1.

OMB No. 1545-1430

Name (as shown on Form 945 or CT-1)

Employer identification number

	January tax liability				February tax liability				March tax liability	
1		17		1		17		1		17
2		18		2		18		2		18
3		19		3		19		3		19
4		20		4		20		4		20
5		21		5		21		5		21
6		22		6		22		6		22
7		23		7		23		7		23
8		24		8		24		8		24
9		25		9		25		9		25
10		26		10		26		10		26
11		27		11		27		11		27
12		28		12		28		12		28
13		29		13		29		13		29
14		30		14				14		30
15		31		15				15		31
16				16				16		
A	Total for month ►			B	Total for month ►			C	Total for month ►	

	April tax liability				May tax liability				June tax liability	
1		17		1		17		1		17
2		18		2		18		2		18
3		19		3		19		3		19
4		20		4		20		4		20
5		21		5		21		5		21
6		22		6		22		6		22
7		23		7		23		7		23
8		24		8		24		8		24
9		25		9		25		9		25
10		26		10		26		10		26
11		27		11		27		11		27
12		28		12		28		12		28
13		29		13		29		13		29
14		30		14		30		14		30
15				15		31		15		
16				16				16		
D	Total for month ►			E	Total for month ►			F	Total for month ►	

Cat. No. 14733M

Form **945-A** (Rev. 8-2003)

Form 945-A (Rev. 8-2003) Page **2**

July tax liability				August tax liability				September tax liability			
1		17		1		17		1		17	
2		18		2		18		2		18	
3		19		3		19		3		19	
4		20		4		20		4		20	
5		21		5		21		5		21	
6		22		6		22		6		22	
7		23		7		23		7		23	
8		24		8		24		8		24	
9		25		9		25		9		25	
10		26		10		26		10		26	
11		27		11		27		11		27	
12		28		12		28		12		28	
13		29		13		29		13		29	
14		30		14		30		14		30	
15		31		15		31		15			
16				16				16			

G Total for month ▶   **H** Total for month ▶   **I** Total for month ▶

October tax liability				November tax liability				December tax liability			
1		17		1		17		1		17	
2		18		2		18		2		18	
3		19		3		19		3		19	
4		20		4		20		4		20	
5		21		5		21		5		21	
6		22		6		22		6		22	
7		23		7		23		7		23	
8		24		8		24		8		24	
9		25		9		25		9		25	
10		26		10		26		10		26	
11		27		11		27		11		27	
12		28		12		28		12		28	
13		29		13		29		13		29	
14		30		14		30		14		30	
15		31		15				15		31	
16				16				16			

J Total for month ▶   **K** Total for month ▶   **L** Total for month ▶

M Total tax liability for year (add lines **A** through **L**). This should equal line 4 on Form 945 (or line 13 on Form CT-1). . . . . ▶

Form **945-A** (Rev. 8-2003)

General Instructions

Purpose of form. Use this form to report nonpayroll income tax withholding on **Form 945,** Annual Return of Withheld Federal Income Tax, **based on the dates the amounts were withheld.**

These nonpayroll items include backup withholding and withholding on pensions, annuities, IRAs, Indian gaming profits, gambling winnings, and military retirement. Also use Form 945-A to report tax liabilities reported on **Form CT-1,** Employer's Annual Railroad Retirement Tax Return.

Note: *Form 945-A is a summary of your tax liability,* **not** *a summary of deposits made. (The IRS gets deposit data from FTD coupons or EFTPS.)*

Who must file. Semiweekly schedule depositors are required to complete and file Form 945-A with Form 945 or CT-1. **Do not** complete this form if you are a monthly schedule depositor, unless you accumulate a tax liability of $100,000 during any month of the year. Monthly schedule depositors who accumulate $100,000 become semiweekly schedule depositors for the remainder of the year and must complete Form 945-A for the entire year. The deposit rules, including the $100,000 next-day deposit rule, are explained in section 11 of **Circular E (Pub. 15),** Employer's Tax Guide, the **Instructions for Form 945,** and the **Instructions for Form CT-1.**

Important. Form 945-A is used by the IRS to match your tax liability reported on this form with your deposits and to determine if you have deposited your withholding tax liabilities on time. Unless Form 945-A is properly completed and filed with Form 945 or CT-1, the IRS will not be able to process your return and will have to contact you for the missing information.

Specific Instructions

If you are required to report your tax liabilities on Form 945-A as discussed above, file it with Form 945 or CT-1. Do not complete entries **A** through **M** of the *Monthly Summary of Federal Tax Liability* (line 8 on Form 945) or the *Monthly Summary of Railroad Retirement Tax Liability* (page 2 of Form CT-1). However, be sure to mark the semiweekly schedule depositor checkbox above line 8 of Form 945.

Each numbered space on Form 945-A corresponds to dates during the year. Report your tax liabilities corresponding to the dates payments were made, **not** when the liabilities accrued. For example, if you became liable for a pension distribution on December 31, 2002, but did not make the distribution until January 3, 2003, the income tax withholding liability for the distribution must be reported on Form 945-A for 2003, on line 3 for January.

Example 1. Cedar Co., which has a semiweekly deposit schedule, makes periodic payments on gambling winnings on the 15th day of each month. On December 24, 2003, in addition to its periodic payments, it withheld from a payment on gambling winnings under the backup withholding rules. Since Cedar Co. is a semiweekly schedule depositor, it **must** record these nonpayroll withholding liabilities on Form 945-A. It must report tax liabilities on line 15 for each month and line 24 for December. Cedar Co. enters the monthly totals on lines **A** through **L.** It adds these monthly subtotals and enters the total tax liability for the year on line **M.** The amount on line **M** should equal line 4 of Form 945.

Example 2. Fir Co. is a semiweekly schedule depositor. During January, it withheld income tax on pension distributions as follows: $52,000 on January 10; $35,000 on January 24. Since Fir Co. is a semiweekly schedule depositor, it **must** record its income tax withholding liabilities on Form 945-A. It must record $52,000 on line 10 and $35,000 on line 24 for January.

Example 3. Because Elm Co. is a new business, it is a monthly schedule depositor for 2003. During January, it withheld income tax on nonpayroll payments as follows: $2,000 on January 10; $99,000 on January 24. The deposit rules require that a monthly schedule depositor begin depositing on a semiweekly deposit schedule when a $100,000 or more tax liability is accumulated on any day within a month (see section 11 of Circular E (Pub. 15) for details). Since Elm Co. accumulated $101,000 ($2,000 + $99,000) on January 24, 2003, it became a semiweekly schedule depositor. Elm Co. must complete Form 945-A and file it with Form 945. It must record $2,000 on line 10 and $99,000 on line 24 for January. **No entries** should be made on line 8 of Form 945 although Elm Co. was a monthly schedule depositor until January 24.

Adjustments. Semiweekly schedule depositors must report adjustments on Form 945-A to correct **administrative errors** on prior Forms 945 and errors on prior Forms CT-1. (**Reminder:** You will not be allowed a refund or credit for any prior year overpayment of income tax that you withheld or deducted from a payee.) For information on correcting administrative errors, see the **Instructions for Form 945,** the **Instructions for Form CT-1,** and section 13 of Circular E (Pub. 15). (The Circular E (Pub. 15) instructions for making adjustments refer to Form 941, but they also apply to Form 945 adjustments.) If the adjustment increases your current liability, report the adjustment on the entry space corresponding to the date the error was discovered.

If the adjustment decreases your current liability, use the adjustment amount as a credit to offset subsequent liabilities on Form 945-A until it is used up. For example, on January 8, 2003, Oak Rail Co. discovered that a mathematical error was made on a prior year return, resulting in a $10,000 overstatement of nonpayroll income tax withholding. Since the correct amounts were withheld and reported on Forms 1099-R, this is an administrative error that can be corrected on Form 945. Oak Rail Co. made payments subject to nonpayroll income tax withholding on January 3, 10, 17, 24, and 31 and had a $5,000 tax liability for each of those pay dates. On Form 945-A, it must report $5,000 on line 3 for January. The adjustment for the $10,000 overstatement is used to offset the January 10 and 17 liabilities, so these two $5,000 liabilities are not deposited or reported on Form 945-A. The $5,000 liabilities for January 24 and 31 must be reported on lines 24 and 31 for January.

Paperwork Reduction Act Notice. We ask for the information on this form to carry out the Internal Revenue laws of the United States. You are required to give us the information. We need it to ensure that you are complying with these laws and to allow us to figure and collect the right amount of tax.

You are not required to provide the information requested on a form that is subject to the Paperwork Reduction Act unless the form displays a valid OMB control number. Books or records relating to a form or its instructions must be retained as long as their contents may become material in the administration of any Internal Revenue law. Generally, tax returns and return information are confidential, as required by Code section 6103.

The time needed to complete and file this form will vary depending on individual circumstances. The estimated average time is:

Recordkeeping . . . . 6 hr., 27 min.

Learning . . . . 6 min.

**Preparing and sending
the form to the IRS** . . . . 12 min.

If you have comments concerning the accuracy of these time estimates or suggestions for making this form simpler, we would be happy to hear from you. You can write to the IRS at the address listed in the **Instructions for Form 945.**

IF YOU WRITE OR CALL US, refer to this information:

Department of The Treasury
Internal Revenue Service
[ADDRESS LINE 1]
[ADDRESS LINE 2]

Notice Number: 972CG
Date of This Notice:
Taxpayer Identification Number: Form:
Tax Period: Penalty Reference Code:

||||||||||||||||||||||||

[taxpayer name]
[address line one]
[address line two]
[city/state/zip]

For General Information,
please call: 1-800-829-1040 TOLL FREE

We're Proposing a Penalty For Your Tax Year 19XX Information Returns

ACTION REQUIRED

Our records show that you didn't file certain information returns as the law requires for the tax period shown above. The law allows us to charge you a penalty for not filing information returns correctly. We're proposing a penalty in the amount of $_____. We won't charge interest on this penalty until after we send you a bill.

Please read this entire notice carefully. It explains why we proposed the penalty and what you should do if you agree or disagree with our proposal. Our explanation of the proposed penalty begins on page 2.

HOW YOU SHOULD RESPOND TO THIS NOTICE

Please review your records related to filing the returns listed on page 2.

--If you AGREE to the full amount of the proposed penalty, do all of the following:

1. Check box (A) on the last page of this notice.
2. Sign and date the consent to the penalty assessment.
3. Enclose your payment in full, if possible. Make your check or money order payable to the *Internal Revenue Service.*
4. Check the box to show if you have or have not enclosed a payment.
5. Return the last page of this notice with your payment in the enclosed envelope.

--If YOU DON'T AGREE with our findings or believe you have a reason why we shouldn't charge all or part of this penalty, do all of the following:

1. Check box (B) or (C) on the last page of this notice.
2. Enclose a signed statement explaining why you disagree.
3. Include any supporting documents you wish us to consider.
4. If you agree to part of penalty, enclose your payment, if possible. Make your check payable to the Internal Revenue Service.
5. Check the box to show if you have or have not enclosed a payment.
6. Return the last page of this notice with your statement and documents in the enclosed envelope. Please include a telephone number, including the area code, and the best time to call you.

It's important that we receive your completed response within 45 days from the date of this notice. You have 60 days to respond if you live outside of the United States. If we don't hear from you within this period, we'll conclude that the proposed penalty is correct. Then we'll send you a bill called "Notice of Penalty Charge" for the amount of the proposed penalty. We'll charge interest from the date of the Notice of Penalty Charge to the date we receive the amount you owe in full. You may contest the Notice of Penalty Charge by sending us proof that the penalty is incorrect.

If you have any questions about this notice, you may write to us at the return address on this notice. If you prefer, you may call the telephone number shown above for general information about this notice. However, the office at the address shown on this notice is most familiar with your case.

Page 1   Notice 972

Appendix

IRS information: service center name, TIN, penalty reference code(s), tax period, date of this notice, notice #)

These information returns were not filed correctly according to our records.

1st name line of payor	Form (1099-INT,MISC,DIV,ETC)	Transmitter Control Code:
2nd name line of payor	Number received:	( )
1st address line of payor	Number amended:	
2nd address line of payor	Date received:	Proposed Penalty Type:
	How received: (paper or tape)	(late filing, magnetic Media, missing or incorrect TINs)

1st name line of payor	Form (1099-INT,MISC,DIV,ETC)	Transmitter Control Code:
2nd name line of payor	Number received:	( )
1st address line of payor	Number amended:	
2nd address line of payor	Date received:	Proposed Penalty Type:
	How received: (paper or tape)	(late filing, magnetic Media, missing or incorrect TINs)

Explanation of Penalty

We propose a penalty for each Form 1098, 1099, W-2G, or W-2 that you didn't file correctly by the due date (including extensions). This penalty may also apply if we sent timely filed returns back to you for changes and you didn't return them to us in the time we requested.

The penalty is:

- $15 for each return filed within 30 days after the due date, up to a maximum of $75,000 per year ($25,000 for small businesses as defined below),

- $30 for each return filed more that 30 days after the due date but by August 1, up to a maximum of $150,000 per year ($50,000 for small businesses), or

- $50 for each return filed after August 1.

The maximum penalty we can charge is $50 per information return, up to $250,000 per year ($100,000 for small businesses).

Lower Penalty for Small Businesses

The lower maximum penalties stated above for small businesses apply if a business had average gross receipts of $5 million or less for the three most recent tax years (or time in business, if shorter) ending before the calendar year the information returns were due. For example, if we charged you a penalty for 1992 information returns due in 1993, the three most recent tax years are 1992, 1991, and 1990. If the penalty on the notice you received is more than the maximum penalty for small businesses, we'll reduce the penalty based on evidence you give us that you're a small business as we define it here.

```
IRS information: service center name, TIN, penalty reference code(s), tax period, date of this notice, notice #)
```

These information returns were not filed correctly according to our records.

```
1st name line of payor        Form (1099-INT,MISC,DIV,ETC)    Transmitter Control Code:
2nd name line of payor        Number received:                (            )
1st address line of payor     Number amended:
2nd address line of payor     Date received:                  Proposed Penalty Type:
                              How received: (paper or tape)    (late filing, magnetic Media,
                                                               missing or incorrect TINs)

1st name line of payor        Form (1099-INT,MISC,DIV,ETC)    Transmitter Control Code:
2nd name line of payor        Number received:                (            )
1st address line of payor     Number amended:
2nd address line of payor     Date received:                  Proposed Penalty Type:
                              How received: (paper or tape)    (late filing, magnetic Media,
                                                               missing or incorrect TINs)
```

Explanation of Penalty

We propose a penalty for each Form 1098, 1099, W-2G, or W-2 that you didn't send to us on magnetic media as the law requires. The law requires you to file on magnetic media if you file more than 250 returns. The penalty for not filing on magnetic media is $50 for each return over 250 that you filed on paper. For example, if you filed 300 paper returns that should have been filed on magnetic media, we would apply the penalty to 50 of them. The maximum penalty we can charge is $50 per information return, up to $250,000 per year ($100,000 for small businesses as defined below).

According to our records, you didn't receive an undue hardship waiver to exempt you from filing returns on magnetic media for 19XX. If you feel that we shouldn't charge this penalty because to file on magnetic media would have caused you an undue hardship, you must send us:

1. An estimate, including the cost of preparation, of what it would have cost you to file paper returns, and

2. An estimate, including the cost of preparation, of what it would have cost you to file on magnetic media, and

3. Cost estimates from two computer service bureaus showing the cost of return preparation.

If you cannot show that an undue hardship existed, you must be able to show reasonable cause to have the penalty waived.

Lower Penalty for Small Businesses

The lower maximum penalty stated above for small businesses applies if a business had average gross receipts of $5 million or less for the three most recent tax years ending before the calendar year in which the information returns were due (or time in business, if shorter). For example, if we charged you a penalty for 1992 information returns due in 1993, the three most recent tax years are 1992, 1991, and 1990. If the penalty on the notice you received is more than the maximum penalty for small businesses, we'll reduce the penalty based on evidence you give us that you are a small business as we define it here.

<table>
<tr><td>Page 2</td><td>Notice 972</td></tr>
</table>

Magnetic Media Penalty

Appendix

These information returns were not filed correctly according to our records.

1st name line of payor	Form (1099-INT,MISC,DIV,ETC)	Transmitter Control Code:
2nd name line of payor	Number received:	( )
1st address line of payor	Number amended:	
2nd address line of payor	Date received:	Proposed Penalty Type:
	How received: (paper or tape)	(late filing, magnetic Media, missing or incorrect TINs)

1st name line of payor	Form (1099-INT,MISC,DIV,ETC)	Transmitter Control Code:
2nd name line of payor	Number received:	( )
1st address line of payor	Number amended:	
2nd address line of payor	Date received:	Proposed Penalty Type:
	How received: (paper or tape)	(late filing, magnetic Media, missing or incorrect TINs)

Explanation of Penalty

We propose a penalty for each information return you filed that had a missing or incorrect taxpayer identification number. The penalty is $50 for each Form 1098, 1099, W-2G or W-2 you sent to us with a missing or incorrect TIN.

The maximum penalty we can charge is $50 per form, up to $250,00 per year ($100,000 for small businesses as defined below).

We've enclosed a list of the information returns you filed that had missing or incorrect TINs. You should check this list against your records to see if you have an acceptable reason why we shouldn't charge the penalty.

The enclosed Publication 1586, Reasonable Cause Regulations and Requirements as they Apply to Missing and Incorrect TINs, explains what actions you must have taken in order to show reasonable cause for missing or incorrect TINs. You should also check the list and follow the guidelines in Publication 1586 to make any required solicitations (requests for TINs) to payee. This may help you establish reasonable cause to avoid penalties in future years.

Publication 1586 also contains:

-Information and guidance needed to comply with the reporting requirements for the Omnibus Budget Reconciliation Act of 1989 and gives special attention to the requirement for requesting TINs from payees.

-Regulations that apply to information returns reporting and the penalties for not filing as the law requires, and

-Regulations which explain how to have the penalties waived based on reasonable cause.

Lower Penalty for Small Businesses

The lower maximum penalty stated above for small businesses applies if a business had average gross receipts of $5 million or less for the three most recent tax years ending before the calendar year in which the information returns were due (or time in business, if shorter). For example, if we charged you a penalty for 1992 information returns due in 1993, the three most recent tax years are 1992, 1991, and 1990. If the penalty on the notice you received is more than the maximum penalty for small businesses, we'll reduce the penalty based on evidence you give us that you are a small business as we define it here.

Page 2   Notice 972

Missing and Incorrect TIN Penalty

(IRS information: service center name, TIN, penalty reference code(s), tax period, date of this notice, notice (

Summary of Proposed Penalty

The summary below shows the information returns on which we proposed the penalty and the amount of penalty for each penalty type. The number of returns shown in the summary may I less than the number you filed because of allowances made in computing the penalty.

PROPOSED PENALTY AMOUNT: $XXX,XXX

TYPE OF RETURNS	PENALTY TYPE AND AMOUNT						
	Late Filing	Number of Returns	Magnetic Media	Number of Returns	Payee Tax ID Number	Number of of Returns	Total Penalty Amount
1099-DIV 1099-B	$XXX,XXX $XXX,XXX	nn,nnn nn,nnn	$XXX,XXX $XXX,XXX	nn,nnn nn,nnn	$XXX,XXX $XXX,XXX	nn,nnn nn,nnn	$XXX,XXX XXX,XXX
Totals	$XXX,XXX	nn,nnn	$XXX,XXX	nn,nnn	$XXX,XXX	nn,nnn	$XXX,XXX

Proposed Penalty-- This amount may be less than the total of the individual penalty amounts shown above if more than one type of penalty applies to any of the returns you filed. For example, if you filed a return late and with a missing taxpayer identificat number, we'll show the returns in both penalty columns. However, the maximum we will charge is $50 for that return. The proposed penalty may also be reduced because the t applicable penalty exceeded the $250,000 per year maximum allowed by law.

Late filing Penalty -- This penalty applies to returns filed after the due date. It ma also apply to returns filed by the due date but not filed correctly.

Magnetic Media penalty -- This penalty applies to the number of paper returns over 250 that you filed.

Payee Tax Identification Number penalty -- This penalty applies to returns filed with a missing or incorrect taxpayer identification number.

If you believe you have an acceptable reason why we should not charge any part of the Total Penalty Amount shown above, please send us an explanation. If you give us an acceptable explanation for only part of the Total Penalty Amount shown, we'll send you bill for any unexplained penalty amounts.

Appendix

Response to Proposed Penalty for Your Tax Year 19XX Information Returns

Please check the box below that applies to you. Return this page in the enclosed envelope and make sure the Internal Revenue Service address appears through the window. We've enclosed an extra copy of this page of the notice so that you will have a complete copy for your records.

Please check only one box:

[ ] (A) TOTAL AGREEMENT WITH THE PROPOSED PENALTY -- I consent to the immediate assessment and collection of the penalty amount shown in this notice, plus interest.
I Have [ ] Have not [ ] enclosed a payment.

_____

Signature   Date

[ ] (B) PARTIAL AGREEMENT WITH THE PROPOSED PENALTY -- I agree with PART of the proposed penalty shown in this notice. I have attached a signed statement and supporting documents explaining which items I disagree with and why I disagree, or why I feel you shouldn't charge part of the proposed penalty.
I Have [ ] Have not [ ] enclosed a payment.

[ ] (C) TOTAL DISAGREEMENT WITH THE PROPOSED PENALTY -- I disagree with all of the proposed penalty shown in this notice. I've attached a signed statement and supporting documents explaining why the proposed penalty is incorrect, or an acceptable reason why you shouldn't charge this proposed penalty.

Telephone number: (   ) _____ Best hours to call: _____
(include area code)

_____

Please Do Not Detach

TIN	Ck digit	NC	MFT(13 or 55)	TINVal.	Chk	9212	640	0000995000

||||||||||||||||||||||||||||

Internal Revenue Service   TIN   Date of notice
Service Center Name   Taxpayer Name
1st Address line   1st Address line
2nd Address line   2nd Address line

Page 4   Notice 972 (JAN. 1994)

A-213

Form 1042

Department of the Treasury
Internal Revenue Service

Annual Withholding Tax Return for U.S. Source Income of Foreign Persons

▶ See instructions.

OMB No. 1545-0096

2005

If this is an amended return, check here . . . . ▶ ☐

Name of withholding agent	Employer identification number	For IRS Use Only	
		CC	FD
Number, street, and room or suite no. (if a P.O. box, see instructions)		RD	FF
		CAF	FP
City or town, province or state, and country (including postal code)		CR	I
		EDC	SIC

If you will not be liable for returns in the future, check here ▶ ☐   Enter date final income paid ▶ ------------------

Check here if you made quarter-monthly deposits using the 90% rule (see **Deposit Requirements** in the instructions) . . . ▶ ☐

Check if you are a: QI/Withholding foreign partnership or trust ☐   NQI/Flow-through entity ☐   (See instructions.)

Record of Federal Tax Liability (Do not show federal tax deposits here.)

Line No.	Period ending		Tax liability for period (including any taxes assumed on Form(s) 1000)	Line No.	Period ending		Tax liability for period (including any taxes assumed on Form(s) 1000)	Line No.	Period ending		Tax liability for period (including any taxes assumed on Form(s) 1000)
1		7		21		7		41		7	
2	Jan.	15		22	May	15		42	Sept.	15	
3		22		23		22		43		22	
4		31		24		31		44		30	
5	Jan. total			25	May total			45	Sept. total		
6		7		26		7		46		7	
7	Feb.	15		27	June	15		47	Oct.	15	
8		22		28		22		48		22	
9		28		29		30		49		31	
10	Feb. total			30	June total			50	Oct. total		
11		7		31		7		51		7	
12	Mar.	15		32	July	15		52	Nov.	15	
13		22		33		22		53		22	
14		31		34		31		54		30	
15	Mar. total			35	July total			55	Nov. total		
16		7		36		7		56		7	
17	Apr.	15		37	Aug.	15		57	Dec.	15	
18		22		38		22		58		22	
19		30		39		31		59		31	
20	Apr. total			40	Aug. total			60	Dec. total		

61 No. of Forms 1042-S filed: **a** On magnetic media .... **b** On paper .... **c** Electronically ....

62 For **all** Form(s) 1042-S and 1000: **a** Gross income paid ....   **b** Taxes withheld or assumed ....

63a	Total tax liability (add monthly total lines from above)	63a	
b	Adjustments (see instructions)	63b	
c	Total **net tax** liability (combine lines 63a and 63b) . . . . . . ▶	63c	
64	Total paid by federal tax deposit coupons or by electronic funds transfer (or with a request for an extension of time to file) for 2005	64	
65	Enter overpayment applied as a credit from 2004 Form 1042 .	65	
66	Credit for amounts withheld by other withholding agents (see inst.)	66	
67	**Total payments.** Add lines 64 through 66 . . . . ▶	67	
68	If line 63c is larger than line 67, enter **balance due** here . . .	68	
69	If line 67 is larger than line 63c, enter **overpayment** here . . .	69	
70	Penalty for failure to deposit tax when due. Also include on line 68 or line 69 (see instructions)	70	
71	Apply overpayment on line 69 to (check one): ☐ **Credit on 2006 Form 1042 or** ☐ **Refund**		

Third Party Designee   Do you want to allow another person to discuss this return with the IRS (see page 4)? ☐ **Yes.** Complete the following. ☐ **No**
Designee's name ▶   Phone no. ▶   Personal identification number (PIN) ▶

Sign Here   Under penalties of perjury, I declare that I have examined this return, including accompanying schedules and statements, and to the best of my knowledge and belief, it is true, correct, and complete. Declaration of preparer (other than withholding agent) is based on all information of which preparer has any knowledge.
Your signature ▶   Date   Capacity in which acting ▶
   Daytime phone number ▶

Paid Preparer's Use Only   Preparer's signature ▶   Date   Check if self-employed ▶ ☐   Preparer's SSN or PTIN
Firm's name (or yours if self-employed), address, and ZIP code ▶   EIN ▶
   Phone no.

For Privacy Act and Paperwork Reduction Act Notice, see the instructions.   Cat. No. 11384V   Form **1042** (2005)

General Instructions

Section references are to the Internal Revenue Code unless otherwise noted.

Purpose of Form

Use Form 1042 to report tax withheld on certain income of foreign persons, including nonresident aliens, foreign partnerships, foreign corporations, foreign estates, and foreign trusts.

Publicly traded partnerships (section 1446 withholding tax). For purposes of reporting on Forms 1042 and 1042-S, new regulations under section 1446 apply to a publicly traded partnership (PTP). These regulations apply to partnership tax years beginning after May 18, 2005. However, the partnership can elect to apply these regulations to partnership tax years beginning after December 31, 2004. To make the election, the partnership must comply with the regulations and attach a statement to Form 1042 filed for the tax year in which the regulations first apply indicating that the partnership is making the election. If the partnership does not make this election, it must follow the procedures in Rev. Proc. 89-31.

Under these regulations, the PTP must withhold section 1446 tax on distributions of effectively connected income to its foreign partners, rather than on the partner's allocable share of the income. The regulations also permit the withholding obligation to be assumed by a domestic nominee holding an interest in the PTP on behalf of one or more foreign partners. For more information, see Regulations section 1.1446-4 and Pub. 515.

Who Must File

Every withholding agent or intermediary (see definitions below) who receives, controls, has custody of, disposes of, or pays any fixed or determinable annual or periodical income must file an annual return for the preceding calendar year on Form 1042.

You must file Form 1042 if either of the following apply.

● You are required to file Form(s) 1042-S (whether or not any tax was withheld or was required to be withheld). File Form 1042 even if you file Forms 1042-S electronically or on magnetic media.

● You pay gross investment income to foreign private foundations that are subject to tax under section 4948(a).

Withholding Agent

Any person required to withhold tax is a withholding agent. A withholding agent may be an individual, trust, estate, partnership, corporation, nominee (under section 1446), government agency, association, or tax-exempt foundation, whether domestic or foreign.

Every person required to deduct and withhold any tax under Chapter 3 of the Code is liable for such tax. See section 1461.

Intermediary

An intermediary is a person who acts as a custodian, broker, nominee, or otherwise as an agent for another person, regardless of whether that other person is the beneficial owner of the amount paid, a flow-through entity, or another intermediary.

Qualified intermediary (QI). A QI is an intermediary that is a party to a withholding agreement with the IRS. An entity must indicate its status as a QI on a Form W-8IMY submitted to a withholding agent. For information on a QI withholding agreement, see Rev. Proc. 2000-12, which is on page 387 of Internal Revenue Bulletin (IRB) 2000-4 at *www.irs.gov/pub/irsirbs/irb00-04.pdf.* Also see Notice 2001-4 (IRB 2001-2); Rev. Proc. 2003-64, Appendix 3 (IRB 2003-32); and Rev. Proc. 2004-21 (IRB 2004-14).

Withholding foreign partnership (WP) or withholding foreign trust (WT). A WP or WT is a foreign partnership or trust that has entered into a withholding agreement with the IRS in which it agrees to assume primary withholding responsibility for all payments that are made to it for its partners, beneficiaries, or owners. For information on these withholding agreements, see Rev. Proc. 2003-64, which is on page 306 of Internal Revenue Bulletin (IRB) 2003-32 at *www.irs.gov/pub/irsirbs/irb03-32.pdf.* Also see Rev. Proc. 2004-21 (IRB 2004-14).

Nonqualified intermediary (NQI). An NQI is any intermediary that is not a U.S. person and that is not a QI.

Where and When To File

File Form 1042 with the Internal Revenue Service Center, Philadelphia, PA 19255-0607, by March 15, 2006. Also send amended returns to this address. Use Form 1042-T to transmit paper Forms 1042-S.

Extension of time to file. If you need more time to file Form 1042, you may submit Form 2758, Application for Extension of Time To File Certain Excise, Income, Information, and Other Returns.

Form 2758 does not extend the time for payment of tax.

Additional Information

For details on withholding of tax, see Pub. 515, Withholding of Tax on Nonresident Aliens and Foreign Entities. You can get Pub. 515 by calling 1-800-TAX-FORM (1-800-829-3676) or by downloading it from the IRS website at *www.irs.gov.*

Income Tax Withholding on Wages, Pensions, Annuities, and Certain Other Deferred Income

Use Form 941, Employer's Quarterly Federal Tax Return, to report income tax withheld and social security and Medicare taxes on wages paid to a nonresident alien employee.

Use Form 945, Annual Return of Withheld Federal Income Tax, to report income tax withheld under section 3405 from pensions, annuities, and certain other deferred income paid to a nonresident alien individual. However, if the recipient has elected under section 3405(a)(2) or (b)(2) not to have withholding under section 3405, these payments are subject to withholding under section 1441 and the tax withheld must be reported using Forms 1042 and 1042-S.

Use Schedule H (Form 1040), Household Employment Taxes, to report income tax withheld and social security and Medicare taxes on wages paid to a nonresident alien household employee.

For more information, see the instructions for these forms.

Deposit Requirements

Generally, if you are not required to use the Electronic Federal Tax Payment System (EFTPS), you must deposit the tax withheld and required to be shown on Form 1042 with an authorized financial institution using your preprinted Form 8109, Federal Tax Deposit Coupon. Do not use anyone else's coupons. If you do not have your coupons when a deposit is due, call 1-800-829-4933, if you are in the United States. If overseas, call 215-516-2000 (not a toll-free number) from 6:00 a.m. to 2:00 a.m. Eastern time. You may also contact your local IRS office. To avoid a penalty, do not mail your deposits directly to the IRS.

The amount of tax you are required to withhold determines the frequency of your deposits. The following rules explain how often deposits must be made.

1. If at the end of any quarter-monthly period the total amount of undeposited taxes is $2,000 or more, you must deposit the taxes within 3 banking days after the end of the quarter-monthly period. (A quarter-monthly period ends on the 7th, 15th, 22nd, and last day of the month.) To determine banking days, do not count Saturdays, Sundays, legal holidays, or any local holidays observed by authorized financial institutions.

This deposit rule is considered met if:

● You deposit at least 90% of the actual tax liability for the deposit period, and

● If the quarter-monthly period is in a month other than December, you deposit any underpayment with your first deposit that is required to be made after the 15th day of the following month. Any underpayment of $200 or more for a quarter-monthly period ending in December must be deposited by January 31.

2. If at the end of any month the total amount of undeposited taxes is at least $200 but less than $2,000, you must deposit the taxes within 15 days after the end of the month. If you make a deposit of $2,000 or more during any month except December under rule 1 above, carry over any end-of-the-month balance of less than $2,000 to the next month. If you make a

deposit of $2,000 or more during December, any end-of-December balance of less than $2,000 should be paid directly to the IRS along with your Form 1042 by March 15, 2006.

3. If at the end of a calendar year the total amount of undeposited taxes is less than $200, you may either pay the taxes with your Form 1042 or deposit the entire amount by March 15, 2006.

Note. If you are requesting an extension of time to file using Form 2758, follow the rules on this page to see if you must make a deposit of any balance due or if you can pay it with Form 2758. See Form 2758 and its instructions for more information.

Electronic deposit requirement. You must make electronic deposits of all depository tax liabilities using the Electronic Federal Tax Payment System (EFTPS) in 2006 if:

● The total deposits of such taxes in 2004 were more than $200,000, or

● You were required to use EFTPS in 2005.

If you are required to use EFTPS and fail to do so, you may be subject to a 10% penalty. If you are not required to use EFTPS, you may participate voluntarily. To enroll in or get more information about EFTPS, call 1-800-555-4477. You can also visit the EFTPS website at *www.eftps.gov.*

Depositing on time. For deposits made by EFTPS to be on time, you must initiate the transaction at least one business day before the date the deposit is due.

Completing Form 8109. If you do not use EFTPS, deposit your income tax payments using Form 8109. In most cases, you will fill out a Form 8109 following the instructions in the coupon book. However, if a deposit liability arises from a distribution reportable on Form 1042 for the prior year, darken the 4th quarter space on Form 8109. If the distribution is reportable for the current year, darken the 1st quarter space. In all cases, follow the coupon book instructions for completing the rest of the deposit coupon. To ensure proper crediting, write your taxpayer identification number, the period to which the tax deposit applies, and "Form 1042" on the check or money order.

Deposits by foreign corporations. Fill in a preprinted Form 8109 showing the "Amount of Deposit" in U.S. dollars. Mail the completed coupon with a bank draft in U.S. dollars to:

Financial Agent
Federal Tax Deposit Processing
P.O. Box 970030
St. Louis, MO 63197 U.S.A.

Interest and Penalties

If you file Form 1042 late, or fail to pay or deposit the tax when due, you may be liable for penalties and interest unless you can show that the failure to file or pay was due to reasonable cause and not willful neglect.

 You do not have to figure the amount of any interest or penalties you may owe. Because figuring these amounts can be complicated, we will do it for you if you want. We will send you a bill for any amount due.

If you include interest or penalties (other than the penalty for failure to deposit tax when due) with your payment, identify and enter the amount in the bottom margin of Form 1042, page 1. Do not include interest or penalties (other than the penalty for failure to deposit tax when due) in the balance due on line 68.

Interest. Interest is charged on taxes not paid by the due date, even if an extension of time to file is granted. Interest is also charged on penalties imposed for failure to file, negligence, fraud, and substantial understatements of tax from the due date (including extensions) to the date of payment. Interest is figured at a rate determined under section 6621.

Late filing of Form 1042. The penalty for not filing Form 1042 when due (including extensions) is 5% of the unpaid tax for each month or part of a month the return is late, up to a maximum of 25% of the unpaid tax.

Late payment of tax. The penalty for not paying tax when due is usually ½ of 1% of the unpaid tax for each month or part of a month the tax is unpaid. The penalty cannot exceed 25% of the unpaid tax.

Failure to deposit tax when due. See the instructions for line 70 on page 4.

Other penalties. Penalties may be imposed for negligence, substantial understatement of tax, and fraud. See sections 6662 and 6663.

Specific Instructions

 File only one Form 1042 consolidating all Form 1042-S recipient information, regardless of the number of different clients, branches, divisions, or types of income for which you are the withholding agent. However, if you are acting in more than one capacity (for example, you are acting as a QI for certain designated accounts and as an NQI for other accounts), file a separate Form 1042 for each capacity in which you are acting.

Rounding off to whole dollars. You may round off cents to whole dollars. If you do round to whole dollars, you must round all amounts. To round off amounts to the nearest whole dollar, drop amounts under 50 cents and increase amounts from 50 to 99 cents to the next dollar. For example, $1.39 becomes $1 and $2.50 becomes $3. If you have to add two or more amounts to figure the amount to enter on a line, include cents when adding and only round off the total.

Employer identification number (EIN). You are generally required to enter your EIN. However, if you are filing Form 1042 as a QI, withholding foreign partnership, or withholding foreign trust, enter your QI-EIN, WP-EIN, or WT-EIN. Also, be sure to check the "QI/Withholding foreign partnership or trust" box. See *QI and NQI checkboxes* below.

If you do not have an EIN, you can apply for one online at *www.irs.gov/smallbiz* or by telephone at 1-800-829-4933. Also, you can file Form SS-4, Application for Employer Identification Number, by fax or mail. File corrected Forms 1042-S when you receive your EIN.

To get a QI-EIN, WP-EIN, or WT-EIN, submit Form SS-4 with your application for that status. Do not send an application for a QI-EIN, WP-EIN, or WT-EIN to the Philadelphia Service Center; it will not be processed.

Address. Include the suite, room, or other unit number after the street address. If your post office does not deliver mail to the street address and you have a P.O. box, show the box number instead of the street address.

QI and NQI checkboxes. See page 2 for definitions of intermediary, qualified intermediary (QI), withholding foreign partnership (WP), withholding foreign trust (WT), and nonqualified intermediary (NQI). See the Form 1042-S instructions for definitions of U.S. branch treated as a U.S. person and flow-through entity.

Check the "QI/Withholding foreign partnership or trust" box on page 1 if you are a QI, WP, WT, or a U.S. branch treated as a U.S. person. Check the "NQI/Flow-through entity" box if you are an NQI or a flow-through entity.

Lines 1 through 60. Do not enter any negative amounts on these lines.

If you are a QI that did not assume primary withholding responsibility, enter the total amount withheld by the U.S. withholding agent(s) on line 59. Report all other amounts (that is, amounts you actually withheld) on the line that corresponds with the date the liability was incurred.

If you repaid the recipient for an amount overwithheld by reducing the amount withheld on a later payment, report the reduced amount on these lines. If you used the reimbursement procedure for overwithheld amounts, see Pub. 515.

Lines 62a and 62b. Enter the amounts requested with respect to all Forms 1042-S (regardless of whether the form was filed electronically, on magnetic media, or on paper) and with respect to all Forms 1000, Ownership Certificate.

 Be sure to reconcile amounts on Form 1042 with amounts on Forms 1042-S (including Forms 1042-S filed electronically and on magnetic media), to avoid unnecessary correspondence with the IRS.

Line 62a. The amount on line 62a should equal the sum of all amounts shown on Forms 1042-S, box 2, and all amounts shown as gross interest paid on Forms 1000.

Line 62b. The amount on line 62b should equal:
- The sum of all Forms 1042-S, box 7, less
- The sum of all Forms 1042-S, box 8, plus
- The tax assumed from Forms 1000.

If it does not, attach a statement to Form 1042 explaining the difference.

Line 63a. The amount on line 63a must equal the sum of the monthly totals as listed on the Record of Federal Tax Liability. Do not make any adjustments on this line. Except for adjustments described in the instructions for line 63b, you may only make adjustments on the appropriate entry line of the Record of Federal Tax Liability.

Line 63b. If you are a regulated investment company (RIC) or a real estate investment trust (REIT) that paid a dividend in January subject to section 852(b)(7) or section 857(b)(9) (relating to certain dividends declared in the preceding October, November, or December), enter your additional tax liability on those dividends declared in 2005 but paid in January 2006 less any additional tax liability on those dividends declared in 2004 but paid in January 2005. Show any negative amount in brackets. Attach a statement showing your calculation.

Line 66. You are permitted to take a credit for amounts withheld by other withholding agents that pertain to the total net tax liability reported on line 63c. For example, you are a QI and the amount you entered on line 63c includes amounts withheld by a U.S. withholding agent. You may take a credit on line 66 for the amounts that were withheld by the U.S. withholding agent.

 If you are a QI requesting a refund, you must attach the corresponding Form(s) 1042-S received to support the amount claimed on line 66. Failure to do so will result in the denial of the refund or credit being claimed.

Lines 69 and 71. You may claim an overpayment shown on line 69 as a refund or a credit. Check the applicable box on line 71 to show which you are claiming. If you claim a credit, it can reduce your required deposits of withheld tax for 2006.

Line 70. The penalty for failure to deposit tax applies to the amount underpaid when the deposit was due. See *Deposit Requirements* on page 2. The penalty rates are 2% for deposits made 1 to 5 days late, 5% for deposits made 6 to 15 days late, and 10% for deposits made 16 or more days late. However, the penalty is 15% if the tax is not deposited within 10 days after the IRS issues the first notice demanding payment. Add the penalty to any tax due and enter the total on line 68. If you are due a refund, subtract the penalty from the overpayment you show on line 69.

 Because this penalty calculation is complicated, if you want to, you can leave line 70 blank and the IRS will figure the penalty and send you a bill. We will not charge you interest on the penalty if you pay by the date specified on the bill.

Third Party Designee

If you want to allow any individual, corporation, firm, organization, or partnership to discuss your 2005 Form 1042 with the IRS, check the "Yes" box in the Third Party Designee section of the return. Also, enter the name, phone number, and any five numbers that the designee chooses as his or her personal identification number (PIN). The authorization applies only to the tax form upon which it appears.

By checking the "Yes" box, you are authorizing the IRS to call the designee to answer any questions relating to the information reported on your tax return. You are also authorizing the designee to:
- Exchange information concerning your tax return with the IRS, and
- Request and receive written tax return information relating to your tax return including copies of specific notices, correspondence, and account transcripts.

You are not authorizing the designee to receive any refund check, bind you to anything (including additional tax liability), or otherwise represent you before the IRS. If you want to expand the designee's authorization, see Pub. 947, Practice Before the IRS and Power of Attorney.

The authorization automatically expires one year from the due date (without regard to extensions) for filing your 2005 Form 1042. If you or your designee desire to terminate the authorization, a written statement conveying your wish to revoke the authorization should be submitted to the IRS service center where the return was processed.

Amended Return

If you have to make changes to your Form 1042 after you submit it, file an amended Form 1042. Use a Form 1042 for the year you are amending. Check the "Amended Return" box at the top of the form. You must complete the entire form, including all filing information for the calendar year, and sign the return. Attach a statement explaining why you are filing an amended return (for example, you are filing because the tax liability for May was incorrectly reported due to a mathematical error).

If you are also amending Form(s) 1042-S, see *Correcting Paper Forms 1042-S* in the Form 1042-S instructions.

Do not amend Form 1042 to recover taxes overwithheld in the prior year. For more information, see *Adjustment for Overwithholding* in Pub. 515.

Privacy Act and Paperwork Reduction Act Notice. We ask for the information on this form to carry out the Internal Revenue laws of the United States. Sections 1441, 1442, and 1446 require withholding agents to report and pay over to the IRS taxes withheld from certain U.S. source income of foreign persons. Form 1042 is used to report the amount of withholding that must be paid over. Form 1042-S is used to report the amount of income and withholding to the payee. Section 6109 requires you to provide your employer identification number. Routine uses of this information include giving it to the Department of Justice for civil and criminal litigation, and cities, states, and the District of Columbia for use in administering their tax laws. We may also disclose this information to other countries under a tax treaty, to federal and state agencies to enforce federal nontax criminal laws, or to federal law enforcement and intelligence agencies to combat terrorism. If you fail to provide this information in a timely manner, you may be liable for penalties and interest.

You are not required to provide the information requested on a form that is subject to the Paperwork Reduction Act unless the form displays a valid OMB control number. Books or records relating to a form or its instructions must be retained as long as their contents may become material in the administration of any Internal Revenue law. Generally, tax returns and return information are confidential, as required by section 6103.

The time needed to complete and file these forms will vary depending on individual circumstances. The estimated average time is: **Recordkeeping,** 9 hr., 48 min.; **Learning about the law or the form,** 2 hr., 25 min.; **Preparing the form,** 4 hr., 33 min.; and **Copying, assembling, and sending the form to the IRS,** 32 min.

If you have comments concerning the accuracy of these time estimates or suggestions for making this form simpler, we would be happy to hear from you. You can write to the Internal Revenue Service, Tax Products Coordinating Committee, SE:W:CAR:MP:T:T:SP, 1111 Constitution Ave. NW, IR-6406, Washington, DC 20224. Do not send the form to this address. Instead, see *Where and When To File* on page 2.

Form 1042-S

Department of the Treasury
Internal Revenue Service

Foreign Person's U.S. Source Income Subject to Withholding

2006

OMB No. 1545-0096

Copy A for Internal Revenue Service

☐ AMENDED   ☐ PRO-RATA BASIS REPORTING

1 Income code	2 Gross income	3 Withholding allowances	4 Net income	5 Tax rate	6 Exemption code	7 U.S. Federal tax withheld	8 Amount repaid to recipient

9 Withholding agent's EIN ▶   ☐ EIN   ☐ QI-EIN

14 Recipient's U.S. TIN, if any ▶   ☐ SSN or ITIN   ☐ EIN   ☐ QI-EIN

10a WITHHOLDING AGENT'S name   Check here if nominee ☐

15 Recipient's country of residence for tax purposes   **16** Country code

10b Address (number and street)

17 NONQUALIFIED INTERMEDIARY'S (NQI's)/ FLOW-THROUGH ENTITY'S name   **18** Country code

10c Additional address line (room or suite no.)

19a NQI's/Flow-through entity's address (number and street)

10d City or town, province or state, and country   **10e** ZIP code or foreign postal code

19b Additional address line (room or suite no.)

11 Recipient's account number (optional)   **12** Recipient code

19c City or town, province or state, and country   **19d** ZIP code or foreign postal code

13a RECIPIENT'S name

20 NQI's/Flow-through entity's TIN, if any ▶

13b Address (number and street)

21 PAYER'S name and TIN (if different from withholding agent's)

13c Additional address line (room or suite no.)

13d City or town, province or state, and country   **13e** ZIP code or foreign postal code

22 State income tax withheld	23 Payer's state tax no.	24 Name of state

For Privacy Act and Paperwork Reduction Act Notice, see page 15 of the separate instructions.   Cat. No. 11386R   Form **1042-S** (2006)

U.S. Income Tax Filing Requirements

Every nonresident alien individual, nonresident alien fiduciary, and foreign corporation with United States income, including income that is effectively connected with the conduct of a trade or business in the United States, must file a United States income tax return. However, no return is required to be filed by a nonresident alien individual, nonresident alien fiduciary, or a foreign corporation if such person was not engaged in a trade or business in the United States at any time during the tax year and if the tax liability of such person was fully satisfied by the withholding of United States tax at the source. (Corporations file Form 1120-F; all others file Form 1040NR (or Form 1040NR-EZ if eligible).) You may get the return forms and instructions at any United States Embassy or consulate or by writing to: National Distribution Center, P.O. Box 8903, Bloomington, IL 61702-8903, U.S.A.

Tout étranger non-résident, tout organisme fidéicommissaire étranger non-résident et toute société étrangère percevant un revenu aux Etats-Unis, y compris tout revenu dérivé, en fait, du fonctionnement ou d'une commerce ou d'une affaire aux Etats-Unis, doit soumettre aux Etats-Unis, une déclaration d'impôt sur le revenu. Cependant aucune déclaration d'impôt sur le revenu n'est exigée d'un étranger non-résident, d'un organisme fidéicommissaire étrange non-résident, ou d'une société étrangère s'ils n'ont pris part à aucun commerce ou affaire aux Etats-Unis à aucun moment pendant l'année fiscale et si les impôts dont ils sont redevables, ont été entièrement acquittés par une retenue à la source, de leur montant. (Les sociétés doivent faire leur déclaration d'impôt en remplissant le formulaire 1120-F; tous les autres redevables doivent remplir le formulaire 1040NR (ou 1040NR-EZ si éligible).) On peut se procurer formulaires de déclarations d'impôts et instructions dans toutes les Ambassades et tous les Consulats des Etats-Unis. L'on peut également s'adresser pour tous renseignements a: National Distribution Center, P.O. Box 8903, Bloomington, IL 61702-8903, U.S.A.

Todo extranjero no residente, todo organismo fideicomisario extranjero no residente y toda sociedad anónima extranjera que reciba ingresos en los Estados Unidos, incluyendo ingresos relacionados con la conducción de un negocio o comercio dentro de los Estados Unidos, deberá presentar una declaración estadounidense de impuestos sobre ingreso. Sin embargo, no se requiere declaración alguna a un individuo extranjero, una sociedad anónima extranjera u organismo fideicomisario extranjero no residente, si tal persona no ha efectuado comercio o negocio en los Estados Unidos durante el año fiscal y si la responsabilidad con los impuestos de tal persona ha sido satisfecha plenamente mediante retención del impuesto de los Estados Unidos en la fuente. (Las sociedades anónimas envian la Forma 1120-F; todos los demás contribuyentes envian la Forma 1040NR (o la Forma 1040NR-EZ si le corresponde).) Se podrán obtener formas e instrucciones en cualquier Embajada o Consulado de los Estados Unidos o escribiendo directamente a: National Distribution Center, P.O. Box 8903, Bloomington, IL 61702-8903, U.S.A.

Jede ausländische Einzelperson, jeder ausländische Bevollmächtigte und jede ausländische Gesellschaft mit Einkommen in den Vereinigten Staaten, einschliesslich des Einkommens, welches direkt mit der Ausübung von Handel oder Gewerbe innerhalb der Staaten verbunden ist, müssen eine Einkommensteuererklärung der Vereinigten Staaten abgeben. Eine Erklärung, muss jedoch nicht von Ausländern, ausländischen Bevollmächtigten oder ausländischen Gesellschaften in den Vereinigten Staaten eingereicht werden, falls eine solche Person während des Steuerjahres kein Gewerbe oder Handel in den Vereinigten Staaten ausgeübt hat und die Steuerschuld durch Einbehaltung der Steuern der Vereinigten Staaten durch die Einkommensquelle abgegolten ist. (Gesellschaften reichen den Vordruck 1120-F ein; alle anderen reichen das Formblatt 1040NR oder wenn passend das Formblatt 1040NR-EZ ein.) Einkommensteuererklärungen und Instruktionen können bei den Botschaften und Konsulaten der Vereinigten Staaten eingeholt werden. Um weitere Informationen wende man sich bitte an: National Distribution Center, P.O. Box 8903, Bloomington, IL 61702-8903, U.S.A.

Appendix

Explanation of Codes

Box 1. Income code.

	Code	Types of Income
Interest	01	Interest paid by U.S. obligors—general
	02	Interest paid on real property mortgages
	03	Interest paid to controlling foreign corporations
	04	Interest paid by foreign corporations
	05	Interest on tax-free covenant bonds
	29	Deposit interest
	30	Original issue discount (OID)
	31	Short-term OID
	33	Substitute payment—interest
Dividend	06	Dividends paid by U.S. corporations—general
	07	Dividends qualifying for direct dividend rate
	08	Dividends paid by foreign corporations
	34	Substitute payment—dividends
Other	09	Capital gains
	10	Industrial royalties
	11	Motion picture or television copyright royalties
	12	Other royalties (e.g., copyright, recording, publishing)
	13	Real property income and natural resources royalties
	14	Pensions, annuities, alimony, and/or insurance premiums
	15	Scholarship or fellowship grants
	16	Compensation for independent personal services[1]
	17	Compensation for dependent personal services[1]
	18	Compensation for teaching[1]
	19	Compensation during studying and training[1]
	20	Earnings as an artist or athlete[2]
	24	Real estate investment trust (REIT) distributions of capital gains
	25	Trust distributions subject to IRC section 1445
	26	Unsevered growing crops and timber distributions by a trust subject to IRC section 1445
	27	Publicly traded partnership distributions subject to IRC section 1446
	28	Gambling winnings[6]
	32	Notional principal contract income[3]
	35	Substitute payment—other
	36	Capital gains distributions
	50	Other income

Box 6. Exemption code (applies if the tax rate entered in box 5 is 00.00).

Code	Authority for Exemption
01	Income effectively connected with a U.S. trade or business
02	Exempt under an Internal Revenue Code section (income other than portfolio interest)
03	Income is not from U.S. sources[4]
04	Exempt under tax treaty
05	Portfolio interest exempt under an Internal Revenue Code section
06	Qualified intermediary that assumes primary withholding responsibility
07	Withholding foreign partnership or withholding foreign trust
08	U.S. branch treated as a U.S. person
09	Qualified intermediary represents income is exempt

Box 12. Recipient code.

Code	Type of Recipient
01	Individual[2]
02	Corporation[2]
03	Partnership other than withholding foreign partnership[2]
04	Withholding foreign partnership or withholding foreign trust
05	Trust
06	Government or international organization
07	Tax-exempt organization (IRC section 501(a))
08	Private foundation
09	Artist or athlete[2]
10	Estate
11	U.S. branch treated as U.S. person
12	Qualified intermediary
13	Private arrangement intermediary withholding rate pool—general[5]
14	Private arrangement intermediary withholding rate pool—exempt organizations[5]
15	Qualified intermediary withholding rate pool—general[5]
16	Qualified intermediary withholding rate pool—exempt organizations[5]
17	Authorized foreign agent
18	Public pension fund
20	Unknown recipient

[1] If compensation that otherwise would be covered under Income Codes 16–19 is directly attributable to the recipient's occupation as an artist or athlete, use Income Code 20 instead.

[2] If Income Code 20 is used, Recipient Code 09 (artist or athlete) should be used instead of Recipient Code 01 (individual), 02 (corporation), or 03 (partnership other than withholding foreign partnership).

[3] Use appropriate Interest Income Code for embedded interest in a notional principal contract.

[4] Non-U.S. source income received by a nonresident alien is not subject to U.S. tax. Use Exemption Code 03 when entering an amount for information reporting purposes only.

[5] May be used only by a qualified intermediary.

[6] Subject to 30% withholding rate unless the recipient is from one of the treaty countries listed under *Gambling winnings (Income Code 28)* in Pub. 515.

Department of the Treasury
Internal Revenue Service

20**06**

Instructions for Form 1042-S

Foreign Person's U.S. Source Income Subject to Withholding

General Instructions

Section references are to the Internal Revenue Code unless otherwise noted.

 Use the 2006 Form 1042-S only for income paid during 2006. Do not use the 2006 Form 1042-S for income paid during 2005.

What's New

Beginning in 2006, processing year 2007, IRS will no longer accept 3 1/2-inch diskettes for filing information returns.

New regulations under section 1446 apply to publicly traded partnerships (PTP) that have effectively connected income. The PTP can no longer elect to withhold tax based on effectively connected income allocable to its foreign partners. The PTP must withhold on the distribution of that income to its foreign partners. See page 5.

Purpose of Form

Use Form 1042-S to report income described under *Amounts Subject to Reporting on Form 1042-S* on page 4 and to report amounts withheld under Chapter 3 of the Internal Revenue Code.

Also use Form 1042-S to report distributions of effectively connected income by a publicly traded partnership or nominee. See *Publicly Traded Partnership (Section 1446 Withholding Tax)* on page 5.

 Every person required to deduct and withhold any tax under Chapter 3 of the Code is liable for such tax.

Copy A is filed with the Internal Revenue Service. Copies B, C, and D are for the recipient. Copy E is for your records.

Do not use Form 1042-S to report an item required to be reported on—
• Form W-2 (wages and other compensation made to employees (other than compensation for dependent personal services for which the beneficial owner is claiming treaty benefits) including wages in the form of group-term life insurance),
• Form 1099, or
• Form 8288-A, Statement of Withholding on Dispositions by Foreign Persons of U.S. Real Property Interests, or Form 8805, Foreign Partner's Information Statement of Section 1446 Withholding Tax. Withholding agents otherwise required to report a distribution partly on a Form 8288-A or Form 8805 and partly on a Form 1042-S may instead report the entire amount on Form 8288-A or Form 8805.

Who Must File

Every withholding agent (defined on page 2) must file an information return on Form 1042-S to report amounts paid during the preceding calendar year that are described under *Amounts Subject to Reporting on Form 1042-S* on page 4. However, withholding agents who are individuals are not required to report a payment on Form 1042-S if they are not making the payment as part of their trade or business and no withholding is required to be made on the payment. For example, an individual making a payment of interest that qualifies for the portfolio interest exception from withholding is not required to report the payment if the portfolio interest is paid on a loan that is not connected to the individual's trade or business. However, an individual paying an amount that has actually been subject to withholding is required to report the payment. Also, an individual paying an amount on which withholding is required must report the payment, whether or not the individual actually withholds. See *Multiple Withholding Agent Rule* beginning on page 10 for exceptions to reporting when another person has reported the same payment to the recipient. Also see *Publicly Traded Partnerships (Section 1446 Withholding Tax)* on page 5.

You must file a Form 1042-S even if you did not withhold tax because the income was exempt from tax under a U.S. tax treaty or the Code, including the exemption for income that is effectively connected with the conduct of a trade or business in the United States, or you released the tax withheld to the recipient. For exceptions, see *Amounts That Are Not Subject to Reporting on Form 1042-S* beginning on page 4.

Amounts paid to bona fide residents of U.S. possessions and territories are not subject to reporting on Form 1042-S if the beneficial owner of the income is a U.S. citizen, national, or resident alien.

 If you are required to file Form 1042-S, you must also file Form 1042, Annual Withholding Tax Return for U.S. Source Income of Foreign Persons. See Form 1042 for more information.

Where, When, and How To File

Forms 1042-S, whether filed on paper, electronically, or on magnetic media, must be filed with the Internal Revenue Service by March 15, 2007. You are also required to furnish Form 1042-S to the recipient of the income on or before March 15, 2007.

Send any paper Forms 1042-S with Form 1042-T, Annual Summary and Transmittal of Forms 1042-S, to the Internal Revenue Service Center, Philadelphia, PA 19255-0607. You must use Form 1042-T to transmit paper Forms 1042-S. Use a separate Form 1042-T to transmit each type of Form 1042-S. See *Payments by U.S. Withholding Agents* beginning on page 5 and the Form 1042-T instructions for more information. If you have 250 or more Forms 1042-S to file, follow the instructions under *Electronic/Magnetic Media Reporting* below.

Extension of time to file. To request an extension of time to file Forms 1042-S, file Form 8809, Application for Extension of Time To File Information Returns. See the Form 8809 instructions for where to file that form. You should request an extension as soon as you are aware that an extension is necessary, but no later than the due date for filing Form 1042-S. By filing Form 8809, you will get an automatic 30-day extension to file Form 1042-S. If you need more time, a second Form 8809 may be submitted before the end of the initial extended due date. See Form 8809 for more information.

 If you are requesting extensions of time to file for more than 50 withholding agents or payers, you must submit the extension requests electronically or magnetically. See Pub. 1187, Specifications for Filing Form 1042-S, Foreign Person's U.S. Source Income Subject to Withholding, Electronically or Magnetically, for more information.

Electronic/Magnetic Media Reporting

If you file 250 or more Forms 1042-S, you are required to submit them electronically or using magnetic media.

Electronic submissions are filed using the Filing Information Returns Electronically (FIRE) System. The FIRE System operates 24 hours a day, 7 days a week, at *http://fire.irs.gov.* For more information, see Pub. 1187.

Acceptable form of magnetic media are tape cartridges that meet the specifications in Pub. 1187.

The electronic/magnetic media filing requirement applies separately to original and amended returns. Any person, including a corporation, partnership,

Cat. No. 64278A

individual, estate, and trust, that is required to file 250 or more Forms 1042-S must file such returns electronically/magnetically. The filing requirement applies individually to each reporting entity as defined by its separate taxpayer identification number (TIN). This requirement applies separately to original and amended returns. For example, if you have 300 original Forms 1042-S, they must be filed electronically/magnetically. However, if 200 of those forms contained erroneous information, the amended returns may be filed on paper forms because the number of amended Forms 1042-S is less than the 250-or-more filing requirement.

 If you file electronically or on magnetic media, do not file the same returns on paper. Duplicate filing may cause penalty notices to be generated.

Note. Even though as many as 249 Forms 1042-S may be submitted on paper to the IRS, the IRS encourages filers to transmit forms electronically/magnetically.

Hardship waiver. To receive a hardship waiver from the required filing of Forms 1042-S electronically or on magnetic media, submit Form 8508, Request for Waiver From Filing Information Returns Magnetically. Waiver requests should be filed at least 45 days before the due date of the returns. See Form 8508 for more information.

Need assistance? For additional information and instructions on filing Forms 1042-S electronically or on magnetic media, extensions of time to file (Form 8809), and hardship waivers (Form 8508), see Pub. 1187. You may also call the Information Reporting Program at 866-455-7438 (toll-free) or 304-263-8700 (not a toll-free number) Monday through Friday from 8:30 a.m. to 4:30 p.m. Eastern time. The Information Reporting Program may also be reached by email at *mccirp@irs.gov* or by fax at 304-264-5602 (not a toll-free number).

 This call site does not answer tax law questions concerning the requirements for withholding of tax on payments of U.S. source income to foreign persons under Chapter 3 of the Code. If you need such assistance, you may call 215-516-2000 (not a toll-free number) from 6:00 a.m. to 2:00 p.m. Eastern time or write to: Internal Revenue Service, International Section, P.O. Box 920, Bensalem, PA 19020-8518.

Additional Information

For more information on withholding of tax, see Pub. 515, Withholding of Tax on Nonresident Aliens and Foreign Entities. To order this publication and other publications and forms, call 1-800-TAX-FORM (1-800-829-3676). You can also download forms and publications from the IRS website at *www.irs.gov*.

Record Retention

Withholding agents should retain a copy of the information returns filed with the IRS, or have the ability to reconstruct the data, for at least 3 years after the reporting due date.

Substitute Forms

The official Form 1042-S is the standard for substitute forms. Because a substitute form is a variation from the official form, you should know the requirements of the official form for the year of use before you modify it to meet your needs. The IRS provides several means of obtaining the most frequently used tax forms. These include the Internet and CD-ROM. For details on the requirements of substitute forms, see Pub. 1179, General Rules and Specifications for Substitute Forms 1096, 1098, 1099, 5498, W-2G, and 1042-S.

 You are permitted to use substitute payee copies of Form 1042-S (that is, copies B, C, and D) that contain more than one income line for boxes 1 through 8. This will reduce the number of Forms 1042-S you send to the recipient. Under no circumstances, however, may the copy of the form filed with the IRS (copy A) contain more than one income line.

Deposit Requirements

For information and rules concerning federal tax deposits, see *Depositing Withheld Taxes* in Pub. 515 or the Form 1042 instructions.

Definitions

Withholding agent. A withholding agent is any person, U.S. or foreign, that has control, receipt, or custody of an amount subject to withholding or who can disburse or make payments of an amount subject to withholding. The withholding agent may be an individual, corporation, partnership, trust, association, or any other entity. The term withholding agent also includes, but is not limited to, a qualified intermediary (QI), a nonqualified intermediary (NQI), a withholding foreign partnership (WP), a withholding foreign trust (WT), a flow-through entity, a U.S. branch of a foreign insurance company or foreign bank that is treated as a U.S. person, a nominee under section 1446, and an authorized foreign agent. A person may be a withholding agent even if there is no requirement to withhold from a payment or even if another person has already withheld the required amount from a payment.

Generally, the U.S. person who pays (or causes to be paid) the item of U.S. source income to a foreign person (or to its agent) must withhold. However, other persons may be required to withhold. For example, if a payment is made by a QI (whether or not it assumes primary withholding responsibility) that knows that withholding was not done by the person from which it received the payment, that QI is required to do the appropriate withholding. In addition, withholding must be done by any QI that assumes primary withholding responsibility under Chapter 3 of the Code, a WP, a WT, a U.S. branch of a foreign insurance company or foreign bank that agrees to be treated as a U.S. person, or an authorized foreign agent.

Finally, if a payment is made by an NQI or a flow-through entity that knows, or has reason to know, that withholding was not done, that NQI or flow-through entity is required to withhold since it also falls within the definition of a withholding agent.

Authorized foreign agent. An agent is an authorized foreign agent only if all four of the following apply.

1. There is a written agreement between the withholding agent and the foreign person acting as agent.

2. The IRS International Section has been notified of the appointment of the agent before the first payment for which the authorized agent acts on behalf of the withholding agent. (This notification must be sent to the following address: Internal Revenue Service, International Section, P.O. Box 920, Bensalem, PA 19020-8518.)

3. The books and records and relevant personnel of the foreign agent are available to the IRS so that the IRS may evaluate the withholding agent's compliance with its withholding and reporting obligations.

4. The U.S. withholding agent remains fully liable for the acts of its agent and does not assert any of the defenses that may otherwise be available.

For further details, see Regulations section 1.1441-7(c).

Beneficial owner. For payments other than those for which a reduced rate of withholding is claimed under an income tax treaty, the beneficial owner of income is, generally, the person who is required under U.S. tax principles to include the income in gross income on a tax return. A person is not a beneficial owner of income, however, to the extent that person is receiving the income as a nominee, agent, or custodian, or to the extent the person is a conduit whose participation in a transaction is disregarded. In the case of amounts paid that do not constitute income, beneficial ownership is determined as if the payment were income.

Foreign partnerships, foreign simple trusts, and foreign grantor trusts are not the beneficial owners of income paid to the partnership or trust. The beneficial owners of income paid to a foreign partnership are generally the partners in the partnership, provided that the partner is not itself a partnership, foreign simple or grantor trust, nominee, or other agent. The beneficial owner of income paid to a foreign simple trust (a foreign trust that is described in section 651(a)) is generally the beneficiary of the trust, if the beneficiary is not a foreign partnership, foreign simple or grantor trust, nominee, or other agent. The beneficial owner of a foreign grantor trust (a foreign trust to the extent that all or a portion of the income of the trust is treated as owned by the grantor or another person under sections 671 through 679) is the person treated as the owner of the trust. The beneficial owner of income paid to a foreign complex trust (a foreign trust that is not a

-2-

foreign simple trust or foreign grantor trust) is the trust itself.

The beneficial owner of income paid to a foreign estate is the estate itself.

A payment to a U.S. partnership, U.S. trust, or U.S. estate is treated as a payment to a U.S. payee that is not subject to 30% foreign-person withholding. A U.S. partnership, trust, or estate should provide the withholding agent with a Form W-9, Request for Taxpayer Identification Number and Certification.

Disregarded entity. A business entity that has a single owner and is not a corporation under Regulations section 301.7701-2(b) is disregarded as an entity separate from its owner.

Exempt recipient. Generally, an exempt recipient is any payee that is not required to provide Form W-9 and is exempt from the Form 1099 reporting requirements. See the Instructions for the Requester of Form W-9 for a list of exempt recipients.

Fiscally transparent entity. An entity is treated as fiscally transparent with respect to an item of income for which treaty benefits are claimed to the extent that the interest holders in the entity must, on a current basis, take into account separately their shares of an item of income paid to the entity, whether or not distributed, and must determine the character of the items of income as if they were realized directly from the sources from which realized by the entity. For example, partnerships, common trust funds, and simple trusts or grantor trusts are generally considered to be fiscally transparent with respect to items of income received by them.

Flow-through entity. A flow-through entity is a foreign partnership (other than a withholding foreign partnership), a foreign simple or grantor trust (other than a withholding foreign trust), or, for any payments for which a reduced rate of withholding under an income tax treaty is claimed, any entity to the extent the entity is considered to be fiscally transparent under section 894 with respect to the payment by an interest holder's jurisdiction.

Foreign person. A foreign person includes a nonresident alien individual, a foreign corporation, a foreign partnership, a foreign trust, a foreign estate, and any other person that is not a U.S. person. The term also includes a foreign branch or office of a U.S. financial institution or U.S. clearing organization if the foreign branch is a QI. Generally, a payment to a U.S. branch of a foreign person is a payment to a foreign person.

Intermediary. An intermediary is a person that acts as a custodian, broker, nominee, or otherwise as an agent for another person, regardless of whether that other person is the beneficial owner of the amount paid, a flow-through entity, or another intermediary.

Qualified intermediary (QI). A QI is an intermediary that is a party to a withholding agreement with the IRS. An entity must indicate its status as a QI on a

Form W-8IMY submitted to a withholding agent. For information on a QI withholding agreement, see Rev. Proc. 2000-12, which is on page 387 of Internal Revenue Bulletin 2000-4 at *www.irs.gov/pub/ irs-irbs/irb00-04.pdf.* Also see Notice 2001-4 (IRB 2001-21); Rev. Proc. 2003-64, Appendix 3 (IRB 2003-32); and Rev. Proc. 2004-21 (IRB 2004-14).

Nonqualified intermediary (NQI). An NQI is any intermediary that is not a U.S. person and that is not a QI.

Private arrangement intermediary (PAI). A QI may enter into a private arrangement with another intermediary under which the other intermediary generally agrees to perform all of the obligations of the QI. See Section 4 of Rev. Proc. 2000-12 for details.

Non-exempt recipient. A non-exempt recipient is any person who is not an exempt recipient.

Nonresident alien individual. Any individual who is not a citizen or resident of the United States is a nonresident alien individual. An alien individual meeting either the "green card test" or the "substantial presence test" for the calendar year is a resident alien. Any person not meeting either test is a nonresident alien individual. Additionally, an alien individual who is a resident of a foreign country under the residence article of an income tax treaty, or an alien individual who is a bona fide resident of Puerto Rico, Guam, the Commonwealth of the Northern Mariana Islands, the U.S. Virgin Islands, or American Samoa, is a nonresident alien individual. See Pub. 519, U.S. Tax Guide for Aliens, for more information on resident and nonresident alien status.

⚠️ **CAUTION** *Even though a nonresident alien individual married to a U.S. citizen or resident alien may choose to be treated as a resident alien for certain purposes (for example, filing a joint income tax return), such individual is still treated as a nonresident alien for withholding tax purposes on all income except wages.*

Payer. A payer is the person for whom the withholding agent acts as a paying agent pursuant to an agreement whereby the withholding agent agrees to withhold and report a payment.

Presumption rules. The presumption rules are those rules prescribed under Chapter 3 and Chapter 61 of the Code that a withholding agent must follow to determine the status of a beneficial owner (for example, as a U.S. person or a foreign person) when it cannot reliably associate a payment with valid documentation. See, for example, Regulations sections 1.1441-1(b)(3), 1.1441-4(a), 1.1441-5(d) and (e), 1.1441-9(b)(3), 1.1446-1(c)(3), and 1.6049-5(d). Also see Pub. 515.

Publicly traded partnership (PTP). A PTP is any partnership in which interests are regularly traded on an established securities market (regardless of the number of its partners). However, it does

not include a PTP treated as a corporation under section 7704.

Recipient. A recipient is any of the following:
• A beneficial owner of income.
• A QI.
• A WP or WT.
• An authorized foreign agent.
• A U.S. branch of certain foreign banks or insurance companies that is treated as a U.S. person.
• A foreign partnership or a foreign trust (other than a WP or WT), but only to the extent the income is effectively connected with its conduct of a trade or business in the United States.
• A payee who is not known to be the beneficial owner, but who is presumed to be a foreign person under the presumption rules.
• A PAI.
• A partner receiving a distribution of effectively connected income from a PTP or nominee.

A recipient does not include any of the following:
• An NQI.
• A nonwithholding foreign partnership, if the income is not effectively connected with its conduct of a trade or business in the United States.
• A disregarded entity.
• A foreign trust that is described in section 651(a) (a foreign simple trust) if the income is not effectively connected with the conduct of a trade or business in the United States.
• A foreign trust to the extent that all or a portion of the trust is treated as owned by the grantor or other person under sections 671 through 679 (a foreign grantor trust).
• A U.S. branch that is not treated as a U.S. person unless the income is, or is treated as, effectively connected with the conduct of a trade or business in the United States.

U.S. branch treated as a U.S. person. The following types of U.S. branches (of foreign entities) may reach an agreement with the withholding agent to treat the branch as a U.S. person: (a) a U.S. branch of a foreign bank subject to regulatory supervision by the Federal Reserve Board or (b) a U.S. branch of a foreign insurance company required to file an annual statement on a form approved by the National Association of Insurance Commissioners with the Insurance Department of a State, Territory, or the District of Columbia.

The U.S. branch must provide a Form W-8IMY evidencing the agreement with the withholding agent.

⚠️ **CAUTION** *A U.S. branch that is treated as a U.S. person is treated as such solely for purposes of determining whether a payment is subject to withholding. The branch is, for purposes of information reporting, a foreign person and payments to such a branch must be reported on Form 1042-S.*

Withholding certificate. The term "withholding certificate" generally refers to Form W-8 or Form W-9.

Note. Throughout these instructions, a reference to or mention of "Form W-8" is a reference to Forms W-8BEN, W-8ECI, W-8EXP, and/or W-8IMY.

Withholding foreign partnership (WP) or withholding foreign trust (WT). A WP or WT is a foreign partnership or trust that has entered into a withholding agreement with the IRS in which it agrees to assume primary withholding responsibility for all payments that are made to it for its partners, beneficiaries, or owners. For information on these withholding agreements, see Rev. Proc. 2003-64, which is on page 306 of Internal Revenue Bulletin 2003-32 at *www.irs.gov/pub/irs-irbs/irb03-32.pdf.* Also see Rev. Proc. 2004-21 (IRB 2004-14).

Amounts Subject to Reporting on Form 1042-S

Amounts subject to reporting on Form 1042-S are amounts paid to foreign persons (including persons presumed to be foreign) that are subject to withholding, even if no amount is deducted and withheld from the payment because of a treaty or Code exception to taxation or if any amount withheld was repaid to the payee. Amounts subject to withholding are amounts from sources within the United States that constitute (a) fixed or determinable annual or periodical (FDAP) income; (b) certain gains from the disposal of timber, coal, or domestic iron ore with a retained economic interest; and (c) gains relating to contingent payments received from the sale or exchange of patents, copyrights, and similar intangible property. Amounts subject to withholding also include distributions of effectively connected income by a publicly traded partnership. Amounts subject to reporting include, but are not limited to, the following U.S. source items.

● **Corporate distributions.** The entire amount of a corporate distribution (whether actual or deemed) must be reported, irrespective of any estimate of the portion of the distribution that represents a taxable dividend. Any distribution, however, that is treated as gain from the redemption of stock is not an amount subject to reporting. For information on dividends paid by a regulated investment company (RIC), see Pub. 515.

● **Interest.** This includes the portion of a notional principal contract payment that is characterized as interest.

● **Rents.**
● **Royalties.**
● **Compensation for independent personal services performed in the United States.**
● **Compensation for dependent personal services performed in the United States for which the beneficial owner is claiming treaty benefits.**
● **Annuities.**
● **Pension distributions and other deferred income.**
● **Most gambling winnings.** However, proceeds from a wager placed in blackjack, baccarat, craps, roulette, or

big-6 wheel are not amounts subject to reporting.

● **Cancellation of indebtedness.** Income from the cancellation of indebtedness must be reported unless the withholding agent is unrelated to the debtor and does not have knowledge of the facts that give rise to the payment.

● **Effectively connected income (ECI).** ECI includes amounts that are (or are presumed to be) effectively connected with the conduct of a trade or business in the United States even if no withholding certificate is required, as, for example, with income on notional principal contracts. Note that bank deposit interest, which generally is not subject to Form 1042-S reporting, is subject to Form 1042-S reporting if it is effectively connected income. ECI of a PTP distributed to a foreign partner must be reported on Form 1042-S.

● **Notional principal contract income.** Income from notional principal contracts that the payer knows, or must presume, is effectively connected with the conduct of a U.S. trade or business is subject to reporting. The amount to be reported is the amount of cash paid on the contract during the calendar year. Any amount of interest determined under the provisions of Regulations section 1.446-3(g)(4) (dealing with interest in the case of a significant non-periodic payment) is reportable as interest and not as notional principal contract income.

● **Students, teachers, and researchers.** Amounts paid to foreign students, trainees, teachers, or researchers as scholarship or fellowship income, and compensation for personal services (whether or not exempt from tax under an income tax treaty), must be reported. However, amounts that are exempt from tax under section 117 are not subject to reporting.

● **Amounts paid to foreign governments, foreign controlled banks of issue, and international organizations.** These amounts are subject to reporting even if they are exempt under section 892 or 895.

● **Foreign targeted registered obligations.** Interest paid on registered obligations targeted to foreign markets paid to a foreign person other than a financial institution or a member of a clearing organization is an amount subject to reporting.

● **Original issue discount (OID) from the redemption of an OID obligation.** The amount subject to reporting is the amount of OID actually includible in the gross income of the foreign beneficial owner of the income, if known. Otherwise, the withholding agent should report the entire amount of OID as if the recipient held the instrument from the date of original issuance. To determine the amount of OID reportable, a withholding agent may rely on Pub. 1212, List of Original Issue Discount Instruments.

● **Certain dispositions of U.S. real property interests.** See *Withholding on Dispositions of U.S. Real Property Interests by Publicly Traded Trusts and*

Real Estate Investment Trusts (REITs) on page 5.

For more details on the types of income that are subject to withholding, see Pub. 515.

Amounts That Are Not Subject to Reporting on Form 1042-S

Interest on deposits. Generally, no withholding (or reporting) is required on interest paid to foreign persons on deposits if such interest is not effectively connected with the conduct of a trade or business in the United States. For this purpose, the term "deposits" means amounts that are on deposit with a U.S. bank, savings and loan association, credit union, or similar institution, and from certain deposits with an insurance company.

Exception for interest payments to Canadian residents who are not U.S. citizens. If you pay $10 or more of U.S. source bank deposit interest to a nonresident alien who is a resident of Canada, you generally must report the interest on Form 1042-S. This reporting requirement applies to interest on a deposit maintained at a bank's office in the United States. However, this reporting requirement does not apply to interest paid on certain bearer certificates of deposit if paid outside the United States. Although you only have to report payments you make to residents of Canada, you can comply by reporting bank deposit interest to all foreign persons if that is easier.

When completing Form 1042-S, use income code 29 in box 1 and exemption code 02 in box 6.

On the statements furnished to the Canadian recipients, you must include an information contact phone number in addition to the name and address in box 10 on Form 1042-S. You must also include a statement that the information on the form is being furnished to the United States Internal Revenue Service and may be provided to the government of Canada.

Interest and OID from short-term obligations. Interest and OID from any obligation payable 183 days or less from the date of original issue should not be reported on Form 1042-S.

Registered obligations targeted to foreign markets. Interest on a registered obligation that is targeted to foreign markets and qualifies as portfolio interest is not subject to reporting if it is paid to a registered owner that is a financial institution or member of a clearing organization and you have received the required certifications.

Bearer obligations targeted to foreign markets. Do not file Form 1042-S to report interest not subject to withholding on bearer obligations if a Form W-8 is not required.

Notional principal contract payments that are not ECI. Amounts paid on a notional principal contract that are not effectively connected with the conduct of a trade or business in the United States should not be reported on Form 1042-S.

Accrued interest and OID. Interest paid on obligations sold between interest payment dates and the portion of the purchase price of an OID obligation that is sold or exchanged in a transaction other than a redemption is not subject to reporting unless the sale or exchange is part of a plan, the principal purpose of which is to avoid tax, and the withholding agent has actual knowledge or reason to know of such plan.

Exception for amounts previously withheld upon. A withholding agent should report on Form 1042-S any amounts, whether or not subject to withholding, that are paid to a foreign payee and that have been withheld upon, including backup withholding, by another withholding agent under the presumption rules.

Example. A withholding agent (WA) makes a payment of bank deposit interest to a foreign intermediary that is a nonqualified intermediary (NQI-B). NQI-B failed to provide any information regarding the beneficial owners to whom the payment was attributable. Under the presumption rules, WA must presume that the amounts are paid to a U.S. non-exempt recipient. WA withholds 28% of the payment under the backup withholding provisions of the Code and files a Form 1099-INT reporting the interest as paid to an unknown recipient. A copy of Form 1099-INT is sent to NQI-B. The beneficial owners of the bank deposit interest are two customers of NQI-B, X and Y. Both X and Y have provided NQI-B with documentary evidence establishing that they are foreign persons and therefore not subject to backup withholding. NQI-B must file a Form 1042-S reporting the amount of bank deposit interest paid to each of X and Y and the proportionate amount of withholding that occurred.

Withholding on Dispositions of U.S. Real Property Interests by Publicly Traded Trusts and Real Estate Investment Trusts (REITs)

Regulations section 1.1445-8 provides rules for withholding required on the disposition of a U.S. real property interest by a publicly traded trust or a REIT. The special rules of Regulations section 1.1445-8 only apply to distributions by a publicly traded trust or a REIT.

In general, when a publicly traded trust or a REIT makes a distribution to a foreign person attributable to the disposition of a U.S. real property interest, it must withhold tax under section 1445. However, this withholding liability is shifted to the person who pays the distribution to a foreign person (or to the account of the foreign person) if the special notice requirement of Regulations

section 1.1445-8(f) and other requirements of Regulations section 1.1445-8(b)(1) are satisfied.

The amount subject to withholding for a distribution by a publicly traded trust is determined under the large trust rules of Regulations section 1.1445-5(c)(3).

The amount subject to withholding for a distribution by a REIT generally is the amount of each share or beneficial interest designated by the REIT as a capital gains dividend, multiplied by the number of shares or certificates of beneficial interests owned by a foreign person. If the withholding liability is shifted to the payer of the distribution under Regulations section 1.1445-8(b), the payer will receive notice as described in Regulations section 1.1445-8(f) of the amount of the distribution subject to withholding.

The rate of withholding is as follows:

1. Distribution by a publicly traded trust that makes recurring sales of growing crops and timber—10%.
2. Distribution by a publicly traded trust not described in (1) above—35%.
3. Distribution by a REIT—35%.

To determine whether an interest holder is a foreign person, see Regulations section 1.1445-8(e).

Any distribution by a REIT on stock regularly traded on a securities market in the United States is not treated as gain from the sale or exchange of a U.S. real property interest if the shareholder did not own more than 5% of that stock at any time during the tax year. These distributions are included in the shareholder's gross income as a dividend (income code 06) from the REIT, not as long-term capital gain.

Use Forms 1042-S and 1042 to report and pay over the withheld amounts. All other withholding required under section 1445 is reported and paid over using Form 8288, U.S. Withholding Tax Return for Dispositions by Foreign Persons of U.S. Real Property Interests, and Form 8288-A, Statement of Withholding on Dispositions by Foreign Persons of U.S. Real Property Interests.

Publicly Traded Partnerships (Section 1446 Withholding Tax)

A publicly traded partnership (PTP) (defined on page 3) that has effectively connected income, gain, or loss must pay a withholding tax on distributions of that income made to its foreign partners and file Form 1042-S. A nominee that receives a distribution of effectively connected income from a PTP is treated as the withholding agent to the extent of the amount specified in the qualified notice received by the nominee. For this purpose, a nominee is a domestic person that holds an interest in a PTP on behalf of a foreign person. See Pub. 515 for details.

Other partnerships that have effectively connected gross income

allocable to foreign partners must pay a withholding tax under section 1446. These amounts are reported on Form 8804, Annual Return for Partnership Withholding Tax (Section 1446), and Form 8805, Foreign Partner's Information Statement of Section 1446 Withholding Tax.

Payments by U.S. Withholding Agents

In general. U.S. withholding agents making payments described under *Amounts Subject to Reporting on Form 1042-S* on page 4 must file a separate Form 1042-S for each recipient who receives the income. Furthermore, withholding agents filing paper Forms 1042-S are not permitted to use multiple income lines on Copy A filed with the IRS. These filers must use a separate Form 1042-S for information reportable on a single income line.

 These filers cannot use a single Form 1042-S to report income if that income is reportable under different income, recipient, or exemption codes, or is subject to different rates of withholding.

A withholding agent may be permitted to use substitute payee copies of Form 1042-S (copies B, C, and D) that contain more than one income line (boxes 1 through 8). See *Substitute Forms* on page 2 for details.

See *Payments Made to Persons Who Are Not Recipients* beginning on page 7 if the payment is made to a foreign person that is not a recipient.

Payments to Recipients

Payments directly to beneficial owners. A U.S. withholding agent making a payment directly to a beneficial owner must complete Form 1042-S and treat the beneficial owner as the recipient. Boxes 17 through 20 should be left blank. A U.S. withholding agent should complete box 21 only if it is completing Form 1042-S as a paying agent acting pursuant to an agreement.

Under a grace period rule, a U.S. withholding agent may, under certain circumstances, treat a payee as a foreign person while the withholding agent waits for a valid withholding certificate. A U.S. withholding agent who relies on the grace period rule to treat a payee as a foreign person must file Form 1042-S to report all payments during the period that person was presumed to be foreign even if that person is later determined to be a U.S. person based on appropriate documentation or is presumed to be a U.S. person after the grace period ends.

In the case of foreign joint owners, you may provide a single Form 1042-S made out to the owner whose status you relied upon to determine the applicable rate of withholding (the owner subject to the highest rate of withholding). If, however, any one of the owners requests its own Form 1042-S, you must furnish a Form 1042-S to the person who requests it. If more than one Form 1042-S is issued for a single payment, the aggregate amount paid and tax withheld that is reported on all Forms 1042-S cannot exceed the total amounts paid to joint owners and the tax withheld on those payments.

Payments to a qualified intermediary, withholding foreign partnership, or withholding foreign trust. A U.S. withholding agent that makes payments to a QI (whether or not the QI assumes primary withholding responsibility), a withholding foreign partnership (WP), or a withholding foreign trust (WT) should generally complete Forms 1042-S treating the QI, WP, or WT as the recipient. However, see *Payments allocated, or presumed made, to U.S. non-exempt recipients* on this page for exceptions. The U.S. withholding agent must complete a separate Form 1042-S for each withholding rate pool of the QI, WP, or WT. For this purpose, a withholding rate pool is a payment of a single type of income, determined in accordance with the income codes used to file Form 1042-S, that is subject to a single rate of withholding. A QI that does not assume primary withholding responsibility provides information regarding the proportions of income subject to a particular withholding rate to the withholding agent on a withholding statement associated with Form W-8IMY. A U.S. withholding agent making a payment to a QI, WP, or WT must use recipient code 12 (qualified intermediary) or 04 (withholding foreign partnership or withholding foreign trust). A U.S. withholding agent must not use recipient code 13 (private arrangement intermediary withholding rate pool—general), 14 (private arrangement intermediary withholding rate pool—exempt organizations), 15 (qualified intermediary withholding rate pool—general), or 16 (qualified intermediary withholding rate pool—exempt organizations). Use of an inappropriate recipient code may cause a notice to be generated.

⚠️ **CAUTION** *A QI, WP, or WT is required to act in such capacity only for designated accounts. Therefore, such an entity may also provide a Form W-8IMY in which it certifies that it is acting as an NQI or flow-through entity for other accounts. A U.S. withholding agent that receives a Form W-8IMY on which the foreign person providing the form indicates that it is not acting as a QI, WP, or WT may not treat the foreign person as a recipient. A withholding agent must not use the EIN that a QI, WP, or WT provides in its capacity as such to report payments that are treated as made to an entity in its capacity as an NQI or flow-through entity. In that case, use the EIN, if any, that is provided by the entity on its Form W-8IMY in which it claims that it is acting as an NQI or flow-through entity.*

Payments allocated, or presumed made, to U.S. non-exempt recipients. You may be given Forms W-9 or other information regarding U.S. non-exempt recipients from a QI together with information allocating all or a portion of the payment to U.S. non-exempt recipients. You must report income allocable to a U.S. non-exempt recipient on the appropriate Form 1099 and not on Form 1042-S, even though you are paying that income to a QI.

You may also be required under the presumption rules to treat a payment made to a QI as made to a payee that is a U.S. non-exempt recipient from which you must withhold 28% of the payment under the backup withholding provisions of the Code. In this case, you must report the payment on the appropriate Form 1099. See the General Instructions for Forms 1099, 1098, 5498, and W-2G.

Example 1. WA, a U.S. withholding agent, makes a payment of U.S. source dividends to QI, a qualified intermediary. QI provides WA with a valid Form W-8IMY with which it associates a withholding statement that allocates 95% of the payment to a 15% withholding rate pool and 5% of the payment to C, a U.S. individual. QI provides WA with C's Form W-9. WA must complete a Form 1042-S, showing QI as the recipient in box 13 and recipient code 12 (qualified intermediary) in box 12, for the dividends allocated to the 15% withholding rate pool. WA must also complete a Form 1099-DIV reporting the portion of the dividend allocated to C.

Example 2. WA, a withholding agent, makes a payment of U.S. source dividends to QI, a qualified intermediary. QI provides WA with a valid Form W-8IMY with which it associates a withholding statement that allocates 40% of the payment to a 15% withholding rate pool and 40% to a 30% withholding rate pool. QI does not provide any withholding rate pool information regarding the remaining 20% of the payment. WA must apply the presumption rules to the portion of the payment (20%) that has not been allocated. Under the presumption rules, that portion of the payment is treated as paid to an unknown foreign payee. WA must complete three Forms 1042-S: one for dividends subject to 15% withholding, showing QI as the recipient in box 13 and recipient code 12 (qualified intermediary) in box 12; one for dividends subject to 30% withholding, showing QI as the recipient in box 13 and recipient code 12 (qualified intermediary) in box 12; and one for dividends subject to 30% withholding, showing QI as the recipient in box 13 and recipient code 20 (unknown recipient) in box 12.

Amounts paid to certain U.S. branches. A U.S. withholding agent making a payment to a "U.S. branch treated as a U.S. person" (defined on page 3) completes Form 1042-S as follows:
- If a withholding agent makes a payment to a U.S. branch that has provided the withholding agent with a Form W-8IMY that evidences its agreement with the withholding agent to be treated as a U.S. person, the U.S. withholding agent treats the U.S. branch as the recipient.

- If a withholding agent makes a payment to a U.S. branch that has provided a Form W-8IMY to transmit information regarding recipients, the U.S. withholding agent must complete a separate Form 1042-S for each recipient whose documentation is associated with the U.S. branch's Form W-8IMY. If a payment cannot be reliably associated with recipient documentation, the U.S. withholding agent must complete Form 1042-S in accordance with the presumption rules.
- If a withholding agent cannot reliably associate a payment with a Form W-8IMY from a U.S. branch, the payment must be reported on a single Form 1042-S treating the U.S. branch as the recipient and reporting the income as effectively connected income.

⚠️ **CAUTION** *The rules above apply only to U.S. branches treated as U.S. persons (defined on page 3). In all other cases, payments to a U.S. branch of a foreign person are treated as payments to the foreign person.*

Amounts paid to authorized foreign agents. If a withholding agent makes a payment to an authorized foreign agent, the withholding agent files Forms 1042-S for each type of income (determined by reference to the income codes used to complete Form 1042-S) treating the authorized foreign agent as the recipient, provided that the authorized foreign agent reports the payments on Forms 1042-S to each recipient to which it makes payments. If the authorized foreign agent fails to report the amounts paid on Forms 1042-S for each recipient, the U.S. withholding agent remains responsible for such reporting.

In box 12, use recipient code 17 (authorized foreign agent).

Amounts paid to an estate or complex trust. If a U.S. withholding agent makes a payment to a foreign complex trust or a foreign estate, a Form 1042-S must be completed showing the complex trust or estate as the recipient. Use recipient code 05 (trust) or 10 (estate). See *Payments Made to Persons Who Are Not Recipients* beginning on page 7 for the treatment of payments made to foreign simple trusts and foreign grantor trusts.

Dual claims. A withholding agent may make a payment to a foreign entity (for example, a hybrid entity) that is simultaneously claiming a reduced rate of tax on its own behalf for a portion of the payment and a reduced rate on behalf of persons in their capacity as interest holders in that entity on the remaining portion. If the claims are consistent and the withholding agent has accepted the multiple claims, a separate Form 1042-S must be filed for the entity for those payments for which the entity is treated as claiming a reduced rate of withholding and separate Forms 1042-S must be filed for each of the interest holders for those payments for which the interest holders are claiming a reduced rate of withholding. If the claims are consistent but the withholding agent has not chosen to accept the multiple claims, or if the

-6-

claims are inconsistent, a separate Form 1042-S must be filed for the person(s) being treated as the recipient(s).

Special instructions for U.S. trusts and estates. Report the entire amount of income subject to reporting, irrespective of estimates of distributable net income.

Payments Made to Persons Who Are Not Recipients

Disregarded entities. If a U.S. withholding agent makes a payment to a disregarded entity but receives a valid Form W-8BEN or W-8ECI from a foreign person that is the single owner of the disregarded entity, the withholding agent must file a Form 1042-S in the name of the foreign single owner. The taxpayer identifying number (TIN) on the Form 1042-S, if required, must be the foreign single owner's TIN.

Example. A withholding agent (WA) makes a payment of interest to LLC, a foreign limited liability company. LLC is wholly-owned by FC, a foreign corporation. LLC is treated as a disregarded entity. WA has a Form W-8BEN from FC on which it states that it is the beneficial owner of the income paid to LLC. WA reports the interest payment on Form 1042-S showing FC as the recipient. The result would be the same if LLC was a domestic entity.

A disregarded entity can claim to be the beneficial owner of a payment if it is a hybrid entity claiming treaty benefits. See Form W-8BEN and its instructions for more information. If a disregarded entity claims on a valid Form W-8BEN to be the beneficial owner, the U.S. withholding agent must complete a Form 1042-S treating the disregarded entity as a recipient and use recipient code 02 (corporation).

Amounts paid to a nonqualified intermediary or flow-through entity. If a U.S. withholding agent makes a payment to an NQI or a flow-through entity, it must complete a separate Form 1042-S for each recipient on whose behalf the NQI or flow-through entity acts as indicated by its withholding statement and the documentation associated with its Form W-8IMY. If a payment is made through tiers of NQIs or flow-through entities, the withholding agent must nevertheless complete Form 1042-S for the recipients to which the payments are remitted. A withholding agent completing Form 1042-S for a recipient that receives a payment through an NQI or a flow-through entity must include in boxes 17 through 20 of Form 1042-S the name, country code, address, and TIN, if any, of the NQI or flow-through entity from whom the recipient directly receives the payment. A copy of the Form 1042-S need not be provided to the NQI or flow-through entity unless the withholding agent must report the payment to an unknown recipient. See *Example 4* beginning on this page.

If a U.S. withholding agent makes payments to an NQI or flow-through entity and cannot reliably associate the payment, or any portion of the payment,

with a valid withholding certificate (Forms W-8 or W-9) or other valid appropriate documentation from a recipient (either because a recipient withholding certificate has not been provided or because the NQI or flow-through entity has failed to provide the information required on a withholding statement), the withholding agent must follow the appropriate presumption rules for that payment. If, under the presumption rules, an unknown recipient of the income is presumed to be foreign, the withholding agent must withhold 30% of the payment and report the payment on Form 1042-S. For this purpose, if the allocation information provided to the withholding agent indicates an allocation of more than 100% of the payment, then no portion of the payment should be considered to be associated with a Form W-8, Form W-9, or other appropriate documentation. The Form 1042-S should be completed by entering "Unknown Recipient" in box 13 and recipient code 20 in box 12.

Pro-rata reporting. If the withholding agent has agreed that an NQI may provide information allocating a payment to its account holders under the alternative procedure of Regulations section 1.1441-1(e)(3)(iv)(D) (no later than February 14, 2007) and the NQI fails to allocate more than 10% of the payment in a withholding rate pool to the specific recipients in the pool, the withholding agent must file Forms 1042-S for each recipient in the pool on a pro-rata basis. If, however, the NQI fails to timely allocate 10% or less of the payment in a withholding rate pool to the specific recipients in the pool, the withholding agent must file Forms 1042-S for each recipient for which it has allocation information and report the unallocated portion of the payment on a Form 1042-S issued to "Unknown Recipient." In either case, the withholding agent must include the NQI information in boxes 17 through 20 on that form. See *Example 6* and *Example 7* on page 8.

The following examples illustrate Form 1042-S reporting for payments made to NQIs and flow-through entities.

Example 1. NQI, a nonqualified intermediary, has three account holders, A, B, and QI. All three account holders invest in U.S. securities that produce interest and dividends. A and B are foreign individuals and have provided NQI with Forms W-8BEN. QI is a qualified intermediary and has provided NQI with a Form W-8IMY and the withholding statement required from a qualified intermediary. QI's withholding statement states that QI has two withholding rate pools: one for interest described by income code 01 (interest paid by U.S. obligors—general) and one for dividends described by income code 06 (dividends paid by U.S. corporations—general). NQI provides WA, a U.S. withholding agent, with its own Form W-8IMY, with which it associates the Forms W-8BEN of A and B and the Form W-8IMY of QI. In addition, NQI provides WA with a complete withholding statement that allocates the

payments of interest and dividends WA makes to NQI among A, B, and QI. All of the interest and dividends paid by WA to NQI is described by income code 01 (interest paid by U.S. obligors—general) and income code 06 (dividends paid by U.S. corporations—general). WA must file a total of six Forms 1042-S: two Forms 1042-S (one for interest and one for dividends) showing A as the recipient, two Forms 1042-S (one for interest and one for dividends) showing B as the recipient, and two Forms 1042-S (one for interest and one for dividends) showing QI as the recipient. WA must show information relating to NQI in boxes 17 through 20 on all six Forms 1042-S.

Example 2. The facts are the same as in Example 1, except that A and B are account holders of NQI2, which is an account holder of NQI. NQI2 provides NQI with a Form W-8IMY with which it associates the Forms W-8BEN of A and B and a complete withholding statement that allocates the interest and dividend payments it receives from NQI to A and B. NQI provides WA with its Form W-8IMY and the Forms W-8IMY of NQI2 and QI and the Forms W-8BEN of A and B. In addition, NQI associates a complete withholding statement with its Form W-8IMY that allocates the payments of interest and dividends to A, B, and QI. WA must file six Forms 1042-S: two Forms 1042-S (one for interest and one for dividends) showing A as the recipient, two Forms 1042-S (one for interest and one for dividends) showing B as the recipient, and two Forms 1042-S (one for interest and one for dividends) showing QI as the recipient. The Forms 1042-S issued to A and B must show information relating to NQI2 in boxes 17 through 20 because A and B receive their payments directly from NQI2, not NQI. The Forms 1042-S issued to QI must show information relating to NQI in boxes 17 through 20.

Example 3. FP is a nonwithholding foreign partnership and therefore a flow-through entity. FP establishes an account with WA, a U.S. withholding agent, from which FP receives interest described by income code 01 (interest paid by U.S. obligors—general). FP has three partners, A, B, and C, all of whom are individuals. FP provides WA with a Form W-8IMY with which it associates the Forms W-8BEN from each of A, B, and C. In addition, FP provides a complete withholding statement with its Form W-8IMY that allocates the interest payments among A, B, and C. WA must file three Forms 1042-S, one each for A, B, and C. The Forms 1042-S must show information relating to FP in boxes 17 through 20.

Example 4. NQI is a nonqualified intermediary. It has four customers: A, B, C, and D. NQI receives Forms W-8BEN from each of A, B, C, and D. NQI establishes an account with WA, a U.S. withholding agent, in which it holds securities on behalf of A, B, C, and D. The securities pay interest that is described by income code 01 (interest paid by U.S. obligors—general) and that may qualify for the portfolio interest exemption from withholding if all of the requirements for that exception are met. NQI provides WA with a Form W-8IMY with which it associates the Forms W-8BEN of A, B, C, and D. However, NQI does not provide WA with a complete withholding statement in association with its Form W-8IMY. Because NQI has not provided WA with a complete withholding statement, WA cannot reliably associate the payments of interest with the documentation of A, B, C, and D, and must apply the presumption rules. Under the presumption rules, WA must treat the interest as paid to an unknown recipient that is a foreign person. The payments of interest are subject to 30% withholding. WA must complete one Form 1042-S, entering "Unknown Recipient" in box 13 and recipient code 20 in box 12. WA must include information relating to NQI in boxes 17 through 20 and must provide the recipient copies of the form to NQI. Because NQI has failed to provide all the information necessary for WA to accurately report the payments of interest to A, B, C, and D, NQI must report the payments on Form 1042-S. See *Amounts Paid by Nonqualified Intermediaries and Flow-Through Entities* on page 10. The results would be the same if WA's account holder was a flow-through entity instead of a nonqualified intermediary.

Example 5. The facts are the same as in Example 4, except that NQI provides the Forms W-8BEN of A and B, but not the Forms W-8BEN of C and D. NQI also provides a withholding statement that allocates a portion of the interest payment to A and B but does not allocate the remaining portion of the payment. WA must file three Forms 1042-S: one showing A as the recipient in box 13, one showing B as the recipient in box 13, and one showing "Unknown Recipient" in box 13 (and recipient code 20 in box 12) for the unallocated portion of the payment that cannot be associated with valid documentation from a recipient. In addition, WA must send the Form 1042-S for the unknown recipient to NQI. All Forms 1042-S must contain information relating to NQI in boxes 17 through 20. The results would be the same if WA's account holder was a flow-through entity instead of a nonqualified intermediary.

Example 6. NQI is a nonqualified intermediary. It has four customers: A, B, C, and D. NQI receives Forms W-8BEN from each of A, B, C, and D. NQI establishes an account with WA, a U.S. withholding agent, in which it holds securities on behalf of A, B, C, and D. The securities pay interest that is described by income code 01 (interest paid by U.S. obligors—general) and that may qualify for the portfolio interest exemption from withholding if all of the requirements for that exception are met. NQI provides WA with a Form W-8IMY with which it associates the Forms W-8BEN of A, B, C, and D. WA and NQI agree that they will apply the alternative procedures of Regulations section 1.1441-1(e)(3)(iv)(D). Accordingly, NQI provides a complete withholding

statement that indicates that it has one 0% withholding rate pool. WA pays $100 of interest to NQI. NQI fails to provide WA with the allocation information by February 14, 2007. Therefore, WA must report 25% of the payment to each of A, B, C, and D using pro-rata basis reporting. Accordingly, for each of the Forms 1042-S, WA must enter $25 in box 2 (gross income),"30.00" in box 5 (tax rate), and $0 in box 7 (U.S. federal tax withheld). In addition, WA must check the PRO-RATA BASIS REPORTING box at the top of the form and include NQI's name, address, country code, and TIN, if any, in boxes 17 through 20. WA must enter "30.00" in box 5 (tax rate) because without allocation information, WA cannot reliably associate the payment of interest with documentation from a foreign beneficial owner and therefore may not apply the portfolio interest exception. See the instructions for box 6 (exemption code) on page 13 for information on completing that box.

Example 7. The facts are the same as in Example 6, except that NQI timely provides WA with information allocating 70% of the payment to A, 10% of the payment to B, and 10% of the payment to C. NQI fails to allocate any of the payment to D. Because NQI has allocated 90% of the payment made to the 0% withholding rate pool, WA is not required to report to NQI's account holders on a pro-rata basis. Instead, WA must file Forms 1042-S for A, B, and C, entering $70, $10, and $10, respectively in box 2 (gross income), "00.00" in box 5 (tax rate), exemption code 05 (portfolio interest) in box 6, and $0 in box 7 (U.S. federal tax withheld). WA must apply the presumption rules to the $10 that NQI has not allocated and file a Form 1042-S showing "Unknown Recipient" in box 13 and recipient code 20 in box 12. On that Form 1042-S, WA must also enter "30.00" in box 5 (tax rate) because the portfolio interest exemption is unavailable and $0 in box 7 (U.S. federal tax withheld) because no amounts were actually withheld from the interest. In addition, WA must send the Form 1042-S for the unknown recipient to NQI. All Forms 1042-S must contain information relating to NQI in boxes 17 through 20.

Payments allocated, or presumed made, to U.S. non-exempt recipients. You may be given Forms W-9 or other information regarding U.S. non-exempt recipients from an NQI or flow-through entity together with information allocating all or a portion of the payment to U.S. non-exempt recipients. You must report income allocable to a U.S. non-exempt recipient on the appropriate Form 1099 and not on Form 1042-S, even though you are paying that income to an NQI or a flow-through entity.

You may also be required under the presumption rules to treat a payment made to an NQI or flow-through entity as made to a payee that is a U.S. non-exempt recipient from which you must withhold 28% of the payment under the backup withholding provisions of the

Code. In this case, you must report the payment on the appropriate Form 1099. See the General Instructions for Forms 1099, 1098, 5498, and W-2G.

Example 1. FP is a nonwithholding foreign partnership and therefore a flow-through entity. FP establishes an account with WA, a U.S. withholding agent, from which FP receives interest described by income code 01 (interest paid by U.S. obligors—general). FP has three partners, A, B, and C, all of whom are individuals. FP provides WA with a Form W-8IMY with which it associates Forms W-8BEN from A and B and a Form W-9 from C, a U.S. person. In addition, FP provides a complete withholding statement in association with its Form W-8IMY that allocates the interest payments among A, B, and C. WA must file two Forms 1042-S, one each for A and B, and a Form 1099-INT for C.

Example 2. The facts are the same as in Example 1, except that FP does not provide any documentation from its partners. Because WA cannot reliably associate the interest with documentation from a payee, it must apply the presumption rules. Under the presumption rules, the interest is deemed paid to an unknown U.S. non-exempt recipient. WA must, therefore, apply backup withholding at 28% to the payment of interest and report the payment on Form 1099-INT. WA must file a Form 1099-INT and send a copy to FP.

Amounts Paid by Qualified Intermediaries

In general. A QI reports payments on Form 1042-S in the same manner as a U.S. withholding agent. However, payments that are made by the QI directly to foreign beneficial owners (or that are treated as paid directly to beneficial owners) may generally be reported on the basis of reporting pools. A reporting pool consists of income that falls within a particular withholding rate and within a particular income code, exemption code, or recipient code as determined on Form 1042-S. A QI may not report on the basis of reporting pools in the circumstances described in *Recipient-by-Recipient Reporting* on page 9. A QI may use a single recipient code 15 (qualified intermediary withholding rate pool—general) for all reporting pools, except for amounts paid to foreign tax-exempt recipients for which recipient code 16 should be used. Note, however, that a QI should only use recipient code 16 for pooled account holders that have claimed an exemption based on their tax-exempt status and not some other exemption (tax treaty or other Code exception). See *Amounts Paid to Private Arrangement Intermediaries* on page 9, if a QI is reporting payments to a PAI.

Example 1. QI, a qualified intermediary, has four direct account holders, A and B, foreign individuals, and X and Y, foreign corporations. A and X are residents of a country with which the United States has an income tax treaty

-8-

and have provided documentation that establishes that they are entitled to a lower treaty rate of 15% on withholding of dividends from U.S. sources. B and Y are not residents of a treaty country and are subject to 30% withholding on dividends. QI receives U.S. source dividends on behalf of its four customers. QI must file one Form 1042-S for the 15% withholding rate pool. This Form 1042-S must show income code 06 (dividends paid by U.S. corporations—general) in box 1, "15.00" in box 5 (tax rate), recipient code 15 (qualified intermediary withholding rate pool—general) in box 12, and "Withholding rate pool" in box 13 (recipient's name). QI must also file one Form 1042-S for the 30% withholding rate pool that contains the same information as the Form 1042-S filed for the 15% withholding rate pool, except that it will show "30.00" in box 5 (tax rate).

Example 2. The facts are the same as in Example 1, except that Y is an organization that has tax-exempt status in the United States and in the country in which it is located. QI must file three Forms 1042-S. Two of the Forms 1042-S will contain the same information as in Example 1. The third Form 1042-S will contain information for the withholding rate pool consisting of the amounts paid to Y. This Form 1042-S will show income code 06 (dividends paid by U.S. corporations—general) in box 1, "00.00" in box 5 (tax rate), exemption code 02 (exempt under an Internal Revenue Code section (income other than portfolio interest)) in box 6, recipient code 16 (qualified intermediary withholding rate pool—exempt organizations) in box 12, and "Zero rate withholding pool—exempt organizations," or similar designation, in box 13 (recipient's name).

Under the terms of its withholding agreement with the IRS, the QI may be required to report the amounts paid to U.S. non-exempt recipients on Form 1099 using the name, address, and TIN of the payee to the extent those items of information are known. These amounts must not be reported on Form 1042-S. In addition, amounts paid to U.S. exempt recipients are not subject to reporting on Form 1042-S or Form 1099.

Amounts Paid to Private Arrangement Intermediaries

A QI generally must report payments made to each private arrangement intermediary (PAI) (defined on page 3) as if the PAI's direct account holders were its own. Therefore, if the payment is made directly by the PAI to the recipient, the QI may report the payment on a pooled basis. A separate Form 1042-S is required for each withholding rate pool of each PAI. The QI must, however, use recipient code 13 or 14 for PAIs and must include the name and address of the PAI in box 13. If the PAI is providing recipient information from an NQI or flow-through entity, the QI may not report the payments on a pooled basis. Instead, it must follow the same procedures as a

U.S. withholding agent making a payment to an NQI or flow-through entity.

Example. QI, a qualified intermediary, pays U.S. source dividends to direct account holders that are foreign persons and beneficial owners. It also pays a portion of the U.S. source dividends to two private arrangement intermediaries, PAI1 and PAI2. The private arrangement intermediaries pay the dividends they receive from QI to foreign persons that are beneficial owners and direct account holders in PAI1 and PAI2. All of the dividends paid are subject to a 15% rate of withholding. QI must file a Form 1042-S for the dividends paid to its own direct account holders that are beneficial owners. QI must also file two Forms 1042-S, one for the dividends paid to the direct account holders of each of PAI1 and PAI2. Each of the Forms 1042-S that QI files for payments made to PAI1 and PAI2 must contain recipient code 13 (private arrangement intermediary withholding rate pool—general) in box 12 and the name and address of PAI1 or PAI2 in box 13 (recipient's name and address).

Amounts Paid to Certain Related Partnerships and Trusts

A QI that is applying the rules of Section 4A.02 of the QI agreement to a partnership or trust must file separate Forms 1042-S reflecting reporting pools for each partnership or trust that has provided reporting pool information in its withholding statement. However, the QI must file separate Forms 1042-S for partners, beneficiaries, or owners of such partnership or trust that are indirect partners, beneficiaries, or owners, and for direct partners, beneficiaries, or owners of such partnership or trust that are intermediaries or flow-through entities.

Recipient-by-Recipient Reporting

If a QI is not permitted to report on the basis of reporting pools, it must follow the same rules that apply to a U.S. withholding agent. A QI may not report the following payments on a reporting pool basis, but rather must complete Form 1042-S for each appropriate recipient.

Payments made to another QI, WP, or WT. The QI must complete a Form 1042-S treating the other QI, WP, or WT as the recipient.

Payments made to an NQI (including an NQI that is an account holder of a PAI). The QI must complete a Form 1042-S for each recipient who receives the payment from the NQI. A QI that is completing Form 1042-S for a recipient that receives a payment through an NQI must include in boxes 17 through 20 the name, country code, address, and TIN, if any, of the NQI from whom the recipient directly receives the payment.

Example. QI, a qualified intermediary, has NQI, a nonqualified intermediary, as an account holder. NQI has two account holders, A and B, both foreign persons

who receive U.S. source dividends from QI. NQI provides QI with a valid Form W-8IMY, with which it associates Forms W-8BEN from A and B and a complete withholding statement that allocates the dividends paid to NQI between A and B. QI must complete two Forms 1042-S, one for A and one for B, and include information relating to NQI in boxes 17 through 20.

Payments made to a flow-through entity. The QI must complete a Form 1042-S for each recipient who receives the payment from the flow-through entity. A QI that is completing a Form 1042-S for a recipient that receives a payment through a flow-through entity must include in boxes 17 through 20 the name, country code, address, and TIN, if any, of the flow-through entity from which the recipient directly receives the payment.

Example. QI, a qualified intermediary, has FP, a nonwithholding foreign partnership, as an account holder. QI pays interest described by income code 01 (interest paid by U.S. obligors—general) to FP. FP has three partners, A, B, and C, all of whom are individuals. FP provides QI with a Form W-8IMY with which it associates the Forms W-8BEN from each of A, B, and C. In addition, FP provides a complete withholding statement in association with its Form W-8IMY that allocates the interest payments among A, B, and C. QI must file three Forms 1042-S, one each for A, B, and C. The Forms 1042-S must show information relating to FP in boxes 17 through 20.

Amounts Paid by Withholding Foreign Partnerships and Trusts

In general. Generally, a withholding foreign partnership (WP) or withholding foreign trust (WT) is required to file a separate Form 1042-S for each direct partner, beneficiary, or owner to whom the WP or WT distributes, or in whose distributive share is included, an amount subject to withholding under Chapter 3 of the Code, in the same manner as a U.S. withholding agent. However, if the WP or WT has made a pooled reporting election in its WP or WT agreement, the WP or WT may instead report payments to such direct partners, beneficiaries, or owners on the basis of reporting pools and file a separate Form 1042-S for each reporting pool. A reporting pool consists of income that falls within a particular withholding rate and within a particular income code, exemption code, and recipient code, as determined on Form 1042-S. A WP or WT may use a single recipient code 15 (qualified intermediary withholding rate pool—general) for all reporting pools, except for amounts paid to foreign tax-exempt recipients for which a separate recipient code 16 must be used. For this purpose, a foreign tax-exempt recipient includes any organization that is not subject to withholding and is not liable to tax in its country of residence because it is a charitable organization, pension fund, or foreign government.

Amounts paid to certain related partnerships and trusts. A WP or WT that is applying the rules of Section 10.02 of the WP or WT agreement to a partnership or trust must file separate Forms 1042-S reflecting reporting pools for each partnership or trust that has provided reporting pool information in its withholding statement. However, the WP or WT must apply the provisions of Regulations sections 1.1441-1 and 1.1441-5 to partners, beneficiaries, or owners of such partnership or trust that are indirect partners, beneficiaries, or owners, and to direct partners, beneficiaries, or owners of such partnership or trust that are intermediaries or flow-through entities.

Amounts Paid by Nonqualified Intermediaries and Flow-Through Entities

An NQI and a flow-through entity are withholding agents and must file Forms 1042-S for amounts paid to recipients. However, an NQI or flow-through entity is not required to file Form 1042-S if it is not required to file Form 1042-S under the *Multiple Withholding Agent Rule* beginning on this page. An NQI or flow-through entity must report payments made to recipients to the extent it has failed to provide to another withholding agent the appropriate documentation and complete withholding statement, including information allocating the payment to each recipient.

Forms 1042-S must be filed in any case where the NQI or flow-through entity is making a payment to a recipient and tax has been withheld on the payment by another withholding agent that did not report the payment on Form 1042-S to the recipient, even if the recipient should have been exempt from taxation. Failure to file Forms 1042-S may not only result in penalties for the NQI or flow-through entity, but may result in the denial of any refund claim made by a recipient.

If another withholding agent has withheld tax on an amount that should have been exempt (for example, where the withholding agent applied the presumption rules because it did not receive proper documentation or other required information from the NQI or flow-through entity), the NQI or flow-through entity should report the correct tax rate and the actual U.S. federal tax withheld in boxes 5 and 7 and should enter the applicable exemption code using the instructions for box 6 on page 13.

NQI or flow-through entity provides correct and complete information to another withholding agent yet the withholding agent underwithholds. In this case, assuming that the NQI or flow-through entity knows that the withholding agent underwithheld, the NQI or flow-through entity must withhold additional amounts to bring the total withholding to the correct amount. Furthermore, the NQI or flow-through

entity must complete Form 1042-S and must include in boxes 5 and 7 the correct tax rate and the combined amount of U.S. federal tax withheld by the NQI or flow-through entity and any other withholding agent in the chain of payment that has withheld on the payment. See *Example 2* on this page.

Example 1. A foreign bank acts as a nonqualified intermediary (NQI) for four different foreign persons (A, B, C, and D) each of whom own securities from which they receive interest. The interest is paid by a U.S. withholding agent (WA) as custodian of the securities for NQI. A, B, C, and D each own a 25% interest in the securities. NQI has furnished WA a Form W-8IMY to which it has attached Forms W-8BEN from A and B. NQI's Form W-8IMY contains an attachment stating that 25% of the securities are allocable to each of A and B, and 50% to undocumented owners. WA pays $100 of interest during the calendar year. WA treats the $25 of interest allocable to A and the $25 of interest allocable to B as portfolio interest and completes a Form 1042-S for A and for B as the recipients. WA includes information relating to NQI in boxes 17 through 20 on the Forms 1042-S for A and B. WA subjects the remaining $50 of interest to 30% withholding under the presumption rules and reports the interest on a Form 1042-S by entering "Unknown Recipient" in box 13 (and recipient code 20 in box 12), "30.00" in box 5 (tax rate), and $15 as the amount withheld in box 7. WA also includes information relating to NQI in boxes 17 through 20 of the Form 1042-S and sends a copy of the form to NQI. Because NQI has not provided WA with beneficial owner information for C and D, NQI must report the interest paid to C and D on Forms 1042-S. (Note that under the multiple withholding agent rule, NQI is not required to file a Form 1042-S for A or B.) The Forms 1042-S for C and D should show $25 in box 2 (gross income) and $7.50 in box 7 (the actual U.S. federal tax withheld). The rate of tax NQI includes on the Form 1042-S for C and D depends on the rate of withholding to which they should be subject. Thus, if C and D provided NQI with documentation prior to the payment of interest that would qualify the interest as portfolio interest, the rate entered in box 5 should be "00.00." If they do not qualify for a reduced rate of withholding, NQI should enter "30.00" in box 5. In any event, NQI must also enter "99" in box 6 (exemption code) of the Forms 1042-S it prepares for C and D. See the instructions for box 6 on page 13.

Example 2. A U.S. withholding agent (WA) makes a $100 dividend payment to a foreign bank (NQI) that acts as a nonqualified intermediary. NQI receives the payment on behalf of A, a resident of a treaty country who is entitled to a 15% rate of withholding, and B, a resident of a country that does not have a tax treaty with the United States and who is subject to 30% withholding. NQI provides WA with its Form W-8IMY to which it associates the Forms W-8BEN from both A and B and a complete withholding

statement that allocates 50% of the dividend to A and 50% to B. A's Form W-8BEN claims a 15% treaty rate of withholding. B's Form W-8BEN does not claim a reduced rate of withholding. WA, however, mistakenly withholds only 15%, $15, from the entire $100 payment. WA completes a Form 1042-S for each A and B as the recipients, showing on each form $50 of dividends in box 2, a withholding rate of "15.00" in box 5 (tax rate), and $7.50 as the amount withheld in box 7. Under the multiple withholding agent rule, NQI is not required to file a Form 1042-S for A. However, because NQI knows (or should know) that B is subject to a 30% rate of withholding, and assuming it knows that WA only withheld 15%, the multiple withholding agent rule does not apply to the dividend paid to B and NQI must withhold an additional 15% from the payment to B. NQI must then file a Form 1042-S for B showing $50 of dividends in box 2, "30.00" in box 5 (the correct tax rate), and $15 withheld in box 7 (the combined amount withheld). NQI must also enter "00" in box 6 (exemption code). See the instructions for box 6 on page 13.

Example 3. A withholding agent (WA) receives a Form W-8IMY from a nonqualified intermediary (NQI). NQI's Form W-8IMY relates to payments of bank deposit interest. NQI collects the bank deposit interest on behalf of A, B, C, and D, but does not associate Forms W-8, W-9, or other documentary evidence with the Form W-8IMY that NQI provides WA. A, B, and C are foreign persons for whom NQI has valid documentation establishing their foreign status. D is a U.S. person and has provided NQI with a Form W-9. Under the presumption rules, WA must treat the bank deposit interest as being paid to an unknown U.S. person and apply backup withholding at 28%. WA must complete one Form 1099 for an unknown payee showing 28% backup withholding. A copy of the form must be sent to NQI. Because NQI failed to provide the requisite documentation to WA and because the amounts have been subject to withholding, NQI must report the amounts paid to A, B, C, and D. Accordingly, NQI must file a Form 1042-S for each A, B, and C showing deposit interest (income code 29) as the type of payment in box 1; "00.00" in box 5 (the correct tax rate); the actual amount withheld from the payment allocable to A, B, and C in box 7; and exemption code 99 in box 6. (See the instructions for box 6 on page 13.) NQI must also file a Form 1099 for D to report the actual amounts paid and withheld.

Multiple Withholding Agent Rule

A withholding agent is not required to file Form 1042-S if a return is filed by another withholding agent reporting the same amount to the same recipient (the multiple withholding agent rule). If an NQI or flow-through entity has provided another withholding agent with the appropriate documentation and complete withholding statement, including information allocating the payment to each recipient, the NQI or flow-through entity may presume that the other withholding agent filed the required Forms 1042-S unless the NQI or flow-through entity knows, or has reason to know, that the required Form 1042-S reporting has not been done.

The multiple withholding agent rule does not relieve withholding agents from Form 1042-S reporting responsibility in the following circumstances.

- Any withholding agent making a payment to a QI, WP, or WT must report that payment as made to the QI, WP, or WT.
- Any U.S. withholding agent making a payment to an authorized foreign agent must report that payment to the authorized foreign agent.
- Any withholding agent making a payment to a U.S. branch treated as a U.S. person must report the payment as made to that branch.
- Any withholding agent making a payment to a flow-through entity must report the payment as made to a beneficial owner, QI, WP, or WT that has a direct or indirect interest in that entity.
- Any withholding agent that withholds an amount from a payment under Chapter 3 of the Code must report that amount to the recipient from whom it was withheld, unless the payment is reportable on another IRS form.

Furthermore, the multiple withholding agent rule does not relieve the following from Form 1042-S reporting responsibility.

- Any QI, WP, or WT required to report an amount to a withholding rate pool.
- An NQI or flow-through entity that has not transmitted a valid Form W-8 or other valid documentation to another withholding agent together with the required withholding statement.

Penalties

The following penalties apply to the person required to file Form 1042-S. The penalties apply to both paper filers and to electronic/magnetic media filers.

Late filing of correct Form 1042-S. A penalty may be imposed for failure to file each correct and complete Form 1042-S when due (including extensions), unless you can show that the failure was due to reasonable cause and not willful neglect. The penalty, based on when you file a correct Form 1042-S, is:

- $15 per Form 1042-S if you correctly file within 30 days; maximum penalty $75,000 per year ($25,000 for a small business). A small business, for this purpose, is defined as having average annual gross receipts of $5 million or less for the 3 most recent tax years (or for the period of its existence, if shorter) ending before the calendar year in which the Forms 1042-S are due.
- $30 per Form 1042-S if you correctly file more than 30 days after the due date but by August 1; maximum penalty $150,000 per year ($50,000 for a small business).
- $50 per Form 1042-S if you file after August 1 or you do not file correct Forms

1042-S; maximum penalty $250,000 per year ($100,000 for a small business).

If you intentionally disregard the requirement to report correct information, the penalty per Form 1042-S is increased to $100 or, if greater, 10% of the total amount of items required to be reported, with no maximum penalty.

Failure to furnish correct Form 1042-S to recipient. If you fail to provide correct statements to recipients and cannot show reasonable cause, a penalty of $50 may be imposed for each failure to furnish Form 1042-S to the recipient when due. The penalty may also be imposed for failure to include all required information or for furnishing incorrect information on Form 1042-S. The maximum penalty is $100,000 for all failures to furnish correct recipient statements during a calendar year. If you intentionally disregard the requirement to report correct information, each $50 penalty is increased to $100 or, if greater, 10% of the total amount of items required to be reported, and the $100,000 maximum does not apply.

Failure to file on electronic/magnetic media. If you are required to file on electronic/magnetic media but fail to do so, and you do not have an approved waiver on record, you may be subject to a $50 penalty per return unless you establish reasonable cause. The penalty applies separately to original returns and amended returns.

Avoid Common Errors

To ensure that your Forms 1042-S can be correctly processed, be sure that you:
- Carefully read the information provided in Pub. 515 and these instructions.
- If you are an electronic or magnetic media filer, comply with the requirements in Pub. 1187.
- Complete all required fields. At a minimum, you must enter information in boxes 1, 2, 5, 6, 7, 9, 10, 12, 13, 15, and 16. Other boxes must be completed if the nature of the payment requires it.

Note. You may leave box 6 blank if you are applying backup withholding to the payment being reported.
- Use only income, recipient, exemption, and country codes specifically listed in these instructions.
- Use only tax rates that are allowed by statute, regulation, or treaty. Do not attempt to "blend" rates. Instead, if necessary, submit multiple Forms 1042-S to show changes in tax rate. Valid tax rates are listed on page 13 under *Box 5, Tax Rate*.

All information you enter when reporting the payment must correctly reflect the intent of statute and regulations. Generally, you should rely on the withholding documentation you have collected (Form W-8 series, Form 8233, etc.) to complete your Form 1042-S submissions.

Also note the following:
- The gross income you report in box 2 cannot be zero.

- The income code you report in box 1 must correctly reflect the type of income you pay to the recipient.
- The withholding agent's name, address, and EIN, QI-EIN, WP-EIN, or WT-EIN must be reported in boxes 9 and 10 in all cases.
- The recipient's name, address, and TIN, if any, must be reported in boxes 13 and 14. You must generally report a foreign address in box 13. See the instructions for box 13 on page 14.
- The recipient code you report in box 12 must correctly identify the recipient's status. Use recipient code 20 only if you do not know who the recipient is.

Note. If you cannot identify the recipient, the tax withheld must be 30%.
- The recipient's country of residence for tax purposes that you report in box 15 must be present and correctly coded and cannot be "US." Additionally, do not use "OC" or "UC" except as specifically allowed in these instructions.
- The exemption code you report in box 6 must correctly identify the proper tax status for the type of income you pay to the recipient.

Note. If you use exemption code 04 (exempt under tax treaty), the recipient's country of residence for tax purposes that you report in box 15 must be a valid treaty country. Countries with which the United States has a tax treaty are shown in bold italics in the country code list beginning on page 15.

 You, the withholding agent, are liable for the tax if you know, or should have known, that underwithholding on a payment has occurred.

Specific Instructions for Withholding Agents

 All amounts must be reported in U.S. dollars.

Rounding Off to Whole Dollars

You may round off cents to whole dollars. If you do round to whole dollars, you must round all amounts. To round off amounts to the nearest whole dollar, drop amounts under 50 cents and increase amounts from 50 to 99 cents to the next dollar. For example, $1.39 becomes $1 and $2.50 becomes $3. If you have to add two or more amounts to figure the amount to enter on a line, include cents when adding and only round off the total.

AMENDED Box at Top of Form

See *Correcting Paper Forms 1042-S* on page 15.

-11-

PRO-RATA BASIS REPORTING Box

Withholding agents must check this box to notify the IRS that an NQI that used the alternative procedures of Regulations section 1.1441-1(e)(3)(iv)(D) failed to properly comply with those procedures. See *Pro-rata reporting* on page 7 for additional information and examples.

Box 1, Income Code

All filers must enter the appropriate 2-digit income code from the list below. Use the income code that is the most specific. For example, if you are paying bank deposit interest, you should use code 29 (deposit interest), not code 01 (interest paid by U.S. obligors—general). If you paid more than one type of income to or on behalf of the same recipient, you must complete a separate Form 1042-S for each income type.

Substitute payment income codes are to be used for all substitute payment transactions. For more information, see Regulations sections 1.861-2(a)(7) and 1.861-3(a)(6) and Notice 97-66.

Note. Although income codes are provided for deposit interest, short-term OID, and notional principal contract income, those items are not always subject to reporting on Form 1042-S. For example, bank deposit interest is reportable if it is effectively connected with the conduct of a U.S. trade or business or is paid to a resident of Canada. Short-term OID or bank deposit interest may need to be reported by an NQI or flow-through entity if those amounts are paid to foreign persons and another withholding agent backup withheld on those amounts under the presumption rules. (See *Example 3* on page 10.) Notional principal contract income is reportable if it is effectively connected with the conduct of a trade or

---

Income Codes, Exemption Codes, and Recipient Codes

Box 1. Enter the appropriate income code.

Code	Interest Income
01	Interest paid by U.S. obligors—general
02	Interest paid on real property mortgages
03	Interest paid to controlling foreign corporations
04	Interest paid by foreign corporations
05	Interest on tax-free covenant bonds
29	Deposit interest
30	Original issue discount (OID)
31	Short-term OID
33	Substitute payment—interest

Code	Dividend Income
06	Dividends paid by U.S. corporations—general
07	Dividends qualifying for direct dividend rate
08	Dividends paid by foreign corporations
34	Substitute payment—dividends

Code	Other Income
09	Capital gains
10	Industrial royalties
11	Motion picture or television copyright royalties
12	Other royalties (e.g., copyright, recording, publishing)
13	Real property income and natural resources royalties
14	Pensions, annuities, alimony, and/or insurance premiums
15	Scholarship or fellowship grants
16	Compensation for independent personal services[1]
17	Compensation for dependent personal services[1]
18	Compensation for teaching[1]
19	Compensation during studying and training[1]
20	Earnings as an artist or athlete[2]
24	Real estate investment trust (REIT) distributions of capital gains
25	Trust distributions subject to IRC section 1445
26	Unsevered growing crops and timber distributions by a trust subject to IRC section 1445
27	Publicly traded partnership distributions subject to IRC section 1446
28	Gambling winnings[6]
32	Notional principal contract income[3]
35	Substitute payment—other
36	Capital gains distributions
50	Other income

Box 6. If the tax rate entered in box 5 is 00.00, you must generally enter the appropriate exemption code from the list below (but see the **Caution** below).

Code	Authority for Exemption
01	Income effectively connected with a U.S. trade or business
02	Exempt under an Internal Revenue Code section (income other than portfolio interest)
03	Income is not from U.S. sources[4]
04	Exempt under tax treaty
05	Portfolio interest exempt under an Internal Revenue Code section
06	Qualified intermediary that assumes primary withholding responsibility
07	Withholding foreign partnership or withholding foreign trust
08	U.S. branch treated as a U.S. person
09	Qualified intermediary represents income is exempt

Caution: *See the instructions for box 6 on page 13 for information on additional codes ("00" and "99") that may be required.*

Box 12. Enter the appropriate recipient code.

Code	Type of Recipient
01	Individual[2]
02	Corporation[2]
03	Partnership other than a withholding foreign partnership[2]
04	Withholding foreign partnership or withholding foreign trust
05	Trust
06	Government or international organization
07	Tax-exempt organization (IRC section 501(a))
08	Private foundation
09	Artist or athlete[2]
10	Estate
11	U.S. branch treated as U.S. person
12	Qualified intermediary
13	Private arrangement intermediary withholding rate pool—general[5]
14	Private arrangement intermediary withholding rate pool—exempt organizations[5]
15	Qualified intermediary withholding rate pool—general[5]
16	Qualified intermediary withholding rate pool—exempt organizations[5]
17	Authorized foreign agent
18	Public pension fund
20	Unknown recipient

---

[1] If compensation that otherwise would be covered under Income Codes 16–19 is directly attributable to the recipient's occupation as an artist or athlete, use Income Code 20 instead.

[2] If Income Code 20 is used, Recipient Code 09 (artist or athlete) should be used instead of Recipient Code 01 (individual), 02 (corporation), or 03 (partnership other than withholding foreign partnership).

[3] Use appropriate Interest Income Code for embedded interest in a notional principal contract.

[4] Non-U.S. source income paid to a nonresident alien is not subject to U.S. tax. Use Exemption Code 03 when entering an amount for information reporting purposes only.

[5] May be used only by a qualified intermediary.

[6] Subject to 30% withholding rate unless the recipient is from one of the treaty countries listed under *Gambling winnings (Income Code 28)* in Pub. 515.

-12-

business in the United States. For more information, see the regulations under Chapter 3 of the Code and Pub. 515.

Box 2, Gross Income

For each income type, enter the gross amount you paid to or on behalf of the recipient during calendar year 2006, including withheld tax. The following special procedures apply to the reporting of gross income.

• You must report the entire amount of a corporate distribution made with respect to stock even if you elect to reduce the amount of withholding on the distribution because all or a portion of the distribution is nontaxable or represents a capital gain dividend or exempt-interest dividend distributed by a regulated investment company.

• You must report the entire amount of a payment if you do not know at the time of payment the amount that is subject to withholding because the determination of the source of the income or the calculation of the amount of income subject to tax depends upon facts that are not known at the time of payment.

• You must report the entire amount of gains relating to the disposal of timber, coal, or domestic iron ore with a retained economic interest and gains relating to contingent payments received from the sale or exchange of patents, copyrights, and similar intangible property.

• You must report only the amount of cash paid on notional principal contracts.

Box 3, Withholding Allowances

This box should only be completed if the income code reported in box 1 is 15 (scholarship or fellowship grants) or 16 (compensation for independent personal services). See Pub. 515 for more information.

Box 4, Net Income

Complete this box only if you entered an amount in box 3. Otherwise, leave it blank.

Box 5, Tax Rate

Enter the correct rate of withholding that applies to the income in box 2 (gross income) or box 4 (net income), as appropriate. (See Valid Tax Rate Table below.) The correct tax rate should be included even if you withheld less than that rate. For example, if an NQI is reporting dividends paid to a beneficial owner who is a resident of a country with which the United States does not have a tax treaty and a U.S. withholding agent paid the dividend and withheld only 15% (rather than the required 30%) and the NQI withholds an additional 15%, the NQI should report "30.00" in box 5. See *Example 2* on page 10.

The tax rate on dividends paid to a corporation created or organized in, or under the law of, the Commonwealth of Puerto Rico may be 10%, rather than 30%. See Pub. 515 for more information.

Enter the tax rate using the following format: two digits, a decimal, and two digits (for example, "30.00" for 30%). However, if the income is exempt from tax under a U.S. tax treaty or the Code, enter "00.00". If the tax rate is less than 10%, enter a zero before the tax rate (for example, "04.00" for 4%).

Valid Tax Rate Table

00.00	07.00	14.00	27.50
04.00	08.00	15.00	28.00
04.90	10.00	17.50	30.00
04.95	12.00	20.00	33.00
05.00	12.50	25.00	35.00

⚠ *If you withheld at more than one tax rate for a specific type of income that you paid to the same recipient, you must file a separate Form 1042-S for each amount to which a separate rate was applied.*

Box 6, Exemption Code

Note. If you are filing a Form 1042-S to correct certain information already provided to you by another withholding agent on a Form 1099 or Form 1042-S (for example, as required under *Amounts Paid by Nonqualified Intermediaries and Flow-Through Entities* on page 10), see item 5 below.

Generally, if the tax rate you entered in box 5 is 00.00, you should enter the appropriate exemption code (01 through 09) from the list on page 12.

If an amount was withheld under Chapter 3 of the Code (the tax rate you entered in box 5 is greater than zero and is not due to backup withholding), enter "00" in box 6. If the tax rate you entered in box 5 is due to backup withholding, leave box 6 blank.

1. If exemption code 01 (income effectively connected with a U.S. trade or business) may apply, you must enter the recipient's U.S. TIN in box 14. If the recipient's U.S. TIN is unknown or unavailable, you must withhold tax at the foreign-person rate of 30% (30.00) and enter "00" in box 6.

2. A withholding agent should use exemption code 06 (qualified intermediary that assumes primary withholding responsibility) only if it is making a payment to a QI that has represented on its Form W-8IMY that it is assuming primary withholding responsibility under Chapter 3 of the Code.

3. A withholding agent should use exemption code 07 (withholding foreign partnership or withholding foreign trust) only if it is making a payment to a foreign partnership or trust that has represented that it is a withholding foreign partnership or trust.

4. A withholding agent should use exemption code 09 (qualified intermediary represents income is exempt) only if it makes a payment to a QI that has not assumed primary withholding responsibility under Chapter 3 of the

Code or primary backup withholding responsibility, but has represented on a withholding statement associated with its Form W-8IMY that the income is exempt from withholding.

5. If you have failed to provide another withholding agent with appropriate information regarding the status of the person to whom you are making a payment, the other withholding agent may be required to withhold on the payment based on the presumption rules. If the income is in fact exempt from withholding, you must submit a Form 1042-S providing the correct information. In this situation, you must:

a. Indicate the correct rate at which the income should have been subject to withholding in box 5 (usually 00.00),

b. Enter "99" in box 6, and

c. Enter the actual amount of U.S. federal tax withheld by the other withholding agent in box 7.

You must also provide the correct recipient code in box 12 and the name and address of the actual recipient in box 13.

Box 7, U.S. Federal Tax Withheld

 Box 7 must be completed in all cases, even if no tax has actually been withheld.

Enter the total amount of U.S. federal tax actually withheld. If no tax has been withheld on the payment by any withholding agent, enter "-0-." If you are a withholding agent filing a Form 1042-S to report income that has already been subject to withholding by another withholding agent, enter the aggregate amount of tax withheld by you and any other withholding agent (see *Amounts Paid by Nonqualified Intermediaries and Flow-Through Entities* on page 10).

Box 8, Amount Repaid to Recipient

This box should be completed only if:

• You repaid a recipient an amount that was overwithheld, and

• You are going to reimburse yourself by reducing, by the amount of tax actually repaid, the amount of any deposit made for a payment period in the calendar year following the calendar year of withholding.

Generally, a QI should not enter an amount in box 8 unless it is a QI that has represented on its Form W-8IMY that it is assuming primary withholding responsibility under Chapter 3 of the Code.

You must also state on a timely filed Form 1042 for the calendar year of overwithholding that the filing of the Form 1042 constitutes a claim for refund.

⚠ *The adjustment for amounts overwithheld do not apply to partnerships or nominees required to withhold under section 1446.*

-13-

Box 9, Withholding Agent's Employer Identification Number (EIN)

You are generally required to enter your EIN. However, if you are filing Form 1042-S as a QI, withholding foreign partnership, or withholding foreign trust, enter your QI-EIN, WP-EIN, or WT-EIN. Enter the number and check the applicable box.

If you do not have an EIN, you can apply for one online at *www.irs.gov/smallbiz* or by telephone at 1-800-829-4933. Also, you can apply for an EIN by filing Form SS-4, Application for Employer Identification Number. File amended Forms 1042-S when you receive your EIN.

To get a QI-EIN, WP-EIN, or WT-EIN, submit Form SS-4 with your application for that status. (See the definitions for *Qualified intermediary (QI)* on page 3 and *Withholding foreign partnership (WP) or withholding foreign trust (WT)* on page 4 for more information.) Do not send an application for a QI-EIN, WP-EIN, or WT-EIN to the Philadelphia Service Center; it will not be processed.

Box 10, Withholding Agent's Name and Address

Enter your name and address. If your post office does not deliver mail to the street address and you have a P.O. box, show the box number instead of the street address.

If you are a nominee that is the withholding agent under section 1446, check the box and enter the PTP's name and other information in boxes 17 through 20.

Note. On statements furnished to Canadian recipients of U.S. source deposit interest, in addition to your name and address, you must include the telephone number of a person to contact. This number must provide direct access to an individual who can answer questions about the statement. The telephone number is not required on Copy A of paper forms or on electronic/magnetic media filed with the IRS. You must also include a statement that the information on the form is being furnished to the United States Internal Revenue Service and may be furnished to Canada.

Box 11, Recipient's Account Number

You may use this box to enter the account number assigned by you to the recipient.

Box 12, Recipient Code

Enter the recipient code from the list on page 12. The following special instructions apply.
• If applicable, use recipient code 09 (artist or athlete) instead of recipient code 01 (individual), 02 (corporation), or 03

(partnership other than a withholding foreign partnership).
• Use recipient code 12 if you are making a payment to a QI and 04 if you are making a payment to a WP or a WT.
• If you are making a payment to an NQI or flow-through entity, you generally must use the recipient code that applies to the type of recipient who receives the income from the NQI or flow-through entity.
• Use recipient code 03 (partnership other than a withholding foreign partnership) only if you are reporting a payment of income that is effectively connected with the conduct of a trade or business of a nonwithholding foreign partnership in the United States. Otherwise, follow the rules that apply to payments to flow-through entities.
• Use recipient code 20 (unknown recipient) only if you have not received a withholding certificate or other documentation for a recipient or you cannot determine how much of a payment is reliably associated with a specific recipient. Do not use this code because you cannot determine the recipient's status as an individual, corporation, etc. The regulations under Chapter 3 of the Code provide rules on how to determine a recipient's status when a withholding agent does not have the necessary information.
• Only QIs may use recipient codes 13 (private arrangement intermediary withholding rate pool—general), 14 (private arrangement intermediary withholding rate pool—exempt organizations), 15 (qualified intermediary withholding rate pool—general), and 16 (qualified intermediary withholding rate pool—exempt organizations). A QI should only use recipient code 14 or 16 for pooled account holders that have claimed an exemption based on their tax-exempt status and not some other exemption (for example, treaty or other Code exception). A U.S. withholding agent making a payment to a QI should use recipient code 12.

Box 13, Recipient's Name and Address

Name. Enter the complete name of the recipient.
• If you do not know the name of the recipient, enter "Unknown Recipient."
• If Form 1042-S is being completed by a QI, WP, or WT for a withholding rate pool, enter "Withholding rate pool" in box 13. No address is necessary.
• A QI reporting payments made to a PAI on a withholding rate pool basis must include the name and address of the PAI in box 13.

Address. You must generally enter a foreign address in box 13. However, there are limited exceptions. For example, you may enter a U.S. address when reporting payments of scholarship or fellowship grants (income code 15).

For addresses outside the United States or its possessions, follow the foreign country's practice for entering the postal code. Do not abbreviate the country name.

For addresses within the United States, use the U.S. Postal Service 2-letter abbreviation for the state name. Do not enter "United States" or "U.S."

Box 14, Recipient's U.S. Taxpayer Identification Number (TIN)

You must obtain and enter a U.S. taxpayer identification number (TIN) for:
• Any recipient whose income is effectively connected with the conduct of a trade or business in the United States.

Note. For these recipients, exemption code 01 should be entered in box 6.
• Any foreign person claiming a reduced rate of, or exemption from, tax under a tax treaty between a foreign country and the United States, unless the income is an unexpected payment (as described in Regulations section 1.1441-6(g)) or consists of dividends and interest from stocks and debt obligations that are actively traded; dividends from any redeemable security issued by an investment company registered under the Investment Company Act of 1940 (mutual fund); dividends, interest, or royalties from units of beneficial interest in a unit investment trust that are (or were, upon issuance) publicly offered and are registered with the Securities and Exchange Commission under the Securities Act of 1933; and amounts paid with respect to loans of any of the above securities.
• Any nonresident alien individual claiming exemption from tax under section 871(f) for certain annuities received under qualified plans.
• A foreign organization claiming an exemption from tax solely because of its status as a tax-exempt organization under section 501(c) or as a private foundation.
• Any QI.
• Any WP or WT.
• Any nonresident alien individual claiming exemption from withholding on compensation for independent personal services.
• Any foreign grantor trust with five or fewer grantors.
• Any U.S. branch of a foreign bank or foreign insurance company that is treated as a U.S. person.

If a foreign person provides a TIN on a Form W-8, but is not required to do so, the withholding agent must include the TIN on Form 1042-S.

Box 15, Recipient's Country of Residence for Tax Purposes

Enter the unabbreviated name of the recipient's country of residence for tax purposes.

Box 16, Recipient's Country Code

You must enter the code (from the list that begins on page 15) for the country of which the recipient claims residency under that country's tax laws. Enter "OC"

-14-

(other country) only when the country of residence does not appear on the list or the payment is made to an international organization (for example, the United Nations). Enter "UC" (unknown country) only if the payment is to an unknown recipient. If you are making a payment to a QI, WP, or WT or if you are a QI, WP, or WT and are making a payment to a QI, WP, or WT withholding rate pool, enter the country code of the QI, WP, or WT.

 If exemption code 04 (exempt under tax treaty) appears in box 6 or if a reduced rate of withholding based on a tax treaty is entered in box 5, the country code entered in box 16 must be a country with which the United States has entered into an income tax treaty.

Boxes 17 Through 20, Nonqualified Intermediary's (NQI's)/ Flow-Through Entity's Name, Country Code, Address, and TIN

If you are reporting amounts paid to a recipient whose withholding certificates or other documentation has been submitted to you with a Form W-8IMY provided by an NQI or flow-through entity, you must include the name, address, and TIN, if any, of the NQI or flow-through entity with whose Form W-8 or other documentation the recipient's Form W-8 or other documentation is associated.

Note. An NQI or flow-through entity will leave these boxes blank unless it is making the payment to an NQI or flow-through entity.

For box 18, you must enter the country code from the list beginning on this page for the country where the NQI or flow-through entity is located.

If you are a nominee that is the withholding agent under section 1446, enter the PTP's name and other information in these boxes.

Box 21, Payer's Name and Taxpayer Identification Number (TIN)

See the definition of a payer on page 3. Include the payer's name and TIN if different from that in boxes 9 and 10.

Boxes 22 Through 24, State Income Tax Withheld and Related Information

Include in these boxes information relating to any state income tax withheld.

Correcting Paper Forms 1042-S

If you filed a Form 1042-S with the IRS and later discover you made an error on it, you must correct it as soon as possible. To correct a previously filed Form 1042-S, you will need to file an amended Form 1042-S. See the *Step-by-Step Instructions* on this page.

To determine whether you are required to submit amended Forms 1042-S electronically or on magnetic media, see *Electronic/Magnetic Media Reporting* beginning on page 1 and Pub. 1187.

 If you fail to correct Form(s) 1042-S, you may be subject to a penalty. See Penalties *on page 11.*

If any information you correct on Form(s) 1042-S changes the information you previously reported on Form 1042, you must also correct the Form 1042 by filing an amended return. To do this, see the Form 1042 instructions.

Step-by-Step Instructions

If you are not filing electronically or on magnetic media, follow these steps to amend a previously filed Form 1042-S.

Step 1. Prepare a paper Form 1042-S.

● Enter all the correct information on the form, including the recipient name and address, money amounts, and codes.
● Enter an "X" in the AMENDED box at the top of the form.

AMENDED box. Enter an "X" in the AMENDED box of Copy A only if you are amending a Form 1042-S you previously filed with the IRS. Enter an "X" in the AMENDED box you give to the recipient only if you are correcting a Form 1042-S previously furnished to the recipient. You must provide statements to recipients showing the corrections as soon as possible.

Step 2. File the amended paper Form 1042-S with a Form 1042-T. See the Form 1042-T instructions for information on filing these forms.

-15-

Appendix

Country Codes

Select the appropriate code from the following list and enter it in box 16 (country code of recipient). Also use the following codes to complete box 18 (country code of NQI), if applicable. See the instructions for box 16 on page 14 (and box 18 above, if applicable) before selecting a country code. **Note.** Countries bolded and italicized are those with which the United States had entered into an income tax treaty at the time these instructions were printed.

Country	Code
Abu Dhabi	TC
Afghanistan	AF
Albania	AL
Algeria	AG
American Samoa	AQ
Andorra	AN
Angola	AO
Anguilla	AV
Antarctica	AY
Antigua and Barbuda	AC
Argentina	AR
Armenia[1]	AM
Aruba	AA
Ashmore and Cartier Islands[2]	AT
Australia	AS
Austria	AU
Azerbaijan[1]	AJ
Azores	PO
Bahamas, The	BF
Bahrain	BA
Baker Island	FQ
Balearic Islands (Mallorca, etc.)	SP
Bangladesh	BG
Barbados	BB
Bassas da India	BS
Belarus[1]	BO
Belgium	BE
Belize	BH
Benin (Dahomey)	BN
Bermuda	BD
Bhutan	BT
Bolivia	BL
Bonaire	NT
Bosnia-Herzegovina	BK
Botswana	BC
Bouvet Island	BV
Brazil	BR
British Indian Ocean Territory	IO
Brunei	BX
Bulgaria	BU
Burkina Faso (Upper Volta)	UV
Burma	BM
Burundi	BY
Cambodia (Kampuchea)	CB
Cameroon	CM
Canada	CA
Canary Islands	SP
Cape Verde	CV
Cayman Islands	CJ
Central African Republic	CT
Chad	CD
Chile	CI
China, People's Republic of (including Inner Mongolia, Tibet, and Manchuria)	CH
Christmas Island (Indian Ocean)[2]	KT
Clipperton Island	IP
Cocos (Keeling) Islands[2]	CK
Colombia	CO
Comoros	CN
Congo (Brazzaville)	CF
Congo, Democratic Republic of (Zaire)	CG
Cook Islands	CW
Coral Sea Islands Territory[2]	CR
Corsica	VP
Costa Rica	CS
Cote D'Ivoire (Ivory Coast)	IV
Croatia	HR
Cuba	CU
Curacao	NT
Cyprus	CY
Czech Republic	EZ
Denmark	DA
Djibouti	DJ
Dominica	DO
Dominican Republic	DR
Dubai	TC
East Timor	TT
Ecuador	EC
Egypt	EG
Eleuthera Island	BF
El Salvador	ES
Equatorial Guinea	EK
Eritrea	ER
Estonia	EN
Ethiopia	ET
Europa Island	EU
Falkland Islands (Islas Malvinas)	FK
Faroe Islands	FO
Fiji	FJ
Finland	FI
France	FR
French Guiana[3]	FG
French Polynesia (Tahiti)	FP
French Southern and Antarctic Lands	FS
Gabon	GB
Gambia, The	GA
Gaza Strip	GZ
Georgia[1]	GG
Germany	GM
Ghana	GH
Gibraltar	GI
Glorioso Islands	GO
Great Britain (United Kingdom)	UK
Greece	GR
Greenland	GL
Grenada (Southern Grenadines)	GJ
Guadeloupe[3]	GP
Guam	GQ
Guatemala	GT
Guernsey	GK
Guinea	GV
Guinea-Bissau	PU
Guyana	GY
Haiti	HA
Heard Island and McDonald Islands	HM
Honduras	HO
Hong Kong[5]	HK
Howland Island	HQ
Hungary	HU
Iceland	IC
India	IN
Indonesia (including Bali, Belitung, Flores, Java, Moluccas, Sumatra, Timor, etc.)	ID
Iran	IR
Iraq	IZ
Ireland, Republic of (Eire)	EI
Isle of Man	IM
Israel	IS
Italy	IT
Jamaica	JM
Jan Mayen	JN
Japan	JA
Jarvis Island	DQ
Jersey	JE
Johnston Atoll	JQ
Jordan	JO
Juan de Nova Island	JU
Kazakhstan	KZ
Kenya	KE
Kingman Reef	KQ
Kiribati (Gilbert Islands)	KR
Korea, Democratic People's Republic of (North)	KN
Korea, Republic of (South)	KS
Kosovo	YO
Kurile Islands	RS
Kuwait	KU
Kyrgyzstan[1]	KG
Laos	LA
Latvia	LG
Lebanon	LE
Lesotho	LT
Liberia	LI
Libya	LY
Liechtenstein	LS
Lithuania	LH
Luxembourg	LU
Macau	MC
Macedonia (former Yugoslav Republic of)	MK
Madagascar (Malagasy Republic)	MA
Malawi	MI
Malaysia	MY
Maldives	MV
Mali	ML
Malta	MT
Marshall Islands	RM
Martinique[3]	MB
Mauritania	MR
Mauritius	MP
Mayotte	MF
Mexico	MX
Micronesia, Federated States of	FM
Midway Islands	MQ
Moldova[1]	MD
Monaco	MN
Mongolia	MG
Montenegro	YO
Montserrat	MH
Morocco	MO
Mozambique	MZ
Namibia	WA
Nauru	NR
Navassa Island	BQ
Nepal	NP
Netherlands	NL
Netherlands Antilles	NT
New Caledonia	NC
New Zealand	NZ
Nicaragua	NU
Niger	NG
Nigeria	NI
Niue	NE
Norfolk Island[2]	NF
Northern Ireland[4]	UK
Northern Mariana Islands	CQ
Norway	NO
Oman	MU
Pakistan	PK
Palau	PS
Palmyra Atoll	LQ
Panama	PM
Papua New Guinea	PP
Paracel Islands	PF
Paraguay	PA
Peru	PE
Philippines	RP
Pitcairn Island	PC
Poland	PL
Portugal	PO
Puerto Rico	RQ
Qatar (Katar)	QA
Redonda	VI
Reunion[3]	RE
Romania	RO
Russia	RS
Rwanda	RW
Ryukyu Islands	JA
St. Helena (Ascension Island and Tristan de Cunha Island Group)	SH
St. Kitts (St. Christopher and Nevis)	SC
St. Lucia	ST
St. Pierre and Miquelon	SB
St. Vincent and the Grenadines (Northern Grenadines)	VC
San Marino	SM
Sao Tome and Principe	TP
Sarawak	MY
Saudi Arabia	SA
Senegal	SG
Serbia	YO
Seychelles	SE
Sierra Leone	SL
Singapore	SN
Slovak Republic (Slovakia)	LO
Slovenia	SI
Solomon Islands	BP
Somalia	SO
South Africa	SF
South Georgia and the South Sandwich Islands	SX
Spain	SP
Spratly Islands	PG
Sri Lanka	CE
Sudan	SU
Suriname	NS
Svalbard (Spitsbergen)	SV
Swaziland	WZ
Sweden	SW
Switzerland	SZ

Syria	SY	Uganda	UG	West Bank	WE
Taiwan	TW	*Ukraine*	UP	Western Sahara	WI
Tajikistan[1]	TI	United Arab Emirates	TC	Western Samoa	WS
Tanzania	TZ	*United Kingdom*		Windward Islands	VC
Thailand	TH	*(England, Wales,*		Yemen (Aden)	YM
Togo	TO	*Scotland, No. Ireland)*	UK	Yugoslavia (Kosovo,	
Tokelau	TL	Uruguay	UY	Montenegro, Serbia)	YO
Tonga	TN	*Uzbekistan*[1]	UZ	Zaire (Democratic	
Tortola	VI	Vanuatu	NH	Republic of Congo)	CG
Trinidad and Tobago	TD	Vatican City	VT	Zambia	ZA
Tromelin Island	TE	*Venezuela*	VE	Zimbabwe	ZI
Tunisia	TS	Vietnam	VM	Other Country	OC
Turkey	TU	Virgin Islands (British)	VI	Unknown Country	UC
Turkmenistan[1]	TX	Virgin Islands (U.S.)	VQ		
Turks and Caicos Islands	TK	Wake Island	WQ		
Tuvalu	TV	Wallis and Futuna	WF		

[1] These countries are parties to the United States treaty with the Commonwealth of Independent States.

[2] These countries are covered under the United States treaty with Australia.

[3] These countries are covered under the United States treaty with France.

[4] Northern Ireland is covered under the United States treaty with the United Kingdom.

[5] Hong Kong is not covered under the United States treaty with China.

DO NOT STAPLE

Form **1042-T** Department of the Treasury Internal Revenue Service	**Annual Summary and Transmittal of Forms 1042-S**	OMB No. 1545-0096 20**05**

Name of withholding agent	Employer identification number

Number, street, and room or suite no.

City or town, province or state, and country (including postal code)

If you are an intermediary (see Form 1042 instructions), check if you are a: ☐ QI/Withholding foreign partnership or trust ☐ NQI/Flow-through entity

1a Type of paper Forms 1042-S attached (check only **one** box): ☐ Original ☐ Voided ☐ Corrected
Also check here if pro-rata (see instructions) ▶ ☐
b Number of paper Forms 1042-S attached ▶ ....

2a Total gross income on all paper Forms 1042-S (box 2) attached . . . . $ ....
b Total U.S. Federal tax withheld on all paper Forms 1042-S (box 7) attached . . . . $ ....

Caution: *If you have already filed a Form 1042 and an attached Form 1042-S causes the gross income or tax withheld information shown on your previously filed Form 1042 to change, you must file an amended Form 1042. See the instructions below.*

If this is your FINAL return, enter an "X" here . . . . ▶ ☐

Please return this entire page to the Internal Revenue Service.

Sign Here Under penalties of perjury, I declare that I have examined this return and accompanying documents, and, to the best of my knowledge and belief, they are true, correct, and complete.

Your signature	Title	Date	Daytime phone number

Instructions

Purpose of form. Use this form to transmit paper Forms 1042-S, Foreign Person's U.S. Source Income Subject to Withholding, to the Internal Revenue Service. Use a separate Form 1042-T to transmit each type of Form 1042-S (see the instructions for line 1a).

 If you file 250 or more Forms 1042-S, you are required to submit them electronically or using magnetic media. You can also use these methods to submit less than 250 Forms 1042-S. If you submit Forms 1042-S using either of these methods, do not use Form 1042-T. If you file electronically or using magnetic media, use Form 4804, Transmittal of Information Returns Reported Magnetically.

Use of this form to transmit paper Forms 1042-S does not affect your obligation to file Form 1042, Annual Withholding Tax Return for U.S. Source Income of Foreign Persons.

If you have not yet filed a Form 1042 for 2005, you may send in more than one Form 1042-T to submit paper Forms 1042-S prior to filing your Form 1042. You may submit corrected and voided Forms 1042-S even though changes reflect differences in gross income and tax withheld information of Forms 1042-S previously submitted with a Form 1042-T.

If you have already filed a Form 1042 for 2005 and an attached Form 1042-S caused the gross income or tax withheld information previously reported on line 62a or 62b of your Form 1042 to change, you must file an amended Form 1042.

Where and when to file. File Form 1042-T (and Copy A of the paper Forms 1042-S being transmitted) with the Internal Revenue Service Center, Philadelphia, PA 19255-0607, by March 15, 2006. Send the forms in a flat mailing (not folded).

Identifying information at top of form. The name, address, and EIN of the withholding agent or intermediary on this form must be the same as those you enter on Forms 1042 and 1042-S. See Form 1042 for definitions of withholding agent and intermediary.

Line 1a. You must file a separate Form 1042-T for each type of paper Form 1042-S you are transmitting. Check only one of the first three boxes. If you are filing pro-rata Forms 1042-S, also check the pro-rata box. As a result, there are six possible types of Form 1042-S that may be transmitted:

- Original
- Voided
- Corrected
- Original pro-rata
- Voided pro-rata
- Corrected pro-rata

Each type would be transmitted with a separate Form 1042-T. For example, you would transmit only original Forms 1042-S with one Form 1042-T, only corrected Forms 1042-S with another Form 1042-T, etc.

Line 2a. Enter the total of the gross income amounts shown on the Forms 1042-S (box 2) being transmitted with this Form 1042-T.

Line 2b. Enter the total of the U.S. federal tax withheld amounts shown on the Forms 1042-S (box 7) being transmitted with this Form 1042-T.

Final return. If you will not be required to file Forms 1042-S in the future (on paper, electronically, or on magnetic media), enter an "X" in the "FINAL return" box.

For more information and the Privacy Act and Paperwork Reduction Act Notice, see Form 1042. Cat. No. 28848W Form **1042-T** (2005)

Do Not Staple   6969

Form **1096**	Annual Summary and Transmittal of U.S. Information Returns	OMB No. 1545-0108

Department of the Treasury
Internal Revenue Service

2006

FILER'S name

Street address (including room or suite number)

City, state, and ZIP code

Name of person to contact	Telephone number ( )	**For Official Use Only**
Email address	Fax number ( )	

1 Employer identification number	2 Social security number	3 Total number of forms	4 Federal income tax withheld $	5 Total amount reported with this Form 1096 $

Enter an "X" in only one box below to indicate the type of form being filed.   If this is your **final return**, enter an "X" here . . . ▶ ☐

W-2G 32	1098 81	1098-C 78	1098-E 84	1098-T 83	1099-A 80	1099-B 79	1099-C 85	1099-CAP 73	1099-DIV 91	1099-G 86	1099-H 71	1099-INT 92	1099-LTC 93
☐	☐	☐	☐	☐	☐	☐	☐	☐	☐	☐	☐	☐	☐

1099-MISC 95	1099-OID 96	1099-PATR 97	1099-Q 31	1099-R 98	1099-S 75	1099-SA 94	5498 28	5498-ESA 72	5498-SA 27
☐	☐	☐	☐	☐	☐	☐	☐	☐	☐

Return this entire page to the Internal Revenue Service. Photocopies are not acceptable.

Under penalties of perjury, I declare that I have examined this return and accompanying documents, and, to the best of my knowledge and belief, they are true, correct, and complete.

Signature ▶   Title ▶   Date ▶

Instructions

Purpose of form. Use this form to transmit paper Forms 1099, 1098, 5498, and W-2G to the Internal Revenue Service. Do not use Form 1096 to transmit electronically or magnetically. For magnetic media, see Form 4804, Transmittal of Information Returns Reported Magnetically; for electronic submissions, see Pub. 1220, Specifications for Filing Forms 1098, 1099, 5498, and W-2G Electronically or Magnetically.

Who must file. The name, address, and TIN of the filer on this form must be the same as those you enter in the upper left area of Forms 1099, 1098, 5498, or W-2G. A filer includes a payer; a recipient of mortgage interest payments (including points) or student loan interest; an educational institution; a broker; a barter exchange; a creditor; a person reporting real estate transactions; a trustee or issuer of any individual retirement arrangement, a Coverdell ESA, an HSA, an Archer MSA (including a Medicare Advantage MSA); certain corporations; certain donees of motor vehicles, boats, and airplanes; and a lender who acquires an interest in secured property or who has reason to know that the property has been abandoned.

Preaddressed Form 1096. If you received a preaddressed Form 1096 from the IRS with Package 1099, use it to transmit paper Forms 1099, 1098, 5498, and W-2G to the Internal Revenue Service. If any of the preprinted information is incorrect, make corrections on the form.

If you are not using a preaddressed form, enter the filer's name, address (including room, suite, or other unit number), and TIN in the spaces provided on the form.

When to file. File Form 1096 with Forms 1099, 1098, or W-2G by February 28, 2007. File Form 1096 with Forms 5498, 5498-ESA, and 5498-SA by May 31, 2007.

Where To File

Except for Form 1098-C, send all information returns filed on paper with Form 1096 to the following:

If your principal business, office or agency, or legal residence in the case of an individual, is located in ▼	Use the following Internal Revenue Service Center address
Alabama, Arizona, Florida, Georgia, Louisiana, Mississippi, New Mexico, North Carolina, Texas, Virginia	Austin, TX 73301
Arkansas, Connecticut, Delaware, Kentucky, Maine, Massachusetts, New Hampshire, New Jersey, New York, Ohio, Pennsylvania, Rhode Island, Vermont, West Virginia	Cincinnati, OH 45999
Illinois, Indiana, Iowa, Kansas, Michigan, Minnesota, Missouri, Nebraska, North Dakota, Oklahoma, South Carolina, South Dakota, Tennessee, Wisconsin	Kansas City, MO 64999

For more information and the Privacy Act and Paperwork Reduction Act Notice, see the 2006 General Instructions for Forms 1099, 1098, 5498, and W-2G.   Cat. No. 14400O   Form **1096** (2006)

| Alaska, California, Colorado, District of Columbia, Hawaii, Idaho, Maryland, Montana, Nevada, Oregon, Utah, Washington, Wyoming | Ogden, UT 84201 |

If your legal residence or principal place of business is outside the United States, file with the Internal Revenue Service Center, Philadelphia, PA 19255.

Form 1098-C. Send all Forms 1098-C filed on paper to the Internal Revenue Service Center, Ogden, UT 84201-0027.

Returns filed magnetically. Send all information returns filed magnetically to Enterprise Computing Center—Martinsburg, Information Reporting Program, 230 Murall Drive, Kearneysville, WV 25430.

Transmitting to the IRS. Send the forms in a flat mailing (not folded). Group the forms by form number and transmit each group with a separate Form 1096. For example, if you must file both Forms 1098 and 1099-A, complete one Form 1096 to transmit your Forms 1098 and another Form 1096 to transmit your Forms 1099-A. You need not submit original and corrected returns separately. Do not send a form (1099, 5498, etc.) containing summary (subtotal) information with Form 1096. Summary information for the group of forms being sent is entered only in boxes 3, 4, and 5 of Form 1096.

Box 1 or 2. Complete only if you are not using a preaddressed Form 1096. Make an entry in either box 1 or 2; not both. Individuals not in a trade or business must enter their social security number (SSN) in box 2; sole proprietors and all others must enter their employer identification number (EIN) in box 1. However, sole proprietors who do not have an EIN must enter their SSN in box 2. Use the same EIN or SSN on Form 1096 that you use on Forms 1099, 1098, 5498, or W-2G.

Box 3. Enter the number of forms you are transmitting with this Form 1096. Do not include blank or voided forms or the Form 1096 in your total. Enter the number of correctly completed forms, not the number of pages, being transmitted. For example, if you send one page of three-to-a-page Forms 5498 with a Form 1096 and you have correctly completed two Forms 5498 on that page, enter "2" in box 3 of Form 1096.

Box 4. Enter the total federal income tax withheld shown on the forms being transmitted with this Form 1096.

Box 5. No entry is required if you are filing Forms 1099-A or 1099-G. For all other forms, enter the total of the amounts from the specific boxes of the forms listed below:

Form W-2G	Box 1
Form 1098	Boxes 1 and 2
Form 1098-C	Box 4c
Form 1098-E	Box 1
Form 1098-T	Boxes 1, 2, 4, 5, 6, and 10
Form 1099-B	Boxes 2 and 3
Form 1099-C	Box 2
Form 1099-CAP	Box 2
Form 1099-DIV	Boxes 1a, 2a, 3, 8, and 9
Form 1099-H	Box 1
Form 1099-INT	Boxes 1 and 3
Form 1099-LTC	Boxes 1 and 2
Form 1099-MISC	Boxes 1, 2, 3, 5, 6, 7, 8, 10, 13, 14, and 15b
Form 1099-OID	Boxes 1, 2, and 6
Form 1099-PATR	Boxes 1, 2, 3, and 5
Form 1099-Q	Box 1
Form 1099-R	Box 1
Form 1099-S	Box 2
Form 1099-SA	Box 1
Form 5498	Boxes 1, 2, 3, 4, 5, 8, 9, and 10
Form 5498-ESA	Boxes 1 and 2
Form 5498-SA	Box 1

Final return. If you will not be required to file Forms 1099, 1098, 5498, or W-2G in the future, either on paper, magnetically, or electronically, enter an "X" in the "final return" box.

Corrected returns. For information about filing corrections, see the 2006 General Instructions for Forms 1099, 1098, 5498, and W-2G. Originals and corrections of the same type of return can be submitted using one Form 1096.

9393 ☐ VOID ☐ CORRECTED

| PAYER'S name, street address, city, state, ZIP code, and telephone no. | **1** Gross long-term care benefits paid $ | OMB No. 1545-1519 **20**06 Form **1099-LTC** | Long-Term Care and Accelerated Death Benefits |
| | **2** Accelerated death benefits paid $ | | |

PAYER'S federal identification number	POLICYHOLDER'S identification number	**3** Check one: ☐ Per diem ☐ Reimbursed amount	INSURED'S social security no.	**Copy A** **For Internal Revenue Service Center**
POLICYHOLDER'S name		INSURED'S name		**File with Form 1096.** For Privacy Act and Paperwork Reduction Act Notice, see the **2006 General Instructions for Forms 1099, 1098, 5498, and W-2G.**
Street address (including apt. no.)		Street address (including apt. no.)		
City, state, and ZIP code		City, state, and ZIP code		
Account number (see instructions)	**4** Qualified contract ☐ (optional)	**5** Check, if applicable: (optional) ☐ Chronically ill ☐ Terminally ill	Date certified	

Form **1099-LTC**   Cat. No. 23021Z   Department of the Treasury - Internal Revenue Service

Do Not Cut or Separate Forms on This Page — Do Not Cut or Separate Forms on This Page

Instructions for Policyholder

A payer, such as an insurance company or a viatical settlement provider, must give this form to you for payments made under a long-term care insurance contract or for accelerated death benefits. Payments include those made directly to you (or to the insured) and those made to third parties.

A long-term care insurance contract provides coverage of expenses for long-term care services for an individual who has been certified by a licensed health care practitioner as chronically ill. A life insurance company or viatical settlement provider may pay accelerated death benefits if the insured has been certified by either a physician as terminally ill or by a licensed health care practitioner as chronically ill.

Long-term care insurance contract. Generally, amounts received under a qualified long-term care insurance contract are excluded from your income. However, if payments are made on a per diem basis, the amount you may exclude is limited. The per diem exclusion limit must be allocated among all policyholders who own qualified long-term care insurance contracts for the same insured. See Pub. 502, Medical and Dental Expenses, and Form 8853, Archer MSAs and Long-Term Care Insurance Contracts, for more information.

Per diem basis. This means the payments were made on a periodic basis without regard to the actual expenses incurred during the period to which the payments relate.

Accelerated death benefits. Amounts paid as accelerated death benefits are fully excludable from your income if the insured has been certified by a physician as terminally ill. Accelerated death benefits paid on behalf of individuals who are certified as chronically ill are excludable from income to the same extent they would be if paid under a qualified long-term care insurance contract.

Account number. May show an account or other unique number the payer assigned to distinguish your account.

Box 1. Shows the gross benefits paid under a long-term care insurance contract during the year.

Box 2. Shows the gross accelerated death benefits paid during the year.

Box 3. Shows if the amount in box 1 or 2 was paid on a per diem basis or was reimbursement of actual long-term care expenses. If the insured was terminally ill, this box may not be checked.

Box 4. May show if the benefits were from a qualified long-term care insurance contract.

Box 5. May show if the insured was certified chronically ill or terminally ill, and the latest date certified.

Instructions for Insured

A payer, such as an insurance company or a viatical settlement provider, must give this form to you and to the policyholder for payments made under a long-term care insurance contract or for accelerated death benefits. Payments include both benefits you received directly and expenses paid on your behalf to third parties.

If you are the insured but are not the policyholder, Copy C is provided to you for information only because these payments are not taxable to you. If you are also the policyholder, you should receive Copy B.

Account number. May show an account or other unique number the payer assigned to distinguish your account.

Box 1. Shows the gross benefits paid under a long-term care insurance contract during the year.

Box 2. Shows the gross accelerated death benefits paid during the year.

Box 3. Shows if the amount in box 1 or 2 was paid on a per diem basis or was reimbursement of actual long-term care expenses. If you are terminally ill, this box may not be checked.

Box 4. May show if the benefits were from a qualified long-term care insurance contract.

Box 5. May show if you were certified chronically ill or terminally ill, and the latest date certified.

Instructions for Payers

General and specific form instructions are provided as separate products. The products you should use to complete Form 1099-LTC are the 2006 General Instructions for Forms 1099, 1098, 5498, and W-2G, and the 2006 Instructions for Form 1099-LTC. A chart in the general instructions gives a quick guide to which form must be filed to report a particular payment. To order these instructions and additional forms, call 1-800-TAX-FORM (1-800-829-3676).

Caution: *Because paper forms are scanned during processing, you cannot file Form 1096, 1098, 1099, or 5498 that you download and print from the IRS website.*

Due dates. Furnish Copy B of this form to the policyholder by January 31, 2007.

Furnish Copy C of this form to the insured by January 31, 2007.

File Copy A of this form with the IRS by February 28, 2007. If you file electronically, the due date is April 2, 2007. To file electronically, you must have software that generates a file according to the specifications in Pub. 1220, Specifications for Filing Forms 1098, 1099, 5498, and W-2G Electronically or Magnetically. IRS does not provide a fill-in form option.

Printed on recycled paper

20**06**

Department of the Treasury
Internal Revenue Service

Instructions for Form 1099-LTC

Section references are to the Internal Revenue Code.

Reminder

In addition to these specific instructions, you should also use the 2006 General Instructions for Forms 1099, 1098, 5498, and W-2G. Those general instructions include information about:
- Backup withholding
- Magnetic media and electronic reporting requirements
- Penalties
- Who must file (nominee/middleman)
- When and where to file
- Taxpayer identification numbers
- Statements to recipients
- Corrected and void returns
- Other general topics

You can get the general instructions from the IRS website at *www.irs.gov* or by calling 1-800-TAX-FORM (1-800-829-3676).

Specific Instructions for Form 1099-LTC

File Form 1099-LTC, Long-Term Care and Accelerated Death Benefits, if you pay any long-term care benefits.

Long-Term Care Benefits

Long-term care benefits means—

1. Any payments made under a product that is advertised, marketed, or offered as long-term care insurance (whether qualified or not) and

2. Accelerated death benefits (excludable in whole or in part from gross income under section 101(g)) paid under a life insurance contract or paid by a viatical settlement provider.

Who Must File

File Form 1099-LTC if you paid any long-term care benefits, including accelerated death benefits. Payers include insurance companies, governmental units, and viatical settlement providers.

Viatical Settlement Providers

A viatical settlement provider is any person who—

1. Is regularly engaged in the trade or business of purchasing or taking assignments of life insurance contracts on the lives of terminally or chronically ill individuals and

2. Is licensed in the state where the insured lives. If licensing is not required in the state, the provider must meet other requirements (including those below) depending on whether the insured is terminally or chronically ill.

   a. If the insured is terminally ill, the provider must meet the requirements of sections 8 and 9 of the Viatical Settlements Model Act of the National Association of Insurance Commissioners (NAIC), relating to disclosure and general rules. The provider must also meet the requirements of the Model Regulations of the NAIC for evaluating the reasonableness of amounts paid in viatical settlement transactions with terminally ill individuals.

   b. If the insured is chronically ill, the provider must meet requirements similar to those of sections 8 and 9 of the Viatical Settlements Model Act of the NAIC and must also meet any standards of the NAIC for evaluating the reasonableness of

amounts paid in viatical settlement transactions with chronically ill individuals.

 However, if a state enacts a licensing requirement but does not permit viatical settlement providers to engage in business until the licenses are granted, the provider will not be considered as licensed under section 101(g)(2)(B)(i)(I). See Rev. Rul. 2002-82, which is on page 978 of Internal Revenue Bulletin 2002-51 at www.irs.gov/pub/irs-irbs/irb02-51.pdf.

Qualified Long-Term Care Insurance Contract

A contract issued after 1996 is a qualified long-term care insurance contract if it meets the requirements of section 7702B, including the requirement that the insured must be a chronically ill individual (see *Chronically ill Individual* below). A contract issued before 1997 generally is treated as a qualified long-term care insurance contract if it met state law requirements for long-term care insurance contracts and it has not been materially changed.

Accelerated Death Benefits

An accelerated death benefit is any amount paid under a life insurance contract for an insured individual who is terminally or chronically ill. It also includes any amount paid by a viatical settlement provider for the sale or assignment of a death benefit under a life insurance contract for a chronically or terminally ill individual.

Chronically ill Individual

A chronically ill individual is someone who has been certified (at least annually) by a licensed health care practitioner as—

1. Being unable to perform, without substantial assistance from another individual, at least two daily living activities (eating, toileting, transferring, bathing, dressing, and continence) for at least 90 days due to a loss of functional capacity or

2. Requiring substantial supervision to protect the individual from threats to health and safety due to severe cognitive impairment.

Terminally ill Individual

A terminally ill individual is someone who has been certified by a physician as having an illness or physical condition that can reasonably be expected to result in death in 24 months or less.

Reporting

Report payments only if the policyholder is an individual. Reportable payments are those made to the policyholder, to the insured, or to a third party.

You may report benefits paid from each contract on a separate Form 1099-LTC. At your option, you may aggregate benefits paid under multiple contracts on one Form 1099-LTC if the same information is reportable on the form for each contract (other than the amount of benefits paid).

Policyholder

The policyholder is the individual who owns the contract, including the owner of a contract sold or assigned to a viatical settlement provider. In the case of a group contract, the term policyholder includes the certificate holder (or similar

Cat. No. 27981Y

participant). You must report long-term care benefits to the policyholder even if the payments were made to the insured or to a third party (for example, a nursing home, caretaker, or physician). The policyholder also may be the insured.

Enter the name, address, and taxpayer identification number (TIN) of the policyholder on Form 1099-LTC. If the policyholder is not an individual, no reporting is required.

Insured

The insured is the chronically or terminally ill individual on whose behalf long-term care benefits are paid.

Enter the name, address, and TIN of the insured on Form 1099-LTC.

Statement to Policyholder and Insured

If you are required to file Form 1099-LTC, you must furnish a statement (or acceptable substitute) to both the policyholder and to the insured as shown.

IF the statement is for the ...	THEN use...
Policyholder	Copy B
Insured	Copy C
Policyholder and the policyholder is the insured	Copy B (Copy C is optional)

For more information about the requirement to furnish a statement to the policyholder and to the insured, see part M in the General Instructions for Forms 1099, 1098, 5498, and W-2G.

Account Number

The account number is required if you have multiple accounts for a recipient for whom you are filing more than one Form 1099-LTC. Additionally, the IRS encourages you to designate an account number for all Forms 1099-LTC that you file. See part L in the 2006 General Instructions for Forms 1099, 1098, 5498, and W-2G.

Box 1. Gross Long-Term Care Benefits Paid

Enter the gross long-term care benefits paid this year (other than accelerated death benefits). These benefits are all amounts paid out on a per diem (or other periodic) basis or on a reimbursed basis. It includes amounts paid to the insured, to the policyholder, and to third parties. You are not required to determine whether any benefits are taxable or nontaxable.

Box 2. Accelerated Death Benefits Paid

Enter the gross accelerated death benefits paid under a life insurance contract this year to or on behalf of an insured who has been certified as terminally or chronically ill. Include the amount paid by a viatical settlement provider for the sale or assignment of the insured's death benefit under a life insurance contract.

Box 3. Check if Per Diem or Reimbursed Amount

Check a box to indicate whether the payments were made on a per diem (or other periodic) basis or on a reimbursed basis. For accelerated death benefits, do not check a box if you made payments on behalf of a terminally ill person. Per diem basis means payments made on any periodic basis without regard to actual expenses. Reimbursed basis means payments made for actual expenses incurred.

Box 4. Qualified Contract (Optional)

Check the box to indicate whether long-term care insurance benefits are paid from a qualified long-term care insurance contract. See *Qualified Long-Term Care Insurance Contract* on page LTC-1.

Box 5. Check if Chronically ill or Terminally ill (Optional)

Check the box to indicate whether the insured was chronically or terminally ill. Also, enter the latest date certified. If the insured was neither chronically nor terminally ill, leave this box blank. See *Chronically ill Individual* and *Terminally ill Individual* on page LTC-1.

LTC-2

9595　☐ VOID　☐ CORRECTED

PAYER'S name, street address, city, state, ZIP code, and telephone no.		**1** Rents $	OMB No. 1545-0115 **2006** Form **1099-MISC**	**Miscellaneous Income**
		2 Royalties $		
		3 Other income $	**4** Federal income tax withheld $	**Copy A**
PAYER'S federal identification number	RECIPIENT'S identification number	**5** Fishing boat proceeds $	**6** Medical and health care payments $	**For Internal Revenue Service Center** File with Form 1096.
RECIPIENT'S name		**7** Nonemployee compensation $	**8** Substitute payments in lieu of dividends or interest $	For Privacy Act and Paperwork Reduction Act
Street address (including apt. no.)		**9** Payer made direct sales of $5,000 or more of consumer products to a buyer (recipient) for resale ▶ ☐	**10** Crop insurance proceeds $	Notice, see the **2006 General Instructions for**
City, state, and ZIP code		**11**	**12**	**Forms 1099, 1098, 5498,**
Account number (see instructions)	2nd TIN not. ☐	**13** Excess golden parachute payments $	**14** Gross proceeds paid to an attorney $	**and W-2G.**
15a Section 409A deferrals $	**15b** Section 409A income $	**16** State tax withheld $ $	**17** State/Payer's state no.	**18** State income $ $

Form **1099-MISC**　　　　Cat. No. 14425J　　　　Department of the Treasury - Internal Revenue Service

Do Not Cut or Separate Forms on This Page — Do Not Cut or Separate Forms on This Page

Instructions for Recipients

Account number. May show an account or other unique number the payer assigned to distinguish your account.

Amounts shown may be subject to self-employment (SE) tax. If your net income from self-employment is $400 or more, you must file a return and compute your SE tax on Schedule SE (Form 1040). See Pub. 334, Tax Guide for Small Business, for more information. If no income or social security and Medicare taxes were withheld and you are still receiving these payments, see Form 1040-ES, Estimated Tax for Individuals. Individuals must report as explained below. Corporations, fiduciaries, or partnerships report the amounts on the proper line of your tax return.

Boxes 1 and 2. Report rents from real estate on Schedule E (Form 1040). If you provided significant services to the tenant, sold real estate as a business, or rented personal property as a business, report on Schedule C or C-EZ (Form 1040). For royalties on timber, coal, and iron ore, see Pub. 544, Sales and Other Dispositions of Assets.

Box 3. Generally, report this amount on the "Other income" line of Form 1040 and identify the payment. The amount shown may be payments received as the beneficiary of a deceased employee, prizes, awards, taxable damages, Indian gaming profits, or other taxable income. See Pub. 525, Taxable and Nontaxable Income. If it is trade or business income, report this amount on Schedule C, C-EZ, or F (Form 1040).

Box 4. Shows backup withholding or withholding on Indian gaming profits. Generally, a payer must backup withhold at a 28% rate if you did not furnish your taxpayer identification number. See Form W-9, Request for Taxpayer Identification Number and Certification, for more information. Report this amount on your income tax return as tax withheld.

Box 5. An amount in this box means the fishing boat operator considers you self-employed. Report this amount on Schedule C or C-EZ (Form 1040). See Pub. 595, Tax Highlights for Commercial Fishermen.

Box 6. For individuals, report on Schedule C or C-EZ (Form 1040).

Box 7. Shows nonemployee compensation. If you are in the trade or business of catching fish, box 7 may show cash you received for the sale of fish. If payments in this box are SE income, report this amount on Schedule C, C-EZ, or F (Form 1040), and complete Schedule SE (Form 1040). You received this form instead of Form W-2 because the payer did not consider you an employee and did not withhold income tax or social security and Medicare taxes. Contact the payer if you believe this form is incorrect or has been issued in error. If you believe you are an employee, report this amount on line 7 of Form 1040 and call the IRS for information on how to report any social security and Medicare taxes.

Box 8. Shows substitute payments in lieu of dividends or tax-exempt interest received by your broker on your behalf as a result of a loan of your securities. Report on the "Other income" line of Form 1040.

Box 9. If checked, $5,000 or more of sales of consumer products was paid to you on a buy-sell, deposit-commission, or other basis. A dollar amount does not have to be shown. Generally, report any income from your sale of these products on Schedule C or C-EZ (Form 1040).

Box 10. Report this amount on line 8 of Schedule F (Form 1040).

Box 13. Shows your total compensation of excess golden parachute payments subject to a 20% excise tax. See the Form 1040 instructions for where to report.

Box 14. Shows gross proceeds paid to an attorney in connection with legal services. Report only the taxable part as income on your return.

Box 15a. Shows current year deferrals as a nonemployee under a nonqualified deferred compensation (NQDC) plan that is subject to the requirements of section 409A. Any earnings on current and prior year deferrals are also reported.

Box 15b. Shows income as a nonemployee under a NQDC plan that does not meet the requirements of section 409A. This amount is also included in box 7 as nonemployee compensation. Any amount included in box 15a that is currently taxable is also included in this box. This income is also subject to a substantial additional tax to be reported on Form 1040. See "Total Tax" in the Form 1040 instructions.

Boxes 16–18. Shows state or local income tax withheld from the payments.

Instructions for Payers

General and specific form instructions are provided as separate products. The products you should use to complete Form 1099-MISC are the 2006 General Instructions for Forms 1099, 1098, 5498, and W-2G and the 2006 Instructions for Form 1099-MISC. A chart in the general instructions gives a quick guide to which form must be filed to report a particular payment. To order these instructions and additional forms, call 1-800-TAX-FORM (1-800-829-3676).

Caution: *Because paper forms are scanned during processing, you cannot file with the IRS Forms 1096, 1098, 1099, or 5498 that you print from the IRS website.*

Due dates. Furnish Copy B of this form to the recipient by January 31, 2007.

File Copy A of this form with the IRS by February 28, 2007. If you file electronically, the due date is April 2, 2007. To file electronically, you must have software that generates a file according to the specifications in Pub. 1220, Specifications for Filing Forms 1098, 1099, 5498, and W-2G Electronically or Magnetically. IRS does not provide a fill-in form option.

 Printed on recycled paper

Department of the Treasury
Internal Revenue Service

20**06**

Instructions for Form 1099-MISC

Section references are to the Internal Revenue Code unless otherwise noted.

Reminder

In addition to these specific instructions, you should also use the 2006 General Instructions for Forms 1099, 1098, 5498, and W-2G. Those general instructions include information about:
- Backup withholding
- Magnetic media and electronic reporting requirements
- Penalties
- Who must file (nominee/middleman)
- When and where to file
- Taxpayer identification numbers
- Statements to recipients
- Corrected and void returns
- Other general topics

You can get the general instructions from the IRS website at *www.irs.gov* or by calling 1-800-TAX-FORM (1-800-829-3676).

Specific Instructions for Form 1099-MISC

File Form 1099-MISC, Miscellaneous Income, for each person to whom you have paid during the year:
- At least $10 in royalties or broker payments in lieu of dividends or tax-exempt interest (see *Box 8* on page MISC-6);
- At least $600 in rents, services (including parts and materials), prizes and awards, other income payments, medical and health care payments, crop insurance proceeds, cash payments for fish (or other aquatic life) you purchase from anyone engaged in the trade or business of catching fish, or, generally, the cash paid from a notional principal contract to an individual, partnership, or estate;
- Any fishing boat proceeds; or
- Gross proceeds to an attorney. See *Payments to attorneys* on page MISC-2.

In addition, use Form 1099-MISC to report that you made direct sales of at least $5,000 of consumer products to a buyer for resale anywhere other than a permanent retail establishment. You must also file Form 1099-MISC for each person from whom you have withheld any federal income tax under the backup withholding rules regardless of the amount of the payment.

> ⚠️ **CAUTION** *Be sure to report each payment in the proper box because the IRS uses this information to determine whether the recipient has properly reported the payment.*

Trade or business reporting only. Report on Form 1099-MISC only when payments are made in the course of your trade or business. Personal payments are not reportable. You are engaged in a trade or business if you operate for gain or profit. However, nonprofit organizations are considered to be engaged in a trade or business and are subject to these reporting requirements. Nonprofit organizations subject to these reporting requirements include trusts of qualified pension or profit-sharing plans of employers, certain organizations exempt from tax under section 501(c) or (d), and farmers' cooperatives that are exempt from tax under section 521. Payments by federal, state, or local government agencies are also reportable.

Exceptions. Some payments are not required to be reported on Form 1099-MISC, although they may be taxable to the recipient. Payments for which a Form 1099-MISC is not required include:
- Generally, payments to a corporation; but see *Reportable payments to corporations* on page MISC-2;
- Payments for merchandise, telegrams, telephone, freight, storage, and similar items;
- Payments of rent to real estate agents, but see Regulations section 1.6041-1(e)(5), Example 5;
- Wages paid to employees (report on Form W-2, Wage and Tax Statement);
- Business travel allowances paid to employees (may be reportable on Form W-2);
- Cost of current life insurance protection (report on Form W-2 or Form 1099-R, Distributions From Pensions, Annuities, Retirement or Profit-Sharing Plans, IRAs, Insurance Contracts, etc.);
- Payments to a tax-exempt organization, the United States, a state, the District of Columbia, a U.S. possession, or a foreign government; and
- Certain payment card transactions if a payment card organization has assigned a merchant/payee a Merchant Category Code (MCC) indicating that reporting is not required. A cardholder/payor may rely on the MCC that the payment card organization assigned to a merchant/payee to determine if a payment card transaction with that merchant/payee is subject to reporting under section 6041 or section 6041A. For more information and a list of merchant types with corresponding MCCs, see Revenue Procedure 2004-43 which is on page 124 of Internal Revenue Bulletin 2004-31 at *www.irs.gov/pub/irs-irbs/irb04-31.pdf*.

Fees paid to informers. A payment to an informer as an award, fee, or reward for information about criminal activity is not required to be reported if the payment is made by a federal, state, or local government agency, or by a nonprofit organization exempt from tax under section 501(c)(3) that makes the payment to further the charitable purpose of lessening the burdens of government. For more information, see Regulations section 1.6041-3(l).

Scholarships. Do not use Form 1099-MISC to report scholarship or fellowship grants. Scholarship or fellowship grants that are taxable to the recipient because they are paid for teaching, research, or other services as a condition for receiving the grant are considered wages and must be reported on Form W-2. Other taxable scholarship or fellowship payments (to a degree or nondegree candidate) are not required to be reported by you to the IRS on any form. See Notice 87-31, 1987-1 C.B. 475 and Regulations section 1.6041-3(n) for more information.

Difficulty-of-care payments. Difficulty-of-care payments that are excludable from the recipient's gross income are not required to be reported. Difficulty-of-care payments to foster care providers are not reportable if paid for not more than 10 children under age 19 and not more than 5 individuals age 19 or older. Amounts paid for more than 10 children or more than 5 individuals are reportable on Form 1099-MISC.

Charitable organizations' reimbursements for certain automobile expenses. Amounts provided as reimbursements for operating expenses of a passenger automobile in providing relief relating to Hurricane Katrina from August 25, 2005, to December 31, 2006, are not reportable if certain requirements

Cat. No. 27982J

are met. See *Box 3. Other Income* on page MISC-4 for additional requirements.

Canceled debt. A canceled debt is not reportable on Form 1099-MISC. Canceled debts are required to be reported on Form 1099-C, Cancellation of Debt, by financial institutions, credit unions, federal government agencies, certain agencies connected with the Federal Government, and an organization where the lending of money (such as finance and credit card companies) is a significant trade or business. See the Instructions for Forms 1099-A and 1099-C.

Reportable payments to corporations. The following payments made to corporations generally must be reported on Form 1099-MISC.
• Medical and health care payments reported in box 6.
• Fish purchases for cash reported in box 7.
• Attorneys' fees reported in box 7.
• Gross proceeds paid to an attorney reported in box 14.
• Substitute payments in lieu of dividends or tax-exempt interest reported in box 8.
• Payments by a federal executive agency for services (vendors) reported in box 7.

 Federal executive agencies may also have to file Form 8596, Information Return for Federal Contracts, if a contracted amount for personal services is more than $25,000. See Rev. Rul. 2003-66, which is on page 1115 of Internal Revenue Bulletin 2003-26 at www.irs.gov/pub/irs-irbs/irb03-26.pdf for details.

Payments to attorneys. The term attorney includes a law firm or other provider of legal services. Attorney's fees of $600 or more paid in the course of your trade or business are reportable in box 7 of Form 1099-MISC.

Gross proceeds paid to attorneys. Under section 6045(f), report in box 14 payments to an attorney made in the course of your trade or business in connection with legal services, for example, as in a settlement agreement, unless the attorney's fees are reportable by you in box 7. Generally, you are not required to report the claimant's attorney's fees. For example, an insurance company pays a claimant's attorney $100,000 to settle a claim. The insurance company reports the payment as gross proceeds of $100,000 in box 14. The insurance company does not have a reporting requirement for the claimant's attorney's fees subsequently paid from these funds.

These rules apply whether or not the legal services are provided to the payer and whether or not the attorney is exclusive payee (for example, the attorney's and claimant's names are on one check). However, these rules do not apply to wages paid to attorneys that are reportable on Form W-2 or to profits distributed by a partnership to its partners that are reportable on:
• Schedule K-1 (Form 1065), Partner's Share of Income, Deductions, Credits, etc., or
• Schedule K-1 (Form 1065-B),Partner's Share of Income (Loss) From an Electing Large Partnership.

Payments to corporations for legal services. The exemption from reporting payments made to corporations does not apply to payments for legal services. Therefore, you must report attorneys' fees (in box 7) or gross proceeds (in box 14) as described above to corporations that provide legal services.

Taxpayer identification numbers (TINs). To report payments to an attorney on Form 1099-MISC, you must obtain the attorney's TIN. You may use Form W-9, Request for Taxpayer Identification Number and Certification, to obtain the attorney's TIN. An attorney is required to promptly supply its TIN whether it is a corporation or other entity, but the attorney is not required to certify its TIN. If the attorney fails to provide its TIN, the attorney may be subject to a penalty under section 6723 and its regulations, and you must backup withhold on the reportable payments.

Fish purchases. If you are in the trade or business of purchasing fish for resale, you must report total cash payments of $600 or more paid during the year to any person who is engaged in the trade or business of catching fish. Report these payments in box 7. You are required to keep records showing

the date and amount of each cash payment made during the year, but you must report only the total amount paid for the year on Form 1099-MISC.

"Fish" means all fish and other forms of aquatic life. "Cash" means U.S. and foreign coin and currency and a cashier's check, bank draft, traveler's check, or money order. Cash does not include a check drawn on your personal or business account.

Deceased employee's wages. If an employee dies during the year, you must report the accrued wages, vacation pay, and other compensation paid after the date of death. If you made the payment in the same year the employee died, you must withhold social security and Medicare taxes on the payment and report them only as social security and Medicare wages on the employee's Form W-2 to ensure that proper social security and Medicare credit is received. On the Form W-2, show the payment as social security wages (box 3) and Medicare wages and tips (box 5) and the social security and Medicare taxes withheld in boxes 4 and 6; do not show the payment in box 1 of Form W-2.

If you made the payment after the year of death, do not report it on Form W-2, and do not withhold social security and Medicare taxes.

Whether the payment is made in the year of death or after the year of death, you also must report the payment to the estate or beneficiary on Form 1099-MISC. Report the payment in box 3 (rather than in box 7 as specified in Rev. Rul. 86-109, 1986-2 C.B. 196). See the *Example* below. Enter the name and TIN of the payment recipient on Form 1099-MISC. For example, if the recipient is an individual beneficiary, enter the name and social security number of the individual; if the recipient is the estate, enter the name and employer identification number of the estate. The general backup withholding rules apply to this payment.

However, death benefits from qualified and nonqualified deferred compensation plans paid to the estate or beneficiary of a deceased employee are not reportable on Form 1099-MISC but are reportable on Form 1099-R. See the Instructions for Forms 1099-R and 5498.

Example. Before Employee A's death on June 15, 2006, A was employed by Employer X and received $10,000 in wages on which federal income tax of $1,500 was withheld. When A died, X owed A $2,000 in wages and $1,000 in accrued vacation pay. The total of $3,000 (less the social security and Medicare taxes withheld) was paid to A's estate on July 20, 2006. Because X made the payment during the year of death, X must withhold social security and Medicare taxes on the $3,000 payment and must complete Form W-2 as follows:
• Box 1—10000.00 (does not include the $3,000 accrued wages and vacation pay)
• Box 2—1500.00
• Box 3—13000.00 (includes the $3,000 accrued wages and vacation pay)
• Box 4—806.00 (6.2% of the amount in box 3)
• Box 5—13000.00 (includes the $3,000 accrued wages and vacation pay)
• Box 6—188.50 (1.45% of the amount in box 5)

Employer X also must complete Form 1099-MISC as follows:
• Boxes for recipient's name, address, and TIN—the estate's name, address, and TIN.
• Box 3—3000.00 (Even though amounts were withheld for social security and Medicare taxes, the gross amount is reported here.)

If Employer X made the payment after the year of death, the $3,000 would not be subject to social security and Medicare taxes and would not be shown on Form W-2. However, the employer would still file Form 1099-MISC.

Employee business expense reimbursements. Do not use Form 1099-MISC to report employee business expense reimbursements. Report payments made to employees under a nonaccountable plan as wages on Form W-2. Generally, payments made to employees under an accountable plan are not reportable on Form W-2, except in certain cases when you

MISC-2

pay per diem or mileage allowance. For more information, see the Instructions for Forms W-2 and W-3, Pub. 463, Travel, Entertainment, Gift, and Car Expenses, and Pub. 1542, Per Diem Rates. For information on reporting employee moving expense reimbursements on Form W-2, see the Instructions for Forms W-2 and W-3.

Independent contractor or employee. Generally, you must report payments to independent contractors on Form 1099-MISC in box 7. See the instructions for box 7 on page MISC-5.

 Section 530 of the Revenue Act of 1978 as extended by section 269(c) of P.L. 97-248, deals with the employment tax status of independent contractors and employees. To qualify for relief under section 530, employers must file Form 1099-MISC. Additional requirements for relief are discussed in Rev. Proc. 85-18, 1985-1 C.B. 518. Also, see Notice 87-19, 1987-1 C.B. 455, for special rules that may apply to certain skilled workers, such as engineers, designers, drafters, computer programmers, and systems analysts.

Transit passes and parking for independent contractors. Although you cannot provide qualified transportation fringes to independent contractors, the working condition and de minimus fringe rules for transit passes and parking apply to independent contractors. Tokens or farecards that enable an independent contractor to commute on a public transit system (not including privately operated van pools) are excludable from the independent contractor's gross income and are not reportable on Form 1099-MISC if their value in any month is $21 or less. However, if the value of a pass provided in a month is greater than $21, the full value is includible in gross income and is reportable on Form 1099-MISC. The value of parking may be excludable from an independent contractor's gross income, and, therefore, not reportable on Form 1099-MISC if certain requirements are met. See Regulations section 1.132-9, Q/A 24.

Directors' fees. You must report directors' fees and other remuneration, including payments made after retirement, on Form 1099-MISC in the year paid. Report them in box 7.

Commissions paid to lottery ticket sales agents. A state that has control over and responsibility for online and instant lottery games must file Form 1099-MISC to report commissions paid, whether directly or indirectly, to licensed sales agents. For example, State X retains control over and liability for online and instant lottery games. For online ticket sales, State X pays commissions by allowing an agent to retain 5% of the ticket proceeds the agent remits to State X. For instant ticket sales, State X pays commissions by providing tickets to the agent for 5% less than the proceeds to be obtained by the agent from the sale of those tickets. If the commissions for the year total $600 or more, they must be reported in box 7 on Form 1099-MISC. See Rev. Rul. 92-96, 1992-2 C.B. 281.

Escrow agent; construction project. When an escrow agent maintains owner-provided funds in an escrow account for a construction project, performs management and oversight functions relating to the construction project, and makes payments for the owner and the general contractor, the escrow agent must file Form 1099-MISC for reportable payments of $600 or more. This requirement applies whether or not the escrow agent is a bank. If the contractor is the borrower of the funds, do not report on Form 1099-MISC any loan payments made to the contractor/borrower.

Indian gaming profits, payments to tribal members. If you make payments to members of Indian tribes from the net revenues of class II or class III gaming activities conducted or licensed by the tribes, you must withhold federal income tax on such payments and file Form 1099-MISC.

File Form 1099-MISC to report the distributions to tribal members. Report the payments in box 3 and the federal income tax withheld in box 4. Pub. 15-A, Employer's Supplemental Tax Guide, contains the necessary "Tables for Withholding on Distributions of Indian Gaming Profits to Tribal Members."

State or local sales taxes. If state or local sales taxes are imposed on the service provider and you (as the buyer) pay them to the service provider, report them on Form 1099-MISC as part of the reportable payment. However, if sales taxes are imposed on you (as the buyer) and collected from you by the service provider, do not report the sales taxes on Form 1099-MISC.

Statements to recipients. If you are required to file Form 1099-MISC, you must provide a statement to the recipient. For more information about the requirement to furnish a statement to each recipient, see part M in the 2006 General Instructions for Forms 1099, 1098, 5498, and W-2G.

2nd TIN not. You may enter an "X" in this box if you were notified by the IRS twice within 3 calendar years that the payee provided an incorrect TIN. If you mark this box, the IRS will not send you any further notices about this account. However, if you received both IRS notices in the same year, or if you received them in different years but they both related to information returns filed for the same year, do not check the box at this time. For purpose of the two notices in 3-year rule, you are considered to have received one notice. You are not required to send a second "B" notice upon receipt of the second notice. See Backup Withholding in the 2006 General Instructions for Forms 1099, 1098, 5498, and W-2G for more information.

 For information on the TIN Matching System offered by the IRS, see the 2006 General Instructions for Forms 1099, 1098, 5498, and W-2G.

Account Number

The account number is required if you have multiple accounts for a recipient for whom you are filing more than one Form 1099-MISC. Additionally, the IRS encourages you to designate an account number for all Forms 1099-MISC that you file. See part L in the 2006 General Instructions for Forms 1099, 1098, 5498, and W-2G.

Box 1. Rents

Enter amounts of $600 or more for all types of rents, such as real estate rentals paid for office space (unless paid to a real estate agent), machine rentals (for example, renting a bulldozer to level your parking lot), and pasture rentals (for example, farmers paying for the use of grazing land). If the machine rental is part of a contract that includes both the use of the machine and the operator, the rental should be prorated between the rent of the machine (reported in box 1) and the operator's charge (reported as nonemployee compensation in box 7).

Public housing agencies must report in box 1 rental assistance payments made to owners of housing projects. See Rev. Rul. 88-53, 1988-1 C.B. 384.

Coin-operated amusements. If an arrangement between an owner of coin-operated amusements and an owner of a business establishment where the amusements are placed is a lease of the amusements or the amusement space, the owner of the amusements or the owner of the space, whoever makes the payments, must report the lease payments in box 1 of Form 1099-MISC if the payments total at least $600. However, if the arrangement is a joint venture, the joint venture must file a Form 1065, U.S. Return of Partnership Income, and provide each partner with the information necessary to report the partner's share of the taxable income. Coin-operated amusements include video games, pinball machines, jukeboxes, pool tables, slot machines, and other machines and gaming devices operated by coins or tokens inserted into the machines by individual users. For more information, see Rev. Rul. 92-49, 1992-1 C.B. 433.

Box 2. Royalties

Enter gross royalty payments of $10 or more before reduction for severance and other taxes that may have been withheld and paid. Use box 2 to report gross royalties (before reduction for fees, commissions, or expenses) paid by a publisher directly to an author or literary agent, unless the agent is a corporation. The literary agent (whether or not a corporation) that receives the royalty payment on behalf of the author must report the

MISC-3

gross amount of royalty payments to the author on Form 1099-MISC whether or not the publisher reported the payment to the agent on its Form 1099-MISC. Do not include surface royalties. They should be reported in box 1. Do not report oil or gas payments for a working interest in box 2; report payments for working interests in box 7. Do not report timber royalties made under a pay-as-cut contract; report these timber royalties on Form 1099-S, Proceeds From Real Estate Transactions.

Box 3. Other Income

Enter other income of $600 or more required to be reported on Form 1099-MISC that is not reportable in one of the other boxes on the form.

 Do not include mileage reimbursements to charitable volunteers to the extent the reimbursement was:

- *For expenses for relief relating to Hurricane Katrina during the period beginning August 25, 2005, and ending December 31, 2006,*
- *For the operating expenses of a passenger automobile that the volunteer has substantiated with adequate records,*
- *Related to expenses that were for the benefit of and reimbursed by a charitable organization as described in section 170(c), including public charities and private foundations,*
- *Not in excess of the standard business mileage rate at the time the automobile was used to provide the relief, and*
- *Not compensation for the performance of services.*

Also enter in box 3 prizes and awards that are not for services performed. Include the fair market value (FMV) of merchandise won on game shows. Also include amounts paid to a winner of a sweepstakes not involving a wager. If a wager is made, report the winnings on Form W-2G, Certain Gambling Winnings.

 If, not later than 60 days after the winner becomes entitled to the prize, the winner can choose the option of a lump sum or an annuity payable over at least 10 years, the payment of winnings is considered made when actually paid. If the winner chooses an annuity, file Form 1099-MISC each year to report the annuity paid during that year.

Do not include prizes and awards paid to your employees. Report these on Form W-2. Do not include in box 3 prizes and awards for services performed by nonemployees, such as an award for the top commission salesperson. Report them in box 7.

Prizes and awards received in recognition of past accomplishments in religious, charitable, scientific, artistic, educational, literary, or civic fields are not reportable if:
- The winners are chosen without action on their part,
- The winners are not expected to perform future services, and
- The payer transfers the prize or award to a charitable organization or governmental unit under a designation made by the recipient. See Rev. Proc. 87-54, 1987-2 C.B. 669.

Other items required to be reported in box 3 include the following:
1. Generally, all punitive damages, any damages for nonphysical injuries or sickness, and any other taxable damages. Report punitive damages even if they relate to physical injury or physical sickness. Generally, report all compensatory damages for nonphysical injuries or sickness, such as employment discrimination or defamation. However, do not report damages (other than punitive damages):
    a. Received on account of personal physical injuries or physical sickness;
    b. That do not exceed the amount paid for medical care for emotional distress; or
    c. Received on account of nonphysical injuries (for example, emotional distress) under a written binding agreement, court decree, or mediation award in effect on or issued by September 13, 1995.
Damages received on account of emotional distress, including physical symptoms such as insomnia, headaches,

and stomach disorders, are not considered received for a physical injury or physical sickness and are reportable unless described in b or c above. However, damages received on account of emotional distress due to physical injuries or physical sickness are not reportable.

Also report liquidated damages received under the Age Discrimination in Employment Act of 1967.

 Taxable back pay damages may be wages and reportable on Form W-2. See Pub. 957, Reporting Back Pay and Special Wage Payments to the Social Security Administration.

2. Payments of $600 or more to any one patient or member in a Department of Veterans Affairs (VA) hospital or domiciliary under the VA's therapeutic or rehabilitative programs. See Rul. 65-18, 1965-1 C.B. 32.

3. Payments as explained on page MISC-2 under *Deceased employee's wages.*

4. Payments as explained on page MISC-3 under *Indian gaming profits, payments to tribal members.*

5. Termination payments to former self-employed insurance salespeople. These payments are not subject to self-employment tax and are reportable in box 3 (rather than box 7) if all the following apply:

    a. The payments are received from an insurance company because of services performed as an insurance salesperson for the company.
    b. The payments are received after termination of the salesperson's agreement to perform services for the company.
    c. The salesperson did not perform any services for the company after termination and before the end of the year.
    d. The salesperson enters into a covenant not to compete against the company for at least 1 year after the date of termination.
    e. The amount of the payments depends primarily on policies sold by the salesperson or credited to the salesperson's account during the last year of the service agreement or to the extent those policies remain in force for some period after termination, or both.
    f. The amount of the payments does not depend at all on length of service or overall earnings from the company (regardless of whether eligibility for payment depends on length of service).
    If the termination payments do not meet all these requirements, report them in box 7.

Box 4. Federal Income Tax Withheld

Enter backup withholding. For example, persons who have not furnished their TIN to you are subject to withholding at a 28% rate on payments required to be reported in boxes 1, 2 (net of severance taxes), 3, 5 (to the extent paid in cash), 6, 7 (except fish purchases for cash), 8, 10, and 14. For more information on backup withholding, see the 2006 General Instructions for Forms 1099, 1098, 5498, and W-2G.

Also enter any income tax withheld from payments to members of Indian tribes from the net revenues of class II or class III gaming activities conducted or licensed by the tribes.

Exception

Regulations section 31.3406(g)-1(f) provides that backup withholding is not required for certain payment card transactions if:
- The payment is made through a payment card organization that is a Qualified Payment Card Agent as described in Rev. Proc. 2004-42, which is on page 121 of Internal Revenue Bulletin 2004-31 at *www.irs.gov/pub/irs-irbs/irb04-31.pdf,*
- The payment is made on or after January 1, 2005, and
- The requirements of Regulations section 31.3406-1(g) are met.

Box 5. Fishing Boat Proceeds

Enter the share of all proceeds from the sale of a catch or the FMV of a distribution in kind to each crew member of fishing boats with normally fewer than 10 crew members. A fishing

---

Illustrated example. The completed Form 1099-MISC illustrates the following example. Z Builders is a contractor that subcontracts drywall work to Ronald Green, a sole proprietor who does business as Y Drywall. During the year, Z Builders pays Mr. Green $5,500. Z Builders must file Form 1099-MISC because they paid Mr. Green $600 or more in the course of their trade or business, and Mr. Green is not a corporation.

9595	☐ VOID	☐ CORRECTED		

PAYER'S name, street address, city, state, ZIP code, and telephone no.	1 Rents $	OMB No. 1545-0115		**Miscellaneous Income**
Z Builders 123 Maple Avenue Oaktown, VA 22000 703-123-4567	2 Royalties $	**2006** Form **1099-MISC**		
	3 Other income $	4 Federal income tax withheld $		**Copy A For Internal Revenue Service Center**
PAYER'S Federal identification number	RECIPIENT'S identification number	5 Fishing boat proceeds $	6 Medical and health care payments $	**File with Form 1096.**
10-9999999	123-00-6789			
RECIPIENT'S name Ronald Green dba/ Y Drywall		7 Nonemployee compensation $ 5500.00	8 Substitute payments in lieu of dividends or interest $	For Privacy Act and Paperwork Reduction Act Notice, see the **2006 General Instructions for Forms 1099, 1098, 5498, and W-2G.**
Street address (including apt. no.) 456 Flower Lane		9 Payer made direct sales of $5,000 or more of consumer products to a buyer (recipient) for resale ► ☐	10 Crop insurance proceeds $	
City, state, and ZIP code Oaktown, VA 22000		11	12	
Account number (see instructions)	2nd TIN not. ☐	13 Excess golden parachute payments $	14 Gross proceeds paid to an attorney $	
15a Section 409A deferrals $	15b Section 409A income $	16 State tax withheld $ _ _ _ $ _ _ _	17 State/Payer's state no. _ _ _ _	18 State income $ _ _ _ $ _ _ _

Form **1099-MISC**   Cat. No. 14425J   Department of the Treasury - Internal Revenue Service

---

boat has normally fewer than 10 crew members if the average size of the operating crew was fewer than 10 on trips during the preceding 4 calendar quarters.

In addition, report cash payments of up to $100 per trip that are contingent on a minimum catch and are paid solely for additional duties (such as mate, engineer, or cook) for which additional cash payments are traditional in the industry. However, do not report on Form 1099-MISC any wages reportable on Form W-2.

Box 6. Medical and Health Care Payments

Enter payments of $600 or more made in the course of your trade or business to each physician or other supplier or provider of medical or health care services. Include payments made by medical and health care insurers under health, accident, and sickness insurance programs. If payment is made to a corporation, list the corporation as the recipient rather than the individual providing the services. Payments to persons providing health care services often include charges for injections, drugs, dentures, and similar items. In these cases the entire payment is subject to information reporting. You are not required to report payments to pharmacies for prescription drugs.

The exemption from issuing Form 1099-MISC to a corporation does not apply to payments for medical or health care services provided by corporations, including professional corporations. However, you are not required to report payments made to a tax-exempt hospital or extended care facility or to a hospital or extended care facility owned and operated by the United States (or its possessions), a state, the District of Columbia, or any of their political subdivisions, agencies, or instrumentalities.

⚠ **CAUTION** *Generally, payments made under a flexible spending arrangement (as defined in section 106(c)(2)) or a health reimbursement arrangement which is treated as employer-provided coverage under an accident or health plan for purposes of section 106 are exempt from the reporting requirements of section 6041.*

Box 7. Nonemployee Compensation

Enter nonemployee compensation of $600 or more. Include fees, commissions, prizes and awards for services performed as a nonemployee, other forms of compensation for services performed for your trade or business by an individual who is not your employee, and fish purchases for cash. Include oil and gas payments for a working interest, whether or not services are performed. Also include expenses incurred for the use of an entertainment facility that you treat as compensation to a nonemployee. Federal executive agencies that make payments to vendors for services, including payments to corporations, must report the payments in this box. See Rev. Rul. 2003-66, which is on page 1115 of Internal Revenue Bulletin 2003-26 at *www.irs.gov/pub/irs-irbs/irb03-26.pdf.*

Exceptions. Do not report in box 7, nor elsewhere on Form 1099-MISC, the cost of current life insurance protection (report on Form W-2 or Form 1099-R); an employee's wages, travel or auto allowance, or bonuses (report on Form W-2); or the cost of group-term life insurance paid on behalf of a former employee (report on Form W-2).

Self-employment tax. Generally, amounts reportable in box 7 are subject to self-employment tax. If payments to individuals are not subject to this tax and are not reportable elsewhere on Form 1099-MISC, report the payments in box 3. However, report section 530 (of the Revenue Act of 1978) worker payments in box 7.

MISC-5

Nonqualified deferred compensation (Section 409A) income. Include in box 7 the amount of all deferrals (plus earnings) reported in box 15b that are includible in gross income because the NQDC plan fails to satisfy the requirements of section 409A. These amounts generally are subject to self-employment tax and are also subject to a substantial additional tax under section 409A that is reported on the nonemployee's Form 1040. See Notice 2005-1, which is available on page 274 of Internal Revenue Bulletin 2005-2 at *www.irs.gov/pub/irs-irbs/irb05-02.pdf.*

When to report. If the following four conditions are met, you must generally report a payment as nonemployee compensation.
● You made the payment to someone who is not your employee;
● You made the payment for services in the course of your trade or business (including government agencies and nonprofit organizations);
● You made the payment to an individual, partnership, estate, or, in some cases, a corporation; and
● You made payments to the payee of at least $600 during the year.

Examples. The following are some examples of payments to be reported in box 7.
● Professional service fees, such as fees to attorneys (including corporations), accountants, architects, contractors, engineers, etc.
● Fees paid by one professional to another, such as fee-splitting or referral fees.
● Payments by attorneys to witnesses or experts in legal adjudication.
● Payment for services, including payment for parts or materials used to perform the services if supplying the parts or materials was incidental to providing the service. For example, report the total insurance company payments to an auto repair shop under a repair contract showing an amount for labor and another amount for parts, if furnishing parts was incidental to repairing the auto.
● Commissions paid to nonemployee salespersons that are subject to repayment but not repaid during the calendar year.
● A fee paid to a nonemployee, including an independent contractor, or travel reimbursement for which the nonemployee did not account to the payer, if the fee and reimbursement total at least $600. To help you determine whether someone is an independent contractor or an employee, see Pub. 15-A.
● Payments to nonemployee entertainers for services. Use Form 1042-S, Foreign Person's U.S. Source Income Subject to Withholding, for payments to nonresident aliens.
● Exchanges of services between individuals in the course of their trades or businesses. For example, an attorney represents a painter for nonpayment of business debts in exchange for the painting of the attorney's law offices. The amount reportable by each on Form 1099-MISC is the FMV of his or her own services performed. However, if the attorney represents the painter in a divorce proceeding, this is an activity that is unrelated to the painter's trade or business. The attorney must report on Form 1099-MISC the value of his or her services. But the painter need not report on Form 1099-MISC the value of painting the law offices because the work is in exchange for legal services that are separate from the painter's business.
● Taxable fringe benefits for nonemployees. For information on the valuation of fringe benefits, see Pub. 15-B, Employer's Tax Guide to Fringe Benefits.
● Gross oil and gas payments for a working interest.
● Payments to an insurance salesperson who is not your common law or statutory employee. See Pub. 15-A for the definition of employee. However, for termination payments to former insurance salespeople, see *5. Termination payments to former self-employed insurance salespeople* on page MISC-4.
● Directors' fees as explained under *Directors' fees* on page MISC-3.
● Commissions paid to licensed lottery ticket sales agents as explained under *Commissions paid to lottery ticket sales agents* on page MISC-3.

● Payments to section 530 (of the Revenue Act of 1978) workers. See the *TIP* on page MISC-3.
● Fish purchases for cash. See *Fish purchases* on page MISC-2.

Golden parachute payments. A parachute payment is any payment that meets all of the following conditions.
1. The payment is in the nature of compensation.
2. The payment is to, or for the benefit of, a disqualified individual.
3. The payment is contingent on a change in the ownership of a corporation, the effective control of a corporation, or the ownership of a substantial portion of the assets of a corporation (a change in ownership or control).
4. The payment has (together with other payments described in 1, 2, and 3 above made to the same individual) an aggregate present value of at least 3 times the individual's base amount.

A disqualified individual is one who at any time during the 12-month period prior to and ending on the date of the change in ownership or control of the corporation (the disqualified individual determination period) was an employee or independent contractor and was in regard to that corporation, a shareholder, an officer, or a highly compensated individual.

For more details, see Regulations section 1.280G-1. Also, see Rev. Proc. 2003-68, which is on page 398 of Internal Revenue Bulletin 2003-34 at *www.irs.gov/pub/irs-irbs/irb03-34.pdf,* concerning the valuation of stock options for purposes of golden parachute payment rules. For the treatment of unvested shares of restricted stock, see Rev. Rul. 2005-39, which is on page 1 of Internal Revenue Bulletin 2005-27 at *www.irs.gov/pub/irs-irbs/irb05-27.pdf*

Independent contractor. Enter in box 7 the total compensation, including any golden parachute payment. For excess golden parachute payments, see box 13 reporting instructions.

For employee reporting of these payments, see Pub. 15-A.

Box 8. Substitute Payments in Lieu of Dividends or Interest
Enter aggregate payments of at least $10 received by a broker for a customer in lieu of dividends or tax-exempt interest as a result of a loan of a customer's securities. For this purpose, a customer includes an individual, trust, estate, partnership, association, company, or corporation. See Notice 2003-67, which is on page 752 of Internal Revenue Bulletin 2003-40 at *www.irs.gov/pub/irs-irbs/irb03-40.pdf.* It does not include a tax-exempt organization, the United States, any state, the District of Columbia, a U.S. possession, or a foreign government. File Form 1099-MISC with the IRS and furnish a copy to the customer for whom you received the payment. Also, file Form 1099-MISC for and furnish a copy to an individual for whom you received a payment in lieu of tax-exempt interest.

Substitute payment means a payment in lieu of (a) a dividend or (b) tax-exempt interest to the extent that interest (including OID) has accrued while the securities were on loan.

Box 9. Payer Made Direct Sales of $5,000 or More
Enter an "X" in the checkbox for sales by you of $5,000 or more of consumer products to a person on a buy-sell, deposit-commission, or other commission basis for resale (by the buyer or any other person) anywhere other than in a permanent retail establishment. Do not enter a dollar amount in this box.

If you are reporting an amount in box 7, you may also check box 9 on the same Form 1099-MISC.

The report you must give to the recipient for these direct sales need not be made on the official form. It may be in the form of a letter showing this information along with commissions, prizes, awards, etc.

MISC-6

Box 10. Crop Insurance Proceeds

Enter crop insurance proceeds of $600 or more paid to farmers by insurance companies unless the farmer has informed the insurance company that expenses have been capitalized under section 278, 263A, or 447.

Boxes 11 and 12. Reserved

Make no entries in these boxes.

Box 13. Excess Golden Parachute Payments

Enter any excess golden parachute payments. An excess parachute payment is the amount of the excess of any parachute payment over the base amount (the average annual compensation for services includible in the individual's gross income over the most recent 5 taxable years). See Q/A-38 through Q/A-44 of Regulations section 1.280G-1 for how to compute the excess amount.

See *Golden parachute payments* on page MISC-6 for more information.

Box 14. Gross Proceeds Paid to an Attorney

Enter gross proceeds paid to an attorney in connection with legal services (regardless of whether the services are performed for the payer). See *Payments to attorneys* on page MISC-2.

Box 15a. Section 409A Deferrals

Enter the amount of the total deferrals during the year of at least $600 for the nonemployee from all nonqualified deferred compensation (NQDC) plans subject to the provisions of section 409A. The deferrals during the year include earnings on the current year and prior year deferrals. For additional information, see Notice 2005-1, which is available on page 274 of Internal Revenue Bulletin 2005-2 at *www.irs.gov/pub/irs-irbs/irb05-02.pdf*.

For deferrals and earnings from NQDC plans for employees, see the Instructions for Forms W-2 and W-3.

Box 15b. Section 409A Income

Enter all amounts of current year and prior year deferrals that are includible in income under section 409A because the NQDC plan fails to satisfy the requirements of section 409A. Include the earnings on the deferrals. Do not include amounts previously included in income. Also, do not include amounts that are considered to be subject to a substantial risk of forfeiture for purposes of section 409A. For additional information, see Notice 2005-1.

The amount included in box 15b is also includible in box 7 and generally is subject to self-employment tax.

Boxes 16–18. State Information

These boxes, and Copies 1 and 2, are provided for your convenience only and need not be completed for the IRS. Use the state information boxes to report payments for up to two states. Keep the information for each state separated by the dash line. If you withheld state income tax on this payment, you may enter it in box 16. In box 17, enter the abbreviated name of the state and the payer's state identification number. The state number is the payer's identification number assigned by the individual state. In box 18, you may enter the amount of the state payment. Use Copy 1 to provide information to the state tax department. Give Copy 2 to the recipient for use in filing the recipient's state income tax return.

MISC-7

Index

9898 ☐ VOID ☐ CORRECTED

PAYER'S name, street address, city, state, and ZIP code		**1** Gross distribution $	OMB No. 1545-0119 20**05** Form **1099-R**	**Distributions From Pensions, Annuities, Retirement or Profit-Sharing Plans, IRAs, Insurance Contracts, etc.**
		2a Taxable amount $		
		2b Taxable amount not determined ☐	Total distribution ☐	**Copy A For**
PAYER'S Federal identification number	RECIPIENT'S identification number	**3** Capital gain (included in box 2a) $	**4** Federal income tax withheld $	**Internal Revenue Service Center** **File with Form 1096.**
RECIPIENT'S name		**5** Employee contributions or insurance premiums $	**6** Net unrealized appreciation in employer's securities $	For Privacy Act and Paperwork Reduction Act Notice, see the
Street address (including apt. no.)		**7** Distribution code(s) IRA/ SEP/ SIMPLE ☐	**8** Other $ %	**2005 General Instructions for Forms 1099, 1098, 5498, and W-2G.**
City, state, and ZIP code		**9a** Your percentage of total distribution %	**9b** Total employee contributions $	
Account number (see instructions)		**10** State tax withheld $ $	**11** State/Payer's state no.	**12** State distribution $ $
		13 Local tax withheld $ $	**14** Name of locality	**15** Local distribution $ $

Form **1099-R**   Cat. No. 14436Q   Department of the Treasury - Internal Revenue Service

Do Not Cut or Separate Forms on This Page — Do Not Cut or Separate Forms on This Page

Instructions for Recipient

Generally, distributions from pensions, annuities, profit-sharing and retirement plans (including section 457 state and local government plans), IRAs, insurance contracts, etc., are reported to recipients on Form 1099-R.

Qualified plans. If your annuity starting date is after 1997, you must use the simplified method to figure your taxable amount if your payer did not show the taxable amount in box 2a. See Pub. 575, Pension and Annuity Income.

IRAs. For distributions from a traditional individual retirement arrangement (IRA), simplified employee pension (SEP), or savings incentive match plan for employees (SIMPLE), generally the payer is not required to compute the taxable amount. Therefore, the amounts in boxes 1 and 2a will be the same most of the time. See the Form 1040 or 1040A instructions to determine the taxable amount. If you are at least age 70½, you must take minimum distributions from your IRA (other than a Roth IRA). If you do not, you may be subject to a 50% excise tax on the amount that should have been distributed. See Pub. 590, Individual Retirement Arrangements (IRAs), and Pub. 560, Retirement Plans for Small Business (SEP, SIMPLE, and Qualified Plans), for more information on IRAs.

Roth IRAs. For distributions from a Roth IRA, generally the payer is not required to compute the taxable amount. You must compute any taxable amount on Form 8606, Nondeductible IRAs. An amount shown in box 2a may be taxable earnings on an excess contribution.

Loans treated as distributions. If you borrow money from a qualified plan, tax-sheltered annuity, or government plan, you may have to treat the loan as a distribution and include all or part of the amount borrowed in your income. There are exceptions to this rule. If your loan is taxable, Code L will be shown in box 7. See Pub. 575.

Account number. May show an account or other unique number the payer assigned to distinguish your account.

Box 1. Shows the total amount you received this year. The amount may have been a direct rollover, a transfer or conversion to a Roth IRA, a recharacterized IRA contribution; or you may have received it as periodic payments, as nonperiodic payments, or as a total distribution. Report the amount on Form 1040 or 1040A on the line for "IRA distributions" or "Pensions and annuities" (or the line for "Taxable amount"), and on Form 8606, whichever applies. However,

if this is a lump-sum distribution, report it on Form 4972, Tax on Lump-Sum Distributions. If you have not reached minimum retirement age, report your disability payments on the line for "Wages, salaries, tips, etc." on your tax return. Also report on that line corrective distributions of excess deferrals, excess contributions, or excess aggregate contributions.

If a life insurance, annuity, or endowment contract was transferred tax free to another trustee or contract issuer, an amount will be shown in this box and Code 6 will be shown in box 7. You need not report this on your tax return.

Box 2a. This part of the distribution is generally taxable. If there is no entry in this box, the payer may not have all the facts needed to figure the taxable amount. In that case, the first box in box 2b should be checked. You may want to get one of the following publications from the IRS to help you figure the taxable amount: Pub. 560, Pub. 571, Tax-Sheltered Annuity Plans (403(b) Plans) for Employees of Public Schools and Certain Tax-Exempt Organizations, Pub. 575, Pub. 590, Pub. 721, Tax Guide to U.S. Civil Service Retirement Benefits, or Pub. 939, General Rule for Pensions and Annuities. For an IRA distribution, see *IRAs* and *Roth IRAs* above. For a direct rollover, zero should be shown, and you must enter zero (-0-) on the "Taxable amount" line of your tax return.

If this is a total distribution from a qualified plan (other than an IRA or tax-sheltered annuity) and you were born before January 2, 1936 (or you are the beneficiary of someone born before January 2, 1936), you may be eligible for the 10-year tax option. See the Instructions for Form 4972 for more information.

Box 2b. If the first box is checked, the payer was unable to determine the taxable amount, and box 2a should be blank. However, if this is a traditional IRA, SEP, or SIMPLE distribution, then see *IRAs* above. If the second box is checked, the distribution was a total distribution that closed out your account.

Box 3. If you received a lump-sum distribution from a qualified plan and were born before January 2, 1936 (or you are the beneficiary of someone born before January 2, 1936), you may be able to elect to treat this amount as a capital gain on Form 4972 (not on Schedule D (Form 1040)). See the Instructions for Form 4972. For a charitable gift annuity, report as a long-term capital gain on Schedule D.

(Continued on the back of Copy C.)

Instructions for Recipient *(Continued)*

Box 4. This is the amount of federal income tax withheld. **Include this on your income tax return as tax withheld, and if box 4 shows an amount (other than zero), attach Copy B to your return.** Generally, if you will receive payments next year that are not eligible rollover distributions, you can change your withholding or elect not to have income tax withheld by giving the payer Form W-4P, Withholding Certificate for Pension or Annuity Payments.

Box 5. Generally, this shows the employee's investment in the contract (after-tax contributions), if any, recovered tax free this year; the part of premiums paid on commercial annuities or insurance contracts recovered tax free; or the nontaxable part of a charitable gift annuity. This box does not show any IRA contributions.

Box 6. If you received a lump-sum distribution from a qualified plan that includes securities of the employer's company, the net unrealized appreciation (NUA) (any increase in value of such securities while in the trust) is taxed only when you sell the securities unless you choose to include it in your gross income this year. See Pub. 575 and the Instructions for Form 4972. If you did not receive a lump-sum distribution, the amount shown is the NUA attributable to employee contributions, which is not taxed until you sell the securities.

Box 7. The following codes identify the distribution you received. **1**—Early distribution, no known exception (in most cases, under age 59½). See the Form 1040/1040A instructions and Form 5329, Additional Taxes on Qualified Plans (Including IRAs) and Other Tax-Favored Accounts. For a rollover of the entire distribution, do not file Form 5329. See the Form 1040/1040A instructions for how to report the rollover. **2**—Early distribution, exception applies (under age 59½)*. **3**—Disability*. **4**—Death*. **5**—Prohibited transaction. **6**—Section 1035 exchange (a tax-free exchange of life insurance, annuity, or endowment contracts). **7**—Normal distribution. **8**—Excess contributions plus earnings/excess deferrals (and/or earnings) taxable in 2005. **9**—Cost of current life insurance protection (premiums paid by a trustee or custodian for current insurance protection, taxable to you currently). **A**—May be eligible for 10-year tax option. See Form 4972. **D**—Excess contributions plus earnings/excess deferrals taxable in 2003. **E**—Excess annual additions under section 415 and certain excess amounts under section 403(b) plans. Report on Form 1040/1040A on the line for taxable pension or annuity income*. **F**—Charitable gift annuity. **G**—Direct rollover to a qualified plan, a tax-sheltered annuity, a governmental 457(b) plan, or an IRA. May also include a transfer from a conduit IRA to a qualified plan*. **J**—Early distribution from a Roth IRA, no known exception (in most cases, under age 59½). Report on Forms 1040 and 8606 and see Form 5329. **L**—Loans treated as distributions. **N**—Recharacterized IRA contribution made for 2005 and recharacterized in 2005. Report on 2005 Form 1040A and Form 8606, if applicable. **P**—Excess contributions plus earnings/excess deferrals taxable in 2004. **Q**—Qualified distribution from a Roth IRA. You are age 59½ or over and meet the 5-year holding period for a Roth IRA. See the Form 1040/1040A instructions*. **R**—Recharacterized IRA contribution made for 2004 and recharacterized in 2005. Report on 2004 Form 1040/1040A and Form 8606, if applicable. **S**—Early distribution from a SIMPLE IRA in first 2 years, no known exception (under age 59½). May be subject to an additional 25% tax. See Form 5329. **T**—Roth IRA distribution, exception applies. You are age 59½ or over, disabled, or are the beneficiary of a participant who died. (You may not meet the 5-year holding period.) See the Form 1040/1040A instructions.

If the IRA/SEP/SIMPLE box is checked, you have received a traditional IRA, SEP, or SIMPLE distribution.

Box 8. If you received an annuity contract as part of a distribution, the value of the contract is shown. It is not taxable when you receive it and should not be included in boxes 1 and 2a. When you receive periodic payments from the annuity contract, they are taxable at that time. If the distribution is made to more than one person, the percentage of the annuity contract distributed to you is also shown. You will need this information if you use the 10-year tax option (Form 4972).

Box 9a. If a total distribution was made to more than one person, the percentage you received is shown.

Box 9b. For a life annuity from a qualified plan or from a tax-sheltered annuity (with after-tax contributions), an amount may be shown for the employee's total investment in the contract. It is used to compute the taxable part of the distribution. See Pub. 575.

Boxes 10–15. If state or local income tax was withheld from the distribution, these boxes may be completed. Boxes 12 and 15 may show the part of the distribution subject to state and/or local tax.

---

*You are not required to file Form 5329.

Instructions for Payers

We provide general and specific form instructions as separate products. The products you should use for 2005 are the General Instructions for Forms 1099, 1098, 5498, and W-2G and the 2005 Instructions for Forms 1099-R and 5498. A chart in the general instructions gives a quick guide to which form must be filed to report a particular payment. To order these instructions and additional forms, call 1-800-TAX-FORM (1-800-829-3676).

Caution: *Because paper forms are scanned during processing, you cannot file with the IRS Forms 1096, 1098, 1099, or 5498 that you print from the IRS website.*

Due dates. Furnish Copies B and C of this form to the recipient by January 31, 2006.

File Copy A of this form with the IRS by February 28, 2006. If you file electronically, the due date is March 31, 2006.

Printed on recycled paper

20**05**

Department of the Treasury
Internal Revenue Service

Instructions for Forms
1099-R and 5498

(Revised December 2005)

Section references are to the Internal Revenue Code unless otherwise noted.

What's New

Form 1099-R

Distribution codes. The explanations to distribution Codes 1, 2, and J have been modified. See *Guide to Distribution Codes* on pages R-10 and R-11.

Deemed IRAs. Regulations section 1.408(q)-1 provides guidance on the treatment of deemed IRAs, traditional and Roth IRAs established as part of a qualified employer plan. See *Deemed IRAs* on page R-2.

Automatic rollover provisions. Notice 2005-5 provides guidance relating to the automatic rollover provisions under section 401(a)(31)(B). These provisions require the direct rollover to an IRA of certain involuntary distributions from qualified plans. See *Automatic rollovers* on page R-3.

Hurricane distributions. The Katrina Emergency Tax Relief Act (KETRA) of 2005 provides for tax-favored distributions from eligible retirement plans (Katrina distributions) made on or after August 25, 2005, and before January 1, 2007, to a qualified individual. Katrina distributions are not subject to the additional tax under section 72(t) and may be eligible for tax-free rollover treatment. KETRA also increases the allowable plan loan amount and permits suspension of payments on outstanding loans on or after August 25, 2005, to qualified individuals. See Notice 2005-92 for information on reporting requirements for Katrina distributions, recontributions, and plan loans. Notice 2005-92 is on page 1165 of Internal Revenue Bulletin 2005-51 available at *www.irs.gov/pub/irs-irbs/irb05-51.pdf*. Also, for additional information on these provisions and similar recently enacted provisions that apply to Hurricanes Rita and Wilma, see Pub. 4492, Information for Taxpayers Affected by Hurricanes Katrina, Rita, and Wilma.

Reminder

In addition, see the 2005 General Instructions for Forms 1099, 1098, 5498, and W-2G for information on:
- Backup withholding
- Magnetic media and electronic reporting requirements
- Penalties
- Who must file (nominee/middleman)
- When and where to file
- Taxpayer identification numbers
- Statements to recipients
- Corrected and void returns
- Other general topics

You can get the general instructions from the IRS website at *www.irs.gov* or call 1-800-TAX-FORM (1-800-829-3676).

Specific Instructions for Form 1099-R

File Form 1099-R, Distributions From Pensions, Annuities, Retirement or Profit-Sharing Plans, IRAs, Insurance Contracts, etc., for each person to whom you have made a designated distribution or are treated as having made a distribution of $10 or more from profit-sharing or retirement plans, any IRAs, annuities, pensions, insurance contracts, survivor income benefit plans, permanent and total disability payments under life insurance contracts, charitable gift annuities, etc.

Also, report on Form 1099-R death benefit payments made by employers that are not made as part of a pension, profit-sharing, or retirement plan. See box 1 on page R-6.

Reportable disability payments made from a retirement plan must be reported on Form 1099-R.

Generally, do not report payments subject to withholding of social security and Medicare taxes on this form. Report such payments on Form W-2, Wage and Tax Statement.

Generally, do not report amounts totally exempt from tax, such as workers' compensation and Department of Veterans Affairs (VA) payments. However, if part of the distribution is taxable and part is nontaxable, report the entire distribution.

Military retirement annuities. Report payments to military retirees or payments of survivor benefit annuities on Form 1099-R. Report military retirement pay awarded as a property settlement to a former spouse under the name and taxpayer identification number (TIN) of the recipient, not that of the military retiree.

Governmental section 457(b) plans. Report on Form 1099-R, not Form W-2, income tax withholding and distributions from a governmental section 457(b) plan maintained by a state or local government employer. Distributions from a governmental section 457(b) plan to a participant or beneficiary include all amounts that are paid from the plan. For more information, see Notice 2003-20 which is on page 894 of Internal Revenue Bulletin 2003-19, available at *www.irs.gov/pub/irs-irbs/irb03-19.pdf*. Also see *Section 457(b) plan distributions* on page R-9 for information on distribution codes.

Nonqualified plans. Report any reportable distributions from commercial annuities. Report distributions to employee plan participants from section 409A nonqualified deferred compensation plans including nongovernmental section 457(b) plans on Form W-2, not on Form 1099-R; for nonemployees, these payments are reportable on Form 1099-MISC. However, report distributions to beneficiaries of deceased plan participants on Form 1099-R. See box 1 on page R-6.

Charitable gift annuities. If cash or capital gain property is donated in exchange for a charitable gift annuity, report distributions from the annuity on Form 1099-R. See *Charitable gift annuities* on page R-7.

Life insurance, annuity, and endowment contracts. Report payments of matured or redeemed annuity, endowment, and life insurance contracts. However, you do not need to file Form 1099-R to report the surrender of a life insurance contract if it is reasonable to believe that none of the payment is includible in the income of the recipient. If you are reporting the surrender of a life insurance contract, see Code 7 on page R-10.

Also report premiums paid by a trustee or custodian for the cost of current life or other insurance protection. Costs of current life insurance protection are not subject to the 10% additional tax under section 72(t). See *Cost of current life insurance protection* on page R-6.

Section 1035 exchange. A tax-free section 1035 exchange is the exchange of (a) a life insurance contract for another life insurance, endowment, or annuity contract, (b) an endowment contract for an annuity contract or for another endowment contract that provides for regular payments to begin no later than they would have begun under the old contract, and (c) an annuity contract for another annuity contract. However, the

Cat. No. 27987M

distribution of other property or the cancellation of a contract loan at the time of the exchange may be taxable and reportable on a separate Form 1099-R.

These exchanges of contracts are generally reportable on Form 1099-R. However, reporting on Form 1099-R is not required if (a) the exchange occurs within the same company, (b) the exchange is solely a contract for contract exchange, as defined above, that does not result in a designated distribution, and (c) the company maintains adequate records of the policyholder's basis in the contracts. For example, a life insurance contract issued by Company X received in exchange solely for another life insurance contract previously issued by Company X does not have to be reported on Form 1099-R as long as the company maintains the required records. See Rev. Proc. 92-26, 1992-1 C.B. 744.

For more information on reporting taxable exchanges, see box 1 on page R-6.

IRA Distributions

 For deemed IRAs under section 408(q), use the rules that apply to traditional IRAs or Roth IRAs as applicable. SEP IRAs and SIMPLE IRAs, however, may not be used as deemed IRAs.

Deemed IRAs. A qualified employer plan may allow employees to make voluntary employee contributions to a separate account or annuity established under the plan. Under the terms of the qualified employer plan, the account or annuity must meet the applicable requirements of section 408 or 408A for a traditional IRA or Roth IRA. Under section 408(q), the "deemed IRA" portion of the qualified employer plan is subject to the rules applicable to traditional and Roth IRAs, and not to those of the applicable plan under section 401(a), 403(a), 403(b), or 457.

Accordingly, the reporting and withholding rules on plan and IRA distributions apply separately depending on whether the distributions are made from the deemed IRA or the qualified employer plan. For example, the reporting rules for required minimum distributions apply separately for the two portions of the plan. A total distribution of amounts held in the qualified employer plan portion and the deemed IRA portion is reported on two separate Forms 1099-R — one for the distribution from the deemed IRA portion and one for the rest of the distribution. Also, the 20% withholding rules of section 3405(c) do not apply to a distribution from the deemed IRA portion but would apply to a distribution from the qualified employer plan portion, and section 72(t) applies separately to the two portions.

IRAs other than Roth IRAs. Distributions from any individual retirement arrangement (IRA), except a Roth IRA, must be reported in boxes 1 and 2a regardless of the amount. You may check the "Taxable amount not determined" box in box 2b. But see the instructions for box 2a on page R-6 for how to report the withdrawal of IRA contributions under section 408(d)(4). Also see *Transfers* on page R-3 for information on trustee-to-trustee transfers, including recharacterizations. The direct rollover provisions on this page do not apply to distributions from any IRA. However, taxable distributions from traditional IRAs and SEP IRAs may be rolled over into an eligible retirement plan. See section 408(d)(3). SIMPLE IRAs may also be rolled over into an eligible retirement plan, but only after the 2-year period described in section 72(t)(6).

An IRA includes all investments under one IRA plan or account. File only one Form 1099-R for distributions from all investments under one plan that are paid in 1 year to one recipient, unless you must enter different codes in box 7. You do not have to file a separate Form 1099-R for each distribution under the plan.

Roth IRAs. For distributions from a Roth IRA, report the gross distribution in box 1 but generally leave box 2a blank. Check the "Taxable amount not determined" box in box 2b. Enter Code J, Q, or T as appropriate in box 7. Do not use any other codes with Code Q or Code T. You may enter Code 8 or P with Code J. For the withdrawal of excess contributions, see *Box 2a* on page R-6. It is not necessary to mark the IRA/SEP/SIMPLE checkbox.

Roth IRA conversions. You must report an IRA that is converted or reconverted this year to a Roth IRA in boxes 1 and 2a, even if the conversion is a trustee-to-trustee transfer or is with the same trustee. Enter Code 2 or 7 in box 7 depending on the participant's age.

Conduit IRAs. If you know the distribution is from a conduit IRA, follow these rules. If a distribution from a conduit IRA is paid to the participant, report the full amount in boxes 1 and 2a, and use Code 1 or 7 in box 7 depending on the participant's age. If a distribution from a conduit IRA is paid to the trustee of, or is transferred to, an employer plan, report the distribution in box 1, enter 0 (zero) in box 2a, and use Code G in box 7.

IRA Revocation

If a traditional or Roth IRA is revoked during its first 7 days (under Regulations section 1.408-6(d)(4)(ii)), the distribution from the IRA must be reported. In addition, Form 5498, IRA Contribution Information, must be filed to report any regular, rollover, Roth IRA conversion, SEP IRA, or SIMPLE IRA contribution to an IRA that is revoked.

If a regular contribution is made to a traditional or Roth IRA that later is revoked, and distribution is made to the taxpayer, enter the gross distribution in box 1. If no earnings are distributed, enter 0 (zero) in box 2a and Code 8 in box 7 for a traditional IRA and Code J for a Roth IRA. If earnings are distributed, enter the amount of earnings in box 2a. For a traditional IRA, enter Code 1 in box 7; for a Roth IRA, enter Code J. These earnings could be subject to the 10% early distribution tax under section 72(t). If a rollover contribution is made to a traditional or Roth IRA that later is revoked, and distribution is made to the taxpayer, enter in boxes 1 and 2a of Form 1099-R the gross distribution and the appropriate code in box 7 (Code J for a Roth IRA). Follow this same procedure for a transfer from a traditional or Roth IRA to another IRA of the same type that later is revoked. The distribution could be subject to the 10% early distribution tax under section 72(t).

If an IRA conversion contribution is made to a Roth IRA that later is revoked, and distribution is made to the taxpayer, enter the gross distribution in box 1 of Form 1099-R. If no earnings are distributed, enter 0 (zero) in box 2a and Code J in box 7. If earnings are distributed, enter the amount of the earnings in box 2a and Code J in box 7. These earnings could be subject to the 10% early distribution tax under section 72(t).

If an employer SEP (simplified employee pension) IRA or SIMPLE (savings incentive match plan for employees) IRA plan contribution is made and the SEP IRA or SIMPLE IRA is revoked by the employee, report the distribution as fully taxable.

For more information on IRAs that have been revoked, see Rev. Proc. 91-70, 1991-2 C.B. 899.

Deductible Voluntary Employee Contributions (DECs)

If you are reporting a total distribution from a plan that includes a distribution of DECs, file two Forms 1099-R—one to report the distribution of DECs, the other to report the distribution from the other part of the plan. Report the distribution of DECs in boxes 1 and 2a on the separate Form 1099-R. However, for the direct rollover (explained below) of funds that include DECs, file only one Form 1099-R to report the direct rollover of the entire amount.

Direct Rollovers

You must report a direct rollover of an eligible rollover distribution. A direct rollover is the direct payment of the distribution from a qualified plan (including a governmental section 457(b) plan) or tax-sheltered annuity to a traditional IRA or other eligible retirement plan. A direct rollover may be made for the employee, for the employee's surviving spouse, or for the spouse or former spouse who is an alternate payee under a qualified domestic relations order (QDRO). If the distribution is paid to the surviving spouse, the distribution is treated in the same manner as if the spouse were the employee.

An eligible rollover distribution is any distribution of all or any portion of the balance to the credit of the employee (including net unrealized appreciation (NUA)) from a qualified plan (including a governmental section 457(b) plan) or a tax-sheltered annuity except:

1. One of a series of substantially equal periodic payments made at least annually over:

R-2

a. The life of the employee or the joint lives of the employee and the employee's designated beneficiary,

b. The life expectancy of the employee or the joint life and last survivor expectancy of the employee and the employee's designated beneficiary, or

c. A specified period of 10 years or more.

2. A required minimum distribution (under section 401(a)(9)). A plan administrator is permitted to assume there is no designated beneficiary for purposes of determining the minimum distribution.

3. Elective deferrals (under section 402(g)(3)) and earnings returned because of the section 415 limits.

4. Corrective distributions of excess deferrals (under section 402(g)) and earnings.

5. Corrective distributions of excess contributions under a qualified cash or deferred arrangement (under section 401(k)) and excess aggregate contributions (under section 401(m)) and earnings.

6. Loans treated as deemed distributions (under section 72(p)). But plan loan offset amounts can be eligible rollover distributions. See Regulations section 1.402(c)-2, Q/A-9.

7. Section 404(k) dividends.

8. Cost of current life insurance protection.

9. Distributions to a payee other than the employee, the employee's surviving spouse, or a spouse or former spouse who is an alternate payee under a QDRO.

10. Any hardship distribution.

Amounts paid under an annuity contract purchased for and distributed to a participant under a qualified plan can qualify as eligible rollover distributions. See Regulations section 1.402(c)-2, Q/A-10.

Automatic rollovers. Eligible rollover distributions may also include involuntary distributions that are more than $1,000 but $5,000 or less and are made from a qualified plan to an IRA on behalf of a plan participant. Involuntary distributions made on or after March 28, 2005, are generally subject to the automatic rollover provisions of section 401(a)(31)(B) and must be paid in a direct rollover to an individual retirement plan. For information on the notification requirements, see *Explanation to Recipients Before Eligible Rollover Distributions (Section 402(f) Notice)* below. For additional information, also see Notice 2005-5 which is available on page 337 of Internal Revenue Bulletin 2005-3 at *www.irs.gov/pub/irs-irbs/irb05-03.pdf*.

Any part of an eligible rollover distribution that is not a direct rollover is subject to 20% income tax withholding. See *Box 4* on page R-7.

Reporting a direct rollover. Report a direct rollover in box 1 and a 0 (zero) in box 2a. You do not have to report capital gain in box 3 or NUA in box 6. Enter Code G in box 7. Prepare the form using the name and social security number (SSN) of the person for whose benefit the funds were rolled over (generally the participant), not those of the trustee of the traditional IRA or other plan to which the funds were rolled.

 Also, use Code G with Code 4 for a surviving spouse who elects a direct rollover to an IRA or a qualified plan. Prepare the form using the name and SSN of the surviving spouse.

If you receive a direct rollover to an IRA, you must prepare Form 5498. If you receive a direct rollover to a qualified plan (including a governmental section 457(b) plan) or tax-sheltered annuity, no report is required.

If part of the distribution is a direct rollover and part is distributed to the recipient, prepare two Forms 1099-R.

For more information on eligible rollover distributions, including substantially equal periodic payments, required minimum distributions, and plan loan offset amounts, see Regulations sections 1.402(c)-2 and 1.403(b)-2. Also, see Rev. Rul. 2002-62 which is on page 710 of Internal Revenue Bulletin 2002-42 at *www.irs.gov/pub/irs-irbs/irb02-42.pdf* for guidance on substantially equal periodic payments that began after December 31, 2002.

 For information on distributions of amounts attributable to rollover contributions separately accounted for by an eligible retirement plan and if permissible timing restrictions apply, see Rev. Rul. 2004-12 which is on page 478

of Internal Revenue Bulletin 2004-7, available at www.irs.gov/pub/irs-irbs/irb04-07.pdf.

Explanation to Recipients Before Eligible Rollover Distributions (Section 402(f) Notice)

For qualified plans, tax-sheltered annuities, and governmental section 457(b) plans, no more than 90 days and no fewer than 30 days before making an eligible rollover distribution (or before the annuity starting date), the plan administrator must provide a written explanation to each recipient (section 402(f) notice). However, if the recipient who has received the section 402(f) notice affirmatively elects a distribution, you will not fail to satisfy the timing requirements merely because you make the distribution fewer than 30 days after you provided the notice as long as you meet the requirements of Regulations section 1.402(f)-1, Q/A-2. You may provide the section 402(f) notice more than 90 days before a distribution if you also provide a summary of the notice during the 90-day/30-day period before the distribution.

The notice must explain the rollover rules, the special tax treatment for lump-sum distributions, the direct rollover option (and any default procedures), the mandatory 20% withholding rules, and an explanation of how distributions from the plan to which the rollover is made may have different restrictions and tax consequences than the plan from which the rollover is made. The notice and summary are permitted to be sent either as a written paper document or through an electronic medium reasonably accessible to the recipient; see Regulations section 1.402(f)-1, Q/A-5.

For periodic payments that are eligible rollover distributions, you must provide the notice before the first payment and at least once a year as long as the payments continue. For tax-sheltered annuities, the payer must provide an explanation of the direct rollover option within the time period described above or some other reasonable period of time.

Notice 2002-3, which is on page 289 of Internal Revenue Bulletin 2002-2 and available at *www.irs.gov/pub/irs-irbs/irb02-02.pdf*, contains model notices that the plan administrator can use to satisfy the notice requirements.

Involuntary distributions. For involuntary distributions paid to an IRA in a direct rollover (automatic rollovers) you may satisfy the notification requirements of section 401(a)(31)(B)(i) either separately or as a part of the section 402(f) notice. The notification must be in writing and may be sent using electronic media in accordance with Q/A 5 of Regulations section 1.402(f)-1. For more information, see Notice 2005-5, Q/A 15.

Transfers

Generally, do not report transfers between trustees or issuers (unless they are direct rollovers from qualified plans) that involve no payment or distribution of funds to the participant, including a trustee-to-trustee transfer from one IRA to another (unless they are recharacterized IRA contributions or Roth IRA conversions) or from one tax-sheltered (section 403(b)) arrangement to another.

IRA recharacterizations. You must report each recharacterization of an IRA contribution. If a participant makes a contribution to an IRA (first IRA) for a year, the participant may choose to recharacterize the contribution by transferring, in a trustee-to-trustee transfer, any part of the contribution (plus earnings) to another IRA (second IRA). The contribution is treated as made to the second IRA (recharacterization). A recharacterization may be made with the same trustee or with another trustee. The trustee of the first IRA must report the recharacterization as a distribution on Form 1099-R and the contribution to the first IRA and its character on Form 5498.

Enter the fair market value (FMV) of the amount recharacterized in box 1, 0 (zero) in box 2a, and Code R in box 7 if reporting a recharacterization of a prior-year (2004) contribution or Code N if reporting a recharacterization of a contribution in the same year (2005). It is not necessary to check the IRA/SEP/SIMPLE checkbox. For more information, see Notice 2000-30 on page 1266 of Internal Revenue Bulletin 2000-25 at *www.irs.gov/pub/irs-irbs/irb00-25.pdf*.

Roth IRA conversions. A Roth IRA conversion is not considered a trustee-to-trustee transfer. You must report a Roth IRA conversion or reconversion as a distribution. Therefore, for an IRA that is converted to a Roth IRA, even with the same trustee, you must report the amount converted in boxes 1 and 2a. Use Code 2 or 7 in box 7 depending on the participant's age.

SIMPLE IRAs. Do not report a trustee-to-trustee transfer from one SIMPLE IRA to another SIMPLE IRA. However, you must report as a taxable distribution in boxes 1 and 2a a trustee-to-trustee transfer from a SIMPLE IRA to an IRA that is not a SIMPLE IRA during the 2-year period beginning on the day contributions are first deposited in the individual's SIMPLE IRA by the employer. Use Code S in box 7 if appropriate.

Section 1035 exchange. You may have to report exchanges of insurance contracts, including an exchange under section 1035, under which any designated distribution may be made. For a section 1035 exchange that is in part taxable, file a separate Form 1099-R to report the taxable amount. See *Section 1035 exchange* on page R-1.

Transfer of an IRA to spouse. If you transfer or re-designate an interest from one spouse's IRA to an IRA for the other spouse under a divorce or separation instrument, the transfer or re-designation as provided under section 408(d)(6) is tax free. Do not report such a transfer on Form 1099-R.

Corrective Distributions

You must report on Form 1099-R corrective distributions of excess deferrals, excess contributions and excess aggregate contributions under section 401(a) plans, section 401(k) cash or deferred arrangements, section 403(a) annuity plans, section 403(b) salary reduction agreements, and salary reduction simplified employee pensions (SARSEPs) under section 408(k)(6). Excess contributions that are recharacterized under a section 401(k) plan are treated as distributed. Corrective distributions of an excess plus earnings are reportable on Form 1099-R for the year of the distribution regardless of when the distribution is taxable to the participant. Enter Code 8, P, or in some cases D, in box 7 to designate the distribution and the year it is taxable.

 The total amount of the elective deferral is reported in Box 12 of Form W-2. See the Instructions for Forms W-2 and W-3 for more information.

If the excess and the earnings are taxable in two different years, you must issue two Forms 1099-R to designate the year each is taxable.

You must advise the plan participant at the time of the distribution of the year(s) in which the distribution is taxable and that it may be necessary to file an amended return for a prior tax year.

For more information about reporting corrective distributions see: the *Guide to Distribution Codes* on pages R-10 and R-11; Notice 89-32, 1989-1 C.B. 671; Notice 88-33, 1988-1 C.B. 513; Notice 87-77, 1987-2 C.B. 385; Rev. Proc. 91-44, 1991-2 C.B. 733 (SARSEPs); and the Regulations under sections 401(k), 401(m), 402(g), and 457.

Excess deferrals. Excess deferrals under section 402(g) can occur in 401(k) plans, 403(b) plans, or SARSEPs. If distributed by April 15 of the year following the year of deferral, the excess is taxable to the participant in the year of deferral, but the earnings are taxable in the year distributed. Except for a SARSEP, if the distribution occurs after April 15, the excess is taxable in the year of deferral and the year distributed. The earnings are taxable in the year distributed. For a SARSEP, excess deferrals not withdrawn by April 15 are considered regular IRA contributions subject to the IRA contribution limits. Corrective distributions of excess deferrals are not subject to federal income tax withholding or social security and Medicare taxes. For losses on excess deferrals, see *Losses* below. See the regulations under section 457 for special rules for excess deferrals under governmental section 457(b) plans.

Excess contributions. Excess contributions can occur in a 401(k) plan or a SARSEP. For a 401(k) plan, if the withdrawal of the excess plus earnings occurs within 2½ months after the close of the plan year, the excess and earnings are taxable to the participant in the year deferred. But if the corrective distribution is made after the 2½-month period, or the excess contribution (not including earnings) (and excess aggregate contributions (not including earnings) in the case of a 401(k)

plan) is less than $100 (de minimus rule), the excess and earnings are taxable in the year distributed. For recharacterized excess contributions, the excess is taxable in the year a corrective distribution would have occurred. No earnings are allocated to recharacterized amounts. For a SARSEP, the employer must notify the participant by March 15 of the year after the year the excess contribution was made that the participant must withdraw the excess and earnings. The excess contribution is taxable to the participant in the year of deferral and the earnings are taxable in the year withdrawn. If the excess contribution (not including earnings) is less than $100, the excess is taxable in the year of notification and the earnings are taxable in the year withdrawn. An excess contribution not withdrawn by April 15 of the year after the year of notification is considered a regular IRA contribution subject to the IRA contribution limits.

Excess contributions distributed within the 2½-month period are not subject to federal income tax withholding or social security and Medicare taxes. But amounts distributed from a 401(k) plan after the 2½-month period are subject to federal income tax withholding under section 3405.

Excess aggregate contributions. Excess aggregate contributions under section 401(m) can occur in 401(a), 401(k), 403(a), and 403(b) plans. A corrective distribution of excess aggregate contributions plus earnings within 2½ months after the close of the plan year is taxable to the participant in the year the contributions were made. A corrective distribution made after the 2½-month period is taxable in the year distributed. Report the gross distribution in box 1 of Form 1099-R. In box 2a, enter the excess and earnings distributed less any after-tax contributions. If the total excess contributions and excess aggregate contributions distributed are less than $100 (excluding earnings), the distribution is taxable in the year of distribution.

A distribution made within 2½ months after the close of the plan year is not subject to federal income tax withholding or social security and Medicare taxes. But amounts distributed after 2½ months are subject to federal income tax withholding under section 3405.

Losses. If a corrective distribution of an excess deferral is made in a year after the year of deferral and a net loss has been allocated to the excess deferral, report the corrective distribution amount in boxes 1 and 2a of Form 1099-R for the year of the distribution with the appropriate distribution code in box 7. However, taxpayers must include the total amount of the excess deferral (unadjusted for loss) in income in the year of deferral, and they may report a loss on the tax return for the year the corrective distribution is made. Therefore, if there are no employer securities distributed, show the actual cash and/or FMV of property distributed in boxes 1 and 2a, and make no entry in box 5. If only employer securities are distributed, show the FMV of the securities in boxes 1 and 2a and make no entry in box 5 or 6. If both employer securities and other property are distributed, show the actual cash and/or FMV of the property distributed in box 1, the gross less any NUA on employer securities in box 2a, no entry in box 5, and any NUA in box 6.

Excess Annual Additions Under Section 415

You must report on Form 1099-R distributions made under Regulations section 1.415-6(b)(6)(iv) of elective deferrals or a return of employee contributions (and gains attributable to such elective deferrals or employee contributions) to reduce excess annual additions arising from the allocation of forfeitures, a reasonable error in estimating a participant's compensation, or a reasonable error in determining the amount of elective deferrals that may be made for an individual under the limits of section 415.

Such distributions are not eligible rollover distributions although they are subject to federal income tax withholding under section 3405. They are not subject to social security, Medicare, or Federal Unemployment Tax Act (FUTA) taxes. In addition, such distributions are not subject to the 10% early distribution tax under section 72(t).

You may report the distribution of elective deferrals and employee contributions (and gains attributable to such elective deferrals and employee contributions) on the same Form 1099-R. However, if you made other distributions during the

R-4

year, report them on a separate Form 1099-R. Because the distribution of elective deferrals is fully taxable in the year distributed (no part of the distribution is a return of the investment in the contract), report the total amount of the distribution in boxes 1 and 2a. Leave box 5 blank, and enter Code E in box 7. For a return of employee contributions plus gains, enter the gross distribution in box 1, the gains attributable to the employee contributions being returned in box 2a, and the employee contributions being returned in box 5. Enter Code E in box 7. For more information, see Rev. Proc. 92-93, 1992-2 C.B. 505.

Certain Excess Amounts Under 403(b) Plans

A corrective distribution under the Employee Plans Compliance Resolution System to the participant of contributions to a 403(b) plan (plus gains attributable to such contributions) that were in excess of the limits under section 415 is treated the same as corrective distributions of elective deferrals to satisfy the limits under section 415. It is taxable to the participant in the year of distribution. See *Excess Annual Additions Under Section 415* on page R-4.

Failing the ADP or ACP Test After a Total Distribution

If you make a total distribution in 2005 and file a Form 1099-R with the IRS and then discover in 2006 that the plan failed either the section 401(k)(3) actual deferral percentage (ADP) test for 2005 and you compute excess contributions or the section 401(m)(2) actual contribution percentage (ACP) test and you compute excess aggregate contributions, you must recharacterize part of the total distribution as excess contributions or excess aggregate contributions. First, file a CORRECTED Form 1099-R for 2005 for the correct amount of the total distribution (not including the amount recharacterized as excess contributions or excess aggregate contributions). Second, file a new Form 1099-R for 2005 for the excess contributions or excess aggregate contributions and allocable earnings.

To avoid a late filing penalty if the new Form 1099-R is filed after the due date, enter in the bottom margin of Form 1096, Annual Summary and Transmittal of U.S. Information Returns, the words "Filed To Correct Excess Contributions."

You must also issue copies of the Forms 1099-R to the plan participant with an explanation of why these new forms are being issued.

Loans Treated as Distributions

A loan from a qualified plan under sections 401 and 403(a) and (b), and a plan maintained by the United States, a state or political subdivision, or any of its subsidiary agencies made to a participant or beneficiary is not treated as a distribution from the plan if the loan satisfies the following requirements:

1. The loan is evidenced by an enforceable agreement,
2. The agreement specifies that the loan must be repaid within 5 years, except for a principal residence,
3. The loan must be repaid in substantially level installments (at least quarterly), and
4. The loan amount does not exceed the limits in section 72(p)(2)(A) (maximum limit is equal to the lesser of 50% of the vested account balance or $50,000).

Certain exceptions, cure periods, and suspension of the repayment schedule may apply.

The loan agreement must specify the amount of the loan, the term of the loan, and the repayment schedule. The agreement may include more than one document.

If a loan fails to satisfy 1, 2, or 3, the balance of the loan is a deemed distribution. The distribution may occur at the time the loan is made or later if the loan is not repaid in accordance with the repayment schedule.

If a loan fails to satisfy 4 at the time the loan is made, the amount that exceeds the amount permitted to be loaned is a deemed distribution.

Deemed distribution. If a loan is treated as a deemed distribution, it is reportable on Form 1099-R using the normal taxation rules of section 72, including tax basis rules. The distribution also may be subject to the 10% early distribution tax

under section 72(t). It is not eligible to be rolled over to an eligible retirement plan nor is it eligible for the 10-year tax option. On Form 1099-R, complete the appropriate boxes, including boxes 1 and 2a, and enter Code L in box 7. Also, enter Code 1, if applicable.

Interest that accrues after the deemed distribution of a loan is not an additional loan, and, therefore, is not reportable on Form 1099-R.

Loans that are treated as deemed distributions or that are actual distributions are subject to federal income tax withholding. If a distribution occurs after the loan is made, you must withhold only if you distributed cash or property (other than employer securities) at the time of the deemed or actual distribution. See section 72(p), 72(e)(4)(A), and Regulations section 1.72(p)-1.

Subsequent repayments. If a participant makes any cash repayments on a loan that was reported on Form 1099-R as a deemed distribution, the repayments increase the participant's tax basis in the plan as if the repayments were after-tax contributions. However, such repayments are not treated as after-tax contributions for purposes of section 401(m) or 415(c)(2)(B).

For a deemed distribution that was reported on Form 1099-R but was not repaid, the deemed distribution does not increase the participant's basis.

If a participant's accrued benefit is reduced (offset) to repay a loan, the amount of the account balance that is offset against the loan is an actual distribution. Report it as you would any other actual distribution. Do not enter Code L in box 7.

Missing Participants

The IRS administers a letter-forwarding program that could help plan administrators contact missing retirement plan participants (or possibly their beneficiaries). To inform individuals of their rights to benefits under a retirement plan, the IRS will forward letters from plan administrators to the missing individuals if the administrators provide the names and social security numbers (SSNs) of the missing individuals. However, the IRS cannot disclose individuals' addresses or give confirmation of letter delivery. All undelivered letters will be destroyed. For further information, see Rev. Proc. 94-22, 1994-1 C.B. 608, or contact your IRS office.

Corrected Form 1099-R

If you filed a Form 1099-R with the IRS and later discover that there is an error on it, you must correct it as soon as possible. For example, if you transmit a direct rollover and file a Form 1099-R with the IRS reporting that none of the direct rollover is taxable by entering 0 (zero) in box 2a, and you then discover that part of the direct rollover consists of required minimum distributions under section 401(a)(9), you must file a corrected Form 1099-R. See part I in the 2005 General Instructions for Forms 1099, 1098, 5498, and W-2G.

Filer

The payer, trustee, or plan administrator must file Form 1099-R using the same name and employer identification number (EIN) used to deposit any tax withheld and to file Form 945, Annual Return of Withheld Federal Income Tax.

Beneficiaries

If you make a distribution to a beneficiary, trust, or estate, prepare Form 1099-R using the name and TIN of the beneficiary, trust, or estate, not that of the decedent. If there are multiple beneficiaries, report on each Form 1099-R only the amount paid to the beneficiary whose name appears on the Form 1099-R, and enter the percentage in box 9a, if applicable.

Alternate Payee Under a Qualified Domestic Relations Order (QDRO)

Distributions to an alternate payee who is a spouse or former spouse of the employee under a QDRO are reportable on Form 1099-R using the name and TIN of the alternate payee. If the alternate payee under a QDRO is a non-spouse, enter the name and TIN of the employee. However, this rule does not apply to IRAs; see *Transfer of an IRA to spouse* on page R-4.

R-5

Nonresident Aliens

If income tax is withheld under section 3405 on a distribution to a nonresident alien, report the distribution and withholding on Form 1099-R. Also file Form 945 to report the withholding. See the Presumption Rules in part O of the 2005 General Instructions for Forms 1099, 1098, 5498, and W-2G.

However, any payments to a nonresident alien from any trust under section 401(a), any annuity plan under 403(a), any annuity, custodial account, or retirement income account under section 403(b), or any IRA account under section 408(a) or (b) are subject to withholding under section 1441. Report the distribution and withholding on Form 1042, Annual Withholding Tax Return for U.S. Source Income of Foreign Persons, and Form 1042-S, Foreign Person's U.S. Source Income Subject to Withholding.

Statements to Recipients

If you are required to file Form 1099-R, you must furnish a statement to the recipient. For more information about the requirement to furnish a statement to each recipient, see part H in the 2005 General Instructions for Forms 1099, 1098, 5498, and W-2G.

 Do not enter a negative amount in any box on Form 1099-R.

Account Number

The account number is required if you have multiple accounts for a recipient for whom you are filing more than one Form 1099-R. Additionally, the IRS encourages you to designate an account number for all Forms 1099-R that you file. See part P in the 2005 General Instructions for Forms 1099, 1098, 5498, and W-2G.

Box 1. Gross Distribution

Enter the total amount of the distribution before income tax or other deductions were withheld. Include direct rollovers, IRA rollovers to accepting employer plans, premiums paid by a trustee or custodian for the cost of current life or other insurance protection, and the gross amount of any IRA distribution, including a recharacterization and a Roth IRA conversion. Also include in this box distributions to plan participants from governmental section 457(b) plans. However, in the case of a distribution by a trust representing CDs redeemed early, report the net amount distributed. Also, see *Box 6* on page R-8.

Include in this box the value of U.S. Savings Bonds distributed from a plan. Enter the appropriate taxable amount in box 2a. Furnish a statement to the plan participant showing the value of each bond at the time of distribution. This will provide him or her with the information necessary to figure the interest income on each bond when it is redeemed.

Include in box 1 amounts distributed from a qualified retirement plan for which the recipient elects to pay health insurance premiums under a cafeteria plan or that are paid directly to reimburse medical care expenses incurred by the recipient (see Rev. Rul. 2003-62, 2003-25 I.R.B. 1034). Also include this amount in box 2a.

In addition to reporting distributions to beneficiaries of deceased employees, report here any death benefit payments made by employers that are not made as part of a pension, profit-sharing, or retirement plan. Also enter these amounts in box 2a; enter Code 4 in box 7.

 Do not report accelerated death benefits on Form 1099-R. Report them on Form 1099-LTC, Long-Term Care and Accelerated Death Benefits.

For section 1035 exchanges that are reportable on Form 1099-R, enter the total value of the contract in box 1, 0 (zero) in box 2a, the total premiums paid in box 5, and Code 6 in box 7.

Employer securities and other property. If you distribute employer securities or other property, include in box 1 the FMV of the securities or other property on the date of distribution. If there is a loss, see *Losses* on page R-7.

If you are distributing worthless property only, you are not required to file Form 1099-R. However, you may file and enter 0

(zero) in boxes 1 and 2a and any after-tax employee contributions in box 5.

Charitable gift annuities. If cash or capital gain property is donated in exchange for a charitable gift annuity, report the total amount distributed during the year in box 1. See *Charitable gift annuities* under box 3 on page R-7.

Box 2a. Taxable Amount

Generally, you must enter the taxable amount in box 2a. However, if you are unable to reasonably obtain the data needed to compute the taxable amount, leave this box blank. Do not enter excludable or tax-deferred amounts reportable in boxes 5, 6, and 8.

For a direct rollover from a qualified plan (including a governmental section 457(b) plan) or tax-sheltered annuity, for a distribution from a conduit IRA that is payable to the trustee of or is transferred to an employer plan, for an IRA recharacterization, or for a nontaxable section 1035 exchange of life insurance, annuity, or endowment contracts, enter 0 (zero) in box 2a.

Cost of current life insurance protection. Include current life insurance protection costs (net premium costs) that were reported in box 1. However, do not report these costs and a distribution on the same Form 1099-R. Use a separate Form 1099-R for each. For the cost of current life insurance protection, enter Code 9 in box 7.

DECs. Include DEC distributions in this box. Also see *Deductible Voluntary Employee Contributions (DECs)* on page R-2.

Annuity starting date in 1998 or later. If you made annuity payments from a qualified plan (under section 401(a), 403(a), or 403(b)) and the annuity starting date is in 1998 or later, you must use the simplified method (under section 72(d)(1)) to figure the taxable amount. Under this method, the expected number of payments you use to figure the taxable amount depends on whether the payments are based on the life of one or more than one person. See Notice 98-2, 1998-1 C.B. 266, and Pub. 575, Pension and Annuity Income, to help you figure the taxable amount to enter in box 2a.

Annuity starting date after November 18, 1996, and before 1998. Under the simplified method for figuring the taxable amount, the expected number of payments is based only on the primary annuitant's age on the annuity starting date. See Notice 98-2.

Annuity starting date before November 19, 1996. If you properly used the rules in effect before November 19, 1996, for annuities that started before that date, continue to report using those rules. No changes are necessary.

Traditional IRA or SEP IRA. Generally, you are not required to compute the taxable amount of a traditional IRA or SEP IRA nor designate whether any part of a distribution is a return of basis attributable to nondeductible contributions. Therefore, report the total amount distributed from a traditional IRA or SEP IRA in box 2a. This will be the same amount reported in box 1. Check the "Taxable amount not determined" box in box 2b.

However, for a distribution by a trust representing CDs redeemed early, report the net amount distributed. Do not include any amount paid for IRA insurance protection in this box.

For a distribution of contributions plus earnings from an IRA before the due date of the return (section 408(d)(4)), report the gross distribution in box 1, only the earnings in box 2a, and enter Code 8 or P, whichever is applicable, in box 7. Enter Code 1 or 4, if applicable.

For a distribution of contributions without earnings after the due date of the individual's return (section 408(d)(5)), enter 0 (zero). Use Code 1 or 7 in box 7 depending on the age of the participant. For a traditional IRA and a SEP IRA rolled over to an accepting employer plan, enter the gross amount in box 1, 0 (zero) in box 2a, and Code G in box 7.

SIMPLE IRA. Enter the total amount distributed from a SIMPLE IRA in box 2a. For a SIMPLE IRA rolled over to an accepting employer plan after the 2-year period (see section 72(t)(6)), enter the gross amount in box 1, 0 (zero) in box 2a, and Code G in box 7.

R-6

Roth IRA. For a distribution from a Roth IRA, report the total distribution in box 1 and leave box 2a blank except in the case of an IRA revocation (see page R-2) and a recharacterization (see page R-3). Use Code J, Q, or T as appropriate in box 7. Use Code 8 or P, if applicable, in box 7 with Code J. Do not combine Code Q or T with any other codes.

However, for the distribution of excess Roth IRA contributions, report the gross distribution in box 1 and only the earnings in box 2a. Enter Code J, and Code 8 or P in box 7.

Roth IRA conversion. Report the total amount converted or reconverted from a traditional IRA, SEP IRA, or SIMPLE IRA to a Roth IRA in boxes 1 and 2a. A conversion or reconversion is considered a distribution and must be reported even if it is with the same trustee and even if the conversion is done by a trustee-to-trustee transfer. For a Roth IRA conversion, use Code 2 in box 7 if the participant is under age 59½ or Code 7 if the participant is at least age 59½. Also check the IRA/SEP/SIMPLE box in box 7.

Losses. If a distribution is a loss, do not enter a negative amount in this box. For example, if stock is distributed from a profit-sharing plan but the value is less than the employee's after-tax contributions, enter the value of the stock in box 1, leave box 2a blank, and enter the employee's contributions in box 5.

For a plan with no after-tax contributions, even though the value of the account may have decreased, there is no loss for reporting purposes. Therefore, if there are no employer securities distributed, show the actual cash and/or FMV of property distributed in boxes 1 and 2a, and make no entry in box 5. If only employer securities are distributed, show the FMV of the securities in boxes 1 and 2a and make no entry in box 5 or 6. If both employer securities and cash or other property are distributed, show the actual cash and/or FMV of the property (including employer securities) distributed in box 1, the gross less any NUA on employer securities in box 2a, no entry in box 5, and any NUA in box 6.

Corrective distributions. Enter in box 2a the amount of excess deferrals, excess contributions, or excess aggregate contributions (other than employee contributions). See *Corrective Distributions* on page R-4.

Box 2b. Taxable Amount not Determined

Enter an "X" in this box only if you are unable to reasonably obtain the data needed to compute the taxable amount. If you check this box, leave box 2a blank unless you are reporting a traditional IRA, SEP IRA, or SIMPLE IRA distribution. Except for IRAs, make every effort to compute the taxable amount. However, see *IRA Revocation* on page R-2 and *Corrective Distributions* on page R-4.

Box 2b. Total Distribution

Enter an "X" in this box only if the payment shown in box 1 is a total distribution. A total distribution is one or more distributions within 1 tax year in which the entire balance of the account is distributed. If periodic or installment payments are made, mark this box in the year the final payment is made.

Box 3. Capital Gain (Included in Box 2a)

If any amount is taxable as a capital gain, report it in box 3.

Charitable gift annuities. Report in box 3 any amount from a charitable gift annuity that is taxable as a capital gain. Report in box 1 the total amount distributed during the year. Report in box 2a the taxable amount. Advise the annuity recipient of any amount in box 3 subject to the 28% rate gain for collectibles and any unrecaptured section 1250 gain. Report in box 5 any nontaxable amount. Enter Code F in box 7. See Regulations section 1.1011-2(c), Example 8.

Special rule for participants born before January 2, 1936 (or their beneficiaries). For lump-sum distributions from qualified plans only, enter the amount in box 2a eligible for the capital gain election under section 1122(h)(3) of the Tax Reform Act of 1986, 1986-3 (Vol. 1) C.B. 1, 387 and section 641(f)(3) of the Economic Growth and Tax Relief Reconciliation Act of 2001. Enter the full amount eligible for the capital gain election. You should not complete this box for a direct rollover.

To compute the months of an employee's active participation before 1974, count as 12 months any part of a calendar year in which an employee actively participated under the plan; for active participation after 1973, count as 1 month any part of a month in which the employee actively participated under the plan. See the *Example* below.

Active participation begins with the first month in which an employee became a participant under the plan and ends with the earliest of:
- The month in which the employee received a lump-sum distribution under the plan;
- For an employee, other than a self-employed person or owner-employee, the month in which the employee separates from service;
- The month in which the employee dies; or
- For a self-employed person or owner-employee, the first month in which the employee becomes disabled within the meaning of section 72(m)(7).

Example for Computing Amount Eligible for Capital Gain Election (See **Box 3.**)

Step 1. Total Taxable Amount

A. Total distribution		XXXXX
B. Less:		
1. Current actuarial value of any annuity	XXXX	
2. Employee contributions (minus any amounts previously distributed that were not includible in the employee's gross income)	XXXX	
3. Net unrealized appreciation in the value of any employer securities that was a part of the lump-sum distribution.	XXXX	
C. Total of lines 1 through 3		XXXXX
D. Total taxable amount. Subtract line C from line A.		XXXXX

Step 2. Capital Gain

$$\text{Line D} \times \frac{\text{Months of active participation before 1974}}{\text{Total months of active participation}} = \text{Capital gain}$$

Box 4. Federal Income Tax Withheld

Enter any federal income tax withheld. This withholding under section 3405 is subject to deposit rules and the withholding tax return is Form 945. Backup withholding does not apply. See Pub. 15-A, Employer's Supplemental Tax Guide, and the Instructions for Form 945 for more withholding information.

Even though you may be using Code 1 in box 7 to designate an early distribution subject to the 10% additional tax specified in section 72(q), (t), or (v), you are not required to withhold that tax.

TIP *The amount withheld cannot be more than the sum of the cash and the FMV of property (excluding employer securities) received in the distribution. If a distribution consists solely of employer securities and cash ($200 or less) in lieu of fractional shares, no withholding is required.*

To determine your withholding requirements for any designated distribution under section 3405, you must first determine whether the distribution is an eligible rollover distribution. See *Direct Rollovers* on page R-2 for a discussion of eligible rollover distributions. If the distribution is not an eligible rollover distribution, the rules for periodic payments or nonperiodic distributions apply. For purposes of withholding, distributions from any IRA are not eligible rollover distributions.

Eligible rollover distribution; 20% withholding. If an eligible rollover distribution is paid directly to an eligible retirement plan in a direct rollover, do not withhold federal income tax. If any part of an eligible rollover distribution is not a direct rollover, you must withhold 20% of the part that is paid to the recipient. The recipient cannot claim exemption from the 20% withholding but may ask to have additional amounts withheld on Form W-4P, Withholding Certificate for Pension or Annuity Payments. If the recipient is not asking that additional amounts be withheld,

R-7

Form W-4P is not required for an eligible rollover distribution because 20% withholding is mandatory.

Employer securities and plan loan offset amounts that are part of an eligible rollover distribution must be included in the amount multiplied by 20%. However, the actual amount to be withheld cannot be more than the sum of the cash and the FMV of property (excluding employer securities and plan loan offset amounts). For example, if the only part of an eligible rollover distribution that is not a direct rollover is employer securities or a plan loan offset amount, no withholding is required. However, any cash that is paid in the distribution must be used to satisfy the withholding on the employer securities or plan loan offset amount.

The payer is required to withhold 20% of eligible rollover distributions from a qualified plan's distributed annuity and on eligible rollover distributions from a governmental section 457(b) plan.

Any NUA excludable from gross income under section 402(e)(4) is not included in the amount of any eligible rollover distribution that is subject to 20% withholding.

You are not required to withhold 20% of an eligible rollover distribution that, when aggregated with other eligible rollover distributions made to one person during the year, is less than $200.

IRAs. The 20% withholding does not apply to distributions from any IRA, but withholding does apply to IRAs under the rules for periodic payments and nonperiodic distributions. For withholding, assume that the entire amount of an IRA distribution is taxable (except for the distribution of contributions under section 408(d)(4), in which only the earnings are taxable, and 408(d)(5), as applicable). Generally, Roth IRA distributions are not subject to withholding except on the earnings portion of excess contributions distributed under section 408(d)(4).

An IRA recharacterization is not subject to income tax withholding.

Periodic payments. For periodic payments that are not eligible rollover distributions, withhold on the taxable part as though the periodic payments were wages, based on the recipient's Form W-4P. The recipient may request additional withholding on Form W-4P or claim exemption from withholding. If a recipient does not submit a Form W-4P, withhold by treating the recipient as married with three withholding allowances. See Circular E, Employer's Tax Guide (Pub. 15), for wage withholding tables.

 Rather than Form W-4P, military retirees should give you Form W-4, Employee's Withholding Allowance Certificate.

Nonperiodic distributions. Withhold 10% of the taxable part of a nonperiodic distribution that is not an eligible rollover distribution. The recipient may request additional withholding on Form W-4P or claim exemption from withholding.

Failure to provide TIN. For periodic payments and nonperiodic distributions, if a payee fails to furnish his or her correct TIN to you in the manner required, or if the IRS notifies you before any distribution that the TIN furnished is incorrect, a payee cannot claim exemption from withholding. For periodic payments, withhold as if the payee was single claiming no withholding allowances. For nonperiodic payments, withhold 10%. Backup withholding does not apply.

Box 5. Employee Contributions or Insurance Premiums

Enter the employee's contributions to a profit-sharing or retirement plan, or insurance premiums that the employee may recover tax free this year. The entry in box 5 may include any of the following: (a) contributions actually made by the employee over the years under the retirement or profit-sharing plan that were required to be included in the income of the employee when contributed (after-tax contributions), (b) contributions made by the employer but considered to have been contributed by the employee under section 72(f), (c) the accumulated cost of premiums paid for life insurance protection taxable to the employee in previous years and in the current year under Regulations section 1.72-16 (cost of current life insurance protection) (only if the life insurance contract itself is distributed), and (d) premiums paid on commercial annuities.

Also report after-tax contributions directly rolled over to an IRA. Do not include contributions to any DEC, 401(k) plan, or any other contribution to a retirement plan that was not an after-tax contribution.

Generally, for qualified plans, tax-sheltered annuities, and nonqualified commercial annuities, enter in box 5 the employee contributions or insurance premiums recovered tax free during the year based on the method you used to determine the taxable amount to be entered in box 2a. If periodic payments began before 1993, you are not required to, but you are encouraged to, report in box 5.

 If you made periodic payments from a qualified plan and the annuity starting date is after November 18, 1996, you must use the simplified method to figure the tax-free amount each year. See Annuity starting date in 1998 or later on page R-6.

If a total distribution is made, the total employee contributions or insurance premiums available to be recovered tax free must be shown only in box 5. If any previous distributions were made, any amount recovered tax free in prior years must not appear in box 5.

If you are unable to reasonably obtain the data necessary to compute the taxable amount, leave boxes 2a and 5 blank, and check the first box in box 2b.

For more information, see Rev. Proc. 92-86, 1992-2 C.B. 495 and section 72(d).

For reporting charitable gift annuities, see *Charitable gift annuities* on page R-6.

Box 6. Net Unrealized Appreciation (NUA) in Employer's Securities

Use this box if a distribution from a qualified plan includes securities of the employer corporation (or a subsidiary or parent corporation) and you can compute the NUA in the employer's securities. Enter all the NUA in employer securities if this is a lump-sum distribution. If this is not a lump-sum distribution, enter only the NUA in employer securities attributable to employee contributions. See Regulations section 1.402(a)-1(b) for the determination of the NUA. Also see Notice 89-25, Q/A-1, 1989-1 C.B. 662. Include the NUA in box 1 but not in box 2a. You do not have to complete this box for a direct rollover.

Box 7. Distribution Code(s)

Enter an "X" in the IRA/SEP/SIMPLE checkbox if the distribution is from a traditional IRA, SEP IRA, or SIMPLE IRA. It is not necessary to check the box for a distribution from a Roth IRA or for an IRA recharacterization.

Enter the appropriate code(s) in box 7. Use the *Guide to Distribution Codes* on pages R-10 and R-11 to determine the appropriate code(s) to enter in box 7 for any amounts reported on Form 1099-R. Read the codes carefully and enter them accurately because the IRS uses the codes to help determine whether the recipient has properly reported the distribution. If the codes you enter are incorrect, the IRS may improperly propose changes to the recipient's taxes.

When applicable, enter a numeric and an alpha code. For example, when using Code P for a traditional IRA distribution under section 408(d)(4), you must also enter Code 1, if it applies. For a normal distribution from a qualified plan that qualifies for the 10-year tax option, enter Codes 7 and A. For a direct rollover to an IRA or a qualified plan for the surviving spouse of a deceased participant, enter Codes 4 and G.

 Only three numeric combinations are permitted on one Form 1099-R: Codes 8 and 1, 8 and 2, or 8 and 4. If two or more other numeric codes are applicable, you must file more than one Form 1099-R. For example, if part of a distribution is premature (Code 1) and part is not (Code 7), file one Form 1099-R for the part to which Code 1 applies and another Form 1099-R for the part to which Code 7 applies. In addition, for the distribution of excess deferrals, excess contributions, or excess aggregate contributions, parts of the distribution may be taxable in 2 or 3 different years. File separate Forms 1099-R using Code 8, D, or P to indicate the year the amount is taxable.

Even if the employee/taxpayer is age 59½ or over, use Code 1 if a series of substantially equal periodic payments was modified within 5 years of the date of the first payment (within the meaning of section 72(q)(3) or (t)(4)). For example, Mr. B began receiving payments that qualified for the exception for part of a series of substantially equal periodic payments under section 72(t)(2)(A)(iv) when he was 57. When he was 61, Mr. B substantially modified the payments. Because the payments were modified within 5 years, use Code 1 in the year the payments were modified, even though Mr. B is over 59½.

For further guidance on what makes a series of substantially equal periodic payments, see Notice 89-25, 1989-1 C.B. 662, as modified by Rev. Rul. 2002-62, 2002-42 I.R.B. 710. Notice 2004-15, available on page 526 of Internal Revenue Bulletin 2004-9 at www.irs.gov/pub/irs-irbs/ irb04-09.pdf, allows taxpayers to use one of three methods in Notice 89-25, as modified by Rev. Rul. 2002-62, to determine whether a distribution from a nonqualified annuity is part of a series of substantially equal periodic payments under section 72(q)(2)(D).

If part of an eligible rollover distribution is paid in a direct rollover and part is not, you must file a separate Form 1099-R for each part showing the appropriate code on each form. If part of a distribution is an eligible rollover distribution and part is not (for example, a minimum distribution required by section 401(a)(9)) and the part that is an eligible rollover distribution is directly rolled over, you must file a separate Form 1099-R to report each part.

Section 457(b) plan distributions. Generally, a distribution from a governmental section 457(b) plan is not subject to the 10% additional tax under section 72(t). However, an early distribution from a governmental section 457(b) plan of an amount that is attributable to a rollover from another type of plan or IRA is subject to the additional tax as if the distribution were from a plan described in section 401(a). See section 72(t)(9). If the distribution consists solely of amounts that are not attributable to such a rollover, enter Code 2 in box 7. If the distribution consists solely of amounts attributable to such a rollover, then enter the appropriate code in box 7 as if the distribution were from a plan described in section 401(a). If the distribution is made up of amounts from both sources, you must file separate Forms 1099-R for each part of the distribution unless Code 2 would be entered on each form.

Box 8. Other

Enter the current actuarial value of an annuity contract that is part of a lump-sum distribution. Do not include this item in boxes 1 and 2a.

To determine the value of an annuity contract, show the value as an amount equal to the current actuarial value of the annuity contract, reduced by an amount equal to the excess of the employee's contributions over the cash and other property (not including the annuity contract) distributed.

If an annuity contract is part of a multiple recipient lump-sum distribution, enter in box 8, along with the current actuarial value, the percentage of the total annuity contract each Form 1099-R represents.

Box 9a. Your Percentage of Total Distribution

If this is a total distribution and it is made to more than one person, enter the percentage received by the person whose name appears on Form 1099-R. You need not complete this box for any IRA distributions or for a direct rollover.

Box 9b. Total Employee Contributions

You are not required to enter the total employee contributions in box 9b. However, because this information may be helpful to the recipient, you may choose to report them.

If you choose to report the total employee contributions, do not include any amounts recovered tax free in prior years. For a total distribution, report the total employee contributions in box 5 rather than in box 9b.

Boxes 10–15. State and Local Information

These boxes and Copies 1 and 2 are provided for your convenience only and need not be completed for the IRS. Use the state and local information boxes to report distributions and taxes for up to two states or localities. Keep the information for each state or locality separated by the broken line. If state or local income tax has been withheld on this distribution, you may enter it in boxes 10 and 13, as appropriate. In box 11, enter the abbreviated name of the state and the payer's state identification number. The state number is the payer's identification number assigned by the individual state. In box 14, enter the name of the locality. In boxes 12 and 15, you may enter the amount of the state or local distribution. Copy 1 may be used to provide information to the state or local tax department. Copy 2 may be used as the recipient's copy in filing a state or local income tax return.

Guide to Distribution Codes		
Distribution Codes	**Explanations**	***Used with code ...(if applicable)**
1—Early distribution, no known exception.	Use Code 1 only if the employee/taxpayer has not reached age 59½, and you do not know if any of the exceptions under Distribution Code 2, 3, or 4 apply. Use Code 1 even if the distribution is made for medical expenses, health insurance premiums, qualified higher education expenses, or a first-time home purchase, under section 72(t)(2)(B), (D), (E), or (F). Code 1 must also be used even if a taxpayer is 59½ or older and he or she modifies a series of substantially equal periodic payments under section 72(q), (t), or (v) prior to the end of the 5-year period.	8, D, L, or P
2—Early distribution, exception applies.	Use Code 2 only if the employee/taxpayer has not reached age 59½ and the distribution is: • A Roth IRA conversion (an IRA converted to a Roth IRA). • A distribution made from a qualified retirement plan or IRA because of an IRS levy under section 6331. • A section 457(b) plan distribution that is not subject to the additional 10% tax. But see *Section 457(b) plan distributions* on page R-9 for information on distributions that may be subject to the 10% additional tax. • A distribution from a qualified retirement plan after separation from service where the taxpayer has reached age 55. • A distribution that is part of a series of substantially equal periodic payments as described in section 72(q), (t), or (v). • Any other distribution subject to an exception under section 72(q), (t), or (v) that is not required to be reported using Code 1, 3, or 4.	8, D, or P
3—Disability.	For these purposes, see section 72(m)(7).	None
4—Death.	Use Code 4 regardless of the age of the employee/taxpayer to indicate payment to a decedent's beneficiary, including an estate or trust. Also use it for death benefit payments made by an employer but not made as part of a pension, profit-sharing, or retirement plan.	8, A, D, G, L, or P
5—Prohibited transaction.	Use Code 5 if there was a prohibited (improper) use of the account. Code 5 means the account is no longer an IRA.	None
6—Section 1035 exchange.	Use Code 6 to indicate the tax-free exchange of life insurance, annuity, or endowment contracts under section 1035.	None
7—Normal distribution.	Use Code 7: (a) for a normal distribution from a plan, including a traditional IRA, if the employee/taxpayer is at least age 59½, (b) for a Roth IRA conversion or reconversion if the participant is at least age 59½, and (c) to report a distribution from a life insurance, annuity, or endowment contract and for reporting income from a failed life insurance contract under sections 7702(g) and (h). See Rev. Rul. 91-17, 1991-1 C.B. 190. Use Code 7 with Code A, if applicable. Generally, use Code 7 if no other code applies. Do not use Code 7 for a Roth IRA distribution. **Note:** Code 1 must be used even if a taxpayer is 59½ or older and he or she modifies a series of substantially equal periodic payments under section 72(q), (t), or (v) prior to the end of the 5-year period.	A
8—Excess contributions plus earnings/ excess deferrals (and/or earnings) taxable in 2005.	Use Code 8 for an IRA distribution under section 408(d)(4), unless Code P applies. Also use this code for corrective distributions of excess deferrals, excess contributions, and excess aggregate contributions, unless Code D or P applies. See *Corrective Distributions* on page R-4 and *IRA Revocation* on page R-2 for more information.	1, 2, 4, or J
9—Cost of current life insurance protection.	Use Code 9 to report premiums paid by a trustee or custodian for current life or other insurance protection. See *Box 2a* on page R-6 for more information.	None
A—May be eligible for 10-year tax option.	Use Code A only for participants born before January 2, 1936, or their beneficiaries to indicate the distribution may be eligible for the 10-year tax option method of computing the tax on lump-sum distributions (on Form 4972, Tax on Lump-Sum Distributions). To determine whether the distribution may be eligible for the tax option, you need not consider whether the recipient used this method (or capital gain treatment) in the past.	4 or 7
D—Excess contributions plus earnings/ excess deferrals taxable in 2003.	See the explanation for Code 8. Generally, do not use Code D for an IRA distribution under section 408(d)(4) or 408(d)(5).	1, 2, or 4
E—Excess annual additions under section 415/certain excess amounts under section 403(b) plans.	See *Excess Annual Additions Under Section 415* on page R-4.	None
F—Charitable gift annuity.	See *Charitable gift annuities* on page R-6.	None

R-10

Appendix

Guide to Distribution Codes		
Distribution Codes	**Explanations**	***Used with code ...(if applicable)**
G—Direct rollover and rollover contribution.	Use Code G for a direct rollover from a qualified plan (including a governmental section 457(b) plan) or tax-sheltered annuity to an eligible retirement plan (another qualified plan, a tax-sheltered annuity, or an IRA). See *Direct Rollovers* on page R-2. Also use Code G for certain distributions from conduit IRAs to an employer plan and IRA rollover contributions to an accepting employer plan. See *Conduit IRAs* on page R-2.	4
J—Early distribution from a Roth IRA.	Use Code J for a distribution from a Roth IRA when Code Q or Code T does not apply. But use Code 2 for an IRS levy and Code 5 for a prohibited transaction.	8 or P
L—Loans treated as deemed distributions under section 72(p).	Do not use Code L to report a loan offset. See *Loans Treated as Distributions* on page R-5.	1 or 4
N—Recharacterized IRA contribution made for 2005.	Use Code N for a recharacterization of an IRA contribution made for 2005 and recharacterized in 2005 to another type of IRA by a trustee-to-trustee transfer or with the same trustee.	None
P—Excess contributions plus earnings/ excess deferrals taxable in 2004.	See the explanation for Code 8. The IRS suggests that anyone using Code P for the refund of an IRA contribution under section 408(d)(4), including excess Roth IRA contributions, advise payees, at the time the distribution is made, that the earnings are taxable in the year in which the contributions were made.	1, 2, 4, or J
Q—Qualified distribution from a Roth IRA.	Use Code Q for a distribution from a Roth IRA if you know that the participant meets the 5-year holding period and: • The participant has reached age 59 ½, or • The participant died, or • The participant is disabled. **Note:** *If any other Code, such as 8 or P applies, use Code J.*	None
R—Recharacterized IRA contribution made for 2004.	Use Code R for a recharacterization of an IRA contribution made for 2004 and recharacterized in 2005 to another type of IRA by a trustee-to-trustee transfer or with the same trustee.	None
S—Early distribution from a SIMPLE IRA in the first 2 years, no known exception.	Use Code S only if the distribution is from a SIMPLE IRA in the first 2 years, the employee/taxpayer has not reached age 59 ½, and none of the exceptions under section 72(t) are known to apply when the distribution is made. The 2-year period begins on the day contributions are first deposited in the individual's SIMPLE IRA. Do not use Code S if Code 3 or 4 applies.	None
T—Roth IRA distribution, exception applies.	Use Code T for a distribution from a Roth IRA if you do not know if the 5-year holding period has been met but: • The participant has reached age 59 ½, or • The participant died, or • The participant is disabled. **Note:** *If any other Code, such as 8 or P applies, use Code J.*	None
*See the **Caution** for box 7 instructions on page R-9.		

R-11

9494   ☐ VOID   ☐ CORRECTED

TRUSTEE'S/PAYER'S name, street address, city, state, and ZIP code			OMB No. 1545-1517 2006 Form **1099-SA**	**Distributions From an HSA, Archer MSA, or Medicare Advantage MSA**
PAYER'S federal identification number	RECIPIENT'S identification number	**1** Gross distribution $	**2** Earnings on excess cont. $	**Copy A** **For**
RECIPIENT'S name		**3** Distribution code	**4** FMV on date of death $	**Internal Revenue Service Center** **File with Form 1096.**
Street address (including apt. no.)		**5** HSA ☐ Archer MSA ☐ MA MSA ☐		For Privacy Act and Paperwork Reduction Act Notice, see the **2006 General Instructions for Forms 1099, 1098, 5498, and W-2G.**
City, state, and ZIP code				
Account number (see instructions)				

Form **1099-SA**   Cat. No. 38471D   Department of the Treasury - Internal Revenue Service

Do Not Cut or Separate Forms on This Page — Do Not Cut or Separate Forms on This Page

Instructions for Recipient

Distributions from a health savings account (HSA), Archer MSA, or Medicare Advantage (MA) MSA are reported to you on Form 1099-SA. File Form 8853, Archer MSAs and Long-Term Care Insurance Contracts, or Form 8889, Health Savings Accounts (HSAs), with your Form 1040 to report a distribution from these accounts even if the distribution is not taxable. The payer is not required to compute the taxable amount of any distribution.

An HSA or Archer MSA distribution is not taxable if you used it to pay qualified medical expenses of the account holder and family or you rolled it over. An HSA may be rolled over to another HSA; an Archer MSA may be rolled over to another Archer MSA or an HSA. An MA MSA is not taxable if you used it to pay qualified medical expenses of the account holder only. If you did not use the distribution from an HSA, Archer MSA, or MA MSA to pay for qualified medical expenses, or in the case of an HSA or Archer MSA, you did not roll it over, you must include the distribution in your income (see Form 8889 or Form 8853). Also, you may owe a penalty.

For more information, see the separate instructions for Form 8853 and Form 8889. Also see Pub. 969, Health Savings Accounts and Other Tax-Favored Health Plans.

Spouse beneficiary. If you inherited an Archer MSA or MA MSA because of the death of your spouse, special rules apply. See Instructions for Form 8853. If you inherited an HSA because of the death of your spouse, see the Instructions for Form 8889.

Estate beneficiary. If the HSA, Archer MSA, or MA MSA account holder dies and the estate is the beneficiary, the fair market value (FMV) of the account on the date of death is includible in the account holder's gross income. Report the amount on the account holder's final income tax return.

Nonspouse beneficiary. If you inherited the HSA, Archer MSA, or MA MSA from someone who was not your spouse, you must report as income on your tax return the FMV of the account as of the date of death. Report the FMV on your tax return for the year the account owner died even if you received the distribution from the account in a later year. See the Instructions for Form 8853 or Form 8889. Any earnings on the account after the date of death (box 1 minus box 4 of Form 1099-SA) are taxable. In the case of an HSA, the amount included on your tax return (other than an estate) is first reduced by any payments from the HSA made for the decedent's qualified medical expenses incurred before the decedent's death and paid within one year after the date of death.

Account number. May show an account or other unique number the payer assigned to distinguish your account.

Box 1. Shows the amount received this year. The amount may have been a direct payment to the medical service provider or distributed to you.

Box 2. Shows the earnings on any excess contributions you withdrew from an HSA or Archer MSA by the due date of your income tax return. If you withdrew the excess, plus any earnings, by the due date of your income tax return, you must include the earnings in your income in the year you received the distribution even if you used it to pay qualified medical expenses. This amount is included in box 1. An excise tax of 6% for each taxable year is imposed on you for excess individual and employer contributions that remain in the account. See Form 5329, Additional Taxes on Qualified Plans (Including IRAs) and Other Tax-Favored Accounts.

Box 3. These codes identify the distribution you received: 1—Normal distribution; 2—Excess contributions; 3—Disability; 4—Death distribution other than code 6; 5—Prohibited transaction; 6—Death distribution after year of death to a nonspouse beneficiary.

Box 4. If the account holder died, shows the FMV of the account on the date of death.

Box 5. Shows the type of account that is reported on this Form 1099-SA.

Instructions for Trustees/Payers

General and specific form instructions are provided as separate products. The products you should use to complete Form 1099-SA are the 2006 General Instructions for Forms 1099, 1098, 5498, and W-2G and the 2006 Instructions for Forms 1099-SA and 5498-SA. A chart in the general instructions gives a quick guide to which form must be filed to report a particular payment. To order these instructions and additional forms, call 1-800-TAX-FORM (1-800-829-3676).

Caution: *Because paper forms are scanned during processing, you cannot file Forms 1096, 1098, 1099, or 5498 that you download and print from the IRS website.*

Due dates. Furnish Copy B of this form to the recipient by January 31, 2007.

File Copy A of this form with the IRS by February 28, 2007. If you file electronically, the due date is April 2, 2007. To file electronically, you must have software that generates a file according to the specifications in Pub. 1220, Specifications for Filing Forms 1098, 1099, 5498, and W-2G Electronically or Magnetically. IRS does not provide a fill-in form option.

 Printed on recycled paper

20**06**

Department of the Treasury
Internal Revenue Service

Instructions for Forms 1099-SA and 5498-SA

Section references are to the Internal Revenue Code unless otherwise noted.

Reminder

In addition to these specific instructions, you should also use the 2006 General Instructions for Forms 1099, 1098, 5498, and W-2G. Those general instructions include information about:
- Backup withholding
- Magnetic media and electronic reporting requirements
- Penalties
- Who must file (nominee/middleman)
- When and where to file
- Taxpayer identification numbers
- Statements to recipients
- Corrected and void returns
- Other general topics

You can get the general instructions from the IRS website at *www.irs.gov* or by calling 1-800-TAX-FORM (1-800-829-3676).

Specific Instructions for Form 1099-SA

File Form 1099-SA, Distributions From an HSA, Archer MSA, or Medicare Advantage MSA, to report distributions made from an HSA, Archer MSA, or Medicare Advantage MSA (MA MSA). The distribution may have been paid directly to a medical service provider or to the account holder. A separate return must be filed for each plan type.

Transfers. Do not report a trustee-to-trustee transfer from one Archer MSA or MA MSA to another Archer MSA or MA MSA, one Archer MSA to an HSA, or from one HSA to another HSA. For reporting purposes, contributions and rollovers do not include transfers.

Mistaken distributions. If amounts were distributed during the year from an HSA because of a mistake of fact due to reasonable cause, the account beneficiary may repay the mistaken distribution no later than April 15 following the first year the account beneficiary knew or should have known the distribution was a mistake. For example, the account beneficiary reasonably, but mistakenly, believed that an expense was a qualified medical expense and was reimbursed for that expense from the HSA. The account beneficiary then repays the mistaken distribution to the HSA.

Under these circumstances, the distribution is not included in gross income, is not subject to the 10 percent additional tax, and the payment is not subject to the excise tax on excess contributions. Do not treat the repayment as a contribution on Form 5498-SA.

TIP *As the trustee or custodian, you do not have to allow beneficiaries to return a mistaken distribution to the HSA. However, if you do allow the return of the mistaken contribution, you may rely on the account beneficiary's statement that the distribution was in fact a mistake. See Notice 2004-50, Q/A 76 which is on page 196 of Internal Revenue Bulletin 2004-33 available at www.irs.gov/pub/irs-irbs/irb04-33.pdf. Do not report the mistaken distribution on Form 1099-SA. Correct any filed Form 1099-SA with the IRS and the account beneficiary as soon as you become aware of the error. See Corrected Returns on Paper Forms in the 2006 General Instructions for Forms 1099, 1098, 5498, and W-2G for more information.*

Death of Account Holder

Archer MSAs and MA MSAs. If the account holder dies and the beneficiary is the spouse:

- The spouse becomes the account holder of the Archer MSA,
- The spouse may continue an MA MSA, but no new contributions may be made to the account, and
- Distributions from an Archer MSA or MA MSA are taxed under the rules that apply to Archer MSAs, not MA MSAs.

If the beneficiary is not the spouse or there is no named beneficiary, the account ceases to be an Archer MSA or MA MSA and the fair market value (FMV) is reported.

Distribution in year of death. If you learn of the account holder's death and make a final distribution to the beneficiary in the year of death, issue a final Form 1099-SA and enter in:
- Box 1, the gross distribution;
- Box 3, code 4 (see page SA-2); and
- Box 4, the FMV of the account on the date of death.

If the beneficiary is the estate, enter the estate's name and taxpayer identification number (TIN) in place of the recipient's on the form.

Distribution after year of death. If you learn of the death of the account holder and make a final distribution after the year of death, issue a final Form 1099-SA in the year you learned of the death of the account holder. Enter in:
- Box 1, the gross distribution;
- Box 3, one of the following codes (see below):
  - 1—if the beneficiary is the spouse,
  - 4—if the beneficiary is the estate, or
  - 6—if the beneficiary is not the spouse or estate;
- Box 4, the FMV of the account on the date of death.

HSAs. If the account holder dies and:
- The named beneficiary is the surviving spouse, the surviving spouse becomes the account holder of the HSA.
- If the HSA passes to a person other than the surviving spouse, the HSA ceases to be an HSA on the date of the account holder's death. If there is no designated beneficiary, or the account passes to the account holder's estate, the FMV of the account as of the date of death is required to be reported in box 4. Follow the rules and coding above under *Distribution in year of death* and *Distribution after year of death*.

Statements to Recipients

If you are required to file Form 1099-SA, you must provide a statement to the recipient. For more information about the requirement to furnish a Form 1099-SA or acceptable substitute statement to recipients, see part M in the 2006 General Instructions for Forms 1099, 1098, 5498, and W-2G.

Account Number

The account number is required if you have multiple accounts for a recipient for whom you are filing more than one Form 1099-SA. Additionally, the IRS encourages you to designate an account number for all Forms 1099-SA that you file. See part L in the 2006 General Instructions for Forms 1099, 1098, 5498, and W-2G.

Box 1. Gross Distribution

Enter the total amount of the distribution. Include any earnings separately reported in box 2. You are not required to determine the taxable amount of a distribution. Do not report a negative amount in box 1.

Cat. No. 38470S

Box 2. Earnings on Excess Contributions

Enter the total earnings distributed with any excess HSA or Archer MSA contributions returned by the due date of the account holder's tax return. Include this amount in box 1. Report earnings on other distributions only in box 1. Do not report excess MA MSA contributions returned to the Secretary of Health and Human Services or his or her representative.

Box 3. Distribution Code

Enter the appropriate distribution code from the list below that shows the type of distribution.

1—Normal distributions	Use this code for normal distributions to the account holder and any direct payments to a medical service provider. Use this code if no other code applies. Also, see *Distribution after year of death* on page SA-1.
2—Excess contributions	Use this code for distributions of excess HSA or Archer MSA contributions. Do not use this code for excess MA MSA contributions returned to the Secretary of Health and Human Services or his or her representative.
3—Disability	Use this code if you made distributions after the account holder was disabled (see section 72(m)(7)).
4—Death distribution other than code 6	Use this code for payments to a decedent's estate in the year of death. Also use this code for payments to an estate after the year of death. Do not use with code 6. See *Death of Account Holder* on page SA-1.
5—Prohibited transaction	See sections 220(e)(2) and 223(e)(2).
6—Death distribution after year of death to a nonspouse beneficiary	Use this code for payments to a decedent's nonspouse beneficiary, other than an estate, after the year of death. Do not use with code 4.

Box 4. FMV on Date of Death

If the account holder died, enter the FMV of the account on the date of death. See *Death of Account Holder* on page SA-1.

Box 5. Checkbox

Check the box to indicate if this distribution was from an HSA, Archer MSA, or MA MSA.

Specific Instructions for Form 5498-SA

File Form 5498-SA, HSA, Archer MSA, or Medicare Advantage MSA Information, with the IRS on or before May 31, 2007, for each person for whom you maintained an HSA, Archer MSA, or Medicare Advantage MSA (MA MSA) during 2006. You are required to file if you are the trustee or custodian of an HSA, Archer MSA, or MA MSA. A separate form is required for each type of plan.

For HSA or Archer MSA contributions made between January 1, 2007, and April 16, 2007, you should obtain the participant's designation of the year for which the contributions are made.

For repayment of a mistaken distribution amount, see *Mistaken distributions* on page SA-1.

Rollovers

You must report the receipt of a rollover from one Archer MSA to another Archer MSA, and receipt of a rollover from an Archer MSA or an HSA to an HSA in box 4.

Transfers

Do not report a trustee-to-trustee transfer from one Archer MSA or MA MSA to another Archer MSA or MA MSA, from an Archer MSA to an HSA, or from one HSA to another HSA. For reporting purposes, contributions and rollovers do not include these transfers.

 Rollovers from an IRA, a health reimbursement arrangement (HRA), or a flexible spending arrangement (FSA) to an HSA are not permitted.

Total Distribution, No Contributions

Generally, if a total distribution was made from an HSA or Archer MSA during the year and no contributions were made for that year, you need not file Form 5498-SA nor furnish a statement to the participant to reflect that the FMV on December 31 was zero.

Death of Account Holder

In the year an HSA, Archer MSA, or MA MSA owner dies, generally you must file a Form 5498-SA and furnish a statement for the decedent. If the beneficiary is the spouse:
● The spouse becomes the account holder of the HSA or Archer MSA,
● The spouse may continue an MA MSA, but no new contributions may be made to the account, and
● Distributions from an Archer MSA or MA MSA are taxed under the rules that apply to Archer MSAs, not MA MSAs. For rules that apply to HSAs, see Notice 2004-2, Q/A-31 which is on page 269 of Internal Revenue Bulletin 2004-2 at *www.irs.gov/pub/irs-irbs/irb04-02.pdf*.

If the beneficiary is not the spouse or there is no named beneficiary, the account ceases to be an HSA, Archer MSA, or MA MSA.

Statements to Participants

If you are required to file Form 5498-SA, you must provide a statement to the participant (generally Copy B) by May 31, 2007. You may, but you are not required to, provide participants with a statement of the December 31, 2006, FMV of the participant's account by January 31, 2007. For more information about statements to participants, see part M in the 2006 General Instructions for Forms 1099, 1098, 5498, and W-2G.

Account Number

The account number is required if you have multiple accounts for a recipient for whom you are filing more than one Form 5498-SA. Additionally, the IRS encourages you to designate an account number for all Forms 5498-SA that you file. See part L in the 2006 General Instructions for Forms 1099, 1098, 5498, and W-2G.

Box 1. Employee or Self-Employed Person's Archer MSA Contributions Made in 2006 and 2007 for 2006

Enter the employee's or self-employed person's regular contributions to the Archer MSA made in 2006 and through April 16, 2007, for 2006. Report gross contributions, including any excess contributions, even if the excess contributions were withdrawn. No HSA information is to be reported in box 1.

Box 2. Total Contributions Made in 2006

Enter the total HSA or Archer MSA contributions made in 2006. Include any contribution made in 2006 for 2005. You may, but you are not required to, report the total MA MSA contributions the Secretary of Health and Human Services or his or her representative made in 2006.

Box 3. Total HSA or Archer MSA Contributions Made in 2007 for 2006

Enter the total HSA or Archer MSA contributions made in 2007 for 2006.

Box 4. Rollover Contributions.

Enter rollover contributions to the HSA or Archer MSA received by you during 2006.

Box 5. Fair Market Value of HSA, Archer MSA, or MA MSA

Enter the FMV of the account on December 31, 2006.

Box 6. Checkbox

Check the box to indicate if this account is an HSA, Archer MSA, or MA MSA.

SA-2

2005

Department of the Treasury
Internal Revenue Service

General Instructions for Forms 1099, 1098, 5498, and W-2G

Section references are to the Internal Revenue Code.

Reminder

Electronic/Magnetic Media Filing. E-filers are reminded that using the FIRE system requires following the specifications contained in Pub. 1220. Also, the IRS does not provide a fill-in form option. See page GEN-5 for information on e-file.

Payee. Throughout these instructions the term "payee" means any recipient of Forms 1099, 1098, 5498, or W-2G including borrowers, debtors, donors, insureds, participants, policyholders, students, transferors, and winners on certain forms.

What's New for 2005

 See the specific form instructions for more information on the changes listed below.

Backup withholding. Certain payment card transactions made by a qualified payment card agent have been added to the list of payments exempt from backup withholding.

New Code section 6043A, Acquisitions and Mergers. New section 6043A was added by the American Jobs Creation Act of 2004 (the Act), P.L. 108-357. At the time this product went to print, the IRS and Treasury were addressing issues relating to information reporting of these corporate transactions. The IRS is expected to release guidance before the end of 2005.

New Form 1098-C. The Act added section 170(f)(12) that requires reporting of charitable contributions of motor vehicles, boats, and airplanes after December 31, 2004. A donee organization must provide an acknowledgment to the donor and file the same information with the Internal Revenue Service. Form 1098-C may be used as the written acknowledgment but must be filed with the IRS. At the time this product went to print, Form 1098-C and its separate instructions had not been released to the public.

Form 1099-C. Final regulations under section 6050P were issued during 2004 that address who is a lender of money for purposes of reporting cancellation of debt. The separate instructions have been revised to reflect this change.

Form 1099-CAP. At the time these instructions went to print, Form 1099-CAP and its separate instructions had not been released to the public. IRS and Treasury were addressing issues relating to development of regulations under sections 6043 and 6043A.

Form 1099-DIV. For tax years beginning after December 31, 2004, the Act repealed provisions of the Internal Revenue Code that specifically excluded distributions from foreign personal holding companies and foreign investment companies from the definition of qualified dividends. The separate instructions have been revised to reflect this change.

Form 1099-G. New Box 5, ATAA Payments, has been added to the form to report payments to eligible individuals under the Demonstration Project for Alternative Trade Adjustment Assistance (ATAA) for Older Workers. Beginning in 2005, the program payments are to be reported on Form 1099-G, not on Form 1099-MISC as in previous years.

Forms 1099-INT and 1099-OID. The Act repealed Code sections 860H through 860L, special rules for FASITs, effective after December 31, 2004. However, the special rules continue to apply to FASITs in existence on October 22, 2004, to the extent that the regular interests issued by the FASIT before that date continue to remain outstanding in accordance with the original terms of issue. The separate instructions have been revised to reflect this change.

Form 1099-MISC. The following changes have been made:
• New Boxes 15a, Section 409A Deferrals, and 15b, Section 409A Income, have been added to Form 1099-MISC. Code section 409A, added by the Act, provides that all amounts deferred under a nonqualified deferred compensation (NQDC) plan for all taxable years are includible in gross income unless certain requirements are satisfied. The reporting rules added to the separate instructions apply to nonemployees as well as employees. Section 409A generally is effective for amounts deferred in tax years beginning after December 31, 2004.
• Added to the list of payments that are not required to be reported on Form 1099-MISC are certain payment card transactions.
• Added to the list of payments exempt from backup withholding are certain payments made through a qualified payment card organization.

Form 1099-PATR. The Act required the following changes to be made.
• Section 199(d)(3) and Notice 2005-14 provide special rules for cooperatives to pass through to their patrons receiving certain patronage dividends or certain qualified per-unit retain allocations from the cooperative a deduction equal to their portion of the cooperative's qualified production activity income (QPAI) that would be deductible by the cooperative and designated by the cooperative in a written notice mailed to its patrons during the payment period. Box 6 on Form 1099-PATR that previously was used to report pass-through credits is revised to report the deduction under section 199. The open box below boxes 8 and 9 is designated as box 10 and will be used to report any pass-through credits not reported in boxes 7 or 8.
• Two credits have been added to the list of pass-through credits available to patrons for 2005: the credit for low sulfur diesel fuel production (Form 8896), and the small ethanol producer credit (Form 6478).

Form 1099-R. The following changes have been made:
• Distribution codes 1, 2, and J have been further modified. See the Guide to Distribution Codes in the Specific Instructions for Form 1099-R.
• Reporting and withholding rules on qualified employer plans and deemed IRA distributions have been added to the instructions based on guidance issued in Regulations section 1.408(q)-1.
• Rules relating to reporting of automatic rollovers of certain mandatory (involuntary) distributions from qualified plans have been added to the instructions based on Notice 2005-5, 2005-3 I.R.B. 337.

Form 1099-SA. Medicare+Choice (M+C) MSAs have been replaced by Medicare Advantage (MA) MSAs each place it appears on Form 1099-SA and its separate instructions.

Cat. No. 27976F

Items You Should Note

Photographs of Missing Children

The Internal Revenue Service is a proud partner with the National Center for Missing and Exploited Children. Photographs of missing children selected by the Center may appear in instructions on pages that would otherwise be blank. You can help bring these children home by looking at the photographs and calling 1-800-THE-LOST(1-800-843-5678) if you recognize a child.

Available Products

In addition to these general instructions, which contain general information concerning Forms 1099, 1098, 5498, and W-2G, we provide specific form instructions as separate products. Get the instructions you need for completing a specific form from the following list of separate instructions:

- Instructions for Forms W-2G and 5754
- Instructions for Form 1098
- Instructions for Form 1098-C
- Instructions for Forms 1098-E and 1098-T
- Instructions for Forms 1099-A and 1099-C
- Instructions for Form 1099-B
- Instructions for Form 1099-CAP
- Instructions for Form 1099-DIV
- Instructions for Form 1099-G
- Instructions for Form 1099-H
- Instructions for Forms 1099-INT and 1099-OID
- Instructions for Form 1099-LTC
- Instructions for Form 1099-MISC
- Instructions for Form 1099-PATR
- Instructions for Form 1099-Q
- Instructions for Forms 1099-R and 5498
- Instructions for Form 1099-S
- Instructions for Forms 1099-SA and 5498-SA
- Instructions for Form 5498-ESA

If you prefer to have all the specific and general instructions in one booklet, the 2005 Instructions for Forms 1099, 1098, 5498, and W-2G is also available. See _How To Get Forms and Publications_ on page GEN-3.

Reporting Backup Withholding on Forms 1099 and W-2G

If you backup withhold on a payment, you must file the appropriate Form 1099 or Form W-2G with the IRS and furnish a statement to the recipient to report the amount of the payment and the amount withheld. This applies even though the amount of the payment may be below the normal threshold for filing Form 1099 or Form W-2G. See _Backup Withholding_ on page GEN-3.

Form 945. Withholding Tax Return

Report backup withholding, voluntary withholding on certain government payments, and withholding from gambling winnings, pensions, annuities, IRAs, military retirement, and Indian gaming profits on Form 945, Annual Return of Withheld Federal Income Tax. Generally, file Form 945 for 2005 by January 31, 2006. For more information, including the deposit requirements for Form 945, see the separate Instructions for Form 945 and Circular E, Employer's Tax Guide (Pub. 15).

Any income tax withholding reported on the following forms must not be reported on Form 945:

- **Form W-2**, Wage and Tax Statement, including withholding on distributions to plan participants from nonqualified plans, must be reported on Form 941, Employer's Quarterly Federal Tax Return.
- **Form 1042-S**, Foreign Person's U.S. Source Income Subject to Withholding, must be reported on Form 1042, Annual Withholding Tax Return for U.S. Source Income of Foreign Persons.

 Pub. 515, Withholding of Tax on Nonresident Aliens and Foreign Entities, has more information on Form 1042 reporting, partnership withholding on effectively connected income, and dispositions of U.S. real property interests by a foreign person.

Use Form 1096 To Send Forms to the IRS

You must send Copies A of all paper Forms 1099, 1098, 5498, and W-2G to the IRS with Form 1096, Annual Summary and Transmittal of U.S. Information Returns. Instructions for completing Form 1096 are contained on Form 1096. Also see part D on page GEN-8.

Substitute Statements to Recipients

If you are using a substitute form to furnish statements to recipients (generally Copy B), be sure your substitute statements comply with the rules in Pub. 1179, General Rules and Specifications for Substitute Forms 1096, 1098, 1099, 5498, W-2G, and 1042-S. Pub. 1179, which is revised annually, explains the requirements for format and content of substitute statements to recipients. If you are using a substitute form to furnish information to recipients, it must comply with the requirements in Pub. 1179.

 All substitute statements to recipients must contain the tax year, form number, and form name prominently displayed together in one area of the statement. For example, they could be shown in the upper right part of the statement.

Guide to Information Returns

See the chart on pages GEN-16 and GEN-17 for a brief summary of information return reporting rules.

Taxpayer Identification Number (TIN) Matching

TIN Matching allows a payer or authorized agent who is required to file Forms 1099-B, DIV, INT, MISC, OID, and/or PATR, which report income subject to backup withholding, to match TIN and name combinations with IRS records before submitting the forms to the IRS. TIN Matching is one of the e-services products that is offered, and is accessible through the IRS website. Go to _www.irs.gov_ and search for "e-services." It is anticipated that payers who validate the TIN and name combinations before filing information returns will receive fewer backup withholding (CP2100) "B" notices and penalty notices. E-services technical support is available by calling 1-866-255-0654, Monday through Friday, from 8:30 a.m. to 7:00 p.m., Eastern time.

Need Help?

Information Reporting Customer Service Site

If you have questions about reporting on Forms 1096, 1098, 1099, 5498, W-2, W-2G, and W-3, you may call a toll-free number, 1-866-455-7438. You may still use the original telephone number, 304-263-8700 (not toll free). For TTY/TDD equipment, call 304-267-3367 (not toll free). The call site can also be reached by email at mccirp@irs.gov. The hours of operation for the call site are Monday through Friday from 8:30 a.m. to 4:30 p.m., Eastern time.

Other tax-related matters. For other tax information related to business returns or accounts, call 1-800-829-4933.

If you have access to TTY/TDD equipment, call 1-800-829-4059 to ask tax account questions or to order forms and publications.

Internal Revenue Bulletin

The Internal Revenue Bulletin (IRB), published weekly, contains newly issued regulations, notices, announcements, legislation, court decisions, and other items of general interest. You may find this publication useful to keep you up to date with current developments. See _How To Get Forms and Publications_ on page GEN-3.

Unresolved Tax Issues

If you have attempted to deal with an IRS problem unsuccessfully, you should contact the Taxpayer Advocate. The

GEN-2

Taxpayer Advocate independently represents your interests and concerns within the IRS by protecting your rights and resolving problems that have not been fixed through normal channels.

While Taxpayer Advocates cannot change the tax law or make a technical decision, they can clear up problems that resulted from previous contacts and ensure that your case is given a complete and impartial review.

Your assigned personal advocate will listen to your point of view and will work with you to address your concerns. You can expect the advocate to provide:
- A "fresh look" at a new or on-going problem.
- Timely acknowledgement.
- The name and phone number of the individual assigned to your case.
- Updates on progress.
- Timeframes for action.
- Speedy resolution.
- Courteous service.

When contacting the Taxpayer Advocate, you should provide the following information:
- Your name, address, and employer identification number (EIN).
- The name and telephone number of an authorized contact person and the hours he or she can be reached.
- The type of tax return and year(s).
- A detailed description of the problem.
- Previous attempts to solve the problem and the office that had been contacted.
- A description of the hardship you are facing and supporting documentation (if applicable).

You may contact a Taxpayer Advocate by calling a toll-free number, 1-877-777-4778. Persons who have access to TTY/TDD equipment may call 1-800-829-4059 and ask for Taxpayer Advocate assistance. If you prefer, you may call, write, or fax the Taxpayer Advocate office for your area. See Pub. 1546, The Taxpayer Advocate Service – How to Get Help With Unresolved Tax Problems, for a list of addresses and fax numbers. You may visit the website at *www.irs.gov/advocate*.

How To Get Forms and Publications

 Because the IRS processes paper forms by machine (optical character recognition equipment), you cannot file with the IRS Form 1096 or Copy A of Forms 1098, 1099, or 5498 that you print from the IRS website or the CD-ROM.

Personal computer. You can access the IRS website 24 hours a day, 7 days a week, at *www.irs.gov* to:

- Access commercial tax preparation and *e-file* services.
- Download forms, instructions, and publications.
- Order IRS products online.
- Research your tax question online.
- Search publications online by topic or keyword.
- Sign up to receive local and national tax news by email.

CD-ROM. Order Pub. 1796, IRS Federal Tax Products CD-ROM, and get:
- Current year forms, instructions, and publications.
- Prior year forms, instructions, and publications.
- Frequently requested tax forms that may be filled in electronically, printed out for submission, and saved for recordkeeping.
- The Internal Revenue Bulletin.

Buy the CD-ROM on the Internet at *www.irs.gov/cdorders* from the National Technical Information Service (NTIS) for $25 (no handling fee) or call 1-877-CDFORMS (1-877-233-6767) toll free to buy the CD-ROM for $25 (plus a $5 handling fee).

By phone and in person. You can order forms and publications 24 hours a day, 7 days a week, by calling 1-800-TAX-FORM (1-800-829-3676). You can pick up some of the most requested forms and publications at many IRS offices, post offices, and libraries.

Backup Withholding

Interest, dividends, rents, royalties, commissions, nonemployee compensation, and certain other payments (including broker and barter exchange transactions, reportable gross proceeds paid to attorneys, and certain payments made by fishing boat operators) may be subject to backup withholding at a 28% rate. To be subject to backup withholding, a payment must be a reportable interest or dividend payment under section 6049(a), 6042(a), or 6044 (if the patronage dividend is paid in money or qualified check), or an "other" reportable payment under section 6041, 6041A(a), 6045, 6050A, or 6050N. If the payment is one of these reportable payments, backup withholding will apply if:

1. The payee fails to furnish his or her taxpayer identification number (TIN) to you,
2. For interest, dividend, and broker and barter exchange accounts opened or instruments acquired after 1983, the payee fails to certify, under penalties of perjury, that the TIN provided is correct,
3. The IRS notifies you to impose backup withholding because the payee furnished an incorrect TIN ("B" notice),
4. For interest and dividend accounts or instruments, you are notified that the payee is subject to backup withholding (under section 3406(a)(1)(C), "C" notice), or
5. For interest and dividend accounts opened or instruments acquired after 1983, the payee fails to certify to you, under penalties of perjury, that he or she is not subject to backup withholding under 4 above.

Except as explained in 2 above, reportable "other" payments are subject to backup withholding only if 1 or 3 above applies.

Some payees are exempt from backup withholding. For a list of exempt payees and other information, see Form W-9, Request for Taxpayer Identification Number and Certification, and the separate Instructions for the Requester of Form W-9.

Examples of payments to which backup withholding does not apply include but are not limited to:
- Wages.
- Distributions from a pension, annuity, profit-sharing or stock bonus plan, any IRA, an owner-employee plan, or other deferred compensation plan.
- Distributions from a medical or health savings account and long-term care benefits.
- Certain surrenders of life insurance contracts.
- Distribution from qualified tuition programs or Coverdell ESAs.
- Gambling winnings if regular gambling winnings withholding is required under section 3402(q). However, if regular gambling winnings withholding is not required under section 3402(q), backup withholding applies if the payee fails to furnish a TIN.
- Real estate transactions reportable under section 6045(e).
- Cancelled debts reportable under section 6050P.
- Fish purchases for cash reportable under section 6050R.
- Certain payment card transactions if the payment is made on or after January 1, 2005, by a qualified payment card agent (as described in Rev. Proc. 2004-42 and Regulations section 31.3406(g)-1(f) and if the requirements under Regulations section 31.3406(g)-1(f) are met. Rev. Proc. 2004-42 is available on page 121 of Internal Revenue Bulletin 2004-31 at *www.irs.gov/pub/irs-irbs/irb04-31*.

When to apply backup withholding. Generally, the period for which the 28% should be withheld is as follows:

1. Failure to furnish TIN in the manner required. Withhold on payments made until the TIN is furnished in the manner required. Special backup withholding rules may apply if the payee has applied for a TIN. The payee may certify to this on Form W-9 by noting "Applied For" in the TIN block and by signing the form. This form then becomes an "awaiting-TIN" certificate, and the payee has 60 days to obtain a TIN and furnish it to you. If you do not receive a TIN from the payee within 60 days and you have not already begun backup withholding, begin backup withholding and continue until the TIN is provided.

GEN-3

The 60-day exemption from backup withholding applies only to interest and dividend payments and certain payments made with respect to readily tradable instruments. Therefore, any other payment, such as nonemployee compensation, is subject to backup withholding even if the payee has applied for and is awaiting a TIN. For information about whether backup withholding applies during the 60-day period, see Regulations section 31.3406(g)-3.

2. Notice from the IRS that payee's TIN is incorrect ("B" notice). You may choose to withhold on any reportable payment made to the account(s) subject to backup withholding after receipt of the "B" notice, but you must withhold on any reportable payment made to the account more than 30 business days after you received the "B" notice. Stop withholding within 30 days after you receive a certified Form W-9 (or other form that requires the payee to certify under penalty of perjury).

 The IRS will furnish a notice to you, and you are required to promptly furnish a copy of such notice, or an acceptable substitute, to the payee. For further information, see Regulations section 31.3406(d)-5 and Rev. Proc. 93-37, 1993-2 C.B. 477.

If you receive two incorrect TIN notices within 3 years for the same account, follow the procedures in Regulations section 31.3406(d)-5(g) and Rev. Proc. 93-37.

3. Notice from the IRS that payee is subject to backup withholding due to notified payee underreporting ("C" notice). You may choose to withhold on any reportable payment made to the account(s) subject to backup withholding after receipt of the "C" notice, but you must withhold on any reportable payment made to the account more than 30 business days after you receive the "C" notice. The IRS will notify you in writing when to stop withholding, or the payee may furnish you a written certification from the IRS stating when the withholding should stop. In most cases, the stop date will be January 1 of the year following the year of the notice.

 You must notify the payee when withholding under this procedure starts. For further information, see Regulations section 31.3406(c)-1(d).

4. Payee failure to certify that he or she is not subject to backup withholding. Withhold on reportable interest and dividends until the certification has been received.

For exceptions to these general timing rules, see section 3406(e).

 For special rules on backup withholding on gambling winnings, see the separate Instructions for Forms W-2G and 5754.

Reporting backup withholding. Report backup withholding on Form 945. For more information, see the Instructions for Form 945. Also, report backup withholding and the amount of the payment on Forms W-2G, 1099-B, DIV, G, INT, MISC, OID, or PATR even if the amount of the payment is less than the amount for which an information return is normally required.

Additional information. For more information about backup withholding, see Pub. 1679, A Guide to Backup Withholding for Missing and Incorrect Name/TIN(s), and Pub. 1281, Backup Withholding for Missing and Incorrect Name/TIN(s) (Including Instructions for Reading Tape Cartridges).

Penalties

The following penalties generally apply to the person required to file information returns. The penalties apply to paper filers as well as to electronic/magnetic media filers.

Failure To File Correct Information Returns by the Due Date (Section 6721)

If you fail to file a correct information return by the due date and you cannot show reasonable cause, you may be subject to a penalty. The penalty applies if you fail to file timely, you fail to include all information required to be shown on a return, or you include incorrect information on a return. The penalty also applies if you file on paper when you were required to file on

magnetic media, you report an incorrect TIN or fail to report a TIN, or you fail to file paper forms that are machine readable.

The amount of the penalty is based on when you file the correct information return. The penalty is:
• $15 per information return if you correctly file within 30 days (by March 30 if the due date is February 28); maximum penalty $75,000 per year ($25,000 for small businesses, defined below).
• $30 per information return if you correctly file more than 30 days after the due date but by August 1; maximum penalty $150,000 per year ($50,000 for small businesses).
• $50 per information return if you file after August 1 or you do not file required information returns; maximum penalty $250,000 per year ($100,000 for small businesses).

 If you do not file corrections and you do not meet any of the exceptions to the penalty described below, the penalty is $50 per information return.

Small businesses—lower maximum penalties. You are a small business if your average annual gross receipts for the 3 most recent tax years (or for the period you were in existence, if shorter) ending before the calendar year in which the information returns were due are $5 million or less.

Exceptions to the penalty. The following are exceptions to the failure to file penalty:

1. The penalty will not apply to any failure that you can show was due to reasonable cause and not to willful neglect. In general, you must be able to show that your failure was due to an event beyond your control or due to significant mitigating factors. You must also be able to show that you acted in a responsible manner and took steps to avoid the failure.

2. An inconsequential error or omission is not considered a failure to include correct information. An inconsequential error or omission does not prevent or hinder the IRS from processing the return, from correlating the information required to be shown on the return with the information shown on the payee's tax return, or from otherwise putting the return to its intended use. Errors and omissions that are never inconsequential are those related to (a) a TIN, (b) a payee's surname, and (c) any money amount.

3. De minimis rule for corrections. Even though you cannot show reasonable cause, the penalty for failure to file correct information returns will not apply to a certain number of returns if you:

    a. Filed those information returns,
    b. Either failed to include all the information required on a return or included incorrect information, and
    c. Filed corrections by August 1.

If you meet all the conditions in a, b, and c above, the penalty for filing incorrect returns (but not for filing late) will not apply to the greater of 10 information returns or ½ of 1% of the total number of information returns you are required to file for the calendar year.

Intentional disregard of filing requirements. If any failure to file a correct information return is due to intentional disregard of the filing or correct information requirements, the penalty is at least $100 per information return with no maximum penalty.

Failure To Furnish Correct Payee Statements (Section 6722)

If you fail to provide correct payee statements and you cannot show reasonable cause, you may be subject to a penalty. The penalty applies if you fail to provide the statement by January 31 (see part H on page GEN-9), you fail to include all information required to be shown on the statement, or you include incorrect information on the statement. "Payee statement" has the same meaning as "statement to recipient" as used in part H on page GEN-9.

The penalty is $50 per statement, no matter when the correct statement is furnished, with a maximum of $100,000 per year. The penalty is not reduced for furnishing a correct statement by August 1.

Exception. An inconsequential error or omission is not considered a failure to include correct information. An inconsequential error or omission cannot reasonably be expected to prevent or hinder the payee from timely receiving correct information and reporting it on his or her income tax return or from otherwise putting the statement to its intended use. Errors and omissions that are never inconsequential are those relating to (a) a dollar amount, (b) a significant item in a payee's address, (c) the appropriate form for the information provided (that is, whether the form is an acceptable substitute for the official IRS form), and (d) whether the statement was furnished in person or by "statement mailing," when required.

Intentional disregard of payee statement requirements. If any failure to provide a correct payee statement is due to intentional disregard of the requirements to furnish a correct payee statement, the penalty is at least $100 per payee statement with no maximum penalty.

Forms 1099-Q, 1099-SA, 5498, 5498-ESA, and 5498-SA

The penalties under sections 6721 and 6722 do not apply to:

Forms	Filed Under Code Section
1099-SA and 5498-SA	220(h) and 223(h)
5498	408(i) and 408(l)
5498-ESA	530(h)
1099-Q	529(d) and 530(h)

The penalty for failure to timely file Forms 1099-SA, 5498-SA, 5498, 5498-ESA, or 1099-Q is $50 per return with no maximum, unless the failure is due to reasonable cause. See section 6693.

Fraudulent Acknowledgments With Respect to Donations of Motor Vehicles, Boats, and Airplanes (Section 6720)

If you are required under section 170(f)(12)(A) to furnish a contemporaneous written acknowledgment to a donor and you knowingly furnish a false or fraudulent Form 1098-C, or knowingly fail to furnish a Form 1098-C within the applicable 30-day period, you may be subject to a penalty. See the 2005 Instructions for Form 1098-C for more detailed information.

Civil Damages for Fraudulent Filing of Information Returns

If you willfully file a fraudulent information return for payments you claim you made to another person, that person may be able to sue you for damages. You may have to pay $5,000 or more.

Electronic/Magnetic Media Reporting

Magnetic media reporting may be required for filing all information returns discussed in this publication (see *Who must file on magnetic media* below). Acceptable forms of magnetic media are IBM 3480, 3490, 3490E, 3590, or 3590E tape cartridges; and 3½-inch diskettes.

 For returns filed after December 31, 2006, Enterprise Computing Center—Martinsburg (ECC-MTB) will no longer accept 3½-inch diskettes for filing information returns.

Pub. 1220, Specifications for Filing Forms 1098, 1099, 5498, and W-2G Electronically or Magnetically, is the revenue procedure for reporting electronically or magnetically. Pub. 1220 is available as Revenue Procedure 2005-49 on page 165 of Internal Revenue Bulletin 2005-31 at *www.gov/pub/irs-irbs/ irb05-31*. Different types of payments, such as interest, dividends, and rents, may be reported on the same tape or other submission.

You can file electronically through the Filing Information Returns Electronically System (FIRE System); however, you must have the software that can produce a file in the proper format according to Pub. 1220. The FIRE system does not provide a fill-in form option. The FIRE system operates 24 hours a day, 7 days a week. You may access the FIRE System via the Internet at *http://FIRE.IRS.gov*. See Pub. 1220 for more information.

Due dates. File Forms 1098, 1099, or W-2G on magnetic media by February 28, 2006. If you file electronically, you may file by March 31, 2006. File Form 5498, 5498-ESA, or 5498-SA by May 31, 2006. See part H on page GEN-9 about providing Forms 1098, 1099, 5498, and W-2G or statements to recipients.

Extension of time to file. For information about requesting an extension of time to file, see *Extension* on page GEN-7.

 If you file electronically or on magnetic media, do not file the same returns on paper.

Who must file on magnetic media. If you are required to file 250 or more information returns, you must file on magnetic media. The 250-or-more requirement applies separately to each type of form. For example, if you must file 500 Forms 1098 and 100 Forms 1099-A, you must file Forms 1098 on magnetic media, but you are not required to file Forms 1099-A on magnetic media.

The magnetic media filing requirement does not apply if you apply for and receive a hardship waiver. See *How to request a waiver from filing on magnetic media* below.

 The IRS encourages you to file on magnetic media or electronically even though you are filing fewer than 250 returns.

Filing requirement applies separately to originals and corrections. The magnetic media filing requirements apply separately to original returns and corrected returns. Originals and corrections are not aggregated to determine whether you are required to file on magnetic media. For example, if you file 400 Forms 1098 on magnetic media and you are making 75 corrections, your corrections can be filed on paper because the number of corrections for Form 1098 is less than the 250 filing requirement. However, if you were filing 250 or more Form 1098 corrections, they would have to be filed on magnetic media.

Reporting incorrect payer name and/or TIN. If a payer discovers an error in reporting the payer name and/or TIN, write a letter to IRS/ECC—MTB (see below) containing the following information:

1. Name and address of the payer,
2. Type of error (including the incorrect payer name/TIN that was reported),
3. Tax year,
4. Payer TIN,
5. Transmitter Control Code (TCC), if applicable,
6. Type of return,
7. Number of payees, and
8. Filing method (paper, electronic, or magnetic media).

Send the letter to Enterprise Computing Center—Martinsburg, Information Reporting Program, 240 Murall Drive, Kearneysville, WV 25430. Also see Pub. 1220, Part A, Section 11.

If a payer realizes duplicate reporting or a large percentage of incorrect information has been filed, contact the information reporting customer service site at 1-866-455-7438 for further instructions.

How to get approval to file on magnetic media. File Form 4419, Application for Filing Information Returns Electronically/ Magnetically, at least 30 days before the due date of the returns. File only one Form 4419 for all types of returns that will be filed on magnetic media. Once you have received approval, you need not reapply each year. The IRS will provide a written reply to the applicant and further instructions at the time of approval, usually within 30 days. A magnetic media reporting package, which includes all the necessary transmittals and instructions, will be mailed to all approved filers.

How to request a waiver from filing on magnetic media. To receive a waiver from the required filing of information returns on magnetic media, submit Form 8508, Request for Waiver From Filing Information Returns Magnetically, at least 45 days before the due date of the returns. You cannot apply for a waiver for more than 1 tax year at a time. If you need a waiver for more than 1 tax year, you must reapply at the appropriate time each year.

If a waiver for original returns is approved, any corrections for the same types of returns will be covered under the waiver. However, if you submit original returns on magnetic media but you want to submit your corrections on paper, a waiver must be approved for the corrections if you must file 250 or more corrections.

If you receive an approved waiver, do not send a copy of it to the service center where you file your paper returns. Keep the waiver for your records only.

Single application. Submit both Forms 4419 and 8508 to apply for approval for filing returns on magnetic media, and if the approval is not granted, to apply for a waiver from the magnetic media requirement.

Penalty. If you are required to file on magnetic media but fail to do so, and you do not have an approved waiver, you may be subject to a penalty of $50 per return for failure to file on magnetic media unless you establish reasonable cause. However, you can file up to 250 returns on paper; those returns will not be subject to a penalty for failure to file on magnetic media.

The penalty applies separately to original returns and corrected returns. See *Filing requirement applies separately to originals and corrections* on page GEN-5.

Paper Document Reporting

If you are required to file 250 or more information returns, see *Electronic/Magnetic Media Reporting* on page GEN-5.

Common errors. Be sure to check your returns to prevent the following common errors:

1. Duplicate filing. Do not send the same information to the IRS more than once. Also see *Multiple filings* below.
2. Filer's name, address, and TIN are not the same on Form 1096 and the attached Forms 1099, 1098, 5498, or W-2G.
3. Decimal point to show dollars and cents omitted. For example, 1230.00 is correct, not 1230.
4. Two or more types of returns submitted with one Form 1096 (for example, Forms 1099-INT and 1099-MISC with one Form 1096). You must submit a separate Form 1096 with each type of return.

Multiple filings. If, after you file Forms 1099, 1098, 5498, or W-2G, you discover additional forms that are required to be filed, file these forms with a new Form 1096. Do not include copies or information from previously filed returns.

Required format. Because paper forms are scanned, all Forms 1096 and Copies A of Forms 1098, 1099, and 5498 must be prepared in accordance with the following instructions. If these instructions are not followed, you may be subject to a penalty of $50 for each incorrectly filed document.

1. Do not cut or separate Copies A of the forms that are printed two or three to a sheet (except Form W-2G). Forms 1098, 1099, and 5498 are printed two or three to an 8 x 11 inch sheet. Form 1096 is printed one to an 8 x 11 inch sheet. These forms must be submitted to the IRS on the 8 x 11 inch sheet. If at least one form on the page is correctly completed, you must submit the entire page. Forms W-2G may be separated and submitted as single forms. Send the forms to the IRS in a flat mailing (not folded).
2. No photocopies of any forms are acceptable. See *How To Get Forms and Publications* on page GEN-3.
3. Do not staple, tear, or tape any of these forms. It will interfere with the IRS's ability to scan the documents.
4. Pinfeed holes on the form are not acceptable. Pinfeed strips outside the 8 x 11 inch area must be removed before submission, without tearing or ripping the form. Substitute forms prepared in continuous or strip form must be burst and stripped to conform to the size specified for a single sheet (8 x 11 inches) before they are filed with the IRS.
5. Do not change the title of any box on any form. Do not use a form to report information that is not properly reportable

on that form. If you are unsure of where to report the data, call the information reporting call site at 866-455-7438 (toll free).

6. Report information only in the appropriate boxes provided on the forms. Make only one entry in each box unless otherwise indicated in the form's specific instructions.
7. Do not submit any copy other than Copy A to the IRS.
8. Do not use prior year forms unless you are reporting prior year information; do not use subsequent year forms for the current year. Because forms are scanned, you must use the current year form to report current year information.
9. Use the official forms or substitute forms that meet the specifications in Pub. 1179. If you submit substitute forms that do not meet the current specifications and that are not scannable, you may be subject to a penalty of $50 for each return for improper format.
10. Do not use dollar signs ($) (they are preprinted on the forms), ampersands (&), asterisks (*), commas (,), or other special characters in money amount boxes.
11. Do not use apostrophes ('), asterisks (*), or other special characters on the payee name line.

Suggested format. Below are suggestions that will allow the IRS to process the submitted forms in the most economical manner:

1. Although handwritten forms are acceptable, the IRS prefers that you type or machine print data entries using 10 pitch (pica) or 12 pitch (elite) black type. Use block print, not script characters. Insert data in the middle of the blocks well separated from other printing and guidelines, and take other measures to guarantee a dark black, clear, sharp image.
2. Do not enter 0 (zero) or "None" in money amount boxes when no entry is required. Leave the boxes blank unless the instructions specifically require that you enter a 0 (zero). For example, in some cases, you must enter 0 (zero) to make corrections. See *Corrected Returns on Paper Forms* on page GEN-11.
3. Do not enter number signs (#); for example, enter RT 2, not Rt. #2.

A. Who Must File

See the separate specific instructions for each form.

Nominee/middleman returns. Generally, if you receive a Form 1099 for amounts that actually belong to another person, you are considered a nominee recipient. You must file a Form 1099 with the IRS (the same type of Form 1099 you received) for each of the other owners showing the amounts allocable to each. You must also furnish a Form 1099 to each of the other owners. File the new Form 1099 with Form 1096 with the Internal Revenue Service Center for your area. On each new Form 1099, list yourself as the "payer" and the other owner as the "recipient." On Form 1096, list yourself as the "filer." A husband or wife is not required to file a nominee return to show amounts owned by the other. The nominee, not the original payer, is responsible for filing the subsequent Forms 1099 to show the amount allocable to each owner.

Successor/predecessor reporting. A successor business (a corporation, partnership, or sole proprietorship) and a predecessor business (a corporation, partnership, or sole proprietorship) may agree that the successor will assume all or some of the predecessor's information reporting responsibilities. This would permit the successor to file one Form 1099, 1098, 5498, or W-2G for each recipient combining the predecessor's and successor's reportable amounts, including any withholding. If they so agree and the successor satisfies the predecessor's obligations and the conditions described on page GEN-7, the predecessor does not have to file the specified information returns for the acquisition year. If the successor and predecessor do not agree, or if the requirements described are not met, the predecessor and the successor each must file Forms 1099, 1098, 5498, and W-2G for their own reportable amounts as they usually would. For more information and the rules that apply to filing combined Forms 1042-S, see Rev. Proc. 99-50, which is available on page 757 of Internal Revenue Bulletin 1999-52 at *www.irs.gov/pub/irs-irbs/irb99-52.*

GEN-6

The combined reporting procedure is available when all the following conditions are met:

1. The successor acquires from the predecessor substantially all the property (a) used in the trade or business of the predecessor, including when one or more corporations are absorbed by another corporation under a merger agreement, or (b) used in a separate unit of a trade or business of the predecessor.

2. The predecessor is required to report amounts, including any withholding, on information returns for the year of acquisition for the period before the acquisition.

3. The predecessor is not required to report amounts, including withholding, on information returns for the year of acquisition for the period after the acquisition.

Combined reporting agreement. The predecessor and the successor must agree on the specific forms to which the combined reporting procedure applies and that the successor assumes the predecessor's entire information reporting obligations for these forms. The predecessor and successor may agree to:

1. Use the combined reporting procedure for all Forms 1099, 1098, 5498, and W-2G, or

2. Limit the use of the combined reporting procedure to (a) specific forms or (b) specific reporting entities, including any unit, branch, or location within a particular business entity that files its own separate information returns. For example, if the predecessor's and successor's only compatible computer or recordkeeping systems are their dividends paid ledgers, they may agree to use the combined reporting procedure for Forms 1099-DIV only. Similarly, if the only compatible systems are in their midwest branches, they may agree to use the combined reporting procedure for only the midwest branches.

Combined reporting procedure. On each Form 1099, 1098, 5498, and W-2G filed by the successor, the successor must combine the predecessor's (before the acquisition) and successor's reportable amounts, including any withholding, for the acquisition year and report the aggregate. For transactional reporting on Form 1099-B, Proceeds From Broker and Barter Exchange Transactions, the successor must report each of the predecessor's transactions and each of its own transactions on each Form 1099-B. The successor may include with the form sent to the recipient additional information explaining the combined reporting.

For purposes of the combined reporting procedure, the sharing of TINs and other information obtained under section 3406 for information reporting and backup withholding purposes does not violate the confidentiality rules in section 3406(f).

Statement required. The successor must file a statement with the IRS indicating the forms that are being filed on a combined basis under Rev. Proc. 99-50. The statement must:

1. Include the predecessor's and successor's names, addresses, telephone numbers, EINs, and the name and telephone number of the person responsible for preparing the statement.

2. Reflect separately the amount of federal income tax withheld by the predecessor and by the successor for each type of form being filed on a combined basis (for example, Form 1099-R or 1099-MISC).

3. Be sent separately from Forms 1099, 1098, 5498, and W-2G by the forms' due date to: Enterprise Computing Center—Martinsburg, Attn: Chief, Information Returns Branch, Mail Stop 360, 230 Murall Dr., Kearneysville, WV 25430. Do not send Form 1042-S statements to this address. Instead, use the address given in the Instructions for Form 1042-S; see Rev. Proc. 99-50.

Qualified settlement funds. A qualified settlement fund must file information returns for distributions to claimants if any transferor to the fund would have been required to file if the transferor had made the distributions directly to the claimants.

For distributions to transferors, a fund is subject to the information reporting requirements of sections 6041 and 6041A and may be required to file Form 1099-MISC. For payments made by the fund on behalf of a claimant or transferor, the fund

is subject to these same rules and may have to file Form 1099-MISC for the payment to a third party. For information reporting purposes, a payment made by the fund on behalf of a claimant or transferor is considered a distribution to the claimant or transferor and is also subject to information reporting requirements.

The same filing requirements, exceptions, and thresholds apply to qualified settlement funds as apply to any other payer. That is, the fund must determine the character of the payment (for example, interest, fixed and determinable income, or gross proceeds from broker transactions) and to whom the payment is made (for example, corporation or individual).

For more information, see Regulations section 1.468B-2(l). In addition, see Proposed Regulations sections 1.468B-1(k) and 1.468B-6 through 1.468B-9 that relate to escrow and other similar funds.

Payments to foreign persons. See the Instructions for Form 1042-S, relating to U.S. source income of foreign persons, for reporting requirements relating to payments to foreign persons.

B. When To File

File Forms 1098, 1099, or W-2G on paper or magnetic media by February 28, 2006 (March 31, 2006, if filing electronically). Also file Form 1096 with paper forms. Brokers may file Forms 1096 and 1099-B anytime after the reporting period they elect to adopt (month, quarter, or year), but not later than the due date. File Form 1096 with Forms 5498, 5498-ESA, and 5498-SA by May 31, 2006.

You will meet the requirement to file if the form is properly addressed and mailed on or before the due date. If the regular due date falls on a Saturday, Sunday, or legal holiday, file by the next business day. A business day is any day that is not a Saturday, Sunday, or legal holiday. See part H on page GEN-9 about providing Forms 1098, 1099, 5498, and W-2G or statements to recipients.

Private delivery services. You can use certain private delivery services designated by the IRS to meet the "timely mailing as timely filing" rule for information returns. The list includes only the following:

• DHL Worldwide Express (DHL): DHL "Same Day" Service; DHL Next Day 10:30 AM; DHL Next Day 12:00 PM; DHL Next Day 3:00 PM; and DHL 2nd Day Service.

• Federal Express (FedEx): FedEx Priority Overnight, FedEx Standard Overnight, FedEx 2 Day, FedEx International Priority, and FedEx International First.

• United Parcel Service (UPS): UPS Next Day Air, UPS Next Day Air Saver, UPS 2nd Day Air, UPS 2nd Day Air A.M., UPS Worldwide Express Plus, and UPS Worldwide Express.

The private delivery service can tell you how to get written proof of the mailing date.

 Private delivery services cannot deliver items to P.O. boxes. You must use the U.S. Postal Service to mail any item to an IRS P.O. box address.

Reporting period. Forms 1098, 1099, and W-2G are used to report amounts received, paid, credited, canceled in the case of Form 1099-C, or contributions in the case of Form 1098-C, during the calendar year. Forms 5498, 5498-ESA, and 5498-SA are used to report amounts contributed and the fair market value of an account for the calendar year.

Extension. For paper or electronic/magnetic media filing, you can get a 30-day extension of time to file by sending Form 8809, Application for Extension of Time To File Information Returns, to the address shown on Form 8809. No signature or explanation is required for the extension. However, you must file Form 8809 by the due date of the returns in order to get the 30-day extension. Under certain hardship conditions you may apply for an additional 30-day extension. See Form 8809 for more information.

 If you are requesting extensions of time to file for more than 50 payers, you must submit the extension requests magnetically or electronically. See Pub. 1220.

GEN-7

For information on extensions for providing statements to recipients, see *Extension* on page GEN-11.

C. Where To File

Except for Form 1098-C, send all information returns filed on paper to the following:

If your principal business, office or agency, or legal residence in the case of an individual, is located in ▼	Use the following Internal Revenue Service Center address ▼
Alabama, Arizona, Florida, Georgia, Louisiana, Mississippi, New Mexico, North Carolina, Texas, Virginia	Austin, TX 73301
Arkansas, Connecticut, Delaware, Kentucky, Maine, Massachusetts, New Hampshire, New Jersey, New York, Ohio, Pennsylvania, Rhode Island, Vermont, West Virginia	Cincinnati, OH 45999
Illinois, Indiana, Iowa, Kansas, Michigan, Minnesota, Missouri, Nebraska, North Dakota, Oklahoma, South Carolina, South Dakota, Tennessee, Wisconsin	Kansas City, MO 64999
Alaska, California, Colorado, District of Columbia, Hawaii, Idaho, Maryland, Montana, Nevada, Oregon, Utah, Washington, Wyoming	Ogden, UT 84201

If your legal residence or principal place of business or principal office or agency is outside the United States, file with the Internal Revenue Service Center, Philadelphia, PA 19255.

Form 1098-C. Send all Forms 1098-C filed on paper to the Internal Revenue Service Center, Ogden, UT 84201-0027.

Returns filed magnetically. Send all information returns filed magnetically to Enterprise Computing Center—Martinsburg, Information Reporting Program, 230 Murall Drive, Kearneysville, WV 25430.

State and local tax departments. Contact the applicable state and local tax department as necessary for reporting requirements and where to file Copy 1 (Forms 1099-MISC and 1099-R). Generally, the state or local tax department you need to contact will be located in the recipient's state of legal residence.

D. Filing Returns With the IRS

The IRS strongly encourages the quality review of data before filing to prevent erroneous notices being mailed to payees (or others for whom information is being reported).

If you must file any Form 1098, 1099, 5498, or W-2G with the IRS and you are filing paper forms, you must send a Form 1096 with each type of form as the transmittal document. You must group the forms by form number and submit each group with a separate Form 1096. For example, if you file Forms 1098, 1099-A, and 1099-MISC, complete one Form 1096 to transmit Forms 1098, another for Forms 1099-A, and a third for Forms 1099-MISC. Specific instructions for completing Form 1096 are included on the form. Also, see *Transmitters, paying agents, etc.* below. For information about filing corrected returns, see *Corrected Returns on Paper Forms* on page GEN-11.

If you are filing on magnetic media, Form 4804, Transmittal of Information Returns Reported Magnetically, must accompany your submissions.

 Form 4804 is no longer required if you file information returns electronically. See Electronic/Magnetic Media Reporting *on page GEN-5.*

For information on the preparation of transmittal documents for magnetic media and paper document reporting (Forms 4804 and 1096), see Rev. Proc. 84-24, 1984-1 C.B. 465.

Report payments on the appropriate form, as explained in the separate specific instructions.

See Pub. 1179 for specifications for private printing of substitute information returns. You may not request special consideration. Only forms that conform with the official form and the specifications in Pub. 1179 are acceptable for filing with the IRS.

Transmitters, paying agents, etc. A transmitter, service bureau, paying agent, or disbursing agent (hereafter referred to as "agent") may sign Form 1096 or Form 4804 on behalf of any person required to file (hereafter referred to as "payer") if the conditions in 1 and 2 below are met:

1. The agent has the authority to sign the form under an agency agreement (oral, written, or implied) that is valid under state law and

2. The agent signs the form and adds the caption "For: (Name of payer)."

Signing of the form by an authorized agent on behalf of the payer does not relieve the payer of the liability for penalties for not filing a correct, complete, and timely Form 1096 or Form 4804 and accompanying returns.

Forms 1098, 1099, 5498, W-2G, or acceptable substitute statements to recipients issued by a service bureau or agent should show the same payer's name as shown on the information returns filed with the IRS.

For information about the election to report and deposit backup withholding under the agent's TIN and how to prepare forms if the election is made, see Rev. Proc. 84-33, 1984-1 C.B. 502.

Keeping copies. Generally, keep copies of information returns you filed with the IRS or have the ability to reconstruct the data for at least 3 years, 4 years for Form 1099-C, from the due date of the returns. Keep copies of information returns for 4 years if backup withholding was imposed.

E. Shipping and Mailing

Send the forms to the IRS in a flat mailing (not folded). If you are sending many forms, you may send them in conveniently sized packages. On each package, write your name, number the packages consecutively, and place Form 1096 in package number one. Postal regulations require forms and packages to be sent by First-Class Mail.

F. Recipient Names and Taxpayer Identification Numbers (TINs)

Recipient name. Show the full name and address in the section provided on the information return. If payments have been made to more than one recipient or the account is in more than one name, show on the first name line the name of the recipient whose TIN is first shown on the return. You may show the names of any other individual recipients in the area below the first line, if desired. Form W-2G filers, see the Instructions for Forms W-2G and 5754.

Sole proprietors. You must show the individual's name on the first name line; on the second name line, you may enter the "doing business as (DBA)" name. You may not enter only the DBA name. For the TIN, enter either the individual's SSN or the EIN of the business (sole proprietorship). The IRS prefers that you enter the SSN.

Limited liability company (LLC). Single-member LLC (including a foreign LLC with a U.S. owner) that is disregarded as an entity separate from its owner under Regulations section 301.7701-3, enter the individual's name only on the first name line and the LLC's name on the second name line. For the TIN, enter the individual's SSN (or EIN, if applicable). If the LLC is a corporation, partnership, etc., enter the entity's EIN.

GEN-8

TINs. TINs are used to associate and verify amounts you report to the IRS with corresponding amounts on tax returns. Therefore, it is important that you furnish correct names, social security numbers (SSNs), individual taxpayer identification numbers (ITINs), or employer identification numbers (EINs) for recipients on the forms sent to the IRS.

Requesting a recipient's TIN. If the recipient is a U.S. person (including a U.S. resident alien), the IRS suggests that you request the recipient complete Form W-9 (or Form W-9S, if appropriate). See the Instructions for the Requester of Form W-9 for more information on how to request a TIN.

If the recipient is a foreign person, the IRS suggests that you request the recipient complete the appropriate Form W-8. See the Instructions for the Requester of Forms W-8BEN, W-8ECI, W-8EXP, and W-8IMY.

 U.S. resident aliens who rely on a "saving clause" of a tax treaty are to complete Form W-9, not Form W-8BEN. See Pub. 515, Withholding of Tax on Nonresident Aliens and Foreign Entities, and Pub. 519.

You may be subject to a penalty for an incorrect or missing TIN on an information return. See *Penalties* on page GEN-4. You are required to maintain the confidentiality of information obtained on a Form W-9/W-9S relating to the taxpayer's identity (including SSNs, EINs, and ITINs), and you may use such information only to comply with the tax laws.

 If the recipient does not provide a TIN, leave the box for the recipient's TIN blank on the Form 1098, 1099, 5498, or W-2G. See Backup Withholding on page GEN-3. Only one recipient TIN can be entered on the form.

The TIN for individual recipients of information returns is the SSN. See the information about sole proprietors on page GEN-8. For other recipients, including corporations, partnerships, and estates, the TIN is the EIN. For LLCs, see the information on LLC on page GEN-8.

SSNs have nine digits separated by two hyphens (000-00-0000), and EINs have nine digits separated by only one hyphen (00-0000000).

Electronic submission of Forms W-9. Requesters may establish a system for payees and payees' agents to submit Forms W-9 electronically, including by fax. A requester is anyone required to file an information return. A payee is anyone required to provide a TIN to the requester.

Payee's agent. A payee's agent can be an investment advisor (corporation, partnership, or individual) or an introducing broker. An investment advisor must be registered with the Securities Exchange Commission (SEC) under The Investment Advisers Act of 1940. The introducing broker is a broker-dealer that is regulated by the SEC and the National Association of Securities Dealers, Inc., and that is not a payer. Except for a broker who acts as a payee's agent for "readily tradable instruments," the advisor or broker must show in writing to the payer that the payee authorized the advisor or broker to transmit the Form W-9 to the payer.

Generally, the electronic system must:

1. Ensure the information received is the information sent and document all occasions of user access that result in the submission.
2. Make reasonably certain the person accessing the system and submitting the form is the person identified on Form W-9.
3. Provide the same information as the paper Form W-9.
4. Be able to supply a hard copy of the electronic Form W-9 if the IRS requests it.
5. Require as the final entry in the submission an electronic signature by the payee whose name is on Form W-9 that authenticates and verifies the submission. The electronic signature must be under penalties of perjury and the perjury statement must contain the language of the paper Form W-9.

 For Forms W-9 that are not required to be signed, the electronic system need not provide for an electronic signature or a perjury statement.

Additional requirements may apply. See Announcement 98-27 that is available on page 30 of Internal Revenue Bulletin 1998-15 at *www.irs.gov/pub/irs-irbs/irb98-15*; and Announcement 2001-91, that is available on page 221 of Internal Revenue Bulletin 2001-36 at *www.irs.gov/pub/irs-irbs/irb01-36*.

Electronic submission of Forms W-9S. See the Instructions for Forms 1098-E and 1098-T.

G. Filer's Name, Identification Number, and Address

The TIN for filers of information returns, including sole proprietors and nominees/middlemen, is the federal EIN. However, sole proprietors and nominees/middlemen who are not otherwise required to have an EIN should use their SSNs. A sole proprietor is not required to have an EIN unless he or she has a Keogh plan or must file excise or employment tax returns. See Pub. 583, Starting a Business and Keeping Records.

The filer's name and TIN should be consistent with the name and TIN used on the filer's other tax returns. The name of the filer's paying agent or service bureau must not be used in place of the name of the filer.

If you do not have an EIN, you may apply for one online. Go to the IRS website *www.irs.gov/businesses/small* and click on the link for EINs. You may also apply by calling 1-800-829-4933 or by faxing or mailing Form SS-4 to the IRS. See Form SS-4 for more information.

Enter your street address including the room, suite, or other unit number on the forms.

H. Statements to Recipients (Borrowers, Debtors, Donors, Insureds, Participants, Payers/Borrowers, Policyholders, Students, Transferors, or Winners on Certain Forms)

If you are required to file Forms 1099, 1098, 5498, or W-2G, you must also furnish statements to recipients containing the information furnished to the IRS and, in some cases, additional information. Be sure that the statements you provide to recipients are clear and legible.

Substitute statements. If you are not using the official IRS form to furnish statements to recipients, see Pub. 1179 for specific rules about providing "substitute" statements to recipients. Generally, a substitute is any statement other than Copy B (and C in some cases) of the official form. You may develop them yourself or buy them from a private printer. However, the substitutes must comply with the format and content requirements specified in Pub. 1179.

Telephone number. You are required to include the telephone number of a person to contact on the following statements to recipients: W-2G, 1098, 1098-C, 1098-E, 1098-T, 1099-A, 1099-B, 1099-CAP, 1099-DIV, 1099-G (excluding state and local income tax refunds), 1099-H, 1099-INT, 1099-LTC, 1099-MISC (excluding fishing boat proceeds), 1099-OID, 1099-PATR, 1099-Q, and 1099-S. You may include the telephone number in any conspicuous place on the statements. This number must provide direct access to an individual who can answer questions about the statement. Although not required, if you report on other Forms 1099 and 5498, you are encouraged to furnish telephone numbers.

Rules for furnishing statements. Different rules apply to furnishing statements to recipients depending on the type of payment (or other information) you are reporting and the form you are filing.

 If you are reporting a payment that includes noncash property, show the fair market value of the property at the time of payment. Although, generally, you are not required to report payments smaller than the minimum described for a form, you may prefer, for economy and your

GEN-9

own convenience, to file Copies A for all payments. The IRS encourages this.

See the heading below for the type of payment or other information you are reporting. The headings are (a) Interest, dividend, and royalty payments; (b) Real estate transactions; and (c) Other information.

Interest, dividend, and royalty payments. For payments of dividends under section 6042 (reported on Form 1099-DIV) or patronage dividends under section 6044 (reported on Form 1099-PATR), interest (including original issue discount) under section 6049 (reported on Form 1099-INT or 1099-OID), or royalties under section 6050N (reported on Form 1099-MISC or 1099-S), you are required to furnish an official IRS Form 1099 or an acceptable substitute Form 1099 to a recipient either in person, by First-Class Mail to the recipient's last known address, or electronically (see *Electronic recipient statements* on page GEN-11). Statements may be sent by intraoffice mail if you use intraoffice mail to send account information and other correspondence to the recipient.

Statement mailing requirements for Forms 1099-DIV, 1099-INT, 1099-OID, and 1099-PATR, and forms reporting royalties only. The following statement mailing requirements apply only to Forms 1099-DIV (except for section 404(k) dividends), 1099-INT (except for interest reportable in the course of your trade or business under section 6041), 1099-OID, 1099-PATR, and timber royalties reported under section 6050N (on Form 1099-MISC or 1099-S). The mailing must contain the official IRS Form 1099 or an acceptable substitute and may also contain the following enclosures: (a) Form W-2, applicable Form W-8, Form W-9, or other Forms W-2G, 1098, 1099, and 5498 statements; (b) a check from the account being reported; (c) a letter explaining why no check is enclosed; (d) a statement of the person's account shown on Forms 1099, 1098, or 5498; and (e) a letter explaining the tax consequences of the information shown on the recipient statement.

A statement of the person's account (year-end account summary) that you are permitted to enclose in a statement mailing may include information similar to the following: (a) tax-exempt interest (including accrued OID) and the part of such interest exempt from the alternative minimum tax or from state or local income tax; (b) the part of a mutual fund distribution that is interest on U.S. Treasury obligations; (c) accrued interest expense on the purchase of a debt obligation; and (d) the cost or other basis of securities and the gain/loss on the sale of securities.

No additional enclosures, such as advertising, promotional material, or a quarterly or annual report, are permitted. Even a sentence or two on the year-end statement describing new services offered by the payer is not permitted. Logos are permitted on the envelope and on any nontax enclosures. See Notice 96-62 which is available on page 8 of Internal Revenue Bulletin 1996-49 at *www.irs.gov/pub/irs-irbs/irb96-49*.

TIP *The IRS intends to amend the regulations to allow the use of certain logos and identifying slogans on substitute statements to recipients that are subject to the statement mailing requirements. Until the new regulations are issued, the IRS will not assess penalties for the use of a logo (including the name of the payer in any typeface, font, or stylized fashion and/or a symbolic icon) or slogan on a statement to a recipient if the logo or slogan is used by the payer in the ordinary course of its trade or business. In addition, use of the logo or slogan must not make it less likely that a reasonable payee will recognize the importance of the statement for tax reporting purposes.*

A recipient statement may be perforated to a check or to a statement of the recipient's specific account. The check or account statement to which the recipient statement is perforated must contain, in bold and conspicuous type, the legend "Important Tax Return Document Attached."

The legend "Important Tax Return Document Enclosed" must appear in a bold and conspicuous manner on the outside of the envelope and on each letter explaining why no check is enclosed, or on each check or account statement that is not

perforated to the recipient statement. The legend is not required on any tax form, tax statement, or permitted letter of tax consequences included in a statement mailing. Further, you need not pluralize the word "document" in the legend simply because more than one recipient statement is enclosed.

TIP *If you provide recipient statements in a "separate mailing" that contains only recipient statements, Forms W-8 and W-9, and a letter explaining the tax consequences of the information shown on a recipient statement included in the envelope, you are not required to include the legend "Important Tax Return Document Enclosed" on the envelope.*

Substitute forms. You may furnish to the recipient Copy B of the official IRS form, or you may use substitute Forms 1099-DIV, 1099-INT, 1099-OID, or 1099-PATR, if they contain the same language as the official IRS forms and they comply with the rules in Pub. 1179, relating to substitute Forms 1099. Applicable box titles and numbers must be clearly identified, using the same wording and numbering as the official IRS form. However, for Form 1099-INT, if your substitute does not contain box 3, "Interest on U.S. Savings Bonds and Treas. obligations," you may omit "not included in box 3" from the box 1 title. For information on substitute Forms 1099-MISC, see *Other information* below. For Forms 1099-S, see *Real estate transactions* below.

TIP *All substitute statements to recipients must contain the tax year, form number, and form name prominently displayed together in one area of the statement. For example, they could be shown in the upper right part of the statement.*

If you are using substitutes, the IRS encourages you to use boxes so that the substitute has the appearance of a form. The substitute form must contain the applicable instructions as on the front and back of Copy B of the official IRS form. See Pub. 1179 for additional requirements. Certain "composite" statements are permitted. See Pub. 1179.

Real estate transactions. You must furnish a statement to the transferor containing the same information reported to the IRS on Form 1099-S. You may use Copy B of the official IRS Form 1099-S or a substitute form that complies with Pub. 1179 and Regulations section 1.6045-4(m). You may use a Uniform Settlement Statement (under RESPA) as the written statement if it is conformed by including on the statement the legend shown on Form 1099-S and by designating which information is reported to the IRS on Form 1099-S. You may furnish the statement to the transferor in person, by mail, or electronically. Furnish the statement at or after closing but by January 31 of the following year.

The statement mailing requirements explained above **do not** apply to statements to transferors for proceeds from real estate transactions reported on Form 1099-S. However, the statement mailing requirements do apply to statements to transferors for timber royalties reportable under section 6050N on Form 1099-S.

Other information. Statements to recipients for Forms 1098, 1098-C, 1098-E, 1098-T, 1099-A, 1099-B, 1099-C, 1099-CAP, 1099-G, 1099-H, 1099-LTC, 1099-MISC, 1099-Q, 1099-R, 1099-SA, 5498, 5498-ESA, 5498-SA, W-2G, 1099-DIV only for section 404(k) dividends reportable under section 6047, 1099-INT only for interest reportable in the course of your trade or business under section 6041, or 1099-S only for royalties need not be, but can be, a copy of the official paper form filed with the IRS. If you do not use a copy of the paper form, the form number and title of your substitute must be the same as the official IRS form. All information required to be reported must be numbered and titled on your substitute in substantially the same manner as on the official IRS form. However, if you are reporting a payment as "Other income" in box 3 of Form 1099-MISC, you may substitute appropriate explanatory language for the box title. For example, for payments of accrued wages to a beneficiary of a deceased employee required to be reported on Form 1099-MISC, you might change the title of box 3 to "Beneficiary payments" or something similar.

GEN-10

Appropriate instructions to the recipient, similar to those on the official IRS form, must be provided to aid in the proper reporting of the items on the recipient's income tax return. For payments reported on Form 1099-B, rather than furnish appropriate instructions with each Form 1099-B statement, you may furnish to the recipient one set of instructions for all statements required to be furnished to a recipient in a calendar year.

Except for royalties reported on Form 1099-MISC, the statement mailing requirements explained earlier do not apply to statements to recipients for information reported on the forms listed on page GEN-10 under *Other information*. You may combine the statements with other reports or financial or commercial notices, or expand them to include other information of interest to the recipient. Be sure that all copies of the forms are legible. Certain "composite" statements are permitted. See Pub. 1179.

When to furnish forms or statements. Generally, you must furnish Forms 1098, 1099, and W-2G information by January 31, 2006. However, you may issue them earlier in some situations, as provided by the regulations. For example, you may furnish Form 1099-INT to the recipient on redemption of U.S. Savings Bonds at the time of redemption. Brokers and barter exchanges may furnish Form 1099-B anytime but not later than January 31, 2006.

Donee organizations required to issue Form 1098-C must furnish the acknowledgment to a donor within 30 days of the sale of the vehicle (if it is sold without material improvements or significant intervening use) or within 30 days of the contribution.

Trustees or issuers of traditional IRAs must furnish participants with a statement of the value of the participant's account, and RMD if applicable, by January 31, 2006. The fair market value of SEP IRAs must also be furnished to the participant by January 31, 2006. Traditional IRA, Roth IRA, SEP, or SIMPLE contribution information must be furnished to the participant by May 31, 2006. However, Coverdell ESA contribution information must be furnished to the beneficiary by May 1, 2006.

Trustees of a SIMPLE must furnish a statement of the account balance and the account activity by January 31, 2006.

For real estate transactions, you may furnish the statement to the transferor at closing or by mail on or before January 31, 2006.

Filers of Form 1099-G who report state or local income tax refunds, credits, or offsets must furnish the statements to recipients during January 2006.

See the *Guide to Information Returns* on pages GEN-16 and GEN-17 for the date other information returns are due to the recipient.

You will meet the requirement to furnish the statement if it is properly addressed and mailed, or posted to a website, on or before the due date. If the regular due date falls on a Saturday, Sunday, or legal holiday, the due date is the next business day. A business day is any day that is not a Saturday, Sunday, or legal holiday.

Electronic recipient statements. If you are required to furnish a written statement (Copy B or an acceptable substitute) to a recipient, then you may furnish the statement electronically instead of on paper. This includes furnishing the statement to recipients of Forms 1098, 1098-E, 1098-T, 1099-A, B, C, CAP, DIV, H, INT, G, LTC, MISC, OID, PATR, Q, R, S, SA, 5498, 5498-ESA, and 5498-SA. It also includes Form W-2G (except for horse and dog racing, jai alai, sweepstakes, wagering pools, and lotteries).

 Until further guidance is issued to the contrary, Form 1098-C may not be furnished electronically.

If you meet the requirements listed below, you are treated as furnishing the statement timely.

Consent. The recipient must consent in the affirmative and not have withdrawn the consent before the statement is furnished. The consent by the recipient must be made

electronically in a way that shows that he or she can access the statement in the electronic format in which it will be furnished.

You must notify the recipient of any hardware or software changes prior to furnishing the statement. A new consent to receive the statement electronically is required after the new hardware or software is put into service.

Prior to furnishing the statements electronically, you must provide the recipient a statement with the following statements prominently displayed:
• If the recipient does not consent to receive the statement electronically, a paper copy will be provided.
• The scope and duration of the consent. For example, whether the consent applies to every year the statement is furnished or only for the January 31 immediately following the date of the consent.
• How to obtain a paper copy after giving consent.
• How to withdraw the consent. The consent may be withdrawn at any time by furnishing the withdrawal in writing (electronically or on paper) to the person whose name appears on the statement. Confirmation of the withdrawal also will be in writing (electronically or on paper).
• Notice of termination. The notice must state under what conditions the statements will no longer be furnished to the recipient.
• Procedures to update the recipient's information.
• A description of the hardware and software required to access, print and retain a statement, and a date the statement will no longer be available on the website.

Format, posting, and notification. Additionally, you must:
• Ensure the electronic format contains all the required information and complies with the applicable revenue procedure for substitute statements to recipients in Pub. 1179.
• Post, on or before the January 31 due date, the applicable statement on a website accessible to the recipient through October 15 of that year.
• Inform the recipient, electronically or by mail, of the posting and how to access and print the statement.

For more information, see Regulations section 31.6051-1. For electronic furnishing of Forms 1098-E and 1098-T, see Regulations section 1.6050S-2. For electronic furnishing of Forms 1099-R, 1099-SA, 1099-Q, 5498, 5498-ESA, and 5498-SA, see Notice 2004-10 that is on page 433 of Internal Revenue Bulletin 2004-6 at *www.irs.gov/pub/irs-irbs/irb04-06.*

Extension. You may request an extension of time to provide the statements to recipients by sending a letter to Enterprise Computing Center—Martinsburg, Information Reporting Program, Attn: Extension of Time Coordinator, 240 Murall Drive, Kearneysville, WV 25430. The letter must include (a) your name, (b) your TIN, (c) your address, (d) type of return, (e) a statement that your extension request is for providing statements to recipients, (f) reason for delay, and (g) the signature of the payer or authorized agent. Your request must be postmarked by the date on which the statements are due to the recipients. If your request for an extension is approved, generally you will be granted a maximum of 30 extra days to furnish the recipient statements. If you are requesting extensions of time to furnish statements for 50 or more recipients, see the TIP on page GEN-7.

I. Corrected Returns on Paper Forms

 To file corrections on magnetic media, see Electronic/Magnetic Media Reporting *on page GEN-5 and Pub. 1220.*

If you filed a return with the IRS and later discover you made an error on it, you must:
• Correct it as soon as possible and file Copy A and Form 1096 with your Internal Revenue Service Center (see *Where To File* on page GEN-8).
• Furnish statements to recipients showing the correction.

When making a correction, complete all required information (see *Filing Corrected Returns on Paper Forms* on page GEN-12).

GEN-11

Filing Corrected Returns on Paper Forms

Identify the correction needed based on **Error Type 1 or 2;** then follow the steps to make the corrections and file the form(s). Also see **Corrected Returns on Paper Forms** on page GEN-11.

Error Type 1	Correction

Incorrect money amount(s), code, or checkbox,
 	
or
 	
Incorrect address,
 	
or
 	
Incorrect payee name,
 	
or
 	
A return was filed when one should not have been filed
 	
These errors require only one return to make the correction.
 	
Caution: *If you must correct a TIN and/or a name and address, follow the instructions under Error 2.*
	A. Form 1098, 1099, 5498, or W-2G
	  1. Prepare a new information return.
	  2. Enter an "X" in the "CORRECTED" box (and date (optional)) at the top of the form.
	  3. Correct any recipient information such as money amounts and address. Report other information as per original return.
	
	B. Form 1096
	  1. Prepare a new transmittal Form 1096.
	  2. Provide all requested information on the form as it applies to Part A, 1 and 2.
	  3. File Form 1096 and Copy A of the return with the appropriate service center.
	  4. Do not include a copy of the original return that was filed incorrectly.

Error Type 2	Correction	
No payee TIN (SSN, EIN, QI-EIN, or ITIN), or **Incorrect payee TIN,** or **Incorrect name and address** **Original return filed using wrong type of return** (for example, a Form 1099-DIV was filed when a Form 1099-INT should have been filed). Two separate returns are required to make the correction properly. Follow all instructions for both Steps 1 and 2. **Note:** *You do not have to file a corrected return for an incorrect payer TIN and/or incorrect payer name and address.*	**Step 1.** Identify incorrect return submitted.	1. Prepare a new information return. 2. Enter an "X" in the "CORRECTED" box (and date (optional)) at the top of the form. 3. Enter the payer, recipient, and account number information exactly as it appeared on the original incorrect return; however, enter 0 (zero) for all money amounts.

	Step 2. Report correct information.	**A. Form 1098, 1099, 5498, or W-2G**
		  1. Prepare a new information return.
		  2. Do not enter an "X" in the "CORRECTED" box at the top of the form. Prepare the new return as though it is an original.
		  3. Include all the correct information on the form including the correct TIN, name, and address.
		
		B. Form 1096
		  1. Prepare a new transmittal Form 1096.
		  2. Enter the words "Filed To Correct TIN," "Filed to Correct Name and Address," or "File to Correct Return" in the bottom margin of the form.
		  3. Provide all requested information on the form as it applies to the returns prepared in Steps 1 and 2.
		  4. File Form 1096 and Copy A of the return with the appropriate service center.
		  5. Do not include a copy of the original return that was filed incorrectly.

GEN-12

• Do not cut or separate forms that are two or three to a page. Submit the entire page even if only one of the forms on the page is completed.
• Do not staple the forms to Form 1096.
• Do not send corrected returns to the IRS if you are correcting state or local information only. Contact the state or local tax department for help with this type of correction.
To correct payer information, see the instructions on page GEN-5.

Form 1096. Use a separate Form 1096 for each type of return you are correcting. For the same type of return, you may use one Form 1096 for both originals and corrections. You do not need to correct a previously filed Form 1096.

CORRECTED checkbox. Enter an "X" in the corrected checkbox only when correcting a form previously filed with the IRS or furnished to the recipient. When the type of error requires two returns to make the correction, see *Filing Corrected Returns on Paper Forms* on page GEN-12 to determine when to mark the "CORRECTED" checkbox.

Account number. If the account number was provided on the original return, the same account number must be included on both the original and corrected return to properly identify and process the correction. If the account number was not provided on the original return, do not include it on the corrected return. See *Account Number Box on Forms* on page GEN-15.

Recipient's statement. You may enter a date next to the "CORRECTED" checkbox. This will help the recipient in the case of multiple corrections.

Filing corrected returns on paper forms. The error charts on page GEN-12 give step-by-step instructions for filing corrected returns for the most frequently made errors. They are grouped under Error Type 1 or 2, based on how the correction is made. Correction of errors may require the submission of more than one return. Be sure to read and follow the steps given.

> ⚠️ **CAUTION** *If you fail to file correct information returns or furnish a correct payee statement, you may be subject to a penalty. See* Penalties *on page GEN-4. Regulations section 301.6724-1 (relating to information return penalties) does not require you to file corrected returns for missing or incorrect TINs if you meet the reasonable cause criteria. You are merely required to include the correct TIN on the next original return you are required to file. However, if you do not meet the reasonable cause criteria, a reduced penalty may be imposed if the corrected returns are filed by August 1.*
>
> *In addition, even if you meet the reasonable cause criteria, the IRS encourages you to file corrections for incorrect or missing TINs so that the IRS can update the payees' records.*

J. Void Returns

An "X" in the "VOID" box at the top of the form will not correct a previously filed return. See *Corrected Returns on Paper Forms* on GEN-12 for instructions for making corrections.

VOID box. If a completed or partially completed Form 1098, 1099, or 5498 is incorrect and you want to void it before submission to the IRS, enter an "X" in the "VOID" box at the top of the form. For example, if you make an error while typing or printing a form, you should void it. The return will then be disregarded during processing by the IRS. Go to the next form on the page, or to another page, and enter the correct information; but do not mark the "CORRECTED" box. Do not cut or separate the forms that are two or three to a page. Submit the entire page even if only one of the forms on the page is a good return.

K. Other Information Returns

The income information you report on the following forms must not be repeated on Forms 1099 or W-2G:
• Form W-2 reporting wages and other employee compensation.
• Forms 1042-S and 1000 reporting income to foreign persons.
• Form 2439 reporting undistributed long-term capital gains of a regulated investment company or real estate investment trust.

• Schedule K-1 of Form 1065 or 1065-B reporting distributive shares to members of a partnership.
• Schedule K-1 of Form 1041 reporting distributions to beneficiaries of trusts or estates.
• Schedule K-1 of Form 1120S reporting distributive shares to shareholders of S corporations.
• Schedule K of Form 1120-IC-DISC reporting actual and constructive distributions to shareholders and deferred DISC income.
• Schedule Q of Form 1066 reporting income from a REMIC to a residual interest holder.

L. Payments to Corporations and Partnerships

Generally, payments to corporations are not reportable. However, you must report payments to corporations for the following:
• Medical and health care payments (Form 1099-MISC),
• Withheld federal income tax or foreign tax,
• Barter exchange transactions (Form 1099-B),
• Substitute payments in lieu of dividends and tax-exempt interest (Form 1099-MISC),
• Interest or original issue discount paid or accrued to a regular interest holder of a REMIC (Form 1099-INT or 1099-OID),
• Acquisitions or abandonments of secured property (Form 1099-A),
• Cancellation of debt (Form 1099-C),
• Payments of attorneys' fees and gross proceeds paid to attorneys (Form 1099-MISC),
• Fish purchases for cash (Form 1099-MISC), and
• Federal executive agency payments for services (Form 1099-MISC). For additional reporting requirements, see Rev. Rul. 2003-66 that is on page 1115 of Internal Revenue Bulletin 2003-26 at *www.irs.gov/pub/irs-irbs/irb03-26*.

Reporting generally is required for all payments to partnerships. For example, payments of $600 or more made in the course of your trade or business to an architectural firm that is a partnership are reportable on Form 1099-MISC. However, see Regulations section 1.6049-4(c)(1)(ii)(A).

M. Earnings on any IRA, Coverdell ESA, Archer MSA, or HSA

Generally, income earned in any IRA, Coverdell ESA, Archer MSA, or HSA, such as interest or dividends, is not reported on Forms 1099. However, distributions must be reported on Form 1099-R, 1099-Q, or 1099-SA.

N. Certain Grantor Trusts

Certain grantor trusts may choose to file Forms 1099 rather than a separate statement attached to Form 1041, U.S. Income Tax Return for Estates and Trusts. If you have filed Form 1041 for a grantor trust in the past and you want to choose the Form 1099 filing method for 2005, you must have filed a final Form 1041 for 2004. To change reporting method, see Regulations section 1.671-4(g) and the Instructions for Form 1041 and Schedules A, B, D, G, I, J, and K-1.

O. Special Rules for Reporting Payments Made Through Foreign Intermediaries and Foreign Flow-Through Entities on Form 1099

If you are the payer and have received a Form W-8IMY, Certificate of Foreign Intermediary, Foreign Flow-Through Entity, or Certain U.S. Branches for United States Tax Withholding, from a foreign intermediary or flow-through entity, follow the instructions on page GEN-14 for completing Form 1099. Definitions of the terms used in these instructions are on page GEN-14.

Presumption Rules

TIP *For additional information including details on the presumption rules, see the Instructions for the Requester of Forms W-8BEN, W-8ECI, W-8EXP, and W-8IMY and Pub. 515. To order, see* How To Get Forms and Publications *on page GEN-3.*

If you are the payer and do not have a Form W-9, appropriate Form W-8, or other valid documentation, or you cannot allocate a payment to a specific payee, prior to payment, you are required to use certain presumption rules to determine the following:
• The status of the payee as a U.S. or foreign person and
• The classification of the payee as an individual, trust, estate, corporation, or partnership.

See Regulations sections 1.1441-1(b)(3), 1.1441-5(d) and (e), 1.6045-1(g)(3)(ii), and 1.6049-5(d).

Under these presumption rules, if you must presume that the payee is a U.S. nonexempt recipient subject to backup withholding, you must report the payment on a Form 1099. However, if before filing Form 1099 with the IRS the recipient is documented as foreign, then report the payment on a Form 1042-S.

On the other hand, if you must presume that the payee is a foreign recipient and prior to filing Form 1042-S with the IRS you discover that the payee is a U.S. nonexempt recipient based on documentation, then report all payments made to that payee during the calendar year on a Form 1099.

If you use the 90-day grace period rule to presume a payee is foreign, you must file a Form 1042-S to report all payments subject to withholding during the grace period. If you later discover that the payee is a U.S. nonexempt recipient subject to backup withholding, you must file a Form 1099 for all payments made to that payee after the discovery of the payee's U.S. status.

Rules for Payments Made to U.S. Nonexempt Recipients Through a QI, NQI, or FTE

If you are the payer making a payment through a QI, NQI, or FTE for a U.S. nonexempt recipient on whose behalf the QI, NQI, or FTE is acting, use the following rules to complete Form 1099.

Known recipient. If you know that a payee is a U.S. nonexempt recipient and have the payee's name, address, and TIN (if a TIN has been provided), you must complete the Form 1099 with that information. Also, on the second name line below the recipient's name enter "IMY" followed by the name of the QI, NQI, or FTE.

For payments made to multiple recipients: (a) enter the name of the recipient whose status you relied on to determine the applicable rate of withholding and (b) on the second name line, enter "IMY" followed by the name of the QI, NQI, or FTE. However, if the QI has assumed primary Form 1099 reporting or backup withholding responsibility, you are not required to issue the Form 1099 or to backup withhold. See *Qualified intermediary* below.

Unknown recipient. If you cannot reliably associate a payment with valid documentation and are required to presume a payee is a U.S. nonexempt recipient:
1. File a Form 1099 and enter "unknown recipient" on the first name line.
2. On the second name line, enter "IMY" followed by the name of the QI, NQI, or FTE.
3. Enter the EIN of the QI, NQI, or FTE, if applicable, in the recipient's identification number box.
4. Furnish a copy of the Form 1099 with "unknown recipient" to the QI, NQI, or FTE who is acting on the recipient's behalf.

! *A payer that is required to report payments made to a U.S. nonexempt recipient account holder but does not receive the necessary allocation information cannot report those payments on a pro rata basis. Report unallocated payments using the presumption rules above.*

Rules for Non-U.S. Payers

Non-U.S. payers (foreign persons that are not U.S. payers) generally have the same reporting obligations as U.S. payers. A U.S. payer is anyone who is:
• A U.S. person,
• Any U.S. governmental agency,
• A controlled foreign corporation (CFC),
• A foreign partnership that has one or more U.S. partners who, in the aggregate hold more than 50 percent of the gross income derived from the conduct of a U.S. trade or business,
• A foreign person who owns 50 percent or more of the gross income that is effectively connected with a U.S. trade or business, or
• A U.S. branch of a foreign bank or a foreign insurance company.

For more information, see Regulations section 1.6049-5(c)(5).

Exceptions. The following payments are **not** subject to reporting by a non-U.S. payer:
1. A foreign source reportable payment paid outside the U.S. For example, see Regulations section 1.6049-5(b)(6).
2. Gross proceeds from a sale effected outside the U.S., see Regulations section 1.6045-1(a).
3. An NQI or QI that provides another payer all the information sufficient for that payer to complete Form 1099 reporting. For example, see Regulations section 1.6049-5(b)(14). However, if an NQI or QI does not provide sufficient information for another payer to report a payment on Form 1099, the intermediary must report the payment.

Rules for Reporting Payments Initially Reported on Form 1042-S

If an NQI or QI receives a Form 1042-S made out to an "unknown recipient" and, the NQI or QI has actual knowledge that the payee of the income is a U.S. nonexempt recipient, it must file a Form 1099 even if the payment has been subject to withholding by another payer. The NQI or QI reports the amount withheld by the other payer on Form 1099 as federal income tax withheld.

Definitions

Foreign intermediary. A foreign intermediary is any person who is not a U.S. person and acts as a custodian, broker, nominee, or otherwise as an agent for another person, regardless of whether that other person is the beneficial owner of the amount paid, a flow-through entity, or another intermediary. The intermediary can be a qualified intermediary or a nonqualified intermediary.

Qualified intermediary (QI). A qualified intermediary is a person that is a party to a withholding agreement with the IRS and is:
• A foreign financial institution or a foreign clearing organization (other than a U.S. branch or U.S. office of the institution or organization),
• A foreign branch or office of a U.S. financial institution or a foreign branch or office of a U.S. clearing organization,
• A foreign corporation for purposes of presenting claims of benefits under an income tax treaty on behalf of its shareholders, or
• Any other person the IRS accepts as a qualified intermediary and who enters into a withholding agreement with the IRS.

For details on QI agreements, see Rev. Proc. 2000-12 that is on page 387 of Internal Revenue Bulletin 2000-4 at *www.irs.gov/pub/irs-irbs/irb00-04*; modified by Rev. Proc. 2003-64, Section 4A (Appendix 3), that is on page 306 of Internal Revenue Bulletin 2003-32 at *www.irs.gov/pub/irs-irbs/ irb03-32*; further modified by Rev. Proc. 2004-21 that is on page 702 of Internal Revenue Bulletin 2004-14 at *www.irs.gov/pub/ irs-irbs/irb04-14*.

Nonqualified intermediary (NQI). A nonqualified intermediary is any intermediary that is not a U.S. person and that is not a qualified intermediary.

Foreign flow-through entity (FTE). A flow-through entity is a foreign partnership (other than a withholding foreign

GEN-14

partnership), a foreign simple trust or foreign grantor trust (other than a withholding foreign trust), or, for payments for which a reduced rate of withholding is claimed under an income tax treaty, any entity to the extent the entity is considered to be fiscally transparent under section 894 with respect to the payment by an interest holder's jurisdiction.

Withholding foreign partnership or withholding foreign trust. A withholding foreign partnership or withholding foreign trust is a foreign partnership or a foreign simple or grantor trust that has entered into a withholding agreement with the IRS in which it agrees to assume primary withholding responsibility for all payments that are made to it for its partners, beneficiaries, or owners. See Rev. Proc. 2003-64 as amended by Rev. Proc. 2004-21, for procedures for entering into a withholding foreign partnership or trust agreement.

Nonwithholding foreign partnership, simple trust, or grantor trust. A nonwithholding foreign partnership is any foreign partnership other than a withholding foreign partnership. A nonwithholding foreign simple trust is any foreign simple trust that is not a withholding foreign trust. A nonwithholding foreign grantor trust is any foreign grantor trust that is not a withholding foreign trust.

Fiscally transparent entity. An entity is treated as fiscally transparent with respect to an item of income to the extent that the interest holders in the entity must, on a current basis, take into account separately their shares of an item of income paid to the entity, whether or not distributed, and must determine the character of the items of income as if they were realized directly from the sources from which they were realized by the entity. For example, partnerships, common trust funds, and simple trusts or grantor trusts are generally considered to be fiscally transparent with respect to items of income received by them.

P. Account Number Box on Forms

Use the account number box, when provided, on Forms 1099, 1098, 5498, and W-2G for an account number designation. The account number is required if you have multiple accounts for a recipient for whom you are filing more than one information return of the same type. Additionally, the IRS encourages you to include the recipient's account number on paper forms if your system of records uses the account number rather than the name or TIN for identification purposes. Also, the IRS will include the account number in future notices to you about backup withholding. If you are filing electronically or magnetically, see Pub. 1220.

The account number may be a checking account number, savings account number, serial number, or any other number you assign to the payee that is unique and will distinguish the specific account. This number must not appear anywhere else on the form, and this box may not be used for any other item unless the separate instructions indicate otherwise. Using unique account numbers ensures that corrected information returns will be processed accurately.

If you are using window envelopes to mail statements to recipients and using reduced rate mail, be sure the account number does not appear in the window. The Postal Service may not accept these for reduced rate mail.

Privacy Act and Paperwork Reduction Act Notice. We ask for the information on these forms to carry out the Internal Revenue laws of the United States. You are required to give us the information. We need it to figure and collect the right amount of tax.

Sections 170(f)(12),199, 220(h), 223, 408, 408A, 529, 530, 6041, 6041A, 6042, 6043, 6044, 6045, 6047, 6049, 6050A, 6050B, 6050D, 6050E, 6050H, 6050J, 6050N, 6050P, 6050Q, 6050R, 6050S, 6050T, and their regulations require you to file an information return with the IRS and furnish a statement to recipients. Section 6109 and its regulations require you to provide your taxpayer identification number on what you file.

Routine uses of this information include giving it to the Department of Justice for civil and criminal litigation, and to cities, states, and the District of Columbia for use in administering their tax laws. We may also disclose this information to other countries under a tax treaty, to federal and state agencies to enforce federal nontax criminal laws, or to federal law enforcement and intelligence agencies to combat terrorism. If you fail to provide this information in a timely manner, you may be subject to penalties.

You are not required to provide the information requested on a form that is subject to the Paperwork Reduction Act unless the form displays a valid OMB control number. Books or records relating to a form or its instructions must be retained as long as their contents may become material in the administration of any Internal Revenue law. Generally, tax returns and return information are confidential, as required by section 6103.

The time needed to complete and file the following forms will vary depending on individual circumstances. The estimated average times are:

Form	Time
1096	13 minutes
1098	7 minutes
1098-C	12 minutes
1098-E	7 minutes
1098-T	13 minutes
1099-A	9 minutes
1099-B	20 minutes
1099-C	10 minutes
1099-CAP	11 minutes
1099-DIV	18 minutes
1099-G	11 minutes
1099-H	18 minutes
1099-INT	13 minutes
1099-LTC	13 minutes
1099-MISC	16 minutes
1099-OID	12 minutes
1099-PATR	15 minutes
1099-Q	11 minutes
1099-R	18 minutes
1099-S	8 minutes
1099-SA	8 minutes
5498	12 minutes
5498-ESA	7 minutes
5498-SA	10 minutes
W-2G	18 minutes

If you have comments concerning the accuracy of these time estimates or suggestions for making these forms simpler, we would be happy to hear from you. You can write to the Internal Revenue Service, Tax Products Coordinating Committee, SE:W:CAR:MP:T:T:SP, 1111 Constitution Ave. NW, IR-6406, Washington, DC 20224. Do not send these forms to this address. Instead, see *Where To File* on page GEN-8.

GEN-15

Appendix

Guide to Information Returns
(If any date shown falls on a Saturday, Sunday, or legal holiday, the due date is the next business day.)

Form	Title	What To Report	Amounts To Report	Due Date To IRS	Due Date To Recipient (unless indicated otherwise)
1042-S	Foreign Person's U.S. Source Income Subject to Withholding	Payments subject to withholding under Chapter 3 of the Code, including interest, dividends, royalties, pensions and annuities, gambling winnings, compensation for personal services, and distributions by publicly traded partnerships of income effectively connected with the conduct of a U.S. trade or business.	All amounts, except $10 or more for interest on U.S. deposits paid to Canadian nonresident aliens	March 15	March 15
1098	Mortgage Interest Statement	Mortgage interest (including points) you received in the course of your trade or business from individuals and reimbursements of overpaid interest.	$600 or more	February 28*	(To Payer/Borrower) January 31
1098-C	Contributions of Motor Vehicles, Boats, and Airplanes	Information regarding a donated motor vehicle, boat, or airplane.	Gross proceeds of more than $500	February 28*	30 days from date of sale or contribution
1098-E	Student Loan Interest Statement	Student loan interest received in the course of your trade or business.	$600 or more	February 28*	January 31
1098-T	Tuition Statement	Qualified tuition and related expenses, reimbursements or refunds, and scholarships or grants (optional).	See instructions	February 28*	January 31
1099-A	Acquisition or Abandonment of Secured Property	Information about the acquisition or abandonment of property that is security for a debt for which you are the lender.	All amounts	February 28*	(To Borrower) January 31
1099-B	Proceeds From Broker and Barter Exchange Transactions	Sales or redemptions of securities, futures transactions, commodities, and barter exchange transactions.	All amounts	February 28*	January 31
1099-C	Cancellation of Debt	Cancellation of a debt owed to a financial institution, the Federal Government, a credit union, RTC, FDIC, NCUA, a military department, the U.S. Postal Service, the Postal Rate Commission, or any organization having a significant trade or business of lending money.	$600 or more	February 28*	January 31
1099-CAP	Changes in Corporate Control and Capital Structure	Information about cash, stock, or other property from an acquisition of control or the substantial change in capital structure of a corporation.	Amounts of stock or property valued at $100 million or more	February 28*	(To Shareholders) January 31
1099-DIV	Dividends and Distributions	Distributions, such as dividends, capital gain distributions, or nontaxable distributions, that were paid on stock, and liquidation distributions.	$10 or more, except $600 or more for liquidations	February 28*	January 31
1099-G	Certain Government Payments	Unemployment compensation, state and local income tax refunds, agricultural payments, and taxable grants.	$10 or more for refunds and unemployment; $600 or more for all others	February 28*	January 31
1099-H	Health Coverage Tax Credit (HCTC) Advance Payments	Health insurance premiums paid on behalf of certain individuals.	All amounts	February 28*	January 31
1099-INT	Interest Income	Interest income.	$10 or more ($600 or more in some cases)	February 28*	January 31
1099-LTC	Long-Term Care and Accelerated Death Benefits	Payments under a long-term care insurance contract and accelerated death benefits paid under a life insurance contract or by a viatical settlement provider.	All amounts	February 28*	(To Insured and Policyholder) January 31
1099-MISC	Miscellaneous Income (Also, use this form to report the occurrence of direct sales of $5,000 or more of consumer goods for resale.)	Rent or royalty payments; prizes and awards that are not for services, such as winnings on TV or radio shows.	$600 or more, except $10 or more for royalties	February 28*	January 31
		Payments to crew members by owners or operators of fishing boats including payments of proceeds from sale of catch.	All amounts		
		Payments to a physician, physicians' corporation, or other supplier of health and medical services. Issued mainly by medical assistance programs or health and accident insurance plans.	$600 or more		
		Payments for services performed for a trade or business by people not treated as its employees. Examples: fees to subcontractors or directors, and golden parachute payments.	$600 or more		
		Fish purchases paid in cash for resale.	$600 or more		
		Substitute dividend and tax-exempt interest payments reportable by brokers.	$10 or more		
		Crop insurance proceeds.	$600 or more		
		Gross proceeds paid to attorneys.	All amounts		
1099-OID	Original Issue Discount	Original issue discount.	$10 or more	February 28*	January 31
1099-PATR	Taxable Distributions Received From Cooperatives	Distributions from cooperatives to their patrons.	$10 or more	February 28*	January 31

*The due date is March 31 if filed electronically.

GEN-16

A-287

Guide to Information Returns (Continued)

Form	Title	What To Report	Amounts To Report	Due Date	
				To IRS	To Recipient (unless indicated otherwise)
1099-Q	Payments From Qualified Education Programs (Under Sections 529 and 530)	Earnings from a qualified tuition program and Coverdell ESAs.	All amounts	February 28*	January 31
1099-R	Distributions From Pensions, Annuities, Retirement or Profit-Sharing Plans, IRAs, Insurance Contracts, etc.	Distributions from retirement or profit-sharing plans, any IRA, insurance contracts, and IRA recharacterizations.	$10 or more	February 28*	January 31
1099-S	Proceeds From Real Estate Transactions	Gross proceeds from the sale or exchange of real estate.	Generally, $600 or more	February 28*	January 31
1099-SA	Distributions From an HSA, Archer MSA, or Medicare Advantage MSA	Distributions from an HSA, Archer MSA, or Medicare Advantage MSA.	All amounts	February 28*	January 31
5471	Information Return of U.S. Persons With Respect To Certain Foreign Corporations	U.S. persons who are officers, directors, or shareholders in certain foreign corporations report information required by sections 6035, 6038, and 6046, and to compute income from controlled foreign corporations under sections 951–964.	See form instructions	Due date of income tax return	None
5472	Information Return of a 25% Foreign-Owned U.S. Corporation or a Foreign Corporation Engaged in a U.S. Trade or Business	Transactions between a 25% foreign-owned domestic corporation or a foreign corporation engaged in a trade or business in the United States and a related party as required by sections 6038A and 6038C.	See form instructions	Due date of income tax return	None
5498	IRA Contribution Information	Contributions (including rollover contributions) to any individual retirement arrangement (IRA) including a SEP, SIMPLE, and Roth IRA; Roth conversions; IRA recharacterizations; and the fair market value (FMV) of the account.	All amounts	May 31	(To Participant) For FMV/RMD Jan.31; For contributions, May 31
5498-ESA	Coverdell ESA Contribution Information	Contributions (including rollover contributions) to a Coverdell ESA.	All amounts	May 31	April 30
5498-SA	HSA, Archer MSA, or Medicare Advantage MSA Information	Contributions to an HSA, Archer MSA and the fair market value of an HSA, Archer MSA, or Medicare Advantage MSA.	All amounts	May 31	(To Participant) May 31
8027	Employer's Annual Information Return of Tip Income and Allocated Tips	Receipts from large food or beverage operations, tips reported by employees, and allocated tips.	See separate instructions	Last day of February*	Allocated tips are shown on Form W-2, due January 31
8300 (IRS/FinCEN form)	Report of Cash Payments Over $10,000 Received in a Trade or Business	Payments in cash (including certain monetary instruments) or foreign currency received in one transaction, or two or more related transactions, in the course of a trade or business. Does not apply to banks and financial institutions filing Form 4789, and casinos that are required to report such transactions on **Form 8362,** Currency Transaction Report by Casinos, or, generally, to transactions outside the United States.	Over $10,000	15 days after date of transaction	(To Payer) January 31
8308	Report of a Sale or Exchange of Certain Partnership Interests	Sale or exchange of a partnership interest involving unrealized receivables or inventory items.	(Transaction only)	Generally, attach to Form 1065 or 1065-B	(To Transferor and Transferee) January 31
W-2G	Certain Gambling Winnings	Gambling winnings from horse racing, dog racing, jai alai, lotteries, keno, bingo, slot machines, sweepstakes, wagering pools, etc.	Generally, $600 or more; $1,200 or more from bingo or slot machines; $1,500 or more from keno	February 28*	January 31
Form 104 (FinCen)	Currency Transaction Report	Each deposit, withdrawal, exchange of currency, or other payment or transfer by, through, or to financial institutions (other than casinos).	Over $10,000	15 days after date of transaction	Not required
926	Return by a U.S. Transferor of Property to a Foreign Corporation	Transfers of property to a foreign corporation and to report information under section 6038B.	See form instructions	Attach to tax return	None
W-2	Wage and Tax Statement	Wages, tips, other compensation; social security, Medicare, withheld income taxes; and advance earned income credit (EIC) payments. Include bonuses, vacation allowances, severance pay, certain moving expense payments, some kinds of travel allowances, and third-party payments of sick pay.	See separate instructions	**To SSA** / Last day of February*	**To Recipient** / January 31
TD F 90-22.1	Report of Foreign Bank and Financial Accounts	Financial interest in or signature or other authority over a foreign bank account, securities account, or other financial account.	Over $10,000	**To Treasury Dept.** / June 30	**To Recipient** / None

*The due date is March 31 if filed electronically.

GEN-17

Appendix

Types of Payments

Below is an alphabetical list of some payments and the forms to file and report them. However, it is not a complete list of all payments, and the absence of a payment from the list does not indicate that the payment is not reportable. For information on a specific type of payment, see the separate instructions for the form(s) listed.

Type of Payment	Report on Form
Abandonment	1099-A
Accelerated death benefits	1099-LTC
Acquisition of control	1099-CAP
Advance earned income credit	W-2
Advance health insurance payments	1099-H
Agriculture payments	1099-G
Allocated tips	W-2
Alternate TAA payments	1099-G
Annuities	1099-R
Archer MSAs:	
Contributions	5498-SA
Distributions	1099-SA
Attorneys, fees and gross proceeds	1099-MISC
Auto reimbursements, employee	W-2
Auto reimbursements, nonemployee	1099-MISC
Awards, employee	W-2
Awards, nonemployee	1099-MISC
Barter exchange income	1099-B
Bonuses, employee	W-2
Bonuses, nonemployee	1099-MISC
Broker transactions	1099-B
Cancellation of debt	1099-C
Capital gain distributions	1099-DIV
Car expense, employee	W-2
Car expense, nonemployee	1099-MISC
Changes in capital structure	1099-CAP
Charitable gift annuities	1099-R
Commissions, employee	W-2
Commissions, nonemployee	1099-MISC
Commodities transactions	1099-B
Compensation, employee	W-2
Compensation, nonemployee	1099-MISC
Contributions of motor vehicles, boats, and airplanes	1098-C
Cost of current life insurance protection	1099-R
Coverdell ESA contributions	5498-ESA
Coverdell ESA distributions	1099-Q
Crop insurance proceeds	1099-MISC
Damages	1099-MISC
Death benefits	1099-R
Accelerated	1099-LTC
Debt cancellation	1099-C
Dependent care payments	W-2
Direct rollovers	1099-Q, 1099-R, 5498
Direct sales of consumer products for resale	1099-MISC
Directors' fees	1099-MISC
Discharge of indebtedness	1099-C
Dividends	1099-DIV
Education loan interest	1098-E
Employee business expense reimbursement	W-2
Employee compensation	W-2
Excess deferrals, excess contributions, distributions of	1099-R
Fees, employee	W-2
Fees, nonemployee	1099-MISC
Fishing boat crew members proceeds	1099-MISC
Fish purchases for cash	1099-MISC
Foreclosures	1099-A
Foreign persons' income	1042-S
401(k) contributions	W-2
404(k) dividend	1099-DIV
Gambling winnings	W-2G
Golden parachute, employee	W-2
Golden parachute, nonemployee	1099-MISC
Grants, taxable	1099-G
Health care services	1099-MISC
Health insurance advance payments	1099-H
Health savings accounts:	
Contributions	5498-SA

Type of Payment	Report on Form
Distributions	1099-SA
Income attributable to domestic production activities, deduction for	1099-PATR
Income tax refunds, state and local	1099-G
Indian gaming profits paid to tribal members	1099-MISC
Interest income	1099-INT
Interest, mortgage	1098
IRA contributions	5498
IRA distributions	1099-R
Life insurance contract distributions	1099-R, 1099-LTC
Liquidation, distributions in	1099-DIV
Loans, distribution from pension plan	1099-R
Long-term care benefits	1099-LTC
Medicare Advantage MSAs:	
Contributions	5498-SA
Distributions	1099-SA
Medical services	1099-MISC
Mileage, employee	W-2
Mileage, nonemployee	1099-MISC
Military retirement	1099-R
Mortgage interest	1098
Moving expense	W-2
Nonemployee compensation	1099-MISC
Nonqualified deferred compensation distribution:	
Beneficiary	1099-R
Employee	W-2
Nonemployee	1099-MISC
Original issue discount (OID)	1099-OID
Patronage dividends	1099-PATR
Pensions	1099-R
Points	1098
Prizes, employee	W-2
Prizes, nonemployee	1099-MISC
Profit-sharing plan	1099-R
Punitive damages	1099-MISC
Qualified plan distributions	1099-R
Qualified tuition program payments	1099-Q
Real estate transactions	1099-S
Recharacterized IRA contributions	1099-R, 5498
Refunds, state and local tax	1099-G
Rents	1099-MISC
Retirement	1099-R
Roth conversion IRA contributions	5498
Roth conversion IRA distributions	1099-R
Roth IRA contributions	5498
Roth IRA distributions	1099-R
Royalties	1099-MISC
Timber, pay-as-cut contract	1099-S
Sales:	
Real estate	1099-S
Securities	1099-B
Section 1035 exchange	1099-R
SEP contributions	W-2, 5498
SEP distributions	1099-R
Severance pay	W-2
Sick pay	W-2
SIMPLE contributions	W-2, 5498
SIMPLE distributions	1099-R
Student loan interest	1098-E
Substitute payments in lieu of dividends or tax-exempt interest	1099-MISC
Supplemental unemployment	W-2
Tax refunds, state and local	1099-G
Tips	W-2
Tuition	1098-T
Unemployment benefits	1099-G
Vacation allowance, employee	W-2
Vacation allowance, nonemployee	1099-MISC
Wages	W-2

GEN-18

Index

Form **2032** (Rev. September 2002) Department of the Treasury Internal Revenue Service	**Contract Coverage Under Title II of the Social Security Act** (For use by an American employer to extend social security coverage to U.S. citizens and resident aliens employed by its foreign affiliates.)	OMB No. 1545-0137 **File three copies of this form**

Name of American employer	Employer identification number
Address number and street (P.O. Box if no mail delivery to street address)	Apt. or suite no.
City, state, and ZIP code	

This Form 2032 is filed as (check applicable box(es)):

1 ☐ An original (new) agreement.

    This agreement is effective for services performed on and after (for original agreements only, check one):

   a ☐ The first day of the calendar quarter in which the service center director signs this agreement.

   b ☐ The first day of the calendar quarter following the calendar quarter in which the service center director signs this agreement.

2 ☐ An amendment to an agreement previously entered into.

3 ☐ An election to apply the rules in effect after April 20, 1983, to agreements in effect on that date. By making this election, U.S. resident aliens as well as U.S. citizens will be covered by social security.

If this is an amended election or agreement, provide the following information:

_____ on _____
(Location where previous Form 2032 was filed)   (Date service center director signed original agreement on Form 2032)

4 This agreement extends the Federal insurance system under Title II of the Social Security Act to certain services performed outside the United States by U.S. citizens and resident aliens employed by any of the foreign affiliates listed below. For an amendment to an agreement without making the election to apply the post-April 20, 1983 rules, this amendment extends Title II social security coverage to certain services performed outside the United States by U.S. citizens employed by any of the foreign affiliates listed below.

Note: *Enter foreign affiliate addresses **below** in the following order: city, province or state, and country. **Do not** abbreviate the country name, and follow the country's practice for entering the postal code. If this agreement includes more than four foreign affiliates, attach a separate sheet of paper identified as a part of this agreement with the name and address of each additional foreign affiliate.*

a Name and address of foreign affiliate	**c** Name and address of foreign affiliate
b Name and address of foreign affiliate	**d** Name and address of foreign affiliate

5 Estimated number of employees to be initially covered by this agreement, amendment, or election:

Nonagricultural employees ▶   Agricultural employees ▶

This agreement applies to all services performed outside the United States by each U.S. citizen or resident alien employed by any of the foreign affiliates named. However, the agreement applies only to the extent that payments to each employee for the services would be considered wages if paid by the employer for services performed in the United States. This agreement does not apply to any service that is considered employment for purposes of the employee tax and the employer tax under the Federal Insurance Contributions Act.

For an original agreement, an amendment to an agreement that was entered into after April 20, 1983, or an election to apply the rules in effect after April 20, 1983, to agreements in effect on that date, the American employer declares that it owns at least a 10% interest (directly or through one or more entities) in the voting stock or profits of each foreign entity named above. It also declares that Code section 3121(l) does not prevent this agreement.

For an amendment to an agreement in effect on April 20, 1983, without making the election to apply the new rules in effect after that date, the domestic corporation declares that **(a)** it owns at least 20% of the voting stock of each foreign corporation named above, or **(b)** it owns at least 20% of the voting stock of a foreign corporation that owns more than 50% of the voting stock of each foreign corporation named above. It also declares that Code section 3121(l) does not prevent this agreement.

The American employer agrees:

1. To pay amounts equal to the taxes that would be imposed by Code sections 3101 and 3111 if the payment for the services were considered wages;

2. To pay, on written notification and demand, amounts equal to the interest, additions to taxes, and penalties that would apply if the payment for the services were considered wages; and

3. To comply with the applicable regulations under Code section 3121(l).

This agreement (or amended agreement or election) is entered into under the provisions of section 3121(l) of the Internal Revenue Code and the applicable regulations.

Signature of individual authorized to enter into this agreement for the American employer	Title	Date
Director, Internal Revenue Service Center	Location	Date

For Privacy Act and Paperwork Reduction Act Notice, see back of form.   Cat. No. 49954D   Form **2032** (Rev. 9-2002)

Form 2032 (Rev. 9-2002)   Page **2**

General Instructions

Section references are to the Internal Revenue Code.

Before April 21, 1983, only domestic corporations could enter into this agreement to cover only U.S. citizens employed by foreign subsidiaries. For this agreement, a foreign subsidiary was defined as **(a)** a foreign corporation in which at least 20% of the voting stock was owned by the domestic corporation, or **(b)** a foreign corporation in which more than 50% of the voting stock was owned by another foreign corporation in which the domestic corporation owned at least 20% of the voting stock.

After April 20, 1983, any American employer (no longer limited to a domestic corporation) can enter into this agreement to cover U.S. resident aliens as well as U.S. citizens employed by a foreign affiliate. For this agreement, a foreign affiliate is any foreign entity (no longer limited to a foreign corporation) in which the American employer owns at least a 10% interest in the voting stock or profits. This interest must be owned directly or through one or more entities.

A domestic corporation having an agreement in effect that was entered into before April 21, 1983, can elect to apply the post-April 20, 1983, rules to such agreements. If a domestic corporation makes this election, social security coverage will be extended to U.S. resident alien employees of any foreign subsidiary for which U.S. citizens are currently covered by an existing agreement. In addition, the election allows a domestic corporation to extend social security and Medicare coverage to U.S. citizens and resident aliens employed by a foreign entity that did not qualify for coverage under the old 20% ownership rules, but that now qualifies under the 10% ownership rules.

Note: *The United States has social security (totalization) agreements with specific countries. These agreements ensure that social security taxes are paid to only one country. However, these agreements may affect the withholding requirements resulting from filing Form 2032. For more information, see Social Security and Medicare Taxes in* **Pub. 54,** *Tax Guide for U.S. Citizens and Resident Aliens Abroad.*

Purpose of form. An American employer uses this form to **(a)** enter into the agreement specified in section 3121(l) to extend coverage under Title II of the Social Security Act to U.S. citizens and resident aliens employed abroad by foreign affiliates, **(b)** amend a previous agreement, or **(c)** elect to apply the rules in effect after April 20, 1983, to agreements in effect on that date.

For this agreement, an American employer is an employer that is **(a)** the United States or any instrumentality thereof, **(b)** an individual who is a resident of the United States, **(c)** a partnership if two-thirds or more of the partners are residents of the United States, **(d)** a trust if all the trustees are residents of the United States, or **(e)** a corporation organized under the laws of the United States or of any state.

Where To File

File three copies of this form with the Internal Revenue Service Center shown below for the state where the American employer's principal place of business is located. **However,** an American employer already filing **Form 941,** Employer's Quarterly Federal Tax Return, should file Form 2032 with the Internal Revenue Service Center where the employer files Form 941 (generally their principal place of business). Also, enter on Form 2032 the employer identification number as shown on Form 941. This will help the IRS process your form faster.

Exceptions. The following exceptions will apply.

1. For exempt organizations and government entities. If you are filing Form 941 for an exempt organization or government entity (Federal, state, local, or Indian tribal government), file Form 2032 with the Internal Revenue Service Center, Ogden, UT 84201-0038.

2. For electronic Form 941 filers. If you file Form 941 electronically, file Form 2032 with the Internal Revenue Service Center, Cincinnati, OH 45999-0038.

If your principal place of business is located in ▼	Use the following Internal Revenue Service Center address ▼
Connecticut, Delaware, District of Columbia, Illinois, Indiana, Kentucky, Maine, Maryland, Massachusetts, Michigan, New Hampshire, New Jersey, New York, North Carolina, Ohio, Pennsylvania, Rhode Island, South Carolina, Vermont, Virginia, West Virginia, Wisconsin	Cincinnati, OH 45999-0038
Alabama, Alaska, Arizona, Arkansas, California, Colorado, Florida, Georgia, Hawaii, Idaho, Iowa, Kansas, Louisiana, Minnesota, Mississippi, Missouri, Montana, Nebraska, Nevada, New Mexico, North Dakota, Oklahoma, Oregon, South Dakota, Tennessee, Texas, Utah, Washington, Wyoming	Ogden, UT 84201-0038
American employers in Guam, American Samoa, the Virgin Islands, or Puerto Rico	Philadelphia, PA 19255-0038

Completing Form 2032

Complete Form 2032 in triplicate. Each copy of the form must be signed and dated by the individual authorized to enter into the agreement, amendment, or election. Attach to each form evidence showing the authority for such individual to sign the form. For example, corporations must include a certified copy of the minutes of the board of director's meeting.

After the director of the Internal Revenue Service Center signs and dates the form, it constitutes the agreement, amendment, or election authorized by section 3121(l). The IRS will return one copy of Form 2032 to the American employer, send one copy to the Social Security Administration, and keep one copy with all related papers.

Original agreements. Check the box on line 1. Also check the applicable box on line 1a or b to designate when the agreement will take effect.

Amending agreements. You may amend an agreement at any time to extend coverage to any foreign affiliate not covered by an existing agreement. File Form 2032 in triplicate, and check the box on line 2. If you amend an agreement entered into on or before April 20, 1983, without making the election to apply the rules in effect after that date, the agreement and amendments will continue to be governed by the rules in effect before April 21, 1983.

Effective date. If you file an amendment to an agreement on Form 2032 to include foreign affiliates not previously covered, and if the service center director signs the amendment during the quarter for which the original agreement is first effective or during the first month following that quarter, the amendment will be effective as of the effective date of the original agreement. But if the amendment is signed by the service center director after the end of the 4th month for which the original

agreement is in effect, the amendment will not be effective until the first day of the quarter following the one in which the service center director signed the amendment.

Election to apply post-April 20, 1983 rules. A domestic corporation having an agreement in effect that was entered into before April 21, 1983 (old agreement), may elect to have the rules in effect after April 20, 1983, apply to the old agreement. File Form 2032 in triplicate, and check the box on line 3.

If you make this election, it will be effective for all foreign entities covered by the agreement. By making the election, U.S. resident alien employees as well as U.S. citizen employees will be covered by the agreement.

To extend coverage to any foreign affiliate not covered by an agreement, indicate the name and address of the foreign affiliate on line 4 in the space provided and check the box on line 2 for the amended agreement, and the box on line 3 for the election.

Effective date. Generally, the election will be effective on the day following the quarter in which the election is signed by the service center director.

No Termination of Agreement

Once you enter into an agreement, you cannot terminate it, either in its entirety or with respect to any foreign affiliate. However, the agreement will terminate for a foreign entity at the end of any quarter in which the foreign entity, at any time in that quarter, ceased to be your foreign affiliate.

Privacy Act and Paperwork Reduction Act Notice. We ask for the information on this form to carry out the Internal Revenue laws of the United States. We need it to figure and collect the right amount of tax. Section 6109 requires you to provide your taxpayer identification number (SSN or EIN). Section 3121 of the Internal Revenue Code allows employees of foreign affiliates to be covered under social security. Routine uses of this information include giving it to the Social Security Adminstration for use in calculating social security benefits, the Department of Justice for civil and criminal litigation, and cities, states and the District of Columbia for use in administering their tax laws. We may also disclose this information to Federal and state agencies to enforce Federal nontax criminal laws and to combat terrorism. We may also give the information to foreign countries under tax treaties. If you want this coverage, you are required to give us this information. If you fail to provide this information in a timely manner, or you provide incorrect or fraudulent information, you may be denied this coverage and you may be liable for penalties and interest.

You are not required to provide the information requested on a form that is subject to the Paperwork Reduction Act unless the form displays a valid OMB control number. Books or records relating to a form or its instructions must be retained as long as their contents may become material in the administration of any Internal Revenue law. Generally, tax returns and return information are confidential, as required by Code section 6103.

The time needed to complete and file this form will vary depending on individual circumstances. The estimated average time is: **Recordkeeping,** 2 hr., 9 min.; **Learning about the law or the form,** 35 min.; **Preparing and sending the form to the IRS,** 39 min. If you have comments concerning the accuracy of these time estimates or suggestions for making this form simpler, we would be happy to hear from you. You can write to the Tax Forms Committee, Western Area Distribution Center, Rancho Cordova, CA 95743-0001. **Do not** send the form to this address. Instead, see **Where To File** above.

Form 2159
(Rev. April 2003)

Department of the Treasury — Internal Revenue Service

Payroll Deduction Agreement

(See Instructions on the back of this page.)

TO: *(Employer name and address)*

Regarding: *(Taxpayer name and address)*

Contact Person's Name   Telephone *(Include area code)*

Social security or employer identification number
(Taxpayer)   *(Spouse)*

EMPLOYER—*See the instructions on the back of Part 2.* The taxpayer identified above on the right named you as an employer. Please read and sign the following statement to agree to withhold amount(s) from the taxpayer's *(employee's)* wages or salary to apply to taxes owed.
I agree to participate in this payroll deduction agreement and will withhold the amount shown below from each wage or salary payment due this employee. I will send the money to the Internal Revenue Service every: *(Check one box.)*

☐ WEEK ☐ TWO WEEKS ☐ MONTH ☐ OTHER *(Specify.)*_____

Signed: _____

Title: _____   Date: _____

Your telephone number *(Include area code)*
(Home)   *(Work or business)*

For assistance, call: **1-800-829-0115** *(Business)* or
1-800-829-8374 *(Individual – Self-Employed/Business Owners)*, or
1-800-829-0922 *(Individuals – Wage Earners)*

Or write: _____ **Campus**
                (City, State, and ZIP Code)

Financial Institution(s) *(Name and address)*

Kinds of taxes *(Form numbers)*	Tax Periods	Amount owed as of _____ $_____ , plus all penalties and interest provided by law.

I am paid every: *(Check one)*: ☐ WEEK ☐ TWO WEEKS ☐ MONTH ☐ OTHER *(Specify.)* _____

I agree to have $_____ deducted from my wage or salary payment beginning _____ until the total liability is paid in full. I also agree and authorize this deduction to be increased or decreased as follows: _____

Date of increase *(or decrease)*	Amount of Increase *(or decrease)*	New installment payment amount

Terms of this agreement—By completing and submitting this agreement, you *(the taxpayer)* agree to the following terms:

- You will make each payment so that we *(IRS)* receive it by the monthly due date stated on the front of this form. *If you cannot make a scheduled payment, contact us immediately.*
- This agreement is based on your current financial condition. We may modify or terminate the agreement if our information shows that your ability to pay has significantly changed. You must provide updated financial information when requested.
- While this agreement is in effect, you must file all federal tax returns and pay any *(federal)* taxes you owe on time.
- We will apply your federal tax refunds or overpayments *(if any)* to the amount you owe until it is fully paid.
- You must pay a $43 user fee, which we have authority to deduct from your first payment(s).
- If you default on your installment agreement, you must pay a $24 reinstatement fee if we reinstate the agreement. We have the

authority to deduct this fee from your first payment(s) after the agreement is reinstated.
- We will apply all payments on this agreement in the best interests of the United States.
- **We can terminate your installment agreement if:**
  - You do not make monthly installment payments as agreed.
  - You do not pay any other federal tax debt when due.
  - You do not provide financial information when requested.
- If we terminate your agreement, we may collect the entire amount you owe by levy on your income, bank accounts or other assets, or by seizing your property.
- We may terminate this agreement at any time if we find that collection of the tax is in jeopardy.
- This agreement may require managerial approval. We'll notify you when we approve or don't approve the agreement.

Additional Terms *(To be completed by IRS)*	**Note:** Internal Revenue Service employees may contact third parties in order to process and maintain this agreement.

Your signature	Title *(If Corporate Officer or Partner)*	Date

Spouse's signature *(If a joint liability)*		Date

Agreement examined or approved by *(Signature, title, function)*		Date

FOR IRS USE ONLY:

AGREEMENT LOCATOR NUMBER: ____ ____ ____ ____
Input Review Suppress Indicator: "1" *(unless specific balance due IA)*
☐ Check box if specific balance due IA; input Review Suppress Indicator "6"
Agreement Review Cycle: __ __ __ __ __ __ Earliest CSED _____
☐ Check box if pre-assessed modules included
Originator's ID:_____ Originator Code:_____
Name:_____ Title:_____

A NOTICE OF FEDERAL TAX LIEN *(Check one box below.)*
☐ **HAS ALREADY BEEN FILED**
☐ **WILL BE FILED IMMEDIATELY**
☐ **WILL BE FILED WHEN TAX IS ASSESSED**
☐ **MAY BE FILED IF THIS AGREEMENT DEFAULTS**

Part 1— Acknowledgement Copy *(Return to IRS)*   Catalog No. 21475H   www.irs.gov   Form **2159** (Rev. 4-2003)

Agreement Locator Number Designations

XX Position *(the first two numbers)* **denotes either the Initiator or Type of Agreement. The XX values are:**

00	Form 433-D initiated by AO on an ACS case
01	Service Center and Toll-free initiated agreements
02	AO Field Territory *(revenue officer)* initiated agreements
03	Direct Debit agreements initiated by any function
06	Exam initiated agreements
07	Submission Processing initiated agreements
08	Agreements initiated by other functions
11	Form 2159 agreement initiated by AO or ACS
12	AO or ACS agreement with multiple conditions
20	Status 22/24 accounts – Call Site/SCCB
90	SCCB initiated agreements – other than status 22 or 26
91	Form 2159 agreement initiated by SCCB
92	SCCB agreement with multiple conditions
99	Up to 120 days extensions

YY Position (the second two numbers) denotes Conditions Affecting the Agreement. The YY values are:

08	Continuous Wage Levy *(from ACS and RO)*
09	All other conditions
12	One year rule *(use for specific BAL DUE module agreements)*
15	In Business Trust Fund *(IBTF)* monitoring required
27	Restricted Interest/Penalty condition present
32	Unassessed modules to be included in agreement
36	Streamlined agreements, less than 60 months, up to $25,000
41	BMF in Business Deferral Level *(SCCB USE ONLY)*
53	*Report Currently Not Collectible (CNC)* if agreement defaults
63	Cross-reference TIN *(Status 63)*
66	File lien in event of default
70	Secondary TP responsible for Joint Liability
80	Review and revise payment amount
99	Up to 120 days extensions

When an agreement has more than one condition, use either 12 or 92 in the "XX" position and assign the primary condition *(YY)* based on the following priorities:

#1-53, #2-08, #3-27, or #4-15

The remaining multiple conditions will be input as a history item on IDRS by SCCB. For example, to construct a history item to record an unassessed module, use the following format:

UM309312 *(Unassessed module, MFT 30, 9312 Tax Period)*; or
UMFILE LIEN *(Unassessed module, file Lien, if appropriate)*

Installment Agreement Originator Codes

20	Collection field function regular agreement
21	Collection field function streamlined agreement
30	Reserved
31	Reserved
50	Field assistance regular agreement
51	Field assistance streamlined agreement
60	Examination regular agreement
61	Examination streamlined agreement
70	Toll-free regular agreement
71	Toll-free streamlined agreement
72	Paper regular agreement
73	Paper streamlined agreement
74	Voice Response Unit (system generated)
75	Automated Collection Branch regular
76	Automated Collection Branch streamlined
77	Automated Collection Branch Voice Response Unit regular *(system generated)*
78	Automated Collection Branch Voice Response Unit streamlined *(system generated)*
80	Other function regular agreement
81	Other function-streamlined agreement
90-91	Reserved for vendors – all streamlined agreements

Catalog No. 21475H   Form **2159** (Rev. 4-2003)

Appendix

Form **2159** (Rev. April 2003)	Department of the Treasury — Internal Revenue Service **Payroll Deduction Agreement** *(See Instructions on the back of this page.)*

TO: *(Employer name and address)*

Regarding: *(Taxpayer name and address)*

Contact Person's Name Telephone *(Include area code)*

Social security or employer identification number
(Taxpayer) *(Spouse)*

EMPLOYER—*See the instructions on the back of Part 2.* The taxpayer identified above on the right named you as an employer. Please read and sign the following statement to agree to withhold amount*(s)* from the taxpayer's *(employee's)* wages or salary to apply to taxes owed.
I agree to participate in this payroll deduction agreement and will withhold the amount shown below from each wage or salary payment due this employee. I will send the money to the Internal Revenue Service every: *(Check one box.)*

☐ WEEK ☐ TWO WEEKS ☐ MONTH ☐ OTHER *(Specify.)*_____

Signed: _____

Title: _____ Date: _____

Your telephone number *(Include area code)*
(Home) *(Work or business)*

For assistance, call: **1-800-829-0115** *(Business)* or
1-800-829-8374 *(Individual – Self-Employed/Business Owners)*, or
1-800-829-0922 *(Individuals – Wage Earners)*

Or write: _____ **Campus**
(City, State, and ZIP Code)

Financial Institution*(s)* *(Name and address)*

Kinds of taxes *(Form numbers)*	Tax Periods	Amount owed as of _____ $_____ , plus all penalties and interest provided by law.

I am paid every: *(Check one)*: ☐ WEEK ☐ TWO WEEKS ☐ MONTH ☐ OTHER *(Specify.)* _____
I agree to have $_____ deducted from my wage or salary payment beginning _____ until the total liability is paid in full. I also agree and authorize this deduction to be increased or decreased as follows: _____

Date of increase *(or decrease)*	Amount of Increase *(or decrease)*	New installment payment amount

Terms of this agreement—By completing and submitting this agreement, you *(the taxpayer)* agree to the following terms:

- You will make each payment so that we *(IRS)* receive it by the monthly due date stated on the front of this form. **If you cannot make a scheduled payment, contact us immediately.**
- This agreement is based on your current financial condition. We may modify or terminate the agreement if our information shows that your ability to pay has significantly changed. You must provide updated financial information when requested.
- While this agreement is in effect, you must file all federal tax returns and pay any *(federal)* taxes you owe on time.
- We will apply your federal tax refunds or overpayments *(if any)* to the amount you owe until it is fully paid.
- You must pay a $43 user fee, which we have authority to deduct from your first payment*(s)*.
- If you default on your installment agreement, you must pay a $24 reinstatement fee if we reinstate the agreement. We have the

authority to deduct this fee from your first payment(s) after the agreement is reinstated.
- We will apply all payments on this agreement in the best interests of the United States.
- **We can terminate your installment agreement if:**
  - You do not make monthly installment payments as agreed.
  - You do not pay any other federal tax debt when due.
  - You do not provide financial information when requested.
- If we terminate your agreement, we may collect the entire amount you owe by levy on your income, bank accounts or other assets, or by seizing your property.
- We may terminate this agreement at any time if we find that collection of the tax is in jeopardy.
- This agreement may require managerial approval. We'll notify you when we approve or don't approve the agreement.

Additional Terms *(To be completed by IRS)*

Note: Internal Revenue Service employees may contact third parties in order to process and maintain this agreement.

Your signature	Title *(If Corporate Officer or Partner)*	Date

Spouse's signature *(If a joint liability)*		Date

Agreement examined or approved by *(Signature, title, function)*	Date

FOR IRS USE ONLY:
AGREEMENT LOCATOR NUMBER: ____ ____ ____ ____
Input Review Suppress Indicator: "1" *(unless specific balance due IA)*
☐ Check box if specific balance due IA; input Review Suppress Indicator "6"
Agreement Review Cycle: __ __ __ __ __ __ Earliest CSED _____
☐ Check box if pre-assessed modules included
Originator's ID:_____ Originator Code:_____
Name:_____ Title:_____

A NOTICE OF FEDERAL TAX LIEN *(Check one box below.)*
☐ **HAS ALREADY BEEN FILED**
☐ **WILL BE FILED IMMEDIATELY**
☐ **WILL BE FILED WHEN TAX IS ASSESSED**
☐ **MAY BE FILED IF THIS AGREEMENT DEFAULTS**

Part 2— Employer's Copy Catalog No. 21475H www.irs.gov Form **2159** (Rev. 4-2003)

INSTRUCTIONS TO EMPLOYER

This payroll deduction agreement requires your approval. If you agree to participate, please complete the spaces provided under the employer section on the front of this form.

WHAT YOU SHOULD DO

- Enter the name and telephone number of a contact person. *(This will allow us to contact you if your employee's liability is satisfied ahead of time.)*

- Indicate when you will forward payments to IRS.

- Sign and date the form.

- After you and your employee have completed and signed the form, please return it *(all parts)* to IRS. Use the IRS address on the letter the employee received with the form or the address shown on the front of the form.

HOW TO MAKE PAYMENTS

☐ Please deduct the amount your employee agreed with the IRS to have deducted from each wage or salary payment due the employee.

☐ Make your check payable to the "United States Treasury." To insure proper credit, please write your employee's name and social security number on each payment.

☐ Send the money to the IRS mailing address printed on the letter that came with the agreement. Your employee should give you a copy of this letter. If there is no letter, use the IRS address shown on the front of the form.

Note: The amount of the liability shown on the form may not include all penalties and interest provided by law. Please continue to make payments unless IRS notifies you that the liability has been satisfied. When the amount owed, as shown on the form, is paid in full and IRS hasn't notified you that the liability has been satisfied, please call the appropriate telephone number below to request the final balance due.

If you need assistance, please call the telephone number on the letter that came with the agreement or write to the address shown on the letter. If there's no letter, please call the appropriate telephone number below or write IRS at the address shown on the front of the form.

For assistance, call: **1-800-829-0115** *(Business),* or
1-800-829-8374 *(Individual – Self-Employed/Business Owners),* or
1-800-829-0922 *(Individuals – Wage Earners)*

THANK YOU FOR YOUR COOPERATION

Catalog No. 21475H   Form **2159** (Rev. 4-2003)

Form **2159**
(Rev. April 2003)

Department of the Treasury — Internal Revenue Service

Payroll Deduction Agreement

(See Instructions on the back of this page.)

TO: *(Employer name and address)*

Regarding: *(Taxpayer name and address)*

Contact Person's Name   Telephone *(Include area code)*

Social security or employer identification number
(Taxpayer)   *(Spouse)*

EMPLOYER—*See the instructions on the back of Part 2.* The taxpayer identified above on the right named you as an employer. Please read and sign the following statement to agree to withhold amount(s) from the taxpayer's *(employee's)* wages or salary to apply to taxes owed.
I agree to participate in this payroll deduction agreement and will withhold the amount shown below from each wage or salary payment due this employee. I will send the money to the Internal Revenue Service every: *(Check one box.)*

☐ WEEK ☐ TWO WEEKS ☐ MONTH ☐ OTHER *(Specify.)* _____

Signed: _____

Title: _____   Date: _____

Your telephone number *(Include area code)*
(Home)   *(Work or business)*

For assistance, call: **1-800-829-0115** *(Business)* or
1-800-829-8374 *(Individual – Self-Employed/Business Owners),* or
1-800-829-0922 *(Individuals – Wage Earners)*

Or write: _____ **Campus** ___
            (City, State, and ZIP Code)

Financial Institution(s) *(Name and address)*

Kinds of taxes *(Form numbers)*	Tax Periods	Amount owed as of _____ $ _____ , plus all penalties and interest provided by law.

I am paid every: *(Check one)*: ☐ WEEK ☐ TWO WEEKS ☐ MONTH ☐ OTHER *(Specify.)* _____

I agree to have $_____ deducted from my wage or salary payment beginning _____ until the total liability is paid in full. I also agree and authorize this deduction to be increased or decreased as follows: _____

Date of increase *(or decrease)*	Amount of Increase *(or decrease)*	New installment payment amount

Terms of this agreement—By completing and submitting this agreement, you *(the taxpayer)* agree to the following terms:

- You will make each payment so that we *(IRS)* receive it by the monthly due date stated on the front of this form. **If you cannot make a scheduled payment, contact us immediately.**
- This agreement is based on your current financial condition. We may modify or terminate the agreement if our information shows that your ability to pay has significantly changed. You must provide updated financial information when requested.
- While this agreement is in effect, you must file all federal tax returns and pay any *(federal)* taxes you owe on time.
- We will apply your federal tax refunds or overpayments *(if any)* to the amount you owe until it is fully paid.
- You must pay a $43 user fee, which we have authority to deduct from your first payment(s).
- If you default on your installment agreement, you must pay a $24 reinstatement fee if we reinstate the agreement. We have the

- authority to deduct this fee from your first payment(s) after the agreement is reinstated.
- We will apply all payments on this agreement in the best interests of the United States.
- **We can terminate your installment agreement if:**
  - You do not make monthly installment payments as agreed.
  - You do not pay any other federal tax debt when due.
  - You do not provide financial information when requested.
- If we terminate your agreement, we may collect the entire amount you owe by levy on your income, bank accounts or other assets, or by seizing your property.
- We may terminate this agreement at any time if we find that collection of the tax is in jeopardy.
- This agreement may require managerial approval. We'll notify you when we approve or don't approve the agreement.

Additional Terms *(To be completed by IRS)*	**Note:** Internal Revenue Service employees may contact third parties in order to process and maintain this agreement.

Your signature	Title *(If Corporate Officer or Partner)*	Date

Spouse's signature *(If a joint liability)*		Date

Agreement examined or approved by *(Signature, title, function)*		Date

FOR IRS USE ONLY:

AGREEMENT LOCATOR NUMBER: ____ ____ ____ ____
Input Review Suppress Indicator: "1" *(unless specific balance due IA)*
☐ Check box if specific balance due IA; input Review Suppress Indicator "6"
Agreement Review Cycle: __ __ __ __ __ __   Earliest CSED _____
☐ Check box if pre-assessed modules included
Originator's ID: _____ Originator Code: _____
Name: _____ Title: _____

A NOTICE OF FEDERAL TAX LIEN *(Check one box below.)*
☐ **HAS ALREADY BEEN FILED**
☐ **WILL BE FILED IMMEDIATELY**
☐ **WILL BE FILED WHEN TAX IS ASSESSED**
☐ **MAY BE FILED IF THIS AGREEMENT DEFAULTS**

Part 3— Taxpayer's Copy   Catalog No. 21475H   www.irs.gov   Form **2159** (Rev. 4-2003)

INSTRUCTIONS TO TAXPAYER

If not already completed by an IRS employee, please fill in the information in the spaces provided on the front of this form for the following items:

- Your employer's name and address

- Your name*(s)* *(plus spouse's name if the amount owed is for a joint return)* and current address.

- Your social security number or employer identification number. *(Use the number that appears on the notice(s) you received.)* Also, enter your spouse's social security number if this is a joint liability.

- Your home and work telephone number*(s)*

- The complete name and address of your financial institution*(s)*

- The kind of taxes you owe *(form numbers)* and the tax periods

- The amount you owe as of the date you spoke to IRS

- When you are paid

- The amount you agreed to have deducted from your pay when you spoke to IRS

- The date the deduction is to begin

- The amount of any increase or decrease in the deduction amount, if you agreed to this with IRS; otherwise, leave BLANK

After you complete, sign *(along with your spouse if this is a joint liability)*, and date this agreement form, give it to your participating employer. If you received the form by mail, please give the employer a copy of the letter that came with it.

Your employer should mark the payment frequency on the form and sign it. Then the employer should return all parts of the form to the IRS address on your letter or the address shown in the "For assistance" box on the front of the form.

If you need assistance, please call the appropriate telephone number below or write IRS at the address shown on the form. However, if you received this agreement by mail, please call the telephone number on the letter that came with it or write IRS at the address shown on the letter.

For assistance, call: 1-800-829-0115 *(Business)*, or
1-800-829-8374 *(Individual – Self-Employed/Business Owners)*, or
1-800-829-0922 *(Individuals – Wage Earners)*

Note: This agreement **will not** affect your liability *(if any)* for backup withholding under Public Law 98-67, the Interest and Dividend Compliance Act of 1983.

Form **2555**

Department of the Treasury
Internal Revenue Service   (99)

Foreign Earned Income

▶ See separate instructions.   ▶ Attach to Form 1040.

OMB No. 1545-0074

2005

Attachment
Sequence No. **34**

For Use by U.S. Citizens and Resident Aliens Only

Name shown on Form 1040

Your social security number

Part I   **General Information**

| 1 | Your foreign address (including country) | 2 | Your occupation |

3	Employer's name ▶
4a	Employer's U.S. address ▶
b	Employer's foreign address ▶
5	Employer is (check any that apply): ▶	**a** ☐ A foreign entity	**b** ☐ A U.S. company	**c** ☐ Self
		d ☐ A foreign affiliate of a U.S. company	**e** ☐ Other (specify) ▶

6a   If, after 1981, you filed Form 2555 or Form 2555-EZ, enter the last year you filed the form. ▶

b   If you did not file Form 2555 or 2555-EZ after 1981 to claim either of the exclusions, check here ▶ ☐ and go to line 7.

c   Have you ever revoked either of the exclusions? . . . . ☐ Yes ☐ No

d   If you answered "Yes," enter the type of exclusion and the tax year for which the revocation was effective. ▶

7   Of what country are you a citizen/national? ▶

8a   Did you maintain a separate foreign residence for your family because of adverse living conditions at your
tax home? See **Second foreign household** on page 3 of the instructions . . . . ☐ Yes ☐ No

b   If "Yes," enter city and country of the separate foreign residence. Also, enter the number of days during your tax year that
you maintained a second household at that address. ▶

9   List your tax home(s) during your tax year and date(s) established. ▶

**Next, complete either Part II or Part III. If an item does not apply, enter "NA." If you do not give
the information asked for, any exclusion or deduction you claim may be disallowed.**

Part II   **Taxpayers Qualifying Under Bona Fide Residence Test** (See page 2 of the instructions.)

10   Date bona fide residence began ▶ , and ended ▶

11   Kind of living quarters in foreign country ▶ **a** ☐ Purchased house   **b** ☐ Rented house or apartment   **c** ☐ Rented room
d ☐ Quarters furnished by employer

12a   Did any of your family live with you abroad during any part of the tax year? . . . . ☐ Yes ☐ No

b   If "Yes," who and for what period? ▶

13a   Have you submitted a statement to the authorities of the foreign country where you claim bona fide residence
that you are not a resident of that country? (See instructions.) . . . . ☐ Yes ☐ No

b   Are you required to pay income tax to the country where you claim bona fide residence? (See instructions.) ☐ Yes ☐ No

**If you answered "Yes" to 13a and "No" to 13b, you do not qualify as a bona fide resident. Do not complete the rest of
this part.**

14   If you were present in the United States or its possessions during the tax year, complete columns **(a)–(d)** below. **Do not**
include the income from column **(d)** in Part IV, but report it on Form 1040.

(a) Date arrived in U.S.	(b) Date left U.S.	(c) Number of days in U.S. on business	(d) Income earned in U.S. on business (attach computation)	(a) Date arrived in U.S.	(b) Date left U.S.	(c) Number of days in U.S. on business	(d) Income earned in U.S. on business (attach computation)

15a   List any contractual terms or other conditions relating to the length of your employment abroad. ▶

b   Enter the type of visa under which you entered the foreign country. ▶

c   Did your visa limit the length of your stay or employment in a foreign country? If "Yes," attach explanation ☐ Yes ☐ No

d   Did you maintain a home in the United States while living abroad? . . . . ☐ Yes ☐ No

e   If "Yes," enter address of your home, whether it was rented, the names of the occupants, and their relationship
to you. ▶

For Paperwork Reduction Act Notice, see page 4 of separate instructions.   Cat. No. 11900P   Form **2555** (2005)

Form 2555 (2005)   Page **2**

Part III   Taxpayers Qualifying Under Physical Presence Test (See page 2 of the instructions.)

16 The physical presence test is based on the 12-month period from ▶ .... through ▶ ....

17 Enter your principal country of employment during your tax year. ▶ --

18 If you traveled abroad during the 12-month period entered on line 16, complete columns **(a)–(f)** below. Exclude travel between foreign countries that did not involve travel on or over international waters, or in or over the United States, for 24 hours or more. If you have no travel to report during the period, enter "Physically present in a foreign country or countries for the entire 12-month period." **Do not** include the income from column **(f)** below in Part IV, but report it on Form 1040.

(a) Name of country (including U.S.)	(b) Date arrived	(c) Date left	(d) Full days present in country	(e) Number of days in U.S. on business	(f) Income earned in U.S. on business (attach computation)

Part IV   All Taxpayers

Note: *Enter on lines 19 through 23 all income, including noncash income, you earned and actually or constructively received during your 2005 tax year for services you performed in a foreign country. If any of the foreign earned income received this tax year was earned in a prior tax year, or will be earned in a later tax year (such as a bonus), see the instructions.* **Do not** *include income from line 14, column* **(d),** *or line 18, column* **(f).** *Report amounts in U.S. dollars, using the exchange rates in effect when you actually or constructively received the income.*

> **If you are a cash basis taxpayer, report on Form 1040 all income you received in 2005, no matter when you performed the service.**

2005 Foreign Earned Income		Amount (in U.S. dollars)
19 Total wages, salaries, bonuses, commissions, etc.	19	
20 Allowable share of income for personal services performed (see instructions):		
a In a business (including farming) or profession	20a	
b In a partnership. List partnership's name and address and type of income. ▶ -------------------		
---	20b	
21 Noncash income (market value of property or facilities furnished by employer—attach statement showing how it was determined):		
a Home (lodging).	21a	
b Meals	21b	
c Car	21c	
d Other property or facilities. List type and amount. ▶ -------------------------	21d	
---		
22 Allowances, reimbursements, or expenses paid on your behalf for services you performed:		
a Cost of living and overseas differential . . . . `22a`		
b Family . . . . `22b`		
c Education . . . . `22c`		
d Home leave . . . . `22d`		
e Quarters . . . . `22e`		
f For any other purpose. List type and amount. ▶ ------------------- `22f`		
g Add lines 22a through 22f	22g	
23 Other foreign earned income. List type and amount. ▶ ---------------------------------	23	
---		
24 Add lines 19 through 21d, line 22g, and line 23	24	
25 Total amount of meals and lodging included on line 24 that is excludable (see instructions) . .	25	
26 Subtract line 25 from line 24. Enter the result here and on line 27 on page 3. This is your **2005 foreign earned income**. . . . . ▶	26	

Form **2555** (2005)

Appendix

Part V   **All Taxpayers**

27 Enter the amount from line 26 . . . . | 27 |
Are you claiming the housing exclusion or housing deduction?
☐ **Yes.** Complete Part VI.
☐ **No.** Go to Part VII.

Part VI   **Taxpayers Claiming the Housing Exclusion and/or Deduction**

28 Qualified housing expenses for the tax year (see instructions) . . . . | 28 |

29 Number of days in your qualifying period that fall within your 2005 tax
year (see instructions) . . . . | 29 | **days** |

30 Multiply $32.59 by the number of days on line 29. If 365 is entered on line 29, enter $11,894.00 here | 30 |

31 Subtract line 30 from line 28. If the result is zero or less, do not complete the rest of this part
or any of Part IX . . . . | 31 |

32 Enter employer-provided amounts (see instructions) . . . . . . | 32 |

33 Divide line 32 by line 27. Enter the result as a decimal (rounded to at least three places), but do
not enter more than "1.000" . . . . | 33 | × . |

34 **Housing exclusion.** Multiply line 31 by line 33. Enter the result but do not enter more than the
amount on line 32. Also, complete Part VIII . . . . ▶ | 34 |
Note: *The housing deduction is figured in Part IX. If you choose to claim the foreign earned
income exclusion, complete Parts VII and VIII before Part IX.*

Part VII   **Taxpayers Claiming the Foreign Earned Income Exclusion**

35 Maximum foreign earned income exclusion . . . . | 35 | $80,000 | 00 |

36 ● If you completed Part VI, enter the number from line 29.
● All others, enter the number of days in your qualifying period that
fall within your 2005 tax year (see the instructions for line 29). | 36 | **days** |

37 ● If line 36 and the number of days in your 2005 tax year (usually 365) are the same, enter "1.000."
● Otherwise, divide line 36 by the number of days in your 2005 tax year and enter the result
as a decimal (rounded to at least three places). | 37 | × . |

38 Multiply line 35 by line 37 . . . . | 38 |

39 Subtract line 34 from line 27 . . . . | 39 |

40 **Foreign earned income exclusion.** Enter the **smaller** of line 38 or line 39. Also, complete Part VIII ▶ | 40 |

Part VIII   **Taxpayers Claiming the Housing Exclusion, Foreign Earned Income Exclusion, or Both**

41 Add lines 34 and 40 . . . . | 41 |

42 Deductions allowed in figuring your adjusted gross income (Form 1040, line 37) that are allocable
to the excluded income. See instructions and attach computation . . . . | 42 |

43 Subtract line 42 from line 41. Enter the result here and in parentheses on **Form 1040, line 21.**
Next to the amount enter "Form 2555." On Form 1040, subtract this amount from your income
to arrive at total income on Form 1040, line 22 . . . . ▶ | 43 |

Part IX   **Taxpayers Claiming the Housing Deduction**—Complete this part only if **(a)** line 31 is more than line
34 and **(b)** line 27 is more than line 41.

44 Subtract line 34 from line 31 . . . . | 44 |

45 Subtract line 41 from line 27 . . . . | 45 |

46 Enter the **smaller** of line 44 or line 45 . . . . | 46 |
Note: *If line 45 is **more than** line 46 and you could not deduct all of your 2004 housing deduction
because of the 2004 limit, use the worksheet on page 4 of the instructions to figure the amount
to enter on line 47. Otherwise, go to line 48.*

47 Housing deduction carryover from 2004 (from worksheet on page 4 of the instructions) . . . | 47 |

48 **Housing deduction.** Add lines 46 and 47. Enter the total here and on Form 1040 to the left of
line 36. Next to the amount on Form 1040, enter "Form 2555." Add it to the total adjustments
reported on that line . . . . ▶ | 48 |

✿ *Printed on recycled paper*   Form **2555** (2005)

20**05**

Department of the Treasury
Internal Revenue Service

Instructions for Form 2555

Foreign Earned Income

Section references are to the Internal Revenue Code.

General Instructions

 Do not include on Form 1040, line 64 (federal income tax withheld), any taxes a foreign employer withheld from your pay and paid to the foreign country's tax authority instead of to the U.S. Treasury.

Purpose of Form

If you are a U.S. citizen or a U.S. resident alien living in a foreign country, you are subject to the same U.S. income tax laws that apply to citizens and resident aliens living in the United States. But if you qualify, use Form 2555 to exclude a limited amount of your foreign earned income. Also, use it to claim the housing exclusion or deduction. You cannot exclude or deduct more than your foreign earned income for the tax year.

You may be able to use Form 2555-EZ, Foreign Earned Income Exclusion, if none of your foreign earned income was from self-employment, your total foreign earned income did not exceed $80,000, you do not have any business or moving expenses, and you do not claim the housing exclusion or deduction. For more details, see Form 2555-EZ and its separate instructions.

Foreign country. A foreign country is any territory (including the air space, territorial waters, seabed, and subsoil) under the sovereignty of a government other than the United States. It does not include U.S. possessions or territories.

Note. Specific rules apply to determine if you are a resident or nonresident alien of the United States. See Pub. 519, U.S. Tax Guide for Aliens, for details.

Who Qualifies

You qualify for the tax benefits available to taxpayers who have foreign earned income if both 1 and 2 apply.

1. You meet the tax home test (see below).

2. You meet either the bona fide residence test (see page 2) or the physical presence test (see page 2).

Note. If your only earned income from work abroad is pay you received from the U.S. Government as its employee, you do not qualify for either of the exclusions or the housing deduction. Do not file Form 2555.

Tax home test. To meet this test, your tax home must be in a foreign country, or countries, throughout your period of bona fide residence or physical presence, whichever applies. For this purpose, your period of physical presence is the 330 full days during which you were present in a foreign country, not the 12 consecutive months during which those days occurred.

Your tax home is your regular or principal place of business, employment, or post of duty, regardless of where you maintain your family residence. If you do not have a regular or principal place of business because of the nature of your trade or business, your tax home is your regular place of abode (the place where you regularly live).

You are not considered to have a tax home in a foreign country for any period during which your abode is in the United States. However, if you are temporarily present in the United States, or you maintain a dwelling in the United States (whether or not that dwelling is used by your spouse and dependents), it does not necessarily mean that your abode is in the United States during that time.

Example. You are employed on an offshore oil rig in the territorial waters of a foreign country and work a 28-day on/28-day off schedule. You return to your family residence in the United States during your off periods. You are considered to have an abode in the

United States and do not meet the tax home test. You cannot claim either of the exclusions or the housing deduction.

Violation of Travel Restrictions

Generally, if you were in a foreign country in violation of U.S. travel restrictions, the following rules applied:

1. Any time spent in that country cannot be counted in determining if you qualify under the bona fide residence or physical presence test,

2. Any income earned in that country is not considered foreign earned income, and

3. Any housing expenses in that country (or housing expenses for your spouse or dependents in another country while you were in that country) are not considered qualified housing expenses.

See the list on this page for countries to which U.S. travel restrictions applied.

Additional Information

Pub. 54, Tax Guide for U.S. Citizens and Resident Aliens Abroad, has more information about the bona fide residence test, the physical presence test, the foreign earned income exclusion, and the housing exclusion and deduction. You can get this publication from most U.S. embassies and consulates or by writing to: National Distribution Center, P.O. Box 8903, Bloomington, IL 61702-8903. You can also download this publication (as well as other forms and publications) from the IRS website at *www.irs.gov.*

Waiver of Time Requirements

If your tax home was in a foreign country and you were a bona fide resident of, or physically present in, a foreign country and had to leave because of war, civil unrest, or similar adverse conditions, the minimum time requirements specified under the bona fide residence and physical presence tests may be waived. You must be able to show that you reasonably could have expected to meet the minimum time requirements if you had not been required to leave. Each year the IRS will publish in the Internal Revenue Bulletin a list of countries and the dates they qualify for the waiver. If you left one of the countries during the period indicated, you can claim the tax benefits on Form 2555, but only for the number of days you were a bona fide resident of, or physically present in, the foreign country.

If you can claim either of the exclusions or the housing deduction

List of Countries To Which Travel Restrictions Applied in 2004 and 2005		
Country	Starting Date	Ending Date
Cuba	January 1, 1987	Still in effect
Iraq*	January 1, 1987	July 29, 2004
Libya*	August 2, 1990	September 20, 2004

*Individuals whose activities in Iraq and Libya are or were permitted by a specific or general license issued by the Department of the Treasury's Office of Foreign Assets Control (OFAC) were not in violation of U.S. law. Accordingly, the restrictions did not apply to such individuals with respect to the activities permitted by the license.

Cat. No. 11901A

because of the waiver of time requirements, attach a statement to your return explaining that you expected to meet the applicable time requirement, but the conditions in the foreign country prevented you from the normal conduct of business. Also, enter "Claiming Waiver" in the top margin on page 1 of your 2005 Form 2555.

When To File

A 2005 calendar year Form 1040 is generally due April 17, 2006.

However, you are automatically granted a 2-month extension of time to file (to June 15, 2006, for a 2005 calendar year return) if, on the due date of your return, you live outside the United States and Puerto Rico and your tax home (defined on page 1) is outside the United States and Puerto Rico. If you take this extension, you must attach a statement to your return explaining that you meet these two conditions.

The automatic 2-month extension also applies to paying the tax. However, interest is charged on the unpaid tax from the regular due date (April 15, 2006, for a 2005 calendar year return) until it is paid.

Special extension of time. The first year you plan to take the foreign earned income exclusion and/or the housing exclusion or deduction, you may not expect to qualify until after the automatic 2-month extension period described earlier. If this occurs, you can apply for an extension to a date after you expect to qualify.

To apply for this extension, complete and file Form 2350, Application for Extension of Time To File U.S. Income Tax Return, with the Internal Revenue Service Center, Philadelphia, PA 19255, before the due date of your return. Interest is charged on the tax not paid by the regular due date as explained earlier.

Choosing the Exclusion(s)

To choose either of the exclusions, complete the appropriate parts of Form 2555 and file it with your Form 1040 or Form 1040X, Amended U.S. Individual Income Tax Return. Your initial choice to claim the exclusion must usually be made on a timely filed return (including extensions) or on a return amending a timely filed return. However, there are exceptions. See Pub. 54 for details.

Once you choose to claim an exclusion, that choice remains in effect for that year and all future years unless it is revoked. To revoke your choice, you must attach a statement to your return for the first year you do not wish to claim the exclusion(s). If you revoke your choice, you cannot claim the exclusion(s) for your next 5 tax years without the approval of the Internal Revenue Service. See Pub. 54 for more information.

Earned income credit. You cannot take the earned income credit if you claim either of the exclusions or the housing deduction.

Specific Instructions

Part II

Bona Fide Residence Test

To meet this test, you must be one of the following:
• A U.S. citizen who is a bona fide resident of a foreign country, or countries, for an uninterrupted period that includes an entire tax year (January 1–December 31, if you file a calendar year return), or
• A U.S. resident alien who is a citizen or national of a country with which the United States has an income tax treaty in effect and who is a bona fide resident of a foreign country, or countries, for an uninterrupted period that includes an entire tax year (January 1–December 31, if you file a calendar year return). See Pub. 901, U.S. Tax Treaties, for a list of countries with which the United States has an income tax treaty in effect.

No specific rule determines if you are a bona fide resident of a foreign country because the determination involves your intention about the length and nature of your stay. Evidence of your intention may be your words and acts. If these conflict, your acts carry more weight than your words. Generally, if you go to a foreign country for a definite, temporary purpose and return to the United States after you accomplish it, you are not a bona fide resident of the foreign country. If accomplishing the purpose requires an extended, indefinite stay, and you make your home in the foreign country, you may be a bona fide resident. See Pub. 54 for more information and examples.

Lines 13a and 13b. If you submitted a statement of nonresidence to the authorities of a foreign country in which you earned income and the authorities hold that you are not subject to their income tax laws by reason of nonresidency in the foreign country, you are not considered a bona fide resident of that country.

If you submitted such a statement and the authorities have not made an adverse determination of your nonresident status, you are not considered a bona fide resident of that country.

Part III

Physical Presence Test

To meet this test, you must be a U.S. citizen or resident alien who is physically present in a foreign country, or countries, for at least 330 full days during any period of 12 months in a row. A full day means the 24-hour period that starts at midnight.

To figure the minimum of 330 full days' presence, add all separate periods you were present in a foreign country during the 12-month period shown on line 16. The 330 full days can be interrupted by periods when you are traveling over international waters or are otherwise not

in a foreign country. See Pub. 54 for more information and examples.

Note. A nonresident alien who, with a U.S. citizen or U.S. resident alien spouse, chooses to be taxed as a resident of the United States can qualify under this test if the time requirements are met. See Pub. 54 for details on how to make this choice.

Part IV

Enter in this part the total foreign earned income you earned and received (including income constructively received) during the tax year. If you are a cash basis taxpayer, report on Form 1040 all income you received during the tax year regardless of when you earned it.

Income is earned in the tax year you perform the services for which you receive the pay. But if you are a cash basis taxpayer and, because of your employer's payroll periods, you received your last salary payment for 2004 in 2005, that income may be treated as earned in 2005. If you cannot treat that salary payment as income earned in 2005, the rules explained under *Income earned in prior year* on page 3 apply. See Pub. 54 for more details.

Foreign earned income for this purpose means wages, salaries, professional fees, and other compensation received for personal services you performed in a foreign country during the period for which you meet the tax home test and either the bona fide residence test or the physical presence test. It also includes noncash income (such as a home or car) and allowances or reimbursements.

Foreign earned income does not include amounts that are actually a distribution of corporate earnings or profits rather than a reasonable allowance as compensation for your personal services. It also does not include the following types of income.
• Pension and annuity income (including social security and railroad retirement benefits treated as social security).
• Interest, ordinary dividends, capital gains, alimony, etc.
• Portion of 2004 moving expense deduction allocable to 2005 that is included in your 2005 gross income. For details, see *Moving Expense Attributable to Foreign Earnings in 2 Years* under *Moving Expenses* in Pub. 54.
• Amounts paid to you by the U.S. Government or any of its agencies if you were an employee of the U.S. Government or any of its agencies.
• Amounts received after the end of the tax year following the tax year in which you performed the services.
• Amounts you must include in gross income because of your employer's contributions to a nonexempt employees' trust or to a nonqualified annuity contract.

Income received in prior year. Foreign earned income received in 2004 for services you performed in 2005 can be excluded from your 2004 gross income if,

-2-

and to the extent, the income would have been excludable if you had received it in 2005. To claim the additional exclusion, you must amend your 2004 tax return. To do this, file Form 1040X.

Income earned in prior year. Foreign earned income received in 2005 for services you performed in 2004 can be excluded from your 2005 gross income if, and to the extent, the income would have been excludable if you had received it in 2004.

If you are excluding income under this rule, do not include this income in Part IV. Instead, attach a statement to Form 2555 showing how you figured the exclusion. Enter the amount that would have been excludable in 2004 on Form 2555 to the left of line 43. Next to the amount enter "Exclusion of Income Earned in 2004." Include it in the total reported on line 43.

Note. If you claimed any deduction, credit, or exclusion on your 2004 return that is definitely related to the 2004 foreign earned income you are excluding under this rule, you may have to amend your 2004 income tax return to adjust the amount you claimed. To do this, file Form 1040X.

Line 20. If you engaged in an unincorporated trade or business in which both personal services and capital were material income-producing factors, a reasonable amount of compensation for your personal services will be considered earned income. The amount treated as earned income, however, cannot be more than 30% of your share of the net profits from the trade or business after subtracting the deduction for one-half of self-employment tax.

If capital is not an income-producing factor and personal services produced the business income, the 30% rule does not apply. Your entire gross income is earned income.

Line 25. Enter the value of meals and/or lodging provided by, or on behalf of, your employer that is excludable from your income under section 119. To be excludable, the meals and lodging must have been provided for your employer's convenience and on your employer's business premises. In addition, you must have been required to accept the lodging as a condition of your employment. If you lived in a camp provided by, or on behalf of, your employer, the camp may be considered part of your employer's business premises. See *Exclusion of Meals and Lodging* in Pub. 54 for details.

Part VI

Line 28. Enter the total reasonable expenses paid or incurred during the tax year by you, or on your behalf, for your foreign housing and the housing of your spouse and dependents if they lived with you. You can also include the reasonable expenses of a second foreign household (defined below). Housing expenses are considered reasonable to the extent they are not lavish or extravagant under the circumstances.

Housing expenses include rent, utilities (other than telephone charges), real and personal property insurance, nonrefundable fees paid to obtain a lease, rental of furniture and accessories, residential parking, and household repairs. You can also include the fair rental value of housing provided by, or on behalf of, your employer if you have not excluded it on line 25.

Do not include deductible interest and taxes, any amount deductible by a tenant-stockholder in connection with cooperative housing, the cost of buying or improving a house, principal payments on a mortgage, or depreciation on the house. Also, do not include the cost of domestic labor, pay television, or the cost of buying furniture or accessories.

Include expenses for housing only during periods for which:
• The value of your housing is not excluded from gross income under section 119 (unless you maintained a second foreign household as defined below), and
• You meet the tax home test and either the bona fide residence or physical presence test.

Second foreign household. If you maintained a separate foreign household for your spouse and dependents at a place other than your tax home because the living conditions at your tax home were dangerous, unhealthful, or otherwise adverse, you can include the expenses of the second household on line 28.

Married couples. The following rules apply if both you and your spouse qualify for the tax benefits of Form 2555:

If you and your spouse lived in the same foreign household and file a joint return, you can figure your housing amounts (line 31) either separately or jointly. If you file separate returns, you must figure your housing amounts separately. In figuring your housing amounts separately, you can allocate your qualified housing expenses (line 28) between yourselves in any proportion you wish, but each spouse claiming a housing amount must use his or her full base amount housing amount (line 30). In figuring your housing amount jointly, either spouse (but not both) can claim the housing exclusion or housing deduction. However, if you and your spouse have different periods of residence or presence and the one with the shorter period of residence or presence claims the exclusion or deduction, you can claim as housing expenses only the expenses for that shorter period. The spouse claiming the exclusion or deduction can aggregate the housing expenses of both spouses and subtract his or her base housing amount.

If you and your spouse lived in separate foreign households, you each can claim qualified expenses for your own household only if:

1. Your tax homes were not within a reasonable commuting distance of each other, and
2. Each spouse's household was not within a reasonable commuting distance of the other spouse's tax home.

Otherwise, only one spouse can claim his or her housing exclusion or deduction. This is true even if you and your spouse file separate returns.

See Pub. 54 for additional information.

Line 29. Enter the number of days in your qualifying period that fall within your 2005 tax year. Your qualifying period is the period during which you meet the tax home test and either the bona fide residence or the physical presence test.

Example. You establish a tax home and bona fide residence in a foreign country on August 14, 2005. You maintain the tax home and residence until January 31, 2007. You are a calendar year taxpayer. The number of days in your qualifying period that fall within your 2005 tax year is 140 (August 14 through December 31, 2005).

Nontaxable U.S. Government allowances. If you or your spouse received a nontaxable housing allowance as a military or civilian employee of the U.S. Government, see Pub. 54 for information on how that allowance may affect your housing exclusion or deduction.

Line 32. Enter any amount your employer paid or incurred on your behalf that is foreign earned income included in your gross income for the tax year (without regard to section 911).

Examples of employer-provided amounts are:
• Wages and salaries received from your employer.
• The fair market value of compensation provided in kind (such as the fair rental value of lodging provided by your employer as long as it is not excluded on line 25).
• Rent paid by your employer directly to your landlord.
• Amounts paid by your employer to reimburse you for housing expenses, educational expenses of your dependents, or as part of a tax equalization plan.

Self-employed individuals. If all of your foreign earned income (Part IV) is self-employment income, skip lines 32 and 33 and enter -0- on line 34. If you qualify, be sure to complete Part IX.

Part VII

Married couples. If both you and your spouse qualify for, and choose to claim, the foreign earned income exclusion, the amount of the exclusion is figured separately for each of you. You each must complete Part VII of your separate Forms 2555.

Community income. The amount of the exclusion is not affected by the income-splitting provisions of community

-3-

property laws. The sum of the amounts figured separately for each of you is the total amount excluded on a joint return.

Part VIII

If you claim either of the exclusions, you cannot claim any deduction (including moving expenses), credit, or exclusion that is definitely related to the excluded income. If only part of your foreign earned income is excluded, you must prorate such items based on the ratio that your excludable earned income bears to your total foreign earned income. See Pub. 54 for details on how to figure the amount allocable to the excluded income.

The exclusion under section 119 and the housing deduction are not considered definitely related to the excluded income.

Line 42. Report in full on Form 1040 and related forms and schedules all deductions allowed in figuring your adjusted gross income (Form 1040, line 37). Enter on line 42 the total amount of those deductions (such as the deduction for moving expenses, the deduction for one-half of self-employment tax, and the expenses claimed on Schedule C or C-EZ (Form 1040)) that are not allowed

because they are allocable to the excluded income. This applies only to deductions definitely related to the excluded earned income. See Pub. 54 for details on how to report your itemized deductions (such as unreimbursed employee business expenses) that are allocable to the excluded income.

IRA deduction. The IRA deduction is not definitely related to the excluded income. However, special rules apply in figuring the amount of your IRA deduction. For details, see Pub. 590, Individual Retirement Arrangements (IRAs).

Foreign taxes. You cannot take a credit or deduction for foreign income taxes paid or accrued on income that is excluded under either of the exclusions.

If all of your foreign earned income is excluded, you cannot claim a credit or deduction for the foreign taxes paid or accrued on that income.

If only part of your income is excluded, you cannot claim a credit or deduction for the foreign taxes allocable to the excluded income. See Pub. 514, Foreign Tax Credit for Individuals, for details on

how to figure the amount allocable to the excluded income.

Part IX

If line 31 is more than line 34 and line 27 is more than line 41, complete this part to figure your housing deduction. Also, complete this part to figure your housing deduction carryover from 2004.

One-year carryover. If the amount on line 44 is more than the amount on line 45, you may carry the difference over to your 2006 tax year. If you cannot deduct the excess in 2006 because of the 2006 limit, you may not carry it over to any future tax year.

Paperwork Reduction Act Notice. We ask for the information on this form to carry out the Internal Revenue laws of the United States. You are required to give us the information. We need it to ensure that you are complying with these laws and to allow us to figure and collect the right amount of tax.

You are not required to provide the information requested on a form that is subject to the Paperwork Reduction Act unless the form displays a valid OMB control number. Books or records relating to a form or its instructions must be retained as long as their contents may become material in the administration of any Internal Revenue law. Generally, tax returns and return information are confidential, as required by section 6103.

The average time and expenses required to complete and file this form will vary depending on individual circumstances. For the estimated averages, see the instructions for your income tax return.

If you have suggestions for making this form simpler, we would be happy to hear from you. See the instructions for your income tax return.

Housing Deduction Carryover Worksheet—Line 47
Keep for Your Records

1 Enter the amount from your 2004 Form 2555, line 44 . . . . 1. _____

2 Enter the amount from your 2004 Form 2555, line 46 . . . . 2. _____

3 Subtract line 2 from line 1. If the result is zero, **stop;** enter -0- on line 47 of your 2005 Form 2555. You do not have any housing deduction carryover from 2004 . . . . 3. _____

4 Enter the amount from your 2005 Form 2555, line 45 . . . . 4. _____

5 Enter the amount from your 2005 Form 2555, line 46 . . . . 5. _____

6 Subtract line 5 from line 4 . . . . 6. _____

7 Enter the **smaller** of line 3 or line 6 here and on line 47 of your 2005 Form 2555. If line 3 is **more than** line 6, you **may not** carry the difference over to any future tax year . . . . ▶ 7. _____

-4-

Form **2555-EZ**

Department of the Treasury
Internal Revenue Service (99)

Foreign Earned Income Exclusion

▶ See separate instructions.   ▶ Attach to Form 1040.

OMB No. 1545-0074

2005

Attachment
Sequence No. **34A**

Name shown on Form 1040

Your social security number

You May Use This Form If You:

- Are a U.S. citizen or a resident alien.
- Earned wages/salaries in a foreign country.
- Had total foreign earned income of $80,000 or less.
- Are filing a calendar year return that covers a 12-month period.

And You:

- Do not have self-employment income.
- Do not have business/moving expenses.
- Do not claim the foreign housing exclusion or deduction.

Part I   Tests To See If You Can Take the Foreign Earned Income Exclusion

1   Bona Fide Residence Test

a Were you a bona fide resident of a foreign country or countries for a period that includes an entire tax year (see page 2 of the instructions)? . . . . ☐ **Yes** ☐ **No**
- If you answered "Yes," you meet this test. Fill in line 1b and then go to line 3.
- If you answered "No," you **do not** meet this test. Go to line 2 to see if you meet the Physical Presence Test.

b Enter the date your bona fide residence began ▶ _____ , and ended (see instructions) ▶ _____ .

2   Physical Presence Test

a Were you physically present in a foreign country or countries for at least 330 full days during—
{ 2005 **or**
{ any other period of 12 months in a row starting or ending in 2005? }   . . . . ☐ **Yes** ☐ **No**

- If you answered "Yes," you meet this test. Fill in line 2b and then go to line 3.
- If you answered "No," you **do not** meet this test. You **cannot** take the exclusion unless you meet the Bona Fide Residence Test above.

b The physical presence test is based on the 12-month period from ▶ _____ through ▶ _____ .

3   Tax Home Test. Was your tax home in a foreign country or countries throughout your period of bona fide residence or physical presence, whichever applies? . . . . ☐ **Yes** ☐ **No**
- If you answered "Yes," you can take the exclusion. Complete Part II below and then go to page 2.
- If you answered "No," you **cannot** take the exclusion. **Do not** file this form.

Part II   **General Information**

4 Your foreign address (including country)

5 Your occupation

6 Employer's name

7 Employer's U.S. address (including ZIP code)

8 Employer's foreign address

9 Employer is (check any that apply):
a A U.S. business . . . . ☐
b A foreign business . . . . ☐
c Other (specify) ▶ _____ ☐

10a If you filed Form 2555 or 2555-EZ after 1981, enter the last year you filed the form. ▶ _____
b If you did not file Form 2555 or 2555-EZ after 1981, check here ▶ ☐ and go to line 11a now.
c Have you ever revoked the foreign earned income exclusion? . . . . ☐ **Yes** ☐ **No**
d If you answered "Yes," enter the tax year for which the revocation was effective. ▶ _____
11a List your tax home(s) during 2005 and date(s) established. ▶ _____
b Of what country are you a citizen/national? ▶ _____

For Paperwork Reduction Act Notice, see page 3 of separate instructions.   Cat. No. 13272W   Form **2555-EZ** (2005)

Form 2555-EZ (2005)

Part III Days Present in the United States—Complete this part if you were in the United States or its possessions during 2005.

12	(a) Date arrived in U.S.	(b) Date left U.S.	(c) Number of days in U.S. on business	(d) Income earned in U.S. on business (attach computation)

Part IV Figure Your Foreign Earned Income Exclusion

13	Maximum foreign earned income exclusion	13	$80,000 00
14	Enter the number of days in your qualifying period that fall within 2005 . **14** **days**		
15	Did you enter 365 on line 14? ☐ **Yes.** Enter "1.000." ☐ **No.** Divide line 14 by 365 and enter the result as a decimal (rounded to at least three places). }	15	× .
16	Multiply line 13 by line 15	16	
17	Enter, in U.S. dollars, the total foreign earned income you earned and received in 2005 (see instructions). Be sure to include this amount on Form 1040, line 7	17	
18	**Foreign earned income exclusion.** Enter the **smaller** of line 16 or line 17 here and in parentheses on **Form 1040, line 21.** Next to the amount enter "2555-EZ." On Form 1040, subtract this amount from your income to arrive at total income on Form 1040, line 22 . . . . ▶	18	

Form **2555-EZ** (2005)

♻ *Printed on recycled paper*

20**05**

Department of the Treasury
Internal Revenue Service

Instructions for Form 2555-EZ

Foreign Earned Income Exclusion

General Instructions

⚠️ **CAUTION** *Do not include on Form 1040, line 64 (federal income tax withheld), any taxes a foreign employer withheld from your pay and paid to the foreign country's tax authority instead of to the U.S. Treasury.*

Purpose of Form

If you qualify, you can use Form 2555-EZ instead of Form 2555, Foreign Earned Income, to exclude a limited amount of your foreign earned income. You cannot exclude more than your foreign earned income for the year.

Remember, U.S. citizens and U.S. resident aliens living in a foreign country are subject to the same U.S. income tax laws that apply to citizens and resident aliens living in the United States.

Foreign country. A foreign country is any territory (including the air space, territorial waters, seabed, and subsoil) under the sovereignty of a government other than the United States. It does not include U.S. possessions or territories.

Note. Specific rules apply to determine if you are a resident or nonresident alien of the United States. See Pub. 519, U.S. Tax Guide for Aliens, for details.

Who Qualifies

You can use Form 2555-EZ to claim the foreign earned income exclusion if all five of the following apply.

1. You meet the seven conditions listed at the top of Form 2555-EZ.
2. Your total foreign earned income received in 2005 is reported on Form 1040, line 7.
3. You do not have a housing deduction carryover from 2004.
4. You meet either the bona fide residence test (see the instructions for

lines 1a and 1b on page 2) or the physical presence test (see the instructions for lines 2a and 2b on page 2).
5. You meet the tax home test (see the instructions for line 3 on page 2).

Note. If your only earned income from work abroad is pay you received from the U.S. Government as its employee, you do not qualify for the foreign earned income exclusion. Do not file Form 2555-EZ.

Married Couples

If both you and your spouse qualify for, and choose to claim, the foreign earned income exclusion, figure the amount of the exclusion separately for each of you. You must each complete separate Forms 2555-EZ.

Community income. The amount of the exclusion is not affected by the income-splitting provisions of community property laws. The sum of the amounts figured separately for each of you is the total amount excluded on a joint return.

Violation of Travel Restrictions

Generally, if you were in a foreign country in violation of U.S. travel restrictions, the following rules applied.

1. Any time spent in that country cannot be counted in determining if you qualify under the bona fide residence or physical presence test, and
2. Any income earned in that country is not considered foreign earned income. See the list below for countries to which U.S. travel restrictions applied.

Additional Information

Pub. 54, Tax Guide for U.S. Citizens and Resident Aliens Abroad, has more information about the bona fide residence test, the physical presence test, and the

foreign earned income exclusion. You can get this publication from most U.S. embassies and consulates or by writing to: National Distribution Center, P.O. Box 8903, Bloomington, IL, 61702-8903. You can also download this publication (as well as other forms and publications) from the IRS website at *www.irs.gov*.

Waiver of Time Requirements

If your tax home was in a foreign country and you were a bona fide resident of, or physically present in, a foreign country and had to leave because of war, civil unrest, or similar adverse conditions, the minimum time requirements specified under the bona fide residence and physical presence tests may be waived. You must be able to show that you reasonably could have expected to meet the minimum time requirements if you had not been required to leave. Each year the IRS will publish in the Internal Revenue Bulletin a list of countries and the dates they qualify for the waiver. If you left one of the countries during the period indicated, you can claim the foreign earned income exclusion on Form 2555-EZ, but only for the number of days you were a bona fide resident of, or physically present in, the foreign country.

If you can claim the foreign earned income exclusion because of the waiver of time requirements, attach a statement to your return explaining that you expected to meet the applicable time requirement, but the conditions in the foreign country prevented you from the normal conduct of business. Also, enter "Claiming Waiver" in the top margin on page 1 of your 2005 Form 2555-EZ.

When To File

Form 1040 is generally due April 17, 2006.

However, you are automatically granted a 2-month extension of time to file (to June 15, 2006) if, on the due date of your return, you live outside the United States and Puerto Rico and your tax home (defined later) is outside the United States and Puerto Rico. If you take this extension, you must attach a statement to your return explaining that you meet these two conditions.

The automatic 2-month extension also applies to paying the tax. However,

List of Countries To Which Travel Restrictions Applied in 2004 and 2005

Country	Starting Date	Ending Date
Cuba	January 1, 1987	Still in effect
Iraq*	January 1, 1987	July 29, 2004
Libya*	August 2, 1990	September 20, 2004

*Individuals whose activities in Iraq and Libya are or were permitted by a specific or general license issued by the Department of the Treasury's Office of Foreign Assets Control (OFAC) were not in violation of U.S. law. Accordingly, the restrictions did not apply to such individuals with respect to the activities permitted by the license.

Cat. No. 14623P

interest is charged on the unpaid tax from the regular due date until it is paid.

Special extension of time. The first year you plan to take the foreign earned income exclusion, you may not expect to qualify until after the automatic 2-month extension period described above. If this occurs, you can apply for an extension to a date after you expect to qualify.

To apply for this extension, complete and file Form 2350, Application for Extension of Time To File U.S. Income Tax Return, with the Internal Revenue Service Center, Philadelphia, PA 19255, before the due date of your return. Interest is charged on the tax not paid by the regular due date as explained earlier.

Choosing the Exclusion

To choose the foreign earned income exclusion, complete the appropriate parts of Form 2555-EZ and file it with your Form 1040 or Form 1040X, Amended U.S. Individual Income Tax Return. Your initial choice to claim the exclusion must usually be made on a timely filed return (including extensions) or on a return amending a timely filed return. However, there are exceptions. See Pub. 54 for more information.

Once you choose to claim the exclusion, that choice remains in effect for that year and all future years unless it is revoked. To revoke your choice, you must attach a statement to your return for the first year you do not wish to claim the exclusion. If you revoke your choice, you cannot claim the exclusion for your next 5 tax years without the approval of the Internal Revenue Service. See Pub. 54 for details.

Earned income credit. You cannot take the earned income credit if you claim the exclusion.

Foreign tax credit or deduction. You cannot claim a credit or deduction for foreign income taxes paid on income you exclude. If all of your foreign earned income is excluded, you cannot claim a credit or deduction for the foreign taxes paid on that income. If only part of your income is excluded, you cannot claim a credit or deduction for the foreign taxes allocable to the excluded income. For details on how to figure the amount allocable to the excluded income, see Pub. 514, Foreign Tax Credit for Individuals.

IRA deduction. If you claim the exclusion, special rules apply in figuring the amount of your IRA deduction. For details, see Pub. 590, Individual Retirement Arrangements (IRAs).

Specific Instructions

Lines 1a and 1b

Bona Fide Residence Test

To meet this test, you must be one of the following:

● A U.S. citizen who is a bona fide resident of a foreign country, or countries, for an uninterrupted period that includes an entire tax year (January 1–December 31), or
● A U.S. resident alien who is a citizen or national of a country with which the United States has an income tax treaty in effect and who is a bona fide resident of a foreign country, or countries, for an uninterrupted period that includes an entire tax year (January 1–December 31). See Pub. 901, U.S. Tax Treaties, for a list of countries with which the United States has an income tax treaty in effect.

No specific rule determines if you are a bona fide resident of a foreign country because the determination involves your intention about the length and nature of your stay. Evidence of your intention may be your words and acts. If these conflict, your acts carry more weight than your words. Generally, if you go to a foreign country for a definite, temporary purpose and return to the United States after you accomplish it, you are not a bona fide resident of the foreign country. If accomplishing the purpose requires an extended, indefinite stay, and you make your home in the foreign country, you may be a bona fide resident. See Pub. 54 for more information and examples.

If you submitted a statement of nonresidence to the authorities of a foreign country in which you earned income and the authorities hold that you are not subject to their income tax laws by reason of nonresidency in the foreign country, you are not considered a bona fide resident of that country.

If you submitted such a statement and the authorities have not made an adverse determination of your nonresident status, you are not considered a bona fide resident of that country.

Line 1b. If you answered "Yes" on line 1a, enter the dates your bona fide residence began and ended. If you are still a bona fide resident, enter "Continues" in the space for the date your bona fide residence ended.

Lines 2a and 2b

Physical Presence Test

To meet this test, you must be a U.S. citizen or resident alien who is physically present in a foreign country, or countries, for at least 330 full days during any period of 12 months in a row. A full day means the 24-hour period that starts at midnight.

To figure the minimum of 330 full days' presence, add all separate periods you were present in a foreign country during the 12-month period in which those days occurred. The 330 full days can be interrupted by periods when you are traveling over international waters or are otherwise not in a foreign country. See Pub. 54 for more information and examples.

Note. A nonresident alien who, with a U.S. citizen or U.S. resident alien spouse,

chooses to be taxed as a resident of the United States can qualify under this test if the time requirements are met. See Pub. 54 for details on how to make this choice.

Line 3

Tax Home Test

To meet this test, your tax home must be in a foreign country, or countries, throughout your period of bona fide residence or physical presence, whichever applies. For this purpose, your period of physical presence is the 330 full days during which you were present in a foreign country, not the 12 consecutive months during which those days occurred.

Your tax home is your regular or principal place of business, employment, or post of duty, regardless of where you maintain your family residence. If you do not have a regular or principal place of business because of the nature of your trade or business, your tax home is your regular place of abode (the place where you regularly live).

You are not considered to have a tax home in a foreign country for any period during which your abode is in the United States. However, if you are temporarily present in the United States, or you maintain a dwelling in the United States (whether or not that dwelling is used by your spouse and dependents), it does not necessarily mean that your abode is in the United States during that time.

Example. You are employed on an offshore oil rig in the territorial waters of a foreign country and work a 28-day on/ 28-day off schedule. You return to your family residence in the United States during your off periods. You are considered to have an abode in the United States and do not meet the tax home test. You cannot claim the foreign earned income exclusion.

Line 12

Complete columns (a) through (d) if you were present in the United States or any of its possessions in 2005. Do not include time spent in the United States or its possessions before your period of bona fide residence or physical presence, whichever applies, began or after it ended.

Column (d). Enter, in U.S. dollars, the amount of income earned in the United States on business (such as meetings or conventions). Attach a statement showing how you determined the amount. Do not include this income on line 17. Even if you live and work in a foreign country, any income earned during the time spent in the United States on business is considered U.S. source income and cannot be excluded.

Line 14

Enter the number of days in your qualifying period that fall within 2005. Your qualifying period is the period during which you meet the tax home test and either the bona fide residence test or the physical presence test.

Example. You establish a tax home and bona fide residence in a foreign country on August 14, 2005. You maintain the tax home and residence until January 31, 2007. The number of days in your qualifying period that fall within 2005 is 140 (August 14 through December 31, 2005).

Line 17

Enter the total foreign earned income you earned and received in 2005. Report the amount in U.S. dollars using the exchange rates in effect when you actually received the income. Be sure to report on Form 1040 all income you received in 2005 regardless of when you earned it.

Income is earned in the year you performed the services for which you received the pay. But if you received your last wage or salary payment for 2004 in 2005 because of your employer's payroll period, that income may be treated as earned in 2005. If you cannot treat that wage or salary payment as earned in 2005, the rules explained on this page under *Income earned in prior year* apply. See Pub. 54 for more details.

Foreign earned income. For purposes of this form, foreign earned income means only the following types of income received for personal services you performed in a foreign country during the period for which you meet the tax home test and either the bona fide residence test or the physical presence test.

- Wages, salaries, tips, and bonuses.
- Noncash income (such as a home or car) if reported as income on Form 1040, line 7.
- Allowances or reimbursements if reported as income on Form 1040, line 7.

Foreign earned income does not include—
- Amounts from line 12, column (d),
- Amounts paid to you by the U.S. Government or any of its agencies if you were an employee of the U.S. Government or any of its agencies,
- Amounts that are actually a distribution of corporate earnings or profits rather than a reasonable allowance as compensation for your personal services, or
- Amounts received after the end of the tax year following the tax year in which you performed the services.

Income earned in prior year. Foreign earned income received in 2005 for services you performed in 2004 can be excluded from your 2005 gross income if, and to the extent, the income would have been excludable if you had received it in 2004.

If you are excluding income under this rule, do not include this income on line 17. Instead, attach a statement to Form 2555-EZ showing how you figured the exclusion. Enter the amount that would have been excludable in 2004 on Form 2555-EZ to the left of line 18. Next to the amount enter "Exclusion of Income Earned in 2004." Include it in the total reported on line 18.

Note. If you claimed any deduction, credit, or exclusion on your 2004 return that is definitely related to the 2004 foreign earned income you are excluding under this rule, you may have to amend your 2004 income tax return to adjust the amount claimed. To do this, file Form 1040X.

Paperwork Reduction Act Notice. We ask for the information on this form to carry out the Internal Revenue laws of the United States. You are required to give us the information. We need it to ensure that you are complying with these laws and to allow us to figure and collect the right amount of tax.

You are not required to provide the information requested on a form that is subject to the Paperwork Reduction Act unless the form displays a valid OMB control number. Books or records relating to a form or its instructions must be retained as long as their contents may become material in the administration of any Internal Revenue law. Generally, tax returns and return information are confidential, as required by Internal Revenue Code section 6103.

The average time and expenses required to complete and file this form will vary depending on individual circumstances. For the estimated averages, see the instructions for your income tax return.

If you have suggestions for making this form simpler, we would be happy to hear from you. See the instructions for your income tax return.

Form **2678** (Rev. June 2002)	Department of Treasury- Internal Revenue Service **Employer Appointment of Agent** Under Section 3504 of the Internal Revenue Code	OMB Number 1545-0748

1. To

Director, Submission Processing

_____ Processing Center

Instructions

Employer or Payer: Please complete this form and give it to the Agent.

Agent: Please attach a letter requesting authority to do either all that is required of the employer for wages you pay on the employer's behalf or all that is required of the payer for requirements of backup withholding. *(See applicable Revenue Procedures 70-6 or 84-33.)* Forward both the letter of request and Form 2678 to the Internal Revenue Service Center Director, Submission Processing where you file your Form 941 returns.

2. Employer's or Payer's Name	3. Employer's or Payer's Address *(Number and street, city, town or post office, State and ZIP Code)*
4. Employer's Identification Number	
5. Agent's Name	6. Agent's Address
7. Agent's Employer Identification Number	

8. Effective For *(Check the box or boxes that apply)*

☐ Employment Taxes *(Rev. Proc 70-6)*
☐ Backup Withholding *(Rev. Proc. 84-33)*

9. If Filing under Rev. Proc. 70-6, does this apply to all employees?

☐ Yes ☐ No

10. Effective Date of Appointment by Employer or Payer

Under Section 3504 of the Internal Revenue Code, please authorize this agent to do all that is required under *(Check the one(s) that apply)*

☐ Chapter 21 *(FICA)*
☐ Chapter 22 *(Railroad Retirement)*
☐ Chapter 24-
  ☐ Withholding and/or
  ☐ Backup Withholding
☐ Chapter 25 *(General Provisions)* of Subtitle C

NOTE: Appointment of an Agent under Section 3504 does NOT apply to Form 940, Employer's Annual Federal Unemployment Return (Chap. 26 of the Internal Revenue Code).

The agent named above has been appointed either to pay wages for employers and/or report and deposit backup withholding amounts for payers. This appointment is effective on the date shown in item 10. It is understood that the Agent and the employer or payer are subject to all provisions of law and regulations *(including penalties)* which apply to employers or payers.

Signature of Employer or Payer

Date

Title of signing official *(Indicate whether the person signing is an owner, partner, member of firm, fiduciary, or a corporate officer)*

For Internal Revenue Service Use Only

Effective Date Granted by IRS

Catalog Number 18770D

Form **2678** (Rev. 6-2002)

Paperwork Reduction Act Notice

We ask for this information to carry out the Internal Revenue laws of the United States. We need it to ensure that taxpayers are complying with these laws and to allow us to figure and collect the right amount of tax. You are required to give us this information. The time needed to complete this form will vary depending on the individual circumstances. The estimated average time is: 30 minutes. If you have comments concerning the accuracy of this time estimate or suggestions for making this form more simple, we would be happy to hear from you. You can write to the Tax Form Committee, Western Area Distribution Center, Rancho Cordova, CA 95743-0001. DO NOT send this form to this address. Instead, send it to the Director of the Internal Revenue Service Center where you file your returns.

**File with the
Internal Revenue Service,
Submission Processing Center at:**

Cincinnati, OH 45999

Ogden, UT 84201

Philadelphia, PA 19255

Catalog Number 18770D

Form **2678** (Rev. 6-2002)

Form 2848
(Rev. March 2004)
Department of the Treasury
Internal Revenue Service

Power of Attorney
and Declaration of Representative

▶ Type or print. ▶ See the separate instructions.

OMB No. 1545-0150

For IRS Use Only
Received by:
Name _____
Telephone _____
Function _____
Date __/__/__

Part I **Power of Attorney**
Caution: *Form 2848 will not be honored for any purpose other than representation before the IRS.*

1 **Taxpayer information.** Taxpayer(s) must sign and date this form on page 2, line 9.

Taxpayer name(s) and address	Social security number(s)	Employer identification number
	Daytime telephone number ( )	Plan number (if applicable)

hereby appoint(s) the following representative(s) as attorney(s)-in-fact:

2 **Representative(s)** must sign and date this form on page 2, Part II.

Name and address	CAF No. .... Telephone No. .... Fax No. .... Check if new: Address ☐ Telephone No. ☐ Fax No. ☐
Name and address	CAF No. .... Telephone No. .... Fax No. .... Check if new: Address ☐ Telephone No. ☐ Fax No. ☐
Name and address	CAF No. .... Telephone No. .... Fax No. .... Check if new: Address ☐ Telephone No. ☐ Fax No. ☐

to represent the taxpayer(s) before the Internal Revenue Service for the following tax matters:

3 **Tax matters**

Type of Tax (Income, Employment, Excise, etc.) or Civil Penalty (see the instructions for line 3)	Tax Form Number (1040, 941, 720, etc.)	Year(s) or Period(s) (see the instructions for line 3)

4 **Specific use not recorded on Centralized Authorization File (CAF).** If the power of attorney is for a specific use not recorded on CAF, check this box. See the instructions for **Line 4. Specific uses not recorded on CAF.** . . . . ▶ ☐

5 **Acts authorized.** The representatives are authorized to receive and inspect confidential tax information and to perform any and all acts that I (we) can perform with respect to the tax matters described on line 3, for example, the authority to sign any agreements, consents, or other documents. The authority does not include the power to receive refund checks (see line 6 below), the power to substitute another representative, the power to sign certain returns, or the power to execute a request for disclosure of tax returns or return information to a third party. See the line 5 instructions for more information.

Exceptions. An unenrolled return preparer cannot sign any document for a taxpayer and may only represent taxpayers in limited situations. See **Unenrolled Return Preparer** on page 2 of the instructions. An enrolled actuary may only represent taxpayers to the extent provided in section 10.3(d) of Circular 230. See the line 5 instructions for restrictions on tax matters partners.

List any specific additions or deletions to the acts otherwise authorized in this power of attorney: ....
....
....
....

6 **Receipt of refund checks.** If you want to authorize a representative named on line 2 to receive, **BUT NOT TO ENDORSE OR CASH,** refund checks, initial here _____ and list the name of that representative below.

Name of representative to receive refund check(s) ▶

For Privacy Act and Paperwork Reduction Notice, see page 4 of the instructions.   Cat. No. 11980J   Form **2848** (Rev. 3-2004)

Form 2848 (Rev. 3-2004)   Page **2**

7   **Notices and communications.** Original notices and other written communications will be sent to you and a copy to the first representative listed on line 2.

   a   If you also want the second representative listed to receive a copy of notices and communications, check this box   .   . ▶ ☐

   b   If you do not want any notices or communications sent to your representative(s), check this box   .   .   .   . ▶ ☐

8   **Retention/revocation of prior power(s) of attorney.** The filing of this power of attorney automatically revokes all earlier power(s) of attorney on file with the Internal Revenue Service for the same tax matters and years or periods covered by this document. If you **do not** want to revoke a prior power of attorney, check here.   .   .   .   . ▶ ☐
   YOU MUST ATTACH A COPY OF ANY POWER OF ATTORNEY YOU WANT TO REMAIN IN EFFECT.

9   **Signature of taxpayer(s).** If a tax matter concerns a joint return, **both** husband and wife must sign if joint representation is requested, otherwise, see the instructions. If signed by a corporate officer, partner, guardian, tax matters partner, executor, receiver, administrator, or trustee on behalf of the taxpayer, I certify that I have the authority to execute this form on behalf of the taxpayer.

   ▶ **IF NOT SIGNED AND DATED, THIS POWER OF ATTORNEY WILL BE RETURNED.**

Signature	Date	Title (if applicable)
☐ ☐ ☐ ☐ ☐		
Print Name PIN Number		Print name of taxpayer from line 1 if other than individual
Signature	Date	Title (if applicable)
☐ ☐ ☐ ☐ ☐		
Print Name PIN Number		

Part II   **Declaration of Representative**

Caution: *Students with a special order to represent taxpayers in Qualified Low Income Taxpayer Clinics or the Student Tax Clinic Program, see the instructions for Part II.*

Under penalties of perjury, I declare that:

   ● I am not currently under suspension or disbarment from practice before the Internal Revenue Service;

   ● I am aware of regulations contained in Treasury Department Circular No. 230 (31 CFR, Part 10), as amended, concerning the practice of attorneys, certified public accountants, enrolled agents, enrolled actuaries, and others;

   ● I am authorized to represent the taxpayer(s) identified in Part I for the tax matter(s) specified there; and

   ● I am one of the following:

   a   Attorney—a member in good standing of the bar of the highest court of the jurisdiction shown below.

   b   Certified Public Accountant—duly qualified to practice as a certified public accountant in the jurisdiction shown below.

   c   Enrolled Agent—enrolled as an agent under the requirements of Treasury Department Circular No. 230.

   d   Officer—a bona fide officer of the taxpayer's organization.

   e   Full-Time Employee—a full-time employee of the taxpayer.

   f   Family Member—a member of the taxpayer's immediate family (i.e., spouse, parent, child, brother, or sister).

   g   Enrolled Actuary—enrolled as an actuary by the Joint Board for the Enrollment of Actuaries under 29 U.S.C. 1242 (the authority to practice before the Service is limited by section 10.3(d) of Treasury Department Circular No. 230).

   h   Unrolled Return Preparer—the authority to practice before the Internal Revenue Service is limited by Treasury Department Circular No. 230, section 10.7(c)(1)(viii). You must have prepared the return in question and the return must be under examination by the IRS. See **Unrolled Return Preparer** on page 2 of the instructions.

▶ **IF THIS DECLARATION OF REPRESENTATIVE IS NOT SIGNED AND DATED, THE POWER OF ATTORNEY WILL BE RETURNED.** See the Part II instructions.

Designation—Insert above letter **(a–h)**	Jurisdiction (state) or identification	Signature	Date

Form **2848** (Rev. 3-2004)

Instructions for Form 2848

(Rev. March 2004)

Department of the Treasury
Internal Revenue Service

Power of Attorney and Declaration of Representative

Section references are to the Internal Revenue Code unless otherwise noted.

General Instructions

What's New

Revocation of an existing power of attorney. The instructions have been revised to allow representatives to use the same procedures as taxpayers for revoking an existing power of attorney. See **Revocation of Power of Attorney/Withdrawal of Representative** on page 2.

Authorization to file Form 2848 electronically. Your representative may be able to file Form 2848 with the IRS electronically. PIN number boxes have been added to the taxpayer's signature section. Entering a PIN number will give your representative authority to file Form 2848 electronically using the PIN number as the electronic signature. You can use any five digits other than all zeros as a PIN number. You may use the same PIN number that you used on other filings with the IRS. See **Where To File** below if completing Form 2848 only for this purpose.

Use of Form 2848 is limited to appointing a representative. If the representative you appoint is not qualified to sign Part II of this form, Form 2848 will not be honored and will be returned to you. As of March 2004, the IRS will no longer treat such invalid forms as authority for the person you named to receive your tax information.

Purpose of Form

Use Form 2848 to authorize an individual to represent you before the IRS. The individual you authorize must be a person eligible to practice before the IRS. The eligible individuals are listed in **Part II**, Declaration of Representative, items **a-h**. You may authorize a student who works in a Qualified Low Income Taxpayer Clinic (QLITC) or Student Tax Clinic Program (STCP) to represent you under a special order issued by the Office of

Professional Responsibility. See page 3. Your authorization of a qualifying representative will also allow that individual to receive and inspect your confidential tax information. See the instructions for line 7 on page 4.

Use **Form 8821,** Tax Information Authorization, if you want to authorize an individual or organization to receive or inspect your confidential tax return information, but do not want to authorize the individual or organization to represent you before the IRS.

Use **Form 56,** Notice Concerning Fiduciary Relationship, to notify the IRS of the existence of a fiduciary relationship. A fiduciary (trustee, executor, administrator, receiver, or guardian) stands in the position of a taxpayer and acts as the taxpayer, not as a representative. If a fiduciary wishes to authorize an individual to represent or perform certain acts on behalf of the entity, then a power of attorney must be filed and signed by the fiduciary who is acting in the position of the taxpayer.

Where To File

Generally, mail or fax Form 2848 directly to the IRS. See the **Where To File Chart** below. Exceptions are listed below.
• If Form 2848 is for a specific use, mail or fax it to the office handling the specific matter. For more information on specific use, see the instructions for line 4 on page 3.
• If you complete Form 2848 only for the purpose of electronic signature authorization, **do not** file Form 2848 with the IRS. Instead, give it to your representative, who will retain the document.

Authority Granted

This power of attorney authorizes the representative to perform any and all acts you can perform, such as signing consents extending the time to assess tax, recording the interview, or executing waivers agreeing to a tax adjustment.

Where To File Chart

IF you live in...	THEN use this address...	Fax number*
Alabama, Arkansas, Connecticut, Delaware, District of Columbia, Florida, Georgia, Illinois, Indiana, Kentucky, Louisiana, Maine, Maryland, Massachusetts, Michigan, Mississippi, New Hampshire, New Jersey, New York, North Carolina, Ohio, Pennsylvania, Rhode Island, South Carolina, Tennessee, Vermont, Virginia, or West Virginia	Internal Revenue Service Memphis Accounts Management Center 5333 Getwell Road Stop 8423 Memphis, TN 38118	901-546-4115
Alaska, Arizona, California, Colorado, Hawaii, Idaho, Iowa, Kansas, Minnesota, Missouri, Montana, Nebraska, Nevada, New Mexico, North Dakota, Oklahoma, Oregon, South Dakota, Texas, Utah, Washington, Wisconsin, or Wyoming	Internal Revenue Service Ogden Accounts Management Center 1973 N. Rulon White Blvd. Mail Stop 6737 Ogden, UT 84404	801-620-4249
All APO and FPO addresses, American Samoa, nonpermanent residents of Guam or the Virgin Islands**, Puerto Rico (or if excluding income under Internal Revenue Code section 933), a foreign country: U.S. citizens and those filing Form 2555, 2555-EZ, or 4563.	Internal Revenue Service Philadelphia Accounts Management Center 11601 Roosevelt Blvd. DPSW 312 Philadelphia, PA 19255	215-516-1017

* These numbers may change without notice.
**Permanent residents of Guam should use Department of Taxation, Government of Guam, P.O. Box 23607, GMF, GU 96921; permanent residents of the Virgin Islands should use: V.I. Bureau of Internal Revenue, 9601 Estate Thomas Charlotte Amalie, St. Thomas, V.I. 00802.

Cat. No. 11981U

Also, you may authorize your representative to substitute another representative or delegate authority to another representative by adding this authority in the space provided on line 5. However, authorizing someone as your power of attorney does not relieve you of your tax obligations.

The power to sign tax returns can be granted only in limited situations. See the instructions for line 5 on page 3.

Unenrolled Return Preparer

An unenrolled return preparer is an individual other than an attorney, CPA, enrolled agent, or enrolled actuary who prepares and signs a taxpayer's return as the preparer, or who prepares a return but is not required (by the instructions to the return or regulations) to sign the return.

An unenrolled return preparer is permitted to represent you only before customer service representatives, revenue agents, and examination officers, with respect to an examination regarding the return he or she prepared.

An unenrolled return preparer **cannot:**
• Represent a taxpayer before other offices of the IRS, such as Collection or Appeals. This includes the Automated Collection System (ACS) unit.
• Execute closing agreements.
• Extend the statutory period for tax assessments or collection of tax.
• Execute waivers.
• Execute claims for refund.
• Receive refund checks.

For more information, see Rev. Proc. 81-38, printed as **Pub. 470,** Limited Practice Without Enrollment.

If the unenrolled return preparer does not meet the requirements for limited representation, you may file Form 8821, which will authorize the unenrolled return preparer to inspect and/or receive your taxpayer information, but will not authorize the unenrolled return preparer to represent you. See Form 8821.

Revocation of Power of Attorney/Withdrawal of Representative

If you want to revoke an existing power of attorney and do not want to name a new representative, or if a representative wants to withdraw from representation, send a copy of the previously executed power of attorney to the IRS, using the **Where To File Chart** on page 1. The copy of the power of attorney must have a current signature of the taxpayer if the taxpayer is revoking, or the representative if the representative is withdrawing, under the original signature on line 9. Write "REVOKE" across the top of Form 2848. If you do not have a copy of the power of attorney you want to revoke or withdraw, send a statement to the IRS. The statement of revocation or withdrawal must indicate that the authority of the power of attorney is revoked, list the tax matters, and must be signed and dated by the taxpayer or representative. If the taxpayer is revoking, list the name and address of each recognized representative whose authority is revoked. If the representative is withdrawing, list the name, TIN, and address (if known) of the taxpayer.

To revoke a specific use power of attorney, send the power of attorney or statement of revocation/withdrawal to the IRS office handling your case, using the above instructions.

Substitute Form 2848

If you want to prepare and use a substitute Form 2848, see **Pub. 1167,** General Rules and Specifications for Substitute Forms and Schedules. If your substitute Form 2848 is approved, the form approval number must be printed in the lower left margin of each substitute Form 2848 you file with the IRS.

Additional Information

Additional information concerning practice before the IRS may be found in:
• **Pub. 216,** Conference and Practice Requirements and
• Treasury Department Circular **No. 230.**

For general information about taxpayer rights, see **Pub. 1,** Your Rights as a Taxpayer.

Specific Instructions

Part I. Power of Attorney

Line 1. Taxpayer Information

Individuals. Enter your name, social security number (SSN), individual taxpayer identification number (ITIN), and/or employer identification number (EIN), if applicable, and your street address or post office box. **Do not** use your representative's address or post office box for your own. If a joint return is, or will be, filed and you and your spouse are designating the same representative(s), also enter your spouse's name and SSN or ITIN, and your spouse's address if different from yours.

Corporations, partnerships, or associations. Enter the name, EIN, and business address. If this form is being prepared for corporations filing a consolidated tax return (Form 1120), do not attach a list of subsidiaries to this form. Only the parent corporation information is required on line 1. Also, for line 3 only list Form 1120 in the Tax Form Number column. A subsidiary must file its own Form 2848 for returns that must be filed separately from the consolidated return, such as **Form 720,** Quarterly Federal Excise Tax Return, and **Form 941,** Employer's Quarterly Federal Tax Return.

Employee plan. Enter the plan name, EIN of the plan sponsor, three-digit plan number, and business address of the sponsor.

Trust. Enter the name, title, and address of the trustee, and the name and EIN of the trust.

Estate. Enter the name, title, and address of the decedent's executor/personal representative, and the name and identification number of the estate. The identification number for an estate includes both the EIN, if the estate has one, and the decedent's SSN or ITIN.

Line 2. Representative(s)

Enter your representative's full name. Only individuals may be named as representatives. Use the identical full name on all submissions and correspondence. If you want to name more than three representatives, indicate so on this line and attach an additional Form(s) 2848.

Enter the nine-digit CAF number for each representative. If a CAF number has not been assigned, enter "None," and the IRS will issue one directly to your representative. The CAF number is a unique nine-digit identification number (not the SSN, EIN, PTIN, or enrollment card number) that the IRS assigns to representatives. The CAF number is not an indication of authority to practice. The representative should use the assigned CAF number on all future powers of attorney. CAF numbers will not be assigned for employee plans and exempt organizations application requests.

Check the appropriate box to indicate if either the address, telephone number, or fax number is new since a CAF number was assigned.

If the representative is a former employee of the Federal Government, he or she must be aware of the postemployment restrictions contained in 18 U.S.C. 207 and in Treasury Department Circular No. 230, section 10.25. Criminal penalties are provided for violation of the statutory restrictions, and the Office of Professional Responsibility is authorized to take disciplinary action against the practitioner.

Students in QLITCs and the STCP. If the lead attorney or CPA will be listed as a representative, list the lead attorney or CPA first on line 2, then the student on the next line. Also see page 4 for how to complete Part II.

Line 3. Tax Matters

Enter the type of tax, the tax form number, and the year(s) or period(s) in order for the power of attorney to be valid. For example, you may list "Income tax, Form 1040" for calendar year "2003" and "Excise tax, Form 720" for the "1st, 2nd, 3rd, and 4th quarters of 2003." For multiple years, you may list "2001 through (thru or a dash (−)) 2003" for an income tax return; for quarterly returns, list "1st, 2nd, 3rd, and 4th quarters of 2001 through 2002" (or 2nd 2002 − 3rd 2003). For fiscal years, enter the ending year and month, using the YYYYMM format. Do not use a general reference such as "All years," "All periods," or "All taxes." Any power of attorney with a general reference will be returned. Representation can only be granted for the years or periods listed on line 3.

You may list any tax years or periods that have already ended as of the date you sign the power of attorney. However, you may include on a power of attorney only future tax periods that end no later than 3 years after the date the power of attorney is received by the IRS. The 3 future periods are determined starting after December 31 of the year the power of attorney is received by the IRS. You must enter the type of tax, the tax form number, and the future year(s) or period(s). If the matter relates to estate tax, enter the date of the decedent's death instead of the year or period.

If the type of tax, tax form number, or years or periods does not apply to the matter (i.e., representation for a penalty or filing a ruling request or determination), specifically describe the matter to which the power of attorney pertains and enter "Not Applicable" in the appropriate column(s).

Civil penalty representation (including the trust fund recovery penalty). Forms 2848 for civil penalty issues will now be recorded on the CAF. Generally, this applies to non-return related civil penalties, such as the penalty for not meeting the due diligence requirement for return preparers of earned income credit and the penalty for failure to file information returns. For example, Joann prepares Form 2848 authorizing Margaret to represent her before the IRS regarding the penalty for failure to file information returns. Margaret will have authority to represent Joann for all non-return related civil penalties. However, Margaret will not be able to represent Joann for any other tax matters, such as Form 941 or Form 1040 issues unless authorized on Form 2848.

Representation for return related civil penalties, such as the accuracy-related penalty or the failure to file penalty is included when representation is authorized for the related tax return. For example, Diana prepares Form 2848 authorizing Susan to represent Diana for an examination of her 2001 and 2002 Form 1040. If the accuracy-related penalty is proposed by the IRS during the examination, Susan would be authorized to discuss the penalty with the IRS.

How to complete line 3. On line 3, enter "Civil penalties" in the type of tax column and the year(s) to which the penalty applies in the year(s) or period(s) column. Enter "Not Applicable" in the tax form number column. You do not have to enter the specific penalty.

Line 4. Specific Uses Not Recorded on CAF

Generally, the IRS records powers of attorney on the CAF system. However, a power of attorney will not be recorded

on the CAF if it does not relate to a specific tax period (except for civil penalties) or if it is for a specific issue. Examples of specific issues include but are not limited to the following:

- Requests for a private letter ruling or technical advice,
- Applications for an EIN,
- Claims filed on **Form 843,** Claim for Refund and Request for Abatement,
- Corporate dissolutions, and
- Requests to change accounting methods or periods.

Check the box on line 4 if the power of attorney is for a use that will not be listed on the CAF. If the box on line 4 is checked, the representative should mail or fax the power of attorney to the IRS office handling the matter. Otherwise, the representative should bring a copy of the power of attorney to each meeting with the IRS.

A specific-use power of attorney will not revoke any prior powers of attorney.

Line 5. Acts Authorized

Use line 5 to modify the acts that your named representative(s) can perform. In the space provided, describe any specific additions or deletions. For example, the representative's authority to substitute another representative or to delegate authority must be specifically stated by you on line 5.

Disclosure of returns to a third party. A representative cannot execute consents that will allow the IRS to disclose your tax return or return information to a third party unless this authority is specifically delegated to the representative on line 5.

Authority to sign your return. Regulations section 1.6012-1(a)(5) permits another person to sign a return for you **only** in the following circumstances:
(a) Disease or injury,
(b) Continuous absence from the United States (including Puerto Rico), for a period of at least 60 days prior to the date required by law for filing the return, or
(c) Specific permission is requested of and granted by the IRS for other good cause.

Authority to sign your income tax return may be granted to **(1)** your representative or **(2)** an agent (a person other than your representative).

Authorizing your representative. Write a statement on line 5 that you are authorizing your representative to sign your income tax return pursuant to Regulations section 1.6012-1(a)(5) by reason of *[enter the specific reason listed under (a), (b), or (c) under **Authority to sign your return** above].*

Authorizing an agent. To authorize an agent you must do **all four** of the following.

1. Complete lines 1-3.
2. Check the box on line 4.
3. Write the following statement on line 5:

"This power of attorney is being filed pursuant to Regulations section 1.6012-1(a)(5), which requires a power of attorney to be attached to a return if a return is signed by an agent by reason of *[enter the specific reason listed under (a), (b), or (c) under **Authority to sign your return** above].* No other acts on behalf of the taxpayer are authorized."

4. Sign and date the form. See the instructions for line 9 for more information on signatures. The agent *does not* complete Part II of Form 2848.

Tax matters partner. The tax matters partner (TMP) (as defined in section 6231(a)(7)) is authorized to perform various acts on behalf of the partnership. The following are examples of acts performed by the TMP that **cannot** be delegated to the representative:
- Binding nonnotice partners to a settlement agreement under section 6224 and, under certain circumstances,

binding all partners to a settlement agreement under Tax Court Rule 248 and
• Filing a request for administrative adjustment on behalf of the partnership under section 6227.

Line 6. Receipt of Refund Checks

If you want to authorize your representative to receive, but not endorse, refund checks on your behalf, you must initial and enter the name of that person in the space provided. Treasury Department Circular No. 230, section 10.31, prohibits an attorney, CPA, or enrolled agent, any of whom is an income tax return preparer, from endorsing or otherwise negotiating a tax refund check that is not issued to him or her.

Line 7. Notices and Communications

Original notices and other written communications will be sent to you and a copy to the first representative listed. If you check:
• **Box (a).** The original will be sent to you and copies to the first two listed representatives.
• **Box (b).** The original will be sent to you. No copies will be sent to any representatives.

Line 8. Retention/Revocation of Prior Power(s) of Attorney

If there is any existing power(s) of attorney that you **do not** want to revoke, check the box on this line and attach a copy of the power(s) of attorney. The filing of a Form 2848 will **not** revoke any Form 8821 that is in effect.

Line 9. Signature of Taxpayer(s)

Individuals. You must sign and date the power of attorney. If a joint return has been filed and both husband and wife will be represented by the same individual(s), both must sign the power of attorney. However, if a joint return has been filed and the husband and wife will be represented by different individuals, each spouse must execute his or her own power of attorney on a separate Form 2848.

Corporations or associations. An officer having authority to bind the taxpayer must sign.

Partnerships. All partners must sign unless one partner is authorized to act in the name of the partnership. A partner is authorized to act in the name of the partnership if, under state law, the partner has authority to bind the partnership. A copy of such authorization must be attached. For purposes of executing Form 2848, the TMP is authorized to act in the name of the partnership. However, see **Tax matters partner** on page 3. For dissolved partnerships, see Regulations section 601.503(c)(6).

All others. If the taxpayer is a dissolved corporation, decedent, insolvent, or a person for whom or by whom a fiduciary (a trustee, guarantor, receiver, executor, or administrator) has been appointed, see Regulations section 601.503(d).

Part II. Declaration of Representative

The representative(s) you name must sign and date this declaration and enter the designation (i.e., items **a-h**) under which he or she is authorized to practice before the IRS. In addition, the representative(s) must list the following in the "Jurisdiction/Identification" column:

a Attorney—Enter the two-letter abbreviation for the state (e.g., "NY" for New York) in which admitted to practice.

b Certified Public Accountant—Enter the two-letter abbreviation for the state (e.g., "CA" for California) in which licensed to practice.

c Enrolled Agent—Enter the enrollment card number issued by the Office of Professional Responsibility.

d Officer—Enter the title of the officer (e.g., President, Vice President, or Secretary).

e Full-Time Employee—Enter title or position (e.g., Comptroller or Accountant).

f Family Member—Enter the relationship to taxpayer (must be a spouse, parent, child, brother, or sister).

g Enrolled Actuary—Enter the enrollment card number issued by the Joint Board for the Enrollment of Actuaries.

h Unenrolled Return Preparer—Enter the two-letter abbreviation for the state (e.g., "KY" for Kentucky) in which the return was prepared and the year(s) or period(s) of the return(s) you prepared.

Students in QLITCs and the STCP. Complete Part II as follows:
1. In the Designation column, enter "Special Orders."
2. In the Jurisdiction column, enter "QLITC" or "STCP."
3. Sign and date Form 2848. Be sure to attach a copy of the letter from the Office of Professional Responsibility authorizing practice before the IRS.

Any individual may represent an individual or entity before personnel of the IRS when such representation occurs outside the United States. Individuals acting as representatives must sign and date the declaration; leave the Designation and Jurisdiction columns blank. See section 10.7(c)(1)(vii) of Circular 230.

Privacy Act and Paperwork Reduction Act Notice. We ask for the information on this form to carry out the Internal Revenue laws of the United States. Form 2848 is provided by the IRS for your convenience and its use is voluntary. If you choose to designate a representative to act on your behalf, under section 6109, you must disclose your SSN, ITIN, or EIN. The principal purpose of this disclosure is to secure proper identification of the taxpayer. We need this information to gain access to your tax information in our files and properly respond to any request. If you do not disclose this information, the IRS may suspend processing of the power of attorney and may not be able to honor your power of attorney until you provide the number.

We may disclose this information to Department of Justice for civil or criminal litigation. We may also disclose this information to other countries under a tax treaty, or to Federal and state agencies to enforce Federal nontax criminal laws and to combat terrorism. The authority to disclose information to combat terrorism expired on December 31, 2003. Legislation is pending that would reinstate this authority.

You are not required to provide the information requested on a form that is subject to the Paperwork Reduction Act unless the form displays a valid OMB control number. Books or records relating to a form or its instructions must be retained as long as their contents may become material in the administration of any Internal Revenue law.

The time needed to complete and file Form 2848 will vary depending on individual circumstances. The estimated average time is: **Recordkeeping,** 6 min.; **Learning about the law or the form,** 31 min.; **Preparing the form,** 26 min.; **Copying and sending the form to the IRS,** 34 min.

If you have comments concerning the accuracy of these time estimates or suggestions for making Form 2848 simpler, we would be happy to hear from you. You can write to the Tax Products Coordinating Committee, Western Area Distribution Center, Rancho Cordova, CA 95743-0001. **Do not** send Form 2848 to this address. Instead, see the **Where To File Chart** on page 1.

-4-

Form **3903**

Department of the Treasury
Internal Revenue Service

Moving Expenses

▶ **Attach to Form 1040.**

OMB No. 1545-0074

20**05**

Attachment
Sequence No. **62**

Name(s) shown on Form 1040	Your social security number

Before you begin: √ See the **Distance Test** and **Time Test** in the instructions to find out if you can deduct your moving expenses.

√ See **Members of the Armed Forces** on back, if applicable.

1	Transportation and storage of household goods and personal effects (see instructions) . .	**1**	
2	Travel (including lodging) from your old home to your new home (see instructions). **Do not** include the cost of meals	**2**	
3	Add lines 1 and 2	**3**	
4	Enter the total amount your employer paid you for the expenses listed on lines 1 and 2 that is **not** included in box 1 of your Form W-2 (wages). This amount should be shown in box 12 of your Form W-2 with code **P**	**4**	
5	Is line 3 **more than** line 4?		
	☐ **No.** You **cannot** deduct your moving expenses. If line 3 is less than line 4, subtract line 3 from line 4 and include the result on Form 1040, line 7.		
	☐ **Yes. Moving expense deduction.** Subtract line 4 from line 3. Enter the result here and on Form 1040, line 26	**5**	

General Instructions

What's New

For 2005, the standard mileage rate for using your vehicle to move to a new home is 15 cents a mile (22 cents a mile after August 31, 2005).

Purpose of Form

Use Form 3903 to figure your moving expense deduction for a move related to the start of work at a new principal place of work (workplace). If the new workplace is outside the United States or its possessions, you must be a U.S. citizen or resident alien to deduct your expenses.

If you qualify to deduct expenses for more than one move, use a separate Form 3903 for each move.

For more details, see Pub. 521, Moving Expenses.

Who Can Deduct Moving Expenses

If you move to a new home because of a new principal workplace, you may be able to deduct your moving expenses whether you are self-employed or an employee. But you must meet both the distance test and time test that follow.

 Members of the Armed Forces may not have to meet these tests. See instructions on back.

Distance Test

Your new principal workplace must be at least 50 miles farther from your old home than your old workplace was. For example, if your old workplace was 3 miles from your old home, your new workplace must be at least 53 miles from that home. If you did not have an old workplace, your new workplace must be at least 50 miles from your old home. The distance between the two points is the shortest of the more commonly traveled routes between them.

You do not have to meet the distance test if you are in the Armed Forces and the move is due to a permanent change of station (see instructions on back).

 To see if you meet the distance test, you can use the worksheet below.

Distance Test Worksheet

Keep a Copy for Your Records

1.	Number of miles from your **old home** to your **new workplace** . . . . **1.**	_____	miles
2.	Number of miles from your **old home** to your **old workplace** . . . . **2.**	_____	miles
3.	Subtract line 2 from line 1. If zero or less, enter -0-. . . . . **3.**	_____	miles
	Is line 3 at least 50 miles?		
	☐ **Yes.** You meet this test.		
	☐ **No.** You do not meet this test. You **cannot** deduct your moving expenses. **Do not** complete Form 3903.		

For Paperwork Reduction Act Notice, see back of form.   Cat. No. 12490K   Form **3903** (2005)

Time Test

If you are an employee, you must work full time in the general area of your new workplace for at least 39 weeks during the 12 months right after you move. If you are self-employed, you must work full time in the general area of your new workplace for at least 39 weeks during the first 12 months and a total of at least 78 weeks during the 24 months right after you move.

What if you do not meet the time test before your return is due? If you expect to meet the time test, you can deduct your moving expenses in the year you move. Later, if you do not meet the time test, you must either:

● Amend your tax return for the year you claimed the deduction by filing Form 1040X, Amended U.S. Individual Income Tax Return, or

● For the year you cannot meet the time test, report as income the amount of your moving expense deduction that reduced your income tax for the year you moved.

If you do not deduct your moving expenses in the year you move and you later meet the time test, you can take the deduction by filing an amended return for the year you moved. To do this, use Form 1040X.

Exceptions to the time test. You do not have to meet the time test if any of the following apply.

● Your job ends because of disability.

● You are transferred for your employer's benefit.

● You are laid off or discharged for a reason other than willful misconduct.

● You are in the Armed Forces and the move is due to a permanent change of station (see below).

● You meet the requirements (explained later) for retirees or survivors living outside the United States.

● You are filing this form for a decedent.

Members of the Armed Forces

If you are in the Armed Forces, you do not have to meet the distance and time tests if the move is due to a permanent change of station. A permanent change of station includes a move in connection with and within 1 year of retirement or other termination of active duty.

How To Complete This Form If You Are In the Armed Forces

Do not include on lines 1 and 2 any expenses for moving services that were provided by the government. If you and your spouse and dependents are moved to or from different locations, treat the moves as a single move.

On line 4, enter the total reimbursements and allowances you received from the government in connection with the expenses you claimed on lines 1 and 2. Do not include the value of moving services provided by the government. Complete line 5 if applicable.

Retirees or Survivors Living Outside the United States

If you are a retiree or survivor who moved to a home in the United States or its possessions and you meet the following requirements, you are treated as if you moved to a new principal workplace located in the United States. You are subject only to the distance test.

Retirees

You can deduct moving expenses for a move to a new home in the United States when you actually retire if both your old principal workplace and your old home were outside the United States.

Survivors

You can deduct moving expenses for a move to a home in the United States if you are the spouse or dependent of a person whose principal workplace at the time of death was outside the United States. The expenses must be for a move (a) that begins within 6 months after the decedent's death, and (b) from a former home outside the United States that you lived in with the decedent at the time of death.

Reimbursements

You can choose to deduct moving expenses in the year you are reimbursed by your employer, even though you paid the expenses in a different year. However, special rules apply. See *When To Deduct Expenses* in Pub. 521.

Filers of Form 2555

If you file Form 2555, Foreign Earned Income, to exclude any of your income or housing costs, report the full amount of your deductible moving expenses on Form 3903 and on Form 1040. Report the part of your moving expenses that is not allowed because it is allocable to the excluded income on the appropriate line of Form 2555. For details on how to figure the part allocable to the excluded income, see Pub. 54, Tax Guide for U.S. Citizens and Resident Aliens Abroad.

Specific Instructions

You can deduct the following expenses you paid to move your family and dependent household members. Do not deduct expenses for employees such as a maid, nanny, or nurse.

Line 1

Moves within or to the United States or its possessions. Enter the amount you paid to pack, crate, and move your household goods and personal effects. You can also include the amount you paid to store and insure household goods and personal effects within any period of 30 days in a row after the items were moved from your old home and before they were delivered to your new home.

Moves outside the United States or its possessions. Enter the amount you paid to pack, crate, move, store, and insure your household goods and personal effects. Also, include the amount you paid to move your personal effects to and from storage and to store them for all or part of the time the new workplace continues to be your principal workplace.

 You do not have to complete this form if (a) you moved in an earlier year, (b) you are claiming only storage fees during your absence from the United States, and (c) any amount your employer paid for the storage fees is included in box 1 of your Form W-2 (wages). Instead, enter the storage fees on Form 1040, line 26, and write "Storage" on the dotted line next to line 26.

Line 2

Enter the amount you paid to travel from your old home to your new home. This includes transportation and lodging on the way. Include costs for the day you arrive. The members of your household do not have to travel together or at the same time. But you can only include expenses for one trip per person. Do not include any temporary living expenses or househunting expenses.

If you use your own vehicle(s), you can figure the expenses by using either:

● Actual out-of-pocket expenses for gas and oil, or

● Mileage at the rate of 15 cents a mile (22 cents a mile after August 31, 2005).

You can add parking fees and tolls to the amount claimed under either method.

Paperwork Reduction Act Notice. We ask for the information on this form to carry out the Internal Revenue laws of the United States. You are required to give us the information. We need it to ensure that you are complying with these laws and to allow us to figure and collect the right amount of tax.

You are not required to provide the information requested on a form that is subject to the Paperwork Reduction Act unless the form displays a valid OMB control number. Books or records relating to a form or its instructions must be retained as long as their contents may become material in the administration of any Internal Revenue law. Generally, tax returns and return information are confidential, as required by Internal Revenue Code section 6103.

The average time and expenses required to complete and file this form will vary depending on individual circumstances. For the estimated averages, see the instructions for your income tax return.

If you have suggestions for making this form simpler, we would be happy to hear from you. See the instructions for your income tax return.

 Printed on recycled paper

Form **4070**
(Rev. August 2005)
Department of the Treasury
Internal Revenue Service

**Employee's Report
of Tips to Employer**

OMB No. 1545-0074

Employee's name and address	Social security number

Employer's name and address (include establishment name, if different)	**1** Cash tips received
	2 Credit and debit card tips received
	3 Tips paid out

Month or shorter period in which tips were received from _____ , _____ , to _____ ,	**4** Net tips (lines **1 + 2 - 3**)
Signature	Date

For Paperwork Reduction Act Notice, see the instructions on the
back of this form.

Cat. No. 41320P

Form **4070** (Rev. 8-2005)

Purpose. Use this form to report tips you receive to your employer. This includes cash tips, tips you receive from other employees, and debit and credit card tips. You must report tips every month regardless of your total wages and tips for the year. However, you do not have to report tips to your employer for any month you received less than $20 in tips while working for that employer.

Report tips by the 10th day of the month following the month that you receive them. If the 10th day is a Saturday, Sunday, or legal holiday, report tips by the next day that is not a Saturday, Sunday, or legal holiday.

See Pub. 531, Reporting Tip Income, for more details.

You can get additional copies of Pub. 1244, Employee's Daily Record of Tips and Report to Employer, which contains both Forms 4070A and 4070, by calling 1-800-TAX-FORM (1-800-829-3676) or by downloading the pub from the IRS website at *www.irs.gov*.

Paperwork Reduction Act Notice. We ask for the information on these forms to carry out the Internal Revenue laws of the United States. You are required to give us the information. We need it to ensure that you are complying with these laws and to allow us to figure and collect the right amount of tax.

You are not required to provide the information requested on a form that is subject to the Paperwork Reduction Act unless the form displays a valid OMB control number. Books or records relating to a form or its instructions must be retained as long as their contents may become material in the administration of any Internal Revenue law. Generally, tax returns and return information are confidential, as required by Code section 6103.

The average time and expenses required to complete and file this form will vary depending on individual circumstances. For the estimated averages, see the instructions for your income tax return.

If you have suggestions for making this form simpler, we would be happy to hear from you. See the instructions for your income tax return.

Instructions

You must keep sufficient proof to show the amount of your tip income for the year. A daily record of your tip income is considered sufficient proof. Keep a daily record for each workday showing the amount of cash and credit card tips received directly from customers or other employees. Also keep a record of the amount of tips, if any, you paid to other employees through tip sharing, tip pooling or other arrangements, and the names of employees to whom you paid tips. Show the date that each entry is made. This date should be on or near the date you received the tip income. You may use Form 4070A, Employee's Daily Record of Tips, or any other daily record to record your tips.

Reporting tips to your employer. If you receive tips that total $20 or more for any month while working for one employer, you must report the tips to your employer. Tips include cash left by customers, tips customers add to debit or credit card charges, and tips you receive from other employees. You must report your tips for any one month by the 10th of the month after the month you receive the tips. If the 10th day falls on a Saturday, Sunday, or legal holiday, you may give the report to your employer on the next business day that is not a Saturday, Sunday, or legal holiday.

You must report tips that total $20 or more every month regardless of your total wages and tips for the year. You may use Form 4070, Employee's Report of Tips to Employer, to report your tips to your employer. See the instructions on the back of Form 4070.

You must include all tips, including tips not reported to your employer, as wages on your income tax return. You may use the last page of this publication to total your tips for the year.

Your employer must withhold income, social security, and Medicare (or railroad retirement) taxes on tips you report. Your employer usually deducts the withholding due on tips from your regular wages.

(continued on inside of back cover)

Instructions *(continued)*

Unreported Tips. If you received tips of $20 or more for any month while working for one employer but did not report them to your employer, you must figure and pay social security and Medicare taxes on the unreported tips when you file your tax return. If you have unreported tips, you must use Form 1040 and Form 4137, Social Security and Medicare Tax on Unreported Tip Income, to report them. You may not use Form 1040A or 1040EZ. Employees subject to the Railroad Retirement Tax Act cannot use Form 4137 to pay railroad retirement tax on unreported tips. To get railroad retirement credit, you must report tips to your employer.

If you do not report tips to your employer as required, you may be charged a penalty of 50% of the social security and Medicare taxes (or railroad retirement tax) due on the unreported tips unless there was reasonable cause for not reporting them.

Additional Information. Get Pub. 531, Reporting Tip Income, and Form 4137 for more information on tips. If you are an employee of certain large food or beverage establishments, see Pub. 531 for tip allocation rules.

Recordkeeping. If you do not keep a daily record of tips, you must keep other reliable proof of the tip income you received. This proof includes copies of restaurant bills and credit card charges that show amounts customers added as tips.

Keep your tip income records for as long as the information on them may be needed in the administration of any Internal Revenue law.

Form **4137**		OMB No. 1545-0074	

Form 4137
Department of the Treasury
Internal Revenue Service (99)

**Social Security and Medicare Tax
on Unreported Tip Income**
▶ See instructions on back.
▶ Attach to Form 1040.

OMB No. 1545-0074
2005
Attachment
Sequence No. **24**

Name of person who received tips (as shown on Form 1040). If married, complete a separate Form 4137 for each spouse with unreported tips.

Social security number

Name(s) of employer(s) to whom you were required to, but did not, report your tips:

---

1 Total cash and charge tips you **received** in 2005 (see instructions) **1**

2 Total cash and charge tips you **reported** to your employer in 2005 . . . . **2**

3 Subtract line 2 from line 1. This amount is income you **must** include in the total on Form 1040, line 7 . . . . . **3**

4 Cash and charge tips you received but did not report to your employer because the total was less than $20 in a calendar month (see instructions) **4**

5 Unreported tips subject to Medicare tax. Subtract line 4 from line 3. Enter here and on line 2 of Schedule U below **5**

6 Maximum amount of wages (including tips) subject to social security tax **6** 90,000 00

7 Total social security wages and social security tips (total of boxes 3 and 7 on Form(s) W-2) or railroad retirement (tier 1) compensation . **7**

8 Subtract line 7 from line 6. If line 7 is more than line 6, enter -0- here and on line 9 and go to line 11 **8**

9 Unreported tips subject to social security tax. Enter the **smaller** of line 5 or line 8 here and on line 1 of Schedule U below. If you received tips as a federal, state, or local government employee, see instructions **9**

10 Multiply line 9 by .062 . . . . **10**

11 Multiply line 5 by .0145 . . . . **11**

12 Add lines 10 and 11. Enter the result here and on Form 1040, line 59 . . . ▶ **12**

For Paperwork Reduction Act Notice, see instructions on back.

Form **4137** (2005)

Do Not Detach

SCHEDULE U (Form 1040)
Department of the Treasury
Internal Revenue Service

U.S. Schedule of Unreported Tip Income
For crediting to your social security record

2005

Note: *The amounts you report below are for your social security record. This record is used to figure any benefits, based on your earnings, payable to you and your dependents or your survivors. Fill in each item accurately and completely.*

Print or type name of person who received tip income (as shown on Form 1040)

Social security number

Address (number, street, and apt. no., or P.O. box if mail is not delivered to your home)

Occupation

City, town or post office, state, and ZIP code

1 Unreported tips subject to social security tax. Enter the amount from line 9 (Form 4137) above . ▶ **1**
2 Unreported tips subject to Medicare tax. Enter the amount from line 5 (Form 4137) above . . ▶ **2**

Please do not write in this space

DLN—

Cat. No. 12626C

Schedule U (Form 1040) 2005

General Instructions

What's New. For 2005, the maximum amount of wages and tips subject to social security tax is $90,000.

Purpose of form. Use Form 4137 to figure the social security and Medicare tax owed on tips you did not report to your employer, including any allocated tips shown on your Form(s) W-2 that you must report as income. Also, use Form 4137 to figure the social security and Medicare tips to be credited to your social security record.

Who must file. You must file Form 4137 if you received cash and charge tips of $20 or more in a calendar month and did not report all of those tips to your employer. You must also file Form 4137 if box 8 of your Form(s) W-2 shows allocated tips that you must report as income.

Allocated tips you must report as income. You must report as income on Form 1040, line 7, at least the amount of allocated tips shown in box 8 of your Form(s) W-2 unless you can prove a smaller amount with adequate records. If you have records that show the actual amount of tips you received, report that amount even if it is more or less than the allocated tips. Although allocated tips are shown on your Form W-2, they are not included in the wages, tips, and other compensation box (box 1) on that form and no income tax, social security tax, or Medicare tax has been withheld from these tips.

Tips you must report to your employer. You must give your employer a written report of cash and charge tips if you received $20 or more in tips during a month. If, in any month, you worked for two or more employers and received tips while working for each, the $20 rule applies separately to the tips you received while working for each employer and not to the total you received. You must report your tips to your employers by the 10th day of the month following the month you received them. If the 10th day of the month falls on a Saturday, Sunday, or legal holiday, give your employer the report by the next business day.

Employees subject to the Railroad Retirement Tax Act. Do not use Form 4137 to report tips received for work covered by the Railroad Retirement Tax Act. In order to get railroad retirement credit, you must report these tips to your employer.

Payment of tax. Tips you reported to your employer are subject to social security and Medicare tax (or railroad retirement tax) and income tax withholding. Your employer collects these taxes from wages (excluding tips) or other funds of yours available to cover them. If your wages were not enough to cover these taxes, you may have given your employer the additional amounts needed. Your Form W-2 will include the tips you reported to your employer and the taxes withheld. If there was not enough money to cover the social security and Medicare tax (or railroad retirement tax), your Form W-2 will also show the tax due in box 12 under codes A and B. See the instructions for line 63 of Form 1040 to find out how to report the tax due.

Penalty for not reporting tips. If you did not report tips to your employer as required, you may be charged a penalty equal to 50% of the social security and Medicare tax due on those tips. You can avoid this penalty if you can show reasonable cause for not reporting these tips to your employer. To do so, attach a statement to your return explaining why you did not report them.

Additional information. See Pub. 531, Reporting Tip Income.

Specific Instructions

Line 1. Include all cash and charge tips received. This includes the following:

● Total tips that you reported to your employer. Tips you reported, as required, by the 10th day of the month following the month you received them are considered income in the month you reported them. For example, tips you received in December 2004 that you reported to your employer after December 31, 2004, and before January 11, 2005, are considered income in 2005 and should be included on your 2005 Form W-2 and reported on line 1 of Form 4137. However, tips you received in December 2005 that you reported to your employer after December 31, 2005, and before January 11, 2006, are considered income in 2006. Do not include these tips on line 1.

● Tips you did not report to your employer on time or did not report at all. These tips are considered income to you in the month you actually received them. For example, tips you received in December 2005 that you reported to your employer after January 10, 2006, are considered income in 2005 because you did not report them to your employer on time.

● Tips you received that you were not required to report to your employer because they totaled less than $20 during the month.

● Allocated tips that you must report as income.

Line 4. Enter only the tips you were not required to report to your employer because the total received was less than $20 in a calendar month. These tips are not subject to social security and Medicare tax.

Line 9. If line 5 includes tips you received for work you did as a federal, state, or local government employee and your pay was subject only to the 1.45% Medicare tax, subtract the amount of those tips from the line 5 amount only for the purpose of comparing lines 5 and 8. Do not reduce the actual entry on line 5. Enter "1.45% tips" and the amount you subtracted on the dotted line next to line 9.

Paperwork Reduction Act Notice. We ask for the information on this form to carry out the Internal Revenue laws of the United States. You are required to give us the information. We need it to ensure that you are complying with these laws and to allow us to figure and collect the right amount of tax.

You are not required to provide the information requested on a form that is subject to the Paperwork Reduction Act unless the form displays a valid OMB control number. Books or records relating to a form or its instructions must be retained as long as their contents may become material in the administration of any Internal Revenue law. Generally, tax returns and return information are confidential, as required by Internal Revenue Code section 6103.

The average time and expenses required to complete and file this form will vary depending on individual circumstances. For the estimated averages, see the instructions for your income tax return.

If you have suggestions for making this form simpler, we would be happy to hear from you. See the instructions for your income tax return.

Printed on recycled paper

(See Instructions on back)

Form **4419** (Rev. May 2002)	Department of the Treasury – Internal Revenue Service **Application for Filing Information Returns** **Electronically/Magnetically** Please type or print in **BLACK** ink.	IRS Use Only	OMB No. 1545-0387

1. Transmitter information

Name _____

Address _____

City _____ State _____ Zip _____

2. Person to contact about this request

Name _____

Title _____

Email address _____

Telephone number ( ) _____

3. Employer Identification Number **(EIN)**	**4.** Foreign Transmitter without an EIN ☐ Yes	**5. Tax year** you wish to begin filing electronically/magnetically

6. Will you be using your TCC only for transmitting requests for extension of time to file? ☐ Yes ☐ No

7. Type of Return To Be Reported
(Check all forms you wish to file)

Important: Form W-2 information is sent to the Social Security Administration only. Do not use Form 4419 to request authorization to file this information electronically/magnetically. Contact SSA for W-2 magnetic/electronic filing information.

☐ Forms 1098 and 1099, 5498 and W-2G (Electronic, Tape Cartridge, 3 ½ " Diskette)	☐ 1042-S (Electronic, Tape Cartridge, 3 ½"Diskette) ☐ 8027 (Electronic, Tape Cartridge, 3 ½" Diskette) ☐ W-4 (Electronic, Tape Cartridge, 3 ½" Diskette)

8. Type of Filing

☐ Electronic Filing   ☐ Tape cartridge   ☐ 3 ½ "Diskette

9. Person responsible for preparation of tax reports	Name (type or print)	Title
	Signature	Date

Catalog Number 41639J   Form **4419** (Rev. 5-2002)

Form **4419** (Rev. May-2002)

General Instructions

Paperwork Reduction Act Notice. We ask for the information on these forms to carry out the Internal Revenue Laws of the United States. You are not required to provide the information requested on a form that is subject to the Paperwork Reduction Act unless the form displays a valid OMB control number. Books or records relating to a form must be retained as long as their contents may become material in the administration of any Internal Revenue law. Generally, tax returns and return information are confidential, as required by Code section 6103.

The time needed to provide this information would vary depending on individual circumstances. The estimated average time is:

Preparing Form 4419 . . . . **20 min.**

If you have comments concerning the accuracy of this time estimate or suggestions for making this form simpler, we would be happy to hear from you. You can write to the Tax Forms Committee, Western Area Distribution Center, Rancho Cordova, CA 95743-0001. DO NOT SEND THE FORM TO THIS OFFICE. Instead, see the instructions below on where to file. **When completing this form, please type or print clearly in BLACK ink.**

Purpose of Form. File Form 4419 to request authorization to file any of the forms shown in Block 6 electronically or magnetically. Please be sure to complete all appropriate blocks. If your application is approved, a five-character alpha-numeric Transmitter Control Code (TCC) will be assigned to your organization.

If any information on the form should change, please write to IRS/Martinsburg Computing Center so we can update our database. It is not necessary to submit a new Form 4419. **NOTE:** Do **NOT** use Form 4419 to request authorization to file Forms W-2 on magnetic media, since Form W-2 information is sent to the Social Security Administration *(SSA)* ONLY. **Contact SSA if you have any questions concerning the filing of Forms W-2 on magnetic media.**

Specific Instructions

Block 1
Enter the name and complete address of the person or organization that will submit the electronic or magnetic media files *(transmitter).*

Block 2
Enter the name, title, email address (if available) and telephone number *(with area code)* of the person to contact about this application if IRS needs additional information. This should be a person who is knowledgeable about electronic/magnetic filing of information returns.

Block 3
Enter the employer identification number *(EIN)* of the organization transmitting the electronic and/or magnetic media files.

Block 4
If you are a foreign transmitter who does not have a nine-digit taxpayer identification number, check this box.

Block 5
Enter the tax year that you wish to start filing electronically and/or magnetically.

Block 6
Indicate if you are requesting this transmitter control code solely for filing electronic and/or magnetic requests for an extension of time to file information returns.

Block 7
Check the box next to all of the returns you will file with IRS electronically and/or magnetically.
A separate TCC will be assigned for each form(s) identified in Block 7. Please make sure you submit your magnetic media files using the correct TCC.
Thereafter, if you need to add any of the forms identified in Block 7, it will be necessary to submit another Form 4419 to IRS so another TCC can be assigned.

Block 8
Check which method you will use to file your information returns. 3 ½-inch diskettes must be MS/DOS, ASCII recording mode. Tape cartridges must be 18, 36, 128, or 256-track.

Block 9
The form must be signed and dated by an official of the company or organization requesting authorization to report electronically and/or magnetically.

Mailing Address:
Send your Form 4419 to the address below:

Internal Revenue Service
Martinsburg Computing Center
Information Reporting Program
230 Murall Drive
Kearneysville, WV 25430

In order to ensure timely filing, submit Form 4419 at least 30 days before the due date of the return.

If your application is approved, IRS will assign a TCC to your organization. We will not issue your TCC without a signed Form 4419 from you, and we will not issue a TCC over the phone. If you do not receive a reply from IRS within 30 days, contact us at the telephone number shown below. Do not submit any files until you receive your TCC.

For further information concerning the filing of information returns with IRS either electronically or magnetically, contact the IRS Martinsburg Computing Center toll-free at (866) 455-7438 between 8:30 a.m. and 4:30 p.m. Eastern Standard Time.

(See Instructions on back)

Form **4804** (Rev. May 2002)	Department of the Treasury – Internal Revenue Service **Transmittal of Information Returns Reported Magnetically** Please type or print in **BLACK** ink **(Use a separate Form 4804 for each file.)**	IRS Use Only	OMB No. 1545-0367

1. Type of file represented by this transmittal ☐ Original ☐ Test ☐ Replacement ☐ Correction	2. **Tax year** for which media is submitted

3. Transmitter Control Code (TCC) (Required)	4. Name of transmitter (Owner of TCC)

5. Name/address of company and name/title of person who should receive correspondence on problem files (should be the same information as in 'T' record)

Company Name _____

Address _____

City _____ State _____ Zip _____

Contact Person _____ Telephone Number (_____) _____

E-mail Address _____

6. Forms 1098, 1099, 5498, W-2G Combined total of payee **'B'** records	7. Form 1042-S Total number of **'Q'** records	8. Form 8027 Total number of establishment(s) reported	9. Transmitter in-house media number(s)

Affidavit

Under penalties of perjury, I declare that I have examined this transmittal, including accompanying documents, and, to the best of my knowledge and belief, it is correct and complete. (Normally, the payer must sign the affidavit above. The authorized agent of the payer may sign if all conditions are met as stated on the back.)

SIGNATURE (Required)		IRS Use Only
Title	Date	

Catalog Number 27210I   Form **4804** (Rev. 5-2002)

Form **4804** (Rev. 5-2002)

General Instructions

Paperwork Reduction Act Notice. We ask for the information on these forms to carry out the Internal Revenue Laws of the United States. You are not required to provide the information requested on a form that is subject to the Paperwork Reduction Act unless the form displays a valid OMB control number. Books or records relating to a form must be retained as long as their contents may become material in the administration of any Internal Revenue law. Generally, tax returns and return information are confidential, as required by Code section 6103.

The time needed to provide this information would vary depending on individual circumstances. The estimated average time is:

Preparing Form 4804 . . . . 15 min.

If you have comments concerning the accuracy of these time estimates or suggestions for making this form simpler, we would be happy to hear from you. You can write to the Tax Forms Committee, Western Area Distribution Center, Rancho Cordova, CA 95743-0001.
DO NOT SEND THE FORMS TO THIS OFFICE. Instead, see the instructions below on where to file. **When completing this form, please type or print clearly in <u>BLACK</u> ink.**

Purpose of Form. Use Form 4804 when submitting the following types of information returns magnetically: Form 1098, 1099, 5498, W-2G, 1042-S, and 8027. You must include Form 4804 with all magnetic media you submit to the Internal Revenue Service.

NOTE: A separate Form 4804 must be submitted for each file.

Specific Instructions

Block 1
Indicate whether the data in this shipment is an original, correction, replacement or test file by checking the appropriate box. Check 'Replacement' only if you are sending media in response to a specific request from IRS/MCC and you have a Form 9267 attached.

Definitions

Correction: A correction is an information return submitted by the payer to correct erroneous information previously sent to and processed by IRS/MCC.

Replacement: A replacement is an information return file sent by the filer at **the request of IRS/MCC** because of errors encountered while processing the filer's original return. Your replacement file may be submitted electronically even if the original file was sent on magnetic media.

Block 2
Indicate the tax year for which media is being submitted.

Block 3
Enter the five-character alpha/numeric Transmitter Control Code assigned by IRS. TCCs for Form 1042-S filing begin with the numbers 22. TCCs for Form 8027 filing begin with the numbers 21.

Block 4
Enter the name of the transmitter. (Reference Affidavit Requirements below.)

Block 5
Enter the name and address of the company, along with the name/title of the person to whom correspondence concerning problem media in need of replacement should be sent. This information should match the information that appears in the Transmitter 'T' Record in your file. Please include an email address if available

NOTE: IRS no longer returns media in need of replacement.

Block 6,7,8
Use only the boxes appropriate to the forms you are reporting. A separate Form 4804 is required for the information returns in box 6, 1042-S Forms in box 7, and 8027 Forms in box 8.

Block 6
Enter the combined number of all payee 'B' records on the media sent with this Form 4804.

Block 7
If reporting Form 1042-S, enter the total number Recipient 'Q' records.

Block 8
If reporting Form 8027, enter the number of establishments reported.

Block 9
If your organization uses an in-house numbering system to identify media, indicate the media number(s) in the appropriate block.

Mailing Address:
Send your media with transmittal Form(s) 4804 to the address below:

IRS, Martinsburg Computing Center
Information Reporting Program
230 Murall Drive
Kearneysville, WV 25430

NOTE: Form 4802, Transmittal of Information Returns Reported Magnetically/Electronically (Continuation) is obsolete.

Affidavit Requirement

A transmitter, service bureau, paying agent, or disbursing agent (all hereafter referred to as "agent") may sign Form 4804 on behalf of the payer (or other person required to file), if the conditions in items 1 and 2 are met:
1. The agent has the authority to sign the form under an agency agreement (oral, written, or implied) that is valid under state law.
2. The agent signs the form and adds the caption "For: (Name of payer or other person required to file)".
he authorized agent's signing of the affidavit on the payer's behalf does not relieve the payer of the responsibility for filing a correct, complete, and timely Form 4804, with attachments, and will not relieve the payer of any penalties for not complying with those requirements.

2727 ☐ VOID   ☐ CORRECTED

TRUSTEE'S name, street address, city, state, and ZIP code	**1** Employee or self-employed person's Archer MSA contributions made in 2006 and 2007 for 2006 $	OMB No. 1545-1518 20**06** Form **5498-SA**	**HSA, Archer MSA, or Medicare Advantage MSA Information**
	2 Total contributions made in 2006 $		
TRUSTEE'S federal identification number	PARTICIPANT'S social security number	**3** Total HSA or Archer MSA contributions made in 2007 for 2006 $	**Copy A** **For** **Internal Revenue Service Center** File with Form 1096.
PARTICIPANT'S name		**4** Rollover contributions $	**5** Fair market value of HSA, Archer MSA, or MA MSA $	
Street address (including apt. no.)		**6** HSA ☐ Archer MSA ☐ MA MSA ☐	For Privacy Act and Paperwork Reduction Act Notice, see the **2006 General Instructions for Forms 1099, 1098, 5498, and W-2G.**
City, state, and ZIP code			
Account number (see instructions)			

Form **5498-SA**   Cat. No. 38467V   Department of the Treasury - Internal Revenue Service

Do Not Cut or Separate Forms on This Page — Do Not Cut or Separate Forms on This Page

Instructions to Participant

This information is submitted to the Internal Revenue Service by the trustee of your health savings account (HSA), Archer MSA, or Medicare Advantage MSA (MA MSA).

Generally, contributions you make to your HSA or Archer MSA are deductible. However, employer contributions to your HSA are not deductible. If your employer makes a contribution to one of your Archer MSAs, you cannot contribute to any Archer MSA for that year. If you made a contribution to your Archer MSA when your employer has contributed, you cannot deduct your contribution, and you will have an excess contribution. If your spouse's employer makes a contribution to your spouse's Archer MSA, you cannot make a contribution to your Archer MSA if your spouse is covered under a high deductible health plan that also covers you.

Contributions that the Social Security Administration makes to your MA MSA are not includible in your gross income nor are they deductible. Neither you nor your employer can make contributions to your MA MSA.

See Form 8853, Archer MSAs and Long-Term Care Insurance Contracts, and its instructions or Form 8889, Health Savings Accounts (HSAs) and its instructions. Any employer contributions made to an Archer MSA are shown on your Form W-2 in Box 12 (code R); employer contributions made to HSAs are shown in Box 12 (code W).

For more information, see Pub. 969, Health Savings Accounts and Other Tax-Favored Health Plans.

Account number. May show an account or other unique number the trustee assigned to distinguish your account.

Box 1. Shows employee or self-employed person's Archer MSA contributions made to your Archer MSA in 2006 and through April 16, 2007, for 2006. You may be able to deduct this amount on your 2006 Form 1040. See the Form 1040 instructions.

Note. The information in boxes 2 and 3 is provided by the trustee for IRS use only.

Box 2. Shows the total employer and employee/self-employed contributions made in 2006 to your HSA or Archer MSA. The trustee of your MA MSA is not required to, but may, show contributions to your MA MSA.

Box 3. Shows the total HSA or Archer MSA contributions made in 2007 for 2006.

Box 4. Shows any rollover contribution you made to this Archer MSA in 2006 after a distribution from another Archer MSA or shows any rollover to this HSA from another HSA or Archer MSA. See Form 8853 or Form 8889 and their instructions for information about how to report distributions and rollovers. This amount is not included in box 1, 2, or 3.

Box 5. Shows the fair market value of your HSA, Archer MSA, or MA MSA at the end of 2006.

Box 6. Shows the type of account that is reported on this Form 5498-SA.

Other information. The trustee of your HSA, Archer MSA, or MA MSA may provide other information about your account on this form.

Note. Do not attach Form 5498-SA to your income tax return. Instead, keep it for your records.

Instructions for Trustees

General and specific form instructions are provided as separate products. The products you should use to complete Form 5498-SA are the 2006 General Instructions for Forms 1099, 1098, 5498, and W-2G, and the 2006 Instructions for Forms 1099-SA and 5498-SA. A chart in the general instructions gives a quick guide to which form must be filed to report a particular payment. To order these instructions and additional forms, call 1-800-TAX-FORM (1-800-829-3676).

Caution: *Because paper forms are scanned during processing, you cannot file Forms 1096, 1098, 1099, or 5498 that you download and print from the IRS website.*

Due dates. Furnish Copy B of this form to the participant by May 31, 2007.

File Copy A of this form with the IRS by May 31, 2007. To file electronically, you must have software that generates a file according to the specifications in Pub. 1220, Specifications for Filing Forms 1098, 1099, 5498, and W-2G Electronically or Magnetically. IRS does not provide a fill-in form option.

 Printed on recycled paper

Form **8027**

Department of the Treasury
Internal Revenue Service

**Employer's Annual Information Return of
Tip Income and Allocated Tips**

▶ See separate instructions.

OMB No. 1545-0714

20**05**

Name of establishment

Number and street (see instructions)

City or town, state, and ZIP code

Employer identification number

Type of establishment (check only one box)

☐ **1** Evening meals only

☐ **2** Evening and other meals

☐ **3** Meals other than evening meals

☐ **4** Alcoholic beverages

Employer's name (same name as on Form 941)

Number and street (P.O. box, if applicable)

Apt. or suite no.

City, state, and ZIP code (if a foreign address, see instructions)

Establishment number
(see instructions)

Does this establishment accept credit cards, debit cards, or other charges?

☐ Yes (lines 1 and 2 **must** be completed)
☐ No

Check **if**: Amended Return ☐
Final Return ☐

1	Total charged tips for calendar year 2005.	**1**
2	Total charge receipts showing charged tips (see instructions)	**2**
3	Total amount of service charges of less than 10% paid as wages to employees	**3**
4a	Total tips reported by indirectly tipped employees	**4a**
b	Total tips reported by directly tipped employees	**4b**

Note: Complete the **Employer's Optional Worksheet for Tipped Employees** on page 5 of the instructions to determine potential unreported tips of your employees.

c	Total tips reported (add lines 4a and 4b)	**4c**
5	Gross receipts from food or beverage operations (not less than line 2—see instructions) .	**5**
6	Multiply line 5 by 8% (.08) or the lower rate shown here ▶ _____ granted by the IRS. (Attach a copy of the IRS determination letter to this return.)	**6**

Note: If you have allocated tips using other than the calendar year (semimonthly, biweekly, quarterly, etc.), mark an **"X"** on line 6 and enter the amount of allocated tips from your records on line 7.

7 Allocation of tips. If line 6 is more than line 4c, enter the excess here **7**

▶ This amount must be allocated as tips to tipped employees working in this establishment. Check the box below that shows the method used for the allocation. (Show the portion, if any, attributable to each employee in box 8 of the employee's Form W-2.)

a Allocation based on hours-worked method (see instructions for restriction) . . . ☐
Note: If you marked the checkbox in line 7a, enter the average number of employee hours worked per business day during the payroll period. (see instructions) _____

b Allocation based on gross receipts method . . . . ☐

c Allocation based on good-faith agreement (Attach a copy of the agreement.). . . ☐

8 Enter the total number of directly tipped employees at this establishment during 2005 ▶

Under penalties of perjury, I declare that I have examined this return, including accompanying schedules and statements, and to the best of my knowledge and belief, it is true, correct, and complete.

Signature ▶   Title ▶   Date ▶

For Privacy Act and Paperwork Reduction Act Notice, see page 6 of the separate instructions.   Cat. No. 49989U   Form **8027** (2005)

Department of the Treasury
Internal Revenue Service

2005

Instructions for Form 8027

Employer's Annual Information Return of Tip Income and Allocated Tips

Section references are to the Internal Revenue Code unless otherwise noted.

General Instructions

Items To Note

● You must check one of the "Yes" or "No" boxes under employer's name and address to indicate whether or not the establishment accepts credit cards, debit cards, or other charges. If the "Yes" box is checked, lines 1 and 2 of Form 8027 must be completed. Also see the instructions for lines 1 and 2 on page 3.

● Complete the *Worksheet for Determining Whether To File Form 8027* (below) to determine if you are required to file Form 8027.

● You may want to use the *Employer's Optional Worksheet for Tipped Employees* on page 5 as a means of determining if your employees are reporting all of their tip income to you.

Purpose of Form

Form 8027 is used by large food or beverage establishments when the employer is required to make annual reports to the IRS on receipts from food or beverage operations and tips reported by employees.

 All employees receiving $20 or more a month in tips must report 100% of their tips to their employer.

Who Must File

If you are an employer who operates a large food or beverage establishment, you must file Form 8027. If you own more than one establishment, you must file Form 8027 for each one. There may be more than one establishment (business activity providing food or beverages) operating within a single building, and, if gross receipts are recorded separately, each activity is required to file a Form 8027.

A return is required only for establishments in the 50 states and the District of Columbia.

 If you are required to report for more than one establishment, you must complete and file Form 8027-T, Transmittal of Employer's Annual Information Return of Tip Income and Allocated Tips, with Forms 8027.

A large food or beverage establishment is one to which all of the following apply:
● Food or beverage is provided for consumption on the premises.
● Tipping is a customary practice.
● More than 10 employees, who work more than 80 hours, were normally employed on a typical business day during the preceding calendar year.

Worksheet for Determining Whether To File Form 8027

Complete the worksheet below to determine if you had more than 10 employees on a typical business day during 2004 and, therefore, are required to file Form 8027 for 2005. It is the **average number of employee hours worked on a typical business day** that determines whether or not you employed more than 10 employees.

1. Enter **one-half** of the **total** employee hours worked during the month in 2004 with the **greatest** aggregate gross receipts from food and beverages . . . . _____

2. Enter the number of **days opened for business** during the month shown in line 1 . . . . _____

3. Enter **one-half** of the **total** employee hours worked during the month in 2004 with the **least** aggregate gross receipts from food and beverages . . . . _____

4. Enter the number of **days opened for business** during the month shown in line 3. _____

5. Divide line 1 by line 2. . . . . _____

6. Divide line 3 by line 4. . . . . _____

7. Add lines 5 and 6. If line 7 is greater than 80 (hours), you are required to file Form 8027 for 2005. . . . . . . _____

Note. The filing requirement (more than 10 employees) is based on the total of all employees who provided services in connection with the provision of food and beverages at the establishment, not just the number of directly tipped employees. Include employees such as waitstaff, bussers, bartenders, seat persons, wine stewards, cooks, and kitchen help. See Regulations section 31.6053-3(j)(10) for more information.

A person who owns 50% or more in value of the stock of a corporation that runs the establishment is not considered an employee when determining whether the establishment normally employs more than 10 individuals.

New large food or beverage establishment. File Form 8027 for a new large food or beverage establishment if, during any 2 consecutive calendar months, the average number of hours worked each business day by all employees is more than 80 hours. To figure the average number of employee hours worked each business day during a month, divide the total hours all employees worked during the month by the number of days the establishment was open for business. After the test is met for 2 consecutive months, you must file a return covering the rest of the year, beginning with the next payroll period.

Exceptions To Filing

A return is not required for:
● Establishments operated for less than 1 month in calendar year 2005.
● Fast food restaurants and operations where tipping is not customary such as cafeterias or operations where 95% of the total sales are carryout sales or sales with a service charge of 10% or more.

When To File

File Form 8027 (and Form 8027-T when filing more than one Form 8027) by February 28, 2006. However, if you file electronically (not by magnetic media), the due date is March 31, 2006.

Cat. No. 61013P

Extension of time to file. Filers of Form 8027 submitted on paper, electronically or magnetically may request an extension of time to file on Form 8809, Application for Extension of Time To File Information Returns. File Form 8809 as soon as you know an extension of time to file is necessary, but not later than February 28, 2006.

Where To File

File with the Internal Revenue Service, Cincinnati, OH 45999.

Reporting on magnetic media. If you are the employer and you file 250 or more Forms 8027, you must file the returns electronically or magnetically. For details, see Regulations section 301.6011-2.

Specifications for filing. See Pub. 1239, Specifications for Filing Form 8027, Employer's Annual Information Return of Tip Income and Allocated Tips, Electronically or Magnetically. This publication provides instructions on how to file and how to request a waiver from magnetic media reporting because of undue hardship. To obtain a copy of Pub. 1239, visit the IRS website at *www.irs.gov* or call 1-800-TAX-FORM (1-800-829-3676).

Penalties

The law provides for a penalty if you do not file Form 8027 (and Form 8027-T) on time unless you can show reasonable cause for the delay. Employers filing late (after the due date including extensions) should attach an explanation to the return to show reasonable cause. You may be charged penalties for each failure to:
● Timely file a correct information return including failure to file electronically or magnetically, if required.
● Timely provide a correct Form W-2 to the employee.

For more information on penalties for untimely or incorrect Forms W-2 or 8027, see Pub. 1239 and the Instructions for Forms W-2 and W-3.

Gross Receipts

Gross receipts include all receipts (other than nonallocable receipts, see definition below) from cash sales, charge receipts, charges to a hotel room (excluding tips charged to the hotel room if your accounting procedures allow these tips to be separated), and the retail value of complimentary food or beverages served to customers as explained below.

Also include charged tips in gross receipts, but only to the extent that you reduced your cash sales by the amount of any cash you paid to tipped employees for any charged tips due them. However, if you did not reduce cash sales for charged tips paid out to employees, do not include those charged tips in gross receipts. Do not include state or local taxes in gross receipts.

 Remind all directly and indirectly tipped employees to include all charged tips and all cash tips received in the tip amount that they must report to you.

Nonallocable receipts. These are receipts for carryout sales and receipts with a service charge added of 10% or more. (Nonallocable receipts generally include all sales on which tipping is not customary).

Complimentary items. Food or beverages served to customers without charge must be included in gross receipts if: (a) tipping for providing them is customary at the establishment, and (b) they are provided in connection with an activity that is engaged in for profit and whose receipts would not be included in the amount on line 5 of Form 8027.

For example, you would have to include in gross receipts the retail value of the complimentary drinks served to customers in a gambling casino because tipping is customary, the gambling casino is an activity engaged in for profit, and the gambling receipts of the casino are not included in the amount on line 5.

However, you would not have to include the retail value of complimentary hors d'oeuvres at your bar or a complimentary dessert served to a regular patron of your restaurant in gross receipts because the receipts of the bar or restaurant would be included in the amount on line 5. You would not have to include the value of a fruit basket placed in a hotel room in gross receipts since, generally, tipping for it is not customary.

Allocation of Tips

You must allocate tips among employees who receive them if the total tips reported to you during any payroll period are less than 8% (or the approved lower rate) of this establishment's gross receipts for that period.

Generally, the amount allocated is the difference between the total tips reported by employees and 8% (or the lower rate) of the gross receipts, other than nonallocable receipts.

Lower rate. You (or a majority of the employees) may request a lower rate (but not lower than 2%) by submitting an application to:

Internal Revenue Service
Compliance Policy Group
S:C:CP:RC:ET, Room 2404
1111 Constitution Ave. NW
Washington, DC 20224

The burden of supplying sufficient information to allow the IRS to estimate with reasonable accuracy the actual tip rate of the establishment rests with the petitioner. Your petition for a lower rate must clearly demonstrate that a rate less than 8% should apply. It must include the following:
● Employer's name, address, and EIN;
● Establishment's name, address, and establishment number;
● Detailed description of the establishment that would help to determine the tip rate. The description should include the type of restaurant, days and hours of operation, type of service including any self-service, the person (waiter or waitress, cashier, etc.) to whom the customer pays the check, whether the check is paid before or after the meal, and whether alcohol is available;
● Past year's information shown on lines 1 through 6 of Form 8027 as well as total carryout sales; total charge sales; percentage of sales for breakfast, lunch, and dinner; average dollar amount of a guest check; service charge, if any, added to the check; and the percentage of sales with a service charge;
● Type of clientele;
● Copy of a representative menu for each meal.

The petition must contain the following statement and be signed by a responsible person who is authorized to make and sign a return, statement, or other document.

"Under penalties of perjury, I declare that I have examined this application, including accompanying documents, and to the best of my knowledge and belief, the facts presented in support of this petition are true, correct, and complete."

You must attach to the petition copies of Form 8027 (if any) filed for the 3 years prior to your petition. If you are petitioning for more than one establishment or you want to know your appeal rights, see Revenue Procedure 86-21, 1986-1 C.B. 560 for additional information. Also include with your petition a check or money order made payable to the "United States Treasury" for the amount of the user fee required for determination letters. For the current user fee amount, contact the IRS at 1-800-829-1040.

A majority of all the directly tipped employees must consent to any petition written by an employee. A "majority of employees" means more than half of all directly tipped employees employed by the establishment at the time the petition is filed. Employee groups must follow the procedures in Regulations section 31.6053-3(h), Pub. 531, Reporting Tip Income, and Revenue Procedure 86-21.

-2-

The IRS will notify you when and for how long the reduced rate is effective.

Reporting Allocated Tips To Employees

Give each employee who has been allocated tips a Form W-2 that shows the allocated amount in box 8. The form must be furnished to the employee by January 31 of the following year. If employment ends before the end of the year and the employee asks for the Form W-2, a tip allocation is not required on the early Form W-2. However, you may include on the early Form W-2 the employee's actual tip allocation or a good-faith estimate of the allocation. Signify a good-faith estimate by writing "estimate" next to the allocated amount in box 8 of the Form W-2.

If no allocation was shown on the early Form W-2 or if the estimated allocation on the early form differs from the actual amount by more than 5%, give the employee Form W-2c, Corrected Wage and Tax Statement, during January of the next year.

If you allocate tips among employees by the methods described in the instructions for lines 7a through 7c, you are not liable to any employee if any amount is improperly allocated. However, if the allocation shown on the employee's Form W-2 differs from the correct allocation by more than 5%, you must adjust that employee's allocation and must review the allocable amount of all other employees in the same establishment to assure that the error did not distort any other employee's share by more than 5%. Use Form W-2c to report the corrected allocation.

You do not need to send to the IRS separate copies of Forms W-2 showing allocated tips. The IRS will use the information shown on the Forms W-2 that you file with the Social Security Data Operations Center.

Tip allocations have no effect on withholding income or social security or Medicare taxes from employees' wages. Allocated tips are not subject to withholding and are not to be included in boxes 1, 3, 5, and 7, of Form W-2.

Specific Instructions

File a separate Form 8027 for each large food or beverage establishment. Use Form 8027-T, Transmittal of Employer's Annual Information Return of Tip Income and Allocated Tips, when filing more than one Form 8027. Do not attach any unrelated correspondence.

Name and address of establishment and employer identification number. If your preprinted name, EIN, or address information on Form 8027 and/or Form 8027-T is not correct, cross out any errors and print the correct information. If Form 8027 and/or Form 8027-T does not have your preprinted information, type or print the name and address of the establishment. They may be different from your mailing address, as in the case of employers who have more than one establishment. If mail is not delivered to the street address of the establishment, enter the P.O. box number. The employer identification number (EIN) should be the same as the number on the Forms W-2 that you give to the employees and the Form 941, Employer's Quarterly Federal Tax Return that you file to report wages and taxes for employees working for the establishment. Once you have filed a return, a preaddressed Form 8027 and/or Form 8027-T will be sent to you annually.

Type of establishment. Check the box (check only one box) on the form that best describes the food or beverage operation at this establishment:
● An establishment that serves evening meals only (with or without alcoholic beverages).
● An establishment that serves evening and other meals (with or without alcoholic beverages).

● An establishment that serves only meals other than evening meals (with or without alcoholic beverages).
● An establishment that serves food, if at all, only as an incidental part of the business of serving alcoholic beverages.

Employer's name and address. Enter the name and address of the entity or individual whose EIN is shown above. Enter foreign addresses as follows: city, province or state, and country. Do not abbreviate the name of the country.

Establishment number. Enter a five-digit number to identify the individual establishments that you are reporting under the same EIN. Give each establishment a separate number. For example, each establishment could be numbered consecutively, starting with 00001.

Lines 1 Through 8

Credit card sales. If the credit or debit charge receipts reflect tips, then you **must** enter on lines 1 and 2 the appropriate amounts shown on the credit card or debit card charge statements. See instructions for line 1 below.

Rounding off to whole dollars. You may round off cents to whole dollars on your return and schedules. If you do round to whole dollars, you must round all amounts. To round, drop amounts under 50 cents and increase amounts from 50 to 99 cents to the next dollar. For example, $1.39 becomes $1 and $2.50 becomes $3.

If you have to add two or more amounts to figure the amount to enter on a line, include cents when adding the amounts and round off only the total.

Line 1 — Total charged tips for calendar year 2005. Enter the total amount of tips that are shown on charge receipts for the year.

Line 2 — Total charge receipts showing charged tips. Enter the total sales (other than nonallocable receipts as defined on page 2) from charge receipts that had a charged tip shown. Include credit card charges and other credit arrangements and charges to a hotel room unless your normal accounting practice consistently excludes charges to a hotel room. Do not include any state or local taxes in the amounts reported.

Line 3 — Total amount of service charges of less than 10% paid as wages to employees. Enter the total amount of service charges of less than 10% that have been added to customers' bills and have been distributed to your employees for the year. In general, service charges added to the bill are not tips since the customer does not have a choice. These service charges are treated as wages and are includible on Form W-2. For details, see Revenue Ruling 69-28, 1969-1 C.B. 270.

Line 4a — Total tips reported by indirectly tipped employees. Enter the total amount of tips reported for the year by indirectly tipped employees, such as cooks, bussers, and service bartenders.

Line 4b — Total tips reported by directly tipped employees. Enter the total amount of tips reported for the year by directly tipped employees, such as bartenders and waitstaff.

⚠ *In figuring the tips you should report for 2005, do not include tips received by employees in December 2004, but not reported until January 2005. However, include tips received by employees in December 2005, but not reported until January 2006.*

Line 5 — Gross receipts from food or beverage operations. Enter the total gross receipts from the provision of food or beverages for this establishment for the year.

If you do not charge separately for providing food or beverages along with other goods or services (such as a package deal for food and lodging), make a good-faith estimate of the gross receipts from the food or beverages. This estimate

-3-

must reflect the cost to the employer for providing the food or beverage plus a reasonable profit factor.

Line 6. Enter the result of multiplying line 5 by 8% (.08) or a lower rate (if the establishment was granted a lower rate by the IRS).

If a lower percentage rate was granted, write the rate in the space provided and attach a copy of the IRS determination letter.

 The 8% rate (or lower rate) is used for tip allocation purposes only. Using this rate does not mean that directly tipped employees must report only 8%. They should report the amount of actual tips received.

TIP *If you have allocated tips using other than the calendar year, put an "X" on line 6 and enter the amount of allocated tips (if any) from your records on line 7. This may occur if you allocated tips based on the time period for which wages were paid or allocated on a quarterly basis.*

Line 7 — Allocation of tips. If the amount shown on line 6 is more than the amount of tips reported by your employees on line 4c, you must allocate the excess to those employees. Enter the excess on line 7. There are three methods by which you may allocate tips. Check the box on line 7a, b, or c to show the method used.

Line 7a — Hours-worked method. Establishments that employ fewer than the equivalent of 25 full-time employees (both tipped and nontipped employees) during a payroll period may use the hours-worked method to allocate tips. You will be considered to have employed fewer than the equivalent of 25 full-time employees during a payroll period if the average number of employee hours worked (both tipped and nontipped employees) per business day during a payroll period is less than 200 hours.

To allocate tips by the hours-worked method, follow the steps explained in *Line 7b — Gross receipts method* below. However, for the fraction in step 3 of the gross receipts method, substitute in the numerator (top number) the number of hours worked by each employee who is tipped directly, and in the denominator (bottom number) the total number of hours worked by all employees who are directly tipped for the payroll period. See Regulations sections 31.6053-3(j)(19) and 31.6053-3(f)(1)(iv) for details.

If you use the hours-worked method, be sure to enter in line 7a the average number of employee (both tipped and nontipped) hours worked per business day during the payroll period. If the establishment has more than one payroll period, you must use the payroll period in which the greatest number of workers (both tipped and nontipped) were employed.

Line 7b — Gross receipts method. If no good-faith agreement (as explained below) applies to the payroll period, you must allocate the difference between total tips reported and 8% of gross receipts using the gross receipts method (or hours-worked method (line 7a)) as follows (see example below):

1. Multiply the establishment's gross receipts (other than nonallocable receipts) for the payroll period by 8% (.08) or the lower rate.

2. Subtract from the amount figured in step 1 the total amount of tips reported by employees who were tipped indirectly for the payroll period. This difference is the directly tipped employees' total share of 8% (or the lower rate) of the gross receipts of the establishment. Indirectly tipped employees do not receive tips directly from customers. Examples are bussers, service bartenders, and cooks. Directly tipped employees, such as waitstaff and bartenders, receive tips directly from customers. Employees, such as maitre d's, who receive tips directly from customers and indirectly through tip splitting or pooling, are treated as directly tipped employees.

3. For each employee who is tipped directly, multiply the result in step 2 by the following fraction: the numerator (top number) is the amount of the establishment's gross receipts attributable to the employee, and the denominator (bottom number) is the gross receipts attributable to all directly tipped employees. The result is each directly tipped employee's share of 8% (or the lower rate) of the gross receipts for the payroll period.

4. From each directly tipped employee's share of 8% or the lower rate of the gross receipts figured in step 3, subtract the tips the employee reported for the payroll period. The result is each directly tipped employee's shortfall (if any) for the period.

5. From the amount figured in step 1, subtract the total tips reported by both directly and indirectly tipped employees. The result is the amount that has to be allocated among the directly tipped employees who had a shortfall for the payroll period as figured in step 4.

6. For each directly tipped employee who had a shortfall for the period as figured in step 4, multiply the amount in step 5 by the following fraction: the numerator is the employee's shortfall (figured in step 4), and the denominator is the total shortfall of all directly tipped employees. The result is the amount of allocated tips for each directly tipped employee.

Line 7c — Good-faith agreement. An allocation can be made under a good-faith agreement. This is a written agreement between you and at least two-thirds of the employees of each occupational category of employees who receive tips (for example, waitstaff, bussers, and maitre d's) working in the establishment when the agreement is adopted. The agreement must:

1. Provide for an allocation of the difference between total tips reported and 8% of gross receipts among employees who receive tips that approximates the actual distribution of tip income among the employees;

2. Be effective the first day of a payroll period that begins after the date the agreement is adopted, but no later than January 1 of the next year;

3. Be adopted when there are employees in each occupational category who would be affected by the agreement; and

4. Allow for revocation by a written agreement adopted by at least two-thirds of the employees in occupational categories affected by the agreement when it is revoked. The revocation is effective only at the beginning of a payroll period.

Line 8 — Total number of directly tipped employees. Enter the total number of directly tipped employees who worked at the establishment during 2005. This is the cumulative total of all directly tipped employees who worked at the establishment at any time during the year. If you have a large turnover of directly tipped employees, this number may be large. Do not use this number to determine if you must file Form 8027. Instead, see the *Worksheet for Determining Whether To File Form 8027* on page 1.

Example for Line 7b — Gross receipts method. A large food or beverage establishment has gross receipts for a payroll period of $100,000 and has tips reported for the payroll period of $6,200. Directly tipped employees reported $5,700, while indirectly tipped employees reported $500.

Directly tipped employees	Gross receipts for payroll period	Tips reported
A	$18,000	$1,080
B	16,000	880
C	23,000	1,810
D	17,000	800
E	12,000	450
F	14,000	680
Total	$100,000	$5,700

1. $100,000 (gross receipts) X .08 = $8,000
2. $8,000 - $500 (tips reported by indirectly tipped employees) = $7,500

3.

Directly tipped employees	Directly tipped employee's share of 8% of the gross	(Times) Gross receipts ratio	Employee's share of 8% of gross
A	$7,500	18,000/100,000 =	$1,350
B	$7,500	16,000/100,000 =	1,200
C	$7,500	23,000/100,000 =	1,725
D	$7,500	17,000/100,000 =	1,275
E	$7,500	12,000/100,000 =	900
F	$7,500	14,000/100,000 =	1,050
			$7,500

4.

Directly tipped employees	Employee's share of 8% of the gross	(Minus) Tips Reported	Employee shortfall
A	$1,350	$1,080 =	$270
B	$1,200	880 =	320
C	$1,725	1,810 =	–
D	$1,275	800 =	475
E	$ 900	450 =	450
F	$1,050	680 =	370
		Total shortfall	$1,885

5. $8,000 less $6,200 (total tips reported) = $1,800 (amount allocable among employees who had a shortfall)

6.

Shortfall employees	Allocable amount	(Times) Shortfall ratio	Amount of allocation
A	$1,800	270/1,885 =	$258
B	$1,800	320/1,885 =	306
D	$1,800	475/1,885 =	454
E	$1,800	450/1,885 =	430
F	$1,800	370/1,885 =	353

Since employee C has no shortfall, there is no allocation to C.

 In this example, the total amount of allocation is $1,801 resulting from the rounding off to whole numbers.

Employer's Optional Worksheet for Tipped Employees

Unreported tip income can lead to additional employer liability for FICA taxes. As a means of determining if your employees are reporting all of their tips to you, please take a few minutes to voluntarily complete the following worksheet. Completing this worksheet is only for the employer's information (it is not sent to the IRS).

1. Enter amount from Form 8027, line 1 . . . . 1. _____
2. Enter amount from Form 8027, line 2 . . . . 2. _____
3. Divide line 1 by line 2, enter as a decimal (at least 4 decimal places). . . . . 3. _____
4. Enter amount from Form 8027, line 4c . . . . . . 4. _____
5. Enter amount from Form 8027, line 5 . . . . 5. _____
6. Divide line 4 by line 5, enter as a decimal (at least 4 decimal places). . . . . 6. _____
7. Subtract line 6 from line 3; if zero or less, stop here 7. _____
8. Potential unreported tips. Multiply line 7 by line 5 8. _____

Once you have completed the worksheet:
● If the entry on line 7 is zero or less, your employees are probably accurately reporting their tips; however,
● If the entry on line 8 is greater than zero, depending on the type of operation you have and whether or not you have allocated tips, it is possible that your employees are not reporting all of their tip income to you.

Another quick method to determine if your employees are properly reporting all of their tips to you is to compare the rate of tips reported on credit sales to the rate of tips reported on cash sales. For example, if line 3 in the worksheet above greatly exceeds the rate determined from dividing reported cash tips by reportable cash receipts (that is, total cash receipts less nonallocable cash receipts), some of your employees may not be reporting all of their tips to you and you generally should be showing an amount on line 7 ("Allocation of tips") of Form 8027.

Need Help?

If it appears that not all tips are being reported to you, the IRS offers a service called the Tip Rate Determination & Education Program. This program can assist you, the employer, in implementing more effective methods of tip income reporting. The program also offers assistance in educating tipped employees concerning their obligations relating to the reporting of any tip income they receive. To find out more about this program or to participate in a voluntary tip compliance agreement, visit *www.irs.gov* and type "restaurant" in the *Keyword* search box. You may also call 1-800-829-4933 or visit *www.irs.gov/localcontacts* for the IRS Taxpayer Assistance Center in your area; or send an email to *TEC.TIP.Program@irs.gov* and request information on this program.

-5-

Privacy Act and Paperwork Reduction Act Notice. We ask for the information on this form to carry out the Internal Revenue laws of the United States. You are required to give us the information. We need it to ensure that you are complying with these laws and to allow us to figure and collect the right amount of tax.

Chapter 61, Information and Returns, of Subtitle F, Procedure and Administration, requires certain employers to report gross receipts, tips reported to them, and any allocated tips; and to furnish the amount of any allocated tips to affected employees. Section 6053 and its related regulations provide the definitions and methodology to be used in completing these forms. If you fail to provide this information in a timely manner you may be liable for penalties as provided by section 6721.

You are not required to provide the information requested on a form that is subject to the Paperwork Reduction Act unless the form displays a valid OMB control number. Books or records relating to a form or its instructions must be retained as long as their contents may become material in the administration of any Internal Revenue law.

Generally, tax returns and return information are confidential, as required by section 6103. However, section 6103 allows or requires the Internal Revenue Service to disclose or give the information shown on your tax return to others as described in the Code. For example, we may disclose your tax information to the Department of Justice for civil and criminal litigation, and to cities, states, and the District of Columbia for use in administering their tax laws. We may also disclose this information to other countries under a tax treaty, to federal and state agencies to enforce federal nontax criminal laws, or to federal law enforcement and intelligence agencies to combat terrorism.

The time needed to complete and file these forms will vary depending on individual circumstances. The estimated average times are:

Forms	8027	8027-T
Recordkeeping	9 hr., 47 min.	43 min.
Learning about the law or the form	53 min.	
Preparing and sending the form to the IRS	1 hr.	

If you have comments concerning the accuracy of these time estimates or suggestions for making these forms simpler, we would be happy to hear from you. You can write to Internal Revenue Service, Tax Products Coordinating Committee, SE:W:CAR:MP:T:T:SP, 1111 Constitution Ave. NW, IR-6406, Washington, DC, 20224. Do not send the tax forms to this address. Instead, see *Where To File* on page 2.

-6-

Form **8027-T**

Department of the Treasury
Internal Revenue Service

**Transmittal of Employer's Annual
Information Return of Tip Income and Allocated Tips**
▶ For Privacy Act and Paperwork Reduction Act Notice, see
the Instructions for Form 8027.

OMB No. 1545-0714

20**05**

Type or print employer's name, address, and employer identification number as shown on Form 941.	Employer's name		Employer identification number
	Number and street (or P.O. box number, if mail is not delivered to street address.)	Apt. or suite no.	Number of accompanying Forms 8027
	City or town, state, and ZIP code		

Use Form 8027-T to send Forms 8027 to the Internal Revenue Service Center if you have more than one establishment for which you have to file Form 8027.

File Form 8027-T along with accompanying Forms 8027 with the Internal Revenue Service, Cincinnati, OH 45999 by February 28, 2006.

Cat. No. 61006A

Form **8027-T** (2005)

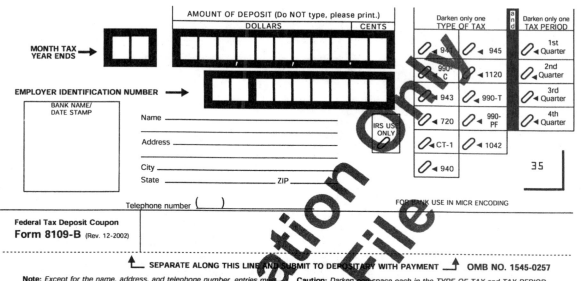

MONTH TAX YEAR ENDS →

AMOUNT OF DEPOSIT (Do NOT type, please print.)

DOLLARS · CENTS

EMPLOYER IDENTIFICATION NUMBER →

BANK NAME/ DATE STAMP

Name _____

Address _____

City _____

State _____ ZIP _____

Telephone number ( )

IRS USE ONLY

Darken only one **TYPE OF TAX**

a n d

Darken only one **TAX PERIOD**

941 · 945
990-C · 1120
943 · 990-T
720 · 990-PF
CT-1 · 1042
940

1st Quarter
2nd Quarter
3rd Quarter
4th Quarter

35

FOR BANK USE IN MICR ENCODING

Federal Tax Deposit Coupon
Form 8109-B (Rev. 12-2002)

- -

↑ **SEPARATE ALONG THIS LINE AND SUBMIT TO DEPOSITARY WITH PAYMENT** ↑ OMB NO. 1545-0257

Note: *Except for the name, address, and telephone number, entries must be made in pencil.* **Use soft lead** *(for example, a #2 pencil) so that the entries can be read more accurately by optical scanning equipment. The name, address, and telephone number may be completed other than by hand.* **You cannot use photocopies of the coupons to make your deposits. Do not staple, tape, or fold the coupons.**

Purpose of form. Use Form 8109-B to make a tax deposit only in the following two situations:

1. You have not yet received your resupply of preprinted deposit coupons (Form 8109); or

2. You are a new entity and have already been assigned an employer identification number (EIN), but you have not received your initial supply of preprinted deposit coupons (Form 8109). If you have not received your EIN, see *Exceptions* below.

Note: *If you do not receive your resupply of deposit coupons and a deposit is due or you do not receive your initial supply within 5-6 weeks of receipt of your EIN, call 1-800-829-4933.*

How to complete the form. Enter your name as shown on your return or other IRS correspondence, address, and EIN in the spaces provided. **Do not** make a name or address change on this form (see **Form 8822,** Change of Address). If you are required to file a Form 1120, 990-C, 990-PF (with net investment income), 990-T, or 2438, enter the month in which your tax year ends in the MONTH TAX YEAR ENDS boxes. For example, if your tax year ends in January, enter 01; if it ends in December, enter 12. Make your entries for EIN and MONTH TAX YEAR ENDS (if applicable) as shown in **Amount of deposit** below.

Exceptions. If you have applied for an EIN, have not received it, and a deposit must be made, **do not** use Form 8109-B. Instead, send your payment to the IRS address where you file your return. Make your check or money order payable to the United States Treasury and show on it your name (as shown on **Form SS-4,** Application for Employer Identification Number), address, kind of tax, period covered, and date you applied for an EIN. **Do not** use Form 8109-B to deposit delinquent taxes assessed by the IRS. Pay those taxes directly to the IRS. See **Circular E,** Employer's Tax Guide, for information on depositing by electronic funds transfer.

Amount of deposit. Enter the amount of the deposit in the space provided. Enter the amount legibly, forming the characters as shown below:

Hand print money amounts without using dollar signs, commas, a decimal point, or leading zeros. If the deposit is for whole dollars only, enter "00" in the CENTS boxes. For example, a deposit of $7,635.22 would be entered like this:

DOLLARS · CENTS

7 6 3 5 · 2 2

Caution: *Darken one space each in the TYPE OF TAX and TAX PERIOD columns as explained below. Darken the space to the left of the applicable tax form and tax period. Darkening the wrong space may delay proper crediting of your account.*

Types of Tax

Form 941 Employer's Quarterly Federal Tax Return (includes Forms **941-M, 941-PR,** and **941-SS**)

Form 943 Employer's Annual Tax Return for Agricultural Employers

Form 945 Annual Return of Withheld Federal Income Tax

Form 720 Quarterly Federal Excise Tax Return

Form CT-1 Employer's Annual Railroad Retirement Tax Return

Form 940 Employer's Annual Federal Unemployment (FUTA) Tax Return (includes Forms **940-EZ** and **940-PR**)

Form 1120 U.S. Corporation Income Tax Return (includes Form **1120** series of returns and Form **2438**)

Form 990-C Farmers' Cooperative Association Income Tax Return

Form 990-T Exempt Organization Business Income Tax Return

Form 990-PF Return of Private Foundation or Section 4947(a)(1) Nonexempt Charitable Trust Treated as a Private Foundation

Form 1042 Annual Withholding Tax Return for U.S. Source Income of Foreign Persons

Marking the Proper Tax Period

Payroll taxes and withholding. For Forms 941, 940, 943, 945, CT-1, and 1042, if your liability was incurred during:

- January 1 through March 31, darken the 1st quarter space
- April 1 through June 30, darken the 2nd quarter space
- July 1 through September 30, darken the 3rd quarter space
- October 1 through December 31, darken the 4th quarter space

Note: *If the liability was incurred during one quarter and deposited in another quarter, darken the space for the quarter in which the tax liability was incurred. For example, if the liability was incurred in March and deposited in April, darken the 1st quarter space.*

Excise taxes. For Form 720, follow the instructions above for Forms 941, 940, etc. For Form 990-PF, with net investment income, follow the instructions below for Form 1120, 990-C, etc.

Income Taxes (Form 1120, 990-C, 990-T, and 2438). To make an estimated tax deposit for any quarter of the current tax year, **darken only the 1st quarter space.**

Example 1. If your tax year ends on December 31, 2003, and a deposit for 2003 is being made between January 1 and December 31, 2003, darken the 1st quarter space.

Department of the Treasury
Internal Revenue Service

Cat. No. 61042S

Form **8109-B** (Rev. 12-2002)

Example 2. If your tax year ends on June 30, 2003, and a deposit for that fiscal year is being made between July 1, 2002, and June 30, 2003, darken the 1st quarter space.

To make a deposit for the prior tax year, **darken only the 4th quarter space.** This includes:

● Deposits of balance due shown on the return (Forms 1120, 990-C, 990-T, and 990-PF).

● Deposits of balance due shown on **Form 7004,** Application for Automatic Extension of Time To File Corporation Income Tax Return (be sure to darken the 1120 or 990-C space as appropriate).

● Deposits of balance due (Forms 990-T and 990-PF filers) shown on **Form 8868,** Application for Extension of Time To File an Exempt Organization Return (be sure to darken the 990-T or 990-PF space as appropriate).

● Deposits of balance due (Form 1042) shown on **Form 2758,** Application for Extension of Time To File Certain Excise, Income, Information, and Other Returns (be sure to darken the 1042 space as appropriate).

● Deposits of tax due shown on **Form 2438,** Undistributed Capital Gains Tax Return (darken the 1120 space).

Example 1. If your tax year ends on December 31, 2003, and a deposit for 2003 is being made after that date, darken the 4th quarter space.

Example 2. If your tax year ends on June 30, 2003, and a deposit for that fiscal year is being made after that date, darken the 4th quarter space.

How to ensure your deposit is credited to the correct account.

   1. Make sure your name and EIN are correct;

   2. Prepare only one coupon for each type of tax deposit;

   3. Darken only one space for the type of tax you are depositing;

   4. Darken only one space for the tax period for which you are making a deposit; and

   5. Use separate FTD coupons for each return period.

Telephone number. We need your daytime telephone number to call if we have difficulty processing your deposit.

Miscellaneous. We use the "IRS USE ONLY" box to ensure proper crediting to your account. **Do not** darken this space when making a deposit.

How to make deposits. Mail or deliver the completed coupon with the appropriate payment for the amount of the deposit to an authorized depositary (financial institution) for Federal taxes. Make checks or money orders payable to that depositary. To help ensure proper crediting of your account, include your EIN, the type of tax (e.g., Form 940), and the tax period to which the payment applies on your check or money order.

Authorized depositaries must accept cash, postal money orders drawn to the order of the depositary, or checks or drafts drawn on and to the order of the depositary. You can deposit taxes with a check drawn on another financial institution only if the depositary is willing to accept that form of payment.

If you prefer, you may mail your coupon and payment to Financial Agent, Federal Tax Deposit Processing, P.O. Box 970030, St. Louis, MO 63197. Make your check or money order payable to the **Financial Agent.**

Timeliness of deposits. The IRS determines whether deposits are on time by the date they are received by an authorized depositary. However, a deposit received by the authorized depositary after the due date will be considered timely if the taxpayer establishes that it was mailed in the United States at least 2 days before the due date.

Note: *If you are required to deposit any taxes more than once a month, any deposit of $20,000 or more must be made by its due date to be timely.*

When to deposit. See the instructions for the applicable return. For deposit rules for employment taxes, see Circular E (Pub. 15). You can get copies of forms and instructions by calling 1-800-TAX-FORM (1-800-829-3676) or by visiting IRS's Web Site at **www.irs.gov.**

Penalties. You may be charged a penalty for not making deposits when due or in sufficient amounts unless you have reasonable cause. This penalty may also apply if you mail or deliver Federal tax deposits to unauthorized institutions or IRS offices, rather than to authorized depositaries. Additionally, a **trust fund recovery penalty** may be imposed on all persons who are determined by the IRS to be responsible for collecting, accounting for, and paying over these taxes, and who acted willfully in not doing so. This penalty may apply to you if these unpaid taxes cannot be immediately collected from the employer or business. For more information on penalties, see Circular E (Pub. 15). See the **instructions for Form 720** for when these penalties apply to excise taxes.

Privacy Act and Paperwork Reduction Act Notice. Internal Revenue Code section 6302 requires certain persons to make periodic deposits of taxes. If you do not deposit electronically, you must provide the information requested on this form. IRC section 6109 requires you to provide your EIN. The information on this form is used to ensure that you are complying with the Internal Revenue laws and to ensure proper crediting of your deposit. Routine uses of this information include providing it to the Department of Justice for civil and criminal litigation, and to cities, states, and the District of Columbia for use in administering their tax laws. We may also disclose this information to Federal and state agencies to enforce Federal nontax criminal laws and to combat terrorism. We may give this information to other countries pursuant to tax treaties. Providing incomplete, incorrect, or fraudulent information may subject you to interest and penalties.

You are not required to provide the information requested on a form that is subject to the Paperwork Reduction Act unless the form displays a valid OMB control number. Books or records relating to a form or its instructions must be retained as long as their contents may become material in the administration of any Internal Revenue law. Generally, tax returns and return information are confidential, as required by IRC section 6103.

The time needed to complete and file this form will vary depending on individual circumstances. The estimated average time is 3 minutes. If you have comments concerning the accuracy of this time estimate or suggestions for making this form simpler, we would be happy to hear from you. You can write to the Tax Forms Committee, Western Area Distribution Center, Rancho Cordova, CA 95743-0001. **Do not** send this form to this address. Instead, see the instructions under **How to make deposits** on this page.

Form **8233**
(Rev. December 2001)

Department of the Treasury
Internal Revenue Service

Exemption From Withholding on Compensation for Independent (and Certain Dependent) Personal Services of a Nonresident Alien Individual

▶ See separate instructions.

OMB No. 1545-0795

Who Should Use This Form?	**IF** you are a nonresident alien individual who is receiving . . .	**THEN,** if you are the beneficial owner of that income, use this form to claim . . .
Note: *For definitions of terms used in this section and detailed instructions on required withholding forms for each type of income, see* **Definitions** *on pages 1 through 3 of the instructions.*	Compensation for independent personal services performed in the United States	A tax treaty withholding exemption for part or all of that compensation and/or to claim the daily personal exemption amount.
	Compensation for dependent personal services performed in the United States	A tax treaty withholding exemption for part or all of that compensation. **Note:** **Do not** use Form 8233 to claim the daily personal exemption amount.
	Noncompensatory scholarship or fellowship income **and** personal services income **from the same withholding agent**	A tax treaty withholding exemption for part or all of **both** types of income.
DO NOT Use This Form. . .	**IF** you are a beneficial owner who is . . .	**INSTEAD,** use . . .
	Receiving compensation for dependent personal services performed in the United States **and** you are **not** claiming a tax treaty withholding exemption for that compensation	Form W-4
	Receiving noncompensatory scholarship or fellowship income **and** you are **not** receiving any personal services income **from the same withholding agent**	Form W-8BEN or, if elected by the withholding agent, Form W-4 for the noncompensatory scholarship or fellowship income
	Claiming only foreign status or treaty benefits with respect to income that is **not** compensation for personal services	Form W-8BEN

This exemption is applicable for compensation for calendar year .... , or other tax year beginning .... and ending ....

Part I   Identification of Beneficial Owner (See instructions.)

1 Name of individual who is the beneficial owner	2 U.S. taxpayer identifying number	3 Foreign tax identifying number, if any (optional)

4   Permanent residence address (street, apt. or suite no., or rural route). **Do not use a P.O. box.**

City or town, state or province. Include postal code where appropriate.	Country (do not abbreviate)

5   Address in the United States (street, apt. or suite no., or rural route). **Do not use a P.O. box.**

City or town, state, and ZIP code

Note: *Citizens of Canada or Mexico are not required to complete lines 7a and 7b.*

6 U.S. visa type	7a Country issuing passport	7b Passport number
8 Date of entry into the United States	9a Current nonimmigrant status	9b Date your current nonimmigrant status expires

10 If you are a foreign student, trainee, professor/teacher, or researcher, check this box . . . . ▶ ☐
    Caution: *See the* **line 10 instructions** *for the required additional statement you must attach.*

For Paperwork Reduction Act Notice, see separate instructions.   Cat. No. 62292K   Form **8233** (Rev. 12-2001)

Form 8233 (Rev. 12-2001)

| **Part II** | **Claim for Tax Treaty Withholding Exemption and/or Personal Exemption Amount** |

11 Compensation for independent (and certain dependent) personal services:

a Description of personal services you are providing ....

....

....

b Total compensation you expect to be paid for these services in this calendar or tax year $ ....

12 If compensation is exempt from withholding based on a tax treaty benefit, provide:

a Tax treaty **and treaty article** on which you are basing exemption from withholding ....

....

b Total compensation listed on line 11b above that is exempt from tax under this treaty $ ....

c Country of permanent residence ....

> **Note:** *Do not complete lines 13a through 13c unless you also received compensation for personal services* **from the same withholding agent.**

13 Noncompensatory scholarship or fellowship income:

a Amount $ ....

b Tax treaty **and treaty article** on which you are basing exemption from withholding ....

....

c Total income listed on line 13a above that is exempt from tax under this treaty $ ....

14 Sufficient facts to justify the exemption from withholding claimed on line 12 and/or line 13 (see instructions) ....

....

....

....

....

....

....

....

....

....

> **Note:** *Lines 15 through 18 are to be completed only for certain independent personal services (see instructions).*

| **15** Number of personal exemptions claimed ▶ | **16** How many days will you perform services in the United States during this tax year? ▶ |

17 Daily personal exemption amount claimed (see instructions) ▶

18 Total personal exemption amount claimed. Multiply line 16 by line 17 ▶

| **Part III** | **Certification** |

Under penalties of perjury, I declare that I have examined the information on this form and to the best of my knowledge and belief it is true, correct, and complete. I further certify under penalties of perjury that:

● I am the beneficial owner (or am authorized to sign for the beneficial owner) of all the income to which this form relates.

● The beneficial owner is not a U.S. person.

● The beneficial owner is a resident of the treaty country listed on line 12a and/or 13b above within the meaning of the income tax treaty between the United States and that country.

● The beneficial owner is not a former citizen or long-term resident of the United States subject to section 877 (relating to certain acts of expatriation) or, if subject to section 877, the beneficial owner is nevertheless entitled to treaty benefits with respect to the amounts received.

Furthermore, I authorize this form to be provided to any withholding agent that has control, receipt, or custody of the income of which I am the beneficial owner or any withholding agent that can disburse or make payments of the income of which I am the beneficial owner.

Sign Here ▶ ....

　　　　　　　Signature of beneficial owner (or individual authorized to sign for beneficial owner)　　　　　　　Date

| **Part IV** | **Withholding Agent Acceptance and Certification** |

Name　　　　　　　　　　　　　　　　　　　　　　　　　　　　　　　　　　| **Employer identification number**

Address (number and street) (Include apt. or suite no. or P.O. box, if applicable.)

City, state, and ZIP code　　　　　　　　　　　　　　　　　　　　　　　　　| Telephone number

Under penalties of perjury, I certify that I have examined this form and any accompanying statements, that I am satisfied that an exemption from withholding is warranted, and that I do not know or have reason to know that the nonresident alien individual is not entitled to the exemption or that the nonresident alien's eligibility for the exemption cannot be readily determined.

Signature of withholding agent ▶ ....　　Date ▶

Instructions for Form 8233

 Department of the Treasury
Internal Revenue Service

(Rev. December 2005)

Exemption From Withholding on Compensation for Independent (and Certain Dependent) Personal Services of a Nonresident Alien Individual

General Instructions

Section references are to the Internal Revenue Code unless otherwise noted.

 If you are a "resident of a treaty country," you must know the terms of the tax treaty between the United States and the treaty country to properly complete Form 8233.

Purpose of Form

In general, section 1441 requires 30% federal income tax withholding on compensation for independent personal services (defined on this page). Sections 1441, 3401, and 3402 require withholding, sometimes at 30% and sometimes at graduated rates, on compensation for dependent personal services (defined beginning on this page). However, some payments may be exempt from withholding because of a tax treaty or the personal exemption amount. Complete and give Form 8233 to your withholding agent if some or all of your compensation is exempt from withholding.

You can use Form 8233 to claim a tax treaty withholding exemption for noncompensatory scholarship or fellowship income only if you are also claiming a tax treaty withholding exemption for compensation for personal services (including compensatory scholarship or fellowship income) received from the same withholding agent.

 Do not use Form 8233 if you have an office in the United States regularly available to you for performing personal services.

Additional information. You can get the complete text of most U.S. tax treaties from the IRS website at *www.irs.gov.* Technical explanations for many of those treaties are also available at that site. Also, see Pub. 901, U.S. Tax Treaties, for a quick reference guide to the provisions of U.S. tax treaties. You can get any of the forms or publications referred to in these instructions by calling 1-800-TAX-FORM (1-800-829-3676) or by downloading them from the website.

Giving Form 8233 to the Withholding Agent

You must complete Form 8233:
● For each tax year (be sure to specify the tax year in the space provided above Part I of the form),
● For each withholding agent, and
● For each type of income. However, you may use one Form 8233 to claim a tax treaty withholding exemption for both compensation for personal services (including compensatory scholarship or

fellowship income) and noncompensatory scholarship or fellowship income received from the same withholding agent.

Example. A nonresident alien is primarily present in the United States as a professor, but also is occasionally invited to lecture at another educational institution. These lectures are not connected with his teaching obligations but are in the nature of self-employment. For each tax year, the professor must complete two Forms 8233 and give one to each withholding agent to claim tax treaty benefits on the separate items of income.

Definitions

Nonresident Alien

If you are an alien individual (that is, an individual who is not a U.S. citizen), specific rules apply to determine if you are a resident alien or a nonresident alien for tax purposes. Generally, you are a resident alien if you meet either the "green card test" or the "substantial presence test" for the calendar year. Any person not meeting either test is generally a nonresident alien. Additionally, an alien individual who qualifies as a "resident of a treaty country" (defined later) or a bona fide resident of Puerto Rico, Guam, the Commonwealth of the Northern Mariana Islands, the U.S. Virgin Islands, or American Samoa is a nonresident alien individual.

For more information on the tests used to determine resident alien or nonresident alien status, see Pub. 519, U.S. Tax Guide for Aliens.

Note. Even though a nonresident alien individual married to a U.S. citizen or resident alien may choose to be treated as a resident alien for certain purposes (for example, filing a joint income tax return), such individual is still treated as a nonresident alien for withholding tax purposes on all income except wages.

U.S. Person

For purposes of this form, a U.S. person is a U.S. citizen or resident alien.

Tax Treaty Withholding Exemption

This term refers to an exemption from withholding permitted by IRS regulations under section 1441 that is based on a tax treaty benefit. See *Resident of a Treaty Country* next for requirements for claiming a tax treaty benefit on this form.

See the instructions for line 4 on page 3 for additional information for determining residence for purposes of claiming a tax treaty withholding exemption on this form.

Resident of a Treaty Country

An alien individual may claim to be a resident of a treaty country if he or she qualifies as a resident of that country under the terms of the residency article of the tax treaty between the United States and that country. See *Nonresident Alien* earlier.

A nonresident alien may claim a tax treaty benefit on this form only if that individual is the beneficial owner of the income and meets the residency requirement and all other requirements for benefits under the terms of the tax treaty.

Compensation for Independent Personal Services

Independent personal services are services performed as an independent contractor in the United States by a nonresident alien who is self-employed rather than an employee. Compensation for such services includes payments for contract labor; payments for professional services, such as fees to an attorney, physician, or accountant, if the payments are made directly to the person performing the services; consulting fees; honoraria paid to visiting professors, teachers, researchers, scientists, and prominent speakers; and generally, payments for performances by public entertainers.

Public entertainers. Special restrictions on exemption from or reduction of withholding apply to nonresident alien public entertainers (such as actors, musicians, artists, and athletes). Generally, such individuals are subject to 30% withholding from gross income paid for personal services performed unless a reduced rate of withholding under a withholding agreement prepared in accordance with Rev. Proc. 89-47, 1989-2 C.B. 598, has been approved by the IRS. In addition, many tax treaties contain separate articles that apply to public entertainers. If present, these articles take precedence over the "independent personal services" and "dependent personal services" articles of the treaties.

Required Withholding Form

For compensation you receive for independent personal services, complete Form 8233 to claim a tax treaty withholding exemption for part or all of that income and/or to claim the daily personal exemption amount.

Compensation for Dependent Personal Services

Dependent personal services are services performed as an employee in the United States by a nonresident alien. Dependent

Cat. No. 22663B

personal services include compensatory scholarship or fellowship income (see definition later). Compensation for such services includes wages, salaries, fees, bonuses, commissions, and similar designations for amounts paid to an employee.

Required Withholding Form(s)

Complete Form 8233 for compensation you receive for dependent personal services only if you are claiming a tax treaty withholding exemption for part or all of that income. Do not use Form 8233 to claim the daily personal exemption amount. For compensation for which you are not claiming a tax treaty withholding exemption, use Form W-4, Employee's Withholding Allowance Certificate.

Completing Form W-4. You should complete Form W-4 as follows:

Line 2. You are required to enter a social security number (SSN) on line 2 of Form W-4. If you do not have an SSN, you must apply for one on Form SS-5, Application for a Social Security Card. You may get Form SS-5 from a Social Security Administration (SSA) Office. Fill in Form SS-5 and return it to the SSA.

 You cannot enter an individual taxpayer identification number (ITIN) on line 2 of Form W-4.

Line 3. Check the single box regardless of your actual marital status.

Line 5. You should generally claim one withholding allowance. However, if you are a resident of Canada, Mexico, or the Republic of (South) Korea; a student from India; or a U.S. national; you may be able to claim additional withholding allowances for your spouse and children. See Pub. 519 for more information.

If you are completing Form W-4 for more than one withholding agent (for example, you have more than one employer), figure the total number of allowances you are entitled to claim (see the previous paragraph) and claim no more than that amount on all Forms W-4 combined. Your withholding usually will be most accurate when all allowances are claimed on the Form W-4 for the highest-paying job and zero allowances are claimed on the others.

Line 6. Write "nonresident alien" or "NRA" above the dotted line on line 6. If you would like to have an additional amount withheld, enter the amount on line 6.

Line 7. Do not claim that you are exempt from withholding on line 7 of Form W-4 (even if you meet both of the conditions listed on that line).

Compensatory Scholarship or Fellowship Income

In general, scholarship or fellowship income is compensatory to the extent it represents payment for past, present, or future services (for example, teaching, research, etc.) performed by a nonresident alien as an employee and the performance of those services is a condition for receiving the scholarship or fellowship (or tuition reduction).

Example. XYZ University awards a scholarship to N, a nonresident alien student. The only condition of the scholarship is that N attends classes and maintains a minimum level of academic performance. The scholarship income is not compensatory because N is not required to perform services as an employee as a condition for receiving the scholarship.

Required Withholding Form(s)

Compensatory scholarship or fellowship income is considered to be dependent personal services income. Therefore, complete Form 8233 for this income only if you are claiming a tax treaty withholding exemption for part or all of that income. Do not complete Form 8233 to claim the daily personal exemption amount.

For any part of this compensatory income for which you are not claiming a tax treaty withholding exemption, use Form W-4. See *Completing Form W-4* earlier.

Noncompensatory Scholarship or Fellowship Income

Noncompensatory scholarship or fellowship income is scholarship or fellowship income that is not compensatory scholarship or fellowship income (defined earlier).

The taxable portion of noncompensatory scholarship or fellowship income (defined below) paid to a nonresident alien is generally subject to withholding at a rate of 30% (the rate is generally 14% in the case of a nonresident alien temporarily present in the United States under an "F," "J," "M," or "Q" visa).

Taxable portion of noncompensatory scholarship or fellowship income. If you were a degree candidate, the amount of this type of income that you used for expenses other than tuition and course-related expenses (fees, books, supplies, and equipment) is generally taxable. For example, amounts used for room, board, and travel are generally taxable. If you were not a degree candidate, the full amount of the scholarship or fellowship income is generally taxable.

Required Withholding Form

You should generally complete Form W-8BEN, Certificate of Foreign Status of Beneficial Owner for United States Tax Withholding, to claim a tax treaty withholding exemption for this type of income. No Form W-8BEN is required unless a treaty benefit is being claimed.

Exception. If you are receiving both compensation for personal services (including compensatory scholarship or fellowship income) and noncompensatory scholarship or fellowship income from the same withholding agent, you may use one Form 8233 for both types of income. However, this exception applies only if you are claiming a tax treaty withholding exemption for both types of income.

Alternate withholding election. A withholding agent may elect to withhold on the taxable portion of noncompensatory scholarship or

fellowship income of a nonresident alien temporarily present in the United States under an "F," "J," "M," or "Q" visa as if it were compensatory scholarship or fellowship income (provided the nonresident alien is not claiming treaty benefits with respect to that income). The withholding agent makes this election by requesting that the nonresident alien complete Form W-4 using the instructions in Rev. Proc. 88-24, 1988-1 C.B. 800.

Withholding Agent

Any person, U.S. or foreign, that has control, receipt, or custody of an amount subject to withholding or who can disburse or make payments of an amount subject to withholding is a withholding agent. The withholding agent may be an individual, corporation, partnership, trust, association, or any other entity, including (but not limited to) any foreign intermediary, foreign partnership, and U.S. branches of certain foreign banks and insurance companies. Generally, the person who pays (or causes to be paid) the amount subject to withholding to the nonresident alien individual (or to his or her agent) must withhold.

Beneficial Owner

For payments other than those for which a reduced rate of withholding is claimed under an income tax treaty, the beneficial owner of income is generally the person who is required under U.S. tax principles to include the income in gross income on a tax return. A person is not a beneficial owner of income, however, to the extent that person is receiving the income as a nominee, agent, or custodian, or to the extent the person is a conduit whose participation in a transaction is disregarded. In the case of amounts paid that do not constitute income, beneficial ownership is determined as if the payment were income.

Avoid Common Errors

To ensure that your Form 8233 is promptly accepted, be sure that you:

• Answer all applicable questions completely.

• Specify the tax year for which this form will be effective in the space provided above Part I of the form.

• Enter your complete name, addresses, and identifying number(s) in Part I.

• Have attached the required statement described in the line 10 instructions if you are a foreign student, trainee, professor/teacher, or researcher.

• Are not trying to claim tax treaty benefits for a country with which the United States does not have a ratified tax treaty.

• Are not trying to claim tax treaty benefits that do not exist in your treaty.

• Complete lines 11 through 14 in sufficient detail to allow the IRS to determine the tax treaty benefit you are claiming.

• Claim the proper number of personal exemptions on line 15.

• Complete the required certification in Part III.

-2-

Specific Instructions

Part I

Line 2

You are required to furnish a U.S. taxpayer identifying number on this form. You are generally required to enter your social security number (SSN) on line 2. To apply for an SSN, get Form SS-5 from a Social Security Administration (SSA) office. Fill in Form SS-5 and return it to the SSA.

If you do not have an SSN and are not eligible to get one, you must get an individual taxpayer identification number (ITIN). To apply for an ITIN, file Form W-7, Application for IRS Individual Taxpayer Identification Number, with the IRS. Generally, you apply for an ITIN when you file your tax return for which the ITIN is needed. However, if the reason for your ITIN request is because you need to provide Form 8233 to the withholding agent, you must file Form W-7 and provide proof that you are not eligible for an SSN (your Form SS-5 was rejected by the SSA) and include a Form 8233. It usually takes about 4-6 weeks to get an ITIN. For more information on requesting an ITIN, see the Form W-7 instructions.

If you have applied for a U.S. taxpayer identifying number but have not yet received it, you may attach a copy of a completed Form W-7 or SS-5 showing that a number has been applied for.

 An ITIN is for tax use only. It does not entitle you to social security benefits or change your employment or immigration status under U.S. law.

Line 3

If your country of residence for tax purposes has issued you a tax identifying number, enter it here. For example, if you are a resident of Canada, enter your Social Insurance Number.

Line 4

Your permanent residence address is the address in the country where you claim to be a resident for purposes of that country's income tax. If you are completing Form 8233 to claim a tax treaty withholding exemption, you must determine your residency in the manner required by the treaty. Do not show the address of a financial institution, a post office box, or an address used solely for mailing purposes. If you are an individual who does not have a tax residence in any country, your permanent residence is where you normally reside.

Most tax treaties that provide for a tax treaty withholding exemption require that the recipient be a resident of the treaty country at the time of, or immediately prior to, entry into the United States. Thus, a student or researcher may generally claim the withholding exemption even if he or she no longer has a permanent address in the treaty country after entry into the United States. If this is the case, you may provide a U.S. address on line 4 and still be eligible for the

withholding exemption if all other conditions required by the tax treaty are met. You must also identify on line 12a and/or line 13b the tax treaty country of which you were a resident at the time of, or immediately prior to, your entry into the United States.

Line 6

Enter your U.S. visa type. For example, foreign students are usually granted an "F-1" visa. Foreign professors, teachers, or researchers are usually granted a "J-1" visa. Business/vocational trainees are usually granted an "M-1" visa; however, some persons granted a "J-1" visa may also be considered business/vocational trainees (for example, a person admitted to complete a postgraduate residency in medicine).

If you do not have, or do not require, a visa, write "None."

 Spouses and dependents admitted on secondary visas (for example, "F-2," "J-2," "H-4," and "O-3" visas) are not usually eligible to claim the same treaty benefits as the primary visa holder.

Line 8

You are generally required to enter your date of entry into the United States that pertains to your current nonimmigrant status. For example, enter the date of arrival shown on your current Immigration Form I-94, Arrival-Departure Record.

Exception. If you are claiming a tax treaty benefit that is determined by reference to more than one date of arrival, enter the earlier date of arrival. For example, you are currently claiming treaty benefits (as a teacher or a researcher) under article 15 of the tax treaty between the United States and Norway. You previously claimed treaty benefits (as a student) under article 16(1) of that treaty. Under article 16(4) of that treaty, the combination of exemptions under articles 15 and 16(1) may not extend beyond 5 tax years from the date you entered the United States. If article 16(4) of that treaty applies, enter on line 8 the date you entered the United States as a student.

Line 9a

Enter your current nonimmigrant status. For example, enter your current nonimmigrant status shown on your current Immigration Form I-94.

Line 9b

Enter the date your current nonimmigrant status expires. For example, you may enter the date of expiration shown on your current Immigration Form I-94. Enter "DS" on line 9b if the date of expiration is based on "duration of status."

Line 10

Nonresident alien students, trainees, professors/teachers, and researchers using Form 8233 to claim a tax treaty withholding exemption for compensation for personal services must attach to Form 8233 a statement. The format and contents of the required statements are shown in Appendix A and Appendix B in Pub. 519.

Part II

Line 11a

For compensation for independent personal services, examples of acceptable descriptions to enter on this line include: "Consulting contract to design software" or "give three lectures at XYZ University."

For compensation for dependent personal services, examples of acceptable descriptions to enter on this line include:
● A nonresident alien student may enter "part-time library assistant," "part-time restaurant worker," or "teaching one chemistry course per semester to undergraduate students."
● A nonresident alien professor or teacher may enter "teaching at ABC University."
● A nonresident alien researcher may enter "research at ABC University's school for liquid crystal research."
● A nonresident alien business/vocational trainee may enter "neurosurgical residency at ABC Hospital" or "one-year internship in hydraulic engineering at XYZ Corporation."

Line 11b

Enter the total amount of compensation for personal services you will receive from this withholding agent during the tax year. Enter an estimated amount if you do not know the exact amount.

Line 12a

Enter the specific treaty and article on which you are basing your claim for exemption from withholding (for example, "U.S./Germany tax treaty, Article 20(4)").

Line 12b

If all income received for the services performed to which this Form 8233 applies is exempt, write "All." If only part is exempt, enter the exact dollar amount that is exempt from withholding.

Line 12c

Generally, you may claim a withholding exemption based on a U.S. tax treaty with the country in which you claim permanent (or indefinite) residence. This is the foreign country in which you live most of the time. It is not necessarily the country of your citizenship. For example, you are a citizen of Pakistan but maintain your home in England. You cannot claim a withholding exemption based on the U.S./Pakistan tax treaty. Any withholding exemption you claim must be based on the U.S./United Kingdom tax treaty.

Line 13b

Enter the specific treaty and article on which you are basing your claim for exemption from withholding (for example, "U.S./Germany tax treaty, Article 20(3)").

Line 14

Provide sufficient facts to justify the exemption from withholding claimed on line 12 and/or line 13. Be sure you provide enough details to allow the IRS to determine the tax treaty benefit you are claiming.

-3-

Lines 15 through 18 (for certain independent personal services)

Do not complete lines 15 through 18 if you are claiming on line 12b that all of the compensation you are receiving for independent personal services is exempt from withholding.

Line 15

For compensation for independent personal services for which an exemption from withholding is not available, 30% must be withheld from that compensation after subtracting the value of one personal exemption. You will generally enter "1" on line 15; however, if the exception below applies to you, enter the total number of personal exemptions you are entitled to on line 15.

Exception. If you are a resident of Canada, Mexico, or the Republic of (South) Korea; a student from India; or a U.S. national; you may be able to claim additional personal exemptions for your spouse and children. For 2005, the new US-Japan treaty does not allow a deduction for additional personal exemptions unless you choose to have the old treaty apply in 2005. See Pub. 519 for more information.

Lines 16 and 17

Each allowable personal exemption must be prorated for the number of days during the tax year you will perform the personal services in the United States. Enter the number of days on line 16 that pertain to the independent personal services described in line 11a. To figure the daily personal exemption amount to enter on line 17, divide the personal exemption amount for the tax year ($3,200 for 2005) by 365 (366 for a leap year) and multiply the result by the amount you entered on line 15. For example, if you are entitled to one personal exemption for 2005, enter $8.77 (that is, $3,200 / 365 days = $8.77 x 1 personal exemption = $8.77) on line 17.

Part IV

Withholding Agent's Responsibilities

When the nonresident alien individual gives you Form 8233, review it to see if you are satisfied that the exemption from withholding is warranted. If you are satisfied, based on the facts presented, complete and sign the certification in Part IV.

You will need three copies of a completed Form 8233. Within 5 days of your acceptance, forward one copy to:
Internal Revenue Service
International Section
P.O. Box 920
Bensalem, PA 19020-8518
Give one copy of the completed Form 8233 to the nonresident alien individual. Keep a copy for your records. Each copy of Form 8233 must include any attachments submitted by the nonresident alien individual.

The exemption from withholding is effective for payments made retroactive to the date of the first payment covered by Form 8233, even though you must wait at least 10 days after you have properly mailed Form 8233 to the IRS to see whether the IRS has any objections to the Form 8233.

You must not accept Form 8233, and you must withhold, if either of the following applies:
• You know, or have reason to know, that any of the facts or statements on Form 8233 may be false or
• You know, or have reason to know, that the nonresident alien's eligibility for the exemption from withholding cannot be readily determined (for example, you know the nonresident alien has a fixed base or permanent establishment in the United States).

If you accept Form 8233 and later find that either of the situations described above applies, you must promptly notify the IRS (by writing to the above address) and you must begin withholding on any amounts not yet paid. Also, if you are notified by the IRS that the nonresident alien's eligibility for the exemption from withholding is in doubt or that the nonresident alien is not eligible for exemption from withholding, you must begin withholding immediately. See Regulations section 1.1441-4(b)(2)(iii) for examples illustrating these rules.

If you submit an incorrect Form 8233, you will be notified by the IRS that the form submitted is not acceptable and that you must begin withholding immediately. Examples of incorrect Forms 8233 include:

• Any Form 8233 that claims a tax treaty benefit that does not exist or is obviously false.
• Any Form 8233 that has not been completed in sufficient detail to allow determination of the correctness of the tax treaty benefit or exemption claimed.

Signature

You or your authorized agent must sign and date Form 8233. See Regulations section 1.1441-7(c) for information about authorized agents.

Paperwork Reduction Act Notice. We ask for the information on this form to carry out the Internal Revenue laws of the United States. If you want to receive exemption from withholding on compensation for independent (and certain dependent) personal services, you are required to give us the information. We need it to ensure that you are complying with these laws and to allow us to figure and collect the right amount of tax.

You are not required to provide the information requested on a form that is subject to the Paperwork Reduction Act unless the form displays a valid OMB control number. Books or records relating to a form or its instructions must be retained as long as their contents may become material in the administration of any Internal Revenue law. Generally, tax returns and return information are confidential, as required by section 6103.

The time needed to complete and file this form will vary depending on individual circumstances. The estimated average time is: **Recordkeeping,** 1 hr. 5 min.; **Learning about the law or the form,** 31 min.; **Preparing and sending the form to IRS,** 57 min.

If you have comments concerning the accuracy of these time estimates or suggestions for making this form simpler, we would be happy to hear from you. You can write to the Internal Revenue Service, Tax Products Coordinating Committee, SE:W:CAR:MP:T:T:SP, 1111 Constitution Ave. NW, IR-6406, Washington, DC 20224. Do not send the tax form to this address. Instead, give it to your withholding agent.

-4-

Form **8508** (Rev. 9-2005) Internal Revenue Service Department of the Treasury	**Request for Waiver From Filing** **Information Returns Electronically/Magnetically** **(Forms W-2, W-2G, 1042-S, 1098 Series, 1099 Series, 5498 Series, and 8027)** *(Please type or print in **black ink** when completing this form - see instructions on back.)*	OMB Number 1545-0957

Note: Only the person required to file electronically/magnetically can file Form 8508. A transmitter cannot file Form 8508 for the payer, unless he or she has a power of attorney. If you have a power of attorney, attach a letter to the Form 8508 stating this fact.

1. Type of submission   ☐ Original   ☐ Reconsideration

2. Waiver requested for tax year (Enter *one year only*)

20 _____

3. Payer name, **complete** address, and contact person. (A **separate** Form 8508 must be filed for *each payer* requesting a waiver.)

Name _____

Address _____

City _____ State _____ ZIP _____

Contact Name _____

4. Taxpayer Identification Number
(9-digit EIN/SSN)

5. Telephone number

(_____) _____

Email Address

6. Waiver Requested for	**Enter the Number of Returns That:**		**Waiver Requested for**	**Enter the Number of Returns That:**	
	(a) You wish to file on paper	(b) You expect to file next tax year		(a) You wish to file on paper	(b) You expect to file next tax year
☐ 1042-S			☐ 1099-PATR		
☐ 1098			☐ 1099-Q		
☐ 1098-C			☐ 1099-R		
☐ 1098-E			☐ 1099-S		
☐ 1098-T			☐ 1099-SA		
☐ 1099-A			☐ 5498		
☐ 1099-B			☐ 5498-ESA		
☐ 1099-C			☐ 5498-SA		
☐ 1099-CAP			☐ 8027		
☐ 1099-DIV			☐ W-2		
☐ 1099-G			☐ W-2AS		
☐ 1099-H			☐ W-2G		
☐ 1099-INT			☐ W-2GU		
☐ 1099-LTC			☐ W-2PR		
☐ 1099-MISC			☐ W-2VI		
☐ 1099-OID					

7. Is this waiver requested for corrections ONLY?   ☐ Yes   ☐ No

8. Is this the first time you have requested a waiver from the electronic/magnetic media filing requirements for any of the forms listed in Block 6?

☐ Yes *(Skip to signature line)*   ☐ No *(Complete Block 9 if your request is due to undue hardship)*

9. Enter **two current cost estimates** given to you by third parties for software, software upgrades or programming for your current system, or costs for preparing your files for you.

Cost estimates for any reason other than the preparation of electronic/magnetic media files will not be acceptable.

$ _____

*Attach these **two written cost estimates** to the Form 8508. Failure to provide **current** cost estimates and/or signature will result in denial of your waiver request.*

$ _____

Under penalties of perjury, I declare that I have examined this document, including any accompanying statements, and, to the best of my knowledge and belief, it is true, correct, and complete.

10. Signature	Title	Date

For Paperwork Reduction Act Notice, see back of this form.   Catalog Number 63499V   Form **8508** (Rev. 9-2005)

General Instructions

Paperwork Reduction Act Notice. We ask for the information on these forms to carry out the Internal Revenue Laws of the United States. You are not required to provide the information requested on a form that is subject to the Paperwork Reduction Act unless the form displays a valid OMB control number. Books or records relating to a form must be retained as long as their contents may become material in the administration of any Internal Revenue law. Generally, tax returns and return information are confidential, as required by Code section 6103.

The time needed to provide this information would vary depending on individual circumstances. The estimated average time is:

Preparing Form 8508 . . . . 15 min.

If you have comments concerning the accuracy of these time estimates or suggestions for making this form simpler, we would be happy to hear from you. You can write to the Internal Revenue Service, Tax Products Coordinating Committee, SE:W:CAR:MP:T:T:SP, 1111 Constitution Ave. NW, IR-6406, Washington, DC 20224. DO NOT SEND THE FORMS TO THIS OFFICE. Instead, see the instructions below on where to file. **When completing this form, please type or print clearly in BLACK ink.**

Purpose of Form. Use this form to request a waiver from filing Forms W-2, W-2AS, W-2G, W-2GU, W-2PR, W-2VI, 1042-S, 1098 Series, 1099 Series, 5498 Series, or 8027 electronically/magnetically for the tax year indicated in Block 2 of this form. Complete a Form 8508 for each Taxpayer Identification Number (TIN). You may use one Form 8508 for multiple types of forms. After evaluating your request, IRS will notify you as to whether your request is approved or denied. The chart below contains types of documents and the acceptable media for each form.

Specific Instructions

Block 1. --Indicate the type of submission by checking the appropriate box. An original submission is your first request for a waiver for the current year. A reconsideration indicates that you are submitting additional information to IRS that you feel may reverse a denial of an originally submitted request.

Block 2. --Enter the tax year for which you are requesting a waiver. Only waiver requests for the current tax year can be processed. If this block is not completed, the IRS will assume the request is for the current tax year.

Block 3. --Enter the name and complete address of the payer and person to contact if additional information is needed by IRS.

Block 4. --Enter the Taxpayer Identification Number *(TIN)* [Employer Identification Number (EIN) or the Social Security Number *(SSN)*] of the payer. The number must contain 9-digits.

Block 5. --Enter the telephone number and Email address of the contact person.

Block 6. --Check the box(es) beside the form(s) for which the waiver is being requested.

Block 6a. -For each type of information return checked, enter the total number of forms you plan to file.

Block 6b. --Provide an estimate of the total number of information returns you plan to file for the following tax year.

Block 7. --Indicate whether or not this waiver is requested for corrections only. If you request a waiver for original documents and it is approved, you will automatically receive a waiver for corrections. However, if you can submit your original returns electronically/magnetically, but not your corrections, a waiver must be requested for corrections only.

Block 8. --If this is the first time you have requested a waiver for any of the forms listed in Block 6, for any tax year, check "YES" and skip to Block 10. However, if you have requested a waiver in the past and check "NO," complete Block 9 to establish undue hardship. Waivers, after the first year, are granted only in case of undue hardship or catastrophic event. *Note: Under Regulations Section 301.6011-2(c)(2), "The principal factor in determining hardship will be the amount, if any, by which the cost of filing the information returns in accordance with this section exceeds the cost of filing the returns on other media."*

Block 9. --Enter the cost estimates from two service bureaus or other third parties. These cost estimates must reflect the total amount that each service bureau will charge for software, software upgrades or programming for your current system, or costs to produce your electronic/magnetic media file only. *If you do not provide two written cost estimates from service bureaus or other third parties, we will automatically deny your request. Cost estimates from prior years will not be accepted. Note: If your request is not due to undue hardship, as defined above, attach a detailed explanation of why you need a waiver.*

Block 10. --The waiver request must be signed by the payer or a person duly authorized to sign a return or other document on his behalf.

Filing Instructions

When to File. -- You should file Form 8508 at least 45 days before the due date of the returns for which you are requesting a waiver. See Publication 1220, Part A for the due dates. Waiver requests will be processed beginning January 1st of the calendar year the returns are due.

Where to File. --

Internal Revenue Service
Enterprise Computing Center -Martinsburg
Information Reporting Program
240 Murall Drive
Kearneysville, WV 25430

For further information concerning the filing of information returns to IRS ectronically/magnetically, contact the IRS Enterprise Computing Center at the address given above or by telephone toll-free at **866-455-743**8 between 8:30 a.m. and 4:30 p.m. Eastern Standard Time.

Penalty. --If you are required to file on magnetic media but fail to do so and you do not have an approved waiver on record, you may be subject to a penalty of $50 per return unless you establish reasonable cause.

Filing Requirements and Acceptable Methods

*If the total number of documents to be filed is below the 250 threshold, you are **not required** to file electronically/magnetically, and you **do not** need to submit Form 8508 to IRS.*

Type of Documents	Acceptable Methods
Forms 1098-series, 1099-series, W-2G, 5498-series	Electronic Filing and Tape Cartridges
Forms W-2, W-2AS, W-2GU, W-2PR, W-2VI *	Electronic Filing
Form 1042-S	Electronic Filing and Tape Cartridges
Form 8027	Electronic Filing and Tape Cartridges

* To file these Forms electronically/magnetically, contact the Social Security Administration *(SSA)* at *1-800-772-6270*. For all other forms listed, contact IRS.

Catalog Number. 63499V   Form **8508** (Rev. 9-2005)

Form **8633**	Application to Participate in the	For Official Use Only
(Rev. July 2003)	IRS *e-file* Program	EFIN: ETIN:
Department of the Treasury Internal Revenue Service		OMB Number 1545-0991

Please check the box(es) that apply to this application:

☐ New ☐ Revised EFIN: .... ☐ Add New Location ☐ Reapply EFIN and /or Previous EFIN ....

1a Please check the box which describes your firm. (Check one box only)

☐ Sole proprietorship ☐ Partnership (number of partners with 5% or more interest) ▶ _____ ☐ Corporation
☐ Limited Liability Company ☐ Limited Liability Partnership ☐ Personal Service Corporation ☐ Federal Government Agency
☐ State Government Agency ☐ Local Government Agency ☐ Credit Union ☐ Association ☐ Volunteer Organization

b Firm's Employer Identification Number (EIN) or Social Security Number (SSN)

c Firm's legal name as shown on firm's tax return

d Doing Business As (DBA) name (if other than the name in item 1c)

e Business location address | Country | Street | City | State | ZIP Code/Country Code

f Business telephone number ( ) Fax Number ( )

g Mailing address of the Firm if different from the location address only (street or P.O. box) | Country | Street | City | State | ZIP Code/Country Code

h Is the firm open 12 months a year? Yes ☐ No ☐
If you answer "No," please give address and telephone number that are available 12 months of the year. | Address | Telephone number ( )

i Primary Contact Name (first, middle initial, last) | Title: | E-mail address (optional):
| | Phone Number: ( ) | Fax Number: ( )

j Alternate Contact Name (first, middle initial, last) | Title: | E-mail address (optional):
| | Phone Number: ( ) | Fax Number: ( )

2 Please answer the following questions by checking the appropriate box or boxes. | Yes | No

a Will you originate the submission of electronic returns to the IRS? **(Electronic Return Originator)** . . . .

b Will you file as a **Reporting Agent** for Forms 940/941 as defined in Revenue Procedure 96-17? **(Reporting Agent)**

Note: If you answer No to 2b, skip to 2c. Check Yes in box 2c if you transmit returns you prepared.

Are you currently listed on the IRS Reporting Agent's File (RAF) for this EIN? . . . .

(If you answer **NO**, you must furnish complete, signed copies of your Forms 8655 for the clients for whom you intend to file returns. You must also furnish a list of your clients containing the Business Name and EIN (Agents List).

c Will you transmit returns prepared by you or those of another ERO? **(Transmitter)** . . . .

d Will you transmit individual or business income tax return information prepared by a taxpayer using commercially purchased software or software you provide through an on-line Internet site? **(On-line Provider)** . . . .

(If you answer **YES**, please follow the instructions on Page 3 for Line 2d.)

e Will you write electronic filing software? **(Software Developer)**

f Will you receive tax return information from EROs, or from taxpayers who have prepared their own returns using commercial software, or on an Internet site, process the information, and either forward it to a transmitter, or send the information back to the ERO? **(Intermediate Service Provider)** . . . . . .

3 If you are a **Not for Profit** service, check the one box that applies below:

☐ VITA ☐ TAC (Tax Assistance Center)
☐ TCE (Tax Counseling for the Elderly)
☐ Military Base ☐ Employee Member Benefit

4 Check the individual and/or business form types you will e-file for:

☐ 940 ☐ 941 ☐ 990 ☐ 1040 ☐ ETD
☐ 1041 ☐ 1065 ☐ 1120 ☐ 1120 POL ☐ State Ack

Check the 1120 box for 1120 and 1120S. Check the 990 box for 990, 990-EZ, and 8868. See instructions for additional information on check boxes State Ack and ETD.

5 If you are a transmitter/software developer and checked the 940 or 941 box, please check the software format which applies:

940 ☐ XML ☐ Non-EDI ☐ On-line Non-EDI
941 ☐ XML ☐ Non-EDI ☐ EDI
☐ On-line ☐ On-line Non-EDI

6 Has the firm failed to file business tax returns, or pay tax liabilities under U.S. Internal Revenue laws? (Please attach an explanation for a "Yes" response.) . . . | Yes | No

See **Paperwork Reduction Act Notice and Privacy Act Notice on page 4.** Cat. No. 64225N Form **8633** (Rev. 7-2003)

7   Principals of Your Firm or Organization

Do not complete this section if you are adding a new location or you checked a box on Line 3, Page 1. If you are a **sole proprietor**, list your name, home address, social security number, and respond to each question. If your firm is a **partnership**, list the name, home address, social security number, and respond to each question for each partner who has a five percent (5%) or more interest in the partnership. If you are a partnership and no partners have at least 5% interest in the partnership, list the name, title, home address, social security number, and respond to each question for at least one individual authorized to act for the firm in legal and/or tax matters. (You may use continuation sheets.) If your firm is a **corporation**, list the name, title, home address, social security number, and respond to each question for the President, Vice-President, Secretary, and Treasurer of the corporation. The signature of each person listed authorizes the Internal Revenue Service to conduct a credit check on that individual.

Type or print name (first, middle, last)	U.S. citizenship?	Are you a/an:	Are you licensed or bonded in accordance with state or local requirements?
Title:	☐ Yes ☐ No ☐ Legal resident alien	☐ attorney ☐ banking official ☐ C.P.A. ☐ enrolled agent ☐ officer of a publicly owned corporation ☐ None apply (Fingerprint Card Required)	☐ Yes ☐ No ☐ Not applicable
Home address	Social Security Number	enrolled agent #_____	
		Have you ever been assessed any preparer penalties, been convicted of a crime, failed to file personal tax returns, or pay tax liabilites, or been convicted of any criminal offense under the U.S. Internal Revenue laws? ☐ Yes ☐ No (Please attach an explanation for a "Yes" response.)	
	Date of birth (month, day, year)	Signature	☐ Add ☐ Delete
E-mail (optional):			

Type or print name (first, middle, last)	U.S. citizenship?	Are you a/an:	Are you licensed or bonded in accordance with state or local requirements?
Title:	☐ Yes ☐ No ☐ Legal resident alien	☐ attorney ☐ banking official ☐ C.P.A. ☐ enrolled agent ☐ officer of a publicly owned corporation ☐ None apply (Fingerprint Card Required)	☐ Yes ☐ No ☐ Not applicable
Home address	Social Security Number	enrolled agent #_____	
		Have you ever been assessed any preparer penalties, been convicted of a crime, failed to file personal tax returns, or pay tax liabilites, or been convicted of any criminal offense under the U.S. Internal Revenue laws? ☐ Yes ☐ No (Please attach an explanation for a "Yes" response.)	
	Date of birth (month, day, year)	Signature	☐ Add ☐ Delete
E-mail (optional):			

8   Responsible Official (Please complete this section and provide signature even if it is the same as Line 7.) A Not for Profit service selected in a box on Line 3, Page 1, must complete this section.

The responsible official is the individual with responsibility for and authority over the operations at designated sites. The responsible official is the first point of contact with the IRS, has the authority to sign revised applications, and is responsible for ensuring that all requirements of the IRS e-file program are adhered to. A responsible official may be responsible for more than one office. A principal listed in Section 7 may also be a responsible official.

Name of responsible official (first, middle initial, last)	U.S. citizenship?	Are you a/an:	Are you licensed or bonded in accordance with state or local requirements?
Title:	☐ Yes ☐ No ☐ Legal resident alien	☐ attorney ☐ banking official ☐ C.P.A. ☐ enrolled agent ☐ officer of a publicly owned corporation ☐ None apply (Fingerprint Card Required)	☐ Yes ☐ No ☐ Not applicable
Home address	Social Security Number	enrolled agent #_____	
		Have you ever been assessed any preparer penalties, been convicted of a crime, failed to file personal tax returns, or pay tax liabilites, or been convicted of any criminal offense under the U.S. Internal Revenue laws? ☐ Yes ☐ No (Please attach an explanation for a "Yes" response.)	
	Date of birth (month, day, year)	Signature	
E-mail (optional):			

Applicant Agreement

Under the penalties of perjury, I declare that I have examined this application and read all accompanying information, and to the best of my knowledge and belief, the information being provided is true, correct, and complete. This firm and employees will comply with all of the provisions of the Revenue Procedure for Electronic Filing of Individual Income Tax Returns and Business Tax Returns, and related publications, for each year of our participation.

Acceptance for participation is not transferable. I understand that if this firm is sold or its organizational structure changes, a new application must be filed. I further understand that noncompliance will result in the firm's and/or the individuals listed on this application, being suspended from participation in the IRS e-file program. I am authorized to make and sign this statement on behalf of the firm.

9 Name and title of Principal, Partner, or Owner (type or print)	10 Signature of Principal, Partner, or Owner	11 Date

Appendix

New! New! This Form 8633 is the new combined form to use to apply to be an authorized *e-file* provider of any of the **Individual** or **Business** *e-file* programs.

Filing Requirements

Who to Contact for Answers: If you have questions and don't know where to get answers, call toll free, 1-866-255-0654. If this is a foreign call, call the non-toll-free number 01-512-416-7750. For additional information about Business *e-file* programs, see the following publications: Publication 1524, Procedures for the Form 1065 *e-file* Programs; Publication 1525, File Specifications for Form 1065 *e-file*; Publication 1855, Technical Specifications Guide for the Electronic Filing of Form 941; Publication 3715, Technical Specifications Guide for the Electronic Filing of Form 940; Publication 1437, Procedures for Electronic Filing of Form 1041; and Publication 1438, File Specifications for Form 1041.

Who Must File Form 8633. (1) New applicants (including foreign filers) and **(2)** Current participants revising a previously submitted Form 8633, in accordance with the IRS *e-file* program requirements outlined in Publication 1345, Handbook For Authorized IRS *e-file* Providers. In some instances, you may **revise** your application by calling 1-866-255-0654.

Note: Those transmitters and software developers who are planning to transmit Forms 990, 990-EZ, 1120, 1120S, 1120-POL, or 8868 through the Internet must apply using the on-line *e-file* application instead of completing Form 8633.

When to File: New Applications— Year Round Application Acceptance. Effective August 1, 2003, paper applications are accepted all year for individuals and business *e-file* programs. This change allows individual and business *e-file* applicants the opportunity to apply to participate in the *e-file* program at any given time. Additionally, the on-line *e-file* application offers the same year round application process. It is recommended that you submit your completed application 45 days prior to the date you intend to begin filing returns electronically (business and/or individual).

Reapply—complete an application to **reapply** to the program if you were suspended and want to be reconsidered or if you were dropped from the program and would like to continue. Please remember to include your previously assigned EFIN.

Where to File. Send Form(s) 8633 to the Andover Campus. (See Page 4 for mailing addresses.)

How to Complete the Form

Page 1

Please check all boxes which apply to this application.

Line 1b.—If your firm is a partnership or a corporation, provide the firm's employer identification number (EIN). If your firm is a sole proprietorship, with employees, provide the business employer identification number (EIN). If you do not have employees, provide your social security number (SSN).

Line 1c.—If your firm is a sole proprietorship, enter the name of the sole proprietor. If your firm is a partnership or corporation, enter the name shown on the firm's tax return. If submitting a revised application, **and the firm's legal name is not changing,** be sure this entry is identical to your original application.

Line 1d.—If, for the purpose of IRS *e-file,* you or your firm use a "doing business as" (DBA) name(s) other than the name on line 1a, include the name(s) on this line. Use an attachment sheet if necessary to list all names.

Line 1e.—Address of the location of the firm. A Post Office box (P.O. box) will not be accepted as the location of your firm.

Line 1g.—Mailing address if different from the business address. Include P.O. box if applicable. You must provide a year-round mailing address.

Lines 1i and 1j.—Contact names must be available on a daily basis to answer IRS questions during testing and throughout the processing year.

Line 2d.—1040 on-line filing applicants must also provide the following information on a separate sheet of paper:

1. The brand name of the software the applicant will be using, has developed, or will be transmitting, including the name of the software developer; the name of the transmitter for the software; the retail cost of the software; any additional costs for transmitting the electronic portion of the taxpayer's return; whether the software can be used for Federal/State returns; whether the software is available on the Internet and if so, the Internet address; the professional package name of the software submitted for testing;

2. The applicant's point of contact (including telephone number) for matters relating to on-line filing, and the applicant's customer service number;

3. The procedures the applicant will use to ensure that no more than five returns are transmitted from one software package or from one e-mail address; and

4. The website URL of the on-line filer

Line 3.—Check the box that applies.

Line 4.— ETD - (Forms 56, 2350, 2688, 4868, 9465) Electronic Transmittted Documents - stand alone documents that are e-filed apart from any other returns but for the purpose of *e-file* application, are grouped together to establish the need for a transmitter communications test.

State Ack (Restricted to Software Developers or Transmitters) - acknowledgement files transmitted by the state taxing agency to the IRS, containing the results of the state e-filed returns for pick-up by the original transmitter of the return.

Line 6.—Misrepresentation when answering this question **will** result in the rejection of your application to participate in the IRS *e-file* Program. If your application is denied, you will be able to apply again for participation two years from the date of the denial letter.

Page 2

Lines 7 and 8.—Each individual listed must be a U.S. citizen or legal resident alien (lawful permanent resident), have attained the age of 21 as of the date of the application, and if applying to be an Electronic Return Originator, meet state and local licensing and/or bonding requirements. Fingerprints must be taken by a trained specialist. Individuals **CANNOT** take their own fingerprints. The *e-file* program **fingerprint cards** are unique and should be obtained by calling the Andover Campus at 1-866-255-0654.

Unless you marked a box on Line 3, Page 1, or your only "Yes" response in section 2 is question e, you must provide a completed fingerprint card for each responsible official, corporate officer, owner, or partner listed on Lines 7 and 8. If a corporate officer, owner, or partner changes, a completed fingerprint card must be provided for each new corporate officer, owner, or partner. If the corporate officer, owner, or partner is an attorney, banking official who is bonded and has been fingerprinted in the last two years, CPA, enrolled agent, or an officer of a publicly owned corporation, evidence of current professional status may be submitted in lieu of the fingerprint card (see Revenue Procedures). **Your application will not be processed if you do not provide a completed fingerprint card or evidence of professional status and the signature of each responsible official, corporate officer, partner, and owner.**

Line 6 instruction also applies to Line 7 and Line 8. Attach an explanation for a "Yes" response to the suitability question.

Lines 9–11—Signature Lines.—A principal, partner, or the owner of the firm must sign new applications. Responsible Officials may sign revised applications.

Mail your application(s) to the address shown below.

Daytime: Internal Revenue Service
Andover Campus
Attn: EFU Acceptance
Testing Stop 983
P.O. Box 4099
Woburn, MA 01888-4099

Overnight Mail: Internal Revenue Service
Andover Campus
Attn: EFU Acceptance
Testing Stop 983
310 Lowell Street
Andover, MA 05501-0001

NOTE: The Andover Campus is a secured building, unauthorized access not permitted. **Applications/Fingerprint cards received/disbursed by MAIL ONLY.**

Call 1-866-255-0654 to obtain fingerprint cards. Approved fingerprint cards can only be obtained at the Andover Campus.

Privacy Act Notice.—The Privacy Act of 1974 requires that when we ask for information we tell you our legal right to ask for the information, why we are asking for it, and how it will be used. We must also tell you what could happen if we do not receive it, and whether your response is voluntary, required to obtain a benefit, or mandatory.

Our legal right to ask for information is 5 U.S.C. 301, 5 U.S.C. 500, 551-559, 31 U.S.C. 330, and Executive Order 9397.

We are asking for this information to verify your standing as a person qualified to participate in the electronic filing program. The information you provide may be disclosed to the FBI and other agencies for background checks, to credit bureaus for credit checks, and to third parties to determine your suitability.

The IRS also may be compelled to disclose information to the public. In response to requests made under 5 U.S.C. 552, the Freedom of Information Act, information that may be released could include your name and business address and whether you are licensed or bonded in accordance with state or local requirements.

Your response is voluntary. However, if you do not provide the requested information, you could be disqualified from participating in the IRS *e-file* program.

If you provide fraudulent information, you may be subject to criminal prosecution.

Paperwork Reduction Act Notice. We ask for the information on this form to carry out the Internal Revenue laws of the United States. You must give us the information if you wish to participate in the IRS *e-file* program. We need it to process your application to file individual income tax returns electronically.

You are not required to provide the information requested on a form that is subject to the Paperwork Reduction Act unless the form displays a valid OMB control number. Books or records relating to a form or its instructions must be retained as long as their contents may become material in the administration of any Internal Revenue law.

Generally, tax returns and return information are confidential, as required by Code section 6103. The time needed to complete this form will vary depending on the individual circumstances. The estimated time is 60 minutes. If you have comments concerning the accuracy of this time estimate or suggestions for making this form simpler, we would be happy to hear from you.

You can write to the Tax Products Coordinating Committee, Western Area Distribution Center, Rancho Cordova, CA 95743-0001. **DO NOT** send this application to this office. Instead, see **Where to File** on page 3.

FORM 8633 ACCURACY CHECKLIST

Please answer this checklist after you have completed your application. Failure to correctly provide all of the information needed on your application can result in the application being returned to you.

1. **Is your Form 8633 the most current application?** _____ Yes _____ No
    If the revision date is not July 2003, your application may be returned.

2. **Did you complete 1e and 1g?** _____ Yes _____ No
    Your application may be returned to you if 1e and 1g are incomplete. However, if your business address in 1e is the same as your mailing address, you are not required to complete 1g.

3. **Did you read all of Section 7? Did you provide us with a fingerprint card for all principals of your firm who are not exempt, evidence of professional status on those who are exempt, and all original signatures?** _____ Yes _____ No
    Acceptable evidence of current professional status consists of the following:
    CPA CERTIFICATION—copy of current state license. (LPAs are not considered exempt/fingerprint cards required)
    ENROLLED AGENT—copy of current enrollment card issued by the IRS
    ATTORNEY—copy of credentials
    BANK OFFICIAL—a copy of the bonding certificate and proof of fingerprinting within the last two years
    OFFICER OF A PUBLICLY OWNED CORPORATION—a copy on corporate letterhead which carries the name of the officer, the stock symbol, the exchange where listed, and the name under which the stock is traded for the individual listed in section 7 or 8 on Form 8633.

4. **Have the principals and responsible officials of your firm reached age 21 as of the date on your application?** _____ Yes _____ No
    Your application will be rejected if anyone listed is under the age of 21.

5. **Have you been suspended from the IRS *e-file* program?** _____ Yes _____ No
    If you answer **Yes**, your suspension period must be complete. Please call the Andover Campus at: 1-866-255-0654 (toll free) to verify this information.

6. **Did you remember to provide original signatures for 7, 8, and 10?** _____ Yes _____ No
    If you failed to provide signatures in the areas listed above, your application will be returned.

Printed on recycled paper

Form **8655**
(Rev. May 2005)

Department of the Treasury
Internal Revenue Service

Reporting Agent Authorization

OMB No. 1545-1058

Taxpayer

1a Name of taxpayer (as distinguished from trade name)	2 Employer identification number (EIN)
1b Trade name, if any	4 If you are a seasonal employer, check here . . . . . . ☐
3 Address (number, street, and room or suite no.)	5 Other identification number
City or town, state, and ZIP code	

6 Contact person	7 Daytime telephone number ( )	8 Fax number ( )

Reporting Agent

9 Name (enter company name or name of business)	10 Employer identification number (EIN)
11 Address (number, street, and room or suite no.)	
City or town, state, and ZIP code	

12 Contact person	13 Daytime telephone number ( )	14 Fax number ( )

Authorization of Reporting Agent To Sign and File Returns

15   Use the entry lines below to indicate the tax return(s) to be filed by the reporting agent. Enter the beginning year of annual tax returns or beginning quarter of quarterly tax returns. See the instructions for how to enter the quarter and year. Once this authority is granted, it is effective until revoked by the taxpayer or reporting agent.

940 _____   941 _____   940-PR _____   941-PR _____   941-SS _____   943 _____

943-PR _____   944 _____   944-PR _____   945 _____   1042 _____   CT-1 _____

Authorization of Reporting Agent To Make Deposits and Payments

16   Use the entry lines below to enter the starting date (the first month and year) of any tax return(s) for which the reporting agent is authorized to make deposits or payments. See the instructions for how to enter the month and year. Once this authority is granted, it is effective until revoked by the taxpayer or reporting agent.

940 _____   941 _____   943 _____   944 _____   945 _____   720 _____   1041 _____

1042 _____   1120 _____   CT-1 _____   990-C _____   990-PF _____   990-T _____

Disclosure of Information to Reporting Agents

17a   Check here to authorize the reporting agent to receive or request copies of tax information and other communications from the IRS related to the authorization granted on line 15 and/or line 16 . . . . ☐

  b   Check here if the reporting agent also wants to receive copies of notices from the IRS . . . . ☐

Form W-2 series or Form 1099 series Disclosure Authorization

18a   The reporting agent is authorized to receive otherwise confidential taxpayer information from the IRS to assist in responding to certain IRS notices relating to the Form W-2 series information returns. This authority is effective for calendar year forms beginning _____.

  b   The reporting agent is authorized to receive otherwise confidential taxpayer information from the IRS to assist in responding to certain IRS notices relating to the Form 1099 series information returns. This authority is effective for calendar year forms beginning _____.

State or Local Authorization

19   Check here to authorize the reporting agent to sign and file state or local returns related to the authorization granted on line 15 and/or line 16 . . . . ☐

Authorization Agreement

I understand that this agreement does not relieve me, as the taxpayer, of the responsibility to ensure that all tax returns are filed and that all deposits and payments are made. If line 15 is completed, the reporting agent named above is authorized to sign and file the return indicated, beginning with the quarter or year indicated. If any starting dates on line 16 are completed, the reporting agent named above is authorized to make deposits and payments beginning with the period indicated. Any authorization granted remains in effect until it is revoked by the taxpayer or reporting agent. I am authorizing the IRS to disclose otherwise confidential tax information to the reporting agent relating to the authority granted on line 15 and/or line 16, including disclosures required to process Form 8655. Disclosure authority is effective upon signature of taxpayer and IRS receipt of Form 8655. The authority granted on Form 8655 will not revoke any Power of Attorney (Form 2848) or Tax Information Authorization (Form 8821) in effect.

Sign Here

I certify I have the authority to execute this form and authorize disclosure of otherwise confidential information on behalf of the taxpayer.

▶ _____   ▶ _____   ▶ _____
 Signature of taxpayer   Title   Date

For Privacy Act and Paperwork Reduction Act Notice, see page 2.   Cat. No. 10241T   Form **8655** (Rev. 5-2005)

General Instructions

What's New

- Magnetic tape is no longer a filing method for the returns on line 15.
- The "Other" box in line 16 has been deleted. Authority to make deposits and payments can only be granted for the forms listed in line 16.
- New Forms 944 and 944-PR have been added to line 15. New Form 944 has been added to line 16. Form 944 should be available for calendar year 2006.
- Lines 18a and 18b have been added to allow taxpayers to grant reporting agents disclosure authority for the Form W-2 series and Form 1099 series information returns.

Purpose of Form

Form 8655 is used to authorize a reporting agent to:

- Sign and file certain returns;
- Make deposits and payments for certain returns;
- Receive duplicate copies of tax information, notices, and other written communication regarding any authority granted; and
- Provide IRS with information to aid in penalty relief determinations related to the authority granted on Form 8655.

Authority Granted

Once Form 8655 is signed, any authority granted is effective beginning with the period indicated on lines 15 or 16 and continues indefinitely unless revoked by the taxpayer or reporting agent. No authorization or authority is granted for periods prior to the period(s) indicated on Form 8655. Disclosure authority by checking the box in line 17a is effective with the dated signature of the taxpayer on Form 8655.

Any authority granted on Form 8655 does not revoke and has no effect on any authority granted on Forms 2848 or 8821, or any third-party designee checkbox authority.

Where To File

Send Form 8655 to:

Internal Revenue Service
Accounts Management Service Center
MS 6748 RAF Team
1973 North Rulon White Blvd.
Ogden, UT 84404

You can fax Form 8655 to the IRS. The number is 801-620-4142.

Additional Information

Additional information concerning reporting agent authorizations may be found in:

- **Pub. 1474,** Technical Specifications Guide for Reporting Agent Authorizations and Federal Tax Depositors, and
- **Rev. Proc. 2003-69.** You can find Rev. Proc. 2003-69 on page 403 of Internal Revenue Bulletin 2003-34 at *www.irs.gov/pub/irs-irbs/irb03-34.pdf*.

Substitute Form 8655

If you want to prepare and use a substitute Form 8655, see Pub. 1167, General Rules and Specifications for Substitute Forms and Schedules. If your substitute Form 8655 is approved, the form approval number must be printed in the lower left margin of each substitute Form 8655 you file with the IRS.

Revoking an Authorization

If you have a valid Form 8655 on file with the IRS, the filing of a new Form 8655 revokes the authority of the prior reporting agent beginning with the period indicated on the new Form 8655. However, the prior reporting agent is still an authorized reporting agent and retains any previously granted disclosure authority for the periods prior to the beginning period of the new reporting agent's authorization unless specifically revoked.

If the taxpayer wants to revoke an existing authorization, send a copy of the previously executed Form 8655 to the IRS at the address under *Where To File,* above. Re-sign the copy of the Form 8655 under the original signature. Write REVOKE across the top of the form. If you do not have a copy of the authorization you want to revoke, send a statement to the IRS. The statement of revocation must indicate that the authority of the reporting agent is revoked and must be signed by the taxpayer. Also, list the name and address of each reporting agent whose authority is revoked.

Withdrawing from reporting authority. A reporting agent can withdraw from authority by filing a statement with the IRS, either on paper or using a delete process. The statement must be signed by the reporting agent (if filed on paper) and identify the name and address of the taxpayer and authorization(s) from which the reporting agent is withdrawing. For information on the delete process, see Pub. 1474.

Specific Instructions

Line 15

Use the "YYYY" format for annual tax returns. Use the "MM/YYYY" format for quarterly tax returns, where "MM" is the ending month of the quarter the named reporting agent is authorized to sign and file tax returns for the taxpayer. For example, enter "03/2005" on the line for "941" to indicate you are authorizing the named reporting agent to sign and file Form 941 for the January–March quarter of 2005 and subsequent quarters.

Line 16

Use the "MM/YYYY" format to enter the starting date, where "MM" is the first month the named reporting agent is authorized to make deposits or payments for the taxpayer. For example, enter "08/2005" on the line for "720" to indicate you are authorizing the named reporting agent to make deposits or payments for Form 720 starting in August 2005 and all subsequent months.

Who Must Sign

Sole proprietorship–The individual owning the business.

Corporation (including an LLC treated as a corporation)–Generally, Form 8655 can be signed by: (a) an officer having legal authority to bind the corporation, (b) any person designated by the board of directors or other governing body, (c) any officer or employee on written request by any principal officer, and (d) any other person authorized to access information under section 6103(e).

Partnership (including an LLC treated as a partnership) or an unincorporated organization–Generally, Form 8655 can be signed by any person who was a member of the partnership during any part of the tax period covered by Form 8655.

Single member limited liability company (LLC) treated as a disregarded entity–The owner of the LLC.

Trust or estate–The fiduciary.

Privacy Act and Paperwork Reduction Act Notice. We ask for the information on this form to carry out the Internal Revenue laws of the United States. Form 8655 is provided by the IRS for your convenience and its use is voluntary. If you choose to authorize a reporting agent to act on your behalf, under section 6109, you must disclose your EIN. The principal purpose of this disclosure is to secure proper identification of the taxpayer. We need this information to gain access to your tax information in our files and properly respond to your request. If you do not disclose this information, the IRS may suspend processing your reporting agent authorization and may not be able to honor your reporting agent authorization until you provide your EIN.

Routine uses of this information include giving it to the Department of Justice for civil and criminal litigation, and to cities, states, and the District of Columbia for use in administering their tax laws. We may also disclose this information to other countries under a tax treaty, to federal and state agencies to enforce federal nontax criminal laws, or to federal law enforcement agencies and intelligence agencies to combat terrorism.

You are not required to provide the information requested on a form that is subject to the Paperwork Reduction Act unless the form displays a valid OMB control number. Books or records relating to a form or instructions must be retained as long as their contents may become material in the administration of any Internal Revenue law.

The time needed to complete and file Form 8655 will vary depending on individual circumstances. The estimated average time is 6 minutes.

If you have comments concerning the accuracy of this time estimate or suggestions for making Form 8655 simpler, we would be happy to hear from you. You can write to the Internal Revenue Service, Tax Products Coordinating Committee, SE:W:CAR:MP:T:T:SP, 1111 Constitution Ave. NW, IR-6406, Washington, DC 20224. **Do not** send Form 8655 to this address. Instead, see *Where To File* above.

Form 8802

(Rev. September 2005)

Department of the Treasury
Internal Revenue Service

Application for United States Residency Certification

▶ **See separate instructions**

OMB No. 1545-1817

☐ **Additional request** (see instructions)	☐ **Foreign claim form attached**
Applicant's name	Applicant's U.S. taxpayer identification number
If a joint return was filed, spouse's name (see instructions)	If a joint return was filed, spouse's U.S. taxpayer identification number

If a separate certification is needed for spouse, check here ▶ ☐

1 Applicant's name and taxpayer identification number as it should appear on the certification if different from above

2 Applicant's address during the calendar year for which certification is requested, including country and ZIP or postal code (see instructions)

3a Mailing Address:

b Appointee Information (see instructions):

Appointee Name ▶ -------------------------------- CAF No. ▶ --------------------------------
Phone No. ▶ ( ) -------------------------------- Fax No. ▶ ( ) --------------------------------

4 Applicant is (check appropriate box(es)):

a ☐ Individual. Check all applicable boxes.
  ☐ U.S. citizen ☐ Sole proprietor ☐ U.S. permanent resident alien (green card holder)
  ☐ Other U.S. resident alien. Type of entry visa ▶ --------------------------------
  Current nonimmigrant status ▶---------------- and date of change (see instructions) ▶ ----------------
  ☐ Dual-status U.S. resident (see instructions). From ▶ ---------------- to ▶ ----------------
  ☐ Partial-year Form 2555 filer (see instructions). U.S. resident from ▶ ---------------- to ▶ ----------------

b ☐ Partnership. Check all applicable boxes. ☐ U.S. ☐ Foreign ☐ LLC

c ☐ Trust. Check if: ☐ Grantor (U.S.) ☐ Simple ☐ Rev. Rul. 81-100 Trust ☐ IRA (for Individual)
  ☐ Grantor (foreign) ☐ Complex ☐ Section 584 ☐ IRA (for Financial Institution)

d ☐ Estate

e ☐ Corporation. If incorporated in the United States, go to line 5. Otherwise, continue.
  Check if: ☐ Section 269B ☐ Section 943(e)(1) ☐ Section 953(d) ☐ Section 1504(d)
  Country of incorporation ▶ --------------------------------
  If a dual-resident corporation, specify other country of residence ▶ --------------------------------
  If included on a consolidated return, attach page 1 of Form 1120 and Form 851.

f ☐ S corporation

g ☐ Employee benefit plan/trust. Plan number, if applicable ▶ ----------------------------
  Check if: ☐ Section 401(a) ☐ Section 403(b) ☐ Section 457(b)

h ☐ Exempt organization. If organized in the United States, check all applicable boxes.
  ☐ Section 501(c) ☐ Section 501(c)(3) ☐ Governmental entity
  ☐ Indian tribe ☐ Other (specify) ▶ ----------------------------

i ☐ Disregarded entity. Check if: ☐ LLC ☐ LP ☐ LLP ☐ Other (specify) ▶ ----------------------------

j ☐ Nominee applicant (must specify the type of entity/individual for whom the nominee is acting) ▶ ----------------------------

5 Was the applicant required to file a U.S. tax form for the tax period(s) on which certification will be based?

Yes. Check the appropriate box for the form filed and **go to line 7.**
  ☐ 990 ☐ 990-T ☐ 1040 ☐ 1041 ☐ 1065 ☐ 1120 ☐ 1120S ☐ 3520-A ☐ 5227 ☐ 5500
  ☐ Other (specify) ▶ --------------------------------

No. Attach explanation (see instructions). Check applicable box and go to line 6.
  ☐ Minor child ☐ QSub ☐ U.S. DRE ☐ Foreign DRE ☐ Section 761(a) election
  ☐ FASIT ☐ Foreign partnership ☐ Other ▶ --------------------------------

For Privacy Act and Paperwork Reduction Act Notice, see instructions.   Cat. No. 10003D   Form **8802** (Rev. 9-2005)

6 Was the applicant's parent, parent organization or owner required to file a U.S. tax form? (**Complete this line only if you checked "No" on line 5.**)

Yes. Check the appropriate box for the form filed by the parent.

☐ 990 ☐ 990-T ☐ 1040 ☐ 1041 ☐ 1065 ☐ 1120 ☐ 1120S ☐ 5500

☐ Other (specify) ▶ ....

Parent's/owner's name and address ▶ ....

....

and U.S. taxpayer identification number ▶ ....

No. Attach explanation (see instructions).

7 Calendar year(s) for which certification is requested (see instructions)

8 Tax period(s) on which certification will be based (see instructions)

9 Purpose of certification. Must check applicable box.

☐ Income tax   ☐ VAT (specify NAICS codes) ▶ ....

☐ Other (must specify) ▶ ....

....

10 Enter the number of certifications needed in the column to the right of each country for which certification is requested (see instructions)

Country	#	Country	#	Country	#	Country	#	Country	#
Armenia		Estonia		Jamaica		Norway		Tajikistan	
Australia		Finland		Japan		Pakistan		Thailand	
Austria		France		Kazakhstan		Philippines		Trinidad & Tobago	
Azerbaijan		Georgia		Rep. of Korea		Poland		Tunisia	
Barbados		Germany		Kyrgyzstan		Portugal		Turkey	
Belarus		Greece		Latvia		Romania		Turkmenistan	
Belgium		Hungary		Lithuania		Russia		Ukraine	
Canada		Iceland		Luxembourg		Slovak Rep.		United Kingdom (see page 2 of the instructions)	
China		India		Mexico		Slovenia		Uzbekistan	
Cyprus		Indonesia		Moldova		South Africa		Venezuela	
Czech Rep.		Ireland		Morocco		Spain		Other(s) (specify below)	
Denmark		Israel		Netherlands		Sweden			
Egypt		Italy		New Zealand		Switzerland			

11 This space can be used to enter additional required information

Sign here

Keep a copy for your records.

Under penalties of perjury, I declare that I have examined this application and accompanying attachments, and to the best of my knowledge and belief, they are true, correct, and complete. If I have designated a third party to receive the residency certification(s), I declare that the certification(s) will be used only for obtaining information or assistance from that person relating to matters designated on line 9.

Applicant's signature (or individual authorized to sign for the applicant)

Applicant's daytime phone no.:

....
Signature and date

....

....
Name and title (print or type)

....
Spouse's signature. If a joint application, **both** must sign.

....
Name (print or type)

Form **8802** (Rev. 9-2005)

Instructions for Form 8802

Department of the Treasury
Internal Revenue Service

(Rev. September 2005)

Application for United States Residency Certification

Section references are to the Internal Revenue Code.

General Instructions

Purpose of Form

Use Form 8802 to request certification of U.S. residency for purposes of claiming benefits under a tax treaty. You can request certification for the current and any prior calendar years.

You can also use Form 8802 to obtain proof of tax status for other purposes, such as obtaining an exemption from a value added tax (VAT) imposed by a foreign country. However, in connection with a VAT request, the United States can certify only certain matters in relation to your U.S. federal income tax status, and not that you meet any other requirements for a VAT exemption in a foreign country.

For more information, see Publication 686, Certification for Reduced Tax Rates in Tax Treaty Countries.

Who Is Not Eligible for Certification

Generally, you are not eligible for U.S. residency certification if, for the tax period on which your certification is to be based, any of the following apply.
• You did not file a required U.S. return.
• You filed a return as a nonresident, including Form 1040NR, U.S. Nonresident Alien Income Tax Return, Form 1040NR-EZ, U.S. Income Tax Return for Certain Nonresident Aliens With No Dependents, Form 1120-F, U.S. Income Tax Return of a Foreign Corporation, Form 1120-FSC, U.S. Income Tax Return of a Foreign Sales Corporation, or any of the U.S. possession tax forms.
• You are a dual resident individual who has made (or intends to make), pursuant to the tie breaker provision within an applicable treaty, a determination that you are not a resident of the United States and are a resident of the other treaty country. For more information and examples, see Reg. section 301.7701(b)-7.
• You are not liable for tax to the United States by reason of your

residence, place of incorporation, or other similar criteria. Accordingly, a U.S. limited liability company (LLC) owned by a foreign corporation, trust, or estate is not eligible for certification if it is a disregarded entity (DRE) separate from its owner or if the LLC has elected to be treated as a partnership for federal tax purposes and all of the partners are foreign.
• The entity requesting certification is a U.S. grantor trust and the owner is a foreign person.
• The entity requesting certification is an exempt organization that is not organized in the United States.

Certification of United States Residency

If you are eligible for certification, you will receive Form 6166, Certification of United States Residency. This form is a computer-generated letter on stationary bearing the U.S. Department of the Treasury letterhead, the U.S. Government watermark, and the facsimile signature of the Field Director, Philadelphia Accounts Management Center.

Note. A U.S. citizen or resident alien must report and pay tax on their worldwide income, regardless of where they reside and whether or not they pay taxes as a resident of a foreign country. If you are a U.S. citizen or resident alien, you may be entitled to treaty benefits, which may reduce or eliminate foreign taxes paid with respect to income derived from a treaty country. You may not claim a foreign tax credit with respect to foreign taxes that have been reduced or eliminated by reason of a treaty. If you receive a refund of foreign taxes paid with the benefit of Form 6166 certification letter, you may need to file an amended return with the IRS adjusting any foreign tax credit previously claimed for those taxes.

 You cannot use Form 6166 to substantiate that U.S. taxes were paid for purposes of claiming a foreign tax credit.

When To File

You should file Form 8802 at least 30 days before the date you need the

certification of U.S. residency. If processing your application will take longer, you should be notified of the delay. If you do not receive Form 6166, a letter rejecting your application, or a notice of delay within 30 days from the date you filed Form 8802, call 215-516-2000 (not a toll-free number).

Early submission for a current year certification. The IRS cannot accept an early submission for a current year certification that has a postmark date before December 1. Requests received with a postmark date earlier than December 1 will be returned to the sender. For example, if you are requesting current year certification for tax year 2006 and you mail your request with a postmark date on or after December 1, 2005, the IRS will accept your application.

Where To File

Form 8802 and required attachments can be either:
• Faxed to the IRS at 215-516-1035 or 215-516-2485 (not toll-free numbers), or
• Mailed to the following address:

   Internal Revenue Service
   Philadelphia Service Center
   U.S. Residency Certification
     Request
   P.O. Box 16347
   Philadelphia, PA 19114-0447
   U.S.A.
• Express mailed to the following address:

   IRS/U.S. Residency Certification
   Unit
   11601 Roosevelt Blvd.
   Philadelphia, PA 19154
   D.P. N322

Confirmations. If you want notice that the IRS has received your Form 8802, you must include a second Form 8802 marked *Copy* with your original request and a self-addressed stamped envelope. The IRS will date stamp your copy and return it.

Federal Express. If you would like to receive your certification by Federal Express, you must supply a Federal Express label indicating your account

Cat. No. 10827V

number with your Form 8802 application.

Special Rules

Form 8802 Filed Before Return Posted by the IRS

If your return has not been posted by the IRS by the time you file Form 8802, you will receive a request to provide a signed copy of your most recent return.

 If you recently filed your return, it may take less time to process your application if you include the return with your Form 8802 instead of waiting for the request.

Third Party Appointee

If the applicant wants to authorize the third party appointee to use the additional request procedure with respect to countries not identified on the Form 8802 signed by the applicant, the applicant should include in box 11 a written statement authorizing the third party appointee to request Form 6166 covering the same tax period for any country. For more information, see *Additional Request*, on page 3.

Individuals With Residency Outside the United States

If you are in any of the following categories for the year for which certification is requested, you must submit a statement and documentation, as described below, with Form 8802.

1. You are a resident under local law of both the United States and the treaty country for which you are requesting certification (you are a dual resident).
2. You are a green card holder or U.S. citizen who filed Form 2555, Foreign Earned Income.
3. You are a bona fide resident of a U.S. possession.

If you are a dual resident described in category 1, above, your request may be denied unless you submit evidence to establish that you are a resident of the United States under the tie breaker provision in the residence article of the treaty of the country for which you are requesting certification.

If you are described in category 2 or 3, please attach a statement and documentation to establish why you believe you should be entitled to certification as a resident of the U.S. for purposes of the relevant treaty. Under many U.S. treaties, a U.S. citizen or green card holder who does not have a substantial presence, permanent home, or habitual abode in the United States

during the tax year is not entitled to treaty benefits. A U.S. citizen or green card holder who resides outside the United States must examine the specific treaty to determine if they are eligible for treaty benefits and U.S. residency certification. See *Exceptions*, below.

Exceptions

You do not need to attach the additional statement or documentation requested if you:
• Are a U.S. citizen or green card holder; and
• Are requesting certification for Cyprus, Hungary, India, Kazakhstan, Russia, South Africa, or Ukraine; and
• The country for which you are requesting certification and your country of residence are not the same.

Form 1116, Foreign Tax Credit

If you have filed or intend to file a Form 1116, Foreign Tax Credit, claiming either a foreign tax credit amount in excess of $5,000 U.S. dollars or a foreign tax credit for any amount of foreign earned income for the tax period in which certification is requested, you must submit evidence that you were (or will be if the request relates to a current year) a resident of the United States and that the foreign taxes paid were not imposed because you were a resident of the foreign country.

In addition, individuals who have already filed must submit a copy of their federal income tax return, including any information return relating to income such as a W-2 or 1099 along with the Form 1116. Your request for U.S. residency certification may be denied if you do not submit the additional materials.

Deceased Taxpayer

If you are filing Form 8802 on behalf of a deceased taxpayer, include proof that you are either the surviving spouse or the executor or administrator of the decedent's estate. A Form 8802 submitted on behalf of a deceased taxpayer can be submitted for the year of death or any prior year.

Note. Proof can include a copy of a joint return filed with the decedent, or a court certificate naming you executor or administrator.

Switzerland

If you are seeking benefits from Switzerland with respect to dividends derived from a Swiss corporation by an

employee benefit plan/trust that is a participant in:
• A group trust arrangement described in Rev. Rul. 81-100, or
• A common trust fund described in section 584, with reference to the special rules under line 4c. For more information regarding the Swiss Pension MAP Agreement, see Announcement 2005-3, 2005-2 I.R.B. 270, or see *http://www.irs.gov/irb/2005-02_IRB/ar12.html*

United Kingdom

If you are applying for relief at source from United Kingdom (U.K.) income tax or filing a claim for repayment of U.K. income tax, you may need to complete a U.K. certification form (US/Individual 2002 or US/Company 2002) in addition to Form 8802. To obtain a copy, contact HM Revenue and Customs:
• On the Internet at *www.hmrc.gov.uk/cnr/usdownload_2002.htm*, or
• By phoning 44-151-210-2222 if calling from outside the U.K., or 0845-070-0040 if calling from the U.K.

Pay close attention to the date your income was paid—a new U.S./U.K. income tax treaty and new U.K. forms apply to taxes on income paid on or after May 1, 2003.

After completing the U.K. form, send it to the IRS with your completed Form 8802.

The IRS sends Form 6166 and the U.K. certification form to the U.K. for you. If you want confirmation that your Form 8802 was processed, send the original and two copies of the U.K. form and a self-addressed stamped envelope with Form 8802.

How To Claim Treaty Benefits

Send Form 6166 to the withholding agent or other appropriate person in the foreign country along with the foreign country's completed certification form, if any. However, if you are applying to the United Kingdom for treaty benefits, you must follow the special procedures discussed earlier on this page.

Comments and Suggestions

Do **not** send Form 8802 to this address. This address is only for comments or suggestions about Form 8802 and its separate instructions.

Internal Revenue Service
Office of Tax Treaty
SE:LM:IN:TT:1
1111 Constitution Avenue NW, MT

Washington, DC 20224
U.S.A.

Specific Instructions

Check Box. Additional Request

Note. Third party appointees cannot use this box to request certifications that were not originally authorized by the taxpayer.

Check this box if you require an additional Form 6166 for a tax period in which the Service has previously issued to you a Form 6166 certification letter. Complete a new Form 8802 to indicate the additional certifications needed. In the signature line of the additional request form, write "See attached original Form 8802." Attach a copy of the original Form 8802. If additional documentation was necessary for the original application, it does not need to be resubmitted with the request for an additional **Form 6166**. An applicant will only be entitled to use this procedure if there are no changes to the applicant's tax information provided on the original application. An applicant may use this procedure to obtain a Form 6166 for a country that was identified on the previously filed Form 8802. An applicant may also use this procedure to obtain a Form 6166 for a country that was not identified on the previously filed Form 8802, but must sign the new Form 8802. An additional request for Form 6166 using this procedure must be made within 12 months of the most recently issued Form 6166 relating to the same tax period.

Note. See the paragraph *Change in taxpayer's name* for more information.

Check Box. Foreign Claim Form

Check the box if you have included with Form 8802 a foreign claim form sent to you by a foreign country. The submission or omission of a foreign claim form will not affect your residency certification. If the IRS does not have an agreement with the foreign country to date stamp, or otherwise process the form, we will not process it and such foreign claim form will be mailed back to you.

Note. For more information about foreign countries with which the IRS has an agreement to process a foreign claim form, call the Philadelphia Service Center at 215-516-2000 (not a toll-free number).

Applicant's Name and U.S. Taxpayer Identification Number

As part of certifying U.S. residency, the IRS must be able to match the name(s) and taxpayer identification number(s) (TIN(s)) on this application to those previously verified on either the U.S. return filed for the tax period on which certification is to be based or on other documentation you provide.

Enter the applicant's name and TIN **exactly** as they appear on the U.S. return filed for the tax period(s) on which certification will be based. If the applicant was not required to file a U.S. return, enter the applicant's name and TIN as they appear on documentation previously provided to the IRS (for example, Form 8832, Entity Classification Election) or on documentation provided by the IRS (for example, a determination letter).

Joint return. If a joint income tax return was filed for a tax period on which certification will be based, enter the spouse's name and TIN **exactly** as they appear on the return filed.

Change in taxpayer's name. If the taxpayer's name has changed since the most recent Form 8802 was filed with the Service, the Form 8802 and tax authorization for each individual or entity must be submitted under the taxpayer's new name. In addition, documentation of the name change must be submitted with Form 8802 (trust agreement, corporate charter).

Note. Certification will not be issued if the name change has not been updated with the IRS database. For information about how to update the IRS on your new name, contact customer service for businesses at 1-800-829-4933 and for individuals at 1-800-829-1040.

Line 2. Applicant's Address

Enter your address for the calendar year for which you seek certification. Certification may be denied if the applicant enters a P.O. Box or C/O address. If you are an individual who lived outside the United States during the year for which certification is requested, the special rules under *Individuals With Residency Outside the United States*, on page 2, may apply to you.

Lines 3a. Mailing Address

Form 6166 may be mailed to you, or to a third party appointee. If you do not indicate a mailing address on line 3a, the Form 6166 will be mailed to your address on line 2.

Line 3b. Appointee's Information

If the mailing address entered on line 3a is for a third party appointee, you must provide written authorization for the IRS to release the certification to the third party. By filling out the appointee's information in lines 3a and 3b (that is, name and address), written authorization will be deemed to have been provided. You are not required to enter a phone number or a fax number of your third party appointee. However, by providing a phone number or fax number, you are authorizing the IRS to call or fax your third party appointee. This may speed the processing of your application.

The Centralized Authorization File (CAF) contains information on third parties authorized to represent taxpayers before the IRS and/or receive and inspect confidential tax information on active tax accounts or those accounts currently under consideration by the IRS. If your appointee has a CAF number, enter it on line 3b.

In general, you do not need to fill out line 3b if you have attached Form 2848, Power of Attorney and Declaration of Representation, or Form 8821, Taxpayer Information Authorization, authorizing the appointee to receive your certification of residence. In line 3b, write "See attached Authorization."

If you appoint more than one third party, attach a Form 8821 for each additional party.

If the applicant is a partnership, S corporation (including a qualified subchapter S subsidiary (Qsub)), simple trust, grantor trust or common trust fund, each partner/shareholder/owner/beneficiary of the entity must provide to the entity Form 8821, or equivalent, authorizing the entity, or its appointee, to receive tax information related to the residency certification program. Pursuant to section 6103(c) and regulations thereunder, authorization on Form 8821, or an equivalent document, will not be accepted if it covers matters other than federal tax matters. See the specific line instructions for each type of entity.

-3-

Line 4a. Individual

Green card holder. If you are a resident alien with lawful permanent resident status who recently arrived in the United States and you have not yet filed a U.S. income tax return, you should provide a copy of your current Form I-551, Alien Registration Receipt Card (green card). Instead of a copy of your green card, you can attach a statement from U.S. Citizenship and Immigration Services (USCIS) that gives your alien registration number, the date and port of entry, date of birth, and classification. For more information in determining your U.S. resident status, see *Chapter 1, Nonresident alien or Resident Alien*, in Pub. 519.

Substantial presence test. An individual who is not a lawful permanent resident of the United States but who meets the "substantial presence test" under section 7701(b) is a resident alien for purposes of U.S. taxation. If you are a resident alien under the substantial presence test and you have not yet filed a U.S. income tax return for the year in which certification is requested, you should provide a copy of your current Form I-94, Arrival-Departure Record. Enter the date (YYYYMMDD) your status changed on the line provided. For information on determining your period of residency, see *Substantial Presence Test* in Publication 519.

Students, teachers, and trainees. If you filed Form 1040, U.S. Individual Income Tax Return, and you are in the United States under an "A1," "F1," "J1," "M1," or "Q1" visa, include the following with Form 8802:

1. A statement explaining why Form 1040 was filed.
2. A statement along with documentation that you reported your worldwide income.

Dual-status alien. An individual is a dual-status alien for U.S. tax purposes if the individual is a part-year resident alien and a part-year nonresident alien during the calendar year(s) for which certification is requested. Dual-status generally occurs in the year an individual acquires status as a U.S. resident or terminates such status. For example, you are a dual-status alien if you are a U.S. citizen or green card holder and you lost citizenship or green card holder status during the same calendar year. You may also be a dual-status alien if you are a non-resident alien but due to meeting the substantial presence test become a resident alien during the same calendar year.

The dual-status alien classification does not occur merely due to a temporary absence from the United States, nor will multiple periods of temporary absence and re-entry into the United States create multiple periods of U.S. resident and non-resident status. For information and examples on the dual-status alien and to determine your period of residency, see Pub. 519.

If you checked the dual-status box, enter the dates (YYYYMMDD) that correspond to the period that you were a resident in the United States during the year(s) for which certification is requested.

First-year election. If you are an individual who has or intends to make the first-year election under section 7701(b)(4) applicable to the year for which certification is requested, enter the date (YYYYMMDD) your status as a U.S. resident for tax purposes will begin. For more information regarding the first-year election and determining your period of residency, see *First-Year Choice* in Pub. 519.

1. If you have made a first-year residence election under section 7701(b)(4) applicable to the year for which you are requesting certification, attach the election statement you were required to file with your income tax return for the taxable year of election with Form 8802.
2. If, for the calendar year for which certification is requested, you have not yet filed a first-year residence election statement, attach a statement that you intend to file such statement and that you are eligible to make the election with Form 8802.

Partial-year Form 2555 filer. Check this box if you filed a Form 2555 that covered only part of a year for which certification is requested. For each year that this applies, enter the eight-digit dates (YYYYMMDD) that correspond to the beginning and ending of the period you were a resident in the United States.

Sole proprietor. Include on line 6 the type of tax return, name, TIN, and any other information that would be required if certification was being requested for the individual owner that filed the Schedule C.

Line 4b. Partnership

Partnerships are not considered U.S. residents within the meaning of the residence article of U.S. income tax treaties. Treaty benefits are only available to a partner who is a U.S. resident.

Note. The Form 6166 requested by partnerships will include an attached list of partners that are U.S. residents. The IRS does not certify the percentage of ownership interest of the listed partners in a particular payment. It is the duty of the partnership to provide such information to the withholding agent.

Include the following with Form 8802:

1. The name and TIN of each partner for which certification is requested and any additional information that would be required if certification were being requested for each of those partners. With respect to a request for certification of a foreign partnership, or foreign entity treated as a partnership, that is not required to file a Form 1065, U.S. Return of Partnership Income, attach a representation (as described in Pub. 686) from each U.S. partner.
2. Authorization (for example, Form 8821) from each partner, including all partners listed within tiered partnerships. Each authorization must explicitly allow the third party requester to receive the partner's tax information and must not address matters other than federal tax matters.
3. An authorization from the partnership, unless the requester is a partner in the partnership during the tax year for which certification is requested.

An LLC that is classified as a partnership follows the above procedures. Members of the LLC are treated as partners.

Nominee partnership. If you are a nominee partnership, do not check the partnership box on line 4b. Rather, complete line 4j, Nominee applicant, and attach the information required by the instructions for line 4j.

Line 4c. Trust

Domestic and foreign grantor trusts and simple trusts can be certified for U.S. residency, to the extent the owner of the grantor trust or beneficiaries of simple trusts are U.S. residents. Domestic complex trusts may be certified without regard to the residence of the settler or beneficiaries.

A trust is domestic if a court within the U.S. is able to exercise primary supervision over the administration of the trust and one or more U.S. persons has authority to control all substantial decisions of the trust.

-4-

Grantor trust. Include the following with Form 8802.

1. The name and TIN of each owner and any information that would be required if certification were being requested for each owner.

2. Authorization (for example, Form 8821) from each owner. Each authorization must explicitly allow the third party requester to receive the owner's tax information and must not address matters other than federal tax matters.

3. An authorization from a trustee of the trust, unless the requester is a trustee of the trust.

If the grantor trust is a foreign trust, also include a copy of Form 3520-A, Annual Information Return of Foreign Trust with a U.S. Owner, and a copy of the foreign grantor trust ownership statement.

Domestic nongrantor trust and simple trust. Include the following with Form 8802.

1. The name and TIN of each beneficiary and any information that would be required if certification were being requested for each beneficiary.

2. Authorizations (for example, Form 8821) from each beneficiary. Each authorization must explicitly allow the third party requester to receive the beneficiary's tax information and must not address matters other than federal tax matters.

3. An authorization from the trustee, unless the requester is a trustee in the trust.

Group trust arrangement, described in Rev. Rul. 81-100. A group trust arrangement that has received a determination letter recognizing its exempt status under section 501(a) must attach a copy of that letter to Form 8802.

A group trust arrangement that is seeking benefits from Switzerland with respect to dividends paid by a Swiss corporation must also attach to Form 8802 the name of each participant and a statement that each participant listed is a trust forming part of a plan described in section 401(a), 403(b), or 457(b).

IRA. Domestic individual retirement arrangements (individual retirement accounts within the meaning of section 408(a) and Roth IRAs within the meaning of section 408A) (collectively referred to as IRAs) may be certified as residents (without regard to the residence of the IRA holder). Either the IRA holder or the trustee of the IRA

may request certification on behalf of the IRA.

An IRA holder requesting certification on behalf of an IRA must provide the IRA account name (that is, the IRA holder's name) and number, the IRA holder's TIN, and a copy of Form 8606, Nondeductible IRAs, or Form 5498, IRA Contribution Information. Complete the remainder of Form 8802 as if certification is being requested by the IRA.

A bank or financial institution acting as the trustee for IRAs may request certification for multiple IRAs grouped by year and by country for which certification is requested. The bank or financial institution must include the following with Form 8802:

1. A list of IRA account names (that is, the IRA holder's name) and account numbers for which certification is requested.

2. A statement that each IRA account name and number listed is an IRA within the meaning of sections 408(a) or 408A.

3. A statement that the bank or financial institution is a trustee of the IRA.

Common trust fund as defined in section 584. Include the following with Form 8802.

1. The name and TIN of each participant and any information that would be required if certification were being requested for each participant.

2. Authorizations (for example, Form 8821) from each participant. Each authorization must explicitly allow the third party requester to receive the participant's tax information and must not address any matters other than federal tax matters. If a pass-through entity is a participant, you must list the partners/shareholders/owners/ participants/members/beneficiaries in the pass-through entity and obtain authorization from each such participant.

3. An authorization from a trustee of the trust, unless the requester is a trustee of the trust.

A common trust fund that is seeking benefits from Switzerland with respect to dividends paid to a Swiss corporation must also attach to Form 8802 the name of each participant and a statement that each participant listed is a trust forming part of a plan that is described in section 401(a), 403(b), or 457(b), or is a trust forming part of a plan described in section 401(a), 403(b), or 457(b) that is within a group

trust arrangement described in IRS Revenue Ruling 81-100.

Line 4e. Corporation

Generally, a corporation that is not incorporated in the United States will not be entitled to U.S. residency certification. However, there are exceptions for certain corporations that are treated as U.S. corporations under sections 269B, 943(e)(1), 953(d), or 1504(d).

Note. Only Canadian and Mexican corporations are eligible to be treated as domestic corporations under section 1504(d).

A corporation that is neither incorporated in the United States nor treated as a U.S. corporation under sections 269B, 943(e)(1), 953(d), or 1504(d), but nevertheless believes it is entitled to U.S. residency certification, must attach a detailed explanation, with documentary evidence, explaining why the corporation is entitled to certification. Prior to seeking certification, request competent authority assistance in accordance with *Revenue Procedure 2002-52, 2002-31 I.R.B. 242.*

Corporations requesting U.S. residency certification on behalf of their subsidiaries should attach a list of the subsidiaries and the Form 851, Affiliations Schedule, filed with the corporation's consolidated return.

Dual-resident corporation. If you are requesting certification for treaty benefits in the other country of residence named on line 4e, you may be denied certification depending on the terms of the residence article of the relevant treaty. If the treaty provides that benefits are available only if the competent authorities reach a mutual agreement to that effect, request competent authority assistance in accordance with Rev. Proc. 2002-52, 2002-31 I.R.B. 242, prior to seeking certification. See also the instructions to line 10.

Line 4f. S Corporation

S corporations are not considered U.S. residents within the meaning of the residence article of U.S. income tax treaties. Treaty benefits will only be available to a shareholder who is a U.S. resident for purposes of the applicable treaty. See Pub. 686 for more information.

Include the following with Form 8802.

1. The name and TIN of each shareholder for which certification is

requested and any additional information that would be required if certification were being requested for each of those shareholders.

2. Authorization (for example, Form 8821) from each shareholder. Each authorization must explicitly allow the third party requester to receive the shareholder's tax information and must not address any matters other than federal tax matters.

3. An authorization from an officer with legal authority to bind the corporation unless the requester is a shareholder in the S corporation during the tax year for which certification is requested.

Line 4g. Employee Benefit Plan/Trust

Trusts that are part of an employee benefit plan that is required to file Form 5500 must include a copy of the following with Form 8802.

1. The signed Form 5500, Annual Return/Report of Employee Benefit Plan.

2. Schedule P, Annual Return of Fiduciary of Employee Benefit Trust, identifying the name and TIN of the entity for which certification is being requested.

An employee plan that is not subject to the Employee Retirement Income Security Act (ERISA) or is not otherwise required to file Form 5500 must include with Form 8802 a copy of the employee benefit plan determination letter.

An employee plan that is not required to file Form 5500 and does not have a determination letter must provide evidence that it is entitled to certification. It must also provide a statement under penalties of perjury explaining why it is not required to file Form 5500 and why it does not have a determination letter.

Line 4h. Exempt Organization

Generally, an organization that is exempt from U.S. income tax must attach to Form 8802 a copy of either the organization's determination letter from the IRS or the determination letter for the parent organization.

An exempt organization that is not required to file a U.S. income tax return and that has not received a determination letter will not be issued a Form 6166, unless such organization has other means of proving U.S. residency for treaty purposes. For such an entity, include the entity's bylaws,

corporate charter, trust agreement, partnership agreement, etc. Submit attachments with Form 8802.

Governmental entity. Federal, state, or local government agencies requesting U.S. residency certification that have not obtained a determination letter, private letter ruling, revenue ruling, etc., can submit in writing, on official government letterhead, a letter under penalties of perjury from a legally authorized government official that the organization is a government agency.

Line 4i. Disregarded Entity

Disregarded entities (DRE) are not considered U.S. residents within the meaning of the residence article of U.S. income tax treaties. Treaty benefits will only be available to a DRE owner who is a U.S. resident. The DRE type must be specified on line 4i.

Note. See line 5 for more information regarding the DRE's owner information that may be required to be included with your Form 8802 application.

Line 4j. Nominee Applicant

If you act as a nominee for another person or entity, you must provide all certification information required for each individual or entity for which you are acting as a nominee. For example, if you are acting as a nominee for a resident alien, you must attach the information required of applicants that are resident aliens. Similarly, if one of the entities for which you are acting as a nominee is a partnership, then you must submit the certification information for each of the partners requesting certification. In addition, you must include the following with Form 8802:

1. Authorization (for example, Form 8821) from each individual or entity. Each authorization must explicitly allow the nominee applicant to receive the individual's or entity's tax information and must not address any matters other than federal tax matters.

2. A statement under penalties of perjury signed by an individual with legal authority to bind the nominee applicant, explicitly stating the nominee applicant is acting as an agent on behalf of the above-named individual(s) or entity(ies) for whom the Form 6166 is being requested.

Note. If you are a nominee partnership, please do not provide information concerning your partners. The

residence of your partners will not be verified.

Line 5. Required to File a U.S. Tax Form

If the applicant was not required to file a U.S. return for the tax periods on which certification will be based, check the applicable box next to "No." If the applicant does not fit in any of the categories listed, check "Other" and on the dotted line that follows, enter the code section that exempts the applicant from the requirement to file a U.S. return.

If the applicant was not required to file a U.S. return and the applicant is:

• An **individual** — attach proof of income (for example, an income statement) and an explanation of why the individual is not required to file a tax return for the tax period(s) on which certification will be based.

• A **minor child** — under the age of 14 whose parent(s) elected to report the child's income on their return, attach a signed copy of the Form 8814, Parents' Election To Report Child's Interest and Dividends.

• A **QSub (qualified subchapter S subsidiary)**, include the parent S corporation information on line 6. Attach proof of the Form 8869 election (Qualified Subchapter S Subsidiary Election) and all other corporate requirements listed in the instructions for line 4f that apply to the parent S corporation.

• A **trust or estate** — attach an explanation of why the trust or estate is not required to file Form 1041.

• A **common trust fund** — attach a copy of the determination letter or proof that a participant is not required to file.

• A **group trust arrangement** — attach a copy of the determination letter or private letter ruling.

• A **partnership described in section 761(a)** — attach a copy of the section 761(a) election submitted with the filing of Form 1065 or a statement as described in Pub. 686. For each partner requesting certification, include all information indicated in the instructions for line 4b.

• A **FASIT (financial asset securitization investment trust)** — include the parent C corporation information on line 6 of Form 8802. Attach a copy of the statement of election made by the parent C corporation requesting that the entity be treated as a FASIT under section 860L(a)(3), the FASIT penalties of perjury statement (as described in Pub. 686) from the parent corporation, and

-6-

all of the other corporate requirements listed in the instructions for line 4e that apply to the corporate parent.

- A **foreign partnership** — include all information indicated in the instructions for line 4b for each partner requesting certification.

- A **domestic DRE (disregarded entity)** — include the entity's single owner information on line 6. Include with Form 8802: the owner's name and entity type (e.g., corporation, partnership), TIN, and all other certification application information required for the owner's type of entity. If the DRE is either newly formed, was established before 2001, or was established by default (no Form 8832 was filed), also include a representation (as described in Pub. 686) from the owner, signed under penalties of perjury.

- A **foreign DRE (foreign disregarded entity)** — For tax years beginning on or after January 1, 2004, if the disregarded entity is organized outside the United States and the owner is a U.S. person or entity, attach a copy of the Form 8858, Information Return of U.S. Persons With Respect to Foreign Disregarded Entities, filed with the U.S. owner's income tax return for the calendar year(s) for which certification is requested. If the owner has not identified the foreign DRE on the Form 8858, the foreign DRE may not be certified. Include the foreign DRE's owner information on line 6. Include with Form 8802, the owner's name and entity type, TIN, and all other certification information required for the owner's type of entity.

Note. If certification is being requested for tax years prior to January 1, 2004, the U.S. owner is not required to attach a copy of the Form 8858, but must attach proof that the foreign DRE is owned by a U.S. resident. For example, if the foreign DRE is owned by a U.S. corporation, attach a copy of Schedule N (Form 1120), Foreign Operations of U.S. Corporations, filed with the owner's income tax return for the calendar year for which certification is requested. If the owner has not identified the DRE on an attachment to its Schedule N, the foreign DRE may not be certified.

Line 6. Parent or Parent Organization

If you answered "Yes" to line 5, do **not** complete line 6.

If you answered "No" to line 5, you must complete line 6.

If you answered "Yes" to line 6, check the appropriate box and enter the parent's, parent organization's or owner's information. If the applicant is a minor child, enter the name, address, and TIN of the parent who reported the child's income.

If you answered "No" to line 6, attach proof of the parent's or parent organization's income and an explanation of why the parent is not required to file a tax return for the tax period(s) on which certification will be based.

Line 7. Calendar Year of Request

 See Publication 686 for the Penalties of Perjury Statements that must be provided with your application.

The certification period is generally 1 year. You can request certification for both the current year and any number of prior years. If certification is requested for the current calendar year or a year for which a return is not yet required to be filed, see Pub. 686 for the penalties of perjury statement that must be provided with your application.

If you entered the most recent prior year on this line, see *Form 8802 Filed Before Return Posted by the IRS* on page 2.

Enter the four-digit (YYYY) calendar year(s) for which you are requesting certification. However, see the *Exception* below.

Exception. If you were a dual-status alien during any year for which you are requesting certification, enter instead the eight-digit dates (YYYYMMDD) that correspond to the beginning and ending of the period you were resident in the United States. You must show the specific period of residence for each year for which you are requesting certification. For information on determining your period of residency, see Pub. 519.

Line 8. Tax Period

Enter the four-digit year and two-digit month (YYYYMM) for the end of the tax period(s) for which you were required to file your return that corresponds to the year(s) for which you are requesting certification (the certification year).

Example 1. A Form 1040 filer who is completing Form 8802 for certification year 2005 on January 1, 2005, would enter 200312 on line 8. This is because on January 1, 2005, the 2003 Form 1040 is the latest return

required to have been filed by an individual requesting certification for 2005.

Example 2. On May 1, 2005, the same Form 1040 filer would enter 200412 as the tax period for a certification year of 2005 (the 2004 Form 1040 was required to have been filed before May 1, 2005).

Example 3. On January 1, 2005, a Form 1040 filer completing Form 8802 for a certification year of 2002 would enter 200212.

VAT. Certification for VAT purposes can be issued only for a year for which a return was filed. Therefore, the tax period entered here must be the same as the certification year (for example, 200412 for the 2004 certification year).

Line 9. Purpose of Certification

The North American Industry Classification System (NAICS) codes can be found in the instructions for your tax return (for example, Form 1120 or Schedule C (Form 1040)). If you do not provide a NAICS code on Form 8802 and one was not provided on the return you filed, one will not be entered automatically. Form 6166 will only be able to certify that you filed a return with a particular NAICS code if it matches the NAICS code on your return. If you provide a code that does not match, Form 6166 will state that you represent that your NAICS code is as stated on Form 8802.

If you fail to indicate the purpose of the certification or you indicate "Income tax" but have requested certification for a non-treaty country, **your application will be returned to you** for correction.

Line 10. Country for Which Certification Is Requested

Generally, the country or countries for which certification is requested will not be identified on Form 6166. However, there are two exceptions.

- In the case of individuals who file Form 2555, or Form 1116 instead of Form 2555, for the calendar year(s) for which certification is requested, and who are requesting certification for Cyprus, Hungary, India, Kazakhstan, Russia, South Africa, and/or Ukraine, the country or countries will be identified on Form 6166.

- In the case of dual-resident corporations that are residents of Australia, Belgium, Canada (only for dual-incorporated entities), China (including dual-resident companies that would be resident in a third country under a treaty with China), Denmark, Estonia, Finland, France, Germany, India, Ireland, Israel, Italy, Jamaica, Kazakhstan, Latvia, Lithuania, Luxembourg, Mexico, Morocco, Netherlands, New Zealand, Pakistan, Portugal, Russia, Slovenia (only for dual-incorporated entities), Spain, Switzerland, Thailand, Trinidad and Tobago, Tunisia, Ukraine, United Kingdom, or Venezuela, the country will not be identified on Form 6166, but the form will prohibit its use in the dual-resident corporation's other country of residence.

Line 11. Attachments and Penalties of Perjury Statement

If additional information is required to be submitted with Form 8802, use the space provided in line 11 or attach the information to the form.

Penalties of perjury statements may be submitted in the space provided under line 11 or as an attachment. Penalties of perjury statements submitted independently of Form 8802 must have a valid signature. For more information regarding penalties of perjury, see Pub. 686.

Note. If any attachment is prepared by someone other than the person signing Form 8802, the attachment must contain the penalties of perjury statement and the signature of the individual signing Form 8802.

Signature

Note. An authorized representative must attach documentation (such as Form 2848, Power of Attorney and Declaration of Representative) showing authorization to sign Form 8802.

If the applicant is:
- A minor child who cannot sign, either parent can sign the child's name in the space provided. Then, add "By (your signature), parent for minor child."
- A minor child under the age of 14 whose parent(s) elected to report the child's income on Form 8814, the parent who filed Form 8814 must sign.
- A deceased individual, either the surviving spouse or personal representative can sign. The personal representative must attach documentation showing authorization. A personal representative can be an executor, administrator, or trustee of the decedent's estate.

- A partnership, either a general partner or the partnership's authorized representative can sign.
- A corporation or an S corporation, either an officer with legal authority to bind the corporation or the corporation's authorized representative can sign.
- A trust, either a trustee or the trust's authorized representative can sign.
- An estate, the personal representative must sign. A personal representative can be an executor, administrator, or trustee of the estate.
- An exempt organization, either an officer with legal authority to bind the organization or the organization's authorized representative can sign.
- An employee benefit plan, either an officer with legal authority to bind the plan or the plan's authorized representative can sign.

TIP *To avoid delays in the processing and possible rejection of Form 8802, if Form 8802 is signed by an individual who is not identified in the instructions, attach a statement in line 11 and any appropriate documentation to indicate such individual's authority to sign Form 8802.*

Daytime Phone Number

Providing your daytime phone number can help speed the processing of Form 8802. We may have questions about items on your application, such as the NAICS code, type of applicant, etc. By answering our questions over the phone, we may be able to continue processing your Form 8802 without mailing you a letter. If you are filing a joint application, you can enter either your or your spouse's daytime phone number.

Privacy Act and Paperwork Reduction Act Notice. We ask for the information on this form under sections 6103 and 6109 of the Internal Revenue Code. You are required to provide the information requested on this form only if you wish to have your U.S. residency for tax purposes confirmed in order to claim certain benefits under a tax treaty between the United States and the foreign country (countries) indicated on line 10 of Form 8802. We need this information to determine if the applicant, in order to obtain benefits under a tax treaty, can be certified as a U.S. resident for tax purposes for the period specified on the application.

Failure to provide a properly completed form or required attachments will result in the applicant not being certified as a U.S. resident for the period specified on the application. Providing false or fraudulent information may subject you to penalties. If you designate an appointee to receive Form 6166, but do not provide all of the information requested, we may be unable to honor the designation.

We may disclose the information to the tax authorities of other countries pursuant to a tax treaty. We may disclose this information to the Department of Justice for civil and criminal litigation. We may also disclose this information to cities, states, and the District of Columbia for use in administering their tax laws, to federal and state agencies to enforce federal nontax criminal laws, or to federal law enforcement and intelligence agencies to combat terrorism.

You are not required to provide the information requested on a form that is subject to the Paperwork Reduction Act unless the form displays a valid OMB control number. Books or records relating to a form or its instructions must be retained as long as their contents may become material in the administration of any Internal Revenue law. Generally, tax returns and return information are confidential, as required by Section 6103.

The time needed to complete and file this form will vary depending on individual circumstances. The estimated average time is:

Recordkeeping	52 min.
Learning about the law or the form	1hr., 3 min.
Preparing the form	56 min.
Copying, assembling, and sending the form to the IRS	34 min.

If you have comments concerning the accuracy of these time estimates or suggestions for making this form simpler, we would be happy to hear from you. You can write to the Internal Revenue Service, Tax Products Coordinating Committee, SE:W:CAR:MP:T:T:SP, 1111 Constitution Ave. NW, IR-6406, Washington, DC 20224. Do **not** send the form to this address. Instead, see *Where To File* on page 1.

-8-

Form **8809**

(Rev. July 2004)

Department of the Treasury
Internal Revenue Service

Application for Extension of Time
To File Information Returns

(For Forms W-2 series, W-2G, 1042-S, 1098 series, 1099 series, 5498 series, and 8027)

▶ **Send to IRS–Martinsburg Computing Center.** See **Where to file** below.

OMB No. 1545-1081

Caution: *Do not use this form to request an extension of time to (1) provide statements to recipients, (2) file Form 1042 (instead use Form 2758), or (3) file Form 1040 (instead use Form 4868).*

Extension Requested for Tax Year

20_____

(Enter one year only.)

1 Filer or transmitter information. **Type or print clearly in black ink.**

Filer/Transmitter Name _____

Address _____

City _____ State _____ ZIP Code _____

Contact Name _____ Telephone number (_____) _____

Email address _____

2 **Taxpayer identification number**
(Enter your nine-digit number. Do not enter hyphens.)

3 Transmitter Control Code (TCC)

4 Check your method of filing information returns (check only one box). Use a separate Form 8809 for each method.

☐ electronic   ☐ magnetic media   ☐ paper

5 If you are requesting an extension for more than one filer, enter the total number of filers and attach a list of names and taxpayer identification numbers. Requests for more than 50 filers must be filed electronically or magnetically. See **How to file** below for details. ▶

6 For extension requests sent electronically/magnetically only, enter the total number of records in your extension file. **Do not** attach a list.
▶

7 Check this box only if you already received the automatic extension and you now need an additional extension. See instructions. ▶ ☐

8 Check the box(es) that apply. **Do not** enter the number of returns.

Form	✓ here	Form	✓ here	Form	✓ here
W-2 series		5498		8027	
1098 series, 1099 series, W-2G		5498-ESA		1099-INT/OID for REMIC	
1042-S		5498-SA			

9 If you checked the box on line 7, state in detail why you need an additional extension of time. You must give a reason or your request will be denied. If you need more space, attach additional sheets.

Under penalties of perjury, I declare that I have examined this form, including any accompanying statements and, to the best of my knowledge and belief, it is true, correct, and complete.

Signature ▶ _____   Title ▶ _____   Date ▶ _____

General Instructions

Purpose of form. Use this form to request an extension of time to file any forms shown in line 8.

Who may file. Filers of returns submitted on paper, on magnetic media, or electronically may request an extension of time to file on this form.

Where to file. Send Form 8809 to IRS-Martinsburg Computing Center, Information Reporting Program, Attn: Extension of Time Coordinator, 240 Murall Dr., Kearneysville, WV 25430. To avoid delays, be sure the attention line is included on all envelopes and packages containing Form 8809.

How to file. When you request extensions of time to file for more than 50 filers for the forms shown in line 8, except Form 8027, you must submit the extension requests magnetically or electronically. For 10–50 filers, you are encouraged to submit the extension request magnetically or electronically.

If filing on paper with 50 or less filers, you must attach a list of the filers' names and taxpayer identification numbers. If you are filing the extension request magnetically or electronically, you do not have to provide a list.

Also, see Pub. 1220, Specifications for Filing Forms 1098, 1099, 5498, and W-2G Electronically or Magnetically and Pub. 1187, Specifications for Filing Form 1042-S, Foreign Person's U.S. Source Income Subject to Withholding, Electronically or Magnetically.

Note. Specifications for filing Forms W-2, Wage and Tax Statements, magnetically or electronically, are only available from the Social Security Administration (SSA). Call 1-800-SSA-6270 for more information.

When to file. File Form 8809 as soon as you know an extension of time to file is necessary. However, Form 8809 must be filed

For Privacy Act and Paperwork Reduction Act Notice, see page 2.

Cat. No. 10322N

Form **8809** (Rev. 7-2004)

Appendix

by the due date of the returns. See the chart below that shows the due dates for filing this form on paper, magnetically, or electronically. IRS will respond in writing beginning in January. Filers and transmitters of Form W-2, Wage and Tax Statement, whose business has terminated, should follow the procedures in the 2004 Instructions for Forms W-2 and W-3 to request an extension.

If you are requesting an extension of time to file several types of forms, you may use one Form 8809, but you must file Form 8809 by the earliest due date. For example, if you are requesting an extension of time to file both 1099 series and 5498 series forms, you must file Form 8809 by February 28 (March 31 if you file electronically). You may complete more than one Form 8809 to avoid this problem. An extension cannot be granted if a request is filed after the due date of the original returns.

The due dates for filing Form 8809 are shown below.

IF you file Form . . .	MAGNETICALLY or on PAPER, then the due date is . . .	ELECTRONICALLY, then the due date is . . .
W-2 Series	Last day of February	March 31
W-2G	February 28	March 31
1042-S	March 15	March 15
1098 Series	February 28	March 31
1099 Series	February 28	March 31
5498 Series	May 31	May 31
8027	Last day of February	March 31

If any due date falls on a Saturday, Sunday, or legal holiday, file by the next business day.

Caution: *You do not have to wait for a response before filing your returns. File your returns as soon as they are ready. For all forms shown in line 8, except Form 8027, if you have received a response, do not send a copy of the letter or Form 8809 with your returns. If you have not received a response by the end of the extension period, file your returns. When filing Form 8027 on paper **only,** attach a copy of your approval letter. If an approval letter has not been received, attach a copy of your timely filed Form 8809.*

Extension period. The automatic extension is 30 days from the original due date. You may request one additional extension of not more than 30 days by submitting a second Form 8809 before the end of the first extension period (see Line 7 below). Requests for an additional extension of time to file information returns are **not** automatically granted. Generally requests for additional time are granted only in cases of extreme hardship or catastrophic event. The IRS will send you a letter of explanation approving or denying your request for an additional extension only.

Note. The automatic and any approved additional request will only extend the due date for filing the returns. It will not extend the due date for furnishing statements to recipients.

Penalty. If you file required information returns late and you have not applied for and received an approved extension of time to file, you may be subject to a late filing penalty. The amount of the penalty is based on when you file the correct information return. For more information on penalties, see the General Instructions for Forms 1099, 1098, 5498, and W-2G.

Specific Instructions

Tax year. You may request an extension for only 1 tax year on this form. If no tax year is shown, the IRS will assume you are requesting an extension for the returns currently due to be filed.

Line 1. Enter the name and complete mailing address, including room or suite number of the filer or transmitter requesting the extension of time. Use the name and address where you want the response sent. For example, if you are a preparer and want to receive the response, enter your client's complete name, care of (c/o) your firm, and your complete mailing address. Enter the name of someone who is familiar with this request whom the IRS

can contact if additional information is required. Please provide your telephone number and e-mail address. If you act as transmitter for a group of filers, enter your name and address here, and see *How to file* on page 1.

Note. Approval or denial notification will be sent only to the person who requested the extension (filer or transmitter).

Line 2. Enter your nine-digit employer identification number (EIN) or qualified intermediary employer identification number (QI-EIN). If you are not required to have an EIN or QI-EIN, enter your social security number. Do not enter hyphens. Failure to provide this number, and the list of numbers if you are acting as a transmitter as explained under Line 1, will result in automatic denial of the extension request.

Line 3. For electronic or magnetic media only. If you filed Form 4419, Application for Filing Information Returns Electronically/ Magnetically, to file Forms 1042-S, 1098, 1099, 5498, W-2G, or 8027, and it was approved, the IRS-Martinsburg Computing Center assigned you a five-character Transmitter Control Code (TCC). Enter that TCC here. Leave this line blank if you (1) are requesting an extension to file any Forms W-2, (2) are requesting an extension to file forms on paper, or (3) have not yet received your TCC.

Line 7. Check this box if you have already received the automatic 30-day extension, but you need an additional extension for the same year and for the same forms. Do not check this box unless you received an original extension.

If you check this box, be sure to complete line 9. Then, sign and date the request.

Signature. No signature is required for the automatic 30-day extension. For an additional extension, Form 8809 must be signed by you or a person who is duly authorized to sign a return, statement, or other document.

Privacy Act and Paperwork Reduction Act Notice. We ask for the information on this form to carry out the Internal Revenue laws of the United States. Form 8809 is provided by the IRS to request an extension of time to file information returns. Regulations section 1.6081-1 requires you to provide the requested information if you desire an extension of time for filing an information return. If you do not provide the requested information, an extension of time for filing an information return may not be granted. Section 6109 requires you to provide your taxpayer identification number (TIN). Routine uses of this information include giving it to the Department of Justice for civil and criminal litigation, and cities, states, and the District of Columbia for use in administering their tax laws. We may also disclose this information to other countries under a tax treaty, or Federal, state, or local agencies to enforce Federal nontax criminal laws and to combat terrorism. The authority to disclose information to combat terrorism expired on December 31, 2003. Legislation is pending that would reinstate this authority.

You are not required to provide the information requested on a form that is subject to the Paperwork Reduction Act unless the form displays a valid OMB control number. Books or records relating to a form or its instructions must be retained as long as their contents may become material in the administration of any Internal Revenue law. Generally, tax returns and return information are confidential, as required by Code section 6103.

The time needed to complete and file this form will vary depending on individual circumstances. The estimated average time is: Recordkeeping, 2 hrs., 10 min.; Learning about the law or the form, 36 min.; Preparing and sending the form to the IRS, 28 min.

If you have comments concerning the accuracy of these time estimates or suggestions for making this form simpler, we would be happy to hear from you. You can write to the Tax Products Coordinating Committee, Western Area Distribution Center, Rancho Cordova, CA 95743-0001. Do not send the form to this address. Instead, see *Where to file* on page 1.

 Printed on recycled paper

Form **8846**	**Credit for Employer Social Security and Medicare Taxes Paid on Certain Employee Tips**	OMB No. 1545-1414

Department of the Treasury
Internal Revenue Service

▶ **Attach to your tax return.**

2005

Attachment Sequence No. **98**

Name(s) shown on return | Identifying number

Note. *Claim this credit* **only** *for social security and Medicare taxes paid by a food or beverage establishment where tipping is customary for providing food or beverages. See the instructions for line 1.*

Part I **Current Year Credit**

1	Tips received by employees for services on which you paid or incurred employer social security and Medicare taxes during the tax year (see instructions)	1	
2	Tips not subject to the credit provisions (see instructions)	2	
3	Creditable tips. Subtract line 2 from line 1	3	
4	Multiply line 3 by 7.65% (.0765). If you had any tipped employees whose wages (including tips) exceeded $90,000, see instructions and check here . . . . ▶ ☐	4	
5	Form 8846 credits from pass-through entities:		

	If you are a—	Then enter the Form 8846 credits from—		
	a Shareholder	Schedule K-1 (Form 1120S) box 13, code F, G, or P	}	5
	b Partner	Schedule K-1 (Form 1065) box 15, code F, G, or P		

| 6 | **Current year credit.** Add lines 4 and 5 . . . . | 6 | |

Part II **Allowable Credit** (See **Who must file Form 3800** to find out if you complete Part II or file Form 3800.)

7	Regular tax before credits:		
	• Individuals. Enter the amount from Form 1040, line 44		
	• Corporations. Enter the amount from Form 1120, Schedule J, line 3; Form 1120-A, Part I, line 1; or the applicable line of your return	7	
	• Estates and trusts. Enter the sum of the amounts from Form 1041, Schedule G, lines 1a and 1b, or the amount from the applicable line of your return		
8	Alternative minimum tax:		
	• Individuals. Enter the amount from Form 6251, line 35		
	• Corporations. Enter the amount from Form 4626, line 14.	8	
	• Estates and trusts. Enter the amount from Form 1041, Schedule I, line 56		
9	Add lines 7 and 8	9	
10a	Foreign tax credit	10a	
b	Credits from Form 1040, lines 48 through 54.	10b	
c	Possessions tax credit (Form 5735, line 17 or 27)	10c	
d	Nonconventional source fuel credit (Form 8907, line 23)	10d	
e	Other specified credits (see instructions)	10e	
f	Add lines 10a through 10e	10f	
11	Net income tax. Subtract line 10f from line 9. If zero, skip lines 12 through 15 and enter -0- on line 16	11	
12	Net regular tax. Subtract line 10f from line 7. If zero or less, enter -0-	12	
13	Enter 25% (.25) of the excess, if any, of line 12 over $25,000 (see instructions)	13	
14	Tentative minimum tax (see instructions):		
	• Individuals. Enter the amount from Form 6251, line 33		
	• Corporations. Enter the amount from Form 4626, line 12 . . .	14	
	• Estates and trusts. Enter the amount from Form 1041, Schedule I, line 54		
15	Enter the greater of line 13 or line 14	15	
16	Subtract line 15 from line 11. If zero or less, enter -0-	16	
17	**Credit allowed for the current year.** Enter the **smaller** of line 6 or line 16 here and on Form 1040, line 55; Form 1120, Schedule J, line 6d; Form 1120-A, Part I, line 2; Form 1041, Schedule G, line 2c; or the applicable line of your return. If line 16 is smaller than line 6, see instructions	17	

For Paperwork Reduction Act Notice, see instructions. | Cat. No. 16148Z | Form **8846** (2005)

Appendix

General Instructions

Section references are to the Internal Revenue Code.

Purpose of Form

Certain food and beverage establishments (see *Who Should File* below) use Form 8846 to claim a credit for social security and Medicare taxes paid or incurred by the employer on certain employees' tips. The credit is part of the general business credit.

You can claim or elect not to claim the credit any time within 3 years from the due date of your return on either your original return or on an amended return.

Who Should File

File Form 8846 if you meet both of the following conditions.

1. You had employees who received tips from customers for providing, delivering, or serving food or beverages for consumption if tipping of employees for delivering or serving food or beverages is customary.

2. During the tax year, you paid or incurred employer social security and Medicare taxes on those tips.

How the Credit Is Figured

Generally, the credit equals the amount of employer social security and Medicare taxes paid or incurred by the employer on tips received by the employee. However, the employer social security and Medicare taxes on tips that are used to meet the Federal minimum wage rate applicable to the employee under the Fair Labor Standards Act are not included in the computation. The Federal minimum wage rate is $5.15 per hour.

For example, an employee worked 100 hours and received $350 in tips for October 2005. The worker received $375 in wages (excluding tips) at the rate of $3.75 an hour. Because the Federal minimum wage rate was $5.15 an hour, the employee would have received wages, excluding tips, of $515 had the employee been paid at the Federal minimum wage rate. Thus, only $210 of the employee's tips for October 2005 is taken into account for credit purposes.

Specific Instructions

Part I

Current Year Credit

Figure the current year credit from your trade or business on lines 1 through 4. Skip lines 1 through 4 if you are only claiming a credit that was allocated to you from an S corporation or a partnership.

S Corporations and Partnerships

S corporations and partnerships figure their current year credit on lines 1 through 4, enter any credit from other flow-through entities on line 5, and allocate the credit on line 6 to the shareholders or partners. Attach Form 8846 to Form 1120S or Form 1065 and show on Schedule K-1 each shareholder's or partner's credit. Electing

large partnerships include this credit in "general credits."

Line 1

Enter the tips received by employees for services on which you paid or incurred employer social security and Medicare taxes during the tax year. Include tips received from customers for providing, delivering, or serving food or beverages for consumption if tipping of employees for delivering or serving food or beverages is customary.

Line 2

If you pay each tipped employee wages (excluding tips) equal to or more than the Federal minimum wage rate, enter zero on line 2.

Figure the amount of tips included on line 1 that are not creditable for each employee on a monthly basis. This is the total amount that would be payable to the employee at the Federal minimum wage rate reduced by the wages (excluding tips) actually paid to the employee during the month. Enter on line 2 the total amounts figured for all employees.

Line 4

If any tipped employee's wages and tips exceeded the 2005 social security tax wage base of $90,000 subject to the 6.2% rate, check the box on line 4 and attach a separate computation showing the amount of tips subject to only the Medicare tax rate of 1.45%. Subtract these tips from the line 3 tips, and multiply the difference by .0765. Then, multiply the tips subject only to the Medicare tax by .0145. Enter the sum of these amounts on line 4.

Reduce the income tax deduction for employer social security and Medicare taxes by the amount on line 4.

Part II

Allowable Credit

The credit allowed for the current year may be limited based on your tax liability. Use Part II to figure the allowable credit unless you must file Form 3800, General Business Credit.

Who must file Form 3800. You must file Form 3800 if you have:

● A credit for employer social security and Medicare taxes paid on certain employee tips from a passive activity;

● More than one credit included in the general business credit (other than a credit from Form 8844, Form 6478, or Section B of Form 8835), or

● A carryback or carryforward of any of those credits.

See the instructions for Form 3800 for a list of credits included in the general business credit.

Line 10e

Include on line 10e any amounts claimed on:

● Form 8834, Qualified Electric Vehicle Credit, line 20;

● Form 8910, Alternative Motor Vehicle Credit, line 18; or

● Form 8911, Alternative Fuel Vehicle Refueling Property Credit, line 19.

Line 13

See section 38(c)(5) for special rules that apply to married couples filing separate returns, controlled corporate groups, regulated investment companies, real estate investment trusts, and estates and trusts.

Line 14

Although you may not owe alternative minimum tax (AMT), you generally must still compute the tentative minimum tax (TMT) to figure your credit. For a small corporation exempt from the AMT under section 55(e), enter zero. Otherwise, complete and attach the applicable AMT form or schedule.

Line 17

If you cannot use all of the credit because of the tax liability limit (line 16 is smaller than line 6), carry the unused credit back 1 year then forward up to 20 years. See the instructions for Form 3800 for details.

Paperwork Reduction Act Notice. We ask for the information on this form to carry out the Internal Revenue laws of the United States. You are required to give us the information. We need it to ensure that you are complying with these laws and to allow us to figure and collect the right amount of tax.

You are not required to provide the information requested on a form that is subject to the Paperwork Reduction Act unless the form displays a valid OMB control number. Books or records relating to a form or its instructions must be retained as long as their contents may become material in the administration of any Internal Revenue law. Generally, tax returns and return information are confidential, as required by section 6103.

The time needed to complete and file this form will vary depending on individual circumstances. The estimated burden for individual taxpayers filing this form is approved under OMB control number 1545-0074 and is included in the estimates shown in the instructions for their individual income tax return. The estimated burden for all other taxpayers who file this form is shown below.

Recordkeeping . . . . 6 hr., 27 min.
**Learning about
the law or the form** . . . . . 18 min.
**Preparing and sending
the form to the IRS** . . . . . 24 min.

If you have comments concerning the accuracy of these time estimates or suggestions for making this form simpler, we would be happy to hear from you. See the instructions for the tax return with which this form is filed.

 Printed on recycled paper

Form 9041
(Rev. May 2002)
Department of the Treasury
Internal Revenue Service

Application/Registration for Electronic/Magnetic Media Filing of Business Returns

OMB No. 1545-1079

This application is: (check one) new ☐ revised ☐

1a Firm's name

b Employer identification number (EIN)
(EIN must be 9 digits.)

c Mailing address (Street, P.O. Box, city, state, ZIP code)

d Contact person's name

Daytime telephone number
(Include area code)   (___) _____

FAX telephone number
(Include area code)   (___) _____

Contact E-mail address(es)
(Optional)   _____

2 Indicate which forms you will file by checking the appropriate box.

☐ **941 e-file** Program

☐ **941 On-Line** Filing Program

☐ **940 e-file** Program

☐ **940 On-Line** Filing Program

☐ **Form 1041,** U.S. Income Tax Return for Estates and Trusts

☐ **Form 1065,** U.S. Return of Partnership Income

☐ **Form** _____

3a List any Electronic Transmitter Identification Number(s) and Magnetic Media Transmitter Identification Number(s) we previously assigned to you or your firm.

3b If you have previously been suspended from any IRS Electronic Filing Program, please check here. ☐

4 Please answer the following questions:
a Will you send return data directly to IRS? . . . . ☐ Yes ☐ No
b Will you develop or modify software that prepares returns for electronic/magnetic media filing? . . . ☐ Yes ☐ No
c Will you file using Magnetic tape? ☐ Floppy Diskette (3 1/2" and 5 1/4")? ☐ Modem? ☐
d **FOR 941 FILERS ONLY:** Will you be transmitting files in . . . Electronic Date Interchange (EDI)? ☐
Non EDI? . . . . ☐
Both? . . . . ☐

If you will be using EDI, please provide the version number here.

5 If you know which software company and/or transmission service you will use, please enter the names, addresses and phone numbers below.

Software Company	Transmitter

6 Estimated tax return volume to be filed:
Form . . . .   K-1 . . . .

7 Comments/Additional Information

Applicant Agreement

Under the penalties of perjury, I declare that I have examined this application/registration and any accompanying information, and to the best of my knowledge and belief it is true, correct, and complete. This firm and its employees will comply with all the provisions of the procedures for electronic/magnetic media filing of Forms 940, 941, 1041 and 1065 as applicable. The firm understands that if it is sold or its organizational structure is changed, acceptance for participation is not transferable; a new application/registration must be filed. The firm further understands that noncompliance will result in the firm no longer being allowed to participate in the program. I am authorized to make and sign this statement on behalf of the firm.

8 Name and title of person responsible for filing this application (Please print or type)

9 Signature of person responsible for this application/registration

Date

10 Name and title of designated PIN Recipient (See instructions)

Date

11 Signature of Designated PIN Recipient (See instructions)

Date

For Privacy Act and Paperwork Reduction Act Notice, see back of this form.   Cat. No. 10333U   Form **9041** (Rev. 5-2002)

Form 9041 (Rev. 5-2002)   Page **2**

Privacy Act Notice.—The Privacy Act of 1974 requires that when we ask you for information we tell you our legal right to ask for the information, why we are asking for it, and how it will be used. We must also tell you what could happen if we do not receive it and whether your response is voluntary, required to obtain a benefit, or mandatory.

Our legal right to ask for the information is Internal Revenue Code sections 6001, 6011, and 6012(a) and their regulations. We are asking for this information to verify your standing as a person qualified to participate in the electronic filing program. Your response is voluntary. Failure to provide the requested information could result in your disqualification from the electronic filing program. If you provide fraudulent information, you may be subject to criminal prosecution.

Paperwork Reduction Act Notice.—We ask for the information on this form to carry out the Internal Revenue laws of the United States. You must give us the information if you wish to participate in the electronic/magnetic media filing program. We need it to process your application/registration to file Business Returns on electronic/magnetic media.

You are not required to provide the information requested on a form that is subject to the Paperwork Reduction Act unless the form displays a valid OMB control number. Books or records relating to a form or its instructions must be retained as long as their contents may become material in the administration of any Internal Revenue law. Generally, tax returns and return information are confidential, as required by Code section 6103.

The time needed to complete this form will vary depending upon individual circumstances. The estimated average time is 18 minutes. If you have comments concerning the accuracy of this time estimate or suggestions for making this form simpler, we would be happy to hear from you. You can write to the Tax Forms Committee, Western Area Distribution Center, Rancho Cordova, CA 95743-0001. **DO NOT** send this application to this office. Instead, see instructions below for **Where to file.**

General Instructions

Who must file.—File Form 9041 if you would like to take part in the electronic/magnetic media filing program for Forms 940, 941, 1041, and 1065. Only those who did not participate in last year's electronic/magnetic media filing program need apply, and those for whom information in item 1 has changed since we last contacted you.

When to file.—To ensure complete and timely review of your application, file Form 9041 at least 60 calendar days before you file electronically. IRS uses the postmark date on the envelope to determine whether the application was filed timely.

Where to file:

Send the completed Form 9041 to:

  Internal Revenue Service
  Austin Submission Processing Center
  Attn: EFU, Stop 6380
  P.O. Box 1231
  Austin, TX 78767
  Phone: 512-460-8900

Reporting Agents Please Note: Your application must be accompanied by your Agent's List, containing the names and EINs of the taxpayers for whom you will be filing returns. In addition, you must have an authorization made on Form 8655, with a revision date of October 1995 or later (or its equivalent), for each taxpayer on the Agent's List. For instructions regarding Form 8655, please refer to Revenue Procedure 96-17.

Specific Line Instructions

Line 1c.—If you have both a post office box and street address, enter both addresses for the firm's main office. We need both addresses in case we need to send information to you by overnight mail.

Line 1d.—If this information changes, please notify the IRS Service Center where you originally filed Form 9041. We need this information in case questions arise and to fax revised documentation or the Acknowledgement Report if it is six pages or less.

Line 2.—If you want to electronically file a form that is not listed and you know we have added it to our electronic filing program since this form's revision date (lower right corner), please enter it on one of the blank lines labeled Form. See Publication 1524, procedures for more information about filing Form 1065 electronically.

Line 5.—If this information changes, please notify the appropriate service center. If you will use your own software or communication equipment, please indicate this in the space provided. Please include the name, address, phone number, and contact person's name, if applicable.

Line 6.—Please enter the approximate number of each return type that you anticipate filing. If you are filing Forms 1065 or 1041, please also indicate the estimated number of Schedules K-1 that you will be filing.

Line 7.—Use this space to include any additional information that you believe we will require to process your application.

Line 10.—Enter the name and title of the individual that is the designated recipient of the Personal Identification Number (PIN). This is the individual who is authorized to sign returns on behalf of the business, or for their clients (Reporting Agents).

Electronic Federal Tax Payment System

Tax Form 9779 with Instructions (OMB 1545-1467)

 **Department of the Treasury**

Business Enrollment Form for EFTPS –
This form contains instructions to complete the Electronic Federal Tax Payment System (EFTPS) Enrollment Form for Business Taxpayers. It is to be used either for initial enrollment in the system or to add financial institution information. If you wish to use multiple accounts in one financial institution, or accounts in multiple financial institutions, you will need to provide multiple copies of the enrollment form.

For *questions* regarding EFTPS or this Enrollment Form please *call:*

Visit our web site at www.EFTPS.gov to enroll online.
24 hours a day, 7 days a week

EFTPS Customer Service	1-800-555-4477 or 1-800-945-8400
For TDD (hearing impaired) support	1-800-733-4829 or 1-800-945-8900
en español	1-800-244-4829 or 1-800-945-8600

When your form is *completed*, please *mail* to:

EFTPS Enrollment Processing Center
P.O. Box 4210
Iowa City, Iowa 52244-4210

You should receive your Confirmation/Update Form and instructions on using EFTPS approximately two to four weeks after we receive your Enrollment Form.

INSTRUCTIONS

1. Employer Identification Number (EIN). Enter your nine-digit Employer Identification Number. *Enter the EIN on the back of the form in the upper right corner as well.*

2. Business Taxpayer Name. Print your business name exactly as it appears on the tax return. The only valid characters are A-Z, 0-9, -, &, and blank.

3. Business Address. This address should be the address as it appears on the business tax return.

 Note: If the address has been pre-printed and is incorrect, it can only be changed by submitting an IRS Change of Address (Form 8822) to the Internal Revenue Service. The address on your EFTPS enrollment will automatically be updated when Form 8822 is submitted. See the back of Form 8822 to determine where the form should be mailed.

4. Primary Contact Name. Print the name of a person, company, or third party who can be contacted in the event questions arise regarding this enrollment or tax payments. All EFTPS mailings will be sent to your primary contact.

5-6. Primary Contact Mailing Address and Phone Number (if different from #3 above). You need not complete the address area if your contact's address is the same as the business address. If an address is provided here, it will be used to mail confirmation materials and instruction booklets.

7. Primary contact E-mail Address. (optional)

Marking Instructions:
- Use black or blue ink only.
- Please print legibly. Use one character per block. **Use only capital letters.** Keep all printing within the boxes.
- Do not make any stray marks on this form.

MARKING EXAMPLE:

| I | A | State
| 5 | 2 | 4 | 7 | 1 | Zip Code

Taxpayer Information

1. Employer Identification Number (EIN) – (Please enter EIN on reverse side also.)

M200590980

2. Business Taxpayer Name:

3. Business Street Address:

City: State: ZIP Code:

International: Province, Country, and Postal Code:

Contact Information

4. Primary Contact Name:

5. Primary Contact Mailing Street Address (if different from #3 above):

City: State: Zip Code:

International: Province, Country, and Postal Code:

6. Primary Contact Phone Number:
US   Area Code   International   Country Code   City Code
                                011-

7. Primary Contact E-mail Address (use as many spaces as needed up to 60):

NCS No. 111104
IRS-136

(over)

EFTPS®
Electronic Federal Tax Payment System

(continued)

For side 2 please fill in
Employer Identification Number (EIN)

EIN: ☐☐ – ☐☐☐☐☐☐☐

Payment Information

8. Payment Method. Choose the payment method(s) by placing an "X" in the box(es). The options available are: EFTPS-Direct and EFTPS-Through A Financial Institution.

When choosing EFTPS-Direct you can use EFTPS-Phone, EFTPS-OnLine or EFTPS-PC Software.★ If you choose EFTPS-PC Software, and after your EFTPS enrollment is successful, you may download the software from our web site (www.EFTPS.gov), or to receive the software via mail, call EFTPS Customer Service at the numbers listed on the front of this form.

8. Payment Method

☐ **EFTPS-Direct:** check here if you will instruct EFTPS to transfer payment from your account. (These EFTPS Payment Input Methods for EFTPS-Direct are interchangeable: EFTPS-Phone, EFTPS-PC Software ★, EFTPS-OnLine)

☐ **EFTPS-Through A Financial Institution:** check here if you will instruct your financial institution to forward the payment to EFTPS. You must check with your financial institution to determine if they are capable of providing this service.

NOTE: If you will only be using EFTPS-Through A Financial Institution as a payment method, skip to item #23.

Note: For EFTPS-Direct, complete the additional information required about your financial institution. Enrollment in the EFTPS-Direct payment method will automatically enroll you for EFTPS-Through A Financial Institution as well as Same-Day Payment.

For EFTPS-Through A Financial Institution, you initiate a tax payment through a financial institution. You must contact your financial institution to insure the institution is capable of making an EFTPS payment through the Automated Clearing House (ACH) or a Same-Day Payment method. If you enroll for EFTPS-Through A Financial Institution or Same-Day Payment, you may also enroll for EFTPS-Direct by providing the financial institution information requested on items 19 through 23.

Tax Form Payment Amount Limits (EFTPS-Direct only)

9-18. Optional Tax Form Payment Amount Limits (For EFTPS-Direct only)

This section is optional. You may set amount limits for each tax type to prevent an overpayment. The system will compare your payment amount against your stated limit and provide a warning if you exceed the limit. You may override the warning if you wish.

9. 720	$	10. 940	$	11. 941	$
12. 943	$	13. 945	$	14. 990C	$
15. 990PF	$	16. 990T	$	17. 1042	$
18. 1120	$				

Financial Institution Information (to be completed if EFTPS-Direct will be used)

(19 through 24 must be completed if EFTPS-Direct will be used)

19. RTN. This is the nine-digit number associated with your financial institution. You may contact your financial institution to verify this number.

20. Account Number. Enter the number of the account you will use to pay your taxes.

21. Type. Please mark one box to indicate whether the account is a checking or savings account.

22. State and ZIP Code. Use the two-character letter abbreviation for the state your financial institution is located in and indicate ZIP Code.

19. RTN: ☐☐☐☐☐☐☐☐☐

20. Account Number: ☐☐☐☐☐☐☐☐☐☐☐☐☐☐☐☐☐

21. Type:
☐ Checking
☐ Savings

22. State: ☐☐

ZIP Code: ☐☐☐☐☐ – ☐☐☐☐

Authorization

23. Authorization. This section authorizes a Financial Agent of the U.S. Treasury to initiate tax payments from the account(s) you designate that you requested the EFTPS-Direct payment method.

24. Taxpayer Signature. The taxpayer *must* sign this section to authorize participation in EFTPS. If there is no signature, a form will be returned.

This section also provides authorization to share the information provided with your financial institution, required for the processing of the Electronic Federal Tax Payment System.

If signed by a corporate officer, partner, or fiduciary on behalf of the taxpayer, the signer certifies that they have the authority to execute this authorization on behalf of the taxpayer.

Remember to sign and mail your enrollment form to the address on reverse side.

23. **For both payment methods:** Please read the following Authorization Agreement:

I (as defined as the taxpayer whose signature is below) hereby authorize the contact person (listed in item #4 of this form) and the financial institutions involved in the processing of my Electronic Federal Tax Payment System (EFTPS) payments to receive confidential information necessary to effect enrollment in EFTPS, electronic payment of taxes, and answer inquiries and resolve issues related to enrollment and payments. This information includes, but is not limited to, passwords, payment instructions, taxpayer name and identifying number, and payment transaction details. If signed by a corporate officer, partner, or fiduciary on behalf of the taxpayer, I certify that I have the authority to execute this authorization on behalf of the taxpayer. This authorization is to remain in full force and effect until the designated Financial Agents of the U.S. Treasury have received notification from me of termination in such time and in such manner to afford a reasonable opportunity to act on it.

Only EFTPS-Direct: Please read the following Authorization Agreement:

By completing the information in boxes 19-22 and signing below, I hereby authorize designated Financial Agents of the U.S. Treasury to initiate EFTPS-Direct debit entries to the financial institution account indicated above, for payment of Federal taxes owed to the IRS upon request by taxpayer or his/her representative, using the Electronic Federal Tax Payment System (EFTPS). I further authorize the financial institution named above to debit such entries to the financial institution account indicated above. All debits initiated by the U.S. Treasury designated Financial Agents pursuant to this authorization shall be made under U.S. Treasury regulations. This authorization is to remain in full force and effect until the designated Financial Agents of the U.S. Treasury have received written notification from me of termination in such time and in such manner as to afford a reasonable opportunity to act on it.

24. Taxpayer Signature

Taxpayer Signature _____ Date _____

Print Name _____ Title _____

Paperwork Reduction Act Notice: In accordance with the Paperwork Reduction Act of 1995, we ask for the information in the Electronic Federal Tax Payment System (EFTPS) Enrollment Form in order to carry out the requirements of 26 United States Code 6001, 6011, and 6109. You are not required to provide information requested on a form that is subject to the Paperwork Reduction Act unless the form displays a valid OMB control number. Books or records relating to a form or its instructions must be retained as long as their contents may become material in the administration of any Internal Revenue law. Generally, tax returns and return information are confidential, as required by Code section 6103. This information is used by the Internal Revenue Service to assure that payment(s) are properly credited to the appropriate account(s). Your response is mandatory if you are required by regulations to use Electronic Funds Transfer to make your Federal Tax Deposits. The time needed to provide this information will vary depending on individual circumstances. The estimated average time is ten minutes. If you have comments concerning the accuracy of this time estimate or suggestions for reducing this burden, we would be happy to hear from you. You can write to the Internal Revenue Service, Tax Forms Committee, Western Area Distribution Center, Rancho Cordova, CA 95743-0001. Please do not send the enrollment form to this address.

The Privacy Act of 1974 requires that when we ask individuals for information about themselves, we state our legal right to ask for the information, why we are asking for the information, and how it will be used. We must also tell you what could happen if we do not receive all or part of it, and whether your response is voluntary, required to obtain a benefit, or mandatory. Our legal right to ask for information is 5 U.S.C. 301 and Internal Revenue Code sections 6001, 6011, 6012, and applicable regulations. The information will be used to enroll you in the Electronic Federal Tax Payment System (EFTPS). The information may not be disclosed except as provided by section 6103 of the Internal Revenue Code. We may give the information to the Department of Justice and to other Federal agencies, as provided by law. We may also give it to cities, states, the District of Columbia, and U.S. commonwealths or possessions to carry out their laws. We may give it to foreign governments because of tax treaties they have with the United States. Your response is mandatory if you are required by regulations to use electronic funds transfer to make your deposits. If you are not required by regulations to use electronic funds transfer; your response is voluntary. If you do not provide all or part of the information, you may not be eligible to participate in the EFTPS. If you are required to use electronic funds transfer by regulation, you may be subject to penalties. If you are not required to use electronic funds transfer to pay taxes owed, you need to pay the taxes due by another method.

U.S. Government Printing Office:
1998–405-503/41607
Cat. No. 21816U

Form 9779 (3/02F)